Introduction to
Operations Research

FOURTH EDITION

Introduction to Operations Research

FOURTH EDITION

Frederick S. Hillier

STANFORD UNIVERSITY

Gerald J. Lieberman

STANFORD UNIVERSITY

HOLDEN-DAY, INC.   OAKLAND, CALIFORNIA

INTRODUCTION TO OPERATIONS RESEARCH
Fourth Edition

Copyright © 1986, 1980, 1974, 1967 by Holden-Day, Inc.
4432 Telegraph Avenue, Oakland, CA 94609

Library of Congress Catalog Card Number: 86-080560
ISBN: 0-8162-3871-5

Printed in the United States of America

To Our Parents

Contents

Preface

The number of students who have "cut their professional teeth" on our *Introduction to Operations Research* by using one of the first three editions is overwhelming, and it leaves us with an enormous sense of responsibility in preparing this new edition. Consequently, we have taken great care to preserve the best of the third edition and improve the rest. This effort has included collecting and evaluating an unusually large volume of feedback from numerous users all over the world, as well as from many of our own students. Although we received many mixed messages, there was near unanimity on a few areas warranting improvement: the initial approach to the simplex method, as well as the treatment of the "fundamental insight," sensitivity analysis, goal programming, and nonlinear programming. We have given special attention to these areas and feel gratified by the results. At the same time, we have been careful not to tamper excessively with many other areas of the book that have been received very well, while updating the material as needed. This is an evolutionary process, and we hope that many more of you will write to us with your comments and suggestions about the current edition.

A long-time user of this book will immediately note that a major reorganization has taken place. The chapter that was formerly last has been moved forward as Chapter 2, with more emphasis placed on modeling. The material on mathematical programming has been brought together in the next twelve chapters. The former five chapters on linear programming have been reorganized into Chapters 3–9 in such a way as to provide greater focus on certain key topics (introductory material, the simplex method, duality theory, sensitivity analysis, and the formulation of linear programming models).

Besides this reorganization, there have been several additions and major revisions for this edition. A new chapter on forecasting (Chapter 19) has been added to provide an up-to-date treatment (including an introduction to the Box-Jenkins technique) of a subject that has become very important to the practitioner. The chapter on nonlinear programming has been completely rewritten and greatly expanded to include recent advances in this important area. Four of the current linear programming chapters (Chapters 4, 5, 6, and 8) have received extensive revision. As in the second edition, the early approach to the simplex method emphasizes geometric insight and an enlightening algebraic development instead of the black box tableau approach, but we believe with considerably more lucidity than the second edition. We also have responded to another widespread request by introducing matrix notation when it can clarify some of the later linear programming material, including the fundamental insight and sensitivity analysis, although without going beyond the primer on matrices presented in Appendix 3.

Other significant changes have also been made. The chapter on integer programming (Chapter 13) has been reorganized to bring the modeling material to the front. Kendall's notation for identifying queueing systems has been incorporated into the queueing theory chapters (Chapters 16–17). We added a useful continuous review stochastic model to the inventory chapter (Chapter 18). Most of the sections of the book also received some polishing.

We have always given considerable attention to the end-of-chapter problems, and this edition is no exception. Many of the old problems have been revised. In addition, approximately 150 new problems have been added, including well over 100 just in the linear and nonlinear programming chapters. The problems have been carefully crafted to stimulate and enlighten the student without requiring an excessive amount of time. The instructor now has a grand total of 555 problems, many with multiple parts, from which to choose.

With all of these additions and expansions, we had to delete some material in order to maintain a reasonably sized volume. Based on considerable feedback that the review of elementary probability theory was not needed, we made that the primary deletion, while retaining the introduction to Markov chains. We also deleted the section on the mathematics of the decomposition principle and the table for the F distribution. In addition, there are a number of places in the book where we have attempted to increase clarity through succinctness.

Another important feature of this edition is that a Study Guide for students is available for the first time. We are delighted to have such a talented operations researcher and author as Dr. Paul A. Jensen of the University of Texas at Austin prepare this Study Guide. As usual, a Solutions Manual is available for instructors. In addition, Dr. Jensen and others have prepared for our publisher sets of microcomputer programs for both instructors and students to serve as an adjunct to this book. Our revision recognizes the growing accessibility of students and practitioners to microcomputers as well as mainframe computers.

We have continued the emphasis of previous editions on motivation and simplicity of explanation rather than rigorous proofs and technical details. We believe that this revision, along with the accompanying Study Guide, should further improve the appeal and readability of the book for the more practically inclined student, even one without much mathematical maturity. However, we still feel that the essential theory of operations research can be best understood and appreciated from a mathematical viewpoint. Therefore, the fourth edition is still aimed at the same audience as the previous editions, namely, the broad spectrum of students in a variety of fields (engineering, business, mathematical sciences, and social sciences), who sometimes prefer a modest use of mathematics to an immoderate amount of verbosity.

However, the mathematics has been kept at a relatively elementary level. Most of Parts Two and Three (Linear Programming and Mathematical Programming, respectively) requires no mathematics beyond high school algebra. Calculus is used only in Chapter 14 (Nonlinear Programming) and in one example in Chapter 11 (Dynamic Programming). Matrix notation is used in Chapter 5 (The Theory of the Simplex Method), Chapter 6 (Duality Theory and Sensitivity Analysis), and Chapter 14, but the only background needed for this is presented in Appendix 3. For Part Four (Probabilistic Models), a previous introduction to probability theory is assumed, and calculus is used in a few places. In general terms, the mathematical maturity that a student achieves through taking an elementary calculus course is useful throughout Part Four and for the more advanced material in Parts Two and Three.

The content of the book is aimed largely at the upper division under-graduate level and at first year (Master's level) graduate students. There are many ways to package the material into a course. The book has great flexibility. Part One is an introduction to the subject of operations research. Part Two (on linear programming) or Parts Two and Three (on mathematical programming) may essentially be covered independently of Part Four (on probabilistic models) and vice versa. Furthermore, the chapters in Parts Two and Three are nearly independent, except that they all use basic material presented in Chapter 3 and perhaps Chapter 4. Chapter 6 also draws upon Chapter 5. Within Part Four, there is considerable flexibility of coverage, although some integration of the material is available.

An elementary survey course covering mathematical programming and some probabilistic models can be presented in a quarter (40 hours) or semester by selectively drawing from material in all four parts of the book. For example, a good survey of the field can be obtained from Chapters 1, 2, 3, 4, 8, 10, 11, 16, 18, 19, 22, and 23. A more extensive elementary survey course can be completed in two quarters (60–80 hours) by excluding just a few chapters, for example, Chapters 9, 12, 20, and 21. Chapters 1 to 9 form an excellent basis for a (one-quarter) course in linear programming. The material in Chapters 10 to 14 covers topics for another (one-quarter) course in other deterministic models. Finally, the material in Chapters 15 to 23 covers the probabilistic (stochastic) models of operations research suitable for presentation in a (one-quarter) course. In fact, these latter three courses (the material in the entire text) can be viewed as a basic one-year sequence in the techniques of operations research, forming the core of a

Master's degree program. Each course outlined is currently being presented at Stanford University, and this text has been used in the manner suggested.

Again, as in previous editions, we thank our wives, Ann and Helen, for their editorial and typing assistance, as well as their encouragement and understanding when we devoted too many evenings and weekends to preparing this fourth edition. As our children, David, John, and Mark Hillier, and Janet, Joanne, Michael, and Diana Lieberman, have come of college age, some have used the text in their own courses, and they (and their friends) have given us more than their share of feedback on the book.

FREDERICK S. HILLIER
GERALD J. LIEBERMAN

Stanford University
January 1986

Acknowledgments

We are deeply indebted to many people for their part in making this revision possible. Those making helpful comments on how to improve the third edition are literally too numerous to mention. However, we would like to acknowledge particularly the advice of Stephen Argyres, Ken Bennett, Iver Bradley, Robert Bulfin, David Butler, Thomas Casstevens, Milton Chen, Richard Cottle, George Dantzig, Cyrus Derman, B. Curtis Eaves, Peter Farquhar, Donald Gross, J. Haddock, J. N. Hool, Donald Iglehart, Henry Jensen, Paul Jensen, William Knight, Judith Liebman, James McFarlane, Bennett Parker, David Ronen, Matthew Rosenshine, Sheldon Ross, Michael Saunders, Don Schneider, Paul Schweitzer, Andrew Shogan, Joel Sobel, David Swanson, Craig Tovey, Richard Turley, Arthur Veinott, Jr., James Wilson, Margaret Wright, and Stanley Zionts. We also thank the dozens of Stanford students who gave us helpful written suggestions at our request.

In addition, we would like to give special thanks to Siegfried Schaible, who devoted several weeks to working personally with us in developing a detailed outline of the material for the nonlinear programming chapter. The writing is ours, but we never could have achieved the present chapter without his expert guidance.

Both Margarida Mello and Scott Schulz provided helpful feedback on both the text and the problems of the fourth edition as they prepared the *Solutions Manual*.

During the last big push, Ann Hillier devoted more than two months to full-time word processing under considerable time pressure—days, nights and weekends—without even complaining about our miscues. Pat Rospendowski also responded with good grace to a series of rush xeroxing and mailing jobs.

We are indebted to the Office of Naval Research and the National Science Foundation for supporting some of the research that led to results included in the chapters on queueing theory and reliability.

Over the past few years, the Holden-Day staff, especially Wallace Shows, Eve Howard, and Ted Riley, have made a special effort to elicit helpful feedback for us. This effort included obtaining many detailed reviews, compiling questionaire results, and arranging for us to talk to a considerable number of thoughtful instructors who shared with us the experiences they had with the third edition. Needless to say, this information was very helpful to us in our preparation of this edition.

In a very real sense then, we feel that this edition represents a joint effort of the operations research/management science community for its own mutual benefit. You have done your part, and now we have done our best to live up to our part of the bargain. Thank you one and all.

PART ONE

Introduction

CHAPTER 1

The Nature of Operations Research

1.1 The Origins of Operations Research

Since the advent of the industrial revolution, the world has seen a remarkable growth in the size and complexity of organizations. The artisans' small shops of an earlier era have evolved into the billion dollar corporations of today. An integral part of this revolutionary change has been a tremendous increase in the division of labor and segmentation of management responsibilities in these organizations. The results have been spectacular. However, along with its blessings, this increasing specialization has created new problems, problems that are still occurring in many organizations. One problem is a tendency for the many components of an organization to grow into relatively autonomous empires with their own goals and value systems, thereby losing sight of how their activities and objectives mesh with those of the overall organization. What is best for one component frequently is detrimental to another, so they may end up working at cross purposes. A related problem is that as the complexity and specialization in an organization increase, it becomes more and more difficult to allocate its available resources to its various activities in a way that is most effective for the organization as a whole. These kinds of problems and the need to find a better way to resolve them provided the environment for the emergence of operations research.

The roots of operations research can be traced back many decades, when early attempts were made to use a scientific approach in the management of organizations. However, the beginning of the activity called *operations research* has generally been attributed to the military services early in World War II. Because of the war effort, there was an urgent need to allocate scarce resources to the various military operations and to the activities within each operation in an effective manner. Therefore the British and then the American military management called upon a large number of scientists to apply a scientific approach to dealing with this and other strategic and tactical problems. In effect they were asked to do research on (military) operations. These teams of scientists were the first operations research teams. Their efforts allegedly were instrumental in winning the Air Battle of Britain, the Island Campaign in the Pacific, the Battle of the North Atlantic, and so on.

Spurred on by the apparent success of operations research in the military, industry gradually became interested in this new field. As the industrial boom following the war was running its course, the problems caused by the increasing complexity and specialization in organizations were again coming to the forefront. It was becoming apparent to a growing number of people, including business consultants who had served on or with the operations research teams during the war, that these were basically the same problems that had been faced by the military but in a different context. In this way operations research began to creep into industry, business, and civil government. By 1951, it had already taken hold in Great Britain and was in the process of doing so in the United States. Since then the field has developed very rapidly, as will be described further in Sec. 1.3.

At least two other factors that played a key role in the rapid growth of operations research during this period can be identified. One was the substantial progress that was made early in improving the techniques available to operations research. After the war, many of the scientists who had participated on operations research teams or who had heard about this work were motivated to pursue research relevant to the field; important advancements in the state of the art resulted. A prime example is the simplex method for solving linear programming problems, developed by George Dantzig in 1947. Many of the standard tools of operations research, e.g., linear programming, dynamic programming, queueing theory, and inventory theory, were relatively well developed before the end of the 1950s. In addition to this rapid advancement in the theory of operations research, a second factor that gave great impetus to the growth of the field was the onslaught of the computer revolution. A large amount of computation is usually required to deal most effectively with the complex problems typically considered by operations research. Doing this by hand would often be out of the question. Therefore the development of the electronic digital computers, with their ability to perform arithmetic calculations thousands or even millions of times faster than a human being can, was a tremendous boon to operations research.

1.2 The Nature of Operations Research

What is operations research? One way of trying to answer this question is to give a definition. For example, operations research may be described as a scientific approach to decision making that involves the operations of organizational systems. However, this description, like earlier attempts at a definition, is so general that it is equally applicable to many other fields as well. Therefore, perhaps the best way of grasping the unique nature of operations research is to examine its outstanding characteristics.

As its name implies, operations research involves "research on operations." This says something about both the approach and the area of application of the field. Thus operations research is applied to problems that concern how to conduct and coordinate the operations or activities within an organization. The nature of the organization is essentially immaterial, and, in fact, operations research has been applied extensively in business, industry, the military, civil government and agencies, hospitals, and so forth. Therefore, the breadth of application is unusually wide. The approach of operations research is that of the scientific method. In particular, the process begins by carefully observing and formulating the problem and then constructing a scientific (typically mathematical) model that attempts to abstract the essence of the real problem. It is then hypothesized that this model is a sufficiently precise representation of the essential features of the situation, so that the conclusions (solutions) obtained from the model are also valid for the real problem. This hypothesis is then modified and verified by suitable experimentation. Thus in a certain sense operations research involves creative scientific research into the fundamental properties of operations. However, there is more to it than this. Specifically, operations research also is concerned with the practical management of the organization. Therefore, to be successful it must also provide positive, understandable conclusions to the decision maker(s) when they are needed.

Still another characteristic of operations research is its broad viewpoint. As implied in the preceding section, operations research adopts an organizational point of view. Thus it attempts to resolve the conflicts of interest among the components of the organization in a way that is best for the organization as a whole. This does not imply that the study of each problem must give explicit consideration to all aspects of the organization; rather, the objectives being sought must be consistent with those of the overall organization. An additional characteristic that was mentioned in passing is that operations research attempts to find the best or optimal solution to the problem under consideration. Rather than being content with merely improving the status quo, the goal is to identify the best possible course of action. Although it must be interpreted carefully, this "search for optimality" is a very important theme in operations research.

All these characteristics lead quite naturally to still another one. It is evident that no single individual should be expected to be an expert on all the many aspects of operations research work or the problems typically considered; this would require a group of individuals having diverse backgrounds and skills. Therefore, when undertaking a full-fledged operations research study of a new problem, it is usually necessary to use a team approach. Such an operations research team typically needs to include individuals who collectively are highly trained in mathematics, statistics and probability theory, economics, business administration, electronic computing, engineering and the physical sciences, the behavioral sciences, and the special techniques of operations research. The team also needs to have the necessary experience and variety of skills to give appropriate consideration to the many ramifications of the problem throughout the organization and to execute effectively all the diverse phases of the operations research study.

In summary, operations research is concerned with optimal decision making in, and modeling of, deterministic and probabilistic systems that originate from real life. These applications, which occur in government, business, engineering, economics, and the natural and social sciences, are largely characterized by the need to allocate limited resources. In these situations, considerable insight can be obtained from scientific analysis such as that provided by operations research. The contribution from the operations research approach stems primarily from:

1. Structuring the real life situation into a mathematical model, abstracting the essential elements so that a solution relevant to the decision maker's objectives can be sought. This involves looking at the problem in the context of the entire system.
2. Exploring the structure of such solutions and developing systematic procedures for obtaining them.
3. Developing a solution, including the mathematical theory, if necessary, that yields an optimal value of the system measure of desirability (or possibly comparing alternative courses of action by evaluating their measure of desirability).

1.3 The Impact of Operations Research

Operations research has had an increasingly great impact on the management of organizations in recent years. Both the number and the variety of its applications continue to grow rapidly, and no slowdown is in sight. In fact, with the exception of the advent of the electronic computer, the extent of this impact seems to be unrivaled by that of any other recent development.

After their success with operations research during World War II, the British and American military services continued to have active operations research groups, often at different levels of command. As a result, there now exists a large number of people called "military operations researchers" who are applying an operations research approach to problems of national defense. For example, they engage in tactical planning for requirements and use of weapon systems as well as consider the larger problems of the allocation and integration of effort. Some of their techniques involve quite sophisticated ideas in political science, mathematics, economics, probability theory, and statistics.

Operations research is also being used widely in other types of organizations, including business and industry. Almost all the dozen or so largest corporations in the world, and a sizable proportion of the small industrial organizations, have well-established operations research groups. Many industries, including aircraft and missile, automobile, communication, computer, electric power, electronics, food, metallurgy, mining, paper, petroleum, and transportation, have made widespread use of operations research. Financial institutions, governmental agencies, and hospitals are rapidly increasing their use of operations research.

To be more specific, consider some of the problems that have been solved by particular techniques of operations research. Linear programming has been used successfully in the solution of problems concerned with assignment of personnel, blending of materials, distribution and transportation, and investment portfolios. Dynamic programming has been applied successfully to such areas as planning advertising expenditures, distributing sales effort, and production scheduling. Queueing theory has had application in solving problems concerned with traffic congestion, servicing machines subject to breakdown, determining the level of a service force, air traffic scheduling, design of dams, production scheduling, and hospital operation. Other techniques of operations research, such as inventory theory, game theory, and simulation, also have been successfully applied to a variety of contexts.

In 1972, Turban[1] reported on a survey of operations research activities that provided a snapshot of activities in 1969. Mail questionnaires were sent to the Directors of Operations Research/Management Science of 475 companies. These companies were selected from *Fortune's* list of the top 500, using the 300 largest industrial corporations, 50 industrial corporations drawn from the companies ranking between 300 and 500, and the 25 largest companies in each of the service categories, banks, utilities, merchandising, life insurance, and transportation. There were 107 questionnaires returned; of these, 47 (or nearly one-half) reported having a special department at their headquarters that is mainly engaged in O.R. activities. In addition, 13 companies indicated that they intended to establish such a department in the near future. Furthermore, the growth rates are impressive in that approximately 4 percent of these companies had departments established prior to 1950, 15 percent between 1951 and 1959, 50 percent between 1960 and 1965, and 30 percent after 1966. Another rather interesting finding is that almost all the departments reported to the company president, vice-president, or controller. The survey also indicated how widely the techniques of operations research had been applied to current projects; the results are shown in Table 1.1.

It is evident that statistical analysis, simulation, and linear programming were currently the most widely used techniques. Furthermore, the survey revealed that the computer was used in the majority of the projects reported.

[1] Turban, E.: "A Sample Survey of Operations Research Activities at the Corporate Level," *Operations Research*, **20**: 708–721, 1972.

Table 1.1 **Use of operations research in current activities (Turban Survey)**

Techniques	No. of projects	Frequency of use (%)
Statistical analysis[†]	63	29
Simulation	54	25
Linear programming	41	19
Inventory theory	13	6
PERT/CPM	13	6
Dynamic programming	9	4
Nonlinear programming	7	3
Queueing	2	1
Heuristic programming	2	1
Miscellaneous	13	6

[†] Includes probability theory, regression analysis, exponential smoothing, statistical sampling, and tests of hypotheses.

In 1977, Ledbetter and Cox[1] reported on a survey of *Fortune's* 500 firms (1975 listing) concerning utilization of operations research techniques in their firms. There were 176 respondents. They concluded that regression analysis, linear programming, and simulation were the most popular, thereby reinforcing the results of the Turban survey. Ledbetter and Cox asked about the comparative use of seven O.R. techniques, and the companies were asked to indicate the frequency of use on a five-point scale. The results are shown in Table 1.2.

Table 1.2 **Relative use of operations research techniques (Ledbetter and Cox Survey)**

Techniques	Number of respondents	Degree of use (%)[†] Never 1	2	3	4	Very Frequently 5	Mean
Regression analysis	74	9.5	2.7	17.6	21.6	48.6	3.97
Linear programming	78	15.4	14.1	21.8	16.7	32.0	3.36
Simulation (in production)	70	11.4	15.7	25.7	24.3	22.9	3.31
Network models	69	39.1	29.0	15.9	10.1	5.8	2.14
Queueing theory	71	36.6	39.4	16.9	5.6	1.4	1.96
Dynamic programming	69	53.6	36.2	7.2	0.0	2.9	1.62
Game theory	67	59.7	25.4	8.9	6.0	0.0	1.61

[†] Percentages shown here are based on the number of responses to each technique.

[1] Ledbetter, W. N. and Cox, J. F.: "Are OR Techniques Being Used," *Industrial Engineering*, pp. 19–21, February 1977.

Table 1.3 **Quality of results reported by firms employing mathematical programming (Fabozzi and Valente Survey)**

Results	Linear Programming		Nonlinear Programming		Dynamic Programming	
	No.	%	No.	%	No.	%
Good	102	76%	38	57%	27	53%
Fair	21	16	19	28	15	29
Poor	6	3	6	9	3	6
Uncertain	7	5	4	6	6	12
Total	133	100%	67	100%	51	100%

In 1976, Fabozzi and Valente[1] reported on the results of a questionnaire mailed to 1,000 firms in the United States in November 1974 concerning the use of mathematical programming (linear, nonlinear, and dynamic). By February 1975, 184 responses had been received. The researchers found that the most important area of application of mathematical programming was production management (determination of product mix, allocation of resources, plant and machine scheduling, and work scheduling). The next largest area of application was financial and investment planning (capital budgeting, cash flow analysis, portfolio management for the employee pension fund, cash management, and merger and acquisitions analysis). The quality of results reported by these firms is given in Table 1.3.

Because of the great impact of operations research, professional societies devoted to this field and related activities have been founded in a number of countries throughout the world. In the United States, the Operations Research Society of America (ORSA), established in 1952, and The Institute of Management Sciences (TIMS), founded in 1953, each has close to 7,000 members. ORSA publishes the journal *Operations Research* and TIMS *Management Science*. The two societies also jointly publish *Mathematics of Operations Research* and *Interfaces*. These four journals contain well over 3,000 pages per year reporting new research and applications in the field. In addition, there are many other similar journals published in such countries as the United States, England, France, India, Japan, Canada, and West Germany. Indeed, there are 29 member countries (including the United States) in the International Federation of Operational Research Societies (IFORS), with each country having a national operations research society.

Operations research also has had considerable impact in the colleges and universities. Today most of the major American universities offer courses in this field, and many offer advanced degrees that are either in or with specialization in

[1] Fabozzi, F. J. and Valente, J.: "Mathematical Programming in American Companies: A Sample Survey," *Interfaces*, **7**(1): 93–98, November 1976.

operations research. As a result, there are now thousands of students taking at least one course in operations research each year. Much of the basic research in the field is also being done in the universities.

1.4 Training for a Career in Operations Research

Because of the great growth of operations research, career opportunities in this field appear to be outstanding. The demand for trained people continues to far exceed the supply, and both attractive starting positions and rapid advancement are readily available. Because of the nature of their work, operations research groups tend to have a prominent staff position, with access to higher level management in the organization. The problems they work on tend to be important, challenging, and interesting. Therefore, any individual with a mathematics and science orientation who is also interested in the practical management of organizations is likely to find a career in operations research very rewarding.

Three complementary types of academic training are particularly relevant for a career in operations research. The first is a basic training in the fundamentals upon which operations research is based. This includes the basic methodology of mathematics and science as well as such topics as linear algebra and matrix theory, probability theory, statistical inference, stochastic processes, computer science, microeconomics, accounting and business administration, organization theory, and the behavioral sciences.

A second important type of training is in operations research per se, including special techniques of the field such as linear and nonlinear programming, dynamic programming, inventory theory, network flow theory, queueing models, reliability, game theory, and simulation. It should also include an introduction to the methodology of operations research, where the various techniques and their role in an operations research study involving specific problem areas would be placed in perspective. Often courses covering certain of these topics are offered in more than one department within a university, including Departments of Business, Industrial Engineering, Mathematics, Statistics, Computer Science, Economics, and Electrical Engineering. This is a natural reflection of the broad scope of application of the field. Since it does spread across traditional disciplinary lines, separate programs or departments in operations research also are being established in some universities.

Finally, it is also good to have specialized training in some field other than operations research, for example, mathematics, statistics, industrial engineering, business, or economics. This additional training provides one with an area of special competence for applying operations research, and it should make that person a more valuable member of an operations research team.

The early operations researchers were people whose primary training and work had been in some traditional field, such as physics, chemistry, mathematics, engineering, or economics. They tended to have little or no formal education in

Table 1.4 **Educational background of operations research personnel (Turban Survey)**

Major field of study	Percentage of total at degree level			
	Bachelors	Masters	Doctorate	All degree levels
Operations research & management science	3	24	32	12
Mathematics & statistics	26	16	21	22
Business administration	20	27	2	22
Engineering	34	17	29	28
Other	17	16	16	16
Percentage of total	27	53	20	

operations research per se. However, as the body of special knowledge has expanded, it has become increasingly more difficult to enter the field without considerable prior education in this area. As a result, although it is still common for new operations researchers to have their college degree(s) in a traditional field, they generally have specialized too in operations research as part of their academic program. The traditional fields that have most commonly served as a vehicle into operations research are indicated in Table 1.4, which is based on the 1972 survey by Turban described in the preceding section. However, present trends indicate that many operations researchers in the future will have both an undergraduate degree in a traditional field and a graduate degree in operations research itself.

Finally, in 1982[1] a survey of TIMS membership provided a profile of its membership, including information on educational training, job activity, and compensation for professionals in industry, government, universities, and consulting. This report reinforced the point that, as the profession has matured, fewer people with formal training in non–operations research fields are entering the profession than occurred in the previous decades.

1.5 The Road Ahead

As an introduction to operations research, this book is designed to acquaint students with the formulation, solution, and implementation of operations research models for analyzing complex systems problems in industry or government. Part 1 introduces the reader to the field of operations research. It provides an overview of the operations research modeling approach and describes the major phases of a typical operations research study. Part 2 presents the topic of linear programming, a prominent area of operations research

[1] Hall, J. R., Jr.: "Career Paths and Compensation in Management Science: Results of a TIMS Membership Survey," *Interfaces*, **14**(3): 15–23, May–June 1984.

concerned largely with how to allocate limited resources among the various activities of an organization. Part 3 deals with the broad topic of mathematical programming, including integer and nonlinear programming. Part 4 considers a number of probabilistic models that take into account the uncertainty associated with future events in order to analyze certain important problems.

Much of the material presented in Parts 2, 3, and 4 can be described in terms of typical examples of situations that are encountered in practice. Synopses of several such examples are presented here with detailed solutions given in successive chapters.

The technique of *linear programming* is illustrated by a company that operates a reclamation center that collects several types of solid waste materials and then treats them so they can be amalgamated into a saleable product. Different grades of this product can be made, depending upon the mix of the materials used. Although there is some flexibility in the mix for each grade, quality standards do specify a minimum or maximum percentage (by weight) of certain materials allowed in that product grade. Data are available on the cost of amalgamation and the selling price for each grade. The reclamation center collects its solid waste materials from some regular sources and so is normally able to maintain a steady production rate for treating these materials. Furthermore, the quantities available for collection and treatment each week, as well as the cost of treatment, for each type of material are known. Using the given information, the company is to determine just how much of each product grade to produce *and* the exact mix of materials to be used for each grade so as to maximize their total weekly profit (total sales income minus the total costs of *both* amalgamation and treatment).

Another example of linear programming concerns a steel producer who is facing an *air pollution problem* caused by pollutants emanating from the manufacturing plant. The three main types of pollutants in the airshed are particulate matter, sulfur oxides, and hydrocarbons. New standards require that the company reduce its annual emission of these pollutants. The steel works has two primary sources of pollution, namely, the blast furnaces for making pig iron and the open-hearth furnaces for changing iron into steel. In both cases the engineers have decided that the most effective types of abatement methods are (1) increasing the height of the smoke stacks, (2) using filter devices (including gas traps) in the smoke stacks, and (3) including cleaner high-grade materials among the fuels for the furnaces. All these methods have known technological limits on how much emission they can eliminate. Fortunately, the methods can be used at any fraction of their abatement capacities. A cost analysis results in estimates of the total annual cost that is incurred by each abatement method when used by blast and open-hearth furnaces (cost of less-than-full-capacity use of a method is essentially proportional to its fractional capacity). Using the aforementioned data, the optimal plan (minimum cost) for pollution abatement is to be determined. This plan would consist of specifying which types of abatement method would be used and at what fractions of their abatement capacities for (1) blast furnaces and (2) open-hearth furnaces.

One of the important special types of linear programming problems is called the *transportation problem*; a typical example deals with a company producing canned peas. The peas are prepared at several distantly located canneries and then shipped by truck to distributing warehouses throughout the western United States. Because the shipping costs are a major expense, management is initiating a study to reduce them as much as possible. For the upcoming season, an estimate has been made of what the output will be from each cannery, and each warehouse has been allocated a certain amount from the total supply of peas. This information (in units of truckloads), along with the shipping cost per truckload for each cannery–warehouse combination, is given. Using the data, the optimal plan for assigning these shipments to the various cannery–warehouse combinations that minimize total shipping costs is to be determined.

In addition to linear programming, there are a number of related mathematical programming techniques for dealing with similar kinds of problems. One of these is *dynamic programming*, which is concerned with making a sequence of interrelated decisions. It is illustrated by a job shop whose workload is subject to considerable seasonal fluctuation. However, machine operators are difficult to hire and costly to train, so the manager is reluctant to lay off workers during the slack seasons. The manager is likewise reluctant to maintain a peak payroll when it is not required. Furthermore, the manager is definitely opposed to overtime work on a regular basis. Because all work is done to custom orders, it is not possible to build up inventories during slack seasons. Therefore, the manager is in a dilemma as to what the policy should be regarding employment levels. Estimates are available for the manpower requirements during the four seasons of the year for the foreseeable future. Employment is not permitted to fall below these levels. Any employment above these levels is wasted. The salaries, hiring costs, and firing costs are known. Assuming that fractional levels of employment are possible because of a few part-time employees, the employment in each season that minimizes the total cost is to be determined.

Among the probabilistic models considered in Part four are some falling into the area of queueing (waiting line) theory. A *queueing theory* model is illustrated by a hospital emergency room. The emergency room provides quick medical care for emergency cases that are brought to the hospital by ambulance or private automobile. At any hour there is always one doctor on duty in the emergency room. However, because of a growing tendency for emergency cases to use these facilities rather than go to a private physician, the hospital has been experiencing a continuing increase in the number of emergency room visits each year. As a result, when patients arrive during peak usage hours (the early evening), they have to wait until it is their turn to be treated by the doctor. Therefore, a proposal has been made that a second doctor should be assigned to the emergency room during these hours so that two emergency cases can be treated simultaneously. By recognizing that the emergency room is a queueing system, several alternative queueing theory models can be applied to predict the waiting characteristics of the system with one doctor and with two doctors. These models will aid the hospital in its evaluation of the proposal to add a second physician.

A similar queueing example in a very different context concerns determining the *optimal number of repairmen* for a group of machines. A company uses 10 identical machines in its production facility. However, because these machines break down and require repair frequently, the company has only enough operators to operate *eight* machines at a time, so two machines are available on a standby basis for use while other machines are down. Thus eight machines are always operating whenever no more than two machines are waiting to be repaired, but the number of operating machines is reduced by one for each additional machine waiting to be repaired. The probability distribution of the time until any given operating machine breaks down and the probability distribution of the time required to repair a machine are known from past history. Up until now the company has had just *one* repairman to repair these machines. However, this has frequently resulted in reduced productivity by having *fewer than eight* operating machines. Therefore, consideration is being given to hiring a *second* repairman so that *two* machines can be repaired simultaneously. Thus the queueing system to be studied has the repairmen as its servers and the machines requiring repair as its customers, where the problem is to choose between having *one* or *two* servers (or possibly more). Given the cost of each repairman and the cost of inoperable machines, the optimal number of repairmen is to be determined.

Inventory theory is illustrated by a television manufacturing company that produces its own speakers, which are used in the production of its television sets. The television sets are assembled on a continuous production line at a known monthly rate. The speakers are produced in batches because they do not warrant setting up a continuous production line and because relatively large quantities can be produced in a short time. The company is interested in determining when and how many to produce. Several costs must be considered. (1) Each time a batch is produced, a setup cost is incurred. This cost includes the cost of "tooling up," administrative costs, record keeping, and so on. (2) The production of speakers in large batch sizes leads to a large inventory, resulting in a monthly cost for keeping a speaker in stock. This cost includes the cost of capital tied up, storage space, insurance, taxes, protection, and so forth. (3) A cost of producing a single speaker (excluding the setup cost) is incurred. (4) Company policy prohibits deliberately planning for shortages of any of its components. However, a shortage of speakers occasionally occurs, resulting in a monthly cost for each speaker unavailable when required. This cost includes the cost of installing speakers after the television set is fully assembled, storage space, delayed revenue, record keeping, and so on. Given data on these costs, the optimal batch size (and period between production) is to be determined.

The use of *Markovian decision processes* can be described in terms of a production process that contains a machine that deteriorates rapidly in both quality and output under heavy usage, so that it is inspected at the end of each day. Immediately after inspection, the condition of the machine is noted and classified into one of four possible states: 0 (as good as new), 1 (operable—minor deterioration), 2 (operable—major deterioration), and 3 (inoperable—output of unacceptable quality). The state of the system is assumed to evolve according to some known probabilistic "laws of motion." At the end of each day, one of three decisions can be made: (1) leave the machine alone, (2) overhaul the machine, which results in leaving it operable with minor deterioration, and (3) replace it, which results in a new machine. As a result of the state of the system found at the end of the day and the decision taken, a cost is incurred. Given these costs and a description of the probabilistic "laws of motion," an optimal maintenance policy is to be found.

■CHAPTER 2

Overview of the Operations Research Modeling Approach

The bulk of this book is devoted to the mathematical methods of operations research. This is quite appropriate because these quantitative techniques form the main part of what is known about operations research. However, it does not imply that practical operations research studies are primarily mathematical exercises. As a matter of fact, the mathematical analysis often represents only a relatively small part of the total effort required. The purpose of this chapter is to place things into better perspective by describing all the major phases of a typical operations research study.

One way of summarizing the usual phases of an operations research study is the following:[1]

1. Formulating the problem.
2. Constructing a mathematical model to represent the system under study.
3. Deriving a solution from the model.
4. Testing the model and the solution derived from it.
5. Establishing controls over the solution.
6. Putting the solution to work: implementation.

Each of these phases will be discussed in turn in the following sections.

[1] Ackoff, Russell L.: "The Development of Operations Research as a Science," *Operations Research*, **4**:265f, 1956.

2.1 Formulating the Problem

In contrast to textbook examples, most practical problems are initially communicated to an operations research team in a vague, imprecise way. Therefore, the first order of business is to study the relevant system and develop a well-defined statement of the problem to be considered. This includes determining such things as the appropriate objectives, the constraints on what can be done, interrelationships between the area to be studied and other areas of the organization, the possible alternative courses of action, time limits for making a decision, and so on. This process of problem formulation is a crucial one because it greatly affects how relevant the conclusions of the study will be. It is difficult to extract a "right" answer from the "wrong" problem! Consequently, this phase should be executed with considerable care, and the initial formulation should be continually reexamined in the light of new insights obtained during the later phases.

The first thing to recognize is that an operations research team is normally working in an *advisory capacity*. The team members are not just given a problem and told to solve it however they see fit. Instead, they are advising management (often one key decision maker). The team performs a detailed technical analysis of the problem and then presents its recommendations to management. Frequently, the report to management will identify a number of alternatives that are particularly attractive under different assumptions or over a different range of values of some policy parameter that can be evaluated only by management (e.g., the tradeoff between *cost* and *benefits*). Management evaluates the study and its recommendations, takes into account a variety of intangible factors, and makes the final decision based on its best judgment. Consequently, it is vital for the operations research team to get on the same wavelength as management, including identifying the "right" problem from management's viewpoint, and to build the support of management for the course that the study is taking.

Determining the *appropriate objectives* is a very important aspect of problem formulation. To do this, it is necessary first to identify the member (or members) of management who actually will be making the decisions concerning the system under study and then to probe into this individual's thinking regarding the pertinent objectives. (Involving the decision maker from the outset also helps to build his or her support for the implementation of the study.) After the decision maker's objectives have been elicited, they should be analyzed and edited to identify the ultimate objectives that encompass the other objectives, to determine the relative importance of these ultimate objectives, and to state them precisely in a way that does not eliminate worthwhile goals and alternatives.

By its nature, operations research is concerned with the welfare of the *entire organization* rather than that of only certain of its components. An operations research study seeks solutions that are optimal for the overall organization rather than suboptimal solutions that are best for only one component. Therefore, the objectives that are formulated should ideally be those of the entire organization. However, this is not always convenient to do. Many problems primarily concern only a portion of the organization, so the analysis would become unwieldy if the stated objectives were too general and if explicit consideration were given to all side effects on the rest of the organization. Granted that operations research takes the viewpoint of the overall organization, this does not imply that each problem should be broadened into a study of the entire organization. Instead, the objectives used in the study should be as specific as they can be while still encompassing the main goals of the decision maker and maintaining a reasonable degree of consistency with the higher level objectives of the organization. Side effects on other segments of the organization must then be considered only to the extent that there are questions of consistency with these higher level objectives.

For profit-making organizations, one possible approach to circumventing the problem of suboptimization is to use *long-run profit maximization* as the sole objective. The adjective *long-run* indicates that this objective provides the flexibility to consider activities that do not translate into profits *immediately* (e.g., research and development projects) but need to do so *eventually* in order to be worthwhile. At first glance, this approach appears to have considerable merit. In particular, this objective is specific enough to be used conveniently, and yet it seems to be broad enough to encompass the basic goal of profit-making organizations. In fact, some people believe that all other legitimate objectives can be translated into this one. However, this is an oversimplification and considerable caution is required! A number of studies of American corporations have found that the goal of *satisfactory profits*, combined with other objectives, is preferred over profit maximization. (In fact, inadequate consideration of long-run profits sometimes is cited as a major reason why American industry may be losing its competitive edge over that of other leading countries.) In particular, typical objectives might be to maintain stable profits, increase (or maintain) one's share of the market, provide for product diversification, maintain stable prices, improve worker morale, maintain family control of the business, and increase company prestige. These objectives might be compatible with long-run profit maximization, but the relationship is sufficiently obscure that it may not be convenient to incorporate them into this one objective. Furthermore, there are additional considerations involving social responsibilities that are distinct from the profit motive. The five parties affected by a business firm located in a single country are: (1) the *owners* (stockholders), who desire profits (dividends, stock appreciation, and so on); (2) the *employees*, who desire steady employment at reasonable wages; (3) the *customers*, who desire a reliable product at a reasonable price; (4) the *vendors*, who desire integrity and a reasonable selling price for their goods; and (5) the *government* and, hence, the *nation*, which desires payment of fair taxes and consideration of the national interest. All five parties make essential contributions to the firm, and the firm should not be viewed as the exclusive servant of any one party for the exploitation of others. By the same token, international corporations acquire additional obligations to follow socially responsible practices. Therefore, although granting that management's prime responsibility is to make profits (which ultimately benefits all five parties), its broader social responsibilities also must be recognized.

2.2 Constructing a Mathematical Model

After formulating the decision maker's problem, the next phase is to reformulate this problem into a form that is convenient for analysis. The conventional operations research approach for doing this is to construct a mathematical model that represents the essence of the problem. Before discussing how to formulate such a model, let us first explore the nature of models in general and of mathematical models in particular.

Models, or idealized representations, are an integral part of everyday life. Common examples include model airplanes, portraits, globes, and so on. Similarly, models play an important role in science and business, as illustrated by models of the atom, models of genetic structure, mathematical equations describing physical laws of motion or chemical reactions, graphs, organization charts, and industrial accounting systems. Such models are invaluable for abstracting the essence of the subject of inquiry, showing interrelationships, and facilitating analysis.

Mathematical models are also idealized representations, but they are expressed in terms of mathematical symbols and expressions. Such laws of physics as $F = ma$ and $E = mc^2$ are familiar examples. Similarly, the mathematical model of a business problem is the system of equations and related mathematical expressions that describe the essence of the problem. Thus, if there are n related quantifiable decisions to be made, they are represented as *decision variables* (say, $x_1, x_2, \ldots, x_n$) whose respective values are to be determined. The composite measure of effectiveness (e.g., profit) is then expressed as a mathematical function of these decision variables (e.g., $P = 3x_1 + 2x_2 + \cdots + 5x_n$). This function is called the *objective function*. Any restrictions on the values that can be assigned to these decision variables are also expressed mathematically, typically by means of inequalities or equations (e.g., $x_1 + 3x_1 x_2 + 2x_2 \leq 10$). Such mathematical expressions for the restrictions often are called *constraints*. The constants (coefficients or right-hand sides) in the constraints and the objective function are called the *input parameters* (or the *parameters of the model*). The mathematical model might then say that the problem is to choose the values of the decision variables so as to maximize the objective function, subject to the specified constraints. Such a model, and minor variations of it, typify the models used in operations research.

You will see numerous examples of mathematical models throughout the remainder of this book. One particularly important type that is studied in Part 2 is the *linear programming model*, where the mathematical functions appearing in both the objective function and the constraints are all linear functions. In the next chapter, specific linear programming models are constructed to fit such diverse problems as determining (1) the mix of products that maximizes profit, (2) the allocation of acreage to crops that maximizes total net return, and (3) the combination of pollution-abatement methods that achieves air quality standards at minimum cost.

Mathematical models have many advantages over a verbal description of the problem. One obvious advantage is that a mathematical model describes a problem much more concisely. This tends to make the overall structure of the problem more comprehensible, and it helps to reveal important cause-and-effect relationships. In this way, it indicates more clearly what additional data are relevant to the analysis. It also facilitates dealing with the problem in its entirety and considering all its interrelationships simultaneously. Finally, a mathematical model forms a bridge to the use of high-powered mathematical techniques and computers to analyze the problem. Indeed, many of the components of the model may entail the use of packaged software.

On the other hand, there are pitfalls to be avoided when using mathematical models. Such a model is necessarily an abstract idealization of the problem, so approximations and simplifying assumptions generally are required if the model is to be *tractable* (capable of being solved). Therefore, care must be taken to ensure that the model remains a valid representation of the problem. The proper criterion for judging the validity of a model is whether or not the model predicts the relative effects of the alternative courses of action with sufficient accuracy to permit a sound decision. Consequently, it is not necessary to include unimportant details or factors that have approximately the same effect for all the alternative courses of action considered. It is not even necessary that the absolute magnitude of the measure of effectiveness be approximately correct for the various alternatives, provided that their relative values (i.e., the differences between their values) are sufficiently precise. Thus all that is required is that there be a high *correlation* between the prediction by the model and what would actually happen in the real world. To ascertain whether this requirement is satisfied or not, it is important to do considerable *testing* and consequent modifying of the model, which will be the subject of Sec. 2.4. Although this testing phase is placed later in the book, much of this *model validation* work actually is conducted during the model building phase of the study to help guide the construction of the mathematical model.

When developing the model, begin with a very simple version and then move in evolutionary fashion toward more elaborate models that more nearly reflect the complexity of the real problem. This process of *model enrichment* continues only as long as the model remains tractable. The basic tradeoff under constant consideration is between the *precision* and the *tractability* of the model. (See Selected Reference 6 for a detailed description of this process.)

A crucial step in formulating the mathematical model is constructing the objective function. This requires developing a quantitative measure of effectiveness relative to each objective. If more than one objective has been formulated for the study, it is then necessary to transform and combine the respective measures into a composite measure of effectiveness. This composite measure would sometimes need to be something tangible (e.g., profit) corresponding to a higher goal of the organization, or it would sometimes need to be abstract (e.g., "utility"). In the latter case, the task of developing this measure tends to be a complex one requiring a careful comparison of the objectives and their relative importance. After developing the composite measure of effectiveness, the objective function is then obtained by expressing this measure as a mathematical function of the decision variables. Alternatively, there also are methods for explicitly considering multiple objectives simultaneously, and one of these (goal programming) is discussed in Chap. 8.

2.3 Deriving a Solution

After formulating a mathematical model for the problem under consideration, the next phase in an operations research study is to derive a solution from this model. You might think that this must be the major part of the study, but actually it is not in most cases. Sometimes, in fact, it is a relatively simple step, in which one of the standard *algorithms* (iterative solution procedures) of operations research is applied on a computer by using one of a number of readily available software packages. For experienced operations research practitioners, finding a solution is the "fun part," whereas the real work comes in the preceding and following steps, including the post-optimality analysis discussed later in this section.

Since much of this book is devoted to the subject of how to obtain solutions for various important types of mathematical models, little needs to be said about it here. However, we do need to discuss the nature of such solutions.

A common theme in operations research is the search for an optimal, or best, solution. Indeed, many procedures have been developed, and are presented in this book, for finding such solutions for certain kinds of problems. However, it needs to be recognized that these solutions are optimal only with respect to the model being used. Since the model necessarily is an idealized rather than an exact representation of the real problem, there cannot be any utopian guarantee that the optimal solution for the model will prove to be the best possible solution that could have been implemented for the real problem. With the many imponderables and uncertainties associated with most real problems, this is only to be expected. However, if the model is well formulated and tested, the resulting solution should tend to be a good approximation to the ideal course of action for the real problem. Therefore, rather than be deluded into demanding the impossible, the test of the practical success of an operations research study should be whether it provides a better guide for action than can be obtained by other means.

The eminent management scientist and Nobel Laureate in Economics, Herbert Simon, has introduced the concept that the goal of an operations research study should be to "satisfice" rather than optimize. In other words, the appropriate goal is to find a good answer, one that the decision maker considers a satisfactory guide for action in a reasonable period of time, rather than to search for an optimal solution. Or to put this in another way that reconciles the two viewpoints, the goal should be to conduct the study in an optimal manner, regardless of whether this involves finding an optimal solution to the model or not. Thus, in addition to considering the composite measure of effectiveness in the model, one should also consider the cost of the study and the disadvantages of delaying its completion, and then attempt to maximize the net benefits resulting from the study. In recognition of this concept, operations research teams occasionally use only heuristic procedures (i.e., intuitively designed procedures that do not guarantee an optimal solution) to find a good suboptimal solution. This is most often the case when the time or cost required to find an optimal solution for an adequate model of the problem would be very large.

The discussion thus far has implied that an operations research study seeks to find only *one* solution, which may or may not be required to be optimal. In fact, this usually is not the case. An optimal solution for the original model may be far from ideal for the real problem. Therefore, *post-optimality analysis* is a very important part of most operations research studies. (Post-optimality analysis in the context of linear programming is the subject of Sec. 4.7.) This involves conducting *sensitivity analysis* to determine which input parameters are most critical in determining the solution, and therefore require more careful estimation, as well as to seek a solution that remains a particularly good one over the entire range of likely values of these critical parameters. (Chap. 6 describes sensitivity analysis for linear programming.) In conjunction with the study phase discussed in the next section (testing the model and the solution), post-optimality analysis also involves obtaining a sequence of solutions that comprises a series of improving approximations to the ideal course of action. Thus the apparent weaknesses in the initial solution are used to suggest improvements in the model, its input data, and perhaps the solution procedure. A new solution is then obtained, and the cycle is repeated. This process continues until the improvements in the succeeding solutions become too small to warrant continuation. Even then, a number of alternative solutions (perhaps solutions that are optimal for one of several plausible versions of the model and its input data) may be presented to management for the final selection. As suggested in Sec. 2.1, this presentation of alternative solutions would normally be done whenever the final choice among these alternatives should be based on considerations that are best left to the judgment of management.

Ways in which the model and its solution are evaluated and improved will be discussed in the next section.

2.4 Testing the Model and the Solution

One of the first lessons of operations research is that it is generally not sufficient to rely solely on one's intuition. This caution applies not only in obtaining a solution to a problem but also in evaluating the model that has been formulated to represent this problem. As indicated in Sec. 2.2, the proper criterion for judging the validity of a model is whether or not it predicts the *relative effects* of the alternative courses of action with sufficient accuracy to permit a sound decision. No matter how plausible the model may appear to be, it should not be accepted on faith that this condition is satisfied. Given the difficulty of communicating and understanding all the aspects and subtleties of a complex operational problem, there is a distinct possibility that the operations research team either has not been given all the true facts of the situation or has not interpreted them properly. For example, an important factor or interrelationship may not have been incorporated into the model or perhaps certain input parameters have not been estimated accurately.

Before undertaking more elaborate tests, it is good to begin by checking for obvious errors or oversights in the model. Reexamining the formulation of the problem and comparing it with the model may help to reveal any such mistakes. Another useful check is to make sure that all the mathematical expressions are *dimensionally consistent* in the units they use. Additional insight into the validity of the model can sometimes be obtained by varying the input parameters and/or the decision variables and checking to see whether the output from the model behaves in a plausible manner. This is often especially revealing when the parameters or variables are assigned extreme values near their maxima or minima. Finally, either the operations research team or management may detect shortcomings in the solution yielded by the model that will suggest particular omissions or errors in the model.

A more systematic approach to testing the model is to use a retrospective test. When it is applicable, this test involves using historical data to reconstruct the past and then determining how well the model and the resulting solution would have performed if it had been used. Comparing the effectiveness of this hypothetical performance with what actually happened then indicates whether using this model tends to yield a significant improvement over current practice. It may also indicate areas where the model has shortcomings and requires modifications. Furthermore, by using alternative solutions from the model and determining their hypothetical historical performances, considerable evidence can be gathered regarding how well the model predicts the relative effects of alternative courses of actions. On the other hand, a disadvantage of retrospective testing is that it uses the same data that guided the formulation of the model. The crucial question is whether or not the past is truly representative of the future. If it is not, then the model might perform quite differently in the future than it would have in the past.

To circumvent this disadvantage of retrospective testing, it is sometimes useful to continue the status quo temporarily. This provides new data that were not available when the model was constructed. These data are then used in the same ways as those described here to evaluate the model.

If the final solution is used repeatedly, it is important to continue checking the model and the solution after the initial implementation to make sure that they remain valid. The establishment of such controls is the subject of the next section.

2.5 Establishing Control over the Solution

Suppose that after a series of tests and consequent improvements, an acceptable model and solution are developed. Suppose further that this solution is to be used repeatedly. (This solution may, in fact, be a well-documented *system*, containing a model and solution procedure that, when installed and implemented, will be called on at regular intervals to provide a specific numerical solution.) It is evident that this solution remains valid for the real problem only as long as this specific model remains valid. However, conditions are constantly changing in the real world. Therefore, changes might well occur that would invalidate this model; e.g., the values of the input parameters might change significantly. If these values should change, it is vital that the change be detected as soon as possible so that the model, its solution, and the resulting course of action can be modified accordingly.

In addition to maintaining a general surveillance of the situation, it is often worthwhile to establish *systematic procedures* for controlling the solution. To do this, it is necessary to identify the critical input parameters for the model, i.e., those parameters subject to changes that would significantly affect the solution. This identification is done by sensitivity analysis (discussed in Sec. 2.3). Next, a procedure is established for detecting *statistically significant changes* in each of these critical parameters. This procedure can sometimes be established by the process control charts used in statistical quality control. Finally, provision is made for adjusting the solution and consequent course of action whenever such a change is detected.

2.6 Implementation

The last phase of an operations research study is to implement the final solution as approved by the decision maker. This phase is a critical one because it is here, and only here, that the benefits of the study are reaped. Therefore, it is important for the operations research team to participate in launching this phase, both to make sure that the solution is accurately translated into an operating procedure and to rectify any flaws in the solution that are then uncovered.

The success of the implementation phase depends a great deal upon the support of both top management and operating management (or their counterparts in nonbusiness organizations). Consequently, as mentioned in Secs. 2.1 and 2.4, the operations research team should encourage the active participation of management in formulating the problem and evaluating the solution. Obtaining the guidance of management is valuable in its own right for identifying relevant special considerations and thereby avoiding potential pitfalls during these phases. However, making management a party to the study also serves to enlist their active support for its implementation.

The implementation phase involves several steps. First, the operations research team gives operating management a careful explanation of the solution to be adopted and how it relates to operating realities. Next, these two parties share the responsibility for developing the procedures required to put this solution into operation. Operating management then sees that a detailed indoctrination is given to the personnel involved, and the new course of action is initiated. If successful, the model and the solution procedure may be used periodically to provide guidance to management. With this in mind, the operations research team monitors the initial experience with the course of action taken and seeks to identify any modifications that should be made in the future.

2.7 Conclusions

Although the remainder of this book focuses primarily on *constructing* and *solving* mathematical models, we have tried to emphasize in the present chapter that this constitutes only a portion of the overall process involved in conducting a typical operations research study. The other phases described here also are very important to the success of the study. Try to keep in perspective the role of the model and the solution procedure in the overall process as you move through the subsequent chapters.

Many of the phases discussed in this chapter entail the use of *software tools*, including *decision support systems*. Operations research is closely intertwined with the use of mainframe computers and, increasingly, microcomputers.

Upon culminating a study, it is appropriate for the operations research team to document its methodology clearly and accurately enough so that the work is *reproducible*. *Replicability* should be part of the professional ethical code of the operations researcher. This condition is especially crucial when controversial public policy issues are being studied.

In concluding this discussion of the major phases of an operations research study, it should be emphasized that there are many exceptions to the "rules" prescribed in this chapter. By its very nature, operations research requires considerable ingenuity and innovation, so it is impossible to write down any standard procedure that should always be followed by operations research teams. Rather, the preceding description may be viewed as a model that roughly represents how successful operations research studies are conducted.

SELECTED REFERENCES

1. Ackoff, Russell L. and Patrick Rivett: *A Manager's Guide to Operations Research*, Wiley, New York, 1963.
2. Ackoff, Russell L. and Maurice W. Sasieni: *Fundamentals of Operations Research*, Wiley, New York, 1968.
3. Churchman, C. West, Russell L. Ackoff, and E. L. Arnoff: *Introduction to Operations Research*, Wiley, New York, 1957.
4. Huysmans, Jan H. B. M.: *The Implementation of Operations Research*, Wiley, New York, 1970.
5. Miller, David W. and Martin K. Starr: *Executive Decisions and Operations Research*, 2d ed., Prentice-Hall, Englewood Cliffs, N.J., 1969.
6. Morris, William T.: "On the Art of Modeling," *Management Science*, **13**:B707–717, 1967.
7. Williams, H. P.: *Model Building in Mathematical Programming*, 2d ed., Wiley, New York, 1985.

PART TWO

Linear Programming

CHAPTER 3

Introduction to Linear Programming

Many people rank the development of linear programming among the most important scientific advances of the mid-twentieth century, and we must agree with this assessment. Its impact since just 1950 has been extraordinary. Today it is a standard tool that has saved many thousands or millions of dollars for most companies or businesses of even moderate size in the various industrialized countries of the world, and its use in other sectors of society has been spreading rapidly. Dozens of textbooks have been written about the subject, and *published* articles describing important applications now number in the hundreds. In fact, a very major proportion of all scientific computation on computers is devoted to the use of linear programming and closely related techniques.[1]

What is the nature of this remarkable tool, and what kinds of problems does it address? You will gain insight into this as you work through subsequent examples. However, a verbal summary may help provide perspective. Briefly, the most common type of application involves the general problem of allocating *limited resources* among *competing activities* in the best possible (i.e., *optimal*) way. This problem of allocation can arise whenever one must select the level of certain activities that compete for scarce resources necessary to perform those activities. The variety of situations to which this description applies is diverse indeed, ranging from the allocation of production facilities to products to the allocation of national resources to domestic needs, from portfolio selection to the selection

---

[1] This proportion was estimated to be 25 percent in a 1970 IBM study of computer usage.

of shipping patterns, from agricultural planning to the design of radiation therapy, and so on. However, the one common ingredient in each of these situations is the necessity for allocating resources to activities.

Linear programming uses a mathematical model to describe the problem of concern. The adjective *linear* means that all the mathematical functions in this model are required to be *linear functions*. The word *programming* does not refer here to computer programming; rather, it is essentially a synonym for planning. Thus linear programming involves the *planning of activities* to obtain an optimal result, i.e., a result that reaches the specified goal best (according to the mathematical model) among all feasible alternatives.

Although allocating resources to activities is the most common type of application, linear programming has numerous other important applications as well. In fact, *any* problem whose mathematical model fits the very general format for the linear programming model is a linear programming problem. Furthermore, a remarkably efficient solution procedure, called the *simplex method*, is available for solving linear programming problems of even enormous size. These are some of the reasons for the tremendous impact of linear programming in recent decades.

Because of its great importance, we devote this and the next six chapters specifically to linear programming. After this chapter introduces the general features of linear programming, Chaps. 4 and 5 focus on the simplex method. Chap. 6 discusses the further analysis of linear programming problems *after* the simplex method has been initially applied. Chap. 7 considers several *special types* of linear programming problems whose importance warrants individual study. Chap. 8 then concentrates on the formulation of linear programming models. Finally, Chap. 9 presents several widely used extensions of the simplex method.

You also can look forward to seeing applications of linear programming to other areas of operations research in several later chapters.

We begin this chapter by developing a miniature prototype example of a linear programming problem. This example is small enough to be solved graphically in a straightforward way. We then present the general *linear programming model* and its basic assumptions. The chapter concludes with some additional examples of linear programming applications.

3.1 Prototype Example

The Wyndor Glass Co. is a producer of high-quality glass products, including windows and glass doors. It has three plants. Aluminum frames and hardware are made in Plant 1, wood frames are made in Plant 2, and Plant 3 is used to produce the glass and assemble the products.

Because of declining earnings, top management has decided to revamp the product line. Several unprofitable products are being discontinued, and this act will release production capacity to undertake one or both of two potential new products that have been in demand. One of these proposed products (product 1) is an 8-foot glass door with aluminum framing. The other product (product 2) is a large (4×6 foot) double-hung wood-framed window. The Marketing Department has concluded that the company could sell as much of either product as could be produced with the available capacity. However, because both products would be competing for the same production capacity in Plant 3, it is not clear which *mix* between the two products would be most profitable. Therefore, management asked the Operations Research Department to study this question.

After some investigation, the O.R. Department determined (1) the percentage of each plant's production capacity that would be available for these products, (2) the percentages required by each product for each unit produced per minute, and (3) the unit profit for each product. This information is summarized in Table 3.1. Because whatever capacity is used by one product in Plant 3 becomes unavailable for the other, the O.R. Department immediately recognized that this was a linear programming problem of the classic **product mix** type, and it next undertook the formulation and solution of the problem.

FORMULATION AS A LINEAR PROGRAMMING PROBLEM To formulate the mathematical (linear programming) model for this problem, let x_1 and x_2 represent the number of units of product 1 and 2, respectively, produced per minute and let Z be the resulting contribution to profit per minute. Thus x_1 and x_2 are the *decision variables* for the model, and the *objective* is to choose their values so as to *maximize*

$$Z = 3x_1 + 5x_2,$$

subject to the restrictions imposed on their values by the limited plant capacities available. Table 3.1 implies that each unit of product 1 produced per minute would use 1 percent of Plant 1 capacity, whereas only 4 percent is available. This restriction is expressed mathematically by the inequality $x_1 \leq 4$. Similarly, Plant 2 imposes the restriction that $2x_2 \leq 12$. The percentage of Plant 3 capacity consumed by choosing x_1 and x_2 as the new products' production rates would be $3x_1 + 2x_2$. Therefore, the mathematical statement of the Plant 3 restriction is $3x_1 + 2x_2 \leq 18$. Finally, since production rates cannot be negative, it is necessary to restrict the decision variables to be nonnegative: $x_1 \geq 0$ and $x_2 \geq 0$.

Table 3.1 **Data for Wyndor Glass Co.**

	Capacity used per unit production rate		*Capacity*
Plant	*Product 1*	*2*	*Available*
1	1	0	4
2	0	2	12
3	3	2	18
Unit profit	$3	$5	

To summarize, in the mathematical language of linear programming, the problem is to choose the values of x_1 and x_2 so as to

$$\text{Maximize} \quad Z = 3x_1 + 5x_2,$$

subject to the restrictions

$$x_1 \qquad\quad \leq 4$$
$$2x_2 \leq 12$$
$$3x_1 + 2x_2 \leq 18$$

and

$$x_1 \geq 0, \quad x_2 \geq 0.$$

(Notice how the layout of the coefficients of x_1 and x_2 in this linear programming model essentially duplicates the information that was summarized in Table 3.1.)

GRAPHICAL SOLUTION This very small problem has only two decision variables, and therefore only two dimensions, so a graphical procedure can be used to solve it. This procedure involves constructing a two-dimensional graph with x_1 and x_2 as the axes. The first step is to identify the values of (x_1,x_2) that are permitted by the restrictions. This is done by drawing the lines that must border the range of permissible values. To begin, note that the nonnegativity restrictions, $x_1 \geq 0$ and $x_2 \geq 0$, require (x_1,x_2) to lie on the positive side of the axes (if not actually on either axis). Next, observe that the restriction $x_1 \leq 4$ means that (x_1,x_2) cannot lie to the right of the line $x_1 = 4$. These results are shown in Fig. 3.1, where the shaded area contains the only values of (x_1,x_2) that are still allowed. In a similar fashion, the line $2x_2 = 12$ would be added to the boundary of the permissible region. The final restriction $3x_1 + 2x_2 \leq 18$ requires plotting the points (x_1,x_2) such that $3x_1 + 2x_2 = 18$ (another line) to complete the boundary. (Note that the

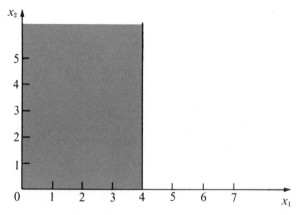

Figure 3.1 Shaded area shows values of (x_1,x_2) allowed by $x_1 \geq 0$, $x_2 \geq 0$, $x_1 \leq 4$.

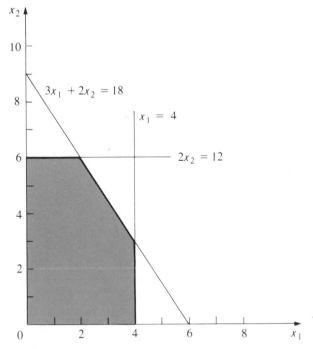

Figure 3.2 **Shaded area shows permissible values of (x_1, x_2).**

points such that $3x_1 + 2x_2 \leq 18$ are those that lie either underneath or on the line $3x_1 + 2x_2 = 18$, so this is the limiting line beyond which the inequality ceases to hold.) The resulting region of permissible values of (x_1, x_2) is shown in Fig. 3.2.

The final step is to pick out the point in this region that maximizes the value of $Z = 3x_1 + 5x_2$. This step becomes automatic after a little practice, but to discover the basis for it, it is instructive to proceed by trial and error. Try, for example, $Z = 10 = 3x_1 + 5x_2$ to see if there are in the permissible region any values of (x_1, x_2) that yield a value of Z as large as 10. By drawing the line $3x_1 + 5x_2 = 10$ you can see that there are many points on this line that lie within the region (see Fig. 3.3). Therefore, try a larger value of Z, say, for example, $Z = 20 = 3x_1 + 5x_2$. Again, Fig. 3.3 reveals that a segment of the line $3x_1 + 5x_2 = 20$ lies within the region, so that the maximum permissible value of Z must be at least 20. Notice that this line giving a larger value of Z is farther up and away from the origin than the first line and that the two lines are parallel. Thus this trial-and-error procedure involves nothing more than drawing a family of parallel lines[1] containing at least one point in the permissible region and selecting

---

[1] After a little practice, a simpler method is actually to draw just *one* of these lines to establish the slope and then *visually* to move this line parallel to itself.

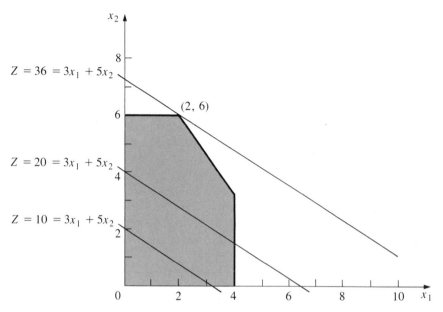

Figure 3.3   **Value of (x_1, x_2) that maximizes $3x_1 + 5x_2$.**

the line that is the greatest distance from the origin (in the direction of increasing values of Z). This line passes through the point $(2,6)$ as indicated in Fig. 3.3, so that the equation is $3x_1 + 5x_2 = 3(2) + 5(6) = 36 = Z$. Hence, the desired solution is $x_1 = 2$, $x_2 = 6$, which indicates that the Wyndor Glass Co. should produce products 1 and 2 at the rate of two per minute and six per minute, respectively, with a resulting profitability of \$36/minute. Furthermore, no other mix of the two products would be so profitable—*according to the model.*

At this point, the O.R. Department is ready to evaluate the validity of the model more critically (to be continued in Sec. 3.3) and to perform a sensitivity analysis on the effect of the estimates in Table 3.1 being inaccurate (to be continued in Sec. 6.7).

3.2 The Linear Programming Model

Let us begin generalizing from the Wyndor Glass Co. problem. In that example there were three limited resources (production capacities at the three plants) to be allocated among two competing activities (the two proposed products). Now suppose that there are any number (call it m) of limited resources of any kind to be allocated among any number (call it n) of competing activities of any kind. Assign number labels to the resources $(1, 2, \ldots, m)$ and activities $(1, 2, \ldots, n)$. Let x_j (a decision variable) be the level of activity j, for $j = 1, 2, \ldots, n$, and let Z be the chosen overall measure of effectiveness. Then let c_j be the increase in Z that would result from each unit increase in x_j (for $j = 1, 2, \ldots, n$). Next, let b_i denote the amount of resource i available for allocation (for $i = 1, 2, \ldots, m$). Finally, define a_{ij}

Table 3.2 **Data for linear programming model**

Resource usage per unit of activity

Resource	Activity 1	2	$\cdots$	n	Amount of resource available
1	a_{11}	a_{12}	$\cdots$	a_{1n}	b_1
2	a_{21}	a_{22}	$\cdots$	a_{2n}	b_2
$\vdots$			$\vdots$		$\vdots$
m	a_{m1}	a_{m2}	$\cdots$	a_{mn}	b_m
ΔZ/unit of activity	c_1	c_2	$\cdots$	c_n	
Level of activity	x_1	x_2	$\cdots$	x_n	

as the amount of resource i consumed by each unit of activity j (for $i = 1,2,\ldots,m$ and $j = 1,2,\ldots,n$). This set of data is summarized in Table 3.2. Notice carefully the complete correspondence between this table (except for the extra row added at the bottom) and Table 3.1.

A STANDARD FORM OF THE MODEL

Proceeding just as for the example, we can now formulate the mathematical model for this general problem of allocating resources to activities. In particular, this model is to select the values for $x_1, x_2, \ldots, x_n$ so as to

Maximize $Z = c_1 x_1 + c_2 x_2 + \cdots + c_n x_n$,

subject to the restrictions

$$a_{11}x_1 + a_{12}x_2 + \cdots + a_{1n}x_n \le b_1$$
$$a_{21}x_1 + a_{22}x_2 + \cdots + a_{2n}x_n \le b_2$$
$$\vdots$$
$$a_{m1}x_1 + a_{m2}x_2 + \cdots + a_{mn}x_n \le b_m,$$

and

$$x_1 \ge 0, \quad x_2 \ge 0, \quad \ldots, \quad x_n \ge 0.$$

We call this *our standard form*[1] for the linear programming problem. Any situation whose mathematical formulation fits this model is a linear programming problem.

Common terminology for the linear programming model can now be summarized. The function being maximized, $c_1 x_1 + c_2 x_2 + \cdots + c_n x_n$, is called the *objective function*. The restrictions normally are referred to as *constraints*. The first m constraints (those with a function $a_{i1}x_1 + a_{i2}x_2 + \cdots + a_{in}x_n$, representing the total usage of resource i, on the left) are sometimes called *functional*

[1] This is called *our* standard form rather than *the* standard form because some textbooks adopt other forms.

constraints. Similarly, the $x_j \geq 0$ restrictions are called *nonnegativity constraints.* As mentioned, the x_j variables are *decision variables.* The input constants—the a_{ij}, b_i, c_j—may be referred to as *parameters* of the model.

OTHER FORMS

We now hasten to add that the preceding model does not actually fit the natural form of some linear programming problems. The other *legitimate forms* are the following:

1. Minimizing rather than maximizing the objective function:

$$\text{Minimize} \quad Z = c_1 x_1 + c_2 x_2 + \cdots + c_n x_n,$$

2. Some functional constraints with a greater-than-or-equal-to inequality:

$$a_{i1} x_1 + a_{i2} x_2 + \cdots + a_{in} x_n \geq b_i, \text{ for some values of } i,$$

3. Some functional constraints in equation form:

$$a_{i1} x_1 + a_{i2} x_2 + \cdots + a_{in} x_n = b_i, \text{ for some values of } i,$$

4. Deleting the nonnegativity constraints for some decision variables:

$$x_j \text{ unrestricted in sign, for some values of } j.$$

Any problem that mixes some or all of these forms with the remaining parts of the preceding model is still a linear programming problem as long as they are the *only* new forms introduced. Our interpretation of allocating *limited resources among competing activities* may no longer apply very well, if at all, but regardless of the interpretation or context, all that is required is that the mathematical statement of the problem fit the allowable forms.

In Sec. 4.6, you will see that all these other four legitimate forms can be rewritten in an equivalent way to fit the model just discussed. Thus every linear programming problem can be put into our standard form if so desired. We shall take advantage of this fact everywhere that procedures for solving linear programming problems are discussed (except Sec. 4.6) by assuming the problems are in our standard form.

TERMINOLOGY FOR SOLUTIONS OF THE MODEL

You may be used to having the term **solution** mean the final answer to a problem, but the convention in linear programming (and its extensions) is quite different. Here, *any* specification of values for the decision variables $(x_1, x_2, \ldots, x_n)$ is called a solution, regardless of whether it is a desirable or even an allowable choice. Different types of solutions are then identified by using an appropriate adjective, as you will see.

A **feasible solution** is a solution for which *all* the constraints are satisfied.

In the example, the feasible solutions are the points within or on the boundary of the shaded area (sometimes called *feasible region*) in Fig. 3.2. Thus (2,3) and (4,1) are feasible solutions, but $(-1,3)$ and (4,4) are infeasible solutions.

It is possible for a problem to have no feasible solutions. This would have happened in the example if the new products had been required to return a net profit of at least \$50/minute to justify discontinuing part of the current product line. The corresponding constraint, $3x_1 + 5x_2 \geq 50$, would eliminate the entire feasible region, so no mix of new products would be superior to the status quo.

Given that there are feasible solutions, the goal of linear programming is to find which one is best, as measured by the value of the objective function in the model.

An **optimal solution** is a feasible solution that has the *most favorable value* of the objective function.

Most favorable value means the largest or smallest value, depending upon whether the objective is maximization or minimization. Thus an optimal solution maximizes/minimizes the objective function over the entire feasible region.

Frequently a problem will have just one optimal solution. This is the case in the example, where only the solution $(x_1, x_2) = (2,6)$ is optimal. However, it is also possible to have *multiple* optimal solutions (more than one). This would occur in the example if the unit profitability of product 2 were changed to \$2, thereby changing the objective function to $Z = 3x_1 + 2x_2$. The lines for constant objective function values in Fig. 3.3 then would be parallel to the constraint line, $3x_1 + 2x_2 = 18$. Therefore, all the points on the line segment connecting (2,6) and (4,3) would be optimal solutions because they all would have the most favorable value of the objective function ($Z = 18$), so the number of optimal solutions in this case is infinite. This actually is a general property; that is, any problem having multiple optimal solutions has an infinite number of them.

The third possibility is that a problem has no optimal solutions. This occurs only if (1) it has no feasible solutions or (2) the constraints do not prevent increasing the value of the objective function (Z) indefinitely in the favorable direction (positive or negative). For example, the latter case would result if the last two functional constraints were mistakenly deleted in the example. A discussion of how the simplex method identifies these unusual cases is included in Secs. 4.5 (for case 2) and 4.6 (for case 1); we assume until then that they do not arise.

3.3 Assumptions of Linear Programming

All the assumptions of linear programming actually are implicit in the model formulation given in Sec. 3.2. However, it is good to highlight these assumptions so you can more easily evaluate how well linear programming applies to any given problem. Furthermore, we still need to see why the O.R. Department of the Wyndor Glass Co. concluded that a linear programming formulation provided a satisfactory representation of their problem.

PROPORTIONALITY

Proportionality is an assumption about *individual* activities considered independently of the others (whereas the subsequent assumption of *additivity* concerns the effect of conducting activities *jointly*). Therefore, consider the case where only one of the n activities is undertaken. Call it activity k, so that $x_j = 0$ for all $j = 1, 2, \ldots, n$ except $j = k$.

The assumption is that (1) the measure of effectiveness Z equals $c_k x_k$ and (2) the usage of each resource i equals $a_{ik} x_k$; that is, both quantities are directly *proportional* to the level of each activity k conducted by itself ($k = 1, 2, \ldots, n$). This implies in particular that there is no extra start-up charge with beginning the activity and that the proportionality holds over the entire range of levels of the activity.

What happens when this assumption does not hold, even as a reasonable approximation? In most cases, this means you must use *nonlinear programming* instead (presented in Chap. 14). However, we do point out in Sec. 14.8 that a certain important kind of nonproportionality can still be handled by linear programming by reformulating the problem appropriately. If the assumption is violated only because of start-up charges, there is an extension of linear programming (*mixed integer programming*) that can be used, as discussed in Sec. 13.2 (the fixed-charge problem).

In the Wyndor Glass Co. problem, the O.R. Department found two ways in which the proportionality assumption is not quite satisfied precisely. One is that there is actually an extra cost associated with arranging the distribution of each new product introduced. Thus the objective function $Z = 3x_1 + 5x_2$ should have the start-up cost (amortized on a per minute basis) subtracted for each product j such that $x_j > 0$ (but not when $x_j = 0$). However, this cost spread over the life of the product was too negligible to warrant inclusion in the model. Second, for each product, production efficiency increases slightly at higher production rates, thereby increasing the marginal unit profit and decreasing the usage of production capacity per unit increase in production rate. Nevertheless, the O.R. Department concluded that, for practical purposes, proportionality could be assumed without serious distortion.

ADDITIVITY

The proportionality assumption is not enough to guarantee that the objective function and constraint functions are linear. Cross-product terms will arise if there are interactions between some of the activities that would change the total measure of effectiveness or the total usage of some resource. Additivity assumes that there are no such interactions between any of the activities. Therefore, the additivity assumption requires that, given any activity levels $(x_1, x_2, \ldots, x_n)$, both the total measure of effectiveness and the total usage of each resource equal the *sum* of the corresponding quantities generated by each activity conducted by itself.

If additivity is not a reasonable assumption, so that some or all of the mathematical functions of the model need to be *nonlinear* (because of the cross-product terms), you definitely enter the realm of nonlinear programming (Chap. 14).

In the Wyndor Glass Co. problem, the two proposed new products are not competitive, so the profits from either product would not be reduced by marketing the other one. They could sometimes be shipped together from Plant 3 to the same distributor, but this would be a very minor cost savings. On the production side, facilities reserved for one product might occasionally be used for the other product during otherwise idle periods, but this again was too negligible a factor to include in the model. Therefore, the O.R. Department did not include any cross-product terms in either the objective function or the constraint functions, thereby adopting the assumption of additivity.

DIVISIBILITY

Sometimes the decision variables have physical significance only if they have integer values. However, the optimal solution obtained by linear programming is often a noninteger one. Therefore, the divisibility assumption is that activity units can be *divided* into *any fractional levels*, so that noninteger values for the decision variables are permissible.

Frequently, linear programming is still applied even when an integer solution is required. If the solution obtained is a noninteger one, then the noninteger variables are merely rounded to integer values. This may be satisfactory, particularly if the decision variables are large, but it does have certain pitfalls (discussed in Sec. 13.3). If this approach cannot be used, then we are in the realm of *integer programming*, which is the topic of Chap. 13. However, it should be noted that linear programming *automatically* will obtain integer solutions to certain special types of problems, including some of those discussed in Chap. 7.

For the Wyndor Glass Co. problem, the decision variables represent production rates, which can have fractional values. Certain fractional values are more convenient than others because they correspond to integer numbers of people and machines working full time on the product. However, the O.R. Department concluded that these minor adjustments could be made easily after using the model to analyze the big picture and to identify approximately what the combination of production rates should be.

CERTAINTY

The certainty assumption is that all the parameters of the model (the a_{ij}, b_i, and c_j values) are *known constants*. In real problems, this assumption is seldom satisfied precisely. Linear programming models usually are formulated to select some future course of action. Therefore, the parameters used would be based on a prediction of future conditions, which inevitably introduces some degree of uncertainty.

For this reason it usually is important to conduct a thorough **sensitivity analysis** after finding a solution that is optimal under the assumed parameter values. The general purpose is to identify the relatively *sensitive* parameters (i.e., those that cannot be changed much without changing the optimal solution), to try to estimate these more closely, and then to select a solution that remains a good one over the ranges of likely values of the sensitive parameters. This is what the O.R. Department will do for the Wyndor Glass Co. problem, as you will see in Sec. 6.7. However, it is necessary to acquire some more background before finishing that story.

Occasionally, the degree of uncertainty in the parameters is too great to be amenable to sensitivity analysis. In this case, it is necessary to treat the parameters explicitly as *random variables*. Formulations of this kind have been developed, but they are beyond the scope of this book.

As you work through the examples in the next section, you will find it good practice to analyze how well each of the preceding assumptions applies to these problems.

3.4 Additional Examples

The Wyndor Glass Co. problem is a prototype example of linear programming in several respects: It involves allocating limited resources among competing activities, its model fits our standard form, and its context is the traditional one of improved business planning. However, the applicability of linear programming is much wider. In this section we begin broadening our horizons. As you study the following examples, note that it is their underlying mathematical model rather than their context that characterizes them as linear programming problems. Then give some thought to how the same mathematical model could arise in many other contexts by merely changing the names of the activities and so forth.

These examples have been kept very small (by linear programming standards) for ease of reading. However, much larger versions of the problems, involving hundreds of constraints and variables, are readily solvable by linear programming.

REGIONAL PLANNING

One of the interesting social experiments in the Mediterranean region is the system of kibbutzim, or communal farming communities, in Israel. It is common for groups of kibbutzim to join together to share common technical services and to coordinate their production. Our first example concerns one such group of three kibbutzim, which we call the *Southern Confederation of Kibbutzim*.

Overall planning for the Southern Confederation of Kibbutzim is done in its Coordinating Technical Office. This office currently is planning agricultural production for the coming year.

Table 3.3 **Resources data for Southern Confederation of Kibbutzim**

Kibbutz	Usable land (acres)	Water allocation (acre feet)
1	400	600
2	600	800
3	300	375

Table 3.4 **Crop data for Southern Confederation of Kibbutzim**

Crop	Maximum quota (acres)	Water consumption (acre feet/acre)	Net return (dollars/acre)
Sugar beets	600	3	400
Cotton	500	2	300
Sorghum	325	1	100

The agricultural output of each kibbutz is limited by both the amount of available irrigable land and by the quantity of water allocated for irrigation by the Water Commissioner (a national government official). These data are given in Table 3.3.

The crops suited for this region include sugar beets, cotton, and sorghum, and these are the three being considered for the upcoming season. These crops differ primarily in their expected net return per acre and their consumption of water. In addition, the Ministry of Agriculture has set a maximum quota for the total acreage that can be devoted to each of these crops by the Southern Confederation of Kibbutzim, as shown in Table 3.4.

The three kibbutzim belonging to the Southern Confederation have agreed that every kibbutz will plant the same proportion of its available irrigable land. However, any combination of the crops may be grown at any of the kibbutzim. The job facing the Coordinating Technical Office is to plan how many acres to devote to each crop at the respective kibbutzim while satisfying the given restrictions. The objective is to maximize the total net return to the Southern Confederation as a whole.

FORMULATION AS A LINEAR PROGRAMMING PROBLEM The quantities to be decided upon are the number of acres to devote to each of the three crops at each of the three kibbutzim. The decision variables, x_j ($j = 1,2,\ldots,9$), represent these nine quantities, as shown in Table 3.5. Since the measure of effectiveness Z is total net return, the resulting linear programming model for this problem is

Table 3.5 **Decision variables for Southern Confederation of Kibbutzim problem**

Allocation (acres)

Crop	Kibbutz		
	1	*2*	*3*
Sugar beets	x_1	x_2	x_3
Cotton	x_4	x_5	x_6
Sorghum	x_7	x_8	x_9

Maximize $Z = 400(x_1 + x_2 + x_3) + 300(x_4 + x_5 + x_6) + 100(x_7 + x_8 + x_9)$,

subject to the following constraints:

1. *Land*:

$$x_1 + x_4 + x_7 \le 400$$
$$x_2 + x_5 + x_8 \le 600$$
$$x_3 + x_6 + x_9 \le 300$$

2. *Water*:

$$3x_1 + 2x_4 + x_7 \le 600$$
$$3x_2 + 2x_5 + x_8 \le 800$$
$$3x_3 + 2x_6 + x_9 \le 375$$

3. *Crop*:

$$x_1 + x_2 + x_3 \le 600$$
$$x_4 + x_5 + x_6 \le 500$$
$$x_7 + x_8 + x_9 \le 325$$

4. *Social*:

$$\frac{x_1 + x_4 + x_7}{400} = \frac{x_2 + x_5 + x_8}{600}$$

$$\frac{x_2 + x_5 + x_8}{600} = \frac{x_3 + x_6 + x_9}{300}$$

$$\frac{x_3 + x_6 + x_9}{300} = \frac{x_1 + x_4 + x_7}{400}$$

Table 3.6 **Optimal solution for Southern Confederation of Kibbutzim problem**

Best allocation (acres)

Crop	Kibbutz		
	1	*2*	*3*
Sugar beets	$133\frac{1}{3}$	100	25
Cotton	100	250	150
Sorghum	0	0	0

5. *Nonnegativity*:

$$x_j \geq 0, \quad \text{for } j = 1, 2, \ldots, 9.$$

This completes the model, except that the social constraints are not yet in an appropriate form for a linear programming model because some of the variables are on the right-hand side. Hence their final form[1] is

4. *Social*:

$$3(x_1 + x_4 + x_7) - 2(x_2 + x_5 + x_8) = 0$$
$$x_2 + x_5 + x_8 - 2(x_3 + x_6 + x_9) = 0$$
$$4(x_3 + x_6 + x_9) - 3(x_1 + x_4 + x_7) = 0.$$

The Coordinating Technical Office formulated this model and then applied the simplex method (developed in the next chapter) to find the best solution. The solution they obtained is

$$(x_1, x_2, x_3, x_4, x_5, x_6, x_7, x_8, x_9) = (133\tfrac{1}{3}, 100, 25, 100, 250, 150, 0, 0, 0),$$

as shown in Table 3.6.

This example illustrates, among other things, how equality constraints can arise naturally in linear programming problems. One feature of the next example is the inclusion of two other nonstandard forms in the model, namely (1) minimizing the objective function and (2) functional constraints with $\geq$ inequalities.

CONTROLLING AIR POLLUTION

The *Nori & Leets Co.*, one of the major producers of steel in its part of the world, is located in the city of Steeltown and is the only large employer there. Steeltown has grown and prospered along with the company, which now employs nearly 50,000 residents. Therefore, the attitude of the townspeople always has been "What's good for Nori & Leets is good for the town." However, this attitude is now changing; uncontrolled air pollution from the company's furnaces is ruining the appearance of the city and endangering the health of its residents.

A recent stockholders' revolt resulted in the election of a new enlightened Board of Directors for the company. These directors are determined to follow socially responsible policies, and they have been discussing with Steeltown city officials and citizens' groups what to do about the air pollution problem. Together they have worked out stringent air quality standards for the Steeltown airshed.

The three main types of pollutants in this airshed are particulate matter, sulfur oxides, and hydrocarbons. The new standards require that the company

---

[1] Actually, any one of these equations is redundant and can be deleted if desired. Because of these equations, any two of the land constraints also could be deleted.

Table 3.7 **Clean air standards for
Nori & Leets Co.**

Pollutant	Required reduction in annual emission rate (million pounds)
Particulates	60
Sulfur oxides	150
Hydrocarbons	125

Table 3.8 **Reduction in emission rate from maximum feasible use of abatement method
for Nori & Leets Co.**

Pollutant	Taller smokestacks		Filters		Better fuels	
	Blast furnaces	Open-hearth furnaces	Blast furnaces	Open-hearth furnaces	Blast furnaces	Open-hearth furnaces
Particulates	12	9	25	20	17	13
Sulfur oxides	35	42	18	31	56	49
Hydrocarbons	37	53	28	24	29	20

reduce its annual emission of these pollutants by the amounts shown in Table 3.7. The Board of Directors has instructed management to have the engineering staff determine how to achieve these reductions in the most economical way.

The steel works has two primary sources of pollution, namely, the blast furnaces for making pig iron and the open-hearth furnaces for changing iron into steel. In both cases the engineers have decided that the most effective types of abatement methods are (1) increasing the height of the smokestacks,[1] (2) using filter devices (including gas traps) in the smokestacks, and (3) including cleaner high-grade materials among the fuels for the furnaces. All these methods have technological limits on how much emission they can eliminate, as shown (in millions of pounds per year) in Table 3.8.

However, the methods can be used at any fraction of their abatement capacities shown in this table. Because they operate independently, the emission reductions achieved by each method are not substantially affected by whether or not the other methods also are used.

After these data were developed, it became clear that no single method by

---

[1] Subsequent to this study, this particular abatement method has become a controversial one. Because its effect is to reduce ground-level pollution by spreading emissions over a greater distance, environmental groups contend that this creates more acid rain by keeping sulfur oxides in the air longer. Consequently, the U.S. Environmental Protection Agency adopted new rules in 1985 to remove incentives for using tall smokestacks.

Table 3.9 **Total annual cost from maximum feasible use of abatement method for Nori & Leets Co.**

Abatement method	Blast furnaces	Open-hearth furnaces
Taller smokestacks	8	10
Filters	7	6
Better fuels	11	9

itself could achieve all the required reductions. On the other hand, combining all three methods at full capacity (which would be prohibitively expensive if the company's products are to remain competitively priced) is much more than adequate. Therefore, the engineers concluded that they would have to use some combination of the methods, perhaps with fractional capacities, based upon their relative costs. Furthermore, because of the differences between the blast and the open-hearth furnaces, the two types probably should not use the same combination.

An analysis was conducted to estimate the total annual cost that would be incurred by each abatement method. In addition to increased operating and maintenance expenses, consideration was given also to the initial costs (converted to an equivalent annual basis) of the method as well as any resulting loss in efficiency of the production process. This analysis led to the total cost estimates (in millions of dollars) given in Table 3.9 for using the methods at their full abatement capacities. It also was determined that the cost of a method being used at a lower level is essentially proportional to its fractional capacity. Thus, for any given fraction used, the total annual cost would be that fraction of the corresponding quantity in Table 3.9.

The stage now was set to develop the general framework of the company's plan for pollution abatement. This plan would consist of specifying which types of abatement methods would be used and at what fractions of their abatement capacities for (1) the blast furnaces and (2) the open-hearth furnaces. Because of the combinatorial nature of the problem of finding a plan that satisfies the requirements with the smallest possible cost, an operations research team was formed to solve the problem. The team adopted a linear programming approach, formulating the model summarized next.

FORMULATION AS A LINEAR PROGRAMMING PROBLEM This problem has six decision variables, x_j ($j = 1, 2, \ldots, 6$), each representing the usage of one of the three abatement methods for one of the two types of furnaces, expressed as a fraction of the abatement capacity. The ordering of these variables is shown in Table 3.10. Because the objective is to minimize total cost while satisfying the emission reduction requirements, the model is

Table 3.10 **Decision variables (fraction of maximum feasible use of abatement method) for Nori & Leets Co.**

Abatement method	Blast furnaces	Open-hearth furnaces
Taller smokestacks	x_1	x_2
Filters	x_3	x_4
Better fuels	x_5	x_6

$$\text{Minimize} \quad Z = 8x_1 + 10x_2 + 7x_3 + 6x_4 + 11x_5 + 9x_6,$$

subject to the following constraints:

1. *Emission reduction*:

$$12x_1 + 9x_2 + 25x_3 + 20x_4 + 17x_5 + 13x_6 \geq 60$$
$$35x_1 + 42x_2 + 18x_3 + 31x_4 + 56x_5 + 49x_6 \geq 150$$
$$37x_1 + 53x_2 + 28x_3 + 24x_4 + 29x_5 + 20x_6 \geq 125$$

2. *Technological*:

$$x_j \leq 1, \quad \text{for } j = 1, 2, \ldots, 6$$

3. *Nonnegativity*:

$$x_j \geq 0, \quad \text{for } j = 1, 2, \ldots, 6.$$

The operations research team used this model[1] to find the minimum cost plan, $(x_1, x_2, x_3, x_4, x_5, x_6) = (1, 0.623, 0.343, 1, 0.048, 1)$. Sensitivity analysis then was conducted, followed by detailed planning and managerial review. Soon after, this program for controlling air pollution was fully implemented by the company, and the citizens of Steeltown breathed deep sighs of relief.

OTHER EXAMPLES

The three linear programming examples you have seen so far are but a small sampling of the uses of this technique. Many more illustrations are given in Chaps. 7 and 8; most involve business and industrial applications, but several others arise in different contexts. Chap. 7 focuses on certain special types of linear programming problems that provide many important applications. Chap. 8 considers some examples that are more difficult to formulate, and it also includes a case study involving the design of school attendance zones to achieve better racial balance. But before considering these topics, we next discuss how to solve linear programming problems.

---

[1] An equivalent formulation can express each decision variable in natural units for its abatement method; for example, x_1 and x_2 could represent the number of *feet* that the heights of the smokestacks are increased.

3.5 Conclusions

Linear programming is a powerful technique for dealing with the problem of allocating limited resources among competing activities as well as other problems having a similar mathematical formulation. It has become a standard tool of great importance for numerous business and industrial organizations. Furthermore, almost any social organization is concerned with allocating resources in some context, and there is a growing recognition of the extremely wide applicability of this technique.

However, not all problems of allocating limited resources can be formulated to fit a linear programming model, even as a reasonable approximation. When one or more of the assumptions of linear programming is violated seriously, it may then be possible to apply another mathematical programming model instead, e.g., the models of integer programming (Chap. 13) or nonlinear programming (Chap. 14).

SELECTED REFERENCES

1. Anderson, David R., Dennis J. Sweeney, and Thomas A. Williams: *An Introduction to Management Science*, 4th ed., chaps. 2, 5, West, St. Paul, Minn., 1985.
2. Cook, Thomas M. and Robert A. Russell: *Introduction to Management Science*, 2d ed., chaps. 2–3, Prentice-Hall, Englewood Cliffs, N.J., 1981.
3. Simmons, Donald M.: *Linear Programming for Operations Research*, Holden-Day, San Francisco, 1972.
4. Spivey, W. Allen and Robert M. Thrall: *Linear Optimization*, Holt, Rinehart & Winston, New York, 1970.
5. Strum, Jay E.: *Introduction to Linear Programming*, Holden-Day, San Francisco, 1972.

PROBLEMS[1]

1. Suppose you have just inherited $6,000 and you want to invest it. Upon hearing this news, two different friends have offered you an opportunity to become a partner in two different entrepreneurial ventures, one planned by each friend. In both cases, this investment would involve expending some of your time next summer as well as putting up cash. Becoming a *full* partner in the first friend's venture would require an investment of $5,000 and 400 hours, and your estimated profit (ignoring the value of your time) would be $4,500. The corresponding figures for the second friend's venture are $4,000 and 500 hours, with an estimated profit to you of $4,500. However, both friends are flexible and would allow you to come in at any fraction of a full partnership you would like; your share of the profit would be proportional to this fraction.

Because you were looking for an interesting summer job anyway (maximum of 600 hours), you have decided to participate in one or both friends ventures in whichever combination would maximize your total estimated profit. You now need to solve the problem of finding the best combination.

---

[1] Some additional *formulation* problems also are given at the end of Chap. 8. Also note that answers to selected problems are given at the back of the book.

(a) Describe the analogy between this problem and the Wyndor Glass Co. problem discussed in Sec. 3.1. Then construct and fill in a table like Table 3.2 for this problem, identifying both the activities and the resources.
(b) Formulate the linear programming model for this problem.
(c) Solve this model graphically. What is your total estimated profit?
(d) Indicate why each of the four assumptions of linear programming (Sec. 3.3) appears to be reasonably satisfied for this problem. Is one assumption more doubtful than the others? If so, what should be done to take this into account?

2. A manufacturing firm has discontinued the production of a certain unprofitable product line. This act created considerable excess production capacity. Management is considering devoting this excess capacity to one or more of three products; call them products 1, 2, and 3. The available capacity on the machines that might limit output is summarized in the following table:

Machine type	Available time (in machine hours per week)
Milling machine	500
Lathe	350
Grinder	150

The number of machine hours required for each unit of the respective products is

Productivity coefficient (in machine hours per unit)

Machine type	Product 1	Product 2	Product 3
Milling machine	9	3	5
Lathe	5	4	0
Grinder	3	0	2

The sales department indicates that the sales potential for products 1 and 2 exceeds the maximum production rate and that the sales potential for product 3 is 20 units per week. The unit profit would be $30, $12, and $15, respectively, on products 1, 2, and 3. The objective is to determine how much of each product the firm should produce to maximize profit.

Formulate the linear programming model for this problem.

3. Use the graphical procedure illustrated in Sec. 3.1 to solve the problem

$$\text{Maximize} \quad Z = 2x_1 + x_2,$$

subject to

$$x_2 \leq 10$$
$$2x_1 + 5x_2 \leq 60$$
$$x_1 + x_2 \leq 18$$
$$3x_1 + x_2 \leq 44$$

and

$$x_1 \geq 0, \quad x_2 \geq 0.$$

4. Use the graphical procedure illustrated in Sec. 3.1 to solve the problem

$$\text{Maximize} \quad Z = 5x_1 + 10x_2,$$

subject to

$$-x_2 + 2x_2 \le 25$$
$$x_1 + x_2 \le 20$$
$$5x_1 + 3x_2 \le 75$$

and

$$x_1 \ge 0, \quad x_2 \ge 0.$$

5. For each of the four assumptions of linear programming discussed in Sec. 3.3, write a one-paragraph analysis of how well you feel it applies to each of the following examples given in Sec. 3.4:

  (a) Regional planning (Southern Confederation of Kibbutzim).
  (b) Controlling air pollution (Nori & Leets Co.).

6. Consider the problem described at the beginning of Sec. 8.5, where the city of Middletown is using linear programming to redesign the school attendance zones for its high schools. The objective function used there is to minimize the total distance that students must travel, subject to constraints on the racial balance in the schools. Now suppose that the school board decides to change the objective function to minimizing the total *cost* of bussing the students. (However, the decision variables continue to be $x_{ij} =$ number of students in tract i assigned to school j.) Each student assigned to a school more than a mile away will be given the opportunity to ride a bus. (However, some of these students may choose to get to and from school in some other way.) Each bus can carry 40 students. The daily cost of providing each bus is estimated to be $50 plus $1 for each student carried. A bus may transport students from more than one tract to try to fill the buses.

  For each of the four assumptions of linear programming discussed in Sec. 3.3, write a one-paragraph analysis of how well it applies to the revised objective function.

7. A farmer is raising pigs for market, and he wishes to determine the quantities of the available types of feed that should be given to each pig to meet certain nutritional requirements at a *minimum cost*. The number of units of each type of basic nutritional ingredient contained within a kilogram of each feed type is given in the following table, along with the daily nutritional requirements and feed costs:

Nutritional ingredient	Kilogram of corn	Kilogram of tankage	Kilogram of alfalfa	Minimum daily requirement
Carbohydrates	90	20	40	200
Protein	30	80	60	180
Vitamins	10	20	60	150
Cost (¢)	35	30	25	

Formulate the linear programming model for this problem.

8. Use the graphical procedure illustrated in Sec. 3.1 to solve the problem

$$\text{Minimize} \quad Z = 4x_1 + 3x_2,$$

subject to

$$2x_1 + x_2 \geq 10$$
$$-3x_1 + 2x_2 \leq 6$$
$$x_1 + x_2 \geq 6$$

and

$$x_1 \geq 0, \quad x_2 \geq 0.$$

9. A certain corporation has three branch plants with excess production capacity. All three plants have the capability for producing a certain product, and management has decided to use some of the excess production capacity in this way. This product can be made in three sizes—large, medium, and small—that yield a net unit profit of \$385, \$330, and \$275, respectively. Plants 1, 2, and 3 have the excess labor and equipment capacity to produce 750, 900, and 450 units per day of this product, respectively, regardless of the size or combination of sizes involved. However, the amount of available in-process storage space also imposes a limitation on the production rates. Plants 1, 2, and 3 have 13,000, 12,000, and 5,000 square feet of in-process storage space available for a day's production of this product. Each unit of the large, medium, and small sizes produced per day requires 20, 15, and 12 square feet, respectively.

Sales forecasts indicate that 900, 1200, and 750 units of the large, medium, and small sizes, respectively, can be sold per day.

To maintain a uniform work load among the plants and to retain some flexibility, management has decided that their additional production assigned to the respective plants must use the same percentage of excess labor and equipment capacities.

Management wishes to know how much of each of the sizes should be produced by each of the plants to maximize profit.

(a) Formulate the linear programming model for this problem.

(b) Use a computer code of the simplex method to solve this problem.

10. A farm family owns 125 acres of land and has \$40,000 in funds available for investment. Its members can produce a total of 3,500 person-hours worth of labor during the winter months (mid-September to mid-May) and 4,000 person-hours during the summer. If any of these person-hours are not needed, younger members of the family will use them to work on a neighboring farm for \$5.00/hour during the winter months and \$6.00/hour during the summer.

Cash income may be obtained from three crops and two types of livestock: dairy cows and laying hens. No investment funds are needed for the crops. However, each cow will require an investment outlay of \$1,200, and each hen will cost \$9.

Each cow will require 1.5 acres of land, 100 person-hours of work during the winter months, and another 50 person-hours during the summer. Each cow will produce a net annual cash income of \$1,000 for the family. The corresponding figures for each hen are: no acreage, 0.6 person-hours during the winter, 0.3 more person-hours during the summer, and an annual net cash income of \$5. The chicken house can accommodate a maximum of 3,000 hens, and the size of the barn limits the herd to a maximum of 32 cows.

Estimated person-hours and income per acre planted in each of the three crops are

	Soybeans	Corn	Oats
Winter person-hours	20	35	10
Summer person-hours	50	75	40
Net annual cash income ($)	500	750	350

The family wishes to determine how much acreage should be planted in each of the crops and how many cows and hens should be kept to maximize its net cash income. Formulate the linear programming model for this problem.

11. A cargo plane has three compartments for storing cargo: front, center, and back. These compartments have capacity limits on both *weight* and *space*, as summarized below:

Compartment	Weight capacity (tons)	Space capacity (cu ft)
Front	12	7,000
Center	18	9,000
Back	10	5,000

Furthermore, the weight of the cargo in the respective compartments must be the same proportion of that compartment's weight capacity to maintain the balance of the airplane.

The following four cargoes have been offered for shipment on an upcoming flight as space is available:

Cargo	Weight (tons)	Volume (cu ft/ton)	Profit ($/ton)
1	20	500	280
2	16	700	360
3	25	600	320
4	13	400	250

Any portion of these cargoes can be accepted. The objective is to determine how much (if any) of each cargo should be accepted and how to distribute each among the compartments to maximize the total profit for the flight.

Formulate the linear programming model for this problem.

12. An investor has money-making activities A and B available at the beginning of each of the next 5 years (call them years 1 to 5). Each dollar invested in A at the beginning of 1 year returns $1.40 (a profit of $0.40) 2 years later (in time for immediate reinvestment). Each dollar invested in B at the beginning of 1 year returns $1.70 3 years later.

In addition, money-making activities C and D will each be available at one time in the future. Each dollar invested in C at the beginning of year 2 returns $1.90 at the end of year 5. Each dollar invested in D at the beginning of year 5 returns $1.30 at the end of year 5.

The investor begins with $50,000 and wishes to know which investment plan maximizes the amount of money that can be accumulated by the beginning of year 6. Formulate the linear programming model for this problem.

CHAPTER 4

Solving Linear Programming Problems: The Simplex Method

We now are ready to begin studying the *simplex method*, the general procedure for solving linear programming problems. Developed by George Dantzig in 1947, it has proven to be a remarkably efficient method that is routinely used to solve huge problems on today's computers. Except for very small problems, this method always is executed on a computer, and sophisticated software packages are widely available for it. Nevertheless, it is important to learn something about how the method works in order to understand how to perform *post-optimality analysis* (including sensitivity analysis) on the model. Therefore, this chapter describes and illustrates the main features of the simplex method.

The first section introduces the general nature of the simplex method, including its geometric interpretation. The following three sections then develop the procedure for solving any linear programming model that is in *our standard form* (as defined in Sec. 3.2) and has only *positive* right-hand sides (b_i) in the functional constraints. Certain details on resolving ties are deferred to Sec. 4.5, and Sec. 4.6 describes how to adapt this method to other model forms. We next discuss post-optimality analysis (Sec. 4.7), and then conclude the chapter with a description of the computer implementation of the simplex method (Sec. 4.8).

4.1 The Essence of the Simplex Method

The simplex method actually is an **algorithm**, the first of many you will see in this book. Although you may not have heard this name used, you undoubtedly have encountered many algorithms before. For example, the familiar procedure for *long division* is an algorithm. So is the procedure for *calculating square roots.* In fact, any *iterative solution procedure* is an algorithm. Thus an algorithm is simply a process where a systematic procedure is repeated (iterated) over and over again until the desired result is obtained. Each time through the systematic procedure is called an *iteration.* (Can you see what the iteration is for the long division algorithm?) Consequently, an algorithm replaces one difficult problem by a series of easy ones.

In addition to iterations, algorithms also include a procedure for getting started and a criterion for determining when to stop, as summarized here.

Structure of Algorithms[1]

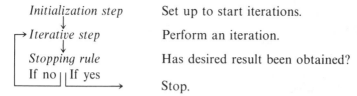

Initialization step	Set up to start iterations.
Iterative step	Perform an iteration.
Stopping rule	Has desired result been obtained?
If no ⌐ If yes	Stop.

For most operations research algorithms, including the simplex method, the desired result mentioned in the stopping rule is that the current solution is optimal. In this case, the stopping rule actually is an *optimality test*, as shown here.

Structure of Most Operations Research Algorithms

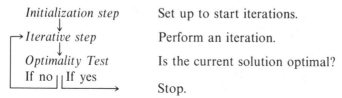

Initialization step	Set up to start iterations.
Iterative step	Perform an iteration.
Optimality Test	Is the current solution optimal?
If no ⌐ If yes	Stop.

The simplex method is an *algebraic* procedure, where each iteration involves solving a system of equations to obtain a new trial solution for the optimality test. However, it also has a very useful *geometric* interpretation. To illustrate the general geometric concepts, we shall use the graphical solution to the Wyndor Glass Co. example presented in Sec. 3.1.

To refresh your memory, the graph for this example is repeated in Fig. 4.1. The five constraint lines and their points of intersection are highlighted in this figure because they are the keys to the analysis. In particular, these points of intersection are the *corner-point solutions* of the problem. The five that lie on the corners of the *feasible region*—(0,0), (0,6), (2,6), (4,3), (4,0)—are the **corner-point**

---

[1] Actually, the stopping rule usually is applied after the initialization step as well to see if *any* iterations are needed.

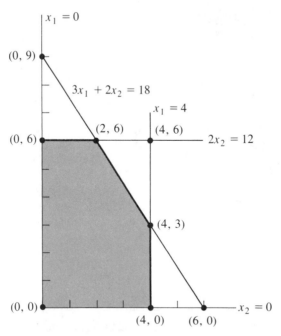

Figure 4.1 **Constraint lines and corner-point solutions for the Wyndor Glass Co. problem.**

feasible solutions. (The other three—(0,9), (4,6), (6,0)—are called *corner-point infeasible solutions*.) Some of these corner-point feasible solutions are **adjacent** to each other in the sense that they are connected by a single edge (line segment) on the boundary of the feasible region; e.g., both (0,6) and (4,3) are adjacent to (2,6).

Sec. 5.1 develops in detail the general properties of corner-point feasible solutions for linear programming problems of any size, as well as the relationships between these properties and the *algebra* of the simplex method presented in the next two sections. The three key properties[1] that form the foundation of the simplex method are summarized as follows.

Properties of Corner-Point Feasible Solutions

1a. If there is exactly one optimal solution, then it *must* be a corner-point feasible solution.

1b. If there are multiple optimal solutions, then at least two *must* be adjacent corner-point feasible solutions.

2. There are only a *finite* number of corner-point feasible solutions.

3. If a corner-point feasible solution is equal to or better than (as measured by Z) all its *adjacent* corner-point feasible solutions, then it

---

[1] The only assumptions required for these properties are (1) the problem has feasible solutions and (2) the problem has a bounded feasible region in the direction of improving Z so that an optimal solution exists.

is equal to or better than all other corner-point feasible solutions; i.e., it is *optimal*.

Property 1 implies that the search for an optimal solution can be reduced to considering *only* the corner-point feasible solutions, so there are only a finite number of solutions to consider (property 2). Property 3 provides a very convenient *optimality test*.

The simplex method exploits these three properties by examining only a relatively few of the promising corner-point feasible solutions and stopping as soon as one of them passes this optimality test. In particular, it repeatedly (iteratively) moves from the current corner-point feasible solution to a better adjacent corner-point feasible solution, which can be done very efficiently, until the current solution does not have any better adjacent corner-point feasible solutions. This procedure is summarized as follows.

Outline of the Simplex Method

1. *Initialization step*: Start at a corner-point feasible solution.
2. *Iterative step*: Move to a better adjacent corner-point feasible solution. (Repeat this step as often as needed.)
3. *Optimality test*: The current corner-point feasible solution is optimal when none of its adjacent corner-point feasible solutions are better.

This outline shows the essence of the simplex method, although the complete description in the next two sections does specify a convenient way of choosing the new solution in both the initialization and iterative steps. Using these choice rules, the simplex method proceeds as follows in the example.

1. *Initialization step*: Start at (0,0).
2a. *Iteration 1*: Move from (0,0) to (0,6).
2b. *Iteration 2*: Move from (0,6) to (2,6).
3. *Optimality test*: Neither (0,6) nor (4,3) is better than (2,6), so stop. (2,6) is optimal.

4.2 Setting Up the Simplex Method

The preceding section stressed the geometric concepts that underlie the simplex method. However, this algorithm normally is run on a computer, which can follow only algebraic instructions. Therefore, it is necessary to translate the conceptually geometric procedure just described into a usable algebraic procedure. In this section, we introduce the *algebraic language* of the simplex method and relate it to the concepts of the preceding section.

In an algebraic procedure, it is much more convenient to deal with equations than with inequality relationships. Therefore, the first step in setting up the simplex method is to convert the functional *inequality constraints* into equivalent *equality constraints*. (The nonnegativity constraints can be left as inequalities because they are used only indirectly by the algorithm.) This conversion is done by introducing **slack variables**. To illustrate, consider the first functional constraint in the Wyndor Glass Co. example of Sec. 3.1,

$$x_1 \leq 4.$$

The slack variable for this constraint is

$$x_3 = 4 - x_1,$$

which is just the slack between the two sides of the inequality. Thus

$$x_1 + x_3 = 4.$$

The original constraint $x_1 \leq 4$ holds whenever $x_3 \geq 0$. Hence $x_1 \leq 4$ is entirely *equivalent* to the set of constraints

$$x_1 + x_3 = 4$$

and

$$x_3 \geq 0,$$

so these more convenient constraints are used instead.

By introducing slack variables in an identical fashion for the other functional constraints, the original linear programming model for the example can now be replaced by the *equivalent* model

$$\text{Maximize} \quad Z = 3x_1 + 5x_2,$$

subject to

(1)		x_1		$+ x_3$			$= 4$

$$
\begin{aligned}
(1) \quad & x_1 && + x_3 && && = 4 \\
(2) \quad & && 2x_2 && + x_4 && && = 12 \\
(3) \quad & 3x_1 + 2x_2 && && && + x_5 && = 18
\end{aligned}
$$

and

$$x_j \geq 0, \quad \text{for } j = 1, 2, \dots, 5.$$

Although this problem is identical to the original, this form is much more convenient for algebraic manipulation and for identification of corner-point feasible solutions. We call this the *equality form* of the problem, as opposed to the original inequality form, in order to introduce the following definition:

> An **augmented solution** is a solution for a problem that was originally in inequality form that has been *augmented* by the corresponding values of the *slack variables* to change the problem into equality form.

For example, augmenting the solution (3,2) in the example yields the augmented solution (3,2,1,8,5) because the corresponding values of the slack variables are $x_3 = 1$, $x_4 = 8$, $x_5 = 5$.

> A **basic solution** is an *augmented* corner-point solution.[1]

---

[1] When the original problem includes equality constraints, the basic solutions are just the augmented corner-point solutions that satisfy all these constraints.

To illustrate, consider the corner-point infeasible solution (4,6) in the example. Augmenting it with the resulting values of the slack variables $x_3 = 0$, $x_4 = 0$, and $x_5 = -6$ yields the corresponding basic solution $(4,6,0,0,-6)$. Basic solutions are allowed to be either feasible or infeasible, which implies the following definition:

A **basic feasible solution** is an *augmented* corner-point feasible solution.

Thus the corner-point feasible solution (0,6) in the example is equivalent to the basic feasible solution (0,6,4,0,6) for the problem in equality form.

Because the terms *basic solution* and *basic feasible solution* are very important parts of the standard vocabulary of linear programming, we now need to clarify their algebraic properties. For the equality form of the example, notice that the system of functional constraints has two more variables (5) than equations (3). This fact gives us two *degrees of freedom* in solving the system, since any two variables can be chosen to be set equal to any arbitrary value in order to solve the three equations in terms of the remaining three variables (barring redundancies). The simplex method uses zero for this arbitrary value. The variables that are currently set to zero by the simplex method are called **nonbasic variables**, and the others are called **basic variables**. The resulting solution is called a *basic solution*. If all of the basic variables are nonnegative, the solution is called a *basic feasible solution*. For any basic solution, the corresponding corner-point solution is obtained simply by deleting the slack variables. (We clarify in Sec. 5.1 why each basic solution obtained in this way still must correspond to a corner-point solution.) Two basic feasible solutions are **adjacent** if *all but one* of their nonbasic variables are the same, and the same statement holds for the basic variables. Thus moving from the current basic feasible solution to an adjacent one involves switching one variable from nonbasic to basic and vice versa for one other variable.

In general terms, the number of *nonbasic variables* in a basic solution always equals the number of *degrees of freedom* in the system of equations, and the number of *basic variables* always equals the number of *functional constraints*.

When dealing with the problem in equality form, it is convenient to consider and manipulate the objective function equation at the same time as the new constraint equations. Therefore, before starting the simplex method, the problem needs to be rewritten once again in an equivalent way as

$$\text{Maximize} \quad Z,$$

subject to

$$
\begin{aligned}
(0) \quad & Z - 3x_1 - 5x_2 && = 0 \\
(1) \quad & x_1 && + x_3 && = 4 \\
(2) \quad & 2x_2 && + x_4 && = 12 \\
(3) \quad & 3x_1 + 2x_2 && + x_5 && = 18,
\end{aligned}
$$

and

$$x_j \geq 0, \quad \text{for } j = 1, 2, \ldots, 5.$$

It is just as if Eq. (0) actually were one of the original constraints, but because it already is in equality form, no slack variable is needed. With this interpretation, the basic solutions would be unchanged except that Z would be viewed as a permanent additional basic variable.

If the original problem had not been in *our standard form* with all $b_i > 0$, then this is the point where the additional adjustments described in Sec. 4.6 would have been needed to set up and apply the simplex method.

4.3 The Algebra of the Simplex Method

The discussion in Sec. 4.1 of the essence of the simplex method did not get into the details of how the steps are performed. In particular, the following questions have not yet been answered completely (the parenthetical phrases restate the questions in the algebraic terminology of Sec. 4.2).

1. *Initialization step*: How is the initial *corner-point feasible solution* (basic feasible solution) selected?
2. *Iterative step*: When seeking to move to a better *adjacent corner-point feasible solution* (adjacent basic feasible solution),
   (a) How is the direction of movement selected? (Which nonbasic variable is selected to become basic?)
   (b) Where do we stop? (Which basic variable becomes nonbasic?)
   (c) How is the new solution identified?
3. *Optimality test*: How do we determine that the *current corner-point feasible solution* (basic feasible solution) has no *adjacent corner-point feasible solutions* (adjacent basic feasible solutions) that are better?

In this section, we answer the preceding questions for any linear programming problem in our standard form that also has $b_i > 0$ for all $i = 1, 2, \ldots, m$. (Other forms are treated in Sec. 4.6.) We continue to use the prototype example of Sec. 3.1, as rewritten at the end of the last section, for illustrative purposes.

INITIALIZATION STEP

As indicated in Sec. 4.1, the simplex method can start at any corner-point feasible solution, so it chooses a convenient one. When the problem is still in the *inequality* form, this choice is the *origin* (all variables equal to zero), or $(x_1, x_2) = (0,0)$ in the example. Consequently, after the introduction of slack variables, the *original* variables are the *nonbasic* variables and the *slack* variables are the *basic* variables for the initial basic feasible solution. This choice is illustrated here where the basic variables are shown in bold type.

$$
\begin{array}{lrcrcrcrl}
(1) & x_1 & & + \mathbf{x_3} & & & & = 4 \\
(2) & & 2x_2 & & + \mathbf{x_4} & & & = 12 \\
(3) & 3x_1 & + 2x_2 & & & + \mathbf{x_5} & & = 18
\end{array}
$$

Because the nonbasic variables are set equal to zero, the remaining solution is read as if they were not there, so $x_3 = 4$, $x_4 = 12$, and $x_5 = 18$, giving the **initial basic feasible solution** (0,0,4,12,18).

Notice that the reason this solution can be read immediately is that each equation has just one basic variable, which has a coefficient of $+1$, and this basic variable does not appear in any other equation. You will soon see that the simplex method manipulates the equations algebraically in such a way that they continue to have this convenient form for reading every subsequent basic feasible solution as well.

ITERATIVE STEP

At each iteration, the simplex method moves from the current basic feasible solution (corner-point feasible solution) to a better *adjacent* basic feasible solution. This movement involves replacing one nonbasic variable (called the *entering basic variable*) by a new one (called the *leaving basic variable*) and identifying the new basic feasible solution.

QUESTION 1: What is the criterion for selecting the *entering basic variable*?

The candidates for the entering basic variable are the n current nonbasic variables. The one chosen would be changed from a nonbasic to a basic variable, so its value would be increased from zero to some positive number (except in degenerate cases), and the others would be kept at zero. Since the new basic feasible solution is required to be an improvement (larger Z) over the current one, it is thus necessary that the net change in Z from increasing the entering basic variable be a positive one. This change is determined by rewriting the objective function just in terms of the nonbasic variables (using the current Eq. (0) in the system of equations), so that the coefficient of each one is the rate at which Z would change as that variable is increased. The one that has the largest coefficient, and so would *increase Z* at the *fastest rate*, is chosen to be the entering basic variable.[1]

To illustrate, the two candidates for entering basic variable in the example are the current nonbasic variables x_1 and x_2. Since the objective function already is written only in terms of these nonbasic variables, it can be considered just as is:

$$Z = 3x_1 + 5x_2.$$

Both variables have positive coefficients, so increasing either one would increase Z, but at the different rates of 3 and 5 per unit increase in the variable. Since $3 < 5$, the choice for **entering basic variable** is x_2.

QUESTION 2: How is the *leaving basic variable* identified?

---

[1] Note that this criterion does not guarantee selecting the variable that would increase Z the most because the constraints may not allow increasing this variable as much as some of the others. However, the extra computations required to check this are not considered worthwhile.

For the problem in *inequality* form, increasing x_2 from zero while keeping x_1 zero means that we are moving up the x_2 axis in Fig. 4.1. The *adjacent* corner-point feasible solution, (0,6), is reached by stopping at the first new *constraint line* ($2x_2 = 12$). We *must* stop there even though there is a corner-point solution at (0,9) because going further would give *infeasible* solutions that violate the $2x_2 \leq 12$ constraint.

For the problem in *equality* form, feasible solutions must satisfy *both* the system of functional constraint equations *and* the nonnegativity constraints on *all* the variables (original variables and slack variables). Increasing x_2 from zero while keeping x_1 zero (nonbasic) means that some or all of the current basic variables (x_3, x_4, x_5) must change their values to keep the system of equations satisfied. Some of these variables will decrease as x_2 increases. The *adjacent* basic feasible solution is reached when the *first* of the basic variables (the *leaving basic variable*) reaches a value of zero. We *must* stop there to avoid going infeasible. Thus, when we have chosen the entering basic variable, the leaving basic variable is not a matter of choice. It must be the current basic variable whose nonnegativity constraint imposes the smallest upper bound on how much the entering basic variable can be increased, as illustrated next.

The possibilities for leaving basic variable in the example are the current basic variables x_3, x_4, and x_5. The most that the entering basic variable x_2 can be increased before each of these variables would become negative is summarized in Table 4.1. Since x_4 (the slack variable for the $2x_2 \leq 12$ constraint) imposes the smallest upper bound on x_2, the **leaving basic variable** is x_4, so $x_4 = 0$ (nonbasic) and $x_2 = 6$ (basic) in the new basic feasible solution.

QUESTION 3: How can the *new basic feasible solution* be identified most conveniently?

After identifying the entering and leaving basic variables (including the new value of the entering basic variable), all that needs to be done to identify the new basic feasible solution is to solve for the new values of the remaining basic variables. This solution could be obtained directly from Table 4.1. However, in order to get

Table 4.1 Calculations for determining first leaving basic variable for Wyndor Glass Co. problem

Basic variable	Equation	Upper bound for x_2
x_3	$x_3 = 4 - x_1$	No limit
x_4	$x_4 = 12 - 2x_2$	$x_2 \leq \dfrac{12}{2} = 6 \leftarrow$ minimum
x_5	$x_5 = 18 - 3x_1 - 2x_2$	$x_2 \leq \dfrac{18}{2} = 9$

set up for the next iteration, the simplex method converts the system of equations into the same convenient form we had in the initialization step (namely, each equation has just one basic variable, which has a coefficient of $+1$, and this basic variable does not appear in any other equation). This conversion can be done by performing the following two kinds of algebraic operations:

   (*a*) Multiplying an equation by a nonzero constant.
   (*b*) Adding a multiple of one equation to another equation.

These operations are legitimate because they involve only (*a*) multiplying equals (both sides of an equation) by the same constant and (*b*) adding equals to equals. Therefore, a solution will satisfy the system of equations after such operations if and only if it did so before.

   To illustrate, consider the original set of equations, where the *new* basic variables are shown in darker type (with Z playing the role of the basic variable in the objective function equation):

(0) $Z - 3x_1 - 5x_2 \qquad\qquad\qquad = 0$

(1) $\qquad\quad x_1 \qquad + x_3 \qquad\qquad = 4$

(2) $\qquad\qquad\quad 2x_2 \qquad + x_4 \quad = 12$

(3) $\qquad\quad 3x_1 + 2x_2 \qquad\qquad + x_5 = 18.$

Thus, x_2 has replaced x_4 as the basic variable in Eq. (2). Since x_2 has a coefficient of $+2$ there, this equation would be multiplied by $\frac{1}{2}$ to give its new basic variable a coefficient of $+1$. The resulting new Eq. (2) is

(2) $$x_2 + \frac{1}{2}x_4 = 6.$$

Next, x_2 must be eliminated from the other equations in which it appears including Eq. (0), to set it up for the optimality test. Using the second kind of algebraic operation just listed, this elimination is done as follows:

   New Eq. (3) = old Eq. (3) $+ (-2) \times$ new Eq. (2)
   New Eq. (0) = old Eq. (0) $+ 5 \times$ new Eq. (2).

This sequence of operations yields the second set of equations (which is completely equivalent algebraically to the first set), as follows:

(0) $Z - 3x_1 \qquad\qquad + \dfrac{5}{2}x_4 \qquad = 30$

(1) $\qquad\quad x_1 \quad + x_3 \qquad\qquad = 4$

(2) $\qquad\qquad\quad x_2 \quad + \dfrac{1}{2}x_4 \qquad = 6$

(3) $\qquad\quad 3x_1 \qquad\qquad - x_4 + x_5 = 6.$

For purposes of illustration, exchange the location of x_2 and x_4.

(0) $$Z - 3x_1 + \frac{5}{2}x_4 = 30$$

(1) $$x_1 + x_3 = 4$$

(2) $$\frac{1}{2}x_4 + x_2 = 6$$

(3) $$3x_1 - x_4 + x_5 = 6.$$

Now compare this last set of equations with the initial set obtained under the initialization step, and notice that it is indeed in the same convenient form for immediately reading the current basic feasible solution after noting that the nonbasic variables (x_1 and x_4) equal zero. Thus we now have our new basic feasible solution, $(x_1,x_2,x_3,x_4,x_5) = (0,6,4,0,6)$, which yields $Z = 30$.[1]

OPTIMALITY TEST

To determine whether the current basic feasible solution is optimal, the current Eq. (0) is used to rewrite the objective function just in terms of the current nonbasic variables,

$$Z = 30 + 3x_1 - \frac{5}{2}x_4.$$

As shown in Sec. 5.1, increasing either of these nonbasic variables from zero (while adjusting the values of the basic variables to continue satisfying the system of equations) would result in moving toward one of the two *adjacent* basic feasible solutions. Because x_1 has a *positive* coefficient, increasing x_1 would lead toward an adjacent basic feasible solution that is better than the current basic feasible solution, so the current solution is not optimal.

In general terms, the current basic feasible solution is optimal if and only if *all* of the nonbasic variables have *nonpositive* coefficients (≤ 0) in the current form of the objective function.

The reason that the *current* form is used instead of the *original* objective function is that the current form contains *all of the nonbasic variables* and *none of the basic variables*. All of the nonbasic variables are needed in order to be able to compare all of the adjacent basic feasible solutions with the current solution. The basic variables must not appear because their values may change when a nonbasic variable is increased from zero, in which case the coefficient of the nonbasic variable no longer indicates the rate of change of Z. Because of the

---

[1] The algebraic method just illustrated for obtaining the simultaneous solution of a system of linear equations is called the *Gauss-Jordan method of elimination*. If it is not yet clear, we suggest you study the method further in Appendix 4.

constraint equations, the two forms of the objective function are *equivalent*, so the one that contains all the desired information is used.

Eq. (0) is included in the algebraic operations at the end of the iterative step so this new more convenient form of the objective function can be obtained.

Before proceeding with the next iteration, it is now possible to give a meaningful summary of the simplex method.

SUMMARY OF THE SIMPLEX METHOD

1. INITIALIZATION STEP: Introduce slack variables. If the model is not in the form being assumed in this section, see Sec. 4.6 for the necessary adjustments. Otherwise, select the original variables to be the nonbasic variables (and thus equal to zero) and the slack variables to be the basic variables (and thus equal to the right-hand side) in the initial basic feasible solution. Go to the optimality test.

2. ITERATIVE STEP:

Part 1. Determine the *entering basic variable*: Select the nonbasic variable that, when increased, would increase Z at the fastest rate. This selection can be made by checking the magnitude of the coefficients in the objective function rewritten just in terms of the nonbasic variables (obtained from the current Eq. (0)) and selecting the nonbasic variable whose coefficient is *largest*.[1] (See Sec. 4.5 regarding ties.)

Part 2. Determine the *leaving basic variable*: Select the basic variable that reaches zero first as the entering basic variable is increased. This selection can be made by checking each equation (except Eq. (0)) to see how much the entering basic variable can be increased before the current basic variable in that equation reaches zero. A formal algebraic procedure for doing this is to let e denote the subscript of the entering basic variable, let a'_{ie} denote its current coefficient in Eq. (i), and let b'_i denote the current right-hand side for this equation ($i = 1, 2, \ldots, m$). Then the upper bound for x_e in Eq. (i) is

$$x_e \leq \begin{cases} +\infty, & \text{if } a'_{ie} \leq 0 \\ \dfrac{b'_i}{a'_{ie}}, & \text{if } a'_{ie} > 0. \end{cases}$$

Therefore, determine the equation with the *smallest* such upper bound, and select the current basic variable in that equation as the leaving basic variable. (See Sec. 4.5 regarding ties, including the case where *all* upper bounds are $+\infty$.)

Part 3. Determine the *new basic feasible solution*: Starting from the current set of equations, solve for the basic variables and Z in terms of the nonbasic variables by the Gauss-Jordan method of elimination (see Appendix 4). Set the

---

[1] Equivalently, the current Eq. (0) can be used directly, in which case the nonbasic variable with the largest *negative* coefficient would be selected. This is what is done in the tabular form of the simplex method presented in Sec. 4.4.

nonbasic variables equal to zero; each basic variable (and Z) equals the new right-hand side of the one equation in which it appears (with a coefficient of $+1$).

3. OPTIMALITY TEST: Determine whether this solution is optimal: Check if Z can be increased by increasing any nonbasic variable. This determination can be made by rewriting the objective function just in terms of the nonbasic variables by bringing these variables to the right-hand side in the current Eq. (0) and then checking the sign of the coefficient of each nonbasic variable. If all these coefficients are nonpositive, then this solution is optimal, so stop.[1] (See Sec. 4.5 to interpret zero coefficients.) Otherwise, go to the iterative step.

To illustrate, apply this summary to the next iteration for the example.

ITERATION 2 FOR EXAMPLE

Part 1. Because the current Eq. (0) yields $Z = 30 + 3x_1 - \frac{5}{2}x_4$, increasing only x_1 would increase Z; that is, x_1 has the largest (and only) positive coefficient. Therefore, x_1 is chosen as the new entering basic variable.

Part 2. The upper limits on x_1 before the basic variable in the respective equations reaches zero are shown in Table 4.2. Therefore, x_5 must be chosen as the leaving basic variable.

Part 3. After eliminating x_1 from all equations in the current set except Eq. (3), where x_1 replaces x_5 as the basic variable, the new set of equations is

$$(0) \qquad Z \qquad\qquad + \frac{3}{2}x_4 + x_5 = 36$$

$$(1) \qquad\qquad\qquad x_3 + \frac{1}{3}x_4 - \frac{1}{3}x_5 = 2$$

$$(2) \qquad\qquad x_2 \quad + \frac{1}{2}x_4 \qquad\quad = 6$$

$$(3) \qquad\quad x_1 \qquad\quad - \frac{1}{3}x_4 + \frac{1}{3}x_5 = 2.$$

Therefore, the next basic feasible solution is $(2,6,2,0,0)$, yielding $Z = 36$.

OPTIMALITY TEST Because the new form of the objective function is $Z = 36 - \frac{3}{2}x_4 - x_5$ so that the coefficient of neither nonbasic variable is positive, the current basic feasible solution just obtained must be optimal. Therefore, the desired solution to the original (inequality) form of the problem is $x_1 = 2, x_2 = 6$, which yields $Z = 36$.

---

[1] Equivalently, the current Eq. (0) can be used directly, in which case all these coefficients have to be nonnegative (≥ 0) for the solution to be optimal. This is what is done in the tabular form of the simplex method presented in Sec. 4.4.

Table 4.2 **Calculations for determining second leaving basic variable for Wyndor Glass Co. problem**

Basic variable	Equation number	Upper bound for x_1
x_3	1	$x_1 \leq \dfrac{4}{1} = 4$
x_2	2	No limit
x_5	3	$x_1 \leq \dfrac{6}{3} = 2 \leftarrow$ minimum

4.4 The Simplex Method in Tabular Form

The algebraic form of the simplex method presented in Sec. 4.3 may be the best one for learning the underlying logic of the algorithm. However, it is not the most convenient form for performing the required calculations. When you need to solve a problem by hand, we recommend the *tabular form* described in this section.[1]

The tabular form of the simplex method is *mathematically equivalent* to the algebraic form. However, instead of writing down each set of equations in full detail, we instead use a **simplex tableau** to record only the essential information, namely, (1) the coefficients of the variables, (2) the constants on the right-hand side of the equations, and (3) the basic variable appearing in each equation. This saves writing the symbols for the variables in each of the equations, but what is even more important is the fact that it permits highlighting the numbers involved in arithmetic calculations and recording the computations compactly.

To introduce the tabular form, we consider the *equality form* of the Wyndor Glass Co. problem as presented at the end of Sec. 4.2. This system of Eqs. (0 to 3) can be expressed as shown in Table 4.3. This table shows the layout for any *simplex tableau*, where the column on the left indicates which basic variable appears in each equation for the current basic feasible solution.

Table 4.3 **Initial simplex tableau for Wyndor Glass Co. problem**

Basic variable	Eq. no.	Coefficient of Z	x_1	x_2	x_3	x_4	x_5	Right side
Z	0	1	-3	-5	0	0	0	0
x_3	1	0	1	0	1	0	0	4
x_4	2	0	0	2	0	1	0	12
x_5	3	0	3	2	0	0	1	18

---

[1] A form more convenient for a *computer* is presented in Sec. 5.2.

Table 4.3 illustrates a key property that all simplex tableaux must possess to be in *proper form*, namely, a special pattern for the coefficients of the basic variables. In particular, note how the x_3, x_4, and x_5 columns (as well as the Z column) each contains exactly one $+1$, located in the row for that particular basic variable (see the first column), and *all* of the other coefficients in that column equal 0. By the same token, each equation contains exactly one basic variable with a nonzero coefficient, where this coefficient is $+1$. The significance of this key property is that the solution for the current basic feasible solution now can be identified immediately from the current tableau; namely, each basic variable *equals* the constant on the right-hand side of its equation. (Remember that the nonbasic variables equal zero.) The initial simplex tableau automatically will be in this proper form (unless the original linear programming problem is not in *our standard form*), but some additional work is required to obtain this proper form in the subsequent simplex tableaux, and this extra work is what part 3 of the iterative step does.

The simplex method develops a simplex tableau for each new basic feasible solution obtained until the optimal solution is reached. The procedure is outlined next for problems in *our standard form*, with $b_i > 0$ for all $i = 1, 2, \ldots, m$.[1] (Other forms are discussed in Sec. 4.6, and tie-breaking considerations are deferred to Sec. 4.5.) We continue to use the Wyndor Glass Co. example for illustrative purposes.

INITIALIZATION STEP Introduce slack variables. Then select the *original variables* to be the *initial nonbasic variables* (set equal to zero) and the *slack variables* to be the *initial basic variables*. This selection yields the initial simplex tableau for the example already shown in Table 4.3. Because this tableau is in *proper form*, the initial basic feasible solution for the example is (0,0,4,12,18). Go next to the optimality test to determine whether this solution is optimal.

OPTIMALITY TEST The current basic feasible solution is optimal if and only if *every* coefficient in Eq. (0) is nonnegative (≥ 0). If it is, stop; otherwise, go to the iterative step to obtain the next basic feasible solution, which involves changing one nonbasic variable to a basic variable (part 1) and vice versa (part 2) and then solving for the new solution (part 3).

The example has two negative coefficients in Eq. (0), -3 for x_1 and -5 for x_2, so go to the iterative step.

ITERATIVE STEP
Part 1. Determine the *entering basic variable* by selecting the variable (automatically a nonbasic variable) with the *negative coefficient* having the largest

---

[1] If you already understand the algebraic form of the simplex method, then you will not need to study carefully the following procedure, which is just a tabular representation of the algebraic procedure presented in Sec 4.3.

Table 4.4 Calculations to determine first leaving basic variable for Wyndor Glass
Co. problem

Basic variable	Eq. no.	Z	Coefficient of x_1	x_2	x_3	x_4	x_5	Right side	Ratio
Z	0	1	-3	-5	0	0	0	0	
x_3	1	0	1	$\boxed{0}$	1	0	0	4	$\dfrac{12}{2} = 6 \leftarrow$ minimum
x_4	2	0	0	$\boxed{2}$	0	1	0	12	
x_5	3	0	3	$\boxed{2}$	0	0	1	18	$\dfrac{18}{2} = 9$

absolute value in Eq. (0). Put a box around the column below this coefficient, and call this the **pivot column**.

In the example, the largest (in absolute terms) negative coefficient is -5 for x_2 ($5 > 3$), so x_2 is to be changed to a basic variable. (This change is indicated in Table 4.4 by the box around the x_2 column below -5.)

Part 2. Determine the *leaving basic variable* by (a) picking out each coefficient in the boxed column that is strictly positive (>0), (b) dividing each of these coefficients into "right side" for the same row, (c) identifying the equation that has the *smallest* of these ratios, and (d) selecting the basic variable for this equation. (This basic variable is the one that reaches zero first as the entering basic variable is increased.) Put a box around this equation's row in the tableau to the right of the Z column, and call the boxed row the **pivot row**. (Hereafter, we continue to use the term **row** to refer just to a row of numbers to the right of the Z column, *including* the right-side number.) Also call the one number that is in *both* boxes the **pivot number**.

The results of parts 1 and 2 for the example (before boxing the row) are shown in Table 4.4, where the **minimum ratio test** for determining the leaving basic variable is shown to the right of the tableau. Thus the leaving basic variable is x_4.

Part 3. Determine the *new basic feasible solution* by constructing a new simplex tableau in *proper form* below the current one. The first three columns are unchanged except that the leaving basic variable in the *Basic variable* column is replaced by the entering basic variable. To change the coefficient of the new basic variable in the pivot row to $+1$, change this pivot row by *dividing* the entire row by the pivot number, so

$$\text{New pivot row} = \frac{\text{old pivot row}}{\text{pivot number}}.$$

The tableaux for the example at this point have the appearance shown in Table 4.5. To obtain a coefficient of 0 for the new basic variable in every other equation for the iteration 1 tableau, every row [including the one for Eq. (0)] *except* the

Table 4.5 **Simplex tableaux for Wyndor Glass Co. problem after revising first pivot row**

Iteration	Basic variable	Eq. no.	Z	x_1	x_2	x_3	x_4	x_5	Right side
					Coefficient of				
0	Z	0	1	-3	-5	0	0	0	0
	x_3	1	0	1	0	1	0	0	4
	x_4	2	0	0	2	0	1	0	12
	x_5	3	0	3	2	0	0	1	18
1	Z	0	1						
	x_3	1	0						
	x_2	2	0	0	1	0	$\frac{1}{2}$	0	6
	x_5	3	0						

pivot row is changed for the new tableau by using the following formula:

New row = old row − (pivot column coefficient × new pivot row),

where *pivot column coefficient* is the number in this row that is also in the pivot column.

To illustrate, the new rows for the example are obtained as follows:

Row 0

$$\begin{array}{c} [-3 \quad -5 \quad 0 \quad 0 \quad 0, \quad 0] \\ -(-5)\begin{bmatrix} 0 & 1 & 0 & \frac{1}{2} & 0, & 6 \end{bmatrix} \\ \hline \text{New row} = \begin{bmatrix} -3 & 0 & 0 & \frac{5}{2} & 0, & 30 \end{bmatrix}. \end{array}$$

Row 1 Unchanged because its pivot column coefficient is zero.

Row 3

$$\begin{array}{c} [3 \quad 2 \quad 0 \quad 0 \quad 1, \quad 18] \\ -(2)\begin{bmatrix} 0 & 1 & 0 & \frac{1}{2} & 0, & 6 \end{bmatrix} \\ \hline \text{New row} = [3 \quad 0 \quad 0 \quad -1 \quad 1, \quad 6]. \end{array}$$

This change yields the new tableau shown in Table 4.6 for iteration 1.

Because each basic variable always equals the right side of its equation, the new basic feasible solution is (0,6,4,0,6), with $Z = 30$.

This work completes the iterative step, so next return to the optimality test. Since the new Eq. (0) still has a negative coefficient (-3 for x_1), the optimality test indicates that the solution is not optimal, and so it directs the algorithm to return to the iterative step to obtain the next basic feasible solution. The iterative step then starts anew from the current tableau to find this new solution. Following the instructions for parts 1 and 2, we find x_1 as the entering basic variable and x_5 as the leaving basic variable, as shown in the tableau for iteration 1 in Table 4.7.

Table 4.6 **First two simplex tableaux for Wyndor Glass Co. problem**

Iteration	Basic variable	Eq. no.	Z	x_1	x_2	x_3	x_4	x_5	Right side
	Z	0	1	-3	-5	0	0	0	0
0	x_3	1	0	1	0	1	0	0	4
	x_4	2	0	0	2	0	1	0	12
	x_5	3	0	3	2	0	0	1	18
	Z	0	1	-3	0	0	$\dfrac{5}{2}$	0	30
1	x_3	1	0	1	0	1	0	0	4
	x_2	2	0	0	1	0	$\dfrac{1}{2}$	0	6
	x_5	3	0	3	0	0	-1	1	6

Table 4.7 **Calculations to determine second leaving basic variable for Wyndor Glass Co. problem**

Iteration	Basic variable	Eq. no.	Z	x_1	x_2	x_3	x_4	x_5	Right side	Ratio
	Z	0	1	-3	0	0	$\dfrac{5}{2}$	0	30	
1	x_3	1	0	1	0	1	0	0	4	$\dfrac{4}{1} = 4$
	x_2	2	0	0	1	0	$\dfrac{1}{2}$	0	6	
	x_5	3	0	3	0	0	-1	1	6	$\dfrac{6}{3} = 2 \leftarrow$ minimum

Using the pivot number 3, the calculations to obtain the rows for the new tableau are

Row 3 Because this is the pivot row,

$$\text{New row} = \frac{1}{3}\begin{bmatrix} 3 & 0 & 0 & -1 & 1, & 6 \end{bmatrix}$$

$$= \begin{bmatrix} 1 & 0 & 0 & -\dfrac{1}{3} & \dfrac{1}{3}, & 2 \end{bmatrix}.$$

Row 0

$$\begin{bmatrix} -3 & 0 & 0 & \dfrac{5}{2} & 0, & 30 \end{bmatrix}$$

$$-(-3)\begin{bmatrix} 1 & 0 & 0 & -\dfrac{1}{3} & \dfrac{1}{3}, & 2 \end{bmatrix}$$

$$\text{New row} = \begin{bmatrix} 0 & 0 & 0 & \dfrac{3}{2} & 1, & 36 \end{bmatrix}.$$

Table 4.8 **Complete set of simplex tableaux for Wyndor Glass Co. problem**

Iteration	Basic variable	Eq. no.	Z	x_1	x_2	x_3	x_4	x_5	Right side
0	Z	0	1	-3	-5	0	0	0	0
	x_3	1	0	1	0	1	0	0	4
	x_4	2	0	0	2	0	1	0	12
	x_5	3	0	3	2	0	0	1	18
1	Z	0	1	-3	0	0	$\frac{5}{2}$	0	30
	x_3	1	0	1	0	1	0	0	4
	x_2	2	0	0	1	0	$\frac{1}{2}$	0	6
	x_5	3	0	3	0	0	-1	1	6
2	Z	0	1	0	0	0	$\frac{3}{2}$	1	36
	x_3	1	0	0	0	1	$\frac{1}{3}$	$-\frac{1}{3}$	2
	x_2	2	0	0	1	0	$\frac{1}{2}$	0	6
	x_1	3	0	1	0	0	$-\frac{1}{3}$	$\frac{1}{3}$	2

$$Row\ 1 \qquad \begin{bmatrix} 1 & 0 & 1 & 0 & 0, & 4 \end{bmatrix}$$

$$-(1)\begin{bmatrix} 1 & 0 & 0 & -\frac{1}{3} & \frac{1}{3}, & 2 \end{bmatrix}$$

$$New\ row = \begin{bmatrix} 0 & 0 & 1 & \frac{1}{3} & -\frac{1}{3}, & 2 \end{bmatrix}.$$

Row 2 Unchanged because its pivot column coefficient is zero.

We now have the set of tableaux shown in Table 4.8. Therefore, the new basic feasible solution is (2,6,2,0,0), with $Z = 36$. Going to the optimality test, we find that this solution is *optimal* because none of the coefficients in Eq. (0) are negative, so the algorithm is finished. Consequently, the optimal solution to the Wyndor Glass Co. problem (before introducing slack variables) is $x_1 = 2$, $x_2 = 6$.

4.5 Tie Breaking in the Simplex Method

You may have noticed in the preceding two sections that we never said what to do if the various choice rules of the simplex method do not lead to a clear-cut decision, either because of ties or other similar ambiguities. We discuss these details now.

TIE FOR THE ENTERING BASIC VARIABLE

Part 1 of the iterative step chooses the nonbasic variable having the *negative* coefficient with the *largest absolute value* in the current Eq. (0) as the entering basic variable. Now suppose that two or more nonbasic variables are tied for having the largest negative coefficient (in absolute terms). For example, this would occur in the first iteration for the Wyndor Glass Co. problem (see Sec. 3.1) if its objective function were changed to $Z = 3x_1 + 3x_2$, so that the initial Eq. (0) becomes $Z - 3x_1 - 3x_2 = 0$. How should this tie be broken?

The answer is that the selection between these contenders may be made *arbitrarily*. The optimal solution will be reached eventually, regardless of the tied variable chosen, and there is no convenient method for predicting in advance which choice will lead there sooner. In this example, the simplex method happens to reach the optimal solution (2,6) in three iterations with x_1 as the initial entering basic variable, versus two iterations if x_2 is chosen.

TIE FOR THE LEAVING BASIC VARIABLE—DEGENERACY

Now suppose that two or more basic variables tie for being the leaving basic variable in part 2 of the iterative step. Does it matter which one is chosen? Theoretically it does, and in a very critical way, because of the following sequence of events that could occur. First, all of the tied basic variables reach zero simultaneously as the entering basic variable is increased. Therefore, the one or ones *not* chosen to be the leaving basic variable also will have a value of zero in the new basic feasible solution. (Basic variables with a value of *zero* are called *degenerate*, and the same term is applied to the corresponding basic feasible solution.) Second, if one of these degenerate basic variables retains its value of zero until it is chosen at a subsequent iteration to be a leaving basic variable, the corresponding entering basic variable must also remain zero (since it cannot be increased without making the leaving basic variable negative), so the value of Z must remain unchanged. Third, if Z may remain the same rather than increase at each iteration, the simplex method may then go around in a loop, repeating the same sequence of solutions periodically rather than eventually increasing Z toward an optimal solution. In fact, examples have been artificially constructed so that they do become entrapped in just such a perpetual loop.

Fortunately, although a perpetual loop is theoretically possible, it has rarely been known to occur in practical problems. If a loop were to occur, one could always get out of it by changing the choice of the leaving basic variable. Futhermore, special rules[1] have been constructed for breaking ties so that such loops are always avoided. However, these rules have been virtually ignored in

[1] See, for example, A. Charnes, "Optimality and Degeneracy in Linear Programming," *Econometrica*, **20**:160–170, 1952.

Table 4.9 **Initial simplex tableau for Wyndor Glass Co. problem without last two functional constraints**

Basic variable	Eq. no.	Z	x_1	x_2	x_3	Right side	Ratio
Z	0	1	−3	−5	0	0	
x_3	1	0	1	$\boxed{0}$	1	4	No minimum

actual application, and they will not be repeated here. For your purposes, just break this kind of tie *arbitrarily* and proceed without worrying about the degenerate basic variables that result.

NO LEAVING BASIC VARIABLE—UNBOUNDED Z

In part 2 of the iterative step there is one other possible outcome that we have not yet discussed, namely, that *no* variable qualifies to be the leaving basic variable.[1] This outcome would occur if the entering basic variable could be increased *indefinitely* without giving negative values to *any* of the current basic variables. In the tabular form, this means that *every* coefficient in the pivot column [excluding Eq. (0)] is either negative or zero. This situation is illustrated in Table 4.9 by deleting the last two functional constraints of the Wyndor Glass Co. problem (note the effect in Fig. 3.2).

The interpretation of a tableau like the one shown in Table 4.9 is that the constraints do not prevent increasing the value of the objective function (Z) indefinitely, so the simplex method would stop with the message that Z is *unbounded*. Because even linear programming has not discovered a way of making infinite profits, the real message for practical problems is that a mistake has been made! The model probably has been misformulated, either by omitting relevant constraints or by stating them incorrectly. Alternatively, a computational mistake may have occurred.

MULTIPLE OPTIMAL SOLUTIONS

We mentioned in Sec 3.2 (under the definition of **optimal solution**) that a problem can have more than one optimal solution. This fact was illustrated by changing the objective function in the Wyndor Glass Co. problem to $Z = 3x_1 + 2x_2$, so that every point on the line segment between (2,6) and (4,3) is optimal. We also noted in Sec. 4.1 that every such problem has at least two optimal corner-point feasible solutions (basic feasible solutions). These solutions can be used to identify every other optimal solution (as described in Prob. 9 of Chap. 5).

For many applications of linear programming, there are intangible factors not incorporated into the model that can be used to make meaningful choices

[1] Note that the analogous case (no *entering* basic variable) cannot occur in part 1 of the iterative step because of the optimality test.

between solutions that are alternative optimal solutions according to the model. After the simplex method finds an optimal basic feasible solution, how does it recognize when there may be others, and how can it be used to find them? The answer is summarized as follows:

> Whenever a problem has more than one optimal basic feasible solution, at least one of the nonbasic variables has a coefficient of *zero* in the final Eq. (0), so increasing any such variable would not change the value of Z. Therefore, these other optimal solutions can be identified by performing additional iterations of the simplex method, each time choosing a nonbasic variable with a zero coefficient as the entering basic variable.

To illustrate, consider the preceding example where the objective function is $Z = 3x_1 + 2x_2$. The simplex method obtains the first three tableaux shown in Table 4.10 and stops with an optimal basic feasible solution. However, because a nonbasic variable (x_3) then has a zero coefficient in Eq. (0), we perform one more iteration in Table 4.10 to identify the other optimal basic feasible solution. Thus

Table 4.10 Complete set of simplex tableaux to obtain all optimal basic feasible solutions for Wyndor Glass Co. problem with $c_2 = 2$

Iteration	Basic variable	Eq. no.	Z	x_1	x_2	x_3	x_4	x_5	Right side	Solution Optimal?
0	Z	0	1	-3	-2	0	0	0	0	No
	x_3	1	0	1	0	1	0	0	4	
	x_4	2	0	0	2	0	1	0	12	
	x_5	3	0	3	2	0	0	1	18	
1	Z	0	1	0	-2	3	0	0	12	No
	x_1	1	0	1	0	1	0	0	4	
	x_4	2	0	0	2	0	1	0	12	
	x_5	3	0	0	2	-3	0	1	6	
2	Z	0	1	0	0	**0**	0	1	18	Yes
	x_1	1	0	1	0	1	0	0	4	
	x_4	2	0	0	0	3	1	-1	6	
	x_2	3	0	0	1	$-\dfrac{3}{2}$	0	$\dfrac{1}{2}$	3	
Extra	Z	0	1	0	0	0	**0**	1	18	Yes
	x_1	1	0	1	0	0	$-\dfrac{1}{3}$	$\dfrac{1}{3}$	2	
	x_3	2	0	0	0	1	$\dfrac{1}{3}$	$-\dfrac{1}{3}$	2	
	x_2	3	0	0	1	0	$\dfrac{1}{2}$	0	6	

the two optimal basic feasible solutions are (4,3,0,6,0) and (2,6,2,0,0), each yielding $Z = 18$. Notice that the last tableau also has a *nonbasic* variable (x_4) with a zero coefficient in Eq. (0). This situation is inevitable because the extra iteration(s) does not change row 0, so each leaving basic variable necessarily retains its zero coefficient. Making x_4 an entering basic variable now would only lead back to the third tableau. (Check this.) Therefore, these two are the only basic feasible solutions that are optimal, and all *other* optimal solutions are a weighted average of these two.

4.6 Adapting to Other Model Forms

Thus far we have presented the details of the simplex method under the assumption that the problem is in *our standard form* (see Sec. 3.2), with $b_i > 0$ for all $i = 1, 2, \ldots, m$. In this section we point out how to make the adjustments required for other legitimate forms of the linear programming model. You will see that all these adjustments can be made in the initialization step, so that the rest of the simplex method can then be applied just as you have learned it already.

The only real problem that the other forms for functional constraints ($=, \geq$, or $b_i \leq 0$) introduce is in identifying an initial basic feasible solution. Before, this initial solution was found very conveniently by letting the slack variables be the initial basic variables, so that each one just equals the *positive* right-hand side of its equation. Now, something else must be done. The standard approach that is used for all these cases is the **artificial variable technique**. This technique constructs a more convenient *revised problem* by introducing into each constraint that needs one a dummy variable (called an *artificial variable*). This new variable is introduced just for the purpose of being the initial basic variable for that equation. The usual nonnegativity constraints are placed on these variables, and the objective function also is modified to impose an exorbitant penalty on their having values larger than zero. The iterations of the simplex method then automatically force the artificial variables to disappear (become zero) one at a time until they are all gone, after which the *real* problem is solved.

To illustrate the artificial variable technique, we first consider the case where the only nonstandard form in the problem is the presence of one or more equality constraints.

EQUALITY CONSTRAINTS

Any equality constraint

$$a_{i1}x_1 + a_{i2}x_2 + \cdots + a_{in}x_n = b_i$$

actually is equivalent to a pair of inequality constraints:

$$a_{i1}x_1 + a_{i2}x_2 + \cdots + a_{in}x_n \leq b_i$$
$$a_{i1}x_1 + a_{i2}x_2 + \cdots + a_{in}x_n \geq b_i.$$

However, rather than making this substitution and thereby increasing the number of constraints, it is more convenient to use the artificial variable technique described next.

Suppose that the Wyndor Glass Co. problem in Sec. 3.1 is modified to *require* that Plant 3 be used at full capacity. The only resulting change in the linear programming model is that the third constraint, $3x_1 + 2x_2 \leq 18$, instead becomes an *equality* constraint,

$$3x_1 + 2x_2 = 18.$$

Therefore, the feasible region for this problem (see Fig. 3.2) now consists of *just* the line segment connecting (2,6) and (4,3).

After introducing the slack variables still needed for the *inequality* constraints, the *equality form* of the problem (see the end of Sec. 4.2) becomes

(0)	$Z - 3x_1 - 5x_2$	$= 0$
(1)	$x_1 \qquad + x_3$	$= 4$
(2)	$2x_2 \qquad + x_4$	$= 12$
(3)	$3x_1 + 2x_2$	$= 18.$

Unfortunately, these equations do not have an obvious initial basic feasible solution because there is no longer a slack variable to use as the initial basic variable for Eq. (3). The artificial variable technique circumvents this difficulty by introducing a nonnegative **artificial variable** (call it $\bar{x}_5$)[1] into this equation, just as if it were a slack variable! Thus the technique *revises* the problem by changing Eq. (3) to

(3) $\qquad\qquad\qquad\qquad 3x_1 + 2x_2 + \bar{x}_5 = 18,$

along with the nonnegativity constraint,

$$\bar{x}_5 \geq 0,$$

just as we had in the original Wyndor Glass Co. problem. Proceeding as before, we now have an initial basic feasible solution (for the *revised problem*) $(x_1, x_2, x_3, x_4, \bar{x}_5) = (0,0,4,12,18)$.

The effect of introducing an artificial variable is to *enlarge* the feasible region. In this case, the feasible region expands from just the line segment connecting (2,6) and (4,3) to the entire shaded area shown in Fig. 3.2. A feasible solution for the *revised* problem is also feasible for the *original* problem if the artificial variable equals zero ($\bar{x}_5 = 0$).

Now suppose that the simplex method is permitted to proceed and obtain an *optimal* solution for the *revised* problem and that this solution happens to be *feasible* for the *original* problem. It can then be concluded that this solution must also be *optimal* for the *original* problem, so we are finished. (The reason is that this

---

[1] We shall always label the artificial variables by putting a bar over them.

solution is the best one in the *entire* feasible region for the revised problem, which includes the feasible region for the original problem.)

Unfortunately, there is no guarantee that the optimal solution to the revised problem also will be feasible for the original problem; that is, there is no guarantee until *another* revision is made. Using the **Big M method**, this new revision amounts to assigning such an *overwhelming penalty* to being outside the feasible region for the original problem that the optimal solution to the revised problem *must* lie within this region. Recall that the revised problem coincides with the original problem when $\bar{x}_5 = 0$. Therefore, if the original objective function, $Z = 3x_1 + 5x_2$, is changed to

$$Z = 3x_1 + 5x_2 - M\bar{x}_5,$$

where M denotes some *huge* positive number, then the maximum value of Z must occur when $\bar{x}_5 = 0$ ($\bar{x}_5$ cannot be negative). After a little more setting up (discussed next), applying the simplex method to *this* revised problem automatically leads to the desired solution.

Using this revised objective function, Eq. (0) becomes

(0) $Z - 3x_1 - 5x_2 + M\bar{x}_5 = 0,$

or in tabular form, the *preliminary* row 0 (call it R_0) becomes

$$R_0 = [-3 \quad -5 \quad 0 \quad 0 \quad M, \quad 0].$$

However, this R_0 *cannot* be used for the initial tableau for applying the simplex method because both the optimality test and part 1 of the iterative step require that *every* basic variable must have a coefficient of zero, and $\bar{x}_5$ is an initial basic variable. This requirement is normally fulfilled by part 3 of the iterative step, and the same method must be used here, proceeding as if the column for the artificial variable ($\bar{x}_5$) were the pivot column and its equality constraint were the pivot row. This method is demonstrated as follows:

Row 0 [	-3	-5	0	0	$M,$	0]
$-M$ [	3	2	0	0	$1,$	18]
New row = [	$(-3M - 3),$	$(-2M - 5),$	0	0	$0,$	$-18M].$

This completes the additional work required in the initialization step for problems of this type, and the rest of the simplex method proceeds just as before. The quantities involving M never appear anywhere except in row 0, so they need to be taken into account only in the optimality test and in part 1 of the iterative step. This could be done by assigning some particular (huge) numerical value to M and working with just the resulting numbers in row 0 in the usual way. However, this approach may result in significant round-off errors that invalidate the optimality test. Therefore, it is better to do what we have just shown, namely, express each coefficient in row 0 as a linear function $aM + b$ of the *symbolic* quantity M by separately recording and updating the current numerical value of (1) the *multiplicative* factor a and (2) the *additive* factor b. Because M is assumed to be so large that b always is negligible compared to aM when $a \neq 0$, the decisions in the optimality test and part 1 of the iterative step are made by using just the *multiplicative* factors in the usual way. The one exception is when this use leads to a tie (where a tie for the optimality test means that the smallest multiplicative factor(s) equals zero), in which case the tie would be broken by using the corresponding *additive* factors.

Using this approach on the example yields the simplex tableaux shown in Table 4.11. Thus the optimal solution is (2,6,2,0,0), so $x_1 = 2$ and $x_2 = 6$, just as for the original Wyndor Glass Co. problem, so the Big M method was not even needed in this case. However, a different sequence of basic feasible solutions was obtained because a comparison of the initial *multiplicative* factors $(3 > 2)$ led to choosing x_1 rather than x_2 as the initial entering basic variable. If the equality constraint had been $3x_1 + 3x_2 = 18$ instead, both multiplicative factors would have been -3, so then a comparison of the *additive* factors $(5 > 3)$ would have led to choosing x_2 as before.

Table 4.11 Complete set of simplex tableaux for Wyndor Glass Co. problem with an equality constraint

Iteration	Basic variable	Eq. no.	Z	x_1	x_2	x_3	x_4	x_5	Right side
					Coefficient of				
0	Z	0	1	$(-3M-3)$	$(-2M-5)$	0	0	0	$-18M$
	x_3	1	0	1	0	1	0	0	4
	x_4	2	0	0	2	0	1	0	12
	$\bar{x}_5$	3	0	3	2	0	0	1	18
1	Z	0	1	0	$(-2M-5)$	$(3M+3)$	0	0	$-6M+12$
	x_1	1	0	1	0	1	0	0	4
	x_4	2	0	0	2	0	1	0	12
	$\bar{x}_5$	3	0	0	2	-3	0	1	6
2	Z	0	1	0	0	$-\dfrac{9}{2}$	0	$\left(M+\dfrac{5}{2}\right)$	27
	x_1	1	0	1	0	1	0	0	4
	x_4	2	0	0	0	3	1	-1	6
	x_2	3	0	0	1	$-\dfrac{3}{2}$	0	$\dfrac{1}{2}$	3
3	Z	0	1	0	0	0	$\dfrac{3}{2}$	$(M+1)$	36
	x_1	1	0	1	0	0	$-\dfrac{1}{3}$	$\dfrac{1}{3}$	2
	x_3	2	0	0	0	1	$\dfrac{1}{3}$	$-\dfrac{1}{3}$	2
	x_2	3	0	0	1	0	$\dfrac{1}{2}$	0	6

This example involved only *one* equality constraint. If a linear programming model has more than one, each would be handled in just this same way.[1] Thus each such constraint would be given an artificial variable to serve as its initial basic variable, each of these variables would be assigned a coefficient of $-M$ in the objective function, and the resulting row 0 would have subtracted from it M times each equality constraint row.

The approach to other kinds of constraints requiring artificial variables is completely analogous. To illustrate the adjustments for a variety of different forms, we modify the Wyndor Glass Co. model as follows.

MODIFIED EXAMPLE

$$\text{Minimize} \quad Z = 3x_1 + 5x_2,$$

subject to

$$
\begin{aligned}
x_1 &\leq 4 \\
2x_2 &= 12 \\
3x_1 + 2x_2 &\geq 18
\end{aligned}
$$

and

$$x_1 \geq 0, \quad x_2 \geq 0.$$

Fig. 4.2 shows the constraint boundaries for this example. The feasible region consists of just the line segment connecting (2,6) and (4,6). Since we are now *minimizing* Z, the optimal solution again lies at (2,6).

Before solving the example in its entirety, we discuss individually the different kinds of adjustments required.

MINIMIZATION

One straightforward way of minimizing Z with the simplex method is to exchange the roles of the positive and negative coefficients in row 0 for both the optimality test and part 1 of the iterative step. However, rather than changing our instructions for the simplex method, we instead present the following simple way of converting any minimization problem into an equivalent maximization problem:

Minimizing $\quad Z = \sum_{j=1}^{n} c_j x_j$ is equivalent to

maximizing $\quad (-Z) = \sum_{j=1}^{n} (-c_j)x_j$; that is, the two formulations yield the

same optimal solution(s).

---

[1] This statement assumes that the equality constraint has a nonnegative right-hand side. Otherwise, multiply it through by (-1) first to satisfy this condition before introducing the artificial variable.

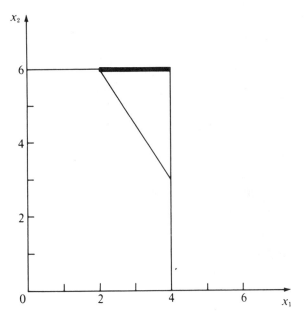

Figure 4.2 **Constraint boundaries for modified example. Darker line segment is feasible region.**

The reason the two formulations are equivalent is that the smaller Z is, the larger $(-Z)$ is, so the solution that gives the *smallest* value of Z in the entire feasible region must also give the *largest* value of $(-Z)$ in this region.

Therefore, in the modified example, we must make the following change in the formulation:

$$\text{Minimize} \quad Z = \quad 3x_1 + 5x_2$$
$$\rightarrow \text{Maximize} \quad (-Z) = -3x_1 - 5x_2.$$

≥ INEQUALITY CONSTRAINTS

The direction of an inequality always is reversed when both sides are multiplied by (-1). As a result, any functional constraint of the $\geq$ form can be converted into an *equivalent* constraint of *our* standard $\leq$ form by changing the signs of all the numbers on both sides.

Using this approach for the third constraint of the example,

$$3x_1 + 2x_2 \quad \geq \quad 18$$
$$\rightarrow -3x_1 - 2x_2 \quad \leq -18$$
$$\rightarrow -3x_1 - 2x_2 + x_5 = -18,$$

where x_5 is the slack variable for this constraint. However, one more change is still needed, as you will see next.

NEGATIVE RIGHT-HAND SIDES

You may recall that the simplex method was presented in the preceding sections under the assumptions that $b_i > 0$ for all $i = 1, 2, \ldots, m$. This assumption enabled us to select the slack variables to be the *initial* basic variables (equal to the right-hand sides) and still obtain a *nondegenerate* basic *feasible* solution. We have since pointed out in Sec. 4.5 that degeneracy (basic variables equal to zero) does not need to be avoided. However, a negative right-hand side, such as in the third constraint,

$$-3x_1 - 2x_2 + x_5 = -18,$$

would give a negative value for the slack variable ($x_5 = -18$) in the initial solution, which violates the nonnegativity constraint for this variable. Multiplying through the equation by (-1) makes the right-hand side positive:

$$3x_1 + 2x_2 - x_5 = 18,$$

but it also changes the coefficient of the slack variable to -1, so the variable still would be negative. However, in this form the constraint can be viewed as an *equality constraint* with a nonnegative right-hand side, so the *artificial variable technique* can be applied just as discussed earlier in this section. (In fact, this constraint is identical to our example of an equality constraint except that it includes one more term on the left-hand side.) If we let $\bar{x}_6$ be the nonnegative artificial variable for this constraint, its final form becomes

$$3x_1 + 2x_2 - x_5 + \bar{x}_6 = 18,$$

where $\bar{x}_6$ is used as the *initial basic variable* ($\bar{x}_6 = 18$) for this equation and x_5 begins as a nonbasic variable. The Big M method also would be applied just as before, as we shall demonstrate shortly.

As usual, introducing this artificial variable enlarges the feasible region. The original constraint allowed only solutions lying above or on the constraint boundary, $3x_1 + 2x_2 = 18$. Now it allows any solution lying below this constraint boundary as well because both x_5 and $\bar{x}_6$ are constrained only to be nonnegative, so their difference ($\bar{x}_6 - x_5$) can be *any* positive or negative number. Therefore, the effect of including $\bar{x}_6$ is to *eliminate* this constraint at the outset (before the Big M method forces $\bar{x}_6$ to be zero). Considering the other constraints as well (see Fig. 4.2), the feasible region for the *revised* problem is expanded to include the entire line segment connecting $(0,6)$ and $(4,6)$.

You may have noticed that we took a somewhat circuitous route in converting the third constraint from its original form, $3x_1 + 2x_2 \geq 18$, to its final version, $3x_1 + 2x_2 - x_5 + \bar{x}_6 = 18$. In fact, we multiplied through the constraint by (-1) twice along the way! Now that you have seen the motivation leading to the final form, we should point out the following shortcut:

$$3x_1 + 2x_2 \geq 18$$
$$\rightarrow 3x_1 + 2x_2 - x_5 = 18 \qquad (x_5 \geq 0)$$
$$\rightarrow 3x_1 + 2x_2 - x_5 + \bar{x}_6 = 18 \qquad (x_5 \geq 0, \bar{x}_6 \geq 0).$$

In this form, x_5 is called a *surplus variable* because it subtracts the surplus of the left-hand side over the right-side to convert the constraint into an equivalent equation.

SOLVING THE MODIFIED EXAMPLE

With the preceding adjustments in the model for the modified example, we now are almost ready to apply the iterative part of the simplex method. All that remains to be done is to make the usual adjustment in the equality constraint, $2x_2 = 12$, and to apply the Big M method. Letting $\bar{x}_4$ be the artificial variable for this constraint, it becomes

$$2x_2 + \bar{x}_4 = 12.$$

Since the entire set of equations now contains two artificial variables, $\bar{x}_4$ and $\bar{x}_6$, the objective function becomes

$$\text{Minimize} \quad Z = 3x_1 + 5x_2 + M\bar{x}_4 + M\bar{x}_6,$$

or in maximization form,

$$\text{Maximize} \quad (-Z) = -3x_1 - 5x_2 - M\bar{x}_4 - M\bar{x}_6.$$

This latter form yields our preliminary Eq. (0):

(0) $$\qquad -Z + 3x_1 + 5x_2 + M\bar{x}_4 + M\bar{x}_6 = 0,$$

or in tabular form,

$$R_0 = [3 \quad 5 \quad 0 \quad M \quad 0 \quad M, \quad 0].$$

Since $\bar{x}_4$ and $\bar{x}_6$ are to be initial basic variables, row 0 needs to be updated to reflect this.

Row 0	[	3	5	0	M	0	M,	0	]
$-M$	[	0	2	0	1	0	0,	12	]
$-M$	[	3	2	0	0	−1	1,	18	]
New row =	[	$(-3M + 3)$,	$(-4M + 5)$,	0	0	M	0,	$-30M$	].

The resulting initial simplex tableau and the subsequent iterations are shown in Table 4.12.

It is interesting to reflect on what the Big M method actually does, as illustrated by this example. Note that it gives an objective function (minimize $Z = 3x_1 + 5x_2 + M\bar{x}_4 + M\bar{x}_6$) such that the coefficients of the original variables (x_1 and x_2) are negligible compared to the huge coefficient M for the artificial variables. Therefore, the Big M method is essentially equivalent to having the simplex method begin by just minimizing the *sum* of the artificial variables, $\bar{x}_4 + \bar{x}_6$, over the feasible region for the *revised* problem (where $\bar{x}_4 \geq 0, \bar{x}_6 \geq 0$). Once the simplex method succeeds in driving this sum down to its minimum possible value of zero, yielding a basic solution that is *feasible* for the *original*

Table 4.12 Complete set of simplex tableaux for modified example

Iteration	Basic variable	Eq. no.	Z	x_1	x_2	x_3	$\bar{x}_4$	x_5	$\bar{x}_6$	Right side
0	Z	0	-1	$(-3M+3)$	$(-4M+5)$	0	0	M	0	$-30M$
	x_3	1	0	1	$\boxed{0}$	1	0	0	0	4
	$\bar{x}_4$	2	0	$\boxed{0}$	2	0	1	0	0	$\boxed{12}$
	$\bar{x}_6$	3	0	3	$\boxed{2}$	0	0	-1	1	18
1	Z	0	-1	$(-3M+3)$	0	0	$\left(2M - \dfrac{5}{2}\right)$	M	0	$-6M-30$
	x_3	1	0	$\boxed{1}$	0	1	0	0	0	4
	x_2	2	0	$\boxed{0}$	1	0	$\dfrac{1}{2}$	0	0	6
	$\bar{x}_6$	3	0	$\boxed{3}$	0	0	-1	-1	1	$\boxed{6}$
2	Z	0	-1	0	0	0	$\left(M - \dfrac{3}{2}\right)$	1	$(M-1)$	-36
	x_3	1	0	0	0	1	$\dfrac{1}{3}$	$\dfrac{1}{3}$	$-\dfrac{1}{3}$	2
	x_2	2	0	0	1	0	$\dfrac{1}{2}$	0	0	6
	x_1	3	0	1	0	0	$-\dfrac{1}{3}$	$-\dfrac{1}{3}$	$\dfrac{1}{3}$	2

problem, it then can start solving this original problem (minimize $Z = 3x_1 + 5x_2$) with this solution as the initial basic feasible solution. For the example, this initial solution (see the last tableau of Table 4.12) also happens to be optimal for the original problem, so no more iterations are needed. In our earlier example just for equality constraints (see Table 4.11), one more iteration was required.

An alternative to the Big M method is the **two-phase method**, which follows the procedure just described *directly*. In *phase 1*, the simplex method is used to *minimize* the *sum* (i.e., maximize the negative of the sum) of the artificial variables over the feasible region for the *revised* problem. The "optimal" solution for phase 1 necessarily has all the artificial variables equal to zero (with the one exception discussed next), so this solution is *feasible* for the *original* problem. *Phase 2* then solves the original problem by the simplex method, starting with this solution as the initial basic feasible solution.

The Big M method and the two-phase method always have the same sequence of basic feasible solutions (with the one possible exception of when a tie for the entering basic variable occurs in phase 1 of the two-phase method), so they are essentially equivalent in terms of computational effort. Because it has better numerical stability than the Big M method (if an actual number is substituted for M), the two-phase method usually is used in computer codes.

NO FEASIBLE SOLUTIONS

So far in this section we have been concerned primarily with the basic problem of identifying an initial basic feasible solution when an obvious one is not available. You have seen how the artificial variable technique constructs an artificial problem and obtains an initial basic feasible solution for this revised problem instead. The Big M method then enables the simplex method to begin its pilgrimage toward the basic feasible solutions, and ultimately toward the optimal solution, for the *original* problem.

However, you should be wary of a certain pitfall with this approach. There may be no obvious choice for the initial basic feasible solution for the very good reason that there are no feasible solutions at all! Nevertheless, by constructing an artificial feasible solution, there is nothing to prevent the simplex method from proceeding as usual and ultimately reporting a supposedly optimal solution.

Fortunately, the artificial variable technique provides the following signpost to indicate when this has happened:

> If the original problem has *no feasible solutions*, then any optimal solution for the *revised* problem with the Big M method has at least one artificial variable *not* equal to zero. Otherwise, they *all* equal zero.

To illustrate, let us change the first constraint in the modified example (see Fig. 4.2) as follows:

$$x_1 \leq 4 \rightarrow x_1 \leq 1,$$

so that the problem no longer has any feasible solutions. Applying the simplex method just as before yields the tableaux shown in Table 4.13. Hence the indicated optimal solution is (1,6,0,0,0,3). However, since an artificial variable $\bar{x}_6 = 3 > 0$, the real message is that the problem has no feasible solutions.

VARIABLES ALLOWED TO BE NEGATIVE

In most practical problems, negative values for the decision variables would have no physical meaning, so it is necessary to include nonnegativity constraints in the formulations of their linear programming models. However, this is not always the case. To illustrate, suppose that the Wyndor Glass Co. problem is changed so that product 1 already is in production, and the first decision variable x_1 represents the *increase* in its production rate. Therefore, a negative value of x_1 would indicate that product 1 is to be cut back by that amount. Such reductions might be desirable to allow a larger production rate for the new more profitable product 2, so negative values should be allowed for x_1 in the model.

Since the iterative step (part 2) of the simplex method requires that all the variables have nonnegativity constraints, any problem containing variables allowed to be negative must be converted into an *equivalent* problem involving only nonnegative variables. Fortunately, this conversion can be done. The

Table 4.13 **Complete set of simplex tableaux for example with no feasible solutions**

Iteration	Basic variable	Eq. no.	Z	x_1	x_2	x_3	$\bar{x}_4$	x_5	$\bar{x}_6$	Right side
						Coefficient of				
0	Z	0	-1	$(-3M+3)$	$(-4M+5)$	0	0	M	0	$-30M$
	x_3	1	0	1	0	1	0	0	0	1
	$\bar{x}_4$	2	0	0	2	0	1	0	0	12
	$\bar{x}_6$	3	0	3	2	0	0	-1	1	18
1	Z	0	-1	$(-3M+3)$	0	0	$\left(2M-\dfrac{5}{2}\right)$	M	0	$-6M-30$
	x_3	1	0	1	0	1	0	0	0	1
	x_2	2	0	0	1	0	$\dfrac{1}{2}$	0	0	6
	$\bar{x}_6$	3	0	3	0	0	-1	-1	1	6
2	Z	0	-1	0	0	$(3M-3)$	$\left(2M-\dfrac{5}{2}\right)$	M	0	$-3M-33$
	x_1	1	0	1	0	1	0	0	0	1
	x_2	2	0	0	1	0	$\dfrac{1}{2}$	0	0	6
	$\bar{x}_6$	3	0	0	0	-3	-1	-1	1	3

modification required for each variable depends upon whether it has a (negative) lower bound on the values allowed or not. Each of these two cases is now discussed.

VARIABLES WITH A BOUND ON THE NEGATIVE VALUES ALLOWED Consider any decision variable x_j that is allowed to have negative values, but only those that satisfy a constraint of the form

$$x_j \geq L_j,$$

where L_j is some negative constant. This constraint can be converted into a nonnegativity constraint by making the change of variables,

$$x'_j = x_j - L_j, \quad \text{so } x'_j \geq 0.$$

Thus $(x'_j + L_j)$ would be substituted for x_j throughout the model, so that the redefined decision variable x'_j cannot be negative.

To illustrate, suppose that the current production rate for product 1 in the Wyndor Glass Co. problem is 10. With the definition of x_1 just given, the complete model at this point is the same as that given in Sec. 3.1 except that the nonnegativity constraint, $x_1 \geq 0$, is replaced by

$$x_1 \geq -10.$$

To obtain the equivalent model needed for the simplex method, this decision variable would be redefined as the *total* production rate of product 1,

$$x_1' = x_1 + 10,$$

which yields the changes in the objective function and constraints as shown:

$Z = 3x_1 + 5x_2$	$Z = 3(x_1' - 10) + 5x_2$	$Z = -30 + 3x_1' + 5x_2$
$x_1 \leq 4$	$(x_1' - 10) \leq 4$	$x_1' \leq 14$
$2x_2 \leq 12$	$2x_2 \leq 12$	$2x_2 \leq 12$
$3x_1 + 2x_2 \leq 18$	$3(x_1' - 10) + 2x_2 \leq 18$	$3x_1' + 2x_2 \leq 48$
$x_1 \geq -10, x_2 \geq 0$	$(x_1' - 10) \geq -10, x_2 \geq 0$	$x_1' \geq 0, x_2 \geq 0$

VARIABLES WITH NO BOUND ON THE NEGATIVE VALUES ALLOWED In the case where x_j does *not* have a lower bound constraint in the model formulated, another approach is required: x_j is replaced throughout the model by the *difference* of two new *nonnegative* variables,

$$x_j = x_j^+ - x_j^-, \quad \text{where } x_j^+ \geq 0, x_j^- \geq 0.$$

Since x_j^+ and x_j^- can have any nonnegative values, this difference $(x_j^+ - x_j^-)$ can have *any* value (positive or negative), so it is a legitimate substitute for x_j in the model. But after such substitutions, the simplex method can proceed with just nonnegative variables.

The new variables, x_j^+ and x_j^-, have a simple interpretation. By the geometric definition of corner-point feasible solution (see Sec. 5.1), each basic feasible solution for the new form of the model necessarily has the property that *either* $x_j^+ = 0$ *or* $x_j^- = 0$ (or both). Therefore, at the optimal solution obtained by the simplex method,

$$x_j^+ = \begin{cases} x_j, & \text{if } x_j \geq 0 \\ 0, & \text{otherwise;} \end{cases}$$

$$x_j^- = \begin{cases} |x_j|, & \text{if } x_j \leq 0 \\ 0, & \text{otherwise;} \end{cases}$$

so that x_j^+ represents the *positive* part of the decision variable x_j and x_j^- its *negative* part (as suggested by the superscripts).

To illustrate this approach, let us use the same example as for the *bounded variable case*. However, now suppose that the $x_1 \geq -10$ constraint was not included in the original model because it clearly would not change the optimal solution. (In some problems, certain variables do not need explicit lower bound constraints because the functional constraints already prevent lower values.) Therefore, before applying the simplex method, x_1 would be replaced by the difference,

$$x_1 = x_1^+ - x_1^-, \quad \text{where } x_1^+ \geq 0, x_1^- \geq 0,$$

as shown:

$$\boxed{\begin{aligned} \text{Maximize} \quad & Z = 3x_1 + 5x_2 \\ & x_1 \qquad\quad \leq 4 \\ & \qquad\quad 2x_2 \leq 12 \\ & 3x_1 + 2x_2 \leq 18 \\ & x_2 \geq 0 \text{ (only)} \end{aligned}} \;\rightarrow\; \boxed{\begin{aligned} \text{Maximize} \quad & Z = 3x_1^+ - 3x_1^- + 5x_2 \\ & x_1^+ - x_1^- \qquad\quad \leq 4 \\ & \qquad\qquad\quad 2x_2 \leq 12 \\ & 3x_1^+ - 3x_1^- + 2x_2 \leq 18 \\ & x_1^+ \geq 0,\, x_1^- \geq 0,\, x_2 \geq 0 \end{aligned}}$$

From a computational viewpoint, this approach has the disadvantage that the new equivalent model to be used has more variables than the original model. In fact, if *all* the original variables lack lower bound constraints, the new model will have *twice* as many variables. Fortunately, the approach can be modified slightly so that the number of variables is increased by only *one*, regardless of how many original variables need to be replaced. This modification is done by replacing each such variable x_j by

$$x_j = x_j' - x'', \quad \text{where } x_j' \geq 0,\, x'' \geq 0,$$

instead, where x'' is the *same* variable for all relevant j. The interpretation of x'' in this case is that $-x''$ is the current value of the *largest* (in absolute terms) negative original variable, so that x_j' is the amount by which x_j exceeds this value. Thus the simplex method now can make some of the x_j' variables larger than zero even when $x'' > 0$.

4.7 Post-Optimality Analysis

We stressed in Secs. 2.3, 2.4, and 2.5 that *post-optimality analysis*—the analysis done *after* an optimal solution is obtained for the initial version of the model—constitutes a very major and very important part of most operations research studies. The fact that post-optimality analysis is very important is particularly true for typical linear programming applications. In this section, we focus on the role of the simplex method in performing this analysis.

Table 4.14 summarizes the typical steps in post-optimality analysis for linear programming studies. The last column of Table 4.14 identifies some algorithmic

Table 4.14 **Post-optimality analysis for linear programming**

Task	Purpose	Technique
Model debugging	Find errors and weaknesses in model	Reoptimization
Model validation	Demonstrate validity of final model	See Sec. 2.4
Final managerial decisions on resource allocations (the b_i)	Make appropriate division of organizational resources between activities under study and other important activities	Shadow prices
Evaluate estimates of model parameters	Determine crucial estimates that may affect optimal solution for further study	Sensitivity analysis
Evaluate tradeoffs between model parameters	Determine best tradeoff	Parametric linear programming

techniques that involve the simplex method. These techniques are introduced briefly here with the technical details deferred to later chapters.

REOPTIMIZATION

After having found an optimal solution for one version of a linear programming model, we frequently must solve again (often many times) for a slightly different version of the model. We nearly always have to solve again several times during the model debugging stage (described in Secs. 2.3 and 2.4), and we usually have to do so a large number of times during the later stages of post-optimality analysis as well.

One approach is simply to reapply the simplex method from scratch for each new version of the model. However, a *much more efficient* approach is to *reoptimize*. Reoptimization involves deducing the changes that get carried along to the *final* simplex tableau (as described in Secs. 5.3 and 6.6) as a result of the changes in the model and then using the optimal solution for the prior model as the *initial basic solution* for solving the new model. If this solution is feasible for the new model, then the simplex method is applied in the usual way, starting from this initial basic feasible solution. If the solution is not feasible, a related algorithm called the *dual simplex method* (described in Sec. 9.2) probably can be applied to find the new optimal solution,[1] starting from this initial basic solution.

The big advantage of this **reoptimization technique** over resolving from scratch is that an optimal solution for the revised model probably is going to be *much* closer to the prior optimal solution than to an initial basic feasible solution constructed in the usual way for the simplex method. Therefore, assuming that the model revisions were modest, only a few iterations should be required to reoptimize instead of the hundreds or thousands that may be required when starting from scratch on a sizeable problem.

SHADOW PRICES

Recall (see Table 3.2) that linear programming problems typically can be interpreted as allocating resources to activities, where the b_i represent the amounts of the respective resources being made available for the activities under consideration. In many cases, there may be some latitude in the amounts that will be made available. If so, the b_i used in the initial (validated) model actually may represent management's *tentative initial decision* on how much of the organization's resources will be provided to the activities considered in the model instead of to other important activities under the purview of management. From this broader perspective, some of the b_i can be increased in a revised model, but

---

[1] The one requirement for using the dual simplex method here is that the *optimality test* still passes when applied to row 0 of the *revised* final tableau. If not, then still another algorithm called the *primal-dual method* can be used instead.

only if a sufficiently strong case can be made to management that this revision would be beneficial.

Consequently, information on the economic contribution of the resources to the measure of performance (Z) for the current study often would be extremely useful. The simplex method provides this information in the form of **shadow prices** for the respective resources.

> The **shadow price** for resource i (denoted by y_i^*) measures the *marginal value* of this resource, that is, the rate at which Z could be increased by (slightly) increasing the amount of this resource (b_i) being made available.[1] The simplex method identifies this shadow price by $y_i^* =$ coefficient of the ith slack variable in Eq. (0) of the final simplex tableau.

To illustrate, for the Wyndor Glass Co. problem (see Sec. 3.1), the final tableau in Table 4.8 yields

$$y_1^* = 0 = \text{shadow price for resource 1,}$$

$$y_2^* = \frac{3}{2} = \text{shadow price for resource 2,}$$

$$y_3^* = 1 = \text{shadow price for resource 3,}$$

where these resources are the available production capacities of Plants 1, 2, and 3, respectively ($b_1 = 4$, $b_2 = 12$, and $b_3 = 18$). You can verify that these numbers are correct by checking in Figs. 3.2 and 3.3 that individually increasing each b_i by 1 indeed would increase the optimal value of Z by y_i^*.[2] For example, Fig. 4.3 shows that this increase happens for resource 2, where the optimal solution, (2,6) with $Z = 36$, changes to (5/3, 13/2) with $Z = 37\frac{1}{2}$ when b_2 is increased by 1 (from 12 to 13), so that

$$y_2^* = \Delta Z = 37\frac{1}{2} - 36 = \frac{3}{2}.$$

Figure 4.3 demonstrates that $y_2^* = \frac{3}{2}$ is the rate at which Z could be increased by increasing b_2 slightly. However, it also demonstrates the common phenomenon that this interpretation holds only for a small increase in b_2. Once b_2 is increased beyond 18, the optimal solution stays at (0,9) with no further increase in Z. (At that point, the set of basic variables in the optimal solution has changed, so a new final simplex tableau would be obtained with new shadow prices, including $y_2^* = 0$.)

Now note in Fig. 4.3 why $y_1^* = 0$. Because the constraint on resource 1,

---

[1] However, note that individually increasing either b_2 or b_3 by more than 6 would result in another set of basic variables becoming optimal, with no further increase in Z, so y_2^* and y_3^* are relevant only for smaller increases in those b_i.

[2] The increase in b_i must be sufficiently small that the current set of basic variables remains optimal since this rate (marginal value) changes if the set of basic variables changes.

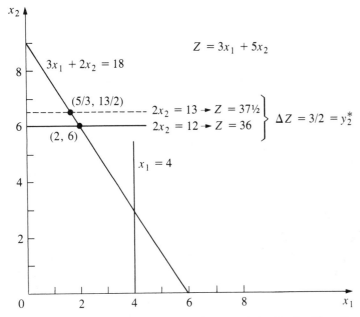

Figure 4.3 *Illustration of shadow price for resource 2 for Wyndor Glass Co. problem.*

$x_1 \leq 4$, is *not binding* on the optimal solution, (2,6), there is a *surplus* of this resource. Therefore, increasing b_1 beyond 4 cannot yield a new optimal solution with a larger value of Z.

The kind of information provided by shadow prices clearly is valuable to management when it considers reallocations of resources within the organization. It also is very helpful when an increase in b_i can be achieved only by going outside the organization to purchase more of the resource in the marketplace. For example, suppose that Z represents *profit* and the unit profits of the activities (the c_j) include the costs (at regular prices) of all the resources consumed. Then a *positive* shadow price of y_i^* for resource i means that the total profit Z can be increased by y_i^* by purchasing one more unit of this resource at its regular price. Alternatively, if a *premium* price must be paid for the resource in the marketplace, then y_i^* represents the *maximum* premium (excess over the regular price) that would be worth paying.

In the Wyndor Glass Co. problem, management has ruled out any expansion of the production capacity in the three plants at this time. Nevertheless, the available capacities allocated to the two new products can be increased by cutting back further on the current product line. The O.R. Department actually investigates this possibility as part of the sensitivity analysis study in Sec. 6.7.

The theoretical foundation for shadow prices is provided by the *duality theory* described in Chap. 6.

SENSITIVITY ANALYSIS

When discussing the *certainty assumption* for linear programming at the end of Sec. 3.3, we pointed out that the values used for the model parameters (the a_{ij}, b_i, and c_j identified in Table 3.2) generally are just *estimates* of quantities whose true values will not become known until the linear programming study is implemented at some time in the future. Therefore, the general purpose of sensitivity analysis is to identify the relatively *sensitive* parameters (i.e., those that cannot be changed much without changing the optimal solution), to try to estimate these parameters more closely, and then to select a solution that remains a good one over the range of likely values of the sensitive parameters.

How are the sensitive parameters identified? In the case of the b_i, you have just seen that this information is given by the shadow prices provided by the simplex method. In particular, if $y_i^* > 0$, then the optimal solution changes if b_i is changed, so b_i is a sensitive parameter. However, $y_i^* = 0$ implies that the optimal solution is not sensitive to at least small changes in b_i. Consequently, if the value used for b_i is an estimate of the amount of the resource that will be available (rather than a managerial decision), then the b_i that need to be estimated more closely are those with *positive* shadow prices—especially those with *large* shadow prices.

When there are just two variables, the sensitivity of the various parameters can be analyzed graphically. For example, in Fig. 4.3 (or Fig. 3.3), you can see that $c_1 = 3$ can be changed to any other value within the range from 0 to $7\frac{1}{2}$ without the optimal solution changing from (2,6). Similarly, if $c_2 = 5$ is the only parameter changed, it can have any value greater than 2 without affecting the optimal solution. Hence neither c_1 nor c_2 is a sensitive parameter. On the other hand, $a_{21} = 0$, $a_{22} = 2$, $a_{31} = 3$, and $a_{32} = 2$ all are sensitive parameters since any individual change in their values would change the optimal solution.

With more than two variables, the same kind of information still can be extracted from the simplex method. Getting this information requires using the *fundamental insight* described in Sec. 5.3 to deduce the changes that get carried along to the final simplex tableau as a result of changing the value of a parameter in the original model. The rest of the procedure is described in Sec. 6.6.

PARAMETRIC LINEAR PROGRAMMING

Sensitivity analysis involves changing one parameter at a time in the original model to check its effect on the optimal solution. By contrast, *parametric linear programming* (or *parametric programming* for short) involves the systematic study of how the optimal solution changes as *many* of the parameters change *simultaneously* over some range. This study can provide a very useful extension of sensitivity analysis, e.g., to check the effect of "correlated" parameters that change together due to exogenous factors such as the state of the economy. However, a more important application is the investigation of *tradeoffs* in parameter values. For example, if the c_j represent the unit profits of the respective activities, it may be possible to increase some of the c_j at the expense of decreasing others by an appropriate shifting of personnel and equipment among activities. Similarly, if the b_i represent the amounts of the respective resources being made available, it may be possible to increase some of the b_i by agreeing to accept decreases in some of the others.

In some applications, the main purpose of the study is to determine the most appropriate tradeoff between two basic factors, such as *costs* and *benefits*. The usual approach is to express one of these factors in the objective function (e.g., minimize total cost) and incorporate the other into the constraints (e.g., benefits $\geq$ minimum acceptable level), as was done for the Nori & Leets Co. air pollution problem in Sec. 3.4. Parametric linear programming then enables systematic investigation of what happens when the initial tentative decision on the tradeoff (e.g., the minimum acceptable level for the benefits) is changed by improving one factor at the expense of the other. This approach is illustrated by the case study in Sec. 8.5, where the two basic factors are the distance traveled by high school students and the degree of racial balance achieved in their schools.

The algorithmic technique for parametric linear programming is a natural extension of that for sensitivity analysis, so it too is based on the simplex method. The procedure is described in Sec. 9.3.

4.8 Computer Implementation

Computer codes for the simplex method now are widely available for essentially all modern computer systems. In fact, major computer manufacturers usually supply their customers with a rather sophisticated linear programming software package (Mathematical Programming System) that also includes many of the special procedures described in Chaps. 6, 7, and 9 (including the algorithmic techniques introduced in the preceding section). Other very good linear programming *systems* also have been developed by independent software development companies and service bureaus, and further progress continues to be made.

These production computer codes do not closely follow either the *algebraic form* or *tabular form* of the simplex method presented in Secs. 4.3 and 4.4. These forms can be streamlined considerably for computer implementation. Therefore, the codes use instead a *matrix form* (usually called the *revised simplex method*) that is especially well suited for the computer. This form accomplishes exactly the same things as the algebraic or tabular forms, but it does this while computing and storing *only* the numbers that actually are needed for the current iteration, and then it carries along the essential data in a more compact form. This *revised simplex method* is described in Sec. 5.2.

The available software packages are used routinely to solve surprisingly large linear programming problems. For example, a problem with 5,000 functional constraints and 10,000 variables usually can be solved in less than an hour on a mainframe computer of recent vintage.[1] Problems with several times this number of constraints and variables also have been successfully solved by the general simplex method. If the problem has some kind of special structure (as described in Chap. 7) that can be solved by a streamlined version of the simplex method, then even *much* larger sizes can sometimes be handled. For example, a problem with 100,000 functional constraints and 500,000 variables has been solved when all but about 1,000 of these constraints were of a special kind (*generalized upper bound constraints* discussed at the end of Sec. 7.5).

Several factors affect how long it will take the general simplex method to solve a linear programming problem. The most important one is the *number of ordinary functional constraints.* In fact, computation time tends to be roughly proportional to the *cube* of this number, so that doubling this number may multiply the computation time by a factor of approximately 8. By contrast, the number of variables is a relatively minor factor.[2] Thus doubling the number of variables probably will not even double the computation time. A third factor of some importance is the *density* of the table of constraint coefficients (i.e., the *proportion* of the coefficients that are *not* zero) because this affects the computation time *per iteration.* One common rule of thumb for the *number of iterations* is that it tends to be roughly twice the number of functional constraints.

One difficulty in dealing with large linear programming problems is the tremendous amount of data involved. For example, a problem with just 1,000 functional constraints and variables would have 1 million constraint coefficients to be specified! Therefore, most experienced practitioners make extensive use of the computer for data-processing purposes both before and after applying the simplex method. Frequently a **matrix generator program** will be written to convert the basic raw data into constraint coefficients in an appropriate format for the simplex method. The matrix generator will do the arithmetic required in this conversion, repeat constraints of a recurring type, and fill in the zero coefficients (most of the coefficients usually are zeroes in large problems). It also should print out the key input data in an easily readable form so they can be shown to various people for checking and correcting. Another useful function of a matrix generator is to scale the coefficients (by changing the units for the activities or resources) to approximately the same order of magnitude to avoid significant round-off error.

For many of the same reasons, it often is helpful to write an **output analyzer program** to convert the output of the simplex method into a useful form. An output analyzer (or **report writer**) has three major functions. Two of these are to compile and summarize relevant information for two of the *post-optimality*

---

[1] On problems of this size, the computation time depends greatly upon the linear programming system being used because large savings can be achieved by using special techniques (e.g., *crashing techniques* for quickly finding an advanced initial basic feasible solution). When problems are resolved periodically after minor updating of the data, much time often is saved by using (or modifying) the last optimal solution to provide the initial basic solution for the new run.

[2] This statement assumes that the *revised* simplex method described in Sec. 5.2 is being used.

analysis tasks introduced in the preceding section, namely, *debugging the model* and *sensitivity analysis*. The third major purpose is to develop a well-organized report presenting the relevant information about the proposed solution in the vernacular of management.

Some codes now are becoming available for solving linear programming problems of modest size on *microcomputers*, which undoubtedly means that the simplex method will be widely used on microcomputers in the relatively near future.

4.9 Conclusions

The simplex method is an efficient and reliable algorithm for solving on a computer linear programming problems that have many hundreds or even thousands of constraints and variables. It also provides the basis for performing the various parts of post-optimality analysis very efficiently.

In 1984, Narendra Karmarkar of AT & T Bell Laboratories announced a completely new algorithm for converging to an optimal solution for linear programming problems (but not for performing post-optimality analysis) by cutting through the interior of the feasible region. Because it was initially reported that certain huge problems were being solved many times faster than by the simplex method, this announcement was accompanied by considerable fanfare in the public press. Since then, independent investigators have reported very mixed results with Karmarkar's algorithm. Consequently, it is unclear what the ultimate role of the new algorithm will be vis-à-vis the simplex method for obtaining the initial optimal solution for various types and sizes of linear programming problems. A considerable number of years may be required to clarify the picture. Meanwhile, the operations research community will be following the new developments with great interest.

Partially because of its crucial role for post-optimality analysis, the simplex method undoubtedly will be an indispensable tool of linear programming for decades to come.

SELECTED REFERENCES

1. Bradley, Stephen P., Arnoldo C. Hax, and Thomas L. Magnanti: *Applied Mathematical Programming*, Addison-Wesley, Reading, Mass., 1977.
2. Dantzig, George B.: *Linear Programming and Extensions*, Princeton University Press, Princeton, N.J., 1963.
3. Orchard-Hays, William: *Advanced Linear Programming Computing Techniques*, McGraw-Hill, New York, 1968.
4. Simmons, Donald M.: *Linear Programming for Operations Research*, Holden-Day, San Francisco, 1972.
5. Spivey, W. Allen and Robert M. Thrall: *Linear Optimization*, Holt, Rinehart & Winston, New York, 1970.
6. Strum, Jay E.: *Introduction to Linear Programming*, Holden-Day, San Francisco, 1972.

PROBLEMS

1. Consider the linear programming model formulated for Prob. 1 of Chap. 3.

(a) Identify all the *corner-point feasible solutions* for this model.
(b) Solve by the simplex method in algebraic form.
(c) Solve by the simplex method in tabular form.
(d) Use the graphical solution to perform sensitivity analysis on this model; i.e., identify the *sensitive* parameters that cannot be changed without changing the optimal solution.

2. Consider the following problem.

$$\text{Maximize} \quad Z = 3x_1 + 2x_2,$$

subject to

$$
\begin{aligned}
x_1 &\leq 12 \quad \text{(resource 1)} \\
x_1 + 3x_2 &\leq 45 \quad \text{(resource 2)} \\
2x_1 + x_2 &\leq 30 \quad \text{(resource 3)}
\end{aligned}
$$

and

$$x_1 \geq 0, \quad x_2 \geq 0.$$

(a) Solve this problem graphically. Identify all the *corner-point feasible solutions* for this model.
(b) Solve by the simplex method in algebraic form.
(c) Solve by the simplex method in tabular form.
(d) Identify the shadow prices for the three resources from the final tableau for the simplex method. Demonstrate graphically that these shadow prices are the correct ones.
(e) Use the graphical solution to perform sensitivity analysis on this model; i.e., identify the *sensitive* parameters that cannot be changed without changing the optimal solution.
(f) Use a computer code of the simplex method to solve this problem.

3. Use the simplex method to solve the following problem.

$$\text{Maximize} \quad Z = -x_1 + x_2 + 2x_3,$$

subject to

$$
\begin{aligned}
x_1 + 2x_2 - x_3 &\leq 10 \\
-2x_1 + 4x_2 + 2x_3 &\leq 40 \\
2x_1 + 3x_2 + x_3 &\leq 30
\end{aligned}
$$

and

$$x_1 \geq 0, \quad x_2 \geq 0, \quad x_3 \geq 0.$$

4. Consider the following problem.

$$\text{Maximize} \quad Z = 4x_1 + 3x_2 + 6x_3,$$

subject to

$$
\begin{aligned}
3x_1 + x_2 + 3x_3 &\leq 30 \\
2x_1 + 2x_2 + 3x_3 &\leq 40,
\end{aligned}
$$

and

$$x_1 \geq 0, \quad x_2 \geq 0, \quad x_3 \geq 0.$$

(a) Solve by the simplex method in algebraic form.
(b) Solve by the simplex method in tabular form.
(c) Use a computer code of the simplex method to solve this problem.

5. Consider the following problem.

$$\text{Maximize} \quad Z = 2x_1 - 2x_2 + 4x_3,$$

subject to

$$
\begin{aligned}
-x_1 + x_2 + x_3 &\leq 20 \quad \text{(resource 1)} \\
2x_1 - x_2 + x_3 &\leq 10 \quad \text{(resource 2)} \\
x_1 + x_2 + 3x_3 &\leq 60 \quad \text{(resource 3)}
\end{aligned}
$$

and

$$x_1 \geq 0, \quad x_2 \geq 0, \quad x_3 \geq 0.$$

(a) Solve by the simplex method.
(b) Identify the shadow prices for the three resources and describe their significance.

6. Consider the following problem.

$$\text{Maximize} \quad Z = 6x_1 + 5x_2 - x_3 + 4x_4,$$

subject to

$$
\begin{aligned}
3x_1 + 2x_2 - 3x_3 + x_4 &\leq 120 \quad \text{(resource 1)} \\
3x_1 + 3x_2 + x_3 + 3x_4 &\leq 180 \quad \text{(resource 2)}
\end{aligned}
$$

and

$$x_1 \geq 0, \quad x_2 \geq 0, \quad x_3 \geq 0, \quad x_4 \geq 0.$$

(a) Solve by the simplex method.
(b) Identify the shadow prices for the two resources and describe their significance.

7. Consider the following problem.

$$\text{Maximize} \quad Z = 2x_1 + 4x_2 + 3x_3,$$

subject to

$$
\begin{aligned}
x_1 + 3x_2 + 2x_3 &\leq 15 \\
x_1 + x_2 + x_3 &\leq 12 \\
3x_1 + 5x_2 + 3x_3 &\leq 30
\end{aligned}
$$

and

$$x_1 \geq 0, \quad x_2 \geq 0, \quad x_3 \geq 0.$$

You are given the information that $x_1 > 0$, $x_2 = 0$, and $x_3 > 0$ in the optimal solution.

(a) Describe how one can use this information in order to *adapt* the simplex method to solve this problem in the minimum possible number of iterations (when starting from the usual initial feasible solution). Do *not* actually perform any iterations.

(b) Use the procedure developed in part (a) to solve this problem.

8. Consider the following problem.

$$\text{Maximize} \quad Z = 15x_1 + 3x_2 + 9x_3 + 12x_4,$$

subject to

$$x_1 - 2x_2 + 4x_3 + 3x_4 \leq 10$$
$$-4x_1 + 6x_2 + 5x_3 - 4x_4 \leq 20$$
$$2x_1 - 3x_2 + 3x_3 + 8x_4 \leq 25$$

and

$$x_1 \geq 0, \quad x_2 \geq 0, \quad x_3 \geq 0, \quad x_4 \geq 0.$$

Use the simplex method to demonstrate that Z is unbounded.

9. Consider the following problem.

$$\text{Maximize} \quad Z = x_1 + x_2 + x_3 + x_4,$$

subject to

$$x_1 + x_2 \leq 10$$
$$x_3 + x_4 \leq 15,$$

and

$$x_j \geq 0, \quad \text{for } j = 1, 2, 3, 4.$$

Use the simplex method to find *all* the optimal basic feasible solutions.

10. Consider the following problem.

$$\text{Maximize} \quad Z = 2x_1 + 3x_2,$$

subject to

$$x_1 + 2x_2 \leq 4$$
$$x_1 + x_2 = 3$$

and

$$x_1 \geq 0, \quad x_2 \geq 0.$$

(a) Solve this problem graphically.

(b) Construct the complete first simplex tableau for the simplex method and identify the corresponding initial (artificial) basic feasible solution. Also identify the initial entering basic variable and the leaving basic variable.

(c) Solve by the simplex method.

11. Consider the following problem.

$$\text{Minimize} \quad Z = 4x_1 + 3x_2,$$

subject to

$$2x_1 + x_2 \geq 25$$
$$-3x_1 + 2x_2 \leq 15$$
$$x_1 + x_2 \geq 15$$

and

$$x_1 \geq 0, \quad x_2 \geq 0.$$

(a) Solve this problem graphically.
(b) Construct the complete first simplex tableau for the simplex method and identify the corresponding initial (artificial) basic feasible solution. Also identify the initial entering basic variable and the leaving basic variable.
(c) Solve by the simplex method.

12. Consider the following problem.

$$\text{Maximize} \quad Z = 2x_1 + 5x_2 + 3x_3,$$

subject to

$$3x_1 - 6x_2 \qquad \geq 30$$
$$6x_1 + 12x_2 + 3x_3 = 75$$

and

$$x_1 \geq 0, \quad x_2 \geq 0, \quad x_3 \geq 0.$$

(a) Construct the complete first simplex tableau for the simplex method and identify the corresponding initial (artificial) basic feasible solution. Also identify the initial entering basic variable and the leaving basic variable.
(b) Solve by the simplex method.
(c) Use a computer code of the simplex method to solve this problem.

13. Consider the following problem.

$$\text{Maximize} \quad Z = -x_1 + 4x_2,$$

subject to

$$-3x_1 + x_2 \leq 6$$
$$x_1 + 2x_2 \leq 4$$
$$x_2 \geq -3$$

(no lower bound constraint for x_1).

(a) Solve this problem graphically.
(b) Reformulate this problem so that it has only two functional constraints and all variables have nonnegativity constraints.
(c) Solve by the simplex method.

14. Consider the following problem.

$$\text{Maximize} \quad Z = -x_1 + 2x_2 + x_3,$$

subject to

$$3x_2 + x_3 \leq 30$$
$$x_1 - x_2 - 4x_3 \leq 20$$
$$-3x_1 + x_2 + 2x_3 \leq 25$$

(no nonnegativity constraints).

    (a) Reformulate this problem so all variables have nonnegativity constraints.

    (b) Solve by the simplex method.

15. Consider the following problem.

$$\text{Minimize} \quad Z = 2x_1 + x_2 + 3x_3,$$

subject to

$$5x_1 + 2x_2 + 7x_3 = 15$$
$$3x_1 + 2x_2 + 5x_3 \geq 10$$

and

$$x_1 \geq 0, \quad x_2 \geq 0, \quad x_3 \geq 0.$$

    (a) Construct the complete first simplex tableau for the simplex method and identify the corresponding initial (artificial) basic feasible solution. Also identify the initial entering basic variable and the leaving basic variable.

    (b) Solve by the simplex method.

    (c) Find a basic feasible solution for the *real* problem by directly using the simplex method to minimize the sum of the artificial variables subject to the constraints as expressed in the simplex tableau obtained in part (a). (This is phase 1 of the two-phase method described in Sec. 4.6.)

    (d) Obtain an optimal solution by using the solution obtained in part (c) as the initial basic feasible solution (deleting all artificial variables) for the simplex method. (This is phase 2 of the two-phase method.)

    (e) Use a computer code of the simplex method to do parts (c) and (d).

16. Consider the following problem.

$$\text{Minimize} \quad Z = 3x_1 + 2x_2 + 4x_3,$$

subject to

$$2x_1 + x_2 + 3x_3 = 10$$
$$3x_1 + 3x_2 + 5x_3 \geq 20$$

and

$$x_1 \geq 0, \quad x_2 \geq 0, \quad x_3 \geq 0.$$

    (a) Construct the complete first simplex tableau for the simplex method and identify the corresponding initial (artificial) basic feasible solution. Also identify the initial entering basic variable and the leaving basic variable.

    (b) Solve by the simplex method.

    (c) Find a basic feasible solution for the *real* problem by directly using the simplex method to minimize the sum of the artificial variables subject to the constraints as expressed in the simplex tableau obtained in part (a). (This is phase 1 of the two-phase method described in Sec. 4.6.)

(d) Obtain an optimal solution by using the solution obtained in part (c) as the initial basic feasible solution (deleting all artificial variables) for the simplex method. (This is phase 2 of the two-phase method.)

(e) Use a computer code of the simplex method to do parts (c) and (d).

17. Consider the following problem.

$$\text{Maximize} \quad Z = 4x_1 + 2x_2 + 3x_3 + 5x_4,$$

subject to

$$2x_1 + 3x_2 + 4x_3 + 2x_4 = 60$$
$$8x_1 + x_2 + x_3 + 5x_4 = 60$$

and

$$x_j \geq 0, \quad \text{for } j = 1, 2, 3, 4.$$

(a) Construct the complete first simplex tableau for the simplex method and identify the corresponding initial (artificial) basic feasible solution. Also identify the initial entering basic variable and the leaving basic variable.

(b) Solve by the simplex method.

(c) Find a basic feasible solution for the *real* problem by directly using the simplex method to minimize the sum of the artificial variables subject to the constraints as expressed in the simplex tableau obtained in part (a). (This is phase 1 of the two-phase method described in Sec. 4.6.)

(d) Obtain an optimal solution by using the solution obtained in part (c) as the initial basic feasible solution (deleting all artificial variables) for the simplex method. (This is phase 2 of the two-phase method.)

(e) Use a computer code of the simplex method to do parts (c) and (d).

18. Consider the following problem.

$$\text{Minimize} \quad Z = 2x_1 + 3x_2 + x_3,$$

subject to

$$x_1 + 4x_2 + 2x_3 \geq 8$$
$$3x_1 + 2x_2 \geq 6$$

and

$$x_1 \geq 0, \quad x_2 \geq 0, \quad x_3 \geq 0.$$

(a) Reformulate this problem to fit our *standard form* for a linear programming model presented in Sec. 3.2.

(b) Construct the complete first simplex tableau for the simplex method and identify the corresponding initial (artificial) basic feasible solution. Also identify the initial entering basic variable and the leaving basic variable.

(c) Solve by the simplex method.

(d) Find a basic feasible solution for the *real* problem by directly using the simplex method to minimize the sum of the artificial variables subject to the constraints as expressed in the simplex tableau obtained in part (b). (This is phase 1 of the two-phase method described in Sec. 4.6.)

(e)   Obtain an optimal solution by using the solution obtained in part (d) as the initial basic feasible solution (deleting all artificial variables) for the simplex method. (This is phase 2 of the two-phase method.)

19.   Consider the following problem.

$$\text{Maximize} \quad Z = -2x_1 + x_2 - 4x_3 + 3x_4,$$

subject to

$$10 \le x_1 + x_2 + 3x_3 + 2x_4 \le 40$$
$$x_1 \quad - x_3 + x_4 \ge -10$$
$$2x_1 + x_2 \qquad \le 20$$
$$x_1 + 2x_2 + x_3 + 2x_4 = 20$$

and

$$x_2 \ge 0, \quad x_3 \ge 0, \quad x_4 \ge 0$$

(no nonnegativity constraint for x_1).

(a)   Reformulate this problem (except for the equality constraint) to fit *our standard form* for a linear programming model presented in Sec. 3.2.
(b)   Construct the complete first simplex tableau for the simplex method and identify the corresponding initial (artificial) basic feasible solution. Also identify the initial entering basic variable and the leaving basic variable.
(c)   Find a basic feasible solution for the *real* problem by applying the simplex method until all the artificial variables are zero.
(d)   Find a basic feasible solution for the *real* problem by directly using the simplex method to minimize the sum of the artificial variables subject to the constraints as expressed in the simplex tableau obtained in part (b). (This is phase 1 of the two-phase method described in Sec. 4.6.)
(e)   Use a computer code of the simplex method to do part (d).
(f)   Starting from the basic feasible solution obtained in part (d), use a computer code of the simplex method to obtain an optimal solution.

20.   Consider the following problem.

$$\text{Maximize} \quad Z = 12x_1 + 15x_2 + 10x_3,$$

subject to

$$x_1 + x_2 + 2x_3 \ge 10$$
$$15x_1 + 6x_2 - 5x_3 \le 30$$
$$x_1 + 3x_2 + 5x_3 \le 18$$

and

$$x_1 \ge 0, \quad x_2 \ge 0, \quad x_3 \ge 0.$$

Use the simplex method to demonstrate that this problem does not possess any feasible solutions.

21.   Consider Prob. 20 of Chap. 8. The linear programming model for this problem has more than 5,000 functional constraints and more than 150,000 variables.

(*a*) There are more than 750,000,000 coefficients for these constraints, which creates a storage problem for a computer solution of the model. Considering that more than 99 percent of these coefficients are zeroes, recommend a way to alleviate this problem.

(*b*) Since the number of *nonzero* coefficients is well over 100,000, manually inputting these data into the computer would be excessively time-consuming. Considering that the number of items of basic raw data is much smaller, recommend a way to alleviate this problem.

CHAPTER 5

The Theory of the Simplex Method

Chapter 4 introduced the basic mechanics of the simplex method. Now we shall delve a little deeper into this method by examining some of its underlying theory. The first section develops the general geometric and algebraic properties that form the foundation of the simplex method. We then describe the *matrix form* of the simplex method (called the *revised simplex method*) that streamlines the procedure considerably for computer implementation. Next, we present a fundamental insight about a property of the simplex method that enables us to deduce how changes that are made in the original model get carried along to the final simplex tableau. This insight will provide the key to the important topics of Chap. 6 (duality theory and sensitivity analysis).

5.1 Foundations of the Simplex Method

Section 4.1 introduced *corner-point feasible solutions* and the key role they play in the simplex method. These geometric concepts were related to the algebra of the simplex method in Sec. 4.2. However, all of this was done in the context of the Wyndor Glass Co. problem, which has only *two variables* and so has a straightforward geometric interpretation. How do these concepts generalize to higher dimensions when we deal with larger problems? We address this question in this section.

We begin by introducing some basic terminology for any linear programming problem with n variables (before introducing slack and artificial variables for initializing the simplex method). While we are doing this, you might find it helpful to refer back to Fig. 4.1 to interpret these definitions in two dimensions.

TERMINOLOGY

It may be quite intuitive to some of you that optimal solutions for any linear programming problem must lie on the boundary of the feasible region, and this is in fact a general property. Because boundary is a geometric concept, our first two definitions clarify how the boundary of the feasible region is identified algebraically.

> The **boundary equation** for any constraint is obtained by replacing its $\leq$, $=$, or $\geq$ sign by an $=$ sign.

Consequently, the form of a *constraint boundary equation* is $a_{i1}x_1 + a_{i2}x_2 + \cdots + a_{in}x_n = b_i$ for functional constraints and $x_j = 0$ for nonnegativity constraints. These equations define a "flat" geometric shape (called a *hyperplane*) in n-dimensional space analogous to the line in two-dimensional space and the plane in three-dimensional space.

> The **boundary** of the feasible region consists of those feasible solutions that satisfy one or more of the constraint boundary equations (i.e., that lie on one or more of the bounding hyperplanes).

Next, we give a general definition of *corner-point feasible solution* in n-dimensional space.

> A **corner-point feasible solution** is a feasible solution that does not lie on *any* line segment[1] connecting two *other* feasible solutions.

With n decision variables ($n > 3$), this definition is not very convenient for identifying corner-point feasible solutions. Therefore, it will prove most helpful to interpret these solutions algebraically. For the Wyndor Glass Co. example, each corner-point feasible solution in Fig. 4.1 lies at the intersection of two ($n = 2$) constraint lines; i.e., it is the *simultaneous solution* of a system of two constraint boundary equations. This situation is summarized in Table 5.1, where **defining equations** refer to the constraint boundary equations that yield (define) the indicated corner-point feasible solution. Similarly, for any linear programming problem, each corner-point feasible solution lies at the intersection of n constraint boundaries; i.e., it is the *simultaneous solution* of a system of n constraint boundary equations. However, this is not to say that *every* set of n boundary equations chosen from among the $(n + m)$ constraints yields a corner-point feasible solution. In particular, the simultaneous solution of such a system of equations might violate one or more of the other m constraints, in which case it is a corner-point *infeasible* solution. The example has three such solutions, as summarized in Table 5.2. (Check to see why they are infeasible.)

---

[1] A formal definition of line segment is given in Appendix 1.

Table 5.1 **Defining equations for each corner-point feasible solution for Wyndor Glass Co. problem**

Corner-point feasible solution	Defining equations
(0,0)	$x_1 = 0$ $x_2 = 0$
(0,6)	$x_1 = 0$ $2x_2 = 12$
(2,6)	$2x_2 = 12$ $3x_1 + 2x_2 = 18$
(4,3)	$3x_1 + 2x_2 = 18$ $x_1 = 4$
(4,0)	$x_1 = 4$ $x_2 = 0$

Table 5.2 **Defining equations for each corner-point infeasible solution for Wyndor Glass Co. problem**

Corner-point infeasible solution	Defining equations
(0,9)	$x_1 = 0$ $3x_1 + 2x_2 = 18$
(4,6)	$2x_2 = 12$ $x_1 = 4$
(6,0)	$3x_1 + 2x_2 = 18$ $x_2 = 0$

Furthermore, a system of n constraint boundary equations might have no solution at all. This occurs twice in the example with the pairs of equations (1) $x_1 = 0$ and $x_1 = 4$; and (2) $x_2 = 0$ and $2x_2 = 12$. Such systems are of no interest to us. The final possibility (which never occurs in the example) is that a system has multiple solutions because of redundant equations. You need not be concerned with this case either, because the simplex method circumvents its difficulties.

We need just one more definition to identify convenient groupings of corner-point feasible solutions for the simplex method:

> Two corner-point feasible solutions are said to be **adjacent** if the line segment connecting them lies on (an edge of)[1] the boundary of the feasible region.

Thus in the example the pairs of adjacent corner-point feasible solutions in Fig. 4.1 are (0,0) and (0,6); (0,6) and (2,6); (2,6) and (4,3); (4,3) and (4,0); and, lastly, (4,0)

---

[1] This parenthetical phrase can be deleted until the next paragraph, where it is explained when it first becomes relevant.

and (0,0). The algebraic interpretation of these pairs is suggested by Table 5.1, which lists adjacent corner-point feasible solutions next to each other except for (4,0) and (0,0). Notice that in each case just *one* defining equation is different for adjacent corner-point solutions. For example, (0,6) is reached from (0,0) by deleting an intersecting line (defining equation) $x_2 = 0$ and moving away from it in the feasible direction ($x_2 \geq 0$) along the other line $x_1 = 0$ until the *first* new constraint boundary (defining equation) $2x_2 = 12$ is reached. As already noted in Sec. 4.3, it is important to stop at the first new constraint boundary because continuing on to the next one ($3x_1 + 2x_2 = 18$) yields a corner-point *infeasible* solution (0,9). Similarly, consider the other corner-point feasible solution that is adjacent to (0,0), namely, (4,0). It is reached from (0,0) by deleting the *other* intersecting line (defining equation) $x_1 = 0$ and moving away from it in the feasible direction ($x_1 \geq 0$) along the line $x_2 = 0$ until the *first* new constraint boundary (defining equation) $x_1 = 4$ is reached. Now convince yourself that each of the other corner-point feasible solutions also has two ($n = 2$) adjacent corner-point feasible solutions that are reached by moving away from one of the two constraint boundaries to the first new one.

These same conclusions also apply when $n > 2$. Recall that a corner-point feasible solution lies at the intersection of n constraint boundaries. Suppose that one of these constraint boundaries (defining equations) is deleted. The intersection of the remaining ($n - 1$) constraint boundaries is a *line*. One *segment* of this line lies on the boundary of the feasible region, and the rest of the line is not allowed by the other constraints. (The technical term used in the preceding definition for such a line segment is **edge**.) Now suppose that you move away from the corner-point feasible solution in the feasible direction along this line until the *first* new constraint boundary (defining equation) is reached. This new point is an *adjacent* corner-point feasible solution. Moving beyond it along the line to other new constraint boundaries would lead only to corner-point *infeasible* solutions. Thus a corner-point feasible solution has just n adjacent corner-point feasible solutions, each of which is reached in the fashion just described by deleting one of the n defining equations for this solution and replacing it by the appropriate new defining equation.

ANALYSIS

In Sec. 4.1, we listed three key properties of corner-point feasible solutions that constitute the underlying principles of the simplex method. We now are in a position to explain why these properties (restated here) do indeed hold in general:

PROPERTY 1 (*a*) If there is exactly one optimal solution, then it *must* be a corner-point feasible solution. (*b*) If there are multiple optimal solutions, then at least two *must* be adjacent corner-point feasible solutions.

Property 1 is a rather intuitive one from a geometric viewpoint. First consider case (*a*), which is illustrated by the example where the one optimal solution (2,6) is indeed a corner-point feasible solution. Note that there is nothing special about the example that led to this result. For *any* problem having just one optimal solution, it always is possible to keep raising the objective function line (hyperplane) until it just touches one point (the optimal solution) at a corner of the feasible region.

The following algebraic viewpoint also clarifies why the property must hold in case (*a*). Let Z^* denote the value of the objective function for the one optimal solution. Using a *proof by contradiction*, assume that case (*a*) holds and that the one optimal solution is *not* a corner-point feasible solution. By definition it must lie on a line segment connecting two other feasible solutions; i.e., it is a weighted average of these other two feasible solutions. Let $\alpha (0 < \alpha < 1)$ and $(1 - \alpha)$ denote the weights on these solutions, and let Z_1 and Z_2 be their values of the objective function. Thus $Z^* = \alpha Z_1 + (1 - \alpha)Z_2$. Since these weights add up to 1, the only possibilities for how Z^*, Z_1, and Z_2 compare are (1) $Z^* = Z_1 = Z_2$, (2) $Z_1 < Z^* < Z_2$, and (3) $Z_1 > Z^* > Z_2$. The first possibility implies that the other two feasible solutions also are optimal, which contradicts the assumption that case (*a*) holds. Both the latter possibilities contradict the assumption that the original solution is optimal. The resulting conclusion is that it is impossible to have a single optimal solution that is not a corner-point feasible solution.

Now consider case (*b*), which was demonstrated in Sec. 3.2 under the definition of *optimal solution* by changing the objective function in the example to $Z = 3x_1 + 2x_2$. What then happens in the graphical solution procedure is that the objective function line keeps getting raised until it contains the line segment connecting the two corner-point feasible solutions (2,6) and (4,3). The same thing would happen in higher dimensions except that now it would be an objective function *hyperplane* that keeps getting raised until it contains the line segment(s) connecting two (or more) adjacent corner-point feasible solutions. As a consequence, *all* optimal solutions can be obtained as weighted averages of optimal corner-point feasible solutions. (This situation is described further in Probs. 8 and 9 at the end of the chapter.)

The real significance of property 1 is that it greatly simplifies the search for an optimal solution because now only corner-point feasible solutions need be considered. The magnitude of this simplification is emphasized in property 2:

PROPERTY 2 There are only a *finite* number of corner-point feasible solutions.

This property certainly holds in the example, where there are just *five* corner-point feasible solutions. To see why the number is finite in general, recall that each corner-point feasible solution is the simultaneous solution of a system of n out of the $(m + n)$ constraint boundary equations. The number of different combinations of $(m + n)$ equations taken n at a time is

$$\frac{(m + n)!}{m!n!},$$

which is a finite number. This number, in turn, is an *upper bound* on the number of corner-point feasible solutions. In the example, $m = 3$ and $n = 2$, so there are 10 different systems of two equations, but only half of them yield corner-point feasible solutions.

Property 2 suggests that an optimal solution can be obtained just by exhaustive enumeration; i.e., find and compare all the finite number of corner-point feasible solutions. Unfortunately, there are finite numbers, and then there are finite numbers that (for all practical purposes) might as well be infinite. For example, a rather small linear programming problem with only $m = 50$ and $n = 50$ would have $(100!)/(50!)^2 \approx 10^{29}$ systems of equations to be solved! By contrast, the simplex method would need to examine only approximately 100 corner-point feasible solutions for a problem of this size. This tremendous saving can be obtained because of the optimality test provided by property 3:

PROPERTY 3 If a corner-point feasible solution is equal to or better than (as measured by Z) all its *adjacent* corner-point feasible solutions, then it is equal to or better than all other corner-point feasible solutions; i.e., it is *optimal*.

The basic reason that property 3 holds is that the feasible region always has the property of being *convex*, as defined in Appendix 1. (It must be convex because the set of solutions satisfying any individual constraint is convex, and any intersection of convex sets is convex, including the intersection over all the constraints that yields the feasible region.) To clarify the significance of a convex feasible region, consider the objective function hyperplane that passes through a corner-point feasible solution that is equal to or better than all of its adjacent corner-point feasible solutions. [In the example, this hyperplane is the line passing through (2,6) in Fig. 3.3.] All of these adjacent solutions [(0,6) and (4,3) in the example)] must either lie on the hyperplane or lie on the unfavorable side (as measured by Z) of the hyperplane. The feasible region being convex means that its boundary cannot "bend outward" beyond an adjacent corner-point feasible solution to give another corner-point feasible solution that lies on the favorable side of the hyperplane. (Check this in Fig. 3.3.)

EXTENSIONS TO THE EQUALITY FORM OF THE PROBLEM

For any linear programming problem in *our standard form* (see Sec. 3.2),[1] the appearance of the functional constraints after slack variables are introduced (see Sec. 4.2) is as follows:

(1) $a_{11}x_1 + a_{12}x_2 + \cdots + a_{1n}x_n + x_{n+1} \qquad\qquad = b_1$

(2) $a_{21}x_1 + a_{22}x_2 + \cdots + a_{2n}x_n \qquad + x_{n+2} \qquad = b_2$

$$\vdots$$

(m) $a_{m1}x_1 + a_{m2}x_2 + \cdots + a_{mn}x_n \qquad\qquad + x_{n+m} = b_m,$

where $x_{n+1}, x_{n+2}, \ldots, x_{n+m}$ are the slack variables. Thus the original solutions

---

[1] The following discussion and definitions assume that nonstandard forms have been converted into our standard form, as discussed in Sec. 4.6.

$(x_1, x_2, \ldots, x_n)$ now are *augmented* by the corresponding values of the slack variables $(x_{n+1}, x_{n+2}, \ldots, x_{n+m})$. This augmentation led in Sec. 4.2 to defining **basic solutions** as *augmented corner-point solutions*, and **basic feasible solutions** as *augmented corner-point feasible solutions*. Consequently, the preceding three properties of corner-point feasible solutions also hold for basic feasible solutions.

Now let us clarify the algebraic relationships between basic solutions and corner-point solutions. Recall that each corner-point solution is the simultaneous solution of a system of n constraint boundary equations, which we called its *defining equations*. The key question is "How do we tell whether a particular constraint boundary equation is one of the defining equations when the problem is in equality form?" The answer, fortunately, is a simple one. Since there now are $(n + m)$ variables, one for each of the $(n + m)$ constraints,[1] each constraint has exactly one variable that completely indicates (by whether its value is zero) whether that constraint's boundary equation is satisfied by the current solution. A summary appears in Table 5.3. Thus whenever a constraint boundary equation is one of the defining equations for a corner-point solution, its indicating variable has a value of zero in the equality form of the problem. Each such indicating variable is called a *nonbasic variable* for the corresponding basic solution. The resulting conclusions and terminology (already introduced in Sec. 4.2) are summarized next.

> Each **basic solution** has n **nonbasic variables** set equal to zero. The values of the remaining m variables (called **basic variables**) are the simultaneous solution of the system of m equations for the problem in equality form (after setting the nonbasic variables to zero). This basic solution is the augmented corner-point solution whose n *defining equations* are those indicated by the nonbasic variables.

Now consider the basic *feasible* solutions. Note that the only requirements for a solution to be feasible in the equality form of the problem are that it satisfy the system of equations and that *all* the variables be *nonnegative*.

> A **basic feasible solution** is a basic solution where all m basic variables are nonnegative (≥ 0). A basic feasible solution is said to be **degenerate** if any of these m variables equals zero.

Thus it is possible for a variable to be zero and still not be a nonbasic variable for the current basic feasible solution. (This case corresponds to a corner-point feasible solution that satisfies another constraint boundary equation in addition to its n defining equations.) Therefore, it is necessary to keep track of which is the current set of nonbasic variables (or the current set of basic variables) rather than relying upon their zero values.

Note again that just as for the corner-point feasible solutions, not every set of n defining variables (nonbasic variables) yields a basic solution. The equations

---

[1] These constraints consist of the m *functional* constraints and the n *nonnegativity* constraints on the original n variables.

Table 5.3 **Indicating variables for constraint boundary equations**

Original constraint (in equality form)	Constraint boundary equation	Indicating variable
$x_j \geq 0 \ (j = 1,2,\dots,n)$	$x_j = 0$	x_j
$\sum_{j=1}^{n} a_{ij}x_j + x_{n+i} = b_i$ $(i = 1,2,\dots,m)$	$\sum_{j=1}^{n} a_{ij}x_j = b_i$	x_{n+i}

Indicating variable $= 0 \Rightarrow$ constraint boundary equation satisfied
Indicating variable $\neq 0 \Rightarrow$ constraint boundary equation violated

may not have a solution, or they may have multiple solutions. However, these cases are avoided by the simplex method.

To illustrate these definitions, consider the example once more. Its constraint boundary equations and indicating variables are shown in Table 5.4.

Augmenting each of the corner-point feasible solutions (see Table 5.1) yields the *basic feasible solutions* listed in Table 5.5, which places *adjacent* basic feasible solutions next to each other, except for the pair consisting of the first and last

Table 5.4 **Indicating variables for constraint boundary equations of Wyndor Glass Co. problem**

	Original constraint (in equality form)	Constraint boundary equation	Indicating variable
	$x_1 \geq 0$	$x_1 = 0$	x_1
	$x_2 \geq 0$	$x_2 = 0$	x_2
(1)	$x_1 + x_3 = 4$	$x_1 = 4$	x_3
(2)	$2x_2 + x_4 = 12$	$2x_2 = 12$	x_4
(3)	$3x_1 + 2x_2 + x_5 = 18$	$3x_1 + 2x_2 = 18$	x_5

Indicating variable $= 0 \Rightarrow$ constraint boundary equation satisfied
Indicating variable $\neq 0 \Rightarrow$ constraint boundary equation violated

Table 5.5 **Basic feasible solutions for Wyndor Glass Co. problem**

Corner-point feasible solution	Defining equations	Basic feasible solution	Nonbasic variables
(0,0)	$x_1 = 0$ $x_2 = 0$	(0,0,4,12,18)	x_1 x_2
(0,6)	$x_1 = 0$ $2x_2 = 12$	(0,6,4,0,6)	x_1 x_4
(2,6)	$2x_2 = 12$ $3x_1 + 2x_2 = 18$	(2,6,2,0,0)	x_4 x_5
(4,3)	$3x_1 + 2x_2 = 18$ $x_1 = 4$	(4,3,0,6,0)	x_5 x_3
(4,0)	$x_1 = 4$ $x_2 = 0$	(4,0,0,12,6)	x_3 x_2

Table 5.6 **Basic infeasible solutions for Wyndor Glass Co. problem**

Corner-point infeasible solution	Defining equations	Basic infeasible solution	Nonbasic variables
$(0,9)$	$x_1 = 0$ $3x_1 + 2x_2 = 18$	$(0,9,4,-6,0)$	x_1 x_5
$(4,6)$	$2x_2 = 12$ $x_1 = 4$	$(4,6,0,0,-6)$	x_4 x_3
$(6,0)$	$3x_1 + 2x_2 = 18$ $x_2 = 0$	$(6,0,-2,12,0)$	x_5 x_2

solution listed. Notice that in each case the nonbasic variables necessarily are the indicating variables for the defining equations. Thus *adjacent* basic feasible solutions differ by having just one different nonbasic variable. Also notice that each basic feasible solution necessarily is the resulting simultaneous solution of the system of equations (1,2,3) for the problem in equality form (see Table 5.4) when the nonbasic variables are set equal to zero.

Similarly, the other three corner-point solutions (see Table 5.2) yield the remaining basic solutions shown in Table 5.6.

The other two sets of defining variables, (1) x_1 and x_3 and (2) x_2 and x_4, do not yield a solution for the system of equations (1,2,3) given in Table 5.4. This conclusion parallels the observation we made early in this section that the corresponding sets of defining equations do not yield a solution.

The *simplex method* starts at a basic feasible solution and then iteratively moves to a better adjacent basic solution until an optimal solution is reached. At each iteration, how is the adjacent basic feasible solution reached? For the inequality form of the problem, recall that an adjacent corner-point solution is reached from the current one by (1) deleting one constraint boundary (defining equation) from the set of n constraint boundaries defining the current solution, (2) moving away from the current solution in the *feasible* direction along the intersection of the remaining $(n-1)$ constraint boundaries, and (3) stopping when the *first* new constraint boundary (defining equation) is reached. Equivalently, in our new terminology, the simplex method reaches an adjacent basic feasible solution from the current one by (1) deleting one variable (the *entering basic variable*) from the set of n nonbasic variables defining the current solution, (2) moving away from the current solution by *increasing* this one variable from zero while keeping the remaining $(n-1)$ nonbasic variables at zero, and (3) stopping when the *first* of the basic variables (the *leaving basic variable*) reaches a value of zero (its constraint boundary).

5.2 The Revised Simplex Method

The simplex method as described in Chap. 4 (hereafter called the *original simplex method*) is a straightforward algebraic procedure. However, this way of executing the algorithm (in either algebraic or tabular form) is not the most efficient computational procedure for digital computers because it computes and stores many numbers that are not needed at the current iteration and that may not even become relevant for decision making at subsequent iterations. The only pieces of information relevant at each iteration are the coefficients of the nonbasic variables in Eq. (0), the coefficients of the entering basic variable in the other equations, and the right-hand side of the equations. It would be very useful to have a procedure that could obtain this information efficiently without computing and storing all the other coefficients.

As mentioned in Sec. 4.8, these considerations motivated the development of the *revised simplex method*. This method was designed to accomplish exactly the same things as the original simplex method, but in a way that is more efficient for execution on a digital computer. Thus it is a streamlined version of the original procedure. It computes and stores only the information that is currently needed, and it carries along the essential data in a more compact form.

The revised simplex method explicitly uses *matrix* manipulations, so it is necessary to describe the problem in matrix notation. (See Appendix 3 for a review of matrices.) To help you distinguish between matrices, vectors, and scalars, we consistently use **boldfaced CAPITAL** letters to represent matrices, **boldfaced lowercase** letters to represent vectors, and *italicized* letters in ordinary print to represent scalars.

If we use the *matrix form*, the general model for linear programming given in Sec. 3.2 becomes

$$
\begin{array}{l}
\text{Maximize} \quad Z = \mathbf{cx}, \\[4pt]
\text{subject to} \\[4pt]
\qquad \mathbf{Ax} \le \mathbf{b} \quad \text{and} \quad \mathbf{x} \ge \mathbf{0},
\end{array}
$$

where **c** is the row vector

$$
\mathbf{c} = [c_1, c_2, \ldots, c_n],
$$

x, **b**, and **0** are the column vectors such that

$$
\mathbf{x} = \begin{bmatrix} x_1 \\ x_2 \\ \vdots \\ x_n \end{bmatrix}, \quad
\mathbf{b} = \begin{bmatrix} b_1 \\ b_2 \\ \vdots \\ b_m \end{bmatrix}, \quad
\mathbf{0} = \begin{bmatrix} 0 \\ 0 \\ \vdots \\ 0 \end{bmatrix},
$$

and **A** is the matrix

$$
\mathbf{A} = \begin{bmatrix}
a_{11} & a_{12} & \cdots & a_{1n} \\
a_{21} & a_{22} & \cdots & a_{2n} \\
\vdots & \vdots & & \vdots \\
a_{m1} & a_{m2} & \cdots & a_{mn}
\end{bmatrix}.
$$

To obtain the *equality form* of the problem, introduce the column vector of slack variables

$$\mathbf{x}_s = \begin{bmatrix} x_{n+1} \\ x_{n+2} \\ \vdots \\ x_{n+m} \end{bmatrix},$$

so that the constraints become

$$[\mathbf{A}, \mathbf{I}] \begin{bmatrix} \mathbf{x} \\ \mathbf{x}_s \end{bmatrix} = \mathbf{b} \quad \text{and} \quad \begin{bmatrix} \mathbf{x} \\ \mathbf{x}_s \end{bmatrix} \geq \mathbf{0},$$

where $\mathbf{I}$ is the $m \times m$ identity matrix, and the vector $\mathbf{0}$ now has $(n + m)$ elements.

SOLVING FOR A BASIC FEASIBLE SOLUTION

Recall that the general approach of the simplex method is to obtain a sequence of *improving basic feasible solutions* until the optimal solution is reached. One of the key features of the revised simplex method involves the way in which it solves for each new basic feasible solution after identifying its basic and nonbasic variables. Given these variables, the resulting basic solution is the solution of the m equations

$$[\mathbf{A}, \mathbf{I}] \begin{bmatrix} \mathbf{x} \\ \mathbf{x}_s \end{bmatrix} = \mathbf{b},$$

in which the n *nonbasic variables* from among the $(n + m)$ elements of

$$\begin{bmatrix} \mathbf{x} \\ \mathbf{x}_s \end{bmatrix}$$

are set equal to *zero*. Eliminating these n variables by equating them to zero leaves a set of m equations in m unknowns (the *basic variables*). This set of equations can be denoted by

$$\mathbf{B}\mathbf{x}_B = \mathbf{b},$$

where the **vector of basic variables**

$$\mathbf{x}_B = \begin{bmatrix} x_{B1} \\ x_{B2} \\ \vdots \\ x_{Bm} \end{bmatrix}$$

is obtained by *eliminating* the *nonbasic variables* from

$$\begin{bmatrix} \mathbf{x} \\ \mathbf{x}_s \end{bmatrix},$$

and the **basis matrix**

$$\mathbf{B} = \begin{bmatrix} B_{11} & B_{12} & \cdots & B_{1m} \\ B_{21} & B_{22} & \cdots & B_{2m} \\ \vdots & \vdots & & \vdots \\ B_{m1} & B_{m2} & \cdots & B_{mm} \end{bmatrix}$$

is obtained by *eliminating* the columns corresponding to *coefficients of nonbasic variables* from $[\mathbf{A},\mathbf{I}]$. (In addition, the elements of $\mathbf{x}_B$ and, therefore, the columns of $\mathbf{B}$ may be placed in a different order when executing the simplex method.) To solve $\mathbf{B}\mathbf{x}_s = \mathbf{b}$, both sides would be premultiplied by $\mathbf{B}^{-1}$:[1]

$$\mathbf{B}^{-1}\mathbf{B}\mathbf{x}_B = \mathbf{B}^{-1}\mathbf{b}.$$

Since $\mathbf{B}^{-1}\mathbf{B} = \mathbf{I}$, the desired solution for the basic variables is

$$\boxed{\mathbf{x}_B = \mathbf{B}^{-1}\mathbf{b}.}$$

Letting $\mathbf{c}_B$ be the vector obtained by *eliminating* the *coefficients* of *nonbasic variables* from $[\mathbf{c},\mathbf{0}]$ and reordering the elements to match $\mathbf{x}_B$, the value of the objective function for this basic solution is then

$$\boxed{Z = \mathbf{c}_B\mathbf{x}_B = \mathbf{c}_B\mathbf{B}^{-1}\mathbf{b}.}$$

EXAMPLE To illustrate this method of solving for a basic feasible solution, consider again the Wyndor Glass Co. problem presented in Sec. 3.1 and solved by the original simplex method in Table 4.8. In this case,

$$\mathbf{c} = [3,5], \quad [\mathbf{A},\mathbf{I}] = \begin{bmatrix} 1 & 0 & 1 & 0 & 0 \\ 0 & 2 & 0 & 1 & 0 \\ 3 & 2 & 0 & 0 & 1 \end{bmatrix}, \quad \mathbf{b} = \begin{bmatrix} 4 \\ 12 \\ 18 \end{bmatrix}, \quad \mathbf{x} = \begin{bmatrix} x_1 \\ x_2 \end{bmatrix}, \quad \mathbf{x}_s = \begin{bmatrix} x_3 \\ x_4 \\ x_5 \end{bmatrix}.$$

Referring to Table 4.8, the sequence of basic feasible solutions obtained by the simplex method (original or revised) is the following:

Iteration 0

$$\mathbf{x}_B = \begin{bmatrix} x_3 \\ x_4 \\ x_5 \end{bmatrix}, \quad \mathbf{B} = \begin{bmatrix} 1 & 0 & 0 \\ 0 & 1 & 0 \\ 0 & 0 & 1 \end{bmatrix} = \mathbf{B}^{-1}, \quad \text{so} \begin{bmatrix} x_3 \\ x_4 \\ x_5 \end{bmatrix} = \begin{bmatrix} 1 & 0 & 0 \\ 0 & 1 & 0 \\ 0 & 0 & 1 \end{bmatrix} \begin{bmatrix} 4 \\ 12 \\ 18 \end{bmatrix} = \begin{bmatrix} 4 \\ 12 \\ 18 \end{bmatrix},$$

$$\mathbf{c}_B = [0,0,0], \quad \text{so } Z = [0,0,0] \begin{bmatrix} 4 \\ 12 \\ 18 \end{bmatrix} = 0.$$

---

[1] The simplex method introduces only basic variables such that $\mathbf{B}$ is *nonsingular*, so that $\mathbf{B}^{-1}$ always will exist.

Iteration 1

$$\mathbf{x}_B = \begin{bmatrix} x_3 \\ x_2 \\ x_5 \end{bmatrix}, \quad \mathbf{B} = \begin{bmatrix} 1 & 0 & 0 \\ 0 & 2 & 0 \\ 0 & 2 & 1 \end{bmatrix}, \quad \mathbf{B}^{-1} = \begin{bmatrix} 1 & 0 & 0 \\ 0 & \frac{1}{2} & 0 \\ 0 & -1 & 1 \end{bmatrix},$$

so

$$\begin{bmatrix} x_3 \\ x_2 \\ x_5 \end{bmatrix} = \begin{bmatrix} 1 & 0 & 0 \\ 0 & \frac{1}{2} & 0 \\ 0 & -1 & 1 \end{bmatrix} \begin{bmatrix} 4 \\ 12 \\ 18 \end{bmatrix} = \begin{bmatrix} 4 \\ 6 \\ 6 \end{bmatrix},$$

$$\mathbf{c}_B = [0, 5, 0], \quad \text{so } Z = [0, 5, 0] \begin{bmatrix} 4 \\ 6 \\ 6 \end{bmatrix} = 30.$$

Iteration 2

$$\mathbf{x}_B = \begin{bmatrix} x_3 \\ x_2 \\ x_1 \end{bmatrix}, \quad \mathbf{B} = \begin{bmatrix} 1 & 0 & 1 \\ 0 & 2 & 0 \\ 0 & 2 & 3 \end{bmatrix}, \quad \mathbf{B}^{-1} = \begin{bmatrix} 1 & \frac{1}{3} & -\frac{1}{3} \\ 0 & \frac{1}{2} & 0 \\ 0 & -\frac{1}{3} & \frac{1}{3} \end{bmatrix},$$

so

$$\begin{bmatrix} x_3 \\ x_2 \\ x_1 \end{bmatrix} = \begin{bmatrix} 1 & \frac{1}{3} & -\frac{1}{3} \\ 0 & \frac{1}{2} & 0 \\ 0 & -\frac{1}{3} & \frac{1}{3} \end{bmatrix} \begin{bmatrix} 4 \\ 12 \\ 18 \end{bmatrix} = \begin{bmatrix} 2 \\ 6 \\ 2 \end{bmatrix},$$

$$\mathbf{c}_B = [0, 5, 3], \quad \text{so } Z = [0, 5, 3] \begin{bmatrix} 2 \\ 6 \\ 2 \end{bmatrix} = 36.$$

MATRIX FORM OF THE CURRENT SET OF EQUATIONS

The last preliminary before summarizing the revised simplex method is to show
the *matrix form* of the set of equations appearing in the simplex tableau for any
iteration of the original simplex method. For the *original* set of equations, the

matrix form is

$$
\begin{bmatrix} 1 & -\mathbf{c} & \mathbf{0} \\ 0 & \mathbf{A} & \mathbf{I} \end{bmatrix} \begin{bmatrix} Z \\ \mathbf{x} \\ \mathbf{x}_s \end{bmatrix} = \begin{bmatrix} 0 \\ \mathbf{b} \end{bmatrix}.
$$

This set of equations also is exhibited in the first simplex tableau of Table 5.7. After any subsequent iteration, $\mathbf{x}_B = \mathbf{B}^{-1}\mathbf{b}$ and $Z = \mathbf{c}_B\mathbf{B}^{-1}\mathbf{b}$, so the right-hand side of these equations has become

$$
\begin{bmatrix} Z \\ \mathbf{x}_B \end{bmatrix} = \begin{bmatrix} 1 & \mathbf{c}_B\mathbf{B}^{-1} \\ 0 & \mathbf{B}^{-1} \end{bmatrix} \begin{bmatrix} 0 \\ \mathbf{b} \end{bmatrix} = \begin{bmatrix} \mathbf{c}_B\mathbf{B}^{-1}\mathbf{b} \\ \mathbf{B}^{-1}\mathbf{b} \end{bmatrix}.
$$

Therefore, the algebraic operations on *both* sides of the original set of equations have been equivalent to premultiplying them by this same matrix. Since

$$
\begin{bmatrix} 1 & \mathbf{c}_B\mathbf{B}^{-1} \\ 0 & \mathbf{B}^{-1} \end{bmatrix} \begin{bmatrix} 1 & -\mathbf{c} & \mathbf{0} \\ 0 & \mathbf{A} & \mathbf{I} \end{bmatrix} = \begin{bmatrix} 1 & \mathbf{c}_B\mathbf{B}^{-1}\mathbf{A} - \mathbf{c} & \mathbf{c}_B\mathbf{B}^{-1} \\ 0 & \mathbf{B}^{-1}\mathbf{A} & \mathbf{B}^{-1} \end{bmatrix},
$$

the desired matrix form of the *set of equations after any iteration* is

$$
\begin{bmatrix} 1 & \mathbf{c}_B\mathbf{B}^{-1}\mathbf{A} - \mathbf{c} & \mathbf{c}_B\mathbf{B}^{-1} \\ 0 & \mathbf{B}^{-1}\mathbf{A} & \mathbf{B}^{-1} \end{bmatrix} \begin{bmatrix} Z \\ \mathbf{x} \\ \mathbf{x}_s \end{bmatrix} = \begin{bmatrix} \mathbf{c}_B\mathbf{B}^{-1}\mathbf{b} \\ \mathbf{B}^{-1}\mathbf{b} \end{bmatrix}.
$$

The second simplex tableau of Table 5.7 also exhibits this same set of equations.

EXAMPLE To illustrate this matrix form for the current set of equations, consider the *final* set of equations resulting from iteration 2 for the Wyndor Glass Co.

Table 5.7 **Initial and later simplex tableaux in matrix form**

Iteration	Basic variable	Eq. no.	Z	Coefficient of Original variables	Coefficient of Slack variables	Right side
0	Z	0	1	$-\mathbf{c}$	$\mathbf{0}$	0
	$\mathbf{x}_B$	$1-m$	0	$\mathbf{A}$	$\mathbf{I}$	$\mathbf{b}$
Any	Z	0	1	$\mathbf{c}_B\mathbf{B}^{-1}\mathbf{A} - \mathbf{c}$	$\mathbf{c}_B\mathbf{B}^{-1}$	$\mathbf{c}_B\mathbf{B}^{-1}\mathbf{b}$
	$\mathbf{x}_B$	$1-m$	0	$\mathbf{B}^{-1}\mathbf{A}$	$\mathbf{B}^{-1}$	$\mathbf{B}^{-1}\mathbf{b}$

problem. Using the $\mathbf{B}^{-1}$ given for iteration 2,

$$\mathbf{B}^{-1}\mathbf{A} = \begin{bmatrix} 1 & \dfrac{1}{3} & -\dfrac{1}{3} \\ 0 & \dfrac{1}{2} & 0 \\ 0 & -\dfrac{1}{3} & \dfrac{1}{3} \end{bmatrix} \begin{bmatrix} 1 & 0 \\ 0 & 2 \\ 3 & 2 \end{bmatrix} = \begin{bmatrix} 0 & 0 \\ 0 & 1 \\ 1 & 0 \end{bmatrix},$$

$$\mathbf{c}_B\mathbf{B}^{-1} = [0,5,3] \begin{bmatrix} 1 & \dfrac{1}{3} & -\dfrac{1}{3} \\ 0 & \dfrac{1}{2} & 0 \\ 0 & -\dfrac{1}{3} & \dfrac{1}{3} \end{bmatrix} = \left[0,\dfrac{3}{2},1\right],$$

$$\mathbf{c}_B\mathbf{B}^{-1}\mathbf{A} - \mathbf{c} = [0,5,3] \begin{bmatrix} 0 & 0 \\ 0 & 1 \\ 1 & 0 \end{bmatrix} - [3,5] = [0,0].$$

Since $\mathbf{x}_B = \mathbf{B}^{-1}\mathbf{b}$ and $Z = \mathbf{c}_B\mathbf{B}^{-1}\mathbf{b}$ have already been found, these results give the following set of equations:

$$\begin{bmatrix} 1 & 0 & 0 & 0 & \dfrac{3}{2} & 1 \\ 0 & 0 & 0 & 1 & \dfrac{1}{3} & -\dfrac{1}{3} \\ 0 & 0 & 1 & 0 & \dfrac{1}{2} & 0 \\ 0 & 1 & 0 & 0 & -\dfrac{1}{3} & \dfrac{1}{3} \end{bmatrix} \begin{bmatrix} Z \\ x_1 \\ x_2 \\ x_3 \\ x_4 \\ x_5 \end{bmatrix} = \begin{bmatrix} 36 \\ 2 \\ 6 \\ 2 \end{bmatrix},$$

as shown in the *final* simplex tableau in Table 4.8.

THE OVERALL PROCEDURE

There are two key implications from the matrix form of the current set of equations. The first is that *only* $\mathbf{B}^{-1}$ needs to be derived to be able to calculate all the numbers in the simplex tableau from the *original parameters* $(\mathbf{A},\mathbf{b},\mathbf{c}_B)$ of the problem. (This implication is the essence of the **fundamental insight** described in the next section.) The second is that *any one* of these numbers (except $Z = \mathbf{c}_B\mathbf{B}^{-1}\mathbf{b}$) can be obtained by performing *only part* of a matrix multiplication. Therefore, the *required numbers* to perform an iteration of the simplex method can be obtained as needed *without* expending the computational effort to obtain *all* the numbers.

Summary of Revised Simplex Method

1. *Initialization step*: Same as for original simplex method.
2. *Iterative step*:

Part 1 Determine the entering basic variable: Same as for original simplex method.

Part 2 Determine the leaving basic variable: Same as for original simplex method, except calculate *only* the numbers required to do this (the coefficients of the entering basic variable in every equation but Eq. (0), and then, for each strictly positive coefficient, the right-hand side of that equation).[1]

Part 3 Determine the new basic feasible solution: Derive $\mathbf{B}^{-1}$ and set $\mathbf{x}_B = \mathbf{B}^{-1}\mathbf{b}$. (Calculating $\mathbf{x}_B$ is optional unless the optimality test finds it to be optimal.)

3. *Optimality test*: Same as for original simplex method, except calculate *only* the numbers required to do this test, i.e., the coefficients of the *nonbasic variables* in Eq. (0).

In part 3 of the iterative step, $\mathbf{B}^{-1}$ could be derived each time by using a standard computer routine for inverting a matrix. However, since $\mathbf{B}$ (and therefore $\mathbf{B}^{-1}$) changes so little from one iteration to the next, it is much more efficient to derive the new $\mathbf{B}^{-1}$ (denote it by $\mathbf{B}_{new}^{-1}$) from the $\mathbf{B}^{-1}$ at the preceding iteration (denote it by $\mathbf{B}_{old}^{-1}$). (For the *initial* basic feasible solution, $\mathbf{B} = \mathbf{I} = \mathbf{B}^{-1}$.) The method for doing this derivation is based directly upon the interpretation of the elements of $\mathbf{B}^{-1}$ (the coefficients of the slack variables in the current equations $1, 2, \ldots, m$) presented in the next section, as well as upon the procedure used by the original simplex method to obtain the new set of equations from the preceding set.

To describe this method formally, let

x_k = entering basic variable

a'_{ik} = coefficient of x_k in current Eq. (i), for $i = 1, 2, \ldots, m$ (calculated in part 2 of the iterative step)

r = number of the equation containing the leaving basic variable.

Recall that the new set of equations [excluding Eq. (0)] can be obtained from the preceding set by subtracting a'_{ik}/a'_{rk} times Eq. (r) from Eq. (i), for all $i = 1, 2, \ldots, m$ *except $i = r$*, and then dividing Eq. (r) by a'_{rk}. Therefore, the element in row i and column j of $\mathbf{B}_{new}^{-1}$ is

$$(\mathbf{B}_{new}^{-1})_{ij} = \begin{cases} (\mathbf{B}_{old}^{-1})_{ij} - \dfrac{a'_{ik}}{a'_{rk}}(\mathbf{B}_{old}^{-1})_{rj}, & \text{if } i \neq r \\[2ex] \dfrac{1}{a'_{rk}}(\mathbf{B}_{old}^{-1})_{rj}, & \text{if } i = r. \end{cases}$$

[1] Because the value of $\mathbf{x}_B$ is the entire vector of right-hand sides except for Eq. (0), the relevant right-hand sides need not be calculated here if $\mathbf{x}_B$ was calculated in part 3 of the preceding iteration.

These formulas are expressed in matrix notation as

$$\mathbf{B}_{new}^{-1} = \mathbf{E}\mathbf{B}_{old}^{-1},$$

where the matrix $\mathbf{E}$ is an identity matrix, except that its rth column is replaced by the vector

$$\boldsymbol{\eta} = \begin{bmatrix} \eta_1 \\ \eta_2 \\ \vdots \\ \eta_m \end{bmatrix}, \quad \text{where } \eta_i = \begin{cases} -\dfrac{a'_{ik}}{a'_{rk}}, & \text{if } i \neq r \\[2ex] \dfrac{1}{a'_{rk}}, & \text{if } i = r. \end{cases}$$

Thus $\mathbf{E} = [\mathbf{U}_1, \mathbf{U}_2, \ldots, \mathbf{U}_{r-1}, \boldsymbol{\eta}, \mathbf{U}_{r+1}, \ldots, \mathbf{U}_m]$, where the m elements of each of the $\mathbf{U}_i$ column vectors are 0 except for a 1 in the ith position.

EXAMPLE We shall illustrate the revised simplex method by applying it to the Wyndor Glass Co. problem. The *initial* basic variables are the slack variables.

$$\mathbf{x}_B = \begin{bmatrix} x_3 \\ x_4 \\ x_5 \end{bmatrix}.$$

Iteration 1

Because the *initial* $\mathbf{B}^{-1} = \mathbf{I}$, no calculations are needed to obtain the numbers required to identify the *entering basic variable* x_2 ($-c_2 = -5 < -3 = -c_1$) and the *leaving basic variable* x_4 ($a_{12} = 0$, $b_2/a_{22} = \frac{12}{2} < \frac{18}{2} = b_3/a_{32}$, so $r = 2$). Thus the new set of basic variables is

$$\mathbf{x}_B = \begin{bmatrix} x_3 \\ x_2 \\ x_5 \end{bmatrix}.$$

To obtain the new $\mathbf{B}^{-1}$,

$$\boldsymbol{\eta} = \begin{bmatrix} -\dfrac{a_{12}}{a_{22}} \\[2ex] \dfrac{1}{a_{22}} \\[2ex] -\dfrac{a_{32}}{a_{22}} \end{bmatrix} = \begin{bmatrix} 0 \\[1ex] \frac{1}{2} \\[1ex] -1 \end{bmatrix},$$

so

$$\mathbf{B}^{-1} = \begin{bmatrix} 1 & 0 & 0 \\ 0 & \frac{1}{2} & 0 \\ 0 & -1 & 1 \end{bmatrix} \begin{bmatrix} 1 & 0 & 0 \\ 0 & 1 & 0 \\ 0 & 0 & 1 \end{bmatrix} = \begin{bmatrix} 1 & 0 & 0 \\ 0 & \frac{1}{2} & 0 \\ 0 & -1 & 1 \end{bmatrix},$$

so that

$$
\begin{bmatrix} x_3 \\ x_2 \\ x_5 \end{bmatrix} = \begin{bmatrix} 1 & 0 & 0 \\ 0 & \dfrac{1}{2} & 0 \\ 0 & -1 & 1 \end{bmatrix} \begin{bmatrix} 4 \\ 12 \\ 18 \end{bmatrix} = \begin{bmatrix} 4 \\ 6 \\ 6 \end{bmatrix}.
$$

To test whether this solution is optimal, we calculate the coefficients of the *nonbasic variables* (x_1 and x_4) in Eq. (0). Performing only the relevant parts of the matrix multiplications,

$$
\mathbf{c}_B \mathbf{B}^{-1} \mathbf{A} - \mathbf{c} = [0, 5, 0] \begin{bmatrix} 1 & 0 & 0 \\ 0 & \dfrac{1}{2} & 0 \\ 0 & -1 & 1 \end{bmatrix} \begin{bmatrix} 1 & - \\ 0 & - \\ 3 & - \end{bmatrix} - [3, -] = [-3, -],
$$

$$
\mathbf{c}_B \mathbf{B}^{-1} = [0, 5, 0] \begin{bmatrix} - & 0 & - \\ - & \dfrac{1}{2} & - \\ - & -1 & - \end{bmatrix} = \left[-, \dfrac{5}{2}, - \right],
$$

so the coefficients of x_1 and x_4 are -3 and $5/2$, respectively. Since x_1 has a negative coefficient, this solution is *not* optimal.

Iteration 2

Using these coefficients of the nonbasic variables, the next iteration begins by identifying x_1 as the *entering basic variable*. To determine the *leaving basic variable*, we must calculate the *other* coefficients of x_1:

$$
\mathbf{B}^{-1}\mathbf{A} = \begin{bmatrix} 1 & 0 & 0 \\ 0 & \dfrac{1}{2} & 0 \\ 0 & -1 & 1 \end{bmatrix} \begin{bmatrix} 1 & - \\ 0 & - \\ 3 & - \end{bmatrix} = \begin{bmatrix} 1 & - \\ 0 & - \\ 3 & - \end{bmatrix}.
$$

Using the right-side column for the current basic feasible solution (the value of $\mathbf{x}_B$) just given for iteration 1, the ratios $4/1 > 6/3$ indicate that x_5 is the leaving basic variable, so the new set of basic variables is

$$
\mathbf{x}_B = \begin{bmatrix} x_3 \\ x_2 \\ x_1 \end{bmatrix}, \quad \text{with } \boldsymbol{\eta} = \begin{bmatrix} -\dfrac{a'_{11}}{a'_{31}} \\[2mm] -\dfrac{a'_{21}}{a'_{31}} \\[2mm] \dfrac{1}{a'_{31}} \end{bmatrix} = \begin{bmatrix} -\dfrac{1}{3} \\[2mm] 0 \\[2mm] \dfrac{1}{3} \end{bmatrix}.
$$

Therefore, the new $\mathbf{B}^{-1}$ is

$$
\mathbf{B}^{-1} =
\begin{bmatrix} 1 & 0 & -\dfrac{1}{3} \\ 0 & 1 & 0 \\ 0 & 0 & \dfrac{1}{3} \end{bmatrix}
\begin{bmatrix} 1 & 0 & 0 \\ 0 & \dfrac{1}{2} & 0 \\ 0 & -1 & 1 \end{bmatrix}
=
\begin{bmatrix} 1 & \dfrac{1}{3} & -\dfrac{1}{3} \\ 0 & \dfrac{1}{2} & 0 \\ 0 & -\dfrac{1}{3} & \dfrac{1}{3} \end{bmatrix},
$$

so that

$$
\begin{bmatrix} x_3 \\ x_2 \\ x_1 \end{bmatrix}
=
\begin{bmatrix} 1 & \dfrac{1}{3} & -\dfrac{1}{3} \\ 0 & \dfrac{1}{2} & 0 \\ 0 & -\dfrac{1}{3} & \dfrac{1}{3} \end{bmatrix}
\begin{bmatrix} 4 \\ 12 \\ 18 \end{bmatrix}
=
\begin{bmatrix} 2 \\ 6 \\ 2 \end{bmatrix}.
$$

Applying the optimality test, we find that the coefficients of the *nonbasic variables* (x_4 and x_5) in Eq. (0) are

$$
\mathbf{c}_B \mathbf{B}^{-1} = [0,5,3]
\begin{bmatrix} -\dfrac{1}{3} & -\dfrac{1}{3} \\ -\dfrac{1}{2} & 0 \\ -\dfrac{1}{3} & \dfrac{1}{3} \end{bmatrix}
= \left[-,\dfrac{3}{2},1 \right].
$$

Because both coefficients ($3/2$ and 1) are nonnegative, the current solution ($x = 2$, $x_2 = 6$, $x_3 = 2$, $x_4 = 0$, $x_5 = 0$) is optimal and the procedure terminates.

GENERAL OBSERVATIONS

Although the preceding pages describe the essence of the revised simplex method, we should point out that minor modifications may be made to improve the efficiency of its execution on computers. For example, $\mathbf{B}^{-1}$ may be obtained as the product of the previous $\mathbf{E}$ matrices. This modification requires storing only the $\boldsymbol{\eta}$ column of $\mathbf{E}$ and the number of the column, rather than the $\mathbf{B}^{-1}$ matrix, at each iteration. If magnetic tape must be used rather than core storage, this "product form" of the basis inverse may be the most efficient.

You should also note that the preceding discussion was limited to the case of linear programming problems fitting *our standard form* given in Sec. 3.2. However, the modifications for other forms are relatively straightforward. The *initialization step* would be conducted just as it would for the original simplex method (see Sec. 4.6). When this step involves introducing artificial variables to obtain an initial basic feasible solution (and thereby to obtain an *identity matrix* as the *initial basis matrix*), these variables would be included among the m elements of $\mathbf{x}_s$.

We shall now summarize the advantages of the revised simplex method over the original simplex method. One advantage is that the number of arithmetic computations may be reduced. This is especially true when the **A** matrix contains a large number of zero elements (which usually is the case for the large problems arising in practice). The amount of information that must be stored at each iteration is less, sometimes considerably so. The revised simplex method also permits the control of the round-off errors inevitably generated by digital computers. This control can be exercised by periodically obtaining the current $\mathbf{B}^{-1}$ by directly inverting **B**. Furthermore, some of the post-optimality problems discussed in Sec. 4.7 can be handled more conveniently with the revised simplex method. For all these reasons, the revised simplex method is usually preferable to the original simplex method for computer execution.

5.3 A Fundamental Insight

We shall now focus on a property of the simplex method (in any form) that has been revealed by the *revised simplex method* in the preceding section. This fundamental insight provides the key to both duality theory and sensitivity analysis (Chap. 6), two very important parts of linear programming. The property involves the coefficients of the slack variables and the information they give. It is a direct result of the initialization step, where the ith slack variable (x_{n+i}) is given a coefficient of $+1$ in Eq. (i) and a coefficient of *zero* in *every other equation* [including Eq. (0)] for $i = 1, 2, \ldots, m$, as shown in the *slack variables* column for iteration 0 in Table 5.7.[1] The other key factor is that subsequent iterations change the initial equations *only* by:

1. multiplying an *entire* equation by a nonzero constant, or
2. adding a multiple of one *entire* equation to another *entire* equation.

As already described in the preceding section, a sequence of these kinds of algebraic operations is equivalent to premultiplying the initial simplex tableau by some matrix. The consequence of combining these two factors is that after any iteration, the coefficients of the slack variables in each equation immediately reveal how that equation has been obtained from the *initial* equations.

Because the primary applications of this property involve the *final* tableau, we shall describe it just in terms of this tableau. Matrix notation, as introduced in the preceding section, will be used since the fundamental insight is most transparent in matrix form. (See Appendix 3 for a review of matrices.) If you

---

[1] We assume throughout this section that the problem is in *our standard form*, with $b_i \geq 0$ for all $i = 1, 2, \ldots, m$, so that no additional adjustments are needed in the initialization step. Problem 23 asks you to adapt our conclusions to nonstandard forms.

haven't read Sec. 5.2, you now need to know that the *parameters* of the model are given by the matrix $\mathbf{A} = \|a_{ij}\|$ and the vectors, $\mathbf{b} = \|b_i\|$ and $\mathbf{c} = \|c_j\|$, as displayed at the beginning of that section.

The only other notation needed is summarized and illustrated in Table 5.8, where *rows* of the simplex tableau refer (as before) to *all* numbers to the right of the Z column (including the right-side number). Notice how the vector $\mathbf{t}$ (representing row 0) and the matrix $\mathbf{T}$ (representing the other rows) together correspond to the rows of the *initial* tableau in Table 4.8, whereas the vector $\mathbf{t}^*$ and matrix $\mathbf{T}^*$ together correspond to the rows of the *final* tableau in Table 4.8.

Now suppose that you are given the initial tableau, $\mathbf{t}$ and $\mathbf{T}$, and just $\mathbf{y}^*$ and $\mathbf{S}^*$ from the final tableau. Is there a way that only this information can be used to calculate the rest of the final tableau? The answer is provided by Table 5.7. This table includes some information not directly relevant to our current discussion, namely, how $\mathbf{y}^*$ and $\mathbf{S}^*$ themselves can be calculated ($\mathbf{y}^* = \mathbf{c}_B \mathbf{B}^{-1}$ and $\mathbf{S}^* = \mathbf{B}^{-1}$) by knowing the current set of basic variables. However, the lower part of this table (which can represent either an intermediate or final simplex tableau) also clearly shows how the rest of the tableau can be obtained from the coefficients of the slack variables, which is summarized as follows.

Fundamental Insight

1. $\mathbf{t}^* = \mathbf{t} + \mathbf{y}^*\mathbf{T} = [\mathbf{y}^*\mathbf{A} - \mathbf{c} \mid \mathbf{y}^* \mid \mathbf{y}^*\mathbf{b}]$.

2. $\mathbf{T}^* = \mathbf{S}^*\mathbf{T} = [\mathbf{S}^*\mathbf{A} \mid \mathbf{S}^* \mid \mathbf{S}^*\mathbf{b}]$.

Table 5.8 General notation for initial and final simplex tableaux in matrix form, illustrated by Wyndor Glass Co. problem

Initial Tableau:

Row 0: $\mathbf{t} = [-3, -5 \mid 0,0,0 \mid 0] = [-\mathbf{c} \mid \mathbf{0} \mid 0]$.

Other rows: $\mathbf{T} = \begin{bmatrix} 1 & 0 & 1 & 0 & 0 & 4 \\ 0 & 2 & 0 & 1 & 0 & 12 \\ 3 & 2 & 0 & 0 & 1 & 18 \end{bmatrix} = [\mathbf{A} \mid \mathbf{I} \mid \mathbf{b}]$.

Combined: $\begin{bmatrix} \mathbf{t} \\ \mathbf{T} \end{bmatrix} = \begin{bmatrix} -\mathbf{c} & \mid \mathbf{0} & \mid 0 \\ \mathbf{A} & \mid \mathbf{I} & \mid \mathbf{b} \end{bmatrix}$.

Final Tableau:

Row 0: $\mathbf{t}^* = [0,0 \mid 0,\frac{3}{2},1 \mid 36] = [\mathbf{z}^* - \mathbf{c} \mid \mathbf{y}^* \mid Z^*]$.

Other rows: $\mathbf{T}^* = \begin{bmatrix} 0 & 0 & 1 & 1/3 & -1/3 & 2 \\ 0 & 1 & 0 & 1/2 & 0 & 6 \\ 1 & 0 & 0 & -1/3 & 1/3 & 2 \end{bmatrix} = [\mathbf{A}^* \mid \mathbf{S}^* \mid \mathbf{b}^*]$.

Combined: $\begin{bmatrix} \mathbf{t}^* \\ \mathbf{T}^* \end{bmatrix} = \begin{bmatrix} \mathbf{z}^* - \mathbf{c} & \mid \mathbf{y}^* & \mid Z^* \\ \mathbf{A}^* & \mid \mathbf{S}^* & \mid \mathbf{b}^* \end{bmatrix}$.

To illustrate, for the Wyndor Glass Co. problem,

$$\mathbf{t}^* = [-3, -5 \mid 0, 0, 0] + [0, \tfrac{3}{2}, 1] \begin{bmatrix} 1 & 0 & 1 & 0 & 0 & 4 \\ 0 & 2 & 0 & 1 & 0 & 12 \\ 3 & 2 & 0 & 0 & 1 & 18 \end{bmatrix}$$

$$= [-3, -5 \mid 0, 0, 0] + [3, 5 \mid 0, \tfrac{3}{2}, 1 \mid 36]$$

$$= [0, 0 \mid 0, \tfrac{3}{2}, 1 \mid 36],$$

as given in Table 5.8. Similarly,

$$\mathbf{T}^* = \begin{bmatrix} 1 & 1/3 & -1/3 \\ 0 & 1/2 & 0 \\ 0 & -1/3 & 1/3 \end{bmatrix} \begin{bmatrix} 1 & 0 & 1 & 0 & 0 & 4 \\ 0 & 2 & 0 & 1 & 0 & 12 \\ 3 & 2 & 0 & 0 & 1 & 18 \end{bmatrix}$$

$$= \begin{bmatrix} 0 & 1 & 1 & 1/3 & -1/3 & 2 \\ 0 & 1 & 0 & 1/2 & 0 & 6 \\ 1 & 0 & 0 & -1/3 & 1/3 & 2 \end{bmatrix}.$$

The logic behind the fundamental insight is relatively straightforward. To derive $\mathbf{T}^*$, note that the sequence of algebraic operations performed by the simplex method (excluding row 0) is equivalent to premultiplying $\mathbf{T}$ by some matrix. What is this matrix? Since part of $\mathbf{T}$ starts as $\mathbf{I}$ and ends up as $\mathbf{S}^*$, this matrix must be $\mathbf{S}^*$ because $\mathbf{S}^*\mathbf{I} = \mathbf{S}^*$.

Similarly, to derive $\mathbf{t}^*$, note that the sequence of algebraic operations involving row 0 amounts to adding some linear combination of the rows in $\mathbf{T}$ to $\mathbf{t}$. Therefore, this sequence of operations is equivalent to adding to $\mathbf{t}$ some vector times $\mathbf{T}$. What is this vector? Since part of $\mathbf{t}$ starts as $\mathbf{0}$ and ends up as $\mathbf{y}^*$, and since the corresponding columns of $\mathbf{T}$ contain $\mathbf{I}$, this vector must be $\mathbf{y}^*$ because $\mathbf{0} + \mathbf{y}^*\mathbf{I} = \mathbf{y}^*$.

Consequently, the coefficients of the slack variables in the final tableau (where the jth slack variable has coefficient y_j^* in row 0 and coefficient s_{ij}^* in row i, for $i = 1, 2, \ldots, m$ and $j = 1, 2, \ldots, m$) have the following interpretation:

y_j^* = multiple of initial row j added to initial row 0 by the simplex method to obtain final row 0 ($j = 1, 2, \ldots, m$).

s_{ij}^* = multiple of initial row j added (over j) by the simplex method to obtain final row i ($i = 1, 2, \ldots, m$; $j = 1, 2, \ldots, m$).

APPLICATIONS

The *fundamental insight* has a variety of important applications in linear programming. One of these applications involves the *revised simplex method*. As described in the preceding section (see Table 5.7), this method used $\mathbf{S}^* = \mathbf{B}^{-1}$ and the initial tableau to calculate all the relevant numbers in the current tableau for *every* iteration. It goes even further than the fundamental insight by using $\mathbf{B}^{-1}$ to calculate $\mathbf{y}^*$ itself as $\mathbf{y}^* = \mathbf{c}_B \mathbf{B}^{-1}$.

Another application involves the interpretation of the *shadow prices* $(y_1^*, y_2^*, \ldots, y_m^*)$ described in Sec. 4.7. The fundamental insight reveals that Z^* (the value of Z for the optimal solution) is

$$Z^* = \mathbf{y^*b} = \sum_{i=1}^{m} y_i^* b_i,$$

so, for example,

$$Z^* = 0b_1 + \frac{3}{2} b_2 + b_3$$

for the Wyndor Glass Co. problem. This equation immediately yields the interpretation for the y_i^* given in Sec. 4.7.

Another group of extremely important applications involves various *post-optimality tasks* (reoptimization technique, sensitivity analysis, parametric linear programming—described in Sec. 4.7) that involve investigating the effect of making one or more changes in the original model. In particular, suppose that the simplex method already has been applied to obtain an optimal solution (as well as $\mathbf{y^*}$ and $\mathbf{S^*}$) for the original model, and then these changes are made. If exactly the same sequence of algebraic operations were to be applied to the revised initial tableau, what would be the resulting changes in the *final* tableau? Because $\mathbf{y^*}$ and $\mathbf{S^*}$ don't change, the fundamental insight reveals the answer immediately.

For example, consider the change from $b_2 = 12$ to $b_2 = 13$ as illustrated in Fig. 4.3 for the Wyndor Glass Co. problem. It isn't necessary to *solve* for the new optimal solution $(x_1, x_2) = (5/3, 13/2)$ because the values of the basic variables in the final tableau ($\mathbf{b^*}$) are immediately revealed by the fundamental insight:

$$\begin{bmatrix} x_3 \\ x_2 \\ x_1 \end{bmatrix} = \mathbf{b^*} = \mathbf{S^*b} = \begin{bmatrix} 1 & 1/3 & -1/3 \\ 0 & 1/2 & 0 \\ 0 & -1/3 & 1/3 \end{bmatrix} \begin{bmatrix} 4 \\ 13 \\ 18 \end{bmatrix} = \begin{bmatrix} 7/3 \\ 13/2 \\ 5/3 \end{bmatrix}.$$

There is an even easier way to make this calculation. Since the only change is in the *second* component of $\mathbf{b}$, which gets premultiplied by only the *second* column of $\mathbf{S^*}$, the *change* in $\mathbf{b^*}$ can be calculated as simply

$$\Delta \mathbf{b^*} = \begin{bmatrix} 1/3 \\ 1/2 \\ -1/3 \end{bmatrix} \Delta b_2 = \begin{bmatrix} 1/3 \\ 1/2 \\ -1/3 \end{bmatrix},$$

so the original values of the basic variables in the final tableau ($x_3 = 2, x_2 = 6, x_1 = 2$) now become

$$\begin{bmatrix} x_3 \\ x_2 \\ x_1 \end{bmatrix} = \begin{bmatrix} 2 \\ 6 \\ 2 \end{bmatrix} + \begin{bmatrix} 1/3 \\ 1/2 \\ -1/3 \end{bmatrix} = \begin{bmatrix} 7/3 \\ 13/2 \\ 5/3 \end{bmatrix}.$$

(If any of these new values were *negative*, and thus infeasible, then the *reoptimization technique* described in Sec. 4.7 would be applied, starting from this revised final tableau.) Applying *incremental analysis* to the preceding equation for Z^* also immediately yields

$$\Delta Z = \Delta Z^* = \frac{3}{2} \Delta b_2 = \frac{3}{2}.$$

The fundamental insight also can be applied to investigating other kinds of changes in the original model in a very similar fashion; it is the crux of the *sensitivity analysis* procedure described in the latter part of Chap. 6.

You also will see in the next chapter that the fundamental insight plays a key role in the very useful *duality theory* for linear programming.

5.4 Conclusions

Although the simplex method is an algebraic procedure, it is based on some fairly simple geometric concepts. These concepts enable the algorithm to examine only a relatively small number of basic feasible solutions before reaching and identifying an optimal solution.

The revised simplex method provides an effective way of adapting the simplex method for computer implementation.

The final simplex tableau includes complete information on how it can be algebraically reconstructed directly from the initial simplex tableau. This fundamental insight has some very important applications, especially for post-optimality analysis.

SELECTED REFERENCES

1. Dantzig, George B.: *Linear Programming and Extensions*, Princeton University Press, Princeton, N.J., 1963.
2. Gass, Saul: *Linear Programming*, 4th ed., McGraw-Hill, New York, 1975.
3. Lasdon, Leon S.: *Optimization Theory for Large Systems*, Macmillan, New York, 1970.
4. Spivey, W. Allen and Robert M. Thrall: *Linear Optimization*, Holt, Rinehart & Winston, New York, 1970.

PROBLEMS

1. Consider the following problem.

$$\text{Maximize} \quad Z = 3x_1 + 2x_2,$$

subject to

$$2x_1 + x_2 \leq 6$$
$$x_1 + 2x_2 \leq 6,$$

and

$$x_1 \geq 0, \quad x_2 \geq 0.$$

(a) Solve this problem graphically. Identify the corner-point feasible solutions by circling them on the graph.

(b) Identify all the sets of two defining equations for this problem. For each one, solve (if a solution exists) for the corresponding corner-point solution, and classify it as a corner-point feasible solution or corner-point infeasible solution.

(c) Introduce slack variables in order to write the functional constraints in *equality form*.

(d) For each set of defining equations from part (b), identify their *indicating variables* from the problem in *equality form*, display the equations from part (c) *after* deleting these nonbasic variables, and give the resulting basic solution.

(e) Without executing the simplex method, use its geometric interpretation (and the objective function) to identify the path (sequence of corner-point feasible solutions) it would follow to reach the optimal solution. For each of these corner-point feasible solutions in turn, rewrite the corresponding information from part (d) and then identify the following decisions being made for the next iteration: (i) which *defining equation* is being deleted and which is being added, (ii) which *indicating variable* is being deleted (the entering basic variable) and which is being added (the leaving basic variable).

2. Repeat Prob. 1 for the linear programming model in Prob. 4 of Chap. 3.

3. Consider the following problem.

$$\text{Maximize} \quad Z = 2x_1 + 3x_2,$$

subject to

$$-3x_1 + x_2 \le 2$$
$$4x_1 + 2x_2 \le 44$$
$$4x_1 - x_2 \le 20$$
$$-x_1 + 2x_2 \le 14,$$

and

$$x_1 \ge 0, \quad x_2 \ge 0.$$

(a) Solve this problem graphically. Identify the corner-point feasible solutions by circling them on the graph.

(b) Develop a table giving each of the corner-point feasible solutions and the corresponding defining equations, basic feasible solution, and nonbasic variables. Calculate Z for each of these solutions and use just this information to identify the optimal solution.

(c) Develop the corresponding table for the corner-point infeasible solutions, and so on. Also identify the sets of defining equations and nonbasic variables that do not yield a solution.

4. Consider the linear programming problem given in Table 6.1 as the *dual problem* for the Wyndor Glass Co. example.

(a) Identify the 10 sets of defining equations for this problem. For each one, solve (if a solution exists) for the corresponding corner-point solution, and classify it as a corner-point feasible solution or corner-point infeasible solution.

(b) For each corner-point solution, give the corresponding basic solution and its set of nonbasic variables. (Compare with Table 6.8.)

5. Consider the following problem.

$$\text{Minimize} \quad Z = x_1 + x_2,$$

subject to

$$-x_1 + x_2 \leq 3$$
$$2x_1 + x_2 \leq 18$$
$$x_2 \geq 6,$$

and

$$x_1 \geq 0, \quad x_2 \geq 0.$$

(a) Solve this problem graphically.
(b) Develop a table giving each of the corner-point feasible solutions and the corresponding defining equations, basic feasible solution, and nonbasic variables.

6. Reconsider Prob. 11 in Chap. 4.

(a) Identify the 10 sets of defining equations for this problem. For each one, solve (if a solution exists) for the corresponding corner-point solution, and classify it as a corner-point feasible solution or a corner-point infeasible solution.
(b) For each corner-point solution, give the corresponding basic solution and its set of nonbasic variables.

7. Reconsider Prob. 3 in Chap. 3.

(a) Identify the 15 sets of defining equations for this problem. For each one, solve (if a solution exists) for the corresponding corner-point solution, and classify it as a corner-point feasible solution or a corner-point infeasible solution.
(b) For each corner-point solution, give the corresponding basic solution and its set of nonbasic variables.

8. A weighted average of N solutions, $\mathbf{x}^{(1)}, \mathbf{x}^{(2)}, \ldots, \mathbf{x}^{(N)}$, is a solution $\mathbf{x}$ such that

$$\mathbf{x} = \sum_{k=1}^{N} \alpha_k \mathbf{x}^{(k)},$$

where the weights $\alpha_1, \alpha_2, \ldots, \alpha_N$ are nonnegative and sum to 1. If the feasible region is bounded, then every feasible solution can be expressed as a weighted average of some of the corner-point feasible solutions (perhaps in more than one way). Similarly, after solutions are augmented with slack variables, every feasible solution can be expressed as a weighted average of some of the basic feasible solutions.

(a) Show that *any* weighted average of *any* set of *feasible* solutions must be a feasible solution (so that any weighted average of *corner-point* feasible solutions must be feasible).
(b) Use the result quoted in part (a) to show that *any* weighted average of basic feasible solutions must be a feasible solution.

9. Using the facts given in Prob. 8, show that the following statements must be true for any linear programming problem that has a bounded feasible region and multiple optimal solutions:

(a) Every weighted average of the optimal basic feasible solutions must be optimal.
(b) No *other* feasible solution can be optimal.

10.   Reconsider Prob. 16 in Chap. 4. Now you are given the information that the basic variables in the optimal solution are x_2 and x_3. Use this information to identify a system of three constraint boundary equations whose simultaneous solution must be this optimal solution. Then solve this system of equations to obtain this solution.

11.   Reconsider Prob. 7 in Chap. 4. Using the given information and the theory of the simplex method, analyze the constraints of the problem in order to identify a system of three constraint boundary equations whose simultaneous solution must be the optimal solution (not augmented). Then solve this system of equations to obtain this solution.

12.   Consider a mathematical programming problem with two variables; it has the feasible region shown on the graph, where the six dots correspond to corner-point feasible solutions. The problem has a linear objective function, and the two dashed lines are objective function lines passing through the optimal solution (4,5) and the second-best corner-point feasible solution (2,5). Note that the nonoptimal solution (2,5) is better than both of its adjacent corner-point feasible solutions, which violates Property 3 in Sec. 5.1 for corner-point feasible solutions in linear programming.

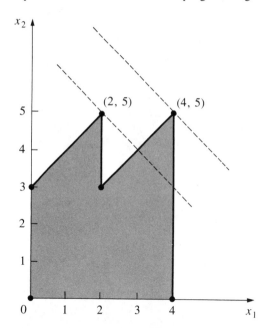

Demonstrate that this problem *cannot* be a linear programming problem by constructing the feasible region that would result if the six line segments on the boundary were constraint boundaries for *linear programming constraints*.

13.   Consider the following problem.

$$\text{Maximize}\quad Z = 5x_1 + 4x_2 + 6x_3 + 3x_4 + 8x_5,$$

subject to

$$
\begin{aligned}
x_1 + 2x_2 + 3x_3 + 3x_4 \quad\;\; &\le 20 && \text{(Resource 1)}\\
4x_1 + 3x_2 + 2x_3 + \;\, x_4 + \;\, x_5 &\le 30 && \text{(Resource 2)}\\
x_1 + 3x_2 \qquad\quad + \;\, x_4 + 3x_5 &\le 20, && \text{(Resource 3)}
\end{aligned}
$$

and

$$x_j \geq 0 \qquad (j = 1, \ldots, 5).$$

You are given the facts that the basic variables in the optimal solution are $x_3, x_1,$ and x_5, and that

$$\begin{bmatrix} 3 & 1 & 0 \\ 2 & 4 & 1 \\ 0 & 1 & 3 \end{bmatrix}^{-1} = \frac{1}{27} \begin{bmatrix} 11 & -3 & 1 \\ -6 & 9 & -3 \\ 2 & -3 & 10 \end{bmatrix}.$$

(a)   Use the given information to identify the optimal solution.

(b)   Use the given information to identify the *shadow prices* for the three resources.

14.   Use the revised simplex method to solve the following problem.

$$\text{Maximize} \quad Z = 5x_1 + 8x_2 + 7x_3 + 4x_4 + 6x_5,$$

subject to

$$2x_1 + 3x_2 + 3x_3 + 2x_4 + 2x_5 \leq 20$$
$$3x_1 + 5x_2 + 4x_3 + 2x_4 + 4x_5 \leq 30,$$

and

$$x_j \geq 0, \quad \text{for } j = 1, 2, 3, 4, 5.$$

15.   Use the revised simplex method to solve the linear programming model given in Prob. 4, Chap. 4.

16.   Reconsider Prob. 1. For the sequence of corner-point solutions identified in part (e), construct the *basis matrix* **B** for each of the corresponding basic feasible solutions. For each one, invert **B** manually and use this $\mathbf{B}^{-1}$ to calculate the current solution and then perform the next iteration (or demonstrate that the current solution is optimal).

17.   Use the revised simplex method to solve the linear programming model given in Prob. 2, Chap. 4.

18.   Use the revised simplex method to solve the linear programming model given in Prob. 5, Chap. 4.

19.   Use the revised simplex method to solve each of the following linear programming models:

(a)   Model given in Prob. 4, Chap. 3.

(b)   Model given in Prob. 6, Chap. 4.

20.   Consider the following problem.

$$\text{Maximize} \quad Z = x_1 - x_2 + 2x_3,$$

subject to

$$2x_1 - 2x_2 + 3x_3 \leq 5$$
$$x_1 + x_2 - x_3 \leq 3$$
$$x_1 - x_2 + x_3 \leq 2,$$

and

$$x_1 \geq 0, \quad x_2 \geq 0, \quad x_3 \geq 0.$$

Let x_4, x_5, and x_6 denote the slack variables for the respective constraints. After applying the simplex method, a portion of the final simplex tableau is as follows:

Basic variable	Eq. no.	Z	Coefficient of						Right side
			x_1	x_2	x_3	x_4	x_5	x_6	
Z	0	1				1	1	0	
x_2	1	0				1	3	0	
x_6	2	0				0	1	1	
x_3	3	0				1	2	0	

(a)   Use the *fundamental insight* presented in Sec. 5.3 to identify the missing numbers in the final simplex tableau.

(b)   Identify the defining equations of the corner-point feasible solution corresponding to the optimal basic feasible solution in the final simplex tableau.

21.   Consider the following problem.

$$\text{Maximize} \quad Z = x_1 - x_2 + 2x_3,$$

subject to

$$x_1 + x_2 + 3x_3 \leq 15$$
$$2x_1 - x_2 + x_3 \leq 2$$
$$-x_1 + x_2 + x_3 \leq 4,$$

and

$$x_1 \geq 0, \quad x_2 \geq 0, \quad x_3 \geq 0.$$

Let x_4, x_5, and x_6 denote the slack variables for the respective constraints. After applying the simplex method, a portion of the final simplex tableau is as follows:

Basic variable	Eq. no.	Z	Coefficient of						Right side
			x_1	x_2	x_3	x_4	x_5	x_6	
Z	0	1				0	3/2	1/2	
x_4	1	0				1	-1	-2	
x_3	2	0				0	1/2	1/2	
x_2	3	0				0	-1/2	1/2	

(a)   Use the *fundamental insight* presented in Sec. 5.3 to identify the missing numbers in the final simplex tableau.

(b)   Identify the defining equations of the corner-point feasible solution corresponding to the optimal basic feasible solution in the final simplex tableau.

22.   Consider the following problem.

$$\text{Maximize} \quad Z = 20x_1 + 6x_2 + 8x_3,$$

subject to

$$8x_1 + 2x_2 + 3x_3 \le 200$$
$$4x_1 + 3x_2 \qquad \le 100$$
$$2x_1 \qquad + x_3 \le 50$$
$$x_3 \le 20,$$

and

$$x_1 \ge 0, \quad x_2 \ge 0, \quad x_3 \ge 0.$$

Let x_4, x_5, x_6, and x_7 denote the slack variables for the first through fourth constraints, respectively. Suppose that after some number of iterations of the simplex method a portion of the current simplex tableau is as follows:

Basic variable	Eq. no.	Z	Coefficient of x_1	x_2	x_3	x_4	x_5	x_6	x_7	Right side
Z	0	1				9/4	1/2	0	0	
x_1	1	0				3/16	−1/8	0	0	
x_2	2	0				−1/4	1/2	0	0	
x_6	3	0				−3/8	1/4	1	0	
x_7	4	0				0	0	0	1	

(a) Use the *fundamental insight* presented in Sec. 5.3 to identify the missing numbers in the current simplex tableau.

(b) Indicate which of these missing numbers would be generated by the *revised simplex method* in order to perform the next iteration.

(c) Identify the defining equations of the corner-point feasible solution corresponding to the basic feasible solution in the current simplex tableau.

23. The description of the *fundamental insight* presented in Sec. 5.3 assumes that the problem is in *our standard form*. Now consider each of the following other forms, where the additional adjustments in the initialization step are those recommended in Sec. 4.6. Describe the resulting adjustments in the *fundamental insight*.

(a) Equality constraints.

(b) Negative right-hand sides.

(c) Variables allowed to be negative (with no lower bound).

24. Consider the following problem.

$$\text{Maximize} \quad Z = 2x_1 + 4x_2 + 3x_3,$$

subject to

$$x_1 + 3x_2 + 2x_3 = 20$$
$$x_1 + 5x_2 \qquad \ge 10,$$

and

$$x_1 \ge 0, \quad x_2 \ge 0, \quad x_3 \ge 0.$$

Let $\bar{x}_4$ be the artificial variable for the first constraint. Let x_5 and $\bar{x}_6$ be the surplus variable and artificial variable, respectively, for the second constraint.

You are now given the information that a portion of the *final* simplex tableau is as follows:

Basic variable	Eq. no.	Z	x_1	x_2	x_3	$\bar{x}_4$	x_5	$\bar{x}_6$	Right side
Z	0	1				$M+2$	0	M	
x_1	1	0				1	0	0	
x_5	2	0				1	1	-1	

Coefficient of

(*a*) Extend the *fundamental insight* presented in Sec. 5.3 to identify the missing numbers in the final simplex tableau.

(*b*) Identify the defining equations of the corner-point feasible solution corresponding to the optimal solution in the final simplex tableau.

25. Reconsider Prob. 12 in Chap. 4. For this model that is not in *our standard form*, construct the complete first simplex tableau for the simplex method, and then identify the columns that will contain **S*** for applying the *fundamental insight* in the *final* tableau. Explain why these are the appropriate columns.

26. Consider the following problem.

$$\text{Maximize} \quad Z = 3x_1 + 5x_2 + 2x_3,$$

subject to

$$-2x_1 + 2x_2 + x_3 \le 5$$
$$3x_1 + x_2 - x_3 \le 10,$$

and

$$x_1 \ge 0, \quad x_2 \ge 0, \quad x_3 \ge 0.$$

You are given the fact that the basic variables in the optimal solution are x_1 and x_3.

(*a*) Introduce slack variables, and then use the given information to find the optimal solution directly by the Gauss-Jordan method of elimination (see Appendix 4).

(*b*) Extend the work in part (*a*) to find the *shadow prices*.

(*c*) Use the given information to identify the defining equations of the optimal corner-point feasible solution, and then solve these equations to obtain the optimal solution.

(*d*) Construct the *basis matrix* **B** for the optimal basic feasible solution, invert **B** manually, and then use this $\mathbf{B}^{-1}$ to solve for the optimal solution and the *shadow prices* (**y***). Then apply the optimality test for the *revised simplex method* to verify that this solution is optimal.

(*e*) Given $\mathbf{B}^{-1}$ and **y*** from part (*d*), use the *fundamental insight* presented in Sec. 5.3 to construct the complete final simplex tableau.

■ CHAPTER 6

Duality Theory and Sensitivity Analysis

One of the most important discoveries in the early development of linear programming was the concept of duality and its many important ramifications. This discovery revealed that every linear programming problem has associated with it another linear programming problem called the *dual*. The relationships between the dual problem and the original problem (called the *primal*) prove to be extremely useful in a variety of ways. For example, you soon will see that the shadow prices described in Sec. 4.7 actually are provided by the optimal solution for the dual problem. We shall describe many other valuable applications of duality theory in this chapter as well.

One of the key roles of duality theory is that of the interpretation and implementation of *sensitivity analysis*. As we already mentioned in Secs. 2.3, 3.3, and 4.7, sensitivity analysis is a very important part of almost every linear programming study. Because some or all of the parameter values used in the original model are just *estimates* of future conditions, the effect on the optimal solution if other conditions prevail instead needs to be investigated. Furthermore, certain parameter values (such as resource amounts) may represent *managerial decisions*, in which case the choice of the parameter values may be the main issue to be studied, and the choice is studied through sensitivity analysis.

For greater clarity, the first three sections discuss duality theory under the assumption that the *primal* linear programming problem is in *our standard form* (but with no restriction that the b_i need to be positive). Other forms are then discussed in Sec. 6.4. We begin the chapter by introducing the essence of duality theory and its applications. We then describe the economic interpretation of the dual problem (Sec. 6.2) and delve deeper into the relationships between the primal and dual problems (Sec. 6.3). Section 6.5 focuses on the role of duality theory in sensitivity analysis. The basic procedure for sensitivity analysis (which is based on the fundamental insight of Sec. 5.3) is summarized in Sec. 6.6 and illustrated in Sec. 6.7.

6.1 The Essence of Duality Theory

Using *our standard form* for the *primal problem* at the left (perhaps after conversion from another form), its *dual problem* has the form shown to the right.

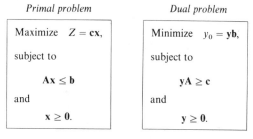

Primal problem

Maximize $Z = \sum_{j=1}^{n} c_j x_j,$

subject to

$\sum_{j=1}^{n} a_{ij} x_j \le b_i,$ for $i = 1, 2, \ldots, m$

and

$x_j \ge 0,$ for $j = 1, 2, \ldots, n.$

Dual problem

Minimize $y_0 = \sum_{i=1}^{m} b_i y_i,$

subject to

$\sum_{i=1}^{m} a_{ij} y_i \ge c_j,$ for $j = 1, 2, \ldots, n$

and

$y_i \ge 0,$ for $i = 1, 2, \ldots, m.$

Thus the dual problem uses exactly the same *parameters* as the primal problem, but in different locations. To highlight the comparison, now see these same two problems in *matrix notation* (as introduced at the beginning of Sec. 5.2), where **c** and $\mathbf{y} = [y_1, y_2, \ldots, y_m]$ are row vectors but **b** and **x** are column vectors.

Primal problem

Maximize $Z = \mathbf{cx},$

subject to

$\mathbf{Ax} \le \mathbf{b}$

and

$\mathbf{x} \ge \mathbf{0}.$

Dual problem

Minimize $y_0 = \mathbf{yb},$

subject to

$\mathbf{yA} \ge \mathbf{c}$

and

$\mathbf{y} \ge \mathbf{0}.$

To illustrate, the primal and dual problems for the Wyndor Glass Co. example of Sec. 3.1 are shown in Table 6.1 in matrix form.

The **primal-dual table** for linear programming (Table 6.2) also helps to highlight the correspondence between the two problems. It shows all the linear programming parameters (the a_{ij}, b_i, and c_j) and how they are used to construct the two problems. All the headings for the primal problem are horizontal, whereas the headings for the dual problem are read by turning the book sideways. We suggest that you begin by looking at each problem *individually* by covering up the headings for the other problem with your hands. Then, after you see what the table is saying for the individual problems, compare them.

Table 6.1 **Primal and dual problems for Wyndor Glass Co. example**

Primal problem

Maximize $Z = [3, 5]\begin{bmatrix} x_1 \\ x_2 \end{bmatrix}$,

subject to

$$\begin{bmatrix} 1 & 0 \\ 0 & 2 \\ 3 & 2 \end{bmatrix}\begin{bmatrix} x_1 \\ x_2 \end{bmatrix} \leq \begin{bmatrix} 4 \\ 12 \\ 18 \end{bmatrix}$$

and

$$\begin{bmatrix} x_1 \\ x_2 \end{bmatrix} \geq \begin{bmatrix} 0 \\ 0 \end{bmatrix}.$$

Dual problem

Minimize $y_0 = [y_1, y_2, y_3]\begin{bmatrix} 4 \\ 12 \\ 18 \end{bmatrix}$,

subject to

$$[y_1, y_2, y_3]\begin{bmatrix} 1 & 0 \\ 0 & 2 \\ 3 & 2 \end{bmatrix} \geq [3, 5]$$

and

$$[y_1, y_2, y_3] \geq [0, 0, 0].$$

Table 6.2 **Primal-dual table for linear programming, illustrated by Wyndor Glass Co. example**

(a) *General Case*

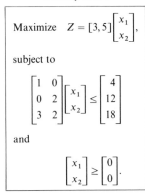

			Primal problem				
			Coefficient of			Right side	
			x_1	x_2 $\cdots$	x_n		
Dual problem	Coefficient of	y_1	a_{11}	a_{12} $\cdots$	a_{1n}	$\leq b_1$	Coefficients for objective function (minimize)
		y_2	a_{21}	a_{22} $\cdots$	a_{2n}	$\leq b_2$	
		y_m	a_{m1}	a_{m2} $\cdots$	a_{mn}	$\leq b_m$	
	Right side		$\leq$ c_1	$\leq$ c_2 $\cdots$	$\leq$ c_n		

Coefficients for
objective function
(maximize)

(b) *Wyndor Glass Co. Example*

	x_1	x_2	
y_1	1	0	≤ 4
y_2	0	2	≤ 12
y_3	3	2	≤ 18
	$\leq$ 3	$\leq$ 5	

Particularly notice in Table 6.2 how (1) the parameters for a *constraint* in either problem are the coefficients of a *variable* in the other problem, and (2) the coefficients for the *objective function* of either problem are the *right sides* for the other problem. Thus there is a direct correspondence between these entities in the

Table 6.3 **Correspondence between entities in primal and dual problems**

One problem	Other problem
Constraint i ⟷	variable i
Objective function ⟷	right sides

two problems, as summarized in Table 6.3. These correspondences are a key to some of the applications of duality theory, including sensitivity analysis.

ORIGIN OF THE DUAL PROBLEM

Duality theory is based directly on the *fundamental insight* (particularly with regard to row 0) presented in Sec. 5.3. To see why, we continue to use the notation introduced in Table 5.8 for row 0 of the *final* tableau, except for replacing Z^* by y_0 and dropping the asterisks from $\mathbf{z}^*$ and $\mathbf{y}^*$ when referring to *any* tableau. Thus, at *any* given iteration of the simplex method for the primal problem, the current numbers in row 0 are denoted as shown in the (partial) tableau given in Table 6.4. Also recall that the fundamental insight led to the following relationships between these quantities and the parameters of the original model:

$$y_0 = \mathbf{y}\mathbf{b} = \sum_{i=1}^{m} b_i y_i,$$

$$\mathbf{z} = \mathbf{y}\mathbf{A}, \quad \text{so } z_j = \sum_{i=1}^{m} a_{ij} y_i, \quad \text{for } j = 1, 2, \ldots, n.$$

The remaining key is to express what the simplex method tries to accomplish (according to the optimality test) in terms of these symbols. Specifically, it seeks a set of basic variables, and the corresponding basic feasible solution, such that *all* coefficients in row 0 are *nonnegative*. It then stops with this optimal solution. This goal is expressed symbolically as follows:

CONDITION FOR OPTIMALITY $z_j - c_j \geq 0, \quad \text{for } j = 1, 2, \ldots, n$
$$y_i \geq 0, \quad \text{for } i = 1, 2, \ldots, m.$$

After substituting the preceding expression for z_j, the condition for optimality says that the simplex method can be interpreted as seeking values for

Table 6.4 Notation for entries in row 0 of simplex tableau

Iteration	Basic variable	Eq. no.	Z	Coefficient of								Right side
				x_1	x_2	$\cdots$	x_n	x_{n+1}	x_{n+2}	$\cdots$	x_{n+m}	
Any	Z	0	1	$(z_1 - c_1)$	$(z_2 - c_2)$	$\cdots$	$(z_n - c_n)$	y_1	y_2	$\cdots$	y_m	y_0

$y_1, y_2, \ldots, y_m$ such that

$$y_0 = \sum_{i=1}^{m} b_i y_i,$$

subject to

$$\sum_{i=1}^{m} a_{ij} y_i \geq c_j, \quad \text{for } j = 1, 2, \ldots, n$$

and

$$y_i \geq 0, \quad \text{for } i = 1, 2, \ldots, m.$$

But, except for lacking an objective for y_0, this problem is precisely the *dual problem*! To complete the formulation, let us now explore what the missing objective should be.

Since y_0 is just the current value of Z, and since the objective for the primal problem is to maximize Z, a natural first reaction is that y_0 should be maximized also. However, this is not correct for the following rather subtle reason: The only *feasible* solutions for this new problem are those that satisfy the condition for *optimality* for the primal problem. Therefore, it is *only* the optimal solution for the primal problem that corresponds to a feasible solution for this new problem. As a consequence, the optimal value of Z in the primal problem is the *minimum* feasible value of y_0 in the new problem, so y_0 should be minimized. (The full justification for this conclusion is provided by the relationships we develop in Sec. 6.3.) Adding this objective of minimizing y_0 gives the *complete* dual problem.

Consequently, the dual problem may be viewed as a restatement in linear programming terms of the *goal* of the simplex method, namely, to reach a solution for the primal problem that *satisfies the optimality test. Before* this goal has been reached, the corresponding **y** in row 0 (coefficients of slack variables) of the final tableau must be *infeasible* for the *dual problem*. However, *after* the goal is reached, the corresponding **y** must be an *optimal solution* (labeled **y***) for the *dual problem*, because it is a feasible solution that attains the minimum feasible value of y_0. This optimal solution $(y_1^*, y_2^*, \ldots, y_m^*)$ provides for the primal problem the *shadow prices* that were described in Sec. 4.7. Furthermore, this optimal y_0 is just the optimal value of Z, so the *optimal objective function values are equal* for the two problems. This fact also implies that $\mathbf{cx} \leq \mathbf{yb}$ for any **x** and **y** that are *feasible* for the primal and dual problems, respectively.

SUMMARY OF PRIMAL-DUAL RELATIONSHIPS

Now let us summarize the newly discovered key relationships between the primal and dual problems.

> **Weak duality property:** If **x** is a *feasible* solution for the *primal problem* and **y** is a *feasible* solution for the *dual problem*, then

$$\mathbf{cx} \leq \mathbf{yb}.$$

Strong duality property: If $\mathbf{x}^*$ is an *optimal* solution for the *primal problem* and $\mathbf{y}^*$ is an *optimal* solution for the *dual problem*, then

$$\mathbf{cx}^* = \mathbf{y}^*\mathbf{b}.$$

Complementary solutions property: At each iteration, the simplex method simultaneously identifies a corner-point feasible solution $\mathbf{x}$ for the *primal problem* and a **complementary solution** $\mathbf{y}$ for the *dual problem* (found in row 0, coefficients of the slack variables), where

$$\mathbf{cx} = \mathbf{yb}.$$

If $\mathbf{x}$ is *not optimal* for the primal problem, then $\mathbf{y}$ is *not feasible* for the dual problem.

To illustrate the *complementary solutions property*, after one iteration for the Wyndor Glass Co. problem, Table 4.8 shows that $\mathbf{x} = [0,6]^T$ and $\mathbf{y} = [0,\frac{5}{2},0]$, with $\mathbf{cx} = 30 = \mathbf{yb}$.

Complementary optimal solutions property: At the final iteration, the simplex method simultaneously identifies an optimal solution $\mathbf{x}^*$ for the *primal problem* and a **complementary optimal solution** $\mathbf{y}^*$ for the *dual problem* (found in row 0, coefficients of the slack variables), where

$$\mathbf{cx}^* = \mathbf{y}^*\mathbf{b}.$$

The y_i^* are the *shadow prices* for the primal problem.

For the example, the last tableau of Table 4.8 shows that $\mathbf{x}^* = [2,6]^T$ and $\mathbf{y}^* = [0,\frac{3}{2},1]$, with $\mathbf{cx}^* = 36 = \mathbf{y}^*\mathbf{b}$.

We will take a closer look at some of these properties in Sec. 6.3. There you will see that the *complementary solutions property* can be extended considerably further. In particular, after slack and surplus variables are introduced for the respective problems, every *basic* solution in the primal problem has a complementary *basic* solution in the dual problem, where the simplex method identifies the values of the surplus variables for the dual problem as the $(z_j - c_j)$ in Table 6.4. This result then leads to an additional *complementary slackness property* that relates the basic variables in one problem to the nonbasic variables in the other (Tables 6.6 and 6.7), but more about that later.

In Sec. 6.4, after describing how to construct the dual problem when the primal problem is *not in our standard form*, we discuss another very useful property, which is summarized as follows:

Symmetry property: For *any* primal problem and its dual problem, all relationships between them must be *symmetric* because the dual of this dual problem is this primal problem.

Therefore, all of the preceding properties hold regardless of which of the two problems is labeled as the primal problem. (The *weak duality property* does require that the *primal* problem be expressed or reexpressed in *maximization* form and the *dual* problem in *minimization* form.) Consequently, the simplex method can be applied to either problem, and it simultaneously will identify complementary solutions (ultimately a complementary optimal solution) for the other problem.

APPLICATIONS

As we have just implied, one important application of duality theory is that the *dual* problem can be solved directly by the simplex method in order to identify an optimal solution for the primal problem. If $m > n$, so that the dual problem has fewer functional constraints (n) than the primal problem (m), then applying the simplex method directly to the dual problem instead of the primal problem probably will achieve a substantial reduction in computational effort (see Sec. 4.8).

The *weak and strong duality properties* describe key relationships between the primal and dual problems. One useful application is for evaluating a proposed solution for the primal problem. For example, suppose $\mathbf{x}$ is a feasible solution that has been proposed for implementation, and that a feasible solution $\mathbf{y}$ has been found by inspection for the dual problem such that $\mathbf{cx} = \mathbf{yb}$. In this case, $\mathbf{x}$ must be *optimal* without even applying the simplex method! Even if $\mathbf{cx} < \mathbf{yb}$, $\mathbf{yb}$ still provides an *upper bound* on the optimal value of Z, so if ($\mathbf{yb} - \mathbf{cx}$) is small, intangible factors favoring $\mathbf{x}$ may lead to its selection without further ado.

One of the key applications of the *complementary solutions property* is its use in the *dual simplex method* presented in Sec. 9.2. This algorithm operates on the *primal* problem exactly as if the *simplex method* were being applied simultaneously to the *dual* problem, which can be done because of this property. Because the roles of *row* 0 and the *right side* in the simplex tableau have been reversed, the dual simplex method requires that row 0 *begins and remains nonnegative* while the right side *begins* with some *negative* values (subsequent iterations strive to reach a nonnegative right side). Consequently, this algorithm occasionally is used because it is more convenient to set up the initial tableau in this form than in the form required by the simplex method. Furthermore, it frequently is used for *reoptimization* (see Sec. 4.7) because changes in the original model lead to the revised final tableau fitting this form. This situation is common for certain types of *sensitivity analysis*, as you will see later in the chapter.

In general terms, duality theory plays a central role in sensitivity analysis. This role is the topic of Sec. 6.5.

Another important application is its use in the economic interpretation of the dual problem and the resulting insights for analyzing the primal problem. You already have seen one example when we discussed *shadow prices* in Sec. 4.7. The next section describes how this interpretation extends to the entire dual problem and then to the simplex method.

6.2 Economic Interpretation of Duality

The economic interpretation of duality is based directly upon the typical interpretation for the primal problem (linear programming problem in *our standard form*) presented in Sec. 3.2. To refresh your memory, we have summarized this interpretation of the primal problem in Table 6.5.

INTERPRETATION OF THE DUAL PROBLEM

To see how this interpretation of the primal problem leads to an economic interpretation for the dual problem,[1] look back at Table 6.4 and the equations immediately following it, as well as at the *complementary solutions property*. Note in Table 6.4 that y_0 is the value of Z (total profit) at the current iteration. Because

$$y_0 = b_1 y_1 + b_2 y_2 + \cdots + b_m y_m,$$

each $b_i y_i$ can thereby be interpreted as the current *contribution to profit* by having b_i units of resource i available for the primal problem. Thus

> y_i is interpreted as the *contribution to profit* per unit of resource i $(i = 1, 2, \ldots, m)$, when the current set of basic variables is used to obtain the primal solution.

In other words, the y_i (or y_i^* in the optimal solution) are just the *shadow prices* discussed in Sec. 4.7.

This interpretation of the dual variables leads to our interpretation of the overall dual problem. Specifically, since each unit of activity j in the primal problem consumes a_{ij} units of resource i,

> $\sum_{i=1}^{m} a_{ij} y_i$ is interpreted as the current *contribution to profit* of that mix of resources that would be consumed if one unit of activity j were used $(j = 1, 2, \ldots, n)$.

Therefore, since c_j is interpreted as the unit profit from activity j, each functional

Table 6.5 **Economic interpretation of primal problem**

Quantity	Interpretation
x_j	Level of activity j $(j = 1, 2, \ldots, n)$
c_j	Unit profit from activity j
Z	Total profit from all activities
b_i	Amount of resource i available $(i = 1, 2, \ldots, m)$
a_{ij}	Amount of resource i consumed by each unit of activity j

[1] Actually, several slightly different interpretations have been proposed. The one presented here seems to us to be the most useful because it also directly interprets what the simplex method does in the primal problem.

constraint in the dual problem is interpreted as follows:

$\sum_{i=1}^{m} a_{ij} y_i \geq c_j$ says that the actual *contribution to profit* of the above mix of resources must be at least as much as if they were used by one unit of activity j; otherwise, we would not be making the best possible use of these resources.

Similarly, the interpretation of the nonnegativity constraints is the following:

$y_i \geq 0$ says that the *contribution to profit* of resource i $(i = 1, 2, \ldots, m)$ must be nonnegative; otherwise, it would be better not to use this resource at all.

The objective,

$$\text{Minimize} \quad y_0 = \sum_{i=1}^{m} b_i y_i,$$

can be viewed as minimizing the total implicit value of the resources consumed by the activities.

This interpretation can be sharpened somewhat by differentiating between *basic* and *nonbasic* variables in the primal problem. Recall that the *basic* variables (the only variables whose values can be nonzero) *always* have a coefficient of *zero* in row 0. Therefore, referring again to Table 6.4 and the accompanying equation for z_j, for any basic feasible solution $(x_1, x_2, \ldots, x_{n+m})$,

$$\sum_{i=1}^{m} a_{ij} y_i = c_j, \quad \text{if } x_j > 0 \qquad (j = 1, 2, \ldots, n),$$

$$y_i = 0, \quad \text{if } x_{n+i} > 0 \qquad (i = 1, 2, \ldots, m).$$

(This is one version of the *complementary slackness property* discussed in the next section.) The economic interpretation of the first statement is that whenever an activity j operates at a strictly positive level $(x_j > 0)$, the marginal value of the resources it consumes *must equal* (as opposed to exceeding) the unit profit from this activity. The second statement implies that the marginal value of resource i is *zero* $(y_i = 0)$ whenever the supply of this resource is not exhausted by the activities $(x_{n+i} > 0)$. In economic terminology, such a resource is a "free good"; the price of goods that are oversupplied must drop to zero by the law of supply and demand. This fact is what justifies interpreting the objective for the dual problem as minimizing the total implicit value of the resources *consumed*, rather than the resources *allocated*.

INTERPRETATION OF THE SIMPLEX METHOD

The interpretation of the dual problem also provides an economic interpretation of what the simplex method does in the primal problem. The *goal* of the simplex method is to find how to use the available resources in the most profitable feasible way. To attain this goal we must reach a basic feasible solution that satisfies all the *requirements* on profitable use of the resources (the constraints of the dual problem). These requirements comprise the *condition for optimality* for the algorithm. For any given basic feasible solution, the requirements (dual constraints) associated with the *basic* variables are automatically satisfied (with equality). However, those associated with *nonbasic* variables may or may not be satisfied.

In particular, if an *original variable* x_j is nonbasic so that activity j is not used, then the *current contribution to profits* of the resources that would be required to undertake each unit of activity j,

$$\sum_{i=1}^{m} a_{ij} y_i,$$

may be either smaller ($<$) or larger ($\geq$) than the unit profit c_j obtainable from the activity. If it is smaller, so $(z_j - c_j) < 0$ in row 0 of the simplex tableau, then these resources can be used more profitably by initiating this activity. If it is larger, then these resources already are being assigned elsewhere in a more profitable way, so they should not be diverted to activity j.

Similarly, if a *slack variable* x_{n+i} is nonbasic so that the total allocation b_i of resource i is being used, then y_i is the *current contribution to profit* of this resource on a marginal basis. Hence, if $y_i < 0$, profit can be increased by cutting back on the use of this resource (i.e., increasing x_{n+i}). If $y_i \geq 0$, it is worthwhile to continue fully using this resource.

Therefore, what the simplex method does is to examine all the nonbasic variables in the current basic feasible solution to see which ones can provide a *more profitable use of the resources* by being increased. If *none* can, so that no feasible shifts or reductions in the current proposed use of the resources can increase profit, the current solution must be optimal. If one or more can, the simplex method selects the variable that, if increased by 1, would *improve the profitability* of the use of the resources the most. It then actually increases this variable (the *entering basic variable*) as much as it can until the marginal values of the resources change. This increase results in a new basic feasible solution with a new row 0 (dual solution), and the whole process is repeated.

To solidify your understanding of this interpretation of the simplex method, we suggest that you apply it to the Wyndor Glass Co. problem, using both Fig. 3.2 and Table 4.8. (See Prob. 6.)

The economic interpretation of the dual problem considerably expands our ability to analyze the primal problem. However, you already have seen in Sec. 6.1 that this interpretation is just one ramification of the relationships between the two problems. In the next section, we delve into these relationships more deeply.

6.3 Primal-Dual Relationships

Because the dual problem is a linear programming problem, it also has corner-point solutions. Furthermore, by using the equality form of the problem, we can express these corner-point solutions as basic solutions. Because the functional constraints have the $\geq$ form, this equality form is obtained by *subtracting* the surplus (rather than adding the slack) from the left-hand side of each constraint j ($j = 1,2,\ldots,n$).[1] This surplus is

$$z_j - c_j = \sum_{i=1}^{m} a_{ij} y_i - c_j, \quad \text{for } j = 1,2,\ldots,n.$$

Thus $(z_j - c_j)$ plays the role of the *surplus variable* for constraint j (or its slack variable if the constraint is multiplied through by -1). Therefore, each corner-point solution $(y_1, y_2, \ldots, y_m)$ yields a basic solution $(y_1, y_2, \ldots, y_m, z_1 - c_1, z_2 - c_2, \ldots, z_n - c_n)$ by using this expression for $(z_j - c_j)$. Since the equality form has n functional constraints and $(n + m)$ variables, each basic solution has n basic variables and m nonbasic variables. (Note how m and n reverse their previous roles here because, as Table 6.3 indicates, dual constraints correspond to primal variables and dual variables correspond to primal constraints.)

COMPLEMENTARY BASIC SOLUTIONS

One of the important relationships between the primal and dual problems is a direct correspondence between their basic solutions. To see this correspondence, look again at the partial tableau shown in Table 6.4. Such a row 0 can be constructed for *any* primal basic solution, feasible or not. This construction is accomplished by using the *Gauss-Jordan method of elimination* (commonly called *Gaussian elimination*), as described in Appendix 4, to solve for this primal basic solution starting from the initial system of equations (1 to m) constructed for the simplex method. Using this method results in an equivalent system of equations where each basic variable has been algebraically eliminated from all but one equation, where each equation thereby contains just one basic variable that has a coefficient of 1. (This form is the *proper form* required for each simplex tableau.) This equivalent system of equations then can be used algebraically to reduce the coefficients of the basic variables in Eq. (0) to zero. (Because part 3 of the iterative step for the simplex method uses *Gaussian elimination* to solve for each basic feasible solution from the preceding one, the procedure just described is equivalent to using part 3 repeatedly, where each "entering basic variable" must be one of the basic variables for the desired basic solution and each "leaving basic variable" must be one of its nonbasic variables.)

   Now note in Table 6.4 how a complete solution for the dual problem (including the surplus variables) can be read directly from row 0. Thus, because of its coefficient in row 0, each variable in the primal problem has an associated variable in the dual problem, as summarized in Table 6.6.

   A key insight here is that the dual solution read from row 0 must also be a basic solution! The reason is that the m basic variables for the primal problem are

---

[1] You might wonder why we do not also introduce *artificial variables* into these constraints as discussed in Sec. 4.6. The reason is that these variables have no purpose other than to change the feasible region temporarily as a convenience in starting the simplex method. We are not interested now in applying the simplex method to the dual problem, and we do not want to change its feasible region.

Table 6.6 **Association between variables in primal and dual problems**

Primal variable	Associated dual variable
(Original variable) x_j	$(z_j - c_j)$ (surplus variable), $j = 1,2,\ldots,n$
(Slack variable) x_{n+i}	y_i (original variable), $i = 1,2,\ldots,m$

required to have a coefficient of *zero* in row 0, which thereby requires the m associated dual variables to be zero, i.e., *nonbasic* variables for the dual problem. The values of the remaining n (basic) variables then will be the simultaneous solution to the system of equations given at the beginning of the section. This system must have a unique simultaneous solution and thus provide a basic solution, because the *fundamental insight* of Sec. 5.3 actually identifies this solution (e.g., see Table 5.7).

Because of the *symmetry property* quoted in Sec. 6.1 (and the direct association between variables shown in Table 6.6), the correspondence between basic solutions in the primal and dual problems is a symmetric one. Furthermore, a pair of complementary basic solutions has the same objective function value, shown as y_0 in Table 6.4.

Let us now summarize our conclusions about the correspondence between primal and dual basic solutions, where the first property extends the *complementary solutions property* of Sec. 6.1 to the *equality forms* of the two problems and then to *any* basic solution (feasible or not) in the primal problem.

> **Complementary Basic Solutions Property:** Each *basic* solution in the *primal problem* has a **complementary basic solution** in the *dual problem*, where their respective objective function values (Z and y_0) are equal. Given row 0 of the simplex tableau for the primal basic solution, the complementary dual basic solution ($\mathbf{y}, \mathbf{z} - \mathbf{c}$) is found as shown in Table 6.4.

The next property shows how to identify the *basic* and *nonbasic* variables in this complementary basic solution.

> **Complementary Slackness Property:** Using the association between variables given in Table 6.6, the variables in the primal basic solution and the complementary dual basic solution satisfy the **complementary**

Table 6.7 **Complementary slackness relationship for complementary basic solutions**

Primal variable	Associated dual variable	
Basic	Nonbasic	(m variables)
Nonbasic	Basic	(n variables)

slackness relationship shown in Table 6.7. Furthermore, this relationship is a symmetric one, so that these two basic solutions are complementary to each other.

The reason for using the name *complementary slackness* for this latter property is that it says (in part) that for each pair of associated variables, if one of them has *slack* in its nonnegativity constraint (a basic variable > 0), then the other one must have *no slack* (a nonbasic variable $= 0$). We mentioned in Sec. 6.2 that this property has a useful economic interpretation for linear programming problems.

EXAMPLE To illustrate these two properties, again consider the Wyndor Glass Co. problem of Sec. 3.1. All eight of its basic solutions (five feasible and three infeasible) are shown in Tables 5.5 and 5.6 along with the corresponding corner-point solutions. Thus its dual problem (see Table 6.1) also must have eight basic solutions, each complementary to one of these primal solutions. This conclusion is indeed true, as summarized in Table 6.8. (You can verify this by finding the eight corner-point solutions for the dual problem; see Prob. 8.)

At this point we ask you to refer back to the complete set of tableaux shown in Table 4.8 for the primal problem for this example. The three basic solutions obtained there are the first, fifth, and sixth primal solutions shown in Table 6.8. Now note how the three complementary basic solutions for the dual problem can be read directly from row 0 in these three tableaux, starting with the coefficients of the slack variables (x_3, x_4, x_5) and then the original variables (x_1, x_2). The other dual basic solutions also could be identified in this way by using part 3 of the iterative step (ignoring the rules in parts 1 and 2 for choosing the entering and leaving basic variables) to iterate to the tableau for the complementary basic

Table 6.8 **Complementary basic solutions for Wyndor Glass Co. example**

	Primal problem			Dual problem	
No.	Basic solution	Feasible?	$Z = y_0$	Feasible?	Basic solution
1	$(0,0,4,12,18)$	Yes	0	No	$(0,0,0, -3, -5)$
2	$(4,0,0,12,6)$	Yes	12	No	$(3,0,0,0, -5)$
3	$(6,0, -2,12,0)$	No	18	No	$(0,0,1,0, -3)$
4	$(4,3,0,6,0)$	Yes	27	No	$\left(-\frac{9}{2},0,\frac{5}{2},0,0\right)$
5	$(0,6,4,0,6)$	Yes	30	No	$\left(0,\frac{5}{2},0, -3,0\right)$
6	$(2,6,2,0,0)$	Yes	36	Yes	$\left(0,\frac{3}{2},1,0,0\right)$
7	$(4,6,0,0, -6)$	No	42	Yes	$\left(3,\frac{5}{2},0,0,0\right)$
8	$(0,9,4, -6,0)$	No	45	Yes	$\left(0,0,\frac{5}{2},\frac{9}{2},0\right)$

solution in the primal problem. For example, try starting from the final tableau, using x_5 as the entering basic variable and x_3 as the leaving basic variable, and you will obtain the next-to-last pair of complementary basic solutions in the table.

Alternatively, for each primal basic solution, the *complementary slackness property* can be used to identify the basic and nonbasic variables for the complementary dual basic solution, so that the system of equations given at the beginning of the section can be solved directly to obtain this complementary solution. For example, consider the next-to-last primal basic solution in Table 6.8, where x_1, x_2, and x_5 are basic variables. Using Tables 6.6 and 6.7, we see that the complementary slackness property implies that $(z_1 - c_1)$, $(z_2 - c_2)$, and y_3 are nonbasic variables for the complementary dual basic solution. Setting these variables equal to zero in the dual problem equations, $y_1 + 3y_3 - (z_1 - c_1) = 3$ and $2y_2 + 2y_3 - (z_2 - c_2) = 5$, immediately yields $y_1 = 3$, $y_2 = \frac{5}{2}$.

Finally, note how the complementary slackness property is satisfied in Table 6.8 for each of these pairs of complementary basic solutions.

RELATIONSHIPS BETWEEN COMPLEMENTARY BASIC SOLUTIONS

We now turn our attention to the relationships between complementary basic solutions, beginning with their *feasibility* relationships. The middle columns in Table 6.8 provide some valuable clues. For the pairs of complementary solutions, notice how the yes or no answers on feasibility also satisfy a complementary relationship in most cases. In particular, with one exception, whenever one solution is feasible, the other is not. (It also is possible for *neither* solution to be feasible, as happened with the third pair.) The one exception is the sixth pair, where the primal solution is known to be *optimal*. The explanation is suggested by the $Z - y_0$ column. Because the sixth dual solution also is optimal (by the *complementary optimal solutions property*), with $y_0 = 36$, then the first five dual solutions *cannot be feasible* because $y_0 < 36$ (remember that the dual problem objective is to *minimize* y_0). By the same token, the last two primal solutions *cannot be feasible* because $Z > 36$.

This explanation is verified by the *strong duality property* given in Sec. 6.1.

Next, let us state the *extension* of the *complementary optimal solutions property* of Sec. 6.1 for the *equality forms* of the two problems.

Complementary Optimal Basic Solutions Property: Each *optimal* basic solution in the *primal problem* has a **complementary optimal basic solution** in the dual problem, where their respective objective function values (Z and y_0) are equal.[1] Given row 0 of the simplex tableau for the optimal

---

[1] Because of the *symmetry property*, it thereby follows that if either problem possesses at least one optimal solution, the other must also. The only ways in which both problems can have no optimal solutions are (1) both problems have no feasible solutions, or (2) one problem has no feasible solutions and the other problem has an unbounded feasible region that permits improving the objective function value indefinitely in the favorable direction.

Table 6.9 **Classification of basic solutions**

| | | Satisfies condition for optimality? | |
		Yes	No
Feasible?	Yes	Optimal	Suboptimal
	No	Superoptimal	Neither feasible nor superoptimal

primal solution, the complementary optimal dual solution $(\mathbf{y}^*, \mathbf{z}^* - \mathbf{c})$ is found as shown in Table 6.4.

To review the reasoning behind this property, note that the dual solution $(\mathbf{y}^*, \mathbf{z}^* - \mathbf{c})$ must be feasible for the dual problem because the *condition for optimality* for the primal problem requires that *all* these dual variables (including surplus variables) be *nonnegative*. Since this solution is *feasible*, it must be *optimal* for the dual problem by the *weak duality property*.

Basic solutions can be classified according to whether or not they satisfy each of two conditions. One is the *condition for feasibility*, namely, whether *all* the variables (including slack variables) in the augmented solution are *nonnegative*. The other is the *condition for optimality*, namely, whether *all* the coefficients in row 0 (i.e., all the variables in the complementary basic solution) are *nonnegative*. Our names for the different types of basic solutions are summarized in Table 6.9. For example, in Table 6.8, primal basic solutions 1, 2, 4, and 5 are suboptimal, 6 is optimal, 7 and 8 are superoptimal, and 3 is neither feasible nor superoptimal.

Using these definitions, the general relationships between complementary basic solutions are summarized in Table 6.10. The resulting range of possible (common) values for the objective functions $(Z = y_0)$ for the first three pairs given in Table 6.10 (the last pair can have any value) is shown in Fig. 6.1. Thus, while the simplex method is dealing directly with suboptimal basic solutions and working toward optimality in the primal problem, it is simultaneously dealing indirectly with complementary superoptimal solutions and working toward feasibility in the dual problem. Conversely, it sometimes is more convenient (or necessary) to work directly with superoptimal basic solutions and to move

Table 6.10 **Relationships between complementary basic solutions**

Primal basic solution	Complementary dual basic solution
Suboptimal	Superoptimal
Optimal	Optimal
Superoptimal	Suboptimal
Neither feasible nor superoptimal	Neither feasible nor superoptimal

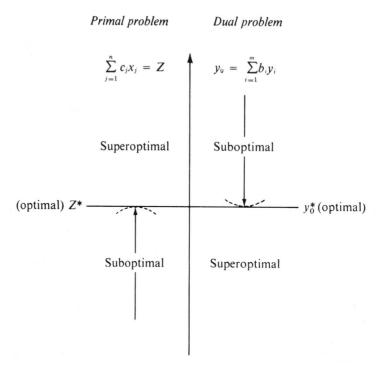

Figure 6.1 **Range of possible values of $Z = y_0$ for certain types of complementary basic solutions.**

toward feasibility in the primal problem, which is the purpose of the dual *simplex method* described in Sec. 9.2. Applying the dual simplex method to the primal problem is equivalent to using the simplex method to deal with suboptimal solutions and to work toward optimality in the dual problem.

These relationships prove very useful, particularly in sensitivity analysis, as you will see later in the chapter.

6.4 Adapting to Other Primal Forms

Thus far it has been assumed that the model for the primal problem is in *our standard form.* However, we indicated at the beginning of the chapter that *any* linear programming problem, whether in our standard form or not, possesses a dual problem. Therefore, this section focuses on how the dual problem changes for other primal forms.

Each *nonstandard* form was discussed in Sec 4.6, and we pointed out how it is possible to convert each one into an *equivalent* standard form if so desired. These conversions are summarized in Table 6.11. Hence you always have the option of converting any model into *our standard form* and *then* constructing its dual problem in the usual way. To illustrate, we do this for our standard *dual problem*

Table 6.11 **Conversions to standard form for linear programming models**

Nonstandard form	Equivalent standard form
Minimize Z	Maximize $(-Z)$
$\sum_{j=1}^{n} a_{ij}x_j \geq b_i$	$-\sum_{j=1}^{n} a_{ij}x_j \leq -b_i$
$\sum_{j=1}^{n} a_{ij}x_j = b_i$	$\sum_{j=1}^{n} a_{ij}x_j \leq b_i$ and $-\sum_{j=1}^{n} a_{ij}x_j \leq -b_i$
x_j unconstrained in sign	$(x_j^+ - x_j^-)$, $x_j^+ \geq 0$, $x_j^- \geq 0$

Table 6.12 **Constructing the dual of the dual problem**

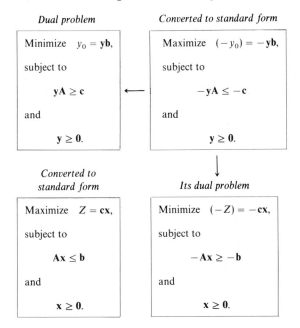

Dual problem

Minimize $y_0 = \mathbf{yb}$,
subject to
$$\mathbf{yA} \geq \mathbf{c}$$
and
$$\mathbf{y} \geq \mathbf{0}.$$

Converted to standard form

Maximize $(-y_0) = -\mathbf{yb}$,
subject to
$$-\mathbf{yA} \leq -\mathbf{c}$$
and
$$\mathbf{y} \geq \mathbf{0}.$$

Converted to standard form

Maximize $Z = \mathbf{cx}$,
subject to
$$\mathbf{Ax} \leq \mathbf{b}$$
and
$$\mathbf{x} \geq \mathbf{0}.$$

Its dual problem

Minimize $(-Z) = -\mathbf{cx}$,
subject to
$$-\mathbf{Ax} \geq -\mathbf{b}$$
and
$$\mathbf{x} \geq \mathbf{0}.$$

(it must have a dual also) in Table 6.12. (If you prefer working with numbers, then do the same thing for the Wyndor Glass Co. dual problem presented in Table 6.1, perhaps replacing y_0 by Z and y_1, y_2, y_3 by x_1, x_2, x_3 if you want; see Prob. 21.) Note that what we end up with is just our standard *primal problem*! Since *any* pair of primal and dual problems can be converted into these forms, this fact demonstrates the following key property of primal-dual relationships:

Symmetry Property: For any primal problem and its dual problem, all relationships between them must be *symmetric* because the dual of this dual problem is this primal problem.

As a result, all the statements made earlier in the chapter about the relationships of the dual problem to the primal problem also hold in reverse.

Another consequence of the symmetry property is that it is immaterial which problem is called the primal and which is called the dual. In practice, you might see a linear programming problem fitting our standard form being referred to as the *dual* problem. The convention is that the model formulated to fit the actual problem is called the *primal problem*, regardless of its form.

Our illustration of how to construct the dual problem for a nonstandard primal problem did not involve either equality constraints or variables unconstrained in sign. Actually, for these two forms, a shortcut is available. It is possible to show [see Probs. 19 and 16(c)] that an *equality constraint* in the primal problem should be treated just like an $\leq$ constraint in constructing the dual problem *except* that the nonnegativity constraint for the corresponding dual variable should be *deleted* (i.e., this variable is unconstrained in sign). By the symmetry property, *deleting a nonnegativity constraint* in the primal problem affects the dual problem only by changing the corresponding constraint into an *equality constraint*.

Because of these shortcuts, it is necessary to convert only the *primal problem* into the form shown in *either* column of Table 6.13. You then construct its *dual problem* in the usual way, using the form shown in the *other* column. However, beware of mixing the forms in the two columns (e.g., maximize Z with $\geq$ constraints) for defining the primal problem. Such mixing is not allowed for the purpose of constructing the dual problem.

To illustrate this procedure, consider the *modified example* presented in Sec. 4.6. Let it be our primal problem. To find its dual problem, we need to convert the model into one of the allowable forms. The form in the second column of Table 6.13 is obtained simply by multiplying through the first constraint $x_1 \leq 4$ by (-1). This work is shown in Table 6.14, along with the resulting dual problem. Equivalently, the form in the first column of the table can be used instead to set up the primal problem. (This form is needed anyway to apply the simplex method as presented in Chap. 4.) This approach leads to the formulation of the two problems shown in Table 6.15. Note that the two versions of the primal and dual problems are *completely equivalent*, where $y_2' = -y_2$. This equivalency

Table 6.13 **Corresponding primal-dual forms**

Primal problem (or dual problem)	Dual problem (or primal problem)
Maximize Z (or y_0)	Minimize y_0 (or Z)
Constraint i	Variable y_i (or x_i)
$\leq$ form	$y_i \geq 0$
= form	$y_i \geq 0$ deleted
Variable x_j (or y_j)	Constraint j
$x_j \geq 0$	$\geq$ form
$x_j \geq 0$ deleted	= form

Table 6.14 **One primal-dual form for modified example of Sec. 4.6**

Primal problem

Minimize $\quad Z = 3x_1 + 5x_2,$
subject to

$$-x_1 \qquad \geq -4$$
$$2x_2 = 12$$
$$3x_1 + 2x_2 \geq 18$$

and

$$x_1 \geq 0, \quad x_2 \geq 0.$$

Dual problem

Maximize $\quad y_0 = -4y_1 + 12y_2 + 18y_3,$
subject to

$$-y_1 \qquad + 3y_3 \leq 3$$
$$2y_2 + 2y_3 \leq 5$$

and

$$y_1 \geq 0, \quad y_3 \geq 0$$

(y_2 unconstrained in sign).

Table 6.15 **The other primal-dual form for modified example of Sec. 4.6**

Primal problem

Maximize $\quad (-Z) = -3x_1 - 5x_2,$
subject to

$$x_1 \qquad \leq \quad 4$$
$$2x_2 = \quad 12$$
$$-3x_1 - 2x_2 \leq -18$$

and

$$x_1 \geq 0, \quad x_2 \geq 0.$$

Dual problem

Minimize $\quad (-y_0) = 4y_1 + 12y_2' - 18y_2,$
subject to

$$y_1 \qquad - 3y_3 \geq -3$$
$$2y_2' - 2y_3 \geq -5$$

and

$$y_1 \geq 0, \quad y_3 \geq 0$$

(y_2' unconstrained in sign).

is inevitable because the differences involve substituting only equivalent forms.

When the simplex method is applied to the nonstandard primal forms, and when the artificial technique (perhaps supplemented by the Big M method) is used to adapt to them, the duality interpretation of row 0 of the simplex tableau must be adjusted somewhat. The reason is that the artificial variables and M's *revise* the primal problem, which thereby changes its dual problem, so the complementary basic solutions shown in row 0 are for this *revised dual problem*. However, *after* the artificial variables have been eliminated (made nonbasic) so that the current solution is a legitimate basic feasible solution for the *original* primal problem, row 0 can still be used to identify the complementary basic solution for the original dual problem. We describe how to do this next.

Suppose that we use the form in the first column of Table 6.13. For each *equality* constraint i, its artificial variable plays the role of a slack variable, *except* that M has been added initially to the coefficient of this variable in row 0. Therefore, the current value of the corresponding dual variable y_i is the current coefficient of this artificial variable *minus* M. If a $\leq$ constraint has a negative right-hand side initially (perhaps because it was converted from a $\geq$ constraint) so that it has been given an artificial variable, the dual variable corresponding to this constraint still equals the coefficient of its *slack* variable. The coefficient of the artificial variable would be ignored in this case. Finally, if a variable x_j is unconstrained in sign so that it has been replaced by the difference of two nonnegativity variables $(x_j^+ - x_j^-)$, then the coefficient of x_j^+, $(z_j^+ - c_j)$, would be used just as for x_j. In other words,

$$z_j^+ = \sum_{i=1}^{m} a_{ij} y_i.$$

The coefficient of x_j^-, $(z_j^- + c_j) = -(z_j^+ - c_j)$, would be ignored. Except for these cases, the coefficients in row 0 would be used just as before (see Sec. 6.3) to give the values of the corresponding dual variables.

To illustrate this procedure, we ask you to refer to the set of simplex tableaux given in Table 4.12 for the modified example. The first two tableaux still have artificial variables as basic variables. However, this is not the case for the *final* tableau, so we can use its row 0 to identify the *optimal* solution for the dual problem shown in Table 6.15. The first primal constraint is a standard one, so y_1 is just the coefficient of the first slack variable (x_3), $y_1 = 0$. The second constraint is an equality constraint, so we refer to the coefficient of its artificial variable $(\bar{x}_4)$ to obtain

$$y_2' = \left(M - \frac{3}{2} \right) - M = -\frac{3}{2}.$$

The third constraint has a negative right-hand side, so we use the coefficient of its slack variable (x_5) to yield $y_3 = 1$. Similarly, the surplus variables are the coefficients of x_1 and x_2, so $(z_1 - c_1) = 0$, $(z_2 - c_2) = 0$. This completes the optimal dual basic solution,

$$(y_1, y_2', y_3, z_1 - c_1, z_2 - c_2) = \left(0, -\frac{3}{2}, 1, 0, 0 \right).$$

6.5 The Role of Duality Theory in Sensitivity Analysis

As described further in the next two sections, *sensitivity analysis* basically involves investigating the effect on the optimal solution of making changes in the values of the model parameters (the a_{ij}, b_i, and c_j). However, changing parameter values in the *primal* problem also changes the corresponding values in the *dual* problem. Therefore, you have your choice of which problem to use to investigate each change. Because of the primal-dual relationships presented in Secs. 6.1 and 6.3 (especially the *complementary basic solutions property*), it is easy to move back and forth between the two problems as desired. In some cases, it is more convenient to analyze the dual problem *directly* in order to determine the complementary effect on the primal problem. We begin by considering two such cases.

CHANGES IN THE COEFFICIENTS OF A NONBASIC VARIABLE

Suppose that the changes made in the original model occur in the coefficients of a variable that was *nonbasic* in the original optimal solution. What is the effect of these changes on this solution? Is it still feasible? Is it still optimal?

Because the variable involved is nonbasic (value of zero), changing its coefficients cannot affect the feasibility of the solution. Therefore, the open question in this case is whether it is still *optimal*. As Tables 6.9 and 6.10 indicate, an *equivalent* question is whether the complementary basic solution for the *dual* problem is still *feasible* after making these changes. Since these changes affect the dual problem by changing only one constraint, this question can be answered simply by checking whether this complementary basic solution still satisfies this revised constraint.

We shall illustrate this case in the corresponding subsection of Sec. 6.7 after developing a relevant example.

INTRODUCTION OF A NEW VARIABLE

As indicated in Table 6.5, the decision variables in the model typically represent the level of the various activities under consideration. In some situations, these activities were selected from a larger group of *possible* activities, where the remaining activities were not included in the original model because they seemed less attractive. Or perhaps these other activities did not come to light until after the original model was formulated and solved. Either way, the key question is whether any of these previously unconsidered activities are sufficiently worthwhile to warrant initiation. In other words, would adding any of these activities to the model change the original optimal solution?

Adding another activity amounts to introducing a new variable, with the appropriate coefficients in the functional constraints and objective function, into the model. The only resulting change in the dual problem is to add a *new* constraint (see Table 6.3).

After these changes are made, would the original optimal solution, along with the new variable equal to *zero* (nonbasic), still be optimal for the primal problem? As for the preceding case, an *equivalent* question is whether the complementary basic solution for the *dual* problem is still *feasible*. And, as before, this question can be answered simply by checking whether this complementary basic solution satisfies *one* constraint, which in this case is the *new* constraint for the dual problem.

To illustrate, suppose for the Wyndor Glass Co. problem of Sec. 3.1 that a possible *third* new product now is being considered for inclusion in the product line. Letting x_{new} represent the production rate for this product, the resulting *revised* model is shown as follows:

$$\text{Maximize} \quad Z = 3x_1 + 5x_2 + 4x_{new},$$

subject to

$$
\begin{aligned}
x_1 \qquad\quad + 2x_{new} &\leq 4 \\
2x_2 + 3x_{new} &\leq 12 \\
3x_1 + 2x_2 + \quad x_{new} &\leq 18
\end{aligned}
$$

and

$$x_1 \geq 0, \quad x_2 \geq 0, \quad x_{new} \geq 0.$$

After introducing slack variables, the *original* optimal solution for this problem without x_{new} (see Table 4.8) was $(x_1, x_2, x_3, x_4, x_5) = (2,6,2,0,0)$. Is this solution, along with $x_{new} = 0$, still optimal?

To answer this question, check the complementary basic solution for the dual problem, which Table 6.8 (and Table 4.8) identifies as

$$(y_1, y_2, y_3, z_1 - c_1, z_2 - c_2) = (0, 3/2, 1, 0, 0).$$

Since this solution was optimal for the original dual problem, it certainly satisfies the original dual constraints shown in Table 6.1. But does it satisfy the one new dual constraint,

$$2y_1 + 3y_2 + y_3 \geq 4?$$

Plugging in this solution,

$$2(0) + 3(3/2) + (1) \geq 4$$

is satisfied, so this dual solution is still *feasible* (and thus still optimal). Consequently, the original primal solution $(2,6,2,0,0)$, along with $x_{new} = 0$, is still *optimal*, so this third possible new product should *not* be added to the product line.

This approach also makes it very easy to conduct sensitivity analysis on the coefficients of the new variable added to the primal problem. By simply checking the new dual constraint, you can immediately see how far any of these parameter values can be changed before they affect the *feasibility* of the dual solution and so the *optimality* of the primal solution.

OTHER APPLICATIONS

Already we have discussed two other key applications of duality theory to sensitivity analysis, namely, *shadow prices* and the *dual simplex method*. As described in Secs. 4.7 and 6.2, the optimal dual solution $(y_1^*, y_2^*, \ldots, y_m^*)$ provides the shadow prices for the respective resources that indicate how Z would change if (small) changes were made in the b_i (the resource amounts). The resulting analysis will be illustrated in some detail in Sec. 6.7.

In more general terms, the economic interpretation of the dual problem and of the simplex method presented in Sec. 6.2 provides some useful insights for sensitivity analysis.

When we investigate the effect of changing the b_i or the a_{ij} (for basic variables), the *original* optimal solution may become a *superoptimal* basic solution instead (see Table 6.9). If you then want to *reoptimize* to identify the new optimal solution, the *dual simplex method* (discussed at the end of Secs. 6.1 and 6.3) should be applied, starting from this basic solution.

We mentioned in Sec. 6.1 that it sometimes is more efficient to solve the *dual* problem directly by the simplex method in order to identify an optimal solution for the *primal* problem. When the solution has been found in this way, sensitivity analysis for the primal problem then is conducted by applying the procedure described in the next two sections directly to the *dual* problem and then inferring the complementary effects on the *primal* problem (e.g., see Table 6.10). This approach to sensitivity analysis is relatively straightforward because of the close primal-dual relationships described in Secs. 6.1 and 6.3. (See Prob. 38.)

6.6 The Essence of Sensitivity Analysis

The work of the operations research team usually is not even nearly done when the simplex method has been successfully applied to identify an optimal solution for the model. As we pointed out at the end of Sec. 3.3, one assumption of linear programming is that all the parameters of the model (the a_{ij}, b_i, and c_j) are *known constants*. Actually, the parameter values used in the model normally are just *estimates* based on a *prediction of future conditions*. The data obtained to develop these estimates often are rather crude or nonexistent, so that the parameters in the original formulation may represent little more than quick rules of thumb provided by harassed line personnel. They may even represent deliberate overestimates or underestimates to protect the interests of the estimators.

Thus the successful manager and operations research staff will maintain a healthy skepticism about the original numbers coming out of the computer and will view them in many cases as only a starting point for further analysis of the problem. An "optimal" solution is optimal only with respect to the specific model being used to represent the real problem, and such a solution becomes a reliable guide for action only after it has been verified as performing well for other reasonable representations of the problem as well. Furthermore, the model parameters (particularly the b_i) sometimes are set as a result of *managerial policy decisions* (e.g., the amount of certain resources to be made available to the activities), and these decisions should be reviewed after seeing their potential consequences.

For these reasons it is important to perform a **sensitivity analysis** to investigate the effect on the optimal solution provided by the simplex method if the parameters take on other possible values. Usually there will be some parameters that can be assigned any reasonable value without affecting the optimality of this solution. However, there may also be parameters with likely values that would yield a new optimal solution. This situation is particularly serious if the original solution would then have a substantially inferior value of the objective function, or perhaps even be infeasible! Therefore, the basic objective of sensitivity analysis is to identify these particularly *sensitive* parameters, so that special care can then be taken to estimate them more closely and to select a solution that performs well for most of their likely values.

Sensitivity analysis would require an exorbitant computational effort if it were necessary to reapply the simplex method from the beginning to investigate each new change in a parameter value. Fortunately, the *fundamental insight* discussed in Sec. 5.3 virtually eliminates computational effort. The basic idea is that the fundamental insight *immediately* reveals just how any changes in the original model would change the numbers in the final simplex tableau (assuming that the *same* sequence of algebraic operations originally performed by the simplex method were to be *duplicated*). Therefore, after making a few simple calculations to revise this tableau, we can check easily whether the original optimal basic feasible solution is now nonoptimal (or infeasible). If so, this solution would be used as the initial basic solution to restart the simplex method (or dual simplex method) to find the new optimal solution, if desired. If the changes in the model are not major, only a very few iterations should be required to reach the new optimal solution from this "advanced" initial basic solution.

To describe this procedure more specifically, consider the following situation. The simplex method already has been used to obtain an optimal solution to a linear programming model with specified values for the b_i, c_j, and a_{ij} parameters. To initiate sensitivity analysis, one or more of the parameters now is changed. After making the changes, let $\bar{b}_i, \bar{c}_j$, and $\bar{a}_{ij}$ denote the values of the various parameters. Thus, in matrix notation,

$$\mathbf{b} \to \bar{\mathbf{b}}, \, \mathbf{c} \to \bar{\mathbf{c}}, \, \mathbf{A} \to \bar{\mathbf{A}},$$

for the *revised* model.

The first step is to revise the *final* simplex tableau to reflect these changes. Continuing to use the notation presented in Table 5.8, as well as the accompanying formulas for the *fundamental insight* [(1) $\mathbf{t}^* = \mathbf{t} + \mathbf{y}^*\mathbf{T}$ and (2) $\mathbf{T}^* = \mathbf{S}^*\mathbf{T}$], the revised final tableau is calculated from $\mathbf{y}^*$ and $\mathbf{S}^*$ (which have not changed) and the new initial tableau, as shown in Table 6.16.

Table 6.16 Revised final simplex tableau resulting from changes in original model

	Eq. no.	Z	Coefficient of		Right side
			Original variables	Slack variables	
New initial tableau	0	1	$-\bar{\mathbf{c}}$	**0**	0
	$1 - m$	**0**	$\bar{\mathbf{A}}$	**I**	$\bar{\mathbf{b}}$
Revised final tableau	0	1	$\mathbf{z}^* - \bar{\mathbf{c}} = \mathbf{y}^*\bar{\mathbf{A}} - \bar{\mathbf{c}}$	$\mathbf{y}^*$	$Z^* = \mathbf{y}^*\bar{\mathbf{b}}$
	$1 - m$	**0**	$\mathbf{A}^* = \mathbf{S}^*\bar{\mathbf{A}}$	$\mathbf{S}^*$	$\mathbf{b}^* = \mathbf{S}^*\bar{\mathbf{b}}$

To illustrate, suppose that the original model for the Wyndor Glass Co. problem of Sec. 3.1 is revised as shown at the right.

Original Model

$$\text{Maximize} \quad Z = [3,5]\begin{bmatrix} x_1 \\ x_2 \end{bmatrix},$$

subject to

$$\begin{bmatrix} 1 & 0 \\ 0 & 2 \\ 3 & 2 \end{bmatrix}\begin{bmatrix} x_1 \\ x_2 \end{bmatrix} \le \begin{bmatrix} 4 \\ 12 \\ 18 \end{bmatrix}$$

and

$$\mathbf{x} \ge \mathbf{0}.$$

Revised Model

$$\text{Maximize} \quad Z = [5,5]\begin{bmatrix} x_1 \\ x_2 \end{bmatrix},$$

subject to

$$\begin{bmatrix} 1 & 0 \\ 0 & 2 \\ 2 & 2 \end{bmatrix}\begin{bmatrix} x_1 \\ x_2 \end{bmatrix} \le \begin{bmatrix} 4 \\ 24 \\ 18 \end{bmatrix}$$

and

$$\mathbf{x} \ge \mathbf{0}.$$

Thus, for the revised model,

$$\bar{\mathbf{c}} = [5,5],$$

$$\bar{\mathbf{A}} = \begin{bmatrix} 1 & 0 \\ 0 & 2 \\ 2 & 2 \end{bmatrix}, \quad \bar{\mathbf{b}} = \begin{bmatrix} 4 \\ 24 \\ 18 \end{bmatrix}.$$

Referring to Table 5.8, $\mathbf{y}^*$ and $\mathbf{S}^*$ for this problem are

$$\mathbf{y}^* = [0, 3/2, 1], \quad \mathbf{S}^* = \begin{bmatrix} 1 & 1/3 & -1/3 \\ 0 & 1/2 & 0 \\ 0 & -1/3 & 1/3 \end{bmatrix}.$$

Consequently, using the formulas in Table 6.16, the numbers in the *final* simplex tableau change from those shown in Table 4.8 to the following.

$$\mathbf{z}^* - \bar{\mathbf{c}} = [0, 3/2, 1]\begin{bmatrix} 1 & 0 \\ 0 & 2 \\ 2 & 2 \end{bmatrix} - [5,5] = [-1,0], \quad z^* = [0, 3/2, 1]\begin{bmatrix} 4 \\ 24 \\ 18 \end{bmatrix} = 54,$$

$$\mathbf{A}^* = \begin{bmatrix} 1 & 1/3 & -1/3 \\ 0 & 1/2 & 0 \\ 0 & -1/3 & 1/3 \end{bmatrix}\begin{bmatrix} 1 & 0 \\ 0 & 2 \\ 2 & 2 \end{bmatrix} = \begin{bmatrix} 1/3 & 0 \\ 0 & 1 \\ 2/3 & 0 \end{bmatrix},$$

$$\mathbf{b}^* = \begin{bmatrix} 1 & 1/3 & -1/3 \\ 0 & 1/2 & 0 \\ 0 & -1/3 & 1/3 \end{bmatrix}\begin{bmatrix} 4 \\ 24 \\ 18 \end{bmatrix} = \begin{bmatrix} 6 \\ 12 \\ -2 \end{bmatrix}.$$

Frequently, only one parameter will be changed at a time in order to check them individually. In this case, the only changes in the final simplex tableau are in the one column that holds the changed parameter in the initial tableau, so that most of the calculations just illustrated would not be needed. Even with multiple changes, any column with no change in the initial tableau (e.g., the x_2 column in the preceding example) would have no changes in the final tableau, so the corresponding calculations can be deleted. Another common shortcut is to adapt the formulas given in Table 6.16 to calculate only the *incremental changes* in the final tableau in terms of the incremental changes in the initial tableau and then to add these increments to the original quantities in the final tableau.

After obtaining the *revised* final simplex tableau, we next *convert the tableau to proper form* (as needed). In particular, the basic variable for row i must have a coefficient of 1 in that row and a coefficient of *zero* in *every* other row (including row 0) for the tableau to be in the proper form for identifying and evaluating the current basic solution. Therefore, if the changes have violated this requirement (which can occur only if the original constraint coefficients of a basic variable have been changed), further changes must be made to restore this form. This restoration is done by using *Gaussian elimination*, i.e., by successively applying part 3 of the iterative step for the simplex method (see Chap. 4) as if each violating basic variable were an entering basic variable. Note that this application may also cause further changes in the right-side column, which gives the value of the current basic solution.

For the example, the revised final simplex tableau shown in the top half of Table 6.17 is not in proper form because of the column for the basic variable x_1. Specifically, the coefficient of x_1 in *its* row (row 3) is 2/3 instead of 1, and it has *nonzero* coefficients (-1 and 1/3) in rows 0 and 1. To restore proper form, row 3 is multiplied by 3/2; then this new row 3 is added to row 0 and 1/3 of the new row 3 is subtracted from row 1. This yields the *proper form* shown in the bottom half of Table 6.17, which now can be used to identify the new values for the current (previously optimal) basic solution,

$$(x_1, x_2, x_3, x_4, x_5) = (-3, 12, 7, 0, 0).$$

Because x_1 is negative, this basic solution no longer is feasible. However, it is

Table 6.17 **Converting the revised final simplex tableau to proper form for the revised Wyndor Glass Co. problem**

	Basic variable	Eq. no.	Z	Coefficient of x_1	x_2	x_3	x_4	x_5	Right side
Revised final tableau	Z	0	1	-1	0	0	3/2	1	54
	x_3	1	0	1/3	0	1	1/3	$-1/3$	6
	x_2	2	0	0	1	0	1/2	0	12
	x_1	3	0	2/3	0	0	$-1/3$	1/3	-2
Converted to proper form	Z	0	1	0	0	0	1	3/2	51
	x_3	1	0	0	0	1	1/2	$-1/2$	7
	x_2	2	0	0	1	0	1/2	0	12
	x_1	3	0	1	0	0	$-1/2$	1/2	-3

superoptimal (see Table 6.9) because *all* the coefficients in row 0 still are *non-negative*. Therefore, the *dual simplex method* can be useful to *reoptimize* (if desired), starting from this basic solution. (It is often used in sensitivity analysis to identify the solutions that are optimal for some set of likely values of the model parameters and then to determine which of these solutions most *consistently* performs well for the various likely parameter values.)

If this basic solution had been *neither* feasible nor superoptimal (i.e., if the tableau had negative entries in *both* the right-side column and row 0), artificial variables could have been introduced to convert the tableau to the proper form for an *initial* simplex tableau.[1]

When testing to see how *sensitive* the original optimal solution is to the various parameters of the model, the common approach is to check each parameter individually, changing its value from the initial estimate to other possibilities in the *range of likely values* (including the endpoints of this range). After the especially *sensitive* parameters have been identified, then some combinations of simultaneous changes of these parameters may be investigated. *Each* time one (or more) of the parameters is changed, the procedure described and illustrated here would be applied. Let us now summarize this procedure.

Summary of Procedure for Sensitivity Analysis

1. *Revision of model:* Make the desired change or changes in the model to be investigated next.
2. *Revision of final tableau:* Use the fundamental insight to determine the resulting changes in the final simplex tableau.
3. *Conversion to proper form:* Convert this tableau to the proper form for identifying and evaluating the current basic solution by applying (as necessary) Gaussian elimination.
4. *Feasibility test:* Test this solution for feasibility by checking whether all its basic variable values in the right-side column of the tableau still are nonnegative.
5. *Optimality test:* Test this solution for optimality (if feasible) by checking whether all its nonbasic variable coefficients in row 0 of the tableau still are nonnegative.
6. *Reoptimization:* If this solution fails either test, the new optimal solution can be obtained (if desired) by using the current tableau as the initial simplex tableau (making any necessary conversions) for the simplex method or dual simplex method.

In the next section, we shall discuss and illustrate the application of this procedure to each of the major categories of revisions in the original model. This discussion will involve, in part, expanding upon the example introduced in this

---

[1] There also exists a primal-dual algorithm that can be directly applied to such a simplex tableau without any conversion.

section for investigating changes in the Wyndor Glass Co. model. In fact, we shall begin by *individually* checking each of the preceding changes. At the same time, we shall integrate some of the applications of duality theory to sensitivity analysis as discussed in Sec. 6.5.

6.7 Applying Sensitivity Analysis

Sensitivity analysis often begins with the investigation of the effect of changes in the b_i, the amount of resource i ($i = 1,2,\ldots,m$) being made available for the activities under consideration. The reason is that there generally is more flexibility in setting and adjusting these values than there is for the other parameters of the model. As already discussed in Secs. 4.7 and 6.2, the economic interpretation of the dual variables (the y_i) as *shadow prices* is extremely useful for deciding which changes should be considered.

CASE 1—CHANGES IN THE b_i

Suppose that the only changes in the current model are that one or more of the b_i parameters ($i = 1,2,\ldots,m$) has been changed. In this case, the *only* resulting changes in the final simplex tableau are in the right-side column. Therefore, both the *conversion to proper form* and *optimality test* steps of the general procedure can be skipped.

EXAMPLE Sensitivity analysis is begun for the *original* Wyndor Glass Co. problem of Sec. 3.1 by examining the optimal values of the y_i dual variables ($y_1^* = 0$, $y_2^* = 3/2$, $y_3^* = 1$). These *shadow prices* give the *marginal value* of each resource i for the activities (two new products) under consideration. As discussed in Sec. 4.7 (see Fig. 4.3), the total profit from these activities can be increased $1.50/minute for each additional unit of resource 2 (production capacity in Plant 2) that is made available. This increase in profit holds for relatively small changes

Table 6.18 **Revised data for Wyndor Glass Co. problem after changing just b_2**

Final simplex tableau

Model parameters	Basic variable	Eq. no.	Z	x_1	x_2	x_3	x_4	x_5	Right side
$c_1 = 3$, $c_2 = 5$ ($n = 2$) $a_{11} = 1$, $a_{12} = 0$, $b_1 = 4$ $a_{21} = 0$, $a_{22} = 2$, $b_2 = 24$ $a_{31} = 3$, $a_{32} = 2$, $b_3 = 18$	Z	0	1	$\frac{9}{2}$	0	0	0	$\frac{5}{2}$	45
	x_3	1	0	1	0	1	0	0	4
	x_2	2	0	$\frac{3}{2}$	1	0	0	$\frac{1}{2}$	9
	x_4	3	0	-3	0	0	1	-1	6

that do not affect the feasibility of the current basic solution (and so do not affect the values of the y_i^*).

Consequently, the O.R. Department has investigated the marginal profitability from the other current uses of this resource to determine if any are less than \$1.50/minute. This investigation reveals that one old product is far less profitable. The production rate for this product already has been reduced to the minimum amount that would justify its marketing expenses. However, it can be discontinued altogether, which would provide an additional 12 units of resource 2 for the new products. Thus the next step is to determine what profit could be obtained from the new products if this shift were to be made. This shift changes b_2 from 12 to 24 in the linear programming model.

When the fundamental insight (Table 6.16) is applied, the effect of this change on the final simplex tableau given in Table 4.8 is found to be that the entries in the right-side column change to the following values:

$$y_0^* = \mathbf{y}^* \bar{\mathbf{b}} = [0, 3/2, 1] \begin{bmatrix} 4 \\ 24 \\ 18 \end{bmatrix} = 54,$$

$$\mathbf{b}^* = \mathbf{S}^* \bar{\mathbf{b}} = \begin{bmatrix} 1 & 1/3 & -1/3 \\ 0 & 1/2 & 0 \\ 0 & -1/3 & 1/3 \end{bmatrix} \begin{bmatrix} 4 \\ 24 \\ 18 \end{bmatrix} = \begin{bmatrix} 6 \\ 12 \\ -2 \end{bmatrix}.$$

Therefore, the current (previously optimal) basic solution has become

$$(x_1, x_2, x_3, x_4, x_5) = (-2, 12, 6, 0, 0),$$

which fails the *feasibility test* because of the negative value. (Note in Fig. 4.1 that this basic solution corresponds to a corner-point solution with defining equations, $2x_2 = 24$ and $3x_1 + 2x_2 = 18$.) The dual simplex method now can be applied, starting with this revised simplex tableau, to find the new optimal solution. This method leads in just one iteration to the new final simplex tableau shown in Table 6.18. (Alternatively, the simplex method could be applied from the beginning, which also would lead to this final tableau in just one iteration in this case.)

Based on these results, the relatively unprofitable old product will be discontinued. Since y_3^* still is positive, a similar study is made of the possibility of changing the allocation of resource 3, but the resulting decision is to retain the current allocation. Therefore, the current linear programming model at this point has the parameter values shown in Table 6.18, where the current optimal solution is

$$(x_1, x_2, x_3, x_4, x_5) = (0, 9, 4, 6, 0).$$

CASE 2a—CHANGES IN THE COEFFICIENTS OF A NONBASIC VARIABLE

Consider a particular variable x_j that is a *nonbasic* variable in the optimal solution shown by the final simplex tableau (so that x_j is *not* included in the list of basic variables in the first column of this tableau). Case 2a is where the only changes in the current model are that one or more of the coefficients of this variable—$c_j, a_{1j}, a_{2j}, \ldots, a_{mj}$—have been changed.

As described at the beginning of Sec. 6.5, duality theory provides a very convenient way of checking these changes. In particular, if the *complementary* basic solution $\mathbf{y}^*$ in the dual problem still satisfies the single dual constraint that has changed, then the original optimal solution in the primal problem *remains optimal* as is.

If the optimal solution has changed ($z_j^* - \bar{c}_j < 0$), and if you wish to find the new one, you can find it rather easily. Simply apply the fundamental insight to revise the x_j column (the only one that has changed) in the final simplex tableau, and then restart the simplex method with x_j as the *initial entering basic variable*. (It has the only negative coefficient in row 0.)

EXAMPLE   Since x_1 is nonbasic in the current optimal solution (see Table 6.18) for the Wyndor Glass Co. problem, the next step in its sensitivity analysis is to check whether any reasonable changes in the estimates of the coefficients of x_1 could still make it advisable to introduce product 1. The set of changes that goes as far as realistically possible to make product 1 more attractive would be to reset $c_1 = 5$ and $a_{31} = 2$ (as was done in Sec. 6.6). The resulting changes in the single revised constraint for the dual problem (see Table 6.1) are shown here along with $\mathbf{y}^*$.

$$y_1 + 3y_3 \geq 3 \rightarrow y_1 + 2y_3 \geq 5,$$
$$y_1^* = 0, \quad y_2^* = 0, \quad y_3^* = 5/2.$$

Note that $\mathbf{y}^*$ *still* satisfies the revised constraint (barely), so the current primal solution (Table 6.18) still is optimal. Because any larger changes in the original estimates of the coefficients of x_1 would be unrealistic, the O.R. Department concludes that these coefficients are not particularly sensitive parameters in the current model.

CASE 2b—INTRODUCTION OF A NEW VARIABLE

After solving for the optimal solution, we may discover that the linear programming formulation did not consider all the attractive alternative activities. Considering a new activity requires introducing a new variable with the appropriate coefficients into the objective function and constraints of the current model—which is case 2b.

The convenient way to deal with this case is to treat it just as if it were case 2a! This is done by pretending that the new variable x_j actually was in the original model with *all* its coefficients equal to *zero* (so that they still are zero in the *final* simplex tableau) and that x_j is a *nonbasic* variable in the current basic feasible solution. Therefore, if we change these zero coefficients to their actual values for the new variable, the procedure (including any reoptimization) does indeed become identical to that for case 2a.

In particular, all you have to do to check whether the current solution still is optimal is check whether the *complementary* basic solution y^* satisfies the one new dual constraint. We already have described this approach and then illustrated it for the Wyndor Glass Co. problem in Sec. 6.5.

CASE 3—CHANGES IN THE COEFFICIENTS OF A BASIC VARIABLE

Now suppose that the variable x_j under consideration is a *basic* variable in the optimal solution shown by the final simplex tableau (so x_j appears in the first column of this tableau). Case 3 assumes that the only changes in the current model are in the coefficients of this variable.

Case 3 differs from case 2a because of the requirements that a basic variable must have a coefficient of 1 in its row of the simplex tableau and a coefficient of *zero* in *every* other row (including row 0). Therefore, after the changes in the x_j column of the *final* simplex tableau have been calculated,[1] it probably will be necessary to apply *Gaussian elimination* to restore this form, as was illustrated in Table 6.17. This step in turn probably will change the value of the current basic solution and may make it either infeasible or nonoptimal. Consequently, all the steps of the overall procedure summarized at the end of Sec. 6.6 are required for case 3.

EXAMPLE Because x_2 is a basic variable in Table 6.18 for the Wyndor Glass Co. problem, sensitivity analysis of its coefficients fits case 3. Given the current optimal solution ($x_1 = 0$, $x_2 = 9$), product 2 is the *only* new product that should be introduced, and its production rate should be relatively large. Therefore, the key question now is whether the initial estimates that led to the coefficients of x_2 in the current model could have *overestimated* the attractiveness of product 2 so much that they invalidate this conclusion. This question can be tested by checking the *most pessimistic* set of reasonable estimates for these coefficients, which turns out to be $\bar{c}_2 = 3$, $\bar{a}_{22} = 3$, and $\bar{a}_{32} = 4$.

Since the *only* resulting changes in the *final* simplex tableau are in the x_2 column, the formulas in Table 6.16 are used to recompute just this column, which gives the *revised* final tableau shown at the top of Table 6.19. Note that the new coefficients of this basic variable do not have the required values, so the *conversion-to-proper-form* step must be applied next. This step involves dividing row 2 by 2, subtracting 7 times the new row 2 from row 0, and adding the new row 2 to row 3. The resulting second tableau in Table 6.19 gives the new value of the current basic solution, namely, $x_3 = 4$, $x_2 = 9/2$, $x_4 = 21/2$ ($x_1 = 0$, $x_5 = 0$). Since all these variables are *nonnegative*, the solution still is *feasible*. However, because of the *negative* coefficient of x_1 in row 0, we know it is *no longer optimal*.

---

[1] For the relatively sophisticated reader, we should point out a possible pitfall for case 3 that would be discovered at this point. Specifically, the changes in the *initial* tableau can destroy the linear independence of the columns of coefficients of basic variables. This event occurs only if the unit coefficient of the basic variable x_j in the *final* tableau has been changed to *zero* at this point, in which case more extensive simplex method calculations must be used for case 3.

Table 6.19 **Sensitivity analysis procedure applied to Case 3 example**

Basic variable	Eq. no.	Z	Coefficient of x_1	x_2	x_3	x_4	x_5	Right side
Revised final tableau								
Z	0	1	$\frac{9}{2}$	7	0	0	$\frac{5}{2}$	45
x_3	1	0	1	0	1	0	0	4
x_2	2	0	$\frac{3}{2}$	2	0	0	$\frac{1}{2}$	9
x_4	3	0	-3	-1	0	1	-1	6
Converted to proper form								
Z	0	1	$-\frac{3}{4}$	0	0	0	$\frac{3}{4}$	$\frac{27}{2}$
x_3	1	0	1	0	1	0	0	4
x_2	2	0	$\frac{3}{4}$	1	0	0	$\frac{1}{4}$	$\frac{9}{2}$
x_4	3	0	$-\frac{9}{4}$	0	0	1	$-\frac{3}{4}$	$\frac{21}{2}$
New final tableau after reoptimization (only one iteration of the simplex method needed in this case)								
Z	0	1	0	0	$\frac{3}{4}$	0	$\frac{3}{4}$	$\frac{33}{2}$
x_1	1	0	1	0	1	0	0	4
x_2	2	0	0	1	$-\frac{3}{4}$	0	$\frac{1}{4}$	$\frac{3}{2}$
x_4	3	0	0	0	$\frac{9}{4}$	1	$-\frac{3}{4}$	$\frac{39}{2}$

Therefore, the simplex method would be applied to this tableau, with this solution as the initial basic feasible solution, to find the new optimal solution. The initial entering basic variable is x_1, with x_3 as the leaving basic variable. Just one iteration is needed in this case to reach the new optimal solution: $x_1 = 4$, $x_2 = 3/2$, $x_4 = 39/2$ ($x_3 = 0$, $x_5 = 0$), as shown in the last tableau of Table 6.19.

This analysis suggests that c_2, a_{22}, and a_{32} are relatively sensitive parameters. However, additional data for estimating them more closely can be obtained only by conducting a pilot run. Therefore, the O.R. Department recommends that production of product 2 be initiated immediately on a small scale ($x_2 = 3/2$) and that this experience be used to guide the decision on whether the remaining production capacity should be allocated to product 2 or product 1.

CASE 4—INTRODUCTION OF A NEW CONSTRAINT

The last case is one in which a new constraint must be introduced into the model after it has already been solved. This case may occur because the constraint was overlooked initially or because new considerations have arisen since the model was formulated originally. Another possibility is that the constraint was deleted purposely to decrease computational effort because it appeared to be less restrictive than other constraints already in the model, but now this impression needs to be checked with the optimal solution actually obtained.

To see if the current optimal solution would be affected by a new constraint, all you have to do is check directly whether the optimal solution satisfies the constraint. If it does, then it would still be the *best feasible solution* (i.e., the optimal solution), even if the constraint were added to the model. The reason is that a new constraint can only eliminate some previously feasible solutions without adding any new ones.

If the new constraint does eliminate the current optimal solution, and if you want to find the new solution, then introduce this constraint into the *final* simplex tableau (as an additional row) *just* as if this were the *initial* tableau, where the usual variable (slack variable or artificial variable) is designated to be the basic variable for this new row. Because the new row probably will have *nonzero* coefficients for some of the other basic variables, the *conversion-to-proper-form* step is applied next, and then the rest of the general procedure is applied in the usual way.

EXAMPLE To illustrate this case, suppose that the new constraint,

$$2x_1 + 3x_2 \leq 24,$$

is introduced into the model given in Table 6.18. Since the current optimal solution $(x_1 = 0, x_2 = 9)$ violates this constraint, it is no longer feasible. To find the new optimal solution, add this constraint to the current final simplex tableau as just described, with the slack variable x_6 as its initial basic variable. This addition yields the first tableau shown in Table 6.20. The *conversion-to-proper-form* step then requires subtracting three times row 2 from the new row, which identifies the current basic solution: $x_3 = 4$, $x_2 = 9$, $x_4 = 6$, $x_6 = -3$ ($x_1 = 0$, $x_5 = 0$), as shown in the second tableau. Applying the dual simplex method to this tableau then leads in just one iteration (more are sometimes needed) to the new optimal solution in the final tableau of Table 6.20.

SYSTEMATIC SENSITIVITY ANALYSIS—PARAMETRIC PROGRAMMING

So far we have described how to test specific changes in the model parameters. Another common approach to sensitivity analysis is to vary one or more parameters continuously over some interval(s) to see when the optimal solution changes. For example, with the Wyndor Glass Co. problem, rather than beginning by testing the specific change from $b_2 = 12$ to $\bar{b}_2 = 24$, we might instead set

$$\bar{b}_2 = 12 + \theta,$$

and then vary θ continuously from 0 to 12 (the maximum value of interest). By using the expressions for Z^* and $\mathbf{b}^*$ given in Table 6.16, we can see from Table 4.8

Table 6.20 **Sensitivity analysis procedure applied to Case 4 example**

	Basic variable	Eq. no.	Z	Coefficient of x_1	x_2	x_3	x_4	x_5	x_6	Right side
Revised final tableau	Z	0	1	$\frac{9}{2}$	0	0	0	$\frac{5}{2}$	0	45
	x_3	1	0	1	0	1	0	0	0	4
	x_2	2	0	$\frac{3}{2}$	1	0	0	$\frac{1}{2}$	0	9
	x_4	3	0	-3	0	0	1	-1	0	6
	x_6	New	0	2	3	0	0	0	1	24
Converted to proper form	Z	0	1	$\frac{9}{2}$	0	0	0	$\frac{5}{2}$	0	45
	x_3	1	0	1	0	1	0	0	0	4
	x_2	2	0	$\frac{3}{2}$	1	0	0	$\frac{1}{2}$	0	9
	x_4	3	0	-3	0	0	1	-1	0	6
	x_6	New	0	$-\frac{5}{2}$	0	0	0	$-\frac{3}{2}$	1	-3
New final tableau after reoptimization (only one iteration of dual simplex method needed in this case)	Z	0	1	$\frac{1}{3}$	0	0	0	0	$\frac{5}{3}$	40
	x_3	1	0	1	0	1	0	0	0	4
	x_2	2	0	$\frac{2}{3}$	1	0	0	0	$\frac{1}{3}$	8
	x_4	3	0	$-\frac{4}{3}$	0	0	1	0	$-\frac{2}{3}$	8
	x_5	New	0	$\frac{5}{3}$	0	0	0	1	$-\frac{2}{3}$	2

that the corresponding optimal solution is

$$Z = 36 + \frac{3}{2}\theta$$

$$x_3 = 2 + \frac{1}{3}\theta$$

$$x_2 = 6 + \frac{1}{2}\theta \qquad (x_4 = 0, x_5 = 0)$$

$$x_1 = 2 - \frac{1}{3}\theta$$

for θ small enough that this solution still is feasible, i.e., for $\theta \leq 6$. For $\theta > 6$, the dual simplex method yields the tableau shown in Table 6.18, with $Z = 45$, $x_3 = 4$, $x_2 = 9$, but $x_4 = -6 + \theta$ ($x_1 = 0$, $x_5 = 0$). This information can then be used (along with other data not incorporated into the model on the effect of increasing b_2) to decide whether to retain the original optimal solution and, if not, how much to increase b_2.

In a similar way, we can investigate the effect on the optimal solution of varying several parameters simultaneously. When we vary just b_i parameters, we need to reset $\bar{b}_i = b_i + \alpha_i \theta$ for $i = 1, 2, \dots, m$, where the α_i are input constants specifying the desired rate of increase of the corresponding right-hand side as θ is increased. For example, it might be possible to shift some of the production of a current Wyndor Glass Co. product from Plant 2 to Plant 3, thereby increasing b_2 by decreasing b_3. If b_3 decreases twice as fast as b_2 increases, then

$$\bar{b}_2 = 12 + \theta$$
$$\bar{b}_3 = 18 - 2\theta,$$

where θ measures the amount of production shifted. (Thus $\alpha_1 = 0$, $\alpha_2 = 1$, and $\alpha_3 = -2$ in this case.)

As we discussed in Sec. 4.7, this way of continuously varying several parameters simultaneously is referred to as **parametric linear programming**. Section 9.3 presents the parametric linear programming procedure when just b_i parameters are being varied as well as the procedure for the analogous case where c_j parameters are being varied. Some mathematical programming computer packages also include routines for varying just the coefficients of a single variable or varying just the parameters of a single constraint. In addition to the other applications discussed in Sec. 4.7, these procedures provide a convenient way of conducting sensitivity analysis systematically.

6.8 Conclusions

Every linear programming problem has associated with it a *dual* linear programming problem. There are a number of very useful relationships between the original (primal) problem and its dual problem that enhance our ability to analyze the primal problem. For example, the economic interpretation of the dual problem gives *shadow prices* that measure the marginal value of the resources in the primal problem, as well as providing an interpretation of the simplex method. Because the simplex method can be applied directly to either problem in order to solve both of them simultaneously, considerable computational effort sometimes can be saved by dealing directly with the dual problem. Duality theory, including the *dual simplex method* for working with superoptimal basic solutions, also plays a major role in *sensitivity analysis*.

The values used for the parameters of a linear programming model generally are just *estimates*. Therefore, sensitivity analysis needs to be performed to investigate what happens if these estimates are wrong. The *fundamental insight* of Sec. 5.3 provides the key for performing this investigation efficiently. The general objectives are to identify the relatively *sensitive* parameters affecting the optimal solution, to try to estimate these sensitive parameters more closely, and then to select a solution that remains good over the range of likely values of the sensitive parameters. This analysis is a very important part of most linear programming studies.

SELECTED REFERENCES

1. Bradley, Stephen P., Arnoldo C. Hax, and Thomas L. Magnanti: *Applied Mathematical Programming*, Addison-Wesley, Reading, Mass., 1977.
2. Dantzig, George B.: *Linear Programming and Extensions*, Princeton University Press, Princeton, N.J., 1963.
3. Gale, David: *The Theory of Linear Economic Models*, McGraw-Hill, New York, 1960.
4. Luenberger, David G.: *Introduction to Linear and Nonlinear Programming*, 2d ed., Addison-Wesley, Reading, Mass., 1984.

PROBLEMS

1. Construct the primal-dual table and the dual problem for each of the following linear programming models fitting our standard form:

(*a*) Model given in Prob. 2 of Chap. 4.
(*b*) Model given in Prob. 6 of Chap. 4.

2. Construct the dual problem for each of the following linear programming models fitting our standard form:

(*a*) Model given in Prob. 4 of Chap. 3.
(*b*) Model given in Prob. 5 of Chap. 4.

3. Consider the linear programming model given in Prob. 8 of Chap. 4.

(*a*) Construct the primal-dual table and the dual problem for this model.
(*b*) What does the fact that Z is unbounded for this model imply about its dual problem?

4. For each of the following linear programming models, give your recommendation on the more efficient way (probably) for obtaining an optimal solution: (1) applying the simplex method directly to this primal problem or (2) applying the simplex method directly to the dual problem instead. Explain.

(*a*) Maximize $Z = 10x_1 - 4x_2 + 7x_3$,

subject to

$$3x_1 - x_2 + 2x_3 \le 25$$
$$x_1 - 2x_2 + 3x_3 \le 25$$
$$5x_1 + x_2 + 2x_3 \le 40$$
$$x_1 + x_2 + x_3 \le 90$$
$$2x_1 - x_2 + x_3 \le 20,$$

and

$$x_1 \ge 0, \quad x_2 \ge 0, \quad x_3 \ge 0.$$

(b) Maximize $Z = 2x_1 + 5x_2 + 3x_3 + 4x_4 + x_5$,

subject to

$$x_1 + 3x_2 + 2x_3 + 3x_4 + x_5 \leq 6$$
$$4x_1 + 6x_2 + 5x_3 + 7x_4 + x_5 \leq 15,$$

and

$$x_j \geq 0, \quad \text{for } j = 1, 2, 3, 4, 5.$$

5. Consider the following problem.

$$\text{Maximize} \quad Z = x_1 - 2x_2 - x_3,$$

subject to

$$x_1 + x_2 + 2x_3 \leq 1$$
$$2x_1 \qquad - x_3 \leq 1,$$

and

$$x_1 \geq 0, \quad x_2 \geq 0, \quad x_3 \geq 0.$$

(a) Construct the dual problem.
(b) Use duality theory to show that the optimal solution to the primal problem has $Z \leq 0$.

6. Consider the simplex tableaux for the Wyndor Glass Co. problem given in Table 4.8. For each tableau, give the economic interpretation of the following items:

(a) Each of the coefficients of the slack variables (x_3, x_4, x_5) in row 0.
(b) Each of the coefficients of the original variables (x_1, x_2) in row 0.
(c) The resulting choice for the entering basic variable (or the decision to stop after the final tableau).

7. Consider the following problem.

$$\text{Maximize} \quad Z = 6x_1 + 8x_2,$$

subject to

$$5x_1 + 2x_2 \leq 20$$
$$x_1 + 2x_2 \leq 10,$$

and

$$x_1 \leq 0, \quad x_2 \geq 0.$$

(a) Construct the dual problem for this primal problem.
(b) Solve both the primal problem and the dual problem graphically. Identify the corner-point feasible solutions and corner-point infeasible solutions for both problems. Calculate the objective function values for all these solutions.
(c) Use the information obtained in part (b) to construct a table listing the complementary basic solutions and so forth for these problems. (Use the same column headings as for Table 6.8.)
(d) Solve the primal problem by the simplex method. After each iteration (including iteration 0), identify the basic feasible solution for this problem and the

complementary basic solution for the dual problem. Also identify the corresponding corner-point solutions.

8. Consider the primal and dual problems for the Wyndor Glass Co. example given in Table 6.1. Using Tables 5.5, 5.6, 6.7, and 6.8, construct a new table giving the eight sets of nonbasic variables for the primal problem in column 1, the corresponding sets of associated variables for the dual problem in column 2, and the set of nonbasic variables for each complementary basic solution of the dual problem in column 3. Explain why this table demonstrates the *complementary slackness property* for this example.

9. Suppose that a primal problem has a *degenerate* basic feasible solution (one or more basic variables equal to zero) as its optimal solution. What does this degeneracy imply about the dual problem? Why? Is the converse also true?

10. Consider the following problem.

$$\text{Maximize} \quad Z = 2x_1 - 4x_2,$$

subject to

$$x_1 - x_2 \leq 1$$

and

$$x_1 \geq 0, \quad x_2 \geq 0.$$

(a) Construct the dual problem, and then find its optimal solution by inspection.

(b) Use the *complementary slackness property* and the optimal solution for the dual problem to find the optimal solution for the primal problem.

(c) Suppose that c_1, the coefficient of x_1 in the primal objective function, actually can have any value in the model. For what values of c_1 does the dual problem have *no* feasible solutions? For these values, what does duality theory then imply about the primal problem?

11. Consider the following problem.

$$\text{Maximize} \quad Z = 4x_1 + 14x_2 + 8x_3,$$

subject to

$$x_1 + 2x_2 + x_3 \leq 10$$
$$3x_1 + 3x_2 + 2x_3 \leq 10,$$

and

$$x_1 \geq 0, \quad x_2 \geq 0, \quad x_3 \geq 0.$$

(a) Construct the dual problem for this primal problem.

(b) Use the dual problem to demonstrate that the optimal value of Z for the primal problem cannot exceed 50.

(c) It has been conjectured that x_2 and x_3 should be the basic variables for the optimal solution of the primal problem. Show that this conjecture is not true by directly deriving this basic solution (and Z) using the *Gauss-Jordan method of elimination* (see Appendix 4) that is employed by part 3 of the iterative step for the simplex method. Simultaneously derive and identify the complementary basic solution for the dual problem.

(d) Solve the dual problem graphically. Use this solution to identify the basic variables and the nonbasic variables for the optimal solution of the primal problem. Directly derive this solution, using the *Gauss-Jordan method of elimination.*

12. Reconsider the model of part (b) of Prob. 4.

(a) Construct its dual problem.
(b) Solve this dual problem graphically.
(c) Use the result from part (b) to identify the nonbasic variables and basic variables for the optimal basic solution for the *primal* problem.
(d) Use the results from part (c) to obtain the optimal basic solution for the primal problem *directly* by using *Gaussian elimination* to solve for its basic variables, starting from the initial system of equations [excluding equation (0)] constructed for the simplex method.
(e) Use the results from part (c) to identify the defining equations (see Sec. 5.1) for the optimal corner-point solution for the primal problem, and then use these equations to find this solution.

13. Consider the model given in Prob. 26 of Chap. 5.

(a) Construct the dual problem.
(b) Use the given information about the basic variables in the optimal primal solution to identify the nonbasic variables and basic variables for the optimal dual solution.
(c) Use the results from part (b) to identify the defining equations (see Sec. 5.1) for the optimal corner-point solution for the dual problem, and then use these equations to find this solution.
(d) Solve the dual problem graphically to verify your results from part (c).

14. Consider the model given in Prob. 3 of Chap. 3.

(a) Construct the dual problem for this model.
(b) Use the fact that $(x_1, x_2) = (13,5)$ is optimal for the primal problem to identify the nonbasic variables and basic variables for the optimal basic solution for the dual problem.
(c) Identify the optimal basic solution for the dual problem by *directly* deriving Eq. (0) corresponding to the optimal primal solution identified in part (b). Derive this equation by using the *Gauss-Jordan method of elimination* (see Appendix 4) that is employed by part 3 of the iterative step for the simplex method.
(d) Use the results from part (b) to identify the defining equations (see Sec. 5.1) for the optimal corner-point solution for the dual problem. Verify your optimal dual solution from part (c) by checking to see that it satisfies this system of equations.

15. Suppose that you also want information about the *dual* problem when you apply the *revised simplex method* (see Sec. 5.2) to the primal problem in *our standard form.*

(a) How would you identify the *optimal solution* for the dual problem?
(b) After obtaining the basic feasible solution at each iteration, how would you identify the *complementary basic solution* in the dual problem?

16. Consider the primal and dual problems in *our standard form* presented in matrix notation at the beginning of Sec. 6.1. Use *only* this definition of the dual problem for a primal problem in this form to prove each of the following results.

(a) The *weak duality property* presented in Sec. 6.1.

(b) If the primal problem has an *unbounded* feasible region that permits increasing Z indefinitely, then the dual problem has *no* feasible solutions.

(c) If the functional constraints for the primal problem, $\mathbf{Ax} \leq \mathbf{b}$, are changed to $\mathbf{Ax} = \mathbf{b}$, the only resulting change in the dual problem is to *delete* the nonnegativity constraints, $\mathbf{y} \geq \mathbf{0}$.

17. Construct the dual problem for the linear programming problem given in Prob. 18 of Chap. 4.

18. For each of the following linear programming models, convert this primal problem into one of the two forms given in Table 6.13 and then construct its dual problem:

(a) Model given in Prob. 11 of Chap. 4.

(b) Model given in Prob. 12 of Chap. 4.

(c) Model given in Prob. 19 of Chap. 4.

19. Consider the model with equality constraints given in Prob. 17 of Chap. 4.

(a) Construct its dual problem by using the corresponding primal-dual form given in Table 6.13.

(b) Demonstrate that the answer in part (a) is correct (i.e., equality constraints yield dual variables without nonnegativity constraints) by first converting the primal problem to *our standard form* (see Table 6.11), then constructing its dual problem, and then converting this dual problem to the form obtained in part (a).

20. Consider the model without nonnegativity constraints given in Prob. 14 of Chap. 4.

(a) Construct its dual problem by using the corresponding primal-dual form given in Table 6.13.

(b) Demonstrate that the answer in part (a) is correct (i.e., variables without nonnegativity constraints yield equality constraints in the dual problem) by first converting the primal problem to *our standard form* (see Table 6.11), then constructing its dual problem, and then converting this dual problem to the form obtained in part (a).

21. Consider the dual problem for the Wyndor Glass Co. example given in Table 6.1. Demonstrate that *its* dual problem is the primal problem given in Table 6.1 by going through the conversion steps given in Table 6.12.

22. Consider the primal and dual problems in *our standard form* presented in matrix notation at the beginning of Sec. 6.1. Let $\mathbf{y}^*$ denote the optimal solution for this dual problem. Suppose that $\mathbf{b}$ is then replaced by $\bar{\mathbf{b}}$. Let $\bar{\mathbf{x}}$ denote the optimal solution for the new primal problem.

Prove that

$$\mathbf{c}\bar{\mathbf{x}} \leq \mathbf{y}^*\bar{\mathbf{b}}.$$

23. Consider the following problem.

$$\text{Maximize} \quad Z = 3x_1 + x_2 + 4x_3,$$

subject to

$$6x_1 + 3x_2 + 5x_3 \leq 25$$
$$3x_1 + 4x_2 + 5x_3 \leq 20$$

and

$$x_1 \geq 0, \quad x_2 \geq 0, \quad x_3 \geq 0.$$

The corresponding *final* set of equations yielding the optimal solution is

(0) $$Z + 2x_2 + \frac{1}{5}x_4 + \frac{3}{5}x_5 = 17.$$

(1) $$x_1 - \frac{1}{3}x_2 + \frac{1}{3}x_4 - \frac{1}{3}x_5 = \frac{5}{3}.$$

(2) $$x_2 + x_3 - \frac{1}{5}x_4 + \frac{2}{5}x_5 = 3.$$

(a) Identify the optimal solution from this set of equations.
(b) Construct the dual problem.
(c) Identify the optimal solution for the dual problem from the final set of equations. Verify this solution by solving the dual problem graphically.
(d) Suppose that the original problem is changed to

$$\text{Maximize} \quad Z = 3x_1 + 3x_2 + 4x_3,$$

subject to

$$6x_1 + 2x_2 + 5x_3 \leq 25$$
$$3x_1 + 3x_2 + 5x_3 \leq 20,$$

and

$$x_1 \geq 0, \quad x_2 \geq 0, \quad x_3 \geq 0.$$

Use duality theory to determine whether the previous optimal solution is still optimal.
(e) Use the *fundamental insight* presented in Sec. 5.3 to identify the new coefficients of x_2 in the final set of equations after it has been adjusted for the changes in the original problem given in part (d).
(f) Now suppose that the only change in the original problem is that a new variable x_{new} has been introduced into the model as follows:

$$\text{Maximize} \quad Z = 3x_1 + x_2 + 4x_3 + 2x_{new},$$

subject to

$$6x_1 + 3x_2 + 5x_3 + 3x_{new} \leq 25$$
$$3x_1 + 4x_2 + 5x_3 + 2x_{new} \leq 20,$$

and

$$x_1 \geq 0, \quad x_2 \geq 0, \quad x_3 \geq 0, \quad x_{new} \geq 0.$$

Use duality theory to determine whether the previous optimal solution, along with $x_{new} = 0$, is still optimal.
(g) Use the *fundamental insight* presented in Sec. 5.3 to identify the coefficient of x_{new} as a nonbasic variable in the final set of equations resulting from the introduction of x_{new} into the original model as shown in part (f).

24. Consider the model of Prob. 30. Use duality theory directly to determine whether the current basic solution remains optimal after each of the following independent changes.

(a) The change in part (e) of Prob. 30.
(b) The change in part (g) of Prob. 30.

25. Consider the model of Prob. 32. Use duality theory directly to determine whether the current basic solution remains optimal after each of the following independent changes.

(a) The change in part (c) of Prob. 32.
(b) The change in part (f) of Prob. 32.

26. Consider the model of Prob. 33. Use duality theory directly to determine whether the current basic solution remains optimal after each of the following independent changes.

(a) The change in part (b) of Prob. 33.
(b) The change in part (d) of Prob. 33.

27. Reconsider the model of Prob. 23. You are now to conduct sensitivity analysis by *independently* investigating each of the following six changes in the original model. For each change, use the sensitivity analysis procedure to revise the given *final* set of equations (in tableau form) and convert it to the proper form for identifying and evaluating the current basic solution. Then test this solution for feasibility and for optimality. (Do not reoptimize.)

(a) Change the right-hand side of constraint 1 to $b_1 = 10$.
(b) Change the right-hand side of constraint 2 to $b_2 = 10$.
(c) Change the coefficient of x_2 in the objective function to $c_2 = 5$.
(d) Change the coefficient of x_3 in the objective function to $c_3 = 2$.
(e) Change the coefficient of x_2 in constraint 2 to $a_{22} = 2$.
(f) Change the coefficient of x_1 in constraint 1 to $a_{11} = 8$.

28. Consider the following problem.

$$\text{Maximize} \quad Z = 2x_1 + 5x_2,$$

subject to

$$x_1 + 2x_2 \le 10$$
$$x_1 + 3x_2 \le 12,$$

and

$$x_1 \ge 0, \quad x_2 \ge 0.$$

Let x_3 and x_4 denote the slack variables for the respective functional constraints. After we apply the simplex method, the final simplex tableau is

Basic variable	Eq. no.	Z	x_1	x_2	x_3	x_4	Right side
				Coefficient of			
Z	0	1	0	0	1	1	22
x_1	1	0	1	0	3	−2	6
x_2	2	0	0	1	−1	1	2

While doing *post-optimality analysis*, you learn that all four b_i and c_j values used in the original model just given should be accurate to within ± 50 percent. Your job now is to perform sensitivity analysis to determine which of these parameters are *sensitive* in the sense that the current basic solution (perhaps with new values) does *not* remain optimal over this range of likely values for the parameter. For each sensitive parameter, also determine the range of values for which this basic solution is *not* optimal (but do not reoptimize).

(a) Perform this sensitivity analysis *graphically* on the original model.
(b) Now perform this sensitivity analysis as described and illustrated in Secs. 6.6 and 6.7 for b_1 and c_1. (*Hint:* For each parameter, begin by checking the two end points of the range of likely values. If the current basic solution is not optimal at either end point, use linear interpolation between the original final tableau and your new final tableau to determine the point at which it ceases to be optimal.)
(c) Repeat part (b) for b_2.
(d) Repeat part (b) for c_2.

29. Consider the following problem.

$$\text{Maximize} \quad Z = 3x_1 + 4x_2 + 8x_3,$$

subject to

$$2x_1 + 3x_2 + 5x_3 \leq 9$$
$$x_1 + 2x_2 + 3x_3 \leq 5,$$

and

$$x_1 \geq 0, \quad x_2 \geq 0, \quad x_3 \geq 0.$$

Let x_4 and x_5 denote the slack variables for the respective functional constraints. After we apply the simplex method, the final simplex tableau is

Basic variable	Eq. no.	Z	x_1	x_2	x_3	x_4	x_5	Right side
				Coefficient of				
Z	0	1	0	1	0	1	1	14
x_1	1	0	1	-1	0	3	-5	2
x_3	2	0	0	1	1	-1	2	1

While doing *post-optimality analysis*, you learn that some of the parameter values used in the original model just given are just rough estimates, where the range of likely values in each case is within ± 50 percent of the value used here. For each of these following parameters, perform sensitivity analysis to determine if the parameter is *sensitive* in the sense that the current basic solution (perhaps with new values) does *not* remain optimal over this range of likely values. If it is sensitive, also determine the range of values for which this basic solution is *not* optimal (but do not reoptimize). (*Hint:* See the hint for part (b) of Prob. 28.)

(a) The parameter b_2.
(b) The parameter c_2.
(c) The parameter a_{22}.
(d) The parameter c_3.
(e) The parameter a_{12}.
(f) The parameter b_1.

30.   Consider the following problem.

$$\text{Maximize}\quad Z = -5x_1 + 5x_2 + 13x_3,$$

subject to

$$-x_1 + x_2 + 3x_3 \le 20$$
$$12x_1 + 4x_2 + 10x_3 \le 90,$$

and

$$x_j \ge 0 \qquad (j = 1,2,3).$$

If we let x_4 and x_5 be the slack variables for the respective constraints, the simplex method yields the following *final* set of equations:

$$(0)\qquad\qquad Z \qquad\qquad + 2x_3 + 5x_4 \qquad\qquad = 100.$$
$$(1)\qquad\qquad -x_1 + x_2 + 3x_3 + x_4 \qquad\quad = 20.$$
$$(2)\qquad\qquad 16x_1 \qquad -2x_3 - 4x_4 + x_5 = 10.$$

Now you are to conduct sensitivity analysis by *independently* investigating each of the following nine changes in the original model. For each change, use the sensitivity analysis procedure to revise this set of equations (in tableau form) and convert it to the proper form for identifying and evaluating the current basic solution. Then test this solution for feasibility and for optimality. (Do not reoptimize.)

(*a*)   Change the right-hand side of constraint 1 to $b_1 = 30$.

(*b*)   Change the right-hand side of constraint 2 to $b_2 = 70$.

(*c*)   Change the right-hand sides to $\begin{bmatrix} b_1 \\ b_2 \end{bmatrix} = \begin{bmatrix} 10 \\ 100 \end{bmatrix}$.

(*d*)   Change the coefficient of x_3 in the objective function to $c_3 = 8$.

(*e*)   Change the coefficients of x_1 to $\begin{bmatrix} c_1 \\ a_{11} \\ a_{21} \end{bmatrix} = \begin{bmatrix} -2 \\ 0 \\ 5 \end{bmatrix}$.

(*f*)   Change the coefficients of x_2 to $\begin{bmatrix} c_2 \\ a_{12} \\ a_{22} \end{bmatrix} = \begin{bmatrix} 6 \\ 2 \\ 5 \end{bmatrix}$.

(*g*)   Introduce a new variable x_6 with coefficients $\begin{bmatrix} c_6 \\ a_{16} \\ a_{26} \end{bmatrix} = \begin{bmatrix} 10 \\ 3 \\ 5 \end{bmatrix}$.

(*h*)   Introduce a new constraint $2x_1 + 3x_2 + 5x_3 \le 50$. (Denote its slack variable by x_6.)

(*i*)   Change constraint 2 to $10x_1 + 5x_2 + 10x_3 \le 100$.

31.   Reconsider the model of Prob. 30. Suppose that we now want to apply parametric linear programming analysis to this problem. Specifically, the right-hand sides of the functional constraints are changed to

$$20 + 2\theta \qquad \text{(for constraint 1)}$$
$$90 - \theta \qquad \text{(for constraint 2)},$$

where θ can be assigned any positive or negative values.

Determine the lower and upper bounds on θ before the "final" basic feasible solution would become infeasible.

32. Consider the following problem.

$$\text{Maximize} \quad Z = 2x_1 - x_2 + x_3,$$

subject to

$$3x_1 + x_2 + x_3 \le 60$$
$$x_1 - x_2 + 2x_3 \le 10$$
$$x_1 + x_2 - x_3 \le 20,$$

and

$$x_1 \ge 0, \quad x_2 \ge 0, \quad x_3 \ge 0.$$

Let $x_4, x_5,$ and x_6 denote the slack variables for the respective constraints. After we apply the simplex method, the final simplex tableau is

Basic variable	Eq. no.	Z	x_1	x_2	x_3	x_4	x_5	x_6	Right side
Z	0	1	0	0	$\frac{3}{2}$	0	$\frac{3}{2}$	$\frac{1}{2}$	25
x_4	1	0	0	0	1	1	-1	-2	10
x_1	2	0	1	0	$\frac{1}{2}$	0	$\frac{1}{2}$	$\frac{1}{2}$	15
x_2	3	0	0	1	$-\frac{3}{2}$	0	$-\frac{1}{2}$	$\frac{1}{2}$	5

Coefficient of is the header spanning Z through x_6.

Now you are to conduct sensitivity analysis by *independently* investigating each of the following six changes in the original model. For each change, use the sensitivity analysis procedure to revise this set of equations (in tableau form) and convert it to the proper form for identifying and evaluating the current basic solution. Then test this solution for feasibility and for optimality. (Do not reoptimize.)

(a) Change the right-hand sides from $\begin{bmatrix} b_1 \\ b_2 \\ b_3 \end{bmatrix} = \begin{bmatrix} 60 \\ 10 \\ 20 \end{bmatrix}$ to $\begin{bmatrix} b_1 \\ b_2 \\ b_3 \end{bmatrix} = \begin{bmatrix} 70 \\ 20 \\ 10 \end{bmatrix}$.

(b) Change the coefficients of x_1 from $\begin{bmatrix} c_1 \\ a_{11} \\ a_{21} \\ a_{31} \end{bmatrix} = \begin{bmatrix} 2 \\ 3 \\ 1 \\ 1 \end{bmatrix}$ to $\begin{bmatrix} c_1 \\ a_{11} \\ a_{21} \\ a_{31} \end{bmatrix} = \begin{bmatrix} 1 \\ 2 \\ 2 \\ 0 \end{bmatrix}$.

(c) Change the coefficients of x_3 from $\begin{bmatrix} c_3 \\ a_{13} \\ a_{23} \\ a_{33} \end{bmatrix} = \begin{bmatrix} 1 \\ 1 \\ 2 \\ -1 \end{bmatrix}$ to $\begin{bmatrix} c_3 \\ a_{13} \\ a_{23} \\ a_{33} \end{bmatrix} = \begin{bmatrix} 2 \\ 3 \\ 1 \\ -2 \end{bmatrix}$.

(d)   Change the objective function to $Z = 3x_1 - 2x_2 + 3x_3$.

(e)   Introduce a new constraint $3x_1 - 2x_2 + x_3 \leq 30$. (Denote its slack variable by x_7).

(f)   Introduce a new variable x_8 with coefficients

$$\begin{bmatrix} c_8 \\ a_{18} \\ a_{28} \\ a_{38} \end{bmatrix} = \begin{bmatrix} -1 \\ -2 \\ 1 \\ 2 \end{bmatrix}.$$

33.   Consider the following problem.

$$\text{Maximize} \quad Z = 2x_1 + 7x_2 - 3x_3,$$

subject to

$$x_1 + 3x_2 + 4x_3 \leq 30$$
$$x_1 + 4x_2 - x_3 \leq 10,$$

and

$$x_1 \geq 0, \quad x_2 \geq 0, \quad x_3 \geq 0.$$

Letting x_4 and x_5 be the slack variables for the respective constraints, the simplex method yields the following *final* set of equations:

(0) $Z + x_2 + x_3 \qquad + 2x_5 = 20.$

(1) $\quad - x_2 + 5x_3 + x_4 - x_5 = 20.$

(2) $x_1 + 4x_2 - x_3 \qquad + x_5 = 10.$

Now you are to conduct sensitivity analysis by *independently* investigating each of the following seven changes in the original model. For each change, use the sensitivity analysis procedure to revise this set of equations (in tableau form) and convert it to the proper form for identifying and evaluating the current basic solution. Then test this solution for feasibility and for optimality. (Do not reoptimize.)

(a)   Change the right-hand sides to $\begin{bmatrix} b_1 \\ b_2 \end{bmatrix} = \begin{bmatrix} 20 \\ 30 \end{bmatrix}.$

(b)   Change the coefficients of x_3 to $\begin{bmatrix} c_3 \\ a_{13} \\ a_{23} \end{bmatrix} = \begin{bmatrix} -2 \\ 3 \\ -2 \end{bmatrix}.$

(c)   Change the coefficients of x_1 to $\begin{bmatrix} c_1 \\ a_{11} \\ a_{21} \end{bmatrix} = \begin{bmatrix} 4 \\ 3 \\ 2 \end{bmatrix}.$

(d)   Introduce a new variable x_6 with coefficients $\begin{bmatrix} c_6 \\ a_{16} \\ a_{26} \end{bmatrix} = \begin{bmatrix} 3 \\ 1 \\ 2 \end{bmatrix}.$

(e)   Change the objective function to $Z = x_1 + 5x_2 - 2x_3$.

(*f*) Introduce a new constraint $3x_1 + 2x_2 + 3x_3 \leq 25$. (Denote its slack variable by x_7.)

(*g*) Change constraint 2 to $x_1 + 2x_2 + 2x_3 \leq 35$.

34. Reconsider the model of Prob. 33. Suppose that we now want to apply parametric linear programming analysis to this problem. Specifically, the right-hand sides of the functional constraints are changed to

$$30 + 3\theta \quad \text{(for constraint 1)}$$
$$10 - \theta \quad \text{(for constraint 2)},$$

where θ can be assigned any positive or negative values.

Determine the lower and upper bounds on θ before the "final" basic feasible solution would become infeasible.

35. Consider the following problem.

$$\text{Maximize} \quad Z = 2x_1 - x_2 + x_3,$$

subject to

$$3x_1 - 2x_2 + 2x_3 \leq 15$$
$$-x_1 + x_2 + x_3 \leq 3$$
$$x_1 - x_2 + x_3 \leq 4,$$

and

$$x_1 \geq 0, \quad x_2 \geq 0, \quad x_3 \geq 0.$$

If we let x_4, x_5, and x_6 be the slack variables for the respective constraints, the simplex method yields the following *final* set of equations:

(0)	$Z \quad 2x_3 + x_4 + x_5 $	$= 18.$
(1)	$x_2 + 5x_3 + x_4 + 3x_5 $	$= 24.$
(2)	$2x_3 \quad + x_5 + x_6 =$	$7.$
(3)	$x_1 + 4x_3 + x_4 + 2x_5 $	$= 21.$

Now you are to conduct sensitivity analysis by *independently* investigating each of the following eight changes in the original model. For each change, use the sensitivity analysis procedure to revise this set of equations (in tableau form) and convert it to the proper form for identifying and evaluating the current basic solution. Then test this solution for feasibility and for optimality. (Do not reoptimize.)

(*a*) Change the right-hand sides to $\begin{bmatrix} b_1 \\ b_2 \\ b_3 \end{bmatrix} = \begin{bmatrix} 10 \\ 4 \\ 2 \end{bmatrix}$.

(*b*) Change the coefficient of x_3 in the objective function to $c_3 = 2$.

(*c*) Change the coefficient of x_1 in the objective function to $c_1 = 3$.

(*d*) Change coefficients of x_3 to $\begin{bmatrix} c_3 \\ a_{13} \\ a_{23} \\ a_{33} \end{bmatrix} = \begin{bmatrix} 4 \\ 3 \\ 2 \\ 1 \end{bmatrix}$.

(e)   Change coefficients of x_1 *and* x_2 to

$$\begin{bmatrix} c_1 \\ a_{11} \\ a_{21} \\ a_{31} \end{bmatrix} = \begin{bmatrix} 1 \\ 1 \\ -2 \\ 3 \end{bmatrix} \quad \text{and} \quad \begin{bmatrix} c_2 \\ a_{12} \\ a_{22} \\ a_{32} \end{bmatrix} = \begin{bmatrix} -2 \\ -1 \\ 3 \\ 2 \end{bmatrix}, \text{respectively.}$$

(f)   Change the objective function to $Z = 5x_1 + x_2 + 3x_3$.

(g)   Change constraint 1 to $2x_1 - x_2 + 4x_3 \le 12$.

(h)   Introduce a new constraint $2x_1 + x_2 + 3x_3 \le 60$. (Denote its slack variable by x_7.)

36.   Reconsider part (d) of Prob. 35. Use duality theory directly to determine whether the original optimal solution is still optimal.

37.   Reconsider the model of Prob. 35. Suppose that you now have the option of making tradeoffs in the profitability of the first two activities, whereby the objective function coefficient of x_1 can be increased by any amount by simultaneously decreasing the objective function coefficient of x_2 by the same amount. Thus the alternative choices of the objective function are

$$Z(\theta) = (2 + \theta)x_1 - (1 + \theta)x_2 + x_3,$$

where any nonnegative value of θ can be chosen.

Determine the upper bound on θ before the original optimal solution would become nonoptimal. Then determine the best choice of θ over this range.

38.   Consider the following problem.

$$\text{Minimize} \quad y_0 = 5y_1 + 4y_2,$$

subject to

$$4y_1 + 3y_2 \ge 4$$
$$2y_1 + y_2 \ge 3$$
$$y_1 + 2y_2 \ge 1$$
$$y_1 + y_2 \ge 2,$$

and

$$y_1 \ge 0, \quad y_2 \ge 0.$$

Because this *primal* problem has more functional constraints than variables, suppose that the simplex method has been applied directly to its *dual* problem. If we let x_5 and x_6 denote the slack variables for this dual problem, the resulting *final* simplex tableau is

Basic variable	Eq. no.	Z	x_1	x_2	x_3	x_4	x_5	x_6	Right side
Z	0	1	3	0	2	0	1	1	9
x_2	1	0	1	1	-1	0	1	-1	1
x_4	2	0	2	0	3	1	-1	2	3

For each of the following independent changes in the original primal model, you now are to conduct sensitivity analysis by *directly* investigating the effect on the *dual* problem and then inferring the complementary effect on the primal problem. For each change, apply the procedure for sensitivity analysis summarized at the end of Sec. 6.6 to the *dual* problem (do *not* reoptimize), and then give your conclusions as to whether the current basic solution for the *primal* problem still is feasible and whether it still is optimal. Then check your conclusions by a direct *graphical* analysis of the *primal* problem.

(a) Change the objective function to $y_0 = 3y_1 + 5y_2$.
(b) Change the right-hand sides of the functional constraints to 3, 5, 2, and 3, respectively.
(c) Change the first constraint to $2y_1 + 4y_2 \geq 7$.
(d) Change the second constraint to $5y_1 + 2y_2 \geq 10$.

39. Consider the Wyndor Glass Co. problem described in Sec. 3.1. Suppose that, in addition to considering the introduction of two new products, management now is also considering changing the production rate of a certain old product that is still profitable. Refer to Table 3.1. The capacity used per unit production rate of this old product is 1, 4, and 3 for Plants 1, 2, and 3, respectively. Therefore, if we let θ denote the *change* (positive or negative) in the production rate of this old product, the right-hand side of the three functional constraints in Sec. 3.1 becomes $(4 - \theta)$, $(12 - 4\theta)$, and $(18 - 3\theta)$, respectively. Thus choosing a negative value of θ would free additional capacity for producing more of the two new products, whereas a positive value would have the opposite effect.

(a) Use a *parametric linear programming* formulation to determine the effect of different choices of θ on the optimal solution for the product mix of the two new products given in the final tableau of Table 4.8. In particular, use the *fundamental insight* of Sec. 5.3 to obtain expressions for Z and the basic variables $(x_3, x_2,$ and $x_1)$ in terms of θ, assuming that θ is sufficiently close to zero that this "final" basic solution still is feasible and thus optimal for the given value of θ.
(b) Now consider the broader question of the choice of θ along with the product mix for the two new products. What is the breakeven unit profit for the old product (in comparison with the two new products) below which its production rate should be decreased $(\theta < 0)$ in favor of the new products and above which its production rate should be increased $(\theta > 0)$ instead?
(c) If the unit profit is above this breakeven point, how much can the old product's production rate be increased before the "final" basic feasible solution would become infeasible?
(d) If the unit profit is below this breakeven point, how much can the old product's production rate be decreased (assuming its previous rate was larger than this decrease) before the "final" basic feasible solution would become infeasible?

40. Consider the following problem.

$$\text{Maximize} \quad Z = 2x_1 - x_2 + 3x_3,$$

subject to

$$x_1 + x_2 + x_3 = 3$$
$$x_1 - 2x_2 + x_3 \geq 1$$
$$2x_2 + x_3 \leq 2,$$

and

$$x_1 \geq 0, \quad x_2 \geq 0, \quad x_3 \geq 0.$$

Suppose that the Big M method (see Sec. 4.6) is used to obtain the initial (artificial) basic feasible solution. Let $\bar{x}_4$ be the artificial slack variable for the first constraint, x_5 the slack (surplus) variable for the second constraint, $\bar{x}_6$ the artificial variable for the second constraint, and x_7 the slack variable for the third constraint. The corresponding *final* set of equations yielding the optimal solution is

$$
\begin{aligned}
Z \quad + 5x_2 \quad\quad + (M+2)\bar{x}_4 \quad\quad + M\bar{x}_6 + x_7 &= 8 \\
x_1 - x_2 \quad\quad + \quad\quad \bar{x}_4 \quad\quad - x_7 &= 1 \\
3x_2 \quad + \quad\quad \bar{x}_4 + x_5 - \quad \bar{x}_6 + x_7 &= 2 \\
2x_2 + x_3 \quad\quad\quad\quad\quad + x_7 &= 2.
\end{aligned}
$$

Suppose that the original objective function is changed to $Z = 2x_1 + 3x_2 + 4x_3$, and that the original third constraint is changed to $2x_2 + x_3 \leq 1$. Use the sensitivity analysis procedure to revise the final set of equations (in tableau form) and convert it to the proper form for identifying and evaluating the current basic solution. Then test this solution for feasibility and for optimality. Reoptimize (if needed), starting from this final tableau, to find the new optimal solution.

41. Consider the transportation problem formulation and solution of the Metro Water District problem presented in Secs. 7.1 and 7.2 (see Tables 7.12 and 7.23). Adapt the sensitivity analysis procedure presented in Sec. 6.6 to conduct sensitivity analysis on this problem by *independently* investigating each of the following four changes in the original model. For each change, revise the final transportation simplex tableau and convert it (if necessary) to the proper form for identifying and evaluating the current basic solution. Then test this solution for feasibility and for optimality. (Do not reoptimize.)

(a) Change c_{34} from 23 to $c_{34} = 20$.
(b) Change c_{23} from 13 to $c_{23} = 16$.
(c) Decrease the supply from source 2 to 50 and decrease the demand at destination 5 to 50.
(d) Increase the supply at source 2 to 80 and increase the demand at destination 2 to 40.

■ CHAPTER 7

Special Types of Linear Programming Problems

Chapter 3 emphasized the wide applicability of linear programming. We continue to broaden our horizons in this chapter by discussing some particularly important types of linear programming problems. These special types share several key characteristics. The first is that they all arise frequently in practice in a variety of contexts. They also tend to require a very large number of constraints and variables, so a straightforward computer application of the simplex method may require an exorbitant computational effort. Fortunately, another characteristic is that most of the a_{ij} coefficients in the constraints are zeros, and the relatively few nonzero coefficients appear in a distinctive pattern. As a result, it has been possible to develop special *streamlined* versions of the simplex method that achieve dramatic computational savings by exploiting this *special structure* of the problem. Therefore, it is important to become sufficiently familiar with these special types of problems so that you can recognize them when they arise and apply the proper computational procedure.

To describe special structures, we shall introduce the table (or matrix) of constraint coefficients shown in Table 7.1, where a_{ij} is the coefficient of the jth variable in the ith functional constraint. Later, portions of the table containing only coefficients equal to zero will be indicated by leaving them blank, whereas blocks containing nonzero coefficients will be shaded darker.

Probably the most important special type of linear programming problem is the so-called *transportation problem*, and we shall describe it first. Its special solution procedure also will be presented, partially to illustrate the kind of streamlining of the simplex method that can be obtained by exploiting special

Table 7.1 **Table of constraint coefficients for linear programming**

$$A = \begin{bmatrix} a_{11} & a_{12} & \cdots & a_{1n} \\ a_{21} & a_{22} & \cdots & a_{2n} \\ \vdots & \vdots & & \vdots \\ a_{m1} & a_{m2} & \cdots & a_{mn} \end{bmatrix}$$

structure in the problem. Next we shall present two special types of linear programming problems (the *transshipment problem* and the *assignment problem*) that are closely related to the transportation problem, and finally we shall describe a special type that frequently arises in multidivisional organizations.

7.1 The Transportation Problem

PROTOTYPE EXAMPLE

One of the main products of the *P & T Company* is canned peas. The peas are prepared at three canneries (near Bellingham, Washington; Eugene, Oregon; and Albert Lea, Minnesota) and then shipped by truck to four distributing warehouses (in Sacramento, California; Salt Lake City, Utah; Rapid City, South Dakota; and Albuquerque, New Mexico) in the western United States, as shown in Fig. 7.1. Because the shipping costs are a major expense, management is initiating a study to reduce them as much as possible. For the upcoming season, an estimate has been made of what the output will be from each cannery, and each warehouse has been allocated a certain amount from the total supply of peas. This information (in units of truckloads), along with the shipping cost per truckload for each cannery-warehouse combination, is given in Table 7.2. Thus there are a total of 300 truckloads to be shipped. The problem now is to determine which plan for assigning these shipments to the various cannery-warehouse combinations would *minimize total shipping costs*.

This is actually a linear programming problem of the *transportation problem* type. To formulate the model, let Z denote total shipping cost, and let x_{ij}

Table 7.2 **Shipping data for P & T Co.**

Shipping cost ($) per truckload

	Warehouse				
	1	2	3	4	Output
Cannery 1	464	513	654	867	75
Cannery 2	352	416	690	791	125
Cannery 3	995	682	388	685	100
Allocation	80	65	70	85	

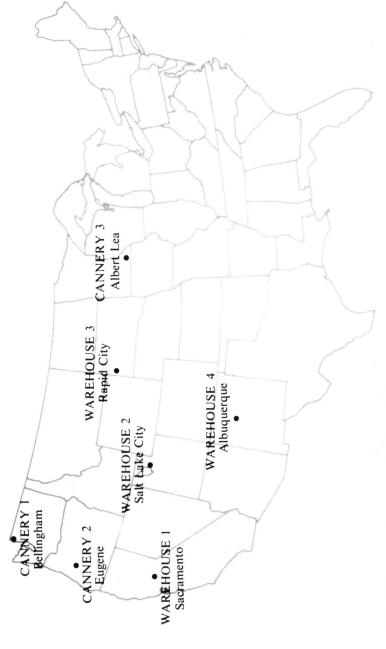

Figure 7.1 **Location of canneries and warehouses for the P & T Co.**

Table 7.3 **Table of constraint coefficients for the P & T Co.**

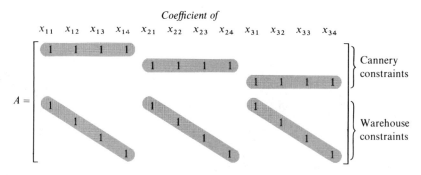

$(i = 1,2,3; j = 1,2,3,4)$ be the number of truckloads to be shipped from cannery i to warehouse j. Thus the objective is to choose the values of these 12 decision variables (the x_{ij}) so as to

$$\text{Minimize } Z = 464x_{11} + 513x_{12} + 654x_{13} + 867x_{14} + 352x_{21} + 416x_{22}$$
$$+ 690x_{23} + 791x_{24} + 995x_{31} + 682x_{32} + 388x_{33} + 685x_{34},$$

subject to the constraints

$$
\begin{array}{llll}
x_{11} + x_{12} + x_{13} + x_{14} & & & = 75 \\
x_{21} + x_{22} + x_{23} + x_{24} & & & = 125 \\
x_{31} + x_{32} + x_{33} + x_{34} & & & = 100 \\
x_{11} & + x_{21} & + x_{31} & = 80 \\
x_{12} & + x_{22} & + x_{32} & = 65 \\
x_{13} & + x_{23} & + x_{33} & = 70 \\
x_{14} & + x_{24} & + x_{34} & = 85,
\end{array}
$$

and

$$x_{ij} \geq 0 \quad (i = 1,2,3; j = 1,2,3,4).$$

Table 7.3 shows the constraint coefficients. As you will see next, it is the special structure in the pattern of these coefficients that distinguishes this problem as a transportation problem, not its context.

By the way, the optimal solution for this problem is $x_{11} = 0$, $x_{12} = 20$, $x_{13} = 0$, $x_{14} = 55$, $x_{21} = 80$, $x_{22} = 45$, $x_{23} = 0$, $x_{24} = 0$, $x_{31} = 0$, $x_{32} = 0$, $x_{33} = 70$, $x_{34} = 30$. When you learn the optimality test that appears in Sec. 7.2, you will be able to verify this yourself (see Prob. 8).

THE TRANSPORTATION PROBLEM MODEL

To describe the general model for the transportation problem, we need to use terms that are considerably less specific than those for the components of the

Table 7.4 **Terminology for the transportation problem**

Prototype example	General problem
Truckloads of canned peas	Units of a commodity
Three canneries	m sources
Four warehouses	n destinations
Output from cannery i	s_i supply from source i
Allocation to warehouse j	d_j demand at destination j
Shipping cost per truckload from cannery i to warehouse j	c_{ij} cost per unit distributed from source i to destination j

prototype example. In particular, the general transportation problem is concerned (literally or figuratively) with distributing *any* commodity from *any* group of supply centers, called **sources**, to *any* group of receiving centers, called **destinations**, in such a way as to minimize total distribution costs. The correspondence in terminology between the prototype example and the general problem is summarized in Table 7.4. Thus, in general, source i ($i = 1,2,\ldots,m$) has a supply of s_i units to distribute to the destinations, and destination j ($j = 1,2,\ldots,n$) has a demand for d_j units to be received from the sources. A basic assumption is that the cost of distributing units from source i to destination j is directly proportional to the number distributed, where c_{ij} denotes the cost per unit distributed. As for the prototype example, these input data can be summarized conveniently in the **cost and requirements table** shown in Table 7.5.

Letting Z be total distribution cost and x_{ij} ($i = 1,2,\ldots,m; j = 1,2,\ldots,n$) be the number of units to be distributed from source i to destination j, the linear programming formulation of this problem becomes

$$\text{Minimize} \quad Z = \sum_{i=1}^{m} \sum_{j=1}^{n} c_{ij} x_{ij},$$

subject to

$$\sum_{j=1}^{n} x_{ij} = s_i, \quad \text{for } i = 1, 2, \ldots, m$$

$$\sum_{i=1}^{m} x_{ij} = d_j, \quad \text{for } j = 1, 2, \ldots, n$$

and

$$x_{ij} \geq 0, \quad \text{for all } i \text{ and } j.$$

Note that the resulting table of constraint coefficients has the special structure shown in Table 7.6. *Any* linear programming problem that fits this special formulation is of the transportation problem type, regardless of its physical context. In fact, there have been numerous applications unrelated to transportation that have been fitted to this special structure, as we shall illustrate in the next example. (The *assignment problem* described in Sec. 7.4 is an additional

Table 7.5 **Cost and requirements table for the transportation problem**

Cost per unit distributed

		Destination				
		1	2	$\cdots$	n	Supply
Source	1	c_{11}	c_{12}	$\cdots$	c_{1n}	s_1
	2	c_{21}	c_{22}	$\cdots$	c_{2n}	s_2
	$\vdots$	$\vdots$	$\vdots$	$\cdots$	$\vdots$	$\vdots$
	m	c_{m1}	c_{m2}	$\cdots$	c_{mn}	s_m
Demand		d_1	d_2	$\cdots$	d_n	

Table 7.6 **Table of constraint coefficients for the transportation problem.**

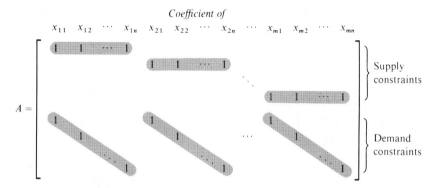

example.) This is one of the reasons why the transportation problem is generally considered the most important special type of linear programming problem.

For many applications, the supply and demand quantities in the model (the s_i and d_j) have integer values, and implementation will require that the distribution quantities (the x_{ij}) also have integer values. Fortunately, because of the special structure shown in Table 7.6, if such a model has any feasible solution, it *always* will have an optimal solution with just integer values, and this solution can be found by the solution procedure described in Sec. 7.2. Therefore, it is unnecessary to add a constraint to the model that the x_{ij} must have integer values.

It should be carefully noted that the model has feasible solutions only if

$$\sum_{i=1}^{m} s_i = \sum_{j=1}^{n} d_j.$$

This fact may be verified by observing that the constraints require that both

$$\sum_{i=1}^{m} s_i \quad \text{and} \quad \sum_{j=1}^{n} d_j \quad \text{equal} \quad \sum_{i=1}^{m}\sum_{j=1}^{n} x_{ij}.$$

This condition that the total supply must equal the total demand merely requires

Table 7.7 **Production scheduling data for Northern Airplane Co.**

Month	Scheduled installations	Maximum production	Unit cost* of production	Unit cost* of storage
1	10	25	1.08	0.015
2	15	35	1.11	0.015
3	25	30	1.10	0.015
4	20	10	1.13	

* Cost is expressed in million of dollars.

that the system be in balance. If the problem has physical significance and this condition is not met, it usually means that either s_i or d_j actually represents a *bound* rather than an exact requirement. If this is the case, a fictitious "source" or "destination" (called the *dummy source* or the *dummy destination*) can be introduced to take up the slack in order to convert the inequalities into equalities and satisfy the feasibility condition. The next two examples illustrate how to do this conversion, as well as how to fit some other common variations into the transportation problem formulation.

EXAMPLE—PRODUCTION SCHEDULING The *Northern Airplane Company* builds commercial airplanes for various airline companies around the world. The last stage in the production process is to produce the jet engines and then to install them (a very fast operation) in the completed airplane frame. The company has been working under some contracts to deliver a considerable number of airplanes in the near future, and the production of the jet engines for these planes must now be scheduled for the next 4 months.

To meet the contracted dates for delivery, the company must supply engines for installation in the quantities indicated in the second column of Table 7.7. Thus the cumulative number of engines produced by the end of months 1, 2, 3, and 4 must be at least 10, 25, 50, and 70, respectively. The facilities that will be available for producing the engines vary according to other production, maintenance, and renovation work scheduled during this period. The resulting monthly differences in the maximum number that can be produced and the cost (in millions of dollars) of producing each one are given in the third and fourth columns of Table 7.7. Because of the variations in production costs, it may well be worthwhile to produce some of the engines a month or more before they are scheduled for installation, and this possibility is being considered. The drawback is that such engines must be stored until the scheduled installation (the airplane frames will not be ready early) at a storage cost of $15,000/month (including interest on expended capital) for each engine,[1] as shown in the last column of Table 7.7. Therefore, the production manager wants a schedule developed for the number

---

[1] For modeling purposes, assume that this storage cost is incurred at the *end of the month* for just those engines that are being held over into the next month. Thus engines that are produced in a given month for installation in the same month are assumed to incur no storage cost.

of engines to be produced in each of the 4 months so that the total of the production and storage costs will be minimized.

If we let x_j ($j = 1,2,3,4$) be the number of jet engines to be produced in month j, it is straightforward to formulate the problem in terms of only these decision variables as a linear programming problem that does not appear to be of the transportation problem type (see Prob. 16). Nevertheless, by adopting a different viewpoint, we can indeed formulate the problem as a transportation problem that requires *much* less effort to solve. This different viewpoint will describe the problem in terms of sources and destinations and then identify the corresponding x_{ij}, c_{ij}, s_i, and d_j. (See if you can do this before reading further.) Specifically, because the units being distributed are jet engines, each of which is to be scheduled for production in a particular month and then installed in a particular (perhaps different) month,

$$\text{Source } i = \text{production of jet engines in month } i \quad (i = 1,2,3,4)$$
$$\text{Destination } j = \text{installation of jet engines in month } j \quad (j = 1,2,3,4)$$

$x_{ij} = $ number of engines produced in month i for installation in month j

$c_{ij} = $ cost associated with each unit of x_{ij}

$$= \begin{cases} \text{cost per unit for production and any storage, if } i \le j \\ ?, \text{ if } i > j \end{cases}$$

$s_i = ?$

$d_j = $ number of scheduled installations in month j.

The corresponding (incomplete) cost and requirements table is given in Table 7.8. Thus it remains to identify the missing costs and the supplies.

Since it is impossible to produce engines in 1 month for installation in an earlier month, x_{ij} must be zero if $i > j$. Therefore, there is no real cost that can be associated with such x_{ij}. Nevertheless, in order to have a well-defined transportation problem to which a standard software package (solution procedure of

Table 7.8 Incomplete cost and requirements table for the Northern Airplane Co.

Cost per unit distributed

		Destination				
		1	*2*	*3*	*4*	*Supply*
	1	1.080	1.095	1.110	1.125	?
Source	2	?	1.110	1.125	1.140	?
	3	?	?	1.100	1.115	?
	4	?	?	?	1.130	?
Demand		10	15	25	20	

Sec. 7.2) can be applied, it is necessary to assign some value for the unidentified costs. Fortunately, we can use the *Big M method* introduced in Sec. 4.6 to assign this value. Thus we assign a *very* large number (denoted by M for convenience) to the unidentified entries in the cost table to force the corresponding values of x_{ij} to be zero in the final solution.

The numbers that need to be inserted into the supply column are not obvious because the "supplies," the amount produced in the respective months, are not fixed quantities. In fact, the objective is to solve for the most desirable values of these production quantities. Nevertheless, as we have said, it is necessary to assign some fixed number to every entry in the table, including those in the supply column, to have a transportation problem. A clue is provided by the fact that although the supply constraints are not present in the usual form, these constraints do exist in the form of upper bounds on the amount that can be supplied, namely,

$$x_{11} + x_{12} + x_{13} + x_{14} \le 25,$$
$$x_{21} + x_{22} + x_{23} + x_{24} \le 35,$$
$$x_{31} + x_{32} + x_{33} + x_{34} \le 30,$$
$$x_{41} + x_{42} + x_{43} + x_{44} \le 10.$$

The only change from the standard model for the transportation problem is that these constraints are in the form of inequalities instead of equations. To convert them to equations, introduce *slack variables* (see Sec. 4.2). In this context, the slack variables are allocations to a single **dummy destination** that represent the *unused production capacity* in the respective months. This change permits the supply in the transportation problem formulation to be the total production capacity in the given month. Furthermore, because the demand for the dummy destination is the total unused capacity, the sum of the supplies equals the sum of the demands, so that a feasible solution is obtainable. The cost entries associated with the dummy destination should be zero because there is no cost incurred by a fictional allocation.

The resulting final cost and requirements table is given in Table 7.9, with the

Table 7.9 Complete cost and requirements table for the Northern Airplane Co.

| | | \multicolumn{6}{c}{Cost per unit distributed} |
| | | \multicolumn{5}{c}{Destination} | |
		1	2	3	4	5(D)	Supply
Source	1	1.080	1.095	1.110	1.125	0	25
	2	M	1.110	1.125	1.140	0	35
	3	M	M	1.100	1.115	0	30
	4	M	M	M	1.130	0	10
Demand		10	15	25	20	30	

Table 7.10 **Water resources data for Metro Water District**

Cost ($) per acre foot

River \ City	Berdoo	Los Devils	San Go	Hollyglass	Supply
Colombo River	16	13	22	17	50
Sacron River	14	13	19	15	60
Calorie River	19	20	23	—	50
Min. needed	30	70	0	10	(in units of
Requested	50	70	30	∞	million acre feet)

dummy destination labeled as destination 5(D). Using this formulation, it is quite easy to find the optimal production schedule by the solution procedure described in Sec. 7.2. (See Prob. 15 and its answer.)

EXAMPLE—DISTRIBUTION OF WATER RESOURCES The *Metro District* is an agency that administers the distribution of water in a certain large geographic region. The region is fairly arid, so the District must purchase and bring in water from outside the region. The sources of this imported water are the Colombo, Sacron, and Calorie Rivers. The District then resells the water to users in its region. Its main customers are the water departments of the cities of Berdoo, Los Devils, San Go, and Hollyglass. It is possible to supply any of these cities with water brought in from any of the three rivers, with one exception that no provision has been made to supply Hollyglass with Calorie River water. However, because of the geographic layouts of the viaducts and the cities in the region, the cost to the District of supplying water depends upon both the source of the water and the city being supplied. The variable cost per acre foot of water (in dollars) for each combination of river and city is given in Table 7.10. Despite these variations, the price per acre foot charged by the District is independent of the source of the water and is the same for all cities.

The management of the District is now faced with the problem of how to allocate the available water during the upcoming summer season. Using units of 1 million acre feet, the amounts available from the three rivers are given in the right-hand column of Table 7.10. The District is committed to providing a certain minimum amount to meet the essential needs of each city (with the exception of San Go, which has an independent source of water), as shown in the *min. needed* row of the table. The *requested* row indicates that Los Devils desires no more than the minimum amount, but that Berdoo would like to buy as much as 20 more, San Go would buy up to 30 more, and Hollyglass will take as much as it can get.

Management wishes to allocate *all* the available water from the three rivers to the four cities in such a way as to at least meet the essential needs of each city while minimizing the total cost to the District.

FORMULATION Table 7.10 already is close to the proper form for a cost and requirements table, with the rivers being the sources and the cities being the destinations. However, the one basic difficulty is that it is not clear what the demands at the destinations should be. The amount to be received at each destination (except Los Devils) actually is a decision variable, with both a lower and an upper bound. (This upper bound is the amount requested unless the request exceeds the total supply remaining after meeting the minimum needs of the other cities, in which case this *remaining supply* becomes the upper bound. Thus insatiably thirsty Hollyglass has an upper bound of $[50 + 60 + 50] - [30 + 70] = 60$ million acre feet.) Unfortunately, the demand quantities in the cost and requirements table of a transportation problem *must be constants*, not bounded decision variables.

To begin resolving this difficulty, temporarily suppose that it is not necessary to satisfy the minimum needs from these rivers, so that the upper bounds are the only constraints on amounts to be allocated to the cities. In this circumstance, can the requested allocations be viewed as the demand quantities for a transportation problem formulation? After one adjustment, yes! (Do you see already what the needed adjustment is?) The situation is analogous to Northern Airplane Company's production scheduling problem, where there was *excess supply capacity*. Now there is *excess demand capacity*. Consequently, rather than introducing a *dummy destination* to "receive" the unused supply capacity, the adjustment needed here is to introduce a **dummy source** to "send" the *unused demand capacity*. The imaginary supply quantity for this dummy source would be the amount by which the sum of the demands exceeds the sum of the real supplies: $(50 + 70 + 30 + 60) - (50 + 60 + 50) = 50$. This formulation yields the cost and requirements table shown in Table 7.11, which uses units of million acre feet and million dollars. (Since Calorie River water cannot be used to supply Hollyglass, the Big M method is used to prevent any such allocation.)

Now let us see how we can take each city's minimum needs into account in this kind of formulation. Because San Go has no minimum need, it is already all set. Similarly, the formulation for Hollyglass does not require any adjustments because its demand (60) exceeds the dummy source's supply (50) by 10, so the

Table 7.11 **Cost and requirements table without minimum needs for Metro Water District**

Cost per unit distributed

		Destination				Supply
		Berdoo	Los Devils	San Go	Hollyglass	
Source	Colombo R.	16	13	22	17	50
	Sacron R.	14	13	19	15	60
	Calorie R.	19	20	23	M	50
	Dummy	0	0	0	0	50
Demand		50	70	30	60	

Table 7.12 **Cost and requirements table for Metro Water District**

Cost per unit distributed

			Destination					
			B.(min.) 1	B.(extra) 2	L.D. 3	S.G. 4	H. 5	Supply
	Col. R.	1	16	16	13	22	17	50
Source	Sac. R.	2	14	14	13	19	15	60
	Cal. R.	3	19	19	20	23	M	50
	Dummy	4(D)	M	0	M	0	0	50
Demand			30	20	70	30	60	

amount supplied to Hollyglass from the *real* sources will be *at least 10* in any feasible solution. Consequently, its minimum need of 10 from the rivers is guaranteed. (If this coincidence had not occurred, Hollyglass would need the same adjustments that we shall have to make for Berdoo.)

Los Devils' minimum need equals its requested allocation, so its *entire* demand of 70 must be filled from the real sources rather than the dummy source. This requirement calls for the Big M method! Assigning a huge unit cost of M to the allocation from the dummy source to Los Devils ensures that this allocation will be zero in an optimal solution.

Finally, consider Berdoo. In contrast to the case of Hollyglass, the dummy source has an adequate (fictional) supply to "provide" at least some of Berdoo's minimum need in addition to its extra requested amount. Therefore, since Berdoo's minimum need is 30, adjustments must be made to prevent the dummy source from contributing more than 20 to Berdoo's total demand of 50. This adjustment is accomplished by splitting Berdoo into two destinations, one having a demand of 30 with a unit cost of M for any allocation from the dummy source and the other having a demand of 20 with a unit cost of zero for the dummy source allocation. This formulation gives the final cost and requirements table shown in Table 7.12.

This problem will be solved in the next section to illustrate the solution procedure presented there.

7.2 A Streamlined Simplex Method for the Transportation Problem

Because the transportation problem is just a special type of linear programming problem, it can be solved by applying the simplex method as described in Chap. 4. However, you will see in this section that some tremendous computational shortcuts can be obtained in this method by exploiting the special structure shown in Table 7.6. We shall refer to this streamlined procedure as the *transportation simplex method*.

As you read on, particularly note how the special structure is exploited to achieve great computational savings. Then bear in mind that comparable savings sometimes can be achieved by exploiting other types of special structures as well, including those described later in the chapter.

SETTING UP THE TRANSPORTATION SIMPLEX METHOD

To highlight the streamlining achieved by the transportation simplex method, let us first review how the general (unstreamlined) simplex method would set up the transportation problem in tabular form. After constructing the table of constraints (see Table 7.6), converting the objective function to maximization form, and using the Big M method to introduce artificial variables $z_1, z_2, \ldots, z_{m+n}$ into the $(m + n)$ respective equality constraints (see Sec. 4.6), typical columns of the simplex tableau would have the form shown in Table 7.13, where all entries *not shown* in these columns are *zeros*. [The one remaining adjustment before the first iteration of the simplex method is algebraically to eliminate the nonzero coefficients of the initial (artificial) basic variables in row 0.] After any subsequent iteration, row 0 then would have the form shown in Table 7.14. Because of the pattern of zeros and ones for the coefficients in Table 7.13, the *fundamental insight* presented in Sec. 5.3 implies that the u_i and v_j would have the interpretation

u_i = multiple of *original* row i that has been subtracted (directly or indirectly) from *original* row 0 by simplex method during all iterations leading to current simplex tableau,

Table 7.13 Original simplex tableau before applying simplex method to transportation problem

Basic variable	Eq. no.	Z	Coefficient of $\cdots x_{ij} \cdots z_i \cdots z_{m+j} \cdots$			Right side
Z	0	-1	c_{ij}	M	M	0
	1					
	$\vdots$					
z_i	i	0	1	1		s_i
	$\vdots$					
z_{m+j}	$m+j$	0	1		1	d_j
	$\vdots$					
	$m+n$					

Table 7.14 Row 0 of simplex tableau when applying simplex method to transportation problem

Basic variable	Eq. no.	Z	Coefficient of $\cdots x_{ij} \cdots z_i \cdots z_{m+j} \cdots$			Right side
Z	0	-1	$c_{ij} - u_i - v_j$	$M - u_i$	$M - v_j$	$-\sum_{i=1}^{m} s_i u_i - \sum_{j=1}^{n} d_j v_j$

v_j = multiple of *original* row $(m + j)$ that has been subtracted (directly or indirectly) from *original* row 0 by simplex method during all iterations leading to current simplex tableau.

You might recognize the u_i and v_j from Chap. 6 as being the *dual variables.*[1] If x_{ij} is a nonbasic variable, $(c_{ij} - u_i - v_j)$ is interpreted as the rate at which Z would change as x_{ij} is increased.

To lay the groundwork for simplifying this setup, recall what information is needed by the simplex method. In the initialization step, an initial basic feasible solution must be obtained, which is done artificially by introducing artificial variables as the initial basic variables and setting them equal to the s_i and d_j. The optimality test and part 1 of the iterative step (selecting an entering basic variable) require knowing the current row 0, which is obtained by subtracting a certain multiple of another row from the preceding row 0. Part 2 (determining the leaving basic variable) must identify the basic variable that reaches zero first as the entering basic variable is increased, which is done by comparing the current coefficients of the entering basic variable and the corresponding right side. Part 3 must determine the new basic feasible solution, which is found by subtracting certain multiples of one row from the other rows in the current simplex tableau.

Now, how does the *transportation simplex method* obtain the same information in much simpler ways? This story will unfold fully in the coming pages, but here are some preliminary answers.

First, *no artificial variables* are needed because a simple and convenient procedure (with several variations) is available for constructing an initial basic feasible solution.

Second, the current row 0 can be obtained *without using any other row* simply by calculating the current values of the u_i and v_j directly. Since each basic variable must have a coefficient of zero in row 0, the current u_i and v_j are obtained by solving the set of equations

$c_{ij} - u_i - v_j = 0$ for each i and j such that x_{ij} is a basic variable,

which can be done in a very straightforward way. (Note how the special structure in Table 7.13 makes this convenient way of obtaining row 0 possible by yielding $c_{ij} - u_i - v_j$ as the coefficient of x_{ij} in Table 7.14.

Third, the leaving basic variable can be identified in a simple way without (explicitly) using the coefficients of the entering basic variable. The reason is that the special structure of the problem makes it very easy to see how the solution must change as the entering basic variable is increased. As a result, the new basic feasible solution also can be identified immediately *without any algebraic manipulations* on the rows of the simplex tableau.

The grand conclusion is that *almost the entire simplex tableau* (and the work of maintaining it) *can be eliminated*! Besides the input data (the c_{ij}, s_i, and d_j

---

[1] It would be easier to recognize these variables as dual variables by relabeling all these variables as y_i and then changing all the signs in row 0 of Table 7.14 by converting the objective function back to its original minimization form.

Table 7.15 **Format of transportation simplex tableau**

		Destination				Supply	u_i
		1	*2*	$\cdots$	*n*		
Source	1	c_{11}	c_{12}	$\cdots$	c_{1n}	s_1	
	2	c_{21}	c_{22}	$\cdots$	c_{2n}	s_2	
	$\vdots$	$\vdots$	$\vdots$	$\vdots$	$\vdots$	$\vdots$	
	m	c_{m1}	c_{m2}		c_{mn}	s_m	
Demand		d_1	d_2	$\cdots$	d_n		
v_j							

Additional information to be added in each cell:

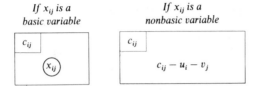

values), the only information needed by the transportation simplex method is the current basic feasible solution,[1] the current values of the u_i and v_j, and the resulting values of $(c_{ij} - u_i - v_j)$ for nonbasic variables x_{ij}. When you solve a problem by hand, it is convenient to record this information for each iteration in a **transportation simplex tableau**, such as shown in Table 7.15. (Note carefully that the values of x_{ij} and $(c_{ij} - u_i - v_j)$ are distinguished in these tableaux by circling the former but not the latter.)

You can gain a fuller appreciation for the great difference in efficiency and convenience between the simplex and the transportation simplex methods by applying them both to the same small problem (see Prob. 18). However, the difference becomes even more pronounced for large problems that must be solved on a computer. This pronounced difference is suggested somewhat by comparing the sizes of the simplex and the transportation simplex tableaux. Thus, for a transportation problem having m sources and n destinations, the simplex tableau would have $(m + n + 1)$ rows and $(m + 1)(n + 1)$ columns (excluding those to the left of the x_{ij} columns), and the transportation simplex tableau would have m rows and n columns (excluding the two extra informational rows and columns). Now try plugging in various values for m and n (for example, $m = 10$ and

---

[1] Since nonbasic variables are automatically zero, the current basic feasible solution is fully identified by recording just the values of the basic variables. We shall use this convention from now on.

$n = 100$ would be a rather typical middle-sized transportation problem), and note how the ratio of the number of cells in the simplex tableau to the number in the transportation simplex tableau increases as m and n increase.

INITIALIZATION STEP

Recall that the objective of the initialization step is to obtain an initial basic feasible solution. Because all the functional constraints in the transportation problem are *equality* constraints, the simplex method would obtain this solution by introducing artificial variables and using them as the initial basic variables, as described in Sec. 4.6. The resulting basic solution actually is feasible only for a revised version of the problem, so a number of iterations then are needed to drive these artificial variables to zero in order to reach the real basic feasible solutions. The transportation simplex method bypasses all this by instead using a simpler procedure to directly construct a real basic feasible solution on a transportation simplex tableau.

Before outlining this procedure we need to point out that the number of basic variables in any basic solution of a transportation problem is one fewer than you might expect. Although there are $(m + n)$ functional constraints, the number of basic variables is just $m + n - 1$. The reason is that these are equality constraints, and this set of $(m + n)$ equations has one *extra* (or *redundant*) equation that can be deleted without changing the feasible region; i.e., any one of the constraints is automatically satisfied whenever the other $m + n - 1$ constraints are satisfied. (This fact can be verified by showing that any supply constraint exactly equals the sum of the demand constraints minus the sum of the *other* supply constraints, and that any demand equation also can be reproduced by summing the supply equations and subtracting the other demand equations. See Prob. 19.) Therefore, any *basic feasible solution* appears on a transportation simplex tableau with exactly $(m + n - 1)$ circled *nonnegative* allocations, where the sum of the allocations for each row or column equals its supply or demand.[1]

The procedure for constructing an initial basic feasible solution selects the $(m + n - 1)$ basic variables one at a time. After each selection, a value that will satisfy one additional constraint (thereby eliminating that constraint's row or column from further consideration for providing allocations) is assigned to that variable. Thus, after $(m + n - 1)$ selections, an entire basic solution has been constructed in such a way as to satisfy all the constraints. A number of different criteria have been proposed for selecting the basic variables. We present and illustrate three of these criteria here after outlining the general procedure.

---

[1] However, note that any feasible solution with $(m + n - 1)$ nonzero variables is *not necessarily* a basic solution because it might be the weighted average of two or more degenerate basic feasible solutions (i.e., basic feasible solutions having some basic variables equal to zero). We need not be concerned about mislabeling such solutions as being basic, however, because the transportation simplex method constructs only legitimate basic feasible solutions.

General Procedure[1] for Constructing an Initial Basic Feasible Solution

To begin: All source rows and destination columns of the transportation simplex tableau are initially under consideration for providing a basic variable (allocation).

Step 1: From among the rows and columns still under consideration, select the next basic variable (allocation) according to some criterion.

Step 2: Make that allocation large enough to exactly use up the remaining supply in its row or the remaining demand in its column (whichever is smaller).

Step 3: Eliminate that row or column (whichever had the smaller remaining supply or demand) from further consideration. (If the row and column have the *same* remaining supply and demand, then arbitrarily select the *row* as the one to be eliminated. The column will be used later to provide a *degenerate* basic variable, i.e., a circled allocation of zero.)

Step 4: If only one row or only one column remains under consideration, then the procedure is completed by selecting every *remaining* variable (i.e., those variables that were neither previously selected to be basic nor eliminated from consideration by eliminating their row or column) associated with that row or column to be basic with the only feasible allocation. Otherwise, return to step 1.

Alternative Criteria for Step 1

1. *Northwest corner rule*: Begin by selecting x_{11} (i.e., start in the *northwest corner* of the transportation simplex tableau). Thereafter, if x_{ij} was the last basic variable selected, then next select $x_{i,j+1}$ (i.e., move one column to the *right*) if source i has any supply remaining. Otherwise, next select $x_{i+1,j}$ (i.e., move one row *down*).

EXAMPLE To make this description more concrete, we now illustrate the general procedure on the Metro Water District problem (see Table 7.12) with the northwest corner rule being used in step 1. Because $m = 4$ and $n = 5$ in this case, the procedure would find an initial basic feasible solution having $m + n - 1 = 8$ basic variables.

As shown in Table 7.16, the first allocation is $x_{11} = 30$, which exactly uses up the demand in column 1 (and eliminates this column from further consideration). This first iteration leaves a supply of 20 remaining in row 1, so next select $x_{1,1+1} = x_{12}$ to be a basic variable. Because this supply is no larger than the demand of 20 in column 2, all of it is allocated, $x_{12} = 20$, and this row is eliminated from further consideration. Therefore, select $x_{1+1,2} = x_{22}$ next. Because the remaining demand of 0 in column 2 is less than the supply of 60 in row 2, allocate $x_{22} = 0$ and eliminate column 2. Continuing in this manner, we

---

[1] In Sec. 4.1 we pointed out that the simplex method is an example of the algorithms (iterative solution procedures) so prevalent in operations research work. Note that this procedure also is an algorithm, where each successive execution of the (four) steps constitutes an iteration.

Table 7.16 **Initial basic feasible solution from northwest corner rule**

		Destination						
		1	*2*	*3*	*4*	*5*	*Supply*	u_i
	1	16 (30)	16 (20)	13	22	17	50	
Source	2	14	14 (0)	13 (60)	19	15	60	
	3	19	19	20 (10)	23 (30)	M (10)	50	
	4(D)	M	O	M	O	O (50)	50	
Demand		30	20	70	30	60		
v_j								

eventually obtain the entire *initial basic feasible solution* shown in Table 7.16 where arrows have been added to show the order in which the basic variables (allocations) were selected.

2. *Vogel's approximation method*: For each row and column remaining under consideration, calculate its **difference**, which is defined as *the arithmetic difference between the smallest and next-to-the-smallest unit cost (c_{ij}) still remaining in that row or column*. In that row or column having the *largest difference*, select the variable having the *smallest remaining unit cost*. (Ties for the largest difference may be broken arbitrarily.)

EXAMPLE Now let us apply the general procedure to the Metro Water District problem by using the criterion for Vogel's approximation method to select the next basic variable in step 1. With this criterion, it is more convenient to work with cost and requirements tables (rather than with complete transportation simplex tableaux), beginning with the one shown in Table 7.12. At each iteration, after calculating and displaying the *difference* for every row and column remaining under consideration, the largest difference is circled and the smallest unit cost in its row or column is enclosed in a box. The resulting selection (and value) of the variable having this unit cost as the next basic variable is indicated in the lower right-hand corner of the current table, along with the row or column thereby being eliminated from further consideration (see steps 2 and 3 of the general procedure). The table for the next iteration is exactly the same except for deleting this row or column and subtracting the last allocation from its supply or demand (whichever remains).

Applying this procedure to the Metro Water District problem yields the sequence of cost and requirements tables shown in Table 7.17, where the resulting initial basic feasible solution consists of the eight basic variables (allocations) given in the lower right-hand corner of the respective cost and requirements tables.

Table 7.17 Initial basic feasible solution from Vogel's approximation method

		Destination						Row
		1	2	3	4	5	Supply	difference
Source	1	16	16	13	22	17	50	3
	2	14	14	13	19	15	60	1
	3	19	19	20	23	M	50	0
	4(D)	M	0	M	$\boxed{0}$	0	50	0
Demand		30	20	70	30	60	Select $x_{44} = 30$	
Column difference		2	14	0	$\boxed{19}$	15	Eliminate column 4	

		Destination					Row
		1	2	3	5	Supply	difference
Source	1	16	16	13	17	50	3
	2	14	14	13	15	60	1
	3	19	19	20	M	50	0
	4(D)	M	0	M	$\boxed{0}$	20	0
Demand		30	20	70	60	Select $x_{45} = 20$	
Column difference		2	14	0	$\boxed{15}$	Eliminate row 4(D)	

		Destination				Row
		1	2	3	5	Supply	difference
Source	1	16	16	$\boxed{13}$	17	50	$\boxed{3}$
	2	14	14	13	15	60	1
	3	19	19	20	M	50	0
Demand		30	20	70	40	Select $x_{13} = 50$	
Column difference		2	2	0	2	Eliminate row 1	

		Destination				Row
		1	2	3	5	Supply	difference
Source	2	14	14	13	$\boxed{15}$	60	1
	3	19	19	20	M	50	0
Demand		30	20	20	40	Select $x_{25} = 40$	
Column difference		5	5	7	$\boxed{M-15}$	Eliminate column 5	

Table 7.17 (continued)

		Destination 1	Destination 2	Destination 3	Supply	Row difference
Source	2	14	14	[13]	20	1
	3	19	19	20	50	0
Demand		30	20	20	Select $x_{23} = 20$	
Column difference		5	5	(7)	Eliminate row 2	

		Destination 1	Destination 2	Destination 3	Supply
Source	3	19	19	20	50
Demand		30	20	0	Select $x_{31} = 30$
					$x_{32} = 20$
					$x_{33} = 0$

This example illustrates two relatively subtle features of the general procedure that warrant special attention. First, note that the final iteration selects *three* variables (x_{31}, x_{32}, and x_{33}) to become basic instead of the single selection made at the other iterations. The reason is that only *one* row (row 3) remains under consideration at this point. Therefore, step 4 of the general procedure says to select *every* remaining variable associated with row 3 to be basic.

Second, note that the allocation of $x_{23} = 20$ at the next-to-last iteration exhausts *both* the remaining supply in its row *and* the remaining demand in its column. However, rather than eliminate both the row and column from further consideration, step 3 says to eliminate *only the row*, saving the column to provide a *degenerate* basic variable later. Column 3 is, in fact, used for just this purpose at the final iteration when $x_{33} = 0$ is selected as one of the basic variables. For another illustration of this same phenomenon, see Table 7.16 where the allocation of $x_{12} = 20$ results in eliminating only row 1, so that column 2 is saved to provide a degenerate basic variable, $x_{22} = 0$, at the next iteration. (Although a zero allocation might seem irrelevant, it actually plays an important role since you will see soon that the transportation simplex method must know *all* $m + n - 1$ basic variables in the current basic feasible solution.)

3. *Russell's approximation method*: For each source row i remaining under consideration, determine its $\bar{u}_i$, which is the *largest* unit cost (c_{ij}) still remaining in that row. For each destination column j remaining under consideration, determine its $\bar{v}_j$, which is the *largest* unit cost (c_{ij}) still remaining in that column. For each variable x_{ij} not previously selected in these rows and columns, calculate $\Delta_{ij} = c_{ij} - \bar{u}_i - \bar{v}_j$. Select the variable having the *largest* (in absolute terms) *negative* value of Δ_{ij}. (Ties may be broken arbitrarily.)

Table 7.18 **Initial basic feasible solution from Russell's approximation method**

Iteration	$\bar{u}_1$	$\bar{u}_2$	$\bar{u}_3$	$\bar{u}_4$	$\bar{v}_1$	$\bar{v}_2$	$\bar{v}_3$	$\bar{v}_4$	$\bar{v}_5$	Largest negative Δ_{ij}	Allocation
1	22	19	M	M	M	19	M	23	M	$\Delta_{45} = -2M$	$x_{45} = 50$
2	22	19	M		19	19	20	23	M	$\Delta_{15} = -5 - M$	$x_{15} = 10$
3	22	19	23		19	19	20	23		$\Delta_{13} = -29$	$x_{13} = 40$
4		19	23		19	19	20	23		$\Delta_{23} = -26$	$x_{23} = 30$
5		19	23		19	19		23		$\Delta_{21} = -24*$	$x_{21} = 30$
6										Irrelevant	$x_{31} = 0$
											$x_{32} = 20$
											$x_{34} = 30$

* Tie with $\Delta_{22} = -24$ broken arbitrarily.

EXAMPLE Using the criterion for Russell's approximation method in step 1, we again apply the general procedure to the Metro Water District problem (see Table 7.12). The results, including the sequence of basic variables (allocations), are shown in Table 7.18. At iteration 1, the largest unit cost in row 1 is $\bar{u}_1 = 22$, the largest in column 1 is $\bar{v}_1 = M$, and so forth. Thus $\Delta_{11} = c_{11} - \bar{u}_1 - \bar{v}_1 = 16 - 22 - M = -6 - M$. Calculating all the Δ_{ij} for $i = 1, 2, 3, 4$ and $j = 1, 2, 3, 4, 5$ shows that $\Delta_{45} = 0 - 2M$ has the *largest negative* value, so $x_{45} = 50$ is selected as the first basic variable (allocation). This allocation exactly uses up the supply in row 4, so this row is eliminated from further consideration. Note that eliminating this row changes $\bar{v}_1$ and $\bar{v}_3$ for the next iteration. Therefore, the second iteration requires recalculating the Δ_{ij} with $j = 1, 3$, as well as eliminating $i = 4$. The largest negative value now is $\Delta_{15} = 17 - 22 - M = -5 - M$, so $x_{15} = 10$ becomes the second basic variable (allocation), eliminating column 5 from further consideration. (The subsequent iterations proceed similarly, but you may want to test your understanding by verifying the remaining allocations given in Table 7.18.)

Comparison of Alternative Criteria for Step 1

Now let us compare these three criteria for selecting the next basic variable. The main virtue of the northwest corner rule is that it is quick and easy. However, because it pays no attention to unit costs (c_{ij}), usually the solution obtained will be far from optimal. (Note in Table 7.16 that $x_{35} = 10$ even though $c_{35} = M$.) Expending a little more effort to find a good initial basic feasible solution might greatly reduce the number of iterations then required by the transportation simplex method to reach an optimal solution (see Probs. 6 and 10). Finding such a solution is the objective of the other two criteria. Vogel's approximation method has been a popular criterion for many years,[1] partially because it is relatively easy to implement by hand. Because *difference* represents the minimum extra unit cost

[1] Reinfeld, N. V. and W. R. Vogel: *Mathematical Programming*, Prentice-Hall, Englewood Cliffs, N.J., 1958.

Table 7.19 **Initial transportation simplex tableau (before obtaining the $c_{ij} - u_i - v_j$) from Russell's approximation method**

Iteration 0		Destination 1	2	3	4	5	Supply	u_i
	1	16	16	13 (40)	22	17 (10)	50	
Source	2	14 (30)	14	13 (30)	19	15	60	
	3	19 (0)	19 (20)	20	23 (30)	M	50	
	4(D)	M	0	M	0	0 (50)	50	
Demand		30	20	70	30	60		
v_j								

incurred by failing to make an allocation to the cell having the smallest unit cost in that row or column, this criterion does take costs into account in an effective way. Russell's approximation method provides another excellent criterion[1] that is still quick to implement on a computer (although not manually). Although more experimentation is required to determine which is more effective *on the average*, this criterion *frequently* does obtain a better solution. (For a large problem, it may be worthwhile to apply *both* criteria and then use the better solution obtained to start the iterations of the transportation simplex method.) One distinct advantage of Russell's approximation method is that it is patterned directly after part 1 of the iterative step for the transportation simplex method (as you will see soon), which somewhat simplifies the overall computer code. In particular, the $\bar{u}_i$ and $\bar{v}_j$ have been defined in such a way that the relative values of the $(c_{ij} - \bar{u}_i - \bar{v}_j)$ *estimate* the relative values of the $c_{ij} - u_i - v_j$ that will be obtained when the transportation simplex method reaches the optimal solution.

We now shall use the initial basic feasible solution obtained in Table 7.18 by Russell's approximation method to illustrate the remainder of the transportation simplex method. Thus our *initial transportation simplex tableau* (before solving for the u_i and v_j) is the one shown in Table 7.19.

The next step is to check whether this initial solution is optimal by applying the *optimality test*.

---

[1] Russell, Edward J.: "Extension of Dantzig's Algorithm to Finding an Initial Near-Optimal Basis for the Transportation Problem," *Operations Research*, **17**: 187–191, 1969.

OPTIMALITY TEST

Using the notation of Table 7.14, we can reduce the standard optimality test for the simplex method (see Sec. 4.3) to the following for the transportation problem:

Optimality test: A basic feasible solution is optimal if and only if $(c_{ij} - u_i - v_j) \geq 0$ for every (i,j) such that x_{ij} is nonbasic.[1]

Thus the only work required by the optimality test is the derivation of the values of the u_i and v_j for the current basic feasible solution and then the calculation of these $(c_{ij} - u_i - v_j)$.

Since $(c_{ij} - u_i - v_j)$ is required to be zero if x_{ij} is a basic variable, the u_i and v_j satisfy the set of equations

$$c_{ij} = u_i + v_j \quad \text{for each } (i,j) \text{ such that } x_{ij} \text{ is basic.}$$

There are $(m + n - 1)$ basic variables, and so there are $(m + n - 1)$ of these equations. Since the number of unknowns (the u_i and v_j) is $(m + n)$, one of these variables can be assigned a value arbitrarily without violating the equations. (The rule we shall adopt is to select the u_i that has the largest number of allocations in its row and assign it the value of zero.) Because of the simple structure of these equations, it is then very simple to solve for the remaining variables algebraically.

To demonstrate, we give each equation that corresponds to a basic variable in our initial basic feasible solution.

$$
\begin{aligned}
&x_{31}: 19 = u_3 + v_1 && x_{23}: 13 = u_2 + v_3 \\
&x_{32}: 19 = u_3 + v_2 && x_{13}: 13 = u_1 + v_3 \\
&x_{34}: 23 = u_3 + v_4 && x_{15}: 17 = u_1 + v_5 \\
&x_{21}: 14 = u_2 + v_1 && x_{45}: \ \ 0 = u_4 + v_5
\end{aligned}
$$

Setting $u_3 = 0$ (since row 3 of Table 7.19 has the largest number of allocations, 3) and moving down the equations one at a time immediately gives $v_1 = 19$; $v_2 = 19$; $v_4 = 23$; $u_2 = 14 - 19 = -5$; $v_3 = 13 - (-5) = 18$; $u_1 = 13 - 18 = -5$; $v_5 = 17 - (-5) = 22$; and $u_4 = -22$.

Once you get the hang of it, you probably will find it even more convenient to solve these equations without writing them down by working directly on the transportation simplex tableau. Thus in Table 7.19, you would begin by writing in the value $u_3 = 0$ and then picking out the circled allocations (x_{31}, x_{32}, x_{34}) in that row. For each one you would set $v_j = c_{3j}$ and then look for circled allocations (except in row 3) in these columns (x_{21}). Mentally calculate $u_2 = c_{21} - v_1$, pick out x_{23}, set $v_3 = c_{23} - u_2$, and so on until you have filled in all the values for the u_i and v_j. (Try it.) Then calculate and fill in the value of $(c_{ij} - u_i - v_j)$

---

[1] The one exception is that two or more equivalent degenerate basic feasible solutions (i.e., identical solutions having different degenerate basic variables equal to zero) can be optimal with only some of these basic solutions satisfying the optimality test. This exception is illustrated later in the example (see the identical solutions in the last two tableaux of Table 7.23, where only the latter solution satisfies the criterion for optimality).

Table 7.20 **Completed initial transportation simplex tableau**

Iteration 0		1	2	3	4	5	Supply	u_i
					Destination			
Source	1	16 +2	16 +2	13 (40)	22 +4	17 (10)	50	−5
	2	14 (30)	14 0	13 (30)	19 +1	15 −2	60	−5
	3	19 (0)	19 (20)	20 +2	23 (30)	M M − 22	50	0
	4(D)	M M + 3	0 +3	M M + 4	0 −1	0 (50)	50	−22
Demand		30	20	70	30	60		
v_j		19	19	18	23	22		

for each nonbasic variable x_{ij} (cell without a circled allocation), and you will have the completed initial transportation simplex tableau shown in Table 7.20.

We are now in a position to apply the optimality test by checking the value of the $(c_{ij} - u_i - v_j)$ given in Table 7.20. Because two of these values, $(c_{25} - u_2 - v_5) = -2$ and $(c_{44} - u_4 - v_4) = -1$, are negative, we conclude that the current basic feasible solution is not optimal. Therefore, the transportation simplex method must next go to the iterative step to find a better basic feasible solution.

ITERATIVE STEP

As with the full-fledged simplex method, the iterative step for this streamlined version must determine an *entering basic variable* (part 1), a *leaving basic variable* (part 2), and then identify the resulting *new basic feasible solution* (part 3).

Part 1: Since $(c_{ij} - u_i - v_j)$ represents the rate at which the objective function would change as the nonbasic variable x_{ij} is increased, the entering basic variable must have a *negative* $(c_{ij} - u_i - v_j)$ to decrease the total cost Z. Thus the candidates in Table 7.20 are x_{25} and x_{44}. To choose between the candidates, select the one having the *largest* (in absolute terms) *negative* value of $(c_{ij} - u_i - v_j)$ to be the *entering basic variable*, which is x_{25} in this case.

Part 2: Increasing the entering basic variable from zero sets off a *chain reaction* of compensating changes in other basic variables (allocations) in order to continue satisfying the supply and demand constraints. The first basic variable to be decreased to zero then becomes the *leaving basic variable*.

With x_{25} as the entering basic variable, the chain reaction in Table 7.20 is the relatively simple one summarized in Table 7.21. (We shall always indicate the entering basic variable by placing a boxed $+$ sign in its cell.) Thus increasing x_{25} requires decreasing x_{15} by the same amount to restore the demand of 60 in column 5, which in turn requires increasing x_{13} by this amount to restore the supply of 50 in row 1, which in turn requires decreasing x_{23} by this amount to restore the demand of 70 in column 3. This decrease in x_{23} successfully completes the chain reaction because it also restores the supply of 60 in row 2. (Equivalently, we could have started the chain reaction by restoring this supply in row 2 with the decrease in x_{23}, and then increase x_{13} and decrease x_{15}.) The net result is that cells (2,5) and (1,3) become **recipient cells**, each receiving its additional allocation from one of the **donor cells**, (1,5) and (2,3). (These cells are indicated in Table 7.21 by the $+$ and $-$ signs.) Note that cell (1,5) had to be the donor cell for column 5 rather than cell (4,5) because cell (4,5) would have no recipient cell in row 4 to continue the chain reaction. [Similarly, if the chain reaction had been started in row 2 instead, cell (2,1) could not be the donor cell for this row because the chain reaction could not then be completed successfully after necessarily choosing cell (3,1) as the next recipient cell and either cell (3,2) or (3,4) as its donor cell.]

Each donor cell decreases its allocation by exactly the same amount that the entering basic variable (and other recipient cells) is increased. Therefore, the donor cell that starts with the smallest allocation—cell (1,5) in this case (since $10 < 30$ in Table 7.21)—must reach a zero allocation first as the entering basic variable x_{25} is increased. Thus x_{15} becomes the *leaving basic variable*.

In general, there always is just *one* chain reaction (in either direction) that can be completed successfully to maintain feasibility when the entering basic

Table 7.21 **Part of initial transportation simplex tableau showing the chain reaction caused by increasing the entering basic variables x_{25}**

variable is increased from zero. This chain reaction can be identified by selecting among the cells having a basic variable: first, the donor cell in the *column* having the entering basic variable, then the recipient cell in the row having this donor cell, then the donor cell in the column having this recipient cell, and so on until the chain reaction yields a donor cell in the *row* having the entering basic variable. When a column or row has more than one additional basic variable cell, it may be necessary to trace them all further to see which one must be selected to be the donor or recipient cell. (All but this one eventually will reach a dead end in a row or column having no additional basic variable cell.) After identifying the chain reaction, the donor cell having the *smallest* allocation automatically provides the leaving basic variable. (In the case of a tie for the donor cell having the smallest allocation, any one can be chosen arbitrarily to provide the leaving basic variable.)

Part 3: The *new basic feasible solution* is identified simply by adding the value of the leaving basic variable (before any change) to the allocation for each recipient cell and subtracting *this same amount* from the allocation for each donor cell. In Table 7.21 the value of the leaving basic variable x_{15} is 10, so this portion of the transportation simplex tableau changes as shown in Table 7.22 for the new solution. (Since x_{15} is nonbasic in the new solution, its new allocation of zero no longer is shown in this new tableau.)

We now are in a position to point out a useful interpretation of the $(c_{ij} - u_i - v_j)$ quantities derived during the optimality test. Because of the shift of 10 allocation units from the donor cells to the recipient cells (shown in Tables 7.21 and 7.22), the total cost changes by $10(15 - 17 + 13 - 13) = 10(-2)$. Thus the effect of increasing the entering basic variable x_{25} from zero has been a cost change at the rate of -2 per unit increase in x_{25}. Now note that $(c_{25} - u_2 - v_3) = -2$ in Table 7.23; obtaining the same value (-2) is no coincidence. In fact, another (but less efficient) way of deriving $(c_{ij} - u_i - v_j)$ for each non-

Table 7.22 **Part of second transportation simplex tableau showing the changes in the basic feasible solution**

		Destination			
		3	4	5	Supply
Source	1 ...	13 (50)	22	17	50
	2 ...	13 (20)	19	15 (10)	60
	...	⋮	⋮	⋮	
Demand		70	30	60	

basic variable x_{ij} is to identify the chain reaction caused by increasing this variable from zero to 1 and then to calculate the resulting cost change. This intuitive interpretation sometimes is useful for checking calculations during the optimality test.

Before completing the solution of the Metro Water District problem, let us now summarize the rules for the transportation simplex method.

Summary of Transportation Simplex Method

Initialization step: Construct an initial basic feasible solution by the procedure outlined earlier in this section. Go to the optimality test.

Iterative step:

  Part 1   Determine the entering basic variable: Select the nonbasic variable x_{ij} having the *largest* (in absolute terms) *negative* value of $(c_{ij} - u_i - v_j)$.

  Part 2   Determine the leaving basic variable: Identify the chain reaction required to retain feasibility when the entering basic variable is increased. From among the donor cells, select the basic variable having the *smallest* value.

  Part 3   Determine the new feasible solution: Add the value of the leaving basic variable to the allocation for each recipient cell. Subtract this value from the allocation for each donor cell.

Optimality test: Derive the u_i and v_j by selecting the row having the largest number of allocations and setting its $u_i = 0$ and then solving the set of equations $c_{ij} = u_i + v_j$ for each (i,j) such that x_{ij} is basic. If $(c_{ij} - u_i - v_j) \geq 0$ for every (i,j) such that x_{ij} is *nonbasic*, then the current solution is optimal, so stop. Otherwise, go to the iterative step.

Continuing to apply this procedure to the Metro Water District problem yields the complete set of transportation simplex tableaux shown in Table 7.23. Since all the $(c_{ij} - u_i - v_j)$ are nonnegative in the fourth tableau, the optimality test identifies the set of allocations in this tableau as being optimal, which concludes the algorithm.

It would be good practice for you to derive the values of the u_i and v_j given in the second, third, and fourth tableaux. Try doing this by working directly on the tableaux. Also check out the chain reactions in the second and third tableaux, which are somewhat more complicated than the one you already have seen in Table 7.21.

You should note three special points that are illustrated by this example. First, the initial basic feasible solution is *degenerate* because the basic variable $x_{31} = 0$, but this fact causes no complication because cell (3,1) becomes a *recipient cell* in the second tableau, which increases x_{31} to a value greater than zero.

Second, another degenerate basic variable (x_{34}) arises in the third tableau because the basic variables for *two* donor cells in the second tableau, cells (2,1) and (3,4), *tie* for having the smallest value (30). (This tie is broken arbitrarily by selecting x_{21} as the leaving basic variable; if x_{34} had been selected instead, then x_{21} would have become the degenerate basic variable.) This degenerate basic

Table 7.23 **Complete set of transportation simplex tableaux for the Metro Water District problem**

Iteration 0

Source	Destination 1	2	3	4	5	Supply	u_i
1	16 +2	16 +2	13 (40)+	22 +4	17 (10)−	50	−5
2	14 (30)	14 0	13 (30)−	19 +1	15 + −2	60	−5
3	19 (0)	19 (20)	20 +2	23 (30)	M M − 22	50	0
4(D)	M M + 3	0 +3	M M + 4	0 −1	0 (50)	50	−22
Demand	30	20	70	30	60		
v_j	19	19	18	23	22		

Iteration 1

Source	Destination 1	2	3	4	5	Supply	u_i
1	16 +2	16 +2	13 (50)	22 +4	17 +2	50	−5
2	14 (30)−	14 0	13 (20)	19 +1	15 (10)+	60	−5
3	19 (0)+	19 (20)	20 +2	23 (30)−	M M − 20	50	0
4(D)	M M + 1	0 +1	M M + 2	0 + −3	0 (50)−	50	−20
Demand	30	20	70	30	60		
v_j	19	19	18	23	20		

Table 7.23 (*continued*)

Iteration 2		Destination 1	2	3	4	5	Supply	u_i
		16	16	13	22	17		
Source	1	+5	+5	(50)	+7	+2	50	−8
		14	14	13	19	15		
	2	+3	+3	(20)−	+4	(40)+	60	−8
		19	19	20	23	M		
	3	(30)	(20)	+ −1	(0)−	M − 23	50	0
		M	0	M	0	0		
	4(D)	M + 4	+4	M + 2	(30)+	(20)−	50	−23
Demand		30	20	70	30	60		
v_j		19	19	21	23	23		

Iteration 3		Destination 1	2	3	4	5	Supply	u_i
		16	16	13	22	17		
Source	1	+4	+4	(50)	+7	+2	50	−7
		14	14	13	19	15		
	2	+2	+2	(20)	+4	(40)	60	−7
		19	19	20	23	M		
	3	(30)	(20)	(0)	+1	M − 22	50	0
		M	0	M	0	0		
	4(D)	M + 3	+3	M + 2	(30)	(20)	50	−22
Demand		30	20	70	30	60		
v_j		19	19	20	22	22		

variable does appear to create a complication subsequently because cell (3,4) becomes a *donor cell* in the third tableau but has nothing to donate! Fortunately, such an event actually gives no cause for concern. Since zero is the amount to be added or subtracted to the allocations for the recipient and donor cells, these allocations do not change. However, the degenerate basic variable does become the leaving basic variable, so it is replaced by the entering basic variable as the circled allocation of zero in the fourth tableau. This change in the set of basic variables changes the values of the u_i and v_j. Therefore, if any of the $(c_{ij} - u_i - v_j)$ had been negative in the fourth tableau, the algorithm would have gone on to make *real* changes in the allocations (whenever all donor cells have nondegenerate basic variables).

Third, because none of the $(c_{ij} - u_i - v_j)$ turned out to be negative in the fourth tableau, the *equivalent* set of allocations in the third tableau is optimal also. Thus the algorithm executed one more iteration than necessary. This extra iteration is a flaw that occasionally arises in both the transportation simplex method and the simplex method because of degeneracy, but it is not sufficiently serious to warrant any adjustments in these algorithms.

7.3 The Transshipment Problem

One requirement of the transportation problem is that the way in which units would be distributed from each source i to each destination j be known in advance, so that the corresponding cost per unit (c_{ij}) can be determined. Sometimes, however, the best method of distribution is not clear because of the possibility of *transshipments*, whereby shipments would go through intermediate transfer points (which might be other sources or destinations). For example, rather than shipping a special cargo directly from port 1 to port 3, it may be cheaper to include it with regular cargoes from port 1 to port 2 and then from port 2 to port 3. Such possibilities could, of course, be investigated in advance to determine the cheapest route from each source to each destination. However, if there are many possible intermediate transfer points, this might be an extremely complicated and time-consuming task. Therefore, it may be much more convenient to let a computer algorithm solve *simultaneously* for the amount to ship from each source to each destination *and* the route to follow for each shipment so as to minimize total shipping costs. This extension of the transportation problem to include the routing decisions is referred to as the *transshipment problem.*

Fortunately, there is a simple way to reformulate the transshipment problem to fit it back into the format of the transportation problem. Thus the transportation simplex method also can be used to solve the transshipment problem.

To clarify the structure of the transshipment problem and the nature of this reformulation, we shall now extend the prototype example for the transportation problem to include transshipments.

PROTOTYPE EXAMPLE

After further investigation, the *P & T Company* (see Sec. 7.1) has found that it can cut costs by discontinuing its own trucking operation and using common carriers instead to truck its canned peas. Since no single trucking company serves the entire area containing all the canneries and warehouses, many of the shipments will need to be transferred to another truck at least once along the way. These transfers can be made at intermediate canneries or warehouses, or at five other locations (Butte, Montana; Boise, Idaho; Cheyenne, Wyoming; Denver, Colorado; and Omaha, Nebraska) referred to as *junctions*, as shown in Fig. 7.2. The shipping cost per truckload between each of these points is given in Table 7.24, where a dash indicates that a direct shipment is not possible.

For example, a truckload of peas can still be sent from cannery 1 to warehouse 4 by direct shipment at a cost of $871. However, another possibility is to ship the truckload from cannery 1 to junction 2, transfer it to a truck going to warehouse 2, and then transfer it again to go to warehouse 4, at a cost of only ($286 + $207 + $341) = $834. This possibility is only one of many indirect ways of shipping a truckload from cannery 1 to warehouse 4 that needs to be considered, if indeed this cannery should send anything to this warehouse. The overall problem is to determine how the output from all the canneries should be shipped to meet the warehouse allocations and minimize total shipping costs.

Now let us see how this *transshipment problem* can be reformulated as a transportation problem. The basic idea is to interpret the individual truck trips (as opposed to complete journeys for truckloads) as being the shipment from a source to a destination, and so label *all* the locations (canneries, junctions, and warehouses) as being *both* potential *destinations* and potential *sources* for these shipments. Thus we have 12 sources and 12 destinations, with the c_{ij} unit costs being given in Table 7.24 (use a huge cost M for the impossible shipments indicated by dashes). The number of truckloads transshipped through a location should be included in both the demand for that location as a destination and the supply for that location as a source. Since we do not know this number in advance, merely add a safe upper bound on this number to *both* the demand and supply for that location and then introduce the *same* slack variable into its demand and supply constraints to be allocated the excess. (This single slack variable thereby serves the role of both a dummy source and a dummy destination.) Since it never would pay to return a truckload to be transshipped through the same location more than once, a safe upper bound on this number for *any* location is the *total number of truckloads* (300), so we shall use 300 as the upper bound. The slack variable for both constraints for location i would be x_{ii}, the (fictional) number of truckloads shipped from this location to itself. Thus, $(300 - x_{ii})$ is the real number of truckloads transshipped through location i. Since x_{ii} represents fictional shipments, let $c_{ii} = 0$ be the corresponding unit cost. This information now gives us the complete cost and requirements table shown in Table 7.25 for the transportation problem formulation of our transshipment problem. Therefore, using the transportation simplex method to obtain an

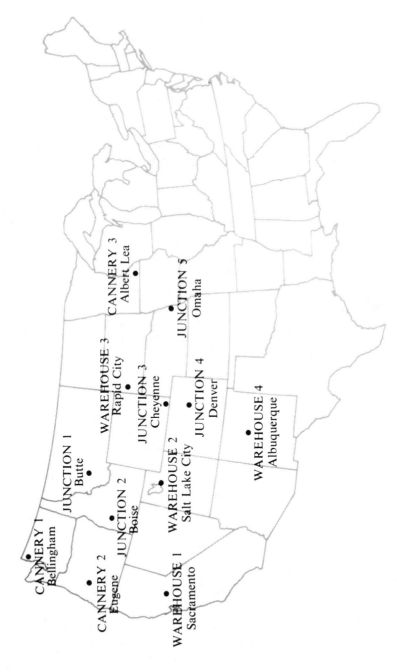

Figure 7.2 Location of canneries, warehouses, and junctions for the P & T Co.

Table 7.24 Independent trucking data for P & T Co.

Shipping cost per truckload

From \ To	Cannery 1	Cannery 2	Cannery 3	Junction 1	Junction 2	Junction 3	Junction 4	Junction 5	Warehouse 1	Warehouse 2	Warehouse 3	Warehouse 4	Output
Cannery 1		$146	—	$324	$286	—	—	—	$452	$505	—	$871	75
Cannery 2	$146		—	$373	$212	$570	$609	—	$335	$407	$688	$784	125
Cannery 3	—	—		$658	—	$405	$419	$158	—	$685	$359	$673	100
Junction 1	$322	$371	$656		$262	$398	$430	—	$503	$234	$329	$558	
Junction 2	$284	$210	—	$262		$406	$421	$644	$305	$207	$464	$282	
Junction 3	—	$569	$403	$398	$406		$81	$272	$597	$253	$171	$229	
Junction 4	—	$608	$418	$431	$422	$81		$287	$613	$280	$236	$482	
Junction 5	—	—	$158	—	$647	$274	$288		$831	$501	$293	$480	
Warehouse 1	$453	$336	—	$505	$307	$599	$615	$831		$359	$706	$587	
Warehouse 2	$505	$407	$683	$235	$208	$254	$281	$500	$357		$362	$341	
Warehouse 3	—	$687	$357	$329	$464	$171	$236	$290	$705	$362		$457	
Warehouse 4	$868	$781	$670	—	$558	$282	$229	$480	$587	$340	$457		
Allocation									80	65	70	85	

Table 7.25 Cost and requirements table for the P & T Co. transshipment problem formulated as a transportation problem

| | | Destination | | | | | | | | | | | | |
| | | (Canneries) | | | (Junctions) | | | | | (Warehouses) | | | | Supply |
		1	2	3	4	5	6	7	8	9	10	11	12	
(Canneries)	1	0	146	M	324	286	M	M	M	452	505	M	871	375
	2	146	0	M	373	212	570	609	M	335	407	688	784	425
	3	M	M	0	658	M	405	419	158	M	685	359	673	400
(Junctions)	4	322	371	656	0	262	398	430	M	503	234	329	M	300
	5	284	210	M	262	0	406	421	644	305	207	464	558	300
	6	M	569	403	398	406	0	81	272	597	253	171	282	300
	7	M	608	418	431	422	81	0	287	613	280	236	229	300
	8	M	M	158	M	647	274	288	0	831	501	293	482	300
(Warehouses)	9	453	336	M	505	307	599	615	831	0	359	706	587	300
	10	505	407	683	235	208	254	281	500	357	0	362	341	300
	11	M	687	357	329	464	171	236	290	705	362	0	457	300
	12	868	781	670	M	558	282	229	480	587	340	457	0	300
Demand		300	300	300	300	300	300	300	300	380	365	370	385	

Source

optimal solution for this transportation problem provides an optimal shipping plan (ignoring the x_{ii}) for the P & T Company (see Prob. 23).

GENERAL COMMENTS This prototype example illustrates all the general features of the transshipment problem and its relationship to the transportation problem. Thus the transshipment problem can be described in general terms as being concerned with how to allocate and route units (truckloads of canned peas in the example) from *supply centers* (canneries) to *receiving centers* (warehouses) via intermediate *transshipment points* (junctions, other supply centers, and other receiving centers). In addition to transshipping units, each supply center generates a given net surplus of units to be distributed, and each receiving center absorbs a given net deficit, whereas the junctions neither generate nor absorb any units. (The problem has feasible solutions only if the total net surplus generated at the supply centers *equals* the total net deficit to be absorbed at the receiving centers.) A positive cost c_{ij} is incurred for each unit sent *directly* from location i (a supply center, junction, or receiving center) to another location j. This direct shipment may be impossible ($c_{ij} = M$) for certain pairs of locations, and, in fact, certain supply centers and receiving centers may not be able to serve as transshipment points at all. The objective is to determine the plan for allocating and routing the units that minimizes total costs.

The resulting mathematical model for the transshipment problem (see Prob. 24) has a special structure slightly different from that for the transportation problem. As in the latter case, it has been found that some applications that have nothing to do with transportation can be fitted to this special structure. However, regardless of the physical context of the application, this model always can be reformulated as an equivalent transportation problem in the manner illustrated by the prototype example.

7.4 The Assignment Problem

The *assignment problem* is the special type of linear programming problem where the resources are being allocated to the activities on a *one-to-one basis*. Thus each resource or *assignee* (e.g., an employee, machine, or time slot) is to be assigned uniquely to a particular activity or *assignment* (e.g., a task, site, or event). There is a cost c_{ij} associated with assignee i ($i = 1,2,\ldots,n$) performing assignment j ($j = 1,2,\ldots,n$), so that the objective is to determine how all the assignments should be made in order to minimize total costs.

PROTOTYPE EXAMPLE

The *Job Shop Company* has purchased three new machines of different types. There are four available locations in the shop where a machine could be installed. Some of these locations are more desirable than others for particular machines because of their proximity to work centers that would have a heavy work flow to and from these machines. Therefore, the objective is to assign the new machines to the available locations to minimize the total cost of materials handling. The

Table 7.26 **Materials-handling cost data for the Job Shop Co.**

		\multicolumn{4}{c}{Location}
		1	2	3	4
	1	13	10	12	11
Machine	2	15	×	13	20
	3	5	7	10	6

Table 7.27 **Cost table for the Job Shop Co. assignment problem**

		\multicolumn{4}{c}{Assignment}
		1	2	3	4
	1	13	10	12	11
	2	15	M	13	20
Assignee	3	5	7	10	6
	4(D)	0	0	0	0

estimated cost per unit time of materials handling involving each of the machines is given in Table 7.26 for the respective locations. Location 2 is not considered suitable for machine 2. There would be no work flow between the new machines.

To formulate this problem as an assignment problem, we must introduce a *dummy machine* for the extra location. Also, an extremely large cost M should be attached to the assignment of machine 2 to location 2 to prevent this assignment in the optimal solution. The resulting assignment problem **cost table** is shown in Table 7.27.

The Job Shop Company can very easily obtain an optimal solution to this problem (or much larger versions of it) by using the *transportation simplex method*! (See Prob. 28.) In fact, this method can be used to solve any assignment problem, as will now be explained.

GENERAL COMMENTS The assignment problem is a special type of linear programming problem; it also turns out to be a special type of transportation problem. In particular, the assignees can be interpreted as transportation problem *sources*, each having a supply of 1. The assignments similarly are interpreted as *destinations* with a demand of 1. Therefore, after introducing any dummy assignees or assignments required to make the number of sources equal to the number of destinations ($m = n$), we would have the cost and requirements table shown in Table 7.28. Every basic feasible solution for this transportation problem would have ($n - 1$) *degenerate* basic variables, but they also would have exactly one nondegenerate basic variable (allocation) $x_{ij} = 1$ for each destination column (as well as for each source row), which identifies the one source (assignee) being "assigned" to that destination (assignment). Therefore, using the transportation simplex method (including the treatment of degenerate basic variables

Table 7.28 **Cost and requirements table for the assignment problem formulated as a transportation problem**

		\multicolumn{5}{c}{*Cost per unit distributed*}
		\multicolumn{4}{c}{*Destination*}	
		1	2	$\cdots$	n	*Supply*
Source	1	c_{11}	c_{12}	$\cdots$	c_{1n}	1
	2	c_{21}	c_{22}	$\cdots$	c_{2n}	1
	$\vdots$	$\vdots$	$\vdots$		$\vdots$	$\vdots$
	m	c_{m1}	c_{m2}	$\cdots$	c_{mn}	1
Demand		1	1	$\cdots$	1	

discussed at the end of Sec. 7.2) to solve this transportation problem provides an optimal solution for the corresponding assignment problem.

Since computer codes for the transportation simplex method are widely available, this method provides a very convenient way of solving any assignment problem. However, we also should point out that this formulation has a *special structure* for a transportation problem (supplies and demands equal to 1) that can be exploited to streamline the solution procedure much further.[1] Therefore, if you need to solve many large assignment problems, it may be worthwhile to obtain or develop a computer code for one of these streamlined procedures.

7.5 Multidivisional Problems

Another important class of linear programming problems having an exploitable special structure consists of *multidivisional problems*. Their special feature is that they involve coordinating the decisions of the separate divisions of a large organization. Because the divisions operate with considerable autonomy, the problem is *almost* decomposable into separate problems, where each division is concerned only with optimizing its own operation. However, some overall coordination is required in order to best divide certain organizational resources among the divisions.

As a result of this special feature, the *table of constraint coefficients* for multidivisional problems has the *block angular structure* shown in Table 7.29. (Recall that shaded blocks represent the only portions of the table that have *any* nonzero a_{ij} coefficients.) Thus each smaller block contains the coefficients of the constraints for one **subproblem**, namely, the problem of optimizing the operation of a division considered by itself. The long block at the top gives the coefficients of the *linking constraints* for the **master problem**, namely, the problem of coordinating the activities of the divisions by dividing organizational resources among them so as to obtain an overall optimal solution for the entire organization.

[1] See Chap. 6 of Selected Reference 6 at the end of this chapter for a description of two special solution procedures for the assignment problem.

Table 7.29 **Table of constraint coefficients for multidivisional problems**

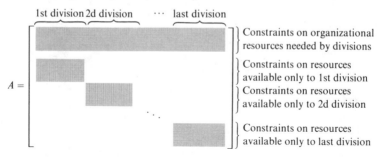

Coefficients of activity variables for

Because of their nature, multidivisional problems frequently are very large, containing many hundreds or even thousands of constraints and variables. Therefore, it may be necessary to exploit the special structure in order to be able to solve such a problem with a reasonable expenditure of computer time, or even to solve it at all! The *decomposition principle* (described in Selected References 1 and 2) provides an effective way of exploiting the special structure. Conceptually, this streamlined version of the simplex method can be thought of as having each division solve its subproblem and sending this solution as its proposal to "headquarters" (the master problem), where negotiators then coordinate the proposals from all the divisions to find an optimal solution for the overall organization. If the subproblems are of manageable size and the master problem is not too large (not more than 50 to 100 constraints), this approach is successful in solving some *extremely* large multidivisional problems. It is particularly worthwhile when the total number of constraints is quite large (at least several hundred) and there are more than a few subproblems.

PROTOTYPE EXAMPLE

The *Good Foods Corp.* is a very large producer and distributor of food products. It has three main divisions: the Processed Foods Division, the Canned Foods Division, and the Frozen Foods Division. Because costs and market prices change frequently in the food industry, Good Foods periodically uses a corporate linear programming model to revise the production rates for its various products in order to use its available production capacities in the most profitable way. This model is similar to that for the Wyndor Glass Co. problem (see Sec. 3.1), but on a much larger scale, having hundreds of constraints and variables. (Since our space is limited, we shall describe a simplified version of this model that combines the products or resources by types.)

The corporation grows its own high-quality corn and potatoes, and these basic food materials are the only ones currently in short supply that are used by all the divisions. Except for these organizational resources, each division uses only its own resources and thus could determine its optimal production rates autonomously. The data for each division and the corresponding *subproblem* involving just its products and resources are given in Table 7.30 (where Z represents profit in millions of dollars per month), along with the data for the organizational resources.

The resulting linear programming problem for the corporation is

$$\text{Maximize} \quad Z = 8x_1 + 5x_2 + 6x_3 + 9x_4 + 7x_5 + 9x_6 + 6x_7 + 5x_8,$$

subject to

$$
\begin{aligned}
5x_1 + 3x_2 \quad + 2x_4 \quad + 3x_6 + 4x_7 + 6x_8 &\le 30 \\
2x_1 \quad + 4x_3 + 3x_4 + 7x_5 \quad + x_7 &\le 20 \\
2x_1 + 4x_2 + 3x_3 &\le 10 \\
7x_1 + 3x_2 + 6x_3 &\le 15 \\
5x_1 \quad + 3x_3 &\le 12 \\
3x_4 + x_5 + 2x_6 &\le 7 \\
2x_4 + 4x_5 + 3x_6 &\le 9 \\
8x_7 + 5x_8 &\le 25 \\
7x_7 + 9x_8 &\le 30 \\
6x_7 + 4x_8 &\le 20,
\end{aligned}
$$

and

$$x_j \ge 0, \quad \text{for } j = 1, 2, \dots, 8.$$

Note how the corresponding table of constraint coefficients shown in Table 7.31 fits the special structure for multidivisional problems given in Table 7.29. Therefore, the Good Foods Corp. can indeed solve this problem (or a more detailed version of it) by the streamlined version of the simplex method provided by the decomposition principle.

IMPORTANT SPECIAL CASES

Some even simpler forms of the special structure exhibited in Table 7.29 arise quite frequently. Two particularly common forms are shown in Table 7.32. The first occurs when some or all of the variables can be divided into groups such that the *sum* of the variables in *each* group must not exceed a specified upper bound for that group (or perhaps must equal a specified constant). Constraints of this form,

$$x_{j_1} + x_{j_2} + \cdots + x_{j_k} \le b_i$$
$$(\text{or} \quad x_{j_1} + x_{j_2} + \cdots + x_{j_k} = b_i),$$

Table 7.30 **Data for the Good Foods Corp. multidivisional problem.**

Divisional data
Processed Foods Division

Subproblem

Product Resource	Resource usage/unit			Amount available
	1	2	3	
1	2	4	3	10
2	7	3	6	15
3	5	0	3	12
ΔZ/unit	8	5	6	
Level	x_1	x_2	x_3	

Maximize $Z_1 = 8x_1 + 5x_2 + 6x_3$,
subject to

$$2x_1 + 4x_2 + 3x_3 \le 10$$
$$7x_1 + 3x_2 + 6x_3 \le 15$$
$$5x_1 \qquad + 3x_3 \le 12$$

and

$$x_1 \ge 0, x_2 \ge 0, x_3 \ge 0.$$

Canned Foods Division

Product Resource	Resource usage/unit			Amount available
	4	5	6	
4	3	1	2	7
5	2	4	3	9
ΔZ/unit	9	7	9	
Level	x_4	x_5	x_6	

Maximize $Z_2 = 9x_4 + 7x_5 + 9x_6$,
subject to

$$3x_4 + x_5 + 2x_6 \le 7$$
$$2x_4 + 4x_5 + 3x_6 \le 9$$

and

$$x_4 \ge 0, x_5 \ge 0, x_6 \ge 0.$$

Frozen Foods Division

Product Resource	Resource usage/unit		Amount available
	7	8	
6	8	5	25
7	7	9	30
8	6	4	20
ΔZ/unit	6	5	
Level	x_7	x_8	

Maximize $Z_3 = 6x_7 + 5x_8$,
subject to

$$8x_7 + 5x_8 \le 25$$
$$7x_7 + 9x_8 \le 30$$
$$6x_7 + 4x_8 \le 20$$

and

$$x_7 \ge 0, x_8 \ge 0.$$

Data for organizational resources

Product Resource	1	2	3	4	5	6	7	8	Available
Corn	5	3	0	2	0	3	4	6	30
Potatoes	2	0	4	3	7	0	1	0	20

Table 7.31 **Table of constraint coefficients for the Good Foods Corp. multidivisional problem**

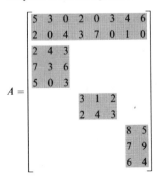

Table 7.32 **Table of constraint coefficients for important special cases of the structure for multidivisional problems given in Table 7.29**

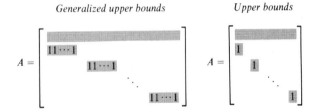

usually are called either *generalized upper bound constraints* (**GUB constraints** for short) or *group constraints*. The second form shown in Table 7.32 occurs when some or all of the *individual* variables must not exceed a specified upper bound for that variable. These constraints,

$$x_j \leq b_i,$$

normally are referred to as **upper bound constraints**.

Either *GUB* or *upper bound constraints* may occur because of the multidivisional nature of the problem. However, we should emphasize that they often arise in many other contexts as well. In fact, you already have seen several examples containing such constraints. Note in Table 7.6 that all the supply constraints in the *transportation problem* actually are *GUB constraints*. (Table 7.6 fits the form in Table 7.32 by placing the supply constraints below the demand constraints.) Alternatively, the demand constraints can be taken to be the *GUB constraints* by reordering the variables. (Therefore, a linear programming problem containing transportation problem constraints within it also fits the special structure in Table 7.32.) Either the land constraints or the crop constraints in the Southern

Confederation of Kibbutzim *regional planning problem* (see Sec. 3.4) also are GUB constraints. The technological constraints in the Nori & Leets Co. *air pollution problem* (see Sec 3.4) are upper bound constraints, as are two of the three functional constraints in the Wyndor Glass Co. *product mix problem* (see Sec. 3.1).

Because of the prevalence of *GUB* and *upper bound constraints*, special techniques have been developed for streamlining the way in which the simplex method deals with them. (The technique for upper bound constraints is described in Sec. 9.1, and the one for GUB constraints[1] is quite similiar.) If there are many such constraints, these techniques can drastically reduce the computation time for a problem.

7.6 Conclusions

The linear programming model encompasses a wide variety of specific types of problems. The general simplex method is a powerful algorithm that can solve surprisingly large versions of any of these problems. However, some of these problem types have such simple formulations that they can be solved much more efficiently by *streamlined* versions of the simplex method which exploit their *special structure.* These streamlined versions can cut down tremendously on the computer time required for large problems, and they sometimes make it computationally feasible to solve huge problems. This is particularly true for *transportation* and *transshipment problems, assignment problems,* and problems with many *upper bound* or *GUB constraints.* For general *multidivisional problems,* the setup times are sufficiently large for the streamlined procedure that it should be used selectively only on large problems.

Much research continues to be devoted to developing streamlined solution procedures for special types of linear programming problems, including some not discussed here. At the same time there is widespread interest in applying linear programming to optimize the operation of complicated large-scale systems, including social systems. The resulting formulations usually have special structures that can be exploited. Recognizing and exploiting special structures has become a very important factor in the successful application of linear programming.

We shall turn our attention in the next chapter to some other important considerations in applying linear programming.

SELECTED REFERENCES

1. Bradley, Stephen P., Arnoldo C. Hax, and Thomas L. Magnanti: *Applied Mathematical Programming*, chap. 12, Addison-Wesley, Reading, Mass., 1977.
2. Dantzig, George B.: *Linear Programming and Extensions*, chaps. 14–23, Princeton University Press, Princeton, N.J., 1963.

[1] George B. Dantzig and Richard M. Van Slyke, "Generalized Upper Bounded Techniques for Linear Programming," *Journal of Computer and Systems Sciences,* **1**, 213–226, 1967.

3. Driebeek, Norman *J.*: *Applied Linear Programming*, Addison-Wesley, Reading, Mass., 1969.

4. Geoffrion, Arthur M.: "Elements of Large-Scale Mathematical Programming," *Management Science*, **16**: 652–691, 1970.

5. Lasdon, Leon S.: *Optimization Theory for Large Systems*, Macmillan, New York, 1970.

6. Spivey, W. Allen and Robert M. Thrall: *Linear Optimization*, chaps. 6, 7, 10, Holt, Rinehart & Winston, New York, 1970.

7. Wismer, David A. (ed.): *Optimization Methods for Large-scale Systems with Applications*, McGraw-Hill, New York, 1971.

PROBLEMS

1. A company has three plants producing a certain product that is to be shipped to four distribution centers. Plants 1, 2, and 3 produce 12, 17, and 11 shipments per month, respectively. Each distribution center needs to receive 10 shipments per month. The distance from each plant to the respective distributing centers is given in miles as follows:

		Distribution center			
		1	*2*	*3*	*4*
	1	800	1,300	400	700
Plant	2	1,100	1,400	600	1,000
	3	600	1,200	800	900

The freight cost for each shipment is $100 plus 50 cents/mile.

How much should be shipped from each plant to each of the distribution centers to minimize the total shipping costs?

(*a*) Formulate this problem as a *transportation problem* by constructing the appropriate cost and requirements table.

(*b*) Use the *northwest corner rule* to obtain an initial basic feasible solution.

(*c*) Starting with the initial basic feasible solution from (*b*), use the *transportation simplex method* to obtain an optimal solution.

2. Tom would like exactly 3 pints of home brew today and at least an additional 4 pints of home brew tomorrow. Dick is willing to sell a maximum of 5 pints total at a price of $2.40/pint today and $2.16/pint tomorrow. Harry is willing to sell a maximum of 4 pints total at a price of $2.31/pint today and $2.25/pint tomorrow.

Tom wishes to know what his purchases should be to minimize his cost while satisfying his minimum thirst requirements.

(*a*) Formulate the *linear programming* model for this problem, and construct the initial simplex tableau (see Chaps. 3 and 4).

(*b*) Formulate this problem as a *transportation problem* by constructing the appropriate cost and requirements table.

(*c*) Starting with the *northwest corner rule*, use the *transportation simplex method* to solve the problem as formulated in (*b*).

3. A corporation has decided to produce three new products. Five branch plants now have excess product capacity. The unit manufacturing cost of the first product would be $31, $29, $32, $28, and $29, in Plants 1, 2, 3, 4, and 5, respectively. The unit manufacturing cost of the second product would be $45, $41, $46, $42, and $43 in Plants 1,

2, 3, 4, and 5, respectively. The unit manufacturing cost of the third product would be $38, $35, and $40 in Plants 1, 2, and 3, respectively, whereas plants 4 and 5 do not have the capability for producing this product. Sales forecasts indicate that 6,000, 10,000 and 8,000 units of products 1, 2, and 3, respectively, should be produced per day. Plants 1, 2, 3, 4, and 5 have the capacity to produce 4,000, 6,000, 4,000, 6,000, and 10,000 units daily, respectively, regardless of the product or combinations of products involved. Assume that any plant having the capability and capacity to produce them can produce any combination of the products in any quantity.

Management wishes to know how to allocate the new products to the plants to minimize total manufacturing cost.

(*a*) Formulate this problem as a *transportation problem* by constructing the appropriate cost and requirements table.

(*b*) Starting with *Vogel's approximation method*, use the *transportation simplex method* to solve the problem as formulated in (*a*).

4. Suppose that England, France, and Spain produce all the wheat, barley, and oats in the world. The world demand for wheat requires 125 million acres of land devoted to wheat production. Similarly, 60 million acres of land are required for barley and 75 million acres of land for oats. The total amount of land available for these purposes in England, France, and Spain is 70 million acres, 110 million acres, and 80 million acres, respectively. The number of hours of labor needed in England, France, and Spain to produce an acre of wheat is 18 hours, 13 hours, and 16 hours, respectively. The number of hours of labor needed in England, France, and Spain to produce an acre of barley is 15 hours, 12 hours, and 12 hours, respectively. The number of hours of labor needed in England, France, and Spain to produce an acre of oats is 12 hours, 10 hours, and 16 hours, respectively. The labor cost per hour in producing wheat is $3.00, $2.40, and $3.30 in England, France, and Spain, respectively. The labor cost per hour in producing barley is $2.70, $3.00, and $2.80 in England, France, and Spain, respectively. The labor cost per hour in producing oats is $2.30, $2.50, and $2.10 in England, France, and Spain, respectively. The problem is to allocate land use in each country so as to meet the world food requirement and minimize the total labor cost.

(*a*) Formulate this problem as a *transportation problem* by constructing the appropriate cost and requirements table.

(*b*) Starting with the *northwest corner rule*, use the *transportation simplex method* to solve this problem.

5. A firm producing a single product has three plants and four customers. The three plants will produce 6, 8, and 4 units, respectively, during the next time period. The firm has made a commitment to sell 4 units to customer 1, 6 units to customer 2, and at least 2 units to customer 3. Both customers 3 and 4 also want to buy as many of the remaining units as possible. The net profit associated with shipping a unit from plant *i* for sale to customer *j* is given by the following table:

		Customer		
	1	*2*	*3*	*4*
Plant 1	6	3	2	4
Plant 2	7	5	4	6
Plant 3	9	8	6	3

Management wishes to know how many units to sell to customers 3 and 4 and how many units to ship from each of the plants to each of the customers to maximize profit.

(a) Formulate this problem as a *transportation problem* by constructing the appropriate cost and requirements table.

(b) Starting with *Vogel's approximation method*, use the *transportation simplex method* to solve the problem as formulated in (a).

6. Plans need to be made for the energy systems for a new building. The three possible sources of energy are electricity, natural gas, and a solar heating unit.

Energy needs in the building are for electricity, water heating, and space heating, where the daily requirements (all measured in the same units) are

Electricity	20 units
Water heating	10 units
Space heating	30 units.

The size of the roof limits the solar heater to 30 units, but there is no limit to the electricity and natural gas available. Electricity needs can be met only by purchasing electricity (at a cost of $200 per unit). Both other energy needs can be met by any source or combination of sources. The unit costs are

	Electricity	*Natural gas*	*Solar heater*
Water heating	$450	$300	$150
Space heating	$400	$250	$200

(a) Formulate this problem as a *transportation problem* by constructing the appropriate cost and requirements table.

(b) Use the *northwest corner rule* to obtain an initial basic feasible solution for the problem as formulated in (a).

(c) Starting with the initial basic feasible solution from (b), use the *transportation simplex method* to obtain an optimal solution.

(d) Use *Vogel's approximation method* to obtain an initial basic feasible solution for the problem as formulated in (a).

(e) Starting with the initial basic feasible solution from (d), use the *transportation simplex method* to obtain an optimal solution. Compare the number of iterations required by the transportation simplex method here and in (c).

7. A company has two plants producing a certain product that is to be shipped to three distribution centers. The unit production costs are the same at the two plants, and the shipping cost (in hundreds of dollars) per unit of the product is shown for each combination of plant and distribution center as follows:

Distribution center

		1	2	3
Plant	A	4	6	3
	B	6	5	2

A total of 60 units is to be produced and shipped per week. Each plant can produce and ship any amount up to a maximum of 50 units per week, so there is considerable flexibility on how to divide the total production between the two plants so as to reduce shipping costs.

Management's objective is to determine how much should be produced at each plant, and then what the overall shipping pattern should be in order to minimize total shipping cost.

(a)   Assume that each distribution center must receive exactly 20 units per week. Formulate this problem as a *transportation problem* by constructing the appropriate cost and requirements table.

(b)   Starting with the *northwest corner rule*, use the *transportation simplex method* to solve the problem as formulated in (a).

(c)   Now assume that any distribution center may receive any quantity between 10 and 30 units per week in order to further reduce total shipping cost, provided only that the total shipped to all three distribution centers must still equal 60 units per week. Formulate this problem as a *transportation problem* by constructing the appropriate cost and requirements table.

(d)   Starting with *Vogel's approximation method*, use the *transportation simplex method* to solve the problem as formulated in (c).

(e)   Now assume that distribution centers 1, 2, and 3 must receive exactly 10, 20, and 30 units per week, respectively. For administrative convenience, management has decided that each distribution center will be supplied totally by a single plant, so that one plant will supply one distribution center and the other plant will supply the other two distribution centers. The choice of these assignments of plants to distribution centers is to be made solely on the basis of minimizing total shipping cost. Formulate this problem as an *assignment problem*.

(f)   Starting with *Russell's approximation method*, use the *transportation simplex method* to solve the problem as formulated in (e).

8.   Consider the prototype example for the transportation problem (the *P & T Company* problem) presented at the beginning of Sec. 7.1. Verify that the claimed optimal solution given there actually is optimal by applying just the *optimality test* portion of the transportation simplex method (see Sec. 7.2) to this solution.

9.   Consider the transportation problem having the following cost and requirements table:

		\multicolumn{5}{c}{Destination}					
		1	*2*	*3*	*4*	*5*	*Supply*
Source	1	8	6	3	7	5	20
	2	5	M	8	4	7	30
	3	6	3	9	6	8	30
	4(D)	0	0	0	0	0	20
Demand		25	25	20	10	20	

After several iterations of the transportation simplex method, the following transportation simplex tableau is obtained:

		Destination					Supply	u_i
		1	2	3	4	5		
Source	1	8	6	3 ⟨20⟩	7	5	20	
	2	5 ⟨25⟩	M	8	4 ⟨5⟩	7	30	
	3	6	3 ⟨25⟩	9	6 ⟨5⟩	8	30	
	4(D)	0	0 ⟨0⟩	0 ⟨0⟩	0	0 ⟨20⟩	20	
Demand		25	25	20	10	20		
v_j								

Continue the transportation simplex method for *two more* iterations. After two iterations, state whether the solution obtained is optimal and, if so, why.

10. Consider the transportation problem having the following cost and requirements table:

		Destination				Supply
		1	2	3	4	
Source	1	3	7	6	4	5
	2	2	4	3	2	2
	3	4	3	8	5	3
Demand		3	3	2	2	

Use each of the following criteria to obtain an initial basic feasible solution. In each case apply the *transportation simplex method*, starting with this initial solution, to obtain an optimal solution. Compare the resulting number of iterations for the transportation simplex method.

(a) Northwest corner rule.
(b) Vogel's approximation method.
(c) Russell's approximation method.

11. Consider the transportation problem having the following cost and requirements table:

		Destination				Supply
		1	2	3	4	
Source	1	5	6	4	2	10
	2	2	M	1	3	20
	3	3	4	2	1	20
	4	2	1	3	2	10
Demand		20	10	10	20	

(a) Use the *northwest corner rule* to construct an initial basic feasible solution.

(b) Starting with the initial basic solution from (a), use the *transportation simplex method* to obtain an optimal solution.

12. Consider the transportation problem having the following cost and requirements table:

		|	Destination			|	
		|	1	2	3	|	Supply
	1	|	4	2	5	|	3
Source	2	|	6	M	3	|	2
	3	|	2	3	2	|	1
Demand		|	2	1	3	|	

(a) Use *Vogel's approximation method* to select the *first* basic variable for an initial basic feasible solution.

(b) Use *Russell's approximation method* to select the *first* basic variable for an initial basic feasible solution.

(c) Use the *northwest corner rule* to construct a complete initial basic feasible solution.

(d) Starting with the initial basic feasible solution from (c), use the *transportation simplex method* to obtain an optimal solution.

13. Consider the transportation problem having the following cost and requirements table:

		|	Destination					|	
		|	1	2	3	4	5	|	Supply
	1	|	2	4	6	5	7	|	4
Source	2	|	7	6	3	M	4	|	6
	3	|	8	7	5	2	5	|	6
	4	|	0	0	0	0	0	|	4
Demand		|	4	4	2	5	5	|	

Use each of the following criteria to obtain an initial basic feasible solution. Compare the values of the objective function for these solutions.

(a) Northwest corner rule.

(b) Vogel's approximation method.

(c) Russell's approximation method.

(d) Use the best of these solutions to initialize the *transportation simplex method* to obtain an optimal solution.

14. Consider the transportation problem having the cost and requirements table at the top of the next page. Use each of the following criteria to obtain an initial basic feasible solution. Compare the values of the objective function for these solutions.

(a) Northwest corner rule.

(b) Vogel's approximation method.

(c) Russell's approximation method.

(d) Use the best of these solutions to initialize the *transportation simplex method* and then obtain the optimal solution.

		Destination						
		1	2	3	4	5	6	Supply
	1	13	10	22	29	18	0	5
	2	14	13	16	21	M	0	6
Source	3	3	0	M	11	6	0	7
	4	18	9	19	23	11	0	4
	5	30	24	34	36	28	0	3
Demand		3	5	4	5	6	2	

15. Use the *transportation simplex method* to solve the *Northern Airplane Company* production scheduling problem as it is formulated in Table 7.9.

16. Consider the Northern Airplane Company production scheduling problem presented in Sec. 7.1 (see Table 7.7). Formulate this problem as a general *linear programming* problem by letting the decision variables be x_j = number of jet engines to be produced in month j ($j = 1,2,3,4$). Construct the *initial simplex tableau* for this formulation, and then contrast the size (number of rows and columns) of this tableau and the *transportation simplex tableaux* for the transportation problem formulation of the problem (see Table 7.9).

17. The *Build-Em-Fast Company* has agreed to supply its best customer with three widgits during *each* of the next three weeks, even though producing them will require some overtime work. The relevant production data are as follows:

Week	Maximum production, regular time	Maximum production, overtime	Production cost per unit, regular time
1	2	2	$6,000
2	2	1	$10,000
3	1	2	$8,000

The cost per unit produced with overtime for each week is $2,000 more than for regular time. The cost of storage is $1,000 per unit for each week it is stored. There is already an inventory of two widgits on hand currently, but the company does not want to retain any widgits in inventory after the three weeks.

Management wants to know how many units should be produced in each week in order to maximize profit.

(a) Formulate this problem as a *transportation problem* by constructing the appropriate cost and requirements table.

(b) Use the *transportation simplex method* to solve this problem.

18. Consider the transportation problem having the following cost and requirements table:

		Destination		
		1	2	Supply
Source	1	8	5	4
	2	6	4	2
Demand		3	3	

(a) Solve this problem by the *transportation simplex method*. (Keep track of your time.)

(b) Reformulate this problem as a general *linear programming* problem, and then solve it by the *simplex method*. [Keep track of how long part (b) takes you, and contrast it with the computation time for part (a).]

19. Consider the general linear programming formulation of the transportation problem (see Table 7.6). Verify the claim in Sec. 7.2 that the set of $(m + n)$ functional constraint equations (m supply constraints and n demand constraints) has one *redundant* equation; i.e., any one equation can be reproduced from a linear combination of the other $(m + n - 1)$ equations.

20. Suppose that the air freight charge per ton between seven particular locations is given by the following table (except where no direct air freight service is available):

Location	1	2	3	4	5	6	7
1	—	21	50	62	93	77	—
2	21	—	17	54	67	—	48
3	50	17	—	60	98	67	25
4	62	54	60	—	27	—	38
5	93	67	98	27	—	47	42
6	77	—	67	—	47	—	35
7	—	48	25	38	42	35	—

A certain corporation must ship a certain perishable commodity from locations 1 to 3 to locations 4 to 7. A total of 70, 80, and 50 tons of this commodity are to be sent from locations 1, 2, and 3, respectively. A total of 30, 60, 50, and 60 tons are to be sent to locations 4, 5, 6, and 7, respectively. Shipments can be sent through intermediate locations at a cost equal to the sum of the costs for each of the legs of the journey. The problem is to determine the shipping plan that minimizes the total freight cost.

(a) Describe how this problem fits into the format of the general *transshipment problem*.
(b) Reformulate this problem as an equivalent *transportation problem* by constructing the appropriate cost and requirements table.
(c) Use *Vogel's approximation method* to obtain an initial basic feasible solution for the problem formulated in (b). Describe the corresponding shipping pattern.
(d) Use the *transportation simplex method* to obtain an optimal solution for the problem formulated in (b). Describe the corresponding optimal shipping pattern.

21. Consider the airline company problem described in Prob. 2 at the end of Chap. 10.

(a) Describe how this problem can be fitted into the format of the *transshipment problem*.
(b) Reformulate this problem as an equivalent *transportation problem* by constructing the appropriate cost and requirements table.
(c) Use *Vogel's approximation method* to obtain an initial basic feasible solution for the problem formulated in (b).
(d) Use the *transportation simplex method* to obtain an optimal solution for the problem formulated in (b).

22. A student about to enter college away from home has decided that she will need an automobile during the next 4 years. But since funds are going to be very limited, she wants to do this in the cheapest possible way. However, considering both the initial purchase price and the operating and maintenance costs, it is not clear whether she should purchase a very old car or just a moderately old car. Furthermore, it is not clear whether she should plan to trade in her car at least once during the 4 years before the costs become too high.

The relevant data *each* time she purchases a car are

	Purchase price	Operating and maintenance costs for ownership year				Trade-in value at end of ownership year			
		1	*2*	*3*	*4*	*1*	*2*	*3*	*4*
Very old car	$1,000	$1,900	$2,200	$2,500	$2,800	$600	$400	$200	0
Moderately old car	$3,800	$1,000	$1,300	$1,700	$2,300	$2,200	$1,600	$1,200	$1,000

If the student trades in a car during the next 4 years, she would do it at the end of a year (during the summer) on another car of one of these two kinds. She definitely plans to trade in her car at the end of the 4 years on a much newer model. However, she needs to determine which plan for purchasing and (perhaps) trading in cars during the 4 years would minimize the *total* net cost for the 4 years.

(a) Describe how this problem can be fitted into the format of the *transshipment problem*.

(b) Reformulate this problem as an equivalent *transportation problem* by constructing the appropriate cost and requirements table.

(c) Use *Russell's approximation method* to obtain an initial basic feasible solution for the problem as formulated in (b).

(d) Use the *transportation simplex method* to obtain an optimal solution for the problem formulated in (b).

23. Consider the *transshipment problem* for the *P & T Company* described in Sec. 7.3 (see Table 7.24). Use a computer code of the *transportation simplex method* to solve this problem as formulated in Table 7.25.

24. Without using x_{ii} variables to introduce fictional shipments from a location to itself, formulate the *linear programming* model for the general *transshipment problem* described at the end of Sec. 7.3. Identify the special structure of this model by constructing its *table of constraint coefficients* (similar to Table 7.6) that shows the location and values of the nonzero coefficients.

25. Four cargo ships will be used for shipping goods from one port to four other ports (labeled 1,2,3,4). Any ship can be used for making any one of these four trips. However, because of differences in the ships and cargoes, the total cost of loading, transporting, and unloading the goods for the different ship–port combinations varies considerably, as shown in the following table:

		Port			
		1	*2*	*3*	*4*
	1	3	5	6	4
Ship	2	5	6	4	5
	3	4	7	5	6
	4	3	6	5	4

The objective is to assign the ships to ports on a one-to-one basis in such a way as to minimize the total cost for all four shipments.

(a) Describe how this problem fits into the general format for the *assignment problem*.

(b) Reformulate this problem as an equivalent *transportation problem* by constructing the appropriate cost and requirements table.

(c) Use the *northwest corner rule* to obtain an initial basic feasible solution for the problem as formulated in (b).

(d) Starting with the initial basic feasible solution from (c), use the *transportation simplex method* to obtain an optimal set of assignments for the original problem.

(e) Are there other optimal solutions in addition to the one obtained in (d)? If so, use the *transportation simplex method* to identify them.

26. Reconsider Prob. 3. Suppose that the sales forecasts have been revised downward to 2,400, 4,000, and 3,200 units per day of products 1, 2, and 3, respectively. Thus each plant now has the capacity to produce all that is required of any one product. Therefore, management has decided that each new product should be assigned to only one plant and that no plant should be assigned more than one product (so that three plants are each to be assigned one product, and two plants are to be assigned none). The objective is to make these assignments so as to minimize the *total* cost of producing these amounts of the three products.

(a) Formulate this problem as an *assignment problem* by constructing the appropriate cost matrix.

(b) Starting with *Vogel's approximation method*, use the *transportation simplex method* to solve the problem as formulated in (a).

27. The coach of a certain swim team needs to assign swimmers to a 200-yard medley relay team to send to the Junior Olympics. Since most of his best swimmers are very fast in more than one stroke, it is not clear which swimmer should be assigned to each of the four strokes. The five fastest swimmers and the best times (in seconds) they have achieved in each of the strokes (for 50 yards) are:

Stroke	Carl	Chris	David	Tony	Ken
Backstroke	37.7	32.9	33.8	37.0	35.4
Breaststroke	43.4	33.1	42.2	34.7	41.8
Butterfly	33.3	28.5	38.9	30.4	33.6
Freestyle	29.2	26.4	29.6	28.5	31.1

The coach wishes to determine how to assign four swimmers to the four different strokes to minimize the sum of the corresponding best times.

(a) Formulate this problem as an *assignment problem*.

(b) Starting with *Vogel's approximation method*, use the *transportation simplex method* to solve this problem.

28. Starting with the *northwest corner rule*, use the *transportation simplex method* to solve the *Job Shop Company* assignment problem as formulated in Table 7.27.

29. Consider the assignment problem having the following cost table:

Job

		1	2	3
	1	6	7	M
Person	2	3	5	6
	3(D)	0	0	0

(a) Reformulate this problem as an equivalent *transportation problem* by constructing the appropriate cost and requirements table.
(b) Use *Vogel's approximation method* to obtain an initial basic feasible solution for the problem as formulated in (a).
(c) Starting with the initial basic feasible solution from (b), use the *transportation simplex method* to obtain an optimal solution for the problem as formulated in (a).

30. Consider the assignment problem having the following cost table:

Assignment

		1	2	3	4
	A	4	1	0	1
Assignee	B	1	3	4	0
	C	3	2	1	3
	D	2	2	3	0

(a) Reformulate this problem as an equivalent *transportation problem* by constructing the appropriate cost and requirements table.
(b) Use the *northwest corner rule* to obtain an initial basic feasible solution for the problem as formulated in (a).
(c) Starting with the initial basic feasible solution from (b), use the *transportation simplex method* to obtain an optimal solution for the problem as formulated in (a).

31. Consider the assignment problem having the following cost table:

Assignment

		1	2	3	4
	A	5	8	7	7
Assignee	B	8	6	7	8
	C	5	9	8	6
	D	6	5	6	9

(a) Reformulate this problem as an equivalent *transportation problem* by constructing the appropriate cost and requirements table.
(b) Use the *northwest corner rule* to obtain an initial basic feasible solution for the problem as formulated in (a).
(c) Starting with the initial basic feasible solution from (b), use the *transportation simplex method* to obtain an optimal solution for the problem formulated in (a).

32. Formulate the *linear programming* model for the general *assignment problem* described at the end of Sec. 7.4. How does its *table of constraint coefficients* differ from the one for the general *transportation problem* (Table 7.6)? In what other ways does it have more *special structure* than the general transportation problem?

33. Describe how the Wyndor Glass Co. problem formulated in Sec. 3.1 can be interpreted as a *multidivisional* linear programming problem. Identify the variables and constraints for the *master problem* and each *subproblem*.

34. Consider the following linear programming problem.

$$\text{Maximize}\quad Z = 2x_1 + 4x_2 + 3x_3 + 2x_4 - 5x_5 + 3x_6,$$

subject to

$$3x_1 + 2x_2 + 3x_3 \le 30$$
$$2x_5 - x_6 \le 20$$
$$5x_1 - 2x_2 + 3x_3 + 4x_4 + 2x_5 + x_6 \le 20$$
$$3 \le x_4 \le 15$$
$$2x_5 + 3x_6 \le 40$$
$$5x_1 - x_3 \le 30$$
$$2x_1 + 4x_2 + 2x_4 + 3x_6 \le 60$$
$$- x_1 + 2x_2 + x_3 \ge 20,$$

and

$$x_j \ge 0, \quad \text{for } j = 1, 2, \ldots, 6.$$

(a) Rewrite this problem in a form that demonstrates that it possesses the special structure for *multidivisional problems*. Identify the variables and constraints for the *master problem* and each *subproblem*.

(b) Construct the corresponding *table of constraint coefficients* having the *block angular structure* shown in Table 7.29. (Include only nonzero coefficients, and draw a box around each block of these coefficients to emphasize this structure.)

35. Consider the following *table of constraint coefficients* for a linear programming problem:

Coefficient of

Constraint	x_1	x_2	x_3	x_4	x_5	x_6	x_7
1		1			1		1
2				1			
3	4	3	-2	2	4		1
4			2			4	
5	1			1			
6		5	3		1	-2	4
7						1	
8		2			1		3
9	2			4			

(a) Show how this table can be converted into the *block angular structure for multidivisional* linear programming as shown in Table 7.29 (with three subproblems in this case) by reordering the variables and constraints appropriately.

(b) Identify the *upper bound constraints* and *GUB constraints* for this problem.

36. A corporation has two divisions (the *Eastern Division* and the *Western Division*) that operate semiautonomously, with each developing and marketing its own products. However, to coordinate their product lines and to promote efficiency, the divisions compete at the corporate level for investment funds for new *product development projects*.

In particular, each division submits its proposals to corporate headquarters in September for new major projects to be undertaken the following year, and available funds are then allocated in such a way as to maximize the estimated total net discounted profits that will eventually result from the projects.

For the upcoming year, each division is proposing three new major projects. Each project can be undertaken at any level, where the estimated net discounted profit would be *proportional* to the level. The relevant data on the projects are summarized as follows:

	Eastern Division project			Western Division project		
	1	*2*	*3*	*1*	*2*	*3*
Level	x_1	x_2	x_3	x_4	x_5	x_6
Required investment (in millions of dollars)	$16x_1$	$7x_2$	$13x_3$	$8x_4$	$20x_5$	$10x_6$
Net profitability	$7x_1$	$3x_2$	$5x_3$	$4x_4$	$7x_5$	$5x_6$
Facility restriction	$10x_1 + 3x_2 + 7x_3 \leq 50$			$6x_4 + 13x_5 + 9x_6 \leq 45$		
Labor restriction	$4x_1 + 2x_2 + 5x_3 \leq 30$			$3x_4 + 8x_5 + 2x_6 \leq 25$		

A total of $130,000,000 is budgeted for investment in these projects.

(a) Formulate this problem as a *multidivisional* linear programming problem.

(b) Construct the corresponding *table of constraint coefficients* having the *block angular structure* shown in Table 7.29.

■ CHAPTER 8

Formulating Linear Programming Models, Including Goal Programming

Chapter 3 introduced the general nature of linear programming problems, and Chaps. 4, 5, and 6 described how to solve and analyze them. Then Chap. 7 discussed some particularly important special types of linear programming problems. However, these chapters have presented only a portion of the story. The most successful users of linear programming report that one of the most crucial areas of their work is *building the model*. Many of the most noteworthy applications of linear programming involve problems whose natural formulation does not even resemble a linear programming model. It is only through some relatively sophisticated *formulation techniques* that the problems can be *reformulated* to fit linear programming and its exceptionally powerful solution procedures. To provide you with a more complete perspective about the application of linear programming, this chapter focuses on describing and illustrating some of the most useful formulation techniques.

The first section describes how to deal with variables and linear functions that can take on either positive or negative values, but with different unit costs for these two cases. This description leads into the key topic of *goal programming* (Sec. 8.2), where the *single objective* that is characteristic of linear programming is *replaced by several goals* toward which we must strive simultaneously. The formulation technique of Sec. 8.1, however, enables us to convert such a problem back into the linear programming format. Section 8.3 deals with a fairly similar problem, where there are *several objective functions* and the one with the *smallest value* is to be maximized. Another formulation technique is introduced to show us how to restore the linear programming format in this case.

All three of these sections also illustrate an additional, widely used formulation technique, namely, the introduction of *auxiliary variables*. In contrast to decision variables, auxiliary variables do not represent the original decisions of the problem. Instead, auxiliary variables simply are extra variables that are helpful for formulating the model. This technique arises again in Sec. 8.4, which presents some examples of relatively difficult formulations. Section 8.5 then concludes with a case study (school rezoning to achieve racial balance) that pulls together some of the key ideas from this chapter and the preceding ones.

8.1 Variables or Linear Functions with Positive and Negative Components

As we discussed at the end of Sec. 4.6, it sometimes is necessary to deal with variables that are allowed to be either positive or negative. When there is no bound on the negative values allowed, each such variable (say x_j) can be replaced throughout the model by the *difference* of two new *nonnegative* variables (say x_j^+ and x_j^-), so that

$$x_j = x_j^+ - x_j^-, \quad \text{where} \quad x_j^+ \geq 0, x_j^- \geq 0.$$

We interpreted x_j^+ as representing the *positive component* of x_j, and x_j^- as its *negative component*. In particular,

$$x_j^+ = \begin{cases} +x_j, & \text{if} \quad x_j \geq 0 \\ 0, & \text{if} \quad x_j \leq 0, \end{cases}$$

$$x_j^- = \begin{cases} 0, & \text{if} \quad x_j \geq 0 \\ -x_j, & \text{if} \quad x_j \leq 0, \end{cases}$$

for all basic feasible solutions, because such solutions necessarily have the property that *either* $x_j^+ = 0$ or $x_j^- = 0$ (or both). (We shall continue to use this notation with plus and minus superscripts throughout the chapter to represent the *positive* and *negative components* of *any* quantity, regardless of whether the quantity is the value of a *variable* or a *function*.)

The effect of the choice of value for x_j may be quite different for positive and negative values. For example, suppose that x_j represents the *inventory level* of a particular product. If $x_j > 0$ (so $x_j^+ > 0$ and $x_j^- = 0$), the costs incurred include storage expenses and interest charges on the capital tied up in this inventory. On the other hand, $x_j < 0$ (so $x_j^- > 0$ and $x_j^+ = 0$) means that a shortage of x_j^- has occurred. The costs in this case result from lost sales, both now (if customers won't wait) and in the future (disgruntled customers won't return). Because of this difference between the positive and negative cases, the cost of x_j is not simply proportional to x_j, so the proportionality assumption of linear programming is violated for this example. The violation of the proportionality assumption is illustrated in Fig. 8.1, where, instead of a single straight line passing through the origin (the proportionality assumption), the unit cost of holding inventory

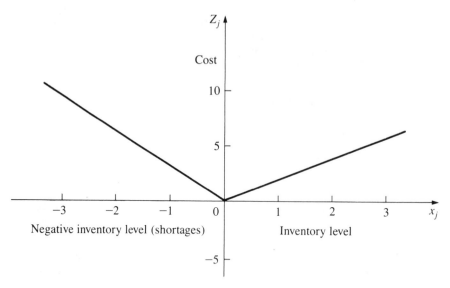

Figure 8.1 **Illustration of inventory cost violating the proportionality assumption of linear programming.**

(positive x_j) per unit time is \$2, whereas the unit cost of shortages (negative x_j) per unit time is \$3 (instead of $-\$2$).

Fortunately, as long as the proportionality assumption holds for the positive and negative cases *considered separately*, the objective function can be reformulated in a linear programming format by using x_j^+ and x_j^-. Let

$$Z_j = \text{contribution of } x_j \text{ to the objective function } Z.$$

For appropriate constants, c_j^+ and c_j^-,

$$\text{if } Z_j = \begin{cases} c_j^+ x_j, & \text{for } x_j \geq 0 \\ c_j^-(-x_j), & \text{for } x_j \leq 0 \end{cases} \quad \text{then } Z_j = c_j^+ x_j^+ + c_j^- x_j^-.$$

For example, in Fig. 8.1, $c_j^+ = 2$ and $c_j^- = 3$, which yields

$$Z_j = \begin{cases} 2x_j, & \text{for } x_j \geq 0 \\ 3(-x_j), & \text{for } x_j \leq 0 \end{cases} \quad \text{so that } Z_j = 2x_j^+ + 3x_j^-.$$

The one restriction on the use of this technique is that c_j^+ and c_j^- must satisfy the following relationship:

$$c_j^+ + c_j^- \geq 0, \quad \text{when minimizing } Z,$$
$$c_j^+ + c_j^- \leq 0, \quad \text{when maximizing } Z.$$

(When this relationship does not hold, the preceding reformulation would create an *unbounded* Z in the favorable direction, simply by adding an increasingly large positive number to both x_j^+ and x_j^-. Adding the same number to x_j^+ and x_j^- does not change the value of $x_j = x_j^+ - x_j^-$.)

An important special case of this technique is where $c_j^+ = c_j^-$ (call this common value c_j), so that Z_j is simply proportional to the absolute value of x_j, $|x_j|$. To satisfy the preceding restriction on c_j^+ and c_j^-, assume that $c_j \geq 0$ when minimizing Z or $c_j \leq 0$ when maximizing Z. Note that

$$|x_j| = x_j^+ + x_j^-.$$

Therefore,

$$\text{if} \quad Z_j = c_j|x_j|, \quad \text{then} \quad Z_j = c_j(x_j^+ + x_j^-).$$

To contrast this case with the one considered in Sec. 4.6 where the proportionality assumption is satisfied,

$$\text{if} \quad Z_j = c_j x_j, \quad \text{then} \quad Z_j = c_j(x_j^+ - x_j^-).$$

The measure of performance also can behave as illustrated in Fig. 8.1 when the abscissa value is given by a *linear function* instead of a single variable. In fact, the *inventory level itself* frequently arises naturally in the model as a linear function of the decision variables. You will see this occur in the second example of Sec. 8.4, where the decision variables for each time period j (or t in Sec. 8.4) are the production level P_j and work force level W_j. However, it is necessary to incorporate the inventory level into the model in order to include the inventory costs in the objective function. To lay the groundwork for doing this incorporation, we introduce an *auxiliary variable* x_j (or I_j in Sec. 8.4) for each time period j to represent the inventory level at the *end* of the period; then we express this variable as a linear function of the appropriate decision variables, and so on. In this case,

$$x_j = x_{j-1} + P_j - S_j,$$

where S_j is the forecasted *sales level* (a given constant) for time period j.

How is this linear function, $x_{j-1} + P_j - S_j$, incorporated into the model? If we use the notation with $+$ and $-$ as superscripts introduced at the beginning of the section, $(x_{j-1} + P_j - S_j)^+$ and $(x_{j-1} + P_j - S_j)^-$ represent the *positive* and *negative components*, respectively, of this function. Therefore, we introduce the additional artificial variables, x_j^+ and x_j^-, defined as

$$x_j^+ = (x_{j-1} + P_j - S_j)^+,$$
$$x_j^- = (x_{j-1} + P_j - S_j)^-.$$

If we define c_j^+ and c_j^- as we have just done (and with the same restriction on their values), the contribution of the inventory cost in period j to the objective function again is

$$Z_j = c_j^+ x_j^+ + c_j^- x_j^-.$$

However, now the one crucial difference is that since the $x_j = x_j^+ - x_j^-$ variables are not the decision variables included in the original model, the *definitions of* x_j^+ and x_j^- (the variables added to the objective function) must be incorporated *directly* into the linear programming model. (It is not enough to simply record the definitions, as we just did, because the simplex method considers only the objective function and constraints that constitute the model.) Because

$$x_j = x_{j-1} + P_j - S_j \quad \text{and} \quad x_j = x_j^+ - x_j^- \quad \text{for each } j,$$

they can be incorporated directly by adding the *equality constraints*,

$$x_j^+ - x_j^- = x_{j-1}^+ - x_{j-1}^- + P_j - S_j \quad \text{for each } j,$$

to the model. (The variables on the right-hand side of these constraints should be moved to the left-hand side for proper form). These additional constraints ensure that x_j^+ and x_j^- will take on appropriate values, given the values assigned to the decision variables by the simplex method. (This technique of introducing *artificial variables*, and then using *equality constraints* to define them in the model, is a very common one in a variety of applications.)

You will see this particular application of the formulation technique worked out in the context of a complete model in Sec. 8.4.

Perhaps the most important application of this technique is to *goal programming*, which is described next in Sec. 8.2.

8.2 Goal Programming

We have assumed throughout the preceding chapters that the objectives of the organization conducting the linear programming study can be encompassed within a single overriding objective, such as maximizing total profit or minimizing total cost. However, this assumption is not always realistic. In fact, as we discussed in Sec. 2.1, studies have found that the management of American corporations frequently focuses on a variety of other objectives—e.g., to maintain stable profits, increase (or maintain) one's share of the market, diversify products, maintain stable prices, improve worker morale, maintain family control of the business, and increase company prestige. *Goal programming* provides a way of striving toward several such objectives *simultaneously*.

The basic idea is to establish a specific numeric *goal* for each of the objectives, formulate an objective function for each objective, and then seek a solution that minimizes the (weighted) sum of deviations of these objective functions from their respective goals. There are two cases to be considered. One, called **nonpreemptive goal programming**, is where all of the goals are of *roughly comparable importance*. The other, called **preemptive goal programming**, is where there is a *hierarchy of priority levels* for the goals, so that the goals of *primary* importance receive first-priority attention, those of *secondary* importance receive second-priority attention, and so forth (if there are more than two priority levels).

We begin with an example that illustrates the basic features of *nonpreemptive* goal programming and then discuss the *preemptive* case.

PROTOTYPE EXAMPLE FOR NONPREEMPTIVE GOAL PROGRAMMING

The *Dewright Company* is considering three new products to replace current models that are being discontinued, so their O. R. Department has been assigned the task of determining which mix of these products should be produced. Management wants primary consideration given to three factors: long-run profit, stability in the work force, and the level of capital investment that would be required now for new equipment. In particular, they have established the goals of (1) achieving a long-run profit (net present value) of at least $125,000,000 from these products, (2) maintaining the current employment level of 4,000 employees, and (3) holding the capital investment to less than $55,000,000. However, they realize that it probably won't be possible to attain all of these goals simultaneously, so they have discussed their priorities with the O. R. Department. This discussion has led to setting penalty weights of 5 for missing the profit goal (per million dollars under), 2 for going over the employment goal (per hundred employees), 4 for going under this same goal, and 3 for exceeding the capital investment goal (per million dollars over).

Each new product's contribution to profit, employment level, and capital investment level is *proportional* to the rate of production that is currently established. These contributions per unit rate of production are shown in Table 8.1, along with the goals and penalty weights.

FORMULATION The Dewright Company problem includes all three possible types of goals: a *lower, one-sided goal* (long-run profit), a *two-sided goal* (employment level), and an *upper, one-sided goal* (capital investment). Letting the decision variables x_1, x_2, x_3 be the production rates of products 1, 2, and 3, respectively, these goals can be stated as

$$12x_1 + 9x_2 + 15x_3 \geq 125 \qquad \text{(Profit goal)}$$
$$5x_1 + 3x_2 + 4x_3 = 40 \qquad \text{(Employment goal)}$$
$$5x_1 + 7x_2 + 8x_3 \leq 55 \qquad \text{(Investment goal)}.$$

Note that these three relationships are *not* constraints. It is not even expected that all of them can be satisfied simultaneously. The right-hand sides are not fixed constants with no flexibility. Instead, they are *managerial goals* to be approached as closely as possible. More precisely, given the penalty weights in

Table 8.1 Data for Dewright Co. nonpreemptive goal programming problem

| | Unit contribution Product | | | | | Penalty |
Factor	1	2	3	Goal	(units)	weight
Long-run profit	12	9	15	≥ 125	(millions of dollars)	5
Employment level	5	3	4	$= 40$	(hundreds of employees)	$2(+)$, $4(-)$
Capital investment	5	7	8	≤ 55	(millions of dollars)	3

the last column of Table 8.1, the overall objective becomes[1]

$$\text{Minimize} \quad Z = \begin{aligned}[t] & 5(12x_1 + 9x_2 + 15x_3 - 125)^- \\ & + 2(\ 5x_1 + 3x_2 + \ 4x_3 - \ 40)^+ \\ & + 4(\ 5x_1 + 3x_2 + \ 4x_3 - \ 40)^- \\ & + 3(\ 5x_1 + 7x_2 + \ 8x_3 - \ 55)^+. \end{aligned}$$

Unfortunately, Z is *not* a linear function because each of the four terms has the *nonlinear* form illustrated in Fig. 8.1 (with a zero slope on one side of the origin), where the value of the abscissa is given by the linear function inside the parentheses. Therefore, the simplex method *cannot* be applied to solve the model in this form. However, it can be applied after the model is *reformulated* to fit the linear programming format. Reformulating requires using the formulation technique presented in the preceding section.

In particular, the first step is to introduce the new *auxiliary variables*,

$$\begin{aligned} y_1 &= 12x_1 + 9x_2 + 15x_3 - 125, \\ y_2 &= \ 5x_1 + 3x_2 + \ 4x_3 - \ 40, \\ y_3 &= \ 5x_1 + 7x_2 + \ 8x_3 - \ 55, \end{aligned}$$

as well as their *positive* and *negative components*,

$$\begin{aligned} y_1 &= y_1^+ - y_1^-, \quad \text{where} \quad y_1^+ \geq 0, y_1^- \geq 0, \\ y_2 &= y_2^+ - y_2^-, \quad \text{where} \quad y_2^+ \geq 0, y_2^- \geq 0, \\ y_3 &= y_3^+ - y_3^-, \quad \text{where} \quad y_3^+ \geq 0, y_3^- \geq 0. \end{aligned}$$

Because there is no penalty for *exceeding* the profit goal of 125 or being *under* the investment goal of 55, neither y_1^+ nor y_3^- should appear in the objective function representing the total penalty for deviations from the goals. However, it is possible (and even desirable) to have $y_1^+ > 0$ and $y_3^- > 0$, so both of these variables should appear (along with $y_1^-, y_2^+, y_2^-,$ and y_3^+) in the *equality constraints* that define the relationship between these six auxiliary variables and the three original decision variables (x_1, x_2, x_3). Using the penalty weights shown in Table 8.1 then leads to the following *linear programming* formulation of this goal programming problem:

$$\text{Minimize} \quad Z = 5y_1^- + 2y_2^+ + 4y_2^- + 3y_3^+,$$

subject to

$$\begin{aligned} 12x_1 + 9x_2 + 15x_3 - (y_1^+ - y_1^-) &= 125 \\ 5x_1 + 3x_2 + \ 4x_3 - (y_2^+ - y_2^-) &= \ 40 \\ 5x_1 + 7x_2 + \ 8x_3 - (y_3^+ - y_3^-) &= \ 55, \end{aligned}$$

---

[1] If you don't recall the significance of using $+$ and $-$ as superscripts, see the definitions at the beginning of Sec. 8.1.

and

$$x_j \geq 0, \, y_k^+ \geq 0, \, y_k^- \geq 0 \qquad (j = 1,2,3; \, k = 1,2,3).$$

(If the original problem had any actual linear programming *constraints*, such as constraints on fixed amounts of certain resources being available, these would be included in the model.)

Applying the simplex method to this formulation yields an optimal solution, $x_1 = 25/3$, $x_2 = 0$, $x_3 = 5/3$, with $y_1^+ = 0$, $y_1^- = 0$, $y_2^+ = 25/3$, $y_2^- = 0$, $y_3^+ = 0$, $y_3^- = 0$. Therefore, $y_1 = 0$, $y_2 = 25/3$, $y_3 = 0$, so the first and third goals are fully satisfied, but the employment level goal of 40 is exceeded by $8\frac{1}{3}$ (833 employees). The resulting penalty for deviating from the goals is $Z = 16\frac{2}{3}$.

PREEMPTIVE GOAL PROGRAMMING

The preceding example assumes that all of the goals are of roughly comparable importance. Now consider the case of *preemptive* goal programming, where there is a hierarchy of priority levels for the goals. Such a case arises when one or more of the goals clearly is far more important than the others. Thus the initial focus should be on achieving as closely as possible these *first-priority* goals. The other goals also might naturally divide further into *second-priority* goals, *third-priority* goals, and so on. After we find an optimal solution with respect to the first-priority goals, we can break any ties for the optimal solution by considering the second-priority goals. Any ties that remain after this reoptimization can be broken by considering the third-priority goals, and so on.

When we deal with goals on the *same* priority level, our approach is just like the one described for *nonpreemptive* goal programming. Any of the same three types of goals (lower one-sided, two-sided, upper one-sided) can arise. Different *penalty weights* for deviations from different goals still can be included, if desired. The formulation technique of Sec. 8.1 again is used to reformulate this portion of the problem to fit the linear programming format.

One way of solving the *overall* problem is to solve a *sequence* of linear programming problems. We shall call this procedure the **sequential procedure**. At the first stage, the only goals included in the linear programming model are the first-priority goals, and the simplex method is applied in the usual way. If the resulting optimal solution is *unique*, we adopt it immediately without considering any additional goals. However, if there are *multiple* optimal solutions with the same optimal value of Z (call it Z^*), we move to the second stage by adding the second-priority goals to the model. If $Z^* = 0$, the *auxiliary variables* representing the *deviations from first-priority goals* now can be completely deleted from the model, where the equality constraints that contain these variables are replaced by the mathematical expressions (inequalities or equations) for these goals to ensure that they continue to be fully achieved. On the other hand, if $Z^* > 0$, the second-stage model simply adds the second-priority goals to the first-stage model (as if these additional goals actually were first-priority goals), but then it also adds the constraint that the *first-stage objective function* must equal Z^* (which enables us to delete these terms from the second-stage objective function). After we apply the simplex method again, we repeat the same process for any lower priority goals.

It also is possible to duplicate the work of the *sequential procedure* with just *one run* of the simplex method if a slight modification is first made in the algorithm. We shall call this procedure the **streamlined procedure**. If there are just *two* priority levels, the modification is one you already have seen, namely, the form of the *Big M method* illustrated throughout Sec. 4.6. In this form, instead of replacing M throughout the model by some huge positive number before running the simplex method, we retain the *symbolic* quantity M in the sequence of simplex tableaux and treat it in the *proper manner*. (As we discussed in Sec. 4.6, the *form* of the Big M method is that each coefficient in row 0 (for each iteration) is some linear function, $aM + b$, where a is the current *multiplicative factor* and b is the current *additive factor*. Treating M in the *proper manner* simply means that the usual decisions based on these coefficients (entering basic variable and optimality test) now are based solely on the *multiplicative* factors, *except* that any ties would be broken by using the *additive* factors.) The linear programming formulation of our current problem (with two priority levels) would include *all* of the goals in the model in the usual manner, but with *basic penalty weights* of M and 1 assigned to deviations from *first-priority* and *second-priority* goals, respectively. If different penalty weights are desired within the same priority level, these basic penalty weights then are multiplied by the individual penalty weights assigned within the level.

When there are more than two priority levels (say p of them), the *streamlined procedure* generalizes in a straightforward way. The *basic penalty weights* for the respective levels now are $M_1, M_2, \ldots, M_{p-1}, 1$, where M_1 represents a number that is vastly larger than M_2, M_2 is vastly larger than $M_3, \ldots$, and M_{p-1} is vastly larger than 1. Each coefficient in row 0 of each simplex tableau is now a linear function of all of these quantities, where the *multiplicative* factor of M_1 is used to make the necessary decisions, with *tie-breakers* beginning with the *multiplicative* factor of M_2 and ending with the *additive* factor.

We shall now illustrate both the *sequential procedure* and the *streamlined procedure* by modifying the *Dewright Company* problem.

EXAMPLE FOR PREEMPTIVE GOAL PROGRAMMING

Faced with the unpleasant recommendation to increase the company's work force by more than 20%, the management of the *Dewright Company* has reconsidered the original formulation of the problem that was summarized in Table 8.1. This increase in the work force probably would be a rather temporary one, so the very high cost of training 833 new employees would be largely wasted, and the large (undoubtedly well-publicized) layoffs would make it more difficult for the company to attract high-quality employees in the future. Consequently, management has concluded that a very high priority should be placed on avoiding an increase in the work force. Furthermore, management has learned that raising *more than* $55,000,000 for capital investment for the new products would be extremely difficult, so a very high priority should be placed on avoiding additional capital investment.

Based on these considerations, management has concluded that a *preemptive goal programming* approach now should be used, where the two goals just discussed should be the *first-priority* goals, and the other two original goals (exceeding $125,000,000 in long-run profit and avoiding a *decrease* in the employment level) should be the *second-priority* goals. Within the two priority levels, the relative penalty weights still should be the same as given in the last column of Table 8.1. This reformulation is summarized in Table 8.2. (The portions of Table 8.1 that are not included in Table 8.2 are *unchanged*.)

SEQUENTIAL PROCEDURE At the first stage of the *sequential procedure*, only the two *first-priority* goals are included in the linear programming model as follows. (For ease of comparison with the *nonpreemptive* model, we have kept the same subscripts on the auxiliary variables.)

$$\text{Minimize} \quad Z = 2My_2^+ + 3My_3^+,$$

subject to

$$5x_1 + 3x_2 + 4x_3 - (y_2^+ - y_2^-) = 40$$
$$5x_1 + 7x_2 + 8x_3 - (y_3^+ - y_3^-) = 55,$$

and

$$x_j \geq 0, \, y_k^+ \geq 0, \, y_k^- \geq 0 \quad (j = 1,2,3; \, k = 2,3).$$

An optimal solution for this model has $y_2^+ = 0$ and $y_3^+ = 0$, with $Z = 0$ (so $Z^* = 0$), because there are innumerable solutions for (x_1, x_2, x_3) that satisfy the relationships,

$$5x_1 + 3x_2 + 4x_3 \leq 40$$
$$5x_1 + 7x_2 + 8x_3 \leq 55,$$

as well as the nonnegativity constraints. Therefore, these two first-priority goals should be used as *constraints* hereafter. Using them as constraints will force y_2^+ and y_3^+ to remain *zero* and thereby disappear from the model automatically.

Table 8.2 **Revised formulation for Dewright Co. preemptive goal programming problem.**

Priority level	Factor	Goal	Penalty weight
First priority	Employment level	≤ 40	2M
	Capital investment	≤ 55	3M
Second priority	Long-run profit	≥ 125	5
	Employment level	≥ 40	4

If we drop y_2^+ and y_3^+ but add the *second-priority* goals, the *second-stage* linear programming model becomes

$$\text{Minimize} \quad Z = 5y_1^- + 4y_2^-,$$

subject to

$$12x_1 + 9x_2 + 15x_3 - (y_1^+ - y_1^-) \qquad\qquad = 125$$
$$5x_1 + 3x_2 + 4x_3 \qquad\qquad + y_2^- \quad = \; 40$$
$$5x_1 + 7x_2 + 8x_3 \qquad\qquad\qquad + y_3^- = \; 55,$$

and

$$x_j \geq 0, \; y_k^+ \geq 0, \; y_k^- \geq 0 \quad (j = 1,2,3; \; k = 1,2,3).$$

Applying the simplex method to this model yields the unique optimal solution, $x_1 = 5$, $x_2 = 0$, $x_3 = 3\frac{3}{4}$, $y_1^+ = 0$, $y_1^- = 8\frac{3}{4}$, $y_2^- = 0$, $y_3^- = 0$, with $Z = 43\frac{3}{4}$. Because this solution is unique (*and* because there are no more priority levels), the procedure can now stop, with $(x_1, x_2, x_3) = (5, 0, 3\frac{3}{4})$ as the optimal solution for the *overall* problem. This solution fully achieves both *first-priority* goals, as well as one of the *second-priority* goals (no decrease in employment level), and it falls short by just $8\frac{3}{4}$ of the other *second-priority* goal (long-run profit ≥ 125).

Streamlined Procedure Using the *streamlined procedure* instead of the *sequential procedure*, we work with just *one* linear programming model that includes *all* of the goals, as follows:

$$\text{Minimize} \quad Z = 5y_1^- + 2My_2^+ + 4y_2^- + 3My_3^+,$$

subject to

$$12x_1 + 9x_2 + 15x_3 - (y_1^+ - y_1^-) = 125$$
$$5x_1 + 3x_2 + 4x_3 - (y_2^+ - y_2^-) = \; 40$$
$$5x_1 + 7x_2 + 8x_3 - (y_3^+ - y_3^-) = \; 55,$$

and

$$x_j \geq 0, \; y_k^+ \geq 0, \; y_k^- \geq 0 \quad (j = 1,2,3; \; k = 1,2,3).$$

Because this model uses M to symbolize a huge positive number, the simplex method should be applied as described and illustrated throughout Sec. 4.6. This application, of course, yields the same optimal solution just obtained by the *sequential procedure*.

8.3 Maximizing the Minimum Progress Toward All Objectives

Goal programming is one very useful tool for dealing with problems where several objectives must be considered simultaneously. However, it does require establishing goals for all of the objectives, and it is not always possible to do this in a meaningful way. In particular, some objectives are *open-ended* and you want to make as much progress toward them as possible. To put it another way, for open-ended objectives there is no minimum standard (goal) such that you would be relatively indifferent about the amount of progress made beyond this standard. (For example, many managers consider the objective of maximizing profit to be of this type.) With open-ended objectives, you may also want to make progress on *all* of the objectives *simultaneously*. In this case, it may be appropriate to *maximize the minimum progress toward all objectives*.

To formulate this approach, suppose that there are K objectives,

$$Z_1 = \sum_{j=1}^{n} c_{j1} x_j \qquad \text{(Objective 1)}$$

$$Z_2 = \sum_{j=1}^{n} c_{j2} x_j \qquad \text{(Objective 2)}$$

$$\vdots$$

$$Z_K = \sum_{j=1}^{n} c_{jK} x_j \qquad \text{(Objective } K\text{).}$$

We wish to increase together the values of all of these individual objective functions. Therefore, the *overall objective function* for the model becomes

$$\text{Maximize} \quad Z = \text{minimum } \{Z_1, Z_2, \ldots, Z_K\},$$

so an optimal solution for $(x_1, x_2, \ldots, x_n)$ is one that makes the *smallest* Z_k $(k = 1, 2, \ldots, K)$ as large as possible.

This overall objective function certainly does not fit into a linear programming format. Now let us see how the problem can be *reformulated* into this format. We begin by introducing an *artificial variable* z to represent the minimum value among the K objectives,

$$z = \text{minimum } \{Z_1, Z_2, \ldots, Z_K\}.$$

Introducing this artificial variable enables us to write the overall objective function as

$$\text{Maximize} \quad Z = z,$$

which is a legitimate linear programming objective function (one variable with a coefficient of $+1$ and all other coefficients zero.) The remaining question is how to incorporate the *definition* of z directly into a linear programming model. The definition implies that

$$z \le \sum_{j=1}^{n} c_{j1} x_j$$

$$z \le \sum_{j=1}^{n} c_{j2} x_j$$

$$\vdots$$

$$z \le \sum_{j=1}^{n} c_{jK} x_j,$$

where these inequalities are legitimate linear programming *constraints* (after bringing all variables to the left-hand side for proper form). Furthermore, the definition also implies that one or more of these constraints (the one with the *smallest* right-hand side) will hold with *equality*. Therefore, z is simply the *largest* quantity that satisfies all K of these constraints, which condition is already ensured by maximizing $Z = z$. Consequently, the *equivalent* linear programming model is

$$\text{Maximize} \quad Z = z,$$

subject to

$$\sum_{j=1}^{n} c_{jk} x_j - z \geq 0, \quad \text{for} \quad k = 1, 2, \ldots, K$$

$$x_j \geq 0, \quad \text{for} \quad j = 1, 2, \ldots, n,$$

and

any other linear programming constraints in the original model.

(If it is clear that z will turn out to be nonnegative, a nonnegativity constraint can be included in the model for this variable as well.)

If the Z_k are not measured in common units, they should be multiplied by the appropriate constants to convert them to a common unit of measurement.

When the objectives are to be minimized rather than maximized, the *overall objective function* for the original model would change to

$$\text{Minimize} \quad Z = \text{maximum} \{Z_1, Z_2, \ldots, Z_K\}.$$

The *equivalent* linear programming model then is

$$\text{Minimize} \quad Z = z,$$

subject to

$$\sum_{j=1}^{n} c_{jk} x_j - z \leq 0, \quad \text{for} \quad k = 1, 2, \ldots, K$$

$$x_j \geq 0, \quad \text{for} \quad j = 1, 2, \ldots, n,$$

and

any other linear programming constraints in the original model.

PROTOTYPE EXAMPLE

An international relief agency, the *Food and Agriculture Organization*, is sending agricultural experts to two underdeveloped countries whose greatest need is to increase their food production by improving their agricultural techniques. Therefore, the experts will be used to develop pilot projects and training programs to demonstrate and teach these techniques. However, the number of such projects that can be undertaken is restricted by the limited availability of three required resources: equipment, experts, and money. The question is how many projects should be undertaken in each of the countries in order to make the best possible use of the resources.

It has been estimated that *each full project* undertaken in country 1 eventually would increase the food production in this country sufficiently to feed 2,000 additional people. The corresponding estimate for country 2 is for an increase that would feed an additional 3,000 people. The two countries differ in the mix of resources needed for projects. These data are summarized in Table 8.3. It is feasible to consider projects at fractional levels as well as whole projects. We assume that fractions of projects will affect the data of Table 8.3 proportionally.

Because both countries are in desperate need, the Food and Agriculture Organization is determined to increase the food production in *both* countries as much as possible. Therefore, it has chosen the overall objective of maximizing the *minimum increase in food production* in the two countries.

FORMULATION The decision variables, x_1 and x_2, are the number of projects to be undertaken in countries 1 and 2, respectively. There are *two* objectives in this case—to increase the food production in country 1 and to increase the food production in country 2. Their objective functions are

$$Z_1 = 2,000x_1 \quad \text{(Objective 1)}$$
$$Z_2 = 3,000x_2 \quad \text{(Objective 2)}.$$

Therefore, using Table 8.3 to construct the constraints, the overall model is

$$\text{Maximize} \quad Z = \text{minimum } \{Z_1, Z_2\}$$
$$= \text{minimum } \{2,000x_1, 3,000x_2\},$$

subject to

$$5x_2 \leq 20$$
$$x_1 + 2x_2 \leq 10$$
$$60x_1 + 20x_2 \leq 300,$$

and

$$x_1 \geq 0, \quad x_2 \geq 0.$$

Table 8.3 **Data for Food and Agriculture Organization problem**

Resource	Amount used per project		Amount available
	Country 1	Country 2	
Equipment	0	5	20
Experts	1	2	10
Money	60	20	300 (thousands of dollars)
People fed	2,000	3,000	

The *equivalent* linear programming model is

$$\text{Maximize} \quad Z = z,$$

subject to

$$
\begin{aligned}
2{,}000x_1 && -z &\geq 0 \\
3{,}000x_2 &- z &&\geq 0 \\
5x_2 && &\leq 20 \\
x_1 + 2x_2 && &\leq 10 \\
60x_1 + 20x_2 && &\leq 300,
\end{aligned}
$$

and

$$x_1 \geq 0, \quad x_2 \geq 0, \quad z \geq 0,$$

where z is an additional *auxiliary* variable for this new model.

Applying the simplex method (which does not differentiate between *decision* variables and *auxiliary* variables) yields the optimal solution,

$$x_1 = \frac{45}{11}, \quad \text{so} \quad Z_1 = 8{,}182$$

$$x_2 = \frac{30}{11}, \quad \text{so} \quad Z_2 = 8{,}182$$

$$z = 8{,}182.$$

Consequently, an additional 8,182 people will be fed in *each* of the two countries.

8.4 Some Formulation Examples

We now present two examples that illustrate the kinds of challenging formulation problems that frequently are encountered in real applications of linear programming.

RECLAIMING SOLID WASTES

The *Save-It Company* operates a reclamation center that collects four types of solid waste materials and then treats them so they can be amalgamated into a saleable product. Three different grades of this product can be made, depending upon the mix of the materials used. Although there is some flexibility in the mix for each grade, quality standards do specify a minimum or maximum percentage (by weight) of certain materials allowed in that product grade. These specifications are given in Table 8.4 along with the cost of amalgamation and the selling price for each grade.

The reclamation center collects its solid waste materials from some regular sources and so is normally able to maintain a steady production rate for treating

Table 8.4 **Product data for Save-It Co.**

Grade	Specification	Amalgamation cost ($) per pound	Selling price ($) per pound
A	Not more than 30% of material 1 Not less than 40% of material 2 Not more than 50% of material 3	3.00	8.50
B	Not more than 50% of material 1 Not less than 10% of material 2	2.50	7.00
C	Not more than 70% of material 1	2.00	5.50

Table 8.5 **Solid waste materials data for Save-It Co.**

Material	Pounds/week available	Treatment cost ($) per pound
1	3,000	3
2	2,000	6
3	4,000	4
4	1,000	5

these materials. Table 8.5 gives the quantities available for collection and treatment each week, as well as the cost of treatment, for each type of material.

The problem facing the company is to determine just how much of each product grade to produce *and* the exact mix of materials to be used for each grade so as to maximize the total weekly profit (total sales income minus the total costs of *both* amalgamation and treatment).

FORMULATION Before attempting to construct a linear programming model, we must give careful consideration to the proper definition of the decision variables. Although this definition is often obvious, it sometimes becomes the crux of the entire formulation. After clearly identifying what information is really desired and the most convenient form for conveying this information by means of decision variables, we can develop the objective function and the constraints on the values of these decision variables.

In this particular problem, the decisions to be made are well defined, but the appropriate means of conveying this information may require some thought. (Try it and see if you first obtain the following *inappropriate* choice of decision variables.) Because one set of decisions concerns the *amount* of each product grade to be produced it would seem natural to define one set of decision variables accordingly. Proceeding tentatively along this line, define y_i ($i = A,B,C$) as the number of pounds of product grade i produced per week. The mixture of each grade is identified by the proportion of each material in the product. This identification would suggest defining the other set of decision variables, z_{ij} ($i = A,B,C; j = 1,2,3,4$), as the *proportion* of material j in product grade i. However, Table 8.5 gives both the treatment cost and the availability of the materials by *quantity* (pounds) rather than *proportion*, and it is the *quantity* information that needs to be recorded in the objective function and in the constraints, respectively. The total quantity of material 1 used, for example, is $z_{A1}y_A + z_{B1}y_B + z_{C1}y_C$. But this is *not* a linear function because it involves products of variables. Therefore, a linear programming model cannot be constructed with these decision variables.

Fortunately, there is another way of defining the decision variables that will fit the linear programming format. (Do you see how to do it?) It is accomplished by merely replacing each *product* of the old decision variables by a single variable! In other words, define $x_{ij} = z_{ij}y_i$ (for $i = A,B,C$; $j = 1,2,3,4$), and then let the x_{ij} be the decision variables. Thus x_{ij} is the total number of pounds of material j allocated to product grade i per week. The total amount of product grade i produced per week is then $x_{i1} + x_{i2} + x_{i3} + x_{i4}$. The proportion of material j in product grade i is $x_{ij}/(x_{i1} + x_{i2} + x_{i3} + x_{i4})$. Therefore, this choice of decision variables conveys all the necessary information and proves to be well suited to the construction of the following linear programming model. (Note particularly how the mixture constraints on the *nonlinear* proportion function are written in a linear form.)

The total profit Z is given by

$$Z = 5.5(x_{A1} + x_{A2} + x_{A3} + x_{A4}) + 4.5(x_{B1} + x_{B2} + x_{B3} + x_{B4})$$
$$+ 3.5(x_{C1} + x_{C2} + x_{C3} + x_{C4}) - 3(x_{A1} + x_{B1} + x_{C1})$$
$$- 6(x_{A2} + x_{B2} + x_{C2}) - 4(x_{A3} + x_{B3} + x_{C3}) - 5(x_{A4} + x_{B4} + x_{C4}).$$

Thus, after combining common terms, the model becomes

Maximize $Z = 2.5x_{A1} - 0.5x_{A2} + 1.5x_{A3} + 0.5x_{A4} + 1.5x_{B1} - 1.5x_{B2} + 0.5x_{B3}$
$$- 0.5x_{B4} + 0.5x_{C1} - 2.5x_{C2} - 0.5x_{C3} - 1.5x_{C4},$$

subject to the following constraints:

1. *Availability of materials*:

$$x_{A1} + x_{B1} + x_{C1} \leq 3,000$$
$$x_{A2} + x_{B2} + x_{C2} \leq 2,000$$
$$x_{A3} + x_{B3} + x_{C3} \leq 4,000$$
$$x_{A4} + x_{B4} + x_{C4} \leq 1,000.$$

2. *Mixture specifications*:

$$x_{A1} \leq 0.3(x_{A1} + x_{A2} + x_{A3} + x_{A4})$$
$$x_{A2} \geq 0.4(x_{A1} + x_{A2} + x_{A3} + x_{A4})$$
$$x_{A3} \leq 0.5(x_{A1} + x_{A2} + x_{A3} + x_{A4}).$$

$$x_{B1} \leq 0.5(x_{B1} + x_{B2} + x_{B3} + x_{B4})$$
$$x_{B2} \geq 0.1(x_{B1} + x_{B2} + x_{B3} + x_{B4}).$$
$$x_{C1} \leq 0.7(x_{C1} + x_{C2} + x_{C3} + x_{C4}).$$

and

3. *Nonnegativity:*

$$x_{ij} \geq 0, \quad \text{for} \quad i = A, B, C; \, j = 1, 2, 3, 4.$$

This formulation completes the model, except that the constraints for the mixture specifications need to be rewritten in the proper form for a linear programming model by bringing all variables to the left-hand side and combining terms, as follows:

2. *Mixture specifications:*

$$0.7x_{A1} - 0.3x_{A2} - 0.3x_{A3} - 0.3x_{A4} \leq 0$$
$$-0.4x_{A1} + 0.6x_{A2} - 0.4x_{A3} - 0.4x_{A4} \geq 0$$
$$-0.5x_{A1} - 0.5x_{A2} + 0.5x_{A3} - 0.5x_{A4} \leq 0.$$

$$0.5x_{B1} - 0.5x_{B2} - 0.5x_{B3} - 0.5x_{B4} \leq 0$$
$$-0.1x_{B1} + 0.9x_{B2} - 0.1x_{B3} - 0.1x_{B4} \geq 0.$$
$$0.3x_{C1} - 0.7x_{C2} - 0.7x_{C3} - 0.7x_{C4} \leq 0.$$

PRODUCTION AND EMPLOYMENT SCHEDULING[1]

The *Boombust Company* faces an unstable sales market and so must frequently make adjustments of some kind to compensate for predicted changes in the level of sales. When sales are increasing, these adjustments take the form of increasing the work force (hiring), having the existing work force work overtime, or using up existing (or future) inventories. Similarly, when sales are dropping, the company decreases its work force (lays people off), underutilizes its current work force, or builds up inventories. All these alternatives are costly in some way, especially when they are used to extremes. Consequently, the company often uses some combination of these possible adjustments. However, it is very difficult to determine just which combination is least expensive, particularly when a series of adjustments is being planned to meet a series of predicted changes in sales. Therefore, management has asked the O.R. Department to study this problem and develop a systematic procedure for production and employment scheduling that will minimize the total cost of meeting the projected sales. The procedure should provide a month-by-month schedule over the upcoming 12 months, for planning purposes, but then the procedure should be *reapplied each month* to update the schedule based on the latest sales forecasts.

The Marketing Division provides updated forecasts each month on the total volume of projected sales for the company in each of the next 12 months. The decisions to be made are concerned with the total *work-force level* (number of employees) and the *production rate* to be scheduled for each of these 12 months. These decisions, in turn, determine the net *inventory level* (amount stored minus

[1] This example is based on a model that was first developed by Fred Hanssmann and Sidney W. Hess in "A Linear Programming Approach to Production and Employment Scheduling," *Management Technology,* **1**:46–52, 1960.

back orders) for these months. These quantities are denoted as follows for month t $(t = 1, 2, \ldots, 12)$:

$$S_t = \text{sales forecast.}$$
$$W_t = \text{work-force level.}$$
$$P_t = \text{production rate.}$$
$$I_t = \text{inventory level at the end of the month.}$$

Because the company produces more than one product, S_t, P_t, and I_t each represents the *total* quantity aggregated over all the products, expressed in the common unit of dollar value.

To relate W_t and P_t, we estimate that ten employees are required on the average to produce one unit of production per month without working overtime, so that

$$W_t = 10P_t, \quad \text{if the work force is fully utilized on regular time only,}$$
$$W_t < 10P_t, \quad \text{if overtime is used,}$$
$$W_t > 10P_t, \quad \text{if the work force is underutilized on regular time.}$$

Various kinds of costs need to be taken into account in the model. Using the notation introduced in Sec. 8.1 ($+$ and $-$ as superscripts), we summarize these costs (in units of thousands of dollars) in Table 8.6.

Note that each of the cost functions in Table 8.6 (except the regular payroll) is a *nonlinear* function of the quantity involved because the function has the form illustrated in Fig. 8.1 (but with a *zero* slope on one side of the origin). Therefore, letting Z be the total cost over all 12 months, the "natural" formulation of the model is the *nonlinear* programming problem.

$$\text{Minimize} \quad Z = \sum_{t=1}^{12} \{ 4(W_t - W_{t-1})^+ + (W_t - W_{t-1})^- + 5W_t + 7(10P_t - W_t)^+ \\ + 2I_t^+ + 3I_t^- \},$$

subject to

$$I_t = I_{t-1} + P_t - S_t$$

and

$$\left. \begin{array}{c} I_t = I_{t-1} + P_t - S_t \\ \\ W_t \geq 0, P_t \geq 0 \end{array} \right\} \quad \text{for} \quad t = 1, 2, \ldots, 12,$$

where the initial inventory level I_0 and work-force level W_0 are given.

Table 8.6 **Cost data for Boombust Co. problem**

Type of cost	Amount	Origin of costs
Hiring cost	$4(W_t - W_{t-1})^+$	Training, reorganization
Layoff cost	$(W_t - W_{t-1})^-$	Severance pay, reorganization, low morale
Regular payroll	$5W_t$	Wages, fringe benefits
Overtime cost	$7(10P_t - W_t)^+$	Premium wages
Inventory cost	$2I_t^+$	Storage expenses, interest on capital tied up
Shortage cost	$3I_t^-$	Customer dissatisfaction, lost future sales

Now let us see how the O.R. Department *reformulated* this problem to fit the linear programming format.

FORMULATION As in the preceding example, the key to achieving a linear programming formulation of the problem is the appropriate definition of the decision variables. In this case, finding the appropriate definition involves combining two formulation techniques that were initially presented in Sec. 8.1. First, we introduce *auxiliary variables* (x_t and y_t) to represent the quantities, $(W_t - W_{t-1})$ and $(10P_t - W_t)$, so

$$x_t = W_t - W_{t-1} \qquad y_t = 10P_t - W_t,$$

for $t = 1, 2, \ldots, 12$. Next, because each of these variables and the I_t are *variables with positive and negative components*, we replace *each* of them by the difference of two new *nonnegative* auxiliary variables as per the following summary:

$$x_t = x_t^+ - x_t^-, \quad \text{so} \quad x_t^+ = (W_t - W_{t-1})^+$$
$$x_t^- = (W_t - W_{t-1})^-,$$
$$y_t = y_t^+ - y_t^-, \quad \text{so} \quad y_t^+ = (10P_t - W_t)^+,$$
$$I_t = I_t^+ - I_t^-,$$

where

$$x_t^+ \geq 0,\ x_t^- \geq 0,\ y_t^+ \geq 0,\ y_t^- \geq 0,\ I_t^+ \geq 0,\ I_t^- \geq 0.$$

The objective function then becomes a *linear* function,

$$Z = \sum_{t=1}^{12} \{4x_t^+ + x_t^- + 5W_t + 7y_t^+ + 2I_t^+ + 3I_t^-\}.$$

You will soon see that W_t also can be expressed as a linear function of the new variables to obtain the final form of the objective function.

The set of constraints for the linear programming formulation can be constructed simply by using the constraints for the preceding nonlinear programming problem (after substituting $I_t^+ - I_t^-$ for I_t for $t = 1, 2, \ldots, 12$), and then incorporating the *definition* of the other nonnegative auxiliary variables into the model by introducing *additional* equality constraints. Consequently, the complete linear programming model[1] is

$$\text{Minimize} \quad Z = \sum_{t=1}^{12} \{4x_t^+ + x_t^- + 5W_t + 7y_t^+ + 2I_t^+ + 3I_t^-\},$$

subject to

$$\left. \begin{array}{l} I_t^+ - I_t^- = I_{t-1}^+ - I_{t-1}^- + P_t - S_t \\ x_t^+ - x_t^- = W_t - W_{t-1} \\ y_t^+ - y_t^- = 10P_t - W_t, \end{array} \right\} \quad \text{for} \quad t = 1, 2, \ldots, 12,$$

---

[1] It is possible to reformulate this model further to reduce the number of variables, but the number of functional constraints remains the same, so the resulting reduction in computational effort turns out to be minor.

and

$$W_t \geq 0, \; P_t \geq 0, \; x_t^+ \geq 0, \; x_t^- \geq 0, \; y_t^+ \geq 0, \; y_t^- \geq 0, \; I_t^+ \geq 0, \; I_t^- \geq 0 \quad (t = 1, 2, \dots, 12),$$

except that the variables appearing in the right-hand sides of the functional constraints still need to be transferred to the left-hand side for proper form. (Also, in the first constraint, when $t = 1$, $I_0^+ - I_0^-$ should be replaced by the known constant I_0.)

8.5 A Case Study—School Rezoning to Achieve Racial Balance[1]

The city of *Middletown* has three high schools, two of them attended primarily by white students and the other attended primarily by black students. Therefore, the Middletown school board has decided to redesign the school attendance zones to reduce the racial isolation in these schools. The new zones will apply only to students entering high school in the future, so the goal is to achieve reasonable racial balance in 3 years without substantially increasing the distances that the students must travel to school.

The school district superintendent has read some articles about how operations research has been used to greatly aid the comprehensive planning of efficient zoning designs. On her recommendation, the school board has hired a team of operations research consultants to conduct the study and make recommendations.

The consultants begin by defining and gathering the relevant data. For this purpose they divide the city geographically into 10 tracts. Since the current junior high population represents the anticipated high school population in 3 years, they then determine the number of white students and black students now in junior high from each tract. The distance the students must travel to school is a fundamental consideration, so they also determine the distance (in miles) from the center of each tract to each school. All this information appears in Table 8.7, along with the maximum number of students that can be assigned to each school.

The consultants next begin formulating a *mathematical model* for the problem. In this case (as for many practical problems), the objective is not too well defined. Instead, only *two basic considerations* have been articulated (racial balance and distance traveled to school), and the goal is to achieve a reasonable *tradeoff* between them. A common approach in this kind of situation is to express one consideration in the objective function and the other in the constraints. Thus there is a choice between optimizing the racial balance subject to constraints on distance traveled or optimizing the distance traveled subject to constraints on racial balance. Because it is easier to express distance traveled in the objective

---

[1] Although this case study is a hypothetical one, it is similar to several actual studies that have been conducted in recent years. The theory is based primarily on a paper by L. B. Hickman and H. M. Taylor, "School Rezoning to Achieve Racial Balance: A Linear Programming Approach," *J. Socio-Econ. Planning Sci.*, 3:127–134, 1969–1970.

Table 8.7 **Data for Middletown study**

Tract	No. of whites	No. of blacks	Distance		
			School 1	School 2	School 3
1	300	150	1.2	1.5	3.3
2	400	0	2.6	4.0	5.5
3	200	300	0.7	1.1	2.8
4	0	500	1.8	1.3	2.0
5	200	200	1.5	0.4	2.3
6	100	350	2.0	0.6	1.7
7	250	200	1.2	1.4	3.1
8	300	200	3.5	2.3	1.2
9	150	250	3.2	1.2	0.7
10	350	100	3.8	1.8	1.0
School capacity:			1,500	2,000	1,300

function, and because it seems more reasonable to (eventually) set minimal standards on racial balance for the constraints, the consultants choose the latter alternative.

However, the objective of "optimizing the distance traveled" needs to be stated more precisely. One possibility is to *minimize the maximum distance* that any student must travel, using the corresponding formulation technique presented in Sec. 8.3, but this objective might lead to many students having to travel the maximum distance. Another more convenient objective that may yield a better overall result is to *minimize the sum of the distances traveled* by all students. If this leads to a few unacceptable inequities, they can be eliminated during the *sensitivity analysis* phase by introducing constraints on distance traveled by groups of students having excessive distances in the original optimal solution. Therefore, the structure chosen for the model is to *minimize total distance traveled* subject to constraints on racial balance and any other required constraints.

Ultimately decisions must be made about which individual students to assign to the respective schools. However, these detailed decisions on how to draw the boundaries of the school attendance zones can be worked out after the broader decisions on how many students from each tract to assign to each school are made. Therefore, the *decision variables* chosen for the model are

$$x_{ij} = \text{number of students in tract } i \text{ assigned}$$
$$\text{to school } j \ (i = 1, 2, \ldots, 10; \ j = 1, 2, 3).$$

Rather than breaking these variables down further into the number of white students and the number of black students to be assigned, the consultants made a *simplifying assumption* that the racial mixture in each tract will be maintained in the assignments to the respective schools. The resulting formulation of the model using Table 8.7 is as follows:

Minimize $Z = 1.2x_{11} + 1.5x_{12} + \cdots + 1.0x_{10,3},$

subject to the following constraints:

1. *Tract assignment*:

$$x_{11} + x_{12} + x_{13} = 450$$
$$x_{21} + x_{22} + x_{23} = 400$$
$$\vdots$$
$$x_{10,1} + x_{10,2} + x_{10,3} = 450.$$

2. *School capacity*:

$$x_{11} + x_{21} + \cdots + x_{10,1} \leq 1{,}500$$
$$x_{12} + x_{22} + \cdots + x_{10,2} \leq 2{,}000$$
$$x_{13} + x_{23} + \cdots + x_{10,3} \leq 1{,}300.$$

3. *Nonnegativity*:

$$x_{ij} \geq 0, \quad \text{for} \quad i = 1, 2, \ldots, 10 \quad \text{and} \quad j = 1, 2, 3.$$

and

4. *Racial balance*:

Still to be developed.

The racial balance constraints need to specify that the fraction of students of a given race in a given school must fall within certain limits. After discussing the issue with the school board and noting that the entire student population is equally divided between whites and blacks, it is decided that the same limits should apply to all the schools and that these limits should be *symmetric* with respect to the races. Thus, for each school and either race, the fraction of students should fall within the limits

$$\frac{1}{2} - \theta \leq \text{fraction} \leq \frac{1}{2} + \theta,$$

so that θ represents the maximum allowable deviation from an equal distribution of races in a school. However, the school board members do not wish to specify a value for θ at this point until they can see the consequences of their decision in terms of the distances that the students must travel. (Remember that they want to achieve a reasonable tradeoff between these two considerations.) Therefore, the consultants conclude that they should use *parametric programming* (see Secs. 4.7, 6.7, and 9.3) to determine how the optimal solution changes over the entire range of possible values of θ ($0 \leq \theta \leq \frac{1}{2}$).

To express the racial balance constraints mathematically, we must first express the fraction of students of each race in each school in terms of the decision variables. For example,

$$\text{Fraction of white students in school 1} = \frac{(\frac{300}{450})x_{11} + (\frac{400}{400})x_{21} + \cdots + (\frac{350}{450})x_{10,1}}{x_{11} + x_{21} + \cdots + x_{10,1}}$$

where each coefficient in the numerator is simply the number of white students in that tract divided by the total number of students in that tract (see Table 8.7). Thus the *lower limit* constraint on this fraction is

$$L \leq \frac{(\frac{2}{3})x_{11} + x_{21} + \cdots + (\frac{7}{9})x_{10,1}}{x_{11} + x_{21} + \cdots + x_{10,1}},$$

where

$$L = \frac{1}{2} - \theta.$$

Because constraints in this form require the use of less efficient *nonlinear* programming algorithms, the consultants next convert these constraints into an equivalent form that fits the *linear* programming format. This conversion is done by multiplying both sides by the denominator of the right-hand side to obtain

$$L(x_{11} + x_{21} + \cdots + x_{10,1}) \leq \frac{2}{3}x_{11} + x_{21} + \cdots + \frac{7}{9}x_{10,1},$$

and then subtracting this right-hand side from both sides to obtain

$$\left(L - \frac{2}{3}\right)x_{11} + (L - 1)x_{21} + \cdots + \left(L - \frac{7}{9}\right)x_{10,1} \leq 0.$$

This same approach is used to develop the lower limit constraints for all six fractions (one for each combination of race and school), which is summarized as follows:

4. *Racial balance*:

$$\left(L - \frac{2}{3}\right)x_{11} + (L - 1)x_{21} + \cdots + \left(L - \frac{7}{9}\right)x_{10,1} \leq 0$$

$$\left(L - \frac{1}{3}\right)x_{11} + (L - 0)x_{21} + \cdots + \left(L - \frac{2}{9}\right)x_{10,1} \leq 0$$

$$\left(L - \frac{2}{3}\right)x_{12} + (L - 1)x_{22} + \cdots + \left(L - \frac{7}{9}\right)x_{10,2} \leq 0$$

$$\left(L - \frac{1}{3}\right)x_{12} + (L - 0)x_{22} + \cdots + \left(L - \frac{2}{9}\right)x_{10,2} \leq 0$$

$$\left(L - \frac{2}{3}\right)x_{13} + (L - 1)x_{23} + \cdots + \left(L - \frac{7}{9}\right)x_{10,3} \leq 0$$

$$\left(L - \frac{1}{3}\right)x_{13} + (L - 0)x_{23} + \cdots + \left(L - \frac{2}{9}\right)x_{10,3} \leq 0.$$

This approach also could be used to develop the corresponding *upper limit* constraints representing the requirement that each fraction $\leq \frac{1}{2} + \theta$. However, because

Fraction of white students = 1 − fraction of black students,

the preceding lower limit constraints on both types of fractions *guarantee* that the upper limit requirements are satisfied also. Therefore, no additional constraints are needed for the model.

One flaw in this formulation is that the x_{ij} (as well as the corresponding numbers of white students and black students from tract i assigned to school j) are allowed to take on *noninteger* values (the *divisibility* assumption of linear programming). However, considering the large numbers of students involved, the consultants feel that there will be no difficulty in adjusting a noninteger optimal solution to integer values during the subsequent analysis. They know from experience that a linear programming formulation has major computational advantages over an *integer programming* formulation, so this approximation seems well worthwhile.

The stage now is set to begin the computational phase of the study. When L is sufficiently small (that is, θ is sufficiently close to $\frac{1}{2}$), the racial balance constraints have no effect and can be deleted. The consultants also note that the problem without these constraints can be formulated as a *transportation problem* (the special type of linear programming problem described in Sec. 7.1), as shown in Table 8.8. Therefore, rather than using the simplex method, they begin by applying the much more efficient *transportation simplex method* (see Sec. 7.2) to

Table 8.8 **Cost and requirements table for transportation problem formulation of Middletown problem without racial balance constraints**

Distance per student

		Destination			
		School 1	School 2	School 3	Supply
Source	Tract 1	1.2	1.5	3.3	450
	Tract 2	2.6	4.0	5.5	400
	Tract 3	0.7	1.1	2.8	500
	Tract 4	1.8	1.3	2.0	500
	Tract 5	1.5	0.4	2.3	400
	Tract 6	2.0	0.6	1.7	450
	Tract 7	1.2	1.4	3.1	450
	Tract 8	3.5	2.3	1.2	500
	Tract 9	3.2	1.2	0.7	400
	Tract 10	3.8	1.8	1.0	450
	Dummy 11(D)	0	0	0	300
Demand		1,500	2,000	1,300	

this formulation. The resulting optimal solution has basic variables $x_{11} = 450$, $x_{21} = 400$, $x_{31} = 500$, $x_{42} = 500$, $x_{52} = 400$, $x_{62} = 450$, $x_{71} = 150$, $x_{72} = 300$, $x_{83} = 500$, $x_{92} = 50$, $x_{93} = 350$, $x_{10,3} = 450$, $x_{11,2} = 300$, with $Z = 4,965$. (Notice that this solution already is an integer solution, which always occurs with transportation problems that have integer supplies and demands.)

The next step is to determine when this solution also is optimal for the original model with the racial balance constraints included. This determination is made by checking how large L can be made before the solution violates any of the racial balance constraints, which turns out to be $L \leq 0.285$. Because the solution is feasible for this range of values of L, it must also be optimal for these values.

Given this information, the consultants next use *parametric programming* to determine how the optimal solution changes as L is increased continuously to $\frac{1}{2}$, beginning with the preceding solution at $L = 0.285$. (This approach can be thought of as applying the *sensitivity analysis procedure* described in Sec. 6.6 on a continuing basis to determine the effect of introducing the racial balance constraints as needed and of changing the coefficients of the variables in these constraints.) However, they feel that the results in this form would be too complex to be considered effectively by the school board. Therefore, after a careful examination of the results, the consultants select a relatively small number of interesting alternatives—$L = 0.285$, 0.30, 0.35, 0.40—that represent a cross section of tradeoffs between racial balance and distance traveled (as summarized in Table 8.9). These alternatives are analyzed in detail and appropriate refinements are made in the "optimal solution" obtained from the model. The consultants then present their basic data and conclusions for the four alternatives to the school board.

After considerable deliberation, the school board members choose the $\theta = 0.15$ alternative. However, they modify this alternative slightly to avoid reassigning a very small proportion of one tract to a new school. The resulting master plan allocates tracts 2, 3, and 7 to school 1, tracts 1, 4, 5, and 6 to school 2, and tracts 8 and 9 to school 3, with tract 10 split as follows: $x_{10,2} = 50$, $x_{10,3} = 400$. Because this plan yields $\theta = 0.155$, the school board officially announces the new policy: that either race should form *at least one-third* the student body of any high school. They then instruct the superintendent to have her staff implement this policy, using the master plan as a basis for detailed planning.

Table 8.9 Summary of results for Middletown problem

θ	Optimal Z	Average distance traveled (miles)	Percentage			
			<1 mile	1.0–1.4 miles	1.5–1.9 miles	≥2 miles
0.215	4965	1.103	37.8	53.3	0	8.9
0.20	4983	1.107	38.9	51.1	1.1	8.9
0.15	5063	1.125	38.9	41.1	11.1	8.9
0.10	5182	1.152	38.9	36.1	16.1	8.9

8.6 Conclusions

This chapter has described and illustrated some particularly useful formulation techniques for building linear programming models. This material provides a good background for you, but the best teacher in this area is experience! Our goal has been to provide you with a solid foundation for dealing with real problems and for *continuing* to learn the art of linear programming.

SELECTED REFERENCES

1. Beale, E. M. L. (ed.): *Applications of Mathematical Programming Techniques*, American Elsevier, New York, 1970.
2. ————: *Mathematical Programming in Practice*, Wiley, New York, 1968.
3. Bradley, Stephen P., Arnoldo C. Hax, and Thomas L. Magnanti: *Applied Mathematical Programming*, Chaps. 5–7, Addison-Wesley, Reading, Mass., 1977.
4. Charnes, Abraham and William W. Cooper: *Management Models and Industrial Applications of Linear Programming*, Wiley, New York, 1961.
5. Driebeek, Norman J.: *Applied Linear Programming*, Addison-Wesley, Reading, Mass., 1969.
6. Ignizio, James P.: *Goal Programming and Extensions*, Heath, Lexington, Mass., 1976.
7. Lee, Sang M.: *Goal Programming for Decision Analysis*, Auerbach, Philadelphia, 1972.
8. Salkin, Harvey M. and Jahar Saha (eds.): *Studies in Linear Programming*, North-Holland/American Elsevier, Amsterdam/New York, 1975.
9. Williams, H. P.: *Model Building in Mathematical Programming*, 2d ed., Wiley, Chichester, England and New York, 1985.

PROBLEMS

1. Consider the following problem.

$$\text{Minimize} \quad Z = |x_1| + 2|x_2|,$$

subject to

$$
\begin{aligned}
x_1 + x_2 &\geq 2 \\
-x_1 + x_2 &\geq 3 \\
-x_1 - 3x_2 &\geq -12
\end{aligned}
$$

(no nonnegativity constraints).

(a) Use the technique presented in Sec. 8.1 to formulate the linear programming model for this problem.

(b) Use the *simplex method* to solve the model as formulated in (a).

(c) Solve the original problem *graphically* by considering *each* of the four quadrants separately.

2. Consider the following problem.

$$\text{Minimize} \quad Z = f_1(x_1) + f_2(x_2),$$

subject to

$$2x_1 + 3x_2 \geq 6$$
$$x_1 + 2x_2 \leq 6$$
$$-x_2 \leq 1$$

(no nonnegativity constraints), where

$$f_1(x_1) = \begin{cases} 3x_1, & \text{if} \quad x_1 \geq 0 \\ x_1, & \text{if} \quad x_1 \leq 0, \end{cases}$$

$$f_2(x_2) = \begin{cases} 4x_2, & \text{if} \quad x_2 \geq 0 \\ 3x_2, & \text{if} \quad x_2 \leq 0. \end{cases}$$

(a) Use the technique presented in Sec. 8.1 to formulate the linear programming model for this problem.

(b) Use the simplex method to solve the problem as formulated in (a).

(c) Solve the original problem graphically by considering *each* of the four quadrants separately.

3. Consider the following problem.

$$\text{Minimize} \quad Z = |x_1 - 2x_2 + x_3|,$$

subject to

$$2x_1 + 3x_2 + 4x_3 \geq 60$$
$$7x_1 + 5x_2 + 3x_3 \geq 105,$$

and

$$x_1 \geq 0, x_2 \geq 0, x_3 \geq 0.$$

Use the technique presented in Sec. 8.1 to formulate the linear programming model for this problem.

4. Consider the following problem.

$$\text{Minimize} \quad Z = f_1(3x_1 - 2x_2) + f_2(3x_2 - 4x_3),$$

subject to

$$10x_1 + 7x_2 + 12x_3 \geq 50$$
$$8x_1 + 9x_2 + 7x_3 \geq 40,$$

and

$$x_1 \geq 0, \quad x_2 \geq 0, \quad x_3 \geq 0,$$

where

$$f_1(3x_1 - 2x_2) = \begin{cases} 3(3x_1 - 2x_2), & \text{if} \quad 3x_1 - 2x_2 \geq 0 \\ -5(3x_1 - 2x_2), & \text{if} \quad 3x_1 - 2x_2 \leq 0, \end{cases}$$

$$f_2(3x_2 - 4x_3) = \begin{cases} 4(3x_2 - 4x_3), & \text{if} \quad 3x_2 - 4x_3 \geq 0 \\ -2(3x_2 - 4x_3), & \text{if} \quad 3x_2 - 4x_3 \leq 0. \end{cases}$$

Use the technique presented in Sec. 8.1 to formulate the linear programming model for this problem.

5. The Research and Development Division of a certain company has developed three new products. The problem is to decide which mix of these products should be produced. Management wants primary consideration given to three factors: long-run profit, stability in the work force, and achieving an increase in the company's earnings next year. In particular, using the units given in the following table, they want to

$$\text{Maximize} \quad Z = P - 3C - 2D,$$

where

P = total (discounted) profit over the life of the new products,

C = change (in either direction) in the current level of employment,

D = decrease (if any) in next year's earnings from the current year's level.

The amount of any increase in earnings does not enter into Z because management is primarily concerned with just achieving some increase to keep the stockholders happy. (It has mixed feelings about a large increase that then would be difficult to surpass in subsequent years.)

The impact of each of the new products (per unit rate of production) on each of these factors is shown in the following table.

Unit contribution

Factor	Product 1	2	3	Goal	(units)
Long-run profit	20	15	25	None	(millions of dollars)
Employment level	6	4	5	$=50$	(hundreds of employees)
Earnings next year	8	7	5	≥ 75	(millions of dollars)

Except for certain additional constraints not described here, use the *goal programming technique* to formulate the linear programming model for this problem.

6. Reconsider the Middletown case study presented in Section 8.5. Suppose that the objective is *changed* to *minimize racial imbalance* subject to a constraint on distance traveled and other necessary constraints. Racial imbalance is defined as the *sum* (over the three high schools) of *the absolute difference between the number of white students and the number of black students at each high school*. The constraint on distance traveled is that the average distance traveled by students to school *must not* exceed 1.15 miles.

Describe how this problem fits into the framework of nonpreemptive goal programming by identifying the goals involved, and then use the *goal programming technique* to formulate the new linear programming model.

7. Consider a *preemptive goal programming* problem with three priority levels, just one goal for each priority level, and just two activities to contribute toward these goals, as summarized in the following table:

Unit contribution

Priority level	Activity 1	2	Goal
First priority	1	2	≤ 20
Second priority	1	1	$=15$
Third priority	2	1	≥ 40

(a) Use the *goal programming technique* to formulate one complete linear programming model for this problem.

(b) Construct the initial simplex tableau for applying the *streamlined procedure*. Identify the *initial basic feasible solution* and the *initial entering basic variable*, but do not proceed further.

(c) Starting from (b), use the *streamlined procedure* to solve the problem *algebraically*.

(d) Use the logic of *preemptive goal programming* to solve the problem *graphically* by focusing on just the two decision variables. Explain the logic used.

(e) Use the *sequential procedure* to solve this problem. After using the *goal programming technique* to formulate the linear programming model (including auxiliary variables) at each stage, solve the model *graphically* by focusing on just the two decision variables. Identify *all* optimal solutions obtained for each stage.

8. Redo Prob. 7 with the following revised table.

Unit contribution

Priority level	Activity 1	2	Goal
First priority	1	1	≤ 10
Second priority	1	1	≥ 15
Third priority	1	2	≥ 30

9. A certain developing country has 15,000,000 acres of publicly controlled agricultural land in active use. Its government currently is planning a way to divide this land among three basic crops (labeled 1, 2, and 3) next year. A certain percentage of each of these crops is exported in order to obtain badly needed foreign capital (dollars), and the rest of each of these crops is used to feed the populace. Raising these crops also provides employment for a significant proportion of the population. Therefore, the main factors to be considered in allocating the land to these crops are (1) the amount of foreign capital generated, (2) the number of citizens fed, and (3) the number of citizens employed in raising these crops. The following table shows how much each 1,000 acres of each crop contributes toward these factors, and the last column gives the goal established by the government for each of these factors.

Contribution per 1,000 acres

Factor	Crop 1	2	3	Goal
Foreign capital	$3,000	$5,000	$4,000	$\geq \$70,000,000$
Citizens fed	150	75	100	$\geq 1,750,000$
Citizens employed	10	15	12	$= 200,000$

(a) In evaluating the relative seriousness of *not* achieving these goals, the government has concluded that the following deviations from the goals should be considered *equally undesirable*: (1) each $100 under the foreign capital goal, (2) each person under the citizens fed goal, and (3) each deviation of one (in either direction) from the citizens employed goal. Use the *goal programming technique* to formulate the linear programming model for this problem.

(*b*)   Now suppose that the government concludes that the importance of the various goals differs greatly so that a *preemptive goal programming* approach should be used. In particular, the first-priority goal is *citizens fed* $\geq 1{,}750{,}000$, the second-priority goal is *foreign capital* $\geq \$70{,}000{,}000$, and the third-priority goal is *citizens employed* $= 200{,}000$. Use the *goal programming technique* to formulate one complete linear programming model for this problem.

(*c*)   Use the *streamlined procedure* to solve the problem as formulated in (*b*).

(*d*)   Use the *sequential procedure* to solve the problem as presented in (*b*).

10.   Reconsider Prob. 9. Suppose now that the third-priority goal actually is a *lower one-sided goal* (desire $\geq 200{,}000$ citizens employed). The government feels that it is critical to come at least close to satisfying *all* of these goals. Therefore, the decision has been made to *reformulate* the problem to adopt the overriding objective of *maximizing the minimum progress* (on a percentage basis) toward all these goals.

Use the technique presented in Sec. 8.3 to formulate the linear programming model for this new problem.

11.   One of the most important problems in the field of *statistics* is the *linear regression problem*. Roughly speaking, this problem involves fitting a straight line to statistical data represented by points—(x_1,y_1), (x_2,y_2), ..., (x_n,y_n)—on a graph. If we denote the line by $y = a + bx$, the objective is to choose the constants a and b to provide the "best" fit according to some criterion. The criterion usually used is the *method of least squares*, but there are other interesting criteria where linear programming can be used to solve for the optimal values of a and b.

For each of the following criteria, formulate the linear programming model for this problem:

(*a*)   Minimize the sum of the absolute deviations of the data from the line; that is,

$$\text{Minimize} \quad \sum_{i=1}^{n} |y_i - (a + bx_i)|.$$

(*Hint*: Note that this problem can be viewed as a nonpreemptive goal programming problem where each data point represents a "goal" for the regression line.)

(*b*)   Minimize the maximum absolute deviation of the data from the line; that is,

$$\text{Minimize} \quad \max_{i=1,2,\ldots,n} |y_i - (a + bx_i)|.$$

12.   Reconsider the Middletown case study described in Sec. 8.5. Suppose that the objective is changed from minimizing the sum of the distances traveled by all students to minimizing the *maximum* over the tracts of the total distance traveled by the students in each respective tract, subject to the same constraints (including racial balance constraints) as before. Formulate the new linear programming model for this problem.

13.   Reconsider the Middletown case study described in Sec. 8.5. Suppose that bussing must be provided for all students traveling more than 1.5 miles (but to no others), and that the school board has adopted the objective of minimizing the total cost of this bussing, subject to the same constraints (including racial balance constraints) as before. Assuming that this cost is proportional to the sum of the distance traveled by all *bussed* students, formulate the new objective function for this problem.

14.   A company desires to blend a new alloy of 40 percent tin, 35 percent zinc, and

25 percent lead from several available alloys having the following properties:

| | Alloy | | | | |
Property	1	2	3	4	5
Percentage tin	60	25	45	20	50
Percentage zinc	10	15	45	50	40
Percentage lead	30	60	10	30	10
Cost ($/lb)	19	17	23	21	25

The objective is to determine the proportions of these alloys that should be blended to produce the new alloy at a minimum cost. Formulate the linear programming model for this problem.

15. At the beginning of the fall semester, the director of the computer facility of a certain university is confronted with the problem of assigning different working hours to his operators. Because all the operators are currently enrolled in the university, his main concern is to make certain that the operators' working times are not so excessive that they would interfere with study times.

There are six operators (four men and two women). They all have different wage rates because of differences in their experience with computers and in their programming ability. The following table shows their wage rates, along with the maximum number of hours each can work each day.

| | | Maximum hours of availability | | | | |
Operator	Wage rate	Mon.	Tue.	Wed.	Thurs.	Fri.
K. C.	$6.00/hour	6	0	6	0	6
D. H.	$6.10/hour	0	6	0	6	0
H. B.	$5.90/hour	4	8	4	0	4
S. C.	$5.80/hour	5	5	5	0	5
K. S.	$6.80/hour	3	0	3	8	0
N. K.	$7.30/hour	0	0	0	6	2

Because of a tight budget, the director has to minimize cost. His decision is that the operators with the highest wage rates should work the least possible number of hours, except this number should not be so low as to impair his or her knowledge of the operation. This level is set arbitrarily at 8 hours per week for the male operators and 7 hours per week for the female operators (K. S., N. K.).

The computer facility is to be open for operation from 8 A.M. to 10 P.M. Monday through Friday with exactly one operator on duty during these hours. On Saturdays and Sundays, the computer is to be operated by other staff.

Formulate a linear programming model so the director can determine the number of hours he should assign to each operator on each day.

16. A lumber company has three sources of wood and five markets to be supplied. The annual availability of wood at sources 1, 2, and 3 are 10, 20, and 15 million board feet, respectively. The amount that can be sold annually at markets 1, 2, 3, 4, and 5 are 7, 12, 9, 10, and 8 million board feet, respectively.

In the past the company has shipped the wood by train. However, because shipping costs have been increasing, the alternative of using ships to make some of the deliveries is being investigated. This alternative would require the company to invest in some ships.

Except for these investment costs, the shipping costs in thousands of dollars per million board feet by rail and by water (when feasible) would be the following for each route:

| | Unit cost by rail | | | | | Unit cost by ship | | | | |
| | Market | | | | | Market | | | | |
Source	1	2	3	4	5	1	2	3	4	5
1	61	72	45	55	66	31	38	24	—	35
2	69	78	60	49	56	36	43	28	24	31
3	59	66	63	61	47	—	33	36	32	26

The capital investment (in thousands of dollars) in ships required for each million board feet to be transported annually by ship along each route is given as follows:

| | Investment for ships | | | | |
| | Market | | | | |
Source	1	2	3	4	5
1	275	303	238	—	285
2	293	318	270	250	265
3	—	283	275	268	240

Considering the expected useful life of the ships and the time value of money, the equivalent uniform annual cost of these investments is one-tenth the amount given in the table. The company is able to raise only $6,750,000 to invest in ships. The objective is to determine the overall shipping plan that minimizes the total equivalent uniform annual cost while meeting this investment budget and the sales demand at the markets. Formulate the linear programming model for this problem.

17. A company needs to lease warehouse storage space over the next 5 months. Just how much space will be required in each of these months is known. However, since these space requirements are quite different, it may be most economical to lease only the amount needed each month on a month-by-month basis. On the other hand, the additional cost for leasing space for additional months is much less than for the first month, so it may be less expensive to lease the maximum amount needed for the entire 5 months. Another option is the intermediate approach of changing the total amount of space leased (by adding a new lease and/or having an old lease expire) at least once but not every month.

The space requirement (in thousands of square feet) and the leasing costs (in hundreds of dollars) for the various leasing periods are as follows:

Month	Required space	Leasing period (months)	Cost ($) per 1,000 sq ft leased
1	30	1	650
2	20	2	1,000
3	40	3	1,350
4	10	4	1,600
5	50	5	1,900

The objective is to minimize the total leasing cost for meeting the space requirements. Formulate the linear programming model for this problem.

18. A spaceship to take astronauts to Mars and back is being designed. This spaceship will have three compartments, each with its own independent life support system. The key element in each of these life support systems is a small *oxidizer* unit that triggers a chemical process for producing oxygen. However, these units cannot be tested in advance, and only some of them succeed in triggering this chemical process. Therefore, it is important to have several backup units for each system. Because the requirements are different for the three compartments, the units needed for each one have somewhat different characteristics. A decision must now be made on the number of units to be provided for each compartment, taking into account design limitations on the *total* amount of *space*, *weight*, and *cost* that can be allocated to these units for the entire spaceship. The following table summarizes these limitations, as well as the characteristics of the individual units for each compartment:

Compartment	Space (cu. in.)	Weight (lb)	Cost ($)	Probability of failure
1	40	15	40,000	0.30
2	50	20	45,000	0.40
3	30	10	35,000	0.20
Limitation	500	200	500,000	

If all the units fail in just one or two of the compartments, the astronauts can occupy the remaining compartment(s) and continue their space voyage but with some loss in the amount of scientific information they can obtain. However, if all units fail in all three compartments, the astronauts can still return the spaceship safely, but the whole voyage must be completely aborted at great expense. Therefore, the objective is to *minimize the probability* of all units failing, subject to the preceding limitations and the further restriction that each compartment has a probability of no more than 0.05 that all its units fail. Formulate the linear programming model for this problem (*Hint*: Use logarithms.)

19. One measure of the quality of the water in a river is its dissolved oxygen (D.O.) concentration. This measure is of interest partly because certain minimum concentration levels of D.O. are necessary to permit fish and other aquatic animals to survive. A large portion of the waste released into streams is organic material. This material is a source of nutrients for many organisms found in streams. In the process of utilizing the organic material, the organisms withdraw the D.O. contained in the stream. Thus the larger the amount of these wastes, the larger the biochemical oxygen demand (B.O.D.).

Consider the following river system consisting of two tributaries leading into the main stream. The daily flow rate of water at cities 1 to 4 is known to be $f_1, f_2, f_1 + f_2,$ $f_1 + f_2$, respectively. Water at city 1 or city 2 requires 1 day to reach city 3 and water at city 3 requires 1 day to reach city 4. Let D_i be the known D.O. concentration of the water just above city i ($i = 1,2$). Similarly, let B_i be the known waste concentration of the water, measured by its B.O.D. concentration, just above city i ($i = 1,2$). Wastes are discharged from cities 1 to 3 into the stream in known amounts w_1, w_2, w_3 per day. (These are negligible in comparison with f_1, f_2.)

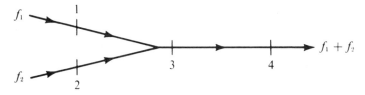

If the waste discharged from city i ($i = 1,2,3$) is untreated, its B.O.D. concentration would be U_i. However, if appropriate treatment processes are used, the B.O.D. concentration can be lowered to any level between L_i and U_i. The cost of reducing the

B.O.D. concentration from U_i is c_i per unit reduction. However, some treatment is necessary at some or all of these cities to achieve at least a minimum standard S for the D.O. concentration at cities 3 and 4. The problem is to choose the B.O.D. concentration of wastes discharged from cities 1 to 3 that minimizes the cost of meeting this standard.

The following biochemical model has been developed to help solve problems of this type. Suppose that river water has a daily flow rate of f and a B.O.D. concentration of b and then has waste discharged at a rate of w per day with a B.O.D. concentration of x. The effect immediately downstream is to raise the B.O.D. concentration of the water to

$$v_0 = \frac{bf + xw}{f + w} \approx b + \left(\frac{w}{f}\right)x.$$

There is no immediate effect on the D.O. concentration. However, both the D.O. concentration and the B.O.D. concentration would change gradually downstream. In particular, if u_0 and v_0 are, respectively, the current D.O. and B.O.D. concentrations of the water at a particular location on a river, and if no waste is added to this water, then the respective concentrations u_1, v_1 of D.O. and B.O.D. in this same water 1 day downstream become

$$u_1 = \alpha + \beta u_0 - \gamma v_0$$
$$v_1 = \delta + \varepsilon v_0,$$

where α, β, γ, δ, ε are positive constants reflecting the various underlying physical and biochemical processes. Formulate the linear programming model for this problem.

20. A large paper manufacturing company has 10 paper mills and a large number (say, 1,000) of customers to be supplied. It uses three alternative types of machines and four types of raw materials to make five different types of paper. Therefore, the company needs to develop a detailed production-distribution plan on a monthly basis, with an objective of minimizing the total cost of producing and distributing the paper during the month. Specifically, it is necessary to determine jointly the amount of each type of paper to be made at each paper mill on each type of machine *and* the amount of each type of paper to be shipped from each paper mill to each customer.

The relevant data can be expressed symbolically as

D_{jk} = numbers of units of paper type k demanded by customer j.

r_{klm} = number of units of raw material m needed to produce one unit of paper type k on machine type l.

R_{im} = number of units of raw material m available at paper mill i.

c_{kl} = number of capacity units of machine type l that will produce one unit of paper type k.

C_{il} = number of capacity units of machine type l available at paper mill i.

P_{ikl} = production cost for each unit of paper type k produced on machine type l at paper mill i.

T_{ijk} = transportation cost for each unit of paper type k shipped from paper mill i to customer j.

(*a*) Using these symbols, formulate the linear programming model for this problem.

(*b*) Considering the special structure of this model, give your recommendation on how it should be solved.

■ CHAPTER 9

Other Algorithms for Linear Programming

The key to the extremely widespread use of linear programming is the availability of an exceptionally efficient algorithm—the simplex method—that will routinely solve the large-sized problems that typically arise in practice. However, the simplex method is only part of the arsenal of algorithms regularly used by linear programming practitioners. Chapter 7 described several special classes of linear programming for which *streamlined* versions of the simplex method are available (as illustrated by the *transportation simplex method* in Sec. 7.2). Section 4.8 mentioned that production computer codes *adapt* the simplex method to a more convenient matrix form. Sections 4.7 and 6.6 pointed out how certain *modifications* or *extensions* of the simplex method are particularly useful for sensitivity analysis. Thus all these algorithms are *variants* of the simplex method as it was presented in Chap. 4. Consequently, they also are exceptionally efficient.

This chapter focuses on three particularly important algorithms based on the simplex method. In particular, the next three sections present the *upper bound technique* (a streamlined version of the simplex method for dealing with variables having upper bounds), the *dual simplex method* (a modification particularly useful for sensitivity analysis), and *parametric programming* (an extension for systematic sensitivity analysis).

9.1 The Upper Bound Technique

At the end of Sec. 7.5 we discussed the fact that it is common for some or all of the *individual* x_j variables to have *upper bound constraints*

$$x_j \le u_j,$$

where u_j is a positive constant representing the maximum *feasible* value of x_j. (The right-hand side of Fig. 7.32 shows the resulting *special structure* of the functional constraints.) However, we also pointed out in Sec. 4.8 that the most important determinant of computation time for the simplex method is the *number of functional constraints*, whereas the number of *nonnegativity* constraints is relatively unimportant. Therefore, having a large number of upper bound constraints among the functional constraints greatly increases computational effort. The *upper bound technique* avoids this increased effort by removing the upper bound constraints from the functional constraints and treating them separately, essentially like nonnegativity constraints. Removing the upper bound constraints in this way causes no problems as long as none of the variables get increased over their upper bounds. The only time the simplex method increases some of the variables is when the entering basic variable is increased to obtain a new basic feasible solution. Therefore, the upper bound technique simply applies the simplex method in the usual way to the *remainder* of the problem (i.e., without the upper bound constraints) but with the one additional restriction that each new basic feasible solution is required to satisfy the upper bound constraints in addition to the usual lower bound (nonnegativity) constraints.

To implement this idea, note that a decision variable x_j with an upper bound constraint $(x_j \le u_j)$ can always be replaced by

$$x_j = u_j - y_j,$$

where y_j would then be the decision variable. In other words, you have a choice between letting the decision variable be the *amount above zero* (x_j) or the *amount below* u_j $(y_j = u_j - x_j)$. (We shall refer to x_j and y_j as *complementary* decision variables.) Because

$$0 \le x_j \le u_j,$$

it also follows that

$$0 \le y_j \le u_j.$$

Thus at any point during the simplex method you can either

1. Use x_j,   where $0 \le x_j \le u_j$

or

2. Replace x_j by $(u_j - y_j)$, where $0 \le y_j \le u_j$.

The upper bound technique uses the following rule to make this choice:

Rule: Begin with choice 1.

Whenever $x_j = 0$, use choice 1, so x_j is *nonbasic*.

Whenever $x_j = y_j$, use choice 2, so $y_j = 0$ is *nonbasic*.

Switch choices only when the other extreme value of x_j is reached.

Therefore, whenever a *basic* variable reaches its upper bound, you should switch choices and use its *complementary* decision variable as the new nonbasic variable (the leaving basic variable) for identifying the new basic feasible solution. Thus the one substantive modification being made in the simplex method is in the rule for selecting the *leaving basic variable*.

Recall that the simplex method selects as the leaving basic variable the one which would be the first to become infeasible by going negative as the entering basic variable is increased. The modification now made is to select instead the variable that would be the first to become infeasible *in any way*, either by going negative or by going over the upper bound, as the entering basic variable is increased. (Notice that one possibility is that the *entering* basic variable may become infeasible first by going over its upper bound, so that its *complementary* variable becomes the leaving basic variable.) If the leaving basic variable reaches zero, then proceed as usual with the simplex method. However, if it reaches its upper bound instead, then switch choices and make its complementary decision variable the leaving basic variable.

To illustrate, consider the problem

$$\text{Maximize} \quad Z = 2x_1 + x_2 + 2x_3,$$

subject to

$$
\begin{aligned}
4x_1 + x_2 \quad\;\; &= 12 \\
-2x_1 \quad\;\; + x_3 &= 4,
\end{aligned}
$$

and

$$
\begin{aligned}
0 \le x_1 &\le 4 \\
0 \le x_2 &\le 15 \\
0 \le x_3 &\le 6.
\end{aligned}
$$

Thus all three variables have upper bound constraints ($u_1 = 4$, $u_2 = 15$, $u_3 = 6$). The two equality constraints are already in the appropriate form for identifying the initial basic feasible solution ($x_1 = 0$, $x_2 = 12$, $x_3 = 4$), and none of the variables in this solution exceed their upper bound, so x_2 and x_3 can be used as the initial basic variables without introducing artificial variables. However, these variables then need to be eliminated algebraically from the objective function to obtain the initial Eq. (0), as follows:

$$
\begin{array}{lrcr}
Z - & 2x_1 - x_2 - 2x_3 &=& 0 \\
+ & (4x_1 + x_2 &=& 12) \\
+2(& -2x_1 \quad\;\; + x_3 &=& 4) \\
\hline
& Z - 2x_1 \quad\;\; &=& 20.
\end{array}
$$

(0)

Thus the initial *entering basic variable* is x_1. Since the upper bound constraints are not to be included, the *entire* initial set of equations and the corresponding calculations for selecting the leaving basic variables are

		Maximum feasible value of x_1
(0)	$Z - 2x_1 \quad\quad\quad = 20$	$x_1 \le 4$ (since $u_1 = 4$)
(1)	$4x_1 + x_2 \quad\quad = 12$	$x_1 \le \dfrac{12}{4} = 3$
(2)	$-2x_1 \quad\quad + x_3 = 4$	$x_1 \le \dfrac{6-4}{2} = 1 \leftarrow$ min
		(because $u_3 = 6$)

The maximum feasible value of the x_1 column shows how much the entering basic variable x_1 can be *increased* from zero before some basic variable (including x_1) becomes infeasible. The maximum value given next to Eq. (0) is just the upper bound constraint for x_1. For Eq. (1), since the coefficient of x_1 is *positive*, *increasing* x_1 to 3 decreases the basic variable in this equation (x_2) from 12 to its *lower* bound of *zero*. For Eq. (2), since the coefficient of x_1 is *negative, increasing* x_1 to 1 *increases* the basic variable in this equation (x_3) from 4 to its *upper* bound of 6. Because this last maximum value of x_1 is the smallest, x_3 provides the *leaving* basic variable. However, because x_3 reached its *upper* bound, replace x_3 by $(6 - y_3)$ so that $y_3 = 0$ becomes the new *nonbasic* variable for the next basic feasible solution and x_1 becomes the new basic variable in Eq. (2). This replacement leads to the following changes in this equation:

$$(2) - 2x_1 \quad\quad + \quad x_3 = \quad 4$$
$$\rightarrow -2x_1 + (6 - \quad y_3) = \quad 4$$
$$\rightarrow -2x_1 \quad\quad - \quad y_3 = -2$$
$$\rightarrow \quad\quad x_1 \quad\quad + \frac{1}{2}y_3 = \quad 1.$$

Therefore, after eliminating x_1 algebraically from the other equations, the *second* complete set of equations becomes

$$(0) \quad\quad\quad\quad Z \quad\quad\quad + \quad y_3 = 22$$
$$(1) \quad\quad\quad\quad\quad\quad\quad x_2 - 2y_3 = \quad 8$$
$$(2) \quad\quad\quad\quad\quad\quad\quad\quad x_1 \quad + \frac{1}{2}y_3 = \quad 1.$$

The resulting basic feasible solution is $x_1 = 1$, $x_2 = 8$, $y_3 = 0$. By the *optimality test*, it also is an optimal solution, so $x_1 = 1$, $x_2 = 8$, $x_3 = 6 - y_3 = 6$ is the desired solution to the original problem.

9.2 The Dual Simplex Method

The *dual simplex method* can be thought of as the *mirror image* of the simplex method. This interpretation is best explained by referring to Tables 6.9 and 6.10 and Fig. 6.1. The simplex method deals directly with *suboptimal* basic solutions and moves toward an optimal solution by striving to satisfy the *optimality test*. By contrast, the dual simplex method deals directly with *superoptimal* basic solutions and moves toward an optimal solution by striving to achieve *feasibility*. Furthermore, the dual simplex method deals with a problem as if the simplex method were being applied simultaneously to its dual problem. If we make their *initial* basic solutions *complementary*, the two methods move in complete sequence, obtaining *complementary* basic solutions with each iteration.

The dual simplex method is very useful in certain special types of situations. Ordinarily it is easier to find an initial basic feasible solution than an initial superoptimal basic solution. However, it is occasionally necessary to introduce many *artificial* variables to construct an initial basic feasible solution artificially. In such cases it may be easier to begin with a superoptimal basic solution and use the dual simplex method. Furthermore, fewer iterations may be required when it is not necessary to drive many artificial variables to zero.

As we mentioned several times in Chap. 6 as well as Sec. 4.7, another important primary application of the dual simplex method is its use in conjunction with sensitivity analysis. Suppose that an optimal solution has been obtained by the simplex method but that it becomes necessary (or of interest for sensitivity analysis) to make minor changes in the model. If the formerly optimal basic solution is *no longer feasible* (but still satisfies the optimality test), you can immediately apply the dual simplex method by starting with this *superoptimal* basic solution. Applying the dual simplex method usually leads to the new optimal solution much more quickly than solving the new problem from the beginning with the simplex method.

The rules for the dual simplex method are very similar to those for the simplex method. In fact, once they are started, the only difference between them is in the criteria used for selecting the entering and the leaving basic variables and for stopping the algorithm. To start the dual simplex method, we must have all the coefficients in Eq. (0) *nonnegative* (so that the basic solution is superoptimal). The basic solutions will be infeasible (except for the last one) only because some of the variables are negative. The method continues to decrease the value of the objective function, always retaining *nonnegative coefficients* in Eq. (0), until all the *variables* are nonnegative. Such a basic solution is feasible (it satisfies all the equations) and is, therefore, optimal by the simplex method criterion of nonnegative coefficients in Eq. (0). The details of the dual simplex method are now summarized.

Summary of Dual Simplex Method

Initialization step: Introduce slack variables as needed to construct a set of equations describing the problem. Find a basic solution such that the coefficients in Eq. (0) are zero for basic variables and nonnegative for nonbasic variables. Go to the optimality test.

Iterative step:

Part 1   Determine the leaving basic variable: Select the basic variable with the *largest negative value.*

Part 2   Determine the entering basic variable: Select the nonbasic variable whose coefficient in Eq. (0) reaches zero first as an increasing multiple of the equation containing the leaving basic variable is added to Eq. (0). This selection is made by checking the nonbasic variables with *negative coefficients* in that equation (the one containing the leaving basic variable) and selecting the one with the smallest ratio of the Eq. (0) coefficient to the absolute value of the coefficient in that equation.

Part 3   Determine the new basic solution: Starting from the current set of equations, solve for the basic variables in terms of the nonbasic variables by the Gauss-Jordan method of elimination (see Appendix 4). When we set the nonbasic variables equal to zero, each basic variable (and Z) equals the new right-hand side of the one equation in which it appears (with a coefficient of $+1$).

Feasibility test: Determine whether this solution is feasible (and therefore optimal): Check to see whether all the basic variables are *nonnegative*. If they are, then this solution is feasible, and therefore optimal, so stop. Otherwise, go to the iterative step.

To fully understand the dual simplex method, you must realize that the method proceeds just as if the *simplex method* were being applied to the complementary basic solutions in the *dual problem*. (In fact, this interpretation was the motivation for constructing the method as it is.) Part 1, determining the leaving basic variable, is equivalent to determining the entering basic variable in the dual problem. The variable with the largest negative value corresponds to the largest negative coefficient in Eq. (0) of the dual problem (see Table 6.3). Part 2, determining the entering basic variable, is equivalent to determining the leaving basic variable in the dual problem. The coefficient in Eq. (0) that reaches zero first corresponds to the variable in the dual problem that reaches zero first. The two criteria for stopping the algorithm are also complementary.

We shall now illustrate the dual simplex method by applying it to the *dual problem* for the Wyndor Glass Co. (see Table 6.1). Normally this method is applied directly to the problem of concern (a primal problem). However, we have chosen this problem because you have already seen the simplex method applied to *its* dual problem (namely, the primal problem[1]) in Table 4.8 so you can compare the two. To facilitate the comparison, we shall continue to denote the decision variables in the problem being solved by y_i rather than x_j.

In *maximization* form, the problem to be solved is

$$\text{Maximize} \quad Z = -4y_1 - 12y_2 - 18y_3,$$

---

[1] Recall that the *symmetry property* in Secs. 6.1 and 6.4 points out that the dual of a dual problem is the original primal problem.

Table 9.1 Dual simplex method applied to Wyndor Glass Co. dual problem

Iteration	Basic variable	Eq. no.	Z	Coefficient of					Right side
				y_1	y_2	y_3	y_4	y_5	
0	Z	0	1	4	12	18	0	0	0
	y_4	1	0	−1	0	−3	1	0	−3
	y_5	2	0	0	−2	−2	0	1	−5
1	Z	0	1	4	0	6	0	6	−30
	y_4	1	0	−1	0	−3	1	0	−3
	y_2	2	0	0	1	1	0	$-\dfrac{1}{2}$	$\dfrac{5}{2}$
2	Z	0	1	2	0	0	2	6	−36
	y_3	1	0	$\dfrac{1}{3}$	0	1	$-\dfrac{1}{3}$	0	1
	y_2	2	0	$-\dfrac{1}{3}$	1	0	$\dfrac{1}{3}$	$-\dfrac{1}{2}$	$\dfrac{3}{2}$

subject to

$$y_1 \qquad + 3y_3 \geq 3$$
$$2y_2 + 2y_3 \geq 5,$$

and

$$y_1 \geq 0, \quad y_2 \geq 0, \quad y_3 \geq 0.$$

After the functional constraints are converted to $\leq$ form and the slack variables are introduced, the initial set of equations is that shown for iteration 0 in Table 9.1. Notice that all the coefficients in Eq. (0) are nonnegative, so the solution is optimal if it is feasible. The initial basic solution is $y_1 = 0$, $y_2 = 0$, $y_3 = 0$, $y_4 = -3$, $y_5 = -5$, with $Z = 0$, which is not feasible because of the negative values. The leaving basic variable is y_5 ($5 > 3$), and the entering basic variable is y_2 ($\frac{12}{2} < \frac{18}{2}$), which leads to the second set of equations shown after iteration 1 in Table 9.1. The corresponding basic solution is $y_1 = 0$, $y_2 = \frac{5}{2}$, $y_3 = 0$, $y_4 = -3$, $y_5 = 0$, with $Z = -30$, which is not feasible. The next leaving basic variable is y_4, and the entering basic variable is y_3 ($\frac{6}{3} < \frac{4}{1}$), which leads to the final set of equations in Table 9.1. The corresponding basic solution is $y_1 = 0$, $y_2 = \frac{3}{2}$, $y_3 = 1$, $y_4 = 0$, $y_5 = 0$, with $Z = -36$, which is feasible and therefore optimal.

Notice that the optimal solution for the *dual* of this problem[1] is $x_1^* = 2$, $x_2^* = 6$, $x_3^* = 2$, $x_4^* = 0$, $x_5^* = 0$, as was obtained in Table 4.8 by the simplex method. We suggest that you now trace through Tables 9.1 and 4.8 simultaneously and compare the complementary steps for the two mirror image methods.

---

[1] The *complementary optimal basic solutions property* presented in Sec. 6.3 indicates how to read the optimal solution for the dual problem from row 0 of the final simplex tableau for the primal problem.

9.3 Parametric Linear Programming

At the end of Sec. 6.7 we described *parametric linear programming* and its use for conducting sensitivity analysis systematically by gradually changing various model parameters simultaneously. We shall now present the algorithmic procedure, first for the case where the c_j parameters are being changed and then where the b_i parameters are varied.

SYSTEMATIC CHANGES IN THE c_j PARAMETERS

For this case, the *objective function* of the ordinary linear programming model,

$$Z = \sum_{j=1}^{n} c_j x_j,$$

is replaced by

$$Z(\theta) = \sum_{j=1}^{n} (c_j + \alpha_j \theta) x_j,$$

where the α_j are given input constants representing the *relative* rates at which the coefficients are being changed. Therefore, gradually increasing θ from zero changes the coefficients at these relative rates. The values assigned to the α_j may represent interesting simultaneous changes of the c_j for systematic sensitivity analysis of the effect of increasing the magnitude of these changes. They may also be based on how the coefficients (e.g., unit profits) would change together with respect to some factor measured by θ. This factor might be uncontrollable, e.g., the *state of the economy*. However, it may also be under the control of the decision maker, e.g., the amount of personnel and equipment to shift from some of the activities to others. For any given value of θ, the optimal solution of the corresponding linear programming problem can be obtained by the simplex method. This solution may have been obtained already for the original problem where $\theta = 0$. However, the objective is to *find the optimal solution* of the modified linear programming problem (maximize $Z(\theta)$ subject to the original constraints) *as a function of* θ. Therefore, the solution procedure needs to be able to determine when and how the optimal solution changes (if it does) as θ increases from zero to any specified positive number. This determination is portrayed graphically in Fig. 9.1, which shows how $Z^*(\theta)$, the objective function value for the optimal solution (given θ), changes as θ increases. $Z^*(\theta)$ always has this *piecewise linear* and *convex*[1] form (see Prob. 20), where the corresponding optimal solution changes (as θ increases) *just* at the values of θ where the slope changes.

The solution procedure is based directly upon the sensitivity analysis procedure for investigating changes in the c_j parameters (cases 2a and 3, Sec. 6.7). The only basic difference is that the changes now are expressed in terms of θ rather than as specific numbers. To illustrate, suppose that $\alpha_1 = 2$ and $\alpha_2 = -1$

---

[1] See Appendix 1 for a definition and discussion of *convex* functions.

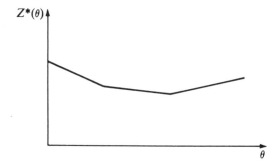

Figure 9.1 **Objective function value for an optimal solution as a function of θ for parametric linear programming with systematic changes in the c_j parameters.**

for the Wyndor Glass Co. problem (see Sec. 3.1 and Table 4.8), so that

$$Z(\theta) = (3 + 2\theta)x_1 + (5 - \theta)x_2.$$

Beginning with the *final* simplex tableau for $\theta = 0$ (Table 4.8), its Eq. (0),

(0)
$$Z + \frac{3}{2}x_4 + x_5 = 36,$$

would first have these changes from the *original* ($\theta = 0$) coefficients added into it on the left-hand side:

(0)
$$Z - 2\theta x_1 + \theta x_2 + \frac{3}{2}x_4 + x_5 = 36.$$

Because both x_1 and x_2 are basic variables (appearing in Eqs. (3) and (2), respectively), they both need to be eliminated algebraically from Eq. (0):

$$Z - 2\theta x_1 + \theta x_2 + \frac{3}{2}x_4 + x_5 = 36$$

$$+2\theta \text{ times Eq. (3)}$$

$$- \ \theta \text{ times Eq. (2)}$$

$$\overline{}$$

(0)
$$Z + \left(\frac{3}{2} - \frac{7}{6}\theta\right)x_4 + \left(1 + \frac{2}{3}\theta\right)x_5 = 36 - 20.$$

The *optimality* test says that the current basic feasible solution will *remain* optimal as long as these coefficients of the nonbasic variables remain *nonnegative*:

$$\frac{3}{2} - \frac{7}{6}\theta \geq 0, \quad \text{for} \quad 0 \leq \theta \leq \frac{9}{7},$$

$$1 + \frac{2}{3}\theta \geq 0, \quad \text{for all} \quad \theta \geq 0.$$

Therefore, after increasing θ past $\theta = \frac{9}{7}$, x_4 would need to be the *entering basic*

Table 9.2 The c_j parametric programming procedure applied to Wyndor Glass Co. example

Range of θ	Basic variable	Eq. no.	Z	x_1	x_2	x_3	x_4	x_5	Right side	Optimal solution
$0 \le \theta \le \dfrac{9}{7}$	$Z(\theta)$	0	1	0	0	0	$\dfrac{9-7\theta}{6}$	$\dfrac{3+2\theta}{3}$	$36-2\theta$	$x_4 = 0$ $x_5 = 0$
	x_3	1	0	0	0	1	$\dfrac{1}{3}$	$-\dfrac{1}{3}$	2	$x_3 = 2$
	x_2	2	0	0	1	0	$\dfrac{1}{2}$	0	6	$x_2 = 6$
	x_1	3	0	1	0	0	$-\dfrac{1}{3}$	$\dfrac{1}{3}$	2	$x_1 = 2$
$\dfrac{9}{7} \le \theta \le 5$	$Z(\theta)$	0	1	0	0	$\dfrac{-9+7\theta}{2}$	0	$\dfrac{5-\theta}{2}$	$27+5\theta$	$x_3 = 0$ $x_5 = 0$
	x_4	1	0	0	0	3	1	-1	6	$x_4 = 6$
	x_2	2	0	0	1	$-\dfrac{3}{2}$	0	$\dfrac{1}{2}$	3	$x_2 = 3$
	x_1	3	0	1	0	1	0	0	4	$x_1 = 4$
$\theta \ge 5$	$Z(\theta)$	0	1	0	$-5+\theta$	$3+2\theta$	0	0	$12+8\theta$	$x_2 = 0$ $x_3 = 0$
	x_4	1	0	0	2	0	1	0	12	$x_4 = 12$
	x_5	2	0	0	2	-3	0	1	6	$x_5 = 6$
	x_1	3	0	1	0	1	0	0	4	$x_1 = 4$

variable for another *iteration* of the simplex method to find the new optimal solution. Then θ would be increased further until another coefficient goes negative, and so on until θ has been increased as far as desired.

This entire procedure is now summarized, and the example is completed in Table 9.2.

Summary of Parametric Programming Procedure for Systematic Changes in the c_j Parameters

Step 1: Solve the problem with $\theta = 0$ by the simplex method.

Step 2: Use the sensitivity analysis procedure (cases 2a and 3, Sec. 6.7) to introduce the $\Delta c_j = \alpha_j \theta$ changes into Eq. (0).

Step 3: Increase θ until one of the nonbasic variables has its coefficient in Eq. (0) go negative (or until θ has been increased as far as desired).

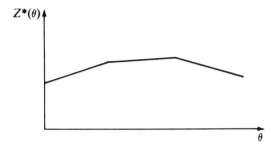

Figure 9.2 **Objective function value for an optimal solution as a function of θ for parametric linear programming with systematic changes in the b_i parameters.**

Step 4: Use this variable as the entering basic variable for an iteration of the simplex method to find the new optimal solution. Return to step 3.

SYSTEMATIC CHANGES IN THE b_i PARAMETERS

For this case, the one modification made in the original linear programming model is that b_i is replaced by $(b_i + \alpha_i\theta)$, for $i = 1, 2, \ldots, m$, where the α_i are given input constants. Thus the problem becomes

$$\text{Maximize} \quad Z(\theta) = \sum_{j=1}^{n} c_j x_j,$$

subject to

$$\sum_{j=1}^{n} a_{ij}x_j \leq b_i + \alpha_i\theta, \quad \text{for} \quad i = 1, 2, \ldots, m,$$

and

$$x_j \geq 0, \quad \text{for} \quad j = 1, 2, \ldots, n.$$

The goal is to identify the optimal solution as a function of θ. With this formulation, the corresponding objective function value $Z^*(\theta)$ always has the *piecewise linear* and *concave*[1] form shown in Fig. 9.2. (See Prob. 21.) The set of basic variables in the optimal solution still changes (as θ increases) *only* where the slope of $Z^*(\theta)$ changes, but now the values of these variables change as a (linear) function of θ between the slope changes.

The following solution procedure summary is very similar to that just presented for systematic changes in the c_j parameters. The reason is that changing the b_i is equivalent to changing the coefficients in the objective function of the *dual* model. Therefore, the procedure for the primal problem is exactly *complementary* to applying simultaneously the procedure for systematic changes in the c_j parameters to the *dual* problem. Consequently, the *dual simplex method*

---

[1] See Appendix 1 for a definition and discussion of *concave* functions.

(see Sec. 9.2) now would be used to obtain each new optimal solution, and the applicable sensitivity analysis case (see Sec. 6.7) now is case 1, but these differences are the only ones.

Summary of Parametric Programming Procedure for Systematic Changes in the b_i Parameters

Step 1: Solve the problem with $\theta = 0$ by the simplex method.

Step 2: Use the sensitivity analysis procedure (case 1, Sec. 6.7) to introduce the $\Delta b_i = \alpha_i \theta$ changes into the right-side column.

Step 3: Increase θ until one of the basic variables has its value in the right-side column go negative (or until θ has been increased as far as desired).

Step 4: Use this variable as the leaving basic variable for an iteration of the dual simplex method to find the new optimal solution. Return to step 3.

To illustrate this procedure in a way that demonstrates its *duality* relationship with the procedure for systematic changes in the c_j parameters, we shall now apply it to the *dual* problem for the Wyndor Glass Co. (see Table 6.1). In particular, suppose that $\alpha_1 = 2$ and $\alpha_2 = -1$ so that the functional constraints become

$$y_1 \quad + 3y_3 \geq 3 + 2\theta, \quad \text{or} \quad -y_1 \quad - 3y_3 \leq -3 - 2\theta$$
$$2y_2 + 2y_3 \geq 5 - \theta, \quad \text{or} \quad -2y_2 - 2y_3 \leq -5 + \theta,$$

Thus the *dual* of this problem is just the example considered in Table 9.2.

This problem with $\theta = 0$ has already been solved in Table 9.1, so we begin with the *final* simplex tableau given there. Using the sensitivity analysis procedure for case 1, Sec. 6.7, we find that the entries in the right-side column of this tableau change to the values given below.

$$y_0^* = \mathbf{y}^* \bar{\mathbf{b}} = [2,6] \begin{bmatrix} -3 & -2\theta \\ -5 & +\theta \end{bmatrix} = -36 + 2\theta,$$

$$\mathbf{b}^* = \mathbf{S}^* \bar{\mathbf{b}} = \begin{bmatrix} -1/3 & 0 \\ 1/3 & -1/2 \end{bmatrix} \begin{bmatrix} -3 & -2\theta \\ -5 & +\theta \end{bmatrix} = \begin{bmatrix} 1 & +2\theta/3 \\ 3/2 & -7\theta/6 \end{bmatrix}.$$

Therefore, the two basic variables

$$y_3 = \frac{3 + 2\theta}{3}$$

and

$$y_2 = \frac{9 - 7\theta}{6}$$

remain nonnegative for $0 \leq \theta \leq \frac{9}{7}$. Increasing θ past $\theta = \frac{9}{7}$ requires making y_2 a

Table 9.3 **The b_i parametric programming procedure applied to dual of Wyndor Glass Co. example**

Range of θ	Basic variable	Eq. no.	Z	y_1	y_2	y_3	y_4	y_5	Right side	Optimal solution
	$Z(\theta)$	0	1	2	0	0	2	6	$-36 + 2\theta$	$y_1 = y_4 = y_5 = 0$
$0 \leq \theta \leq \dfrac{9}{7}$	y_3	1	0	$\dfrac{1}{3}$	0	1	$-\dfrac{1}{3}$	0	$\dfrac{3 + 2\theta}{3}$	$y_3 = \dfrac{3 + 2\theta}{3}$
	y_2	2	0	$-\dfrac{1}{3}$	1	0	$\dfrac{1}{3}$	$-\dfrac{1}{2}$	$\dfrac{9 - 7\theta}{6}$	$y_2 = \dfrac{9 - 7\theta}{6}$
	$Z(\theta)$	0	1	0	6	0	4	3	$-27 - 5\theta$	$y_2 = y_4 = y_5 = 0$
$\dfrac{9}{7} \leq \theta \leq 5$	y_3	1	0	0	1	1	0	$-\dfrac{1}{2}$	$\dfrac{5 - \theta}{2}$	$y_3 = \dfrac{5 - \theta}{2}$
	y_1	2	0	1	-3	0	-1	$\dfrac{3}{2}$	$\dfrac{-9 + 7\theta}{2}$	$y_1 = \dfrac{-9 + 7\theta}{2}$
	$Z(\theta)$	0	1	0	12	6	4	0	$-12 - 8\theta$	$y_2 = y_3 = y_4 = 0$
$\theta \geq 5$	y_5	1	0	0	-2	-2	0	1	$-5 + \theta$	$y_5 = -5 + \theta$
	y_1	2	0	1	0	3	-1	0	$3 + 2\theta$	$y_1 = 3 + 2\theta$

leaving basic variable for another *iteration* of the dual simplex method, and so on, as summarized in Table 9.3.

We suggest that you now trace through Tables 9.2 and 9.3 simultaneously to note the *duality* relationship between the two procedures.

9.4 Conclusions

This chapter has presented three particularly important algorithms for linear programming practitioners. Mathematical programming computer packages usually include them, and they are widely used. Because their basic structure is largely based upon the simplex method as presented in Chap. 4, they retain the exceptional computational efficiency to handle very large problems of the sizes described in Sec. 4.8.

The *dual simplex method* and *parametric linear programming* are especially valuable for sensitivity analysis, although they also can be very useful in other contexts as well.

The *upper bound technique* provides a way of streamlining the simplex method for the common situation in which many or all of the variables have explicit upper bounds. It can greatly reduce the computational effort for large problems. Various other special-purpose algorithms also have been developed to exploit the special structure of particular types of linear programming problems (such as those discussed in Chap. 7). Much research is currently being done in this area.

SELECTED REFERENCES

1. Bradley, Stephen P., Arnoldo C. Hax, and Thomas L. Magnanti: *Applied Mathematical Programming*, Addison-Wesley, Reading, Mass., 1977.

2. Dantzig, George B.: *Linear Programming and Extensions*, Princeton University Press, Princeton, N.J., 1963.

3. Lasdon, Leon S.: *Optimization Theory for Large Systems*, Macmillan, New York, 1970.

4. Orchard-Hays, William: *Advanced Linear-Programming Computing Techniques*, McGraw-Hill, New York, 1968.

PROBLEMS

1. Use the *upper bound technique* to solve the Wyndor Glass Co. problem presented in Sec 3.1.

2. Consider the following problem.

$$\text{Maximize} \quad Z = 15x_1 + 10x_2,$$

subject to

$$x_1 - x_2 \leq 1$$
$$x_1 \qquad \leq 2$$
$$x_2 \leq 2,$$

and

$$x_1 \geq 0, \quad x_2 \geq 0.$$

(*a*) Solve this problem graphically.

(*b*) Use the *upper bound technique* to solve this problem.

(*c*) Trace graphically the path taken by the upper bound technique.

3. Use the *upper bound technique* to solve the following problem.

$$\text{Maximize} \quad Z = x_1 + 3x_2 - 2x_3,$$

subject to

$$x_2 - 2x_3 \leq 1$$
$$2x_1 + x_2 + 2x_3 \leq 8$$
$$x_1 \leq 1$$
$$x_2 \leq 3$$
$$x_3 \leq 2,$$

and

$$x_1 \geq 0, \quad x_2 \geq 0, \quad x_3 \geq 0.$$

4. Use the *upper bound technique* to solve the following problem.

$$\text{Maximize} \quad Z = 2x_1 + 3x_2 - 2x_3 + 5x_4,$$

subject to

$$2x_1 + 2x_2 + x_3 + 2x_4 \le 5$$
$$x_1 + 2x_2 - 3x_3 + 4x_4 \le 5,$$

and

$$0 \le x_j \le 1, \quad \text{for} \quad j = 1, 2, 3, 4.$$

5. Use the *upper bound technique* to solve the linear programming model given in Prob. 4b, Chap 6.

6. Consider the following problem.

$$\text{Maximize} \quad Z = -x_1 - x_2,$$

subject to

$$x_1 + x_2 \le 6$$
$$x_2 \ge 2$$
$$-x_1 + x_2 \le 1,$$

and

$$x_1 \ge 0, \quad x_2 \ge 0.$$

  (a) Solve this problem graphically.
  (b) Use the *dual simplex method* to solve this problem.
  (c) Trace graphically the path taken by the dual simplex method.

7. Use the *dual simplex method* to solve each of the following linear programming models:

  (a) Model given in Prob. 11, Chap. 4.
  (b) Model given in Prob. 18, Chap. 4.

8. Use the *dual simplex method* to solve the following problem.

$$\text{Minimize} \quad Z = 5x_1 + 2x_2 + 4x_3,$$

subject to

$$3x_1 + x_2 + 2x_3 \ge 4$$
$$6x_1 + 3x_2 + 5x_3 \ge 10,$$

and

$$x_1 \ge 0, \quad x_2 \ge 0, \quad x_3 \ge 0.$$

9. Use the *dual simplex method* to solve the following problem.

$$\text{Minimize} \quad Z = 42x_1 + 12x_2 + 30x_3 + 24x_4,$$

subject to

$$2x_1 + 4x_2 + 7x_3 + x_4 \ge 25$$
$$8x_1 + 4x_2 + 6x_3 + 4x_4 \ge 40$$
$$3x_1 + 8x_2 + x_3 + 4x_4 \ge 20,$$

and

$$x_j \ge 0, \quad \text{for} \quad j = 1, \dots, 4.$$

10. Consider the following problem.

$$\text{Maximize} \quad Z = 3x_1 + 2x_2,$$

subject to

$$3x_1 + x_2 \le 40$$
$$x_1 + x_2 \le 20$$
$$5x_1 + 3x_2 \le 90,$$

and

$$x_1 \ge 0, x_2 \ge 0.$$

(a) Solve by the *original simplex method* (in tabular form). Identify the *complementary* basic solution for the dual problem obtained at each iteration.
(b) Solve the *dual* of this problem by the *dual simplex method*. Compare the resulting sequence of basic solutions with the complementary basic solutions obtained in part (a).

11. Consider the example for case 1 of sensitivity analysis given in Sec. 6.7, where the initial simplex tableau of Table 4.8 is modified by changing b_2 from 12 to 24, thereby changing the respective entries in the right-side column of the *final* simplex tableau to 54, 6, 12, and -2. Starting from this revised final simplex tableau, use the *dual simplex method* to obtain the new optimal solution shown in Table 6.18. Show your work.

12. Consider Prob. 30 (a) and (b), Chap. 6. Use the *dual simplex method* to obtain the new optimal solution for each of these two cases.

13. Use *both* the *upper bound technique* and the *dual simplex method* to solve the following problem.

$$\text{Minimize} \quad Z = 2x_1 + 4x_2 + 3x_3,$$

subject to

$$x_1 + x_2 \qquad \ge 2$$
$$x_2 + x_3 \ge 3,$$

and

$$0 \le x_1 \le 3, \quad 0 \le x_2 \le 1, \quad 0 \le x_3 \le 5.$$

14. Use *both* the *upper bound technique* and the *dual simplex method* to solve the Nori & Leets Co. problem given in Sec. 3.4 for controlling air pollution.

15. Consider the following problem.

$$\text{Maximize} \quad Z = 8x_1 + 24x_2,$$

subject to

$$x_1 + 2x_2 \le 10$$
$$2x_1 + x_2 \le 10,$$

and

$$x_1 \ge 0, \quad x_2 \ge 0.$$

Suppose that Z represents profit and that it is possible to modify the objective function somewhat by an appropriate shifting of key personnel between the two activities. In particular, suppose that the unit profit of activity 1 can be increased above 8 (to a maximum of 18) at the expense of decreasing the unit profit of activity 2 below 24 by twice the amount. Thus Z can actually be represented as

$$Z(\theta) = (8 + \theta)x_1 + (24 - 2\theta)x_2,$$

where θ is also a decision variable such that $0 \le \theta \le 10$.

(a) Solve the original form of this problem graphically. Then extend this graphical procedure to solve the parametric extension of the problem; i.e., find the optimal value of $Z(\theta)$ as a function of θ, for $0 \le \theta \le 10$.

(b) Find the optimal solution to the original form of the problem by the simplex method. Then use *parametric linear programming* to find the optimal solution and the optimal value of $Z(\theta)$ as a function of θ, for $0 \le \theta \le 10$. Plot $Z(\theta)$.

(c) Determine the optimal value of θ. Then indicate how this optimal value could have been identified directly by solving only two ordinary linear programming problems. (*Hint:* A convex function achieves its maximum at an end point.)

16. Use *parametric linear programming* to find the optimal solution of the following problem as a function of θ, for $0 \le \theta \le 20$:

$$\text{Maximize} \quad Z(\theta) = (300 + 60\theta)x_1 + (450 - 45\theta)x_2 + 75x_3,$$

subject to

$$
\begin{aligned}
3x_1 + 3x_2 + x_3 &\le 30 \\
8x_1 + 6x_2 + 4x_3 &\le 80 \\
6x_1 + x_2 + x_3 &\le 45,
\end{aligned}
$$

and

$$x_1 \ge 0, \quad x_2 \ge 0, \quad x_3 \ge 0.$$

17. Consider the following problem.

$$\text{Maximize} \quad Z(\theta) = (10 - \theta)x_1 + (7 + 2\theta)x_2 + (12 + \theta)x_3,$$

subject to

$$
\begin{aligned}
x_1 + 2x_2 + 2x_3 &\le 30, \\
x_1 + x_2 + x_3 &\le 20,
\end{aligned}
$$

and

$$x_1 \ge 0, \quad x_2 \ge 0, \quad x_3 \ge 0.$$

(a) Use *parametric linear programming* to find the optimal solution for this problem as a function of θ, for $\theta \ge 0$.

(b) Construct the dual model for this problem. Then find the optimal solution for this dual problem as a function of θ, for $\theta \ge 0$, by the method described in the latter part of Sec. 9.3. Indicate graphically what this algebraic procedure is doing. Compare the basic solutions obtained with the complementary basic solutions obtained in part (a).

18. Use the *parametric linear programming* procedure for making systematic changes in the b_i parameters to find the optimal solution for the following problem as a function of θ, for $0 \le \theta \le 25$.

$$\text{Maximize} \quad Z(\theta) = 2x_1 + x_2,$$

subject to

$$
\begin{aligned}
x_1 &\le 10 + 2\theta \\
x_1 + x_2 &\le 25 - \theta \\
x_2 &\le 10 + 2\theta,
\end{aligned}
$$

and

$$x_1 \ge 0, \quad x_2 \ge 0.$$

Indicate graphically what this algebraic procedure is doing.

19. Use the *parametric linear programming* procedure for making systematic changes in the b_i parameters to find the optimal solution for the following problem as a function of θ, for $0 \le \theta \le 20$.

$$\text{Maximize} \quad Z(\theta) = 20x_1 + 24x_2 + 16x_3 + 28x_4,$$

subject to

$$
\begin{aligned}
3x_1 - 2x_2 + x_3 + 3x_4 &\le 135 - 2\theta \\
2x_1 + 4x_2 - x_3 + 2x_4 &\le 78 - \theta \\
x_1 + 2x_2 + x_3 + 2x_4 &\le 30 + \theta,
\end{aligned}
$$

and

$$x_j \ge 0, \quad \text{for} \quad j = 1, 2, 3, 4.$$

Then identify the value of θ that gives the largest optimal value of $Z(\theta)$.

20. Consider the $Z^*(\theta)$ function shown in Fig. 9.1 for *parametric linear programming* with systematic changes in the c_j parameters.

(a) Explain why this function is *piecewise linear*.
(b) Show that this function must be *convex*.

21. Consider the $Z^*(\theta)$ function shown in Fig. 9.2 for *parametric linear programming* with system changes in the b_i parameters.

(a) Explain why this function is *piecewise linear*.
(b) Show that this function must be *concave*.

22. Let

$$Z^* = \max \left\{ \sum_{j=1}^{n} c_j x_j \right\},$$

subject to

$$\sum_{j=1}^{n} a_{ij} x_j \le b_i, \quad \text{for} \quad i = 1, 2, \ldots, m,$$

and

$$x_j \geq 0, \quad \text{for} \quad j = 1, 2, \dots, n,$$

(where the a_{ij}, b_i, and c_j are fixed constants), and let $(y_1^*, y_2^*, \dots, y_m^*)$ be the corresponding optimal dual solution. Then let

$$Z^{**} = \max \left\{ \sum_{j=1}^{n} c_j x_j \right\},$$

subject to

$$\sum_{j=1}^{n} a_{ij} x_j \leq b_i + k_i, \quad \text{for} \quad i = 1, 2, \dots, m,$$

and

$$x_j \geq 0, \quad \text{for} \quad j = 1, 2, \dots, n,$$

where $k_1, k_2, \dots, k_m$ are given constants. Show that

$$Z^{**} \leq Z^* + \sum_{i=1}^{m} k_i y_i^*.$$

Mathematical Programming

■ CHAPTER 10

Network Analysis, Including PERT-CPM

Network analysis has long played an important role in electrical engineering. In recent decades, there has been a growing awareness that certain concepts and tools of network theory are also very useful in many other contexts. For example, important applications of network analysis have been made in *information theory, cybernetics*, the study of *transportation systems*, and the planning and control of *research and development projects*. Other areas of application include social-group structures, communication systems, production schedules, chemical-bond structures, and language structures. The network representation provides a powerful conceptual aid for portraying the relationships between the components of the complicated systems frequently studied by operations researchers. As a result, certain aspects of network analysis (commonly called *network flow theory*) have become an extremely useful tool of operations research.

One basic problem of network theory that commonly arises in the study of transportation systems is finding the *shortest route* through a network. A similar problem is to choose a set of connections that provides a route between any two points of a network in such a way as to *minimize the total length of these connections*. Another fundamental problem involves allocating flows to *maximize the flow* through a network connecting a source and a destination. *Project planning and control* is a fourth problem area that has been attacked by network techniques, especially PERT (Program Evaluation and Review Technique) and CPM (Critical Path Method).

The first section introduces a prototype example that will be used subsequently to illustrate the approach to the first three of these problems. Section 10.2 presents some basic terminology for networks. The remainder of the chapter is then devoted to the four problems: the shortest-route problem, the minimal spanning tree problem, the maximal flow problem, and project planning and control with PERT-CPM.

10.1 Prototype Example

Seervada Park has recently been set aside for a limited amount of sightseeing and backpack hiking. Cars are not allowed into the park, but there is a narrow, winding road system for trams and for jeeps driven by the park rangers. This road system is shown (without the curves) in Fig. 10.1, where location O is the entrance into the park; other letters designate the locations of ranger stations (and other limited facilities). The numbers give the distances of these winding roads in miles.

The park contains a scenic wonder at station T. A small number of trams are used to transport sightseers from the park entrance to station T and back.

The park management currently faces three problems. One is to determine which route from the park entrance to station T has the *smallest total distance* for the operation of the trams. (This is an example of the *shortest-route problem* to be discussed in Sec. 10.3.)

A second problem is that telephone lines must be installed under the roads to establish telephone communication between all the stations (including the park entrance). Because the installation is both expensive and disruptive to the natural environment, lines will be installed under just enough roads to provide some connection between every pair of stations. The question is where the lines should be laid to accomplish this with a *minimum* total number of miles of line installed. (This is an example of the *minimal spanning tree problem* to be discussed in Sec. 10.4.)

The third problem is that more people want to take the tram ride from the park entrance to station T than can be accommodated during the peak season. To

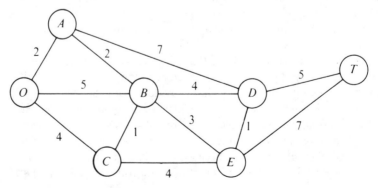

Figure 10.1 **The road system for Seervada Park.**

avoid unduly disturbing the ecology and wildlife of the region, a strict ration has been placed on the number of tram trips that can be made on each of the roads per day. (These limits differ for the different roads, as we shall describe in detail in Sec. 10.5.) Therefore, during the peak season, various routes might be followed regardless of distance to increase the number of tram trips that can be made each day. The question is how to route the various trips to *maximize* the number of trips that can be made per day without violating the limits on any individual road. (This is an example of the *maximal flow problem* to be discussed in Sec. 10.5.)

You will see later in the chapter how each of these problems is solved.

10.2 The Terminology of Networks

According to the terminology of the *theory of graphs*, a **graph** consists of a set of junction points called **nodes**, with certain pairs of the nodes being joined by lines called **branches** (or arcs or links or edges). Thus Fig. 10.1 is an example of a graph, where the circles designating stations are the nodes and the roads connecting them are the branches. A **network** is considered to be a graph with a flow of some type in its branches. There are numerous examples of systems satisfying this definition of network, as suggested by Table 10.1.

Additional terminology has been developed to describe graphs. A **chain** between nodes i and j is a sequence of branches connecting these two nodes. For example, one of the chains connecting nodes O and T in Fig. 10.1 is the sequence of branches OB, BD, DT, or vice versa. When the direction of travel along the chain is also specified, it is called a **path**. A **cycle** is a chain connecting a node to itself without retracing its steps. Thus AD, DB, and BA form a cycle in Fig. 10.1.

A graph is said to be a **connected graph** if there is a chain connecting every pair of nodes. Thus the graph of Fig. 10.1 is a connected graph, but it would not be if branches AD, BD, BE, and CE were removed. A **tree** is a connected graph (for some set of nodes) containing no cycles. For example, Fig. 10.1 would be a tree if the only branches were OB, BD, DT, BA, BC, and DE. One of the theorems of graph theory states that a graph having n nodes is connected if it has $(n - 1)$ branches and no cycles (so that such a graph is a tree). A graph having these properties is referred to as a **spanning tree**.

A branch of a graph is said to be **oriented** (or directed) if a sense of direction is attributed to the branch such that one node is considered the point of origin and the other node the point of destination. An **oriented graph** is one in which all

Table 10.1 **Components of typical networks**

Nodes	Branches	Flow
Intersections	Roads	Vehicles
Airports	Air lanes	Aircraft
Switching points	Wires, channels	Messages
Pumping stations	Pipes	Fluid
Work centers	Materials-handling routes	Jobs

the branches are oriented. If an oriented graph is a network, the orientation of a branch is the feasible direction of flow along the branch. However, a network need not be oriented because it may be feasible to have flow in either direction along a branch. The **flow capacity** of a branch in a specified direction is the upper limit to the feasible amount of flow (expressed either as a rate or a total quantity) in the branch in that direction. The flow capacity may be any nonnegative quantity, including infinity. A branch is oriented if the flow capacity is zero in one direction. A node may also have a limited flow capacity—although that possibility is ignored here.

A node in a network is referred to as a **source** if every one of its branches has an orientation such that the flow moves away from that node. Similarly, it is called a **sink** if each of its branches is oriented toward that node. Thus sources may be thought of as the generators of the flow, and sinks may be thought of as the absorbers of that flow.

10.3 The Shortest-Route Problem

The shortest-route problem is concerned with finding the *shortest route from an origin to a destination through a connecting network*, given the nonnegative distance associated with the respective branches of the network. Although various similar solution procedures (algorithms) have been proposed, the version described here is perhaps the shortest and simplest. The essence of this procedure is that it fans out from the origin, successively identifying the shortest route to each of the nodes of the network in the ascending order of their (shortest) distances from the origin, thereby solving the problem when the destination node is reached. We shall first outline the method and then illustrate it by solving the shortest-route problem encountered by the *Seervada Park* management in Sec. 10.1.

Algorithm for Shortest-Route Problem

Objective of nth iteration: Find nth nearest node to origin. (To be repeated for $n = 1, 2, \ldots$ until nth nearest node is the destination.)

Input for nth iteration: $(n - 1)$ nearest nodes to origin (solved for at previous iterations), including their shortest route and distance from the origin. (These nodes, plus the origin, will be called *solved nodes*; the others are *unsolved nodes*.)

Candidates for nth nearest node: Each solved node that is directly connected by a branch to one or more unsolved nodes provides *one* candidate—the unsolved node with the *shortest* connecting branch. (Ties provide additional candidates.)

Calculation of nth nearest node: For each such solved node and its candidate, add the distance between them and the distance of the shortest route from the origin to this solved node. The candidate with the smallest such total distance is the nth nearest node (ties provide additional solved nodes), and its shortest route is the one generating this distance.

Table 10.2 **Applying algorithm for shortest-route problem to Seervada Park problem**

n	Solved nodes directly connected to unsolved nodes	Closest connected unsolved node	Total distance involved	nth nearest node	Minimum distance	Last connection
1	O	A	2	A	2	OA
2	O	C	4	C	4	OC
	A	B	2 + 2 = 4	B	4	AB
4	A	D	2 + 7 = 9			
	B	E	4 + 3 = 7	E	7	BE
	C	E	4 + 4 = 8			
5	A	D	2 + 7 = 9			
	B	D	4 + 4 = 8	D	8	BD
	E	D	7 + 1 = 8	D	8	ED
6	D	T	8 + 5 = 13	T	13	DT
	E	T	7 + 7 = 14			

EXAMPLE The Seervada Park management needs to find the shortest route from the park entrance (node O) to the scenic wonder (node T) through the road system shown in Fig. 10.1. Applying the preceding algorithm to this problem yields the results shown in Table 10.2 (where the tie for the second nearest node allows skipping directly to seeking the fourth nearest node next). The first column (n) indicates the iteration count. The second column simply lists the *solved nodes* for beginning the current iteration after deleting the irrelevant ones (those not directly connected to any unsolved node). The third column then gives the *candidates* for the nth nearest node (the unsolved nodes with the *shortest* connecting branch to a solved node). The fourth column calculates the distance of the shortest route from the origin to each of these candidates (namely, the distance to the solved node plus the branch distance to the candidate). The candidate with the smallest such distance is the nth nearest node to the origin, as listed in the fifth column. The last two columns summarize the information for this *newest solved node* that is needed to proceed to subsequent iterations (namely, the distance of the shortest route from the origin to this node and the last branch on this shortest route).

The shortest route *from the destination to the origin* can now be traced back through the last column of Table 10.2 as *either* $T \to D \to E \to B \to A \to O$ or $T \to D \to B \to A \to O$. Therefore, the two alternates for the shortest route *from the origin to the destination* have been identified as $O \to A \to B \to E \to D \to T$ and $O \to A \to B \to D \to T$, with a total distance of 13 miles on either route.

OTHER APPLICATIONS

Before concluding this discussion of the shortest-route problem, we need to emphasize one point. The problem thus far has been described in terms of minimizing the *distance* from an origin to a destination. However, in actuality the network problem being solved is finding which path connecting two specified nodes minimizes the sum of the *branch values* on the path. There is no reason that these branch values need to represent *distances*, even indirectly. For example, the branches might correspond to *activities* of some kind, where the value associated with each branch is the *cost* of that activity. The problem then would be to find which sequence of activities that accomplishes a specified objective minimizes the total *cost* involved. (See Prob. 2.) Another alternative is that the value associated with each branch is the *time* required for that activity. The problem then would be to find which sequence of activities that accomplishes a specified objective minimizes the total *time* involved. (See Prob. 4.) Thus some of the most important applications of the shortest-route problem have nothing to do with *routes* in the usual sense of the word.

10.4 The Minimal Spanning Tree Problem

Now consider a variation of the shortest-route problem known as the *minimal spanning tree* problem. As before, a set of nodes and the distances[1] between pairs of these nodes are given. However, the branches between the nodes are no longer specified. Thus, rather than finding a shortest route through a fully defined network, the problem involves *choosing* for the network the *branches* that have the *shortest total length* while providing a route between each pair of nodes. The branches need to be chosen in such a way that the resulting network forms a *tree* (as defined in Sec. 10.2) that spans (i.e., connects to) all the given nodes. In short, the problem is to find the *spanning tree* with a minimum total length of the branches.

    Figure 10.2 illustrates this concept of a *spanning tree* for the Seervada Park problem (see Sec. 10.1). Thus Fig. 10.2a is *not* a *spanning* tree because the (O,A,B,C) nodes are not connected with the (D,E,T) nodes. It needs another branch to make this connection. This network actually consists of *two* trees, one for each of these two sets of nodes. The branches in Fig. 10.2b do *span* the network (i.e., it is a *connected graph* as defined in Sec. 10.2), but it is *not a tree* because there are two cycles (O–A–B–C–O and D–T–E–D). It has too many branches. Because the Seervada Park problem has $n = 7$ nodes, Sec. 10.2 indicates that the network must have exactly $(n - 1) = 6$ branches, with *no cycles*, to qualify as a spanning tree. This condition is achieved in Fig. 10.2c, so this network is a *feasible* solution (with a value of 24 miles for the total length of the branches) for the minimal spanning tree problem. (You soon will see that this solution is not *optimal* because it is possible to construct a spanning tree with only 14 miles of branches.)

    This problem has a number of important practical applications. For example, it can sometimes be helpful in planning *transportation networks* that will not be used much, where the primary consideration is to provide *some* connecting route between all pairs of nodes in the *most economical* way. (See Prob. 6.) The

---

[1] Once again, "distance" instead can be cost, time, or some other quantity.

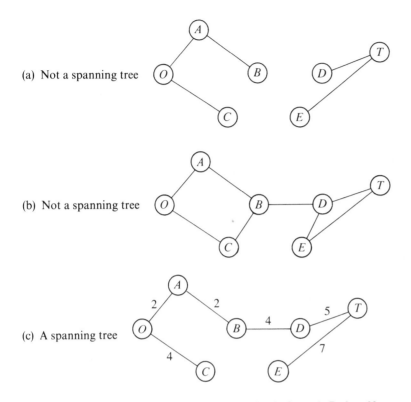

Figure 10.2 **Illustrations of the spanning tree concept for the Seervada Park problem.**

nodes would be the locations that require access to the other locations, the branches would be transportation lanes (highways, railroad tracks, air lanes, and so forth), and the "distances" (branch values) would be the costs of providing the transportation lanes. In this context, the minimal spanning tree problem is to determine which transportation lanes would service all the locations with a minimum total cost. Other examples where a comparable decision arises include the planning of large-scale *communication networks* and *distribution networks*. Both represent important application areas.

The minimal spanning tree problem can be solved in a very straightforward way because it happens to be one of the few operations research problems where being *greedy* at each stage of the solution procedure still leads to an overall optimal solution at the end! Thus, beginning with any node, the first stage involves choosing the shortest possible branch to another node, without worrying about the effect this choice would have on subsequent decisions. The second stage involves identifying the unconnected node that is closest to either of these connected nodes and then adding the corresponding branch to the network. This process would be repeated, as per the following summary, until all the nodes have been connected. The resulting network is guaranteed to be a minimal spanning tree.

Algorithm for Minimal Spanning Tree Problem

1. Select any node arbitrarily, and then connect it to the nearest distinct node.

2. Identify the unconnected node that is closest to a connected node, and then connect these two nodes. Repeat this procedure until all nodes have been connected.

TIE BREAKING Ties for the nearest distinct node (step 1) or the closest unconnected node (step 2) may be broken arbitrarily and the algorithm must still yield an optimal solution. However, such ties are a signal that there may be (but need not be) multiple optimal solutions. All such optimal solutions can be identified by pursuing all ways of breaking ties to their conclusion.

The fastest way of executing this algorithm manually is the graphical approach illustrated as follows.

EXAMPLE The Seervada Park management (see Sec. 10.1) needs to determine under which roads telephone lines should be installed to connect all stations with a minimum total length of line. Using the data given in Fig. 10.1, we outline the step-by-step solution of this problem next.

Nodes and distances for the problem are

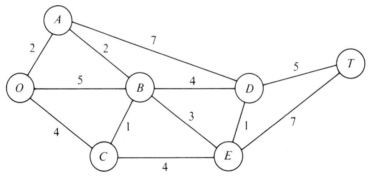

Arbitrarily select node O to start. The unconnected node closest to node O is node A. Connect node A to node O.

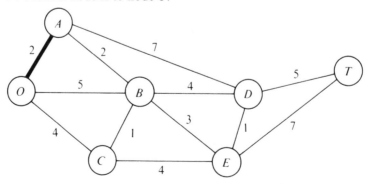

The unconnected node closest to either node O or A is node B (closest to A). Connect node B to node A.

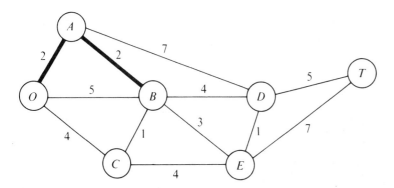

The unconnected node closest to node O, A, or B is node C (closest to B). Connect node C to node B.

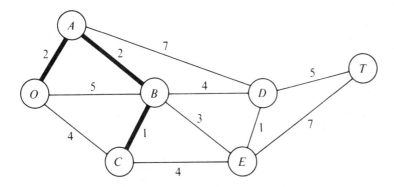

The unconnected node closest to node O, A, B, or C is node E (closest to B). Connect node E to node B.

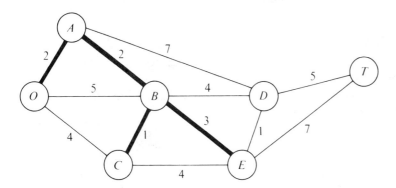

The unconnected node closest to node O, A, B, C, or E is node D (closest to E). Connect node D to node E.

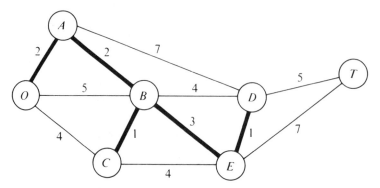

The only remaining unconnected node is node T. It is closest to node D. Connect node T to node D.

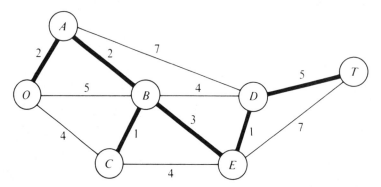

All nodes are now connected, so this solution to the problem is the desired (optimal) one. The total length of the branches is 14 miles.

Although it may appear at first glance that the choice of the initial node will affect the resulting final solution (and its total branch length) with this procedure, it really doesn't. We suggest you verify this fact for the example by reapplying the algorithm, starting with nodes other than node O.

10.5 The Maximal Flow Problem

Now recall that the third problem facing the Seervada Park management (see Sec. 10.1) during the peak season is to determine how to route the various tram trips from the park entrance (station O in Fig. 10.1) to the scenic wonder (station T) to maximize the number of trips per day. (Each tram will return by the same route it took on the outgoing trip, so the analysis focuses on outgoing trips only.) Strict upper limits have been imposed on the number of outgoing trips allowed in each direction on each individual road. These limits are shown in Fig. 10.3, where the numbers next to each station and road give the limit for that road in the direction leading away from that station. For example, only *one* loaded trip per day is

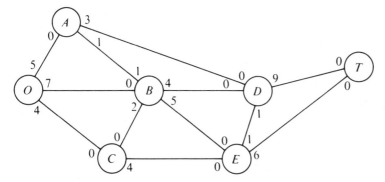

Figure 10.3 Limits on the number of trips per day for the Seervada Park problem.

allowed from station A to station B, but one other also is allowed from station B to station A. Given the limits, one *feasible solution* is to send seven trams per day, with five using the route $O \to B \to E \to T$, one using $O \to B \to C \to E \to T$, and one using $O \to B \to C \to E \to D \to T$. However, because this solution blocks the use of any routes starting with $O \to C$ (because the $E \to T$ and $E \to D$ capacities are fully used), it is easy to find better feasible solutions. Many *combinations* of routes (and the number of trips to assign to each one) need to be considered to find the one(s) maximizing the number of trips made per day. This kind of problem is called a *maximal flow problem*.

Using the terminology introduced in Sec. 10.2, the maximal flow problem can be described formally as follows. Consider a connected network having a single *source* and a single *sink*. Assume *conservation of flow* (i.e., flow into the node equals flow out of the node) at each node other than the source and the sink. Suppose that the rate (or total quantity) of flow along branch (i, j) from node i to node j can be any nonnegative quantity not exceeding the specified *flow capacity* c_{ij}. The objective is to determine the feasible pattern of flows through the network that *maximizes the total flow* from the source to the sink.

The maximal flow problem actually can be formulated as a *linear programming problem* (see Prob. 9), so it can be solved by the simplex method. However, an even more efficient algorithm is available for solving this problem. Except for one refinement, the procedure is simply to select repeatedly *any* path from the source to the sink and assign the maximum feasible flow to that path, continuing this process until no more paths still have *strictly positive flow capacity*. (The flow capacity of a path equals the *smallest remaining flow capacity* for any branch on that path, which is just the maximum feasible flow that can be assigned to the path.) Because this indiscriminate selection of paths for assigning flows may prevent the use of a better combination of flow assignments, the purpose of the refinement is to *undo* a previous assignment to make room for a better one. It accomplishes this goal by merely modifying the process just described to permit assigning fictional flows in the "wrong" direction along a branch *also* (i.e., in a direction having zero flow capacity) when the real effect of this assignment is only to cancel out part or all of the previously assigned flow in the "right" direction. To permit this cancellation, whenever some amount of flow is assigned to a branch in one direction (thereby decreasing the remaining flow capacity by that amount), the remaining flow capacity in the *opposite* direction for that branch should be *increased* by the same amount. Therefore, each *iteration* of the algorithm consists of the following three steps.

Algorithm for Maximal Flow Problem[1]

1. Find a path from source to sink with *strictly positive flow capacity*. (If none exists, the net flows already assigned constitute an optimal flow pattern.)

2. Search this path for the branch with the *smallest remaining flow capacity* (denote this capacity as c^*), and *increase* the flow in this path by c^*.

3. *Decrease* by c^* the *remaining flow capacity* of each branch in the path. *Increase* by c^* the *remaining flow capacity* in the opposite direction for each branch in the path. Return to step 1.

EXAMPLE Applying this algorithm to the Seervada Park problem (with an arbitrary selection of the path at each iteration) yields the results summarized next, where the numbers on the branches represent *remaining flow capacities.* (For the original network, see Fig. 10.3.)

Iteration 1   Assign a flow of 5 to $O \rightarrow B \rightarrow E \rightarrow T$. The resulting network is

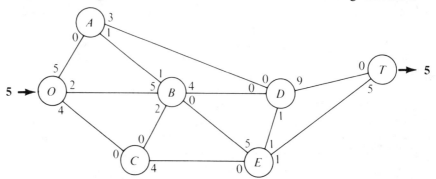

Iteration 2   Assign a flow of 3 to $O \rightarrow A \rightarrow D \rightarrow T$. The resulting network is

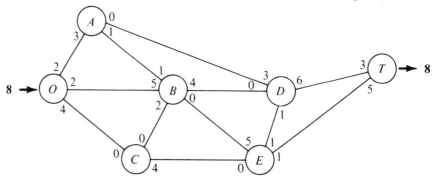

[1] It is assumed that the flow capacities are either integers or rational numbers.

Iteration 3 Assign a flow of 1 to $O \to A \to B \to D \to T$.

Iteration 4 Assign a flow of 2 to $O \to B \to D \to T$. The resulting network is

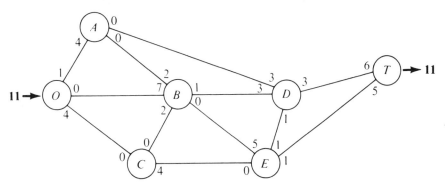

Iteration 5 Assign a flow of 1 to $O \to C \to E \to D \to T$.

Iteration 6 Assign a flow of 1 to $O \to C \to E \to T$. The resulting network is

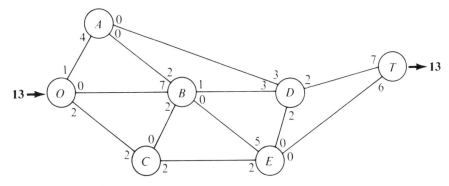

Iteration 7 Assign a flow of 1 to $O \to C \to E \to B \to D \to T$. The resulting network is

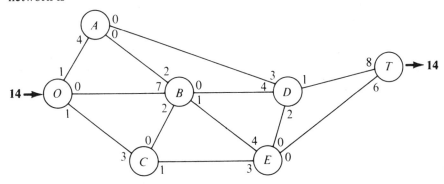

No paths with strictly positive flow capacity remain.
The current flow pattern is optimal.

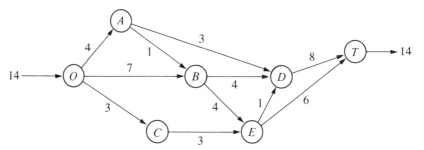

Figure 10.4 **Optimal solution for the Seervada Park maximal flow problem.**

The current flow pattern may be identified by either cumulating the flow assignments or by comparing the remaining flow capacities with the original flow capacities. If we use the latter method, the direction of net flow in a branch is in the direction of a branch whose remaining flow capacity is less than the original capacity. The magnitude of this flow equals the amount by which this original flow capacity has been decreased. Applying this method by comparing the network obtained from the last iteration with Fig. 10.3 yields the optimal flow pattern shown in Fig. 10.4.

This example nicely illustrates the role of the *refinement* in the solution procedure just discussed. Without the refinement, the first six iterations would be unchanged. However, at that point it would appear that no paths with strictly positive flow capacity remain (because the real flow capacity for $E \to B$ is *zero*). Therefore, the refinement permits adding the flow assignment of 1 for $O \to C \to E \to B \to D \to T$ in *iteration 7*. In effect, this additional flow assignment cancels out one unit of flow assigned at *iteration 1* ($O \to B \to E \to T$) and replaces it by assignments of one unit of flow to *both* $O \to B \to D \to T$ and $O \to C \to E \to T$.

The most difficult part of this algorithm when *large* networks are involved is finding a path from source to sink with positive flow capacity. This task may be simplified by the following systematic procedure. Begin by determining all nodes that can be reached from the source along a (single) branch with positive flow capacity. Then, for each of these nodes that were reached, determine all *new* nodes (those not yet reached) that can be reached from this node along a branch with positive flow capacity. Repeat this successively with the new nodes as they are reached. The result will be the identification of a tree of all the nodes that can be reached from the source along a path with positive flow capacity. Hence this *fanning-out procedure* will always identify a path from source to sink with positive flow capacity, if one exists. The procedure is illustrated in Fig. 10.5 for the network that results from *iteration 6* in the preceding example.

Although the procedure illustrated in Fig. 10.5 is a relatively straightforward one, it would be helpful to be able to recognize when optimality has been reached without an exhaustive search for a nonexistent path. It is sometimes possible to recognize this event because of an important theorem of network theory known

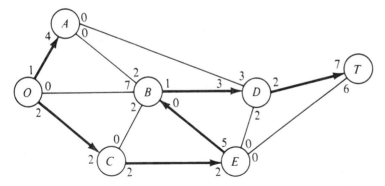

Figure 10.5 **Procedure for finding a path from source to sink with positive flow capacity for iteration 7 of the Seervada Park example.**

as the *max-flow min-cut theorem*. A *cut* may be defined as *any set of oriented branches containing at least one branch from every path from source to sink*. The *cut value* is the *sum of the flow capacities of the branches (in the specified direction) of the cut*. The **max-flow min-cut theorem** states that, for any network with a single source and sink, the *maximum feasible flow* from source to sink *equals* the *minimum cut value* for all of the cuts of the network. Thus, if we let F denote the amount of flow from source to sink for any feasible flow pattern, the value of any cut provides an upper bound to F, and the smallest of the cut values is equal to the maximum value of F. Therefore, if a cut whose value equals the value of F currently attained by the solution procedure can be found in the original network, the current flow pattern must be *optimal*. Equivalently, optimality has been attained whenever there exists a cut whose value is zero with respect to the *remaining* flow capacities in the current network.

To illustrate, consider the cut in the network of Fig. 10.3 that is indicated in Fig. 10.6. Notice that the value of the cut is $(3 + 4 + 1 + 6) = 14$, which was found to be the maximum value of F, so this cut is a *minimal cut*. Notice also that,

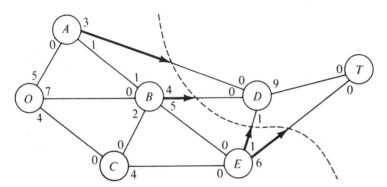

Figure 10.6 **A minimal cut for the Seervada Park problem.**

in the network resulting from *iteration 7*, where $F = 14$, the corresponding cut has a value of *zero* with respect to the *remaining* flow capacities. If this had been noticed, it would not have been necessary to search for additional paths from source to sink with positive flow capacity.

10.6 Project Planning and Control with PERT-CPM

The successful management of large-scale projects requires careful *planning*, *scheduling*, and *coordinating* of numerous interrelated activities. To aid in these tasks, formal procedures based on the use of *networks* and *network techniques* were developed beginning in the late 1950s. The most prominent of these procedures are PERT (Program Evaluation and Review Technique) and CPM (Critical Path Method), although there have been many variants under different names. As you will see later, there are a few important differences between these two procedures. However, in recent years the trend has been to merge the two approaches into what is usually referred to as a *PERT-type system*.

Although the original application of PERT-type systems was for evaluating a schedule for a research and development program, it is also used to measure and control progress on numerous other types of special projects. Examples of these project types include construction programs, programming of computers, preparation of bids and proposals, maintenance planning, and the installation of computer systems. This kind of approach has even been applied to the production of motion pictures, political campaigns, and complex surgery.

A PERT-type system is designed to *aid* in planning and control, so it may not involve much direct *optimization*. Sometimes one of the primary objectives is to determine the probability of meeting specified deadlines. It also identifies the activities that are most likely to be bottlenecks and, therefore, the places where the greatest effort should be made to stay on schedule. A third objective is to evaluate the effect of changes in the program. For example, it will evaluate the effect of a contemplated shift of resources from the less critical activities to the activities identified as probable bottlenecks. Other resource and performance tradeoffs may also be evaluated. Another important use is to evaluate the effect of deviations from schedule.

All PERT-type systems use a **project network** to portray graphically the interrelationships among the elements of a project. This network representation of the project plan shows all the *precedence relationships* regarding the order in which tasks must be performed. This feature is illustrated by Fig. 10.7, which shows the initial project network for building a house.

In the terminology of PERT, each *branch* of the project network represents an **activity** that is one of the tasks required by the project. Each *node* represents an **event** that usually is defined as the point in time when all activities leading into that node are completed. The *arrowheads* indicate the sequences in which the events must be achieved. Furthermore, an event must precede the initiation

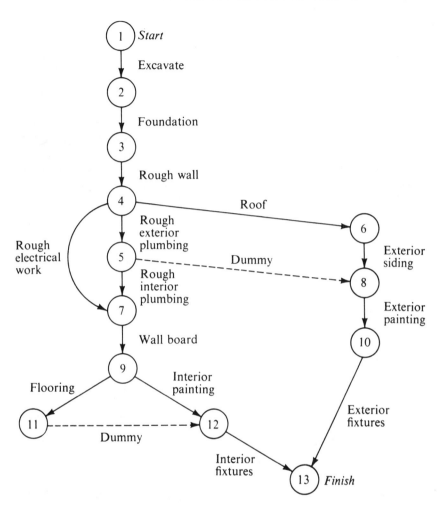

Figure 10.7 **Initial *project network* for constructing a house.**

of the activities leading out of that node. (In reality, it is often possible to over-lap successive phases of a project, so the network may represent an approximate idealization of the project plan.) The node toward which all activities lead (the *sink* of the network) is the event that corresponds to the completion of the currently planned project. The network may represent either the plan for the project from its inception or, if the project has already begun, the plan for the completion of the project. In the latter case, each *source* of the network represents either the event of continuing a current activity or the event of initiating a new activity that may begin at any time.

Dashed-line arrows, called **dummies**, show precedence relationships only; they do not represent real activities. For example, there is a dummy branch from node 5 to node 8 in Fig. 10.7 because the rough exterior plumbing must be completed before the exterior painting can begin. A common rule for constructing these project networks is that two nodes can be directly connected by *no more than one* branch. Dummy activities can also be used to avoid violating this rule when there are two or more concurrent activities, as illustrated by the dummy branch from node 11 to node 12 in Fig. 10.7.

After the network for a project has been developed, the next step is to estimate the *time* required for each of the activities. These estimates for the house-construction example of Fig. 10.7 are shown by the darker numbers (in units of *work days*) next to the branches in Fig. 10.8. These times are used to calculate two basic quantities for *each event*, namely, its *earliest time* and its *latest time*.

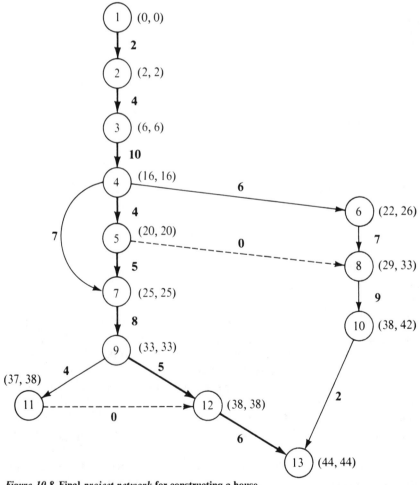

Figure 10.8 Final *project network* for constructing a house.

Table 10.3 **Calculation of earliest times for house-construction example**

Event	Immediately preceding event	Earliest + Activity time time	Maximum = earliest time
1	—	—	0
2	1	0 + 2	2
3	2	2 + 4	6
4	3	6 + 10	16
5	4	16 + 4	20
6	4	16 + 6	22
7	4	16 + 7	25
	5	20 + 5	
8	5	20 + 0	29
	6	22 + 7	
9	7	25 + 8	33
10	8	29 + 9	38
11	9	33 + 4	37
12	9	33 + 5	38
	11	37 + 0	
13	10	38 + 2	44
	12	38 + 6	

The **earliest time** for an event is the (estimated) time at which the event will occur if the *preceding* activities are started *as early as possible.*

The *earliest times* are obtained by making a *forward pass* through the network, starting with the initial events and working forward in time toward the final events, successively calculating the time at which each event will occur if each immediately preceding event occurs at its earliest time and each intervening activity consumes exactly its estimated time. The initiation of the project should be labeled as time 0. This process is shown in Table 10.3 for the example considered in Figs. 10.7 and 10.8. The resulting earliest times are recorded in Fig. 10.8 as the *first* of the two numbers given by each node.

The **latest time** for an event is the (estimated) last time at which the event can occur *without delaying the completion of the project* beyond its earliest time.

In this case, the latest times are obtained successively for the events by making a *backward pass* through the network, starting with the final events and working backward in time toward the initial events, each time calculating the final time the event can occur in order for each immediately *following* event to occur at its latest time if each intervening activity consumes exactly its estimated time. This process is illustrated in Table 10.4, with 44 as the earliest time *and* latest time for the completion of the house-construction project. The resulting latest times are recorded in Fig. 10.8 as the *second* of the two numbers given by each node.

Table 10.4 **Calculation of latest times for house-construction example**

Event	Immediately following event	Latest — Activity time — time	Minimum = latest time
13	—	—	44
12	13	44–6	38
11	12	38–0	38
10	13	44–2	42
9	12	38–5	33
	11	38–4	
8	10	42–9	33
7	9	33–8	25
6	8	33–7	26
5	8	33–0	20
	7	25–5	
4	7	25–7	16
	6	26–6	
	5	20–4	
3	4	16–10	6
2	3	6–4	2
1	2	2–2	0

Let activity (i, j) denote the activity going from event i to event j in the project network.

> The **slack for an event** is the *difference* between its latest and its earliest time. The **slack for an activity** (i, j) is the *difference* between [the latest time of event j] and [the earliest time of event i plus the estimated activity time].

Thus, assuming everything else remains on schedule, the *slack for an event* indicates how much delay in reaching the event can be tolerated without delaying the project completion, and the *slack for an activity* indicates the same thing regarding a delay in the completion of that activity. The calculation of these slacks is illustrated in Table 10.5 for the house-construction project.

> A **critical path** for a project is a path through the network such that the activities on this path have *zero slack*. (*All* activities and events having zero slack must lie on a critical path, but no others can.)

If we check the activities in Table 10.5 that have zero slack, we find that the house-construction example has one critical path, $1 \rightarrow 2 \rightarrow 3 \rightarrow 4 \rightarrow 5 \rightarrow 7 \rightarrow 9 \rightarrow 12 \rightarrow 13$, as shown in Fig. 10.8 by the dark arrows. Thus this sequence of critical activities must be kept strictly on schedule in order to avoid slippage in completing the project. Other projects may have more than one such critical path; e.g., note what would happen in Fig. 10.6 if the estimated time for activity (4,6) were changed from 6 to 10.

Table 10.5 **Calculation of slacks for house-construction example**

Event	Slack	Activity	Slack
1	$0 - 0 = 0$	(1,2)	$2 - (0 + 2) = 0$
2	$2 - 2 = 0$	(2,3)	$6 - (2 + 4) = 0$
3	$6 - 6 = 0$	(3,4)	$16 - (6 + 10) = 0$
4	$16 - 16 = 0$	(4,5)	$20 - (16 + 4) = 0$
5	$20 - 20 = 0$	(4,6)	$26 - (16 + 6) = 4$
6	$26 - 22 = 4$	(4,7)	$25 - (16 + 7) = 2$
7	$25 - 25 = 0$	(5,7)	$25 - (20 + 5) = 0$
8	$33 - 29 = 4$	(6,8)	$33 - (22 + 7) = 4$
9	$33 - 33 = 0$	(7,9)	$33 - (25 + 8) = 0$
10	$42 - 38 = 4$	(8,10)	$42 - (29 + 9) = 4$
11	$38 - 37 = 1$	(9,11)	$38 - (33 + 4) = 1$
12	$38 - 38 = 0$	(9,12)	$38 - (33 + 5) = 0$
13	$44 - 44 = 0$	(10,13)	$44 - (38 + 2) = 4$
		(12,13)	$44 - (38 + 6) = 0$

It is interesting to observe in Table 10.5 that, whereas every event on the critical path (including events 4 and 7) necessarily has zero slack, activity (4,7) does not because its estimated time is less than the sum of the estimated times for activities (4,5) and (5,7). Consequently, the latter activities are on the critical path but activity (4,7) is not.

This information on earliest and latest times, slack, and the critical path is invaluable for the project manager. Among other things, it enables the manager to investigate the effect of possible improvements in the project plan, to determine where special effort should be expended to stay on schedule, and to assess the impact of schedule slippages.

THE PERT THREE-ESTIMATE APPROACH

Thus far we have implicitly assumed that reasonably accurate estimates can be made of the time required for each *activity* of the project. In actuality, there frequently is considerable uncertainty about what the time will be; it really is a *random variable* having some probability distribution. The original version of PERT took this uncertainty into account by using *three* different types of estimates of the activity time to obtain basic information about its probability distribution. This information for all the activity times is then used to estimate the *probability* of completing the project by the scheduled date.

The three time estimates used by PERT for each activity are a *most likely* estimate, an *optimistic* estimate, and a *pessimistic* estimate. The **most likely estimate** (denoted by m) is intended to be the *most realistic* estimate of the time the activity might consume. Statistically speaking, it is an estimate of the *mode* (the highest point) of the probability distribution for the activity time. The **optimistic estimate** (denoted by a) is intended to be the *unlikely but possible time if everything goes well*. Statistically speaking, it is an estimate of essentially the *lower bound* of

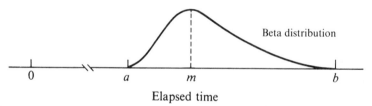

Elapsed time

Figure 10.9 **Model of the probability distribution of activity times for the PERT three-estimate approach: *m* = most likely estimate, *a* = optimistic estimate, and *b* = pessimistic estimate.**

the probability distribution. The **pessimistic estimate** (denoted by *b*) is intended to be the *unlikely but possible time if everything goes badly*. Statistically speaking, it is an estimate of essentially the *upper bound* of the probability distribution. The intended location of these three estimates with respect to the probability distribution is shown in Fig. 10.9.

Two assumptions are made to convert *m*, *a*, and *b* into estimates of the *expected value* (t_e) and *variance* (σ^2) of the elapsed time required by the activity. One assumption is that σ, the standard deviation (square root of the variance), equals one-sixth the *range* of reasonably possible time requirements; that is,

$$\sigma^2 = \left[\frac{1}{6}(b - a) \right]^2$$

is the desired estimate of the variance. The rationale for this assumption is that the tails of many probability distributions (such as the normal distribution) are considered to lie about 3 standard deviations from the mean, so that there is a spread of about 6 standard deviations between the tails. For example, the control charts commonly used for statistical quality control are constructed so that the spread between the control limits is estimated to be 6 standard deviations.

To obtain the estimated *expected value* (t_e), we also need an assumption about the *form* of the probability distribution. This assumption is that the distribution is (at least approximately) a **beta distribution**. This type of distribution is shown in Fig. 10.9.

If we use the model illustrated in Fig. 10.9, the expected value of the activity time is approximately

$$t_e = \frac{1}{3}\left[2m + \frac{1}{2}(a + b) \right].$$

Notice that the midrange $(a + b)/2$ lies midway between *a* and *b*, so that t_e is the weighted arithmetic mean of the mode and the midrange, the mode carrying two-thirds of the entire weight. Although the assumption of a beta distribution is an arbitrary one, it serves its purpose of locating the expected value with respect to *m*, *a*, and *b* in what seems to be a reasonable way.

After calculating the estimated *expected value* and *variance* for each of the activity times, we need three additional assumptions (or approximations) to enable us to calculate the probability of completing the project on schedule. One is that the activity times are *statistically independent*. A second is that the *critical path* (in terms of expected times) *always* requires a longer total elapsed time than any other path. The resulting implication is that the expected value and variance of *project time* are just the *sum* of the expected values and variances (respectively) of the times for the activities on the critical path. The third assumption is that the project time has a *normal distribution*. The rationale for this assumption is that this time is the sum of many independent random variables, and the general version of the *central limit theorem* implies that the probability distribution of such a sum is approximately *normal* under a wide range of conditions. Given the mean and variance, it is then straightforward (see Table A5.1) to find the probability that this *normal* random variable (project time) will be less than the scheduled completion time.[1]

To illustrate, suppose that the house-construction project of Fig. 10.7 is scheduled to be completed after 50 working days and that *both* the expected value and variance of each activity time happen to equal the estimated time given for that activity in Fig. 10.8. Therefore, when we add these quantities (separately) over the critical path, both the expected value and variance of *project time* are 44, so its standard deviation is $\sqrt{44} \approx 6.63$. Thus the scheduled completion time is approximately 0.9 standard deviations above the *expected* project time. Table A5.1 then gives an approximate probability of $1 - 0.1841 \approx 0.82$ that this schedule will be met.

THE CPM METHOD OF TIME-COST TRADEOFFS

The original versions of CPM and PERT differ in two important ways. First, CPM assumes that activity times are *deterministic* (i.e., they can be reliably predicted without significant uncertainty), so that the three-estimate approach just described is not needed. Second, rather than primarily emphasizing time (explicitly), CPM places equal emphasis on *time and cost*. This emphasis is achieved by constructing a **time-cost curve** for *each activity*, such as the one shown in Fig. 10.10. This curve plots the relationship between the budgeted *direct cost*[2] for the activity and its resulting *duration time*. The plot normally is based on two points:[3] the *normal* and the *crash*. The **normal point** gives the cost and time involved when the activity is performed in the *normal* way *without* any extra costs (overtime labor, special time-saving materials or equipment, and so on) being expended to speed up the activity. By contrast, the **crash point** gives the time and

---

[1] The same procedure can also be used to find the probability that an *intermediate* event will be accomplished before a scheduled time.

[2] *Direct* cost includes the cost of the material, equipment, and direct labor required to perform the activity but *excludes* indirect project costs such as supervision and other customary overhead costs, interest charges, and so forth.

[3] More than two points can be used under certain circumstances.

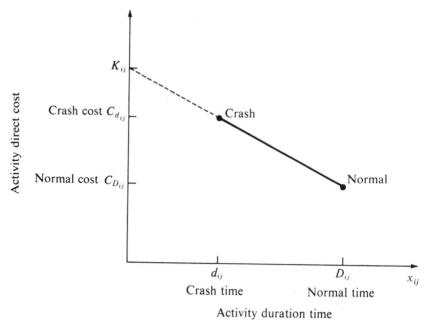

Figure 10.10 **Time-cost curves for activity** (i, j)**.**

cost involved when the activity is performed on a *crash basis*; i.e., it is *fully expedited* with no cost spared to reduce the duration time as much as possible. As an approximation, it is then assumed that *all* intermediate *time-cost tradeoffs* also are possible and that they lie on the *line segment* between these two points (see the solid-line segment shown in Fig. 10.10). Thus the only estimates that need to be obtained from the project personnel are the cost and time for the two points.

The basic objective of CPM is to determine just *which* time-cost tradeoff should be used for each activity to *meet the scheduled project completion time at a minimum cost*. One way of determining the optimal combination of time-cost tradeoffs is to use *linear programming*. To describe this approach, we need to introduce considerable notation, some of which is summarized in Fig. 10.10. Let

$$D_{ij} = normal\ time\ \text{for activity } (i, j).$$
$$C_{D_{ij}} = normal\ (direct)\ cost\ \text{for activity } (i, j).$$
$$d_{ij} = crash\ time\ \text{for activity } (i, j).$$
$$C_{d_{ij}} = crash\ (direct)\ cost\ \text{for activity } (i, j).$$

The *decision variables* for the problem are the x_{ij}, where

$$x_{ij} = duration\ time\ \text{for activity } (i, j).$$

Thus there is one decision variable x_{ij} for each activity, but there is none for those values of i and j that do not have a corresponding activity. To express the direct cost for activity (i,j) as a (linear) function of x_{ij}, let

$$C_{ij} = \frac{C_{d_{ij}} - C_{D_{ij}}}{D_{ij} - d_{ij}},$$

which is the *incremental direct cost* for activity (i,j) *per unit decrease* in x_{ij}. Also define K_{ij} as the *intercept* with the *direct cost axis* of the line through the normal and crash points for activity (i,j), as shown in Fig. 10.10. Therefore,

$$\text{Direct cost for activity } (i,j) = K_{ij} - C_{ij}x_{ij}.$$

Consequently,

$$\text{Total direct cost for the project} = \sum_{(i,j)} (K_{ij} - C_{ij}x_{ij}),$$

where the summation is over *all* activities (i,j). We are now ready to state and formulate the problem mathematically.

THE PROBLEM   For a given (maximum) project completion time T, choose the x_{ij} to *minimize total direct cost* for the project.

LINEAR PROGRAMMING FORMULATION To take the project completion time into account, we need one more variable for each event in the linear programming formulation of the problem. This additional variable is

y_k = (unknown) *earliest time* for event k, which is a deterministic function of the x_{ij}.

Each y_k is an *auxiliary variable*, i.e., a variable that is introduced into the model as a convenience in the formulation rather than representing a decision. However, the simplex method treats auxiliary variables just like the regular decision variables (the x_{ij}). To see how the y_k are worked into the formulation, consider event 7 in Fig. 10.7. By definition, its earliest time is

$$y_7 = \max\{y_4 + x_{47}, y_5 + x_{57}\}.$$

In other words, y_7 is the *smallest* quantity such that *both* of the following constraints hold:

$$y_4 + x_{47} \leq y_7$$
$$y_5 + x_{57} \leq y_7,$$

so that these two constraints can be incorporated directly into the linear programming formulation (after bringing y_7 to the left-hand side for proper form). Furthermore, we shall soon describe why the optimal solution obtained by the simplex method for the overall model *automatically* will have y_7 at the *smallest* quantity that satisfies these constraints, so no further constraints are needed to incorporate the definition of y_7 into the model.

In the process of adding these constraints for all the events, *every* variable x_{ij} will appear in exactly one constraint of this type,

$$y_i + x_{ij} \leq y_j.$$

To continue the preparations for writing down the complete linear programming model, label

$$\text{Event } 1 = \text{project start}$$
$$\text{Event } n = \text{project completion,}$$

so

$$y_1 = 0$$
$$y_n = \text{(unknown) project completion time.}$$

Also note that $\sum K_{ij}$ is just a fixed constant that can be dropped from the objective function, so that minimizing total direct cost for the projects is *equivalent* (see Sec. 4.6) to *maximizing* $\sum C_{ij}x_{ij}$. Therefore, the linear programming problem is to find the x_{ij} (and the corresponding y_k) that

$$\text{Maximize} \quad Z = \sum_{(i,j)} C_{ij}x_{ij},$$

subject to

$$\left. \begin{array}{c} x_{ij} \geq d_{ij} \\ x_{ij} \leq D_{ij} \\ y_i + x_{ij} - y_j \leq 0 \end{array} \right\} \quad \text{for all activities } (i,j)$$
$$y_n \leq T.$$

From a computational viewpoint, this formulation can be improved somewhat by replacing each x_{ij} by

$$x_{ij} = d_{ij} + x'_{ij}$$

throughout the model, so that the first set of functional constraints ($x_j \geq d_{ij}$) would be replaced by simple *nonnegativity constraints*

$$x'_{ij} \geq 0.$$

As a convenience we can also introduce nonnegativity constraints for the other variables:

$$y_k \geq 0,$$

although these variables already are forced to be nonnegative by setting $y_1 = 0$ because of the $x'_{ij} \geq 0$ and $y_j \geq y_i + d_{ij} + x'_{ij}$ constraints.

The key to this formulation is the way that the y_k are introduced into the model in order to assign to y_n the value that it should have for any given values of the x_{ij}. Note that there is *no possible benefit* to making y_j any larger than it is forced to be in each of the $y_i + x_{ij} - y_j \leq 0$ constraints in the linear programming formulation. In fact, having y_j larger can only be a *disadvantage* because its larger value might ultimately force y_n to be larger than it need be, which would increase the cost of satisfying the $y_n \leq T$ constraint. Therefore, the optimal solution or solutions to the model will include a basic feasible solution with *all* y_j no larger than they are forced to be by the optimal x_{ij}; that is, these y_j will be true *earliest*

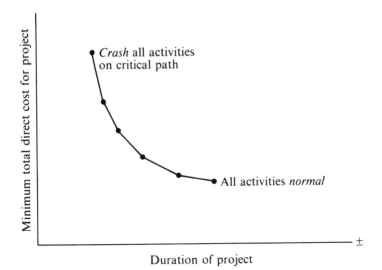

Figure 10.11 **Time-cost curve for the overall project.**

times for the events. In particular, the optimal solution obtained by the simplex method will have this property.

The problem as stated here assumes that a specified *deadline T* has been fixed (perhaps by contract) for the completion of the project. In fact, some projects do not have such a deadline, in which case it is not clear what value should be assigned to T in the linear programming formulation. In such situations, the decision on T (which turns out to be the *duration* of the project in the optimal solution) actually is a question of what is the *best tradeoff* between the *total cost* and the *total time* for the project. The basic information we need to address this question is how the *minimum total direct cost* changes as T is changed in the preceding formulation, as illustrated in Fig. 10.11, where t is the time parameter that represents the duration of the project. This information can be obtained by using *parametric linear programming* (see Secs. 4.7, 6.7, and 9.3) to solve for the optimal solution *as a function of t* over its entire range.[1] However, an even more efficient procedure is available for obtaining this information that is commonly used instead. This procedure exploits the *special structure* of the problem by reducing the *dual problem* to a variation of the *maximal flow problem* described in the preceding section.[2] Computer codes for this procedure are quite widely available.

Figure 10.11 provides a useful basis for a managerial decision on T (and the corresponding optimal solution for the x_{ij}) when the important effects of the project duration (other than direct costs) are largely intangible. However, when

[1] The *slope* of the time-cost curve changes at the points shown in Fig. 10.11 because the set of basic variables that give the optimal solution changes at these values of t. This fact is discussed further in a more general context in Sec. 9.3.

[2] See Selected Reference 9, pages 218 to 235, for details on this procedure.

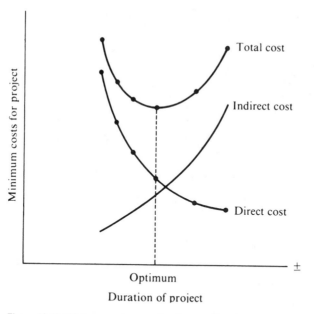

Figure 10.12 **Minimum cost curves for the overall project.**

these other effects are primarily financial (indirect costs), it is appropriate to combine the minimum total direct cost curve of Fig. 10.11 with a curve of *minimum total indirect cost* (supervision, facilities, clerical, interest, contractual penalties) versus t, as shown in Fig. 10.12. The *sum* of these curves thereby gives the *minimum total project cost* curve for the various values of t. The *optimal* value of t is then the one that minimizes this total cost curve.

CHOOSING BETWEEN PERT AND CPM

The choice between the PERT *three-estimate approach* and the CPM *method of time-cost tradeoffs* depends primarily upon the *type of project* and the *managerial objectives*. PERT is particularly appropriate when there is considerable uncertainty in predicting activity times and when it is important to effectively *control* the project schedule; for example, most *research and development* projects fall into this category. On the other hand, CPM is particularly appropriate when activity times can be predicted well (perhaps based on previous experience) but these times can be adjusted readily (e.g., by changing crew sizes), and when it is important to plan an appropriate tradeoff between project *time* and *cost*. This latter type is typified by most *construction* and *maintenance* projects.

Actually, differences between *current* versions of PERT and CPM are not necessarily as pronounced as we have described them. Most versions of PERT now allow using only a *single* estimate (the most likely estimate) of each activity time and thus omit the probabilistic investigation. A version called *PERT/Cost* also considers *time-cost tradeoffs* in a manner similar to CPM.

10.7 Conclusions

Networks of some type arise in a wide variety of contexts. *Network analysis* provides useful techniques (especially optimization techniques) for the design and operation of network systems. Because of their combinatorial nature, network problems often are extremely difficult to solve. However, great progress is being made in developing powerful modeling techniques and solution methodologies that are opening up new vistas for important applications. In fact, recent algorithmic advances are enabling us to solve successfully some complex network problems of enormous size.

The most widely used network technique has been the *PERT-type system* for project planning and control. It has been very valuable for organizing planning effort, testing alternative plans, revealing the overall dimensions and details of the project plan, establishing well-understood management responsibilities, and identifying realistic expectations for the project. It also lays the foundation for *anticipatory* management action against potential trouble spots during the course of the project. Although it is not a panacea, and although its serious pitfalls have not always been avoided,[1] it has greatly aided project management on numerous occasions.

SELECTED REFERENCES

1. Bazaraa, Mokhtar S. and John J. Jarvis: *Linear Programming and Network Flows*, Wiley, New York, 1977.
2. Elmaghraby, S. E.: *Activity Networks: Project Planning and Control by Network Models*, Wiley, New York, 1977.
3. Ford, L. R., Jr., and D. R. Fulkerson: *Flows in Networks*, Princeton University Press, Princeton, N.J., 1962.
4. Fulkerson, D. R.: "Flow Networks and Combinatorial Operations Research" and Dreyfus, S. E.: "An Appraisal of Some Shortest-Path Algorithms," reprinted in Arthur M. Geoffrion (ed.), *Perspectives on Optimization: A Collection of Expository Articles*, pp. 197–238, Addison-Wesley, Reading, Mass., 1972.
5. Jensen, Paul A. and J. Wesley Barnes: *Network Flow Programming*, Wiley, New York, 1980.
6. Kennington, Jeff L. and Richard V. Helgason: *Algorithms for Network Programming*, Wiley-Interscience, Somerset, N.J., 1980.
7. Lawler, E.: *Combinatorial Optimization*, Holt, Rinehart & Winston, New York, 1976.
8. Minieka, Edward: *Optimization Algorithms for Networks and Graphs*, Dekker, New York, 1978.
9. Moder, Joseph J. and Cecil R. Phillips: *Project Management with CPM and PERT*, 2d ed., Van Nostrand, New York, 1970.
10. Weist, Jerome D. and Ferdinand K. Levy: *Management Guide to PERT/CPM*, 2d ed., Prentice-Hall, Englewood Cliffs, N.J., 1977.

[1] For example, see J. W. Pocock, "PERT as an Analytical Aid for Program Planning—Its Payoff and Problems," *Operations Research*, **10**:893–903, 1962.

PROBLEMS

1. Use the algorithm described in Sec. 10.3 to find the *shortest route* through networks (*a*) and (*b*), where the numbers represent actual distances between the corresponding nodes.

(*a*)

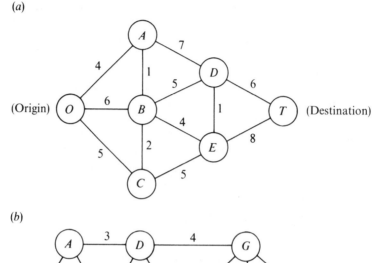

(*b*)

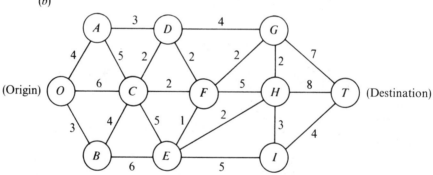

2. At a small but growing airport, the local airline company is purchasing a new tractor for a tractor-trailer train to bring luggage to and from the airplanes. A new mechanized luggage system will be installed in 3 years, so the tractor will not be needed after that. However, because it will receive heavy use, so that the running and maintenance costs will increase rapidly as it ages, it may still be more economical to replace the tractor after 1 or 2 years. The following table gives the total net discounted cost associated with purchasing a tractor (purchase price minus trade-in allowance, plus running and maintenance costs) at the end of year i and trading it in at the end of year j (where year 0 is now).

	j		
	1	*2*	*3*
0	8	18	31
i 1		10	21
2			12

The problem is to determine at what times (if any) the tractor should be replaced to minimize the total cost for the tractors over the 3 years.

  (a) Formulate this problem as a shortest-route problem.
  (b) Use the algorithm described in Sec. 10.3 to solve this shortest-route problem.

  3. Reconsider the student's "car problem" described in Prob. 22 at the end of Chap. 7.

  (a) Formulate the student's problem as a shortest-route problem.
  (b) Use the algorithm described in Sec. 10.3 to solve this shortest-route problem.

  4. A company has learned that a competitor is planning to come out with a new kind of product with a great sales potential. This company has been working on a similar product, and research is nearly complete. It now wishes to rush the product out to meet the competition. There are four nonoverlapping phases left to be accomplished, including the remaining research that currently is being conducted at a normal pace. However, each phase can instead be conducted at a priority or crash level to expedite completion. The times required (in months) at these levels are

Time

Level	Remaining research	Development	Design of manufacturing system	Initiate production and distribution
Normal	5			
Priority	4	3	5	2
Crash	2	2	3	1

$30,000,000 is available for these four phases. The cost (in millions of dollars) at the different levels is

Cost

Level	Remaining research	Development	Design of manufacturing system	Initiate production and distribution
Normal	3			
Priority	6	6	9	3
Crash	9	9	12	6

The problem is to determine at which level to conduct each of the four phases to minimize the total time until the product can be marketed subject to the budget restriction.

  (a) Formulate this problem as a shortest-route problem.
  (b) Use the algorithm described in Sec. 10.3 to solve this shortest-route problem.

  5. Reconsider the networks shown in Prob. 1. Assume that the nodes and actual distances between nodes are as shown there (where unspecified distances between nodes are greater than any of the given distances), but assume that the branches have not yet been specified. Use the algorithm described in Sec. 10.4 to find the *minimal spanning tree* for each of these networks.

  6. A logging company will soon begin logging eight groves of trees in the same general area. Therefore, it must develop a system of dirt roads that makes each grove accessible from every other grove. The distance (in miles) between every pair of groves is

Distance between pairs of groves

Grove	1	2	3	4	5	6	7	8
1	—	1.3	2.1	0.9	0.7	1.8	2.0	1.5
2	1.3	—	0.9	1.8	1.2	2.6	2.3	1.1
3	2.1	0.9	—	2.6	1.7	2.5	1.9	1.0
4	0.9	1.8	2.6	—	0.7	1.6	1.5	0.9
5	0.7	1.2	1.7	0.7	—	0.9	1.1	0.8
6	1.8	2.6	2.5	1.6	0.9	—	0.6	1.0
7	2.0	2.3	1.9	1.5	1.1	0.6	—	0.5
8	1.5	1.1	1.0	0.9	0.8	1.0	0.5	—

The problem is to determine between which pairs of groves the roads should be constructed to connect all groves with a minimum total length of road.

(a) Describe how this problem fits the network description of the minimal spanning tree problem.

(b) Use the algorithm described in Sec. 10.4 to solve the problem.

7. A bank soon will be hooking up computer terminals at each of its branch offices to the computer at its main office using special phone lines with telecommunications devices. The phone line from a branch office need not be connected directly to the main office. It can be connected indirectly by being connected to another branch office that is connected (directly or indirectly) to the main office. The only requirement is that every branch office be connected by some route to the main office.

The charge for the special phone lines is directly proportional to the mileage involved, where the distance (in miles) between every pair of offices is

Distance between pairs of offices

	Main	B.1	B.2	B.3	B.4	B.5
Main office	—	190	70	115	270	160
Branch 1	190	—	100	240	215	50
Branch 2	70	100	—	140	120	220
Branch 3	115	240	140	—	175	80
Branch 4	270	215	120	175	—	310
Branch 5	160	50	220	80	310	—

The problem is to determine which pair of offices should be connected by special phone lines in order to connect every branch office (directly or indirectly) to the main office at a minimum total cost.

(a) Describe how this problem fits the network description of the minimal spanning tree problem.

(b) Use the algorithm described in Sec. 10.4 to solve the problem.

8. For networks (a) and (b), find the *maximal flow* from the source to the sink, given that the flow capacity from node i to node j is the number along branch (i, j) nearest node i.

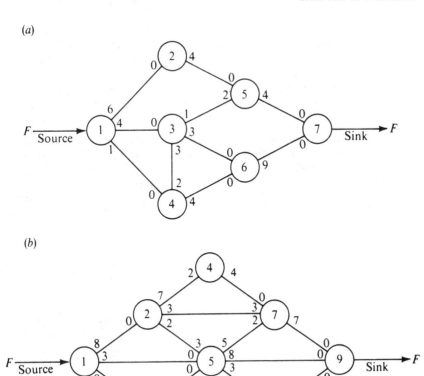

(a)

(b)

9. Formulate the maximal flow problem as a linear programming problem.

10. One track of the Eura Railroad system runs from the major industrial city of Faireparc to the major port city of Portstown. This track is heavily used by both express passenger and freight trains. The passenger trains are carefully scheduled and have priority over the slower freight trains (this is a European railroad), so that the freight trains must pull over onto a siding whenever a passenger train is scheduled to pass them soon. It is now necessary to increase the freight service, so the problem is to schedule the freight trains so as to maximize the number that can be sent each day without interfering with the fixed schedule for passenger trains.

Consecutive freight trains must maintain a schedule differential of at least 0.1 hours, and this is the time unit used for scheduling them (so that the daily schedule indicates the status of each freight train at times $0.0, 0.1, 0.2, \ldots, 23.9$). There are S sidings between Faireparc and Portstown, where siding i is long enough to hold n_i freight trains $(i = 1, \ldots, S)$. It requires t_i time units (rounded up to an integer) for a freight train to travel from siding i to siding $i + 1$ (where t_0 is the time from the Faireparc station to siding 1 and t_s is the time from siding S to the Portstown station). A freight train is allowed to pass or leave siding i $(i = 0, 1, \ldots, S)$ at time j $(j = 0.0, 0.1, \ldots, 23.9)$ only if it would not be overtaken by a scheduled passenger train before reaching siding $i + 1$ (let $\delta_{ij} = 1$ if it would not be overtaken, and let $\delta_{ij} = 0$ if it would be). A freight train also is required to stop at a siding if there will not be room for it at all subsequent sidings that it would reach before being overtaken by a passenger train.

Formulate this problem as a maximal flow problem by identifying every node (including the source and sink) as well as every branch and its flow capacity for the network representation of the problem. (*Hint:* Use a different set of nodes for each of the 240 times.)

11. Consider the following project network. Assume that the time required (in weeks) for each activity is a predictable constant and that it is given by the number along the corresponding branch. Find the earliest time, latest time, and slack for each event, as well as the slack for each activity. Also identify the critical path.

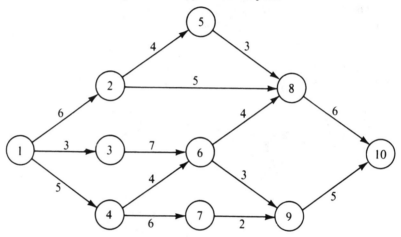

12. Consider the following project network. Assume that the time required (in days) for each activity is a predictable constant and that it is given by the number along the

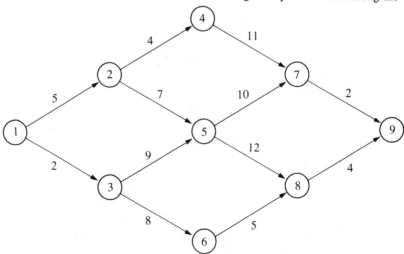

corresponding branch. Find the earliest time, latest time, and slack for each event, as well as the slack for each activity. Also identify the critical path.

13. You and several friends are about to prepare a lasagne dinner. The tasks to be performed, their times (in minutes), and the precedence constraints are as follows:

Task #	Task	Time	Tasks that must precede
1	Buy the mozzarella cheese*	30	
2	Slice the mozzarella	5	1
3	Beat 2 eggs	2	
4	Mix eggs and ricotta cheese	3	3
5	Cut up onions and mushrooms	7	
6	Cook the tomato sauce	25	5
7	Boil large quantity of water	15	
8	Boil the lasagne noodles	10	7
9	Drain the lasagne noodles	2	8
10	Assemble all the ingredients	10	9,6,4,2
11	Preheat the oven	15	
12	Bake the lasagne	30	10,11

* There is none in the refrigerator.

(*a*) Formulate this problem as a *PERT-type system* by drawing the project network. Use one event to represent the simultaneous initiation of the initial tasks. On one side of each branch, identify the number of the task being performed in parentheses, e.g., (Task 7). On the other side, show the times required.

(*b*) Find the earliest time, latest time, and slack for each event, as well as the slack for each activity. Also identify the critical path.

(*c*) Because of a phone call you were interrupted for 6 minutes when you should have been cutting the onions and mushrooms. By how much will the dinner be delayed? If you use your food processor, which reduces the cutting time from 7 minutes to 2 minutes, will the dinner still be delayed?

14. Using the PERT three-estimate approach, the three estimates for one of the activities are as follows: Optimistic estimate = 30 days, most likely estimate = 36 days, pessimistic estimate = 48 days. What are the resulting estimates of the *expected value* and *variance* of the time required by the activity?

15. Consider the following project network.

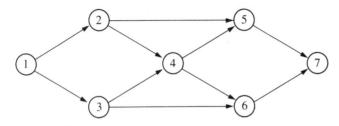

The PERT three-estimate approach has been used, and it has led to the following estimates of the *expected value* and *variance* of the time required (in months) for the respective activities.

Activity times

Activity	Estimated expected value	Estimated variance
1 → 2	4	5
1 → 3	6	10
2 → 4	4	8
2 → 5	8	12
3 → 4	3	6
3 → 6	7	14
4 → 5	5	12
4 → 6	3	5
5 → 7	5	8
6 → 7	5	7

The scheduled project completion time is 22 months after the start of the project.

(a)   Using expected values, determine the *critical path* for the project.

(b)   Using the procedure described in Sec. 10.6, find the approximate probability that the project will be completed by the scheduled time.

(c)   In addition to the critical path, there are five other paths through the network. For each of these other paths, find the approximate probability that the sum of the activity times along the path is not more than 22 months.

16.   Consider the following project network.

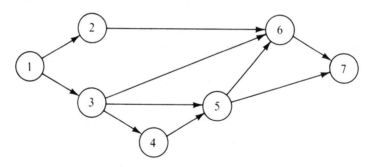

Using the PERT three-estimate approach, suppose that the usual three estimates for the time required (in weeks) for each of these activities are

Activity	Optimistic estimate	Most likely estimate	Pessimistic estimate
1 → 2	28	32	36
1 → 3	22	28	32
2 → 6	26	36	46
3 → 4	14	16	18
3 → 5	32	32	32
3 → 6	40	52	74
4 → 5	12	16	24
5 → 6	16	20	26
5 → 7	26	34	42
6 → 7	12	16	30

The project is ready to start now and the deadline for completing the project is 100 weeks hence.

(a) On the basis of the estimates just listed, calculate the *expected value* and *standard deviation* of the time required for each activity.

(b) Using expected times, determine the *critical path* for the project.

(c) Using the procedure described in Sec. 10.6, find the approximate probability that the project will be completed by the deadline.

17. Reconsider the project network shown in Prob. 16. Suppose that the CPM method of time-cost tradeoffs is to be used to determine how to meet the project deadline (100 weeks hence) in the most economical way. Also suppose that the *crash time* and *normal time* for each of the activities corresponds to the times shown in the *Optimistic estimate* and *Pessimistic estimate* columns of the table for Prob. 16 (except that activity 3 → 5 has a crash time of 28 and a normal time of 36) and that the difference between the *crash cost* and *normal cost* is 10 (in units of thousands of dollars) for *every* activity. Formulate the linear programming model for this problem.

18. Suppose that the scheduled completion time for the house-construction project described in Figs. 10.7 and 10.8 has been moved forward to 40. Therefore, the CPM method of time-cost tradeoffs is to be used to determine how to accelerate the project to meet this deadline in the most economical way. The relevant data are

Activity	Normal time	Crash time	Normal cost, $	Crash cost, $
1 → 2	2	1	1,800	2,300
2 → 3	4	2	3,200	3,600
3 → 4	10	7	6,200	7,300
4 → 5	4	3	4,100	4,900
4 → 6	6	4	2,600	3,000
4 → 7	7	5	2,100	2,400
5 → 7	5	3	1,800	2,200
6 → 8	7	4	9,000	9,600
7 → 9	8	6	4,300	4,600
8 → 10	9	6	2,000	2,500
9 → 11	4	3	1,600	1,800
9 → 12	5	3	2,500	3,000
10 → 13	2	1	1,000	1,500
12 → 13	6	3	3,300	4,000

Formulate the linear programming model for this problem.

CHAPTER 11

Dynamic Programming

Dynamic programming is a useful mathematical technique for making a sequence of interrclated decisions. It provides a systematic procedure for determining the combination of decisions that maximizes overall effectiveness.

In contrast to linear programming, there does not exist a standard mathematical formulation of "the" dynamic programming problem. Rather, dynamic programming is a general type of approach to problem solving, and the particular equations used must be developed to fit each individual situation. Therefore, a certain degree of ingenuity and insight into the general structure of dynamic programming problems is required to recognize when a problem can be solved by dynamic programming procedures and how it can be done. These abilities can best be developed by an exposure to a wide variety of dynamic programming applications and a study of the characteristics that are common to all this situations. A large number of illustrative examples are presented for this purpose.

11.1 Prototype Example

The **stagecoach problem** is a problem especially constructed[1] to illustrate the features and to introduce the terminology of dynamic programming. It concerns a mythical salesman who had to travel west by stagecoach about 125 years ago

---

[1] This problem was developed by Professor Harvey M. Wagner while he was at Stanford University.

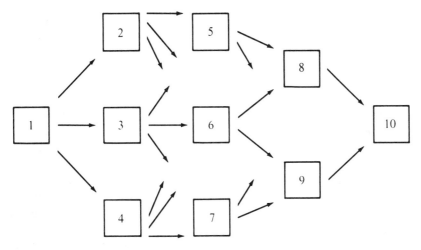

Figure 11.1 **The road system for the stagecoach problem.**

when there was a serious danger of attack by marauders. Although his starting point and destination were fixed, he had considerable choice as to which **states** (or territories that subsequently became states) to travel through en route. The possible routes are shown in Fig. 11.1, where each state is represented by a numbered block. Thus four **stages** (*stage*coach runs) were required to travel from his point of embarkation in state 1 to his destination in state 10.

This salesman was a prudent man who was quite concerned about his safety. After some thought, he came up with a rather clever way of determining the safest route. Life insurance policies were offered to stagecoach passengers. Because the cost of the **policy** for taking any given stagecoach run was based on a careful evaluation of the safety of that run, the safest route should be the one with the cheapest total life insurance policy.

The cost for the standard policy on the stagecoach run from state i to state j, which will be denoted by c_{ij}, is

	2	3	4
1	2	4	3

	5	6	7
2	7	4	6
3	3	2	4
4	4	1	5

	8	9
5	1	4
6	6	3
7	3	3

	10
8	3
9	4

Which route minimizes the total cost of the policy?

SOLUTION First note that the shortsighted approach of selecting the cheapest run offered by each successive stage need not yield an overall optimal decision. Following this strategy would give the route $1 \rightarrow 2 \rightarrow 6 \rightarrow 9 \rightarrow 10$ at a total cost of 13. However, sacrificing a little on one stage may permit greater savings thereafter. For example, $1 \rightarrow 4 \rightarrow 6$ is cheaper overall than $1 \rightarrow 2 \rightarrow 6$.

One possible approach to solving this problem is to use trial and error.[1] However, the number of possible routes is large (18) and having to calculate the total cost for each route is not an appealing task.

Fortunately, dynamic programming provides a solution with much less effort than exhaustive enumeration. (The computational savings are enormous for larger versions of this problem.) Dynamic programming starts with a small portion of the original problem and finds the optimal solution for this smaller problem. It then gradually enlarges the problem, finding the current optimal solution from the preceding one, until the original problem is solved in its entirety. For the stagecoach problem, we start with the smaller problem where the salesman has nearly completed his journey and has only one more stage (stagecoach run) to go. The obvious optimal solution for this smaller problem is to go from his current state (whatever it is) to his ultimate destination (state 10). At each subsequent iteration, the problem is enlarged by increasing by one the number of stages left to go to complete the journey. For this enlarged problem, the optimal solution for where to go next from each possible state can be found relatively easily from the results obtained at the preceding iteration. The details involved in implementing this approach are as follows.

Let the decision variables x_n ($n = 1,2,3,4$) be the immediate destination on stage n (the nth stagecoach run to be taken). Thus the route selected is $1 \to x_1 \to x_2 \to x_3 \to x_4$, where $x_4 = 10$. Let $f_n(s,x_n)$ be the total cost of the best overall *policy* for the *remaining* stages, given that the salesman is in state s ready to start stage n and selects x_n as the immediate destination. Given s and n, let x_n^* denote the value of x_n that minimizes $f_n(s,x_n)$, and let $f_n^*(s)$ be the corresponding minimum value of $f_n(s,x_n)$. Thus

$$f_n^*(s) = \min_{x_n} f_n(s,x_n) = f_n(s,x_n^*),$$

where

$f_n(s,x_n) =$ immediate cost (stage n) + minimum future cost (stages $n + 1$ onward)

$$= c_{sx_n} + f_{n+1}^*(x_n),$$

where the value of c_{sx_n} is given by the preceding tables for c_{ij} by setting $i = s$ (the current state) and $j = x_n$ (the immediate destination). Because the ultimate destination (state 10) is reached at the end of stage 4, $f_5^*(10) = 0$. The objective is to find $f_1^*(1)$ and the corresponding route. Dynamic programming finds it by successively finding $f_4^*(s)$, $f_3^*(s)$, $f_2^*(s)$ for each of the possible states s and then using $f_2^*(s)$ to solve for $f_1^*(s)$.[2]

When the salesman has only one more stage to go ($n = 4$), his route here-

---

[1] This problem also can be formulated as a *shortest-route problem* (see Sec. 10.3), where the branch values represent *costs* rather than *distances*. The solution procedure presented in Sec. 10.3 actually uses the philosophy of dynamic programming. However, because the present problem has a fixed number of stages, the dynamic programming approach presented here is even better.

[2] Because this procedure involves moving *backward* stage by stage, some writers also count n backward to denote the number of *remaining stages* to the destination. We use the more natural *forward counting* for greater simplicity.

after is entirely determined by his current state s (either 8 or 9) and his final destination, $x_4 = 10$, so the route for this final stagecoach run is $s \rightarrow 10$. Therefore, since $f_4^*(s) = f_4(s,10) = c_{5,10}$, the immediate solution to the $n = 4$ problem is

$n = 4$	s	$f_4^*(s)$	x_4^*
	8	3	10
	9	4	10

When the salesman has two more stages to go ($n = 3$), the solution requires a few calculations. For example, assume that the salesman is in state 5. He must next go to either state 8 or 9 at a cost of $c_{5,8} = 1$ or $c_{5,9} = 4$, respectively. If he chooses state 8, the minimum additional cost after he reaches there is given in the preceding table as $f_4^*(8) = 3$, so that the total cost for this decision would be $1 + 3 = 4$. Similarly, if he chooses state 9, the total cost is $4 + 4 = 8$. Therefore, he would choose state 8, $x_3^* = 8$, because it gives the minimum cost, $f_3^*(5) = 4$. Proceeding similarly for $s = 6$ and $s = 7$ yields the following results for the $n = 3$ problem.

		$f_2(s,x_3) = c_{sx_3} + f_4^*(x_3)$			
	x_3				
$n = 3$	s	8	9	$f_3^*(s)$	x_3^*
	5	4	8	4	8
	6	9	7	7	9
	7	6	7	6	8

The solution for the three-stage problem ($n = 2$) is obtained in a similar fashion. In this case, $f_2(s,x_2) = c_{sx_2} + f_3^*(x_2)$. For example, if the salesman is in state 2 and chooses to go to state 5 next, the minimum total cost $f_2(2,5)$ is the cost of the first stage $c_{25} = 7$ plus the minimum cost from state 5 onward, $f_3^*(5) = 4$, so that $f_2(2,5) = 7 + 4 = 11$. Similarly, $f_2(2,6) = 4 + 7 = 11$ and $f_2(2,7) = 6 + 6 = 12$, so that the minimum total cost from state 2 onward is $f_2^*(2) = 11$, and the immediate destination should be $x_2^* = 5$ or 6. The complete results for the $n = 2$ problem are

		$f_2(s,x_2) = c_{sx_2} + f_3^*(x_2)$				
	x_2					
$n = 2$	s	5	6	7	$f_2^*(s)$	x_2^*
	2	11	11	12	11	5 or 6
	3	7	9	10	7	5
	4	8	8	11	8	5 or 6

Moving to the four-stage problem ($n = 1$), the cost of the optimal policy given the immediate destination is again the sum of the cost of the first stage plus the minimum cost thereafter. The consequent results are

		$f_1(s,x_1) = c_{sx_1} + f_2^*(x_1)$				
	x_1					
$n = 1$	s	2	3	4	$f_1^*(s)$	x_1^*
	1	13	11	11	11	3 or 4

The optimal solution can now be identified. The results for the $n = 1$ problem indicate that the salesman should go initially to either state 3 or state 4. Suppose that he chooses $x_1^* = 3$. For $n = 2$, the result for $s = 3$ is $x_2^* = 5$. This result leads to the $n = 3$ problem, which gives $x_3^* = 8$ for $s = 5$, and the $n = 4$ problem yields $x_4^* = 10$ for $s = 8$. Hence one optimal route is $1 \to 3 \to 5 \to 8 \to 10$. Choosing $x_1^* = 4$ leads to the other two optimal routes, $1 \to 4 \to 5 \to 8 \to 10$ and $1 \to 4 \to 6 \to 9 \to 10$. They all yield a total cost of $f_1^*(1) = 11$.

You will see in the next section that the *special terms* describing the particular context of this problem—*stage, state, policy*—actually are part of the *general terminology* of dynamic programming with an analogous interpretation in other contexts.

11.2 Characteristics of Dynamic Programming Problems

The stagecoach problem is a literal prototype of dynamic programming problems. In fact, this example was purposely designed to provide a literal physical interpretation of the rather abstract structure of such problems. Therefore, one way to recognize a situation that can be formulated as a dynamic programming problem is to notice that its basic structure is analogous to that of the stagecoach problem.

These basic features that characterize dynamic programming problems are presented and discussed here.

1. The problem can be divided into **stages**, with a **policy decision** required at each stage.

The stagecoach problem was literally divided into its four stages (stagecoaches) that correspond to the four legs of the journey. The policy decision at each stage was the destination for that particular stagecoach (i.e., which life insurance policy to choose). Similarly, other dynamic programming problems require making a *sequence of interrelated decisions*, where each decision corresponds to one stage of the problem.

2. Each stage has a number of **states** associated with it.

The states associated with each stage in the stagecoach problem were the states (or territories) in which the salesman could be located when embarking on that particular leg of the journey. In general, the states are the various *possible conditions* in which the system might be at that stage of the problem. The number of states may be either *finite* (as in the stagecoach problem) or *infinite* (as in some subsequent examples).

3. The effect of the policy decision at each stage is to *transform the current state into a state associated with the next stage* (possibly according to a probability distribution).

The salesman's decision as to his next destination led him from his current state to the next state on his journey. This procedure suggests that dynamic programming problems can be interpreted in terms of the *networks* described in

Chap. 10. Each *node* would correspond to a *state*. The network would consist of columns of nodes, with each *column* corresponding to a *stage*, so that the flow from a node can go only to a node in the next column to the right. The value assigned to each branch connecting two nodes can sometimes be interpreted as the contribution to the objective function made by going from one state to the next state that correspond to these nodes. If this is the case, the objective would be to find either the *shortest* or the *longest route* through the network.

4. The solution procedure is designed to find an **optimal policy** for the overall problem, i.e., a prescription of the optimal policy decision at each stage for *each* of the possible states.

For the stagecoach problem, the solution procedure constructed a table for each stage (n) that prescribes the optimal decision (x_n^*) for *each* possible state (s). Thus, in addition to identifying three *optimal solutions* (optimal routes) for the overall problem, the results also show the salesman how he should proceed if he gets detoured to a state that is not on an optimal route. This kind of additional information can be very helpful for sensitivity analysis and so forth.

5. Given the current state, an *optimal policy for the remaining stages* is *independent* of the policy adopted in *previous stages*.

Given the state in which the salesman is currently located, the optimal life insurance policy (and its associated route) from this point onward is independent of how he got there. For dynamic programming problems in general, knowledge of the current state of the system conveys all the information about its previous behavior necessary for determining the optimal policy henceforth. (This property is the *Markovian property* discussed in Sec. 15.3.) It is sometimes referred to as the *principle of optimality* for dynamic programming.

6. The solution procedure begins by finding the *optimal policy for the last stage*.

The optimal policy for the last stage prescribes the optimal policy decision for *each* of the possible states at that stage. The solution of this one-stage problem is usually trivial, as it was for the stagecoach problem.

7. A **recursive relationship** that identifies the optimal policy for stage n, given the optimal policy for stage ($n + 1$), is available.

For the stagecoach problem, this recursive relationship was

$$f_n^*(s) = \min_{x_n} \{c_{sx_n} + f_{n+1}^*(x_n)\}.$$

Therefore, finding the *optimal policy decision* when starting in state s at stage n requires finding the minimizing value of x_n. The corresponding minimum cost is achieved by using this value of x_n and then following the optimal policy when starting in state x_n at stage ($n + 1$).

The precise form of the recursive relationship differs somewhat among dynamic programming problems. However, notation analogous to that introduced in the preceding section will continue to be used here. Thus let the variable (or vector) x_n be the decision variable at stage n ($n = 1, 2, \ldots, N$). Let $f_n(s, x_n)$ be the maximizing (or minimizing) value of the objective function, given that the system starts in state s at stage n and x_n is selected. Let $f_n^*(s)$ be the maximum (or minimum) value of $f_n(s,x_n)$ over all possible values of x_n. The recursive relationship will always be of the form

$$f_n^*(s) = \max_{x_n} \{ f_n(s,x_n) \}$$

or

$$f_n^*(s) = \min_{x_n} \{ f_n(s,x_n) \},$$

where $f_n(s,x_n)$ would be written in terms of s, x_n, $f_{n+1}^*(\cdot)$ and probably some measure of the first-stage effectiveness (or ineffectiveness) of x_n.

8. When we use this recursive relationship, the solution procedure moves *backward* stage by stage—each time finding the optimal policy for that stage—until it finds the optimal policy starting at the *initial* stage.

This backward movement was demonstrated by the stagecoach problem, where the optimal policy was found successively beginning in each state at stages 4, 3, 2, and 1, respectively.[1] For all dynamic programming problems, a table such as the following one would be obtained for each stage ($n = N$, $N-1,\ldots,1$).

s	$f_n^*(s)$	x_n^*

When this table is finally obtained for the initial stage ($n = 1$), the problem of interest is solved. Because the initial state is known, the initial decision is specified by x_1^* in this table. The optimal value of the other decision variables is then specified by the other tables in turn according to the state of the system that results from the preceding decisions.

11.3 Deterministic Dynamic Programming

This section further elaborates upon the dynamic programming approach to *deterministic* problems, where the *state* at the *next stage* is *completely determined* by the *state* and *policy decision* at the *current stage*. The *probabilistic* case, where there is a probability distribution for what the next state will be, is discussed in the next section.

Deterministic dynamic programming can be described diagrammatically as shown in Fig. 11.2. Thus at stage n the process will be in some state s_n. Making policy decision x_n then moves the process to some state s_{n+1} at stage $(n+1)$. From that point onward the objective function value for the optimal policy has been previously calculated to be $f_{n+1}^*(s_{n+1})$. The policy decision x_n also makes some contribution to the objective function. Combining these two quantities in

[1] Actually, for this problem the solution procedure can move *either* backward or forward. However, for many problems (especially when the stages correspond to *time periods*), the solution procedure *must* move backwards.

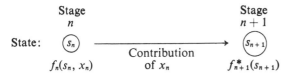

Figure 11.2 **The basic structure for deterministic dynamic programming.**

an appropriate way provides the objective function value $f_n(s_n,x_n)$ beginning at stage n. Optimizing with respect to x_n then gives $f_n^*(s_n) = f_n(s_n,x_n^*)$. After finding x_n^* and $f_n^*(s_n)$ for each possible value of s_n, the solution procedure is ready to move back one stage.

One way of categorizing deterministic dynamic programming problems is by the *form of the objective function.* For example, the objective might be to *minimize* the *sum* of the contributions from the individual stages (as for the stagecoach problem), or to *maximize* such a sum, or to minimize a *product* of such terms, and so on. Another categorization is in terms of the nature of the *set of states* for the respective stages. In particular, the states s_n might be representable by a *discrete* state variable (as for the stagecoach problem), or by a *continuous* state variable, or perhaps a state *vector* (more than one variable) is required.

Several examples are presented to illustrate these various possibilities. More importantly, they illustrate that these apparently major differences are actually quite inconsequential (except in terms of computational difficulty) because the underlying basic structure shown in Fig. 11.2 always remains the same.

The first example arises in a much different context from the stagecoach problem, but it has the same *mathematical formulation* except that the objective is to *maximize* rather than minimize a sum.

EXAMPLE 2 The *World Health Council* is devoted to improving health care in the underdeveloped countries of the world. It now has five *medical teams* available to allocate among three such countries to improve their medical care, health education, and training programs. Therefore, the council needs to determine how many teams (if any) to allocate to each of these countries to maximize the total effectiveness of the five teams. The measure of effectiveness being used is *additional person-years of life.* (For a particular country, this measure equals the country's *increased life expectancy* in years times its population.) Table 11.1 gives the estimated additional person-years of life (in multiples of 1,000) for each country for each possible allocation of medical teams.

SOLUTION This problem requires making three *interrelated decisions,* namely, how many medical teams to allocate to each of the three countries. Therefore, even though there is no fixed sequence, these three countries can be considered as the three *stages* in a dynamic programming formulation. The decision variables x_n ($n = 1,2,3$) would be the number of teams to allocate to stage (country) n.

The identification of the *states* may not be readily apparent. To determine the states, we ask questions such as the following. What is it that changes from

Table 11.1 **Data for World Health Council**

No. of medical teams	Thousands of additional person-years of life		
	Country		
	1	2	3
0	0	0	0
1	45	20	50
2	70	45	70
3	90	75	80
4	105	110	100
5	120	150	130

one stage to the next? Given that the decisions have been made at the previous stages, how can the status of the situation at the current stage be described? What information about the current state of affairs is necessary to determine the optimal policy hereafter? On these bases, an appropriate choice for the "state of the system" is the *number of medical teams still available for allocation* (i.e., the number not already allocated at previous stages).

Let $p_i(x_i)$ be the measure of effectiveness from allocating x_i medical teams to country i, as given in Table 11.1. Thus the objective is to choose x_1, x_2, x_3 so as to

$$\text{Maximize } \sum_{i=1}^{3} p_i(x_i),$$

subject to

$$\sum_{i=1}^{3} x_i = 5,$$

and

the x_i are nonnegative integers.

Using the notation presented in Sec. 11.2, $f_n(s_n, x_n)$ then is

$$f_n(s, x_n) = p_n(x_n) + \text{maximum} \sum_{i=n+1}^{3} p_i(x_i),$$

subject to

$$\sum_{i=n}^{3} x_i = s,$$

and

the x_i are nonnegative integers,

for $n = 1, 2, 3$. In addition,

$$f_n^*(s) = \max_{x_n = 0, 1, \ldots, s} f_n(s, x_n).$$

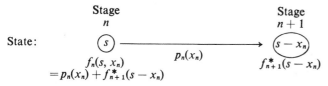

Figure 11.3 The basic structure for the World Health Council problem.

Therefore,

$$f_n(s,x_n) = p_n(x_n) + f^*_{n+1}(s - x_n)$$

(with f^*_4 defined to be *zero*). These basic relationships are summarized in Fig. 11.3.

Consequently, the *recursive relationship* relating the f^*_1, f^*_2, and f^*_3 functions for this problem is

$$f^*_n(s) = \max_{x_n = 0,1,\dots,s} \{p_n(x_n) + f^*_{n+1}(s - x_n)\}, \quad \text{for} \quad n = 1, 2.$$

For the last stage ($n = 3$),

$$f^*_3(s) = \max_{x_3 = 0,1,\dots,s} p_3(x_3).$$

The resulting dynamic programming calculations are given as follows, beginning with the last stage ($n = 3$) and proceeding backward to the first stage ($n = 1$).

$n = 3$

s	$f^*_3(s)$	x^*_3
0	0	0
1	50	1
2	70	2
3	80	3
4	100	4
5	130	5

$n = 2$

s	$f_2(s,x_2) = p_2(x_2) + f^*_3(s - x_2)$						$f^*_2(s)$	x^*_2
x_2	0	1	2	3	4	5		
0	0						0	0
1	50	20					50	0
2	70	70	45				70	0 or 1
3	80	90	95	75			95	2
4	100	100	115	125	110		125	3
5	130	120	125	145	160	150	160	4

$n = 1$

s	$f_1(s,x_1) = p_1(x_1) + f^*_2(s - x_1)$						$f^*_1(s)$	x^*_1
x_1	0	1	2	3	4	5		
5	160	170	165	160	155	120	170	1

Thus the optimal solution has $x_1^* = 1$, which makes $s = 5 - 1 = 4$ for $n = 2$, so $x_2^* = 3$, which makes $s = 4 - 3 = 1$ for $n = 3$, so $x_3^* = 1$. Since $f_1^*(5) = 170$, this (1,3,1) allocation of medical teams to the three countries will yield an estimated total of 170,000 *additional person-years of life*, which is at least 5,000 more than for any other allocation.

The preceding example illustrates a particularly common type of dynamic programming problem called the **distribution of effort problem**. For this type of problem, there is just one kind of *resource* that is to be allocated to a number of *activities*.[1] The objective is to determine how to *distribute the effort* (the resource) among the activities most effectively. For the World Health Council example, the resource involved is the *medical teams*, and the three activities are the health care work in the three *countries*. In the dynamic programming formulation of *any* distribution of effort problem, the *stages* correspond to the *activities*, where the *policy decision* at each stage is the *amount of the resource* to be allocated to that activity. The current *state* at any stage always can be defined as the *amount of the resource still remaining* to be distributed to the current and remaining stages (activities), i.e., the original total amount available minus the amount allocated to the previous stages.

The *context* of the next example is somewhat similar to the one for the World Health Council because it too is a *distribution of effort problem*. However, its *mathematical formulation* differs in that its objective is to minimize a *product* of terms for the respective stages. At first glance this example may appear *not* to be a *deterministic* dynamic programming problem because probabilities are involved. However, it does indeed fit our definition because the state at the next stage is completely determined by the state and policy decision at the current stage.

EXAMPLE 3 A government space project is conducting research on a certain engineering problem that must be solved before people can fly safely to Mars. Three research teams are currently trying three different approaches for solving this problem. The estimate has been made that, under present circumstances, the probability that the respective teams—call them 1, 2, and 3—will not succeed is 0.40, 0.60, and 0.80, respectively. Thus the current probability that all three teams will fail is $(0.40)(0.60)(0.80) = 0.192$. Because the objective is to minimize the probability of failure, two more top scientists have been assigned to the project.

Table 11.2 gives the estimated probability that the respective teams will fail when 0, 1, or 2 additional scientists are added to that team. The problem is to determine how to allocate the two additional scientists to minimize the probability that all three teams will fail.

---

[1] Note the strong analogy to the typical interpretation for linear programming problems given at the beginning of Chap. 3, namely, allocating limited resources among competing activities. The differences here are (1) only *one resource* (one linear functional constraint) is involved and (2) except for *additivity* (or its analogue for functions involving a *product* of terms), none of the assumptions of linear programming outlined in Sec. 3.3 are needed for dynamic programming.

Table 11.2 **Data on government space project problem**

No. of new scientists	Probability of failure		
	Team		
	1	*2*	*3*
0	0.40	0.60	0.80
1	0.20	0.40	0.50
2	0.15	0.20	0.30

SOLUTION Because both Examples 2 and 3 are *distribution of effort* problems, their underlying structure is actually very similar. In this case, scientists replace medical teams as the resource involved, and research teams replace countries as the activities. Therefore, instead of medical teams being allocated to countries, scientists are being allocated to research teams. The only basic difference between the two problems is in their objective functions.

With so few scientists and teams involved, this problem could be solved very easily by a process of exhaustive enumeration. However, the dynamic programming solution is presented for illustrative purposes. In this case, the *stages* correspond to the research teams, and the *state s* is the number of new scientists *still available* for assignment at the current and remaining stages. The decision variables x_n ($n = 1,2,3$) are the number of additional scientists allocated to stage (team) n. Let $p_i(x_i)$ denote the probability of failure for team i if it is assigned x_i additional scientists, as given by Table 11.2. Letting Π denote multiplication, the government's objective is to choose x_1, x_2, x_3 so as to

$$\text{Minimize} \quad \prod_{i=1}^{3} p_i(x_i) = p_1(x_1)p_2(x_2)p_3(x_3),$$

subject to

$$\sum_{i=1}^{3} x_i = 2$$

and

the x_i are nonnegative integers.

Consequently,

$$f_n(s,x_n) = p_n(x_n) \cdot \text{minimum} \prod_{i=n+1}^{3} p_i(x_i),$$

subject to

$$\sum_{i=n}^{3} x_i = s,$$

and

the x_i are nonnegative integers,

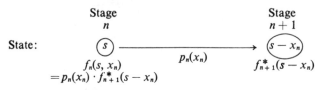

Figure 11.4 **The basic structure for the government space project problem.**

for $n = 1, 2, 3$. Thus

$$f_n^*(s) = \min_{x_n \le s} f_n(s, x_n).$$

Hence

$$f_n(s, x_n) = p_n(x_n) \cdot f_{n+1}^*(s - x_n)$$

(with f_4^* defined to be *one*). Fig. 11.4 summarizes these basic relationships.

Thus the *recursive relationship* relating the f_1^*, f_2^*, and f_3^* functions in this case is

$$f_n^*(s) = \min_{x_n \le s} \{p_n(x_n) \cdot f_{n+1}^*(s - x_n)\}, \quad \text{for } n = 1, 2,$$

and, when $n = 3$,

$$f_3^*(s) = \min_{x_3 \le s} p_3(x_3).$$

The resulting dynamic programming calculations are

$n = 3$

s	$f_3^*(s)$	x_3^*
0	0.80	0
1	0.50	1
2	0.30	2

$n = 2$

s	$f_2(s,x_2) = p_2(x_2) \cdot f_3^*(s - x_2)$ x_2 = 0	1	2	$f_2^*(s)$	x_2^*
0	0.48			0.48	0
1	0.30	0.32		0.30	0
2	0.18	0.20	0.16	0.16	2

$n = 1$

s	$f_1(s,x_1) = p_1(x_1) \cdot f_2^*(s - x_1)$ x_1 = 0	1	2	$f_1^*(s)$	x_1^*
2	0.064	0.060	0.072	0.060	1

Therefore, the optimal solution must have $x_1^* = 1$, which makes $s = 1$ at stage 2, so that $x_2^* = 0$, which makes $s = 1$ at stage 3, so that $x_3^* = 1$. Thus teams 1 and 3 should each receive one additional scientist. The new probability that all three teams will fail would then be 0.060.

All the examples thus far have had a *discrete* state variable *s*. Furthermore, they all have been *reversible* in the sense that the solution procedure actually could have moved *either* backward or forward stage by stage.[1] The next example is different in both respects; rather than being restricted to *integer* values, its state variable *s* is a *continuous* variable that can take on *any* value over certain intervals. Since *s* now has an infinite number of values, it is no longer possible to consider each of its feasible values individually. Rather, the solution for $f_n^*(x)$ and x_n^* must be expressed as *functions* of *s*. Furthermore, this example is *not* reversible because its stages correspond to *time periods*, so the solution procedure *must* proceed backward.

EXAMPLE 4 The work load for the *Local Job Shop* is subject to considerable seasonal fluctuation. However, machine operators are difficult to hire and costly to train, so the manager is reluctant to lay off workers during the slack seasons. He is likewise reluctant to maintain his peak season payroll when it is not required. Furthermore, he is definitely opposed to overtime work on a regular basis. Since all work is done to custom orders, it is not possible to build up inventories during slack seasons. Therefore, the manager is in a dilemma as to what his policy should be regarding employment levels.

The following estimates are given for the work force requirements during the four seasons of the year for the foreseeable future:

Season	Spring	Summer	Autumn	Winter	Spring
Requirements	255	220	240	200	255

Employment will not be permitted to fall below these levels. Any employment above these levels is wasted at an approximate cost of $2,000/person/season. It is estimated that the hiring and firing costs are such that the total cost of changing the level of employment from one season to the next is $200 times the square of the difference in employment levels. Fractional levels of employment are possible because of a few part-time employees, and the cost data also apply on a fractional basis.

The manager needs to determine what the employment level should be in each season to minimize total cost.

SOLUTION On the basis of the data available, it is not worthwhile to have the employment level go above the peak season requirements of 255. Therefore, spring employment should be at 255, and the problem is reduced to finding the employment level for the other three seasons.

For a dynamic programming formulation, the seasons should be the *stages*. There are actually an indefinite number of stages because the problem extends into the indefinite future. However, each year begins an identical cycle, and

---

[1] This is a general characteristic of *distribution of effort problems* such as Examples 2 and 3, since the activities (stages) can be ordered in any desired manner.

because spring employment is known, it is possible to consider only one cycle of four seasons ending with the spring season.

The decision variables x_n ($n = 1,2,3,4$) are the employment levels at stage n. It is necessary that the spring season be the last stage because the optimal value of the decision variable for each state at the last stage must be either known or obtainable without considering other stages. For every other season, the solution for the optimal employment level must consider the effect on costs in the following season. Therefore, x_1, x_2, x_3, and x_4 are the employment levels for summer, autumn, winter, and spring, respectively, where $x_4 = 255$.

The cost at the current stage depends only upon the current decision x_n and the employment in the preceding season. The preceding employment level is all the information about the current state of affairs that we need to determine the optimal policy henceforth. Therefore, the *state* s is described by the employment level at the preceding stage. Thus at stage n the state $s = x_{n-1}$ (where $x_0 = x_4 = 255$).

Let r_n denote the minimum work force requirement at stage n, so that $r_1 = 220$, $r_2 = 240$, $r_3 = 200$, and $r_4 = 255$. Thus the only feasible values for x_n are $r_n \le x_n \le 255$. Furthermore, the only states that need be considered at stage n are $r_{n-1} \le s \le 255$ (or $s = 255$ for $n = 1$).

The objective for the problem is to choose x_1, x_2, x_3, x_4 so as to

$$\text{Minimize } \sum_{i=1}^{4} [200(x_i - x_{i-1})^2 + 2{,}000(x_i - r_i)],$$

subject to

$$r_i \le x_i \le 255, \quad \text{for} \quad i = 1, 2, 3, 4.$$

Thus for stage n onward ($n = 1,2,3,4$),

$$f_n(s,x_n) = 200(x_n - s)^2 + 2{,}000(x_n - r_n)$$

$$+ \text{minimum} \sum_{\substack{r_i \le x_i \le 255 \\ i=n+1}}^{4} [200(x_i - x_{i-1})^2 + 2{,}000(x_i - r_i)],$$

because $s = x_{n-1}$. Also,

$$f_n^*(s) = \min_{r_n \le x_n \le 255} f_n(s,x_n).$$

Hence

$$f_n(s,x_n) = 200(x_n - s)^2 + 2{,}000(x_n - r_n) + f_{n+1}^*(x_n)$$

(with f_5^* defined to be *zero* because costs after stage 4 are irrelevant to the analysis). A summary of these basic relationships is given in Fig. 11.5.

Consequently, the *recursive relationship* relating the f_n^* functions is

$$f_n^*(s) = \min_{r_n \le x_n \le 255} \{200(x_n - s)^2 + 2{,}000(x_n - r_n) + f_{n+1}^*(x_n)\}.$$

The dynamic programming approach uses this relationship to identify succes-

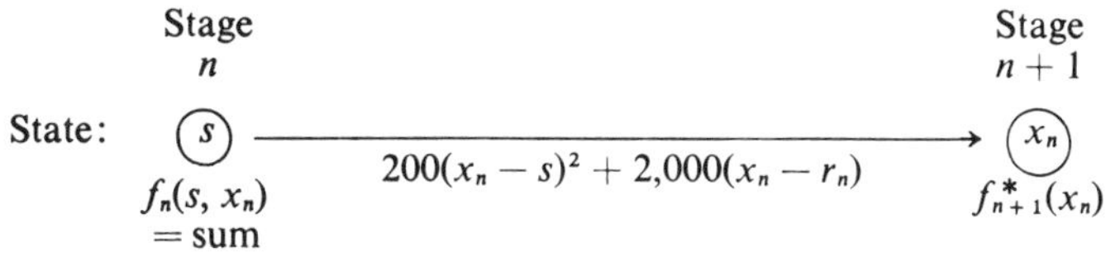

Stage
n

Stage
$n+1$

State: $\;\;\;(s)$ $\xrightarrow{\hspace{1cm} 200(x_n - s)^2 + 2,000(x_n - r_n) \hspace{1cm}}$ (x_n)

$f_n(s, x_n)$
$=$ sum

$f^*_{n+1}(x_n)$

Figure 11.5 **The basic structure for the Local Job Shop problem.**

sively these functions—$f^*_4(s)$, $f^*_3(s)$, $f^*_2(s)$, $f^*_1(255)$—and the corresponding minimizing x_n.

Beginning at the *last* stage ($n = 4$), we already know that $x^*_4 = 255$, so the necessary results are

$n = 4$	s	$f^*_4(s)$	x^*_4
	$200 \le s \le 255$	$200(255 - s)^2$	255

For the problem consisting of just the last *two* stages ($n = 3$), this recursive relationship reduces to

$$f^*_3(s) = \min_{200 \le x_3 \le 255} f_3(s, x_3)$$
$$= \min_{200 \le x_3 \le 255} \{200(x_3 - s)^2 + 2,000(x_3 - 200) + 200(255 - x_3)^2\}.$$

One way to solve for the minimum of $f_3(s, x_3)$ for any particular value of s is the graphical approach illustrated in Fig. 11.6. However, a faster way is to use *calculus*. In particular, equate to zero the first (partial) derivative of $f_3(s, x_3)$ with

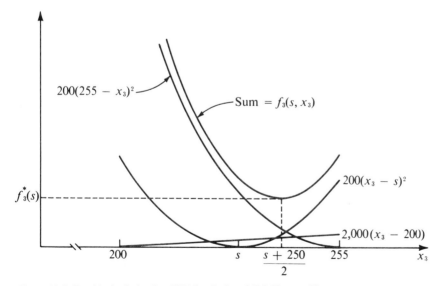

Figure 11.6 **Graphical solution for $f^*_3(s)$ for the Local Job Shop problem.**

respect to x_3,

$$\frac{\partial}{\partial x_3} f_3(s,x_3) = 400(x_3 - s) + 2{,}000 - 400(255 - x_3)$$

$$= 400(2x_3 - s - 250) = 0,$$

which yields

$$x_3^* = \frac{s + 250}{2}.$$

Because the second derivative is positive, and because this solution lies in the feasible interval for x_3, it is indeed the desired minimum. Using

$$f_3^*(s) = f_3(s,x_3^*) = 200\left(\frac{s + 250}{2} - s\right)^2 + 200\left(255 - \frac{s + 250}{2}\right)^2$$

$$+ 2{,}000\left(\frac{s + 250}{2} - 200\right)$$

and reducing this expression algebraically completes the required results for the two-stage problem summarized as follows:

$n = 3$	s	$f_3^*(s)$	x_3^*
	$240 \le s \le 255$	$50(250 - s)^2 + 50(260 - s)^2 + 1{,}000(s - 150)$	$\dfrac{s + 250}{2}$

The three-stage ($n = 2$) and four-stage problems ($n = 1$) are solved in a similar fashion. Thus for $n = 2$,

$$f_2(s,x_2) = 200(x_2 - s)^2 + 2{,}000(x_2 - r_2) + f_3^*(x_2)$$

$$= 200(x_2 - s)^2 + 2{,}000(x_2 - 240)$$

$$+ 50(250 - x_2)^2 + 50(260 - x_2)^2 + 1{,}000(x_2 - 150)$$

in the feasible region $240 \le x_2 \le 255$. The problem is to find the minimizing value of x_2 in this region, so that

$$f_2^*(s) = \min_{240 \le x_2 \le 255} f_2(s,x_2).$$

Setting

$$\frac{\partial}{\partial x_2} f_2(s,x_2) = 0$$

$$= 400(x_2 - s) + 2{,}000 - 100(250 - x_2) - 100(260 - x_2) + 1{,}000$$

$$= 200(3x_2 - 2s - 240)$$

yields

$$x_2 = \frac{2s + 240}{3}.$$

Because

$$\frac{\partial^2}{\partial x_2^2} f_2(s,x_2) = 600 > 0,$$

this value of x_2 is the desired minimizing value if $s \geq 240$. If $s < 240$ (so that this value of x_2 is *infeasible*), then

$$\frac{\partial}{\partial x_2} f_2(s,x_2) > 0, \quad \text{for } 240 \leq x_2 \leq 255,$$

so that $x_2 = 240$ would be the minimizing value. The next step is to plug these values of x_2 into $f_2(s,x_2)$ to obtain $f_2^*(s)$ for $s \geq 240$ and $s < 240$. After considerable algebraic manipulation, the following results are obtained:

$n = 2$	s	$f_2^*(s)$	x_2^*
	$220 \leq s \leq 240$	$200(240 - s)^2 + 115{,}000$	240
	$240 \leq s \leq 255$	$\dfrac{200}{9}[2(250 - s)^2 + (265 - s)^2 + 30(3s - 575)]$	$\dfrac{2s + 240}{3}$

For the four-stage problem $(n = 1)$,

$$f_1(s,x_1) = 200(x_1 - s)^2 + 2{,}000(x_1 - r_1) + f_2^*(x_1).$$

Because $r_1 = 220$, the feasible region is $220 \leq x_1 \leq 255$. The expression for $f_2^*(x_1)$ will differ in the two portions $220 \leq x_1 \leq 240$ and $240 \leq x_1 \leq 255$ of this region. Therefore,

$$f_1(s,x_1) = \begin{cases} 200(x_1 - s)^2 + 2{,}000(x_1 - 220) + 200(240 - x_1)^2 + 115{,}000, \\ \qquad\qquad\qquad\qquad\qquad\qquad\qquad \text{if } 220 \leq x_1 \leq 240 \\[2ex] 200(x_1 - s)^2 + 2{,}000(x_1 - 220) + \dfrac{200}{9}[2(250 - x_1)^2 \\[1ex] \qquad\qquad + (265 - x_1)^2 + 30(3x_1 - 575)], \quad \text{if } 240 \leq x_1 \leq 255. \end{cases}$$

Considering first the case where $x_1 \leq 240$,

$$\frac{\partial}{\partial x_1} f_1(s,x_1) = 400(x_1 - s) + 2{,}000 - 400(240 - x_1)$$

$$= 400(2x_1 - s - 235).$$

It is known that $s = 255$ (spring employment), so that

$$\frac{\partial}{\partial x_1} f_1(s,x_1) = 800(x_1 - 245) < 0$$

for all $x_1 \leq 240$. Therefore, $x_1 = 240$ is the minimizing value of $f_1(s,x_1)$ over the region $x_1 \leq 240$.

When $240 \leq x_1 \leq 255$,

$$\frac{\partial}{\partial x_1} f_1(s,x_1) = 400(x_1 - s) + 2{,}000 - \frac{200}{9}[4(250 - x_1) + 2(265 - x_1) - 90]$$

$$= \frac{400}{3}(4x_1 - 3s - 225).$$

Because

$$\frac{\partial^2}{\partial x_1^2} f_1(s,x_1) > 0, \quad \text{for all } x_1,$$

set

$$\frac{\partial}{\partial x_1} f_1(s,x_1) = 0,$$

which yields

$$x_1 = \frac{3s + 225}{4}.$$

Because $s = 255$, it follows that $x_1 = 247.5$ minimizes $f_1(s,x_1)$ over the region $240 \leq x_1 \leq 255$. Because this region includes $x_1 = 240$, which minimizes $f_1(s,x_1)$ over the region where $x_1 \leq 240$, we conclude that $x_1 = 247.5$ also minimizes $f_1(s,x_1)$ over the entire feasible region $220 \leq x \leq 255$. Hence

$$f_1^*(255) = 200(247.5 - 255)^2 + 2{,}000(247.5 - 220)$$

$$+ \frac{200}{9}[2(250 - 247.5)^2 + (265 - 247.5)^2 + 30(742.5 - 575)]$$

$$= 185{,}000.$$

These results are summarized as follows:

$n = 1$	s	$f_1^*(s)$	x_1^*
	255	185,000	247.5

Therefore, tracing back through the tables for $n = 2$, $n = 3$, and $n = 4$, respectively, and setting $s = x_{n-1}^*$ each time, the resulting optimal solution is $x_1^* = 247.5$, $x_2^* = 245$, $x_3^* = 247.5$, $x_4^* = 255$, with a total estimated cost per cycle of $185,000.

To conclude our illustrations of deterministic dynamic programming, we give one example that requires *more than one* variable to describe the state at each stage.

EXAMPLE 5 Consider the following linear programming problem.

$$\text{Maximize} \quad Z = 3x_1 + 5x_2,$$

subject to

$$x_1 \qquad \leq 4$$
$$2x_2 \leq 12$$
$$3x_1 + 2x_2 \leq 18,$$

and

$$x_1 \geq 0, x_2 \geq 0.$$

(You might recognize this model as the one for the Wyndor Glass Co. problem—the prototype example for linear programming in Chap. 3.) One way of solving small linear (or nonlinear) programming problems like this one is by dynamic programming, which is illustrated below.

SOLUTION This problem requires making two interrelated decisions, namely, the level of activity 1, x_1, and the level of activity 2, x_2. Therefore, these two activities can be interpreted as the two *stages* in a dynamic programming formulation. Although they can be taken in either order, let stage n = activity n (n = 1,2). Thus x_n is the decision variable at stage n.

What are the states? In other words, given that the decision had been made at stage 1, what information is needed about the current state of affairs before the decision can be made at stage 2? Reflection might suggest that the required information is the *amount of slack* left in the functional constraints. Interpret the right-hand side of these constraints (4, 12, and 18) as the total available amount of resources 1, 2, and 3, respectively (as described in Sec. 3.1). Then the state s is the amount of the respective resources remaining to be allocated. (Note that this definition of the state is analogous to that for Examples 2 and 3 except that there are now three resources to be allocated instead of just one.) Thus

$$s = (R_1, R_2, R_3),$$

where R_i is the amount of resource i remaining to be allocated (i = 1,2,3).

Therefore, in contrast to the preceding examples, this problem has *three* state variables (i.e., a state vector with three components) rather than one. From a theoretical standpoint, this difference is not particularly serious. It only means that, instead of considering all possible values of the one state variable, we must consider all possible *combinations* of values of the several state variables. However, from the standpoint of computational efficiency, this difference tends to be a very serious complication. Because the number of combinations, in general, can be as large as the *product* of the number of possible values of the respective variables, the number of required calculations tends to "blow up" rapidly when additional state variables are introduced. (This phenomenon has been given the apt name of *the curse of dimensionality*.)

Each of the three state variables is *continuous*. Therefore, rather than consider each possible combination of values separately, we must use the approach introduced in Example 4 of solving for the required information as a *function* of the state of the system.

Despite these complications, this problem is small enough that it can still be solved without great difficulty. To solve it, we need to introduce the usual dynamic programming notation. Thus, interpreting Z as profit, $f_n(R_1,R_2,R_3,x_n)$ is the maximum total profit from stage n onward, *given* that the state and policy decision at stage n are (R_1,R_2,R_3) and x_n, respectively. Using the *general notation* of linear programming (see Sec. 3.2),

$$f_n(R_1,R_2,R_3,x_n) = c_n x_n + \text{maximum} \sum_{j=n+1}^{2} c_j x_j,$$

subject to

$$\sum_{j=n}^{2} a_{ij} x_j \le R_i \quad (i = 1,2,3),$$

and

$$\text{the } x_j \ge 0,$$

for $n = 1, 2$. In addition,

$$f_n^*(R_1,R_2,R_3) = \max_{x_n} f_n(R_1,R_2,R_3,x_n),$$

where this maximum is taken over the *feasible* values of x_n. Therefore,

$$f_n(R_1,R_2,R_3,x_n) = c_n x_n + f_{n+1}^*(R_1 - a_{1n}x_n, R_2 - a_{2n}x_n, R_3 - a_{3n}x_n)$$

(with f_3^* defined to be *zero*). These basic relationships are summarized in Fig. 11.7.

Because the last two equations together define the *recursive relationship* relating f_1^* and f_2^*, the preparations for performing the dynamic programming calculations are complete. To solve at the last stage ($n = 2$), note that

$$f_2(R_1,R_2,R_3,x_2) = 5x_2,$$

where the feasible values of x_2 are those that satisfy the set of restrictions $2x_2 \le R_2, 2x_2 \le R_3, x_2 \ge 0$. Therefore,

$$f_2^*(R_1,R_2,R_3) = \max_{\substack{2x_2 \le R_2 \\ 2x_2 \le R_3 \\ x_2 \ge 0}} \{5x_2\}.$$

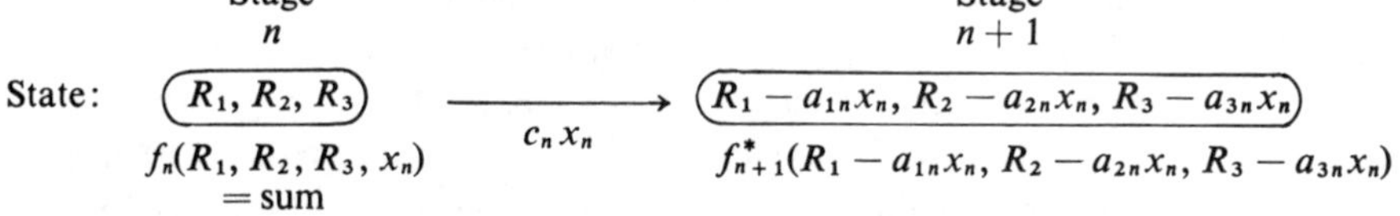

Figure 11.7 **The basic structure for the Wyndor Glass Co. linear programming problem.**

Thus the resulting solution is

$n = 2$	R_1,R_2,R_3	$f_2^*(R_1,R_2,R_3)$	x_2^*
	$R_i \geq 0$	$5\min\left\{\dfrac{R_2}{2},\dfrac{R_2}{2}\right\}$	$\min\left\{\dfrac{R_2}{2},\dfrac{R_3}{2}\right\}$

For the two-stage problem ($n = 1$),

$$f_1(R_1,R_2,R_3,x_1) = 3x_1 + f_2^*(R_1 - x_1, R_2, R_3 - 3x_1),$$

where the feasible values of x_1 are those that satisfy the set of restrictions $x_1 \leq R_1, 3x_1 \leq R_3, x_1 \geq 0$. Therefore, because it is known that $R_1 = 4, R_2 = 12$, $R_3 = 18$ at the first stage, the desired recursive relationship is

$$f_1^*(4,12,18) = \max_{\substack{x_1 \leq 4 \\ 3x_1 \leq 18 \\ x_1 \geq 0}} \{3x_1 + f_2^*(4 - x_1, 12, 18 - 3x_1)\}$$

$$= \max_{0 \leq x_1 \leq 4} \left\{3x_1 + 5\min\left\{\frac{12}{2}, \frac{18 - 3x_1}{2}\right\}\right\}.$$

Notice that

$$\min\left\{\frac{12}{2}, \frac{18 - 3x_1}{2}\right\} = \begin{cases} 6, & \text{if } 0 \leq x_1 \leq 2 \\ 9 - \dfrac{3}{2}x_1, & \text{if } 2 \leq x_1 \leq 4, \end{cases}$$

so that

$$3x_1 + 5\min\left\{\frac{12}{2}, \frac{18 - 3x_1}{2}\right\} = \begin{cases} 3x_1 + 30, & \text{if } 0 \leq x_1 \leq 2 \\ 45 - \dfrac{9}{2}x_1, & \text{if } 2 \leq x_1 \leq 4. \end{cases}$$

Because both

$$\max_{0 \leq x_1 \leq 2} \{3x_1 + 30\} \quad \text{and} \quad \max_{2 \leq x_1 \leq 4} \left\{45 - \frac{9}{2}x_1\right\}$$

achieve their maximum at $x_1 = 2$, it follows that $x_1^* = 2$, as given in the following table.

$n = 1$	R_1,R_2,R_3	$f_1^*(R_1,R_2,R_3)$	x_1^*
	4,12,18	36	2

Because $x_1^* = 2$ leads to

$$R_1 = 4 - 2 = 2, R_2 = 12, R_3 = 18 - 3(2) = 12$$

for stage 2, the $n = 2$ table yields $x_2^* = 6$. Consequently, $x_1^* = 2, x_2^* = 6$ is the optimal solution for this problem (as originally found in Sec. 3.1), and the $n = 1$ table shows that the resulting total profit is 36.

11.4 Probabilistic Dynamic Programming

Probabilistic dynamic programming differs from deterministic dynamic programming in that the state at the next stage is *not* completely determined by the state and policy decision at the current stage. Rather, there is a *probability distribution* for what the next state will be. However, this probability distribution still is completely determined by the state and policy decision at the current stage. The resulting basic structure for probabilistic dynamic programming is described diagrammatically in Fig. 11.8, where N denotes the number of possible states at stage $n + 1$; $(p_1, p_2, \ldots, p_N)$ is the probability distribution of what the state will be, given the state s_n and decision x_n at stage n; and C_i is the resulting contribution to the objective function from stage n if the state turns out to be state i.

When Fig. 11.8 is expanded to include all the possible states and decisions at all the stages, it is sometimes referred to as a **decision tree**. If the decision tree is not too large, it provides a useful way of summarizing the various possibilities that may occur.

Because of the probabilistic structure, the relationship between $f_n(s_n, x_n)$ and the $f^*_{n+1}(s_{n+1})$ necessarily is somewhat more complicated than for deterministic dynamic programming. The precise form of this relationship will depend upon the form of the overall objective function. To illustrate, suppose that the objective is to *minimize* the *expected sum* of the contributions from the individual stages. In this case, $f_n(s_n, x_n)$ would represent the minimum expected sum from stage n onward, *given* that the state and policy decision at stage n are s_n and x_n, respectively. Consequently,

$$f_n(s_n, x_n) = \sum_{i=1}^{N} p_i [C_i + f^*_{n+1}(i)],$$

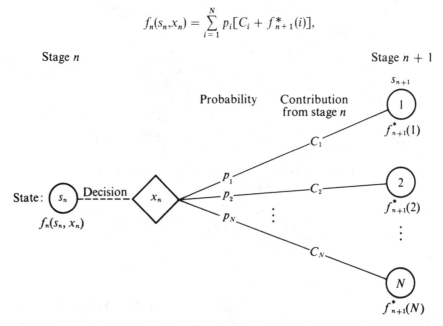

Figure 11.8 The basic structure for probabilistic dynamic programming.

with

$$f_{n+1}^*(s_{n+1}) = \min_{x_{n+1}} f_{n+1}(s_{n+1}, x_{n+1}),$$

where this minimization is taken over the *feasible* values of x_{n+1}.

Example 6 has this same form; Example 7 will illustrate another form.

EXAMPLE 6 The *Hit-and-Miss Manufacturing Company* has received an order to supply one item of a particular type. However, the customer has specified such stringent quality requirements that the manufacturer may have to produce more than one item to obtain an item that is acceptable. The manufacturer estimates that each item of this type that is produced will be *acceptable* with probability $\frac{1}{2}$ and *defective* (without possibility for rework) with probability $\frac{1}{2}$. Thus the number of acceptable items produced in a lot of size L will have a binomial distribution; that is, the probability of producing *zero* acceptable items in such a lot is $(\frac{1}{2})^L$.

Marginal production costs for this product are estimated to be $100 per item (even if defective), and excess items are worthless. In addition, a setup cost of $300 must be incurred whenever the production process is set up for this product. If inspection reveals that a completed lot has not yielded an acceptable item, the production process must be set up at an additional cost of $300. The manufacturer has time to make no more than three production runs. If an acceptable item has not been obtained by the end of the third production run, the cost to the manufacturer in lost sales income and in penalty costs would be $1,600.

The objective is to determine the policy regarding the lot size for the required production run(s) that minimizes total expected cost for the manufacturer.

SOLUTION The dynamic programming *stages* are the production runs. The decision variables x_n ($n = 1,2,3$) are the production lot size at stage n. The number of acceptable items still to be obtained (one or zero) will serve to describe the *state* of the system at any stage. Thus the state $s = 1$ at stage 1. If at least one acceptable item is obtained subsequently, the state changes to $s = 0$, after which no additional costs need to be incurred.

Although a complicated expression can be given for the overall objective function, it is more straightforward to define $f_n(s,x_n)$ directly. In this case, $f_n(s,x_n)$ is the *minimum total expected cost* for stage n onward, *given* that the state and policy decision at stage n are s and x_n, respectively. Furthermore,

$$f_n^*(s) = \min_{x_n=0,1,\dots} f_n(s,x_n),$$

where $f_n^*(0) = 0$. Using $100 as the unit of money, the contribution to cost from stage n is $(K + x_n)$ regardless of the next state, where

$$K = \begin{cases} 0, & \text{if } x_n = 0 \\ 3, & \text{if } x_n > 0. \end{cases}$$

Therefore, for $s = 1$,

$$f_n(1, x_n) = K + x_n + \left(\frac{1}{2}\right)^{x_n} f_{n+1}^*(1) + \left[1 - \left(\frac{1}{2}\right)^{x_n}\right] f_{n+1}^*(0)$$

$$= K + x_n + \left(\frac{1}{2}\right)^{x_n} f_{n+1}^*(1)$$

(where $f_4^*(1)$ is defined to be 16, the terminal cost if no acceptable items have been obtained). A summary of these basic relationships is given in Fig. 11.9.

Consequently, the *recursive relationship* for the dynamic programming calculations is

$$f_n^*(1) = \min_{x_n = 0,1,\dots} \left\{ K + x_n + \left(\frac{1}{2}\right)^{x_n} f_{n+1}^*(1) \right\}$$

for $n = 1, 2, 3$. These calculations are summarized as follows:

$n = 3$

$$f_3(1, x_3) = K + x_3 + 16\left(\frac{1}{2}\right)^{x_3}$$

s \ x_3	0	1	2	3	4	5	$f_3^*(s)$	x_3^*
0	0						0	0
1	16	12	9	8	8	$8\frac{1}{2}$	8	3 or 4

$n = 2$

$$f_2(1, x_2) = K + x_2 + \left(\frac{1}{2}\right)^{x_2} f_3^*(1)$$

s \ x_2	0	1	2	3	4	$f_2^*(s)$	x_2^*
0	0					0	0
1	8	8	7	7	$7\frac{1}{2}$	7	2 or 3

$n = 1$

$$f_1(1, x_1) = K + x_1 + \left(\frac{1}{2}\right)^{x_1} f_3^*(1)$$

s \ x_1	0	1	2	3	4	$f_2^*(s)$	x_1^*
1	7	$7\frac{1}{2}$	$6\frac{3}{4}$	$6\frac{7}{8}$	$7\frac{7}{16}$	$6\frac{3}{4}$	2

Thus the optimal policy is to produce *two* items on the first production run; if none are acceptable, then produce either *two* or *three* items on the second production run; if none are acceptable, then produce either *three* or *four* items on the third production run. The *total expected cost* for this policy is $675.

EXAMPLE 7 An enterprising young statistician believes that she has developed a system for winning a popular Las Vegas game. Her colleagues do not believe that her system works, so they have made a large bet with her that, starting with three chips, she will not have five chips after three plays of the game. Each play of the game involves betting any desired number of available chips and then either winning or losing this number of chips. The statistician believes that her system will give her a probability of $\frac{2}{3}$ of winning a given play of the game.

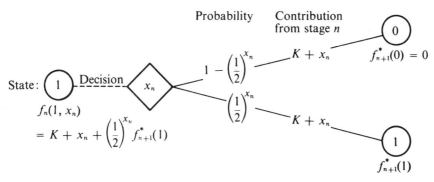

Figure 11.9 **The basic structure for the Hit-and-Miss Manufacturing Co. problem.**

Assuming the statistician is correct, determine her optimal policy regarding how many chips to bet (if any) at each of the three plays of the game. The decision at each play should take into account the results of earlier plays. The objective is to maximize the probability of winning her bet with her colleagues.

SOLUTION The plays of the game constitute the *stages* in the dynamic programming formulation. The decision variables x_n ($n = 1,2,3$) are the number of chips to bet at stage n. The *state* of the system at any stage is the number of chips available for betting at that stage because this is the information that is required for making an optimal decision on how many chips to bet.

Because the objective is to maximize the probability that the statistician will win her bet, the objective function to be maximized at each stage must be the probability of finishing the three plays with at least five chips. Therefore, $f_n(s,x_n)$ is the maximum of this probability *given* that the statistician is starting play (stage) n with s chips available. Furthermore,

$$f_n^*(s) = \max_{x_n = 0,1,\dots,s} f_n(s,x_n).$$

The expression for $f_n(s,x_n)$ must reflect the fact that it may still be possible to accumulate five chips eventually even if the statistician should lose the next play. If she should lose, the state at the next stage would be $(s - x_n)$, and the probability of finishing with at least five chips would then be $f_{n+1}^*(s - x_n)$. If she should win the next play instead, the state would become $(s + x_n)$, and the corresponding probability would be $f_{n+1}^*(s + x_n)$. Because the alleged probability of winning a given play is $\frac{2}{3}$, it now follows that

$$f_n(s,x_n) = \frac{1}{3} f_{n+1}^*(s - x_n) + \frac{2}{3} f_{n+1}^*(s + x_n)$$

(where $f_4^*(s)$ is defined to be *zero* for $s < 5$ and 1 for $s \geq 5$). Thus there is no direct contribution to the objective function from stage n in addition to the effect of being in the next state. These basic relationships are summarized in Fig. 11.10.

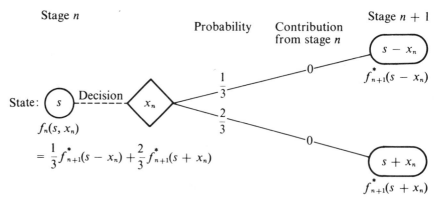

Figure 11.10 The basic structure for the Las Vegas problem.

Therefore, the *recursive relationship* for this problem is

$$f_n^*(s) = \max_{x_n = 0,1,\ldots,s} \left\{ \frac{1}{3} f_{n+1}^*(s - x_n) + \frac{2}{3} f_{n+1}^*(s + x_n) \right\},$$

for $n = 1, 2, 3$, with $f_4^*(s)$ as just defined. This recursive relationship leads to the following computational results.

$n = 3$	s	$f_3^*(s)$	x_3^*
	0	0	—
	1	0	—
	2	0	—
	3	$\frac{2}{3}$	2 (or more)
	4	$\frac{2}{3}$	1 (or more)
	≥ 5	1	0 (or $\leq s - 5$)

$n = 2$	s	$f_2(s,x_2) = \frac{1}{3} f_3^*(s - x_2) + \frac{2}{3} f_3^*(s + x_2)$					$f_2^*(s)$	x_2^*
		x_2						
		0	1	2	3	4		
	0	0					0	—
	1	0	0				0	—
	2	0	$\frac{4}{9}$	$\frac{4}{9}$			$\frac{4}{9}$	1 or 2
	3	$\frac{2}{3}$	$\frac{4}{9}$	$\frac{2}{3}$	$\frac{2}{3}$		$\frac{2}{3}$	0, 2, or 3
	4	$\frac{2}{3}$	$\frac{8}{9}$	$\frac{2}{3}$	$\frac{2}{3}$	$\frac{2}{3}$	$\frac{8}{9}$	1
	≥ 5	1					1	0 (or $\leq s - 5$)

	$f_1(s,x_1) = \frac{1}{3} f_2^*(s - x_1) + \frac{2}{3} f_2^*(s,x_1)$					
$n = 1$	x_1					
s	0	1	2	3	$f_1^*(s)$	x_1^*
3	$\frac{2}{3}$	$\frac{20}{27}$	$\frac{2}{3}$	$\frac{2}{3}$	$\frac{20}{27}$	1

Therefore, the optimal policy is

$$x_1^* = 1 \begin{cases} \text{if win, } x_2^* = 1 \begin{cases} \text{if win, } x_3^* = 0 \\ \text{if lose, } x_3^* = 2 \text{ or } 3. \end{cases} \\ \\ \text{if lose, } x_2^* = 1 \text{ or } 2 \begin{cases} \text{if win, } x_3^* = \begin{cases} 2 \text{ or } 3 \text{ (for } x_2^* = 1) \\ 1, 2, 3, \text{ or } 4 \text{ (for } x_2^* = 2) \end{cases} \\ \text{if lose, bet is lost.} \end{cases} \end{cases}$$

This policy gives the statistician a probability of $\frac{20}{27}$ of winning her bet with her colleagues.

11.5 Conclusions

Dynamic programming is a very useful technique for making a *sequence of interrelated decisions*. It requires formulating an appropriate *recursive relationship* for each individual problem. However, it provides a great computational savings over using exhaustive enumeration to find the best combination of decisions, especially for large problems. For example, if a problem has 10 stages with 10 states and 10 possible decisions at each stage, then exhaustive enumeration must consider up to 10^{10} combinations, whereas dynamic programming need make no more than 10^3 calculations (10 for each state at each stage).

This chapter has considered only dynamic programming with a *finite* number of stages. Chapter 20 is devoted to a general kind of model for probabilistic dynamic programming where the stages continue to recur indefinitely—namely, *Markovian decision processes*.

SELECTED REFERENCES

1. Bellman, Richard and Stuart Dreyfus: *Applied Dynamic Programming*, Princeton University Press, Princeton, N.J., 1962.
2. Cooper, Leon L. and Mary W. Cooper: *Introduction to Dynamic Programming*, Pergamon Press, Elmsford, N.Y., 1981.
3. Denardo, Eric V.: *Dynamic Programming Models and Applications*, Prentice-Hall, Englewood Cliffs, N.J., 1982.
4. Dreyfus, Stuart E. and Averill M. Law: *The Art and Theory of Dynamic Programming*, Academic Press, New York, 1977.
5. Howard, Ronald A.: "Dynamic Programming," *Management Science*, **12**: 317–345, 1966.

PROBLEMS

1. Consider the following network, where each number along a branch represents the actual distance between the pair of nodes connected by that branch.

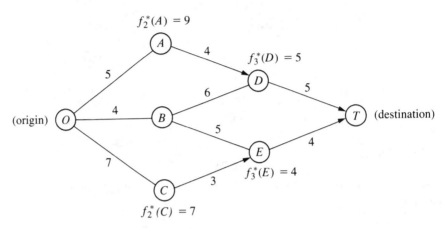

$f_2^*(A) = 9$

$f_3^*(D) = 5$

(origin) O

$f_3^*(E) = 4$

$f_2^*(C) = 7$

T (destination)

The objective is to find the shortest route from the origin to the destination.

(a) What are the stages and states for the dynamic programming formulation of this problem?

(b) Use dynamic programming to solve this problem. However, instead of using the usual tables, show your work graphically. In particular, redraw the preceding network, where the answers already are given for $f_n^*(s)$ for four of the nodes; then solve for and fill in $f_2^*(B)$ and $f_1^*(O)$. Draw an arrowhead that shows the optimal branch to take out of each of the latter two nodes. Finally, identify the optimal route by following the arrows from node O onward to node T.

(c) Use dynamic programming to solve this problem by constructing the usual tables for $n = 3$, $n = 2$, and $n = 1$.

(d) Use the shortest-route algorithm presented in Sec. 10.3 to solve this problem. Compare and contrast this approach with the one in parts (b) and (c).

2. The sales manager for a publisher of college textbooks has six traveling salesmen to assign to three different regions of the country. She has decided that each region should be assigned at least one salesman and that each individual salesman should be restricted to one of the regions, but now she wants to determine how many salesmen should be assigned to the respective regions in order to maximize sales.

The following table gives the estimated increase in sales (in appropriate units) in each region if it were allocated various numbers of salesmen.

Number of salesmen	Region 1	2	3
1	4	3	5
2	6	6	7
3	9	8	10
4	11	10	12

(*a*)   Use dynamic programming to solve this problem. Instead of using the usual tables, show your work graphically by constructing and filling in a network such as the one shown for Prob. 1. Proceed as in part (*b*) of Prob. 1 by solving for $f_n^*(s)$ for each node (except the terminal node) and writing its value by the node. Draw an arrowhead to show the optimal branch (or branches in the case of a tie) to take out of each node. Finally, identify the resulting optimal route (or routes) through the network and the corresponding optimal solution (or solutions).

(*b*)   Use dynamic programming to solve this problem by constructing the usual tables for $n = 3$, $n = 2$, and $n = 1$.

3.   The owner of a chain of three grocery stores has purchased five crates of fresh strawberries. The estimated probability distribution of potential sales of the strawberries before spoilage differs among the three stores. Therefore, the owner wants to know how he should allocate the five crates to the three stores to maximize expected profit.

For administrative reasons, the owner does not wish to split crates between stores. However, he is willing to distribute zero crates to any of his stores.

The following table gives the estimated expected profit at each store when it is allocated various numbers of crates:

Number	Stores		
of crates	1	2	3
0	0	0	0
1	5	6	4
2	9	11	9
3	14	15	13
4	17	19	18
5	21	22	20

Use dynamic programming to determine how many of the five crates should be assigned to each of the three stores to maximize the total expected profit.

4.   A college student has 7 days remaining before final examinations begin in her four courses, and she wants to allocate this study time as effectively as possible. She needs at least 1 day on each course, and she likes to concentrate on just one course each day, so she wants to allocate 1, 2, 3, or 4 days to each course. Having recently taken an operations research course, she decides to use dynamic programming to make these allocations to maximize the total grade points to be obtained from the four courses. She estimates that the alternative allocations for each course would yield the number of grade points shown in the following table:

Estimated grade points

Number of	Course			
study days	1	2	3	4
1	4	3	5	2
2	4	5	6	4
3	5	6	8	7
4	8	7	8	8

Solve this problem by dynamic programming.

5. A county chairwoman of a certain political party is making plans for an upcoming presidential election. She has received the services of six volunteer workers for precinct work, and she wants to assign them to four precincts in such a way as to maximize their effectiveness. She feels that it would be inefficient to assign a worker to more than one precinct, but she is willing to assign no workers to any one of the precincts if they can accomplish more in other precincts.

The following table gives the estimated increase in the number of votes for the party's candidate in each precinct if it were allocated various numbers of workers:

Number of workers	Precinct 1	2	3	4
0	0	0	0	0
1	4	7	5	6
2	9	11	10	11
3	15	16	15	14
4	18	18	18	16
5	22	20	21	17
6	24	21	22	18

Use dynamic programming to determine how many of the six workers should be assigned to each of the four precincts to maximize the total estimated increase in the plurality of the party's candidate.

6. Use dynamic programming to solve the Northern Airplane Company production scheduling problem presented in Sec. 7.1 (see Table 7.7). Assume that production quantities must be integer multiples of 5.

7. Reconsider the Build-Em-Fast Company problem described in Prob. 17 of Chap. 7 (also see Prob. 51 of Chap. 14). Use dynamic programming to solve this problem.

8. A company will soon be introducing a new product into a very competitive market and is currently planning its marketing strategy. The decision has been made to introduce the product in three phases. Phase 1 will feature making a special introductory offer of the product to the public at a greatly reduced price to attract first-time buyers. Phase 2 will involve an intensive advertising campaign to persuade these first-time buyers to continue purchasing the product at a regular price. It is known that another company will be introducing a new competitive product at about the time phase 2 will end. Therefore, phase 3 will involve a follow-up advertising and promotion campaign to try to keep the regular purchasers from switching to the competitive product.

A total of $4 million has been budgeted for this marketing campaign. The problem now is to determine how to allocate this money most effectively to the three phases. Let m denote the initial share of the market (expressed as a percentage) attained in phase 1, f_2 the fraction of this market share that is retained in phase 2, and f_3 the fraction of the remaining market share that is retained in phase 3. Given the following data, use dynamic programming to determine how to allocate the $4 million to maximize the *final share* of the market for the new product, i.e., to maximize mf_2f_3.

(a) Assume that the money must be spent in integer multiples of $1 million in each phase, where the minimum permissible multiple is 1 for phase 1 and 0 for phases 2 and 3. The following table gives the estimated effect of expenditures in each phase:

Millions of dollars expended	Effect on market share		
	m	f_2	f_3
0	—	0.2	0.3
1	20	0.4	0.5
2	30	0.5	0.6
3	40	0.6	0.7
4	50	—	—

(b) Now assume that *any* amount within the total budget can be spent in each phase, where the estimated effect of spending an amount x_i (in units of *millions* of dollars) in phase i ($i = 1,2,3$) is

$$m = 10x_1 - x_1^2$$
$$f_2 = 0.40 + 0.10x_2$$
$$f_3 = 0.60 + 0.07x_3.$$

[*Hint:* After solving for the $f_2^*(s)$ and $f_3^*(s)$ functions analytically, solve for x_1^* graphically.]

9. Consider the following linear programming problem.

$$\text{Maximize} \quad Z = 3x_1 + 2x_2,$$

subject to

$$x_1 + 2x_2 \le 6$$
$$3x_1 + x_2 \le 8,$$

and

$$x_1 \ge 0, \quad x_2 \ge 0.$$

Use dynamic programming to solve this problem.

10. Consider the following nonlinear programming problem.

$$\text{Maximize} \quad Z = x_1^2 x_2,$$

subject to

$$x_1^2 + x_2 \le 2.$$

(Note that there are no nonnegativity constraints.) Use dynamic programming to solve this problem.

11. Consider an electronic system consisting of four components, each of which must function for the system to function. The reliability of the system can be improved by installing several parallel units in one or more of the components. The following table gives the probability that the respective components will function if they consist of one, two, or three parallel units:

Number of parallel units	Probability of functioning			
	Component 1	Component 2	Component 3	Component 4
1	0.5	0.6	0.7	0.5
2	0.6	0.7	0.8	0.7
3	0.8	0.8	0.9	0.9

The probability that the system will function is the product of the probabilities that the respective components will function.

The cost (in hundreds of dollars) of installing one, two, or three parallel units in the respective components is given by the following table:

Number of parallel units	Cost, $			
	Component 1	Component 2	Component 3	Component 4
1	2	3	2	3
2	3	5	4	4
3	4	6	5	5

Because of budget limitations, a maximum of $1,400 can be expended.

Use dynamic programming to determine how many parallel units should be installed in each of the four components to maximize the probability that the system will function.

12. Resolve the *Local Job Shop* employment scheduling problem (Example 4) when the total cost of changing the level of employment from one season to the next is changed to $100 times the square of the difference in employment levels.

13. Consider the following nonlinear programming problem.

$$\text{Maximize} \quad Z = 36x_1 + 9x_1^2 - 6x_1^3 + 36x_2 - 3x_2^3,$$

subject to

$$x_1 + x_2 \leq 3$$

and

$$x_1 \geq 0, \quad x_2 \geq 0.$$

Use dynamic programming to solve this problem.

14. Consider the following integer nonlinear programming problem.

$$\text{Maximize} \quad Z = x_1 x_2^2 x_3^3,$$

subject to

$$x_1 + 2x_2 + 3x_3 \leq 10,$$
$$x_1 \geq 1, \quad x_2 \geq 1, \quad x_3 \geq 1,$$

and

$$x_1, x_2, x_3 \text{ are integers.}$$

Use dynamic programming to solve this problem.

15. Consider the following "fixed-charge" problem.

$$\text{Maximize} \quad Z = 3x_1 + 7x_2 + f(x_3),$$

subject to

$$x_1 + 3x_2 + 2x_3 \leq 6$$
$$x_1 + x_2 \qquad \leq 5,$$

and

$$x_1 \geq 0, \quad x_3 \geq 0, \quad x_3 \geq 0,$$

where

$$f(x_3) = \begin{cases} 0, & \text{if } x_3 = 0 \\ -6 + 6x_3, & \text{if } x_3 > 0. \end{cases}$$

Use dynamic programming to solve this problem.

16. Consider the *Food and Agriculture Organization* example presented in Sec. 8.3. Suppose that large additional amounts of equipment and money become available, so that the constraint on experts, $x_1 + 2x_2 \le 10$, is the *only* relevant functional constraint. After deleting the other two functional constraints, use dynamic programming to solve directly the first model presented for this example (ignore the equivalent linear programming model) under the following alternative assumptions.

(a) Assume that x_1 and x_2 are required to be integer.
(b) Assume that the divisibility assumption (see Sec. 3.3) holds, so that the only restrictions on x_1 and x_2 are the one functional constraint and the nonnegativity constraints.

17. A backgammon player will be playing three consecutive matches with friends tonight. For each match, he will have the opportunity to place an even bet that he will win; the amount bet can be *any* quantity of his choice between zero and the amount of money he still has left after the bets on the preceding matches. For each match, the probability is $1/2$ that he will win the match and thus win the amount bet, whereas the probability is $1/2$ that he will lose the match and thus lose the amount bet. He will begin with $30, and his goal is to have $40 at the end. (Because these are friendly matches, he does not want to end up with more than $40.) Therefore, he wants to find the optimal betting policy (including all ties) that maximizes the probability that he will have exactly $40 after the three matches.

Use dynamic programming to solve this problem.

18. Imagine that you have $5,000 to invest and that you will have an opportunity to invest that amount in either of two investments (A or B) at the beginning of each of the next 3 years. Both investments have uncertain returns. For investment A you will either lose your money entirely or (with higher probability) get back $10,000 (a profit of $5,000) at the end of the year. For investment B you will either get back just your $5,000 or (with low probability) $10,000 at the end of the year. The probabilities for these events are

Investment	Amount returned ($)	Probability
A	0	0.4
	10,000	0.6
B	5,000	0.9
	10,000	0.1

You are allowed to make only (at most) *one* investment each year, and can invest only $5,000 each time. (Any additional money accumulated is left idle.)

(a) Use dynamic programming to find the investment policy that maximizes the *expected amount of money* you will have after the 3 years.
(b) Use dynamic programming to find the investment policy that maximizes the *probability* that you will have at least $10,000 after the 3 years.

19. Suppose that the situation for the Hit-and-Miss Manufacturing Co. problem (Example 6) has changed somewhat. After a more careful analysis, you now estimate that each item produced will be *acceptable* with probability $\frac{2}{3}$, rather than $\frac{1}{2}$, so that the probability of producing *zero* acceptable items in a lot of size L is $(\frac{1}{3})^L$. Furthermore, there now is only enough time available to make *two* production runs. Use dynamic programming to determine the new optimal policy for this problem.

20. Reconsider Example 7. Suppose that the bet is changed to "Starting with two chips, he will not have five chips after *five* plays of the game." By referring to the previous computational results, make additional calculations to determine what the new optimal policy is for the enterprising young statistician.

21. The Profit & Gambit Company has a major product that has been losing money recently because of declining sales. In fact, during the current quarter of the year, sales will be 4 million units below the *break-even point*. Because the *marginal* revenue for each unit sold exceeds the *marginal* cost by $1, this amounts to a loss of $4 million for the quarter. Therefore, management must take action quickly to rectify this situation. Two alternative courses of action are being considered. One is to abandon the product immediately, incurring a cost of $4 million for shutting down. The other alternative is to undertake an intensive advertising campaign to increase sales and then abandon the product (at the cost of $4 million) only if the campaign is not sufficiently successful. Tentative plans for this advertising campaign have been developed and analyzed. It would extend over the next three quarters (subject to early cancellation), and the cost would be $6 million in each of the three quarters. It is estimated that the increase in sales would be approximately 3 million units in the first quarter, another 2 million units in the second quarter, and another 1 million units in the third quarter. However, because of a number of unpredictable market variables, there is considerable uncertainty as to what impact the advertising actually would have, and careful analysis indicates that the estimate for each quarter could turn out to be off by as much as 2 million units in either direction. (To quantify this uncertainty, assume that the additional increases in sales in the three quarters are independent random variables having a uniform distribution with a range from 1 to 5 million, from 0 to 4 million, and from -1 to 3 million, respectively.) If the actual increases are too small, the advertising campaign can be discontinued and the product abandoned at the end of either of the next two quarters.

If the intensive advertising campaign were to be initiated and continued to its completion, it is estimated that the sales for some time thereafter would continue to be at about the same level as in the third (last) quarter of the campaign. Therefore, if the sales in that quarter still are below the break-even point, the product would be abandoned. Otherwise, it is estimated that the expected discounted profit thereafter would be $8 for each unit sold over the break-even point in the third quarter.

Use dynamic programming to determine the optimal policy maximizing expected profit.

■ CHAPTER 12

Game Theory

12.1 Introduction

Life is full of conflict and competition. Numerous examples involving adversaries in conflict include parlor games, military battles, political campaigns, advertising and marketing campaigns by competing business firms, and so forth. A basic feature in many of these situations is that the final outcome depends primarily upon the combination of strategies selected by the adversaries. *Game theory* is a mathematical theory that deals with the general features of competitive situations like these in a formal, abstract way. It places particular emphasis on the decision-making processes of the adversaries.

As briefly surveyed in Sec. 12.6, research on game theory continues to delve into rather complicated types of competitive situations. However, the focus in this chapter is on the simplest case, called **two-person zero-sum games**. As the name implies, these games involve only two adversaries or *players* (who may be armies, teams, firms, and so on). They are called *zero-sum* games because one player wins whatever the other one loses, so that the sum of their net winnings is zero.

To illustrate the basic characteristics of a game theory model, consider the game called *Odds and Evens*. This game consists simply of each player simultaneously showing either one finger or two fingers. If the number of fingers matches, then the player taking Evens (say player I) wins the bet (say $1) from the player taking Odds (player II). If the number does not match, player I would pay $1 to player II. Thus each player has two *strategies*: to show either one finger or

Table 12.1 **Payoff table for the Odds and Evens game**

		II	
		1	*2*
I	*1*	1	−1
	2	−1	1

two fingers. The resulting payoff to player I in dollars is shown in the *payoff table* given in Table 12.1.

In general, a two-person game is characterized by

1. The strategies of player I.
2. The strategies of player II.
3. The payoff table.

A *strategy* may involve only a simple action, as in this example. On the other hand, in more complicated games involving a series of moves, a **strategy** is a *predetermined rule that specifies completely how one intends to respond to each possible circumstance at each stage of the game.* Before the game begins, each player knows the strategies he or she has available, the ones the opponent has available, and the payoff table. The actual play of the game consists of the players simultaneously choosing a strategy without knowing the opponent's choice.

The *payoff table* usually is given only for player I because the table for player II is just the negative of this one, due to the zero-sum nature of the game. The entries in the table may be in any units desired, such as dollars, provided that they accurately represent the *utility* to player I of the corresponding outcome. It should be noted that utility is not necessarily proportional to the amount of money (or any other commodity) when large quantities are involved. For example, $2 million (after taxes) is probably worth much less than twice as much as $1 million to a poor person. In other words, given the choice between (1) a 50 percent chance of receiving $2 million rather than nothing and (2) being sure of getting $1 million, such an individual probably would much prefer the latter. On the other hand, the outcome corresponding to an entry of 2 in a payoff table should be "worth twice as much" to player I as the outcome corresponding to an entry of 1. Thus, given the choice, he or she should be indifferent between a 50 percent chance of receiving the former outcome (rather than nothing) and definitely receiving the latter outcome instead.[1]

A primary objective of game theory is the development of *rational criteria* for selecting a strategy. This development is done under two key assumptions:

1. *Both* players are *rational.*

---

[1] See Sec. 22.5 for a further discussion of the concept of *utility.*

2. *Both* players choose their strategies solely to *promote their own welfare* (no compassion for the opponent).

Game theory contrasts with *decision analysis* (see Chap. 22), where the assumption is that the decision maker is playing a game with a passive opponent, nature, which chooses its strategies in some random fashion.

We shall develop the standard game theory criteria for choosing strategies by means of illustrative examples. In particular, the next section presents a prototype example that illustrates the formulation of a game and its solution in some simple situations. A more complicated variation of this game is then carried into Sec. 12.3 to develop a more general criterion. Sections 12.4 and 12.5 describe a *graphical procedure* and a *linear programming formulation* for solving such games. Extensions of game theory to cover situations other than two-person zero-sum games are then discussed briefly in Sec. 12.6.

12.2 Solving Simple Games—A Prototype Example

Two politicians are running against each other for the United States Senate. Campaign plans must now be made for the final 2 days before the election; this time is expected to be crucial because of the closeness of the race. Therefore, both politicians want to spend these days campaigning in two key cities: *Bigtown* and *Megalopolis*. To avoid wasting campaign time they plan to travel at night and spend either one full day in each city or two full days in just one of the cities. However, since the necessary arrangements must be made in advance, neither politician will learn his (or her) opponent's campaign schedule until after he has finalized his own. Therefore each politician has asked his campaign manager in each of these cities to assess what the impact would be (in terms of votes won or lost) from the various possible combinations of days spent there by himself and by his opponent. He then wishes to use this information to choose his best strategy on how to use these 2 days.

FORMULATION To formulate this problem as a two-person zero-sum game, we must identify the two *players* (obviously the two politicians), the *strategies* for each player, and the *payoff table*.

As the problem has been stated, each player has the following three strategies:

Strategy 1 = spend 1 day in each city.

Strategy 2 = spend both days in Bigtown.

Strategy 3 = spend both days in Megalopolis.

However, by contrast, these strategies would *not* be the ones used if each politician could learn where his opponent will spend his first day before he finalizes his own plans for his second day. In that case, each politician would have *eight* strategies (because two choices of city for the first day *and* two choices for

Table 12.2 **Formulation of payoff table for the political campaign problem**

		Total net votes won by politician I (in units of 1,000 votes)		
	Strategy	Politician II		
Strategy		*1*	*2*	*3*
Politician I 1				
2				
3				

the second day given *each* of the two possible first-day choices by his opponent provides $2 \times 2 \times 2 = 8$ combinations).

Each entry in the payoff table for player I represents the *utility* to player I (or the negative utility to player II) of the outcome resulting from the corresponding strategies used by the two players. From the politician's viewpoint, the objective is to *win votes*, and each additional vote (before learning the outcome of the election) is of equal value to him. Therefore, the appropriate entries for the payoff table are the *total net votes won* from the opponent (i.e., the sum of the net vote changes in the two cities) resulting from these 2 days of campaigning. This formulation is summarized in Table 12.2.

However, we should also point out that this payoff table would *not* be appropriate if additional information were available to the politicians. In particular, if they knew exactly how the populace was planning to vote 2 days before the election, the only significance of the data prescribed by Table 12.2 would be to indicate which politician would win the election with each combination of strategies. Because the ultimate goal is to win the election, and because the size of the plurality is relatively inconsequential, the utility entries in the table then should be some positive constant (say, $+\frac{1}{2}$) when politician I would win and $-\frac{1}{2}$ when he would lose. Even if only a *probability* of winning can be determined for each combination of strategies, the appropriate entries would be these probabilities minus $\frac{1}{2}$ because they then would represent *expected* utilities. However, sufficiently accurate data to make such determinations usually are not available.

Using the form given in Table 12.2, three alternative sets of data for the payoff table are given here to illustrate how to solve three different kinds of games.

VARIATION 1

Given that Table 12.3 is the payoff table for the two politicians (players), which strategy should each of them select? This situation is a rather special one where the answer can be obtained just by applying the concept of **dominated strategies** to rule out a succession of inferior strategies until only one choice remains.

Table 12.3 **Payoff table for variation 1 of the political campaign problem**

		II		
		1	*2*	*3*
	1	1	2	4
I	2	1	0	5
	3	0	1	−1

Specifically, a strategy can be eliminated from further consideration if it is *dominated* by another strategy, i.e., if there is another strategy that is *always at least as good* regardless of what the opponent does.

At the outset, Table 12.3 includes *no* dominated strategies for player II. However, for player I, strategy 3 is dominated by strategy 1 because the latter has larger payoffs ($1 \geq 0$, $2 \geq 1$, $4 \geq -1$) regardless of what player II does. Eliminating strategy 3 from further consideration yields the following reduced payoff table:

	1	*2*	*3*
1	1	2	4
2	1	0	5

Because both players are assumed to be rational, player II also can deduce that player I has only these two strategies remaining under consideration. Therefore, player II now *does* have a dominated strategy—strategy 3, which is dominated by both strategies 1 and 2 because they always have smaller losses (payoffs to player I) in this reduced payoff table ($1 \leq 4$, $1 \leq 5$ *and* $2 \leq 4$, $1 \leq 5$). Eliminating this strategy yields

	1	*2*
1	1	2
2	1	0

At this point, strategy 2 for player I becomes dominated by strategy 1 because the latter is better in column 2 ($2 \geq 0$) and equally good in column 1 ($1 \geq 1$). Eliminating the dominated strategy leads to

	1	*2*
1	1	2

where strategy 2 for player II is dominated by strategy 1 ($1 \leq 2$). Consequently, both players should select their strategy 1.

With this solution, player I will receive a payoff of 1 from player II (i.e., politician I will gain 1,000 votes from politician II), so that the *value of the game* is said to be 1. It is only when a game has a value of zero that it is said to be a **fair game**.

Thus the concept of a *dominated strategy* is a very useful one for reducing the size of the payoff table that needs to be considered and, in unusual cases like this one, actually identifying the optimal solution for the game.

VARIATION 2

Now suppose that the current data give Table 12.4 as the payoff table for the politicians (players). This game does not have dominated strategies, so it is not obvious what the players should do. What line of reasoning does game theory say they should use?

Consider player I: By selecting strategy 1, he could win 6 or he could lose as much as 3. However, because player II is rational and thus will protect himself from large payoffs to I, it seems probable that playing strategy 1 would result in a loss to player I. Similarly, by selecting strategy 3, player I could win 5, but more probably his rational opponent would avoid this loss and instead administer him a loss, which could be as large as 4. On the other hand, if player I selects strategy 2, he is guaranteed not to lose anything, and he could even win something. Therefore, because it provides a *better guarantee* than the others, strategy 2 seems to be a "rational" choice for player I against his rational opponent. By arguing in a similar manner, player II would see that he could lose as much as 5, 0, and 6 by using strategies 1, 2, and 3, respectively, so the apparent rational choice is strategy 2. Furthermore, even when either player learns the other's strategy, he cannot improve by changing his own, so this strategy can be used safely and (given the opportunity) repeatedly.

The end product of this line of reasoning is that each player should play in such a way as to *minimize his maximum losses* whenever the resulting choice of strategy cannot be exploited by the opponent to then improve his position. This so-called **minimax criterion** is a standard criterion proposed by game theory for selecting a strategy. In terms of the payoff table, it implies that *player I* should select the strategy whose *minimum payoff* is *largest*, whereas *player II* should choose the one whose *maximum payoff to player I* is the *smallest*. This criterion is

Table 12.4 **Payoff table for variation 2 of the political campaign problem**

		II 1	2	3	Minimum
I	1	−3	−2	6	−3
	2	2	0	2	0 ← Maximum strategy for I
	3	5	−2	−4	−4
	Maximum:	5	0	6	

Minimax strategy for II

illustrated in Table 12.4, where strategy 2 is identified as the "maximin" strategy for player I, and strategy 2 is the minimax strategy for player II. The maximin and minimax values, which are both zero here, are referred to as the *lower value* and the *upper value* of the game, respectively. When they are equal, the common quantity is called the **value of the game**. It is zero here, so this is a *fair game*.

Notice the interesting fact that the same entry in this payoff table yields both the lower and the upper values. The reason is that this entry is both the minimum in its row and the maximum in its column. The position of any such entry is called a **saddle point**.

The fact that this game possesses a saddle point was actually crucial in determining how it should be played. Because of the saddle point, neither player can take advantage of the opponent's strategy to improve his own position. In particular, when player II predicts or learns that player I is using strategy 2, player II would only increase his losses if he were to change from his original plan of using his strategy 2. Similarly, player I would only worsen his position if he were to change his plan. Thus neither player has any motive to consider changing strategies, either to take advantage of his opponent or to prevent the opponent from taking advantage of him. Therefore, since this is a **stable solution**, players I and II should exclusively use their maximin and minimax strategies, respectively.

As the next variation illustrates, some games do not possess a saddle point, in which case a more complicated analysis is required.

VARIATION 3

Late developments in the campaign result in the *final* payoff table for the two politicians (players) given by Table 12.5. How should this game be played?

Suppose that both players attempt to apply the *minimax criterion* in the same way as in variation 2. Player I would notice that the lower value of the game is −2, so he can guarantee that he will lose no more than 2 by playing strategy 1. Similarly, because the upper value of the game is 2, player II can guarantee that he will lose no more than 2 by playing strategy 3.

However, notice that there is *no value of the game* and therefore *no saddle point*. What are the resulting consequences if both players should plan to use the

Table 12.5 **Payoff table for variation 3 of the political campaign problem**

		II 1	II 2	II 3	Minimum
	1	0	−2	2	−2 ← Lower value of the game
I	2	5	4	−3	−3
	3	2	3	−4	−4
Maximum:		5	4	2	

Upper value of the game

strategies just derived? It can be seen that player I would win 2 from player II, which would make player II unhappy. Because player II is rational and can therefore foresee this outcome, he would then conclude that he can do much better, actually winning 2 rather than losing 2, by playing strategy 2 instead. Because player I is also rational, he would anticipate this switch and conclude that he can improve considerably, from -2 to 4, by changing to strategy 2. Realizing this, player II would then consider switching back to strategy 3 to convert a loss of 4 to a gain of 3. This possibility of a switch would cause player I to consider again using strategy 1, after which the whole cycle would start over again. In short, the originally suggested solution (player I to play strategy 1 and player II to play strategy 3) is *unstable*, so it is necessary to develop a more satisfactory solution. But what kind of solution should it be?

The key fact seems to be that whenever one player's strategy is predictable, the opponent here can take great advantage of this information to improve his position. Therefore, an essential feature of a rational plan for playing a game such as this one is that neither player should be able to deduce which strategy the other will use. Hence, rather than applying some known criterion for determining a single strategy that will definitely be used, it is necessary to choose among alternative acceptable strategies on some kind of random basis. By doing this, neither player knows in advance which of his own strategies will be used, let alone what his opponent will do.

This suggests, in very general terms, the kind of approach that is required for games lacking a saddle point. The next section discusses this approach more fully. Given this foundation, we turn our attention to procedures for finding an optimal way of playing such games. This particular variation of the political campaign problem will continue to be used to illustrate these ideas as they are developed.

12.3 Games with Mixed Strategies

Whenever a game does not possess a saddle point, game theory advises each player to assign a probability distribution over his or her[1] set of strategies. To express this mathematically, let

x_i = probability that player I will use strategy i ($i = 1, 2, \ldots, m$),

y_j = probability that player II will use strategy j ($j = 1, 2, \ldots, n$),

where m and n are the respective numbers of available strategies. Thus player I would specify his plan for playing the game by assigning values to $x_1, x_2, \ldots, x_m$. Because these values are probabilities, they would need to be nonnegative and add up to 1. Similarly, the plan for player II would be described by the values he assigns to his decision variables $y_1, y_2, \ldots, y_n$. These plans $(x_1, x_2, \ldots, x_m)$ and $(y_1, y_2, \ldots, y_n)$ are usually referred to as **mixed strategies**, and the original strategies would then be called *pure strategies*. When actually playing the game it

---

[1] We use only *his* or *her* in our examples and problems for ease of reading; we do not mean to imply that only men or women are engaged in the various activities.

is necessary for each player to use one of his pure strategies. However, this pure strategy would be chosen by using some random device to obtain a random observation from the probability distribution specified by the mixed strategy, where this observation would indicate which particular pure strategy to use.

To illustrate, suppose that players I and II in *variation* 3 of the political campaign problem (see Table 12.5) select the mixed strategies $(x_1, x_2, x_3) = (\frac{1}{2}, \frac{1}{2}, 0)$ and $(y_1, y_2, y_3) = (0, \frac{1}{2}, \frac{1}{2})$, respectively. This selection would say that player I is giving an equal chance (probability of $\frac{1}{2}$) to choosing either (pure) strategy 1 or 2, but he is discarding strategy 3 entirely. Similarly, player II is randomly choosing between his last two pure strategies. To play the game, each player could then flip a coin to determine which of his two acceptable pure strategies he will actually use.

Although no completely satisfactory measure of performance is available for evaluating mixed strategies, a very useful one is the *expected payoff*. Applying the probability theory definition of expected value, this quantity would be

$$\text{Expected payoff} = \sum_{i=1}^{m} \sum_{j=1}^{n} p_{ij} x_i y_j,$$

where p_{ij} is the payoff if player I uses pure strategy i and player II uses pure strategy j. It does not disclose anything about the risks involved in playing the game, but it does indicate what the average payoff will tend to be if the game is played many times. Thus, in the example of mixed strategies just given, there are four possible payoffs $(-2, 2, 4, -3)$, each occurring with a probability of $\frac{1}{4}$, so the expected payoff is $\frac{1}{4}(-2 + 2 + 4 - 3) = \frac{1}{4}$.

The time has now come to extend the concept of the minimax criterion to games that lack a saddle point and thus need mixed strategies. In this context, the **minimax criterion** says that a given player should select the mixed strategy that *maximizes the minimum expected payoff* (i.e., that minimizes the maximum expected loss) to himself. By *minimum expected payoff* we mean the smallest possible expected payoff that can result from any mixed strategy with which the opponent can counter. Thus the mixed strategy for player I that is *optimal* according to this criterion is the one that *guarantees* him the largest possible expected payoff, regardless of which mixed strategy player II might use. The value of this maximin *expected* payoff is called the *lower value* of the game and is denoted by $\underline{v}$. Similarly, the *optimal* strategy for player II is the one that guarantees him the smallest possible expected loss, regardless of what player I does. The corresponding value of the *expected* payoff to player I is the *upper value* of the game, $\bar{v}$.

Recall that when only pure strategies were used, games not having a saddle point turned out to be unstable. The reason was essentially that $\underline{v} < \bar{v}$, so that the players would want to change their strategies to improve their positions. Similarly, for games with mixed strategies, it is necessary that $\underline{v} = \bar{v}$ for the optimal solution to be stable. Fortunately, according to the *minimax theorem* of game theory this condition always holds for such games.

MINIMAX THEOREM *If mixed strategies are allowed, there always exists a value of the game; that is, $\underline{v} = \bar{v} = v$.*

Thus if both players use the mixed strategy that is optimal according to the minimax criterion, the expected payoff would be v, and neither player can do better by unilaterally changing his strategy. One proof of this theorem is included in Sec. 12.5.

Although the concept of mixed strategies becomes quite intuitive if the game is played *repeatedly*, it requires some interpretation when the game is to be played just *once*. In this case, using a mixed strategy still involves selecting and using *one* pure strategy (randomly selected from the specified probability distribution), so it might seem more sensible to ignore this randomization process and just choose the one "best" pure strategy to be used. However, we have already illustrated for variation 3 in the preceding section that a player must *not* allow his opponent to deduce what his strategy will be (i.e., the solution procedure under the rules of game theory must not *definitely* identify which pure strategy will be used when the game is unstable). Furthermore, even if the opponent is able to use only his knowledge of the tendencies of the first player to deduce *probabilities* (for the pure strategy chosen) that are different from those for the *optimal* mixed strategy, then he still can take advantage of this knowledge to reduce the expected payoff to the first player. Therefore, the only way to *guarantee* attaining the optimal *expected* payoff v is to *randomly* select the pure strategy to be used from the probability distribution for the optimal mixed strategy. (Valid statistical procedures for making such a random selection are discussed in Sec. 23.2.)

Now we must show how to find the optimal mixed strategy for each player. There are several methods of doing this. One is a graphical procedure that may be used whenever one of the players has only two (undominated) pure strategies; this approach is described in the next section. When larger games are involved, the usual method is to transform the problem into a linear programming problem that would then be solved by the simplex method on a computer; Sec. 12.5 discusses this approach.

12.4 Graphical Solution Procedure

Consider any game with mixed strategies such that, after eliminating dominated strategies, one of the players has only two pure strategies. To be specific, let this player be player I. Because his mixed strategies are (x_1, x_2) and $x_2 = 1 - x_1$, it is necessary for him to solve only for the optimal value of x_1. However, it is straightforward to plot the expected payoff as a function of x_1 for each of his opponent's pure strategies. This graph can then be used to identify the point that maximizes the minimum expected payoff. The opponent's minimax mixed strategy can also be identified from the graph.

To illustrate this procedure, consider *variation 3* of the political campaign problem (see Table 12.5). Notice that the third pure strategy for player I is dominated by his second, so the payoff table can be reduced to the form given in

Table 12.6 **Reduced payoff table for variation 3 of the political campaign problem**

			II		
	Probability		y_1	y_2	y_3
Probability	*Pure strategy*		*1*	*2*	*3*
x_1	1		0	-2	2
$1 - x_1$	2		5	4	-3

I

Table 12.6. Therefore, for each of the pure strategies available to player II the expected payoff for player I will be

(y_1, y_2, y_3)	*Expected payoff*
$(1, 0, 0)$	$0x_1 + 5(1 - x_1) = 5 - 5x_1$
$(0, 1, 0)$	$-2x_1 + 4(1 - x_1) = 4 - 6x_1$
$(0, 0, 1)$	$2x_1 - 3(1 - x_1) = -3 + 5x_1$

Now plot these expected payoff lines on a graph, as shown in Fig. 12.1. For any given value of x_1 and of (y_1, y_2, y_3), the expected payoff will be the appropriate weighted average of the corresponding points on these three lines. In particular,

$$\text{Expected payoff} = y_1(5 - 5x_1) + y_2(4 - 6x_1) + y_3(-3 + 5x_1).$$

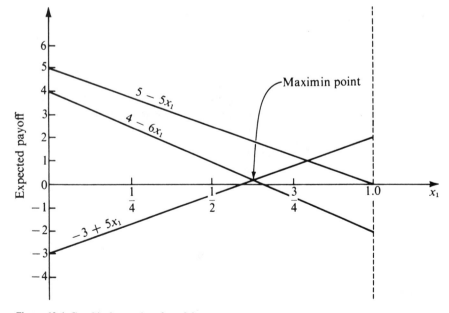

Figure 12.1 **Graphical procedure for solving games.**

Thus, given x_1, the minimum expected payoff is given by the corresponding point on the "bottom" line. According to the minimax (or maximin) criterion, player I should select the value of x_1 giving the *largest* minimum expected payoff, so that

$$\underline{v} = v = \max_{0 \le x_1 \le 1} \{\min(-3 + 5x_1, 4 - 6x_1)\}.$$

Therefore, the optimal value of x_1 is the one at the intersection of the two lines $(-3 + 5x_1)$ and $(4 - 6x_1)$. Solving algebraically,

$$-3 + 5x_1 = 4 - 6x_1,$$

so that $x_1 = \frac{7}{11}$; thus $(x_1, x_2) = (\frac{7}{11}, \frac{4}{11})$ is the *optimal mixed strategy* for player I, and

$$\underline{v} = v = -3 + 5\left(\frac{7}{11}\right) = \frac{2}{11}$$

is the value of the game.

To find the corresponding optimal mixed strategy for player II, one would now reason as follows. According to the definition of upper value and the minimax theorem, the expected payoff resulting from this strategy $(y_1, y_2, y_3) = (y_1^*, y_2^*, y_3^*)$ will satisfy the condition,

$$y_1^*(5 - 5x_1) + y_2^*(4 - 6x_1) + y_3^*(-3 + 5x_1) \le \bar{v} = v = \frac{2}{11}$$

for all values of x_1 ($0 \le x_1 \le 1$); furthermore, when player I is playing optimally (that is, $x_1 = \frac{7}{11}$), this inequality will be an equality, so that

$$\frac{20}{11} y_1^* + \frac{2}{11} y_2^* + \frac{2}{11} y_3^* = v = \frac{2}{11}.$$

Because (y_1, y_2, y_3) is a probability distribution, it is also known that

$$y_1^* + y_2^* + y_3^* = 1.$$

Therefore, $y_1^* = 0$ because $y_1^* > 0$ would violate the next-to-last equation; i.e., the expected payoff on the graph at $x_1 = \frac{7}{11}$ would be above the maximin point. (In general, any line that does not pass through the maximin point must be given a zero weight to avoid increasing the expected payoff above this point.) Hence

$$y_2^*(4 - 6x_1) + y_3^*(-3 + 5x_1) \begin{cases} \le \dfrac{2}{11}, & \text{for } 0 \le x_1 \le 1 \\[2mm] = \dfrac{2}{11}, & \text{for } x_1 = \dfrac{7}{11}. \end{cases}$$

But y_2^* and y_3^* are numbers, so the left-hand side is the equation of a straight line, which is a fixed weighted average of the two "bottom" lines on the graph. Because the ordinate of this line must equal $\frac{2}{11}$ at $x_1 = \frac{7}{11}$, and because it must never exceed $\frac{2}{11}$, the line necessarily is horizontal. (This conclusion is always true unless the optimal value of x_1 is either zero or 1, in which case player II also should use a single pure strategy.) Therefore,

$$y_2^*(4 - 6x_1) + y_3^*(-3 + 5x_1) = \frac{2}{11}, \quad \text{for } 0 \le x_1 \le 1.$$

Hence, to solve for y_2^* and y_3^*, select two values of x_1 (say, zero and 1), and solve the resulting two simultaneous equations. Thus

$$4y_2^* - 3y_3^* = \frac{2}{11},$$

$$-2y_2^* + 2y_3^* = \frac{2}{11},$$

so that $y_3^* = \frac{6}{11}$ and $y_2^* = \frac{5}{11}$. Therefore, the *optimal mixed strategy* for player II is $(y_1, y_2, y_3) = (0, \frac{5}{11}, \frac{6}{11})$.

If, in another problem, there should happen to be more than two lines passing through the maximin point, so that more than two of the y_j^* can be greater than zero, this condition would imply that there are many ties for the optimal mixed strategy for player II. One such strategy can then be identified by arbitrarily setting all but two of these y_j^* equal to zero and solving for the remaining two in the manner just described.

Although this graphical procedure has been illustrated for only one particular problem, essentially the same reasoning can be used to solve any game with mixed strategies that has only two undominated pure strategies for one of the players.

12.5 Solving by Linear Programming

Any game with mixed strategies can be solved rather easily by transforming the problem into a linear programming problem. As you will see, this transformation requires little more than applying the definitions of lower value and upper value and the minimax theorem.

First, consider how to find the optimal mixed strategy for player I. As indicated in Sec. 12.3,

$$\text{Expected payoff} = \sum_{i=1}^{m} \sum_{j=1}^{n} p_{ij} x_i y_j$$

and the strategy $(x_1, x_2, \ldots, x_m)$ is optimal if

$$\sum_{i=1}^{m} \sum_{j=1}^{n} p_{ij} x_i y_j \ge \underline{v} = v$$

for all opposing strategies $(y_1, y_2, \ldots, y_n)$. Thus this inequality will need to hold, for example, for each of the pure strategies of player II, i.e., for each of the strategies $(y_1, y_2, \ldots, y_m)$ where one $y_j = 1$ and the rest equal zero. Substituting these values into the inequality yields

$$\sum_{i=1}^{m} p_{ij} x_i \ge v, \quad \text{for } j = 1, 2, \ldots, n,$$

so that the inequality *implies* this set of n inequalities. Furthermore, this set of n inequalities *implies* the original inequality (rewritten),

$$\sum_{j=1}^{n} y_j \left(\sum_{i=1}^{m} p_{ij} x_i \right) \geq \sum_{j=1}^{n} y_j v = v,$$

because

$$\sum_{j=1}^{n} y_j = 1.$$

Because the implication goes in both directions, it follows that imposing this set of n linear inequalities is *equivalent* to requiring the original inequality to hold for all strategies $(y_1, y_2, \ldots, y_n)$. But these n inequalities are legitimate linear programming constraints, as are the additional constraints

$$x_1 + x_2 + \cdots + x_m = 1$$
$$x_i \geq 0, \quad \text{for } i = 1, 2, \ldots, m$$

that are required to ensure that the x_i are probabilities. Therefore, any solution $(x_1, x_2, \ldots, x_m)$ that satisfies this entire set of linear programming constraints is the desired optimal mixed strategy.

Consequently, the problem of finding an optimal mixed strategy has been reduced to finding a *feasible solution* for a *linear programming* problem, which can be done as described in Chap. 4. The two remaining difficulties are (1) v is unknown and (2) the linear programming problem has no objective function. Fortunately, both these difficulties can be resolved at one stroke by replacing the unknown constant v by the variable x_{m+1} and then *maximizing* x_{m+1}, so that x_{m+1} automatically will equal v (by definition) at the *optimal* solution for the linear programming problem!

To summarize, player I would find his optimal mixed strategy by using the simplex method to solve the *linear programming* problem

$$\text{Minimize} \quad (-x_{m+1}),$$

subject to

$$p_{11} x_1 + p_{21} x_2 + \cdots + p_{m1} x_m - x_{m+1} \geq 0$$
$$p_{12} x_1 + p_{22} x_2 + \cdots + p_{m2} x_m - x_{m+1} \geq 0$$
$$\vdots$$
$$p_{1n} x_1 + p_{2n} x_2 + \cdots + p_{mn} x_m - x_{m+1} \geq 0$$
$$-(x_1 + x_2 + \cdots + x_m) = -1,$$

and

$$x_i \geq 0, \quad \text{for } i = 1, 2, \ldots, m.$$

(The objective function and equality constraint have been rewritten here in an equivalent way for later convenience.) Note that x_{m+1} is not restricted to be nonnegative, whereas the simplex method can be applied only after *all* the variables have nonnegativity constraints. However, this matter can be easily rectified, as will be discussed shortly.

Now consider player II. He could find his optimal mixed strategy by rewriting the payoff table as the payoff to himself rather than to player I and then by proceeding exactly as just described. However, it is enlightening to summarize his formulation in terms of the original payoff table. By proceeding in a way that is completely analogous to the one just described, player II would conclude that his optimal mixed strategy is given by the optimal solution to the *linear programming* problem

$$\text{Maximize} \quad (-y_{n+1}),$$

subject to

$$p_{11}y_1 + p_{12}y_2 + \cdots + p_{1n}y_n - y_{n+1} \leq 0$$
$$p_{21}y_1 + p_{22}y_2 + \cdots + p_{2n}y_n - y_{n+1} \leq 0$$
$$\vdots$$
$$p_{m1}y_1 + p_{m2}y_2 + \cdots + p_{mn}y_n - y_{n+1} \leq 0$$
$$-(y_1 + y_2 + \cdots + y_n) = -1,$$

and

$$y_j \geq 0, \quad \text{for } j = 1, 2, \ldots, n.$$

Notice the key fact that this linear programming problem and the one given for player I are *dual* to each other in the sense described in Secs. 6.1 and 6.4. (In particular, this problem is in the form given for the primal problem, and the one for player I is the corresponding dual problem.) This fact has several important implications. One implication is that the optimal mixed strategies for both players can be found by solving only one of the linear programming problems because the optimal dual solution is an automatic by-product of the simplex method calculations to find the optimal primal solution. A second implication is that this brings all *duality theory* (described in Chap. 6) to bear upon the interpretation and analysis of games. A related implication is that this provides a very simple proof of the minimax theorem. Let x_{m+1}^* and y_{n+1}^* denote the value of x_{m+1} and y_{n+1} in the optimal solution of the respective linear programming problems. It is known from the *strong duality property* given in Sec. 6.1 that $-x_{m+1}^* = -y_{n+1}^*$, so that $x_{m+1}^* = y_{n+1}^*$. However, it is evident from the definition of lower value and upper value that $\underline{v} = x_{m+1}^*$ and $\bar{v} = y_{n+1}^*$, so it follows that $\underline{v} = \bar{v}$ as claimed by the minimax theorem.

The objective functions of these two linear programming problems have been written as minimize $(-x_{m+1})$ and maximize $(-y_{n+1})$ simply to demonstrate that the two problems are *dual* to each other. Hereafter, these objective functions will be written in the more natural *equivalent* forms, maximize x_{m+1} and minimize y_{n+1}. For the same reason, the negative sign now should be deleted from both sides of the equality constraint in each problem.

One remaining loose end needs to be tied up, namely, what to do about x_{m+1} and y_{n+1} being unrestricted in sign in the linear programming formulations. If it is clear that $v \geq 0$ so that the optimal values of x_{m+1} and y_{n+1} are nonnegative, then it is safe to introduce nonnegativity constraints for these variables for purposes of applying the simplex method. However, if $v < 0$, then an adjustment needs to be made. One possibility is to use the approach described in Sec. 4.6 for replacing a variable without a nonnegativity constraint by the difference of two nonnegative variables. Another is to reverse players I and II so that the payoff table would be rewritten as the payoff to the original player II, which would make the corresponding value of v positive. A third, and the most commonly used, procedure is to add a sufficiently large fixed constant to all the entries in the payoff table so that the new value of the game will be positive. (For example, setting this constant equal to the absolute value of the largest negative entry will suffice.) Because this same constant is added to every entry, this adjustment cannot alter the optimal mixed strategies in any way, so they can now be obtained in the usual manner. The indicated value of the game would be increased by the amount of the constant, but this value can be readjusted after the solution has been obtained.

To illustrate this linear programming approach, consider again variation 3 of the political campaign problem after eliminating dominated strategy 3 for player I (see Table 12.6). Because there are some negative entries in the reduced payoff table, it is unclear at the outset whether the *value* of the game v is *nonnegative* (it turns out to be). For the moment, let us assume that $v \geq 0$ and proceed without making any of the adjustments discussed in the preceding paragraph. To write out the linear programming model for player I shown earlier in this section, we note that p_{ij} is the entry in row i and column j of Table 12.6, for $i = 1, 2$ and $j = 1, 2, 3$. Using maximize x_{m+1} instead of the equivalent minimize $(-x_{m+1})$, with $m = 2$ and $n = 3$, the resulting model is

$$\text{Maximize} \quad x_3,$$

subject to

$$5x_2 - x_3 \geq 0$$
$$-2x_1 + 4x_2 - x_3 \geq 0$$
$$2x_1 - 3x_2 - x_3 \geq 0$$
$$x_1 + x_2 = 1,$$

and

$$x_1 \geq 0, \quad x_2 \geq 0, \quad x_3 \geq 0.$$

Applying the simplex method to this linear programming problem yields $x_1^* = \frac{7}{11}$, $x_2^* = \frac{4}{11}$, $x_3^* = \frac{2}{11}$ as the optimal solution. (See Probs. 15 and 16.) Consequently, the optimal *mixed* strategy for player I according to the minimax criterion is $(x_1, x_2) = (\frac{7}{11}, \frac{4}{11})$, and the *value* of the game is $v = x_3^* = \frac{2}{11}$. The simplex method also yields the optimal solution to the *dual* (given next) of this problem, namely, $y_1^* = 0$, $y_2^* = \frac{5}{11}$, $y_3^* = \frac{6}{11}$, $y_4^* = \frac{2}{11}$, so the optimal *mixed* strategy for player II is $(y_1, y_2, y_3) = (0, \frac{5}{11}, \frac{6}{11})$.

The *dual* of the preceding problem is just the linear programming model for player II (the one with variables $y_1, y_2, \ldots, y_n, y_{n+1}$) shown earlier in this section. Plugging in the values of p_{ij} from Table 12.6, this model (in minimization form) is

$$\text{Minimize} \quad y_4,$$

subject to

$$-2y_2 + 2y_3 - y_4 \le 0$$
$$5y_1 + 4y_2 - 3y_3 - y_4 \le 0$$
$$y_1 + y_2 + y_3 \qquad = 1,$$

and

$$y_1 \ge 0, \quad y_2 \ge 0, \quad y_3 \ge 0, \quad y_4 \ge 0.$$

Applying the simplex method directly to this model yields the optimal solution: $y_1^* = 0$, $y_2^* = \frac{5}{11}$, $y_3^* = \frac{6}{11}$, $y_4^* = \frac{2}{11}$ (as well as the optimal *dual* solution, $x_1^* = \frac{7}{11}$, $x_2^* = \frac{4}{11}$, $x_3^* = \frac{2}{11}$). Thus the optimal *mixed* strategy for player II is $(y_1, y_2, y_3) = (0, \frac{5}{11}, \frac{6}{11})$, and the *value* of the game is again seen to be $v = y_2^* = \frac{2}{11}$.

Because we already had found the optimal *mixed* strategy for player II while dealing with the first model, we did not have to solve the second one. In general, you always can find the optimal mixed strategies for *both* players by choosing just one of the models (either one) and then using the simplex method to solve for *both* the optimal solution and the optimal *dual* solution.

Both of these linear programming models assumed that $v \ge 0$. If this assumption were violated, what would happen is that both models would have *no feasible solutions*, so the simplex method would stop quickly with this message. To avoid this risk, we could have added a positive constant, say 3 (the absolute value of the largest negative entry), to all of the entries in Table 12.6. This then would increase by 3 all of the coefficients of $x_1, x_2, y_1, y_2,$ and y_3 in the inequality constraints of the two models. (See Prob. 12.)

12.6 Extensions

Although this chapter has considered only *two-person zero-sum games* with a *finite* number of pure strategies, it would be incorrect to conclude that game theory is limited solely to this kind of game. In fact, extensive research has been done on a number of more complicated types of games, including the ones summarized in this section.

One such type is the *n-person game*, where more than two players may participate in the game. This generalization is particularly important because, in many kinds of competitive situations, there frequently are more than two competitors involved, which is often the case, for example, in competition among business firms, in international diplomacy, and so forth. Unfortunately, the existing theory for such games is less satisfactory than it is for two-person games.

Another generalization is the *nonzero-sum game*, where the sum of the payoffs to the players need not be zero (or any other fixed constant). This case reflects the fact that many competitive situations include noncompetitive aspects that contribute to the mutual advantage or mutual disadvantage of the players. For example, the advertising strategies of competing companies can affect not only how they will split the market but also the total size of the market for their competing products. Because mutual gain is possible, nonzero-sum games are further classified in terms of the degree to which the players are permitted to cooperate. At one extreme is the *noncooperative game*, where there is no preplay communication between the players. At the other extreme is the *cooperative game*, where preplay discussions and binding agreements are permitted. For example, competitive situations involving trade regulations between countries, or collective bargaining between labor and management, might be formulated as cooperative games. When there are more than two players, cooperative games also allow some or all of the players to form coalitions.

Still another extension is to the class of *infinite games*, where the players have an infinite number of pure strategies available to them. These games are designed for the kind of situation where the strategy to be selected can be represented by a *continuous* decision variable. For example, this decision variable might be the time at which to take a certain action, or the proportion of one's resources to allocate to a certain activity, in a competitive situation. Much research has been concentrated on such games in recent years.

However, the analysis required in these extensions beyond the two-person zero-sum finite game is relatively complex and will not be pursued further here.

12.7 Conclusions

The general problem of how to make decisions in a competitive environment is a very common and important one. The fundamental contribution of game theory is that it provides a basic conceptual framework for formulating and analyzing such problems in simple situations. However, there is a considerable gap between what the theory can handle and the complexity of most competitive situations arising in practice. Therefore, the conceptual tools of game theory usually play just a supplementary role in dealing with these situations.

Because of the importance of the general problem, research is continuing with some success to extend the theory to more complex situations.

SELECTED REFERENCES

1. Begley, Sharon with David Grant: "The Games Scholars Play," *Newsweek*, Sept. 6, 1982, p. 72.
2. Davis, M.: *Game Theory: A Nontechnical Introduction*, Basic Books, New York, 1970.
3. Kaplan, E. L.: *Mathematical Programming and Games*, Wiley, New York, 1982.
4. Luce, R. Duncan and Howard Raiffa: *Games and Decisions*, Wiley, New York, 1957.
5. May, Francis B.: *Introduction to Games of Strategy*, Allyn and Bacon, Boston, 1970.
6. Owen, Guillermo: *Game Theory*, 2d ed., Academic Press, New York, 1982.

7. Shubik, M.: *The Uses and Methods of Game Theory*, American Elsevier, New York, 1975.

8. Williams, J. D.: *The Compleat Strategyst*, rev. ed., McGraw-Hill, New York, 1966.

PROBLEMS

1. For each of the following payoff tables, determine the optimal strategy for each player by successively eliminating dominated strategies. (Indicate the order in which you eliminated strategies.)

(a)

		II 1	II 2	II 3
	1	−3	1	2
I	2	1	2	1
	3	1	0	−2

(b)

		II 1	II 2	II 3
	1	0	4	1
I	2	−1	−2	3
	3	1	3	2

2. Consider the game having the following payoff table.

		II 1	II 2	II 3	II 4
	1	2	−2	1	−1
I	2	3	−1	2	−1
	3	1	−1	−3	2

Determine the optimal strategy for each player by successively eliminating dominated strategies. Give a list of the dominated strategies (and the corresponding dominating strategies) in the order in which you were able to eliminate them.

3. Find the saddle point for the game having the following payoff table.

		II 1	II 2	II 3	II 4
	1	2	−2	−4	−8
I	2	0	4	−2	2
	3	−8	−4	−6	6

4. Two companies share the bulk of the market for a particular kind of product. Each is now planning its new marketing plans for the next year in an attempt to wrest some sales away from the other company. (The total sales for the product are relatively fixed, so that one company can only increase its sales by winning them away from the other.) Each company is considering three possibilities: (1) better packaging of the product, (2) increased advertising, and (3) a slight reduction in price. The costs of the three alternatives are quite comparable and sufficiently large that each company will select just one. The estimated effect of each combination of alternatives on the *increased percentage of the sales* for company I is

		II 1	II 2	II 3
	1	−1	3	0
I	2	−2	−3	2
	3	0	2	1

Each company must make its selection before learning the decision of the other company.

(*a*)   Without eliminating dominated strategies, use the minimax (or maximin) criterion to determine the best strategy for each side.

(*b*)   Now identify and eliminate dominated strategies as far as possible. Make a list of the dominated strategies showing the order in which you were able to eliminate them. Then show the resulting reduced payoff table with no remaining dominated strategies.

5.   The labor union and management of a particular company have been negotiating a new labor contract. However, negotiations have now come to an impasse, with management making a "final" offer of a wage increase of \$1.20/hour and the union making a "final" demand of a \$1.70/hour increase. Therefore, both sides have agreed to have an impartial arbitrator set the wage increase somewhere between \$1.20/hour and \$1.70/hour (inclusively).

The arbitrator has asked each side to submit to her a confidential proposal for a fair and economically reasonable wage increase (rounded to the nearest dime). From past experience both sides know that this arbitrator normally accepts the proposal of the side that gives the most from its "final" figure. If neither side changes its final figure, or if they both give in the same amount, then the arbitrator normally compromises halfway between (\$1.45 in this case). Each side now needs to determine what wage increase to propose for its own maximum advantage.

(*a*)   Formulate this problem as a *two-person zero-sum game*.

(*b*)   Use the concept of dominated strategies to determine the best strategy for each side.

(*c*)   Without eliminating dominated strategies, use the minimax criterion to determine the best strategy for each side.

6.   Two politicians soon will be starting their campaigns against each other for a certain political office. Each must now select the main issue he will emphasize as the theme of his campaign. Each has three advantageous issues from which to choose, but the relative effectiveness of each one would depend upon the issue chosen by his opponent. In particular, the estimated increase in the vote for politician I (expressed as a percentage of the total vote) resulting from each combination of issues is

		Issue for politician II		
		1	*2*	*3*
	1	7	−1	3
Issue for politician I	*2*	1	0	2
	3	−5	−3	1

However, because considerable staff work is required to research and formulate the issue chosen, each politician must make his own choice before learning his opponent's choice. Which issue should he choose?

For each of the situations described here, formulate this problem as a *two-person zero-sum game*, and then determine which issue should be chosen by each politician according to the specified criterion.

(*a*)   The current preferences of the voters are very uncertain, so each additional percent of votes won by one of the politicians has the same value to him. Use the *minimax* criterion.

(*b*) A reliable poll has found that the percentage of the voters currently preferring politician I (before the issues have been raised) lies between 45 and 50 percent. (Assume a uniform distribution over this range.) Use the concept of *dominated strategies*, beginning with the strategies for politician I.

(*c*) Suppose that the percentage described in part (*b*) actually were 45 percent. Should politician I use the minimax criterion? Explain. Which issue would you recommend? Why?

7. Two manufacturers currently are competing for sales in two different but equally profitable product lines. In both cases the sales volume for manufacturer II is three times as large as that for manufacturer I. Because of a recent technological breakthrough, both manufacturers will be making a major improvement in both products. However, they are uncertain as to what development and marketing strategy they should follow.

If both product improvements are developed simultaneously, either manufacturer can have them ready for sale in 12 months. Another alternative is to have a "crash program" to develop only one product first to try to get it marketed ahead of the competition. By doing this, manufacturer II could have one product ready for sale in 9 months, whereas manufacturer I would require 10 months (because of previous commitments for its production facilities). For either manufacturer, the second product could then be ready for sale in an additional 9 months.

For either product line, if both manufacturers market their improved models simultaneously, it is estimated that manufacturer I would increase its share of the total future sales of this product by 8 percent of the total (from 25 to 33 percent). Similarly, manufacturer I would increase its share by 20, 30, and 40 percent of the total if it markets the product sooner than manufacturer II by 2, 6, and 8 months, respectively. On the other hand, manufacturer I would lose 4, 10, 12, and 14 percent of the total if manufacturer II markets it sooner by 1, 3, 7, and 10 months, respectively.

Formulate this problem as a two-person zero-sum game, and then determine which strategy the respective manufacturers should use according to the minimax criterion.

8. Consider the following parlor game to be played between two players. Each player begins with three chips: one red, one white, and one blue. Each chip can be used only once.

To begin, each player selects one of his chips and places it on the table, concealed. Both players then uncover the chips and determine the payoff to the winning player. In particular, if both players play the same kind of chip, it is a draw; otherwise, the following table indicates the winner and how much he receives from the other player. Next, each player selects one of his two remaining chips and repeats the procedure, resulting in another payoff according to the following table. Finally, each player plays his one remaining chip, resulting in the third and final payoff.

Winning chip	Payoff
Red beats White	$20
White beats Blue	$15
Blue beats Red	$10
Matching colors	0

Formulate this problem as a two-person zero-sum game by identifying the form of the strategies and payoffs.

9. Consider the game having the following payoff table.

		II	
		1	*2*
I	*1*	−1	4
	2	3	−1

Use the graphical procedure described in Sec. 12.4 to determine the value of the game and the optimal *mixed* strategy for each player according to the minimax criterion. Check your answer for player II by constructing *his* payoff table and applying the graphical procedure directly to this table.

10. For each of the following payoff tables, use the graphical procedure described in Sec. 12.4 to determine the value of the game and the optimal *mixed* strategy for each player according to the minimax criterion:

(a)

		II		
		1	*2*	*3*
I	*1*	4	3	1
	2	0	1	2

(b)

		II		
		1	*2*	*3*
	1	4	−1	6
I	*2*	−2	7	−1
	3	2	0	3
	4	1	5	3

11. Consider the following parlor game between two players. It begins when a referee flips a coin, notes whether it comes up heads or tails, and then shows this result to only player I. Player I may then either (1) pass and thereby pay $5 to player II or (2) he may bet. If player I passes, the game is terminated. However, if he bets, the game continues, in which case player II may then either (1) pass and thereby pay $5 to player I or (2) he may call. If player II calls, the referee then shows him the coin; if it came up heads, player II pays $10 to player I; if it came up tails, player II receives $10 from player I.

(a) Give the pure strategies for each player. (*Hint:* Player I will have four pure strategies, each one specifying how he would respond to each of the two results the referee can show him; player II will have two pure strategies, each one specifying how he will respond if player I bets.)

(b) Develop the payoff table for this game, using expected values for the entries when necessary. Determine whether it has a saddle point or not.

(c) Use the graphical procedure described in Sec. 12.4 to determine the optimal *mixed* strategy for each player according to the minimax criterion. Also give the corresponding value of the game.

12. Referring to the last paragraph of Sec. 12.5, suppose that 3 were added to all of the entries of Table 12.6 in order to ensure that the corresponding linear programming models for both players have feasible solutions with $x_3 \geq 0$ and $y_4 \geq 0$. Write out these two models. Based on the information given in Sec. 12.5, what are the optimal solutions for these two models? What is the relationship between x_3^* and y_4^*? What is the relationship between the *value* of the original game v and the values of x_3^* and y_4^*?

13. Consider the game having the following payoff table.

	II			
I	1	2	3	4
1	5	0	3	1
2	2	4	3	2
3	3	2	0	4

Use the approach described in Sec. 12.5 to formulate the problem of finding the optimal *mixed* strategies according to the minimax criterion as a *linear programming* problem.

14. For each of the following payoff tables, transform the problem of finding the minimax *mixed* strategies into an equivalent *linear programming* problem.

(a)

	II		
I	1	2	3
1	2	-3	1
2	-1	2	-2
3	1	-4	3

(b)

	II				
1	1	2	3	4	5
1	-2	-4	1	-1	3
2	-3	1	-2	-5	-1
3	1	-3	0	2	-4
4	-1	2	-3	1	2

15. Consider variation 3 of the political campaign problem (see Table 12.6). Refer to the resulting *linear programming* model for player I given near the end of Sec. 12.5. Ignoring the objective function variable (x_3), plot the *feasible region* for x_1 and x_2 graphically (as described in Sec. 3.1). (*Hint*: This feasible region consists of a single line segment.) Next, write an algebraic expression for the maximizing value of x_3 for any point in this feasible region. Finally, use this expression to demonstrate that the optimal solution must, in fact, be the one given in Sec. 12.5.

16. Consider the *linear programming* model for player I given near the end of Sec. 12.5 for variation 3 of the political campaign problem (see Table 12.6). Verify the optimal *mixed* strategies for both players given in Sec. 12.5 by applying a computer code of the simplex method to this model to find *both* its optimal solution and its optimal *dual* solution.

17. The A. J. Swim Team soon will have an important swim meet with the G. N. Swim Team. Each team has a star swimmer (John and Mark, respectively) who can swim very well in the 100-yard butterfly, backstroke, and breaststroke events. However, the rules prevent them from being used in more than *two* of these events. Therefore, their coaches now need to decide how to use them to maximum advantage.

Each team will enter three swimmers per event (the maximum allowed). For each event, the following table gives the best time previously achieved by John and Mark as well as the best time for each of the other swimmers who will definitely enter that event. (Whichever event John or Mark does not swim, his team's third entry for that event will be slower than the two shown in the table.)

	A. J. Swim Team			G. N. Swim Team		
	Entry			Entry		
Event	1	2	John	Mark	1	2
Fly	1:01.6	59.1	57.5	58.4	1:03.2	59.8
Back	1:06.8	1:05.6	1:03.3	1:02.6	1:04.9	1:04.1
Breast	1:13.9	1:12.5	1:04.7	1:06.1	1:15.3	1:11.8

The points awarded are 5 points for 1st place, 3 for 2d place, 1 for 3d place, and none for lower places. Both coaches believe that all swimmers will essentially equal their best times in this meet. Thus John and Mark each will definitely be entered in two of these three events.

(a) The coaches must submit all their entries before the meet without knowing the entries for the other team, and no changes are permitted later. The outcome of the meet is very uncertain, so each additional point has equal value for the coaches. Formulate this problem as a *two-person zero-sum* game. Eliminate dominated strategies, and then use the graphical procedure described in Sec. 12.4 to find the optimal *mixed* strategy for each team according to the minimax criterion.

(b) The situation and assignment are the same as in part (a), except that both coaches now believe that the A. J. Swim Team will win the swim meet if they can win 13 or more points in these three events, but will lose with less than 13 points. [Compare the resulting optimal mixed strategies with those obtained in part (a).]

(c) Now suppose that the coaches submit their entries during the meet one event at a time. When submitting his entries for an event, the coach does not know who will be swimming that event for the other team, but he does know who has swum *preceding* events. The three key events just discussed are swum in the order listed in the table. Once again, the A. J. Swim Team needs 13 points in these events to win the swim meet. Formulate this problem as a *two-person zero-sum* game. Then use the concept of dominated strategies to determine the best strategy for the G. N. team that actually "guarantees" they will win under the assumptions being made.

(d) The situation is the same as in part (c). However, assume now that the coach for the G. N. team does not know about game theory and so may, in fact, choose any of his available strategies that have Mark swimming two events. Use the concept of dominated strategies to determine the best strategies from which the coach for the A. J. team should choose. If this coach knows that the other coach has a tendency to enter Mark in the butterfly and the backstroke more often than in the breaststroke, which strategy should he choose?

18. Consider the general $m \times n$ two-person zero-sum game. Let p_{ij} denote the payoff to player I if he plays his strategy i ($i = 1, \dots, m$) and player II plays his strategy j ($j = 1, \dots, n$). Strategy 1 (say) for player I is said to be *weakly dominated* by strategy 2 (say) if $p_{1j} \le p_{2j}$ for $j = 1, \dots, n$ and $p_{1j} = p_{2j}$ for one or more values of j.

(a) Assume that the payoff table possesses one or more *saddle points*, so that the players have corresponding optimal pure strategies under the minimax criterion. Prove that eliminating *weakly dominated* strategies from the payoff table cannot eliminate all these saddle points and cannot produce any new ones.

(b) Assume that the payoff table does not possess any saddle points, so that the optimal strategies under the minimax criterion are *mixed* strategies. Prove that eliminating weakly dominated pure strategies from the payoff table cannot eliminate all optimal mixed strategies and cannot produce any new ones.

19. Briefly describe what you feel are the advantages and disadvantages of the minimax criterion.

CHAPTER 13

Integer
Programming

In Part Two, you saw several examples of the numerous diverse applications of *linear programming*. However, one key limitation that prevents many more applications is the assumption of *divisibility* (see Sec. 3.3), which requires that *noninteger* values be permissible for decision variables. In many practical problems, the decision variables actually make sense only if they have *integer* values. For example, it is often necessary to assign people, machines, and vehicles to activities in integer quantities. If requiring integer values is the only way in which a problem deviates from a linear programming formulation, then it is an **integer programming (IP)** problem. (The more complete name is *integer linear programming*, but the adjective *linear* normally is dropped except when contrasting this problem to the more esoteric *integer nonlinear programming* problem, which is beyond the scope of this book.)

The mathematical model for integer programming is simply the linear programming model (see Sec. 3.2) with the one additional restriction that the variables must have integer values. If only *some* of the variables are required to have integer values (so the divisibility assumption holds for the rest), this model is referred to as **mixed integer programming (MIP)**. When distinguishing the all-integer problem from this mixed case, we call the former *pure* integer programming.

For example, the Wyndor Glass Co. problem presented in Sec. 3.1 actually would have been an IP problem if the two decision variables, x_1 and x_2, had represented the total number of units to be produced of products 1 and 2, respectively, instead of the production rates. Because both products (glass doors and wood-framed windows) necessarily come in whole units, x_1 and x_2 would have to be restricted to integer values.

There have been numerous such applications of integer programming that involve a direct extension of linear programming where the divisibility assumption must be dropped. However, another area of application may be of even greater importance, namely, problems involving a number of interrelated "yes-or-no decisions." In such decisions, the only two possible choices are *yes* or *no*. For example, should we undertake a particular fixed project? Should we make a particular fixed investment? Should we locate a facility in a particular site?

With just two choices, we can represent such decisions by decision variables that are restricted to just two values, say zero and 1. Thus the jth yes-or-no decision would be represented by, say, x_j, such that

$$x_j = \begin{cases} 1, & \text{if decision } j \text{ is yes} \\ 0, & \text{if decision } j \text{ is no.} \end{cases}$$

Such variables are called **binary variables** (or 0–1 variables). Consequently, IP problems that contain only binary variables sometimes are called **binary integer programming (BIP)** problems.

Section 13.1 presents a miniature version of a typical **BIP** problem. Additional formulation possibilities with binary variables are discussed in Sec. 13.2. The remaining sections then deal with ways to solve *IP* problems, including both *BIP* (Sec. 13.5) and *MIP* (Sec. 13.6) problems.

13.1 Prototype Example

The *California Manufacturing Company* has decided to expand by building a new factory in *either* Los Angeles *or* San Francisco. It also is considering building a new warehouse in whichever city is selected for the new factory. The *net present value* (total profitability considering the time value of money) of each of these alternatives is shown in the fourth column of Table 13.1. The last column gives the capital required for the respective investments, where the total capital available is $25,000,000. The objective is to find the feasible combination of alternatives that maximizes the total net present value.

Although this problem is small enough that it can be solved very quickly by inspection (build the factory *and* a warehouse in San Francisco), let us formulate

Table 13.1 **Data for California Manufacturing Company example**

Decision number	Yes-or-no question	Decision variable	Net present value	Capital required
1	Build factory in L.A.?	x_1	$7 million	$20 million
2	Build factory in S.F.?	x_2	$5 million	$15 million
3	Build warehouse in L.A.?	x_3	$4 million	$12 million
4	Build warehouse in S.F.?	x_4	$3 million	$10 million

Capital Available: $25 million

the IP model for illustrative purposes. All of the decision variables have the *binary* form,

$$x_j = \begin{cases} 1, & \text{if decision } j \text{ is yes} \\ 0, & \text{if decision } j \text{ is no} \end{cases} \quad (j = 1,2,3,4).$$

Because the first two decisions represent *mutually exclusive alternatives* (the company wants to build only *one* new factory), they need the constraint

$$x_1 + x_2 = 1.$$

Similarly, the last two decisions also represent mutually exclusive alternatives (the company wants *at most* one new warehouse), which implies the constraint

$$x_3 + x_4 \leq 1.$$

Furthermore, decisions 3 and 4 are *contingent decisions*, because they are contingent on decisions 1 and 2, respectively (the company would consider building a warehouse in a city only if the new factory also is going there). This contingency is taken into account by the constraints

$$x_3 - x_1 \leq 0$$
$$x_4 - x_2 \leq 0,$$

which force $x_3 = 0$ if $x_1 = 0$ and $x_4 = 0$ if $x_2 = 0$. Therefore, the complete BIP model is

$$\text{Maximize} \quad Z = 7x_1 + 5x_2 + 4x_3 + 3x_4,$$

subject to

$$
\begin{aligned}
20x_1 + 15x_2 + 12x_3 + 10x_4 &\leq 25 \\
x_1 + x_2 &= 1 \\
x_3 + x_4 &\leq 1 \\
-x_1 + x_3 &\leq 0 \\
-x_2 + x_4 &\leq 0 \\
x_j &\leq 1 \\
x_j &\geq 0,
\end{aligned}
$$

and

$$x_j \text{ is an integer}, \quad \text{for } j = 1,2,3,4.$$

Equivalently, the last three lines of this model can be replaced by the single restriction

$$x_j \text{ is binary}, \quad \text{for } j = 1,2,3,4.$$

In addition, the third constraint, $x_3 + x_4 \leq 1$, can be deleted as a *redundant* constraint, because it is implied by the second, fourth, and fifth constraints.

Except for its small size, this example is typical of many real applications of integer programming where the basic decisions to be made are of the yes-or-no type. Like the two pairs of decisions for this example, groups of yes-or-no decisions often constitute groups of **mutually exclusive alternatives** such that *only one* decision in the group can be yes. Each group requires a constraint that the sum of the corresponding binary variables must be $= 1$ (if *exactly one* decision in the group must be yes) or ≤ 1 (if *at most one* decision in the group can be yes). Occasionally, decisions of the yes-or-no type are **contingent decisions**, i.e., decisions depend upon previous decisions. In particular, one decision is said to be *contingent* on another decision if it is allowed to be yes *only if* the other is yes. This situation occurs when the contingent decision involves a follow-up action that would become irrelevant, or even impossible, if the other decision is no. The form that the resulting constraint takes always is that illustrated by the fourth and fifth constraints in the example.

13.2 Some Other Formulation Possibilities with Binary Variables

You have just seen a prototype example where the *basic decisions* of the problem are of the *yes-or-no type*, so that *binary variables* are introduced to represent these decisions. In addition, binary variables also can be very useful in other ways for formulating difficult problems in a tractable manner. In particular, these variables sometimes enable us to take a problem whose natural formulation is intractable and *reformulate* it as a pure or mixed IP problem.

This kind of situation arises when the original formulation of the problem fits either an IP or a linear programming format *except* for certain minor disparities involving combinatorial relationships in the model. By expressing these combinatorial relationships in terms of questions that must be answered yes or no, *auxiliary* binary variables can be introduced into the model to represent these yes-or-no decisions. Introducing these variables reduces the problem to an MIP problem (or a *pure* IP problem if all of the original variables also are required to have integer values).

Some cases that can be handled by this approach are discussed next, where the x_j denote the *original* variables of the problem (they may be either continuous or integer variables), and the y_i denote the *auxiliary* binary variables that are introduced for the reformulation.

EITHER-OR CONSTRAINTS

Consider the important case where a choice can be made between two constraints, so that *only one* must hold. For example, there may be a choice as to which of two resources to use for a certain purpose, so that it is necessary for only one of the two resource availability constraints to hold mathematically. To illustrate the approach to such situations, suppose that one of the requirements in the overall problem is that

$$\text{Either} \quad 3x_1 + 2x_2 \leq 18$$
$$\text{or} \quad x_1 + 4x_2 \leq 16.$$

This requirement must be reformulated to fit it into the linear programming format where *all* specified constraints must hold. Let M be an *extremely* large positive number. Then this requirement can be rewritten as

$$\text{Either} \begin{cases} 3x_1 + 2x_2 \leq 18 \\ \text{and} \quad x_1 + 4x_2 \leq 16 + M \end{cases}$$
$$\text{or} \begin{cases} 3x_1 + 2x_2 \leq 18 + M \\ \text{and} \quad x_1 + 4x_2 \leq 16, \end{cases}$$

because adding M to the right-hand side of such constraints has the effect of eliminating them, because they automatically would be satisfied by any solutions that satisfy the other constraints of the problem. (This formulation assumes that the set of feasible solutions for the overall problem is a bounded set and that M is large enough so that it will not eliminate any feasible solutions.) This formulation is equivalent to the set of constraints

$$3x_1 + 2x_2 \leq 18 + yM$$
$$x_1 + 4x_2 \leq 16 + (1 - y)M.$$

Because the *auxiliary variable* y must be either zero or 1, this formulation guarantees that one of the original constraints must hold while the other one is in effect eliminated. This new set of constraints would then be appended to the other constraints in the overall model to give a pure or mixed IP problem (depending on whether the x_j are integer or continuous variables).

This approach is directly related to our earlier discussion about expressing combinatorial relationships in terms of questions that must be answered yes or no. The combinatorial relationship involved concerns the combination of the *other* constraints of the model with the *first* of the two *alternative* constraints and then with the *second*. Which of these two combinations of constraints is *better* (in terms of the value of the objective function that then can be achieved)? To rephrase this question in yes-or-no terms, we ask two complementary questions:

1. Should $x_1 + 4x_2 \leq 16$ be selected as the constraint that must hold?
2. Should $3x_1 + 2x_2 \leq 18$ be selected as the constraint that must hold?

Because exactly one of these questions is to be answered affirmatively, we let the binary terms, y and $(1 - y)$, respectively, represent these yes-or-no decisions, so that $y + (1 - y) = 1$ (*one* yes) automatically. If instead separate binary variables, y_1 and y_2, had been used to represent these yes-or-no decisions, then an additional constraint, $y_1 + y_2 = 1$, would have been needed to make them mutually exclusive.

A formal presentation of this approach is given next for a more general case.

K OUT OF N CONSTRAINTS MUST HOLD

Consider the case where the overall model includes a set of N possible constraints such that only some K of these constraints *must* hold. (Assume $K < N$.) Part of the optimization process is to choose *which combination* of K constraints permits the objective function to reach its best possible value. The $(N - K)$ constraints *not* chosen are, in effect, eliminated from the problem, although feasible solutions might coincidentally still satisfy some of them.

This case is a direct generalization of the preceding case, which had $K = 1$ and $N = 2$. Denote the N possible constraints by

$$f_1(x_1, x_2, \ldots, x_n) \leq d_1$$
$$f_2(x_1, x_2, \ldots, x_n) \leq d_2$$
$$\vdots$$
$$f_N(x_1, x_2, \ldots, x_n) \leq d_N.$$

Then, applying the same logic as for the preceding case, we find that an equivalent formulation of the requirement that some K of these constraints *must* hold is

$$f_1(x_1, x_2, \ldots, x_n) \leq d_1 + My_1$$
$$f_2(x_1, x_2, \ldots, x_n) \leq d_2 + My_2$$
$$\vdots$$
$$f_N(x_1, x_2, \ldots, x_n) \leq d_N + My_N$$
$$\sum_{i=1}^{N} y_i = N - K,$$

and

$$y_i \text{ is binary, } \quad \text{for } i = 1, 2, \ldots, N,$$

where M is an extremely large positive number. Because the constraints on the y_i guarantee that K of these variables will equal zero and those remaining will equal 1, K of the original constraints will be unchanged and the rest will, in effect, be eliminated. The choice of *which K* of these constraints should be retained is made by applying the appropriate algorithm to the overall problem so it finds an optimal solution for *all* of the variables simultaneously.

FUNCTIONS WITH N POSSIBLE VALUES

Consider the situation where a given function is required to take on any one of N given values. Denote this requirement by

$$f(x_1, x_2, \ldots, x_n) = d_1, \quad \text{or} \quad d_2, \ldots, \quad \text{or} \quad d_N.$$

One special case is where this function is

$$f(x_1, x_2, \ldots, x_n) = \sum_{j=1}^{n} a_j x_j,$$

as on the left-hand side of a linear programming constraint. Another special case is where $f(x_1, x_2, \ldots, x_n) = x_j$ for a given value of j, so the requirement becomes that x_j must take on any one of N given values.

The equivalent IP formulation of this requirement is the following:

$$f(x_1, x_2, \ldots, x_n) = \sum_{i=1}^{N} d_i y_i$$

$$\sum_{i=1}^{N} y_i = 1$$

and

$$y_i \text{ is binary}, \quad \text{for} \quad i = 1, 2, \ldots, N,$$

so this new set of constraints would replace this requirement in the statement of the overall problem. This set of constraints provides an *equivalent* formulation because exactly one y_i must equal 1 and the others must equal zero, so exactly one d_i is being chosen as the value of the function. In this case, there are N yes-or-no questions being asked, namely, should d_i be the value chosen ($i = 1, 2, \ldots, N$)? Because the y_i respectively represent these *yes-or-no decisions*, the second constraint makes them *mutually exclusive alternatives*.

To illustrate how this case can arise, reconsider the Wyndor Glass Co. problem presented in Sec. 3.1. Eighteen percent of the total production capacity of Plant 3 currently is unused and available for the two new products *or* for certain future products that will be ready for production soon. In order to leave any remaining capacity in usable blocks for these future products, management now wants to impose the restriction that the amount of capacity used by the two current new products must be 6 percent *or* 12 percent *or* 18 percent. Thus the third constraint of the original model ($3x_1 + 2x_2 \leq 18$) now becomes

$$3x_1 + 2x_2 = 6 \quad \text{or} \quad 12 \quad \text{or} \quad 18.$$

In the preceding notation, $N = 3$ with $d_1 = 6$, $d_2 = 12$, and $d_3 = 18$. Consequently, management's new requirement should be formulated as follows:

$$3x_1 + 2x_2 = 6y_1 + 12y + 18y_3$$
$$y_1 + y_2 + y_3 = 1$$

and

$$y_1, y_2, y_3 \text{ are binary}.$$

The overall model for this new version of the problem then consists of the original model (see Sec. 3.1) plus this new set of constraints that replaces the original third constraint. This replacement yields a very tractable MIP formulation.

THE FIXED-CHARGE PROBLEM

It is quite common to incur a fixed charge or setup cost when undertaking an activity. For example, such a charge occurs when a production run to produce a small batch of a particular product is undertaken and the required production facilities must be set up to initiate the run. In such cases the total cost of the activity is the sum of a variable cost related to the level of the activity and the setup cost required to initiate the activity. Frequently the variable cost will be at least roughly proportional to the level of the activity. If it is, the *total cost* of the activity (say activity j) can be represented by a function of the form

$$f_j(x_j) = \begin{cases} k_j + c_j x_j, & \text{if } x_j > 0 \\ 0, & \text{if } x_j = 0 \end{cases}$$

where x_j denotes the level of activity j ($x_j \geq 0$), k_j denotes the setup cost, and c_j denotes the cost for each incremental unit. Were it not for the setup cost k_j, this cost structure would suggest the possibility of a *linear programming* formulation to determine the optimal levels of the competing activities. Fortunately, even with the k_j, IP can still be used.

To formulate the overall model, suppose that there are n activities, each with the preceding cost structure (with $k_j \geq 0$ in every case and $k_j > 0$ for some $j = 1, 2, \ldots, n$), and that the problem is to

$$\text{Minimize} \quad Z = f_1(x_1) + f_2(x_2) + \cdots + f_n(x_n),$$

subject to

given linear programming constraints.

To convert this problem into an MIP format, we begin by posing n questions that must be answered yes or no; namely, for each $j = 1, 2, \ldots, n$, should activity j be undertaken ($x_j > 0$)? Each of these *yes-or-no decisions* is then represented by an auxiliary *binary variable* y_j, so that

$$Z = \sum_{j=1}^{n} (c_j x_j + k_j y_j),$$

where

$$y_j = \begin{cases} 1, & \text{if } x_j > 0 \\ 0, & \text{if } x_j = 0. \end{cases}$$

Therefore, the y_j can be viewed as *contingent decisions* similar to (but not identical to) the type considered in Sec. 13.1. Let M be an extremely large positive number that exceeds the maximum feasible value of any x_j ($j = 1, 2, \ldots, n$). Then the constraints,

$$x_j \leq M y_j, \quad \text{for} \quad j = 1, 2, \ldots, n,$$

will ensure that $y_j = 1$ rather than zero whenever $x_j > 0$. The one difficulty remaining is that these constraints leave y_j free to be either zero or 1 when $x_j = 0$. Fortunately, this difficulty is automatically resolved because of the nature of the objective function. The case where $k_j = 0$ can be ignored because y_j can then be deleted from the formulation. So we consider the only other case; namely, where $k_j > 0$. When $x_j = 0$, so that the constraints permit a choice between $y_j = 0$ and $y_j = 1$, $y_j = 0$ must yield a smaller value of Z than $y_j = 1$. Therefore, because the objective is to minimize Z, an algorithm yielding an optimal solution would always choose $y_j = 0$ when $x_j = 0$.

To summarize, the MIP formulation of the fixed-charge problem is

$$\text{Minimize} \quad Z = \sum_{j=1}^{n} (c_j x_j + k_j y_j),$$

subject to

the original constraints, plus
$$x_j - My_j \leq 0$$

and

$$y_j \text{ is binary}, \quad \text{for } j = 1, 2, \ldots, n.$$

If the x_j also had been restricted to be integer, then this would be a *pure* IP problem.

To illustrate this approach, look again at Sec. 3.4 at the air pollution problem faced by the *Nori & Leets Co.* The first of the abatement methods considered—increasing the height of the smokestacks—actually would involve a substantial *fixed charge* to get ready for *any* increase in addition to a variable cost that would be roughly proportional to the amount of increase. After conversion to the equivalent annual costs used in the formulation, this fixed charge would be $2,000,000 each for the blast furnaces and the open-hearth furnaces, whereas the variable costs are those identified in Table 3.9. Thus, in the preceding notation, $k_1 = 2$, $k_2 = 2$, $c_1 = 8$, and $c_2 = 10$. Because the other abatement methods do not involve any fixed charges, $k_j = 0$ for $j = 3, 4, 5, 6$. Consequently, the new MIP formulation of this problem is

$$\text{Minimize} \quad Z = 8x_1 + 10x_2 + 7x_3 + 6x_4 + 11x_5 + 9x_6 + 2y_1 + 2y_2,$$

subject to

the constraints given in Sec. 3.4, plus
$$x_1 - My_1 \leq 0$$
$$x_2 - My_2 \leq 0,$$

and

$$y_1, y_2 \text{ are binary}.$$

Before concluding this discussion of formulation possibilities with (auxiliary) binary variables, we need to strike one note of caution. This approach sometimes requires adding a relatively large number of such variables, which can make the model *computationally infeasible*. In fact, as the next section explains, you may even be in trouble with a few dozen binary variables.

13.3 Some Perspectives on Solving Integer Programming Problems

It may seem that IP problems should be relatively easy to solve. After all, *linear programming* problems can be solved extremely efficiently, and the only difference is that IP problems have far fewer solutions to be considered. In fact, *pure* IP problems with a bounded feasible region are guaranteed to have just a *finite* number of feasible solutions.

Unfortunately, there are two fallacies in this line of reasoning. One is that having a finite number of feasible solutions ensures that the problem is readily solvable. Finite numbers can be astronomically large. For example, consider the simple case of BIP problems. With n variables, there are 2^n solutions to be considered (where some of these solutions can subsequently be discarded because they violate the functional constraints). Thus, each time n is increased by *one*, the number of solutions is *doubled*. This pattern is referred to as the **exponential growth** of the difficulty of the problem. With $n = 10$, there are more than a *thousand* solutions (1,024); with $n = 20$, there are more than a *million*; with $n = 30$, there are more than a *billion*, and so forth. Therefore, even the fastest computers are incapable of performing *exhaustive enumeration* (checking each solution for feasibility and, if it is feasible, calculating the value of the objective value) for BIP problems with a few dozen variables, let alone for *general* IP problems with the same number of integer variables. Sophisticated algorithms, such as those developed in subsequent sections, can do somewhat better. However, because of *exponential growth*, even these algorithms sometimes can handle only a few dozen binary or integer variables.

The second fallacy is that removing some feasible solutions (the noninteger ones) from a linear programming problem will make it easier to solve. To the contrary, it is only because all of these feasible solutions are there that the guarantee can be given (see Sec. 5.1) that there will be a corner-point feasible solution (basic feasible solution) that is optimal for the overall problem. *This* guarantee is the key to the remarkable efficiency of the simplex method. As a result, linear programming problems generally are *much* easier to solve than IP problems.

Consequently, most successful algorithms for integer programming incorporate the simplex method (or dual simplex method) as much as they can by relating portions of the IP problem under consideration to the corresponding linear programming problem (i.e., the same problem except that the integer restriction is deleted). For any given IP problem, this corresponding linear programming problem commonly is referred to as its **LP-relaxation**. The algorithm presented in Sec. 13.6 illustrates how a sequence of LP-relaxations for portions of an IP problem can be used to solve the overall IP problem effectively.

There is one special situation where solving an IP problem is no more difficult than solving its LP-relaxation once by the simplex method, namely, when the optimal solution to the latter problem turns out to satisfy the integer restriction of the IP problem. When this situation occurs, this solution *must* be optimal for the IP problem as well, because it is the best solution among all the feasible solutions for the LP-relaxation, which includes all the feasible solutions for the IP problem. Therefore, it is common for an IP algorithm to begin by applying the simplex method to the LP-relaxation to check whether this fortuitous outcome has occurred.

Although it generally is quite fortuitous indeed for the optimal solution to the LP-relaxation to be integer as well, there actually exist several *special types* of IP problems for which this outcome is *guaranteed*. You already have seen two of these special types in Chap. 7, namely, the *Transportation Problem* (when all of the supply and demand quantities are integer) and the *Assignment Problem*. The reason that this guarantee can be given for these types of problems is that they possess a certain *special structure* (e.g., see Table 7.6) that ensures that every basic feasible solution is integer. Consequently, these special types of IP problems can be treated like linear programming problems (which is why two of them appear in Chap. 7), because they can be solved completely by a streamlined version of the simplex method.

Although this much simplification is somewhat unusual, in practice IP problems frequently have *some* special structure that can be exploited to simplify the problem. Sometimes, very large versions of these problems can be solved successfully. *Special-purpose algorithms* that are specifically designed to exploit certain kinds of special structures are becoming increasingly important in integer programming.

Thus the two primary determinants of *computational difficulty* for an IP problem are (1) the *number of integer variables* and (2) the *structure* of the problem. This situation is in contrast to *linear programming*, where the number of (functional) constraints is much more important than the number of variables. In integer programming, the number of constraints is of *some* importance (especially if LP-relaxations are being solved), but it is strictly secondary to the other two factors. In fact, there occasionally are cases where *increasing* the number of constraints *decreases* the computation time because the number of feasible solutions has been reduced. For MIP problems, it is the number of *integer* variables rather than the *total* number of variables that is important, because the *continuous* variables have almost no effect on computational effort.

Because IP problems are, in general, much more difficult to solve than linear programming problems, it sometimes is tempting to use the approximate procedure of simply applying the simplex method to the LP-relaxation and then *rounding* the noninteger values to integers in the resulting solution. This approach may be adequate for some applications, especially if the values of the variables are quite large so that rounding creates relatively little error. However, you should beware of two pitfalls involved in this approach.

One pitfall is that the optimal linear programming solution is *not necessarily feasible* after it is rounded. Often it is difficult to see in which way the rounding should be done to retain feasibility. It may even be necessary to change the value of some variables by 1 or more units after rounding. To illustrate, suppose that some of the constraints are

$$-x_1 + x_2 \leq 3\tfrac{1}{2}$$
$$x_1 + x_2 \leq 16\tfrac{1}{2}$$

and that the simplex method has identified the optimal solution for the LP-relaxation as $x_1 = 6\tfrac{1}{2}$, $x_2 = 10$. Notice that it is impossible to round x_1 to 6 or 7 (or any other integer) and retain feasibility. Feasibility can be retained only by also changing the integer value of x_2. It is easy to imagine how such difficulties can be compounded when there are tens or hundreds of constraints and variables.

Even if the optimal solution for the LP-relaxation is rounded successfully, there remains another pitfall. There is no guarantee that this rounded solution will be the optimal integer solution. In fact, it may even be far from optimal in terms of the value of the objective function. This fact is illustrated by the following problem:

$$\text{Maximize} \quad Z = x_1 + 5x_2,$$

subject to the restrictions

$$x_1 + 10x_2 \leq 20$$
$$x_1 \qquad\quad \leq 2,$$

and

$$x_1 \geq 0, \qquad x_2 \geq 0$$
$$x_1, x_2 \text{ are integers.}$$

Because there are only two decision variables, this problem can be depicted graphically as shown in Fig. 13.1. Either the graph or the simplex method may be used to find that the optimal solution for the LP-relaxation is $x_1 = 2$, $x_2 = 9/5$,

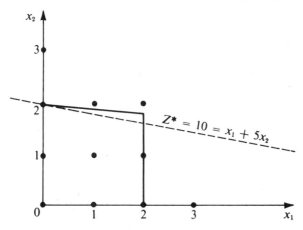

Figure 13.1 **Illustrative integer programming problem.**

with $Z = 11$. If a graphical solution were not available (which it would not be with more decision variables), then the variable with the noninteger value $x_2 = \frac{9}{5}$ would normally be rounded in the feasible direction to $x_2 = 1$. The resulting integer solution is $x_1 = 2$, $x_2 = 1$, which yields $Z = 7$. Notice that this solution is far from the optimal solution $(x_1, x_2) = (0, 2)$, where $Z = 10$.

Because of these two pitfalls, a better approach for dealing with IP problems that are too large to be solved exactly is to use one of the available *heuristic algorithms*. These algorithms are extremely efficient for large problems, but they are not guaranteed to find an optimal solution. However, they do tend to be considerably more effective than the rounding approach just discussed in finding very good feasible solutions.

For IP problems that are small enough to be solved to optimality, a considerable number of algorithms now are available. Unfortunately, none possess computational efficiency that is even remotely comparable to the *simplex method* (except on special types of problems). Therefore, developing IP algorithms remains an active area of research, and progress continues to be made in developing more efficient algorithms.

The most popular mode for IP algorithms is to use the *branch-and-bound technique* and related ideas to *implicitly enumerate* the feasible integer solutions, and we shall focus on this approach. The next section presents the branch-and-bound technique in a general context. Section 13.5 then describes a branch-and-bound algorithm for BIP problems, and Sec. 13.6 presents another algorithm of the same type for MIP problems.

13.4 The Branch-and-Bound Technique

Because any bounded *pure* IP problem has only a finite number of feasible solutions, it is natural to consider using some kind of *enumeration procedure* for finding an optimal solution. Unfortunately, as we discussed in the preceding section, this finite number can be, and usually is, very large. Therefore, it is imperative that any enumeration procedure be cleverly structured so that only a tiny fraction of the feasible solutions actually need be examined. For example, dynamic programming (see Chap. 11) provides one such kind of procedure for many problems having a finite number of feasible solutions (although it is not particularly efficient for most IP problems). Another such approach is provided by the *branch-and-bound technique*. This technique and variations of it have been applied with some success to a variety of operations research problems, but it is especially well known for its application to IP problems.

The basic idea of the branch-and-bound technique is the following. Suppose (to be specific) that the objective function is to be *minimized*. Assume that an *upper bound* (to be labeled Z_U) on the optimal value of the objective function is available. This upper bound normally is the value of the objective function for the *best feasible solution identified thus far*. (This solution is referred to as the **incumbent solution**.) The first step is to *partition* the set of all feasible solutions *into several subsets*, and then, for each one, a *lower bound* (to be labeled Z_L) is obtained for the value of the objective function of the solutions within that subset. Those subsets whose lower bounds exceed the current upper bound on the objective function value are then excluded from further consideration. Other subsets also are discarded if they are found to be of no further interest, either because the subset has no feasible solutions or because its best feasible solution has been found (so that this solution can be recorded and the rest of the subset eliminated). A subset that is excluded from further consideration for any of these reasons is said to be **fathomed**. After the appropriate subsets have been fathomed, one of the *remaining subsets*, say, the one with the smallest lower bound, is then *partitioned* further *into several subsets*. Their lower bounds are obtained in turn and used as before to exclude some of these subsets from further consideration. From *all* the *remaining* subsets, another one is selected for further partitioning, and so on. This process is repeated again and again until a feasible solution whose objective function value is no greater than the lower bound for any remaining subset is found. Such a feasible solution must be optimal because none of the subsets can contain a better solution.

Summary of Branch-and-Bound Technique

Initialization step Set $Z_U = \infty$. Begin with the *entire set* of solutions under consideration (including any *infeasible* solutions that cannot conveniently be eliminated) as the only remaining subset. Before beginning the regular iterations through the following steps, apply just the bound step, the fathoming step, and the optimality test to this one subset. (We shall refer to this as *iteration 0*.)

Branch step Use some *branch rule* to select *one* of the *remaining* subsets (those neither fathomed nor partitioned) and partition it into two or more new subsets of solutions.

Bound step For each new subset, obtain a *lower bound* Z_L on the value of the objective function for the feasible solutions in the subset.

Fathoming step For each new subset, exclude it from further consideration (i.e., *fathom* it) if

  Fathoming Test 1. $Z_L \geq Z_U$,

or

  Fathoming Test 2. The subset is found to contain no feasible solutions,

or

  Fathoming Test 3. The best feasible solution in the subset has been identified (so Z_L corresponds to its objective function value); if this situation occurs and $Z_L < Z_U$, then reset $Z_U = Z_L$, store this solution as the new *incumbent* solution, and reapply Fathoming Test 1 to *all remaining* subsets.

Optimality test Stop when there are *no remaining* (unfathomed) subsets; the current *incumbent* solution is *optimal.*[1] Otherwise, return to the branch step.

---

[1] If there is no incumbent solution (that is, if Z_U still equals ∞), then the problem possesses no feasible solutions.

If the objective is to *maximize* rather than minimize the objective function, the procedure is unchanged *except* that the roles of the upper and lower bounds are reversed. Thus Z_U would be replaced by Z_L and vice versa, ∞ would become $-\infty$, and the directions of the inequalities would be reversed.

The *branch* and *bound steps* allow considerable flexibility in designing a specific algorithm for the problem of interest, and they have an important effect on the computational efficiency of the algorithm. The two most popular *branch rules* for selecting a subset to partition are the *best bound rule* and the *newest bound rule*. The **best bound rule** says to select the subset having the *most favorable bound* (the smallest lower bound in the case of minimization) because this subset would seem to be the most promising one to contain an optimal solution. This rule tends to minimize the number of iterations required by the algorithm. The **newest bound rule** says to select the *most recently created* subset that has not been fathomed, breaking a tie between subsets created at the same time by taking the one with the most favorable bound. The advantages of this rule are less cumbersome bookkeeping and greater opportunity to obtain the bounds efficiently (as you will see in Secs. 13.5 and 13.6). The method selected for obtaining the bounds should represent a careful compromise between the *tightness* of the bounds and *computational effort*.

EXAMPLE WITH BEST BOUND RULE

We now illustrate the branch-and-bound technique with the *best bound rule* by applying it to an *assignment problem* (see Sec. 7.4) having the *cost table* shown in Table 13.2. Thus the objective is to assign each of the four assignees to its unique assignment in such a way as to *minimize* the sum of the four corresponding entries in the cost matrix. There are 4! ($=24$) *feasible* solutions.

SPECIFICATION OF BRANCH STEP In addition to selecting a branch rule (the best bound rule in this case), we must specify how the *remaining subset* selected by this rule will be *partitioned* into two or more new subsets of solutions. A natural way of partitioning for the assignment problem is to enumerate the different ways of making one of the remaining assignments. For example, the entire set of 24

Table 13.2 **Cost table for assignment problem illustrating branch-and-bound technique**

		Assignment			
		1	2	3	4
Assignee	A	9	5	4	5
	B	4	3	5	6
	C	3	1	3	2
	D	2	4	2	6

feasible solutions can be partitioned into four subsets of 6 feasible solutions each by respectively assigning A, B, C, and D to assignment 1. Each of these subsets can be partitioned further (as needed) into three subsets of 2 feasible solutions each by respectively assigning each of the three unassigned assignees to assignment 2. Finally, each of these new subsets of 2 feasible solutions can be partitioned further (as needed) into two subsets of 1 feasible solution each by respectively assigning each of the two unassigned assignees to assignment 3 (and thus the other unassigned assignee to assignment 4). This procedure is the one that will be used, where each subset generated will be identified by listing its assigned assignees in order.

SPECIFICATION OF BOUND STEP For each new subset of feasible solutions generated by the branch step, the bound step must efficiently establish a tight *lower bound* Z_L on the total cost for any of the solutions in the subset. The method we have chosen is to add the *minimum* possible cost of the respective assignments (i.e., the sum of *minimum column entries* in the cost table)[1] without worrying about whether the corresponding solution is a feasible solution. For example, such a lower bound over the entire set of *all* feasible solutions is the sum of the minimum of the respective columns of Table 13.2, or $2 + 1 + 2 + 2 = 7$. (This cost of 7 does *not* correspond to a feasible solution, because it involves assigning assignees C and D *twice* each to assignments and *never* assigning A and B, but it still provides a valid lower bound.) When calculating Z_L for a subset where one or more assignments already has been made, we need to make two modifications in this procedure: (1) The costs of these actual assignments are used in place of the minimum entries in these columns, and (2) the rows for the assignees already assigned are deleted before we find the minimum entry in each of the other columns. For example, if assignee C were assigned to assignment 1, then the lower bound for the resulting C subset of six feasible solutions would be the cost of this assignment plus the sum of the minimum costs (ignoring row C) for the last three columns, or $3 + (3 + 2 + 5) = 13$. (This coincidently happens to correspond to a feasible solution whose respective assignments are $CBDA$.)

SPECIFICATION OF FATHOMING STEP The fathoming step will be executed just as outlined under Summary of Branch-and-Bound Technique, *except* that Fathoming Test 2 (subset found to contain no feasible solutions) will be deleted because the new subsets generated by the branch step just specified always contain feasible solutions. For Fathoming Test 3, the best feasible solution in the subset has been identified only when the assignments made to obtain the lower bound Z_L in the bound step correspond to a *feasible* solution.

---

[1] Note that we could just as well have used the sum of minimum *row* entries instead. In fact, we could do *both* and then take the maximum of the two sums as the lower bound. This latter procedure tends to give a better bound at the expense of somewhat more computational effort—the inevitable tradeoff to be considered in designing the bound step.

ITERATION 0 Consider the *entire* set of all 24 feasible solutions. Its lower bound already has been obtained (when illustrating the bound step) as $Z_L = 7$. Because this bound corresponds to an *infeasible* solution ($DCDC$), Fathoming Test 3 fails. With $Z_U = \infty$ at this point, Fathoming Test 1 also fails. Therefore, this set continues to be the one *remaining subset*, ready to be partitioned into new subsets to begin the first complete iteration.

ITERATION 1 The entire set of all 24 feasible solutions is partitioned into the four subsets corresponding to the four possible ways in which assignment 1 can be made. The corresponding lower bounds (Z_L) are $9 + (1 + 2 + 2) = 14$ for the A subset, $4 + (1 + 2 + 2) = 9$ for the B subset, 13 (as obtained above) for the C subset, and $2 + (1 + 3 + 2) = 8$ for the D subset. Because this lower bound of 13 for the C subset happens to correspond to a *feasible* solution, $CBDA$, 13 also is an *upper bound* Z_U on the total cost for the optimal solution, and this solution becomes the current *incumbent* solution. Therefore, the C subset is fathomed by Fathoming Test 3. Furthermore, this leads to fathoming the A subset by reapplying Fathoming Test 1 ($14 \geq 13$) with the new Z_U, so this leaves the B and D subsets as the only *remaining* subsets at this point. These results are summarized by the *tree* (defined in Sec. 10.2) shown in Fig. 13.2, where the numbers give the lower bound Z_L for each subset, and the solution following each number in parentheses is the solution (frequently infeasible) that generated this lower bound.

ITERATION 2 With only two *remaining* subsets, the best bound rule selects the D subset as the one to *partition* into new subsets, because it has a smaller value of

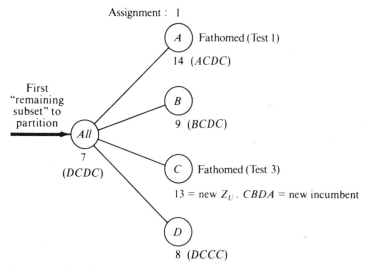

Figure 13.2 **Results from the first iteration of the branch-and-bound technique (with the best bound rule) for the assignment problem example.**

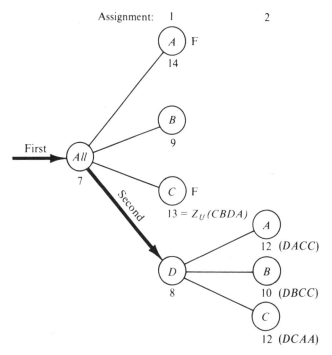

Figure 13.3 **Results from the second iteration of the branch-and-bound technique (with the best bound rule) for the assignment problem example.**

Z_L (8 < 9) than the B subset. The partitioning is done by continuing to assign assignee D to assignment 1 and then making assignment 2 in the three possible ways (A, B, or C), thereby obtaining the DA, DB, and DC subsets. Because the DA subset is the set of the (two) feasible solutions that include assigning D to 1 and A to 2, its lower bound is $Z_L = 2 + 5 + (3 + 2) = 12$. Similarly, the lower bound for the DB subset is $Z_L = 2 + 3 + (3 + 2) = 10$, and for the DC subset it is $Z_L = 2 + 1 + (4 + 5) = 12$. None of the fathoming tests succeed in fathoming any of these new subsets, so the *remaining* subsets are B, DA, DB, and DC. The tree shown in Fig. 13.3 has now been obtained.

ITERATION 3 Among the four *remaining* subsets, the one with the smallest lower bound Z_L now is subset B, so it is partitioned into the three new subsets, BA, BC, and BD. Their lower bounds are, respectively, $Z_L = 4 + 5 + (2 + 2) = 13$, $Z_L = 4 + 1 + (2 + 5) = 12$, and $Z_L = 4 + 4 + (3 + 2) = 13$. Because the first two bounds correspond to feasible solutions, and the last bound (as well as the first) equals Z_U, all of these subsets immediately are fathomed. Furthermore, this feasible solution ($BCDA$) for the BC subset has an objective function value that is better (12 < 13) than for the *current incumbent* solution, so $BCDA$ becomes the *new incumbent* solution. Because the new $Z_U = 12$ equals Z_L for the DA and DC

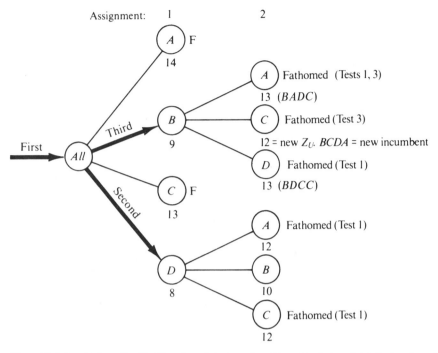

Figure 13.4 **Results from the third iteration of the branch-and-bound technique (with the best bound rule) for the assignment problem example.**

subsets, they now are fathomed as well. This result leaves *only* subset *DB* as the one *remaining* subset. All of these results are summarized in Fig. 13.4.

ITERATION 4 The one *remaining* subset *DB* next is partitioned into the new subsets, *DBA* and *DBC*, having lower bounds, $Z = 2 + 3 + 4 + (2) = 11$ and $Z = 2 + 3 + 3 + (5) = 13$, respectively. Because both of these bounds correspond to *feasible* solutions, both new subsets are fathomed. Furthermore, the feasible solution (*DBAC*) for the *DBA* subset is better than the incumbent solution ($11 < 12$), so it becomes the *new incumbent* solution. But there now are no *remaining* subsets still to be fathomed (see Fig. 13.5), so this new *incumbent* solution (*DBAC*) also must be *optimal*, and the algorithm stops.

SAME EXAMPLE WITH NEWEST BOUND RULE

Now let us contrast the preceding results with what happens when the *newest bound rule* is used instead to select the *remaining* subset to partition at each iteration.

Iteration 1 proceeds as before (Fig. 13.2) because there is only one possible choice. There again is no change at iteration 2 (Fig. 13.3), because all four *remaining* subsets (*A,B,C,D*) were created at the same time (iteration 1), so the tie is

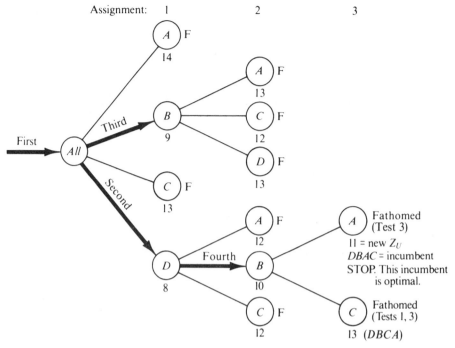

Assignment: 1   2   3

Figure 13.5 **Results from the fourth (final) iteration of the branch-and-bound technique (with the best bound rule) for the assignment problem example.**

broken by selecting the one with the *best* bound (subset D with $Z_L = 8$) just as for the *best bound rule*.

The first change occurs at iteration 3 (Fig. 13.4), where the *remaining* subsets (see Fig. 13.3) are B, DA, DB, and DC. Because subset B was created at iteration 1, whereas subsets DA, DB, and DC were created later at iteration 2, the selection must be made from among these latter three. Subset DB has a better bound ($Z_L = 10$) than subsets DA and DC ($Z_L = 12$), so it is the one chosen for partitioning, as depicted in the upper portion of Fig. 13.6. This partitioning leads to a new *incumbent* solution ($DBAC$ with $Z_U = 11$), and the subsequent fathoming leaves just subset B as the only *remaining* subset, so it becomes the automatic choice to be partitioned for iteration 4 (see the lower portion of Fig. 13.6). This iteration yields no *remaining* subsets, so the algorithm once again terminates with $DBAC$ as the optimal solution.

In this particular example, the newest bound rule happens to require the *same* number of iterations (four) as the best bound rule to find and verify an optimal solution. However, this is not always the case. The newest bound rule can use fewer iterations, but the tendency is to require more because the selection of which *remaining* subset to partition is not based primarily on which one seems most promising (based on Z_L) for containing an optimal solution. Furthermore,

Iteration 1: Same as Fig. 13.2.

Iteration 2: Same as Fig. 13.3.

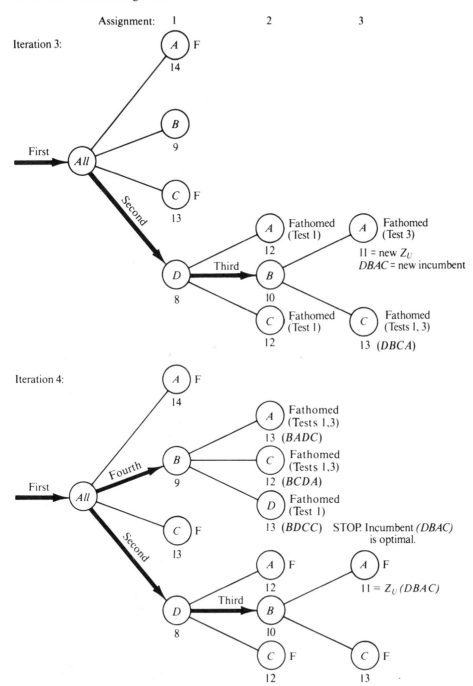

Figure 13.6 **Results from applying the branch-and-bound technique with the *newest bound rule* to the assignment problem example.**

the newest bound rule has no significant compensating advantages for solving assignment problems, so the *best bound rule* is the preferable bound rule for this kind of problem. However, you will see in Secs. 13.5 and 13.6 that the newest bound rule can have important compensating advantages for other types of problems.

GENERAL OBSERVATIONS

In general, the branch-and-bound technique can be described in terms of a tree such as those shown in Figs. 13.2 to 13.6. The origin corresponds to the set of *all* feasible solutions. This set is partitioned into several subsets, usually by designating the respective values of one of the decision variables. Each value corresponds to a node at the end of a branch out of the origin. Associated with each node is a lower bound on the value of the objective function for the feasible solutions that can be reached from that node. Assuming that the best bound rule is used, the branches out of the node with the smallest lower bound are then constructed, and a lower bound is obtained for the node at the end of each of these branches. From among all the nodes that form the end points of the tree, the one with the smallest lower bound is chosen for constructing the next set of branches and associated bounds. This process of branching and bounding is repeated again and again, each time adding new branches to the tree, until the end-point node having the *smallest* lower bound is known to lead to a *complete feasible solution* that achieves this lower bound. This solution is then known to be an *optimal solution*, and the algorithm terminates.

So far we have described how to use the branch-and-bound technique to find only *one* optimal solution. However, in the case of ties for the optimal solution, it is sometimes desirable to identify *all* of these optimal solutions so that the final choice among them can be made on the basis of intangible factors not incorporated into the mathematical model. To find them all, you need to make only two slight alterations in the *fathoming step*. First, change Fathoming Test 1 from $Z_L \geq Z_U$ to $Z_L > Z_U$. Second, in Fathoming Test 3, if the best feasible solution in the subset has been identified and $Z_L = Z_U$, store this solution as *another* (tied) incumbent solution. Then, when the *optimality test* finds that there are *no remaining* (unfathomed) subsets, *all* of the current *incumbent* solutions will be the *optimal* solutions.

Finally, it should be noted that rather than finding an optimal solution, the branch-and-bound technique can also be used to find a *nearly optimal* solution, generally with much less computational effort. Such a solution can be found merely by terminating the procedure the first time that the smallest lower bound Z_L is within a prespecified percentage (or quantity) of the current upper bound Z_U for the problem (in the case of minimization). The feasible solution corresponding to the upper bound is then the desired *suboptimal* solution whose objective function value is guaranteed to be within the prespecified amount of the optimal value.

13.5 A Branch-and-Bound Algorithm for Pure Binary Integer Programming

As illustrated in Sec. 13.1, many IP problems have the special feature that *all* variables are *binary* (0-1) variables. Furthermore, when a few of the original decision variables require more than two possible values, they are sometimes replaced by a *binary representation* to reduce the entire problem to a binary (BIP) form. Specifically, if the bounds on an integer variable x are

$$0 \le x \le u, \quad \text{where } 2^{N-1} < u \le 2^N,$$

then each feasible value of x can be expressed uniquely as

$$x = \sum_{i=0}^{N} 2^i y_i,$$

where the y_i variables are (auxiliary) binary variables. Therefore, the x variable can be replaced throughout the problem by this summation involving $(N + 1)$ *binary variables*.

For these reasons, considerable attention has been focused in recent years on developing efficient algorithms for the pure BIP problem. A convenient form in which to treat this problem is

$$\text{Minimize} \quad Z = \sum_{j=1}^{n} c_j x_j,$$

subject to

$$\sum_{j=1}^{n} a_{ij} x_j \ge b_i, \quad \text{for } i = 1, 2, \ldots, m,$$

and

$$x_j \text{ is binary}, \quad \text{for } j = 1, 2, \ldots, n,$$

where $0 \le c_1 \le c_2 \le \cdots \le c_n$. This condition on the c_j parameters actually is not restrictive because if $c_j < 0$, originally, then x_j can be replaced by $(1 - x_j')$ where x_j' also is binary, so that x_j' will have a *positive* coefficient in the objective function. All the variables can then be reordered as needed to place these coefficients in increasing order.

Roughly speaking, with the problem in this form the general objective of an algorithm should be to make as many of the variables *zero* as the constraints will allow but to give preference to using the variables with the smallest subscripts when it is necessary to set some variables equal to 1. Therefore, it would seem sensible to check first whether it is feasible (and thus optimal) to set *all* the variables to zero; if not, then check just setting $x_1 = 1$, then just $x_1 = 1$ and $x_2 = 1$, and so forth.

Using roughly this idea, we shall now describe the individual steps of a *branch-and-bound* algorithm for the BIP problem. (See Summary of Branch-and-Bound Technique in the preceding section for the overall flow of the algorithm.)

It is a slightly simplified version of Balas' **additive algorithm**,[1] which has formed the basis for much of the algorithmic development on this problem. (The name *additive* comes from the fact that all the arithmetic operations are simple additions or subtractions.)

SPECIFICATION OF BRANCH STEP This algorithm defines subsets of solutions by *assigning values* to some of the variables, say $(x_1, x_2, \ldots, x_N)$. [We shall always let N denote the number of assigned variables for the subset currently under consideration and refer to the value of $(x_1, x_2, \ldots, x_N)$ as the *current* **partial solution**. Any complete solution $(x_1, x_2, \ldots, x_N, x_{N+1}, \ldots x_n)$ starting out in this way is then called a **completion** of this partial solution, so that the subset of solutions defined by the current partial solution is just the set of all completions for this partial solution.] The *newest bound rule* is used to select the next partial solution (subset) to partition. If $(x_1, x_2, \ldots x_N)$ is the one selected, it is partitioned into *two* new subsets (partial solutions) by additionally setting $x_{N+1} = 1$ and then $x_{N+1} = 0$ (after which N is reset equal to this $N + 1$ for these two new partial solutions).

SPECIFICATION OF BOUND STEP For the *bound step*, the lower bound Z_L for a partial solution $(x_1, x_2, \ldots, x_N)$ is just

$$Z_L = \begin{cases} \displaystyle\sum_{j=1}^{N} c_j x_j, & \text{if } x_N = 1 \quad (\text{or if } N = 0 \text{ or } n) \\[2ex] \displaystyle\sum_{j=1}^{N-1} c_j x_j + c_{N+1}, & \text{if } x_N = 0. \end{cases}$$

[The reason for adding c_{N+1} if $x_N = 0$ is that the algorithm would be calculating this bound only if it had previously found that $(x_1, x_2, \ldots, x_{N-1}, x_N = 0, \ldots, x_n = 0)$ is *infeasible*. This situation occurs while conducting Fathoming Test 3 (described next) for the previous partial solution $(x_1, x_2, \ldots, x_M)$, where $M = \max\{j \mid x_j = 1\}$.] Because $c_N \leq c_{N+1}$, the bound always is *smaller* (or equal) for $x_N = 1$ than $x_N = 0$, so the newest bound rule *always* selects the $x_N = 1$ partial solution first for partitioning if neither has been fathomed.[2]

SPECIFICATION OF FATHOMING STEP The *fathoming step* allows us to *fathom* (discard from further consideration) the *current partial solution* if it passes any one of the usual three fathoming tests presented in the preceding section. In this context, these tests are conducted as follows.

[1] Egon Balas, "An Additive Algorithm for Solving Linear Programs with Zero-One Variables," *Operations Research*, **13**(4): 517–546, July–August, 1965.

[2] Consequently, the original version of Balas' additive algorithm does not even bother to apply the *fathoming step* to the $x_N = 0$ partial solution until after the $x_N = 1$ partial solution has been fathomed (perhaps by fathoming all its subsequent subsets at later iterations). However, for consistency with the preceding section, we shall continue to apply the fathoming step immediately to *both* new partial solutions (subsets) generated by the branch step at each iteration.

Fathoming Test 1. $\quad Z_L \geq Z_U$,

where Z_U again is the value of the objective function for the best complete feasible solution (the *incumbent* solution) identified by the algorithm so far ($Z_U = \infty$ if none found yet).

Fathoming Test 2 (the subset is found to contain no feasible solutions) is conducted by seeing whether any *individual* constraint cannot be satisfied by completions of the partial solution. Therefore, the partial solution is fathomed by this test if

Fathoming Test 2. $\quad \displaystyle\sum_{j=1}^{N} a_{ij} x_j + \sum_{j=N+1}^{n} \max\{a_{ij}, 0\} < b_i$,

$$\text{for some } i = 1, 2, \ldots, m,$$

because $\max\{a_{ij}, 0\} = \max\{a_{ij} x_j | x_j = 0 \text{ or } 1\}$.

Fathoming Test 3 (the best feasible solution in the subset has been identified) is conducted by seeing whether the solution corresponding to the lower bound Z_L (namely, the current partial solution plus $x_{N+1} = 1 - x_N$ and the rest of the variables equal to zero) actually is feasible. Therefore, the third way in which the partial solution can be fathomed is if

Fathoming Test 3. $\quad \displaystyle\sum_{j=1}^{N} a_{ij} x_j + a_{i,N+1}(1 - x_N) \geq b_i, \quad \text{for all } i = 1, 2, \ldots, m.$

If this occurs and $Z_L < Z_U$, then the instructions for the branch-and-bound technique would be followed in resetting $Z_U = Z_L$ and storing this solution as the current *incumbent* solution.

EXAMPLE We shall now illustrate this algorithm by applying it to the problem

$$\text{Minimize} \quad Z = 3x_1 + 5x_2 + 6x_3 + 9x_4 + 10x_5 + 10x_6,$$

subject to

$$-2x_1 + 6x_2 - 3x_3 + 4x_4 + x_5 - 2x_6 \geq +2$$
$$-5x_1 - 3x_2 + x_3 + 3x_4 - 2x_5 + x_6 \geq -2$$
$$5x_1 - x_2 + 4x_3 - 2x_4 + 2x_5 - x_6 \geq +3,$$

and

$$x_j \text{ is binary for } j = 1, 2, \ldots, 6.$$

The results are summarized in Fig. 13.7, where the ordering of the boldfaced arrows (First, Second, and so on) indicates the order in which subsets of solutions (partial solutions) are partitioned into new subsets. Thus the *entire* set of solutions cannot be fathomed at iteration 0 [$Z_L \leq Z_U$, each constraint can be satisfied, but $(0, 0, \ldots, 0)$ is infeasible], so iteration 1 begins by partitioning this set into the two new subsets corresponding to the two partial solutions, $x_1 = 0$ and $x_1 = 1$. Neither of these partial solutions can be fathomed because Tests 1 and 2 immediately fail, and, for Test 3, $(0, 1, 0, 0, 0, 0)$ and $(1, 0, 0, 0, 0, 0)$, respectively, are

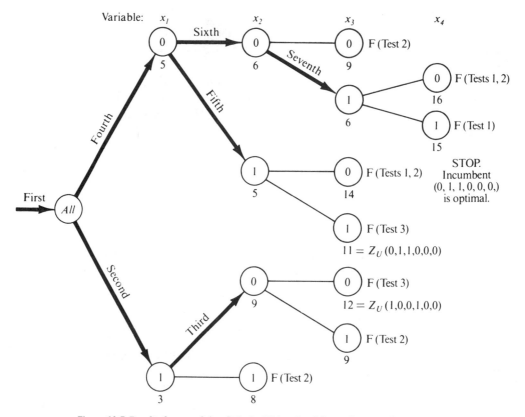

Figure 13.7 **Results from applying** *Balas' additive algorithm* **to the example.**

found to be infeasible. For iteration 2, the $x_1 = 1$ partial solution is selected to be partitioned further into the new partial solutions, $(x_1, x_2) = (1, 0)$ and $(x_1, x_2) = (1, 1)$.

However, the partial solution $(x_1, x_2) = (1, 1)$ is fathomed by Test 2 because it has *no* completions, even $(1, 1, 1, 1, 0, 1)$, that satisfy the second constraint. Because the other new partial solution $(1, 0)$ cannot be fathomed, it is selected next (iteration 3) by the newest bound rule to be partitioned into two new partial solutions, both of which can be fathomed. One of these, $(x_1, x_2, x_3) = (1, 0, 1)$, is fathomed by Test 2 again because none of its completions, even $(1, 0, 1, 1, 1, 0)$, satisfies constraint 1. For the other new partial solution, $(x_1, x_2, x_3) = (1, 0, 0)$, its *best* possible completion (except the one ruled out earlier when Fathoming Test 3 failed for the $x_1 = 1$ partial solution)—$(1, 0, 0, 1, 0, 0)$—is *feasible*, so this provides the first *incumbent* solution with objective function value $Z_U = 12$.

This process exhausts the $x_1 = 1$ branch of the tree, so the remaining iterations (4 through 7) search down the $x_1 = 0$ branch. At iteration 4, the $x_1 = 0$ partial solution is partitioned into the new partial solutions, $(x_1, x_2) = (0, 0)$ and

$(x_1, x_2) = (0, 1)$, but neither of these partial solutions are fathomed. Iteration 5 leads to a new partial solution, $(x_1, x_2, x_3) = (0, 1, 1)$, whose best possible completion—$(0, 1, 1, 0, 0, 0)$—also is feasible, with a lower objective function value (11) than for the incumbent, so this completion becomes the *new incumbent* solution (with $Z_U = 11$). The final two iterations [partitioning the partial solutions, $(x_1, x_2) = (0, 0)$ and then $(x_1, x_2, x_3) = (0, 0, 1)$] find that the only *remaining* (unfathomed) partial solution. $(x_1, x_2) = (0, 0)$, cannot lead to better feasible solutions, so the optimal solution is $x_1 = 0$, $x_2 = 1$, $x_3 = 1$, $x_4 = 0$, $x_5 = 0$, $x_6 = 0$.

We now are in a position to comment on the reason why the *bound rule* chosen for this algorithm was the *newest bound rule* rather than the *best bound rule*. For this particular example, the required number of iterations is the same (with a different order) for the two rules (although the latter rule tends to do a little better on the average for other problems). However, the *newest bound rule substantially* reduces the computational effort for many of the iterations. In particular, if the *current partial solution* is not fathomed and then is partitioned immediately (as happens much more frequently with the newest bound rule), then the quantities needed for Fathoming Tests 1, 2, and 3 for each of the new partial solutions can be obtained from their *current values* by a single addition or subtraction. (Theoretically, these quantities also could be obtained in a similar way with the best bound rule by storing the corresponding quantities for all of the unfathomed partial solutions until they are partitioned, but the storage requirements would become prohibitive for large problems.)

It has been found that Fathoming Test 2 is not always very effective in finding that a partial solution has no feasible completions, particularly when the problem has a considerable number of constraints. Frequently, different completions of a partial solution will satisfy individual constraints even though *no* completion satisfies all of them. Therefore, much of the more recent algorithmic development has been concerned with improving this part of the fathoming step. The most notable improvement has involved using *linear programming* to obtain a single *surrogate constraint* that effectively combines the m original functional constraints.[1]

13.6 A Branch-and-Bound Algorithm for Mixed Integer Programming

We shall now consider the general MIP problem, where *some* of the variables (say I of them) are restricted to integer values (but not necessarily just 0 and 1), but the rest are ordinary continuous variables. In *minimization form*, this problem is

$$\text{Minimize} \quad Z = \sum_{j=1}^{n} c_j x_j,$$

[1] A. M. Geoffrion, "An Improved Implicit Enumeration Approach for Integer Programming," *Operations Research*, **17**(3): 437–454, May–June, 1969.

subject to

$$\sum_{j=1}^{n} a_{ij}x_j \geq b_i, \quad \text{for } i = 1, 2, \ldots, m,$$

and

$$x_j \geq 0, \quad \text{for } j = 1, 2, \ldots, n,$$
$$x_j \text{ is integer}, \quad \text{for } j = 1, 2, \ldots, I(I \leq n).$$

(When $I = n$, this problem becomes the *pure* IP problem.)

Section 13.5 described how the *additive algorithm* is able to solve a *special case* of this problem ($I = N$ and all $x_j \leq 1$) by making just a few simple calculations for each partial solution. Without this special structure, it is no longer possible to obtain a reasonable lower bound Z_L and conduct strong fathoming tests with so little computational effort. However, this same information *can* still be obtained in a reasonably efficient way by using linear programming (the simplex or dual simplex method). We now describe one version of an algorithm that uses linear programming that was developed by R. J. Dakin,[1] based on a pioneering branch-and-bound algorithm by A. H. Land and A. G. Doig.[2]

This algorithm is quite similar in structure to the additive algorithm. It again fits directly into the format for the branch-and-bound technique presented in Sec. 13.4. It also uses the *newest bound rule* to select the next subset of solutions for partitioning. It then partitions this subset into *two* new subsets. However, because the variables now may have more than two possible values, this partitioning is done by dividing the possible values of some variable into two *intervals*. (Consequently, the *same variable* can eventually be partitioned more than once.)

The algorithm begins (iteration 0) by ignoring the integer restriction and using the simplex method to solve the *LP-relaxation*. If the resulting solution has integer values for all the x_j for $j = 1, 2, \ldots, I$, then it is the desired optimal solution. Otherwise, the *branch step* (at each iteration) finds the first such variable that is not integer valued, say x_j, so that

$$k < x_j < k + 1,$$

where k is an integer. It then partitions the current subset of solutions into the two new subsets:

1. Solutions in which $x_j \leq k$,
2. Solutions in which $x_j \geq k + 1$,

where these solutions also must satisfy all of the constraints defining the current

[1] R. J. Dakin, "A Tree Search Algorithm for Mixed Integer Programming Problems," *Computer Journal*, **8**(3): 250–255, 1965.

[2] A. H. Land and A. G. Doig, "An Automatic Method of Solving Discrete Programming Problems," *Econometrica*, **28**: 497–520, 1960.

subset (namely, any similar bounds on individual variables from previous partitions plus the original constraints of the problem). The *bound step* then obtains the lower bound Z_L for each of these subsets by again ignoring the integer restriction and solving the resulting *LP-relaxation* (including the new constraint bounding x_j) to obtain the optimal value of the objective function. However, rather than resolving each of these problems from the beginning, it uses just the sensitivity analysis procedure (see case 4 in Sec. 6.7) by applying the *dual simplex method* (see Sec. 9.2) starting from the basic solution that was optimal before introducing the new constraint. (Note that the *newest bound rule* increases the opportunity for reoptimizing efficiently in this way.) The *fathoming step* then merely checks the optimal solution for the current LP-relaxation as obtained by the dual simplex method. In particular, the new subset is *fathomed* if

Fathoming Test 1. $Z_L \geq Z_U$,

or

Fathoming Test 2.   The dual simplex method finds that no feasible solutions exist,

or

Fathoming Test 3.   The optimal solution obtained has integer values for all the x_j such that $j = 1, 2, \ldots, I$.

If Fathoming Test 3 succeeds *and* $Z_L < Z_U$, then reset $Z_U = Z_L$ and store this solution as the new *incumbent* solution. [However, Fathoming Test 1 does not need to be reapplied to the *remaining* subsets until they would otherwise be selected by the newest bound rule.] When all the unpartitioned subsets have been fathomed, the current incumbent solution then is the desired optimal solution.

EXAMPLE Suppose that this algorithm is applied to the *pure* IP problem considered in Sec. 13.3 (see Fig. 13.1), so that $I = n = 2$. Because this problem is in *maximization* form, whereas the preceding discussion assumes *minimization*, let us first convert it (see Sec. 4.6) into the *equivalent* minimization problem:

$$\text{Minimize} \quad Z = -x_1 - 5x_2,$$

subject to the original constraints.

For iteration 0, the optimal solution for the LP-relaxation of this problem is found to be $(x_1, x_2) = (2, \frac{9}{5})$, so that

$$1 < x_2 < 2$$

for this solution. Therefore, iteration 1 begins by partitioning the *entire* set of solutions into the two subsets:

1. Solutions in which $x_2 \leq 1$,
2. Solutions in which $x_2 \geq 2$.

For the first subset, its LP-relaxation has the optimal solution, $(x_1, x_2) = (2,1)$, which is integer valued, so this subset is fathomed by Test 3 and this solution becomes the first *incumbent* solution with $Z_U = Z_L = -7$. For the second subset, its LP-relaxation has only one feasible solution, $(x_1, x_2) = (0,2)$, but it is integer valued, so this subset is also fathomed by Test 3. Furthermore, this solution is better $(Z = Z_L = -10 < Z_U)$ than the incumbent solution, so it becomes the *new incumbent* solution (reset $Z_U = -10$). However, there now are no unpartitioned subsets left that have not been fathomed, so $(x_1, x_2) = (0, 2)$ must be optimal for the original IP problem.

13.7 Conclusions

IP problems arise frequently because some or all of the decision variables must be restricted to integer values. There also are many applications involving yes-or-no decisions (including combinatorial relationships expressible in terms of such decisions) that can be represented by binary (0-1) variables. These problems are more difficult than they would be without the integer restriction, so the algorithms available for integer programming are generally much less efficient than the simplex method. The most important determinants of computation time are the *number of integer variables* and the *structure* of the problem. Some very large problems have been solved successfully when they contain some special structure that can be exploited. However, unless the problem has a relatively simple special structure, it may be solvable only if it has no more than a few dozen integer variables (somewhat more with just binary variables).

Computer codes for IP algorithms now are commonly available in mathematical programming software packages. These algorithms usually are based on the *branch-and-bound* technique and variations thereof. Some of the early algorithms used another approach involving the successive introduction of additional constraints (cutting planes) that would eliminate more and more noninteger solutions (including the optimal solution for the current LP-relaxation) but not any integer solutions, until finally the optimal solution for the new LP-relaxation is integer valued. However, these *cutting plane* algorithms met with only limited success, and that success depended strongly upon the special structure of the problem. (On the other hand, there is growing evidence that *combining* cutting planes with the branch-and-bound approach occasionally can be very helpful.) A related approach involving the application of *mathematical group theory* also has been explored, again with limited success.

Practical problems often are too large to be handled by any of these algorithms. In these cases, it is common to simply apply the simplex method to the LP-relaxation and then round the optimal solution to a feasible integer solution. However, this approach is sometimes quite unsatisfactory because it may be difficult (or impossible) to find a feasible integer solution in this way, and the solution found may be far from optimal. Considerable progress has been made in developing *efficient heuristic algorithms* for finding feasible integer solutions for these problems that are not necessarily optimal but usually are better than those that can be found by simple rounding.

In recent years, there has been considerable investigation into the development of algorithms for integer *nonlinear* programming, and this area continues to be a very active area of research.

SELECTED REFERENCES

1. Crowder, H., E. L. Johnson, and M. Padberg: "Solving Large-Scale Zero-One Linear Programming Problems," *Operations Research*, **31**(5): 803–834, 1983.
2. Garfinkel, Robert S., and George L. Nemhauser: *Integer Programming*, Wiley, New York, 1972.
3. Geoffrion, A. M., and R. E. Marsten: "Integer Programming Algorithms: A Framework and State-of-the-Art Survey," *Management Science*, **18**(9): 465–491, May 1972.
4. Johnson, E. L., M. M. Kostreva, and U. H. Suhl: "Solving 0-1 Integer Programming Problems Arising from Large Scale Planning Models," *Operations Research*, **33**(4): 803–819, 1985.
5. Lawler, E. L., and D. E. Wood: "Branch-and-Bound Methods: A Survey," *Operations Research*, **14**(4): 699–719, 1966.
6. Mitten, L. G.: "Branch-and-Bound Methods: General Formulation and Properties," *Operations Research*, **18**(1): 24–34, January-February 1970.
7. Salkin, Harvey M.: *Integer Programming*, Addison-Wesley, Reading, Mass., 1975.
8. Taha, Hamdy A.: *Integer Programming: Theory, Applications, and Computations*, Academic Press, New York, 1975.
9. Zionts, Stanley: *Linear and Integer Programming*, Prentice-Hall, Englewood Cliffs, N.J., 1974.

PROBLEMS

1. A young couple, Eve and Steven, want to divide their main household chores (marketing, cooking, dishwashing, and laundering) between them so that each has two tasks but the total time they spend on household duties is kept to a minimum. Their efficiencies on these tasks differ, where the time each would need to perform the task is given by the following table.

	Marketing	*Cooking*	*Dishwashing*	*Laundering*
		Hours per week needed		
Eve	4.5	7.8	3.6	2.9
Steven	4.9	7.2	4.3	3.1

(*a*) Formulate a BIP model for this problem.

(*b*) Use the *branch-and-bound technique* (with the *best bound rule*) to solve this problem.

2. The Board of Directors of the *General Wheels Co.* is considering seven large capital investments. These investments differ in the estimated long-run profit (net present value) they will generate, as well as in the amount of capital required, as shown by the following table (in units of millions of dollars).

	Investment opportunity						
	1	2	3	4	5	6	7
Estimated profit	17	10	15	19	7	13	9
Capital required	43	28	34	48	17	32	23

The total amount of capital available for these investments is $100,000,000. Investment opportunities 1 and 2 are mutually exclusive, and so are 3 and 4. Furthermore, neither 3 nor 4 can be undertaken unless either 1 or 2 is undertaken. There are no such restrictions on investment opportunities 5, 6, and 7. The objective is to select the combination of capital investments that will maximize the total estimated long-run profit (net present value).

(a) Formulate a BIP model for this problem.

(b) Reformulate this BIP model in the proper form for applying *Balas' additive algorithm* presented in Sec. 13.5. (Do not actually solve.)

3. Reconsider Prob. 27, Chap. 7. Formulate a BIP model for this problem.

4. Consider the following special type of *shortest-route problem* (see Sec. 10.3) where the nodes are in columns and the only routes considered always move forward one column at a time.

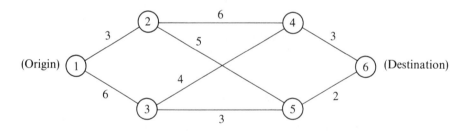

The numbers along the branches represent distances, and the objective is to find the shortest route from the origin to the destination.

This problem also can be formulated as a BIP model involving both mutually exclusive alternatives and contingent decisions. Formulate this model.

5. A new planned community is being developed, and one of the decisions to be made is where to locate the two fire stations that have been allocated to the community. For planning purposes, the community has been divided into five tracts, with no more than one fire station to be located in any given tract. Each station is to respond to *all* of the fires that occur in the tract in which it is located as well as in the other tracts that are assigned to this station. Thus the decisions to be made consist of (1) the tracts to receive a fire station and (2) the assignment of each of the other tracts to one of the fire stations. The objective is to minimize the overall average of the *response times* to fires.

The following table gives the average response time (in minutes) to a fire in each tract (the columns) if that tract is served by a station in a given tract (the rows). The bottom row gives the forecasted average number of fires that will occur in each of the tracts each day.

		Response times				
		Fire in tract				
		1	*2*	*3*	*4*	*5*
Assigned station located in tract	1	5	12	30	20	15
	2	20	4	15	10	25
	3	15	20	6	15	12
	4	25	15	25	4	10
	5	10	25	15	12	5
Frequency of emergencies		2	1	3	1	3

Formulate a complete BIP model for this problem. Identify any constraints that correspond to *mutually exclusive alternatives* or *contingent decisions*.

6. Reconsider the Middletown racial balance study presented in Sec. 8.5. Suppose that the school board changes the current policy by prohibiting the splitting of a tract among different schools, so that an entire tract must be assigned to the same school. However, they will continue to require that the fraction of students in a school who are white (or who are black) must be between $\frac{1}{3}$ and $\frac{2}{3}$. Formulate a BIP model for this problem under this new policy.

7. Suppose that a state sends R persons to the U.S. House of Representatives. There are D counties in the state ($D > R$), and the state legislature wants to group these counties into R distinct electoral districts, each of which sends a delegate to Congress. The total population of the state is P, and the legislature wants to form districts whose population approximates $p = P/R$. Suppose that the appropriate legislative committee studying the electoral districting problem generates a long list of N *candidates* to be districts ($N > R$). Each of these candidates contains contiguous counties and a total population p_j ($j = 1, 2, \ldots, N$) that is acceptably close to p. Define $c_j = |p_j - p|$. Each county i ($i = 1, 2, \ldots, D$) is included in at least one candidate and typically will be included in a considerable number of candidates (in order to provide many feasible ways of selecting a set of R candidates that includes each county exactly once). Define

$$a_{ij} = \begin{cases} 1, & \text{if county } i \text{ is included in candidate } j \\ 0, & \text{if not.} \end{cases}$$

Given the values of the c_j and the a_{ij}, the objective is to select R of these N possible districts such that each county is contained in a single district and such that the largest of the associated c_j is as small as possible.

Formulate a BIP model for this problem.

8. An airline company is considering the purchase of new long-, medium-, and short-range jet passenger airplanes. The purchase price would be $33,500,000 for each long-range plane, $25,000,000 for each medium-range plane, and $17,500,000 for each short-range plane. The Board of Directors has authorized a maximum commitment of $750,000,000 for these purchases. Regardless of which airplanes are purchased, air travel of all distances is expected to be sufficiently large enough so that these planes would be utilized at essentially maximum capacity. It is estimated that the net annual profit (after subtracting capital recovery costs) would be $2,100,000 per long-range plane, $1,500,000 per medium-range plane, and $1,150,000 per short-range plane.

It is predicted that enough trained pilots will be available to the company to man 30 new airplanes. If only short-range planes were purchased, the maintenance facilities would be able to handle 40 new planes. However, each medium-range plane is equivalent to $1\frac{1}{3}$ short-range planes, and each long-range plane is equivalent to $1\frac{2}{3}$ short-range planes in terms of their use of the maintenance facilities.

The information given here was obtained by a preliminary analysis of the problem. A more detailed analysis will be conducted subsequently. However, using the preceding data as a first approximation, management wishes to know how many planes of each type should be purchased to maximize profit.

(a) Formulate the IP model for this problem.
(b) Use *Dakin's algorithm* presented in Sec. 13.6 to solve this model.
(c) Use a binary representation of the variables to reformulate the IP model in part (a) as a BIP problem.

9. The Research and Development Division of a company has been developing four possible new product lines. Management must now make a decision as to which of these four products actually will be produced and at what levels. Therefore, they have asked the Operations Research Department to formulate a mathematical programming model to find the most profitable product mix.

A substantial cost is associated with beginning the production of any product, as given in the first row of the following table. The marginal net revenue from each unit produced is given in the second row of the table.

	Product			
	1	*2*	*3*	*4*
Start-up cost	$50,000	$40,000	$70,000	$60,000
Marginal revenue	$70	$60	$90	$80

Let the continuous decision variables x_1, x_2, x_3, and x_4 be the production levels of products 1, 2, 3, and 4, respectively. Management has imposed the following policy constraints on these variables:

1. No more than two of the products can be produced.
2. Either product 3 or 4 can be produced only if either product 1 or 2 is produced.
3. Either $5x_1 + 3x_2 + 6x_3 + 4x_4 \leq 6000$
   or $4x_1 + 6x_2 + 3x_3 + 5x_4 \leq 6000$.

Introduce auxiliary binary variables to formulate an MIP model for this problem.

10. Consider the following mathematical model.

$$\text{Minimize} \quad Z = f_1(x_1) + f_2(x_2),$$

subject to the restrictions

1. Either $x_1 \geq 3$ or $x_2 \geq 3$.
2. At least one of the following inequalities holds:

$$2x_1 + x_2 \geq 7$$
$$x_1 + x_2 \geq 5$$
$$x_1 + 2x_2 \geq 7.$$

3. $|x_1 - x_2| = 0$, or 3, or 6.
4. $x_1 \geq 0, x_2 \geq 0$,

where

$$f_1(x_1) = \begin{cases} 7 + 5x_1, & \text{if } x_1 > 0 \\ 0, & \text{if } x_1 = 0, \end{cases}$$

$$f_2(x_2) = \begin{cases} 5 + 6x_2, & \text{if } x_2 > 0 \\ 0, & \text{if } x_2 = 0. \end{cases}$$

Formulate this problem as an MIP problem.

11. Consider the following mathematical model.

$$\text{Maximize} \quad Z = 3x_1 + 2f(x_2) + 2x_3 + 3g(x_4),$$

subject to the restrictions

1. $2x_1 - x_2 + x_3 + 3x_4 \leq 15$.
2. At least one of the following two inequalities holds:

$$x_1 + x_2 + x_3 + x_4 \leq 4$$
$$3x_1 - x_2 - x_3 + x_4 \leq 3.$$

3. At least two of the following four inequalities hold:

$$5x_1 + 3x_2 + 3x_3 - x_4 \leq 10$$
$$2x_1 + 5x_2 - x_3 + 3x_4 \leq 10$$
$$-x_1 + 3x_2 + 5x_3 + 3x_4 \leq 10$$
$$3x_1 - x_2 + 3x_3 + 5x_4 \leq 10.$$

4. $x_3 = 1$, or 2, or 3.
5. $x_j \geq 0 \ (j = 1, 2, 3, 4)$,

where

$$f(x_2) = \begin{cases} -5 + 3x_2, & \text{if } x_2 > 0 \\ 0, & \text{if } x_2 = 0, \end{cases}$$

and

$$g(x_4) = \begin{cases} -3 + 5x_4, & \text{if } x_4 > 0 \\ 0, & \text{if } x_4 = 0. \end{cases}$$

Formulate this problem as an MIP problem.

12. Consider the following IP problem.

$$\text{Maximize} \quad Z = 5x_1 + x_2,$$

subject to

$$-x_1 + 2x_2 \leq 4$$
$$x_1 - x_2 \leq 1$$
$$4x_1 + x_2 \leq 12,$$

and

$$x_1 \geq 0, \qquad x_2 \geq 0$$
$$x_1, x_2 \text{ are integers.}$$

(a) Solve this problem graphically.

(b) Solve the LP-relaxation graphically. Round this solution to the *nearest* integer solution and check whether it is feasible. Then enumerate *all* of the rounded solutions (rounding each noninteger value *either* up or down), check them for feasibility, and calculate Z for those that are feasible. Are any of these feasible rounded solutions optimal for the IP problem?

(c) Solve this problem *graphically* by *Dakin's algorithm* presented in Sec. 13.6. Describe what is being done at each iteration.

13. Consider the following IP problem.

$$\text{Maximize} \quad Z = 220x_1 + 80x_2,$$

subject to

$$-x_1 + 2x_2 \leq 4$$
$$5x_1 + 2x_2 \leq 16$$
$$2x_1 - x_2 \leq 4,$$

and

$$x_1 \geq 0, \qquad x_2 \geq 0$$
$$x_1, x_2 \text{ are integers.}$$

(a) Solve this problem graphically.

(b) Solve the LP-relaxation graphically. Round this solution to the *nearest* integer solution and check whether it is feasible. Then enumerate *all* of the rounded solutions (rounding each noninteger value *either* up or down), check them for feasibility, and calculate Z for those that are feasible. Are any of these feasible rounded solutions optimal for the IP problem?

(c) Solve this problem *graphically* by *Dakin's algorithm* presented in Sec. 13.6. Describe what is being done at each iteration.

14. Consider the assignment problem with the following cost table:

		Assignment				
		1	*2*	*3*	*4*	*5*
	1	39	65	69	66	57
	2	64	84	24	92	22
Assignee	*3*	49	50	61	31	45
	4	48	45	55	23	50
	5	59	34	30	34	18

Use the *branch-and-bound technique* to find the set of assignments that minimizes total cost.

(a) Use the *best bound rule.*

(b) Use the *newest bound rule.*

15. Consider the assignment problem having the following cost table:

Assignment

		1	2	3	4
	A	4	1	0	1
Assignee	B	1	3	4	0
	C	3	2	1	3
	D	2	2	3	0

(a) Use the *branch-and-bound technique* (with the *best bound rule*) to find *all* optimal solutions for this problem.

(b) Now adapt the *branch-and-bound technique* (with the *best bound rule*) to find all *good* solutions whose objective function value is no more than 1 above that for an optimal solution.

(c) Now suppose that the numbers in the cost table actually represent profits, so that the objective is to determine how all the assignments should be made in order to *maximize* total profits. Use the *branch-and-bound technique* (with the best *bound rule*) to find *all* optimal solutions for this new version of the problem.

16. Reconsider the assignment problem given in Prob. 31, Chap. 7.

(a) Use the *branch-and-bound technique* (with the *newest bound rule*) to find *all* optimal solutions for this problem.

(b) Now suppose that the numbers in the cost table actually represent profits, so that the objective is to determine how all the assignments should be made in order to *maximize* total profits. Use the *branch-and-bound technique* (with the *newest bound rule*) to find *all* optimal solutions for this new version of the problem.

17. Use the *branch-and-bound technique* (with the *best bound rule*) to solve the following assignment problems:

(a) Prob. 26, Chap. 7.
(b) Prob. 27, Chap. 7.

18. Five jobs need to be done on a certain machine. However, the setup time for each job depends upon which job immediately preceded it, as shown by the following table:

Setup time

Job

		1	2	3	4	5
	None	4	5	8	9	4
	1	—	7	12	10	9
Immediately	2	6	—	10	14	11
preceding job	3	10	11	—	12	10
	4	7	8	15	—	7
	5	12	9	8	16	—

The objective is to schedule the *sequence* of jobs that minimizes the sum of the resulting setup times.

(a) Design a *branch-and-bound algorithm* for sequencing problems of this type by specifying how the branch, bound, and fathoming steps would be performed.

(b)   Use this algorithm to solve this problem.

19.   Consider the following IP problem.

$$\text{Maximize} \quad Z = 80x_1 + 60x_2 + 40x_3 + 20x_4 - (7x_1 + 5x_2 + 3x_3 + 2x_4)^2,$$

subject to

$$x_j \text{ is binary,} \quad \text{for } j = 1, 2, 3, 4.$$

Given the values of the first k variables $(x_1, \ldots, x_k)$, where $k = 0, 1, 2,$ or 3, an upper bound on the value of Z that can be achieved by the corresponding feasible solutions is

$$\sum_{j=1}^{k} c_j x_j - \left(\sum_{j=1}^{k} d_j x_j\right)^2 + \sum_{j=k+1}^{4} \max\left\{0, c_j - \left[\left(\sum_{i=1}^{k} d_i x_i + d_j\right)^2 - \left(\sum_{i=1}^{k} d_i x_i\right)^2\right]\right\},$$

where $c_1 = 80, c_2 = 60, c_3 = 40, c_4 = 20, d_1 = 7, d_2 = 5, d_3 = 3, d_4 = 2$. Use this bound and the *best bound rule* to solve the problem by the *branch-and-bound technique*.

20.   Use *Balas' additive algorithm* presented in Sec. 13.5 to solve the *California Manufacturing Company* problem discussed in Sec. 13.1.

21.   Use *Balas' additive algorithm* presented in Sec. 13.5 to solve the following problem.

$$\text{Minimize} \quad Z = 5x_1 + 6x_2 + 7x_3 + 8x_4 + 9x_5,$$

subject to

$$3x_1 - x_2 + x_3 + x_4 - 2x_5 \geq 2$$
$$x_1 + 3x_2 - x_3 - 2x_4 + x_5 \geq 0$$
$$-x_1 - x_2 + 3x_3 + x_4 + x_5 \geq 1,$$

and

$$x_j \text{ is binary,} \quad \text{for } j = 1, 2, \ldots, 5.$$

22.   Use *Balas' additive algorithm* presented in Sec. 13.5 to solve the following problem.

$$\text{Maximize} \quad Z = 2x_1 - x_2 + 5x_3 - 3x_4 + 4x_5,$$

subject to

$$3x_1 - 2x_2 + 7x_3 - 5x_4 + 4x_5 \leq 6$$
$$x_1 - x_2 + 2x_3 - 4x_4 + 2x_5 \leq 0,$$

and

$$x_j \text{ is binary,} \quad \text{for } j = 1, 2, \ldots, 5.$$

23.   Consider the illustrative IP problem discussed in Sec. 13.3 (see Fig. 13.1).

(a)   Use a *binary representation* of the variables to reformulate the problem as a BIP problem.

(b)   Use *Balas' additive algorithm* presented in Sec. 13.5 to solve this BIP problem.

24.   Consider the following IP problem.

$$\text{Maximize} \quad Z = -3x_1 + 5x_2,$$

subject to

$$5x_1 - 7x_2 \geq 3$$

and

$$x_j \leq 3$$
$$x_j \geq 0$$
$$x_j \text{ is integer,} \quad \text{for } j = 1, 2.$$

(a) Use the binary representation for integer variables and so forth to reformulate this problem as a **BIP** problem in the proper form for applying *Balas' additive algorithm* presented in Sec. 13.5.

(b) Use *Balas' additive algorithm* to solve the problem as reformulated in part (a).

25. Use *Balas' additive algorithm* presented in Sec. 13.5 to solve the following problem.

$$\text{Maximize} \quad Z = 2x_1 + 2x_2 + 3x_3 - x_4 - 2x_5,$$

subject to

$$-2x_1 + 3x_2 - 4x_3 + 5x_4 + 5x_5 \geq 5$$
$$x_1 + 2x_2 \quad\quad - x_4 - 3x_5 \leq 0,$$

and

$$x_j \text{ is binary,} \quad \text{for } j = 1, 2, \ldots, 5.$$

26. Use *Dakin's algorithm* presented in Sec. 13.6 to solve the following problem.

$$\text{Minimize} \quad Z = 2x_1 + 3x_2,$$

subject to

$$x_1 + x_2 \geq 3$$
$$x_1 + 3x_2 \geq 6,$$

and

$$x_1 \geq 0, \quad\quad x_2 \geq 0$$
$$x_1, x_2 \text{ are integers.}$$

27. Consider the following IP problem.

$$\text{Maximize} \quad Z = 4x_1 - 2x_2 + 7x_3,$$

subject to

$$x_1 \quad\quad + 5x_3 \leq 10$$
$$x_1 + x_2 - x_3 \leq 1$$
$$6x_1 - 5x_2 \quad\quad \leq 0,$$

and

$$x_1 \geq 0, \quad\quad x_2 \geq 0, \quad\quad x_3 \geq 0$$
$$x_1, x_2, x_3 \text{ are integers.}$$

Suppose that the simplex method has been applied to its LP-relaxation. The resulting final set of equations is the following:

(0) $\qquad Z \quad + \dfrac{17}{12}x_4 + \dfrac{1}{12}x_5 + \dfrac{5}{12}x_6 = 14\tfrac{1}{4}$

(1) $\qquad x_3 + \dfrac{11}{60}x_4 - \dfrac{1}{12}x_5 - \dfrac{1}{60}x_6 = 1\tfrac{3}{4}$

(2) $\qquad x_2 + \dfrac{1}{10}x_4 + \dfrac{1}{2}x_5 - \dfrac{1}{10}x_6 = 1\tfrac{1}{2}$

(3) $\qquad x_1 + \dfrac{1}{12}x_4 + \dfrac{5}{12}x_5 + \dfrac{1}{12}x_6 = 1\tfrac{1}{4}.$

Thus the optimal solution for the LP-relaxation is $(x_1, x_2, x_3) = (1\tfrac{1}{4}, 1\tfrac{1}{2}, 1\tfrac{3}{4})$.

    (a) Demonstrate by trial and error that a feasible (integer) solution cannot be obtained by rounding this solution in any way.

    (b) Solve this problem by *Dakin's algorithm* presented in Sec. 13.6.

28. Use *Dakin's algorithm* presented in Sec. 13.6 to solve the following MIP problem.

$$\text{Minimize} \quad Z = 5x_1 + x_2 + x_3 + 2x_4 + 3x_5,$$

subject to

$$
\begin{aligned}
x_2 - 5x_3 + x_4 + 2x_5 &\geq -2 \\
5x_1 - x_2 \qquad\qquad + x_5 &\geq 7 \\
x_1 + x_2 + 6x_3 + x_4 \qquad &\geq 4,
\end{aligned}
$$

and

$$
\begin{aligned}
x_j &\geq 0, && \text{for } j = 1, 2, 3, 4, 5 \\
x_j &\text{ is integer,} && \text{for } j = 1, 2, 3.
\end{aligned}
$$

■ CHAPTER 14

Nonlinear Programming

The fundamental role of *linear programming* in operations research is accurately reflected by the fact that it is the focus of *seven* chapters of this book, and it is used in several other chapters. A key assumption of linear programming is that *all its functions* (objective function and constraint functions) *are linear*. Although this assumption essentially holds for numerous practical problems, it frequently does not hold. In fact, many economists have found that some degree of nonlinearity is the rule and not the exception in economic planning problems.[1] Therefore, it often is necessary to deal directly with *nonlinear programming problems*, so we turn our attention to this important area.

In one general form,[2] the *nonlinear programming problem* is to find $\mathbf{x} = (x_1, x_2, \ldots, x_n)$ so as to

$$\text{Maximize} \quad f(\mathbf{x}),$$

subject to

$$g_i(\mathbf{x}) \leq b_i, \quad \text{for } i = 1, 2, \ldots, m$$

and

$$\mathbf{x} \geq \mathbf{0},$$

[1] For example, see W. J. Baumol and R. C. Bushnell: "Error Produced by Linearization in Mathematical Programming," *Econometrica*, **35**:447–471, 1967.

[2] The other *legitimate forms* correspond to those for *linear programming* listed in Sec. 3.2. Section 4.6 describes how to convert these other forms into the form given here.

where $f(\mathbf{x})$ and the $g_i(\mathbf{x})$ are given functions of the n decision variables.[1]

No algorithm that will solve *every* specific problem fitting this format is available. However, substantial progress has been made for some important special cases of this problem by making various assumptions about these functions, and research is continuing very actively. This area is a large one, and we do not have space to survey it completely. However, we do present a few sample applications and then introduce some of the basic ideas for solving certain important types of nonlinear programming problems.

Both Appendixes 1 and 2 provide useful background for this chapter, and we recommend that you review these appendixes as you study the next few sections.

14.1 Sample Applications

The following examples illustrate a few of the many important types of problems to which nonlinear programming has been applied.

THE PRODUCT MIX PROBLEM WITH PRICE ELASTICITY

In *product mix* problems, such as the Wyndor Glass Co. problem of Sec. 3.1, the goal is to determine the optimal mix of production levels for a firm's products, given limitations on the resources needed to produce those products, in order to maximize the firm's total profit. In some cases, there is a fixed unit profit associated with each of the products, so the resulting objective function will be linear. However, in many product mix problems, certain factors introduce *nonlinearities* into the objective function. For example, a large manufacturer may encounter *price elasticity*, whereby the amount of a product that can be sold has an inverse relationship to the price charged. Thus the *price-demand curve* might look like the one shown in Fig. 14.1, where $p(x)$ is the price required in order to be able to sell x units. If the unit cost for producing the product is fixed at c (see the dashed line in Fig. 14.1), the firm's profit for producing and selling x units is given by the nonlinear function,

$$P(x) = x\, p(x) - cx,$$

as plotted in Fig. 14.2. If *each* of the firm's n products has a similar profit function, say $P_j(\mathbf{x}_j)$ for producing and selling x_j units of product j ($j = 1, 2, \ldots, n$), then the overall objective function is

$$f(\mathbf{x}) = \sum_{j=1}^{n} P_j(x_j),$$

a sum of nonlinear functions.

---

[1] For simplicity, we assume throughout the chapter that *all* of these functions are *differentiable* everywhere.

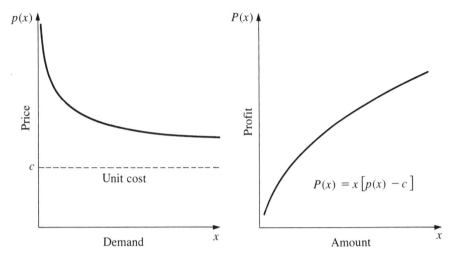

Figure 14.1 Price-demand curve. **Figure 14.2** Profit function.

Another reason that nonlinearities can arise in the objective function is due to the fact that the *marginal cost* of producing another unit of a given product varies with the production level. For example, the marginal cost may decrease when the production level is increased because of a *learning curve effect* (more efficient production with more experience). On the other hand, it may increase instead because special measures such as overtime or more expensive production facilities may be needed to increase production further.

Nonlinearities also may arise in the $g_i(\mathbf{x})$ constraint functions in a similar fashion. For example, if there is a budget constraint on total production cost, the cost function will be nonlinear if the marginal cost of production varies as just described. For constraints on the other kinds of resources, $g_i(\mathbf{x})$ will be nonlinear whenever the use of the corresponding resource is not strictly proportional to the production levels of the respective products.

THE TRANSPORTATION PROBLEM WITH VOLUME DISCOUNTS ON SHIPPING COSTS

As illustrated by the P & T Company example in Sec. 7.1, a typical application of the *transportation problem* is to determine an optimal plan for shipping goods from various sources to various destinations, given supply and demand constraints, in order to minimize total shipping cost. It was assumed in Chapter 7 that the *cost per unit shipped* from a given source to a given destination is *fixed*, regardless of the amount shipped. In actuality, this cost may not be fixed. *Volume discounts* sometimes are available for large shipments, so that the *marginal cost* of shipping one more unit might follow a pattern like the one shown in Fig. 14.3. The resulting cost of shipping x units then is given by a *nonlinear* function $C(x)$, which is a *piecewise linear function* with slope equal to the marginal cost, like the one

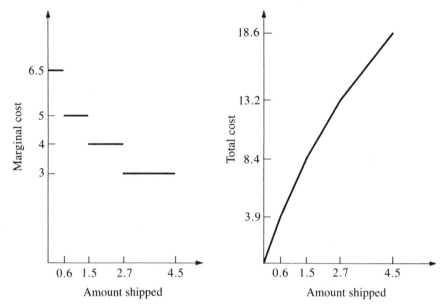

Figure 14.3 **Marginal shipping cost.**   *Figure 14.4* **Shipping cost function.**

shown in Fig. 14.4. Consequently, if *each* combination of source and destination has a similar shipping cost function, so that the cost of shipping x_{ij} units from source i ($i = 1,2,\ldots,m$) to destination j ($j = 1,2,\ldots,n$) is given by a nonlinear function $C_{ij}(x_{ij})$, then the overall objective function to be *minimized* is

$$f(\mathbf{x}) = \sum_{i=1}^{m} \sum_{j=1}^{n} C_{ij}(x_{ij}).$$

Even with this nonlinear objective function, the constraints normally are still the special linear constraints that fit the transportation problem model in Sec. 7.1.

PORTFOLIO SELECTION WITH RISKY SECURITIES

It now is common practice for professional managers of large stock portfolios to use computer models based partially on nonlinear programming to guide them. Because investors are concerned about both the expected return (gain) and the risk associated with their investments, nonlinear programming is used to determine a portfolio which, under certain assumptions, provides an optimal tradeoff between these two factors.

A nonlinear programming model can be formulated for this problem as follows. Suppose that n stocks (securities) are being considered for inclusion in the portfolio, and let the decision variables x_j ($j = 1, 2, \ldots, n$) be the number of shares of stock j to be included. Let μ_j and σ_{jj} be the (estimated) *mean* and *variance* of the return on each share of stock j, where σ_{jj} measures the risk of this stock. For

$i = 1, 2, \ldots, n \, (i \neq j)$, let σ_{ij} be the *covariance* of the return on one share each of stock i and stock j. (Because it would be difficult to estimate all of the σ_{ij}, the usual approach is to make certain assumptions about market behavior that enable us to calculate σ_{ij} directly from σ_{ii} and σ_{jj}.) Then the expected value $R(\mathbf{x})$ and the variance $V(\mathbf{x})$ of the total return from the entire portfolio are

$$R(\mathbf{x}) = \sum_{j=1}^{n} \mu_j x_j,$$

$$V(\mathbf{x}) = \sum_{i=1}^{n} \sum_{j=1}^{n} \sigma_{ij} x_i x_j,$$

where $V(\mathbf{x})$ measures the risk associated with the portfolio. The device used to consider the tradeoff between these two factors is to combine them together in the objective function to be maximized,

$$f(\mathbf{x}) = R(\mathbf{x}) - \beta V(\mathbf{x}),$$

where the parameter β is a nonnegative constant that reflects the investor's desired tradeoff between expected return and risk. Thus choosing $\beta = 0$ implies that risk should be ignored completely, whereas choosing a large value for β places a heavy weight on minimizing risk [by maximizing the negative of $V(\mathbf{x})$].

The complete nonlinear programming model might be

$$\text{Maximize} \quad f(\mathbf{x}) = \sum_{j=1}^{n} \mu_j x_j - \beta \sum_{i=1}^{n} \sum_{j=1}^{n} \sigma_{ij} x_i x_j,$$

subject to

$$\sum_{j=1}^{n} P_j x_j \leq B$$

and

$$x_j \geq 0, \quad \text{for } j = 1, 2, \ldots, n,$$

where P_j is the price for each share of stock j and B is the amount of money budgeted for the portfolio. Under certain assumptions about the investor's *utility function* (measuring the relative value to the investor of different total returns), it can be shown that an optimal solution for this nonlinear programming maximizes the investor's *expected utility*.[1]

One drawback of the preceding formulation is that, because $R(\mathbf{x})$ and $V(\mathbf{x})$ are somewhat incommensurable, it is relatively difficult to choose an appropriate value for β. Therefore, rather than stopping with one choice of β, it is common to use a *parametric* (nonlinear) programming approach to generate the optimal solution as a function of β over a wide range of values of β and then to analyze these solutions further before choosing one. This procedure often is referred to as generating the solutions on the *efficient frontier* because, when the $(R(\mathbf{x}), V(\mathbf{x}))$

---

[1] See Selected Reference 2, pp. 21–22, for further details.

points are plotted for all feasible solutions, these particular solutions lie on the *frontier* (boundary) of the attainable region, and they are *efficient* in the sense that no other feasible solution is at least equally good with one measure (R or V) and strictly better with the other measure (smaller V or larger R).

14.2 Graphical Illustration of Nonlinear Programming Problems

When a nonlinear programming problem has just one or two variables, it can be represented graphically much like the Wyndor Glass Co. example for linear programming in Sec. 3.1. Because such a graphical representation gives considerable insight into the properties of optimal solutions for linear and nonlinear programming, let us look at a few examples. In order to highlight these differences, we shall use some *nonlinear* variations of the Wyndor Glass Co. problem.

Figure 14.5 shows what happens to this problem if the only changes in the model shown in Sec. 3.1 are that both the second and third functional constraints are replaced by the single nonlinear constraint, $9x_1^2 + 5x_2^2 \leq 216$. Compare Fig. 14.5 with Fig. 3.3. The optimal solution still happens to be $(x_1, x_2) = (2,6)$. Furthermore, it still lies on the boundary of the feasible region. However, it is *not* a corner-point feasible solution. The optimal solution could have been a corner-

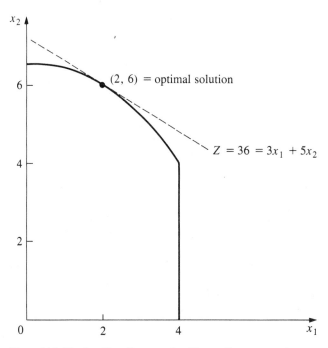

Figure 14.5 **Wyndor Glass Co. example with a nonlinear constraint.**

point feasible solution with a different objective function (check $Z = 3x_1 + x_2$), but the fact that it need not be one means that we no longer have the tremendous simplification used in linear programming of limiting the search for an optimal solution to just the corner-point feasible solutions.

Now suppose that the linear constraints of Sec. 3.1 are kept unchanged, but the objective function is made nonlinear. For example, if $Z = 126x_1 - 9x_1^2 + 182x_2 - 13x_2^2$, then the graphical representation in Fig. 14.6 indicates that the optimal solution is $x_1 = \frac{8}{3}$, $x_2 = 5$, which again lies on the boundary of the feasible region. On the other hand, if

$$Z = 54x_1 - 9x_1^2 + 78x_2 - 13x_2^2,$$

then the optimal solution turns out to be $(x_1, x_2) = (3,3)$, which lies *inside* the boundary of the feasible region. (You can check that this solution is optimal by using calculus to derive it as the unconstrained global maximum; because it also satisfies the constraints, it must be optimal for the constrained problem.) Therefore, a general algorithm for solving similar problems needs to consider *all* solutions in the feasible region, not just those on the boundary.

Another complication that arises in nonlinear programming is that a *local* maximum need not be a *global* maximum (the overall optimal solution). For example, consider the function of a single variable plotted in Fig. 14.7. Over the

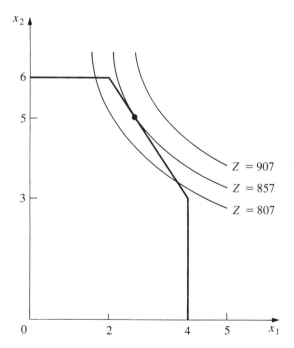

Figure 14.6 **Wyndor Glass Co. example with a nonlinear objective function.**

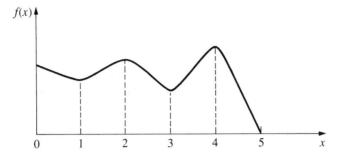

Figure 14.7 **A function with several local maxima.**

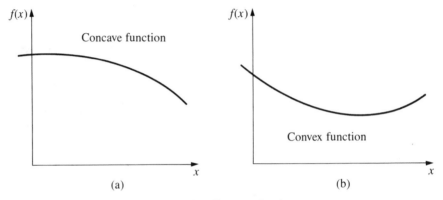

Figure 14.8 **Examples of (a)** *concave* **function, (b)** *convex* **function.**

interval, $0 \leq x \leq 5$, this function has three local maxima—$x = 0, x = 2, x = 4$—but only one of these, $x = 4$, is a *global maximum*. (Similarly, there are local minima at $x = 1, 3,$ and 5, but only $x = 5$ is a *global minimum*.)

Because nonlinear programming algorithms generally are only able to find local maxima (or local minima), it becomes crucial to know when a local maximum is *guaranteed* to be a global maximum over the feasible region. You may recall from calculus that when we maximize an ordinary (doubly differentiable) function of a single variable $f(x)$ without any constraints, this guarantee can be given when

$$\frac{d^2f}{dx^2} \leq 0 \quad \text{for all } x.$$

Such a function that is always "curving downward" (or not curving at all) is called a **concave** function.[1] Similarly, if $\leq$ is replaced by $\geq$, so that the function is always "curving upward" (or not curving at all), it is called a **convex** function.[2] (Thus a *linear* function is both concave and convex.) See Fig. 14.8 for examples.

---

[1] *Concave* functions sometimes are referred to as *concave downward*.

[2] *Convex* functions sometimes are referred to as *concave upward*.

Then note that Fig. 14.7 illustrates a function that is *neither* concave nor convex because it alternates between curving upward and curving downward.

Functions of multiple variables also can be characterized as *concave* or *convex* if they always curve downward or curve upward. For example, consider a function consisting of a sum of terms. If *each* term is *concave* (we can check to see if it is from its second derivative when the term involves just one of the variables), then the function is concave. Similarly, the function is *convex* if *each* term is *convex*. These intuitive definitions are restated in precise terms, along with further elaboration on these concepts, in Appendix 1.

If a nonlinear programming problem has no constraints, the objective function being *concave* guarantees that a local maximum is a *global maximum*. (Similarly, the objective function being *convex* ensures that a local minimum is a *global minimum*.) If there are constraints, then one more condition will provide this guarantee—namely, that the *feasible region* is a **convex set**. As discussed in Appendix 1, a convex set is simply a set of points such that, for each pair of points in the collection, the entire line segment joining these two points is also in the collection. Thus the feasible region in Fig. 14.7, $0 \leq x \leq 5$, is a convex set, as is the feasible region in Fig. 3.3 (or the feasible region for any other linear programming problem). Similarly, the feasible region in Fig. 14.5 is a convex set, which occurs whenever all of the $g_i(\mathbf{x})$ [for the constraints $g_i(\mathbf{x}) \leq b_i$] are convex.

14.3 Types of Nonlinear Programming Problems

Nonlinear programming problems come in many different shapes and forms. Unlike the simplex method for linear programming, no single algorithm that will solve all of these different types of problems exists. Instead, algorithms have been developed for various individual *classes* (special types) of nonlinear programming problems. The most important classes are introduced next, and then the subsequent sections describe how some problems of these types can be solved.

UNCONSTRAINED OPTIMIZATION

Unconstrained optimization problems have *no* constraints, so the objective is simply

$$\text{Maximize} \quad f(\mathbf{x})$$

over *all* values of $\mathbf{x} = (x_1, x_2, \ldots, x_n)$. As reviewed in Appendix 2, the *necessary* condition that a particular solution $\mathbf{x} = \mathbf{x}^*$ be optimal when $f(\mathbf{x})$ is a differentiable function is

$$\frac{\partial f}{\partial x_j} = 0 \quad \text{at } \mathbf{x} = \mathbf{x}^*, \text{ for } j = 1, 2, \ldots, n.$$

When $f(\mathbf{x})$ is *concave*, this condition also is *sufficient*, so then solving for $\mathbf{x}^*$ reduces to solving the system of n equations obtained by setting the n partial derivatives equal to zero. Unfortunately, for *nonlinear* functions $f(\mathbf{x})$, these equations often are going to be *nonlinear* as well, in which case you are unlikely to be able to solve analytically for their simultaneous solution. What then? Sections 14.4 and 14.5 describe *algorithmic search procedures* for finding $\mathbf{x}^*$, first for $n = 1$ and then for $n > 1$. These procedures also play an important role in solving many of the problem types described next where there are constraints. The reason is that many algorithms for *constrained* problems are designed so that they can focus on an *unconstrained* version of the problem during a portion of each iteration.

When a variable x_j does have a nonnegativity constraint, $x_j \geq 0$, the preceding necessary and (perhaps) sufficient condition changes slightly to

$$\frac{\partial f}{\partial x_j} \begin{cases} \leq 0 & \text{at } \mathbf{x} = \mathbf{x}^*, \text{if } x_j^* = 0 \\ = 0 & \text{at } \mathbf{x} = \mathbf{x}^*, \text{if } x_j^* > 0 \end{cases}$$

for each such j. A problem that has some such nonnegativity constraints but no functional constraints is one special case ($m = 0$) of the next class of problems.

LINEARLY CONSTRAINED OPTIMIZATION

Linearly constrained optimization problems are characterized by constraints that completely fit linear programming, so that *all* of the $g_i(\mathbf{x})$ constraint functions are *linear*, but the objective function $f(\mathbf{x})$ is *nonlinear*. The problem is considerably simplified by having just one nonlinear function to take into account, along with a linear programming feasible region. A number of special algorithms based upon *extending* the simplex method to consider the nonlinear objective function have been developed.

One important special case, which we consider next, is *quadratic programming*.

QUADRATIC PROGRAMMING

Quadratic programming problems again have linear constraints, but now the objective function $f(\mathbf{x})$ must be *quadratic*. Thus, the only difference between them and a linear programming problem is that some of the terms in the objective function involve the *square* of a variable or the *product* of two variables.

Many algorithms have been developed for this case under the additional assumption that $f(\mathbf{x})$ is *concave*. Section 14.7 presents an algorithm that involves a direct extension of the simplex method.

Quadratic programming is very important, partially because such formulations arise naturally in many applications. For example, the problem of portfolio selection with risky securities described in Sec. 14.1 fits into this format. However, another major reason for its importance is that a common approach to solving general linearly constrained optimization problems is to solve a sequence of quadratic programming approximations.

CONVEX PROGRAMMING

Convex programming covers a broad class of problems that actually encompasses as special cases all of the preceding types when $f(\mathbf{x})$ is concave. The assumptions are

1. $f(\mathbf{x})$ is concave,
2. Each $g_i(\mathbf{x})$ is convex.

As discussed at the end of Sec. 14.2, these assumptions are enough to ensure that a *local maximum* is a *global maximum*. You will see in Sec. 14.6 that the necessary and sufficient conditions for such an optimal solution are a natural generalization of the conditions just given for *unconstrained optimization* and its extension to include *nonnegativity constraints*. Section 14.9 then describes algorithmic approaches to solving convex programming problems.

SEPARABLE PROGRAMMING

Separable programming is a special case of *convex programming*, where the one additional assumption is

3. All of the $f(\mathbf{x})$ and $g_i(\mathbf{x})$ functions are *separable functions*.

A **separable function** is simply a function where *each term* involves just a *single variable*, so that the function is *separable* into a sum of functions of individual variables. For example, if $f(\mathbf{x})$ is a *separable function*, it can be expressed as

$$f(\mathbf{x}) = \sum_{j=1}^{n} f_j(x_j),$$

where each $f_j(x_j)$ function includes only the terms involving just x_j. In the terminology of linear programming (see Sec. 3.3), separable programming problems satisfy the assumption of *additivity* but not the assumption of *proportionality* (for nonlinear functions).

It is important to distinguish these problems from other convex programming problems, because any separable programming problem can be closely approximated by a *linear programming* problem so that the extremely efficient simplex method can be used. This approach is described in Sec. 14.8. (For simplicity, we focus there on the *linearly constrained* case where the special approach is needed only on the objective function.)

NONCONVEX PROGRAMMING

Nonconvex programming encompasses all nonlinear programming problems that do not satisfy the assumptions of convex programming. Now, even if you are successful in finding a *local maximum*, there is no assurance that it also will be a *global maximum*. Therefore, there is no algorithm that will guarantee finding an optimal solution for all such problems. However, there do exist some algorithms that are relatively well suited for finding *local maxima*, especially when the forms of the nonlinear functions do not deviate too strongly from those assumed for convex programming. One such algorithm is presented in Sec. 14.10.

However, certain specific types of nonconvex programming problems can be solved without great difficulty by special methods. Two especially important such types are discussed briefly next.

GEOMETRIC PROGRAMMING

When we apply nonlinear programming to engineering design problems, the objective function and the constraint functions frequently take the form

$$g(\mathbf{x}) = \sum_{i=1}^{N} c_i P_i(\mathbf{x}),$$

where

$$P_i(\mathbf{x}) = x_1^{a_{i1}} x_2^{a_{i2}} \cdots x_n^{a_{in}}, \quad \text{for } i = 1, 2, \ldots, N.$$

In such cases, the c_i and a_{ij} typically represent physical constants and the x_j are design variables. These functions generally are neither convex nor concave, so the techniques of convex programming cannot be applied directly to these *geometric programming problems*. However, there is one important case where the problem can be *transformed* into an *equivalent* convex programming problem. This case is where *all* of the c_i coefficients in each function are strictly positive, so that the functions are *generalized positive polynomials* (now called **posynomials**), and the objective function is to be minimized. The *equivalent* convex programming problem with decision variables $y_1, y_2, \ldots, y_n$ is then obtained by setting

$$x_j = e^{y_j}, \quad \text{for } j = 1, 2, \ldots, n$$

throughout the original model, so now a convex programming algorithm can be applied. Alternative solution procedures also have been developed for solving these *posynomial programming problems*, as well as for geometric programming problems of other types.[1]

FRACTIONAL PROGRAMMING

Suppose that the objective function is in the form of a *fraction*, i.e., the *ratio* of two functions,

$$\text{Maximize} \quad f(\mathbf{x}) = \frac{f_1(\mathbf{x})}{f_2(\mathbf{x})}.$$

Such *fractional programming* problems arise, for example, when maximizing the

---

[1] Duffin, Richard J., Elmur L. Peterson, and Clarence M. Zehner: *Geometric Programming*, Wiley, New York, 1967; Beightler, Charles, and Donald T. Phillips: *Applied Geometric Programming*, Wiley, New York, 1976.

ratio of *output* to *manhours expended* (productivity), or *profit* to *capital expended* (rate of return), or *expected value* to *standard deviation* of some measure of performance for an investment portfolio (return/risk). Some special solution procedures have been developed for certain forms of $f_1(\mathbf{x})$ and $f_2(\mathbf{x})$.[1]

When it can be done, the most straightforward approach to solving a fractional programming problem is to *transform* it into an *equivalent* problem of a standard type for which effective solution procedures already are available. To illustrate, suppose that $f(\mathbf{x})$ is of the *linear fractional programming* form

$$f(\mathbf{x}) = \frac{\mathbf{cx} + c_0}{\mathbf{dx} + d_0},$$

where $\mathbf{c}$ and $\mathbf{d}$ are row vectors, $\mathbf{x}$ is a column vector, and c_0 and d_0 are scalars. Also assume that the constraint functions $g_i(\mathbf{x})$ are linear, so that the constraints in matrix form are $\mathbf{Ax} \le \mathbf{b}$ and $\mathbf{x} \ge \mathbf{0}$.

Under mild additional assumptions, we can transform the problem into an equivalent *linear programming problem* by letting

$$\mathbf{y} = \frac{\mathbf{x}}{\mathbf{dx} + d_0} \quad \text{and} \quad t = \frac{1}{\mathbf{dx} + d_0},$$

so that $\mathbf{x} = \mathbf{y}/t$. This result yields

$$\text{Maximize} \quad Z = \mathbf{cy} + c_0 t,$$

subject to

$$\mathbf{Ay} - \mathbf{b}t \le \mathbf{0}$$
$$\mathbf{dy} + d_0 t = 1,$$

and

$$\mathbf{y} \ge \mathbf{0}, \qquad t \ge 0,$$

which can be solved by the simplex method. More generally, the same kind of transformation can be used to convert a fractional programming problem with concave $f_1(\mathbf{x})$, convex $f_2(\mathbf{x})$, and convex $g_i(\mathbf{x})$ into an equivalent convex programming problem.

THE COMPLEMENTARITY PROBLEM

When we deal with quadratic programming in Sec. 14.7, you will see one example of how solving certain nonlinear programming problems can be reduced to solving the complementarity problem. Given variables $w_1, w_2, \ldots, w_p$ and $z_1, z_2, \ldots, z_p$, the **complementarity problem** is to find a *feasible* solution for

[1] The pioneering work on fractional programming was done by Charnes, A., and W. W. Cooper: "Programming with Linear Fractional Functionals," *Naval Research Logistics Quarterly*, 9: 181–186, 1962. Also see Schaible, Siegfried: "A Survey of Fractional Programming," in Schaible, Siegfried, and William T. Ziemba (eds.): *Generalized Concavity in Optimization and Economics*, Academic Press, New York, 1981, pp. 417–440.

the set of constraints,

$$\mathbf{w} = F(\mathbf{z}), \qquad \mathbf{w} \geq \mathbf{0}, \qquad \mathbf{z} \geq \mathbf{0},$$

that also satisfies the **complementarity constraint**,

$$\mathbf{w}^T \mathbf{z} = 0.$$

Here, $\mathbf{w}$ and $\mathbf{z}$ are column vectors, F is a given vector-valued function, and the superscript T denotes *transpose* (see Appendix 3). The problem has no objective function, so technically it is not a full-fledged nonlinear programming problem. It is called the *complementarity problem* because of the complementary relationships that *either*

$$w_i = 0 \quad \text{or} \quad z_i = 0 \quad \text{(or both) for each } i = 1, 2, \ldots, p.$$

An important special case is the **linear complementarity problem** where

$$F(\mathbf{z}) = \mathbf{q} + \mathbf{Mz},$$

where $\mathbf{q}$ is a given column vector and $\mathbf{M}$ is a given $p \times p$ matrix. Efficient algorithms have been developed for solving this problem under suitable assumptions about the properties of the matrix $\mathbf{M}$.[1] One type involves pivoting from one basic feasible solution to the next, much like the simplex method for linear programming.

In addition to having applications in nonlinear programming, complementarity problems have applications in game theory, economic equilibrium problems, and engineering equilibrium problems.

14.4 One-Variable Unconstrained Optimization

We now begin discussing how to solve some of the types of problems just described by considering the simplest case—*unconstrained optimization* with just a single variable x ($n = 1$), where the differentiable function $f(x)$ to be maximized is *concave*.[2] Thus the *necessary and sufficient condition* for a particular solution $x = x^*$ to be optimal (a *global maximum*) is

$$\frac{df}{dx} = 0 \quad \text{at } x = x^*,$$

as depicted in Fig. 14.9. If this equation can be solved directly for x^*, you are done. However, if $f(x)$ is not a particularly simple function, so the derivative is not just a linear or quadratic function, you may not be able to solve the equation *analytically*. If not, the *one-dimensional search procedure* provides a straightforward way of solving the problem *numerically*.

---

[1] See Cottle, R. W., and G. B. Dantzig: "Complementary Pivot Theory of Mathematical Programming," *Linear Algebra and Its Applications*, **1**:103–125, 1966, and Murty, K. G.: *Linear and Combinatorial Programming*. Wiley, New York, 1976, chap. 16.

[2] See the beginning of Appendix 2 for a review of the corresponding case when $f(x)$ is not concave.

THE ONE-DIMENSIONAL SEARCH PROCEDURE

Like other *search procedures* in nonlinear programming, this one finds a sequence of *trial solutions* that lead toward an optimal solution. At each iteration, you begin at the current trial solution to conduct a systematic search that culminates by identifying a new *improved* (hopefully substantially improved) trial solution.

The idea behind the one-dimensional search procedure is a very intuitive one, namely, that whether the *slope* (derivative) is positive or negative at a *trial solution* definitely indicates whether this solution needs to be made larger or smaller to move toward an optimal solution. Thus, if the derivative evaluated at a particular value of x is *positive*, then x^* must be larger than this x (see Fig. 14.9), so this x becomes a *lower bound* on the trial solutions that need to be considered thereafter. Conversely, if the derivative is *negative*, then x^* must be *smaller* than this x, so x would become an *upper bound*. Therefore, after both types of bounds have been identified, each new trial solution selected between the current bounds provides a new *tighter* bound of one type, thereby narrowing the search further. As long as a reasonable rule is used to select each trial solution in this way, the resulting *sequence* of trial solutions must *converge* to x^*. In practice, this means continuing the sequence until the distance between the bounds is sufficiently small that the next trial solution must be within a prespecified *error tolerance* of x^*.

This entire process is summarized next, using the notation

$$x' = \text{current trial solution,}$$
$$\underline{x} = \text{current lower bound on } x^*,$$
$$\bar{x} = \text{current upper bound on } x^*,$$
$$\varepsilon = \text{error tolerance for } x^*.$$

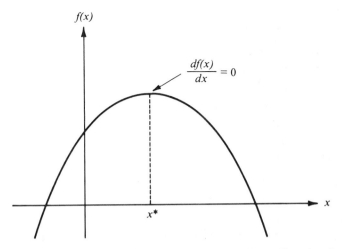

Figure 14.9 **The one-variable unconstrained programming problem when the function is concave.**

Although there are several reasonable rules for selecting each new trial solution, the one used in the following procedure is the **midpoint rule** (traditionally called the *Bolzano search plan*), which says simply to select the *midpoint* between the two current bounds.

Summary of One-Dimensional Search Procedure

Initialization step   Select ε. Find an initial $\underline{x}$ and $\bar{x}$ by inspection (or by respectively finding any value of x at which the derivative is positive and then negative). Select an initial trial solution,

$$x' = \frac{\underline{x} + \bar{x}}{2}.$$

Iterative step   1.   Evaluate $\dfrac{df(x)}{dx}$ at $x = x'$.

2.   If $\dfrac{df(x)}{dx} \geq 0$, reset $\underline{x} = x'$.

3.   If $\dfrac{df(x)}{dx} \leq 0$, reset $\bar{x} = x'$.

4.   Select a new $x' = \dfrac{\underline{x} + \bar{x}}{2}$.

Stopping rule   If $(\bar{x} - \underline{x}) \leq 2\varepsilon$, so the new x' must be within ε of x^*, stop. Otherwise, return to the iterative step.

We shall now illustrate this procedure by applying it to the following example.

EXAMPLE Suppose that the function to be maximized is

$$f(x) = 12x - 3x^4 - 2x^6,$$

as plotted in Fig. 14.10. Its first two derivatives are

$$\frac{df(x)}{dx} = 12(1 - x^3 - x^5),$$

$$\frac{d^2f(x)}{dx^2} = -12(3x^2 + 5x^4).$$

Because the second derivative is nonpositive everywhere, $f(x)$ is a concave function, so the one-dimensional search procedure can be applied safely to find its global maximum. A quick inspection of this function (without even constructing its graph as shown in Fig. 14.10) indicates that $f(x)$ is positive for small positive values of x, but it is negative for $x < 0$ or $x > 2$. Therefore, $\underline{x} = 0$ and $\bar{x} = 2$ can be used as the initial bounds, with their midpoint, $x' = 1$, as the initial trial solution.

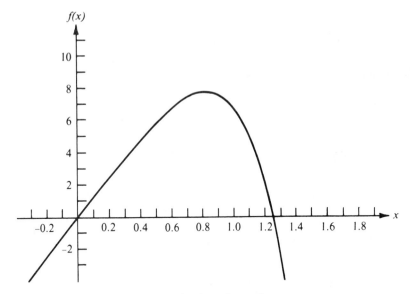

Figure 14.10 **Example for one-dimensional search procedure.**

Let 0.01 be the error tolerance for x^* in the stopping rule, so the final $(\bar{x} - \underline{x}) \leq 0.02$ with the final x' at the midpoint. Applying the one-dimensional search procedure then yields the sequence of results shown in Table 14.1. (This table includes both the function and derivative values for your information, where the derivative is evaluated at the trial solution generated at the *preceding* iteration. However, note that the algorithm actually doesn't need to calculate $f(x')$ at all and that it only needs to calculate the derivative far enough to determine its sign.) The conclusion is that

$$x^* \approx 0.836,$$
$$0.828125 < x^* < 0.84375.$$

Table 14.1 **Application of one-dimensional search procedure to example**

Iteration	$\dfrac{df(x)}{dx}$	$\underline{x}$	$\bar{x}$	New x'	$f(x')$
0	0	0	2	1	7.0000
1	−12	0	1	0.5	5.7812
2	+10.12	0.5	1	0.75	7.6948
3	+4.09	0.75	1	0.875	7.8439
4	−2.19	0.75	0.875	0.8125	7.8672
5	+1.31	0.8125	0.875	0.84375	7.8829
6	−0.34	0.8125	0.84375	0.828125	7.8815
7	+0.51	0.828125	0.84375	0.8359375	7.8839
Stop					

14.5 Multivariable Unconstrained Optimization

Now consider the problem of maximizing a *concave* function $f(\mathbf{x})$ of *multiple* variables, $\mathbf{x} = (x_1, x_2, \ldots, x_n)$, when there are no constraints on the feasible values. Suppose again that the *necessary and sufficient condition* for optimality, given by the system of equations obtained by setting the respective partial derivatives equal to zero (see Sec. 14.3), cannot be solved *analytically*, so that a *numerical* search procedure must be used. How can the preceding *one-dimensional* search procedure be extended to this *multidimensional* problem?

In Sec. 14.4, the value of the *ordinary* derivative was used to select one of just *two* possible directions (increase x or decrease x) in which to move from the current trial solution to the next one. The goal was to reach a point eventually where this derivative is (essentially) *zero*. Now, there are *innumerable* possible directions in which to move; they correspond to the possible *proportional rates* at which the respective variables can be changed. The goal is to reach a point eventually where all of the partial derivatives are (essentially) *zero*. Therefore, extending the one-dimensional search procedure requires using the values of the *partial* derivatives to select the specific direction in which to move. This selection involves using the *gradient* of the objective function, as described next.

Because the objective function $f(\mathbf{x})$ is assumed to be differentiable, it possesses a *gradient* denoted by $\nabla f(\mathbf{x})$ at each point $\mathbf{x}$. In particular, the **gradient** at a specific point $\mathbf{x} = \mathbf{x}'$ is the *vector* whose elements are the respective *partial derivatives* evaluated at $\mathbf{x} = \mathbf{x}'$, so that

$$\nabla f(\mathbf{x}') = \left(\frac{\partial f}{\partial x_1}, \frac{\partial f}{\partial x_2}, \ldots, \frac{\partial f}{\partial x_n} \right) \quad \text{at } \mathbf{x} = \mathbf{x}'.$$

The significance of the gradient is that the (infinitesimal) change in $\mathbf{x}$ that *maximizes* the rate at which $f(\mathbf{x})$ increases is the change that is *proportional* to $\nabla f(\mathbf{x})$. To express this idea geometrically, the "direction" of the gradient, $\nabla f(\mathbf{x}')$, is interpreted as the *direction* of the directed line segment (arrow) from the origin $(0, 0, \ldots, 0)$ to the point $(\partial f/\partial x_1, \partial f/\partial x_2, \ldots, \partial f/\partial x_n)$, where $\partial f/\partial x_j$ is evaluated at $x_j = x_j'$. Therefore, it may be said that the rate at which $f(\mathbf{x})$ increases is maximized if (infinitesimal) changes in $\mathbf{x}$ are in the *direction* of the gradient $\nabla f(\mathbf{x})$. Because the objective is to find the feasible solution *maximizing* $f(\mathbf{x})$, it would seem expedient to attempt to move in the direction of the gradient as much as possible.

THE GRADIENT SEARCH PROCEDURE

Because the current problem has *no* constraints, this interpretation of the gradient suggests that an efficient *search procedure* should keep moving in the direction of the gradient until it (essentially) reaches an optimal solution $\mathbf{x}^*$, where $\nabla f(\mathbf{x}^*) = \mathbf{0}$. However, it normally would not be practical to change $\mathbf{x}$ *continuously* in the direction of $\nabla f(\mathbf{x})$ because this series of changes would require continuously *reevaluating* the $\partial f/\partial x_j$ and changing the direction of the path.

Therefore, a better approach is to keep moving in a *fixed* direction from the current trial solution, not stopping until $f(\mathbf{x})$ stops increasing. This stopping point would be the next trial solution, so the gradient then would be recalculated to determine the new direction in which to move. With this approach, each *iteration* involves changing the *current* trial solution $\mathbf{x}'$ as follows:

$$\text{Reset} \quad \mathbf{x}' = \mathbf{x}' + t^* \nabla f(\mathbf{x}),$$

where t^* is the positive value of t that *maximizes* $f(\mathbf{x}' + t \nabla f(\mathbf{x}'))$; that is,

$$f(\mathbf{x}' + t^* \nabla f(\mathbf{x}')) = \max_{t \geq 0} f(\mathbf{x}' + t \nabla f(\mathbf{x}')).$$

[Note that $f(\mathbf{x}' + t \nabla f(\mathbf{x}'))$ is simply $f(\mathbf{x})$ where

$$x_j = x'_j + t \left[\frac{\partial f}{\partial x_j} \right]_{\mathbf{x} = \mathbf{x}'}, \quad \text{for } j = 1, 2, \ldots, n,$$

and that these expressions for the x_j involve only constants and t, so $f(\mathbf{x})$ becomes a function of just the single variable t.] The iterations of this gradient search procedure continue until $\nabla f(\mathbf{x}) = \mathbf{0}$ within a small tolerance ε, i.e., until

$$\left[\frac{\partial f}{\partial x_j} \right] \leq \varepsilon \quad \text{for } all \ j = 1, 2, \ldots, n.$$

An analogy may help to clarify this procedure. Suppose that you need to climb to the top of a hill. You are near-sighted, so you can't see the top of the hill in order to walk directly in that direction. However, when you stand still, you can see the ground around your feet well enough to determine the direction in which the hill is sloping upward most sharply. You are able to walk in a straight line. While walking you also are able to tell when you stop climbing (zero slope in your direction). Assuming that the hill is *concave*, you now can use the *gradient search procedure* for climbing to the top efficiently. This problem is a *two-variable* problem, where (x_1, x_2) represents the coordinates (ignoring height) of your current location. The function $f(x_1, x_2)$ gives the height of the hill at (x_1, x_2). You start each iteration at your current location (current trial solution) by determining the direction [in the (x_1, x_2) coordinate system] in which the hill is sloping upward most sharply (the direction of the gradient) at this point. You then begin walking in this fixed direction and continue as long as you still are climbing. You eventually stop at a new trial location (solution) when the hill becomes level in your direction, at which point you prepare to do another iteration in another direction. You continue these iterations, following a zig-zag path up the hill, until you reach a trial location where the slope is essentially zero in all locations. Under the assumption that the hill $[f(x_1, x_2)]$ is concave, you must then be essentially at the top of the hill.

The most difficult part of the gradient search procedure usually is to find t^*, the value of t that maximizes f in the direction of the gradient, at each iteration. Because $\mathbf{x}$ and $\nabla f(\mathbf{x})$ have fixed values for the maximization, and because $f(\mathbf{x})$ is concave, this problem should be viewed as maximizing a *concave* function of a *single variable t.* Therefore, it can be solved by the *one-dimensional search procedure* of Sec. 14.4 (where the initial lower bound on t must be nonnegative because of the $t \geq 0$ constraint). Alternatively, if f is a simple function, it may be possible to obtain an analytical solution by setting the derivative with respect to t equal to zero and solving.

Summary of Gradient Search Procedure

Initialization step   Select ε and any initial trial solution $\mathbf{x}'$. Go first to the stopping rule.

Iterative step   1.   Express $f(\mathbf{x}' + t\,\nabla f(\mathbf{x}'))$ as a function of t by setting

$$x_j = x_j' + t\left(\frac{\partial f}{\partial x_j}\right)\Bigg|_{\mathbf{x}=\mathbf{x}'} \quad \text{for } j = 1, 2, \ldots, n,$$

and then substituting these expressions and t into $f(\mathbf{x})$.

2.   Use the one-dimensional search procedure (or calculus) to find $t = t^*$ that maximizes $f(\mathbf{x}' + t\,\nabla f(\mathbf{x}'))$ over $t \geq 0$.

3.   Reset $\mathbf{x}' = \mathbf{x}' + t^*\,\nabla f(\mathbf{x}')$. Then go to the stopping rule.

Stopping rule   Evaluate $\nabla f(\mathbf{x}')$ at $\mathbf{x} = \mathbf{x}'$. Check if

$$\left|\frac{\partial f}{\partial x_j}\right| \leq \varepsilon \quad \text{for all } j = 1, 2, \ldots, n.$$

If so, stop with the current $\mathbf{x}'$ as the desired approximation of an optimal solution $\mathbf{x}^*$. Otherwise, go to the iterative step.

Now let us illustrate this procedure.

EXAMPLE   Consider the following two-variable problem.

$$\text{Maximize} \quad f(\mathbf{x}) = 2x_1 x_2 + 2x_2 - x_1^2 - 2x_2^2.$$

Thus

$$\frac{\partial f}{\partial x_1} = 2x_2 - 2x_1,$$

$$\frac{\partial f}{\partial x_2} = 2x_1 + 2 - 4x_2.$$

We also can verify (see Appendix 1) that $f(\mathbf{x})$ is *concave*. To begin the gradient search procedure, suppose that $\mathbf{x} = (0,0)$ is selected as the initial trial solution. Because the respective partial derivatives are 0 and 2 at this point, the gradient is

$$\nabla f(0,0) = (0,2).$$

Therefore, to begin the first iteration, set

$$x_1 = 0 + t(0) = 0,$$
$$x_2 = 0 + t(2) = 2t,$$

and then substitute these expressions into $f(\mathbf{x})$ to obtain

$$f(\mathbf{x}' + t\nabla f(\mathbf{x}')) = f(0, 2t)$$
$$= 2(0)(2t) + 2(2t) - (0)^2 - 2(2t)^2$$
$$= 4t - 8t^2.$$

Because

$$f(0, 2t^*) = \max_{t \geq 0} f(0, 2t) = \max_{t \geq 0} \{4t - 8t^2\},$$

and

$$\frac{d}{dt}\{4t - 8t^2\} = 4 - 16t = 0,$$

it follows that

$$t^* = \frac{1}{4},$$

so

$$\text{Reset} \quad \mathbf{x}' = (0, 0) + \frac{1}{4}(0, 2) = \left(0, \frac{1}{2}\right).$$

For this new trial solution, the gradient is

$$\nabla f\left(0, \frac{1}{2}\right) = (1, 0).$$

Thus for the second iteration, set

$$\mathbf{x} = \left(0, \frac{1}{2}\right) + t(1, 0) = \left(t, \frac{1}{2}\right),$$

so

$$f(\mathbf{x}' + t\nabla f(\mathbf{x}')) = f\left(0 + t, \frac{1}{2} + 0t\right) = f\left(t, \frac{1}{2}\right)$$
$$= (2t)\frac{1}{2} + 2\left(\frac{1}{2}\right) - t^2 - 2\left(\frac{1}{2}\right)^2$$
$$= t - t^2 + \frac{1}{2}.$$

Because

$$f\left(t^*, \frac{1}{2}\right) = \max_{t \geq 0} f\left(t, \frac{1}{2}\right) = \max_{t \geq 0}\left\{t - t^2 + \frac{1}{2}\right\},$$
$$\frac{d}{dt}\left\{t - t^2 + \frac{1}{2}\right\} = 1 - 2t = 0,$$

Table 14.2 **Application of gradient search procedure to example**

Iteration	$\mathbf{x}'$	$\nabla f(\mathbf{x}')$	$\mathbf{x}' + t\,\nabla f(\mathbf{x}')$	$f(\mathbf{x}' + t\,\nabla f(\mathbf{x}'))$	t^*	$\mathbf{x}' + t^*\,\nabla f(\mathbf{x}')$
1	$(0,0)$	$(0,2)$	$(0,2t)$	$4t - 8t^2$	$\frac{1}{4}$	$(0,\frac{1}{2})$
2	$(0,\frac{1}{2})$	$(1,0)$	$(t,\frac{1}{2})$	$t - t^2 + \frac{1}{2}$	$\frac{1}{2}$	$(\frac{1}{2},\frac{1}{2})$

then

$$t^* = \frac{1}{2},$$

so

$$\text{Reset} \quad \mathbf{x}' = \left(0,\frac{1}{2}\right) + \frac{1}{2}(1,0) = \left(\frac{1}{2},\frac{1}{2}\right).$$

A nice way of organizing this work is to write out a table such as Table 14.2, which summarizes the preceding two iterations. At each iteration, the second column shows the current trial solution, and the last column shows the eventual new trial solution, which then is carried down into the second column for the next iteration. The fourth column gives the expressions for the x_j in terms of t that need to be substituted into $f(\mathbf{x})$ to give the fifth column.

Continuing in this fashion, the subsequent trial solutions would be $(\frac{1}{2},\frac{3}{4})$, $(\frac{3}{4},\frac{3}{4})$, $(\frac{3}{4},\frac{7}{8})$, $(\frac{7}{8},\frac{7}{8})$,..., as shown in Fig. 14.11. Because these points are converging to $\mathbf{x}^* = (1,1)$, this solution is the optimal solution, as verified by the fact that

$$\nabla f(1,1) = (0,0).$$

However, because this converging sequence of trial solutions never *reaches* its limit, the procedure actually will stop somewhere (depending on ε) slightly below $(1,1)$ as its final approximation of $\mathbf{x}^*$.

As Fig. 14.11 suggests, the gradient search procedure *zig zags* to the optimal solution rather than moving in a straight line. Some modifications of the procedure have been developed that *accelerate* movement toward the optimum by taking this zig-zag behavior into account.

If $f(\mathbf{x})$ were *not* a *concave* function, the gradient search procedure still would converge to a *local* maximum. The only change in the description of the procedure for this case is that t^* now would correspond to the *first local maximum* of $f(\mathbf{x} + t\,\nabla f(\mathbf{x}))$ as t is increased from zero.

If the objective were to *minimize* $f(\mathbf{x})$ instead, one change in the procedure would be to move in the *opposite* direction of the gradient at each iteration. In other words, the rule for obtaining the next point now would be

$$\text{Reset} \quad \mathbf{x}' = \mathbf{x}' - t^*\,\nabla f(\mathbf{x}').$$

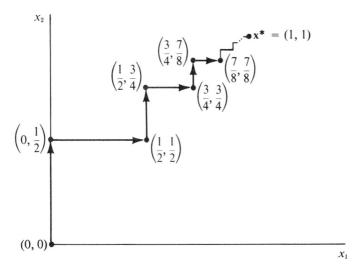

Figure 14.11 Illustration of the gradient search procedure.

The only other change is that t^* now would be the nonnegative value of t that *minimizes* $f(\mathbf{x}' - t\,\nabla f(\mathbf{x}'))$; that is,

$$f(\mathbf{x}' - t^*\,\nabla f(\mathbf{x}')) = \min_{t \geq 0} f(\mathbf{x}' - t\,\nabla f(\mathbf{x}')).$$

14.6 The Karush-Kuhn-Tucker (KKT) Conditions for Constrained Optimization

We now focus on the question of how to recognize an *optimal solution* for a nonlinear programming problem (with differentiable functions). What are the necessary and (perhaps) sufficient conditions that such a solution must satisfy?

In the preceding sections we already have noted these conditions for *unconstrained optimization*, as summarized in the first two lines of Table 14.3. Early in Sec. 14.3 we also gave these conditions for the slight *extension* of unconstrained optimization where the *only* constraints are nonnegativity constraints. These conditions are shown in the third line of Table 14.3 in another *equivalent* form that is suggestive of their generalization for *general* constrained optimization. As indicated in the last line of the table, the conditions for the general case are called the **Karush-Kuhn-Tucker conditions** (or **KKT conditions**), because they were derived independently by Karush[1] and by Kuhn and Tucker.[2] Their basic result is embodied in the following theorem.

[1] Karush, W.: "Minima of Functions of Several Variables with Inequalities as Side Conditions," M.S. Thesis, Department of Mathematics, University of Chicago, 1939.

[2] Kuhn, H. W., and A. W. Tucker: "Nonlinear Programming," in Jerzy Neyman (ed.), *Proceedings of the Second Berkeley Symposium*, University of California Press, Berkeley, 1951, pp. 481–492.

Table 14.3 **Necessary and sufficient conditions for optimality**

Problem	Necessary conditions for optimality	Also sufficient if
One-variable unconstrained	$\dfrac{df}{dx} = 0$	$f(\mathbf{x})$ concave
Multivariable unconstrained	$\dfrac{\partial f}{\partial x_j} = 0 \quad (j = 1, 2, \ldots, n)$	$f(\mathbf{x})$ concave
Constrained, nonnegativity constraints only	$\dfrac{\partial f}{\partial x_j} \leq 0$ $\quad (j = 1, 2, \ldots, n)$ $x_j \dfrac{\partial f}{\partial x_j} = 0$	$f(\mathbf{x})$ concave
General constrained problem	Karush-Kuhn-Tucker conditions	$f(\mathbf{x})$ concave $g_i(\mathbf{x})$ convex $(i = 1, 2, \ldots, m)$

THEOREM Assume that $f(\mathbf{x})$, $g_1(\mathbf{x})$, $g_2(\mathbf{x})$, ..., $g_m(\mathbf{x})$ are *differentiable* functions satisfying certain regularity conditions.[1] Then

$$\mathbf{x}^* = (x_1^*, x_2^*, \ldots, x_n^*)$$

can be an *optimal solution* for the nonlinear programming problem only if there exist m numbers, $u_1, u_2, \ldots, u_m$, such that *all* of the *following conditions* are satisfied:

$$\left. \begin{array}{l} \textbf{1.} \ \dfrac{\partial f}{\partial x_j} - \displaystyle\sum_{i=1}^{m} u_i \dfrac{\partial g_i}{\partial x_j} \leq 0 \\[3mm] \textbf{2.} \ x_j^* \left(\dfrac{\partial f}{\partial x_j} - \displaystyle\sum_{i=1}^{m} u_i \dfrac{\partial g_i}{\partial x_j} \right) = 0 \end{array} \right\} \ \text{at } \mathbf{x} = \mathbf{x}^*, \quad \text{for } j = 1, 2, \ldots, n.$$

$$\left. \begin{array}{l} \textbf{3.} \ g_i(\mathbf{x}^*) - b_i \leq 0 \\ \textbf{4.} \ u_i(g_i(\mathbf{x}^*) - b_i) = 0 \end{array} \right\} \ \text{for } i = 1, 2, \ldots, m.$$

5. $x_j^* \geq 0$, $\qquad$ for $j = 1, 2, \ldots, n.$
6. $u_i \geq 0$, $\qquad$ for $i = 1, 2, \ldots, m.$

In the preceding *KKT conditions*, the u_i correspond to the *dual variables* of linear programming (we expand on this correspondence at the end of the section), and they have a comparable economic interpretation. (However, the u_i actually arose in the mathematical derivation as Lagrange multipliers.) Conditions 3 and 5 do nothing more than help ensure the feasibility of the solution. The other

[1] Ibid., p. 483.

conditions eliminate most of the feasible solutions as possible candidates to be an optimal solution. However, it should be noted that satisfying these conditions does not guarantee that the solution is optimal. As summarized in the last column of Table 14.3, certain additional *convexity* assumptions are needed to obtain this guarantee. These assumptions are spelled out in the following extension of the theorem.

COROLLARY Assume that $f(\mathbf{x})$ is a *concave function* and that $g_1(\mathbf{x})$, $g_2(\mathbf{x}), \dots, g_m(\mathbf{x})$ are *convex functions* (i.e., this problem is a *convex programming problem*), where all of these functions satisfy the regularity conditions. Then $\mathbf{x}^* = (x_1^*, x_2^*, \dots, x_n^*)$ is an *optimal solution* if and only if *all* the conditions of the theorem are satisfied.

EXAMPLE To illustrate the formulation and application of the *KKT conditions*, we consider the following two-variable nonlinear programming problem.

$$\text{Maximize} \quad f(\mathbf{x}) = \ln(x_1 + 1) + x_2,$$

subject to

$$2x_1 + x_2 \le 3$$

and

$$x_1 \ge 0, \qquad x_2 \ge 0,$$

where ln denotes *natural logarithm*. Thus $m = 1$ and $g_1(\mathbf{x}) = 2x_1 + x_2$, so $g_1(\mathbf{x})$ is *convex*. Furthermore, it can be easily verified (see Appendix 1) that $f(\mathbf{x})$ is *concave*. Hence the corollary applies, so any optimal solution can definitely be obtained by solving the KKT conditions.

These conditions are

$1(a).\ \dfrac{1}{x_1 + 1} - 2u_1 \le 0.$

$2(a).\ x_1\left(\dfrac{1}{x_1 + 1} - 2u_1\right) = 0.$

$1(b).\ 1 - u_1 \le 0.$
$2(b).\ x_2(1 - u_1) = 0.$
$\quad 3.\ 2x_1 + x_2 \le 3.$
$\quad 4.\ u_1(2x_1 + x_2 - 3) = 0.$
$\quad 5.\ x_1 \ge 0, x_2 \ge 0.$
$\quad 6.\ u_1 \ge 0.$

To solve these conditions, note that $u_1 \ge 1$ from condition $1(b)$. Because $(x_1 + 1)^{-1} \le 1$ from the $x_1 \ge 0$ condition, $u_1 \ge 1$ implies that $(x_1 + 1)^{-1} - 2u_1 < 0$, so $x_1 = 0$ from condition $2(a)$. Similarly, $u_1 \ge 1$ implies that $2x_1 + x_2 - 3 = 0$

from condition 4, so $x_2 = 3$. Consequently, $\mathbf{x}^* = (0, 3)$ is an optimal solution for this problem.

For problems more complicated than this example, it may be difficult, if not essentially impossible, to derive an optimal solution *directly* from the KKT conditions. Nevertheless, these conditions still provide valuable clues as to the identity of an optimal solution, and they also permit us to check whether a proposed solution may be optimal.

There also are many valuable *indirect* applications of the KKT conditions. One of these applications arises in the *duality theory* that has been developed for nonlinear programming to parallel the duality theory for linear programming presented in Chapter 6. In particular, for any given constrained maximization problem (call it the *primal problem*), the KKT conditions can be used to define a closely associated dual problem which is a constrained minimization problem. The variables in the dual problem consist of both the Lagrange multipliers, u_i $(i = 1, 2, \ldots, m)$, and the primal variables, x_j $(j = 1, 2, \ldots, n)$.[1] In the special case where the primal problem is a linear programming problem, the x_j variables drop out of the dual problem and it becomes the familiar dual problem of linear programming (where the u_i variables here correspond to the y_i variables in Chap. 6). When the primal problem is a convex programming problem, it is possible to establish between the primal problem and the dual problem relationships that are similar to those for linear programming. For example, the *strong duality property* of Sec. 6.1, which states that the optimal objective function values of the two problems are equal, also holds here. Furthermore, the values of the u_i variables in an optimal solution for the dual problem can again be interpreted as *shadow prices* (see Secs. 4.7 and 6.2); i.e., they give the rate at which the optimal objective function value for the primal problem could be increased by (slightly) increasing the right-hand side of the corresponding constraint. Because duality theory for nonlinear programming is a relatively advanced topic, the interested reader is referred elsewhere for further information.[2]

You will see another indirect application of the KKT conditions in the next section.

14.7 Quadratic Programming

As indicated in Sec. 14.3, the *quadratic programming* problem differs from the linear programming problem only in that the *objective function* also includes x_j^2 and $x_j x_k$ $(j \neq k)$ terms. Thus, if we use matrix notation like that introduced in Sec. 5.2, the problem is to find $\mathbf{x}$ so as to

$$\text{Maximize} \quad f(\mathbf{x}) = \mathbf{c}\mathbf{x} - \tfrac{1}{2}\mathbf{x}^\mathrm{T}\mathbf{Q}\mathbf{x},$$

[1] For details on this formulation, see Mangasarian, Olvi T.: *Nonlinear Programming*, McGraw-Hill, New York, 1969, Chap. 8. For a unified survey of various approaches to duality in nonlinear programming, see Geoffrion, A.M.: "Duality in Nonlinear Programming: A Simplified Applications-Oriented Development," *SIAM Review*, **13**:1–37, 1971.

[2] Ibid.

subject to

$$\mathbf{Ax} \le \mathbf{b} \quad \text{and} \quad \mathbf{x} \ge \mathbf{0},$$

where $\mathbf{c}$ is a row vector, $\mathbf{x}$ and $\mathbf{b}$ are column vectors, $\mathbf{Q}$ and $\mathbf{A}$ are matrices, and the superscript T denotes *transpose* (see Appendix 3). The q_{ij} (elements of Q) are given constants such that $q_{ij} = q_{ji}$ (which is the reason for the factor of $1/2$ in the objective function).

Several algorithms have been developed for the special case of the quadratic programming problem where the objective function is a *concave* function. (A way to verify that the objective function is concave is to verify the equivalent condition that

$$\mathbf{x}^{\mathrm{T}}\mathbf{Qx} \ge 0$$

for all $\mathbf{x}$, i.e., that $\mathbf{Q}$ is a *positive semidefinite* matrix.) We shall describe one[1] of these algorithms that has been quite popular because it requires using only the *simplex method* with a slight modification.

THE MODIFIED SIMPLEX METHOD

The first step for this algorithm is to formulate the *KKT conditions* for the problem. A convenient form for expressing them for this case is

$$\mathbf{Qx} + \mathbf{A}^{\mathrm{T}}\mathbf{u} - \mathbf{y} = \mathbf{c}^{\mathrm{T}},$$
$$\mathbf{Ax} + \mathbf{v} = \mathbf{b},$$
$$\mathbf{x} \ge \mathbf{0}, \quad \mathbf{u} \ge \mathbf{0}, \quad \mathbf{y} \ge \mathbf{0}, \quad \mathbf{v} \ge \mathbf{0},$$
$$\mathbf{x}^{\mathrm{T}}\mathbf{y} + \mathbf{u}^{\mathrm{T}}\mathbf{v} = \mathbf{0},$$

where the elements of the column vector $\mathbf{u}$ are the u_i of the preceding section, and the elements of the column vectors $\mathbf{y}$ and $\mathbf{v}$ are slack variables. (You are asked in Prob. 40 to verify that this form indeed is one form of the KKT conditions). Notice that the last two lines of conditions imply the complementary relationships that *either* $x_j = 0$ or $y_j = 0$ (or both) for each $j = 1, 2, \ldots, n$, and that *either* $u_i = 0$ or $v_i = 0$ (or both) for each $i = 1, 2, \ldots, m$. Consequently, the two variables in each of these pairs are referred to as **complementary variables**.

Because the objective function of the original problem is assumed to be concave and because the constraint functions are linear and therefore convex, the corollary to the theorem of Sec. 14.6 applies. Thus $\mathbf{x}$ is *optimal* if and only if there exist values of $\mathbf{y}$, $\mathbf{u}$, and $\mathbf{v}$ such that all four vectors together satisfy all these conditions. The original problem is thereby reduced to the equivalent problem of finding a *feasible solution* to these *constraints*.

---

[1] Wolfe, Philip.: "The Simplex Method for Quadratic Programming," *Econometrics*, **37**:382–398, 1959. This paper develops both a short form and a long form of the algorithm. We present a version of the *short form*, which assumes further that *either* $\mathbf{c} = \mathbf{0}$ *or* the objective function is *strictly* concave.

It is of interest to note that this equivalent problem is one example of the **linear complementarity problem** introduced in Sec. 14.3 (see Prob. 13), where the last preceding equation is the **complementarity constraint**.

Now notice the key fact that, with the exception of the complementarity constraint, these KKT conditions are nothing more than *linear programming constraints* involving $2(n + m)$ variables. Furthermore, the complementarity constraint simply implies that it is not permissible for *both* complementary variables of any pair to be *basic variables* when considering (nondegenerate) basic feasible solutions. Therefore, the problem reduces to finding an *initial basic feasible solution* to any linear programming problem that has these constraints, subject to this additional restriction on the identity of the basic variables. (This initial basic feasible solution may be the only feasible solution in this case.)

As we discussed in Sec. 4.6, finding such an initial basic feasible solution is relatively straightforward. In the simple case where $\mathbf{c}^T \leq \mathbf{0}$ (unlikely) and $\mathbf{b} \geq \mathbf{0}$, the initial basic variables are the elements of $\mathbf{y}$ and $\mathbf{v}$ (multiply through the first set of equations by -1), so that the desired solution is $\mathbf{x} = \mathbf{0}, \mathbf{u} = \mathbf{0}, \mathbf{y} = -\mathbf{c}^T, \mathbf{v} = \mathbf{b}$. Otherwise, you need to revise the problem by introducing an *artificial variable* into each of the equations where $c_j > 0$ (add the variable on the left) or $b_i < 0$ (subtract the variable on the left and then multiply through by -1) in order to use these artificial variables (call them z_1, z_2, and so on) as initial basic variables for the revised problem. (Note that this choice of initial basic variables satisfies the *complementarity constraint*, because as nonbasic variables $\mathbf{x} = \mathbf{0}$ and $\mathbf{u} = \mathbf{0}$ automatically.) Next, use *phase 1* of the *two-phase method* (see Sec. 4.6) to find a basic feasible solution for the real problem; i.e., apply the simplex method (with one modification) to the following linear programming problem.

$$\text{Minimize} \quad Z = \sum_j z_j,$$

subject to the preceding linear programming constraints with these artificial variables included. The one modification is the following change in the procedure for selecting an *entering basic variable*.

RESTRICTED ENTRY RULE When choosing an entering basic variable, exclude from consideration any nonbasic variable whose *complementary variable* already is a basic variable; the choice should be made from among the *other* nonbasic variables according to the usual criterion for the simplex method.

This rule keeps the complementarity constraint satisfied throughout the course of the algorithm. When an optimal solution

$$\mathbf{x}^*, \mathbf{u}^*, \mathbf{y}^*, \mathbf{v}^*, z_1 = 0, \dots, z_n = 0$$

is obtained for this problem, $\mathbf{x}^*$ is the desired optimal solution for the original quadratic programming problem.

EXAMPLE We shall now illustrate this approach on the following problem.

$$\text{Maximize} \quad f(x_1, x_2) = 15x_1 + 30x_2 + 4x_1x_2 - 2x_1^2 - 4x_2^2,$$

subject to

$$x_1 + 2x_2 \le 30$$

and

$$x_1 \ge 0, \qquad x_2 \ge 0.$$

As we can verify from the results in Appendix 1 [see Prob. 41(a)], $f(x_1, x_2)$ is *strictly concave*; i.e.,

$$\mathbf{Q} = \begin{bmatrix} 4 & -4 \\ -4 & 8 \end{bmatrix}$$

is *positive definite*, so the algorithm can be applied. If we calculate the KKT conditions and introduce the needed artificial variables, the linear programming problem to be addressed *explicitly* by the *modified simplex method* is

$$\text{Minimize} \quad Z = z_1 + z_2,$$

subject to

$$
\begin{aligned}
4x_1 - 4x_2 + u_1 - y_1 & & + z_1 & = 15 \\
-4x_1 + 8x_2 + 2u_1 & - y_2 & + z_2 & = 30 \\
x_1 + 2x_2 & & + v_1 & = 30,
\end{aligned}
$$

and

$$x_1 \ge 0, x_2 \ge 0, u_1 \ge 0, y_1 \ge 0, y_2 \ge 0, v_1 \ge 0, z_1 \ge 0, z_2 \ge 0.$$

The additional *complementarity constraint*,

$$x_1 y_1 + x_2 y_2 + u_1 v_1 = 0,$$

is not included explicitly, because the algorithm *automatically* enforces this constraint because of the *restricted entry rule*. In particular, for each of the three pairs of *complementary variables*—(x_1, y_1), (x_2, y_2), (u_1, v_1)—whenever one of the two variables already is a basic variable, the other variable is *excluded* as a candidate to be the entering basic variable. Remember that the only *nonzero* variables are basic variables. Because the initial set of basic variables for the linear programming problem—z_1, z_2, v_1—gives an initial basic feasible solution that satisfies the complementarity constraint, there is no way that this constraint can be violated by any subsequent basic feasible solution.

Table 14.4 shows the results of applying the *modified simplex method* to this problem. The first simplex tableau exhibits the initial system of equations *after* converting from minimizing Z to maximizing $(-Z)$ *and* algebraically eliminating the initial basic variables from Eq. (0), just as was done for the *modified example* in Sec. 4.6. The three iterations proceed just as for the regular simplex method, *except* for eliminating certain candidates to be the entering basic variable because of the *restricted entry rule*. In the first tableau, u_1 is eliminated as a candidate because its *complementary variable* (v_1) already is a basic variable (but x_2 would

Table 14.4 **Application of modified simplex method to quadratic programming example**

Iteration	Basic variable	Eq. no.	Z	x_1	x_2	u_1	y_1	y_2	v_1	z_1	z_2	Right side
0	Z	0	-1	0	-4	-3	1	1	0	0	0	-45
	z_1	1	0	4	-4	1	-1	0	0	1	0	15
	z_2	2	0	-4	8	2	0	-1	0	0	1	30
	v_1	3	0	1	2	0	0	0	1	0	0	30
1	Z	0	-1	-2	0	-2	1	$\frac{1}{2}$	0	0	$\frac{1}{2}$	-30
	z_1	1	0	2	0	2	-1	$-\frac{1}{2}$	0	1	$\frac{1}{2}$	30
	x_2	2	0	$-\frac{1}{2}$	1	$\frac{1}{4}$	0	$-\frac{1}{8}$	0	0	$\frac{1}{8}$	$3\frac{3}{4}$
	v_1	3	0	2	0	$-\frac{1}{2}$	0	$\frac{1}{4}$	1	0	$-\frac{1}{4}$	$22\frac{1}{2}$
2	Z	0	-1	0	0	$-\frac{5}{2}$	1	$\frac{3}{4}$	1	0	$\frac{1}{4}$	$-7\frac{1}{2}$
	z_1	1	0	0	0	$\frac{5}{2}$	-1	$-\frac{3}{4}$	-1	1	$\frac{3}{4}$	$7\frac{1}{2}$
	x_2	2	0	0	1	$\frac{1}{8}$	0	$-\frac{1}{16}$	$\frac{1}{4}$	0	$\frac{1}{16}$	$9\frac{3}{8}$
	x_1	3	0	1	0	$-\frac{1}{4}$	0	$\frac{1}{8}$	$\frac{1}{2}$	0	$-\frac{1}{8}$	$11\frac{1}{4}$
3	Z	0	-1	0	0	0	0	0	0	1	1	0
	u_1	1	0	0	0	1	$-\frac{2}{5}$	$-\frac{3}{10}$	$-\frac{2}{5}$	$\frac{2}{5}$	$\frac{3}{10}$	3
	x_2	2	0	0	1	0	$\frac{1}{20}$	$-\frac{1}{40}$	$\frac{3}{10}$	$-\frac{1}{20}$	$\frac{1}{40}$	9
	x_1	3	0	1	0	0	$-\frac{1}{10}$	$\frac{1}{20}$	$\frac{2}{5}$	$\frac{1}{10}$	$-\frac{1}{20}$	12

have been chosen anyway because $-4 < -3$). In the second tableau, both u_1 and y_2 are eliminated as candidates (because v_1 and x_2 are basic variables), so x_1 automatically is chosen as the only candidate with a negative coefficient in row 0 (whereas the *regular* simplex method would have permitted choosing *either* x_1 or u_1 because they are tied for having the largest negative coefficient). In the third tableau, both y_1 and y_2 are eliminated (because x_1 and x_2 are basic variables). However, u_1 is *not* eliminated because v_1 no longer is a basic variable, so u_1 is chosen as the entering basic variable in the usual way.

The resulting optimal solution for this problem is $x_1 = 12$, $x_2 = 9$, $u_1 = 3$, with the rest of the variables zero. (Prob. 41c asks you to verify that this solution is optimal by showing that $x_1 = 12, x_2 = 9, u_1 = 3$ satisfy the KKT conditions for the original problem when they are written in the form given in Sec. 14.6.) Therefore, the optimal solution for the quadratic programming problem (which includes only the x_1 and x_2 variables) is $(x_1, x_2) = (12, 9)$.

14.8 Separable Programming

The preceding section showed how one class of nonlinear programming problems can be solved by an extension of the *simplex method*. We now consider another class, called *separable programming*, that actually can be solved by the simplex method itself, because any such problem can be approximated as closely as desired by a *linear programming* problem with a larger number of variables.

As indicated in Sec. 14.3, separable programming assumes that the objective function $f(\mathbf{x})$ is *concave*, that *each* of the constraint functions $g_i(\mathbf{x})$ is *convex*, and that *all* of these functions are *separable functions* (functions where *each* term involves just a *single* variable). However, in order to simplify the discussion, we focus here on the special case where the convex and separable $g_i(\mathbf{x})$ are, in fact, *linear functions*, just as for linear programming. Thus only the objective function requires special treatment.

Under the preceding assumptions, the objective function can be expressed as a *sum* of *concave* functions of individual variables,

$$f(\mathbf{x}) = \sum_{j=1}^{n} f_j(x_j),$$

so that each $f_j(x_j)$ has a shape such as the one shown in Fig. 14.12 (either case) over the feasible range of values of x_j.[1] Because $f(\mathbf{x})$ represents the measure of performance (say *profit*) for all of the activities together, $f_j(x_j)$ represents the *contribution to profit* from activity j when it is conducted at the level x_j. The condition of $f(\mathbf{x})$ being *separable* simply implies *additivity* (see Sec. 3.3); i.e., there are no interactions between the activities (no cross-product terms) that affect total profit beyond their independent contributions. The assumption that each $f_j(x_j)$ is concave says that the *marginal profitability* (slope of the profit curve) either stays the same or decreases (*never* increases) as x_j is increased.

Concave profit curves occur quite frequently. For example, it may be possible to sell a limited amount of some product at a certain price, and then a further amount at a lower price, and perhaps finally a further amount at a still lower price. Similarly, it may be necessary to purchase raw materials from increasingly expensive sources. Another common situation is where a more expensive production process must be used (e.g., overtime rather than regular-time work) to increase the production rate beyond a certain point.

These kinds of situations can lead to either type of profit curve shown in Fig. 14.12. In case 1, the slope decreases only at certain *breakpoints*, so that $f_j(x_j)$ is a *piecewise linear function* (a sequence of connected line segments). For case 2, the slope may decrease continuously as x_j increases, so that $f_j(x_j)$ is a general concave function. Any such function can be approximated as closely as desired by a piecewise linear function, and this kind of approximation is used as needed for separable programming problems. (Figure 14.12 shows an approximating function that consists of just three line segments, but the approximation can be made even better just by introducing additional breakpoints.) This approximation is very convenient because a piecewise linear function of a single variable can be rewritten as a *linear function* of several variables, with one special restriction on the values of these variables, as described next.

REFORMULATION AS A LINEAR PROGRAMMING PROBLEM

The key to rewriting a piecewise linear function as a linear function is to use a separate variable for each line segment. To illustrate, consider the piecewise linear

---

[1] $f(\mathbf{x})$ is concave if any only if *every* $f_j(x_j)$ is concave.

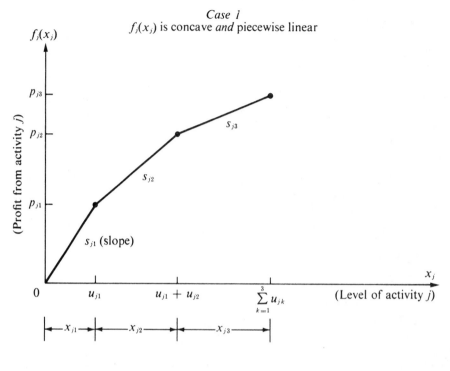

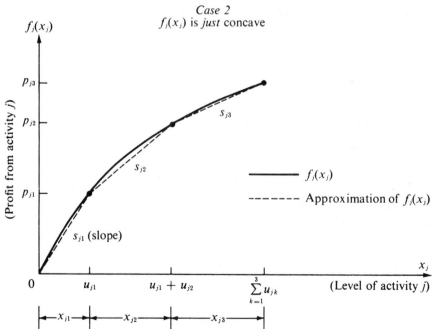

Figure 14.12 **Shape of profit curves for separable programming.**

function $f_j(x_j)$ shown in Fig. 14.12, case 1 (or its approximation for case 2), which has three line segments over the feasible range of values of x_j. Introduce the three new variables—x_{j1}, x_{j2}, x_{j3}—and set

$$x_j = x_{j1} + x_{j2} + x_{j3},$$

where

$$0 \le x_{j1} \le u_{j1}, \qquad 0 \le x_{j2} \le u_{j2}, \qquad 0 \le x_{j3} \le u_{j3}.$$

Then use the slopes—s_{j1}, s_{j2}, s_{j3}—to rewrite $f_j(x_j)$ as

$$f_j(x_j) = s_{j1}x_{j1} + s_{j2}x_{j2} + s_{j3}x_{j3},$$

with the *special restriction* that

$$x_{j2} = 0 \quad \text{whenever} \quad x_{j1} < u_{j1},$$
$$x_{j3} = 0 \quad \text{whenever} \quad x_{j2} < u_{j2}.$$

To see why this special restriction is required, suppose that $x_j = 1$, where $u_{jk} > 1$ ($k = 1,2,3$), so that $f_j(1) = s_{j1}$. Note that

$$x_{j1} + x_{j2} + x_{j3} = 1$$

permits

$$x_{j1} = 1, \qquad x_{j2} = 0, \qquad x_{j3} = 0 \Rightarrow f_j(1) = s_{j1},$$
$$x_{j1} = 0, \qquad x_{j2} = 1, \qquad x_{j3} = 0 \Rightarrow f_j(1) = s_{j2},$$
$$x_{j1} = 0, \qquad x_{j2} = 0, \qquad x_{j3} = 1 \Rightarrow f_j(1) = s_{j3},$$

and so on, where

$$s_{j1} > s_{j2} > s_{j3}.$$

However, the special restriction permits only the first possibility, which is the only one giving the correct value for $f_j(1)$.

Unfortunately, the *special restriction* does not fit into the required format for linear programming constraints, so *some* piecewise linear functions cannot be rewritten in a linear programming format. However, *our* $f_j(x_j)$ are assumed to be concave, so $s_{j1} > s_{j2} > \dots$, so that an algorithm for maximizing $f(\mathbf{x})$ *automatically* gives the highest priority to using x_{j1} when (in effect) increasing x_j from zero, the next highest priority to using x_{j2}, and so on, without even including the special restriction explicitly in the model. This observation leads to the following key property.

KEY PROPERTY OF SEPARABLE PROGRAMMING When $f(\mathbf{x})$ and the $g_i(\mathbf{x})$ satisfy the assumptions of separable programming, and when the resulting piecewise linear functions are rewritten as linear functions, deleting the *special restriction* gives a *linear programming model* whose optimal solution automatically satisfies the special restriction.

We shall elaborate further on the logic behind this key property later in this section in the context of a specific example. (Also see Prob. 50a.)

To write down the complete linear programming model using the above notation, let n_j be the number of line segments in $f_j(x_j)$ (or the piecewise linear function approximating it), so that

$$x_j = \sum_{k=1}^{n_j} x_{jk}$$

would be substituted throughout the original model and

$$f_j(x_j) = \sum_{k=1}^{n_j} s_{jk} x_{jk}$$

would be substituted into the objective function for $j = 1, 2, \ldots, n$.[1] The resulting model is

$$\text{Maximize} \quad Z = \sum_{j=1}^{n} \left(\sum_{k=1}^{n_j} s_{jk} x_{jk} \right),$$

subject to

$$\sum_{j=1}^{n} a_{ij} \left(\sum_{k=1}^{n_j} x_{jk} \right) \le b_i, \quad \text{for } i = 1, 2, \ldots, m$$

$$x_{jk} \le u_{jk}, \quad \text{for } k = 1, 2, \ldots, n_j \quad \text{and} \quad j = 1, 2, \ldots, n,$$

and

$$x_{jk} \ge 0, \quad \text{for } k = 1, 2, \ldots, n_j \quad \text{and} \quad j = 1, 2, \ldots, n.$$

(The $\sum_{k=1}^{n_j} x_{jk} \ge 0$ constraints are deleted because they are ensured by the $x_{jk} \ge 0$ constraints.) If some original variable x_j has no upper bound, then $u_{jn_j} = \infty$, so the constraint involving this quantity would be deleted.

The most efficient way of solving this model is to use the streamlined version of the simplex method for dealing with *upper bound constraints* mentioned at the end of Sec. 7.5 (and described in Sec. 9.1). After obtaining an optimal solution for this model, you then would calculate

$$x_j = \sum_{k=1}^{n_j} x_{jk},$$

for $j = 1, 2, \ldots, n$ in order to identify an optimal solution for the original separable programming program (or its piecewise linear approximation).

EXAMPLE The Wyndor Glass Co. (see Sec. 3.1) has received a special order for handcrafted goods to be made in Plants 1 and 2 throughout the next 4 months. Filling this order will require borrowing certain employees from the work crews

---

[1] If one or more of the $f_j(x_j)$ already are *linear functions*, $f_j(x_j) = c_j x_j$, then $n_j = 1$ so neither of these substitutions would be made for the j.

for the regular products, so the remaining workers would need to work overtime to utilize the full production capacity of the plant's machinery and equipment for these regular products. In particular, for the two new regular products discussed in Sec. 3.1, overtime would be required to utilize the last 25 percent of the production capacity available in Plant 1 for product 1, and for the last 50 percent of the capacity available in Plant 2 for product 2. The additional cost of using overtime work would reduce the profit for each unit involved from $3 to $2 for product 1, and from $5 to $1 for product 2, giving the *profit curves* of Fig. 14.13, both of which fit the form for case 1 of Fig. 14.12.

Management has decided to go ahead and use overtime work rather than hire additional workers during this temporary situation. However, it does insist that the work crew for each product be fully utilized on regular time before any overtime is used. Furthermore, it feels that the current production rates ($x_1 = 2$ for product 1 and $x_2 = 6$ for product 2) should be changed temporarily if this would improve overall profitability. Therefore, it has instructed the O.R. Department to review products 1 and 2 again to determine the most profitable product mix during the next 4 months.

FORMULATION At first glance it may appear straightforward to modify the Wyndor Glass Co. linear programming model in Sec. 3.1 to fit this new situation. In particular, let the production rate for product 1 be $x_1 = x_{1R} + x_{1O}$, where x_{1R} is the production rate achieved on regular time and x_{1O} is the incremental

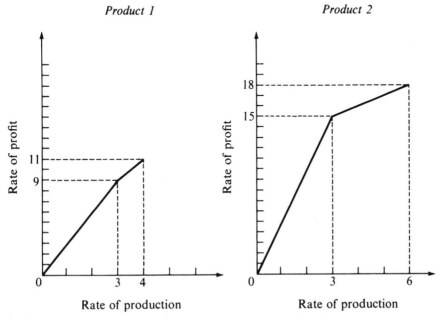

Figure 14.13 **Profit data during the next 4 months for the Wyndor Glass Co.**

production rate from using overtime. Define $x_2 = x_{2R} + x_{2O}$ in the same way for product 2. Thus $n = 2$, $n_1 = 2$, and $n_2 = 2$ in the preceding general model. The new linear programming problem is to determine the values of $x_{1R}, x_{1O}, x_{2R}, x_{2O}$ so as to

$$\text{Maximize} \quad Z = 3x_{1R} + 2x_{1O} + 5x_{2R} + x_{2O},$$

subject to

$$
\begin{aligned}
x_{1R} & \quad & \leq 3 \\
& x_{1O} & \leq 1 \\
& 2x_{2R} & \leq 6 \\
& 2x_{2O} \leq 6 \\
3(x_{1R} + x_{1O}) + 2(x_{2R} + x_{2O}) & \leq 18
\end{aligned}
$$

and

$$x_{1R} \geq 0, \qquad x_{1O} \geq 0, \qquad x_{2R} \geq 0, \qquad x_{2O} \geq 0.$$

However, there is one important factor that is not taken into account explicitly in this formulation. Specifically, there is nothing in the model that requires all available regular time for a product to be fully utilized before any overtime is used for that product. In other words, it may be feasible to have $x_{1O} > 0$ even when $x_{1R} < 3$ and to have $x_{2O} > 0$ even when $x_{2R} < 3$. Such solutions would not, however, be acceptable to management. (Prohibiting such solutions is the *special restriction* discussed earlier in this section.)

Now we come to the *key property of separable programming.* Even though the model does not take this factor into account explicitly, the model does take it into account implicitly! Despite the model having excess "feasible" solutions that actually are unacceptable, any *optimal* solution for the model is *guaranteed* to be a legitimate one that does not replace any available regular-time work with overtime work. (The reasoning here is analogous to that for the *Big M method* discussed in Sec. 4.6, where excess feasible but *nonoptimal* solutions also were allowed in the model as a matter of convenience.) Therefore, the simplex method can be safely applied to this model to find the most profitable acceptable product mix. The reason is twofold. First, the two decision variables for each product *always* appear together as a *sum*, $(x_{1R} + x_{1O})$ or $(x_{2R} + x_{2O})$, in *each* functional constraint (one in this case) other than the upper bound constraints on individual variables. Therefore, it *always* is possible to convert an unacceptable feasible solution to an acceptable one having the same total production rates, $x_1 = x_{1R} + x_{1O}$ and $x_2 = x_{2R} + x_{2O}$, merely by replacing overtime production by regular-time production as much as possible. Secondly, overtime production is less profitable than regular-time production (i.e., the *slope* of each profit curve in Fig. 14.13 is a monotonically *decreasing* function of the rate of production), so converting an unacceptable feasible solution to an acceptable one in this way *must* increase the total rate of profit Z. Consequently, any feasible solution that uses overtime production for a product when regular-time production is still available *cannot* be optimal with respect to the model.

For example, consider the unacceptable feasible solution $x_{1R} = 1$, $x_{1O} = 1$, $x_{2R} = 1$, $x_{2O} = 3$, which yields a total rate of profit $Z = 13$. The acceptable way of achieving the same total production rates $x_1 = 2$ and $x_2 = 4$ is $x_{1R} = 2$, $x_{1O} = 0$, $x_{2R} = 3$, $x_{2O} = 1$. This latter solution is still feasible, but it also increases Z by $(3 - 2)(1) + (5 - 1)(2) = 9$.

Similarly, the optimal solution for this model turns out to be $x_{1R} = 3$, $x_{1O} = 1$, $x_{2R} = 3$, $x_{2O} = 0$, which is an acceptable feasible solution.

Notice that most of the functional constraints in the model are *upper bound constraints*, i.e., constraints that simply specify the maximum value allowed for an individual variable. When a computer code is available for the special streamlined version of the simplex method for dealing with such constraints (see Secs. 7.5 and 9.1), it provides a very efficient way of solving even extremely large problems of this type.

EXTENSIONS

Thus far we have focused on the special case of separable programming where the only nonlinear function is the objective function $f(\mathbf{x})$. Now consider briefly the general case where the constraint functions $g_i(\mathbf{x})$ need not be linear, but are convex and separable, so that each $g_i(\mathbf{x})$ can be expressed as a sum of functions of individual variables,

$$g_i(\mathbf{x}) = \sum_{j=1}^{n} g_{ij}(x_j),$$

where each $g_{ij}(x_j)$ is a *convex* function. Once again, each of these new functions may be approximated as closely as desired by a *piecewise linear* function (if it is not already in that form). The one new restriction is that for each variable x_j ($j = 1, 2, \ldots, n$), all of the piecewise linear approximations of the functions of this variable $[f_j(x_j), g_{1j}(x_j), \ldots, g_{mj}(x_j)]$ must have the *same* breakpoints so that the same new variables $(x_{j1}, x_{j2}, \ldots, x_{jn_j})$ can be used for all of these piecewise linear functions. This formulation leads to a linear programming model just like the one given for the special case except that for each i and j, and x_{jk} variables now have different coefficients in constraint i [where these coefficients are the corresponding slopes of the piecewise linear function approximating $g_{ij}(x_j)$]. Because the $g_{ij}(x_j)$ are required to be convex, essentially the same logic as before implies that the *key property of separable programming* still must hold. (See Prob. 50(b).)

One drawback of approximating functions by piecewise linear functions as described in this section is that achieving a close approximation requires a large number of line segments (variables), whereas such a fine grid for the breakpoints is needed only in the immediate neighborhood of an optimal solution. Therefore, more sophisticated approaches that use a succession of *two-segment* piecewise linear functions have been developed[1] to obtain *successively closer*

---

[1] Meyer, R.R.: "Two-Segment Separable Programming," *Management Science*, **25**:385–395, 1979.

approximations within this immediate neighborhood. This kind of approach tends to be both *faster* and *more accurate* in closely approximating an optimal solution.

14.9 Convex Programming

We already have discussed some special cases of convex programming in Secs. 14.4 and 14.5 (unconstrained problems), 14.7 (quadratic objective function with linear constraints), and 14.8 (separable functions). You also have seen some theory for the general case (necessary and sufficient conditions for optimality) in Sec. 14.6. In this section, we briefly discuss some of the types of approaches used to solve the general convex programming problem (where the objective function $f(\mathbf{x})$ to be maximized is concave and the $g_i(\mathbf{x})$ constraint functions are convex) and then present one example of an algorithm for convex programming.

There is no single standard algorithm that always is used to solve convex programming problems. Many different algorithms have been developed, each with its own advantages and disadvantages, and research continues to be active in this area. Roughly speaking, most of these algorithms fall into one of the following three categories.

One category is **gradient algorithms**, where the *gradient search procedure* of Sec. 14.5 is modified in some way to keep the search path from penetrating any constraint boundary. For example, one popular gradient method is the *generalized reduced gradient* (GRG) method.[1]

The second category—**sequential unconstrained algorithms**—includes *penalty function* and *barrier function* methods. These algorithms convert the original constrained optimization problem into a sequence of *unconstrained optimization* problems whose optimal solutions converge to the optimal solution for the original problem. Each of these unconstrained optimization problems can be solved by the *gradient search procedure* of Sec. 14.5. This conversion is accomplished by incorporating the constraints into a *penalty function* (or *barrier function*) that is subtracted from the objective function in order to impose large penalties for violating constraints (or even being near constraint boundaries). You will see one example of this category of algorithms in the next section.

A third category—**sequential-approximation algorithms**—includes *linear-approximation* and *quadratic-approximation* methods. These algorithms replace the nonlinear objective function by a succession of linear or quadratic approximations. For linearly constrained optimization problems, these approximations allow repeated application of linear or quadratic programming algorithms. This work is accompanied by other analysis that yields a sequence of solutions that converges to an optimal solution for the original problem. Although these algorithms are particularly suitable for linearly constrained

[1] Lasdon, L. S., and A. D. Warren: "Generalized Reduced Gradient Software for Linearly and Nonlinearly Constrained Problems," in H. G. Greenberg (ed.), *Design and Implementation of Optimization Software*, Sijthoff and Noordhoff, Alphem aan den Rijn, The Netherlands, 1978.

optimization problems, some of them also can be extended to problems with nonlinear constraint functions by the use of appropriate linear approximations.

As one example of a *sequential-approximation* algorithm, we present here the **Frank-Wolfe algorithm**[1] for the case of *linearly constrained* convex programming (so the constraints are $\mathbf{Ax} \le \mathbf{b}$, $\mathbf{x} \ge \mathbf{0}$ in matrix form). This procedure is particularly straightforward; it combines *linear* approximations of the objective function (enabling us to use the simplex method) with the one-dimensional search procedure of Sec. 14.4.

A SEQUENTIAL-LINEAR-APPROXIMATION ALGORITHM (FRANK-WOLFE)

Given a feasible trial solution $\mathbf{x}'$, the linear approximation used for the objective function $f(\mathbf{x})$ is the first-order Taylor's series expansion of $f(\mathbf{x})$ around $\mathbf{x} = \mathbf{x}'$, namely,

$$f(\mathbf{x}) \approx f(\mathbf{x}') + \sum_{j=1}^{n} \frac{\partial f(\mathbf{x}')}{\partial x_j}(x_j - x'_j) = f(\mathbf{x}') + \nabla f(\mathbf{x}')(\mathbf{x} - \mathbf{x}').$$

Because $f(\mathbf{x}')$ and $\nabla f(\mathbf{x}')\mathbf{x}'$ have fixed values, they can be dropped to give an equivalent linear objective function,

$$g(\mathbf{x}) = \nabla f(\mathbf{x}')\mathbf{x}.$$

The simplex method (or the graphical procedure if $n = 2$) then is applied to the resulting *linear programming* problem to find *its* optimal solution $\mathbf{x}_{LP}$. Note that the linear objective function necessarily increases steadily as one moves along the line segment from $\mathbf{x}'$ to $\mathbf{x}_{LP}$ (which is on the boundary of the feasible region). However, the linear approximation may not be a particularly close one for $\mathbf{x}$ far from $\mathbf{x}'$, so the *nonlinear* objective function may not continue to increase all the way from $\mathbf{x}'$ to $\mathbf{x}_{LP}$. Therefore, rather than just accepting $\mathbf{x}_{LP}$ as the next trial solution, we choose the point that maximizes the nonlinear objective function along this line segment. This point may be found by conducting the *one-dimensional search procedure* of Sec. 14.4, where the one variable for purposes of this search is the fraction t of the total distance from $\mathbf{x}'$ to $\mathbf{x}_{LP}$. This point then becomes the new trial solution for initiating the next iteration of the algorithm, as just described. The sequence of trial solutions generated by repeated iterations converges to an optimal solution for the original problem, so the algorithm stops as soon as the successive trial solutions are close enough together to have essentially reached this optimal solution.

Summary of Frank-Wolfe Algorithm

Initialization step Find a feasible initial trial solution $\mathbf{x}^{(0)}$, e.g., by applying linear programming procedures to find an initial basic feasible solution. Set $k = 1$.

---

[1] Frank, M., and P. Wolfe: "An Algorithm for Quadratic Programming," *Naval Research Logistics Quarterly*, **3**:95–110, 1956. Although originally designed for quadratic programming, this algorithm is easily adapted to the case of a general concave objective function considered here.

Iterative step

Part 1.   For $j = 1, 2, \ldots, n$, evaluate

$$\frac{\partial f(\mathbf{x})}{\partial x_j} \quad \text{at } \mathbf{x} = \mathbf{x}^{(k-1)} \quad \text{and set} \quad c_j = \frac{\partial f(\mathbf{x})}{\partial x_j}.$$

Part 2.   Find an optimal solution $\mathbf{x}_{LP}^{(k)}$ to the following linear programming problem.

$$\text{Maximize} \quad g(\mathbf{x}) = \sum_{j=1}^{n} c_j x_j,$$

subject to

$$\mathbf{Ax} \leq \mathbf{b} \quad \text{and} \quad \mathbf{x} \geq \mathbf{0}.$$

Part 3.   For the variable t ($0 \leq t \leq 1$), set

$$h(t) = f(\mathbf{x}) \quad \text{for } \mathbf{x} = \mathbf{x}^{(k-1)} + t(\mathbf{x}_{LP}^{(k)} - \mathbf{x}^{(k-1)}).$$

Use some procedure such as the one-dimensional search procedure (see Sec. 14.4) to maximize $h(t)$ over $0 \leq t \leq 1$, and set $\mathbf{x}^{(k)}$ equal to the corresponding $\mathbf{x}$. Go to the stopping rule.

Stopping rule   If $\mathbf{x}^{(k-1)}$ and $\mathbf{x}^{(k)}$ are sufficiently close, stop and use $\mathbf{x}^{(k)}$ (or some extrapolation of $\mathbf{x}^{(0)}, \mathbf{x}^{(1)}, \ldots, \mathbf{x}^{(k-1)}, \mathbf{x}^{(k)}$) as your estimate of an optimal solution. Otherwise, reset $k = k + 1$ and return to the iterative step.

Now let us illustrate this procedure.

EXAMPLE   Consider the following linearly constrained convex programming problem.

$$\text{Maximize} \quad f(\mathbf{x}) = 5x_1 - x_1^2 + 8x_2 - 2x_2^2,$$

subject to

$$3x_1 + 2x_2 \leq 6$$

and

$$x_1 \geq 0, \quad x_2 \geq 0.$$

Note that

$$\frac{\partial f}{\partial x_1} = 5 - 2x_1, \quad \frac{\partial f}{\partial x_2} = 8 - 4x_2,$$

so that the *unconstrained* maximum, $\mathbf{x} = (\frac{5}{2}, 2)$, violates the functional constraint. Thus more work is needed to find the *constrained* maximum.

Because $\mathbf{x} = (0, 0)$ is clearly feasible (and corresponds to the initial basic feasible solution for the linear programming constraints), let us choose it as the initial trial solution $\mathbf{x}^{(0)}$ for the Frank-Wolfe algorithm. Plugging $x_1 = 0$ and

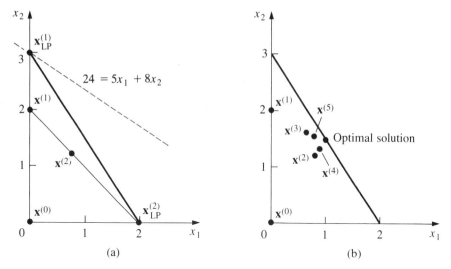

Figure 14.14 **Illustration of the Frank-Wolfe algorithm.**

$x_2 = 0$ into the expressions for the partial derivatives gives $c_1 = 5$ and $c_2 = 8$, so that $g(\mathbf{x}) = 5x_1 + 8x_2$ is the initial linear approximation of the objective function. Graphically solving this linear programming problem (see Fig. 14.14a) yields $\mathbf{x}_{LP}^{(1)} = (0, 3)$. For part 3 of the iterative step, the points on the line segment between $(0, 0)$ and $(0, 3)$ shown in Fig. 14.14a are expressed by

$$(x_1, x_2) = (0, 0) + t[(0, 3) - (0, 0)] \quad \text{for} \quad 0 \le t \le 1$$
$$= (0, 3t) \quad \text{for} \quad 0 \le t \le 1.$$

as shown in the sixth column of Table 14.5. This expression then gives

$$h(t) = f(0, 3t) = 8(3t) - 2(3t)^2$$
$$= 24t - 18t^2,$$

so that the value $t = t^*$ that maximizes $h(t)$ over $0 \le t \le 1$ may be obtained in this case by setting

$$\frac{dh(t)}{dt} = 24 - 36t = 0,$$

Table 14.5 **Application of Frank-Wolfe algorithm to example**

k	$\mathbf{x}^{(k-1)}$	c_1	c_2	$\mathbf{x}_{LP}^{(k)}$	$\mathbf{x}$ for $h(t)$	$h(t)$	t^*	$\mathbf{x}^{(k)}$
1	$(0, 0)$	5	8	$(0, 3)$	$(0, 3t)$	$24t - 18t^2$	$\dfrac{2}{3}$	$(0, 2)$
2	$(0, 2)$	5	0	$(2, 0)$	$(2t, 2 - 2t)$	$8 + 10t - 12t^2$	$\dfrac{5}{12}$	$\left(\dfrac{5}{6}, \dfrac{7}{6}\right)$

so that $t^* = \frac{2}{3}$. This result yields the next trial solution,

$$\mathbf{x}^{(1)} = (0,0) + \tfrac{2}{3}[(0,3) - (0,0)]$$
$$= (0,2),$$

which completes the first iteration.

To sketch the calculations that lead to the results in the second row of Table 14.5, note that $\mathbf{x}^{(1)} = (0,2)$ gives

$$c_1 = 5 - 2(0) = 5,$$
$$c_2 = 8 - 2(2)^2 = 0.$$

For the objective function, $g(\mathbf{x}) = 5x_1$, graphically solving the problem over the feasible region in Fig. 14.14a gives $\mathbf{x}_{LP}^{(2)} = (2,0)$. Therefore, the expression for the line segment between $\mathbf{x}^{(1)}$ and $\mathbf{x}_{LP}^{(2)}$ (see Fig. 14.14a) is

$$\mathbf{x} = (0,2) + t[(2,0) - (0,2)]$$
$$= (2t, 2 - 2t),$$

so that

$$h(t) = f(2t, 2 - 2t)$$
$$= 5(2t) - (2t)^2 + 8(2 - 2t) - 2(2 - 2t)^2$$
$$= 8 + 10t - 12t^2.$$

Setting

$$\frac{dh(t)}{dt} = 10 - 24t = 0$$

yields $t^* = \frac{5}{12}$. Hence

$$\mathbf{x}^{(2)} = (0,2) + \frac{5}{12}[(2,0) - (0,2)]$$

$$= \left(\frac{5}{6}, \frac{7}{6}\right).$$

You can see in Fig. 14.14b how the trial solutions keep alternating between two trajectories that appear to intersect at approximately the point $\mathbf{x} = (1, \frac{3}{2})$. This point is, in fact, the optimal solution, as can be verified by applying the *KKT conditions* from Sec. 14.6.

This example illustrates a common feature of the Frank-Wolfe algorithm, namely, that the trial solutions alternate between two (or more) trajectories. When they alternate in this way, we can extrapolate the trajectories to their approximate point of intersection to estimate an optimal solution. This estimate tends to be better than using the last trial solution generated. The reason is that the trial solutions tend to converge rather slowly toward an optimal solution, so the last trial solution may still be quite far from optimal.

In conclusion, we should emphasize that the Frank-Wolfe algorithm is just one example of sequential-approximation algorithms. Many of these algorithms use *quadratic* instead of *linear* approximations at each iteration because quadratic approximations provide a considerably closer fit to the original problem and thus enable the sequence of solutions to converge considerably more rapidly toward an optimal solution than was the case in Fig. 14.14*b*. For this reason, even though sequential-linear-approximation methods such as the Frank-Wolfe algorithm are relatively straightforward to use, *sequential-quadratic-approximation methods*[1] now are generally preferred in actual applications. Popular among these are the so-called *quasi-Newton* (or *variable metric*) methods, which compute a quadratic approximation to the curvature of a nonlinear function without explicitly calculating second (partial) derivatives. (For linearly constrained optimization problems, this nonlinear function is just the objective function, whereas with nonlinear constraints, it is the Lagrangian function described in Appendix 2.) Some quasi-Newton algorithms don't even explicitly form and solve an approximating quadratic programming problem at each iteration, but instead incorporate some of the basic ingredients of *gradient algorithms*.

For further information about the state-of-the-art in convex programming algorithms, see Selected References 6 and 7.

14.10 Nonconvex Programming

The assumptions of convex programming are very convenient ones, because they ensure that any *local maximum* also is a *global maximum*. Unfortunately, the nonlinear programming problems that arise in practice frequently only come fairly close to satisfying these assumptions, but they have some relatively minor disparities. What kind of approach can be used to deal with such *nonconvex programming* problems?

A common approach is to apply an algorithmic *search procedure* that will stop when it finds a *local maximum* and then to restart it a number of times from a variety of initial trial solutions in order to find as many distinct local maxima as possible. The best of these local maxima is then chosen for implementation. Normally, the search procedure is one that has been designed to find a global maximum when all of the assumptions of convex programming hold, but it also can operate to find a local maximum when they do not.

One such search procedure that has been widely used since its development in the 1960s is the *Sequential Unconstrained Minimization Technique* (or *SUMT* for short).[2] There actually are two main versions of SUMT, one of which is as an

---

[1] For a survey of these methods, see Powell, M. J. D.: "Variable Metric Methods for Constrained Optimization," pp. 288–311, in Bachem, A., M. Grotschel, and B. Korte (eds.): *Mathematical Programming: The State of the Art*, Springer-Verlag, Berlin, Heidelberg, New York, and Tokyo, 1983.

[2] Fiacco, Anthony V., and Garth P. McCormick: *Nonlinear Programming: Sequential Unconstrained Minimization Techniques*, Wiley, New York, 1968.

exterior point algorithm that deals with *infeasible* solutions while using a *penalty function* to force convergence to the feasible region. We shall describe the other version, which is as an *interior point* algorithm that deals directly with *feasible* solutions while using a *barrier function* to force staying inside the feasible region. Although SUMT was originally presented as a *minimization* technique, we shall convert it to a maximization technique in order to be consistent with the rest of the chapter. Therefore, we continue to assume that the problem is in the form given at the beginning of the chapter, and that all of the functions are differentiable.

SEQUENTIAL UNCONSTRAINED MINIMIZATION TECHNIQUE (SUMT)

As the name implies, SUMT replaces the original problem by a *sequence* of *unconstrained* optimization problems whose solutions *converge* to a solution (local maximum) of the original problem. This approach is very attractive because unconstrained optimization problems are much easier to solve (see the *gradient search procedure* in Sec. 14.5) than those with constraints. Each of the unconstrained problems in this sequence involves choosing a (successively smaller) strictly positive value of a scalar r and then solving for $\mathbf{x}$ so as to

$$\text{Maximize} \quad P(\mathbf{x};r) = f(\mathbf{x}) - rB(\mathbf{x}).$$

$B(\mathbf{x})$ is a **barrier function** that has the properties (for $\mathbf{x}$ that are feasible for the original problem) that

1. $B(\mathbf{x})$ is *small* when $\mathbf{x}$ is *far* from the boundary of the feasible region,
2. $B(\mathbf{x})$ is *large* when $\mathbf{x}$ is *close* to the boundary of the feasible region,
3. $B(\mathbf{x}) \to \infty$ as the distance from the (nearest) boundary of the feasible region $\to 0$.

Thus, by starting the search procedure with a *feasible* initial trial solution and then attempting to increase $P(\mathbf{x};r)$, $B(\mathbf{x})$ provides a *barrier* that prevents the search from ever crossing (or even reaching) the boundary of the feasible region for the original problem.

The most common choice of $B(\mathbf{x})$ is

$$B(\mathbf{x}) = \sum_{i=1}^{m} \frac{1}{b_i - g_i(\mathbf{x})} + \sum_{j=1}^{n} \frac{1}{x_j}.$$

For feasible values of $\mathbf{x}$, note that the denominator of each term is proportional to the distance of $\mathbf{x}$ from the constraint boundary for the corresponding functional or nonnegativity constraint. Consequently, *each* term is a *boundary repulsion term* that has all of preceding three properties with respect to this particular constraint boundary. Another attractive feature of this $B(\mathbf{x})$ is that, when all the assumptions of *convex programming* are satisfied, $P(\mathbf{x};r)$ is a *concave* function.

Because $B(\mathbf{x})$ keeps the search away from the boundary of the feasible region, you probably are asking the very legitimate question: What happens if the desired solution lies there? This concern is the reason that SUMT involves solving a *sequence* of these unconstrained optimization problems for successively smaller values of r approaching zero (where the final trial solution from each one becomes the initial trial solution for the next). For example, each new r might be obtained from the preceding one by multiplying by a constant θ ($0 < \theta < 1$), where a typical value is $\theta = 0.01$. As r approaches zero, $P(\mathbf{x};r)$ approaches $f(\mathbf{x})$, so the corresponding local maximum of $P(\mathbf{x};r)$ converges to a local maximum of the original problem. Therefore, it is necessary to solve only enough unconstrained optimization problems to permit extrapolating their solutions to this limiting solution.

How many are enough to permit this extrapolation? When the original problem satisfies the assumptions of *convex programming*, useful information is available to guide us in this decision. In particular, if $\bar{x}$ is a global maximum of $P(\mathbf{x};r)$, then

$$f(\bar{\mathbf{x}}) \leq f(\mathbf{x}^*) \leq f(\bar{\mathbf{x}}) + rB(\bar{\mathbf{x}}),$$

where $\mathbf{x}^*$ is the (unknown) *optimal* solution for the original problem. Thus, $rB(\bar{\mathbf{x}})$ is the *maximum error* (in the value of the objective function) that can result by using $\bar{\mathbf{x}}$ to approximate $\mathbf{x}^*$, and extrapolating beyond $\bar{\mathbf{x}}$ to increase $f(\mathbf{x})$ further decreases this error. If an *error tolerance* is established in advance, then you can stop as soon as $rB(\bar{\mathbf{x}})$ is less than this quantity.

Unfortunately, no such guarantee for the maximum error can be given for *nonconvex programming* problems. However, $rB(\bar{\mathbf{x}})$ still is *likely* to exceed the actual error when $\bar{x}$ and $\mathbf{x}^*$ now are corresponding *local maxima of* $P(\mathbf{x};r)$ and the original problem, respectively.

Summary of SUMT

Initialization step   Identify a *feasible* initial trial solution $\mathbf{x}^{(0)}$ that is not on the boundary of the feasible region. Set $k = 1$ and choose appropriate strictly positive values for the initial r and for $\theta < 1$ (say $r = 1$ and $\theta = 0.01$).[1]

Iterative step   Starting from $\mathbf{x}^{(k-1)}$, apply the *gradient search procedure* described in Sec. 14.5 (or some similar method) to find a *local maximum*, $\mathbf{x}^{(k)}$, of

$$P(\mathbf{x};r) = f(\mathbf{x}) - r\left[\sum_{i=1}^{m} \frac{1}{b_i - g_i(\mathbf{x})} + \sum_{j=1}^{n} \frac{1}{x_j} \right].$$

Stopping rule   If the change from $\mathbf{x}^{(k-1)}$ to $\mathbf{x}^{(k)}$ is negligible, stop and use $\mathbf{x}^{(k)}$ (or an extrapolation of $\mathbf{x}^{(0)}, \mathbf{x}^{(1)}, \ldots, \mathbf{x}^{(k-1)}, \mathbf{x}^{(k)}$) as your estimate of a *local maximum* of the original problem. Otherwise, reset $k = k + 1$ and $r = \theta r$ and return to the iterative step.

When the assumptions of *convex programming* are not satisfied, this algorithm should be repeated a number of times by starting from a variety of

---

[1] A reasonable criterion for choosing the initial r is one that makes $rB(\mathbf{x})$ about the same order of magnitude as $f(\mathbf{x})$ for feasible solutions $\mathbf{x}$ that are not particularly close to the boundary.

feasible initial trial solutions. The best of the *local maxima* thereby obtained for the original problem should be used as the best available approximation of a *global maximum*.

EXAMPLE To illustrate *SUMT*, consider the following two-variable problem.

$$\text{Maximize} \quad f(\mathbf{x}) = x_1 x_2,$$

subject to

$$x_1^2 + x_2 \leq 3$$

and

$$x_1 \geq 0, \qquad x_2 \geq 0.$$

Even though $g_1(\mathbf{x}) = x_1^2 + x_2$ is convex (because each term is convex), this problem is a *nonconvex programming* problem because $f(\mathbf{x}) = x_1 x_2$ is *not* concave (see Appendix 1).

For the initialization step, $(x_1, x_2) = (1, 1)$ is one obvious feasible solution that is not on the boundary of the feasible region, so we can set $\mathbf{x}^{(0)} = (1, 1)$. Reasonable choices for r and θ are $r = 1$ and $\theta = 0.01$.

For the iterative step,

$$P(\mathbf{x};r) = x_1 x_2 - r\left(\frac{1}{3 - x_1^2 - x_2} + \frac{1}{x_1} + \frac{1}{x_2}\right).$$

With $r = 1$, applying the *gradient search procedure* starting from $(1, 1)$ to maximize this expression eventually leads to $\mathbf{x}^{(1)} = (0.90, 1.36)$. Resetting $r = 0.01$ and restarting the gradient search procedure from $(0.90, 1.36)$ then leads to $\mathbf{x}^{(2)} = (0.983, 1.933)$. One more iteration with $r = 0.01(0.01) = 0.00001$ leads from $\mathbf{x}^{(2)}$ to $\mathbf{x}^{(3)} = (0.998, 1.994)$. This sequence of points, summarized in Table 14.6, quite clearly is converging to $(1, 2)$. Applying the *KKT conditions* to this solution verifies that it does indeed satisfy the necessary condition for optimality. Graphical analysis demonstrates that $(x_1, x_2) = (1, 2)$ is, in fact, a *global maximum*. [See Prob. 56(b).]

Table 14.6 **Illustration of SUMT**

k	r	$x_1^{(k)}$	$x_2^{(k)}$
0		1	1
1	1	0.90	1.36
2	10^{-2}	0.983	1.933
3	10^{-4}	0.998	1.994
		$\downarrow$	$\downarrow$
		1	2

For this problem, there are no local maxima other than $(x_1, x_2) = (1, 2)$,[1] so reapplying SUMT from various feasible initial trial solutions always leads to this same solution.

Finally, note that SUMT also can be easily extended to deal with *equality* constraints, $g_i(\mathbf{x}) = b_i$. One standard way is as follows. For each equality constraint,

$$\frac{-[b_i - g_i(\mathbf{x})]^2}{\sqrt{r}} \quad \text{replaces} \quad \frac{-r}{b_i - g_i(\mathbf{x})}$$

in the expression for $P(\mathbf{x}; r)$ given under Summary of SUMT, and then the same procedure is used. The numerator, $-[b_i - g_i(\mathbf{x})]^2$, imposes a large penalty for deviating substantially from satisfying the equality constraint, and then the denominator tremendously increases this penalty as r is decreased to a tiny amount, thereby forcing the sequence of trial solutions to converge toward a point that satisfies the constraint.

SUMT has been widely used because of its simplicity and versatility. However, numerical analysts have found that it is relatively prone to *numerical instability*, so considerable caution is advised. For further information on this issue, as well as similar analyses for alternative algorithms, see Selected Reference 7.

14.11 Conclusions

Practical optimization problems frequently involve *nonlinear* behavior that must be taken into account. It is sometimes possible to *reformulate* these nonlinearities to fit into a linear programming format, as can be done for *separable programming* problems. However, it is frequently necessary to use a *nonlinear programming* formulation.

In contrast to the case of the simplex method for linear programming, there is no efficient all-purpose algorithm that can be used to solve *all* nonlinear programming problems. In fact, some of these problems cannot be solved in a very satisfactory manner by *any* method. However, considerable progress has been made for some important classes of problems, including *quadratic programming*, *convex programming*, and certain special types of *nonconvex programming*. A variety of algorithms that frequently perform well are available for these cases. Some of these algorithms incorporate highly efficient procedures for *unconstrained optimization* for a portion of each iteration, and some use a succession of linear or quadratic approximations to the original problem.

There has been a strong emphasis in recent years on developing high-quality, reliable *software packages* for general use in applying the best of these

---

[1] The technical reason is that $f(\mathbf{x})$ is a (strictly) *quasiconcave* function that shares the property of concave functions that a local maximum always is a global maximum. For further information, see Avriel, Mordecai, W. Erwin Diewert, Siegfried Schaible, and Israel Zang: *Generalized Concavity*, Plenum Publishing Corp., New York, 1985.

algorithms on mainframe computers. (See Selected References 6 and 7.) For example, a highly refined package called MINOS 5.0 has been developed at Stanford University[1] and widely used elsewhere for solving many of the types of problems discussed in this chapter (as well as linear programming problems). The steady improvements being made in both algorithmic techniques and software now are bringing some rather large problems into the range of computational feasibility.

With the current rapid growth in the use and power of personal computers, the next few years should see similar progress in software development for microcomputers.

Research in nonlinear programming remains very active.

SELECTED REFERENCES

1. Avriel, Mordecai: *Nonlinear Programming*: *Analysis and Methods*, Prentice-Hall, Englewood Cliffs, N.J., 1976.
2. Bazaraa, Mokhtar S., and C. M. Shetty: *Nonlinear Programming*: *Theory and Algorithms*, Wiley, New York, 1979.
3. Beightler, Charles S., Don T. Phillips, and Douglas J. Wilde: *Foundations of Optimization*, 2d ed., Prentice-Hall, Englewood Cliffs, N. J., 1979.
4. Bracken, Jerome, and Garth P. McCormick: *Selected Applications of Nonlinear Programming*, Wiley, New York, 1968.
5. Fletcher, R.: *Practical Methods of Optimization, Volume 2, Constrained Optimization*, Wiley, New York, 1981.
6. Gill, Philip E., Walter Murray, Michael A. Saunders, and Margaret H. Wright: "Trends in Nonlinear Programming Software," *European Journal of Operational Research*, **17**: 141–149, 1984.
7. Gill, Philip E., Walter Murray, and Margaret H. Wright: *Practial Optimization*, Academic Press, London, 1981.
8. Luenberger, David G.: *Introduction to Linear and Nonlinear Programming*, 2d ed., Addison-Wesley, Reading, Mass., 1984.
9. McCormick, G. P.: *Nonlinear Programming—Theory, Algorithms and Applications*, Wiley, New York, 1983.
10. Schittkowski, Klaus: *Nonlinear Programming Codes*, Lecture Notes in Economics and Mathematical Systems No. 183, Springer-Verlag, Berlin, Heidelberg, New York, 1980.
11. Shapiro, Jeremy F.: *Mathematical Programming*: *Structures and Algorithms*, chaps. 5–7, Wiley, New York, 1979.
12. Zangwill, Willard I.: *Nonlinear Programming*: *A Unified Approach*, Prentice-Hall, Englewood Cliffs, N.J., 1969.

PROBLEMS

1. Consider the *product mix* problem described in Prob. 2, Chap. 3. Suppose that this manufacturing firm actually encounters *price elasticity* in selling the three products, so

---

[1] Murtagh, Bruce A., and Michael A. Saunders: "MINOS 5.0 User's Guide," Technical Report SOL 83–20, Systems Optimization Laboratory, Department of Operations Research, Stanford University, December, 1983.

that the profits would be different from those stated in Chap. 3. In particular, suppose that the unit costs for producing products 1, 2, and 3 are \$15, \$6, and \$8, respectively, and that the price required (in dollars) in order to be able to sell x_1, x_2, and x_3 units are $(10 + 40x_1^{-1/3})$, $(5 + 15x_2^{-1/4})$, and $(10 + 20x_3^{-1/2})$, respectively.

    (a) Formulate a *linearly constrained optimization* model for the problem of determining how many units of each product the firm should produce to maximize profit.

    (b) Verify that this problem is a *convex programming* problem.

    (c) Starting from the initial trial solution $(x_1, x_2, x_3) = (0,0,0)$, apply two iterations of the *Frank-Wolfe algorithm*. For parts 2 and 3 of each iteration, use computer codes of the *simplex method* and the *one-dimensional search procedure*.

    2. For the P & T Company problem described in Sec. 7.1, suppose that there is a 10% discount in the shipping cost for all truckloads *beyond* the first 40 for each combination of cannery and warehouse. Show that this situation leads to a *nonconvex programming* problem.

    3. Consider the following example of the *portfolio selection* problem with risky securities described in Sec. 14.1. Just two stocks are being considered for inclusion in the portfolio. The estimated mean and variance of the return on each share of stock 1 are 5 and 4, respectively, whereas the corresponding quantities for stock 2 are 10 and 100, respectively. The covariance of the return on one share each of the two stocks is 5. The price per share is 20 for stock 1 and 30 for stock 2, where the total amount budgeted for the portfolio is 50.

    (a) Without assigning a specific numerical value to β, formulate the *quadratic programming* model for this problem.

    (b) Verify that the model in part (a) is a *convex programming* problem by using the test in Appendix 1 to show that the objective function is *concave*.

    (c) Starting from the initial trial solution $(x_1, x_2) = (0,0)$, apply five iterations of the *Frank-Wolfe algorithm* to this problem with $\beta = 0.1$.

    (d) Repeat part (c) for $\beta = 0.02$ (low aversion to risk) and $\beta = 0.5$ (high aversion to risk). Also solve by inspection the extreme cases of $\beta = 0$ (no aversion to risk) and $\beta = \infty$ (complete aversion to risk), where the latter case means to minimize $V(\mathbf{x})$. Characterize the solutions for the five values of β in terms of the relative concentration on the conservative investment (stock 1) or the risky investment (stock 2).

    4. Consider the variation of the Wyndor Glass Co. example represented in Fig. 14.5, where the second and third functional constraints of the original problem (see Sec. 3.1) have been replaced by $9x_1^2 + 5x_2^2 \le 216$.

    (a) Demonstrate that $(x_1, x_2) = (2,6)$ with $Z = 36$ is indeed optimal by showing that the objective function line, $36 = 3x_1 + 5x_2$, is *tangent* to this constraint boundary at $(2, 6)$. (*Hint:* Express x_2 in terms of x_1 on this boundary, and then differentiate this expression with respect to x_1 to find the slope of the boundary.)

    (b) Starting from the initial trial solution $(x_1, x_2) = (2, 3)$, apply *SUMT* to this problem. Use a computer code of the *gradient search procedure* to obtain the maximizing solution of $P(\mathbf{x}; r)$ at each iteration, with $r = 1, 10^{-2}, 10^{-4}, 10^{-6}$.

    5. Consider the variation of the Wyndor Glass Co. problem represented in

Fig. 14.6, where the original objective function (see Sec. 3.1) has been replaced by $Z = 126x_1 - 9x_1^2 + 182x_2 - 13x_2^2$. Demonstrate that $(x_1, x_2) = (\frac{8}{3}, 5)$ with $Z = 857$ is indeed optimal by showing that the ellipse, $857 - 126x_1 - 9x_1^2 + 182x_2 - 13x_2^2$, is *tangent* to the constraint boundary, $3x_1 + 2x_2 = 18$, at $(\frac{8}{3}, 5)$. (*Hint*: Solve for x_2 in terms of x_1 for the ellipse, and then differentiate this expression with respect to x_1 to find the slope of the ellipse.)

6. Consider the following function.

$$f(x) = 48x - 60x^2 + x^3.$$

(*a*) Use the first and second derivatives to find the *local maxima* and *local minima* of $f(x)$.

(*b*) Use the first and second derivatives to show that $f(x)$ has neither a *global maximum* nor a *global minimum* because it is unbounded in both directions.

7. For each of the following functions, show whether it is convex, concave, or neither.

(*a*) $f(x) = 10x - x^2$.
(*b*) $f(x) = x^4 + 6x^2 + 12x$.
(*c*) $f(x) = 2x^3 - 3x^2$.
(*d*) $f(x) = x^4 + x^2$.
(*e*) $f(x) = x^3 + x^4$.

8. For each of the following functions, use the test given in Appendix 1 to determine whether it is convex, concave, or neither.

(*a*) $f(\mathbf{x}) = x_1 x_2 - x_1^2 - x_2^2$.
(*b*) $f(\mathbf{x}) = 3x_1 + 2x_1^2 + 4x_2 + x_2^2 - 2x_1 x_2$.
(*c*) $f(\mathbf{x}) = x_1^2 + 3x_1 x_2 + 2x_2^2$.
(*d*) $f(\mathbf{x}) = 20x_1 + 10x_2$.
(*e*) $f(\mathbf{x}) = x_1 x_2$.

9. Consider the following function.

$$f(\mathbf{x}) = 5x_1 + 2x_2^2 + x_3^2 - 3x_3 x_4 + 4x_4^2 + 2x_5^4 + x_5^2 + 3x_5 x_6 + 6x_6^2 + 3x_6 x_7 + x_7^2.$$

Show that $f(\mathbf{x})$ is *convex* by expressing it as a *sum* of functions of one or two variables and then showing (see Appendix 1) that all of these functions are convex.

10. Consider the following nonlinear programming problem.

$$\text{Maximize} \quad f(\mathbf{x}) = x_1 + x_2,$$

subject to

$$x_1^2 + x_2^2 \leq 1$$

and

$$x_1 \geq 0, \qquad x_2 \geq 0.$$

(*a*) Verify that this is a *convex programming* problem.
(*b*) Solve this problem graphically.
(*c*) Use the *KKT conditions* to verify that the solution you obtained in part (*b*) is optimal.

11. Consider the following *constrained optimization problem.*

$$\text{Maximize} \quad f(x) = -6x + 3x^2 - 2x^3,$$

subject to

$$x \geq 0.$$

Use just the first and second derivatives of $f(x)$ to derive an optimal solution.

12. Consider the following nonlinear programming problem.

$$\text{Minimize} \quad Z = x_1^4 + 2x_1^2 + 2x_1 x_2 + 4x_2^2,$$

subject to

$$2x_1 + x_2 \geq 10$$
$$x_1 + 2x_2 \geq 10,$$

and

$$x_1 \geq 0, \qquad x_2 \geq 0.$$

(a) Of the special types of nonlinear programming problems described in Sec. 14.3, to which type or types can this particular problem be fitted? Justify your answer.

(b) What are the *KKT conditions* for this problem? Use these conditions to determine whether $(x_1, x_2) = (0, 10)$ can be optimal.

(c) If *SUMT* were to be applied directly to this problem, what is the unconstrained function $P(\mathbf{x}; r)$ to be *minimized* at each iteration?

(d) Setting $r = 100$ and using $(x_1, x_2) = (5, 5)$ as the initial trial solution, apply one iteration of the *gradient search procedure* to minimize the function $P(\mathbf{x}; r)$ you obtained in part (c). To find t^*, use the *one-dimensional search procedure* with initial bounds $\underline{t} = 0, \bar{t} = 0.02$ and with an error tolerance $\varepsilon = 0.0005$.

(e) Now suppose that the problem were changed slightly by replacing the nonnegativity constraints by $x_1 \geq 1$, $x_2 \geq 1$. Convert this new problem into an *equivalent* problem that has just two functional constraints, two variables, and two nonnegativity constraints.

13. Consider the expression given in Sec. 14.7 for the *KKT conditions* for the quadratic programming problem. Show that the problem of finding a *feasible solution* for these conditions is a *linear complementarity problem*, as introduced in Sec. 14.3, by identifying $\mathbf{w}, \mathbf{z}, \mathbf{q},$ and $\mathbf{M}$ in terms of the vectors and matrices in Sec. 14.7.

14. Consider the following *geometric programming* problem.

$$\text{Minimize} \quad f(\mathbf{x}) = 2x_1^{-2} x_2^{-1} + x_1^{-1} x_2^{-2},$$

subject to

$$4x_1 x_2 + x_1^2 x_2^2 \leq 12$$

and

$$x_1 \geq 0, \qquad x_2 \geq 0.$$

(a) Transform this problem into an equivalent *convex programming* problem.

(b) Use the test given in Appendix 1 to verify that the model formulated in part (a) is indeed a convex programming problem.

15. Consider the following *linear fractional programming* problem.

$$\text{Maximize} \quad f(\mathbf{x}) = \frac{10x_1 + 20x_2 + 10}{3x_1 + 4x_2 + 20},$$

subject to

$$x_1 + 3x_2 \le 50$$
$$3x_1 + 2x_2 \le 80,$$

and

$$x_1 \ge 0, \qquad x_2 \ge 0.$$

(a) Transform this problem into an equivalent *linear programming* problem.
(b) Use a computer code of the simplex method to solve the model formulated in part (a). What is the resulting optimal solution for the original problem?

16. Use the *one-dimensional search procedure* to solve (approximately) the following problem.

$$\text{Maximize} \quad f(x) = x^3 + 2x - 2x^2 - 0.25x^4.$$

Use an error tolerance $\varepsilon = 0.04$ and initial bounds $\underline{x} = 0$, $\bar{x} = 2.4$.

17. Use the *one-dimensional search procedure* with an error tolerance $\varepsilon = 0.04$ and with the following initial bounds to solve (approximately) each of the following problems.

(a) Maximize $f(x) = 6x - x^2$, with $\underline{x} = 0$, $\bar{x} = 4.8$.
(b) Minimize $f(x) = 6x + 7x^2 + 4x^3 + x^4$, with $\underline{x} = -4$, $\bar{x} = 1$.

18. Use the *one-dimensional search procedure* to solve (approximately) the following problem.

$$\text{Maximize} \quad f(x) = 48x^5 + 42x^3 + 3.5x - 16x^6 - 61x^4 - 16.5x^2.$$

Use an error tolerance $\varepsilon = 0.08$ and initial bounds $\underline{x} = -1$, $\bar{x} = 4$.

19. Use the *one-dimensional search procedure* to solve (approximately) the following problem.

$$\text{Maximize} \quad f(x) = x^3 + 30x - x^6 - 2x^4 - 3x^2.$$

Use an error tolerance $\varepsilon = 0.07$ and find appropriate initial bounds by inspection.

20. Consider the following convex programming problem.

$$\text{Minimize} \quad Z = x^4 + x^2 - 4x,$$

subject to

$$x \le 2$$

and

$$x \ge 0.$$

(a) Use one simple calculation *just* to check whether the optimal solution lies in the interval $0 \le x \le 1$ or the interval $1 \le x \le 2$. (Do *not* actually solve for the optimal solution in order to determine in which interval it must lie.) Explain your logic.

(b) Use the *one-dimensional search procedure* with initial bounds $\underline{x} = 0$, $\bar{x} = 2$ and with an error tolerance $\varepsilon = 0.02$ to solve (approximately) this problem.

(c) Use the *KKT conditions* to derive the optimal solution.

21. Consider the problem of maximizing a differentiable function $f(x)$ of a single unconstrained variable x. Let $\underline{x}_0$ and $\bar{x}_0$ respectively be a valid lower bound and upper bound on the same global maximum (if one exists). Prove the following general properties of the *one-dimensional search procedure* (as presented in Sec. 14.4) for attempting to solve such a problem.

(a) Given $\underline{x}_0$, $\bar{x}_0$, and $\varepsilon = 0$, the sequence of trial solutions selected by the *midpoint rule* must *converge* to a limiting solution. (*Hint:* First show that $\lim_{n \to \infty} (\bar{x}_n - \underline{x}_n) = 0$, where $\bar{x}_n$ and $\underline{x}_n$ are the upper and lower bound identified at iteration n.)

(b) If $f(x)$ is *concave* $\left(\text{so } \dfrac{df(x)}{dx} \text{ is a monotone decreasing function of } x\right)$, then the limiting solution in part (a) must be a global maximum.

(c) If $f(x)$ is not concave everywhere, but would be concave if its domain were restricted to the interval between $\underline{x}_0$ and $\bar{x}_0$, then the limiting solution in part (a) must be a global maximum.

(d) If $f(x)$ is not concave even over the interval between $\underline{x}_0$ and $\bar{x}_0$, then the limiting solution in part (a) need not be a global maximum. (Prove this by graphically constructing a counterexample.)

(e) If $\dfrac{df(x)}{dx} < 0$ for all x, then no $\underline{x}_0$ exists. If $\dfrac{df(x)}{dx} > 0$ for all x, then no $\bar{x}_0$ exists. In either case, $f(x)$ does not possess a global maximum.

(f) If $f(x)$ is concave and $\lim\limits_{x \to -\infty} \dfrac{df(x)}{dx} < 0$, then no $\underline{x}_0$ exists. If $f(x)$ is concave and $\lim\limits_{x \to \infty} \dfrac{df(x)}{dx} > 0$, then no $\bar{x}_0$ exists. In either case, $f(x)$ does not possess a global maximum.

22. Consider the following *unconstrained optimization* problem.

$$\text{Maximize} \quad f(\mathbf{x}) = 2x_1 x_2 + x_2 - x_1^2 - 2x_2^2.$$

(a) Starting from the initial trial solution $(x_1, x_2) = (1,1)$, apply the *gradient search procedure* with $\varepsilon = 0.25$ to obtain an approximate solution.

(b) Solve the system of linear equations obtained by setting $\nabla f(\mathbf{x}) = \mathbf{0}$ to obtain the exact solution.

(c) Referring to Fig. 14.11 as a sample for a similar problem, draw the path of trial solutions you obtained in part (a). Then show the apparent *continuation* of this path with your best guess for the next three trial solutions [based on the pattern in part (a) and in Fig. 14.11]. Also show the exact solution from part (b) toward which this sequence of trial solutions is converging.

23. Repeat the three parts of Prob. 22 (except with $\varepsilon = 0.5$) for the following *unconstrained optimization* problem.

$$\text{Maximize} \quad f(\mathbf{x}) = 2x_1 x_2 - 2x_1^2 - x_2^2.$$

24. Starting from the initial trial solution $(x_1, x_2) = (0,0)$, do two iterations of the *gradient search procedure* to begin solving the following problem.

$$\text{Maximize} \quad f(\mathbf{x}) = 6x_1 + 2x_1x_2 - 2x_2 - 2x_1^2 - x_2^2.$$

Then solve $\nabla f(\mathbf{x}) = \mathbf{0}$ directly to obtain the exact solution.

25. Starting from the initial trial solution $(x_1, x_2) = (0,0)$, use the *gradient search procedure* with $\varepsilon = 0.3$ to obtain an approximate solution for the following problem.

$$\text{Maximize} \quad f(\mathbf{x}) = 8x_1 - x_1^2 - 12x_2 - 2x_2^2 + 2x_1x_2.$$

Then solve $\nabla f(\mathbf{x}) = \mathbf{0}$ directly to obtain the exact solution.

26. Starting from the initial trial solution $(x_1, x_2) = (0,0)$, apply *two* iterations of the *gradient search procedure* to the following problem.

$$\text{Maximize} \quad f(\mathbf{x}) = 4x_1 + 2x_2 - x_1^2 - x_1^4 - 2x_1x_2 - x_2^2.$$

For each of these iterations, approximately solve for t^* by applying *two* iterations of the *one-dimensional search procedure* with initial bounds $t = 0, \bar{t} = 1$.

27. Starting from the initial trial solution $(x_1, x_2, x_3) = (1, 1, 1)$, use the *gradient search procedure* with $\varepsilon = 0.05$ to solve (approximately) the following problem.

$$\text{Maximize} \quad f(\mathbf{x}) = 3x_1x_2 + 3x_2x_3 - x_1^2 - 6x_2^2 - x_3^2.$$

28. Starting from the initial trial solution $(x_1, x_2) = (0,0)$, use the *gradient search procedure* with $\varepsilon = 1$ to solve (approximately) each of the following problems.

(*a*) Maximize $f(\mathbf{x}) = x_1x_2 + 3x_2 - x_1^2 - x_2^2.$
(*b*) Minimize $f(\mathbf{x}) = x_1^2x_2^2 - 2x_1x_2^2 + 2x_1^2x_2 - 4x_1x_2$
$\qquad\qquad\qquad + 2x_1^2 + 2x_2^2 - 4x_1 + 4x_2.$

29. Consider the following *linearly constrained optimization* problem.

$$\text{Maximize} \quad f(\mathbf{x}) = \ln(x_1 + x_2),$$

subject to

$$x_1 + 2x_2 \leq 5$$

and

$$x_1 \geq 0, \qquad x_2 \geq 0,$$

where ln denotes *natural logarithm*.

(*a*) Verify that this problem is a *convex programming* problem.
(*b*) Use the *KKT conditions* to derive an optimal solution.
(*c*) Use intuitive reasoning to demonstrate that the solution obtained in part (*b*) is indeed optimal. [*Hint*: Note that $\ln(x_1 + x_2)$ is a monotone strictly increasing function of $(x_1 + x_2)$.]
(*d*) Starting from the initial trial solution $(x_1, x_2) = (1, 1)$, use one iteration of the *Frank-Wolfe algorithm* to obtain exactly the same solution you found in part (*b*), and then use a second iteration to verify that it is an optimal solution (because it is replicated exactly). Explain why exactly the same results would be obtained on these two iterations with any other initial trial solution except (0,0). What complication arises with (0, 0)?

30. Consider the following *linearly constrained optimization* problem.

$$\text{Maximize} \quad f(\mathbf{x}) = \ln(x_1 + 1) - x_2^2,$$

subject to

$$x_1 + 2x_2 \leq 3$$

and

$$x_1 \geq 0, \qquad x_2 \geq 0,$$

where ln denotes *natural logarithm*.

(a) Verify that this problem is a *convex programming* problem.
(b) Use the *KKT conditions* to derive an optimal solution.
(c) Use intuitive reasoning to demonstrate that the solution obtained in part (b) is indeed optimal.
(d) Starting from the initial trial solution $(x_1, x_2) = (0, 0)$, use one iteration of the *Frank-Wolfe algorithm* to obtain exactly the same solution you found in part (b), and then use a second iteration to verify that it is an optimal solution (because it is replicated exactly).

31. Consider the following *convex programming* problem.

$$\text{Maximize} \quad f(\mathbf{x}) = 10x_1 - 2x_1^2 - x_1^3 + 8x_2 - x_2^2,$$

subject to

$$x_1 + x_2 \leq 2$$

and

$$x_1 \geq 0, \qquad x_2 \geq 0.$$

(a) Use the *KKT conditions* to demonstrate that $(x_1, x_2) = (1, 1)$ is *not* an optimal solution.
(b) Use the *KKT conditions* to derive an optimal solution.

32. Consider the nonlinear programming problem given in Prob. 13, Chap. 11. Determine whether $(x_1, x_2) = (1, 2)$ can be optimal by applying the *KKT conditions*.

33. Consider the following *convex programming* problem.

$$\text{Maximize} \quad f(\mathbf{x}) = 24x_1 - x_1^2 + 10x_2 - x_2^2,$$

subject to

$$x_1 \leq 8$$
$$x_2 \leq 7,$$

and

$$x_1 \geq 0, \qquad x_2 \geq 0.$$

(a) Use the *KKT conditions* for this problem to derive an optimal solution.
(b) Decompose this problem into two separate constrained optimization problems involving just x_1 and just x_2, respectively. For each of these two problems, plot the objective function over the feasible region in order to

demonstrate that the value of x_1 or x_2 derived in part (*a*) is indeed optimal. Then *prove* that this value is optimal by using just the first and second derivatives of the objective function and the constraints for the respective problems.

34. Consider the following nonlinear programming problem.

$$\text{Maximize} \quad f(\mathbf{x}) = \frac{x_1}{x_2 + 1},$$

subject to

$$x_1 - x_2 \le 2$$

and

$$x_1 \ge 0, \qquad x_2 \ge 0.$$

(*a*) Use the *KKT conditions* to demonstrate that $(x_1, x_2) = (4, 2)$ is *not* optimal.
(*b*) Derive a solution that does satisfy the *KKT conditions*.
(*c*) Show that this problem is *not* a *convex programming* problem.
(*d*) Despite the conclusion in part (*c*), use *intuitive* reasoning to show that the solution obtained in part (*b*) is, in fact, optimal. (The theoretical reason is that $f(\mathbf{x})$ is *pseudoconcave*.)
(*e*) Use the fact that this problem is a *linear fractional programming* problem to transform it into an equivalent *linear programming* problem. Solve the latter problem and thereby identify the optimal solution for the original problem. (*Hint*: Use the equality constraint in the linear programming problem to substitute one of the variables out of the model, and then solve the model graphically.)

35. Use the *KKT conditions* to derive an optimal solution for each of the following problems.

(*a*) $\qquad\qquad$ Maximize $\quad f(\mathbf{x}) = x_1 + 2x_2 - x_2^3,$

subject to

$$x_1 + x_2 \le 1$$

and

$$x_1 \ge 0, \qquad x_2 \ge 0.$$

(*b*) $\qquad\qquad$ Maximize $\quad f(\mathbf{x}) = 20x_1 + 10x_2,$

subject to

$$x_1^2 + x_2^2 \le 1$$
$$x_1 + 2x_2 \le 2,$$

and

$$x_1 \ge 0, \qquad x_2 \ge 0.$$

36. What are the *KKT conditions* for nonlinear programming problems of the following form?

$$\text{Minimize} \quad f(\mathbf{x}),$$

subject to

$$g_i(\mathbf{x}) \ge b_i, \quad \text{for } i = 1, 2, \ldots, m$$

and

$$\mathbf{x} \geq \mathbf{0}.$$

(*Hint*: Convert this form into our standard form assumed in this chapter by using the techniques presented in Sec. 4.6, and then applying the *KKT conditions* as given in Sec. 14.6.)

37. Consider the following *convex programming* problem.

$$\text{Minimize} \quad Z = x_1^2 - 6x_1 + x_2^3 - 3x_2,$$

subject to

$$x_1 + x_2 \leq 1$$

and

$$x_1 \geq 0, \qquad x_2 \geq 0.$$

(a) Obtain the *KKT conditions* for this problem.
(b) Use the *KKT conditions* to check whether $(x_1, x_2) = (\frac{1}{2}, \frac{1}{2})$ is an optimal solution.
(c) Use the *KKT conditions* to derive an optimal solution.
(d) Starting from the initial trial solution $(x_1, x_2) = (0,0)$, use one iteration of the *Frank-Wolfe algorithm* to obtain exactly the same solution you found in part (c), and then use a second iteration to verify that it is an optimal solution (because it is replicated exactly). Explain why exactly the same results would be obtained on these two iterations with any other trial solution as well.

38. Consider the following *linearly constrained convex programming* problem.

$$\text{Maximize} \quad f(\mathbf{x}) = 8x_1 - x_1^2 + 2x_2 + x_3,$$

subject to

$$x_1 + 3x_2 + 2x_3 \leq 12$$

and

$$x_1 \geq 0, \qquad x_2 \geq 0, \qquad x_3 \geq 0.$$

(a) Use the *KKT conditions* to demonstrate that $(x_1, x_2, x_3) = (2, 2, 2)$ is *not* an optimal solution.
(b) Use the *KKT conditions* to derive an optimal solution. (*Hint*: Do some preliminary intuitive analysis to determine the most promising case regarding which variables are nonzero and which are zero.)
(c) Starting from the initial trial solution $(x_1, x_2, x_3) = (0, 0, 0)$, apply three iterations of the *Frank-Wolfe algorithm*. (*Hint*: The resulting linear programming problems can be solved immediately by choosing the variable x_j having the largest values of c_j/a_{1j} to be the only basic variable, with $x_j = 12/a_{1j}$.)

39. Use the *KKT conditions* to determine whether $(x_1, x_2, x_3) = (1, 1, 1)$ can be optimal for the following problem.

$$\text{Minimize} \quad Z = 2x_1 + x_2^3 + x_3^2,$$

subject to

$$x_1^2 + 2x_2^2 + x_3^2 \geq 4$$

and

$$x_1 \geq 0, \qquad x_2 \geq 0, \qquad x_3 \geq 0.$$

40. Derive the *KKT conditions* for the *quadratic programming* problem. Show that they can be expressed as given in Sec. 14.7.

41. Consider the *quadratic programming* example presented in Sec. 14.7.

(*a*) Use the test given in Appendix 1 to show that the objective function is *strictly concave*.

(*b*) Verify that the objective function is *strictly concave* by demonstrating that $\mathbf{Q}$ is a *positive definite* matrix; i.e., $\mathbf{x}^T\mathbf{Q}\mathbf{x} > \mathbf{0}$ for all $\mathbf{x} \neq \mathbf{0}$. (*Hint*: Reduce $\mathbf{x}^T\mathbf{Q}\mathbf{x}$ to a sum of squares.)

(*c*) Show that $x_1 = 12, x_2 = 9$, and $u_1 = 3$ satisfy the *KKT conditions* when they are written in the form given in Sec. 14.6.

(*d*) Starting from the initial trial solution $(x_1, x_2) = (5, 5)$, apply three iterations of the *Frank-Wolfe algorithm*.

42. Consider the following *quadratic programming* problem.

$$\text{Maximize} \quad f(\mathbf{x}) = 8x_1 - x_1^2 + 4x_2 - x_2^2,$$

subject to

$$x_1 + x_2 \leq 2$$

and

$$x_1 \geq 0, \qquad x_2 \geq 0.$$

(*a*) Use the *KKT conditions* to derive an optimal solution.

(*b*) Now suppose that this problem is to be solved by the *modified simplex method*. Formulate the *linear programming* problem that is to be addressed *explicitly*, and then identify the additional *complementarity* constraint that is enforced automatically by the algorithm.

(*c*) Apply the *modified simplex method* to the problem as formulated in part (*b*).

43. Consider the following *quadratic programming* problem.

$$\text{Maximize} \quad f(\mathbf{x}) = 20x_1 - 20x_1^2 + 50x_2 - 5x_2^2 + 20x_1x_2,$$

subject to

$$x_1 + \ x_2 \leq \ 6$$
$$x_1 + 4x_2 \leq 18,$$

and

$$x_1 \geq 0, \qquad x_2 \geq 0.$$

Suppose that this problem is to be solved by the *modified simplex method*.

(*a*) Formulate the *linear programming* problem that is to be addressed *explicitly*, and then identify the additional *complementarity* constraint that is enforced automatically by the algorithm.

(*b*) Apply the *modified simplex method* to the problem as formulated in part (*a*).

44. Consider the following *quadratic programming* problem.

$$\text{Maximize} \quad f(\mathbf{x}) = 2x_1 + 3x_2 - x_1^2 - x_2^2,$$

subject to

$$x_1 + x_2 \le 2$$

and

$$x_1 \ge 0, \qquad x_2 \ge 0.$$

(a) Starting from the initial trial solution $(x_1, x_2) = (0,0)$, use the *Frank-Wolfe algorithm* (six iterations) to solve the problem (approximately).

(b) Show graphically how the sequence of trial solutions obtained in part (a) can be extrapolated to obtain a closer approximation of an optimal solution. What is your resulting estimate of this solution?

(c) Use the *KKT conditions* to derive an optimal solution directly.

(d) Now suppose that this problem is to be solved by the *modified simplex method*. Formulate the *linear programming* problem that is to be addressed *explicitly*, and then identify the additional *complementarity constraint* that is enforced automatically by the algorithm.

(e) Without applying the *modified simplex method*, show that the solution derived in part (c) is indeed optimal ($Z = 0$) for the equivalent problem formulated in part (d).

(f) Apply the *modified simplex method* to the problem as formulated in part (d).

45. Repeat parts (a) (three iterations only), (c), (d), (e), and (f) of Prob. 44 for the first *quadratic programming* variation of the *Wyndor Glass Co.* problem presented in Sec. 14.2 (see Fig. 14.6); i.e.,

$$\text{Maximize} \quad Z = 126x_1 - 9x_1^2 + 182x_2 - 13x_2^2,$$

subject to the linear constraints given in Sec. 3.1.

46. A certain corporation is planning to produce and market three different products. Let x_1, x_2 and x_3 denote the number of units of the three respective products to be produced. The preliminary estimates of their potential profitability are as follows.

For the first 15 units produced of product 1, the unit profit would be approximately $36. The unit profit would only be $3 for any additional units of product 1. For the first 20 units produced of product 2, the unit profit is estimated at $24. The unit profit would be $12 for each of the next 20 units and $9 for any additional units. For the first 10 units of product 3, the unit profit would be $45. The unit profit would be $30 for each of the next 5 units and $18 for any additional units.

Certain limitations on the use of needed resources impose the following constraints on the production of the three products:

$$
\begin{aligned}
x_1 + \; x_2 + \; x_3 &\le \; 60 \\
3x_1 + 2x_2 \qquad\;\; &\le 200 \\
x_1 \qquad\; + 2x_3 &\le \;\; 70.
\end{aligned}
$$

Management wants to know what values of x_1, x_2, and x_3 should be chosen to maximize total profit.

(a) Use the *separable programming* formulation presented in Sec. 14.8 to formulate a linear programming model for this problem.

(b)   Use a computer code of the simplex method to solve the model formulated in part (a). Verify that the optimal solution satisfies the *special restriction* for the model.

47.   Consider the following *convex programming* problem.

$$\text{Maximize} \quad f(\mathbf{x}) = 4x_1 + 6x_2 - x_1^3 - 2x_2^2,$$

subject to

$$x_1 + 3x_2 \leq 8$$
$$5x_1 + 2x_2 \leq 14,$$

and

$$x_1 \geq 0, \qquad x_2 \geq 0.$$

(a)   Verify that $(x_1, x_2) = (\frac{2}{\sqrt{3}}, \frac{3}{2})$ is an optimal solution by applying the KKT conditions.
(b)   Treat this problem as a *separable programming* problem by formulating an *approximate* mathematical model that could be solved by the simplex method. Use the integers as the breakpoints of the piecewise linear functions.
(c)   Use a computer code of the simplex method to solve the approximate model formulated in part (b). Verify that the optimal solution satisfies the *special restriction* for the model. Compare this solution with the exact optimal solution for the original problem [see part (a)].

48.   Consider the following *linearly constrained convex programming* problem.

$$\text{Maximize} \quad f(\mathbf{x}) = 32x_1 + 50x_2 - 10x_2^2 + x_2^3 - x_1^4 - x_2^4,$$

subject to

$$3x_1 + x_2 \leq 11$$
$$2x_1 + 5x_2 \leq 16,$$

and

$$x_1 \geq 0, \qquad x_2 \geq 0.$$

(a)   Treat this problem as a *separable programming* problem by formulating an *approximate* mathematical model that can be solved by the simplex method. Use $x_1 = 0, 1, 2, 3$ and $x_2 = 0, 1, 2, 3$ as the breakpoints of the piecewise linear functions.
(b)   Use the KKT *conditions* to determine whether $(x_1, x_2) = (2, 2)$ can be optimal for this original problem (not the approximate model).
(c)   Starting from the initial trial solution $(x_1, x_2) = (0, 0)$, use the *Frank-Wolfe algorithm* (four iterations) to solve the original problem (approximately).
(d)   Ignore the constraints and solve the resulting two *one-variable unconstrained optimization* problems. Use calculus to solve the problem involving x_1 and use the *one-dimensional search procedure* with $\varepsilon = 0.1$ and initial bounds 0 and 4 to solve the problem involving x_2. Show that the resulting solution for (x_1, x_2) satisfies all of the constraints, so it is actually optimal for the original problem.

49.   Suppose that the *separable programming* technique has been applied to a certain problem (the "original problem") to convert it into the following equivalent linear programming problem.

$$\text{Maximize} \quad Z = 5x_{11} + 4x_{12} + 2x_{13} + 4x_{21} + x_{22},$$

subject to

$$3x_{11} + 3x_{12} + 3x_{13} + 2x_{21} + 2x_{22} \le 25$$
$$2x_{11} + 2x_{12} + 2x_{13} - x_{21} - x_{22} \le 10,$$

and

$$0 \le x_{11} \le 2$$
$$0 \le x_{12} \le 3$$
$$0 \le x_{13}$$
$$0 \le x_{21} \le 3$$
$$0 \le x_{22} \le 1.$$

What was the mathematical model for the original problem? (You may define the objective function either algebraically or graphically, but express the constraints algebraically.)

50. For each of the following cases, *prove* that the *key property of separable programming* given in Sec. 14.8 must hold. (*Hint*: Assume that there exists an optimal solution that violates this property, and then contradict this assumption by showing that there exists a better feasible solution.)

(*a*) The special case of separable programming where all of the $g_i(\mathbf{x})$ are linear functions.

(*b*) The general case of separable programming where all of the functions are nonlinear functions of the designated form. (*Hint*: Think of the functional constraints as constraints on resources, where $g_{ij}(x_j)$ represents the amount of resource i used by running activity j at level x_j, and then use what the convexity assumption implies about the slopes of the approximating piecewise linear function.)

51. Reconsider the production scheduling problem of the Build-Em-Fast Company described in Prob. 17 of Chap. 7. The *special restriction* for such a situation is that overtime should not be used in any particular period unless regular time in that period is completely used up. Explain why the logic of *separable programming* implies that this restriction will be satisfied automatically by any optimal solution for the transportation problem formulation of the problem.

52. The *MFG Company* produces a certain subassembly in each of two separate plants. These subassemblies are then brought to a third nearby plant where they are used in the production of a certain product. The peak season of demand for this product is approaching, so in order to maintain the production rate within a desired range, it is necessary to use temporarily some overtime in making the subassemblies. The cost per subassembly on regular time (RT) and on overtime (OT) is shown in the following table for both plants, along with the maximum number of subassemblies that can be produced on RT and on OT each day.

	Unit Cost		Capacity	
	RT	OT	RT	OT
Plant 1	$15	$25	2,000	1,000
Plant 2	$16	$24	1,000	500

Let x_1 and x_2 denote the total number of subassemblies produced per day at plants 1 and 2, respectively. Suppose that the objective is to maximize $Z = x_1 + x_2$, subject to the constraint that the total daily cost should not exceed $60,000. Note that the mathematical programming formulation of this problem (with x_1 and x_2 as decision variables) has the same form as the main case of the *separable programming* model described in Sec. 14.8, except that the separable functions appear in a constraint function rather than the objective function. However, if it is allowable to use OT even when the RT capacity at that plant is not fully used, the same approach can be used to reformulate the problem as a linear programming problem.

(a) Formulate this linear programming problem.

(b) Explain why the logic of *separable programming* also applies here to guarantee that an optimal solution for the model formulated in part (a) never uses OT unless the RT capacity at that plant has been fully used.

53. Consider the following *linearly constrained convex programming* problem.

$$\text{Maximize} \quad f(\mathbf{x}) = 3x_1x_2 + 40x_1 + 30x_2 - 4x_1^2 - x_1^4 - 3x_2^2 - x_2^4,$$

subject to

$$4x_1 + 3x_2 \leq 12$$
$$x_1 + 2x_2 \leq 4,$$

and

$$x_1 \geq 0, \qquad x_2 \geq 0.$$

Starting from the initial trial solution $(x_1, x_2) = (0,0)$, apply two iterations of the *Frank-Wolfe algorithm*.

54. Consider the following *linearly constrained convex programming* problem.

$$\text{Maximize} \quad f(\mathbf{x}) = 3x_1 + 4x_2 - x_1^3 - x_2^2,$$

subject to

$$x_1 + x_2 \leq 1$$

and

$$x_1 \geq 0, \qquad x_2 \geq 0.$$

(a) Starting from the initial trial solution $(x_1, x_2) = (\frac{1}{4}, \frac{1}{4})$, apply three iterations of the *Frank-Wolfe algorithm*.

(b) Use the *KKT conditions* to check whether the solution obtained in part (a) is, in fact, optimal.

(c) Starting from the initial trial solution $(x_1, x_2) = (\frac{1}{4}, \frac{1}{4})$, apply *SUMT*. Use a computer code of the *gradient search procedure* to obtain the maximizing solution of $P(\mathbf{x}; r)$ at each iteration, with $r = 1, 10^{-2}, 10^{-4}$.

55. Consider the following *linearly constrained convex programming* problem.

$$\text{Maximize} \quad f(\mathbf{x}) = 4x_1 - x_1^4 + 2x_2 - x_2^2,$$

subject to

$$4x_1 + 2x_2 \le 5$$

and

$$x_1 \ge 0, \qquad x_2 \ge 0.$$

(*a*) Starting from the initial trial solution $(x_1, x_2) = (\frac{1}{2}, \frac{1}{2})$, apply four iterations of the *Frank-Wolfe algorithm.*

(*b*) Show graphically how the sequence of trial solutions obtained in part (*a*) can be extrapolated to obtain a closer approximation of an optimal solution. What is your resulting estimate of this solution?

(*c*) Use the *KKT conditions* to check whether the solution you obtained in part (*b*) is, in fact, optimal. If not, use these conditions to derive the exact optimal solution.

(*d*) Starting from the initial trial solution $(x_1, x_2) = (\frac{1}{2}, \frac{1}{2})$, apply *SUMT*. Use a computer code of the *gradient search procedure* to obtain the maximizing solution of $P(\mathbf{x}; r)$ at each iteration, with $r = 1, 10^{-2}, 10^{-4}, 10^{-6}$.

56. Consider the example for applying SUMT given in Sec. 14.10.

(*a*) Show that $(x_1, x_2) = (1, 2)$ satisfies the *KKT conditions.*

(*b*) Display the feasible region graphically, and then plot the locus of points, $x_1 x_2 = 2$, to demonstrate that $(x_1, x_2) = (1, 2)$ with $f(1, 2) = 2$ is, in fact, a *global maximum.*

57. Use SUMT to solve the following *convex programming* problem.

$$\text{Maximize} \quad f(\mathbf{x}) = -2x_1 - (x_2 - 3)^2,$$

subject to

$$x_1 \ge 3$$
$$x_2 \ge 3.$$

Derive the maximizing solution of $P(\mathbf{x}; r)$ analytically, and use $r = 1, 10^{-2}, 10^{-4}, 10^{-6}$.

58. Use SUMT to solve the following *convex programming* problem.

$$\text{Minimize} \quad f(\mathbf{x}) = \frac{(x_1 + 1)^3}{3} + x_2,$$

subject to

$$x_1 \ge 1$$
$$x_2 \ge 0.$$

Derive the minimizing solution of $P(\mathbf{x}; r)$ analytically, and use $r = 1, 10^{-2}, 10^{-4}, 10^{-6}$.

59. Use SUMT to solve the following *convex programming* problem.

$$\text{Maximize} \quad f(\mathbf{x}) = x_1 x_2 - x_1 - x_1^2 - x_2 - x_2^2,$$

subject to

$$x_2 \geq 0.$$

Use the *gradient search procedure* to obtain the maximizing solution of $P(\mathbf{x};r)$ at each iteration, with $r = 1, 10^{-2}, 10^{-4}$. Begin with the initial trial solution $(x_1, x_2) = (1, 1)$.

60. Apply SUMT to Prob. 44. Use the *gradient search procedure* to obtain the maximizing solution of $P(\mathbf{x};r)$ at each iteration, with $r = 1, 10^{-2}, 10^{-4}$. Begin with the initial trial solution $(x_1, x_2) = (\frac{1}{2}, \frac{1}{2})$.

61. Apply SUMT to Prob. 45. Use a computer code of the *gradient search procedure* to obtain the maximizing solution of $P(\mathbf{x};r)$ at each iteration, with $r = 10^2, 1, 10^{-2}, 10^{-4}$. Begin with the initial trial solution $(x_1, x_2) = (2, 3)$.

62. Consider the following *nonconvex programming* problem.

$$\text{Maximize} \quad f(x) = 1000x - 400x^2 + 40x^3 - x^4,$$

subject to

$$x^2 + x \leq 500$$

and

$$x \geq 0.$$

(a) Identify the feasible values for x. Obtain general expressions for the first three derivatives of $f(x)$. Use this information to help you draw a rough sketch of $f(x)$ over the feasible region for x. Without calculating their values, mark the points on your graph that correspond to *local maxima* and *local minima*.

(b) Use the *one-dimensional search procedure* with $\varepsilon = 0.05$ to find each of the local maxima. Use your sketch from part (a) to identify appropriate initial bounds for each of these searches. Which of the local maxima is a *global maximum*?

(c) Use SUMT with $\varepsilon = 25$ and $r = 10^4, 10^2, 1$ to find each of the local maxima. Use $x = 3$ and $x = 15$ as the initial trial solutions for these searches. To find the maximizing solution of $P(\mathbf{x};r)$ each time, use the *one-dimensional search procedure* as described in part (b). Which of the local maxima is a *global maximum*?

63. Consider the following *nonconvex programming* problem.

$$\text{Maximize} \quad f(\mathbf{x}) = 3x_1 x_2 - 2x_1^2 - x_2^2,$$

subject to

$$x_1^2 + 2x_2^2 \leq 4$$
$$2x_1 - x_2 \leq 0$$
$$x_1 x_2^2 + x_1^2 x_2 = 2,$$

and

$$x_1 \geq 0, \qquad x_2 \geq 0.$$

(a) If SUMT were to be applied to this problem, what would be the unconstrained function $P(\mathbf{x};r)$ to be maximized at each iteration?

(b) Starting from the initial trial solution $(x_1, x_2) = (1, 1)$, apply SUMT. Use a computer code of the *gradient search procedure* to obtain the maximizing solution of $P(\mathbf{x};r)$ at each iteration, with $r = 1, 10^{-2}, 10^{-4}$.

64. Consider the following *nonconvex programming* problem.

$$\text{Minimize} \quad f(\mathbf{x}) = \sin 3x_1 + \cos 3x_2 + \sin(x_1 + x_2),$$

subject to

$$x_1^2 - 10x_2 \geq -1$$
$$10x_1 + x_2^2 \leq 100,$$

and

$$x_1 \geq 0, \qquad x_2 \geq 0.$$

(*a*) If SUMT were to be applied to this problem, what would be the unconstrained function $P(\mathbf{x};r)$ to be *minimized* at each iteration?

(*b*) Apply SUMT to find as many *local minima* as you can. For each initial trial solution, use a computer code of the *gradient search procedure* to obtain the *minimizing* solution of $P(\mathbf{x};r)$ at each iteration, with $r = 1, 10^{-2}, 10^{-4}$. Based upon your results, which solution or solutions appear to be optimal (a *global minimum*)? (*Hint*: Choose your initial trial solutions by performing a preliminary analysis to identify the promising regions for searching for local minima.)

PART FOUR

Probabilistic Models

■ CHAPTER 15

Stochastic Processes

■ 15.1 Introduction

In decision-making problems, we often are faced with making decisions based upon phenomena that have uncertainty associated with them. This uncertainty is caused by inherent variation due to sources of variation that elude control or due to the inconsistency of natural phenomena. Rather than treat this variability qualitatively, we can incorporate it into the mathematical model and thus handle it quantitatively. This treatment generally can be accomplished if the natural phenomena exhibit some degree of regularity, so that their variation can be described by a probability model. We assume that the reader has a basic knowledge of probability theory. The ensuing sections are concerned with special types of probability models.

15.2 Stochastic Process

A **stochastic process** is defined to be simply *an indexed collection of random variables* $\{X_t\}$, *where the index t runs through a given set T.* Often T is taken to be the set of nonnegative integers, and X_t represents a measurable characteristic of interest at time t. For example, the stochastic process, $X_1, X_2, X_3,\ldots$, can represent the collection of weekly (or monthly) inventory levels of a given product, or it can represent the collection of weekly (or monthly) demands for this product.

There are many stochastic processes that are of interest. A consideration of the behavior of a system operating for some period of time often leads to the analysis of a stochastic process with the following structure. At particular points of time t labeled $0, 1, \ldots$, the system is found in exactly one of a finite number of mutually exclusive and exhaustive categories or *states* labeled $0, 1, \ldots, M$. The points in time may be spaced equally, or their spacing may depend upon the overall behavior of the physical system in which the stochastic process is *imbedded*, e.g., the time between occurrences of some phenomenon of interest. Although the states may constitute a qualitative as well as a quantitative characterization of the system, no loss of generality is entailed by the numerical labels, $0, 1, \ldots, M$, which are used henceforth to denote the possible states of the system. Thus the mathematical representation of the physical system is that of a stochastic process $\{X_t\}$, where the random variables are observed at $t = 0, 1, 2, \ldots$, and where each random variable may take on any one of the $(M + 1)$ integers $0, 1, \ldots, M$. These integers are a characterization of the $(M + 1)$ states of the process.

As an example, consider the following inventory problem. A camera store stocks a particular model camera that can be ordered weekly. Let $D_1, D_2, \ldots$, represent the demand for this camera during the first week, second week, $\ldots$, respectively. It is assumed that the D_i are independent and identically distributed random variables having a known probability distribution. Let X_0 represent the number of cameras on hand at the outset, X_1 the number of cameras on hand at the end of week one, X_2 the number of cameras on hand at the end of week two, and so on. Assume that $X_0 = 3$. On Saturday night the store places an order that is delivered in time for the opening of the store on Monday. The store uses the following (s,S) ordering policy:[1] If the number of cameras on hand at the end of the week is less than $s = 1$ (no cameras in stock), the store orders (up to) $S = 3$. Otherwise, the store does not order (if there are any cameras in stock, no order is placed). It is assumed that sales are lost when demand exceeds the inventory on hand. Thus $\{X_t\}$ for $t = 0, 1, \ldots$, is a stochastic process of the form just described. The possible states of the process are the integers $0, 1, 2, 3$ representing the possible number of cameras on hand at the end of the week. In fact, the random variables X_t are clearly dependent and may be evaluated iteratively by the expression

$$X_{t+1} = \begin{cases} \max\{(3 - D_{t+1}),0\}, & \text{if } X_t < 1 \\ \max\{(X_t - D_{t+1}),0\}, & \text{if } X_t \geq 1, \end{cases}$$

for $t = 0, 1, 2, \ldots$. This example is used for illustrative purposes throughout many of the following sections. Section 15.3 further defines the type of stochastic process considered in this chapter.

---

[1] In general, an (s,S) policy is a periodic review policy that calls for ordering up to S units whenever the inventory level dips below s $(S \geq s)$. If the inventory level is s or greater, then no order is placed. These policies are discussed in detail in Chap. 18.

15.3 Markov Chains

Assumptions regarding the joint distribution of X_0, $X_1,\ldots$, are necessary to obtain analytical results. One assumption that leads to analytical tractability is that the stochastic process is a Markov chain (defined later), which has the following key property: A stochastic process $\{X_t\}$ is said to have the *Markovian property* if $P\{X_{t+1} = j \,|\, X_0 = k_0, X_1 = k_1, \ldots, X_{t-1} = k_{t-1}, X_t = i\} = P\{X_{t+1} = j \,|\, X_t = i\}$, for $t = 0, 1, \ldots$ and every sequence $i, j, k_0, k_1, \ldots, k_{t-1}$.

This Markovian property can be shown to be equivalent to stating that the conditional probability of any future "event," given any past "event" and the present state $X_t = i$, is *independent* of the past event and depends upon only the present state of the process. The conditional probabilities $P\{X_{t+1} = j \,|\, X_t = i\}$ are called transition probabilities. If, for each i and j,

$$P\{X_{t+1} = j \,|\, X_t = i\} = P\{X_1 = j \,|\, X_0 = i\}, \quad \text{for all } t = 0, 1, \ldots,$$

then the (one-step) transition probabilities are said to be *stationary* and are usually denoted by p_{ij}. Thus having stationary transition probabilities implies that the transition probabilities do not change in time. The existence of stationary (one-step) transition probabilities also implies that, for each i, j, and n ($n = 0, 1, 2, \ldots$),

$$P\{X_{t+n} = j \,|\, X_t = i\} = P\{X_n = j \,|\, X_0 = i\},$$

for all $t = 0, 1, \ldots$. These conditional probabilities are usually denoted by $p_{ij}^{(n)\dagger}$ and are called *n*-step transition probabilities. Thus $p_{ij}^{(n)}$ is just the conditional probability that the random variable X, starting in state i, will be in state j after exactly n steps (time units).

Because the $p_{ij}^{(n)}$ are conditional probabilities, they must satisfy the properties

$$p_{ij}^{(n)} \geq 0, \quad \text{for all } i \text{ and } j, \text{ and } \quad n = 0, 1, 2, \ldots$$

$$\sum_{j=0}^{M} p_{ij}^{(n)} = 1, \quad \text{for all } i, \text{ and } \quad n = 0, 1, 2, \ldots.$$

A convenient notation for representing the transition probabilities is the matrix form

$$
\mathbf{P}^{(n)} =
\begin{array}{c|ccc}
State & 0 & 1 & M \\
\hline
0 & p_{00}^{(n)} & \cdots & p_{0M}^{(n)} \\
1 & & & \\
\vdots & \vdots & & \vdots \\
M & p_{M0}^{(n)} & \cdots & p_{MM}^{(n)}
\end{array}
\quad, \quad \text{for } n = 0, 1, 2, \ldots
$$

or equivalently

$$
\mathbf{P}^{(n)} =
\begin{bmatrix}
p_{00}^{(n)} & \cdots & p_{0M}^{(n)} \\
\vdots & & \\
p_{M0}^{(n)} & & p_{MM}^{(n)}
\end{bmatrix}.
$$

$\dagger$ For $n = 0$, $p_{ij}^{(0)}$ is just $P\{X_0 = j \,|\, X_0 = i\}$ and hence is 1 when $i = j$ and 0 when $i \neq j$. For $n = 1$, $p_{ij}^{(1)}$ is just the (one-step) transition probability and is denoted by p_{ij}.

It is now possible to define a Markov chain. A stochastic process $\{X_t\}$ ($t = 0,1,\ldots$) is said to be a *finite-state Markov chain*[1] if it has the following:

1. A finite number of states.
2. The Markovian property.
3. Stationary transition probabilities.
4. A set of initial probabilities $P\{X_0 = i\}$ for all i.

Returning to the inventory example developed in the preceding section, it is easily seen that $\{X_t\}$, where X_t is the number of cameras in stock at the end of the tth week (before an order is received), is a Markov chain. Now consider how to obtain the (one-step) transition probabilities, i.e., the elements of the (one-step) *transition matrix*

$$\mathbf{P} = \begin{bmatrix} p_{00} & p_{01} & p_{02} & p_{03} \\ p_{10} & p_{11} & p_{12} & p_{13} \\ p_{20} & p_{21} & p_{22} & p_{23} \\ p_{30} & p_{31} & p_{32} & p_{33} \end{bmatrix},$$

assuming that each D_t has a Poisson distribution with parameter $\lambda = 1$.

To obtain p_{00} it is necessary to evaluate $P\{X_t = 0 \mid X_{t-1} = 0\}$. If $X_{t-1} = 0$, then $X_t = \max\{(3 - D_t),0\}$. Therefore, if $X_t = 0$, then the demand during the week has to be 3 or more. Hence $p_{00} = P\{D_t \geq 3\}$. This transition probability is just the probability that a Poisson random variable with parameter $\lambda = 1$ takes on a value of 3 or more, which is obtained from Table A5.4 of Appendix 5, so that $p_{00} = 0.08$. $p_{10} = P\{X_t = 0 \mid X_{t-1} = 1\}$ can be obtained in a similar way. If $X_{t-1} = 1$, then $X_t = \max\{(1 - D_t),0\}$. To have $X_t = 0$, the demand during the week has to be 1 or more. Hence $p_{10} = P\{D_t \geq 1\} = 0.632$ (from Table A5.4 of Appendix 5). To find $p_{21} = P\{X_t = 1 \mid X_{t-1} = 2\}$, note that $X_t = \max\{(2 - D_t),0\}$ if $X_{t-1} = 2$. Therefore, if $X_t = 1$, then the demand during the week has to be exactly 1. Hence $p_{21} = P\{D_t = 1\} = 0.368$ (from Table A5.4 of Appendix 5). The remaining entries are obtained in a similar manner, which yield the following (one-step) transition matrix:

$$\mathbf{P} = \begin{bmatrix} 0.080 & 0.184 & 0.368 & 0.368 \\ 0.632 & 0.368 & 0 & 0 \\ 0.264 & 0.368 & 0.368 & 0 \\ 0.080 & 0.184 & 0.368 & 0.368 \end{bmatrix}$$

15.4 Chapman-Kolmogorov Equations

Section 15.3 introduced the n-step transition probability $p_{ij}^{(n)}$. This transition probability can be useful when the process is in state i and the probability that

---

[1] The definitions of Markovian property and Markov chain are more restrictive than the usages of these terms in the literature because the discussion is confined to a discrete time parameter and finite-state space.

the process will be in state j after n periods is desired. The *Chapman-Kolmogorov equations* provide a method for computing these n-step transition probabilities:

$$p_{ij}^{(n)} = \sum_{k=0}^{M} p_{ik}^{(v)} p_{kj}^{(n-v)}, \quad \text{for all } i, j, n, \text{ and } \quad 0 \le v \le n.$$

These equations merely point out that in going from state i to state j in n steps, the process will be in some state k after exactly v (less than n) steps. Thus $p_{ik}^{(v)} p_{kj}^{(n-v)}$ is just the conditional probability that, starting from state i, the process goes to state k after v steps and then to state j in $n - v$ steps. Therefore, summing these conditional probabilities over all possible k must yield $p_{ij}^{(n)}$. The special cases of $v = 1$ and $v = n - 1$ lead to the expressions

$$p_{ij}^{(n)} = \sum_{k=0}^{M} p_{ik} p_{kj}^{(n-1)}$$

and

$$p_{ij}^{(n)} = \sum_{k=0}^{M} p_{ik}^{(n-1)} p_{kj},$$

for all i, j, n. It then becomes evident that the n-step transition probabilities can be obtained from the one-step transition probabilities recursively. This recursive relationship is best explained in matrix notation (see Appendix 3). For $n = 2$, these expressions become

$$p_{ij}^{(2)} = \sum_{k=0}^{M} p_{ik} p_{kj}, \quad \text{for all } i, j.$$

Note that the $p_{ij}^{(2)}$ are the elements of the matrix $\mathbf{P}^{(2)}$. However, it must also be noted that these elements

$$\sum_{k=0}^{M} p_{ik} p_{kj}$$

are obtained by multiplying the matrix of one-step transition probabilities by itself; that is,

$$\mathbf{P}^{(2)} = \mathbf{P} \cdot \mathbf{P} = \mathbf{P}^2.$$

More generally, it follows that the matrix of n-step transition probabilities can be obtained from the expression

$$\mathbf{P}^{(n)} = \mathbf{P} \cdot \mathbf{P} \cdots \mathbf{P} = \mathbf{P}^n$$
$$= \mathbf{P}\mathbf{P}^{n-1} = \mathbf{P}^{n-1}\mathbf{P}.$$

Thus the n-step transition probability matrix can be obtained by computing the nth power of the one-step transition matrix. For values of n that are not too large, the n-step transition matrix can be calculated in the manner just described. However, when n is large, such computations are often tedious, and furthermore, round-off errors may cause inaccuracies.

Returning to the inventory example, the two-step transition matrix is given by

$$
\mathbf{P}^{(2)} = \mathbf{P}^2 = \begin{bmatrix} 0.080 & 0.184 & 0.368 & 0.368 \\ 0.632 & 0.368 & 0 & 0 \\ 0.264 & 0.368 & 0.368 & 0 \\ 0.080 & 0.184 & 0.368 & 0.368 \end{bmatrix} \begin{bmatrix} 0.080 & 0.184 & 0.368 & 0.368 \\ 0.632 & 0.368 & 0 & 0 \\ 0.264 & 0.368 & 0.368 & 0 \\ 0.080 & 0.184 & 0.368 & 0.368 \end{bmatrix}
$$

$$
= \begin{bmatrix} 0.249 & 0.286 & 0.300 & 0.165 \\ 0.283 & 0.252 & 0.233 & 0.233 \\ 0.351 & 0.319 & 0.233 & 0.097 \\ 0.249 & 0.286 & 0.300 & 0.165 \end{bmatrix}. \dagger
$$

Thus, given that there is one camera left in stock at the end of a week, the probability is 0.283 that there will be no cameras in stock 2 weeks later; that is, $p_{10}^{(2)} = 0.283$. Similarly, given that there are two cameras left in stock at the end of a week, the probability is 0.097 that there will be three cameras in stock 2 weeks later; that is, $p_{23}^{(2)} = 0.097$.

The four-step transition matrix can also be obtained as follows:

$$
\mathbf{P}^{(4)} = \mathbf{P}^4 = \mathbf{P}^{(2)} \cdot \mathbf{P}^{(2)}
$$

$$
= \begin{bmatrix} 0.249 & 0.286 & 0.300 & 0.165 \\ 0.283 & 0.252 & 0.233 & 0.233 \\ 0.351 & 0.319 & 0.233 & 0.097 \\ 0.249 & 0.286 & 0.300 & 0.165 \end{bmatrix} \begin{bmatrix} 0.249 & 0.286 & 0.300 & 0.165 \\ 0.283 & 0.252 & 0.233 & 0.233 \\ 0.351 & 0.319 & 0.233 & 0.097 \\ 0.249 & 0.286 & 0.300 & 0.165 \end{bmatrix}
$$

$$
= \begin{bmatrix} 0.289 & 0.286 & 0.261 & 0.164 \\ 0.282 & 0.285 & 0.268 & 0.166 \\ 0.284 & 0.283 & 0.263 & 0.171 \\ 0.289 & 0.286 & 0.261 & 0.164 \end{bmatrix}.
$$

Thus, given that there is one camera left in stock at the end of a week, the probability is 0.282 that there will be no cameras in stock 4 weeks later; that is, $p_{10}^{(4)} = 0.282$. Similarly, given that there are two cameras left in stock at the end of a week, the probability is 0.171 that there will be three cameras in stock 4 weeks later; that is, $p_{23}^{(4)} = 0.171$.

It was pointed out that the one- or n-step transition probabilities are conditional probabilities; for example, $P\{X_n = j \mid X_0 = i\} = p_{ij}^{(n)}$. If the unconditional probability $P\{X_n = j\}$ is desired, it is necessary to have specified the probability distribution of the initial state. Denote this probability distribution by $Q_{X_0}(i)$, where

$$
Q_{X_0}(i) = P\{X_0 = i\}, \quad \text{for } i = 0, 1, \ldots, M.
$$

---

† Note that round-off errors already appear in the row corresponding to state 1.

It then follows that

$$P\{X_n = j\} = Q_{X_0}(0)p_{0j}^{(n)} + Q_{X_0}(1)p_{1j}^{(n)} + \cdots + Q_{X_0}(M)p_{Mj}^{(n)}.$$

In the inventory example it was assumed that initially there were 3 units in stock; that is, $X_0 = 3$. Thus

$$Q_{X_0}(0) = Q_{X_0}(1) = Q_{X_0}(2) = 0,$$

and

$$Q_{X_0}(3) = 1.$$

Hence the (unconditional) probability that there will be three cameras in stock 2 weeks after the inventory system began is 0.165; that is, $P\{X_2 = 3\} = (1)p_{33}^{(2)}$. If, instead, it were given that $Q_{X_0}(i) = \frac{1}{4}$, for $i = 0, 1, 2, 3$, then

$$P\{X_2 = 3\} = \left(\frac{1}{4}\right)0.165 + \left(\frac{1}{4}\right)0.233 + \frac{1}{4}(0.097) + \frac{1}{4}(0.165) = 0.165.$$

The fact that the same answer is obtained using these two initial probability distributions is purely coincidental.

15.5 First Passage Times

Section 15.4 dealt with finding n-step transition probabilities [i.e., given that the process is in state i, determining the (conditional) probability that the process will be in state j after n periods]. It is often desirable to make probability statements about the number of transitions made by the process in going from state i to state j *for the first time*. This length of time is called the *first passage time* in going from state i to state j. When $j = i$, this first passage time is just the number of transitions until the process returns to the initial state i. In this case, the first passage time is called the *recurrence time* for state i.

To illustrate these definitions, reconsider the inventory example developed in the preceding sections. Recall that the initial inventory (X_0) contains three cameras. Suppose that it turns out that there are two cameras at the end of the first week (X_1 takes on the value 2), one camera at the end of the second week (X_2 takes on the value 1), no cameras in stock at the end of the third week (X_3 takes on the value 0), three cameras at the end of the fourth week (X_4 takes on the value 3), and one camera at the end of the fifth week (X_5 takes on the value 1). In this case, the first passage time in going from state 3 to state 1 is 2 weeks, the first passage time in going from state 3 to state 0 is 3 weeks, and the recurrence time of state 3 is 4 weeks.

In general, the first passage times are random variables and hence have probability distributions associated with them. These probability distributions depend upon the transition probabilities of the process. In particular, let $f_{ij}^{(n)}$ denote the probability that the first passage time from state i to j is equal to n. It can be shown that these probabilities satisfy the following recursive relationships:

$$f_{ij}^{(1)} = p_{ij}^{(1)} = p_{ij},$$
$$f_{ij}^{(2)} = p_{ij}^{(2)} - f_{ij}^{(1)} p_{jj},$$
$$\vdots$$
$$f_{ij}^{(n)} = p_{ij}^{(n)} - f_{ij}^{(1)} p_{jj}^{(n-1)} - f_{ij}^{(2)} p_{jj}^{(n-2)} \cdots - f_{ij}^{(n-1)} p_{jj}.$$

Thus the probability of a first passage time from state i to state j in n steps can be computed recursively from the one-step transition probabilities. In the inventory example, the probability distribution of the first passage time in going from state 3 to state 0 is obtained as follows:

$$f_{30}^{(1)} = 0.080$$
$$f_{30}^{(2)} = (0.249) - (0.080)(0.080) = 0.243$$
$$\vdots$$

For fixed i and j, the $f_{ij}^{(n)}$ are nonnegative numbers such that

$$\sum_{n=1}^{\infty} f_{ij}^{(n)} \leq 1.$$

Unfortunately, this sum may be strictly less than 1, which implies that a process initially in state i may never reach state j. When the sum does equal 1, $f_{ij}^{(n)}$ (for $n = 1,2,\ldots$) can be considered as a probability distribution for the random variable, the first passage time.

If $i = j$ and

$$\sum_{n=1}^{\infty} f_{ii}^{(n)} = 1,$$

then state i is called a *recurrent state* because this condition implies that once the process is in state i, it will return to state i. A special case of a recurrent state is an *absorbing state*. A state i is said to be an *absorbing state* if the (one-step) transition probability p_{ii} equals 1. Thus, if a state is an absorbing state, the process will never leave it once it enters.

If

$$\sum_{n=1}^{\infty} f_{ii}^{(n)} < 1,$$

then state i is called a *transient state* because this condition implies that once the process is in state i, there is a strictly positive probability that it will never return to state i.

It is not generally possible to calculate the probabilities of first passage time for all n, so it is not always evident whether a state should be classified as recurrent or transient. For example, although all states in the inventory example are recurrent (as shown in Sec. 15.6), it is not simple to prove that

$$\sum_{n=1}^{\infty} f_{ii}^{(n)} = 1.$$

As another example, suppose that a Markov process has the following transition matrix:

$$
\mathbf{P} = \begin{array}{c} \\ \\ \\ \text{State} \\ \\ \\ \end{array}
\begin{array}{cc}
 & \text{State} \\
 & \begin{array}{ccccc} 0 & 1 & 2 & 3 & 4 \end{array} \\
\begin{array}{c} 0 \\ 1 \\ 2 \\ 3 \\ 4 \end{array} &
\left[\begin{array}{ccccc}
\frac{1}{4} & \frac{3}{4} & 0 & 0 & 0 \\
\frac{1}{2} & \frac{1}{2} & 0 & 0 & 0 \\
0 & 0 & 1 & 0 & 0 \\
0 & 0 & \frac{1}{3} & \frac{2}{3} & 0 \\
1 & 0 & 0 & 0 & 0
\end{array} \right].
\end{array}
$$

It is evident that state 2 is an absorbing state (and hence a recurrent state) because once the process enters state 2 (third row of the matrix), it will never leave. States 3 and 4 are transient states because once the process is in state 3, there is a positive probability that it will never return. The probability is $\frac{1}{3}$ that the process will go from state 3 to state 2 on the first step. Once the process is in state 2, it remains in state 2. Once a process leaves state 4, it can never return. States 0 and 1 are recurrent states. As indicated earlier, to show that states 0 and 1 are recurrent it is sufficient to show that

$$
\sum_{n=1}^{\infty} f_{00}^{(n)} = 1 \quad \text{and} \quad \sum_{n=1}^{\infty} f_{11}^{(n)} = 1.
$$

This is generally difficult, and an alternative test is desired. A necessary and sufficient condition that state i be recurrent is that

$$
\sum_{n=1}^{\infty} p_{ii}^{(n)}
$$

should diverge. Unfortunately, this criterion is also difficult to apply, so that another criterion is given in Sec. 15.6. However, observe that the n-step transition matrix of the preceding example always has the appearance

$$
\mathbf{P}^{(n)} = \begin{bmatrix}
* & * & 0 & 0 & 0 \\
* & * & 0 & 0 & 0 \\
0 & 0 & 1 & 0 & 0 \\
0 & 0 & * & * & 0 \\
* & * & 0 & 0 & 0
\end{bmatrix},
$$

where the symbol $*$ represents positive numbers. Hence it is intuitively evident that once the process is in state 0, it will return to state 0 (possibly passing through state 1) after some number of steps. A similar argument holds for state 1.

Whereas calculating $f_{ij}^{(n)}$ for all n may be difficult, it is relatively simple to obtain the expected first passage time from state i to state j. Denote this expectation by μ_{ij}, which is defined by the expressions

$$
\mu_{ij} =
\begin{cases}
\infty, & \text{if } \sum_{n=1}^{\infty} f_{ij}^{(n)} < 1 \\
\sum_{n=1}^{\infty} n f_{ij}^{(n)}, & \text{if } \sum_{n=1}^{\infty} f_{ij}^{(n)} = 1.
\end{cases}
$$

Whenever

$$
\sum_{n=1}^{\infty} f_{ij}^{(n)} = 1,
$$

then μ_{ij} satisfies uniquely the equation

$$
\mu_{ij} = 1 + \sum_{k \neq j} p_{ik} \mu_{kj}.
$$

For the inventory example, these equations can be used to compute the expected time until the cameras are out of stock, assuming the process is started when three cameras are available; i.e., the expected first passage time, μ_{30}, can be obtained. Assuming that all the states are recurrent (as is shown soon), the system of equations leads to the expressions

$$
\mu_{30} = 1 + p_{31}\mu_{10} + p_{32}\mu_{20} + p_{33}\mu_{30},
$$
$$
\mu_{20} = 1 + p_{21}\mu_{10} + p_{22}\mu_{20} + p_{23}\mu_{30},
$$
$$
\mu_{10} = 1 + p_{11}\mu_{10} + p_{12}\mu_{20} + p_{13}\mu_{30},
$$

or

$$
\mu_{30} = 1 + 0.184\mu_{10} + 0.368\mu_{20} + 0.368\mu_{30},
$$
$$
\mu_{20} = 1 + 0.368\mu_{10} + 0.368\mu_{20},
$$
$$
\mu_{10} = 1 + 0.368\mu_{10}.
$$

The simultaneous solution to this system of equations is

$$
\mu_{10} = 1.58 \text{ weeks,}
$$
$$
\mu_{20} = 2.51 \text{ weeks,}
$$
$$
\mu_{30} = 3.50 \text{ weeks,}
$$

so that the expected time until the cameras are out of stock is 3.50 weeks. In making these calculations, we also obtain μ_{20} and μ_{10}.

When $j = i$, the expected first passage time is called the *expected recurrence time*. The recurrent state is called a *null recurrent* state if $\mu_{ii} = \infty$, and it is called a *positive recurrent* state if $\mu_{ii} < \infty$. In a finite-state Markov chain there are no null recurrent states (only positive recurrent states and transient states).

15.6 Classification of States of a Markov Chain

Section 15.5 classified states of a Markov chain as recurrent (positive or null) or transient. Some further concepts and definitions concerning these states are required.

State j is said to be *accessible* from state i if $p_{ij}^{(n)} > 0$ for some $n \geq 0$. Recall that $p_{ij}^{(n)}$ is just the conditional probability of being in state j after n steps, starting in state i. It is easily shown then that state j is accessible from state i if, and only if, it is possible for the system to enter state j starting from state i. In the inventory example, $p_{ij}^{(2)} > 0$ for all i, j, so that every state is accessible from every other state. Obviously a sufficient condition for *all* states to be accessible is that there exists a value of n, not dependent upon i and j, for which $p_{ij}^{(n)} > 0$ for all i and j.

If state j is accessible from state i, and, in addition, state i is accessible from state j, then states i and j are said to *communicate*. In the inventory example, all states communicate. In general, (1) any state communicates with itself [because $p_{ii}^{(0)} = P\{X_0 = i \mid X_0 = i\} = 1$]; (2) if state i communicates with state j, then state j communicates with state i; and furthermore, (3) if state i communicates with state j, and state j communicates with state k, then state i communicates with state k.

As a result of these three properties of communication, the state space may be partitioned into disjoint classes, with two states communicating said to belong in the same class. Thus the states of a Markov chain may consist of one or more disjoint classes (a class may consist of a single state). If there is only one class, i.e., all the states communicate, the Markov chain is said to be *irreducible*. In the inventory example, the Markov chain is irreducible. The transition matrix presented in Sec. 15.5 contains four classes. States 0 and 1, recurrent states, form one class in that they communicate with one another. State 2 is an absorbing (and recurrent) state and hence forms a class because it communicates with itself. State 3, a transient state, communicates with itself and also forms a class. State 4, also a transient state, forms the final class.

In a finite-state Markov chain, the members of a class are either all transient states or all positive recurrent states. Many Markov chains encountered in practice consist entirely of states that all communicate with each other; these irreducible Markov chains contain only positive recurrent states.[1] As we have just indicated, to determine whether all states of a chain communicate with each other, it is sufficient to show that there exists a value of n not dependent upon i and j for which $p_{ij}^{(n)} > 0$ for all i and j. This criterion is, then, the alternative criterion alluded to in Sec. 15.5 for determining whether states are recurrent. In the inventory example, $p_{ij}^{(2)}$ is positive for all i and j, so that all states communicate, and hence is an irreducible Markov chain. Therefore, this chain must contain states that are all positive recurrent.

A final property of Markov chains that is to be considered is the property of *periodicities*. A state i is said to have period t ($t > 1$) if $p_{ii}^{(n)} = 0$ whenever n is not divisible by t, and t is the largest integer with this property. For example, it may be possible for the process to enter state i only at the time $0, 2, 4, \ldots$, in which case this state has period 2. If there are two consecutive numbers, s and $(s + 1)$, such that the process can be in state i at times s and $(s + 1)$, the state is said to have

---

[1] The only possible alternative for such a chain is that it contains all transient states, which is not possible for a finite-state Markov chain.

period 1 and is called an *aperiodic* state. If state i in a class is aperiodic, then all states in the class are aperiodic. Positive recurrent states that are aperiodic are called *ergodic* states.

15.7 Long-Run Properties of Markov Chains

STEADY-STATE PROBABILITIES

In Sec. 15.4 the four-step transition matrix for the inventory example was obtained. It will now be instructive to examine the eight-step transition probabilities given by the matrix

$$\mathbf{P}^{(8)} = \mathbf{P}^8 = \mathbf{P}^4 \cdot \mathbf{P}^4 = \begin{bmatrix} 0.286 & 0.285 & 0.264 & 0.166 \\ 0.286 & 0.285 & 0.264 & 0.166 \\ 0.286 & 0.285 & 0.264 & 0.166 \\ 0.286 & 0.285 & 0.264 & 0.166 \end{bmatrix}$$

Notice the rather remarkable fact that each of the four rows has identical entries. This implies that the probability of being in state j after 8 weeks appears to be independent of the initial level of inventory. In other words, it appears that there is a limiting probability that the system will be in state j after a large number of transitions, and this probability is independent of the initial state. An important result related to the long-run behavior of finite-state Markov processes follows.

For an irreducible ergodic Markov chain, it can be shown that $\lim_{n \to \infty} p_{ij}^{(n)}$ exists and is independent of i. Furthermore,

$$\lim_{n \to \infty} p_{ij}^{(n)} = \pi_j,$$

where the π_j's uniquely satisfy the following steady-state equations:

$$\pi_j > 0,$$

$$\pi_j = \sum_{i=0}^{M} \pi_i p_{ij}, \quad \text{for } j = 0, 1, \dots, M,$$

$$\sum_{j=0}^{M} \pi_j = 1.$$

The π_j's are called the *steady-state probabilities* of the Markov chain and are equal to the reciprocal of the expected recurrence time; that is,

$$\pi_j = \frac{1}{\mu_{jj}}, \quad \text{for } j = 0, 1, \dots, M.$$

The term *steady-state* probability means that the probability of finding the process in a certain state, say j, after a large number of transitions tends to the value π_j, independent of the initial probability distribution defined over the states. It is important to note that steady-state probability does *not* imply that the process settles down into one state. On the contrary, the process continues to make transitions from state to state, and at any step n the transition probability from state i to state j is still p_{ij}.

The π_j's can also be interpreted as stationary probabilities (not to be confused with stationary transition probabilities). If the initial absolute probability of being in state j is given by π_j (that is, $P\{X_0 = j\} = \pi_j$) for all j, then the absolute probability of finding the process in state j at time $n = 1, 2, \ldots$, is also given by π_j (that is, $P\{X_n = j\} = \pi_j$).

It should be noted that the steady-state equations consist of $(M + 2)$ equations in $(M + 1)$ unknowns. Because it has a unique solution, at least one equation must be redundant and can, therefore, be deleted. It cannot be the equation

$$\sum_{j=0}^{M} \pi_j = 1$$

because $\pi_j = 0$ for all j will satisfy the other $(M + 1)$ equations. Furthermore, the solutions to the other $(M + 1)$ steady-state equations have a unique solution up to a multiplicative constant, and it is the final equation that forces the solution to be a probability distribution.

Returning to the inventory example, the steady-state equations can be expressed as

$$\pi_0 = \pi_0 p_{00} + \pi_1 p_{10} + \pi_2 p_{20} + \pi_3 p_{30},$$
$$\pi_1 = \pi_0 p_{01} + \pi_1 p_{11} + \pi_2 p_{21} + \pi_3 p_{31},$$
$$\pi_2 = \pi_0 p_{02} + \pi_1 p_{12} + \pi_2 p_{22} + \pi_3 p_{32},$$
$$\pi_3 = \pi_0 p_{03} + \pi_1 p_{13} + \pi_2 p_{23} + \pi_3 p_{33},$$
$$1 = \pi_0 \quad + \pi_1 \quad + \pi_2 \quad + \pi_3.$$

Substituting values for p_{ij} into these equations leads to the equations

$$\pi_0 = (0.080)\pi_0 + (0.632)\pi_1 + (0.264)\pi_2 + (0.080)\pi_3,$$
$$\pi_1 = (0.184)\pi_0 + (0.368)\pi_1 + (0.368)\pi_2 + (0.184)\pi_3,$$
$$\pi_2 = (0.368)\pi_0 \quad\quad\quad + (0.368)\pi_2 + (0.368)\pi_3,$$
$$\pi_3 = (0.368)\pi_0 \quad\quad\quad\quad\quad\quad\quad + (0.368)\pi_3,$$
$$1 = \quad \pi_0 + \quad \pi_1 + \quad \pi_2 + \quad \pi_3.$$

Solving the last four equations provides the simultaneous solutions

$$\pi_0 = 0.285,$$
$$\pi_1 = 0.285,$$
$$\pi_2 = 0.264,$$
$$\pi_3 = 0.166,$$

which are essentially the results that appear in the matrix $\mathbf{P}^{(8)}$. Thus after many weeks the probability of finding zero, one, two, and three cameras in stock tends to 0.285, 0.285, 0.264, and 0.166, respectively. The corresponding expected recurrence times are

$$\mu_{00} = \frac{1}{\pi_0} = 3.51 \text{ weeks},$$

$$\mu_{11} = \frac{1}{\pi_1} = 3.51 \text{ weeks},$$

$$\mu_{22} = \frac{1}{\pi_2} = 3.79 \text{ weeks},$$

$$\mu_{33} = \frac{1}{\pi_3} = 6.02 \text{ weeks}.$$

There are other important results concerning steady-state probabilities. In particular, if i and j are recurrent states belonging to different classes, then

$$p_{ij}^{(n)} = 0, \quad \text{for all } n.$$

This result follows from the definition of a class.

Similarly, if j is a transient state, then

$$\lim_{n \to \infty} p_{ij}^{(n)} = 0, \quad \text{for all } i.$$

This result implies that the probability of finding the process in a transient state after a large number of transitions tends to zero.

EXPECTED AVERAGE COST PER UNIT TIME

The previous subsection dealt with Markov chains whose states were ergodic (positive recurrent and aperiodic). If the requirement that the states be aperiodic is relaxed, then the limit

$$\lim_{n \to \infty} p_{ij}^{(n)}$$

may not exist. To illustrate this point, consider the two-state transition matrix

$$\mathbf{P} = \begin{bmatrix} 0 & 1 \\ 1 & 0 \end{bmatrix}.$$

If the process starts in state 0 at time 0, it will be in state 0 at times $2, 4, 6, \ldots$, and in state 1 at times $1, 3, 5, \ldots$. Thus $p_{00}^{(n)} = 1$ if n is even and $p_{00}^{(n)} = 0$ if n is odd, so that

$$\lim_{n \to \infty} p_{00}^{(n)}$$

does not exist. However, the following limit always exists: For an irreducible Markov chain with positive recurrent states, e.g., a finite-state chain, then

$$\lim_{n \to \infty} \left\{ \frac{1}{n} \sum_{k=1}^{n} p_{ij}^{(k)} \right\} = \pi_j,$$

where the π_j's satisfy the steady-state equations presented on p. 510.

This result is extremely important in computing the long-run average cost per unit time associated with a Markov chain. Suppose that a cost (or other penalty function) $C(X_t)$ is incurred when the process is in state X_t at time t, for $t = 0, 1, 2, \ldots$. Note that $C(X_t)$ is a random variable which takes on any one of the values $C(0), C(1), \ldots, C(M)$, and the function $C(\cdot)$ is independent of t. The expected average cost incurred over the first n periods is given by the expression

$$E\left[\frac{1}{n}\sum_{t=1}^{n} C(X_t)\right].$$

Using the result that

$$\lim_{n \to \infty}\left\{\frac{1}{n}\sum_{k=1}^{n} p_{ij}^{(k)}\right\} = \pi_j,$$

it is simple to show that the (long-run) *expected average cost per unit time* is given by

$$\lim_{n \to \infty}\left\{E\left[\frac{1}{n}\sum_{t=1}^{n} C(X_t)\right]\right\} = \sum_{j=0}^{M} C(j)\pi_j.$$

As an example, suppose the camera store finds that a storage charge is being allocated for each camera remaining on the shelf at the end of the week. The cost is charged as follows: If $X_t = 0$, then $C(0) = 0$. If $X_t = 1$, then $C(1) = 2$. If $X_t = 2$, then $C(2) = 8$. Finally, if $X_t = 3$, then $C(3) = 18$. The long-run expected average holding cost per week can then be obtained from the preceding equation; that is,

$$\lim_{n \to \infty}\left\{E\left[\frac{1}{n}\sum_{t=1}^{n} C(X_t)\right]\right\} = 0(0.285) + 2(0.285) + 8(0.264) + 18(0.166) = 5.67.$$

It should be noted that an alternative measure to the (long-run) expected average cost per unit time is the (long-run) *actual average cost per unit time*. It can be shown that this latter measure is given by

$$\lim_{n \to \infty}\left\{\frac{1}{n}\sum_{t=1}^{n} C(X_t)\right\} = \sum_{j=0}^{M} \pi_j C(j)$$

for almost all paths of the process. Thus either measure leads to the same result. These results can also be used to interpret the meaning of the π_j's. To interpret them, let

$$C(X_k) = \begin{cases} 1, & \text{if } X_k = j \\ 0, & \text{if } X_k \neq j. \end{cases}$$

The (long-run) expected fraction of times the system is in state j is then given by

$$\lim_{n \to \infty}\left\{E\left[\frac{1}{n}\sum_{t=1}^{n} C(X_t)\right]\right\} = \lim_{n \to \infty}\{E[\text{fraction of times system is in state } j]\} = \pi_j.$$

Similarly, π_j can also be interpreted as the (long-run) actual fraction of times that the system is in state j.

EXPECTED AVERAGE COST PER UNIT TIME FOR COMPLEX COST FUNCTIONS

In the preceding subsection, the cost function was based solely on the state that the process is in at time t. In many important problems encountered in practice, the cost may depend upon another random variable as well as upon the state that the process is in. For example, in the inventory example developed in this chapter, suppose that the costs to be considered are the ordering cost and the penalty cost for unsatisfied demand (storage costs will be ignored). It is reasonable to assume that the number of cameras ordered depends only upon the state of the process (the number of cameras in stock) when the order is placed. The cost for unsatisfied demand may be assumed to depend upon the demand during the week as well as upon the state of the process at the beginning of the week. The charges for period t will be made at the end of the week and will include the cost of the order delivered on the Monday of that week and the cost of unsatisfied demand during the week. Thus the cost incurred for period t can be described as a function of X_{t-1} and D_t, that is, $C(X_{t-1}, D_t)$. Note that the demands D_t, $D_{t+1}, \ldots$, during successive weeks are assumed to be independent and identically distributed random variables. Furthermore, recall that the (s, S) policy $(1, 3)$ is being used. X_{t-1}, the stock level at the end of period $t - 1$ (before ordering), is defined iteratively by the expression given in Sec. 15.2. Thus it follows that $(X_0, X_1, X_2, \ldots, X_{t-1})$ and D_t are independent random variables because X_0, $X_1, X_2, \ldots, X_{t-1}$ are functions only of $X_0, D_1, \ldots, D_{t-1}$, which are independent of D_t. Under these conditions, it can be shown that the (long-run) *expected average cost per unit time* is given by

$$\lim_{n \to \infty} \left\{ E\left[\frac{1}{n} \sum_{t=1}^{n} C(X_{t-1}, D_t) \right] \right\} = \sum_{j=0}^{M} k(j)\pi_j,$$

where

$$k(j) = E[C(j, D_t)].$$

and this latter (conditional) expectation is taken with respect to the probability distribution of the random variable D_t (given the state). Similarly, the (long-run) actual average cost per unit time is given by

$$\lim_{n \to \infty} \left\{ \frac{1}{n} \sum_{t=1}^{n} C(X_{t-1}, D_t) \right\} = \sum_{j=0}^{M} k(j)\pi_j.$$

Suppose that the following costs are associated with the (s, S) inventory policy given earlier (storage charges are now neglected). If $z > 0$ cameras are ordered, the cost incurred is $10 + 25z$ dollars. If no cameras are ordered, no ordering cost is incurred. For each unit of unsatisfied demand (lost sales), there is a penalty of $50 per unit. If the $(s = 1, S = 3)$ ordering policy is followed, then the cost in week t is given by $C(X_{t-1}, D_t)$, where

$$C(X_{t-1}, D_t) = \begin{cases} 10 + (25)(3) + 50 \max\{(D_t - 3), 0\}, & \text{if } X_{t-1} < 1 \\ 50 \max\{(D_t - X_{t-1}), 0\}, & \text{if } X_{t-1} \geq 1 \end{cases}$$

for $t = 1, 2, \ldots$. Hence

$$C(0, D_t) = 85 + 50 \max\{(D_t - 3), 0\},$$

so that

$$k(0) = E[C(0, D_t)] = 85 + 50E[\max\{(D_t - 3), 0\}]$$
$$= 85 + 50[1P_D(4) + 2P_D(5) + 3P_D(6) + \cdots],$$

where $P_D(i)$ is the probability that the demand equals i and has been assumed to have a Poisson distribution with parameter $\lambda = 1$. Hence $k(0) = 86.2$. Similar calculations lead to the results

$$k(1) = E[C(1, D_t)] = 50E[\max\{(D_t - 1), 0\}]$$
$$= 50[1P_D(2) + 2P_D(3) + 3P_D(4) + \cdots]$$
$$= 18.4,$$

$$k(2) = E[C(2, D_t)] = 50E[\max\{(D_t - 2), 0\}]$$
$$= 50[1P_D(3) + 2P_D(4) + 3P_D(5) + \cdots]$$
$$= 5.2,$$

and

$$k(3) = E[C(3, D_t)] = 50E[\max\{(D_t - 3), 0\}]$$
$$= 50[1P_D(4) + 2P_D(5) + \cdots]$$
$$= 1.2.$$

Thus the (long-run) expected average inventory cost per week is given by

$$\sum_{j=0}^{3} k(j)\pi_j = (86.2)(0.285) + (18.4)(0.285) + (5.2)(0.264) + (1.2)(0.166) = 31.4.$$

This cost is the cost associated with the (s, S) policy, $(s, S) = (1, 3)$. The cost of other (s, S) policies can be evaluated in a similar way to identify the policy that minimizes the expected average inventory cost per week.

The results of this section were presented only in terms of the inventory example. However, the (nonnumerical) results still hold for other problems as long as the following conditions are satisfied:

1. $\{X_t\}$ is an irreducible Markov chain whose states are positive recurrent.
2. Associated with this Markov chain is a sequence of random variables $\{D_t\}$, each of which is independent and identically distributed.
3. For a fixed $m = 0, \pm 1, \pm 2, \ldots$, a cost $C(X_t, D_{t+m})$ is incurred at time t, for $t = 0, 1, 2, \ldots$.
4. The sequence $(X_0, X_1, X_2, \ldots, X_t)$ must be independent of D_{t+m}.

In particular, if these conditions are satisfied then

$$\lim_{n \to \infty} \left\{ E\left[\frac{1}{n} \sum_{t=1}^{n} C(X_t, D_{t+m}) \right] \right\} = \sum_{j=0}^{M} k(j)\pi_j,$$

where

$$k(j) = E[C(j, D_{t+m})],$$

and this latter conditional expectation is taken with respect to the probability distribution of the random variable D_t (given the state). Furthermore,

$$\lim_{n \to \infty} \left\{ \frac{1}{n} \sum_{t=1}^{n} C(X_t, D_{t+m}) \right\} = \sum_{j=0}^{M} k(j)\pi_j$$

for almost all paths of the process.

15.8 Absorption States

It was pointed out that a state k is called an *absorbing state* if $p_{kk} = 1$, so that once the chain visits k it remains there forever. If k is an absorbing state, the first passage probability from i to k is called the probability of absorption into k, having started at i. When there are two or more absorbing states in a chain, and when it is evident that the process will be absorbed into one of these states, it is desirable to find these probabilities of absorption. These probabilities can be obtained by solving a system of linear equations. Suppose that the Markov chain is such that ultimately one of the absorbing states will be reached. If the state k is an absorbing state, then the set of absorption probabilities f_{ik} satisfies the system of equations

$$f_{ik} = \sum_{j=0}^{M} p_{ij} f_{jk}, \quad \text{for } i = 0, 1, \ldots, M,$$

subject to the conditions

$$f_{kk} = 1,$$
$$f_{ik} = 0, \quad \text{if state } i \text{ is recurrent and } i \neq k.$$

Absorption probabilities are important in "random walks." A *random walk* is a Markov chain with the property that if the system is in a state i, then in a single transition the system either remains at i or moves to one of the states immediately adjacent to i. For example, a random walk often is used as a model for situations involving gambling. To illustrate, suppose that two players, each having \$2, agree to keep playing a game and betting \$1 at a time until one is broke. The amount of money that player A has after n plays of the game forms a Markov chain with transition matrix

$$\mathbf{P} = \begin{bmatrix} 1 & 0 & 0 & 0 & 0 \\ 1-p & 0 & p & 0 & 0 \\ 0 & 1-p & 0 & p & 0 \\ 0 & 0 & 1-p & 0 & p \\ 0 & 0 & 0 & 0 & 1 \end{bmatrix}.$$

If p represents the probability of A winning a single encounter, then the probability of absorption into state 0 (A losing all his money) can be obtained from the preceding system of equations. It can be shown that these equations then result in the alternate expressions (for general M rather than $M = 4$ as in this example),

$$1 - f_{i0} = \frac{\sum_{m=0}^{i-1} \rho^m}{\sum_{m=0}^{M-1} \rho^m}, \quad \text{for } i = 1, 2, \ldots, M,$$

where $\rho = (1 - p)/p$. For $M = 4$ and $i = 2$, the probability of A going broke is given by

$$f_{20} = \frac{\rho^2 + \rho^3}{1 + \rho + \rho^2 + \rho^3}.$$

15.9 Continuous Parameter Markov Chains

All the previous sections assumed that the time parameter t was discrete (that is, $t = 0, 1, 2, \ldots$). Such an assumption is suitable for many problems, but there are certain cases (such as for some queueing models) where a continuous time parameter is required.

Let $\{X(t)\}$, where $t \geq 0$, be a Markov chain with $M + 1$ discrete states $0, 1, \ldots, M$ and stationary transition probability function

$$p_{ij}(t) = P\{X(t + s) = j \,|\, X(s) = i\}, \quad \text{for } i, j = 0, 1, \ldots, M.$$

This function is assumed to be continuous at $t = 0$ with

$$\lim_{t \to 0} p_{ij}(t) = \begin{cases} 1, & \text{if } i = j \\ 0, & \text{if } i \neq j. \end{cases}$$

Just as the discrete time parameter models satisfy the Chapman-Kolmogorov equations, the continuous time transition probability function also satisfies these equations; i.e., for any state i and j, and positive numbers t and v ($0 \leq v \leq t$),

$$p_{ij}(t) = \sum_{k=0}^{M} p_{ik}(v) p_{kj}(t - v).$$

A pair of states i and j are said to communicate if there are times t_1 and t_2 such that $p_{ij}(t_1) > 0$ and $p_{ji}(t_2) > 0$. All states that communicate are said to form a class. If all states in a chain form a single class (irreducible chain), then

$$p_{ij}(t) > 0, \quad \text{for all } t > 0 \text{ and all states } i \text{ and } j.$$

Furthermore,

$$\lim_{t \to \infty} p_{ij}(t) = \pi_j$$

always exists and is independent of the initial state of the chain, for $i = 0$,

$1,\ldots,M$. The π_j satisfy the equations

$$\pi_j = \sum_{i=0}^{M} \pi_i p_{ij}(t), \quad \text{for } j = 0, 1, \ldots, M, \text{ and for every } t \geq 0.$$

Just as the one-step transition probabilities played a major role in describing the Markov process for a discrete time parameter chain, the analogous role for a continuous time parameter chain is played by the transition intensities. The *transition intensity* is defined by

$$u_j = -\frac{d}{dt}p_{jj}(0) = \lim_{t \to 0}\frac{1 - p_{jj}(t)}{t}, \quad \text{for } j = 0, 1, \ldots, M,$$

and

$$u_{ij} = \frac{d}{dt}p_{ij}(0) = \lim_{t \to 0}\frac{p_{ij}(t)}{t}, \quad \text{for all } i \neq j,$$

provided that these limits exist and are finite. μ_j is called the *intensity of passage*, given that the Markov chain is in state j, and μ_{ij} is called the *intensity of transition to state j* from the state i.

These transition intensities also satisfy the equation

$$\pi_j u_j = \sum_{i \neq j} \pi_i u_{ij}, \quad \text{for } j = 0, 1, \ldots, M.$$

The transition intensities can be interpreted as follows. The probability of transition from state i to j during the interval of length Δt, $p_{ij}(\Delta t)$, is equal to $u_{ij}\Delta t$ plus a remainder that, when divided by Δt, tends to zero as $\Delta t \to 0$. Similarly, $1 - p_{jj}(\Delta t)$, the probability of a transition from a state j to some other state during the interval of length Δt, is equal to $u_j\Delta t$ plus a remainder that, when divided by Δt, tends to zero as $\Delta t \to 0$. Thus, for small Δt, the probabilities of transition within a time interval of length Δt are essentially proportional to Δt, the proportionality constants being the transition intensities.

As an example, consider the following repairman problem that is discussed in detail in Chap. 16 (Queueing Theory). There are M machines serviced by a single repairman. A machine that breaks down (with mean rate λ) is serviced immediately (with service rate μ) unless the repairman is servicing another machine, in which case a waiting line is formed. A system is said to be in state n if n machines are not working. If the process is in state n, where $1 \leq n \leq M$, this state means that one machine is being serviced and $(n - 1)$ are in the waiting line waiting to be repaired. If the process is in state 0, then all machines are working, and the repairman is idle. Let $X(t)$ be the number of machines not working at time t. Suppose the transition intensities satisfy the condition that if i and j are states such that $|i - j| \geq 2$, than $u_{ij} = 0$. It can be shown that $\{X(t)\}$ is a continuous parameter Markov process that changes states only through transitions from a state to its immediate neighbors. The transition intensities can be written as

$$u_{j,j+1} = (M-j)\lambda, \qquad \text{if } j = 0,1,2,\dots,M,$$

$$u_{j,j-1} = \begin{cases} \mu, & \text{if } j = 1,2,\dots,M \\ 0, & \text{if } j = 0, \end{cases}$$

$$u_j = \begin{cases} (M-j)\lambda + \mu, & \text{if } j = 1,\dots,M \\ M\lambda, & \text{if } j = 0. \end{cases}$$

More explicitly,

$$\lim_{t \to 0} \left\{ \frac{p_{j,j+1}(t)}{t} \right\} = (M-j)\lambda, \qquad \text{for } j = 0,1,2,\dots,M,$$

$$\lim_{t \to 0} \left\{ \frac{p_{j,j-1}(t)}{t} \right\} = \begin{cases} \mu, & \text{for } j = 1,2,\dots,M \\ 0, & \text{for } j = 0, \end{cases}$$

$$\lim_{t \to 0} \left\{ \frac{1 - p_{jj}(t)}{t} \right\} = \begin{cases} (M-j)\lambda + \mu, & \text{for } j = 1,2,\dots,M \\ M\lambda, & \text{for } j = 0. \end{cases}$$

Thus these equations indicate that in a small time interval the number of machines not working either increases by 1, decreases by 1, or stays the same. The conditional probability of an increase of 1 is denoted by $(M-j)\lambda$; the conditional probability of a decrease by 1 is denoted by μ. Substituting these results into the system of equations that the π_j satisfy, that is,

$$\pi_j u_j = \sum_{i \neq j} \pi_i u_{ij},$$

the following system of equations is obtained:

$$\pi_0 M\lambda = \pi_1 \mu,$$

$$\pi_j[(M-j)\lambda + \mu] = \pi_{j-1}(M-j+1)\lambda + \pi_{j+1}\mu, \quad \text{for } j = 1,\dots,M-1.$$

$$\pi_M \mu = \pi_{M-1}\lambda, \qquad\qquad\qquad \text{for } j = M.$$

Solving this system of equations (together with the condition that $\Sigma \pi_i = 1$) leads to the steady-state probability distribution of $X(t)$ which is given in Sec. 16.6 (basic model with a limited source); that is,

$$P_0 = 1 \bigg/ \sum_{j=0}^{M} \left[\frac{M!}{(M-j)!} \left(\frac{\lambda}{\mu}\right)^j \right],$$

$$P_j = \frac{M!}{(M-j)!} \left(\frac{\lambda}{\mu}\right)^j P_0, \quad \text{for } j = 1,2,\dots,M.$$

SELECTED REFERENCES

1. Chung, K. L.: *Markov Chains with Stationary Transition Probabilities*, Springer-Verlag, Berlin, 1960.
2. Feller, W.: *An Introduction to Probability Theory and Its Applications*, vol. 1, 2d ed., Wiley, New York, 1957.

3. Heyman, D., and M. Sobel: *Stochastic Models in Operations Research*, vol. 1, McGraw-Hill, New York, 1982.
4. Karlin, S., and H. Taylor: *First Course in Stochastic Processes*, 2d ed., Academic Press, New York, 1975.
5. Ross, S.: *Introduction to Probability Models*, 3d ed., Academic Press, New York, 1985.
6. Ross, S.: *Stochastic Processes*, John Wiley, New York, 1983.

PROBLEMS

1. Assume that the probability of rain tomorrow is 0.6 if it is raining today, and assume that the probability of its being clear tomorrow is 0.9 if it is clear today.

  (a) Determine the one-step transition matrix of the Markov chain.
  (b) Find the steady-state probabilities.

2. Determine the classes of the Markov chains and whether or not they are recurrent.

$$
\begin{bmatrix}
0 & 0 & \frac{1}{3} & \frac{2}{3} \\
1 & 0 & 0 & 0 \\
0 & 1 & 0 & 0 \\
0 & 1 & 0 & 0
\end{bmatrix}
\begin{bmatrix}
1 & 0 & 0 & 0 \\
0 & \frac{1}{2} & \frac{1}{2} & 0 \\
0 & \frac{1}{2} & \frac{1}{2} & 0 \\
\frac{1}{2} & 0 & 0 & \frac{1}{2}
\end{bmatrix}
$$

3. Consider the following gambler's ruin problem. A gambler bets one unit on each play of a game. She has a probability p of winning and $q = 1 - p$ of losing. She will continue to play until she goes broke or nets a fortune of T units. Let X_n denote the gambler's fortune on the nth play of the game. Then

$$
X_{n+1} =
\begin{cases}
X_n + 1, \text{ with probability } p \\
X_n - 1, \text{ with probability } q = 1 - p
\end{cases},
\quad \text{for } 0 < X_n < T.
$$

$$
X_{n+1} = X_n, \qquad\qquad\qquad\qquad\qquad \text{for } X_n = 0 \text{ or } T.
$$

$\{X_n\}$ is a Markov chain. Assume that successive plays of the game are independent and that the gambler has an initial fortune of X_0.

  (a) Determine the one-step transition matrix of the Markov chain.
  (b) Find the classes of the Markov chain.
  (c) Let $T = 3$ and $p = 0.3$. Find $f_{10}, f_{1T}, f_{20}, f_{2T}$.
  (d) Let $T = 3$ and $p = 0.7$. Find $f_{10}, f_{1T}, f_{20}, f_{2T}$.
  What can you conclude from (c) and (d)?

4. Suppose that a communications network transmits binary digits, 0 or 1. In passing through the network, there is a probability q that the binary digit will be received incorrectly at the next stage. If X_0 denotes the binary digit entering the system, X_1 the binary digit recorded after the first transmission, X_2 the binary digit recorded after the second transmission, ..., then $\{X_n\}$ is a Markov chain. Find the one-step and steady-state transition matrices.

5. A transition matrix $\mathbf{P}$ is said to be doubly stochastic if the sum over each column equals 1; that is,

$$
\sum_{i=0}^{M} p_{ij} = 1, \quad \text{for all } j.
$$

If such a chain is irreducible, aperiodic, and consists of $M + 1$ states, show that

$$\pi_j = \frac{1}{M + 1}, \quad \text{for } j = 0, 1, \ldots, M.$$

6. A particle moves on a circle through points that have been marked 0, 1, 2, 3, 4 (in a clockwise order). The particle starts at point 0. At each step it has probability q of moving one point clockwise (0 follows 4) and $1 - q$ of moving one point counterclockwise. Let $X_n(n \geq 0)$ denote its location on the circle. $\{X_n\}$ is a Markov chain.

(a) Find the transition probability matrix.
(b) Find the steady-state probabilities.

7. Using ordering costs and unsatisfied demand costs, evaluate the expected average inventory cost per week for the inventory example introduced in Sec. 15.7, using the (s, S) policy, $(s, S) = (2, 3)$.

8. Consider the inventory example introduced in Sec. 15.2. Instead of following an (s,S) policy, we use a (q,Q) policy. If the stock level at the end of each period is less than $q = 2$ units, $Q = 2$ additional units will be ordered. Otherwise, no ordering will take place. This policy is a (q,Q) policy with $q = 2$ and $Q = 2$. Let X_t denote the number of units on hand at the end of the tth period. Assume that demand which is not filled results in lost sales. $\{X_n\}$ is a Markov chain (assume $X_0 = 0$). Using the cost values and demand distribution given for the inventory example in the text,

(a) Find the steady-state probabilities.
(b) Find the long-run expected average cost per unit time.

9. Consider the following (k,Q) inventory policy. Let $D_1, D_2, \ldots,$ be the demand for a product in periods $1, 2, \ldots,$ respectively. If the demand during a period exceeds the number of items available, this unsatisfied demand is backlogged; i.e., it is filled when the next order is received. Let Z_n $(n = 0,1,\ldots)$ denote the amount of inventory on hand minus the number of units backlogged before ordering at the end of period n ($Z_0 = 0$). If Z_n is zero or positive, no orders are backlogged. If Z_n is negative, then $-Z_n$ represents the number of backlogged units and no inventory is on hand. If at the end of period $n, Z_n < k = 1$, an order is placed for $2m$ (Qm in general) units, where m is the smallest integer such that $Z_n + 2m \geq 1$. (The amount ordered is the smallest integral multiple of 2, which brings the level to at least 1 unit.) Let D_n be independent and identically distributed random variables taking on the values, 0, 1, 2, 3, 4, each, with probability $\frac{1}{5}$. Let X_n denote the amount of stock on hand *after* ordering at the end of period n ($X_0 = 2$). It is evident that

$$X_n = \begin{cases} X_{n-1} - D_n + 2m, & \text{if } X_{n-1} - D_n < 1 \\ X_{n-1} - D_n, & \text{if } X_{n-1} - D_n \geq 1 \end{cases} \quad (n = 1,2,\ldots),$$

and $\{X_n\}$ $(n = 0,1,\ldots)$ is a Markov chain with only two states: 1 and 2. [The only time that ordering will take place is when $Z_n = 0, -1, -2,$ or $-3,$ in which case 2, 2, 4, and 4 units are ordered, respectively, leaving $X_n = 2, 1, 2, 1,$ respectively. In general, for any (k,Q) policy, the possible states are $k, k + 1, k + 2, \ldots, k + Q - 1.$]

(a) Find the one-step transition matrix.
(b) Find the stationary probabilities (see Prob. 5).
(c) Suppose that the ordering cost is given by $(2 + 2m)$ if an order is placed and zero otherwise. The holding cost per period is Z_n if $Z_n \geq 0$ and zero otherwise. The

shortage cost per period is $-4Z_n$ if $Z_n < 0$ and zero otherwise. Find the (long-run) expected average cost per unit time.

10. An important unit consists of two components placed in parallel. The unit performs satisfactorily if one of the two components is operating. A component breaks down in a given period with probability q. Assume that the component breaks down only at the end of a period. When this occurs, the parallel component takes over, if available, beginning at the next period. Only one serviceman is assigned to service each component in need of repair, and it takes two periods to complete the servicing. Let X_t be a vector consisting of two elements U and V. U represents the number of components operating at the end of the tth period. V takes on the value 1 if the serviceman requires only one additional period to complete a repair, if he is so engaged, and zero otherwise. Thus the state space consists of the four states $(2,0)$, $(1,0)$, $(0,1)$, and $(1,1)$. For example, the state $(1,1)$ implies that one component is operative and the other component needs an additional period for repair before becoming operative. Denote these four states by 0, 1, 2, 3, respectively. $\{X_t\}$ $(t = 0, 1, \ldots)$ is a Markov chain [assume that X_0 is the vector $(2,0)$; that is, $X_0 = 0$] with transition matrix,

$$\mathbf{P} = \begin{bmatrix} 1-q & q & 0 & 0 \\ 0 & 0 & q & 1-q \\ 0 & 1 & 0 & 0 \\ 1-q & q & 0 & 0 \end{bmatrix}.$$

(a) What is the probability that there is a waiting line of length 1 (a component needing service but not being worked on) at the end of a current period?

(b) What are the steady-state probabilities?

(c) If it costs \$30,000 per period when the unit is inoperable (both components down) and zero otherwise, what is the (long-run) expected average cost per period?

11. Consider a single-server queueing system, in which customers arrive according to a Poisson input process with parameter λ (see Sec. 16.6), and the service times for the respective calling units are independent and identically distributed random variables. For $n = 1, 2, \ldots$, let X_n denote the number of calling units in the system at the moment t_n when the nth calling unit to be served (over a certain time interval) has finished being served. The sequence of time $\{t_n\}$ corresponding to the moments when successive calling units depart service are called *regeneration points*. Furthermore, $\{X_n\}$, which represents the number of calling units in the system at the corresponding sequence of time $\{t_n\}$, is a Markov chain and is known as an *imbedded Markov chain*. Imbedded Markov chains are useful for studying the properties of continuous time parameter stochastic processes.

Now consider the particular special case where the service time of successive calling units is a fixed constant, say, 10 minutes, and the mean arrival rate is one every 50 minutes. To obtain a *finite* number of states, assume as an approximation that, if there are 4 calling units in the system, the system becomes saturated so that additional arrivals are turned away. Therefore, $\{X_n\}$ is an imbedded Markov chain with states 0, 1, 2, or 3. (Because there are never more than 4 calling units in the system, there can never be more than 3 in the system at a regeneration point.) Because the system is observed at successive departures, X_n can never decrease by more than 1. Furthermore, the probabilities of transitions that result in increases in X_n are obtained directly from the Poisson distribution.

(a) Find the one-step transition matrix. (In obtaining the transition probability from state 3 to state 3, use the probability of one or more arrivals rather than just one arrival, and similarly for other transitions to state 3.)

(b) Find the steady-state probabilities for the number of calling units in the system at regeneration points.

(c) Compute the expected number of calling units in the queueing system at regeneration points, and compare it to the value of L for the single-server model in Sec. 16.7.

12. Suppose that E_1, $E_2, \ldots, E_m$ are mutually exclusive events such that $E_1 \cup E_2 \cup \cdots \cup E_m = \Omega$; that is, exactly one of the E events will occur. Denote by F any event in the sample space. Note that

$$F = FE_1 \cup FE_2 \cup \cdots \cup FE_m,^\dagger$$

and that $FE_i, i = 1, 2, \ldots, m$ are also mutually exclusive.

(a) Show that $P\{F\} = \sum_{i=1}^{m} P\{FE_i\} = \sum_{i=1}^{m} P\{F \mid E_i\} P\{E_i\}$.

(b) Show that $P\{E_i \mid F\} = P\{F \mid E_i\} P\{E_i\} \Big/ \sum_{i=1}^{m} P\{F \mid E_i\} P\{E_i\}$.

(This result is called *Bayes' formula* and is useful when it is known that the event F has occurred and there is interest in determining which one of the E_i also occurred.)

---

† Recall that FE_1 is the same as $F \cap E_1$, that is, the intersection of the two events F and E_1.

■ CHAPTER 16

Queueing Theory

■ Queueing theory involves the mathematical study of queues, or waiting lines. The formation of waiting lines is, of course, a common phenomenon that occurs whenever the current demand for a service exceeds the current capacity to provide that service. Decisions regarding the amount of capacity to provide must be made frequently in industry and elsewhere. However, because it is often impossible to predict accurately when units will arrive to seek service and/or how much time will be required to provide that service, these decisions often are difficult ones. Providing too much service involves excessive costs. On the other hand, not providing enough service capacity causes the waiting line to become excessively long at times. Excessive waiting also is costly in some sense, whether it be a social cost, the cost of lost customers, the cost of idle employees, or some other important cost. Therefore, the ultimate goal is to achieve an economic balance between the cost of service and the cost associated with waiting for that service. Queueing theory itself does not directly solve this problem; however, it does contribute vital information required for such decisions by predicting such various characteristics of the waiting line as the average waiting time.

Queueing theory provides a large number of alternative mathematical models for describing a waiting-line situation. Mathematical results that predict some of the characteristics of the waiting line often are available for these models. After some general discussion, this chapter presents most of the more elementary models and their basic results. Chapter 17 discusses how the information provided by queueing theory might be used for making decisions.

16.1 Prototype Example

The emergency room of *County Hospital* provides quick medical care for emergency cases brought to the hospital by ambulance or private automobile. At any hour there is always one doctor on duty in the emergency room. However, because of a growing tendency for emergency cases to use these facilities rather than go to a private physician, the hospital has been experiencing a continuing increase in the number of emergency room visits each year. As a result, it has become quite common for patients arriving during peak usage hours (the early evening) to have to wait until it is their turn to be treated by the doctor. Therefore, a proposal has been made that a second doctor should be assigned to the emergency room during these hours, so that two emergency cases can be treated simultaneously. The hospital's Management Engineer has been assigned to study this question.[1]

The Management Engineer began by gathering the relevant historical data and then projecting these data into the next year. Recognizing that the emergency room is a queueing system, he applied several alternative queueing theory models to predict the waiting characteristics of the system with one doctor and with two doctors—as you will see in the latter sections of this chapter (see Tables 16.2, 16.3, and 16.4).

16.2 Basic Structure of Queueing Models

THE BASIC QUEUEING PROCESS

The basic process assumed by most queueing models is the following. *Customers* requiring service are generated over time by an *input source*. These customers enter the *queueing system* and join a *queue*. At certain times a member of the queue is selected for service by some rule known as the *queue discipline* (or *service discipline*). The required service is then performed for the customer by the *service mechanism*, after which the customer leaves the queueing system. This process is depicted in Fig. 16.1.

Many alternative assumptions can be made about the various elements of the queueing process; they are discussed next.

INPUT SOURCE (CALLING POPULATION)

One characteristic of the input source is its size. The *size* is the total number of customers that might require service from time to time, i.e., the total number of distinct potential customers. This population from which arrivals come is referred to as the **calling population**. The size may be assumed to be either *infinite* or *finite* (so that the input source also is said to be either *unlimited* or *limited*).

---

[1] For one actual case study of this kind, see Bolling, W. Blaker: "Queueing Model of a Hospital Emergency Room," *Industrial Engineering*, pp. 26–31, September 1972.

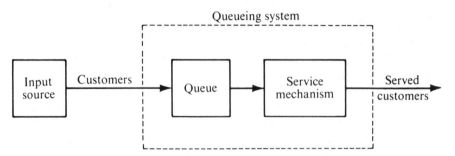

Figure 16.1 **The basic queueing process.**

Because the calculations are far easier for the infinite case, this assumption often is made even when the actual size is some relatively large finite number, and it should be taken to be the implicit assumption for any queueing model that does not state otherwise. The finite case is more difficult analytically because the number of customers in the queueing system affects the number of potential customers outside the system at any time. However, the finite assumption must be made if the rate at which the input source generates new customers is significantly affected by the number of customers in the queueing system.

The statistical pattern by which customers are generated over time must also be specified. The common assumption is that they are generated according to a *Poisson process*; i.e., the number of customers generated until any specific time has a Poisson distribution. As we discuss in Sec. 16.4, this case is the one where arrivals to the queueing system occur randomly but at a certain fixed mean rate, regardless of how many customers already are there (so the *size* of the input source is *infinite*). An equivalent assumption is that the probability distribution of the time between consecutive arrivals is an *exponential* distribution. (The properties of this distribution are described in Sec. 16.4.) The time between consecutive arrivals is referred to as the **interarrival time**.

Any unusual assumptions about the behavior of the customers must also be specified. One example is *balking*, where the customer refuses to enter the system and is lost if the queue is too long.

QUEUE

A queue is characterized by the maximum permissible number of customers that it can contain. Queues are called *infinite* or *finite*, according to whether this number is infinite or finite. The assumption of an *infinite queue* is the standard one for most queueing models, even for situations where there actually is a (relatively large) finite upper bound on the permissible number of customers, because dealing with such an upper bound would be a complicating factor in the analysis. However, for queueing systems where this upper bound is small enough that it actually would be reached with some frequency, it becomes necessary to assume a *finite queue*.

QUEUE DISCIPLINE

The queue discipline refers to the order in which members of the queue are selected for service. For example, it may be first-come-first-served, random, according to some priority procedure, or some other order. First-come-first-served usually is assumed by queueing models unless stated otherwise.

SERVICE MECHANISM

The service mechanism consists of one or more *service facilities*, each of which contains one or more *parallel service channels*, called **servers**. If there is more than one service facility, the customer may receive service from a sequence of these (*service channels in series*). At a given facility, the customer enters one of the parallel service channels and is completely serviced by that server. A queueing model must specify the arrangement of the facilities and the number of servers (parallel channels) at each one. Most elementary models assume one service facility with either one or a finite number of servers.

The time elapsed from the commencement of service to its completion for a customer at a service facility is referred to as the **service time** (or *holding time*). A model of a particular queueing system must specify the probability distribution of service times for each server (and possibly for different types of customers), although it is common to assume the *same* distribution for all servers (all models in this chapter make this assumption). The service-time distribution that is most frequently assumed in practice (largely because it is far more tractable than any other) is the *exponential* distribution discussed in Sec. 16.4, and most of our models will be of this type. Other important service-time distributions are the *degenerate* distribution (constant service time) and the *Erlang* (gamma) distribution, as illustrated by models in Sec. 16.7.

AN ELEMENTARY QUEUEING PROCESS

As we have already suggested, queueing theory has been applied to many different types of waiting-line situations. However, the most prevalent type of situation is the following: A single waiting line (which may be empty at times) forms in the front of a single service facility, within which are stationed one or more servers. Each customer generated by an input source is serviced by one of the servers, perhaps after some waiting in the queue (waiting line). The queueing system involved is depicted in Fig. 16.2.

Notice that the queueing process in the illustrative example of Sec. 16.1 is of this type. The input source generates customers in the form of emergency cases requiring medical care. The emergency room is the service facility, and the doctors are the servers.

A server need not be a single individual; it may be a group of persons, e.g., a repair crew that combines forces to perform simultaneously the required service for a customer. Furthermore, servers need not even be people. In many cases, a

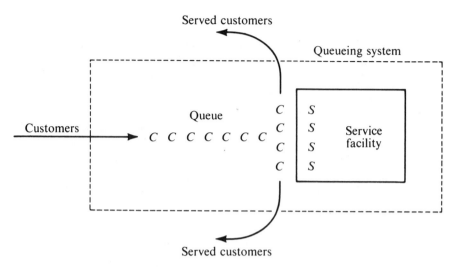

Served customers

Queueing system

Customers

Queue

C C C C C C C

C	S
C	S
C	S
C	S

Service facility

Served customers

Figure 16.2 An elementary queueing system (each customer is indicated by a *C* and each server by an *S*).

server may be a machine or a piece of equipment, e.g., a forklift that performs a given service on call (although probably with human guidance). By the same token, the customers in the waiting line need not be people. For example, they may be items waiting for a certain operation by a given type of machine, or they may be cars waiting in front of a toll booth.

It is not necessary that there actually be a physical waiting line forming in front of a physical structure that constitutes the service facility; that is, the members of the queue may be scattered throughout an area waiting for a server to come to them, e.g., machines waiting to be repaired. The server or group of servers assigned to a given area constitute the service facility for that area. Queueing theory still gives the average number waiting, the average waiting time, and so on because it is irrelevant whether or not the customers wait together in a group. The only essential requirement for queueing theory to be applicable is that changes in the number of customers waiting for a given service occur just as though the physical situation described in Fig. 16.2 (or a legitimate counterpart) prevails.

Except for Sec. 16.9, all the queueing models discussed in this chapter are of the elementary type depicted in Fig. 16.2. Many of these models further assume that all *interarrival times* are independent and identically distributed and that all *service times* are independent and identically distributed. Such models conventionally are labeled as follows:

Distribution of service times

—/—/— Number of servers

Distribution of interarrival times,

where

M = exponential distribution (Markovian), as described in Sec. 16.4,

D = degenerate distribution (constant times), as discussed in Sec. 16.7,

E_k = erlang distribution (shape parameter = k), as described in Sec. 16.7,

G = general distribution (any arbitrary distribution allowed),[1] as discussed in Sec. 16.7.

For example, the M/M/s model discussed in Sec. 16.6 assumes that both interarrival times and service times have an exponential distribution and that the number of servers is s (any positive integer). The M/G/1 model discussed again in Sec. 16.7 assumes that interarrival times have an exponential distribution, but it places no restriction on what the distribution of service times must be, whereas the number of servers is restricted to be exactly one. Various other models that fit this labeling scheme also are introduced in Sec. 16.7.

TERMINOLOGY AND NOTATION

Unless otherwise noted, the following standard terminology and notation will be used:

State of the system = number of customers in queueing system.

Queue length = number of customers waiting for service
= state of system minus number of customers being served.

$N(t)$ = number of customers in queueing system at time t ($t \geq 0$).

$P_n(t)$ = probability that exactly n customers are in queueing system at time t, given number at time 0.

s = number of servers (parallel service channels) in queueing system.

λ_n = mean arrival rate (expected number of arrivals per unit time) of new customers when n customers are in system.

μ_n = mean service rate for overall system (expected number of customers completing service per unit time) when n customers are in system. *Note*: μ_n represents *combined* rate at which all *busy* servers (those serving customers) achieve service completions.

λ, μ, ρ: see following paragraph.

---

[1] When referring to interarrival times, we conventionally replace the symbol G by GI = General Independent distribution.

When λ_n is a constant for all n, this constant is denoted by λ. When the mean service rate *per busy server* is a constant for all $n \geq 1$, this constant is denoted by μ. (In this case, $\mu_n = s\mu$ when $n \geq s$, i.e., when all s servers are busy.) Under these circumstances, $1/\lambda$ and $1/\mu$ are the *expected interarrival time* and the *expected service time*, respectively. Also, $\rho = \lambda/s\mu$ is the **utilization factor** for the service facility, i.e., the expected fraction of time the individual servers are busy because $\lambda/s\mu$ represents the fraction of the system's service capacity ($s\mu$) that is being *utilized* on the average by arriving customers (λ).

Certain notation also is required to describe *steady-state* results. When a queueing system has recently begun operation, the state of the system (number of customers in the system) will be greatly affected by the initial state and the time that has since elapsed. The system is now said to be a **transient condition**. However, after sufficient time has elapsed, the state of the system becomes essentially independent of the initial state and the elapsed time (except under unusual circumstances).[1] The system has now essentially reached a **steady-state condition**, where the probability distribution of the state of the system remains the same (the *steady-state* or *stationary* distribution) over time. Queueing theory has tended to focus largely on the steady-state condition, partially because the transient case is more difficult analytically. (Some transient results exist, but they are generally beyond the technical scope of this book.) The following notation assumes that the system is in a *steady-state condition*:

P_n = probability that exactly n customers are in queueing system.

L = expected number of customers in queueing system.

L_q = expected queue length (excludes customers being served).

$\mathscr{W}$ = waiting time in system (includes service time) for each individual customer.

$W = E(\mathscr{W})$.

$\mathscr{W}_q$ = waiting time in queue (excludes service time) for each individual customer.

$W_q = E(\mathscr{W}_q)$.

RELATIONSHIPS BETWEEN L, W, L_q, AND W_q

Assume that λ_n is a constant λ for all n. It has been proven that in a steady-state queueing process,

$$L = \lambda W.$$

(Because John D. C. Little[2] provided the first rigorous proof, this equation

---

[1] When λ and μ are defined, these unusual circumstances are that $\rho \geq 1$, in which case the state of the system tends to grow continually larger as time goes on.

[2] Little, John D. C.: "A Proof for the Queueing Formula: $L = \lambda W$," *Operations Research,* **9**(3): 383–387, 1961; also see Stidham, Jr., Shaler: "A Last Word on $L = \lambda W$," *Operations Research,* **22**(2): 417–421, 1974.

sometimes is referred to as **Little's formula**.) Furthermore, the same proof also shows that

$$L_q = \lambda W_q.$$

If the λ_n are not equal, then λ can be replaced in these equations by $\bar{\lambda}$, the *average* arrival rate over the long run. (We shall show later how $\bar{\lambda}$ can be determined for some basic cases.)

Now assume that the mean service time is a constant, $1/\mu$, for all $n \geq 1$. It then follows that

$$W = W_q + \frac{1}{\mu}.$$

These relationships are extremely important because they enable all four of the fundamental quantities—L, W, L_q, and W_q—to be immediately determined as soon as one of them is found analytically. This situation is fortunate because some of these quantities often are much easier to find than others when solving a queueing model from basic principles.

16.3 Examples of Real Queueing Systems

It may appear that our description of queueing systems in the preceding section is relatively abstract and applicable to only rather special practical situations. To the contrary—queueing systems are surprisingly prevalent in a wide variety of contexts. To broaden your horizons on the applicability of queueing theory, we shall briefly mention various examples of real queueing systems.

One important class of queueing systems that we all encounter in our daily lives is **commercial service systems**, where outside customers receive service from commercial organizations. Many of these involve person-to-person service at a fixed location, such as a *barber shop* (the barbers are the servers), *bank teller* service, *checkout stands* at a grocery store, and a *cafeteria line* (service channels in series). However, many others do not, such as *home appliance repairs* (the server travels to the customers), a *vending machine* (the server is a machine), and a *gas station* (the cars are the customers).

Another important class is **transportation service systems**. For some of these systems, the vehicles are the customers, such as *cars* waiting at a *toll booth* or *traffic light* (the server), a *truck* or *ship* waiting to be loaded or unloaded by a *crew* (the server), and *airplanes* waiting to land or take off from a *runway* (the server). (An unusual example of this kind is a *parking lot*, where the cars are the customers and the parking spaces are the servers, but there is no queue because arriving customers go elsewhere to park if the lot is full.) In other cases, the vehicles are the servers, such as *taxicabs*, *fire trucks*, and *elevators*.

In recent years, queueing theory probably has been applied most to **business-industrial internal service systems**, where the customers receiving service are *internal* to the organization. Examples include *materials-handling systems*, where materials-handling units (the servers) move loads (the customers); *maintenance systems*, where maintenance crews (the servers) repair machines (the customers); and *inspection stations*, where quality control inspectors (the servers) inspect items (the customers). *Employee facilities* and *typing pools* also fit into this category. In addition, *machines* can be viewed as servers whose customers are the jobs being processed. A related example of great importance is a *computer facility*, where the computer is viewed as the server.

There is now growing recognition that queueing theory also is applicable to **social service systems**. For example, a *judicial system* is a queueing network, where the courts are service facilities, the judges (or panels of judges) are the servers, and the cases waiting to be tried are the customers. A *legislative system* is a similar queueing network, where the customers are the congressional bills waiting to be processed. Various *health-care systems* also are queueing systems. You already have seen one example in Sec. 16.1 (a hospital emergency room), but you can also view *ambulances*, *x-ray machines*, and *hospital beds* as servers in their own queueing systems. Similarly, families waiting for low- and moderate-income housing, or other social services, can be viewed as customers in a queueing system.

Although these are four broad classes of queueing systems, they still do not exhaust the list. In fact, queueing theory first began early in this century with applications to *telephone engineering* (the founder of queueing theory, A. K. Erlang, was an employee of the Danish Telephone Company in Copenhagen), and telephone engineering still is an important application. Furthermore, we all have our own *personal queues*—homework assignments, books to be read, and so forth. However, these examples are sufficient to suggest that queueing systems do indeed pervade many areas of society.

16.4 The Role of the Exponential Distribution

The operating characteristics of queueing systems are largely determined by two statistical properties, namely, the probability distribution of *interarrival times* (see Input Source in Sec. 16.2) and the probability distribution of *service times* (see Service Mechanism in Sec. 16.2). For real queueing systems, these distributions can take on almost any form. (The only restriction is that negative values cannot occur.) However, to formulate a queueing-theory *model* as a representation of the real system, it is necessary to specify the assumed form of each of these distributions. To be useful, the assumed form should be *sufficiently realistic*, so that the model provides *reasonable predictions* while, at the same time, being *sufficiently simple*, so that the model is *mathematically tractable*. Based on these considerations, the most important probability distribution in queueing theory is the *exponential distribution*.

Suppose that a random variable T represents either *interarrival* or *service times*. (We shall refer to the occurrences marking the end of these times—arrivals or service completions—as *incidents*.) T is said to have an *exponential dis-*

tribution with parameter α if its probability density function is

$$f_T(t) = \begin{cases} \alpha e^{-\alpha t}, & \text{for } t \ge 0 \\ 0, & \text{for } t < 0, \end{cases}$$

as shown in Fig. 16.3. In this case, the cumulative probabilities are

$$\begin{aligned} P\{T \le t\} &= 1 - e^{-\alpha t}, \\ P\{T > t\} &= e^{-\alpha t}, \end{aligned} \quad (t \ge 0)$$

and the expected value and variance of T are

$$E(T) = \frac{1}{\alpha},$$

$$\text{var}(T) = \frac{1}{\alpha^2}.$$

What are the implications of assuming that T has an exponential distribution for a queueing model? To explore this question, let us examine five key properties of the exponential distribution.

PROPERTY 1 $f_T(t)$ is a strictly *decreasing* function of t $(t \ge 0)$.

One consequence of property 1 is that

$$P\{0 \le T \le \Delta t\} > P\{t \le T \le t + \Delta t\}$$

for any strictly positive values of Δt and t. [This consequence follows from the fact that these probabilities are the area under the $f_T(t)$ curve over the indicated interval of length Δt, and the average height of the curve is less for the second probability than for the first.] Therefore, it is not only possible but relatively likely that T will take on a small value near zero. In fact,

$$P\left\{0 \le T \le \frac{1}{2}\frac{1}{\alpha}\right\} = 0.393,$$

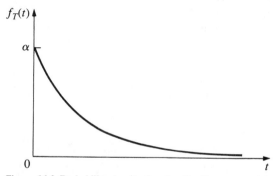

Figure 16.3 Probability density function for the exponential distribution.

whereas

$$P\left\{\frac{1}{2}\frac{1}{\alpha} \le T \le \frac{3}{2}\frac{1}{\alpha}\right\} = 0.383,$$

so that the value T takes on is more likely to be "small" [i.e., less than half of $E(T)$] than "near" its expected value [i.e., no further away than half of $E(T)$], even though the second interval is twice as wide as the first.

Is this really a reasonable property for T in a queueing model? If T represents *service times*, the answer depends upon the general nature of the service involved, as discussed here.

If the service required is essentially identical for each customer, with the server always performing the same sequence of service operations, then the actual service times tend to be near the expected service time. Small deviations from the mean may occur, but usually because of only minor variations in the efficiency of the server. A small service time far below the mean is essentially impossible because a certain minimum amount of time is needed to perform the required service operations even when the server is working at top speed. The exponential distribution clearly does not provide a close approximation to the service-time distribution for this type of situation.

On the other hand, consider the type of situation where the specific tasks required of the server differ among the customers. The broad nature of the service may be the same, but the specific type and amount of service differ. For example, this would be the case in the *County Hospital* emergency room problem discussed in Sec. 16.1. The doctors encounter a wide variety of medical problems. In most cases, they can provide the required treatment rather quickly, but an occasional patient requires extensive care. Similarly, bank tellers and grocery store checkout clerks are other servers of this general type, where the required service is often brief but must occasionally be extensive. An exponential service-time distribution would seem quite plausible for this type of service situation.

If T represents *interarrival times*, property 1 rules out situations where potential customers approaching the queueing system tend to postpone their entry if they see another customer entering ahead of them. On the other hand, it is entirely consistent with the common phenomenon of arrivals occurring "randomly," described by subsequent properties.

PROPERTY 2 Lack of memory.

This property can be stated mathematically as

$$P\{T > t + \Delta t \mid T > \Delta t\} = P\{T > t\}$$

for any positive quantities t and Δt. In other words, the probability distribution of the *remaining* time until the incident (arrival or service completion) occurs always is the same, regardless of how much time (Δt) already has passed. In effect, the process "forgets" its history. This surprising phenomenon occurs with the exponential distribution because

$$P\{T > t + \Delta t \,|\, T > \Delta t\} = \frac{P\{T > \Delta t, T > t + \Delta t\}}{P\{T > \Delta t\}}$$

$$= \frac{P\{T > t + \Delta t\}}{P\{T > \Delta t\}}$$

$$= \frac{e^{-\alpha(t + \Delta t)}}{e^{-\alpha \Delta t}}$$

$$= e^{-\alpha t}.$$

For *interarrival times*, this property describes the common situation where the time until the next arrival is completely uninfluenced by when the last arrival occurred. For *service times*, the property is more difficult to interpret. We should not expect it to hold in a situation where the server must perform the same fixed sequence of operations for each customer, because then a long elapsed service should imply that probably little remains to be done. On the other hand, in the type of situation where the required service operations differ among the customers, the mathematical statement of the property may be quite realistic. For this case, if considerable service has already elapsed for a customer, the only implication may be that this particular customer requires more extensive service than most.

PROPERTY 3 The *minimum* of several independent exponential random variables has an exponential distribution.

To state this property mathematically, let $T_1, T_2, \ldots, T_n$ be *independent* exponential random variables with parameters $\alpha_1, \alpha_2, \ldots, \alpha_n$, respectively. Also let U be the random variable that takes on the value equal to the *minimum* of the values actually taken on by $T_1, T_2, \ldots, T_n$; that is,

$$U = \text{minimum}\,\{T_1, T_2, \ldots, T_n\}.$$

Thus, if T_i represents the time until a particular kind of incident will occur, then U represents the time until the *first* of the n different incidents will occur. Now note that for any $t \geq 0$,

$$P\{U > t\} = P\{T_1 > t, T_2 > t, \ldots, T_n > t\}$$

$$= P\{T_1 > t\}P\{T_2 > t\} \cdots P\{T_n > t\}$$

$$= e^{-\alpha_1 t} e^{-\alpha_2 t} \cdots e^{-\alpha_n t}$$

$$= \exp\left\{-\sum_{i=1}^{n} \alpha_i t\right\},$$

so that U indeed has an exponential distribution with parameter

$$\alpha = \sum_{i=1}^{n} \alpha_i.$$

This property has some implications for *interarrival times* in queueing models. In particular, suppose that there are several (*n*) *different* types of customers, but the interarrival times for *each* type (type *i*) have an exponential distribution with parameter α_i ($i = 1, 2, \ldots, n$). By property 2, the *remaining* time from any specified instant until the next arrival of a customer of type *i* would have this same distribution. Therefore, let T_i be this remaining time measured from the instant a customer of *any* type arrives. Property 3 then tells us that *U*, the interarrival times for the queueing system as a whole, has an exponential distribution with parameter α defined by the last equation. As a result, you can choose to ignore the distinction between customers and still have exponential interarrival times for the queueing model.

However, the implications are even more important for *service times* in queueing models having more than one server than they are for interarrival times. For example, consider the situation where all the servers have the same exponential service-time distribution with parameter μ. For this case, let *n* be the number of servers *currently* providing service, and let T_i be the *remaining* service time for server *i* ($i = 1, 2, \ldots, n$), which also has an exponential distribution with parameter $\alpha_i = \mu$. It then follows that *U*, the time until the *next* service completion from any of these servers, has an exponential distribution with parameter $\alpha = n\mu$. In effect, the queueing system *currently* would be performing just like a *single*-server system, where service times have an exponential distribution with parameter $n\mu$. We shall make frequent use of this implication for analyzing multiple-server models later in the chapter.

PROPERTY 4 Relationship to the Poisson distribution.

Suppose that the *time* between consecutive occurrences of some particular kind of incident (e.g., arrivals or service completions by a continuously busy server) has an *exponential distribution* with parameter α. Property 4 then has to do with the resulting implication about the probability distribution of the *number* of times this kind of incident occurs over a specified length of time. In particular, let *X(t)* be the number of occurrences by time *t* ($t > 0$), where time 0 designates the instant at which the count begins. The implication is that

$$P\{X(t) = n\} = \frac{(\alpha t)^n e^{-\alpha t}}{n!}, \quad \text{for } n = 0, 1, 2, \ldots;$$

that is, *X(t)* has a *Poisson distribution* with parameter αt. For example, with $n = 0$,

$$P\{X(t) = 0\} = e^{-\alpha t},$$

which is just the probability from the exponential distribution that the *first* incident occurs after time *t*. The mean of this Poisson distribution is

$$E\{X(t)\} = \alpha t,$$

so that the expected number of incidents *per unit time* is α. Thus α is said to be the *mean rate* at which the incidents occur. When the incidents are counted on a continuing basis, the counting process $\{X(t); t > 0\}$ is said to be a **Poisson process** with parameter α (the mean rate).

This property provides useful information about *service completions* when service times have an exponential distribution with parameter μ. We obtain this information by defining $X(t)$ as the number of service completions achieved by a *continuously busy* server in elapsed time t, where $\alpha = \mu$. For *multiple*-server queueing models, $X(t)$ can also be defined as the number of service completions achieved by n continuously busy servers in elapsed time t, where $\alpha = n\mu$.

The property is particularly useful for describing the probabilistic behavior of *arrivals* when interarrival times have an exponential distribution with parameter λ. In this case, $X(t)$ would be the *number* of arrivals in elapsed time t, where $\alpha = \lambda$ is the *mean arrival rate*. Therefore, arrivals occur according to a *Poisson input process*. Such queueing models also are described as assuming a *Poisson input*.

Arrivals sometimes are said to occur *randomly*, meaning that they occur in accord with a Poisson input process. One intuitive interpretation of this phenomenon is that every time period of fixed length has the *same* chance of having an arrival regardless of when the preceding arrival occurred, as suggested by the following property.

PROPERTY 5 For all positive values of t, $P\{T \leq t + \Delta t \mid T > t\} \approx \alpha \Delta t$, for small Δt.

Continuing to interpret T as the time from the last incident of a certain type (arrival or service completion) until the *next* such incident, suppose that a time t already has elapsed without the incident occurring. We know from property 2 that the probability that the incident will occur within the next time interval of fixed length Δt is a *constant* (identified in the next paragraph), regardless of how large or small t is. Property 5 goes further to say that, when the value of Δt is small, this constant probability can be approximated very closely by $\alpha \Delta t$. Furthermore, when considering different small values of Δt, this probability is essentially *proportional* to Δt, with proportionality factor α. In fact, α is the *mean rate* at which the incidents occur (see property 4), so that the *expected number* of incidents in the interval of length Δt is *exactly* $\alpha \Delta t$. The only reason that the probability of an incident occurring differs slightly from this value is the possibility that *more than one* incident will occur, which has negligible probability when Δt is small.

To see why property 5 holds mathematically, note that the constant value of our probability (for a fixed value of $\Delta t > 0$) is just

$$P\{T \leq t + \Delta t \mid T > t\} = P\{T \leq \Delta t\}$$
$$= 1 - e^{-\alpha \Delta t}$$

for any $t \geq 0$. Therefore, because the series expansion of e^x for any exponent x is

$$e^x = 1 + x + \sum_{n=2}^{\infty} \frac{x^n}{n!},$$

it follows that

$$P\{T \leq t + \Delta t \mid T > t\} = 1 - 1 + \alpha \, \Delta t - \sum_{n=2}^{\infty} \frac{(-\alpha \, \Delta t)^n}{n!}$$

$$\approx \alpha \, \Delta t, \text{ for small } \Delta t,{}^1$$

because the summation terms become relatively negligible for sufficiently small values of $\alpha \, \Delta t$.

Because T can represent either *interarrival* or *service times* in queueing models, this property provides a convenient approximation of the probability that the incident of interest occurs in the next small interval (Δt) of time. An analysis based on this approximation also can be made exact by taking appropriate limits as $\Delta t \to 0$.

16.5 The Birth-and-Death Process

Most elementary queueing models assume that the inputs (arriving customers) and outputs (leaving customers) of the queueing system occur according to the *birth-and-death process*. This important process in probability theory has applications in various areas. However, in the context of queueing theory, the term **birth** refers to the *arrival* of a new customer into the queueing system, and **death** refers to the *departure* of a served customer. The *state* of the system at time t ($t \geq 0$), $N(t)$, is the number of customers in the queueing system at time t. The birth-and-death process describes *probabilistically* how $N(t)$ changes as t increases. Broadly speaking, it says that *individual* births and deaths occur *randomly*, where their mean occurrence rates depend only upon the current state of the system. More precisely, the assumptions of the birth-and-death process are the following:

ASSUMPTION 1 Given $N(t) = n$, the current probability distribution of the *remaining* time until the next *birth* (arrival) is *exponential* with parameter λ_n ($n = 0, 1, 2, \ldots$).

ASSUMPTION 2 Given $N(t) = n$, the current probability distribution of the *remaining* time until the next *death* (service completion) is *exponential* with parameter μ_n ($n = 1, 2, \ldots$).

---

[1] More precisely,

$$\lim_{\Delta t \to 0} \frac{P\{T \leq t + \Delta t \mid T > t\}}{\Delta t} = \alpha.$$

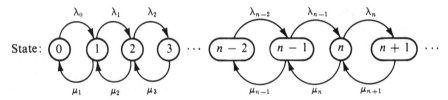

Figure 16.4 **Rate diagram for the birth-and-death process.**

ASSUMPTION 3 Only *one* birth or death can occur at a time.

Because of assumptions 1 and 2, the birth-and-death process is a special type of *continuous parameter Markov chain* (see Sec. 15.8). Queueing models that can be represented by a continuous parameter Markov chain are far more tractable analytically than any other, and assumption 3 simplifies the analysis considerably further.

Because property 4 for the exponential distribution (see Sec. 16.4) implies that the λ_n and μ_n are *mean rates*, we can summarize these assumptions by the *rate diagram* shown in Fig. 16.4. The arrows in this diagram show the only possible *transitions* in the state of the system (as specified by assumption 3), and the entry for each arrow gives the mean rate for that transition (as specified by assumptions 1 and 2) when the system is in the state at the base of the arrow.

Except for a few special cases, analysis of the birth-and-death process is very difficult when the system is in a *transient* condition. Some results about the probability distribution of $N(t)$[1] have been obtained, but they are too complicated to be of much practical use. On the other hand, it is relatively straightforward to derive this distribution *after* the system has reached a *steady-state* condition (assuming that this condition can be reached). This derivation can be done directly from the rate diagram, as outlined next.

Consider any particular state of the system n ($n = 0, 1, 2, \ldots$). Suppose that we were to start counting the number of times that the process *enters* this state and the number of times it *leaves* this state. Because the two types of incidents (entering and leaving) must alternate, these two numbers must always be either *equal* or differ by just 1. This possible difference of 1 will *eventually* cause only a *negligible* difference in the *average rates* (total number of occurrences per unit time) at which these two types of incidents occur; that is, $1/t \to 0$ as $t \to \infty$). Therefore, these two rates *must* be *equal* in the long run. This conclusion yields the following key principle:

RATE IN = RATE OUT PRINCIPLE For any state of the system n ($n = 0, 1, 2, \ldots$), the mean rate (expected number of occurrences per unit time) at which the *entering incidents* occur must equal the mean rate at which the *leaving incidents* occur.

[1] Karlin, S., and J. McGregor: "Many Server Queueing Processes with Poisson Input and Exponential Service Times," *Pacific Journal of Mathematics*, **8**: 87–118, 1958.

The *equation* expressing this principle is called the **balance equation** for state n. After constructing the balance equations for *all* the states in terms of the *unknown* P_n probabilities, we can solve this system of equations to find these probabilities.

To illustrate a balance equation, consider state 0. The process enters this state *only* from state 1. Thus the steady-state probability of being in state 1 (P_1) represents the proportion of time that it would be *possible* for the process to enter state 0. *Given* that the process is in state 1, the mean rate of entering state 0 is μ_1. (In other words, for each cumulative unit of time that the process spends in state 1, the expected number of times that it would leave state 1 to enter state 0 is μ_1.) From any *other* state, this mean rate is 0. Therefore, the overall mean rate at which the process leaves its current state to enter state 0 (the *mean occurrence rate* of the entering incidents) is

$$\mu_1 P_1 + 0(1 - P_1) = \mu_1 P_1.$$

By the same reasoning, the mean occurrence rate of the leaving incidents must be $\lambda_0 P_0$, so the balance equation for state 0 is

$$\mu_1 P_1 = \lambda_0 P_0.$$

For every other state there are *two* possible transitions both into and out of the state. Therefore, each side of the balance equations for these states represents the *sum* of the mean rates for the two transitions involved. Otherwise, the reasoning is just the same as for state 0. These balance equations are summarized in Table 16.1.

Notice that the first balance equation contains two variables for which to solve (P_0 and P_1), the first two equations contain three variables (P_0, P_1, and P_2), and so on, so that there always is one "extra" variable. Therefore, the procedure in solving these equations is to solve in terms of one of the variables, the most convenient one being P_0. Thus the first equation is used to solve for P_1 in terms of P_0; this result and the second equation are then used to solve for P_2 in terms of P_0, and so forth. At the end, the requirement that the sum of all the probabilities must equal 1 can be used to evaluate P_0.

Table 16.1 **Balance equations for birth-and-death process**

State	Rate in = rate out
0	$\mu_1 P_1 = \lambda_0 P_0$
1	$\lambda_0 P_0 + \mu_2 P_2 = (\lambda_1 + \mu_1)P_1$
2	$\lambda_1 P_1 + \mu_3 P_3 = (\lambda_2 + \mu_2)P_2$
$\vdots$	$\vdots$
$n-1$	$\lambda_{n-2}P_{n-2} + \mu_n P_n = (\lambda_{n-1} + \mu_{n-1})P_{n-1}$
n	$\lambda_{n-1}P_{n-1} + \mu_{n+1} P_{n+1} = (\lambda_n + \mu_n)P_n$
$\vdots$	$\vdots$

Applying this procedure yields the following results:

State

0: $P_1 = \dfrac{\lambda_0}{\mu_1} P_0$

1: $P_2 = \dfrac{\lambda_1}{\mu_2} P_1 + \dfrac{1}{\mu_2}(\mu_1 P_1 - \lambda_0 P_0)$ $\qquad = \dfrac{\lambda_1}{\mu_2} P_1 \qquad = \dfrac{\lambda_1 \lambda_0}{\mu_2 \mu_1} P_0$

2: $P_3 = \dfrac{\lambda_2}{\mu_3} P_2 + \dfrac{1}{\mu_3}(\mu_2 P_2 - \lambda_1 P_1)$ $\qquad = \dfrac{\lambda_2}{\mu_3} P_2 \qquad = \dfrac{\lambda_2 \lambda_1 \lambda_0}{\mu_3 \mu_2 \mu_1} P_0$

$\vdots \qquad \vdots$

$n-1: P_n = \dfrac{\lambda_{n-1}}{\mu_n} P_{n-1} + \dfrac{1}{\mu_n}(\mu_{n-1} P_{n-1} - \lambda_{n-2} P_{n-2}) = \dfrac{\lambda_{n-1}}{\mu_n} P_{n-1} = \dfrac{\lambda_{n-1} \lambda_{n-2} \cdots \lambda_0}{\mu_n \mu_{n-1} \cdots \mu_1} P_0$

$n: P_{n+1} = \dfrac{\lambda_n}{\mu_{n+1}} P_n + \dfrac{1}{\mu_{n+1}}(\mu_n P_n - \lambda_{n-1} P_{n-1}) \qquad = \dfrac{\lambda_n}{\mu_{n+1}} P_n = \dfrac{\lambda_n \lambda_{n-1} \cdots \lambda_0}{\mu_{n+1} \mu_n \cdots \mu_1} P_0$

$\vdots \qquad \vdots$

To simplify notation, let

$$C_n = \frac{\lambda_{n-1} \lambda_{n-2} \cdots \lambda_0}{\mu_n \mu_{n-1} \cdots \mu_1}, \quad \text{for } n = 1, 2, \dots.$$

Thus the steady-state probabilities are

$$P_n = C_n P_0, \quad \text{for } n = 1, 2, \dots.$$

The requirement that

$$\sum_{n=0}^{\infty} P_n = 1$$

implies that

$$\left[1 + \sum_{n=1}^{\infty} C_n \right] P_0 = 1,$$

so that

$$P_0 = \frac{1}{1 + \sum_{n=1}^{\infty} C_n}.$$

Given this information,

$$L = \sum_{n=0}^{\infty} n P_n.$$

Also, because the number of servers s represents the number of customers that can be served (and thus are not in the queue) simultaneously,

$$L_q = \sum_{n=s}^{\infty} (n - s)P_n.$$

Furthermore, the relationships given in Sec. 16.2 yield

$$W = \frac{L}{\bar{\lambda}}, \qquad W_q = \frac{L_q}{\bar{\lambda}},$$

where $\bar{\lambda}$ is the *average* arrival rate over the long run. Because λ_n is the mean arrival rate while the system is in state n ($n = 0, 1, 2, \ldots$), and P_n is the proportion of time that the system is in this state,

$$\bar{\lambda} = \sum_{n=0}^{\infty} \lambda_n P_n.$$

Several of the expressions just given involve summations with an infinite number of terms. Fortunately, these summations have analytic solutions for a number of interesting special cases,[1] as seen in the next section. Otherwise, they can be approximated by summing a finite number of terms on an electronic computer.

These steady-state results have been derived under the assumption that the λ_n and μ_n parameters have values such that the process actually can *reach* a steady-state condition. This assumption *always* holds if $\lambda_n = 0$ for some value of n greater than the initial state, so that only a finite number of states (those less than this n) are possible. It also *always* holds when λ and μ are defined (see terminology and notation in Sec. 16.2) and $\rho = \lambda/s\mu < 1$. It does *not* hold if $\sum_{n=1}^{\infty} C_n = \infty$.

The following section describes several queueing models that are just *special cases* of the birth-and-death process. Therefore, the *general* steady-state results just given in boxes will be used over and over again to obtain the *specific* steady-state results for these models.

16.6 Queueing Models Based on the Birth-and-Death Process

Because each of the mean rates $\lambda_0, \lambda_1, \ldots$ and $\mu_1, \mu_2, \ldots$ for the birth-and-death process can be assigned any nonnegative value, we have great flexibility in modeling a queueing system. Probably the most widely used models in queueing theory are based directly upon this process. Because of assumptions 1 and 2 (and

---

[1] These solutions are based on the following known results for the sum of any geometric series:

$$\sum_{n=0}^{N} x^n = \frac{1 - x^{N+1}}{1 - x}, \quad \text{for any } x,$$

$$\sum_{n=0}^{\infty} x^n = \frac{1}{1 - x}, \quad \text{if } |x| < 1.$$

property 4 for the exponential distribution), these models are said to have a **Poisson input** and **exponential service times**. The models differ only in their assumptions about how the λ_n and the μ_n change with n. We present four of these models in this section for four important types of queueing systems.

THE M/M/s MODEL

As described in Sec. 16.2, the M/M/s model assumes that all *interarrival times* are independently and identically distributed according to an exponential distribution (i.e., the input process is Poisson), that all *service times* are independent and identically distributed according to another exponential distribution, and that the number of servers is s (any positive integer). Consequently, this model is just the special case of the birth-and-death process where the queueing system's *mean arrival rate* and *mean service rate per busy server* are constant (λ and μ, respectively) regardless of the state of the system. When the system has just a *single server* ($s = 1$), the implication is that the parameters for the birth-and-death process are $\lambda_n = \lambda$ ($n = 0, 1, 2, \ldots$) and $\mu_n = \mu$ ($n = 1, 2, \ldots$). The resulting *rate diagram* is shown in Fig. 16.5a.

However, when the system has *multiple servers* ($s > 1$), the μ_n cannot be expressed this simply. Keep in mind that μ_n represents the mean service rate for the *overall* queueing system (i.e., the mean rate at which service completions occur, so that customers leave the system) when there are n customers currently in the system. As mentioned for property 4 of the exponential distribution (see Sec. 16.4), when the mean service rate per busy server is μ, the overall mean service rate for n busy servers must be $n\mu$. Therefore, $\mu_n = n\mu$ when $n \le s$, whereas $\mu_n = s\mu$ when $n \ge s\mu$, so that all s servers are busy. The rate diagram for this case is shown in Fig. 16.5b.

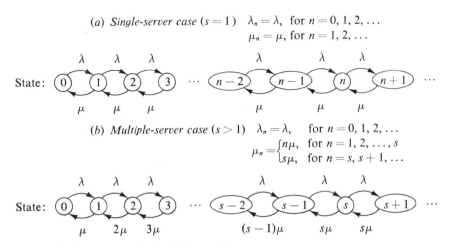

(a) Single-server case ($s = 1$) $\lambda_n = \lambda$, for $n = 0, 1, 2, \ldots$
$\mu_n = \mu$, for $n = 1, 2, \ldots$

(b) Multiple-server case ($s > 1$) $\lambda_n = \lambda$,   for $n = 0, 1, 2, \ldots$
$\mu_n = \begin{cases} n\mu, & \text{for } n = 1, 2, \ldots, s \\ s\mu, & \text{for } n = s, s + 1, \ldots \end{cases}$

Figure 16.5 **Rate diagrams for the M/M/s model.**

When the maximum mean service rate $(s\mu)$ exceeds the mean arrival rate (λ), that is, when

$$\rho = \frac{\lambda}{s\mu} < 1,$$

a queueing system fitting this model will eventually reach a steady-state condition. In this situation, the steady-state results derived in Sec. 16.5 for the general birth-and-death process are directly applicable. However, these results simplify considerably for this model and yield closed form expressions for the P_n, L, L_q, and so forth, as shown next.

RESULTS FOR THE SINGLE-SERVER CASE $(M/M/1)$ For $s = 1$, the C_n factors for the birth-and-death process reduce to

$$C_n = \left(\frac{\lambda}{\mu}\right)^n = \rho^n, \quad \text{for } n = 1, 2, \dots.$$

Therefore,

$$P_n = \rho^n P_0, \quad \text{for } n = 1, 2, \dots,$$

where

$$P_0 = \frac{1}{1 + \sum_{n=1}^{\infty} \rho^n}$$

$$= \left(\sum_{n=0}^{\infty} \rho^n\right)^{-1}$$

$$= \left(\frac{1}{1-\rho}\right)^{-1}$$

$$= 1 - \rho.$$

Thus

$$P_n = (1 - \rho)\rho^n, \quad \text{for } n = 0, 1, 2, \dots.$$

Consequently,

$$L = \sum_{n=0}^{\infty} n(1 - \rho)\rho^n$$

$$= (1 - \rho)\rho \sum_{n=0}^{\infty} \frac{d}{d\rho}(\rho^n)$$

$$= (1 - \rho)\rho \frac{d}{d\rho}\left(\sum_{n=0}^{\infty} \rho^n\right)$$

$$= (1 - \rho)\rho \frac{d}{d\rho}\left(\frac{1}{1-\rho}\right)$$

$$= \frac{\rho}{1-\rho} = \frac{\lambda}{\mu - \lambda}.$$

Similarly,

$$
\begin{aligned}
L_q &= \sum_{n=1}^{\infty} (n-1)P_n \\
&= L - 1(1 - P_0) \\
&= \frac{\lambda^2}{\mu(\mu - \lambda)}.
\end{aligned}
$$

When $\lambda \geq \mu$, so that the mean arrival rate exceeds the mean service rate, the preceding solution "blows up" (because the summation for computing P_0 diverges). For this case, the queue would "explode" and grow without bound.

Assuming again that $\lambda < \mu$, we now can derive the probability distribution of the waiting time in the system (*including* service) $\mathscr{W}$ for a random arrival when the queue discipline is first-come-first-served. If this arrival finds n customers already in the system, he will have to wait through $(n + 1)$ exponential service times, including his own. (For the customer currently being served, recall the lack of memory property for the exponential distribution discussed in Sec. 16.4.) Therefore, let $T_1, T_2, \ldots$ be independent service time random variables having an exponential distribution with parameter μ, and let

$$
S_{n+1} = T_1 + T_2 + \cdots + T_{n+1}, \quad \text{for } n = 0, 1, 2, \ldots,
$$

so that S_{n+1} represents the *conditional* waiting time given n customers already in the system. As discussed in Sec. 16.7, S_{n+1} is known to have an *Erlang distribution*.[1] Because the probability that the random arrival will find n customers in the system is P_n, it follows that

$$
P\{\mathscr{W} > t\} = \sum_{n=0}^{\infty} P_n P\{S_{n+1} > t\},
$$

which reduces after considerable algebraic manipulation to

$$
P\{\mathscr{W} > t\} = e^{-\mu(1-\rho)t}, \quad \text{for } t \geq 0.
$$

The surprising conclusion is that $\mathscr{W}$ has an *exponential* distribution with parameter $\mu(1 - \rho)$. Therefore,

$$
\begin{aligned}
W = E(\mathscr{W}) &= \frac{1}{\mu(1 - \rho)} \\
&= \frac{1}{\mu - \lambda}.
\end{aligned}
$$

These results *include* service time in the waiting time. In some contexts (e.g., the County Hospital emergency room problem), the more relevant waiting time is just until service begins. Thus consider the waiting time in the queue (so *excluding* service time) $\mathscr{W}_q$ for a random arrival when the queue discipline is first-come-first-served. If this arrival finds *no* customers already in the system, he is served

---

[1] Outside of queueing theory, this distribution is known as the *gamma distribution*.

immediately, so that

$$P\{\mathscr{W}_q = 0\} = P_0 = 1 - \rho.$$

If he finds $n > 0$ customers already there instead, then he has to wait through n exponential service times until his own service begins, so that

$$P\{\mathscr{W}_q > t\} = \sum_{n=1}^{\infty} P_n P\{S_n > t\}$$

$$= \sum_{n=1}^{\infty} (1 - \rho)\rho^n P\{S_n > t\}$$

$$= \rho \sum_{n=0}^{\infty} P_n P\{S_{n+1} > t\}$$

$$= \rho P\{\mathscr{W} > t\}$$

$$= \rho e^{-\mu(1-\rho)t}, \quad \text{for } t \geq 0.$$

By deriving the mean of this distribution [or applying either $L_q = \lambda W_q$ or $W_q = W - (1/\mu)$],

$$W_q = E(\mathscr{W}_q) = \frac{\lambda}{\mu(\mu - \lambda)}.$$

RESULTS FOR THE MULTIPLE-SERVER CASE ($s > 1$) When $s > 1$, the C_n factors become

$$C_n = \frac{(\lambda/\mu)^n}{n!}, \quad \text{for } n = 1, 2, \ldots, s,$$

and

$$C_n = \frac{(\lambda/\mu)^s}{s!}\left(\frac{\lambda}{s\mu}\right)^{n-s} = \frac{(\lambda/\mu)^n}{s!s^{n-s}}, \quad \text{for } n = s, s+1, \ldots.$$

Consequently, if $\lambda < s\mu$, then

$$P_0 = 1 \left/ \left[\sum_{n=0}^{s-1} \frac{(\lambda/\mu)^n}{n!} + \frac{(\lambda/\mu)^s}{s!} \sum_{n=s}^{\infty} \left(\frac{\lambda}{s\mu}\right)^{n-s}\right]\right.$$

$$= 1 \left/ \left[\sum_{n=0}^{s-1} \frac{(\lambda/\mu)^n}{n!} + \frac{(\lambda/\mu)^s}{s!} \frac{1}{1 - (\lambda/s\mu)}\right]\right.$$

and

$$P_n = \begin{cases} \dfrac{(\lambda/\mu)^n}{n!} P_0, & \text{if } 0 \leq n \leq s \\[3mm] \dfrac{(\lambda/\mu)^n}{s!s^{n-s}} P_0, & \text{if } n \geq s. \end{cases}$$

Using the notation $\rho = \lambda/\mu s$,

$$L_q = \sum_{n=s}^{\infty} (n-s)P_n$$

$$= \sum_{j=0}^{\infty} jP_{s+j}$$

$$= \sum_{j=0}^{\infty} j \frac{(\lambda/\mu)^s}{s!} \rho^j P_0$$

$$= P_0 \frac{(\lambda/\mu)^s}{s!} \rho \sum_{j=0}^{\infty} \frac{d}{d\rho}(\rho^j)$$

$$= P_0 \frac{(\lambda/\mu)^s}{s!} \rho \frac{d}{d\rho}\left(\sum_{j=0}^{\infty} \rho^j\right)$$

$$= P_0 \frac{(\lambda/\mu)^s}{s!} \rho \frac{d}{d\rho}\left(\frac{1}{1-\rho}\right)$$

$$= \frac{P_0(\lambda/\mu)^s \rho}{s!(1-\rho)^2}.$$

$$W_q = \frac{L_q}{\lambda};$$

$$W = W_q + \frac{1}{\mu};$$

$$L = \lambda\left(W_q + \frac{1}{\mu}\right) = L_q + \frac{\lambda}{\mu}.$$

Figures 16.6 and 16.7 show how P_0 and L change with ρ for various values of s.

The single-server method for finding the probability distribution of waiting times also can be extended to the multiple-server case. This yields[1] (for $t \geq 0$)

$$P\{\mathscr{W} > t\} = e^{-\mu t}\left[1 + \frac{P_0(\lambda/\mu)^s}{s!(1-\rho)}\left(\frac{1 - e^{-\mu t(s-1-\lambda/\mu)}}{s-1-\lambda/\mu}\right)\right]$$

and

$$P\{\mathscr{W}_q > t\} = [1 - P\{\mathscr{W}_q = 0\}]e^{-s\mu(1-\rho)t},$$

where

$$P\{\mathscr{W}_q = 0\} = \sum_{n=0}^{s-1} P_n.$$

---

[1] When $s - 1 - \lambda/\mu = 0$, $(1 - e^{-\mu t(s-1-\lambda/\mu)})/(s - 1 - \lambda/\mu)$ should be replaced by μt.

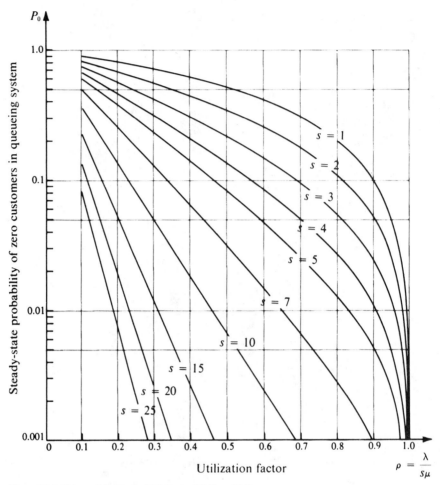

Figure 16.6 **Values of P_0 for the M/M/s model (Sec. 16.6).**

If $\lambda \geq s\mu$, so that the mean arrival rate exceeds the maximum mean service rate, the queue grows without bound, so the preceding steady-state solutions are not applicable.

EXAMPLE For the *County Hospital* emergency room problem (see Sec. 16.1), the Management Engineer has concluded that the emergency cases arrive pretty much at random (a *Poisson input process*), so that interarrival times have an exponential distribution. He also has concluded that the time spent by a doctor treating the cases approximately follows an *exponential distribution*. Therefore, he has chosen the M/M/s model for a preliminary study of this queueing system.

By projecting the available data for the early evening shift into next year, he estimates that patients will arrive at an *average* rate of one every half-hour. A

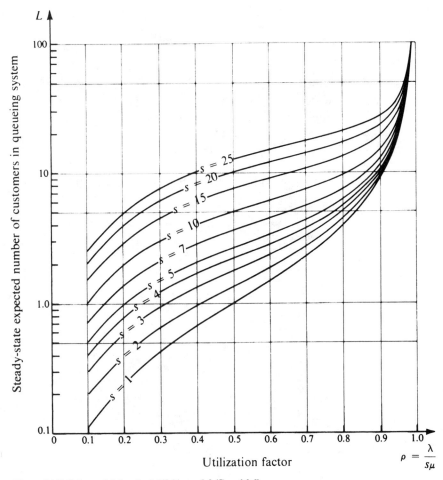

Figure 16.7 **Values of L for the M/M/s model (Sec. 16.6).**

doctor requires an average of 20 minutes to treat each patient. Thus, using an hour as the unit of time,

$$\frac{1}{\lambda} = \frac{1}{2} \text{hour per customer}$$

$$\frac{1}{\mu} = \frac{1}{3} \text{hour per customer,}$$

so that

$$\lambda = 2 \text{ customers per hour}$$
$$\mu = 3 \text{ customers per hour.}$$

The two alternatives being considered are to continue having just one doctor during this shift ($s = 1$) or to add a second doctor ($s = 2$). In both cases,

$$\rho = \frac{\lambda}{s\mu} < 1,$$

so that the system should approach a steady-state condition. (Actually, because λ is somewhat different during other shifts, the system will never truly reach a steady-steady condition, but the Management Engineer feels that steady-state results will provide a good approximation.) Therefore, the preceding equations are used to obtain the results shown in Table 16.2.

On the basis of these results, he tentatively concluded that a single doctor would be inadequate next year for providing the relatively prompt treatment

Table 16.2 **Steady-state results from M/M/s model for County Hospital problem**

	$s = 1$	$s = 2$
ρ	$\dfrac{2}{3}$	$\dfrac{1}{3}$
P_0	$\dfrac{1}{3}$	$\dfrac{1}{2}$
P_1	$\dfrac{2}{9}$	$\dfrac{1}{3}$
P_n for $n \geq 2$	$\dfrac{1}{3}\left(\dfrac{2}{3}\right)^n$	$\left(\dfrac{1}{3}\right)^n$
L_q	$\dfrac{4}{3}$	$\dfrac{1}{12}$
L	2	$\dfrac{3}{4}$
W_q	$\dfrac{2}{3}$	$\dfrac{1}{24}$ (in hours)
W	1	$\dfrac{3}{8}$ (in hours)
$P\{W_q > 0\}$	0.667	0.167
$P\left\{W_q > \dfrac{1}{2}\right\}$	0.404	0.022
$P\{W_q > 1\}$	0.245	0.003
$P\{W_q > t\}$	$\dfrac{2}{3}e^{-t}$	$\dfrac{1}{6}e^{-4t}$
$P\{W > t\}$	e^{-t}	$\dfrac{1}{2}e^{-3t}(3 - e^{-t})$

needed in a hospital emergency room. You will see later how the Management Engineer checked this conclusion by applying two other queueing models that provide better representations of the real queueing system in some ways.

THE FINITE QUEUE VARIATION OF THE M/M/s MODEL

We mentioned in the discussion of queues in Sec. 16.2 that queueing systems sometimes have a *finite queue*; i.e., the number of customers in the system is not permitted to exceed some specified number (denoted by K). Any customer that arrives while the queue is "full" is refused entry into the system and so leaves forever. From the viewpoint of the birth-and-death process, the *mean input rate* into the system becomes zero at these times. Therefore, the one modification needed in the M/M/s model to introduce a finite queue is to change the λ_n parameters to

$$\lambda_n = \begin{cases} \lambda, & \text{for } n = 0, 1, 2, \ldots, K - 1 \\ 0, & \text{for } n \geq K. \end{cases}$$

Because $\lambda_n = 0$ for some values of n, a queueing system that fits this model will eventually reach a steady-state condition.

This model commonly is labeled as M/M/s/K, where the presence of the fourth symbol distinguishes it from the M/M/s model. The single difference in the formulation of these two models is that K is finite for the M/M/s/K model and $K = \infty$ for the M/M/s model.

The usual physical interpretation for the M/M/s/K model is that there is only *limited waiting room* that will accommodate a maximum of K customers in the system. For example, for the *County Hospital* emergency room problem, this system actually would have a finite queue if there were only K cots for the patients and if the policy were to send arriving patients to another hospital whenever there were no empty cots.

Another possible interpretation is that arriving customers will leave and "take their business elsewhere" whenever they find too many customers (K) ahead of them in the system because they are not willing to incur a long wait. This *balking* phenomenon is quite common in *commercial service systems*. However, there are other models available (e.g., see Prob. 5) that fit this interpretation even better.

The *rate diagram* for this model is identical to that shown in Fig. 16.5 for the M/M/s model, *except* that it stops with state K.

RESULTS FOR THE SINGLE-SERVER CASE (M/M/1/K) For this case,

$$C_n = \begin{cases} \left(\dfrac{\lambda}{\mu}\right)^n = \rho^n, & \text{for } n = 1, 2, \ldots, K \\ 0, & \text{for } n > K. \end{cases}$$

Therefore, for $\rho \neq 1$,[1]

$$P_0 = \frac{1}{\sum_{n=0}^{K} (\lambda/\mu)^n}$$

$$= 1 \Big/ \left[\frac{1 - (\lambda/\mu)^{K+1}}{1 - (\lambda/\mu)} \right]$$

$$= \frac{1 - \rho}{1 - \rho^{K+1}},$$

so that

$$P_n = \left(\frac{1 - \rho}{1 - \rho^{K+1}} \right) \rho^n, \quad \text{for } n = 0, 1, 2, \ldots, K.$$

Hence

$$L = \sum_{n=0}^{K} n P_n$$

$$= \frac{1 - \rho}{1 - \rho^{K+1}} \rho \sum_{n=0}^{K} \frac{d}{d\rho} (\rho^n)$$

$$= \frac{1 - \rho}{1 - \rho^{K+1}} \rho \frac{d}{d\rho} \left(\sum_{n=0}^{K} \rho^n \right)$$

$$= \left(\frac{1 - \rho}{1 - \rho^{K+1}} \right) \rho \frac{d}{d\rho} \left(\frac{1 - \rho^{K+1}}{1 - \rho} \right)$$

$$= \rho \frac{-(K+1)\rho^K + K\rho^{K+1} + 1}{(1 - \rho^{K+1})(1 - \rho)}$$

$$= \frac{\rho}{1 - \rho} - \frac{(K+1)\rho^{K+1}}{1 - \rho^{K+1}}.$$

As usual (when $s = 1$),

$$L_q = L - (1 - P_0).$$

Notice that the preceding results do not require that $\lambda < \mu$ (i.e., that $\rho < 1$).

When $\rho < 1$, it can be verified that the second term in the final expression for L converges to zero as $K \to \infty$, so that *all* of the preceding results do indeed converge to the corresponding results given earlier (see p. 544) for the M/M/1 model.

The waiting-time distributions can be derived by using the same reasoning as for the M/M/1 model (see Prob. 15). However, no simple expressions are

[1] If $\rho = 1$, then $P_n = 1/(K + 1)$ for $n = 0, 1, 2, \ldots, K$, so that $L = K/2$.

obtained in this case, so computer calculations are required. Fortunately, even though $L \neq \lambda W$ and $L_q \neq \lambda W_q$ for the current model because the λ_n are not equal for all n (see the end of Sec. 16.2), the *expected* waiting times for customers entering the system still can be obtained directly from the expressions given at the end of Sec. 16.5,

$$W = \frac{L}{\bar{\lambda}}, \qquad W_q = \frac{L_q}{\bar{\lambda}},$$

where

$$
\begin{aligned}
\bar{\lambda} &= \sum_{n=0}^{\infty} \lambda_n P_n \\
&= \sum_{n=0}^{K-1} \lambda P_n \\
&= \lambda (1 - P_K).
\end{aligned}
$$

RESULTS FOR THE MULTIPLE-SERVER CASE ($s > 1$) Because this model does not allow more than K customers in the system, K is the maximum number of servers that could ever be used. Therefore, assume that $s \leq K$. In this case, C_n becomes

$$C_n = \frac{(\lambda/\mu)^n}{n!}, \qquad \text{for } n = 1, 2, \ldots, s,$$

$$C_n = \frac{(\lambda/\mu)^s}{s!} \left(\frac{\lambda}{s\mu}\right)^{n-s} = \frac{(\lambda/\mu)^n}{s! s^{n-s}}, \quad \text{for } n = s, s+1, \ldots, K,$$

$$C_n = 0, \qquad \text{for } n > K.$$

Hence

$$
P_n = \begin{cases}
\dfrac{(\lambda/\mu)^n}{n!} P_0, & \text{for } n = 1, 2, \ldots, s \\[2ex]
\dfrac{(\lambda/\mu)^n}{s! s^{n-s}} P_0, & \text{for } n = s, s+1, \ldots, K \\[2ex]
0, & \text{for } n > K,
\end{cases}
$$

where

$$P_0 = 1 \Big/ \left[1 + \sum_{n=1}^{s} \frac{(\lambda/\mu)^n}{n!} + \frac{(\lambda/\mu)^s}{s!} \sum_{n=s+1}^{K} \left(\frac{\lambda}{s\mu}\right)^{n-s} \right].$$

Adapting the derivation of L_q for the M/M/s model (see p. 547) to this case (see Prob. 19) yields

$$L_q = \frac{P_0 (\lambda/\mu)^s \rho}{s! (1-\rho)^2} [1 - \rho^{K-s} - (K-s)\rho^{K-s}(1-\rho)],$$

where $\rho = \lambda/s\mu$.[1] It can then be shown (see Prob. 29) that

$$L = \sum_{n=0}^{s-1} nP_n + L_q + s\left(1 - \sum_{n=0}^{s-1} P_n\right).$$

W and W_q are obtained from these quantities just as shown for the single-server case.

THE FINITE CALLING POPULATION VARIATION OF THE M/M/s MODEL

Now assume that the only deviation from the M/M/s model is that (as defined in Sec. 16.2) the *input source* is *limited*; i.e., the size of the *calling population* is *finite*. For this case, let N denote the size of the calling population. Thus, when the number of customers in the queueing system is n ($n = 0, 1, 2, \ldots, N$), there are only $(N - n)$ *potential* customers remaining in the input source.

The most important application of this model has been to the *machine repair problem*, where one or more repairmen are assigned the responsibility of maintaining in operational order a certain group of N machines by repairing each one that breaks down. The repairmen are considered to be individual servers in the queueing system if they work individually on different machines, whereas

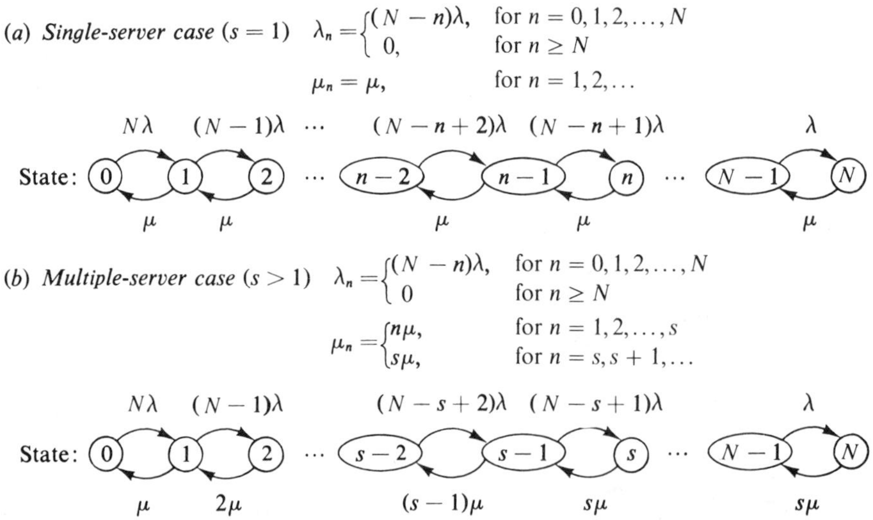

(a) *Single-server case* ($s = 1$) $\lambda_n = \begin{cases} (N - n)\lambda, & \text{for } n = 0, 1, 2, \ldots, N \\ 0, & \text{for } n \geq N \end{cases}$

$\mu_n = \mu,$ for $n = 1, 2, \ldots$

(b) *Multiple-server case* ($s > 1$) $\lambda_n = \begin{cases} (N - n)\lambda, & \text{for } n = 0, 1, 2, \ldots, N \\ 0 & \text{for } n \geq N \end{cases}$

$\mu_n = \begin{cases} n\mu, & \text{for } n = 1, 2, \ldots, s \\ s\mu, & \text{for } n = s, s + 1, \ldots \end{cases}$

Figure 16.8 Rate diagrams for the finite calling population variation of the M/M/s model.

[1] If $\rho = 1$, it is necessary to apply L'Hôpital's rule twice to this expression for L_q. Otherwise, all of these multiple-server results hold for all $\rho > 0$. The reason that this queueing system can reach a steady-state condition even when $\rho \geq 1$ is that $\lambda_n = 0$ for $n \geq K$, so that the number of customers in the system cannot continue growing indefinitely.

the entire crew is considered to be a single server if they work together on each machine. The machines constitute the calling population. Each one is considered to be a customer in the queueing system when it is down waiting to be repaired, whereas it is outside the queueing system while it is operational.

Note that each member of the calling population alternates between being *inside* and *outside* the queueing system. Therefore, the analog of the M/M/s model that fits this situation assumes that *each* member's *outside time* (i.e., the elapsed time from leaving the system until returning for the next time) has an *exponential distribution* with parameter λ. When n of the members are *inside*, and so $(N - n)$ members are *outside*, the current probability distribution of the *remaining* time until the next arrival to the queueing system is the distribution of the *minimum* of the *remaining outside times* for the latter $(N - n)$ members. Properties 2 and 3 for the exponential distribution imply that this distribution must be exponential with parameter $\lambda_n = (N - n)\lambda$. Hence this model is just the special case of the birth-and-death process that has the rate diagram shown in Fig. 16.8.

Because $\lambda_n = 0$ for $n = N$, any queueing system that fits this model will eventually reach a steady-state condition. The available steady-state results are summarized as follows:

RESULTS FOR THE SINGLE-SERVER CASE ($s = 1$) When $s = 1$, the C_n factors in Sec. 16.5 reduce to

$$C_n = N(N - 1)\cdots(N - n + 1)\left(\frac{\lambda}{\mu}\right)^n = \frac{N!}{(N - n)!}\left(\frac{\lambda}{\mu}\right)^n, \quad \text{for } n = 1, 2, \ldots, N$$

$$C_n = 0, \quad \text{for } n > N,$$

for this model. Therefore,

$$P_0 = 1 \bigg/ \sum_{n=0}^{N}\left[\frac{N!}{(N - n)!}\left(\frac{\lambda}{\mu}\right)^n\right];$$

$$P_n = \frac{N!}{(N - n)!}\left(\frac{\lambda}{\mu}\right)^n P_0, \quad \text{if } n = 1, 2, \ldots, N;$$

$$L_q = \sum_{n=1}^{N}(n - 1)P_n,$$

which can be reduced to

$$L_q = N - \frac{\lambda + \mu}{\lambda}(1 - P_0);$$

$$L = \sum_{n=0}^{N} nP_n = L_q + (1 - P_0)$$

$$= N - \frac{\mu}{\lambda}(1 - P_0).$$

Finally,

$$W = \frac{L}{\bar{\lambda}}, \qquad W_q = \frac{L_q}{\bar{\lambda}},$$

where

$$\bar{\lambda} = \sum_{n=0}^{\infty} \lambda_n P_n = \sum_{n=0}^{N} (N-n)\lambda P_n = \lambda(N-L).$$

RESULTS FOR THE MULTIPLE-SERVER CASE ($s > 1$) For $s > 1$,

$$C_n = \begin{cases} \dfrac{N!}{(N-n)!n!}\left(\dfrac{\lambda}{\mu}\right)^n, & \text{for } n = 1, 2, \ldots, s \\[3mm] \dfrac{N!}{(N-n)!s!s^{n-s}}\left(\dfrac{\lambda}{\mu}\right)^n, & \text{for } n = s, s+1, \ldots, N \\[3mm] 0, & \text{for } n > N. \end{cases}$$

Hence

$$P_n = \begin{cases} P_0 \dfrac{N!}{(N-n)!n!}\left(\dfrac{\lambda}{\mu}\right)^n, & \text{if } 0 \le n \le s \\[3mm] P_0 \dfrac{N!}{(N-n)!s!s^{n-s}}\left(\dfrac{\lambda}{\mu}\right)^n, & \text{if } s \le n \le N \\[3mm] 0, & \text{if } n > N, \end{cases}$$

where

$$P_0 = 1 \Big/ \left[\sum_{n=0}^{s-1} \frac{N!}{(N-n)!n!}\left(\frac{\lambda}{\mu}\right)^n + \sum_{n=s}^{N} \frac{N!}{(N-n)!s!s^{n-s}}\left(\frac{\lambda}{\mu}\right)^n \right].$$

Finally,

$$L_q = \sum_{n=s}^{N} (n-s)P_n,$$

$$L = \sum_{n=0}^{s-1} nP_n + L_q + s\left(1 - \sum_{n=0}^{s-1} P_n\right),$$

which then yield W and W_q by the same equations as in the single-server case.

Extensive tables of computational results are available[1] for this model for both the single-server and multiple-server cases.

For both cases, it has been shown[2] relatively recently that the preceding formulas for P_n and P_0 (and so for L_q, L, W, and W_q) *also* hold for a generalization of this model. In particular, we can *drop* the assumption that the times spent *outside* the queueing system by the members of the calling population have an

[1] Peck, L. G., and R. N. Hazelwood: *Finite Queueing Tables*, Wiley, New York, 1958.

[2] Bunday, B. D., and R. E. Scraton: "The G/M/r Machine Interference Model," *European Journal of Operational Research*, **4**:399–402, 1980.

exponential distribution, even though this takes the model outside the realm of the birth-and-death process. As long as these times are identically distributed with mean $1/\lambda$ (and the assumption of exponential service times still holds), these outside times can have *any* probability distribution!

A MODEL WITH STATE-DEPENDENT SERVICE RATE AND/OR ARRIVAL RATE

All the models thus far have assumed that the mean service rate is always a constant, regardless of how many customers are in the system. Unfortunately, this rate often is not a constant in real queueing systems, particularly when the servers are people. When there is a large backlog of work (i.e., a long queue), it is quite likely that such servers will tend to work faster than they do when the backlog is small or nonexistent. This increase in the service rate may result merely because the servers increase their effort when they are under the pressure of a long queue. However, it may also result partly because the quality of the service is compromised or because assistance is obtained on certain service phases.

Given that the mean service rate does increase as the queue size increases, it would be desirable to develop a theoretical model that seems to describe the pattern by which it increases. This model not only should be a reasonable approximation of the actual pattern but also should be simple enough to be practical for implementation. One such model is formulated next. (You have the flexibility to formulate many similar models within the framework of the birth-and-death process.) We then show how the same results apply when the *arrival rate* is affected by the queue size in an analogous way.

FORMULATION FOR THE SINGLE-SERVER CASE ($s = 1$) Let

$$\mu_n = n^c \mu_1, \quad \text{for } n = 1, 2, \ldots,$$

where n = number of customers in system.

μ_n = mean service rate when there are n customers in system.

$1/\mu_1$ = expected "normal" service time—expected time to service customer when that customer is the only one in system.

c = "pressure coefficient"—positive constant that indicates degree to which service rate of system is affected by system state.

Thus, selecting $c = 1$, for example, hypothesizes that the mean service rate is directly proportional to n; $c = \frac{1}{2}$ implies that the mean service rate is proportional to the square root of n; and so on. The preceding queueing models in this section have implicitly assumed that $c = 0$.

Now assume additionally that the queueing system has a Poisson input with $\lambda_n = \lambda$ (for $n = 0, 1, 2, \ldots$) and exponential service times with μ_n as just given. This case is now a special case of the birth-and-death process, where

$$C_n = \frac{(\lambda/\mu_1)^n}{(n!)^c}, \quad \text{for } n = 1, 2, \ldots.$$

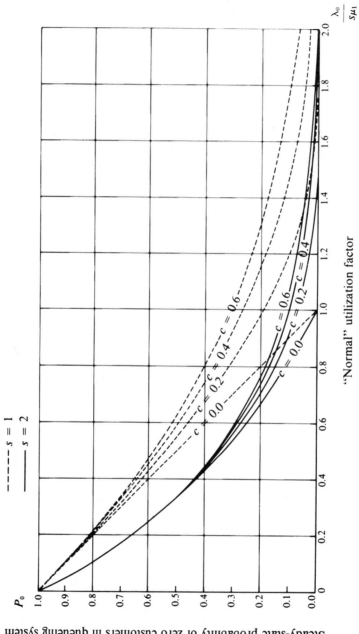

Figure 16.9 Values of P_0 for the state-dependent model (Sec. 16.6).

Thus all the steady-state results given in Sec. 16.5 are applicable to this model. (A steady-state condition always can be reached when $c > 0$.) Unfortunately, analytical expressions are not available for the summations involved. However, nearly exact values of P_0 and L have been tabulated[1] for various values of c and λ/μ_1 by summing a finite number of terms on a computer. A small portion of these results also is shown in Figs. 16.9 and 16.10.

A queueing system may react to a long queue by decreasing the arrival rate instead of increasing the service rate. (The arrival rate may be decreased, for example, by diverting some of the customers requiring service to another service facility.) The corresponding model for describing mean arrival rates for this case is to let

$$\lambda_n = (n + 1)^{-b}\lambda_0, \quad \text{for } n = 0, 1, 2, \ldots,$$

where b is a constant whose interpretation is analogous to that for c. The C_n values for the birth-and-death process with these λ_n (and with $\mu_n = \mu$ for $n = 1$, $2, \ldots$) are *identical* to those just shown (replacing λ by λ_0) for the state-dependent service rate model when $c = b$ and $\lambda/\mu_1 = \lambda_0/\mu$, so the steady-state results also are the same.

A more general model that combines these two patterns can also be used when both the mean arrival and the mean service rates are state-dependent. Thus let

$$\mu_n = n^a\mu_1, \quad \text{for } n = 1, 2, \ldots,$$
$$\lambda_n = (n + 1)^{-b}\lambda_0, \quad \text{for } n = 0, 1, 2, \ldots.$$

Once again, the C_n values for the birth-and-death process with these parameters are identical to those shown for the state-dependent service rate model when $c = a + b$ and $\lambda/\mu_1 = \lambda_0/\mu_1$, so the tabulated steady-state results actually are applicable to this general model.

FORMULATION FOR THE MULTIPLE-SERVER CASE $(s > 1)$ To generalize this combined model further to the multiple-server case, it would seem natural to have the μ_n and λ_n vary with the number of customers *per server* (n/s) in essentially the same way they vary with n for the single-server case. Thus let

$$\mu_n = \begin{cases} n\mu_1, & \text{if } n \leq s \\ \left(\dfrac{n}{s}\right)^a s\mu_1, & \text{if } n \geq s, \end{cases}$$

$$\lambda_n = \begin{cases} \lambda_0, & \text{if } n \leq s - 1 \\ \left(\dfrac{s}{n+1}\right)^b \lambda_0, & \text{if } n \geq s - 1. \end{cases}$$

[1] Conway, Richard W. and William L. Maxwell: "A Queueing Model with State Dependent Service Rate," *Journal of Industrial Engineering*, **12**: 132–136, 1961.

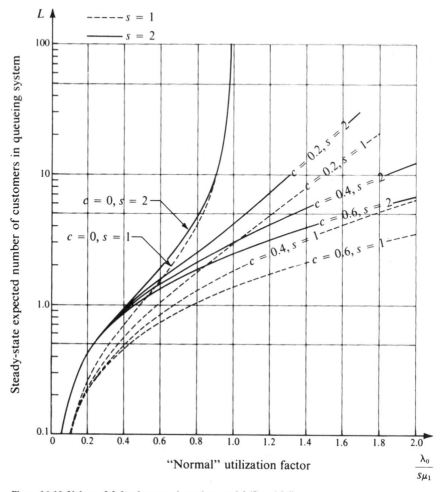

Figure 16.10 **Values of *L* for the state-dependent model (Sec. 16.6).**

Therefore, the birth-and-death process with these parameters has

$$
C_n = \begin{cases}
\dfrac{(\lambda_0/\mu_1)^n}{n!}, & \text{for } n = 1, 2, \ldots, s \\[2mm]
\dfrac{(\lambda_0/\mu_1)^n}{s!(n!/s!)^c s^{(1-c)(n-s)}}, & \text{for } n = s, s+1, \ldots,
\end{cases}
$$

where $c = a + b$.

Computational results for P_0, L_q, and L have been tabulated[1] for various values of c, (λ_0/μ_1), and s. Some of these results also are given in Figs. 16.9 and 16.10.

---

[1] Hillier, F. S., R. W. Conway, and W. L. Maxwell: "A Multiple Server Queueing Model with State Dependent Service Rate," *Journal of Industrial Engineering*, **15**: 153–157, 1964.

EXAMPLE After gathering additional data for the *County Hospital* emergency room, the Management Engineer found that the time a doctor spends with a patient tends to decrease as the number of patients waiting increases. Part of the explanation is simply that the doctor works faster, but the main reason is that more of the treatment is turned over to a nurse for completion. The pattern of the μ_n (the mean rate at which a doctor treats patients while there are a total of n patients to be treated in the emergency room) seems to fit reasonably the *state-dependent service rate model* presented here. Therefore, the Management Engineer has decided to apply this model.

The new data indicate that the average time a doctor spends treating a patient is 24 minutes if no other patients are waiting, whereas this average becomes 12 minutes when each doctor has six patients (so five are waiting their turn). Thus, with a single doctor on duty,

$$\mu_1 = 2\tfrac{1}{2} \text{ customers per hour,}$$
$$\mu_6 = 5 \text{ customers per hour.}$$

Therefore, the pressure coefficient c (or a in the general model) must satisfy the relationship

$$\mu_6 = 6^c \mu_1, \quad \text{so } 6^c = 2.$$

Using logarithms to solve for c yields $c = 0.4$. Because $\lambda = 2$ from before, this solution for c completes the specification of parameter values for this model.

To compare the two alternatives of having *one* doctor ($s = 1$) or *two* doctors ($s = 2$) on duty, the Management Engineer developed the various measures of performance shown in Table 16.3. The values of P_0, L, and (for $s = 2$) L_q were obtained directly from the tabulated results for this model. (Except for this L_q, you can approximate the same values from Figs. 16.9 and 16.10.) These values

Table 16.3 **Steady-state results from state-dependent service rate model for County Hospital problem**

	$s = 1$	$s = 2$	
$\dfrac{\lambda}{s\mu_1}$	0.8	0.4	
$\dfrac{\lambda}{s\mu_{6s}}$	0.4	0.2	
P_0	0.367	0.440	
P_1	0.294	0.352	
L_q	0.618	0.095	
L	1.251	0.864	
W_q	0.309	0.048	(in hours)
W	0.626	0.432	(in hours)
$P\{\mathcal{W}_q > 0\}$	0.633	0.208	

were then used to calculate

$$P_1 = C_1 P_0,$$
$$L_q = L - (1 - P_0), \quad \text{if} \quad s = 1,$$
$$[L_q = (L - P_1) - 2(1 - P_0 - P_1), \quad \text{if} \quad s = 2]$$
$$W_q = \frac{L_q}{\lambda}, \qquad W = \frac{L}{\lambda},$$

$$P\{\mathcal{W}_q > 0\} = 1 - \sum_{n=0}^{s-1} P_n.$$

The fact that some of the results in Table 16.3 do not deviate substantially from those in Table 16.2 reinforce the tentative conclusion that a single doctor will be inadequate next year.

16.7 Queueing Models Involving Nonexponential Distributions

Because all the queueing theory models in the preceding section (except for one generalization) are based on the birth-and-death process, both their interarrival and service times are required to have *exponential* distributions. As discussed in Sec. 16.4, this type of probability distribution has many convenient properties for queueing theory, but it provides a reasonable fit for only certain kinds of queueing systems. In particular, the assumption of exponential *interarrival times* implies that arrivals occur *randomly* (a Poisson input process), which is a reasonable approximation in many situations but *not* when the arrivals are carefully scheduled or regulated. Furthermore, the *actual service-time distribution* frequently deviates greatly from the exponential form, particularly when the service requirements of the customers are quite similar. Therefore, it is important to have available other queueing models that use alternative distributions.

Unfortunately, the mathematical analysis of queueing models with non-exponential distributions is much more difficult. However, it has been possible to obtain some useful results for a few such models. This analysis is beyond the level of this book, but in this section we shall summarize the models and describe their results.

THE M/G/1 MODEL

As introduced in Sec. 16.2, the M/G/1 model assumes that the queueing system has a *single server* and a *Poisson input process* (exponential interarrival times) with a *fixed* mean arrival rate λ. As usual, it is assumed that the customers have *independent* service times with the *same* probability distribution. However, *no* restrictions are imposed on what this service-time distribution can be. In fact, it is only necessary to know (or estimate) the mean $1/\mu$ and variance σ^2 of this distribution.

Any such queueing system can eventually reach a *steady-state condition* if

$\rho = \lambda/\mu < 1$. The readily available steady-state results[1] for this general model are the following:

$$P_0 = 1 - \rho,$$

$$L_q = \frac{\lambda^2\sigma^2 + \rho^2}{2(1 - \rho)},$$

$$L = \rho + L_q,$$

$$W_q = \frac{L_q}{\lambda},$$

$$W = W_q + \frac{1}{\mu}.$$

Considering the complexity involved in analyzing a model that permits *any* service-time distribution, it is remarkable that such a simple formula can be obtained for L_q. This formula is one of the most important results in queueing theory because of its ease of use and the prevalence of $M/G/1$ queueing systems in practice. This equation for L_q (or its counterpart for W_q) commonly is referred to as the **Pollaczek-Khintchine formula**, named after the Frenchman and the Russian who derived it more than 50 years ago.

For any fixed expected service time $1/\mu$, notice that L_q, L, W_q, and W all increase as σ^2 is increased. This result is important because it indicates that the consistency of the server has a major bearing on the performance of the service facility—not just his average speed. This key point is illustrated in the next subsection.

When the service-time distribution is exponential, $\sigma^2 = 1/\mu^2$, and the preceding results will reduce to the corresponding results for the $M/M/1$ model given at the beginning of Sec. 16.6.

The complete flexibility in the service-time distribution provided by this model is extremely useful, so it is unfortunate that efforts to derive similar results for the *multiple-server* case have been unsuccessful. However, some multiple-server results have been obtained for the important special cases described by the following two models.

THE M/D/s MODEL

When the service consists of essentially the same routine task to be performed for all customers, there tends to be little variation in the service time required. The $M/D/s$ model often provides a reasonable representation for this kind of situation, because it assumes that all service times actually equal some fixed *constant* (the *degenerate* service-time distribution) and that we have a *Poisson* input process with a fixed mean arrival rate λ.

---

[1] A recursion formula also is available for calculating the probability distribution of the number of customers in the system; see Hordijk, A. and H. C. Tijms: *Statistica Neerlandica*, **30**: 97–100, 1976.

When there is just a *single* server, the M/D/1 model is just the special case of the M/G/1 model where $\sigma^2 = 0$, so that the **Pollaczek-Khintchine formula** reduces to

$$L_q = \frac{\rho^2}{2(1 - \rho)},$$

where L, W_q, and W are obtained from L_q as just shown. Notice that this L_q and W_q are exactly *half* as large as for the exponential service-time case of Sec. 16.6 (the M/M/1 model), where $\sigma^2 = 1/\mu^2$, so decreasing σ^2 can *greatly* improve the measures of performance of a queueing system.

For the multiple-server version of this model (M/D/s), a complicated method is available[1] for deriving the steady-state probability distribution of the number of customers in the system and its mean (assuming $\rho = \lambda/s\mu < 1$). However, these results have been tabulated for numerous cases,[2] and the means (L) also are given graphically in Fig. 16.11.

THE $M/E_k/s$ MODEL

The M/D/s model assumes *zero* variation in the service times ($\sigma = 0$), whereas the *exponential* service-time distribution assumes a very large variation ($\sigma = 1/\mu$). Between these two rather extreme cases lies a long middle ground ($0 < \sigma < 1/\mu$), where most *actual* service-time distributions fall. Another kind of theoretical service-time distribution that fills this middle ground is the **Erlang distribution** (named after the founder of queueing theory).

The probability density function for the Erlang distribution is

$$f(t) = \frac{(\mu k)^k}{(k - 1)!} t^{k-1} e^{-k\mu t}, \quad \text{for } t \geq 0,$$

where μ and k are strictly positive parameters of the distribution, and k is further restricted to be *integer*. (Except for this integer restriction, and the definition of the parameters, this distribution is *identical* to the *gamma* distribution.) Its mean and standard deviation are

$$\text{Mean} = \frac{1}{\mu},$$

$$\text{Standard deviation} = \frac{1}{\sqrt{k}} \frac{1}{\mu}.$$

Thus k is the parameter that specifies the degree of variability of the service times relative to the mean. It usually is referred to as the *shape parameter*.

[1] See Prabhu, N. U.: *Queues and Inventories*, pp. 32–34, Wiley, New York, 1965; also see pp. 344–346 in Selected Reference 2.

[2] Hillier, F. S., and O. S. Yu, with D. Avis, L. Fossett, F. Lo, and M. Reiman: *Queueing Tables and Graphs*, Elsevier North-Holland, New York, 1981.

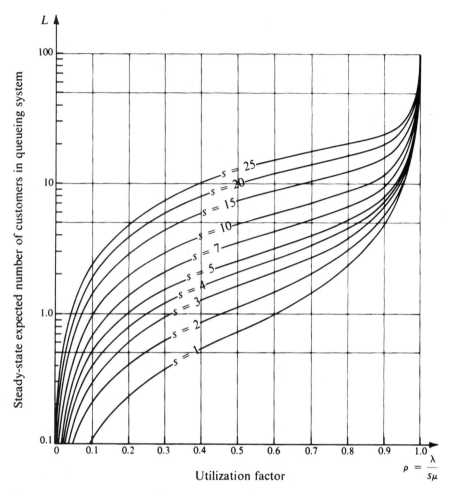

Figure 16.11 Values of L for the M/D/s model (Sec. 16.7).

The Erlang distribution is a very important distribution in queueing theory for two reasons. To describe the first one, suppose that T_1, T_2,..., T_k are k independent random variables with an identical *exponential* distribution whose mean is $1/k\mu$. Then their sum,

$$T = T_1 + T_2 + \cdots + T_k,$$

has an *Erlang* distribution with parameters μ and k. The discussion of the exponential distribution in Sec. 16.4 suggested that the time required to perform certain kinds of tasks might well have an exponential distribution. However, the total service required by a customer may involve the server performing not just one specific task but a sequence of k tasks. If the respective tasks have an identical exponential distribution for their duration, the total service time would have an

Erlang distribution, which would be the case, for example, if the server must perform the *same* exponential task k times for each customer.

The Erlang distribution also is very useful because it is a large (two-parameter) family of distributions permitting only nonnegative values. Hence empirical service-time distributions can usually be reasonably approximated by an Erlang distribution. In fact, both the *exponential* and the *degenerate* (constant) distributions are special cases of the Erlang distribution, with $k = 1$ and $k = \infty$, respectively. Intermediate values of k provide intermediate distributions with mean $= 1/\mu$, mode $= (k - 1)/\mu k$, and variance $= 1/k\mu^2$, as suggested by Fig. 16.12.

Now consider the $M/E_k/1$ model, which is just the special case of the $M/G/1$ model where service times have an *Erlang* distribution with shape parameter $= k$. Applying the *Pollaczek-Khintchine formula* with $\sigma^2 = 1/k\mu^2$ (and the accompanying results given for $M/G/1$) yields

$$L_q = \frac{\lambda^2/k\mu^2 + \rho^2}{2(1 - \rho)} = \frac{1 + k}{2k} \frac{\lambda^2}{\mu(\mu - \lambda)},$$

$$W_q = \frac{1 + k}{2k} \frac{\lambda}{\mu(\mu - \lambda)},$$

$$W = W_q + \frac{1}{\mu},$$

$$L = \lambda W.$$

With *multiple* servers ($M/E_k/s$), the relationship of the Erlang distribution to the exponential distribution just described can be exploited to formulate a *modified* birth-and-death process (continuous parameter Markov chain) in terms

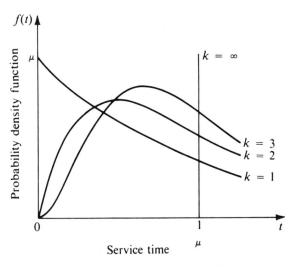

Figure 16.12 **A family of Erlang distributions with constant mean $1/\mu$.**

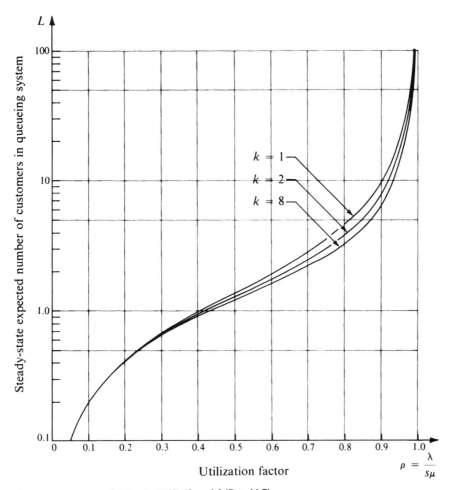

Figure 16.13 Values of L for the M/E_k/2 model (Sec. 16.7).

of individual exponential service phases (k per customer) rather than complete customers. However, it has not been possible to derive a general steady-state solution (when $\rho = \lambda/s\mu < 1$) for the probability distribution of the number of customers in the system as we did in Sec. 16.5. Instead, advanced theory is required to solve individual cases numerically. Once again, these results have been obtained and tabulated for numerous cases.[1] The means (L) also are given graphically in Fig. 16.13 for some cases where $s = 2$.

MODELS WITHOUT A POISSON INPUT

All the queueing models presented thus far have assumed a Poisson input process (exponential interarrival times). However, this assumption is violated if the

[1] Ibid.

arrivals are scheduled or regulated in some way that prevents them from occurring randomly, in which case another model is needed.

As long as the service times have an *exponential* distribution with a fixed parameter, three such models are readily available. These models are obtained by merely *reversing* the assumed distributions of the *interarrival* and *service times* in the preceding three models. Thus the first new model (GI/M/s) imposes no restriction on what the *interarrival time* distribution can be. In this case, there are some steady-state results available[1] (particularly in regard to waiting-time distributions) for *both* the single-server and multiple-server versions of the model, but these results are not nearly as convenient as the simple expressions given for the M/G/1 model. The second new model (D/M/s) assumes that all interarrival times equal some fixed *constant*, which would represent a queueing system where arrivals are *scheduled* at regular intervals. The third new model (E_k/M/s) assumes an *Erlang* interarrival time distribution, which provides a middle ground between *regularly scheduled* (constant) and *completely random* (exponential) arrivals. Extensive computational results have been tabulated[2] for these latter two models, including the values of L given graphically in Figs. 16.14 and 16.15.

If *neither* the interarrival times nor the service times for a queueing system have an *exponential* distribution, then there are three additional queueing models for which computational results also are available.[3] One of these models (E_m/E_k/s) assumes an *Erlang* distribution for *both* these times. The other two models (E_k/D/s and D/E_k/s) assume that *one* of these times has an *Erlang* distribution and the *other* time equals some fixed *constant*.

OTHER MODELS

Although you have seen in this section a large number of queueing models that involve nonexponential distributions, we have far from exhausted the list. For example, another distribution that occasionally is used for either interarrival times or service times is the **hyperexponential distribution**. The key characteristic of this distribution is that, even though only nonnegative values are allowed, its standard deviation, σ, actually is larger than its mean, $1/\mu$. This characteristic is in contrast to the *Erlang* distribution, where $\sigma < 1/\mu$ in *every* case except $k = 1$ (exponential distribution), which has $\sigma = 1/\mu$. To illustrate a typical situation where $\sigma > 1/\mu$ can occur, we suppose that the service involved in the queueing system is the repair of some kind of machine or vehicle. If many of the repairs turn out to be routine (small service times) but occasional repairs require an extensive overhaul (very large service times), then the standard deviation of service times will tend to be quite large relative to the mean, in which case the hyperexponential distribution may be used to represent the service-time distribution.

[1] For example, see pp. 304–320 of Selected Reference 2.

[2] F. S. Hillier and O. S. Yu, op. cit.

[3] Ibid.

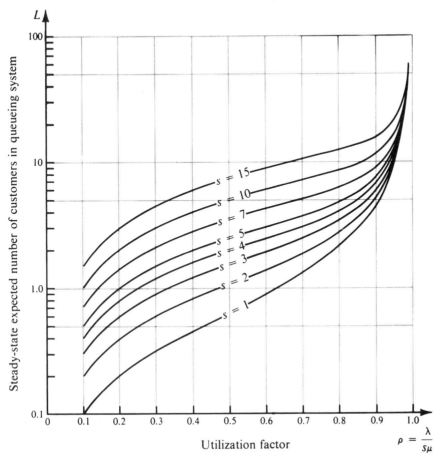

Figure 16.14 **Values of *L* for the D/M/s model (Sec. 16.7).**

Another family of distributions coming into general use consists of **phase-type distributions** (some of which also are called *generalized Erlangian distributions*). These distributions are obtained by breaking down the total time into a number of *phases*, each having an *exponential* distribution, where the parameters of these exponential distributions may be different and the phases may be either *in series* or *in parallel* (or both). A group of phases being *in parallel* means that the process randomly selects *one* of the phases to go through each time according to specified probabilities. This approach is, in fact, how the *hyperexponential* distribution is derived, so this distribution is a special case of the phase-type distributions. Another special case is the *Erlang* distribution, which has the restrictions that all of its *k* phases are *in series* and that these phases have the *same* parameter for their exponential distributions. Removing these restrictions means that phase-type distributions in general can provide considerably more flexibility than the Erlang distribution in fitting the *actual* distribution of interarrival times

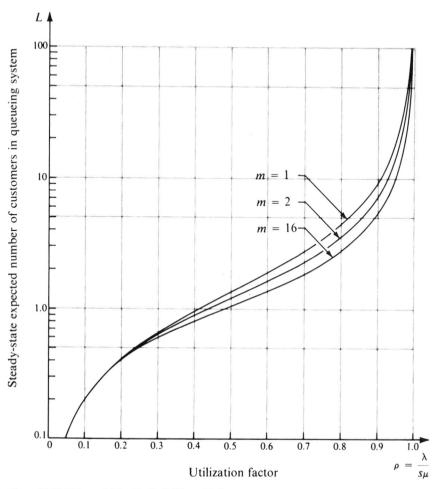

Figure 16.15 Values of *L* for the $E_k/M/2$ model (Sec. 16.7).

or service times observed in a real queueing system. This flexibility is especially valuable when using the actual distribution directly in the model is not analytically tractable, whereas the ratio of the *mean* to the *standard deviation* for the actual distribution does not closely match the available ratios ($\sqrt{k}$ for $k = 1, 2, \ldots$) for the Erlang distribution.

Because they are built up from combinations of exponential distributions, queueing models using phase-type distributions still can be represented by a *continuous parameter Markov chain*. This Markov chain generally will have an infinite number of states, so solving for the steady-state distribution of the state of the system requires solving an infinite system of linear equations that have a relatively complicated structure. Solving such a system is far from a routine thing, but recent theoretical advances have enabled us to solve these queueing models numerically in some cases. An extensive tabulation of these results for models with various phase-type distributions (including the hypergeometric distribution) now is available in a recently published book.[1]

16.8 A Priority-Discipline Queueing Model

Priority-discipline queueing models are those where the queue discipline is based on a *priority system*. Thus the order in which members of the queue are selected for service is on the basis of their assigned priorities.

Many real queueing systems fit these priority-discipline models much more closely than other available models. Rush jobs are taken ahead of other jobs, and important customers may be given precedence over others. Therefore, the use of priority-discipline models often provides a very welcome refinement over the more usual queueing models.

Unfortunately, the inclusion of priorities makes the mathematical analysis fairly complicated, so that only limited results are available. Almost all these results are for the single-server case. However, usable results are available for one *multiple-server* model. This model assumes that there are N *priority classes* (class 1 has the highest priority and class N the lowest) and that, whenever a server becomes free to begin serving a new customer from the queue, the one selected is that member of the *highest* priority class represented in the queue who has waited longest. In other words, customers are selected to begin service in the order of their priority classes, but on a first-come-first-served basis within each priority class. A *Poisson* input process and *exponential* service times are assumed for each priority class. The model also makes the somewhat restrictive assumption that the mean service time is the *same* for all priority classes. However, it does permit the mean arrival rate to differ among the priority classes.

Notice that if this distinction between customers in different priority classes is ignored, this model actually fits the M/M/s model studied in Sec. 16.6. Therefore, when we count just the *total* number of customers in the system, the steady-state distribution given there still applies here. Consequently, the formulas for L and L_q also carry over, as do the expected waiting-time results (by Little's formula), W and W_q, for a randomly selected customer. What changes is the *distribution* of waiting times, which was derived in Sec. 16.6 under the assumption of a first-come-first-served queue discipline. With a priority discipline, this distribution has a much larger *variance*, because the waiting times of customers in the highest priority classes tend to be much smaller than under a first-come-first-served discipline, whereas the waiting times in the lowest priority classes tend to be much larger. By the same token, the breakdown of the total number of customers in the system tends to be disproportionately weighted toward the lower priority classes. But this condition is just the reason for imposing priorities on the queueing system in the first place. We want to *improve* the *measures of performance* for each of the higher priority classes at the expense

[1] Seelen, L. P., H. C. Tijms, and M. H. Van Hoorn: *Tables for Multi-Server Queues*, North-Holland, Amsterdam, 1985.

of performance for the lower priority classes. To determine how much improvement is being made, we need to obtain such measures as *expected waiting time in the system* and *expected number of customers in the system* for the individual priority classes. We obtain these measures next for this priority-discipline model.

First consider the case of **nonpreemptive priorities**, where a customer being served cannot be ejected back into the queue (preempted) if a higher priority customer enters the queueing system. Therefore, once a server has begun serving a customer, the service must be completed without interruption. Under this assumption for the priority-discipline model, W_k, the steady-state *expected waiting time in the system* (including service time) for a member of priority class k, is

$$W_k = \frac{1}{A \cdot B_{k-1} \cdot B_k} + \frac{1}{\mu}, \quad \text{for } k = 1, 2, \ldots, N,$$

where

$$A = s! \left(\frac{s\mu - \lambda}{\rho^s} \right) \sum_{j=0}^{s-1} \frac{\rho^j}{j!} + s\mu,$$

$$B_0 = 1,$$

$$B_k = 1 - \frac{\sum_{i=1}^{k} \lambda_i}{s\mu}, \quad \text{for } k = 1, 2, \ldots, N,$$

and

s = number of servers,

μ = mean service rate per busy server,

λ_i = mean arrival rate for priority class i, for $i = 1, 2, \ldots, N$,

$$\lambda = \sum_{i=1}^{N} \lambda_i,$$

$$\rho = \frac{\lambda}{\mu}.$$

(These results assume

$$\sum_{i=1}^{k} \lambda_i < \mu,$$

so that priority class k can reach a steady-state condition.) *Little's formula* still applies to individual priority classes, so L_k, the steady-state *expected number of members of priority class k in the queueing system* (including those being served), is

$$L_k = \lambda_k W_k, \quad \text{for } k = 1, 2, \ldots, N.$$

To determine the *expected waiting time in the queue* (excluding service time) for priority class k, merely subtract $1/\mu$ from W_k; the corresponding *expected queue length* is again obtained by multiplying by λ_k. For the special case where $s = 1$, the expression for A reduces to $A = \mu^2/\lambda$.

Now consider the case of **preemptive priorities**, whereby the lowest priority customer being served is *preempted* (ejected back into the queue) whenever a higher priority customer enters the queueing system. A server is thereby freed to begin servicing the new arrival immediately. (When a server does succeed in *finishing* a service, the next customer to begin receiving service is selected in just the same way as described earlier, so a preempted customer normally will get back into service again and, after enough tries, eventually finish.) If the other assumptions of the preceding model are retained, this preemption feature changes the *total* expected waiting time in the system (including total service time) to

$$W_k = \frac{1/\mu}{B_{k-1} \cdot B_k}, \quad \text{for } k = 1, 2, \ldots, N$$

for the *single-server* case ($s = 1$). When $s > 1$, the W_k can be calculated by an iterative procedure that will be illustrated soon by the County Hospital example. The L_k just defined continue to satisfy the relationship

$$L_k = \lambda_k W_k, \quad \text{for } k = 1, 2, \ldots, N.$$

The corresponding results for the *queue* (excluding customers in service) also can be obtained from W_k and L_k as just described for the case of nonpreemptive priorities. Because of the lack of memory property of the exponential distribution (see Sec. 16.4), preemptions do not affect the service process (occurrence of service completions) in any way. The expected *total* service time for any customer still is $1/\mu$. This lack of memory property also implies that we don't need to worry about defining the point at which service begins when a preempted customer returns to service; the distribution of the *remaining* service time *always* is the same. (For any *other* service-time distribution, it becomes important to distinguish between *preemptive-resume* systems, where service for a preempted customer resumes at the point of interruption, and *preemptive-repeat* systems, where service must start at the beginning again.)

Some results are also available[1] for a few other single-server, priority-discipline models involving other service-time distributions and/or unequal expected service times.

EXAMPLE For the *County Hospital* emergency room problem, the Management Engineer has noticed that the patients are not treated on a first-come-first-served basis. Rather, the admitting nurse seems to divide the patients into roughly three categories: (1) *critical* cases, where prompt treatment is vital for survival; (2) *serious* cases, where early treatment is important to prevent further deterioration; and (3) *stable* cases, where treatment can be delayed without adverse medical consequences. Patients are then treated in this order of priority, where those

---

[1] See Selected Reference 3.

Table 16.4 **Steady-state results from priority-discipline model for County Hospital problem**

	Preemptive priorities		Nonpreemptive priorities	
	s = 1	s = 2	s = 1	s = 2
A	—	—	4.5	36
B_1	0.933	—	0.933	0.967
B_2	0.733	—	0.733	0.867
B_3	0.333	—	0.333	0.667
$W_1 - \dfrac{1}{\mu}$	0.024	0.00037	0.238	0.029
$W_2 - \dfrac{1}{\mu}$	0.154	0.00793	0.325	0.033
$W_3 - \dfrac{1}{\mu}$	1.033	0.06542	0.889	0.048

in the same category are normally taken on a first-come-first-served basis. A doctor will interrupt treatment of a patient if a new case in a higher priority category arrives. Approximately 10 percent of the patients fall into the first category, 30 percent into the second, and 60 percent into the third. Because the more serious cases will be sent into the hospital for further care after receiving emergency treatment, the average treatment time by a doctor in the emergency room actually does not differ greatly among these categories.

The Management Engineer has decided to use the priority-discipline queueing model just described as a reasonable representation of this queueing system, where the three categories of patients constitute the three priority classes in the model. Because treatment is interrupted by the arrival of a higher priority case, the *preemptive priorities* version of this model is the appropriate one. Given the previously available data ($\mu = 3$ and $\lambda = 2$), the preceding percentages yield $\lambda_1 = 0.2, \lambda_2 = 0.6, \lambda_3 = 1.2$. Table 16.4 gives the resulting expected waiting times in the queue (so *excluding* treatment time) in *hours* for the respective priority classes[1] when there is one doctor ($s = 1$) or two doctors ($s = 2$) on duty. (The corresponding results for the *nonpreemptive priorities* version of the model also are given in Table 16.4 to show the effect of preempting.)

These preemptive priority results for $s = 2$ were obtained as follows. Because the waiting times for priority class 1 customers are completely unaffected by the presence of customers in lower priority classes, W_1 would be the same for any other values of λ_2 and λ_3, including $\lambda_2 = 0, \lambda_3 = 0$. Therefore, W_1 must equal W for the corresponding *one-class* model (the M/M/s model in Sec. 16.6) with $s = 2$,

---

[1] Note that these expected times can no longer be interpreted as the expected time before treatment begins when $k > 1$, because treatment may be interrupted at least once, causing additional waiting time, before being completed.

$\mu = 3$, and $\lambda = \lambda_1 = 0.2$, which yields

$$W_1 = W \quad \text{for } \lambda = 0.2$$
$$= 0.33370,$$

so

$$W_1 - \frac{1}{\mu} = 0.33370 - 0.33333 = 0.00037.$$

Now consider the first *two* priority classes. Again note that customers in these classes are completely unaffected by lower priority classes (just priority class 3 in this case), which can therefore be ignored in the analysis. Let $\bar{W}_{1-2}$ be the expected waiting time in the system (so including service time) of a *random arrival* in *either* of these two classes, so the probability is $\lambda_1/(\lambda_1 + \lambda_2) = \frac{1}{4}$ that this arrival is in class 1 and $\lambda_2/(\lambda_1 + \lambda_2) = \frac{3}{4}$ that it is in class 2. Therefore, $\bar{W}_{1-2} = \frac{1}{4}W_1 + \frac{3}{4}W_2$. Furthermore, because *expected* waiting time is the same for *any* queue discipline, $\bar{W}_{1-2}$ must also equal W for the M/M/s model in Sec. 16.6, with $s = 2$, $\mu = 3$, and $\lambda = \lambda_1 + \lambda_2 = 0.8$, which yields

$$\bar{W}_{1-2} = W \quad \text{for } \lambda = 0.8$$
$$= 0.33937.$$

Combining these facts gives

$$W_2 = \frac{4}{3}\left[0.33937 - \frac{1}{4}(0.33370)\right] = 0.34126.$$

$$\left(W_2 - \frac{1}{\mu} = 0.00793.\right)$$

Finally, let $\bar{W}_{1-3}$ be the expected waiting time in the system (so including service time) for a *random arrival* in *any* of the three priority classes, so the probabilities are 0.1, 0.3, and 0.6 that it is in class 1, 2, and 3, respectively. Therefore,

$$\bar{W}_{1-3} = 0.1W_1 + 0.3W_2 + 0.6W_3.$$

Furthermore, $\bar{W}_{1-3}$ must also equal W for the M/M/s model in Sec. 16.6, with $s = 2$, $\mu = 3$, and $\lambda = \lambda_1 + \lambda_2 + \lambda_3 = 2$, so that (from Table 16.2),

$$\bar{W}_{1-3} = W \quad \text{for } \lambda = 2$$
$$= 0.375.$$

Consequently,

$$W_3 = \frac{1}{0.6}[0.375 - 0.1(0.33370) - 0.3(0.34126)]$$

$$= 0.39875.$$

$$\left(W_3 - \frac{1}{\mu} = 0.06542.\right)$$

The corresponding W_q results for the M/M/s model in Sec. 16.6 also could have been used in exactly the same way to derive the $[W_k - (1/\mu)]$ quantities directly.

When $s = 1$, the $[W_k - 1/\mu]$ values in Table 16.4 for the preemptive priorities case indicate that providing just a single doctor would cause *critical* cases to wait about $1\frac{1}{2}$ minutes (0.024 hour) on the average, *serious* cases to wait more than 9 minutes, and *stable* cases to wait more than an hour. (Contrast these results with the average wait of $W_q = 2/3$ hour for all patients that was obtained in Table 16.2 under the first-come-first-served queue discipline.) However, these values represent *statistical expectations*, so some patients have to wait considerably longer than the average for their priority class. This wait would not be tolerable for the critical and serious cases, where a few minutes can be vital. By contrast, the $s = 2$ results in Table 16.4 (preemptive priorities case) indicate that adding a second doctor would virtually eliminate waiting for all but the stable cases. Therefore, the Management Engineer recommended that there be two doctors on duty in the emergency room during the early evening hours next year. The Board of Directors for County Hospital adopted this recommendation and simultaneously raised the charge for using the emergency room!

16.9 Queueing Networks

Thus far we have considered only queueing systems that have a *single* service facility with one or more servers. However, queueing systems encountered in operations research studies are sometimes actually *queueing networks*, i.e., networks of service facilities where customers must receive service at some or all of these facilities. For example, orders being processed through a job shop must be routed through a sequence of machine groups (service facilities). It is therefore necessary to study the entire network to obtain such information as expected total waiting time, expected number of customers in the entire system, and so forth.

Analytical results on queueing networks have been quite limited because of the difficulty of the problem. Most of the work has been confined to cases with a Poisson input process and exponential service times. Many of the results that have been obtained[1] have necessarily been quite involved and unsuitable for general routine use.

However, there is available one simple result that is of such fundamental importance for queueing networks that it warrants special attention here. This result is the following *equivalence property* for the *input process* of arriving customers and the *output process* of departing customers for certain queueing systems.

EQUIVALENCE PROPERTY Assume that a service facility with s servers has a Poisson input with parameter λ and the same exponential service-time distribu-

[1] For a survey, see Lemoine, Austin J.: "Networks of Queues—A Survey of Equilibrium Analysis," *Management Science*, **24**(4): 464–481, 1977.

tion for each server (the M/M/s model), where $s\mu > \lambda$. Then the steady-state *output* of this service facility is also a Poisson process with parameter λ.[1]

Notice that this property makes no assumption about the type of queue discipline used. Whether it be first-come-first-served, random, or even a priority discipline as in Sec. 16.8, the served customers will leave the service facility according to a Poisson process. The crucial implication of this fact for queueing networks is that if these units must then go to another service facility for further service, this second facility *also* will have a *Poisson* input. Suppose that customers must all receive service at a series of service facilities in a fixed sequence. Assume further that the customers arrive at the first facility according to a Poisson process with parameter λ and that each facility has the same exponential service-time distribution for its servers. It then follows from the equivalence property that (under steady-state conditions) *each* service facility has a Poisson input with parameter λ. Therefore, the elementary M/M/s model of Sec. 16.6 (or its priority-discipline counterpart in Sec. 16.8) can be used to analyze each service facility independently of the others! (The equivalence property can even be used to draw essentially the same conclusion when the customers pass through a network of service facilities in different sequences according to transition probabilities.[2]) The expected total waiting time and the expected number of customers in the entire system can then be obtained by merely summing the corresponding quantities obtained at the respective facilities.

Unfortunately, the equivalence property and its implications do not hold for the case of *finite* queues discussed in Sec. 16.6. This case is actually quite important in practice, because there is often a definite limitation on the queue length in front of service facilities in networks. The facilities must be analyzed jointly in this case, and only limited results have been obtained.

16.10 Conclusions

Queueing systems are prevalent throughout society. The adequacy of these systems can have an important effect on the quality of life and productivity.

Queueing theory studies queueing systems by formulating mathematical models of their operation and then using these models to derive measures of performance. This analysis provides vital information for effectively designing queueing systems that achieve an appropriate balance between the cost of providing a service and the cost associated with waiting for that service.

This chapter presented the most basic models of queueing theory for which particularly useful results are available. However, many other interesting models could be considered if space permitted. In fact, *several thousand* research papers

[1] For a proof, see Burke, P. J.; "The Output of a Queueing System," *Operations Research*, **4**(6): 699–704, 1956.

[2] See Jackson, James R.: "Jobshop-Like Queueing Systems," *Management Science*, **10**(1): 131–142, 1963.

formulating and/or analyzing queueing models have already appeared in the technical literature, and many more are being published each year!

The *exponential distribution* plays a fundamental role in queueing theory for representing the distribution of interarrival and service times, because this assumption enables us to represent the queueing system as a *continuous parameter Markov chain*. For the same reason, *phase-type distributions* such as the *Erlang distribution*, where the total time is broken down into individual phases having an exponential distribution, are very useful. Useful analytical results have been obtained for only a relatively few queueing models making other assumptions.

When no tractable model that provides a reasonable representation of the queueing system under study is available, a common approach is to obtain relevant performance data by developing a computer program for *simulating* the operation of the system. This technique is discussed in Chap. 23.

Chapter 17 describes how queueing theory can be used to help design effective queueing systems.

SELECTED REFERENCES

1. Cooper, Robert B.: *Introduction to Queueing Theory*, 2d ed., Macmillan, New York, 1981.
2. Gross, Donald, and Carl M. Harris: *Fundamentals of Queueing Theory*, 2d ed., Wiley, New York, 1985.
3. Jaiswell, N. K.: *Priority Queues*, Academic Press, New York, 1968.
4. Kleinrock, Leonard: *Queueing Systems, Vol. I: Theory*, Wiley, New York, 1975.
5. Neuts, M. F.: *Matrix-Geometric Solutions in Stochastic Models*, Johns Hopkins University Press, Baltimore, 1981.
6. White, J. A., J. W. Schmidt, and G. K. Bennett: *Analysis of Queueing Systems*, Academic Press, New York, 1975.

PROBLEMS[1]

1. Consider a typical barber shop. Demonstrate that it is a queueing system by describing its components.

2. Identify the customers and the servers in the queueing system in each of the following situations:

(*a*) The checkout stand in a grocery store.
(*b*) A fire station.
(*c*) The toll booth for a bridge.
(*d*) A bicycle repair shop.
(*e*) A shipping dock.
(*f*) A group of semiautomatic machines assigned to one operator.
(*g*) The materials-handling equipment in a factory area.

---

[1] See also the end of Chap. 17 for problems involving the application of queueing theory.

(*h*)   A plumbing shop.
(*i*)   A job shop producing custom orders.
(*j*)   A secretarial typing pool.

3. Suppose that a queueing system has *two* servers, an *exponential* interarrival time distribution with a mean of 2 hours, and an *exponential* service-time distribution with a mean of 2 hours. Furthermore, a customer has just arrived at 12:00 noon.

(*a*)   What is the probability that the *next* arrival will come before 1:00 P.M.? Between 1:00 and 2:00 P.M.? After 2:00 P.M.?
(*b*)   Suppose that *no* additional customers arrive before 1:00 P.M. Now what is the probability that the next arrival will come between 1:00 and 2:00 P.M.?
(*c*)   What is the probability that the *number* of arrivals between 1:00 and 2:00 P.M. will be *zero*? *One*? *Two or more*?
(*d*)   Suppose that both servers are serving customers at 1:00 P.M. What is the probability that *neither* customer will have service completed before 2:00 P.M.? Before 1:10 P.M.? Before 1:01 P.M.?

4. The jobs to be performed on a particular machine arrive according to a Poisson input process with a mean rate of two per hour. Suppose that the machine breaks down and will require 1 hour to be repaired. What is the probability that the number of new jobs that will arrive during this time is (*a*) zero, (*b*) two, (*c*) five or more?

5. A service station has one gasoline pump. Cars wanting gasoline arrive according to a *Poisson* process at a mean rate of 15 per hour. However, if the pump already is being used, these potential customers may *balk* (drive on to another service station). In particular, if there are *n* cars already at the service station, the probability that an arriving potential customer will balk is $n/3$ for $n = 1, 2, 3$. The time required to service a car has an *exponential* distribution with a mean of 4 minutes.

(*a*)   Construct the rate diagram for this queueing system.
(*b*)   Develop the balance equations.
(*c*)   Solve these equations to find the steady-state probability distribution of the number of cars at the station. Verify that this solution is the same as that given by the general solution for the *birth-and-death process*.
(*d*)   Find the expected waiting time (including service) for those cars that stay.

6. Consider a variation of the M/M/1 model where customers *renege* (leave the queueing system without being served) if their waiting time in the queue grows too large. In particular, assume that the time each customer is willing to wait in the queue before reneging has an exponential distribution with a mean of $1/\theta$.

(*a*)   Construct the rate diagram for this queueing system.
(*b*)   Develop the balance equations.

7. A certain small grocery store has a single checkout stand with a full-time cashier. Customers arrive at the stand "randomly" (i.e., a Poisson input process) at a mean rate of 30 per hour. When there is only one customer at the stand, he is processed by the cashier alone, with an expected service time of 1.5 minutes. However, the stock boy has been given standard instructions that whenever there is more than one customer at the stand, he is to help the cashier by bagging the groceries. This help reduces the expected time required to process a customer to 1 minute. In both cases, the service-time distribution is exponential.

(a)   Construct the rate diagram for this queueing system.
(b)   What is the steady-state probability distribution of the number of customers at the checkout stand?
(c)   Derive L for this system. Use this information to determine L_q, W, and W_q.

8.   For each of the following models, write the *balance equations* and show that they are satisfied by the solution given in Sec. 16.6.

(a)   The M/M/1 model.
(b)   The *finite queue variation* of the M/M/1 model, with $K = 2$.
(c)   The *finite calling population variation* of the M/M/1 model, with $N = 2$.

9.   Consider the M/M/s model.

(a)   Suppose there is *one* server and the expected service time is exactly 1 minute. Compare L for the cases where the mean arrival rate is 0.5, 0.9, and 0.99 customers per minute, respectively. Do the same for L_q, W, W_q, and $P\{\mathcal{W} > 5\}$.
(b)   Now suppose there are *two* servers and the expected service time is exactly 2 minutes. Make the same comparisons as for part (a).

10.   A bank employs four tellers to serve its customers. Customers arrive according to a *Poisson* process at a mean rate of three per minute. If a customer finds all tellers busy, he joins a queue that is serviced by all tellers; that is, there are no lines in front of each teller, but rather one line waiting for the first available teller. The transaction time between the teller and customer has an exponential distribution with a mean of 1 minute.

(a)   Construct the rate diagram for this queueing system.
(b)   Find the steady-state probability distribution of the number of customers in the bank.
(c)   Find L_q, W_q, W, and L.

11.   Jobs arrive at a particular work center according to a Poisson input process at a mean rate of two per day, and the operation time has an exponential distribution with a mean of $\frac{1}{4}$ day. Enough in-process storage space is provided at the work center to accommodate three jobs in addition to the one being processed, whereas excess jobs are stored temporarily in a less convenient location. For what proportion of the time will this storage space at the work center be adequate to accommodate all waiting jobs?

12.   It is necessary to determine how much in-process storage space to allocate to a particular work center in a new factory. Jobs arrive at this work center according to a *Poisson* process with a mean rate of three per hour, and the time required to perform the necessary work has an *exponential* distribution with a mean of 0.25 hour. Whenever the waiting jobs require more in-process storage space than has been allocated, the excess jobs are stored temporarily in a less convenient location. If each job requires 1 square foot of floor space while it is in in-process storage at the work center, how much space must be provided to accommodate all waiting jobs (a) 50 percent of the time? (b) 90 percent? (c) 99 percent? *Hint*: The sum of a geometric series is

$$\sum_{n=0}^{N} x^n = \frac{1 - x^{N+1}}{1 - x}.$$

13.   Section 16.6 gives the following equations for the M/M/1 model:

(1) $$P\{\mathcal{W} > t\} = \sum_{n=0}^{\infty} P_n P\{S_{n+1} > t\}.$$

(2)
$$P\{\mathcal{W} > t\} = e^{-\mu(1-\rho)t}.$$

Show that Eq. (1) reduces algebraically to Eq. (2).

14. Derive W_q directly for the following cases by developing and reducing an expression analogous to Eq. (1), Prob. 13. (*Hint:* Use the *conditional* expected waiting time in the queue given that a random arrival finds n customers already in the system.)

    (*a*)   The M/M/1 model.
    (*b*)   The M/M/s model.

15. For the *finite queue variation* of the M/M/1 model, develop an expression analogous to Eq. (1) in Prob. 13 for the following probabilities:

    (*a*) $P\{\mathcal{W} > t\}$.
    (*b*) $P\{\mathcal{W}_q > t\}$.

16. An airline ticket office has two ticket agents answering incoming phone calls for flight reservations. In addition, one caller can be put on hold until one of the agents is available to take the call. If all three phone lines (both agent lines and the hold line) are busy, a potential customer gets a busy signal, and it is assumed that the call goes to another ticket office and that the business is lost. The calls and attempted calls occur *randomly* (i.e., according to a *Poisson* process) at a mean rate of 15 per hour. The length of a telephone conversation has an *exponential* distribution with a mean of 4 minutes.

    (*a*)   Construct the rate diagram for this queueing system.
    (*b*)   Find the steady-state probability that

        (i)   A caller will get to talk to an agent immediately,
        (ii) The caller will be put on hold,
        (iii) The caller will get a busy signal.

17. The Copy Shop is open 5 days per week for copying materials that are brought to the shop. It has three identical copying machines, but only two operators are kept on duty to run the machines, so the third machine is a spare that is used only when one of the other machines breaks down. When a machine is being used, the time until it breaks down has an exponential distribution with a mean of 2 weeks. If a machine breaks down while the other two are operational, a repairman is called in to repair it, in which case the total time from the breakdown until the repair is completed has an exponential distribution with a mean of 0.2 week. However, if a second machine breaks down before the first one has been repaired, the third machine is shut off while the two operators work together to repair this second machine quickly, in which case its repair time has an exponential distribution with a mean of only 1/15 week. If the repairman finishes repairing the first machine before the two operators complete the repair of the second, the operators go back to running the two operational machines while the repairman finishes the second repair, in which case the remaining repair time has an exponential distribution with a mean of 0.2 week.

    (*a*)   Letting the state of the system be the number of machines not working, construct the rate diagram for this queueing system.
    (*b*)   Find the steady-state distribution of the number of machines not working.
    (*c*)   What is the expected number of operators available for copying?

18. Plans are being made to open a small car-wash operation, and the owner must decide how much space to provide for waiting cars. It is estimated that customers would arrive randomly (i.e., a *Poisson* input process) with a mean rate of one every 4 minutes, unless the waiting area is full, in which case the arriving customers would take their cars elsewhere. The time that can be attributed to washing one car has an exponential distribution with a mean of 3 minutes. Compare the expected fraction of potential customers that would be *lost* because of inadequate waiting space if (*a*) zero spaces (not including the car being washed) were to be provided. (*b*) Two spaces. (*c*) Four spaces.

19. Consider the *finite queue variation* of the M/M/s model. Derive the expression for L_q given in Sec. 16.6 for this model.

20. Suppose that one repairman has been assigned the responsibility of maintaining three machines. For each machine, the probability distribution of the running time before a breakdown is *exponential*, with a mean of 9 hours. The repair time also has an *exponential* distribution, with a mean of 2 hours.

(*a*)   Calculate the steady-state probability distribution and the expected number of machines that are not running.

(*b*)   As a crude approximation, assume that the calling population is infinite, so that the input process is *Poisson* with a mean arrival rate of three every 9 hours. Compare the result from part (*a*) with that obtained by making this approximation using (1) the corresponding infinite queue model and (2) the corresponding finite queue model.

(*c*)   Now suppose that a second repairman is available whenever more than one of these three machines requires repair. Calculate the information specified in part (*a*).

21. Plans are currently being developed for a new factory. One department has been allocated a large number of automatic machines of a certain type, and we need to determine how many machines should be assigned to each operator for servicing (loading, unloading, adjusting, setup, and so on). For the purpose of this analysis, the following information has been provided.

The running time (time between completing service and the machine requiring service again) of each machine has an *exponential* distribution, with a mean of 150 minutes. The service time has an *exponential* distribution, with a mean of 15 minutes. Each operator attends to his own machines; he does not give help to or receive help from other operators. For the department to achieve the required production rate, the machines must be running at least 89 percent of the time on the average.

(*a*)   What is the maximum number of machines that can be assigned to an operator while still achieving the required production rate?

(*b*)   Given that the maximum number found in part (*a*) is assigned to each operator, what is the expected fraction of time that the operators will be busy servicing machines?

22. Consider a single-server queueing system. It has been observed that this server seems to speed up as the number of customers in the system increases, and that the pattern of acceleration seems to fit the *state-dependent model* presented at the end of Sec. 16.6. Furthermore, it is estimated that the expected service time is 8 minutes when there is only *one* customer in the system. Determine the pressure coefficient c for this model for the following cases:

(*a*)   The expected service time is estimated to be 4 minutes when there are *four* customers in the system.

(*b*) The expected service time is estimated to be 5 minutes when there are *four* customers in the system.

23. For the *state-dependent model* presented at the end of Sec. 16.6, show the effect of the *pressure coefficient c* by using Fig. 16.10 to construct a table giving the *ratio* (expressed as a decimal number) of L for this model to L for the corresponding M/M/s model (that is, with $c = 0$). Tabulate these ratios for $\lambda_0/s\mu_1 = 0.5, 0.9, 0.99$ when $c = 0.2$, 0.4, 0.6, and $s = 1, 2$.

24. Consider the M/G/1 model.

(*a*) Compare the expected waiting time in the queue if the service-time distribution is (i) exponential, (ii) constant, (iii) Erlang with the amount of variation (i.e., the standard deviation) halfway between the constant and exponential cases.

(*b*) What is the effect on the expected waiting time in the queue and on the expected queue length if both λ and μ are doubled and the scale of the service-time distribution is changed accordingly?

25. Consider a queueing system with a *Poisson* input, where the server must perform two distinguishable tasks in sequence for each customer, so the total service time is the sum of the two task times (which are statistically independent).

(*a*) Suppose that the first task time has an *exponential* distribution with a mean of 3 minutes and the second task time has an *Erlang* distribution with a mean of 9 minutes and with the shape parameter $k = 3$. Which queueing theory model should be used to represent this system?

(*b*) Suppose that part (*a*) is modified so that the first task time also has an *Erlang* distribution with the shape parameter $k = 3$ (but with the mean still equal to 3 minutes). Which queueing theory model should be used to represent this system?

26. An airline maintenance base has facilities for overhauling only one airplane engine at a time. Therefore, to return the airplanes to use as soon as possible, the policy has been to stagger the overhauling of the four engines of each airplane. In other words, only one engine is overhauled each time an airplane comes into the shop. Under this policy, airplanes have arrived according to a *Poisson* process at a mean rate of one per day. The time required for an engine overhaul (once work has begun) has an *exponential* distribution with a mean of $\frac{1}{2}$ day.

A proposal has been made to change the policy so that all four engines are overhauled consecutively each time an airplane comes into the shop. Although this would quadruple the expected service time, each plane would need to come into the shop only one-fourth as often.

Use queueing theory to compare the two alternatives on a meaningful basis.

27. Consider a shoe repair shop with a single repairman. Pairs of shoes are brought in to be repaired (on a first-come-first-served basis) according to a Poisson process at a mean rate of one pair per hour. The time required to repair each individual shoe has an exponential distribution with a mean of 15 minutes.

(*a*) Consider the formulation of this queueing system where the *individual* shoes (not pairs of shoes) are considered to be the customers. For this formulation, construct the rate diagram and develop the balance equations, but do not solve further.

(b)   Now consider the formulation of this queueing system where the *pairs* of shoes are considered to be the customers. Identify the specific queueing model that fits this formulation, and then use the available results for this model to calculate the expected waiting time W. (Interpret W to be the expected waiting time until *both* shoes in a pair have been repaired.)

28.   Consider a single-server queueing system with *any* service-time distribution and *any* distribution of interarrival times (the G1/G/1 model). Use only basic definitions and the relationships given in Sec. 16.2 to verify the following general relationships:

(a) $L = L_q + (1 - P_0)$.
(b) $L = L_q + \rho$.
(c) $P_0 = 1 - \rho$.

29.   Show that

$$L = \sum_{n=0}^{s-1} nP_n + L_q + s\left(1 - \sum_{n=0}^{s-1} P_n\right)$$

by using the statistical definitions of L and L_q in terms of the P_n.

30.   A company currently has *two* tool cribs, each with a *single* clerk, in its manufacturing area. One tool crib handles only the tools for the heavy machinery; the second one handles all other tools. However, for each crib the mechanics arrive to obtain tools at a mean rate of 24 per hour, and the expected service time is 2 minutes.

Because of complaints that the mechanics coming to the tool cribs have to wait too long, it has been proposed that the two tool cribs be combined so that either clerk can handle either kind of tool as the demand arises. It is believed that the mean arrival rate to the combined two-clerk tool crib would double to 48 per hour, and the expected service time would continue to be 2 minutes. However, information is not available on the *form* of the probability distributions for *interarrival* and *service times*, so it is not clear which queueing model would be most appropriate.

Compare the status quo and the proposal with respect to the total expected number of mechanics at the tool crib(s) and the expected waiting time (including service) for each mechanic. Do this by tabulating these data for the four queueing models considered in Figs. 16.7, 16.11, 16.13, and 16.14 (use $k = 2$ when an *Erlang* distribution is appropriate).

31.   Consider the model with *nonpreemptive priorities* presented in Sec. 16.8. Suppose there are just two priority classes, with $\lambda_1 = 4$ and $\lambda_2 = 4$. In designing this queueing system, you are offered the choice between the following two alternatives: (1) one fast server ($\mu = 10$) and (2) two slow servers ($\mu = 5$).

Compare these alternatives with the usual four mean measures of performance (W, L, W_q, L_q) for the individual priority classes $(W_1, W_2, L_1, L_2,$ and so forth). Which alternative is preferred if your primary concern is expected waiting time in the *system* for priority class 1 (W_1)? Which is preferred if your primary concern is expected waiting time in the *queue* for priority class 1?

32.   A particular work center in a job shop can be represented as a single-server queueing system, where jobs arrive according to a *Poisson* process, with a mean rate of eight per day. Although the arriving jobs are of three distinct types, the time required to perform any of these jobs has the same *exponential* distribution, with a mean of 0.1 working day. The practice has been to work on arriving jobs on a first-come-first-served basis. However, it is important that jobs of type 1 do not have to wait very long, whereas the wait is only moderately important for jobs of type 2 and relatively unimportant for jobs of type 3. These three types arrive with a mean rate of two, four, and two per day, respectively. Because all three types have experienced rather long delays on the average, it has been proposed that the jobs be selected according to an appropriate priority discipline instead.

Compare the expected waiting time (including service) for each of the three types of jobs if the queue discipline is (a) first-come-first-served, (b) nonpreemptive priority, or (c) preemptive priority.

33. Reconsider the *County Hospital* emergency room problem as analyzed in Sec. 16.8. Suppose that the definitions of the three categories of patients are tightened somewhat in order to move marginal cases into a lower category. Consequently, only 5% of the patients will qualify as *critical* cases, 20% as *serious* cases, and 75% as *stable* cases. Develop a table showing the data presented in Table 16.4 for this revised problem.

34. One inspector has been assigned the full-time task of inspecting the output from a group of 10 identical machines. Jobs to be done by any one of the machines arrive according to a *Poisson* process at a mean rate of 70 per hour. The time required by a machine to perform each job has an *exponential* distribution with a mean of 6 minutes. Thus, whenever all 10 machines are busy, the jobs are being completed ready for inspection at a mean rate of 100 per hour. Unfortunately, the inspector is able to inspect them at a mean rate of only 80 per hour. (In particular, his inspection time has an *Erlang* distribution with a mean of 0.75 minute and a shape parameter $k = 25$.) This inspection rate has resulted in a substantial average amount of in-process inventory at the inspection station (i.e., the expected number of jobs waiting to be inspected is fairly large), in addition to that already found at the group of machines. Management feels that there is too much capital tied up in in-process inventory, so it has instructed the production manager to cut down on such inventory. Therefore, the production manager has made two alternative proposals to reduce the average level of in-process inventory. Proposal 1 is to use slightly less power for the machines (which would increase their expected time to perform a job to 7 minutes), so that the inspector can keep up with their output better. Proposal 2 is to substitute a certain younger inspector for this task. He is somewhat faster (albeit more variable in his inspection times because of less experience), so he should keep up better. (His inspection time would have an *Erlang* distribution with a mean of 0.72 minute and a shape parameter $k = 2$.)

The production manager has asked you to "use the latest O.R. techniques to see how much each proposal would cut down on in-process inventory."

(a) What would be the effect of proposal 1? Why? How would you explain this outcome to the production manager?

(b) Determine the effect of proposal 2. How would you explain this outcome to the production manager?

(c) What suggestions would you make for reducing the average level of in-process inventory at the inspection station? At the group of machines?

35. Consider the queueing-theory model with a *preemptive priority* queue discipline presented in Sec. 16.8. Suppose that $s = 1$, $N = 2$, and $(\lambda_1 + \lambda_2) < \mu$, and let P_{ij} be the steady-state probability that there are i members of the higher priority class and j members of the lower priority class in the queueing system ($i = 0,1,2,\ldots; j = 0,1,2,\ldots$). Use a method analogous to that presented in Sec. 16.5 to derive a system of linear equations whose simultaneous solution is the P_{ij}. Do not actually obtain this solution.

36. Consider a single-server queueing system with a *Poisson* input, *Erlang* service times, and a *finite* queue. In particular, suppose that $k = 2$, the mean arrival rate is two customers per hour, the expected service time is 0.25 hour, and the maximum permissible number of customers in the system is two. Derive the steady-state probability distribution of the number of customers in the system, and then calculate the expected number. Compare this result with the corresponding results when the service-time distribution is *exponential*.

37. Consider the $E_2/M/1$ model with $\lambda = 4$ and $\mu = 3$.

(a) How should the states of the system be defined in order to formulate this model as a *continuous parameter Markov chain*?

(b) Construct the corresponding rate diagram.

38. A shop contains three identical machines that are subject to a failure of a certain kind. Therefore, a maintenance system is provided to perform the maintenance operation (recharging) required by a failed machine. The time required by each operation has an exponential distribution with a mean of 30 minutes. However, with probability 1/3, the operation must be performed a second time (with the same distribution of time) in order to bring the failed machine back to a satisfactory operational state. The maintenance system works on only one failed machine at a time, performing all of the operations (one or two) required by that machine, on a first-come-first-served basis. After a machine is repaired, the time until its next failure has an exponential distribution with a mean of 3 hours.

(a) How should the states of the system be defined in order to formulate this queueing system as a *continuous parameter Markov chain*? (*Hint*: Given that a first operation is being performed on a failed machine, completing this operation *successfully* and completing it *unsuccessfully* are two separate incidents of interest. In both cases, the time remaining until an incident of this kind occurs has an exponential distribution.)

(b) Construct the corresponding rate diagram.

(c) Develop the balance equations.

39. A company has one repairman to keep a large group of machines in running order. Treating this group as an infinite calling population, individual breakdowns occur according to a *Poisson* process at a mean rate of one per hour. For each breakdown, the probability is 0.9 that only a *minor repair* is needed, in which case the repair time has an *exponential* distribution with a mean of 1/2 hour. Otherwise, a *major repair* is needed, in which case the repair time has an *exponential* distribution with a mean of 5 hours. Because both of these *conditional* distributions are exponential, the *unconditional* (combined) distribution of repair times is *hyperexponential*.

(a) Compute the mean and standard deviation of this hyperexponential distribution. (*Hint*: Use the general relationships from probability theory that, for any random variable X and any pair of mutually exclusive events, E_1 and E_2, $E(X) = E(X \mid E_1)P(E_1) + E(X \mid E_2)P(E_2)$ and $\text{Var}(X) = E(X^2) - E(X)^2$). Compare this standard deviation with that for an *exponential* distribution having this mean.

(b) What are $P_0, L_q, L, W_q,$ and W for this queueing system?

(c) What is the *conditional* value of W, *given* that the machine involved requires a *major repair*? A *minor repair*? What is the division of L between machines requiring the two types of repairs? (*Hint*: *Little's formula* still applies for the individual categories of machines.)

(*d*) How should the states of the system be defined in order to formulate this queueing system as a *continuous parameter Markov chain*? (*Hint*: Consider what additional information must be given, besides the number of machines down, for the conditional distribution of the time remaining until the next incident of each kind to be exponential.)

(*e*) Construct the corresponding rate diagram.

The Application of Queueing Theory

Queueing theory has enjoyed a prominent place among the modern analytical techniques of operations research. However, the emphasis thus far has been on developing a *descriptive* mathematical theory. Thus queueing theory is not directly concerned with achieving the goal of operations research: *optimal decision making*. Rather, it develops *information* on the *behavior* of queueing systems. This theory provides *part* of the information needed to conduct an operations research study attempting to find the *best design* for a queueing system.

This chapter discusses the *application* of queueing theory in the broader context of an overall operations research study. It begins by introducing three examples that will be used for illustration throughout the chapter. Section 17.2 discusses the basic considerations for *decision making* in this context. The following two sections then develop *decision models* for the *optimal* design of queueing systems. The last model requires the incorporation of *travel-time models*, which are presented in Sec. 17.5.

17.1 Examples

EXAMPLE 1—HOW MANY REPAIRMEN?

Simulation, Inc., a small company that makes gidgets for analog computers, has 10 gidget-making machines. However, because these machines break down and require repair frequently, the company has only enough operators to operate *eight* machines at a time, so two machines are available on a standby basis for use while other machines are down. Thus eight machines are always operating whenever no more than two machines are waiting to be repaired, but the number of operating machines is reduced by one for each additional machine waiting to be repaired.

The time until any given operating machine breaks down has an exponential distribution, with a mean of 20 days. The time required to repair a machine also has an exponential distribution, with a mean of 2 days. Until now the company has had just *one* repairman to repair these machines, which has frequently resulted in reduced productivity because *fewer than eight* machines are operating. Therefore, the company is considering hiring a *second* repairman, so that *two* machines can be repaired simultaneously.

Thus the queueing system to be studied has the repairmen as its servers and the machines requiring repair as its customers, where the problem is to choose between having *one* or *two* servers. (Notice the analogy between this problem and the *County Hospital* emergency room problem described in Sec. 16.1.) With one slight exception, this system fits the *finite calling population variation* of the M/M/s model presented in Sec. 16.6, where $N = 10$ machines, $\lambda = 1/20$ customer per day (for each operating machine), and $\mu = 1/2$ customer per day. The exception is that the λ_0 and λ_1 parameters of the birth-and-death process are changed from $\lambda_0 = 10\lambda$ and $\lambda_1 = 9\lambda$ to $\lambda_0 = 8\lambda$ and $\lambda_1 = 8\lambda$. (All the other parameters are the same as those given in Sec. 16.6.) Therefore, the C_n factors for calculating the P_n probabilities change accordingly (see Sec. 16.5).

Each repairman costs the company approximately \$70/day. However, the estimated *lost profit* from having fewer than eight machines operating to produce gidgets is \$100/day for each machine down. (The company can sell the full output from eight operating machines, but not much more.)

The analysis of this problem will be pursued in Secs. 17.3 and 17.4.

EXAMPLE 2—WHICH COMPUTER?

Emerald University currently has one large computer that is shared by everyone on campus. Because students have been experiencing long turnaround times, the university now is planning to lease an additional small batch-processing computer for the exclusive use of its students, while reserving the large computer for the other users. Two models are being considered: one from the MBI Corporation and the other from the EG Company. The MBI computer costs more but is somewhat faster than the EG computer. In particular, if a sequence of typical student programs were run continuously for 1 hour, the number completed would have a Poisson distribution with a mean of 30 and 25 for the MBI and the EG computers, respectively. A statistical study has shown that the student population actually submits programs to be run every 3 minutes on the average during all operating hours and that the time from one submission to the next has an exponential distribution with this mean. The leasing cost per operating hour would be $100 for the MBI computer and $75 for the EG computer.

Thus the queueing system of concern has the new small computer as its (single) server and the students' programs as its customers. Furthermore, this system fits the M/M/1 model presented at the beginning of Sec. 16.6. With 1 hour as the unit of time, $\lambda = $ (60 minutes per hour)/(3 minutes per customer) $= 20$ customers per hour, and $\mu = 30$ and 25 customers per hour with the MBI and the EG computers, respectively. You will see in Secs. 17.3 and 17.4 how the decision was made between the two computers.

EXAMPLE 3—HOW MANY TOOL CRIBS?

The *Mechanical Company* is designing a new plant. This plant will need to include one or more tool cribs in the factory area to store tools required by the shop mechanics. The tools will be handed out by clerks as the mechanics arrive and request them and returned to the clerks when they are no longer needed. In existing plants, there have been frequent complaints from foremen that their mechanics have had to waste too much time traveling to tool cribs and waiting to be served, so it appears that there should be *more* tool cribs and *more* clerks in the new plant. On the other hand, management is exerting pressure to reduce overhead in the new plant, and this reduction would lead to *fewer* tool cribs and *fewer* clerks. To resolve these conflicting pressures, an operations research study is to be conducted to determine just how many tool cribs and clerks the new plant should have.

Each tool crib constitutes a queueing system, with the clerks as its servers and the mechanics as its customers. Based on previous experience, it is estimated that the time required by a tool crib clerk to service a mechanic has an exponential distribution, with a mean of $\frac{1}{2}$ minute. Judging from the anticipated number of mechanics in the entire factory area, it is also predicted that they would require this service *randomly* but at a mean rate of two mechanics per minute. Therefore, it was decided to use the M/M/s model of Sec. 16.6 to represent each queueing system. With 1 hour as the unit of time, $\mu = 120$. If only one tool crib were to be provided, λ also would be 120. With more than one tool crib, this mean arrival rate would be divided among the different queueing systems.

The total cost to the company of each tool crib clerk is about $10/hour. The capital recovery costs, upkeep costs, and so forth associated with each tool crib provided are estimated to be $8/working hour. While a mechanic is busy, the value to the company of his output averages about $24/hour.

Sections 17.3 and 17.5 include discussions of how this (and additional) information was used to make the required decisions.

17.2 Decision Making

Queueing-type situations that require decision making arise in a wide variety of contexts. For this reason, it is not possible to present a meaningful decision-making procedure that is applicable to all these situations. Instead, this section attempts to give a broad conceptual picture of the general approach to a predominant group of waiting-line problems.

A large proportion of waiting-line problems that arise in practice involve making one or a combination of the following decisions:

1. Number of servers at a service facility.
2. Efficiency of the servers.
3. Number of service facilities.

When such problems are formulated in terms of a queueing model, the corresponding decision variables usually would be s (number of servers at each facility), μ (mean service rate per busy server), and λ (mean arrival rate at each facility). The *number of service facilities* is directly related to λ because, assuming a uniform work load among the facilities, λ equals the total mean arrival rate to all facilities divided by the number of facilities.

Refer back to Sec. 17.1 and note how the three examples there respectively illustrate situations involving these three decisions. In particular, the decision facing *Simulation, Inc.* is *how many repairmen* (servers) to provide. The problem for *Emerald University* is *how fast a computer* (server) is needed. The problem facing *Mechanical Company* is *how many tool cribs* (service facilities) to install, as well as *how many clerks* (servers) to provide at each facility.

The first kind of decision is particularly common in practice. However, the other two also arise frequently, particularly for the *business-industrial internal service systems* described in Sec. 16.3. One example illustrating a decision on the *efficiency of the servers* is the selection of the type of materials-handling equipment (the servers) to purchase to transport certain kinds of loads (the customers). Another such example is the determination of the size of a maintenance crew (where the entire crew is one server). Other decisions concern the *number of service facilities*, such as restrooms, first-aid centers, drinking fountains, storage areas, and so on, to distribute throughout an area.

All the specific decisions discussed here involve the general question of the *appropriate level of service* to provide in a queueing system. As mentioned at the beginning of Chap. 16, decisions regarding the amount of service capacity to provide usually are based primarily on two considerations: (1) the cost incurred by providing the service, as shown in Fig. 17.1, and (2) the amount of waiting for that service, as suggested in Fig. 17.2. Figure 17.2 can be obtained by using the appropriate waiting-time equation from queueing theory.

It is readily apparent that these two considerations create conflicting pressures on the decision maker. The objective of reducing service costs recommends a minimal level of service. On the other hand, long waiting times are undesirable, which recommends a high level of service. Therefore, it is necessary to strive for some type of compromise. To assist us in finding this compromise, Figs. 17.1 and 17.2 may be combined, as shown in Fig. 17.3. The problem is thereby reduced to selecting the point on the curve of Fig. 17.3 that gives the best balance between the average delay in being serviced and the cost of

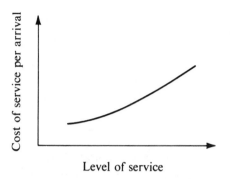

Figure 17.1 **Service cost as a function of service level.**

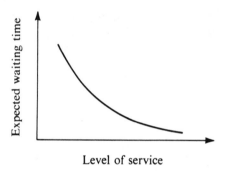

Figure 17.2 **Expected waiting time as a function of service level.**

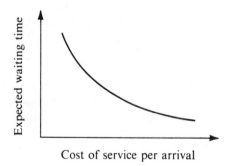

Figure 17.3 **Relationship between average delay and service cost.**

providing that service. Reference to Figs. 17.1 and 17.2 indicates the corresponding level of service.

Unfortunately, it is all too easy to terminate further analysis and make a quick subjective judgment on the basis of Fig. 17.3. Actually, the most crucial portion of the analysis still lies ahead. An intelligent decision on the proper balance between delays and service costs can be made only after the relative seriousness of delays and service costs has been established. Obtaining the proper balance requires answers to such questions as "How much expenditure on service is equivalent (in its detrimental impact) to a customer being delayed one unit of time?" Thus, to compare service costs and waiting times, it is necessary to adopt (explicitly or implicitly) a common measure of their impact. The natural choice for this common measure is cost, so that it becomes necessary to estimate the cost of waiting. This cost probably cannot be identified entirely with expenditures on the accounting books. Nevertheless, a given amount of waiting can be considered to be equivalent in its long-run impact (from the viewpoint of the decision maker) to an expenditure of a certain amount. If it is reasonable to assume that this cost of waiting is proportional to the total amount of waiting, it is sufficient to estimate the cost of waiting per unit time per arrival.

A common viewpoint in practice is that the cost of waiting is often too intangible to be amenable to estimation; hence the decision must instead be based on more tangible, even if less fundamental, criteria, such as the desired expected waiting time in Fig. 17.3. The fallacy in this viewpoint is that it is impossible to avoid the equivalent of estimating waiting costs when analyzing the problem rationally. Any comparison of waiting times and service costs must inevitably reduce to estimating the cost that is equivalent to the waiting. The only question is whether the estimation should be done explicitly or implicitly. The answer to this question depends, in part, upon the time and cost required to develop a reasonable explicit estimate. Will the time and cost incurred be more or less than the potential savings? It seems evident that performing the penetrating analysis required to obtain this explicit estimate should provide a sounder basis for the required decision than superficial criteria that are ultimately based on these same cost considerations in a very imprecise and intuitive way. In addition to using a better estimate, this explicit procedure permits using rigorous mathematical analysis to identify accurately the decision that minimizes the total estimated expected cost.

Granted that an explicit estimate of the cost of waiting is desirable, the next question is how to develop this estimate. Because of the diversity of waiting-line situations, no single estimating process is generally applicable. However, we shall discuss the basic considerations involved for several types of situations.

One broad category is where the customers are *external* to the organization providing the service; i.e., they are *outsiders* bringing their business to the organization. To discuss this category meaningfully, we need to divide it further in terms of whether the service is being provided *for profit* or *not for profit* (on a nonprofit basis). Consider first the case of *profit-making* organizations (typified by the *commercial service systems* described in Sec. 16.3). From the viewpoint of the decision maker, the cost of waiting probably consists primarily of the *lost profit* from *lost business*. This loss of business may occur immediately (because the customer grows impatient and leaves) and/or in the future (because the customer is sufficiently irritated that he does not come again). This kind of cost is quite difficult to estimate, and it may be necessary to revert to other criteria, such as a tolerable probability distribution of waiting times. When the customer is not a human being, but a job being performed on order, there may be more readily identifiable costs incurred, such as those caused by idle in-process inventories or increased expediting and administrative effort.

Now consider the type of situation where service is provided on a *nonprofit* basis to customers *external* to the organization (typical of *social service systems* and some *transportation service systems* described in Sec. 16.3). In this case, the cost of waiting usually is a *social cost* of some kind. Thus it is necessary to evaluate the consequences of the waiting for the individuals involved and/or for society as a whole and to try to impute a monetary value to avoiding these consequences. (We shall illustrate this process in the next section with Example 2—the Emerald University computer problem—the example that most closely fits this type of situation.) Once again, this kind of cost is quite difficult to estimate, and it may be necessary to revert to other criteria.

A situation may be more amenable to estimating waiting costs if the customers are *internal* to the organization providing the service (as for *business-industrial internal service systems*). For example, the customers may be machines (as in Example 1) or employees (as in Example 3) of a firm. Therefore, it may be possible to identify directly some or all of the costs associated with the idleness of these customers. (A detailed discussion of the estimating process for this situation is available elsewhere.[1]) To illustrate the underlying rationale (and to warn against a common pitfall), we consider the case where the customers are machine operators. At first glance, it is easy to jump to the conclusion that the relevant cost to the firm if such an employee waits in a queue is his wage during the waiting time. However, this conclusion implies that the net reduction in the earnings of the firm because an operator has to wait is equal to his wage. There is no reason why this particular relationship should hold in general. Perhaps one reason this approach is sometimes used in practice is the misconception that what is being wasted by the waiting is the operator's wage. The operator actually will receive the same wage regardless of the waiting, and what is really lost is the contribution to the firm's earnings that the operator would have made otherwise. Furthermore, the worker does not work in a vacuum; rather, he is the catalyst that causes the efforts of all the economic resources involved (machinery and equipment, materials, managerial skill, capital, and so on) to result in one of the changes in the product necessary to make it salable. Thus, although the output of the machine operator and his colleagues is essential if a salable product is to be produced, the sale of that product must not only pay their wages but also pay for the other necessary economic resources. Therefore, when the operator is idle because he is waiting in a queue, what is being wasted is productive output that would have helped pay the fixed expenses of the firm in addition to the operator's wage. In short, rather than focusing solely on the value of the one economic resource that physically waits in the queue, the emphasis instead should be on

[1] Hillier, Frederick S.: "Cost Models for the Application of Priority Waiting Line Theory to Industrial Problems," *Journal of Industrial Engineering*, **16**(3):178–185, 1965.

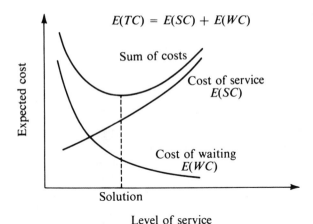

$$E(TC) = E(SC) + E(WC)$$

Sum of costs

Cost of service
$E(SC)$

Cost of waiting
$E(WC)$

Solution

Level of service

Figure 17.4 **Conceptual solution procedure for many waiting-line problems.**

finding the value of all the economic resources that would be idled as a consequence of this waiting. This approach frequently boils down to evaluating the *lost profit* from *all lost productivity*.

Given that the cost of waiting has been evaluated explicitly, the remainder of the analysis is conceptually straightforward. The objective is to determine the level of service that minimizes the total of the expected cost of service and the expected cost of waiting for that service. This concept is depicted in Fig. 17.4, where *WC* denotes *waiting cost*, *SC* denotes *service cost*, and *TC* denotes *total cost*. Thus the mathematical statement of the objective is to

$$\text{Minimize} \quad E(TC) = E(SC) + E(WC).$$

Sections 17.3 to 17.5 are concerned with the *application* of this concept to various types of problems. Thus Sec. 17.3 describes how $E(WC)$ can be expressed mathematically. Section 17.4 then focuses on $E(SC)$ to formulate the overall objective function $E(TC)$ for several basic design problems (including some with multiple decision variables, so that the level of the service axis in Fig. 17.4 actually requires more than one dimension). This section also introduces the fact that when a decision on the number of service facilities is required, time spent in traveling to and from a facility should be included in the analysis (as part of the total time waiting for service). Section 17.5 discusses how to determine the expected value of this travel time.

17.3 Formulation of Waiting-Cost Functions

To express $E(WC)$ mathematically, we must first formulate a *waiting-cost function* that describes how the actual waiting cost being incurred varies with the current behavior of the queueing system. The form of this function depends on the context of the individual problem. However, most situations can be represented by one of the two basic forms described next.

THE $g(N)$ FORM

Consider first the situation discussed in the preceding section where the queueing system *customers* are *internal* to the organization providing the service, and so the primary cost of waiting may be the *lost profit from lost productivity*. The *rate* at which productive output is lost sometimes is essentially *proportional* to the number of customers in the queueing system. However, in many cases there is not enough productive work available to keep all the members of the calling population continuously busy. Therefore, little productive output may be lost by having just a few members idle waiting for service in the queueing system, whereas the loss may increase greatly if a few more members are made idle because they require service. Consequently, the primary property of the queueing system that determines the *current rate* at which waiting costs are being incurred is N, the *number of customers* in the system. Thus the form of the waiting-cost function for this kind of situation is that illustrated in Fig. 17.5, namely, a function of N. We shall denote this form by $g(N)$.

The $g(N)$ function would be constructed for a particular situation by estimating $g(n)$, the waiting cost rate incurred when $N = n$, for $n = 1, 2, \ldots$, where $g(0) = 0$. After computing the P_n probabilities for a given design of the queueing system, we can calculate

$$E(WC) = E\{g(N)\}.$$

Because N is a random variable, this calculation is made by using the equation for the expected value of a *function* of a *discrete* random variable,

$$E(WC) = \sum_{n=0}^{\infty} g(n)P_n.$$

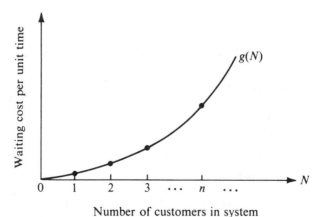

Figure 17.5 **The waiting-cost function as a function of N.**

When $g(N)$ is a *linear* function (i.e., when the waiting-cost rate is proportional to N), then

$$g(N) = C_w N,$$

where C_w is the cost of waiting per unit time for each customer. In this case, $E(WC)$ reduces to

$$E(WC) = C_w \sum_{n=0}^{\infty} n P_n = C_w L.$$

EXAMPLE 1—HOW MANY REPAIRMEN? For Example 1 of Sec. 17.1, *Simulation, Inc.* has two *standby* gidget-making machines, so there is *no* lost productivity as long as the number of customers (machines requiring repair) in the system does not exceed *two*. However, for each *additional* customer (up to the maximum of 10 total), the estimated lost profit is $100/day. Therefore,

$$g(n) = \begin{cases} 0, & \text{for } n = 0, 1, 2 \\ 100(n-2), & \text{for } n = 3, 4, \dots, 10, \end{cases}$$

as shown in Table 17.1. Consequently, $E(WC)$ is calculated by summing the last column of Table 17.1 for each of the two cases of interest, namely, having *one* repairman ($s = 1$) or *two* repairmen ($s = 2$).

THE $h(W)$ FORM

Now consider the cases discussed in Sec. 17.2 where the queueing system *customers* are *external* to the organization providing the service. Three major types of queueing systems described in Sec. 16.3—commercial service systems, transportation service systems, and social service systems—typically fall into this

Table 17.1 Calculation of $E(WC)$ for Example 1

$N = n$	$g(n)$	$s = 1$		$s = 2$	
		P_n	$g(n)P_n$	P_n	$g(n)P_n$
0	0	0.271	0	0.433	0
1	0	0.217	0	0.346	0
2	0	0.173	0	0.139	0
3	100	0.139	14	0.055	6
4	200	0.097	19	0.019	4
5	300	0.058	17	0.006	2
6	400	0.029	12	0.001	0
7	500	0.012	6	3×10^{-4}	0
8	600	0.003	2	4×10^{-5}	0
9	700	7×10^{-4}	0	4×10^{-6}	0
10	800	7×10^{-5}	0	2×10^{-7}	0
	$E(WC)$		$70/day		$12/day

category. In the case of *commercial service systems*, the primary cost of waiting may be the *lost profit from lost future business*. For *transportation service systems* and *social systems*, the primary cost of waiting may be in the form of a *social cost*. However, for either type of cost, its magnitude tends to be affected greatly by the size of the waiting times experienced by the customers. Thus the primary property of the queueing system that determines the waiting cost currently being incurred is $\mathscr{W}$, the waiting time in the system for the *individual* customers. Consequently, the form of the waiting-cost function for this kind of situation is that illustrated in Fig. 17.6, namely, a function of $\mathscr{W}$. We shall denote this form by $h(\mathscr{W})$.

One way of constructing the $h(\mathscr{W})$ function is to estimate $h(w)$ (the waiting cost incurred when a customer's waiting time $\mathscr{W} = w$) for several different values of w and then to fit a polynomial to these points. The expectation of this *function* of a *continuous* random variable is then defined as

$$E\{h(\mathscr{W})\} = \int_0^\infty h(w)f_{\mathscr{W}}(w)\,dw,$$

where $f_{\mathscr{W}}(w)$ is the probability density function of $\mathscr{W}$. However, because $E\{h(\mathscr{W})\}$ is the expected waiting cost *per customer* and $E(WC)$ is the expected waiting cost *per unit time*, these two quantities are not equal in this case. To relate them it is necessary to multiply $E\{h(\mathscr{W})\}$ by the expected *number of customers per unit time* entering the queueing system. In particular, if the mean arrival rate is a constant λ, then

$$E(WC) = \lambda E\{h(\mathscr{W})\} = \lambda \int_0^\infty h(w)f_{\mathscr{W}}(w)\,dw.$$

EXAMPLE 2—WHICH COMPUTER? Because the students of *Emerald University* would experience different turnaround times with the two computers under

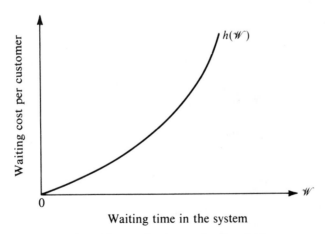

Figure 17.6 **The waiting-cost function as a function of** $\mathscr{W}$.

consideration (see Sec. 17.1), the choice between the computers required an evaluation of the *consequences* of making students wait for their programs to be run. This evaluation led to the following conclusions.

From the university's viewpoint, there are two primary consequences of making students wait. First, it decreases the time available for the student to pursue other academic endeavors because little effective studying can be done during the wait. Second, it detracts from the efficiency and academic value of the computer assignment because it breaks the continuity in dealing with the problem, and it may prevent the student from completing the assignment satisfactorily.

To evaluate the first consequence, an estimate was made that an average student studies at only one-third of full efficiency during the wait. Furthermore, by calculating the total expenditures from all sources for a student's college education, a monetary figure of $15/hour was placed on the value of being able to study at *full* efficiency. Therefore, this component of waiting cost was estimated to be $10/hour, that is, $10\mathcal{W}$, where $\mathcal{W}$ is expressed in units of hours.

To evaluate the second consequence, two groups of students were interviewed just after experiencing turnaround times of $\frac{1}{2}$ hour and 1 hour, respectively. They were asked to estimate how much additional time working on the assignment had been caused by the break in the continuity, as well as the effect of the wait on their ability to complete the assignment satisfactorily. On this basis, averages of $2 and $8 were imputed to the value of a student being able to avoid this consequence entirely rather than having a wait of $\frac{1}{2}$ hour and 1 hour, respectively. Therefore, this component of the waiting cost was estimated to be $8\mathcal{W}^2$.

This analysis yields

$$h(\mathcal{W}) = 10\mathcal{W} + 8\mathcal{W}^2.$$

Because

$$f_{\mathcal{W}}(w) = \mu(1 - \rho)e^{-\mu(1-\rho)w}$$

for the M/M/1 model (see Sec. 16.6) fitting this single-server queueing system,

$$E\{h(\mathcal{W})\} = \int_0^\infty (10w + 8w^2)\mu(1 - \rho)e^{-\mu(1-\rho)w}\,dw.$$

Using the fact that $\mu(1 - \rho) = \mu - \lambda$ for a single-server system, the values of μ and λ presented in Sec. 17.1 give

$$\mu(1 - \rho) = \begin{cases} 10, & \text{for the MBI computer} \\ 5, & \text{for the EG computer.} \end{cases}$$

Evaluating the integral for these two cases yields

$$E\{h(\mathcal{W})\} = \begin{cases} 1.16, & \text{for the MBI computer} \\ 2.64, & \text{for the EG computer.} \end{cases}$$

This result represents the expected waiting cost (in dollars) for each student arriving with a computer program to be run. Because $\lambda = 20$, the total expected waiting cost per hour becomes

$$E(WC) = \begin{cases} \$23.20/\text{hr}, & \text{for the MBI computer} \\ \$52.80/\text{hr}, & \text{for the EG computer.} \end{cases}$$

THE LINEAR CASE When $h(\mathcal{W})$ is a *linear* function,

$$h(\mathcal{W}) = C_w \mathcal{W},$$

$E(WC)$ reduces to

$$E(WC) = \lambda E(C_w \mathcal{W}) = C_w(\lambda W) = C_w L.$$

Note that this result is identical to the result when $g(N)$ is a linear function. Consequently, when the total waiting cost incurred by the queueing system is simply *proportional* to the total waiting time, it does not matter whether the $g(N)$ or the $h(\mathcal{W})$ form is used for the waiting-cost function.

EXAMPLE 3—HOW MANY TOOL CRIBS? As indicated in Sec. 17.1, the value to the *Mechanical Company* of a busy mechanic's output averages about $24/hour. Thus $C_w = 24$. Consequently, *for each tool crib* the expected waiting cost per hour is

$$E(WC) = 24L,$$

where L represents the expected number of mechanics waiting (or being served) at the tool crib.

17.4 Decision Models

We mentioned in Sec. 17.2 that three common decision variables in designing queueing systems are s (number of servers), μ (mean service rate for each server), and λ (mean arrival rate at each service facility). We shall now formulate models for making some of these decisions.

MODEL 1—UNKNOWN s

Model 1 is designed for the case where both μ and λ are fixed at a particular service facility, but where a decision must be made on the number of servers to have on duty at the facility.

FORMULATION OF MODEL 1

Definition: C_s = marginal cost of a server per unit time.
Given: μ, λ, C_s.
To find: s.
Objective: Minimize $E(TC) = sC_s + E(WC)$.

Table 17.2 **Calculation of** $E(TC)$ **for Example 1**

s	sC_s	$E(WC)$	$E(TC)$
1	70	70	\$140/day ← minimum
2	140	12	\$152/day
≥ 3	≥ 210	≥ 0	$\geq$ \$210/day

Because only a few alternative values of s normally need to be considered, the usual way of solving this model is to calculate $E(TC)$ for these values of s and select the minimizing one.

EXAMPLE 1—HOW MANY REPAIRMEN? For Example 1 of Sec. 17.1, each repairman (server) costs *Simulation Inc.* approximately \$70/day. Thus, with a day as the unit of time, $C_s = 70$. Using the values of $E(WC)$ calculated in Table 17.1 then yields the results shown in Table 17.2, which indicate that the company should continue having just *one* repairman.

MODEL 2—UNKNOWN μ AND s

Model 2 is designed for the case where both the *efficiency* of service, measured by μ, and the *number* of servers s at a service facility need to be selected. Alternative values of μ may be available because there is a choice on the *quality* of the servers. (In one example, both the *type* and *quantity* of materials-handling equipment to transport certain kinds of loads must be selected for purchase.) Another possibility is that the *speed* of the servers can be adjusted mechanically. (For example, the speed of machines frequently can be adjusted by changing the amount of power consumed, which also changes the cost of operation.) Still another type of example is the selection of the number of crews (the servers) and the size of each crew (which determines μ) for jointly performing a certain task, e.g., maintenance work, loading and unloading operations, inspection work, setup of machines, and so forth. In many cases, only a few alternative values of μ are available, e.g., the efficiency of the alternative types of materials-handling equipment or the efficiency of the alternative crew sizes.

FORMULATION OF MODEL 2

Definitions: $f(\mu)$ = marginal cost of server per unit time when mean service rate is μ.

A = set of feasible values of μ.

Given: $\lambda, f(\mu), A$.

To find: μ, s.

Objective: Minimize $E(TC) = sf(\mu) + E(WC)$, subject to $\mu \in A$.

EXAMPLE 2—WHICH COMPUTER? As indicated in Sec. 17.1, $\mu = 30$ for the *MBI computer* and $\mu = 25$ for the *EG computer*, where 1 hour is the unit of time. These computers are the only two being considered by Emerald University, so

$$A = \{25,30\}.$$

Because the leasing cost per operating hour would be \$75 for the EG computer ($\mu = 25$) and \$100 for the MBI computer ($\mu = 30$),

$$f(\mu) = \begin{cases} 75, & \text{for } \mu = 25 \\ 100, & \text{for } \mu = 30. \end{cases}$$

The computer chosen will be the only one available for student use, so the number of servers (computers) for this queueing system is restricted to be $s = 1$. Hence

$$E(TC) = f(\mu) + E(WC),$$

where $E(WC)$ is given in Sec. 17.3 for the two alternatives. Thus

$$\begin{aligned} E(TC) &= 75 + 52.80 \\ &= \$127.80/\text{hr}, \quad \text{for EG computer,} \\ E(TC) &= 100 + 23.20 \\ &= \$123.20/\text{hr}, \quad \text{for MBI computer.} \end{aligned}$$

Consequently, the decision was made to lease the MBI computer.

This example illustrates a case where the number of feasible values of μ is *finite* but the value of s is fixed. If s were not fixed, a two-stage approach could be used to solve such a problem. First, for each individual value of μ, set $C_s = f(\mu)$, and solve for the value of s that minimizes $E(TC)$ for model 1. Second, compare these minimum $E(TC)$ for the alternative values of μ, and select the one giving the overall minimum.

When the number of feasible values of μ is *infinite* (as when mechanically setting the speed of a machine or piece of equipment within some feasible interval), another two-stage approach sometimes can be used to solve the problem. First, for each individual value of s, *analytically* solve for the value of μ that minimizes $E(TC)$. [This approach requires setting to zero the derivative of $E(TC)$ with respect to μ and then solving this equation for μ, which can be done only when analytical expressions are available for both $f(\mu)$ and $E(WC)$.] Second, compare these minimum $E(TC)$ for the alternative values of s, and select the one giving the overall minimum.

This analytical approach frequently is relatively straightforward for the case of $s = 1$ (see Prob. 13). However, because far fewer and less convenient analytical results are available for *multiple-server* versions of queueing models, this approach is either difficult (requiring computer calculations with numerical methods to solve the equation for μ) or completely impossible when $s > 1$. Therefore, a more practical approach is to consider only a relatively small

Table 17.3 **Comparison of service efficiency for model 2 solutions.**

	Mean rate of service completions
$N = n$	(s^*, μ^*) vs. $(1, s^*\mu^*)$ for (s, μ), where $s^* > 1$
$n = 0$	$0 = 0$
$n = 1, 2, \ldots, s^* - 1$	$n\mu^* < s^*\mu^*$
$n \geq s^*$	$s^*\mu^* = s^*\mu^*$

number of representative values of μ and to use available tabulated results for the appropriate queueing model to obtain (or approximate) $E(TC)$ for these μ.

Fortunately, under certain fairly common circumstances described next, $s = 1$ (and its minimizing value of μ) *must* yield the overall minimum $E(TC)$ for model 2, so $s > 1$ cases need not be considered at all.

OPTIMALITY OF A SINGLE SERVER Under certain conditions, $s = 1$ necessarily is *optimal* for model 2.

The primary conditions[1] are

1. The value of μ minimizing $E(TC)$ for $s = 1$ is feasible,
2. $f(\mu)$ is either a *linear* function or a *concave* function (as defined in Appendix 1).

In effect, this optimality result indicates that it is better to concentrate service capacity into one *fast* server rather than dispersing it among several *slow* servers. Condition 2 says that this concentrating of a given amount of service capacity can be done without increasing the cost of service. Condition 1 says that it must be possible to make μ sufficiently large so that a single server can be used to full advantage.

To understand why this result holds, consider *any* other solution to model 2, $(s, \mu) = (s^*, \mu^*)$, where $s^* > 1$. The service capacity of this system (as measured by the mean rate of service completions when all servers are working) would be $s^*\mu^*$. We shall now compare this solution with the corresponding *single-server* solution $(s, \mu) = (1, s^*\mu^*)$ having the *same* service capacity. In particular, Table 17.3 compares the *mean rate* at which service completions occur for each given number of customers in the system $N = n$. Table 17.3 shows that the service efficiency of the (s^*, μ^*) solution sometimes is worse but never is better than for the $(1, s^*\mu^*)$ solution because it can use the full service capacity only when there are at least s^* customers in the system, whereas the single-server solution uses the full service capacity whenever there are *any* customers

---

[1] There also are minor restrictions on the queueing model and the waiting-cost function. However, any of the constant service-rate queueing models presented in Chap. 16 for $s \geq 1$ are allowed. If the $g(N)$ form is used for the waiting-cost function, it can be any *increasing* function. If the $h(W)$ form is used, it can be any *linear* function or any *convex* function (as defined in Appendix 1), which fits most cases of interest.

in the system. Because this lower service efficiency can only increase waiting in the system, $E(WC)$ must be *larger* for (s^*, μ^*) than $(1, s^*\mu^*)$. Furthermore, the expected service cost must be *at least as large* because condition 2 [and $f(0) = 0$] imply that

$$s^* f(\mu^*) \geq f(s^*\mu^*).$$

Therefore, $E(TC)$ is *larger* for (s^*, μ^*) than $(1, s^*\mu^*)$. Finally, note that condition 1 implies that there is a *feasible* solution with $s = 1$ that is *at least as good* as $(1, s^*\mu^*)$. The conclusion is that *any* $s > 1$ solution *cannot* be optimal for model 2, so $s = 1$ must be optimal.[1]

This result is still of some use even when one or both conditions fail to hold. If μ cannot be made sufficiently large to permit a single server, it still suggests that a *few* fast servers should be preferred to many slow ones. If condition 2 does not hold, we still know that $E(WC)$ is minimized by concentrating any given amount of service capacity into a single server, so the best $s = 1$ solution must be at least nearly optimal unless it causes a *substantial* increase in service cost.

MODEL 3—UNKNOWN λ AND s

Model 3 is designed especially for the case where it is necessary to select both the *number of service facilities* and the *number of servers* (s) at each facility. The typical situation would be where a population (such as the employees in an industrial building) must be provided with a certain service, so a decision must be made as to what proportion of the population (and therefore what value of λ) should be assigned to each service facility. Examples of such facilities include *employee facilities* (drinking fountains, vending machines, and restrooms), *storage facilities*, and *reproduction equipment facilities*. It may sometimes be clear that only a single server should be provided at each facility (e.g., one drinking fountain or one copy machine), but s often is also a decision variable.

To simplify our presentation, we shall require in model 3 that λ and s must be the same for all service facilities. However, it should be recognized that a slight improvement in the indicated solution might be achieved by permitting minor deviations in these parameters at individual facilities. This should be investigated as part of the detailed analysis that generally follows the application of the mathematical model.

FORMULATION OF MODEL 3

Definitions: C_s = marginal cost of server per unit time.
C_f = fixed cost of service per service facility per unit time.
λ_p = mean arrival rate for entire population.
n = number of service facilities = λ_p / λ.

---

[1] For a rigorous proof of this result, see Stidham, Jr., Shaler: "On the Optimality of Single-Server Queueing Systems," *Operations Research*, **18**: 708–732, 1970.

Given: μ, C_s, C_f, λ_p.

To find: λ, s.

Objective: Minimize $E(TC)$, subject to $\lambda = \lambda_p/n$, where $n = 1, 2, \ldots$.

It might appear at first glance that the appropriate expression for the expected total cost per unit time of all the facilities should be

$$E(TC) \overset{?}{=} n[(C_f + sC_s) + E(WC)],$$

where $E(WC)$ here represents the expected waiting cost per unit time for *each* facility. However, if this expression actually were valid, it would imply that $n = 1$ *necessarily* is optimal for model 3. [The reasoning is completely analogous to that for the optimality of a single-server result for model 2, namely, any solution $(n, s) = (n^*, s^*)$ with $n^* > 1$ has higher service costs than the $(n, s) = (1, n^*s^*)$ solution, and it *also* has a higher expected waiting cost because it sometimes makes less effective use of the available service capacity. In particular, it sometimes has idle servers at one facility while customers are waiting at another facility, so the mean rate of service completions would be less than it would be if the customers had access to *all* the servers at one common facility.] Because there are many situations where it obviously would *not* be optimal to have just *one* service facility (e.g., the number of restrooms in the Pentagon), something must be wrong with this expression. Its deficiency is that it considers only the cost of service and the cost of waiting *at the service facilities* and totally ignores the cost of the time wasted in *traveling to and from* the facilities. Because travel time would be prohibitive with only one service facility for a large population, enough separate facilities must be distributed throughout the population to hold travel time down to a reasonable level.

Thus, letting the *random variable T* be the round trip *travel time* for a customer coming to and going back from one of the service facilities, the *total time lost* by the customer actually is $(\mathcal{W} + T)$. (Recall from Chap. 16 that $\mathcal{W}$ is the waiting time in the queueing system *after* the customer arrives.) Therefore, a customer's *total* cost for time lost should be based on $(\mathcal{W} + T)$ rather than just $\mathcal{W}$. To simplify the analysis, we shall separate this total cost into the *sum* of the *waiting-time cost* based on $\mathcal{W}$ (or N) and the *travel-time cost* based on T. We shall also assume that the travel-time cost is *proportional* to T, where C_t is the cost of each unit of travel time for each customer. For ease of presentation, suppose that the probability distribution of T is the same for each service facility, so that $C_t E(T)$ is the *expected travel cost* for each arrival at any of the service facilities. The resulting expression for $E(TC)$ would be

$$E(TC) = n[(C_f + sC_s) + E(WC) + \lambda C_t E(T)]$$

because λ is the expected number of arrivals *per unit time* at each facility. Consequently, if $E(T)$ could be evaluated for each case of interest, model 3 can be solved by calculating $E(TC)$ for various values of s for each n and then selecting the solution giving the overall minimum. The next section discusses how to evaluate $E(T)$ and also solves an example (Example 3 of Sec. 17.1) fitting model 3.

17.5 The Evaluation of Travel Time

$E(T)$ can be interpreted as the *average travel time* spent by customers in coming both to and from a given service facility. Therefore, the value of $E(T)$ depends very much upon the characteristics of the individual situation. However, we shall illustrate a rather general approach to evaluating $E(T)$ by developing a basic travel-time model and then calculating $E(T)$ for a particular example involving a more complicated situation. In both cases it is assumed that the portion of the population assigned to the service facility under consideration is *distributed uniformly* throughout the assigned area, that each arrival returns to its *original location* after receiving service, and that the average speed of travel does *not* depend upon the distance traveled. Another basic assumption is that all travel is *rectilinear*, i.e., it progresses along a system of *orthogonal* paths (aisles, streets, highways, and so on) that are *parallel* to the main sides of the area under consideration.

A BASIC TRAVEL-TIME MODEL

Description: Rectangular area and rectilinear travel, as shown in Fig. 17.7.

Definitions: T = travel time (round trip) for an arrival.

v = average velocity (speed) of customers in traveling to and from facility.

a, b, c, d = respective distances from facility to boundary of area assigned to facility, as shown in Fig. 17.7.

Given: v, a, b, c, d.

To find: Expected value of T, $E(T)$.

Using an orthogonal (x,y) coordinate system, Fig. 17.7 shows the coordinates (x,y) of the location of a *particular* customer. The x and y coordinates of the location from which a *random* arrival comes actually are *random variables* X and Y, where X ranges from $-a$ to c and Y ranges from $-b$ to d. Because

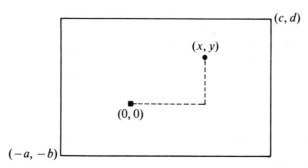

Figure 17.7 **Graphical representation of a basic travel-time model, where the service is at $(0,0)$ and a random arrival comes from (and returns to) some location (x, y).**

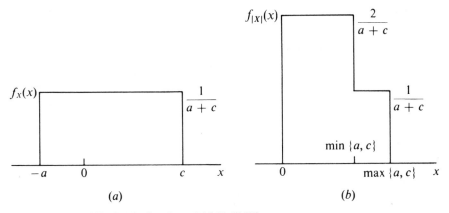

Figure 17.8 **Probability density functions of (a) X; (b) $|X|$.**

the total round trip distance traveled by the random arrival is

$$D = 2(|X| + |Y|)$$

and

$$T = \frac{D}{v},$$

it follows that

$$E(T) = \frac{2}{v}(E\{|X|\} + E\{|Y|\}).$$

Thus the problem is reduced to identifying the probability distributions of $|X|$ and $|Y|$ and then calculating their means.

First consider $|X|$. Its probability distribution can be obtained directly from the probability of X. Because the customers are assumed to be distributed uniformly throughout the assigned area, and because the *height* of the rectangular area is the *same* for all possible values of $X = x$, X must have a *uniform distribution* between $-a$ and c, as shown in Fig. 17.8a. Because $|x| = |-x|$, adding the probability density function values at x and $-x$ then yields the probability distribution of $|X|$ shown in Fig. 17.8b.

Therefore, noting that $|x| = x$ for $x \geq 0$,

$$E\{|X|\} = \int_0^{max\{a, c\}} x f_{|X|}(x)\, dx$$

$$= \int_0^{min\{a, c\}} \frac{2x}{a + c}\, dx + \int_{min\{a, c\}}^{max\{a, c\}} \frac{x}{a + c}\, dx$$

$$= \frac{1}{2} \frac{1}{a + c} [(min\{a, c\})^2 + (max\{a, c\})^2]$$

$$= \frac{a^2 + c^2}{2(a + c)}.$$

The analysis for $|Y|$ is completely analogous, where the *width* of the rectangular area for possible values of $Y = y$ now determines the probability distribution of Y. The result is that

$$E\{|Y|\} = \frac{b^2 + d^2}{2(b + d)}.$$

Consequently,

$$E(T) = \frac{1}{v}\left(\frac{a^2 + c^2}{a + c} + \frac{b^2 + d^2}{b + d}\right).$$

EXAMPLE 3—HOW MANY TOOL CRIBS? For the new plant being designed for the *Mechanical Company* (see Sec. 17.1), the layout of the portion of the factory area where the mechanics will work is shown in Fig. 17.9. The three *possible* locations for tool cribs are identified as Locations 1, 2, and 3, where access to these locations will be provided by a system of orthogonal aisles parallel to the sides of the indicated area. The coordinates are given in units of *feet*. The mechanics will be distributed quite uniformly throughout the area shown, and each mechanic will be assigned to the *nearest* tool crib. It is estimated that the mechanics will walk to and from a tool crib at an average speed of slightly less than 3 miles/hour, so v is set at $v = 15,000$ feet/hour.

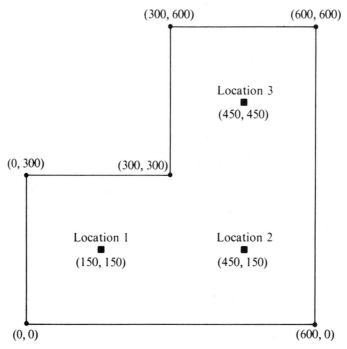

Figure 17.9 Layout for Example 3.

The three basic alternatives being considered are

Alternative 1: Have *three* tool cribs—use Locations 1, 2, and 3;
Alternative 2: Have *one* tool crib—use Location 2;
Alternative 3: Have *two* tool cribs—use Locations 1 and 3.

The calculation of $E(T)$ for each alternative is given next, followed by the use of model 3 to make the choice among them.

Alternative 1 (n = 3)   If all three locations were used, *each* tool crib would service a 300×300 foot *square* area. Therefore, this case is just a special case of the basic travel-time model just presented, where $a = c = 150$ and $b = d = 150$. Consequently,

$$E(T) = \frac{1}{15,000 \text{ ft/hr}} \left(\frac{150^2 + 150^2}{150 + 150} + \frac{150^2 + 150^2}{150 + 150} \right) \text{ft}$$

$$= \frac{1}{15,000 \text{ ft/hr}} (300 \text{ ft})$$

$$= 0.02 \text{ hr.}$$

Alternative 2 (n = 1)   With just *one* tool crib (in Location 2) to service the entire area shown in Fig. 17.9, the derivation of $E(T)$ is a little more complicated than it is for the basic travel-time model. The first step is to relabel Location 2 as the origin $(0,0)$ for an (x,y) coordinate system, so that 450 would be subtracted from the first coordinates shown and 150 would be subtracted from the second coordinates. The probability density function for X is then obtained by dividing the *height* for each possible value of $X = x$ by the total area (so that the area under the probability density function curve equals 1), as given in Fig. 17.10*a*. Combining the values for x and $-x$ then yields the probability distribution of $|X|$ shown in 17.10*b*.
    Hence

$$E\{|X|\} = \int_0^{450} x f_{|X|}(x) \, dx$$

$$= \int_0^{150} x \left(\frac{1}{225} \right) dx + \int_{150}^{450} x \left(\frac{1}{900} \right) dx$$

$$= \frac{150^2}{450} + \frac{450^2 - 150^2}{1,800} = 150.$$

    We suggest that you now try the same approach (using the *width* of the area rather than the height) to derive $E\{|Y|\}$. You will find that the probability distribution of $|Y|$ is *identical* to that for $|X|$, so $E\{|Y|\} = 150$. As a result,

$$E(T) = \frac{2}{15,000} (150 + 150)$$

$$= 0.04 \text{ hr.}$$

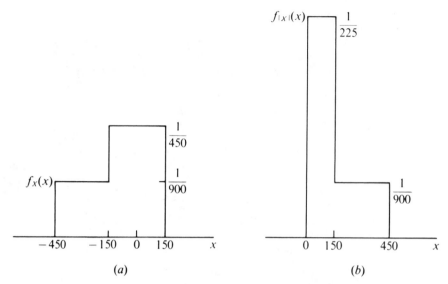

Figure 17.10 Probability density functions of (a) X and (b) $|X|$ for a tool crib at Location 2 of Fig. 17.9 under Alternative 2 (no other tool cribs).

Alternative 3 ($n = 2$)   With tool cribs in just Locations 1 and 3, the areas assigned to them would be divided by a line segment between $(300, 300)$ and $(600, 0)$ in Fig. 17.9. Notice that the two areas and their tool cribs are located symmetrically with respect to this line segment. Therefore, $E(T)$ is the same for both, so we shall derive it just for the tool crib in Location 1. (You might try it for the other tool crib for practice—see Prob. 17.)

Proceeding just as for Alternative 2, relabel Location 1 as the origin $(0,0)$ for an (x,y) coordinate system, so that 150 would be subtracted from all coordinates shown in Fig. 17.9. This relabeling leads directly to the probability density function of X, and then of $|X|$, shown in Fig. 17.11.

As a result,

$$
\begin{aligned}
E\{|X|\} &= \frac{1}{225} \int_0^{150} x\,dx + \frac{1}{300} \int_{150}^{450} \left(1 - \frac{x}{450}\right) x\,dx \\
&= \frac{1}{225}\left[\frac{x^2}{2}\right]_0^{150} + \frac{1}{300}\left[\frac{x^2}{2} - \frac{x^3}{1{,}350}\right]_{150}^{450} \\
&= \frac{1}{225}\frac{150^2}{2} + \frac{1}{300}\left[\frac{450^2}{2} - \frac{450^3}{1{,}350}\right] - \frac{1}{300}\left[\frac{150^2}{2} - \frac{150^3}{1{,}350}\right] \\
&= 133\tfrac{1}{3}.
\end{aligned}
$$

Next, the probability density function of Y is obtained by using the *width* of the area assigned to the tool crib at Location 1 for each possible value of $Y = y$ and then dividing by the size of the area, as given in Fig. 17.12a. This result then

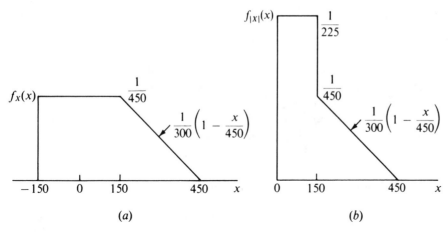

Figure 17.11 Probability density functions of (a) X and (b) $|X|$ for a tool crib at Location 1 of Fig. 17.9 under Alternative 3 (the only other tool crib is at Location 3).

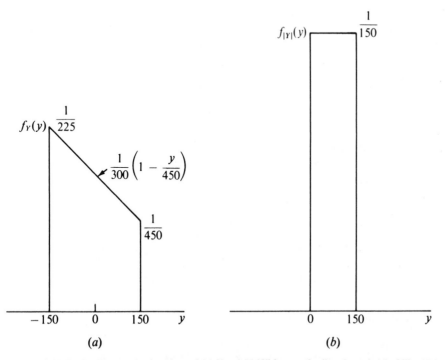

Figure 17.12 Probability density functions of (a) Y and (b) $|Y|$ for a tool crib at Location 1 of Fig. 17.9 under Alternative 3 (the only other tool crib is at Location 3).

Table 17.4 **Calculation of $E(TC)$ in \$/hr for Example 3**

n	λ	s	L	$E(T)$	$C_f + sC_s$	$E(WC)$	$\lambda C_t E(T)$	$E(TC)$
1	120	1	∞	0.04	18.00	∞	115.20	∞
1	120	2	1.333	0.04	28.00	32.00	115.20	175.20
1	120	3	1.044	0.04	38.00	25.06	115.20	178.26
2	60	1	1.000	0.0278	18.00	24.00	40.00	164.00
2	60	2	0.534	0.0278	28.00	12.82	40.00	161.64
3	40	1	0.500	0.02	18.00	12.00	19.20	147.60
3	40	2	0.344	0.02	28.00	8.26	19.20	166.38

yields the *uniform* distribution of $|Y|$ shown in Fig. 17.12b. Thus

$$E\{|Y|\} = \frac{1}{150}\int_0^{150} y\, dy$$
$$= 75.$$

Consequently,

$$E(T) = \frac{2}{15,000}(133\tfrac{1}{3} + 75)$$
$$= 0.0278 \text{ hr.}$$

Applying model 3 Because $E(T)$ now has been evaluated for the three alternatives under consideration, the stage is set for using model 3 from Sec. 17.4 to choose among these alternatives. Most of the data required for this model are given in Sec. 17.1, namely,

$$\mu = 120/\text{hr}, \qquad C_f = \$8/\text{hr},$$
$$C_s = \$10/\text{hr},$$
$$\lambda_p = 120/\text{hr}, \qquad C_t = \$24/\text{hr},$$

where the M/M/s model given in Sec. 16.6 would be used to calculate L, and so on. In addition, the end of Sec. 17.3 gives $E(WC) = 24L$ in dollars per hour. Therefore,

$$E(TC) = n\left[(8 + 10s) + 24L + \frac{120}{n}24E(T)\right].$$

The resulting calculation of $E(TC)$ for various s for each n is given in Table 17.4, which indicates that the *overall minimum $E(TC)$* is obtained by having *three* tool cribs (so $\lambda = 40$ for each), with *one* clerk at *each* tool crib.

17.6 Conclusions

This chapter has discussed the application of queueing theory for *designing* queueing systems. Every individual problem has its own special characteristics, so no standard procedure can be prescribed to fit every situation. Therefore, the emphasis has been on introducing fundamental considerations and approaches that can be adapted to most cases. We have focused on three particularly common decision variables (s, μ, and λ) as a vehicle for introducing and illustrating these concepts. However, there are many other possible decision variables (e.g., the size of a waiting room for a queueing system) and many more complicated situations (e.g., designing a *priority* queueing system) that can also be analyzed in a similar way.

The time required to *travel* to and from a service facility sometimes is an important consideration. A rather general approach to evaluating expected travel time has been introduced by applying it to some relatively simple cases. However, once again, many more complicated situations can also be analyzed quite similarly. We have discussed the incorporation of travel-time information into the overall analysis only in the context of determining the *number* of service facilities to provide when *customers* must travel to the nearest facility. But travel-time models also can be very useful when the *servers* must travel to the customer from the service facility (e.g., fire trucks and ambulances), as well as in other contexts.

Another potentially useful area for the application of queueing theory is the development of policies for *controlling* queueing systems, e.g., for *dynamically* adjusting the number of servers or the service rate to compensate for changes in the number of customers in the system. Considerable research is being conducted in this area.

Queueing theory has proven to be a very useful tool, and we anticipate that its use will continue to grow as recognition of the many guises of queueing systems grows.

SELECTED REFERENCES

1. Allen, Arnold O.: *Probability, Statistics, and Queueing Theory with Computer Science Applications*, chaps. 5–6, Academic Press, New York, 1978.
2. Kleinrock, Leonard: *Queueing Systems, Vol. II: Computer Applications*, Wiley, New York, 1976.
3. Kobayashi, Hisashi: *Modeling and Analysis: An Introduction to System Performance Evaluation Methodology*, chap. 3, Addison-Wesley, Reading, Mass., 1978.
4. Lee, Alec M.: *Applied Queueing Theory*, St. Martin's Press, New York, 1966.
5. Newell, Gordon F.: *Applications of Queueing Theory*, 2d ed., Chapman and Hall, London, 1982.

PROBLEMS

1. For each kind of queueing system listed in Prob. 2, Chap. 16, briefly describe the nature of the *cost of service* and the *cost of waiting* that would need to be considered in designing the system.

2. Suppose that a queueing system fits the M/M/1 model described in Sec. 16.6, with $\lambda = 2$ and $\mu = 4$. Evaluate the expected waiting cost per unit time $E(WC)$ for this system when its waiting cost function has the form

(a) $g(N) = 10N + 2N^2$.

(b) $g(N) = \begin{cases} 10N, & \text{for } N = 0, 1, 2 \\ 6N^2, & \text{for } N = 3, 4, 5 \\ N^3, & \text{for } N > 5. \end{cases}$

(c) $h(\mathscr{W}) = 25\mathscr{W} + \mathscr{W}^3$.

(d) $h(\mathscr{W}) = \begin{cases} \mathscr{W}, & \text{for } 0 \le \mathscr{W} \le 1 \\ \mathscr{W}^2, & \text{for } \mathscr{W} \ge 1. \end{cases}$

3. A certain queueing system has a *Poisson* input, with a mean arrival rate of four customers per hour. The service-time distribution is *exponential*, with a mean of 0.2 hour. The marginal cost of providing each server is $20/hour, where it is estimated that the cost that is incurred by having each customer *idle* (i.e., in the queueing system) is $120/hour for the first customer and $180/hour for each additional customer. Determine the *number of servers* that should be assigned to the system to minimize the expected total cost per hour. (*Hint*: Express $E(WC)$ in terms of L, P_0, and ρ, and then use Figs. 16.6 and 16.7.)

4. A certain small grocery store has a single checkout stand with a full-time cashier. Customers arrive at the stand according to a *Poisson* process at a mean rate of 30 per hour. The service-time distribution is *exponential*, with a mean of 1.5 minutes. This situation has resulted in occasional long lines and complaints from customers. Therefore, because there is no room for a second checkout stand, the proposal has been made that another person be hired to help the cashier by bagging the groceries. This help would reduce the expected time required to process a customer to 1 minute, but the distribution still would be exponential.

The total compensation for the new employee would be $5 per hour, which is just half that for the cashier. It is estimated that the grocery store incurs lost profit due to lost future business of 5¢ for each minute that each customer has to wait (including service time). The manager wants to determine on an expected total cost basis whether it would be worthwhile to hire the new person.

(a)   Which decision model presented in Sec. 17.4 applies to this problem? Why?
(b)   Use this model to determine whether to continue the status quo or to adopt the proposal.

5. The problem is to choose between two types of materials-handling equipment, *A* and *B*, for transporting certain types of goods between certain producing centers in a job shop. Calls for the materials-handling unit to move a load would come essentially at random (i.e., according to a *Poisson* input process) at a mean rate of four per hour. The total time required to move a load has an *exponential* distribution, where the expected time is 12 minutes for *A* and 9 minutes for *B*. The total equivalent uniform hourly cost (capital recovery cost plus operating cost) would be $50 for *A* and $150 for *B*. The estimated cost of idle goods (waiting to be moved or in transit) because of increased in-process inventory is $20/load/hour. Furthermore, the scheduling of the work at the producing centers allows for just 1 hour from the completion of a load at one center to the arrival of that load at the next center. Therefore, an additional $100/load/hour of delay (including transit time) *after the first hour* is to be charged for lost production because of idle personnel and equipment, extra costs of expediting and supervision, and so forth.

Assuming that only one materials-handling unit is to be purchased, which type of unit should be selected?

6. A railroad company paints its own railroad cars as needed. Alternative 1 is to provide two paint shops, where painting is done by hand (one car at a time in each shop), for a total annual cost of $300,000. The painting time for a car is 6 hours. Alternative 2 is to provide one spray shop involving an annual cost of $400,000. In this case, the painting time for a car (again done one at a time) is 3 hours. For both alternatives, the cars arrive according to a *Poisson* input, with a mean arrival rate of one every 5 hours. The cost of idle time per car is $50/hour. Which alternative should the railroad choose? Assume that the paint shops are always open; i.e., they work $(24)(365) = 8,760$ hours per year.

7. An airline maintenance base wants to make a change in its overhaul operation. The present situation is that only one airplane can be repaired at a time, and the expected repair time is 36 hours, whereas the expected time between arrivals is 45 hours. This situation has led to frequent and prolonged delays in repairing incoming planes, even though the base operates continuously. The average cost of an idle plane to the airline is $3,000/hour. It is estimated that each plane goes into the maintenance shop five times per year. It is believed that the input process for the base is essentially *Poisson* and that the probability distribution of repair times is *Erlang*, with shape parameter $k = 2$. Alternative *A* is to provide a duplicate maintenance shop, so that two planes can be repaired simultaneously. The cost, amortized over a period of 5 years, is $400,000 per airplane per year.

Alternative *B* is to replace the present maintenance equipment by the most efficient (and expensive) equipment available, thereby reducing the expected repair time to 18 hours. The cost, amortized over a period of 5 years, is $550,000/airplane/year.

Which alternative should the airline choose?

8. A particular in-process inspection station is used to inspect subassemblies of a certain kind. At present there are two inspectors at the station, and they work together to inspect each subassembly. The inspection time has an *exponential* distribution, with a mean of 15 minutes. The cost of providing this inspection system is $20/hour.

A proposal has been made to streamline the inspection procedure so that it can be handled by only one inspector. This inspector would begin by visually inspecting the exterior of the subassembly, and he would then use new efficient equipment to complete the inspection. The times required for these two phases of the inspection have independent *Erlang* distributions, with shape parameter $k = 2$ and means of 6 and 12 minutes, respectively. The capitalized cost of providing this inspection system would be $15/hour.

The subassemblies arrive at the inspection station according to a Poisson process at a mean rate of three per hour. The cost of having the subassemblies wait at the inspection station (thereby increasing in-process inventory and disrupting subsequent production) is estimated to be $10/hour for each subassembly.

Determine whether to continue the status quo or adopt the proposal in order to minimize expected total cost per hour.

9. A car rental agency has been subcontracting for the maintenance and repair of its cars. However, due to long delays in getting its cars back, the agency has decided to open its own maintenance shop to do this work more quickly. This shop will operate 42 hours per week.

Alternative 1 is to hire two mechanics (at a cost of $1,000/week each), so that two cars can be worked on at a time. The time required by a mechanic to service a car would have an *exponential* distribution with a mean of 5 hours.

Alternative 2 is to hire just one mechanic but to provide some additional special equipment (at a capitalized cost of $500 per week) to speed up his work. In this case, the maintenance work on each car would be done in stages, where the time required for *each* stage has an *Erlang* distribution with the shape parameter $k = 4$, where the mean is 2 hours for the first stage and 1 hour for the second stage.

For both alternatives, the cars would arrive according to a *Poisson* process, with a mean arrival rate of 0.3 car per hour (during work hours). The agency estimates that its net lost revenue due to having its cars unavailable for rental is $100/week/car.

Which alternative should the agency choose to minimize expected total cost per week?

10.   A certain small car-wash business is currently being analyzed to see if costs can be reduced. Customers arrive according to a *Poisson* process at a mean rate of 15 per hour, and only one car can be washed at a time. At present the time required to wash a car has an *exponential* distribution, with a mean of 4 minutes. It also has been noticed that if there are already four cars waiting (including the one being washed), then any additional arriving customers leave and take their business elsewhere. The lost incremental profit from each such lost customer is $3.

Two proposals have been made. Proposal 1 is to add certain equipment, at a capitalized cost of $3/hour, which would reduce the expected washing time to 3 minutes. In addition, each arriving customer would be given a guarantee that if he has to wait longer than $\frac{1}{2}$ hour (according to a time slip he receives upon arrival) before his car is ready, then he receives a free car wash (at a marginal cost of $2 for the company). This guarantee would be well posted and advertised, so it is believed that no arriving customers would be lost.

Proposal 2 is to obtain the most advanced equipment available, at an increased cost of $10/hour, where each car would be sent through two cycles of the process in succession. The time required for a cycle has an *exponential* distribution, with a mean of 1 minute, so total expected washing time would be 2 minutes. Because of the increased speed and effectiveness, it is believed that essentially no arriving customers would be lost.

The owner also feels that because of the loss of customer goodwill (and consequent lost future business) when customers have to wait, a cost of 10 cents for each minute that a customer has to wait before his car wash begins should be included in the analysis of all alternatives.

Evaluate the expected total cost per hour $E(TC)$ of the status quo, proposal 1, and proposal 2 to determine which one should be chosen.

11.   A single crew is provided for unloading and/or loading each truck that arrives at the loading dock of a warehouse. These trucks arrive according to a *Poisson* input process at a mean rate of one per hour. The time required by a crew to unload and/or load a truck has an *exponential* distribution (regardless of the crew size). The expected time required by a one-man crew would be 1 hour.

The cost of providing each additional member of the crew is $10/hour. The cost that is attributable to having a truck not in use (i.e., a truck standing at the loading dock) is estimated to be $15/hour.

(*a*)   Assume that the mean service rate of the crew is proportional to its size. What should the size be to minimize the expected total cost per hour?

(b) Assume that the mean service rate of the crew is proportional to the square root of its size. What should the size be to minimize expected total cost per hour?

12. A machine shop contains a grinder for sharpening the machine cutting tools. A decision must now be made on the speed at which to set the grinder.

The grinding time required by a machine operator to sharpen his cutting tool has an *exponential* distribution, where the mean $1/\mu$ can be set at anything from $\frac{1}{2}$ minute to 2 minutes, depending upon the speed of the grinder. The running and maintenance costs go up rapidly with the speed of the grinder, so the estimated cost per minute for providing a mean of $1/\mu$ is $\$(0.10\mu^2)$.

The machine operators arrive to sharpen their tools according to a *Poisson* process at a mean rate of one every 2 minutes. The estimated cost of an operator being away from his machine to the grinder is $\$0.20$/minute.

Plot the expected total cost per minute $E(TC)$ vs. μ over the feasible range for μ to solve graphically for the minimizing value of μ.

13. Consider the special case of model 2 where (1) any $\mu > \lambda/s$ is feasible and (2) both $f(\mu)$ and the waiting-cost function are *linear* functions, so that

$$E(TC) = sC_r\mu + C_wL,$$

where C_r is the marginal cost per unit time for each unit of a server's mean service rate and C_w is the cost of waiting per unit time for each customer. The optimal solution is $s = 1$ (by the optimality of a single server result), and

$$\mu = \lambda + \sqrt{\frac{\lambda C_w}{C_r}}$$

for any queueing system fitting the M/M/1 model presented in Sec. 16.6.

Show that this μ is indeed optimal for the M/M/1 model.

14. Consider a harbor with a single dock for unloading ships. The ships arrive according to a *Poisson* process at a mean rate of λ ships per week, and the service-time distribution is *exponential* with a mean rate of μ unloadings per week. Assume the harbor facilities are owned by the shipping company, so that the objective is to balance the cost associated with idle ships with the cost of running the dock. The shipping company has no control over the arrival rate λ (i.e., λ is fixed); however, by changing the size of the unloading crew, and so on, the shipping company can adjust the value of μ as desired.

Suppose that the expected cost per unit time of running the unloading dock is $D \cdot \mu$. The waiting cost for each idle ship is some constant (C) times the *square* of the total waiting time (including loading time). The shipping company wishes to adjust μ so that the expected *total* cost (including the waiting cost for idle ships) per unit time is minimized. Derive this optimal value of μ in terms of D and C.

15. Reconsider Prob. 21 in Chap. 16.

(a) Formulate part (a) to fit as closely as possible a special case of one of the decision models presented in Sec. 17.4. (Do not solve.)

(b) Because the answer for part (b) reveals a very low utilization of the machine operators (who are relatively expensive employees), the department manager has asked you to analyze each of the following alternative ways of organizing the work of the operators: (i) pool the operators so that *any* idle operator can take the next machine needing servicing, (ii) combine the operators into small *crews* to work together on any machine needing servicing within their assigned group of machines, and (iii) keep each operator assigned to his own group of machines but allow idle operators to assist busy operators on their machines. Describe each of these alternatives in queueing theory terms, including their relationship (if any) to the decision models presented in Sec. 17.4. Briefly indicate why each of these alternatives might decrease the total number of operators (thereby increasing their utilization) needed to achieve the required production rate. Also point out any dangers that might prevent this decrease.

16. Consider a factory whose floor area is a square with 600 feet on each side. Suppose that one service facility of a certain kind is provided in the center of the factory. The employees are distributed uniformly throughout the factory, and they walk to and from the facility at an average speed of 3 miles/hour along a system of orthogonal aisles. Compute the expected travel time $E(T)$ per arrival.

17. Consider *Alternative 3* (tool cribs in Locations 1 and 3) for the example illustrated in Fig. 17.9. Derive $E(T)$ for the tool crib in Location 3 by using the probability density functions of X and Y directly for this tool crib.

18. Suppose that the calling population for a particular service facility is uniformly distributed over *each* area shown, where the service facility is located at (0,0). Making the same assumptions as in Sec. 17.5, derive the expected round trip travel time per arrival $E(T)$ in terms of the average velocity v and the distance r.

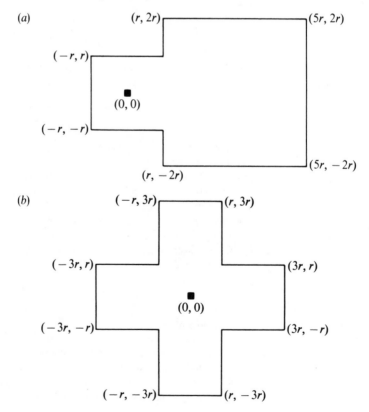

(c)

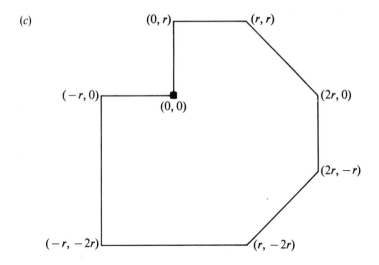

(d)

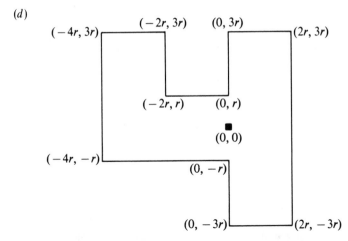

19. A certain large shop doing light fabrication work uses a single central storage facility (dispatch station) for material in in-process storage. The typical procedure is that each employee personally delivers his finished work (by hand, tote box, or hand cart) and receives new work and materials at the facility. Although this procedure had worked well in earlier years when the shop was smaller, it appears that it may now be advisable to divide the shop into two semi-independent parts, with a separate storage facility for each one. You have been assigned the job of comparing the use of two facilities and of one facility from a cost standpoint.

The factory has the shape of a rectangle 150 by 100 yards. Thus, letting 1 yard be the unit of distance, the (x, y) coordinates of the corners would be $(0, 0)$, $(150, 0)$, $(150, 100)$, and $(0, 100)$. With this coordinate system, the existing facility is located at $(50, 50)$, and the location available for the second facility is $(100, 50)$.

Each facility would be operated by a single clerk. The time required by a clerk to service a caller has an *exponential* distribution, with a mean of 2 minutes. Employees arrive at the present facility according to a *Poisson* input process at a mean rate of 24 per hour.

The employees are rather uniformly distributed throughout the shop, and if the second facility were installed, each employee would normally use the nearer of the two facilities. Employees walk at an average speed of about 5,000 yards per hour. All aisles are parallel to the outer walls of the shop. The net cost of providing each facility is estimated to be about $20/hour, plus $15/hour for the clerk. The estimated total cost of an employee being idled by traveling or waiting at the facility is $25/hour.

Given the preceding cost factors, which alternative minimizes expected total cost?

20. A job shop is being laid out in a square area with 600 feet on a side, and one of the decisions to be made is the *number* of facilities for the storage and shipping of final inventory. The capitalized cost associated with providing each facility would be $10/hour. There are just four potential locations available for these facilities, one in the middle of each of the four sides of the square area as shown in the figure.

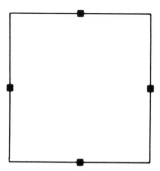

The loads to be moved to a storage and shipping facility would be distributed uniformly throughout the shop area, and they become available according to a *Poisson* process at a mean rate of 90 per hour. Each time a load becomes available, an appropriate materials-handling vehicle would be sent from the *nearest* facility to pick it up (with an expected loading time of 3 minutes) and bring it there, where the cost would be $40/hour for time spent in traveling, loading, and waiting to be unloaded. The vehicles would travel at a speed of 20,000 feet per hour along a system of orthogonal aisles parallel to the sides of the shop area.

Another decision to be made is the number of men (m) to provide at each storage and shipping facility for unloading an arriving vehicle. These m men would work together on each vehicle, and the time required to unload it would have an *exponential* distribution, with a mean of $2/m$ minutes. The cost of providing each man is $15/hour.

Determine the number of facilities and the value of m at each that will minimize expected total cost per hour.

21. Consider the formulation of the *County Hospital* emergency room problem as a preemptive priority queueing system, as presented in Sec. 16.8. Suppose that the following imputed costs are assigned to making patients wait (*excluding* treatment time): $10/hour for *stable* cases, $1,000/hour for *serious* cases, and $100,000/hour for *critical* cases. The cost associated with having an additional doctor on duty would be $40/hour. Determine on an expected total cost basis whether there should be *one* or *two* doctors on duty.

22. A certain job shop has been experiencing long delays in jobs going through the turret lathe department because of inadequate capacity. The foreman contends that five machines are required, as opposed to the three machines that he now has. However, because of pressure from management to hold down capital expenditures, only one additional machine will be authorized unless there is solid evidence that a second one is necessary.

This shop does three kinds of jobs, namely, government jobs, commercial jobs, and standard products. Whenever a turret lathe finishes a job, it starts a government job if one is waiting; if not, it starts a commercial job if any are waiting; if not, it starts on a standard product if any are waiting. Jobs of the same type are taken on a first-come-first-served basis.

Although much overtime work is required currently, management wants the turret lathe department to operate on an 8-hour, 5-day-a-week basis. The probability distribution of the time required by a turret lathe for a job appears to be approximately *exponential*, with a mean of 10 hours. Jobs come into the shop according to a *Poisson* input process, but at a mean rate of 6 per week for government jobs, 4 per week for commercial jobs, and 2 per week for standard products. (These figures are expected to remain the same for the indefinite future.)

It is worth about $750, $450, and $150 to avoid a delay of one additional (working) day in a government, commercial, and standard job, respectively. The incremental capitalized cost of providing each turret lathe (including the operator and so on) is estimated to be $250/working day.

Determine the number of *additional* turret lathes that should be obtained to minimize expected total cost.

CHAPTER 18

Inventory Theory

18.1 Introduction

Keeping an inventory (stock of goods) for future sale or use is very common in business. Retail firms, wholesalers, manufacturing companies—and even blood blanks—generally have a stock of goods on hand. How does such a facility decide upon its "inventory policy"; i.e., when and how much does it replenish? In a small firm the manager may keep track of his inventory and make these decisions. However, since this may not be feasible even in small firms, many companies have saved large sums of money by using "scientific inventory management." In particular, they

1. Formulate a mathematical model describing the behavior of the inventory system,
2. Derive an optimal inventory policy with respect to this model,
3. Frequently use a computer to maintain a record of the inventory levels and to signal when and how much to replenish.

There are several basic considerations involved in determining an inventory policy that must be reflected in the mathematical inventory model; these are illustrated in the following examples.

EXAMPLE 1 A television manufacturing company produces its own speakers, which are used in the production of its television sets. The television sets are assembled on a continuous production line at a rate of 8,000 per month. The speakers are produced in batches because they do not warrant setting up a continuous production line, and relatively large quantities can be produced in a short time. The company is interested in determining when and how many to produce. Several costs must be considered:

1. Each time a batch is produced, a setup cost of $12,000 is incurred. This cost includes the cost of "tooling up," administrative costs, record keeping, and so forth. Note that the existence of this cost argues for producing speakers in large batches.

2. The production of speakers in large batches leads to a large inventory. The estimated cost of keeping a speaker in stock is 30 cents/month. This cost includes the cost of capital tied up, storage space, insurance, taxes, protection, and so on. The existence of a storage or holding cost argues for producing small batches.

3. The production cost of a single speaker (excluding the setup cost) is $10 and can be assumed to be a unit cost independent of the batch size produced. (In general, however, the unit production cost need not be constant and may decrease with batch size.)

4. Company policy prohibits deliberately planning for shortages of any of its components. However, a shortage of speakers occasionally crops up and it has been estimated that each speaker that is not available when required costs $1.10/month. This cost includes the cost of installing speakers after the television set is fully assembled, storage space, delayed revenue, record keeping, and so forth.

EXAMPLE 2 A wholesale distributor of bicycles is having trouble with shortages of the most popular inexpensive 10-speed model and is currently reviewing the inventory policy for this model. The distributor purchases this model bicycle from the manufacturer monthly and then supplies them to various bicycle shops in the western United States. Upon request from shops, the distributor wholesales bicycles to the individual shops in its region. The distributor has analyzed his costs and has determined that the following are important:

1. The shortage cost, i.e., the cost of not having a bicycle on hand when needed. Most models are easily reordered from the manufacturer, and stores usually accept a delay in delivery. Still, although shortages are permissible, the distributor feels that he incurs a loss, which he estimates to be $15 per bicycle. This cost represents an evaluation of the cost of the loss of goodwill, additional clerical costs incurred, and the cost of the delay in revenue received. On a very few competitive (in price) models, stores do not accept a delay, which results in lost sales. In this case, the cost of lost revenue must be included in the shortage cost.

2. The holding cost, i.e., the cost of maintaining an inventory, is $1 per bicycle remaining at the end of the month. This cost represents the costs of capital tied up, warehouse space, insurance, taxes, and so on.

3. The ordering cost, i.e., the cost of placing an order plus the cost of the bicycle, consists of two components: The paperwork involved in placing an order is estimated as $200, and the actual cost of a bicycle is $35.

These two examples indicate that there exists a tradeoff between the costs involved; the next section discusses the basic cost components of inventory models.

18.2 Components of Inventory Models

Because inventory policies obviously affect profitability, the choice among policies depends upon their relative profitability. Some of the costs that determine this profitability are (1) the costs of ordering or manufacturing, (2) holding or storage costs, (3) unsatisfied demand or shortage penalty costs, (4) revenues, (5) salvage costs, and (6) discount rates. [Costs (1) to (3) were encountered in Examples 1 and 2.]

The cost of ordering or manufacturing an amount z can be represented by a function $c(z)$. The simplest form of this function is one that is directly proportional to the amount ordered, that is, $c \cdot z$, where c represents the unit price paid. Another common assumption is that $c(z)$ is composed of two parts: a term that is directly proportional to the amount ordered and a term that is constant K for z positive and zero for $z = 0$. For this case, if z is positive, the ordering, or production cost, is given by $K + c \cdot z$. The constant K is often referred to as the setup cost and generally includes the administrative cost of ordering, the preliminary labor, and other expenses of starting a production run. There are other assumptions that can be made about this ordering function, but this chapter is restricted to the two cases just described. In Example 1, the speakers are manufactured, and the setup cost for the production run is $12,000. Furthermore, each speaker costs $10, so that the *production* cost is given by

$$c(z) = 12,000 + 10z, \quad \text{for } z > 0.$$

In Example 2, the distributor orders bicycles from the manufacturer, and the *ordering* cost is given by

$$c(z) = 200 + 35z, \quad \text{for } z > 0.$$

The holding or storage costs represent the costs associated with the storage of the inventory until it is sold or used. They may include the cost of capital tied up, space, insurance, protection, and taxes attributed to storage. These costs may be a function of the maximum quantity held during a period, the average amount held, or the cumulated excess of supply over the amount required (demand). The latter viewpoint is usually taken in this chapter. In the bicycle example, the holding cost was $1 per bicycle remaining at the end of the month. This cost can be interpreted as the interest lost in keeping capital tied up in an "unnecessary" bicycle for a month, cost of extra storage space, insurance, and so forth.

The unsatisfied demand or shortage penalty cost is incurred when the amount of the commodity required (demand) exceeds the available stock. This cost depends upon the structure of the model. One such case occurs when (1) the demand exceeds the available inventory, and it is met by a priority shipment, or (2) it is not met at all. In (1) the penalty cost can be viewed as the entire cost of the priority shipment that is used to meet the excess demand. In (2), the situation where the unsatisfied demand is lost, the penalty cost can be viewed as the loss in revenue. Either situation is known as "no backlogging of unsatisfied demand." The scenario of the bicycle example implies that there exist a few competitive (in price) bicycle models where unsatisfied demand is lost, thereby resulting in lost revenue, and hence the example is one where unsatisfied demand is not backlogged. The second case of demand not being fulfilled out of stock assumes that it is satisfied when the commodity next becomes available. The penalty cost can be interpreted as the loss of customers' goodwill, his subsequent reluctance to do business with the firm, the cost of delayed revenue, and extra record keeping. This case is known as "backlogging of unsatisfied demand." The speaker example calls for backlogging of unsatisfied demand. If a shortage occurs, the final assembly of the television set awaits the production of the next batch of speakers. Usually the unsatisfied demand cost is a function of the excess of demand over supply.

The revenue cost may or may not be included in the model. If it is assumed that both the price and the demand for the product are not under the control of the company, the revenue from sales is independent of the firm's inventory policy and may be neglected. However, if revenue is neglected in the model, the *loss in revenue* must then be included in the unsatisfied demand penalty cost whenever the firm cannot meet the demand and the sale is lost. This point is discussed at length in the 10-speed bicycles example presented on page 644. Furthermore, even in the case where demand is backlogged, the cost of the delay in revenue must also be included in the unsatisfied demand cost. With these interpretations, revenue will not be considered as a separate cost in the remainder of this chapter.

The salvage value of an item is the value of a leftover item at the termination of the inventory period. If the inventory policy is carried on for an indefinite number of periods, and if there is no obsolescence, there are no leftover items. What is left over at the end of one period is the amount available at the beginning of the next period. On the other hand, if the policy is to be carried out for only one period, the salvage value represents the disposal value of the item to the firm, say, the selling price. The negative of the salvage value is called the salvage cost. If there is a cost associated with the disposal of an item, the salvage cost may be positive. Because the storage costs generally are assumed to be a function of excess of supply over demand, the salvage costs can be combined with this cost and hence they are usually neglected in this chapter.

Finally, the discount rate takes into account the time value of money. When a firm ties up capital in inventory, it is prevented from using this money for alternative purposes. For example, it could invest this money in secure investments, say, government bonds, and have a return on investment a year hence of, say, 7 percent. Thus a dollar invested today would be worth $1.07 a year hence, or alternatively, a dollar profit a year hence is equivalent to $\alpha = 1/\$1.07$ today. The quantity α is known as the discount factor. Thus, in considering the profitability of an inventory policy, the profit or costs a year hence should be multiplied by α; 2 years hence, by α^2; and so on.

Of course, the convention of choosing a discount factor α that is based upon the current value of a dollar delivered *1 year* hence is arbitrary, and any time period could have been used, for example, 1 month. It is also evident that in problems having short-time horizons, α may be assumed to be 1 (and thereby neglected) because the current value of a dollar delivered during this short-time horizon does not change very much. However, in problems having long-time horizons, the discount factor must be included.

In using quantitative techniques to seek optimal inventory policies, we use the criterion of minimizing the total (expected) discounted cost. Under the assumptions that the price and demand for the product are not under the control of the company and that the lost or delayed revenue is included in the shortage penalty cost, minimizing cost is equivalent to maximizing net income. Another criterion to be considered, although it is nonquantitative but nevertheless important in practice, is that the resultant inventory policy be simple; i.e., the rule for indicating *when to order* and *how much to order* must be able to be easily described. Most of the policies considered possess this property.

Inventory models are usually classified according to whether the demand for a period is known (deterministic demand) or whether it is a random variable having a known probability distribution (nondeterministic or random demand). The production of batches of speakers is an example of deterministic demand because it is assumed that they are used in television assemblies at a rate of 8,000 per month. The bicycle shops' purchases of bicycles from the distributor is an example of random demand. This classification is frequently coupled with whether or not there exist time lags in the delivery of the items ordered or produced. In both the speaker and the bicycle examples, there was an implication that the items appeared immediately after an order was placed. In fact, the production of speakers may require some time, and similarly, the delivery of bicycles may not be instantaneous, so that time lags may have to be incorporated into the inventory model.

Another possible classification relates to the way the inventory is reviewed, either continuously or periodically. In continuous review, an order is placed as soon as the stock level falls below the prescribed reorder point, whereas in the periodic review case, the inventory level is checked at discrete intervals, e.g., at the end of each week, and ordering decisions are made only at these times even if the inventory level dips below the reorder point during the preceding period. The production of speakers is an example of a continuous review, whereas the bicycle problem is an example of periodic review. Incidentally, in practice, a periodic review policy can be used to approximate a continuous review policy by making the time interval sufficiently small.

In this chapter inventory policies are classified according to whether the demand is deterministic or random, and models are developed for continuous and periodic review policies. Instantaneous delivery will be assumed throughout.[1]

18.3 Deterministic Models

This section is concerned with inventory problems where the actual demand is assumed to be known. Several models are considered, including the well-known economic lot-size formulation.

CONTINUOUS REVIEW—UNIFORM DEMAND

The most common inventory problem faced by manufacturers, retailers, and wholesalers is concerned with the case where stock levels are depleted with time and then are replenished by the arrival of new items. A simple model representing this situation is given by the economic lot-size model. Items are assumed to be withdrawn continuously at a known constant rate denoted by a; that is, a units are required per unit time, say, per month. It is further assumed that items are produced (or ordered) in equal numbers, Q at a time, and all Q items arrive simultaneously when desired (fixed delivery lags will be considered later). The only costs to be considered are the setup cost K, charged at the time of the production (or ordering), a production cost (or purchase cost) of c dollars per item, and an inventory holding cost of h dollars per item per unit of time. The inventory problem is to determine how often to make a production run and what size it should be so that the cost per unit of time is a minimum. This is a continuous review inventory policy. We will first assume that shortages are not allowed, and then we will relax this assumption. The example of the production of speakers in television sets satisfies this model.

SHORTAGES NOT PERMITTED A cycle can be viewed as the time between production runs. Thus, if 24,000 speakers are produced at each production run and are used at the rate of 8,000 per month, then the cycle length is $24,000/8,000 = 3$ months. In general, the cycle length is Q/a. Figure 18.1 illustrates how the inventory level varies over time.

The cost per unit time is obtained as follows: The production cost per cycle is given by

$$\begin{cases} 0, & \text{if } Q = 0 \\ K + cQ, & \text{if } Q > 0. \end{cases}$$

The holding cost per cycle is easily obtained. The average inventory level during a

---

[1] Results for the delivery-lag case often can be obtained from the corresponding instantaneous delivery model by a simple modification in the calculation of some of the inventory costs.

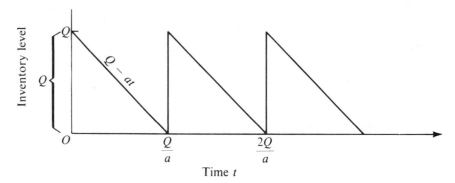

Figure 18.1 **Diagram of inventory level as a function of time—no shortages permitted.**

cycle is $(Q + 0)/2 = Q/2$ items per unit of time, and the corresponding cost is $hQ/2$ per unit of time. Because the cycle length is Q/a, the holding cost per cycle is given by

$$\frac{hQ^2}{2a}.$$

Therefore, the total cost per cycle is

$$K + cQ + \frac{hQ^2}{2a},$$

and the total cost per unit of time is

$$T = \frac{K + cQ + hQ^2/2a}{Q/a} = \frac{aK}{Q} + ac + \frac{hQ}{2}.$$

It is evident that the value of Q, say Q^*, that minimizes T is found from $dT/dQ = 0$. $dT/dQ = -aK/Q^2 + h/2 = 0$, so that

$$Q^* = \sqrt{\frac{2aK}{h}}$$

(because $d^2T/dQ^2 > 0$), which is the well-known economic lot-size result. Similarly the time it takes to withdraw this optimum value of Q^*, say, t^*, is given by

$$t^* = \frac{Q^*}{a} = \sqrt{\frac{2K}{ah}}.$$

These results will now be applied to the speaker example. The appropriate parameters are

$$K = 12{,}000$$
$$h = 0.30$$
$$a = 8{,}000,$$

so that

$$Q^* = \sqrt{\frac{(2)(8,000)(12,000)}{0.30}} = 25,298$$

and

$$t^* = \frac{25,298}{8,000} = 3.2 \text{ months}.$$

Hence the production line is to be set up every 3.2 months and produce 25,298 speakers. Incidentally, the cost curve is rather flat near this optimal value, so that any production between 20,000 and 30,000 speakers is acceptable; this fact can be seen in Fig. 18.3.

SHORTAGES PERMITTED It may be profitable to permit shortages to occur because the cycle length can be increased with a resultant saving in setup costs. However, this benefit may be offset by the cost that is incurred when shortages occur, and hence a detailed analysis is required.

  If shortages are allowed and are priced out at a cost of p dollars for each unit of demand unfilled for one unit of time, results similar to the no shortage case can be obtained. Denote by S the stock on hand at the beginning of a cycle. The problem is summarized in Fig. 18.2.

  The cost per unit time is obtained as follows: The production cost per cycle is given by

$$\begin{cases} 0, & \text{if } Q = 0 \\ K + cQ, & \text{if } Q > 0. \end{cases}$$

The holding cost per cycle is easily obtained. Note that the inventory level is positive for a time of S/a. The average inventory level *during this time* is $(S + 0)/2 = S/2$ items per unit of time, and the corresponding cost is $hS/2$ per unit of time. Hence the total holding cost incurred over the time the inventory

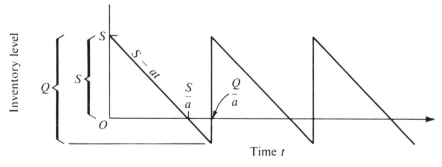

Figure 18.2 **Diagram of inventory level as a function of time—shortages permitted.**

level is positive is the holding cost per cycle, which is given by

$$\frac{hS}{2}\frac{S}{a} = \frac{hS^2}{2a}.$$

Similarly, shortages occur for a time $(Q - S)/a$. The average amount of shortages *during this time* is $[0 + (Q - S)]/2 = (Q - S)/2$ items per unit of time, and the corresponding cost is $p(Q - S)/2$ per unit of time. Hence the total shortage cost incurred over the time shortages exist is the shortage cost per cycle, which is given by

$$\frac{p(Q - S)}{2}\frac{(Q - S)}{a} = \frac{p(Q - S)^2}{2a}.$$

Therefore, the total cost per cycle is

$$K + cQ + \frac{hS^2}{2a} + \frac{p(Q - S)^2}{2a},$$

and the total cost per unit of time is

$$T = \frac{K + cQ + hS^2/2a + p(Q - S)^2/2a}{Q/a}$$

$$= \frac{aK}{Q} + ac + \frac{hS^2}{2Q} + \frac{p(Q - S)^2}{2Q}.$$

In this model there are two decision variables (S and Q), so the optimum values (S^* and Q^*) are found by setting the partial derivatives $\partial T/\partial S$ and $\partial T/\partial Q$ equal to zero. Thus

$$\frac{\partial T}{\partial S} = \frac{hS}{Q} - \frac{p(Q - S)}{Q} = 0.$$

$$\frac{\partial T}{\partial Q} = -\frac{aK}{Q^2} - \frac{hS^2}{2Q^2} + \frac{p(Q - S)}{Q} - \frac{p(Q - S)^2}{2Q^2} = 0.$$

Solving these equations simultaneously leads to

$$S^* = \sqrt{\frac{2aK}{h}}\sqrt{\frac{p}{p + h}}, \qquad Q^* = \sqrt{\frac{2aK}{h}}\sqrt{\frac{p + h}{p}}.$$

The optimal period length t^* is given by

$$t^* = \frac{Q^*}{a} = \sqrt{\frac{2K}{ah}}\sqrt{\frac{p + h}{p}}.$$

The maximum shortage is expressed as

$$Q^* - S^* = \sqrt{\frac{2aK}{p}}\sqrt{\frac{h}{p + h}}.$$

Further, from Fig. 18.2, the fraction of time that no shortage exists is given by

$$\frac{S*/a}{Q*/a} = \frac{p}{p+h},$$

which is independent of K.

If shortages are permitted in the speaker example, the cost is estimated as $p = \$1.10$ per speaker. Again

$$K = 12,000$$
$$h = 0.30$$
$$a = 8,000,$$

so that

$$S* = \sqrt{\frac{(2)(8,000)(12,000)}{0.30}} \sqrt{\frac{1.1}{1.1 + 0.3}} = 22,424,$$

$$Q* = \sqrt{\frac{(2)(8,000)(12,000)}{0.30}} \sqrt{\frac{1.1 + 0.3}{1.1}} = 28,540,$$

and

$$t* = \frac{28,540}{8,000} = 3.6 \text{ months.}$$

Hence, when shortages are permitted, the production line is to be set up every 3.6 months to produce 28,540 speakers. A shortage of 6,116 speakers is permitted. Note that $Q*$ and $t*$ are not very different from the no shortage case.

QUANTITY DISCOUNTS, SHORTAGES NOT PERMITTED The models considered have assumed that the unit cost of an item is the same, independent of the quantity produced. In fact, this assumption resulted in the optimal solutions being independent of this unit cost. Suppose, however, that there exist cost breaks; i.e., the unit cost varies with the quantity ordered. For example, suppose the unit cost of producing a speaker is $c_1 = \$11$ if less than 10,000 speakers are produced, $c_2 = \$10$ if production falls between 10,000 and 80,000 speakers, and $c_3 = \$9.50$ if production exceeds 80,000 speakers. What is the optimal policy? The solution to this specific problem will reveal the general method.

From the results of the previously considered economic lot-size model (shortages not permitted), the total cost per unit time if the production cost is c_j is given by

$$T_j = \frac{aK}{Q} + ac_j + \frac{hQ}{2}, \quad \text{for } j = 1, 2, 3.$$

A plot of T_j versus Q is shown in Fig. 18.3.

The feasible values of Q are shown by the solid lines, and it is only these regions that must be investigated. For each curve, the value of Q that minimizes

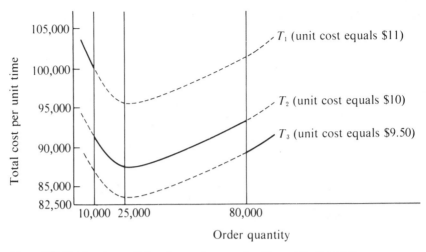

Figure 18.3 **Total cost per unit time for speaker example with quantity discounts.**

T_j is easily found by the methods used in the previously considered economic lot-size model. For $K = 12,000$, $h = 0.30$, and $a = 8,000$, this value is

$$\sqrt{\frac{(2)(8,000)(12,000)}{0.30}} = 25,298.$$

This number is a feasible value for the cost function T_2. Because it is evident that for fixed Q, $T_j < T_{j-1}$ for all j, T_1 can be eliminated from further consideration. However, T_3 cannot be immediately discarded. Its minimum feasible value (which occurs at $Q = 80,000$) must be compared to T_2 evaluated at 25,298 (which is $87,589). Because T_3 evaluated at 80,000 equals $89,200, it is better to produce in quantities of 25,298, and thus this quantity is the optimal value for this set of quantity discounts. If the quantity discount led to a cost of $9 (instead of $9.50) when production exceeded 80,000, then T_3 evaluated at 80,000 would equal 85,200, and the optimal production quantity would become 80,000.

Although this analysis concerned a very specific problem, its extension to a general problem is evident. Furthermore, a similar analysis can be made for other types of quantity discounts such as incremental quantity discounts, where a cost c_0 is incurred for the first q_0 items, c_1 for the next q_1 items, and so on.

Remarks. Several remarks can be made about economic lot-size models:

1. If it is assumed that the production (or purchase) cost of an item is constant throughout time, it does not appear in the optimal solution. This result is evident because no matter what policy is used, the same quantity is required, and hence this cost is fixed.
2. It was previously assumed that Q, the number of units produced, was constant from cycle to cycle. A little reflection will reveal that this assumption is really a result rather than an assumption.

3. These models can be viewed as a special case of an (s,S) policy. An (s,S) policy is usually used in the context of a periodic review policy, where at review time an order is placed to bring the inventory level up to S if the current inventory is less than or equal to s. Otherwise, no order is placed.[1] The symbol S then denotes the reorder level, and s denotes the reorder point. In the economic lot-size models, s denotes the inventory level when items are ordered, so that when shortages are not permitted the reorder point s is zero, and when shortages are permitted, s is equal to the negative of the maximum shortage; that is,

$$s = -\sqrt{\frac{2aK}{p}} \sqrt{\frac{h}{p+h}}.$$

Furthermore, because the economic lot-size models are continuously reviewed, when the inventory level equals s an order is placed, bringing the inventory up to the reorder level S. Hence, for economic lot-size models the (s,S) policy can be described as follows: When the inventory level reaches the reorder point s, place an order to bring the inventory level up to reorder level S; that is, order $Q = S - s$.

4. It is evident from the analysis presented that the reorder point will never be positive. A policy that calls for $s > 0$ cannot be optimal because it is dominated by a policy that calls for ordering the same Q, but only when the reorder point reaches zero. It is dominated in that the latter policy has the same setup and purchase costs but a uniformly smaller holding cost.

5. A known fixed delivery lag is easily accommodated. Denote by λ the lead time between the placing and receiving of the order. It is assumed that λ is constant over time and independent of the size of the order. It is evident that if it is desired to have the order arrive the moment the inventory level reaches s, then the order must be placed λ periods earlier. Thus the reorder point is simply

$$s + \lambda a,$$

where s is determined for the no-lag situation.[2]

PERIODIC REVIEW—A GENERAL MODEL FOR PRODUCTION PLANNING

The last section explored the economic lot-size model. The results were dependent upon the assumption of a constant demand rate. When this assumption is relaxed, i.e., when the amounts required from period to period are allowed to vary, the square root formula no longer ensures a minimum cost solution.

---

[1] Usually (s,S) policies are described as ordering when the inventory level is less than s rather than when the inventory level is less than or equal to s. However, the costs are often the same if an optimal policy is followed.

[2] This result holds only when $\lambda a < Q$.

Consider the following model due to Wagner and Whitin.[1] As before, the only costs to be considered are the setup cost K, charged at the beginning of the period, a production cost (or purchase cost) of c dollars per item, and an inventory holding cost of h dollars per item, which is charged (arbitrarily) at the end of the time period. The choice of charging the inventory at the end of the period, and hence as a function of the excess of the supply over the requirement, is somewhat different from the holding charge incurred in the economic lot-size models. In the latter case, the average cost per unit of time was charged. Clearly, different policies can result from alternative ways of dealing with holding costs. In addition, $r_i = 1, 2, \ldots, n$ represents the requirements at time i, and it is assumed that these requirements must be met. Initially there is no stock on hand. For a horizon of n periods, the inventory problem is to determine how much should be produced at the beginning of each time period (assumed to be instantaneous) to minimize the total cost incurred over the n periods.

The model can be illustrated by the following variation of the speaker example.

EXAMPLE A market survey conducted by the television manufacturer has indicated that the demand for television sets is seasonal rather than uniform. In particular, a sales of 30,000 sets is forecast for the Christmas season (October to December), 20,000 for the winter slack season (January to March), 30,000 for the "new model" season (April to June), and 20,000 for the summer season (July to September). Because of the necessity of meeting the increased demand during the peak seasons, the television set production line was revamped. This revised production line enabled the company to introduce new equipment as well as to redesign some of its components, including the speakers. Hence the setup cost for speaker production is now $20,000, but the unit cost is down to $1. Furthermore, the holding cost of a speaker has been reduced to 20 cents per (3-month) period. Finally, the labor and equipment costs are such that the speakers must be produced in increments of 10,000. It is assumed that production of the television sets is completed and ready for shipment in the 3-month period prior to the season in which it is required. Thus the 30,000 sets required for the Christmas season are to be assembled during the July to September period. The speaker is the last component added to the television set, and it is easily installed. Furthermore, large quantities of speakers can be produced in a very short time period so that their production and subsequent installation can be viewed as instantaneous. The problem is to determine how many to produce in each period while satisfying the requirements and minimizing the total cost. A solution, though not an optimal one, is given in Fig. 18.4; this policy calls for producing 30,000 speakers at the beginning of the first period (Christmas season), 60,000 speakers at the beginning of the second period, and 10,000 speakers at the beginning of the fourth period.

[1] H. M. Wagner and T. M. Whitin, "Dynamic Version of the Economic Lot-Size Model," *Management Science*, **5**(1): 89–96, 1958.

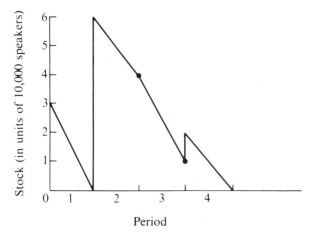

Figure 18.4 **Production schedule that satisfies requirements.**

One approach to the solution of this model is to enumerate, for each of the 2^{n-1} combinations of either producing or not producing in each period, the possible quantities that can be produced. This approach is rather cumbersome, even for moderate-sized n. Hence a more efficient method is desirable. In particular, the method of dynamic programming introduced in Chap. 11 will be applied, followed by the introduction of an algorithm (in the ensuing section) that exploits the structure. Finally, a mathematical programming solution will be presented.

THE DYNAMIC PROGRAMMING SOLUTION Following the notation introduced for dynamic programming (Chap. 11) and interpreting the variables in the inventory context, the ith stage corresponds to the ith period; the state corresponds to the inventory entering period i and will be denoted by x_i; and the decision variable corresponds to the quantity produced (or ordered) at the beginning of period i and will be denoted by z_i.[1]

Let $B_i(x_i, z_i)$ denote the costs incurred in period i, given the entering inventory and the quantity produced. Recall that the only costs considered are the setup cost K, charged at the beginning of the period, a production cost (or purchase cost) of c dollars per item, and an inventory holding cost of h dollars per item charged at the end of the time period. The requirement for period i is r_i. Then $B_i(x_i, z_i)$ is given by

$$B_i(x_i, z_i) = \begin{cases} K + cz_i + h(x_i + z_i - r_i), & \text{if } z_i > 0 \\ h(x_i - r_i), & \text{if } z_i = 0. \end{cases}$$

Denote by $C_i(x_i, z_i)$ the total cost of the best overall policy from the beginning of period i to the end of the planning horizon, given that the inventory

[1] For the notation in this chapter to be consistent with that used in inventory theory in general, it may differ somewhat from the notation introduced in Chap. 11.

level entering period i is x_i and z_i is chosen to be produced; and let $C_i^*(x_i)$ denote the corresponding minimum value of $C_i(x_i, z_i)$, subject to the constraints that $z_i \geq 0$ and that the requirements for the periods are met. Therefore,

$$C_i^*(x_i) = \underset{\substack{z_i \geq 0 \\ z_i \geq r_i - x_i}}{\text{minimum}} [B_i(x_i, z_i) + C_{i+1}^*(x_i + z_i - r_i)],$$

for $i = 1, 2, \ldots, n$, and $C_{n+1}^*(\cdot)$ is defined to be zero. In the speaker example, there are four periods to be considered. (All calculations have been reduced in scale by a factor of 10,000.) The first iteration corresponds to $i = 4$, that is, a description of the optimal policy at the beginning of period 4. For this case,

$$C_4^*(x_4) = \underset{\substack{z_4 \geq 0 \\ z_4 \geq 2 - x_4}}{\text{minimum}} [B_4(x_4, z_4)],$$

so that the immediate solution to the fourth-period problem is as follows:

x_4	z_4	$C_4^*(x_4)$	z_4^*
0	2	4	2
1	1	3	1
2	0	0	0

The second iteration requires finding the optimal policy from the beginning of period 3 to the end of period 4. For this case,

$$C_3^*(x_3) = \underset{\substack{z_3 \geq 0 \\ z_3 \geq 3 - x_3}}{\text{minimum}} [B_3(x_3, z_3) + C_4^*(x_3 + z_3 - 3)],$$

so that the solution to the problem beginning at period 3 is as follows:

			$B_3(x_3, z_3) + C_4^*(x_3 + z_3 - 3)$					
x_3 $\backslash$ z_3	0	1	2	3	4	5	$C_3^*(x_3)$	z_3^*
0	—	—	—	9.0	9.2	7.4	7.4	5
1	—	—	8	8.2	6.4	—	6.4	4
2	—	7	7.2	5.4	—	—	5.4	3
3	4.0	6.2	4.4	—	—	—	4.0	0
4	3.2	3.4	—	—	—	—	3.2	0
5	0.4	—	—	—	—	—	0.4	0

A typical entry can be verified. Let $x_3 = 2$ and $z_3 = 3$. Then 3 units are produced, given an initial inventory of 2. The cost of production is then $2 + 1(3) = 5$, and the inventory holding cost is $\frac{1}{5}(2 + 3 - 3) = 0.4$. The entering inventory in period 4 is then 2, so that $C_4^*(2) = 0$. Hence the total cost is given by $5 + 0.4 = 5.4$, which is the value given.

The third iteration requires finding the optimal policy from the beginning of period 2 to the end of period 4. For this case,

$$C_2^*(x_2) = \underset{\substack{z_2 \geq 0 \\ z_2 \geq 2 - x_2}}{\text{minimum}} [B_2(x_2, z_2) + C_3^*(x_2 + z_2 - 2)],$$

so that the solution to the problem beginning at period 2 is as follows:

x_2 \\ z_2	0	1	2	3	4	5	6	7	$C_2^*(x_2)$	z_2^*
			$B_2(x_2,z_2) + C_3^*(x_2 + z_2 - 2)$							
0	—	—	11.4	11.6	11.8	11.6	12.0	10.4	10.4	7
1	—	10.4	10.6	10.8	10.6	11.0	9.4	—	9.4	6
2	7.4	9.6	9.8	9.6	10.0	8.4	—	—	7.4	0
3	6.6	8.8	8.6	9.0	7.4	—	—	—	6.6	0
4	5.8	7.6	8.0	6.4	—	—	—	—	5.8	0
5	4.6	7.0	5.4	—	—	—	—	—	4.6	0
6	4.0	4.4	—	—	—	—	—	—	4.0	0
7	1.4	—	—	—	—	—	—	—	1.4	0

Finally, the last iteration requires finding the optimal policy from the beginning of period 1 to the end of period 4. For this case,

$$C_1^*(0) = \underset{z_1 \geq 3}{\text{minimum}} \, [B_1(0, z_1) + C_2^*(z_1 - 3)],$$

so that the solution to the production planning problem is as follows:

x_1 \\ z_1	0	1	2	3	4	5	6	7	8	9	10	$C_1^*(x_1)$	z_1^*
				$B_1(0, z_1) + C_2^*(z_1 - 3)$									
0	—	—	—	15.4	15.6	14.8	15.2	15.6	15.6	16.2	14.8	14.8	5 or 10

Therefore, the optimal production schedule is to produce all the speakers at the beginning of the first period, or produce 50,000 speakers (5 units) at the beginning of the first period and 50,000 speakers (5 units) at the beginning of the third period. The minimum cost is $148,000.

It should be noted that the unit cost c is irrelevant to the problem because over all the time periods, all policies use the same number of items at the same total cost. Hence this cost could have been neglected, and the same optimal policies would have been obtained. Different costs in different periods are easily handled by this method of solution. For example, during the peak production periods (when 30,000 speakers are produced), the workers are fully engaged in the assembly of television sets, so that the speakers must be produced during overtime hours. Hence the unit cost is increased. This increase would be reflected in the calculations of $C_3^*(x_3)$ and $C_1^*(x_1)$.

PERIODIC REVIEW—PRODUCTION PLANNING—AN ALGORITHM

In the previous section, dynamic programming was applied to solve the production planning model. Alternatively, by streamlining the dynamic programming approach, we shall develop an algorithm that exploits the structure of the model. Initially the production planning model we consider will be the same as that presented in the previous section, i.e., arbitrary demand requirement, a fixed setup cost, and linear production and holding costs.

The following result characterizes an optimal policy:

For an arbitrary demand requirement, a fixed setup cost, and linear production and holding costs, there is an optimum policy that produces only when the inventory level is zero.

To show why this result is true, choose any policy. Consider the time period that begins when production is made with zero stock level and ends with the first time production is made when the stock is not at zero level. For the policy given in Fig. 18.4, this interval starts at the beginning of period 2 and ends at the beginning of period 4, when one item is produced. This time period is also shown by the solid lines in Fig. 18.5.

Consider the alternative policy, which implies production of 50,000 speakers at the beginning of period 2 and production of 20,000 speakers at the beginning of period 4. This policy is shown by the dotted lines in Fig. 18.5. This policy, B, dominates policy A in that the total cost is smaller. The setup and the production costs for both policies are the same. It is evident that the holding cost for B is smaller than that for A because there is always less stock on hand at the end of a period. Therefore, B is better than A, so that A cannot be optimal.

This characterization of optimal policies can be used to determine which policies are not optimal. In addition, because it implies that the amount produced at the beginning of the ith period must be either 0, r_i, $r_i + r_{i+1}, \ldots,$ $r_i + r_{i+1} + \cdots + r_n$, it can be exploited to obtain an efficient algorithm.

Suppose an optimal policy is presented. Consider the time from the initial production at the beginning of the first period to the first time the inventory level is again zero. The total cost of the subsequent periods must be a minimum for this reduced problem because the overall policy is optimal. Therefore, in the context

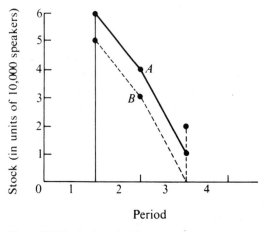

Figure 18.5 **Production schedules.**

of the speaker example, if the inventory level is zero for the first time (after the initial production) at the end of the second period, and if an optimal policy is being followed, all that remains to be done is to determine the optimal policy for the last two periods (periods 3 and 4) that have a requirement of 30,000 speakers for period 3 and 20,000 speakers for period 4.

Let C_i denote the total cost of the best overall policy from the beginning of period i, when no stock is available, to the end of the planning horizon, $i = 1, 2, \ldots, n$. A recursive relationship for C_i is given by

$$C_i = \operatorname*{minimum}_{j=i, i+1, \ldots, n} [C_{j+1} + K + c(r_i + r_{i+1} + \cdots + r_j)$$
$$+ h(r_{i+1} + 2r_{i+2} + 3r_{i+3} + \cdots + (j - i)r_j)],$$

where j can be viewed as an index that denotes the (end of the) period when the inventory reaches a zero level for the first time after the production at the beginning of period i. The cost C_{n+1} is 0, $c(r_i + r_{i+1} + \cdots + r_j)$ is the cost of the production from period i until the inventory level next reaches zero, and the quantity $h(\ )$ is the total holding cost of the inventory that results from the production from period i and remaining until the inventory level next reaches zero. This latter cost is charged at the end of every period as a function of the excess, if any, over the requirement.

The solution of this algorithm is much simpler than the dynamic programming approach. As in dynamic programming, $C_n, C_{n-1}, \ldots, C_2$ must be found before C_1 is obtained. However, the number of calculations is much smaller, and the number of possible production values is greatly reduced.

EXAMPLE Returning to the speaker example, first consider the case of finding C_4, the cost of the optimal policy from the beginning of period 4 to the end of the planning horizon:

$$C_4 = C_5 + 2 + 1(2) = 0 + 2 + 2 = 4.0.$$

To find C_3 we must consider two cases; i.e., the first time after period 3 when the inventory reaches a zero level can occur at (1) the end of the third period or (2) the end of the fourth period. In the recursive relationship j may range over period 3 or 4, resulting in the costs $C_3^{(3)}$ or $C_3^{(4)}$, respectively. The cost C_3 is then the minimum of $C_3^{(3)}$ and $C_3^{(4)}$. These cases are reflected by the policies given in Fig. 18.6.

$$C_3^{(3)} = C_4 + 2 + 1(3) = 4 + 2 + 3 = 9$$

and

$$C_3^{(4)} = C_5 + 2 + 1(3 + 2) + \frac{1}{5}(2) = 0 + 2 + 5 + 0.4 = 7.4.$$

Hence

$$C_3 = \min(7.4, 9.0) = 7.4.$$

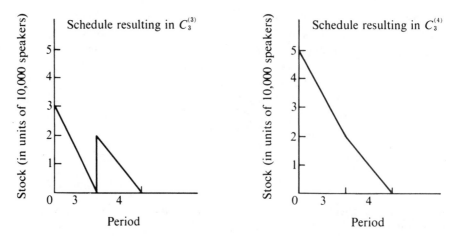

Figure 18.6 **Alternative production schedules when production is required at the beginning of period 3.**

To find C_2 we must consider three cases; i.e., the first time after period 2 when the inventory reaches a zero level can occur at (1) the end of the second period, (2) the end of the third period, or (3) the end of the fourth period. In the recursive relationship j may range over period 2, 3, or 4, resulting in costs $C_2^{(2)}$, $C_2^{(3)}$, or $C_2^{(4)}$, respectively. The cost C_2 is then the minimum of $C_2^{(2)}$, $C_2^{(3)}$, and $C_2^{(4)}$.

$$C_2^{(2)} = C_3 + 2 + 1(2) \qquad\qquad = 7.4 + 2 + 2 = 11.4,$$

$$C_2^{(3)} = C_4 + 2 + 1(2 + 3) + \frac{1}{5}(3) \qquad = 4 + 2 + 5 + 0.6 = 11.6,$$

and

$$C_2^{(4)} = C_5 + 2 + 1(2 + 3 + 2) + \frac{1}{5}[3 + 2(2)] = 0 + 2 + 7 + 1.4 = 10.4.$$

Hence

$$C_2 = \min(11.4, 11.6, 10.4) = 10.4.$$

Finally, to find C_1 we must consider four cases; i.e., the first time after period 1 when the inventory reaches zero can occur at (1) the end of the first period, (2) the end of the second period, (3) the end of the third period, or (4) the end of the fourth period. In the recursive relationship j may range over period 1, 2, 3, or 4, resulting in the costs $C_1^{(1)}, C_1^{(2)}, C_1^{(3)}, C_1^{(4)}$. The cost C_1 is then the minimum of $C_1^{(1)}$, $C_1^{(2)}$, $C_1^{(3)}$, and $C_1^{(4)}$.

$$C_1^{(1)} = C_2 + 2 + 1(3) \qquad\qquad\qquad = 10.4 + 2 + 3 = 15.4,$$

$$C_1^{(2)} = C_3 + 2 + 1(3 + 2) + \frac{1}{5}(2) \qquad\qquad = 7.4 + 2 + 5 + 0.4 = 14.8,$$

$$C_1^{(3)} = C_4 + 2 + 1(3 + 2 + 3) + \frac{1}{5}[2 + 2(3)] \qquad = 4 + 2 + 8 + 1.6 = 15.6,$$

and

$$C_1^{(4)} = C_5 + 2 + 1(3 + 2 + 3 + 2) + \frac{1}{5}[2 + 2(3) + 3(2)]$$

$$= 0 + 2 + 10 + 2.8 = 14.8.$$

Hence

$$C_1 = \min(15.4, 14.8, 15.6, 14.8) = 14.8,$$

so that the optimal production schedule is to produce all the speakers at the beginning of the first period or to produce 50,000 speakers at the beginning of the first period and 50,000 speakers at the beginning of the third period (the same solution as obtained previously).

Again it should be noted that the unit cost c is irrelevant to the problem because over all the time periods, all policies use the same number of items at the same total cost. Hence this cost could have been neglected, and the same optimal policies would have been obtained.

The characterization of the optimal policy, and the subsequent algorithm for finding an optimal policy, depended upon the assumption that the holding and production costs were linear. This constraint can be relaxed to include *concave production and holding costs*. In fact, any increasing function of the holding cost will serve as an alternative condition if the production cost is linear. However, these alternate conditions require a modification in the algorithm for finding an optimal policy. If the production cost function is denoted by $c[\cdot]$ and holding cost function $h[\cdot]$, the recursive relationship for C_i becomes

$$\begin{aligned}
C_i = \underset{j=i,i+1,\dots,n}{\text{minimum}} \{ &C_{j+1} + K + c[r_i + r_{i+1} + \cdots + r_j] \\
&+ h[r_{i+1} + r_{i+2} + r_{i+3} + \cdots + r_j] \\
&+ h[r_{i+2} + r_{i+3} + \cdots + r_j] + \cdots + h[r_j]\},
\end{aligned}$$

where $C_{n+1} = 0$.[1]

A natural extension of the production planning model permits shortages to occur. This extension has been studied by Zangwill[2] and differs from the production planning model studied in that shortage costs are incurred for each unit of demand unfilled for one unit of time. Zangwill characterizes the form of the optimal policy and gives an efficient recursive relationship for finding the optimal policy. These results apply when the production, holding, and shortage costs, per period, are concave functions (thereby including the case of linear costs).

Other results have been obtained for this production planning model under the assumption that the production, holding, and shortage costs are convex. Convex production costs arise, for example, when there are several sources of

---

[1] In the expression for C_i there is no holding cost when $j = i$.

[2] W. I. Zangwill, "A Deterministic Multi-Period Production Scheduling Model with Backlogging," *Management Science*, **13**(1): 105–119, 1966.

limited production at different unit costs in a period. If ones uses these sources up to capacity in order of ascending unit cost (as is optimal), the resulting production cost is convex in the total amount produced. Such an assumption about the production cost precludes the use of the setup charge.

PERIODIC REVIEW—PRODUCTION PLANNING— INTEGER PROGRAMMING FORMULATION

The final technique for solving the production planning model is to formulate it as an integer programming problem. Instead of presenting the general solution, we shall again solve the speaker production example.

Again, let z_i denote the quantity produced at the beginning of period i.[1] The costs to be considered are

$$\text{Production costs} = \text{setup costs} + c(z_1 + z_2 + z_3 + z_4)$$

and

$$\begin{aligned} \text{Holding costs} &= h(z_1 - r_1) + h(z_1 + z_2 - r_1 - r_2) \\ &\quad + h(z_1 + z_2 + z_3 - r_1 - r_2 - r_3) \\ &= 3h(z_1 - r_1) + 2h(z_2 - r_2) + h(z_3 - r_3) \\ &= 0.20[3(z_1 - 3) + 2(z_2 - 2) + z_3 - 3)]. \end{aligned}$$

Hence the problem to be solved is to minimize the sum of the production and holding costs; that is,

$$\begin{aligned} \text{Minimize} \quad W &= \text{setup cost} + 1(z_1 + z_2 + z_3 + z_4) \\ &\quad + 0.20[3(z_1 - 3) + 2(z_2 - 2) + (z_3 - 3)], \end{aligned}$$

subject to

$$z_1 \leq r_1 + r_2 + r_3 + r_4 = 10$$
$$z_2 \leq r_2 + r_3 + r_4 = 7$$
$$z_3 \leq r_3 + r_4 = 5$$
$$z_4 \leq r_4 = 2.$$

$$z_1 \geq r_1 = 3$$
$$z_1 + z_2 \geq r_1 + r_2 = 5$$
$$z_1 + z_2 + z_3 \geq r_1 + r_2 + r_3 = 8$$
$$z_1 + z_2 + z_3 + z_4 = r_1 + r_2 + r_3 + r_4 = 10,$$

and

$$z_1 \geq 0, \quad z_2 \geq 0, \quad z_3 \geq 0, \quad z_4 \geq 0, \quad \text{and integer valued.}$$

[1] Again, all values are expressed in units of 10,000 speakers.

Unfortunately, this model is not an integer linear programming model because the objective function is not linear because of the "setup costs" term that appears in the objective function. However, this problem can be resolved as follows:

Define variables v_1, v_2, v_3, and v_4 such that

$$v_1 \leq 1, \qquad v_2 \leq 1, \qquad v_3 \leq 1, \qquad v_4 \leq 1,$$
$$v_1 \geq 0, \qquad v_2 \geq 0, \qquad v_3 \geq 0, \qquad v_4 \geq 0,$$

and

$$v_1, v_2, v_3, \text{ and } v_4 \text{ are integers } (v_i \text{ is then } 0 \text{ or } 1).$$

Add the following constraints to the problem:

$$z_1 \leq \left(\sum_{i=1}^{4} r_i \right) v_1 = 10v_1$$

$$z_2 \leq \left(\sum_{i=2}^{4} r_i \right) v_2 = 7v_2$$

$$z_3 \leq \left(\sum_{i=3}^{4} r_i \right) v_3 = 5v_3$$

$$z_4 \leq r_4 v_4 = 2v_4.$$

Thus if $v_i = 0$, then $z_i = 0$, and if $v_i = 1$, then z_i is less than or equal to the maximum production in period i. The objective function can now be written as a linear function subject to linear constraints; that is,

Minimize $\quad W = K(v_1 + v_2 + v_3 + v_4) + 1(z_1 + z_2 + z_3 + z_4)$
$$+ 0.20[3(z_1 - 3) + 2(z_2 - 2) + (z_3 - 3)],$$

subject to

$$z_1 \leq 10v_1$$
$$z_2 \leq 7v_2$$
$$z_3 \leq 5v_3$$
$$z_4 \leq 2v_4$$
$$z_1 \geq 3$$
$$z_1 + z_2 \geq 5$$
$$z_1 + z_2 + z_3 \geq 8$$
$$z_1 + z_2 + z_3 + z_4 = 10$$

and

$$\begin{cases} z_1 \geq 0, & z_2 \geq 0, & z_3 \geq 0, & z_4 \geq 0, & \text{and integer valued,} \\ v_1 \geq 0, & v_2 \geq 0, & v_3 \geq 0, & v_4 \geq 0, & \\ v_1 \leq 1, & v_2 \leq 1, & v_3 \leq 1, & v_4 \leq 1, & \text{and integer valued.} \end{cases}$$

The solution to this problem may be obtained by using an integer programming algorithm; it yields the same solution as obtained previously, i.e., produce 100,000 speakers at the beginning of the first period ($z_1 = 10, v_1 = 1$, and all other z_i and v_i equal zero), or produce 50,000 speakers at the beginning of the first period and 50,000 speakers at the beginning of the third period ($z_1 = z_3 = 5$, $v_1 = v_3 = 1$, and all other z_i and v_i equal zero).

18.4 Stochastic Models

This section is concerned with inventory problems where the demand for a period is a random variable having a known probability distribution. Both single-period and multiperiod models are analyzed.

A SINGLE-PERIOD MODEL WITH NO SETUP COST

The second example discussed in Sec. 18.1 is concerned with a wholesale distributor of 10-speed bicycles. Suppose that this distributor is offered very favorable terms on the purchase of a model of a name-brand bicycle whose production is to be discontinued. This opportunity appears to be ideal for the forthcoming Christmas season, where, because production has been discontinued, the stores have been informed that no reorders are possible. The cost of each bicycle is $20, and it will be assumed that there is no setup cost incurred. The cost of maintaining an inventory is $-$9$ per bicycle. This cost includes $1, which represents the cost of capital tied up, warehouse space, and so on, and $-$10$, which is what the distributor can get for each bicycle remaining in the inventory after the Christmas season (the salvage value). Note that this cost of maintaining an inventory is obtained by combining the bicycle storage cost with the bicycle salvage value and results in a negative holding cost. Each bicycle is sold for $45 for a profit of $25.

Two remaining cost components still require discussion, i.e., the unsatisfied demand cost and the revenue. If the demand exceeds the supply, those customers who fail to purchase a bicycle may bear some ill will, thereby resulting in a "cost" to the distributor. This unsatisfied demand cost is simply the per item quantification of the loss of goodwill times the unsatisfied demand whenever a shortage occurs. In the bicycle example, this cost is considered to be negligible.

If we adopt the criterion of maximizing net income, we must include revenue in the model. Indeed, net income is equal to total revenue minus the costs incurred (ordering, inventory holding, and unsatisfied demand). The total revenue component is simply the sales price of a bicycle ($45) times the demand *minus* the sales price times the unsatisfied demand whenever a shortage occurs. The former is independent of the inventory policy, and, hence, can be neglected, whereas the latter is just the lost revenue when a shortage exists. This latter term behaves just like the aforementioned description of the unsatisfied demand cost, and, hence, the two (the loss of goodwill and the lost revenue) can be combined (added) and considered to be the resultant *unsatisfied demand cost*. The unsatisfied demand cost will be so interpreted throughout this chapter. Thus, in the bicycle example, the unsatisfied demand is simply $45[1] times the unsatisfied demand whenever a shortage exists.

Because the revenue times the demand term is independent of the inventory policy chosen, its omission from the net income expression results in terms that are the negative of total cost. Hence maximizing net income in this model is equivalent to minimizing total cost.

The discussion about the interpretation of the unsatisfied demand cost assumed that the unsatisfied demand was lost. For the case where this unsatisfied demand is met by a priority shipment, the same principles prevail. The total revenue component becomes the sales price of a bicycle ($45) times the demand *minus* the unit cost of the priority shipment times the unsatisfied demand whenever a shortage occurs. If the West Coast distributor is forced to meet the unsatisfied demand by purchasing bicycles from the Midwest distributor at the same cost that bicycles are sold to the retail outlets ($45) plus an air freight charge of, say, $2, then the appropriate unsatisfied demand cost is $47 per bicycle. Of course, any costs associated with loss of goodwill, if present, would be added to this amount.

The previous discussion concerned the costs involved in the model, and little attention was paid to the concept of the demand for the bicycles. Unfortunately, the distributor does not know what the demand for these bicycles will be from the stores in the western United States, i.e., the demand is a random variable, and hence he does not know how many bicycles will be required. However, an optimal inventory policy can be obtained if information about the probability distribution of demand is available. Let D represent the random variable demand, and denote by $P_D(d)$ the probability that the demand equals d; that is,

$$P_D(d) = P\{D = d\}.$$

It will be assumed that $P_D(d)$ is known for all values of d; that is, the probability distribution is specified.

In general, we consider the following inventory model. Items are purchased (or produced) for a *single period* at a cost of c dollars per item. The holding cost, the net unit cost of storing leftover items minus their salvage value, is given by h dollars per item and charged as a function of excess stock over the amount required. The cost of unsatisfied demand, e.g., lost revenue from sales or the cost of supplying a required unit, is given by p dollars per unit ($p > c$). It is assumed that there is no initial inventory on hand. Denote by y the quantity purchased (or

---

[1] In general, the cost of the loss of goodwill, assumed to be negligible in the bicycle example, must be added to the revenue to determine the complete *unsatisfied demand cost*.

produced) at the beginning of the period,[1] and let D be a random variable that denotes the demand during the period.

This single-period model may represent the inventory of an item that (1) becomes obsolete quickly, such as the bicycle in the example or a daily newspaper; (2) spoils quickly, such as vegetables; (3) is stocked only once, such as spare parts for a single production run of a new model airplane; or (4) has a future that is uncertain beyond a single period.

With the aforementioned structure, the question of how much inventory to have becomes relevant. More than the expected demand is probably desirable, but certainly less than the maximum demand is required. A tradeoff is needed between (1) the risk of being short and thereby incurring shortage costs and (2) the risk of having an excess and thereby incurring wasted costs of ordering and holding excess units. One reasonable criterion is to choose the inventory level that minimizes the expected value (in the statistical sense) of the sums of these costs.

The amount sold is given by

$$\begin{cases} D, & \text{if } D < y \\ y, & \text{if } D \geq y \end{cases} = \min(D,y).$$

Hence the cost incurred if the demand is D and y is stocked is given by

$$C(D,y) = cy + p\max(0,D - y) + h\max(0,y - D).$$

Because the demand is a random variable [with probability distribution $P_D(d)$], this cost is also a random variable. The expected cost is then given by $C(y)$, where

$$C(y) = E[C(D,y)] = \sum_{d=0}^{\infty} [cy + p\max(0,d - y) + h\max(0,y - d)]P_D(d)$$

$$= cy + \sum_{d=y}^{\infty} p(d - y)P_D(d) + \sum_{d=0}^{y-1} h(y - d)P_D(d).$$

It is evident that $C(y)$ depends upon the probability distribution $P_D(d)$. Frequently a representation of this probability distribution is difficult to find, particularly when the demand ranges over a large number of possible values. Hence this discrete random variable is often approximated by a continuous random variable. Furthermore, when demand ranges over a large number of possible values, this approximation will generally yield small differences in numerical values in the optimal amounts of inventory to stock. In addition, when discrete demand is used the resulting expressions may become slightly more difficult to solve analytically. Hence, unless otherwise stated, continuous demand is assumed throughout the remainder of this chapter. The probability *density*

---

[1] In the previous models the symbol z was used to denote the quantity produced, and x represented the inventory level at the beginning of the period. The symbol y is introduced here to denote the inventory level to be achieved after the ordering decision is made; that is, y is the amount ordered up to, so that $y = x + z$. Because the initial inventory level is assumed to be zero—that is, $x = 0$—y and z are the same.

function of this *continuous* random variable will be denoted by $\varphi_D(\xi)$. The expected cost $C(y)$ is then expressed as

$$C(y) = E[C(D,y)] = \int_0^\infty [cy + p\max(0,\xi - y) + h\max(0,y - \xi)]\varphi_D(\xi)\,d\xi$$

$$= cy + \int_y^\infty p(\xi - y)\varphi_D(\xi)\,d\xi + \int_0^y h(y - \xi)\varphi_D(\xi)\,d\xi^\dagger$$

$$= cy + L(y),$$

where $L(y)$ is often called the expected shortage plus holding cost. It then becomes necessary to find the value of y, say y^0, which minimizes $C(y)$. *The optimal quantity to order, y^0, is that value which satisfies*

$$\Phi(y^0) = \frac{p - c}{p + h},$$

where the function $\Phi(a)$ is the cumulative distribution function of the demand random variable; that is,

$$\Phi(a) = \int_0^a \varphi_D(\xi)\,d\xi.$$

The derivation of this solution is given on page 650.

If D is assumed to be a discrete random variable having cumulative distribution function

$$F_D(b) = \sum_{d=0}^b P_D(d),$$

a similar result for the optimal order quantity is obtained. In particular, *the optimal quantity to order, y^0, is the smallest integer such that*

$$F_D(y^0) \geq \frac{p - c}{p + h}.$$

EXAMPLE Returning to the bicycle example described in this section, assume that the demand has an exponential distribution given by

$$\varphi_D(\xi) = \begin{cases} \dfrac{1}{10,000} e^{-\xi/10,000}, & \xi \geq 0 \\ 0, & \text{otherwise.} \end{cases}$$

---

† The standard notation of probability theory is being followed. If X is a random variable having density function $f_X(y)$, and $g(X)$ is a function of X, then

$$E[g(X)] = \int_{-\infty}^\infty g(y)f_X(y)\,dy.$$

Thus the expected cost is given by $C(y)$.

From the data given,

$$c = 20$$
$$p = 45$$
$$h = -9.$$

Because the demand density is exponential,

$$\Phi(a) = \int_0^a \frac{1}{10,000} e^{-\xi/10,000} d\xi = 1 - e^{-a/10,000}.$$

The optimum quantity to order, y^0, is that value which satisfies

$$1 - e^{-y^0/10,000} = \frac{45 - 20}{45 - 9} = 0.6944,$$

$$y^0 = 11,856.$$

Therefore, the distributor should stock 11,856 bicycles in the Christmas season. Note that this number is slightly more than the expected demand.

Whenever the demand is exponential with expectation λ, y^0 can easily be obtained from the relation

$$y^0 = -\lambda \ln\left(\frac{c + h}{p + h}\right).$$

MODEL WITH INITIAL STOCK LEVEL As a slight variation of the previous model, suppose that the distributor has 500 bicycles of the aforementioned type on hand. How does this stock influence the optimal inventory policy? In particular, suppose that the initial stock level is given by x, and the problem is to determine how much is to be made available, y, at the beginning of the period. Thus $(y - x)$ is to be ordered so that

Amount available (y) = initial stock (x) + amount ordered $(y - x)$.

The cost equation presented earlier remains identical except for the term that was previously cy. This term now becomes $c(y - x)$, so that minimizing the expected cost is given by

$$\underset{y \geq x}{\text{Minimum}} \left[c(y - x) + \int_y^\infty p(\xi - y)\varphi_D(\xi)\,d\xi + \int_0^y h(y - \xi)\varphi_D(\xi)\,d\xi \right].$$

The constraint $y \geq x$ must be added because it is assumed that items on hand at the beginning of the period cannot be depleted or returned. The optimum policy is described as follows.

The inventory policy which satisfies, for $p > c$,

$$\underset{y \geq x}{\text{Minimum}} \left[-cx + \left\{ \int_y^\infty p(\xi - y)\varphi_D(\xi)\,d\xi + \int_0^y h(y - \xi)\varphi_D(\xi)\,d\xi + cy \right\} \right]$$

is given by $y = \{^{y^0}_x$, *so that*

> If $x < y^0$, *order up to* y^0 (*order* $y^0 - x$),
>
> If $x \geq y^0$, *do not order*,

where y^0 *satisfies*

$$\Phi(y^0) = \frac{p - c}{p + h}.$$

Thus, in the bicycle example, if there are 500 bicycles on hand, the optimal policy is to order up to 11,856 bicycles (which implies ordering 11,356 additional bicycles). On the other hand, if there are 12,000 bicycles already on hand, the optimal policy is not to order.

MODEL WITH NONLINEAR PENALTY COSTS Similar results for these models can be obtained for other than linear holding and shortage penalty costs. Denote the holding cost by

$$\begin{cases} h[y - D], & \text{if } y \geq D \\ 0 & \text{if } y < D, \end{cases}$$

where $h[\cdot]$ is a mathematical function, not necessarily linear.

Similarly, the shortage penalty cost can be denoted by

$$\begin{cases} p[D - y], & \text{if } D \geq y \\ 0, & \text{if } D < y, \end{cases}$$

where $p[\cdot]$ is also a function, not necessarily linear.

Thus the total expected cost is given by

$$c(y - x) + \int_y^\infty p[\xi - y]\varphi_D(\xi)\,d\xi + \int_0^y h[y - \xi]\varphi_D(\xi)\,d\xi,$$

where x is the amount on hand.

If $L(y)$ is defined as the expected shortage plus holding cost, that is,

$$L(y) = \int_y^\infty p[\xi - y]\varphi_D(\xi)\,d\xi + \int_0^y h[y - \xi]\varphi_D(\xi)\,d\xi,$$

then the total expected cost can be written as

$$c(y - x) + L(y).$$

The optimal policy is obtained by minimizing this expression, subject to the constraint that $y \geq x$, that is,

$$\underset{y \geq x}{\text{Minimum}}\, [c(y - x) + L(y)].$$

If $L(y)$ *is strictly convex*[1] [*a sufficient condition being that the shortage and*

---

[1] See Appendix 1 for the definition of a convex function.

holding costs each are convex and $\varphi_D(\xi) > 0$], then the optimal policy is given by

$$\begin{cases} \text{if } x < y^0, \text{ order up to } y^0, \\ \text{if } x \geq y^0, \text{ do not order,} \end{cases}$$

where y^0 is the value of y that satisfies the expression

$$\frac{dL(y)}{dy} + c = 0.$$

DERIVATION OF RESULTS FOR THE SINGLE-PERIOD MODEL WITH NO SETUP COST AND LINEAR SHORTAGE AND HOLDING COSTS[1] A useful result for finding policies that minimize the expected cost is as follows:

Let D be a random variable having a density function

$$\begin{cases} \varphi_D(\xi), & \text{if } \xi \geq 0 \\ 0, & \text{otherwise.} \end{cases}$$

Denote by $\Phi(a)$ the cumulative distribution function; that is,

$$\Phi(a) = \int_0^a \varphi_D(\xi) \, d\xi.$$

Let $g(\xi, y)$ be defined as

$$g(\xi, y) = \begin{cases} c_1(y - \xi), & \text{if } y > \xi, c_1 > 0 \\ c_2(\xi - y), & \text{if } y \leq \xi, c_2 > 0, \end{cases}$$

and

$$G(y) = \int_0^\infty g(\xi, y) \varphi_D(\xi) \, d\xi + cy,$$

where $c > 0$. Then $G(y)$ is minimized at $y = y^0$, where y^0 is the solution to

$$\Phi(y^0) = \frac{c_2 - c}{c_2 + c_1}.$$

To see why this value of y^0 minimizes $G(y)$, note that by definition

$$G(y) = c_1 \int_0^y (y - \xi) \varphi_D(\xi) \, d\xi + c_2 \int_y^\infty (\xi - y) \varphi_D(\xi) \, d\xi + cy.$$

Taking the derivative (see Appendix 2) and setting it equal to zero leads to

$$\frac{dG(y)}{dy} = c_1 \int_0^y \varphi_D(\xi) \, d\xi - c_2 \int_y^\infty \varphi_D(\xi) \, d\xi + c = 0.$$

This expression implies that

$$c_1 \Phi(y^0) - c_2[1 - \Phi(y^0)] + c = 0$$

---

[1] This section may be omitted by the less mathematically inclined reader.

because

$$\int_0^\infty \varphi_D(\xi)\, d\xi = 1.$$

Solving this expression results in

$$\Phi(y^0) = \frac{c_2 - c}{c_2 + c_1}.$$

Checking the second derivative indicates that

$$\frac{d^2 G(y)}{dy^2} = (c_1 + c_2)\varphi_D(y) \geq 0$$

for all y, so that the result is obtained.

To apply this result, it is sufficient to show that

$$C(y) = cy + \int_y^\infty p(\xi - y)\varphi_D(\xi)\, d\xi + \int_0^y h(y - \xi)\varphi_D(\xi)\, d\xi$$

has the form of $G(y)$.

Clearly, $c_1 = h$, $c_2 = p$, and $c = c$, so that the optimal quantity to order, y^0, is that value which satisfies

$$\Phi(y^0) = \frac{p - c}{p + h}.$$

To derive the results for the case where the initial stock level is x, recall that it is necessary to solve the relationship

$$\min_{y \geq x}\left[-cx + \left\{ \int_y^\infty p(\xi - y)\varphi_D(\xi)\, d\xi + \int_0^y h(y - \xi)\varphi_D(\xi)\, d\xi + cy \right\} \right].$$

Note that the expression in braces has the form of a $G(y)$, with $c_1 = h$, $c_2 = p$, and $c = c$. Hence the cost function to be minimized can be written as

$$\min_{y \geq x}[-cx + G(y)].$$

It is clear that $-cx$ is a constant, so that it is sufficient to find the y that satisfies the expression

$$\min_{y \geq x} G(y).$$

Hence the value of y^0 that minimizes $G(y)$ satisfies

$$\Phi(y^0) = \frac{p - c}{p + h}.$$

Furthermore, $G(y)$ must be a convex function because

$$\frac{d^2 G(y)}{dy^2} \geq 0.$$

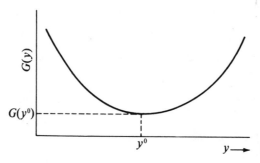

Figure 18.7 Graph of $G(y)$.

Also,

$$\lim_{y \to 0} \frac{dG(y)}{dy} = c - p,$$

which is negative,[1] and

$$\lim_{y \to \infty} \frac{dG(y)}{dy} = h + c,$$

which is positive. Hence $G(y)$ must be as shown in Fig. 18.7. Thus the optimal policy must be given by the following:

If $x < y^0$, order up to y^0 because y^0 can be achieved together with the minimum value $G(y^0)$,
If $x \geq y^0$, do not order because any $G(y)$, with $y > x$, must exceed $G(x)$.

A similar argument can be constructed for obtaining optimal policies with nonlinear penalty costs when $L(y)$ is strictly convex.

A SINGLE-PERIOD MODEL WITH A SETUP COST

In discussing the bicycle example in this section, it was assumed that there was no fixed cost incurred in ordering the bicycles for the Christmas season. In actual fact, the cost of placing this special order is $800, and this cost should be included in the analysis of the model. In fact, inclusion of the setup cost generally causes major changes in the results.

In general, the setup cost will be denoted by K. To begin with, the shortage and holding costs will each be assumed to be linear. Their resultant effect is then given by $L(y)$, where

$$L(y) = p \int_y^\infty (\xi - y)\varphi_D(\xi)\,d\xi + h \int_0^y (y - \xi)\varphi_D(\xi)\,d\xi.$$

---

[1] If $c - p$ is nonnegative, $G(y)$ will be a monotone increasing function. This implies that the item should not be stocked; that is, $y^0 = 0$.

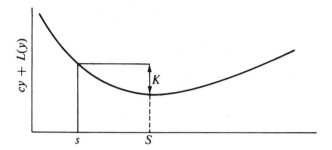

Figure 18.8 **Graph of** *cy + L(y).*

Thus the total expected cost incurred if one orders up to y is given by

$$\begin{cases} K + c(y - x) + L(y), & \text{if } y > x \\ L(x), & \text{if } y = x. \end{cases}$$

Note that $cy + L(y)$ is the same expected cost considered in the previous section when the setup cost was omitted. If $cy + L(y)$ is drawn as a function of y, it will appear as shown in Fig. 18.8.[1] Define S as the value of y that minimizes $cy + L(y)$, and define s as the smallest value of y for which $cs + L(s) = K + cS + L(S)$. From Fig. 18.8 it is evident that if $x > S$, then $K + cy + L(y) > cx + L(x)$, for all $y > x$. Hence $K + c(y - x) + L(y) > L(x)$, where the left-hand side of the inequality represents the expected total cost if one orders up to y, and the right-hand side of the inequality represents the expected total cost if no ordering occurs. Hence the optimum policy indicates that if $x > S$, do not order. If $s \le x \le S$, it is again evident from Fig. 18.8 that

$$K + cy + L(y) \ge cx + L(x), \quad \text{for all } y > x,$$

so that

$$K + c(y - x) + L(y) \ge L(x).$$

Again, no ordering is less expensive than ordering. Finally, if $x < s$, it follows from Fig. 18.8 that

$$\min_{y \ge x} [K + cy + L(y)] = K + cS + L(S) < cx + L(x),$$

or

$$\min_{y \ge x} [K + c(y - x) + L(y)] = K + c(S - x) + L(S) < L(x),$$

so that it pays to order. The minimum cost is incurred if one orders up to S.

---

[1] In the derivation of results for the single-period model with no setup cost and linear shortage and holding costs, $cy + L(y)$ was denoted by $G(y)$ and rigorously shown to be a convex function of the form plotted in Fig. 18.8.

Thus the optimum ordering policy can be summarized as follows:

$$\begin{cases} if \ x < s, \ order \ up \ to \ S \\ if \ x \geq s, \ do \ not \ order. \end{cases}$$

The value of S is obtained from

$$\Phi(S) = \frac{p - c}{p + h},$$

and s is the smallest value that satisfies the expression

$$cs + L(s) = K + cS + L(S).$$

This policy is an (s,S) policy mentioned previously, and it has had extensive use in industry.

EXAMPLE Referring to the bicycle example of the previous section,

$$y^0 = S = 11,856.$$

If $K = 800$, $c = 20$, $p = 45$, and $h = -9$, s is obtained from

$$20s + 45 \int_s^\infty (\xi - s) \frac{1}{10,000} e^{-\xi/10,000} \, d\xi - 9 \int_0^s (s - \xi) \frac{1}{10,000} e^{-\xi/10,000} \, d\xi$$

$$= 800 + 20(11,856) + 45 \int_{11,856}^\infty (\xi - 11,856) \frac{1}{10,000} e^{-\xi/10,000} \, d\xi$$

$$- 9 \int_0^{11,856} (11,856 - \xi) \frac{1}{10,000} e^{-\xi/10,000} \, d\xi,$$

so that

$$s = 10,674.$$

Hence the optimal policy calls for ordering up to $S = 11,856$ bicycles if the amount on hand is less than $s = 10,674$. Otherwise, no order is placed.

SOLUTION WHEN THE DEMAND DISTRIBUTION IS EXPONENTIAL It may be of interest to solve this model, in general, when the distribution of demand, D, is exponential; that is,

$$\varphi_D(\xi) = \frac{1}{\lambda} e^{-\xi/\lambda}, \quad for \ \xi > 0.$$

If Δ is defined as $S - s$, then Δ is the solution to the equation

$$e^{\Delta/\lambda} = \frac{K}{\lambda(c + h)} + \frac{\Delta}{\lambda} + 1.$$

Furthermore, a good approximation for Δ is given by

$$\Delta \simeq \sqrt{\frac{2\lambda K}{c + h}}.$$

Note that

$$s = S - \Delta.$$

These results are easily obtained. From the no-setup cost results,

$$1 - e^{-S/\lambda} = \frac{p - c}{p + h}$$

or

$$S = \lambda \ln\left(\frac{h + p}{h + c}\right).$$

For any y,

$$cy + L(y) = cy + h \int_0^y (y - \xi)\frac{1}{\lambda}e^{-\xi/\lambda}\,d\xi + p \int_y^\infty (\xi - y)\frac{1}{\lambda}e^{-\xi/\lambda}\,d\xi$$
$$= (c + h)y + \lambda(h + p)e^{-y/\lambda} - \lambda h.$$

Evaluating $cy + L(y)$ at the point $y = s$ and $y = S$ leads to

$$(c + h)s + \lambda(h + p)e^{-s/\lambda} - \lambda h = K + (c + h)S + \lambda(h + p)e^{-S/\lambda} - \lambda h,$$

or

$$(c + h)s + \lambda(h + p)e^{-s/\lambda} = K + (c + h)S + \lambda(c + h).$$

By letting $\Delta = S - s$, the last equation yields

$$e^{\Delta/\lambda} = \frac{K}{\lambda(c + h)} + \frac{\Delta}{\lambda} + 1.$$

If Δ/λ is close to zero, $e^{\Delta/\lambda}$ can be expanded into a Taylor series around zero. If the terms beyond the quadratic term are neglected, the result becomes

$$1 + \frac{\Delta}{\lambda} + \frac{\Delta^2}{2\lambda^2} \simeq \frac{K}{\lambda(c + h)} + \frac{\Delta}{\lambda} + 1,$$

so that

$$\Delta \simeq \sqrt{\frac{2\lambda K}{c + h}}.$$

Using the approximation in the bicycle example results in

$$\Delta = \sqrt{\frac{(2)(10{,}000)(800)}{20 - 9}} = 1{,}206,$$

which is quite close to the exact value of $\Delta = 1{,}182$.

MODEL WITH NONLINEAR PENALTY COSTS Again it is evident that these results can be extended easily to any strictly convex expected shortage plus holding cost, $L(y)$. This extension results in a strictly convex $cy + L(y)$, similar to Fig. 18.8. Hence the optimal ordering policy is of the form

$$\begin{cases} \textit{if } x < s, \textit{ order up to } S \\ \textit{if } x \geq s, \textit{ do not order,} \end{cases}$$

where S is the value of y that satisfies

$$c + \frac{dL(y)}{dy} = 0,$$

and s is the smallest value that satisfies the expression

$$cs + L(s) = K + cS + L(S).$$

A TWO-PERIOD INVENTORY MODEL WITH NO SETUP COST

The single-period model was illustrated with a bicycle example where the distributor had only one opportunity to place an order. In many situations an opportunity to place an order occurs periodically, e.g., monthly, and the inventory manager must make a decision about whether and how much to stock. He may be interested in these decisions for a horizon of the next 2 months, 12 months, 18 months, or even possibly forever. Even for a horizon of 2 months, the periodic review policy of using the optimal one-period solution twice is not generally the optimal policy for the two-period problem. Smaller costs can usually be achieved by viewing the problem from a two-period viewpoint and then using the methods of dynamic programming introduced in Chap. 11 to obtain the best inventory policy. In fact, the only difference in concept in the dynamic programming approach for solving the inventory problem compared to the material in Chap. 11 is the probabilistic aspects that are introduced by the random demand.

TWO-PERIOD MODEL—NO SETUP COST Suppose that the bicycle distributor is permitted to make at most one reorder, to occur on November 15, after placing his initial order for the special type 10-speed bicycle on October 15. The assumptions about the costs are similar to those presented before. Assume that the purchase leads to immediate delivery; shortages at the end of the first period are to be made up, if they exist (backlogging of orders is possible at the end of the first period, but not at the end of the second period); no disposal of stock is permitted. Furthermore, the demands D_1, D_2 for the two periods are independent, identically distributed random variables having density $\varphi_D(\xi)$. The purchase cost is linear, that is, cz, where z is the amount ordered (no setup cost), and the shortage and holding costs are also linear with respective unit costs denoted by p and h.

As indicated earlier, the solution to this problem is not to use the optimal one-period solution twice. Smaller costs can be achieved by viewing the problem from a two-period dynamic programming viewpoint. Order the time periods so that the beginning of time period 1 implies that there are two periods left in the horizon. Similarly, the beginning of time period 2 implies that there is one period left in the horizon (the last period is beginning). The problem is to find critical numbers that describe the optimum ordering policy. It will be shown that these numbers are single critical numbers for each period. These numbers will be denoted by y_1^0 and y_2^0. Furthermore, y_1 and y_2 (without the superscript) represent any amount of stock ordered up to at the beginning of the respective period.

Denote by $C_1(x_1)$ the expected cost of following an optimum policy (minimum cost) from the beginning of period 1 to the end of period 2, given that there are x_1 units on hand. Similarly, denote by $C_2(x_2)$ the expected cost of following an optimum policy (minimum cost) from the beginning of period 2, given that there are x_2 units on hand. $C_1(x_1)$ is the expression sought because this expression is obtained by following the optimum policy for the entire (two-period) horizon. To obtain $C_1(x_1)$ it is necessary to first find $C_2(x_2)$. From the results for the single-period model, the optimal policy for a one-period problem is given by a single critical number found from

$$\Phi(y_2^0) = \frac{p - c}{p + h};$$

that is, if x_2 is the amount available at the beginning of the last period, then

$$\begin{cases} \text{order } (y_2^0 - x_2^0), & \text{if } x_2 < y_2^0 \\ \text{do not order,} & \text{if } x_2 \geq y_2^0. \end{cases}$$

The cost of this optimum policy can be expressed as

$$C_2(x_2) = \begin{cases} L(x_2), & \text{if } x_2 \geq y_2^0 \\ c(y_2^0 - x_2) + L(y_2^0), & \text{if } x_2 < y_2^0, \end{cases}$$

where y_2^0 is the single critical number just determined, and $L(z)$ is the expected shortage plus holding cost for a single period when there are z units available. $L(z)$ can be expressed as

$$L(z) = \int_z^\infty p(\xi - z)\varphi_D(\xi)\,d\xi + \int_0^z h(z - \xi)\varphi_D(\xi)\,d\xi.$$

At the beginning of period 1, the costs incurred consist of the purchase cost $c(y_1 - x_1)$, the expected shortage plus holding cost $L(y_1)$, and the costs associated with following an optimal policy during the second period. Thus the expected cost of following the optimal policy for two periods is given by

$$C_1(x_1) = \underset{y_1 \geq x_1}{\text{minimum}} \{c(y_1 - x_1) + L(y_1) + E[C_2(x_2)]\},$$

where $E[C_2(x_2)]$ is obtained as follows: Note that x_2 is a random variable that depends upon the amount of stock on hand at the beginning of period 2; that is, $x_2 = y_1 - D_1$. Thus

$$C_2(x_2) = C_2(y_1 - D_1) = \begin{cases} L(y_1 - D_1), & \text{if } y_1 - D_1 \geq y_2^0 \\ c(y_2^0 - y_1 + D_1) + L(y_2^0), & \text{if } y_1 - D_1 < y_2^0. \end{cases}$$

Hence $C_2(x_2)$ is a random variable, and its expected value is given by

$$E[C_2(x_2)] = \int_0^\infty C_2(y_1 - \xi)\varphi_D(\xi)\,d\xi = \int_0^{y_1 - y_2^0} L(y_1 - \xi)\varphi_D(\xi)\,d\xi$$

$$+ \int_{y_1 - y_2^0}^\infty [c(y_2^0 - y_1 + \xi) + L(y_2^0)]\varphi_D(\xi)\,d\xi.$$

Note that because shortages are permitted, $(y_1 - \xi)$ can be negative; further note that $E[C_2(x_2)]$ is just a function of y_1 and y_2^0, with y_2^0 obtained from the solution to the single-period problem. Thus $C_1(x_1)$ can now be expressed as

$$C_1(x_1) = \underset{y_1 \geq x_1}{\text{minimum}} \left\{ c(y_1 - x_1) + L(y_1) + \int_0^{y_1 - y_2^0} L(y_1 - \xi)\varphi_D(\xi)\,d\xi \right.$$

$$\left. + \int_{y_1 - y_2^0}^\infty [c(y_2^0 - y_1 + \xi) + L(y_2^0)]\varphi_D(\xi)\,d\xi \right\}.$$

It can easily be shown that $C_1(x_1)$ has a unique minimum so that the optimal value of y_1, denoted by y_1^0, satisfies the equation

$$-p + (p + h)\Phi(y_1^0) + (c - p)\Phi(y_1^0 - y_2^0)$$

$$+ (p + h)\int_0^{y_1^0 - y_2^0} \Phi(y_1^0 - \xi)\varphi_D(\xi)\,d\xi = 0,$$

where $\Phi(a)$ denotes the cumulative distribution function; that is,

$$\Phi(a) = \int_0^a \varphi_D(\xi)\,d\xi.$$

If the density function of demand is uniform over the range 0 to t, i.e.,

$$\varphi_D(\xi) = \begin{cases} 1/t, & \text{if } 0 \leq \xi \leq t \\ 0, & \text{otherwise}, \end{cases}$$

then y_1^0 can be obtained from the expression

$$y_1^0 = \sqrt{(y_2^0)^2 + \left[\frac{2t(c - p)}{p + h}\right]y_2^0 + \frac{t^2[2p(p + h) + (h + c)^2]}{(p + h)^2}} - \frac{t(h + c)}{p + h}.$$

Finally, if the density function of demand is exponential, that is

$$\varphi_D(\xi) = \frac{1}{\lambda}e^{-\xi/\lambda}, \quad \text{for } \xi > 0,$$

the optimal value of y_1^0 satisfies the relationship

$$(h + c)e^{-(y_1^0 - y_2^0)/\lambda} + (p + h)e^{-y_1^0/\lambda} + \frac{(p + h)(y_1^0 - y_2^0)}{\lambda}e^{-y_1^0/\lambda} = 2h + c.$$

An alternative way of finding y_1^0 is to let z_0 denote $(y_1^0 - y_2^0)/\lambda$. Then z_0 satisfies the relationship

$$e^{-z^0}[(h + c) + (p + h)e^{-y_2^0/\lambda} + z^0(p + h)e^{-y_2^0/\lambda}] = 2h + c,$$

and

$$y_1^0 = \lambda z_0 + y_2^0.$$

EXAMPLE Consider the following example: The cost of producing an item is $10 per item ($c = 10$). If any excess inventory remains at the end of a period, it is charged at $10 per item ($h = 10$); if no excess appears, there is no holding charge. If a shortage occurs within a period, there is a penalty cost of $15 per item ($p = 15$). The density function of demand is given by

$$\varphi_D(\xi) = \begin{cases} \dfrac{1}{10}, & \text{if } 0 \le \xi \le 10 \\ 0, & \text{otherwise.} \end{cases}$$

It is necessary to find the optimum two-period policy. For linear costs, the equation for the optimal single-period model becomes

$$\Phi(y_2^0) = \frac{p - c}{p + h} = \frac{15 - 10}{15 + 10} = \frac{1}{5}.$$

Hence, because $\Phi(y_2^0) = y_2^0/10$,

$$y_2^0 = 2.$$

Because the distribution of demand is uniform (with parameter $t = 10$), the optimal value of y_1^0 is found from

$$y_1^0 = \sqrt{(2)^2 + \left[\frac{2(10)(10 - 15)}{(15 + 10)}\right]2 + (10)^2\left[\frac{2(15)(15 + 10) + (10 + 10)^2}{(15 + 10)^2}\right]}$$

$$- \frac{10(10 + 10)}{15 + 10}$$

$$= \sqrt{4 - 8 + 184} - 8 = 13.42 - 8 = 5.42.$$

Substituting $y_1^0 = 5$ and $y_1^0 = 6$ into $C_1(x_1)$ leads to a smaller value, with $y_1^0 = 5$. Thus the optimal policy can be described as follows: If the initial amount of stock on hand does not exceed 5, order up to 5 units (order $5 - x_1$ units). Otherwise, do not order. After a period has elapsed, and at the beginning of the last period, if the amount on hand does not exceed 2 units, order up to 2 units (order $2 - x_2$ units, where x_2 may be negative).

This two-period model has been solved by using the same penalty shortage cost for each of the two periods, even though unsatisfied demand is backlogged at the end of the first period and lost at the end of the second period. This is a deficiency of the model as presented, but it can be remedied by using different penalty shortage costs in each period. The computational procedure of the modified model is similar, and no additional difficulties are added.

MULTIPERIOD MODELS—AN OVERVIEW

The two-period model can be extended to several periods or to an infinite number of periods. This section presents a summary of multiperiod results that have practical importance.

MULTIPERIOD MODEL—NO SETUP COST This model is an extension of the two-period problem. Suppose there exists a horizon of n periods, for which we need to determine the optimal inventory policy. As before, assume that production leads to immediate delivery; shortages are to be backlogged except at the final period when they are lost; no disposal of stock is permitted. Furthermore, the demands for the n periods are independent, identically distributed random variables having density $\varphi_D(\xi)$. The purchase cost is linear, that is, cz, where z is the amount ordered (no setup cost), and the expected (one-period) shortage plus holding penalty cost $L(y)$ is strictly convex [which is the case if each cost is linear and $\varphi_D(\xi) > 0$]. A cost discounting factor is included; it is denoted by α; $0 < \alpha < 1$.

Again the time periods are ordered so that the beginning of time period 1 implies that there are n periods left in the horizon. Similarly, the beginning of time period n implies there is one period left in the horizon (the last period is beginning). The problem is to find critical numbers that describe the optimal ordering policy. As in the two-period model, the numbers $y_1^0, y_2^0, \ldots, y_n^0$ are difficult to obtain numerically, but it can be shown that the optimal policy has the form

At the beginning of period i, $i = 1, 2, \ldots, n$

$$\begin{cases} \text{order up to } y_i^0 \ (order \ y_i^0 - x_i), & \text{if } x_i < y_i^0 \\ \text{do not order}, & \text{if } x_i \geq y_i^0. \end{cases}$$

Furthermore,

$$y_n^0 \leq y_{n-1}^0 \leq \cdots \leq y_2^0 \leq y_1^0.$$

For the infinite-period model (where the inventory decisions are made indefinitely), there exists a single critical period number, y^0, so that the optimal policy now has the form

At the beginning of period i, $i = 1, 2, \ldots$

$$\begin{cases} \text{order up to } y^0 \ (order \ y^0 - x_i), & \text{if } x_i < y^0 \\ \text{do not order}, & \text{if } x_i \geq y^0. \end{cases}$$

Furthermore, y^0 is easily obtained because y^0 is the value of y that satisfies the expression

$$\frac{dL(y)}{dy} + c(1 - \alpha) = 0.$$

For the case of linear shortage and holding costs, unit costs of p and h respectively, y^0 simply satisfies

$$\Phi(y^0) = \frac{p - c(1 - \alpha)}{p + h}.$$

A VARIATION OF THE MULTIPERIOD INVENTORY MODEL—NO SETUP COST A slight modification of the aforementioned model leads to some simple, but interesting, results.[1] Consider the n-period model, but now assume that stock left over at the end of the final period can be salvaged with a return of the initial purchase cost c. Similarly, if there is a shortage at this time, the items are supplied also at the purchase price c. These two changes may lead to more realism in the model, but, what is equally important, they lead to rather simple optimal policies. In particular, the same single critical number y^0 is used for *all* periods, and, furthermore, the optimal policy is the same as that just presented in the infinite-period model; i.e.,

At the beginning of period i, i = 1, 2, ..., n

$$\begin{cases} order\ up\ to\ y^0\ (order\ y^0 - x_i), & x_i < y^0 \\ do\ not\ order, & x_i \geq y^0, \end{cases}$$

where y^0 satisfies the expression

$$\frac{dL(y)}{dy} + c(1 - \alpha) = 0.$$

Of course, this same result also holds for the infinite-period model. For the case of linear shortage and holding costs, unit costs of p and h, respectively, y^0 simply satisfies

$$\Phi(y^0) = \frac{p - c(1 - \alpha)}{p + h}.$$

EXAMPLE OF A MULTIPERIOD MODEL Example 2, Sec. 18.1, concerned the western distributor of bicycles who is having trouble with shortages of the most popular 10-speed model. The unit shortage cost p was estimated to be \$15. The holding cost h was determined to be \$1 per bicycle remaining at the end of the month. The actual cost of a bicycle is \$35. Orders may be placed on the first working day of each month. The distributor always places an order for some model bicycles each

[1] This formulation is due to A. F. Veinott, Jr., "The Optimal Inventory Policy for Batch Orderings," *Operations Research*, **13**(3):424–432, 1965.

month, so that he is willing to assume that the marginal setup cost is zero for this most popular model. The discount factor may be assumed to be $\alpha = 0.995$. From past history, the distribution of demand can be approximated by a uniform distribution given by

$$\varphi_D(\xi) = \begin{cases} \dfrac{1}{800}, & \text{if } 0 \le \xi \le 800 \\ 0, & \text{otherwise.} \end{cases}$$

The distributor expects to stock this model indefinitely, so that the infinite-period model is appropriate.

Because the shortage and holding costs are linear, y^0 satisfies

$$\Phi(y^0) = \frac{p - c(1 - \alpha)}{p + h}.$$

Because the demand distribution is uniform

$$\Phi(y^0) = y^0/800,$$

and

$$\frac{p - c(1 - \alpha)}{p + h} = \frac{15 - 35(1 - 0.995)}{15 + 1} = 0.927,$$

so that $y_0 = 741$. Thus, if the number of bicycles on hand, x, at the first of each month is fewer than 741, the optimal policy calls for ordering up to 741 (ordering $741 - x$ bicycles). Otherwise, no order is placed. Note that if this policy is to be in effect for only a finite number of months, say, 24, and if (1) bicycles remaining in stock after 24 months can be salvaged at $35 per bicycle and (2) unsatisfied demand remaining at the end of 24 months can be supplied to the western distributor from, say, the eastern distributor, at $35 per bicycle, then the policy of ordering up to 741 bicycles each month is still optimal.

MULTIPERIOD MODEL WITH SETUP COST The introduction of a fixed setup cost K that is incurred when ordering often adds more realism to the model. Unfortunately, however, the mathematics becomes very cumbersome, and the results available are primarily those that characterize the form of the optimal policy. In particular, if the ordering cost is assumed to be $K + cz$ for $z > 0$ and zero for $z = 0$, and if $L(y)$ is strictly convex, then the optimal policy has the form

At the beginning of period i, $i = 1, 2, \ldots, n$

$$\begin{cases} \textit{order up to } S_i \textit{ (order } S_i - x_i\text{)}, & \textit{if } x_i < s_i \\ \textit{do not order}, & \textit{if } x_i \ge s_i. \end{cases}$$

This policy is the familiar (s, S) policy alluded to earlier in the discussion of one-period models. As previously mentioned, unfortunately exact computations of s_i and S_i for the finite- or infinite-horizon model are extremely difficult. However, the importance of this result cannot be minimized. Even if the exact s_i

and S_i are unknown, it is important to know that one should consider using policies of this form rather than a policy from another class.

(k,Q) POLICIES FOR A MULTIPERIOD MODEL WITHOUT SETUP COST In the discussion of the previous models, any quantity could be ordered at the time of inventory review. Suppose that an additional constraint is placed on the ordering policy; i.e., each order for stock must be some nonnegative integral multiple of Q, a fixed positive constraint.

As before, the demands for the n periods are assumed to be independent, identically distributed random variables having density $\varphi_D(\xi)$. The purchase cost is linear, and the expected (one-period) shortage plus holding penalty cost $L(y)$ is strictly convex. α is the cost discounting factor, $0 < \alpha < 1$. At the beginning of each period the system is reviewed. An order may be placed for any nonnegative integral multiple of Q, a fixed positive number. Thus orders must be placed in multiples of some standard batch size, e.g., a case or a truckload. When the demand exceeds the inventory on hand, the excess demand is backlogged until it is subsequently filled by a delivery. In addition, it is assumed that stock left over at the end of the final period n can be salvaged with a return of the initial purchase cost c. Similarly, if there is a shortage at this time, the items are backlogged also at the purchase price c. This model was introduced by Veinott, Jr.[1] He shows that a (k,Q) policy is optimal. A (k,Q) policy is described as follows:

> If at the beginning of a period the stock on hand is less than k, an order should be placed for the smallest multiple of Q that will bring the stock level to at least k (and probably higher); otherwise, an order should not be placed. The same parameter k is used in each period.

The parameter k is chosen as follows: Let y^0 be the minimizer of $G(y) = (1 - \alpha)cy + L(y)$. $G(y)$ must be of the shape (convex) shown in Fig. 18.9. Then k is any number for which $k \le y^0 \le k + Q$ and $G(k) = G(k + Q)$. Refer to Fig. 18.9. If a "ruler" of length Q is placed horizontally into the "valley," k is found to be that value of the abscissa to the left of y^0 where the ruler intersects the valley. Note that if the initial inventory on hand lies in R_1, then Q is ordered; if it lies in R_2, then $2Q$ is ordered; and so on.

It should be noted that the same value of parameter k is used for each period of a finite-horizon model as well as for the infinite-horizon model. In the latter situation, this policy is the same optimal policy that would have been obtained if salvage costs and backlogging *at the last period* were omitted.

CONTINUOUS REVIEW MODEL WITH FIXED DELIVERY LAG In Section 18.3, a deterministic continuous review model, i.e., the economic lot-size model, was considered. The demand was assumed to be continuous, and required at a known constant rate. This model was classified as *continuous review* in that the inventory was continuously monitored, and orders were placed at any time, i.e., orders were

[1] This formulation is due to A. F. Veinott, Jr., "The Optimal Inventory Policy for Batch Orderings," *Operations Research*, **13**(3):424–432, 1965.

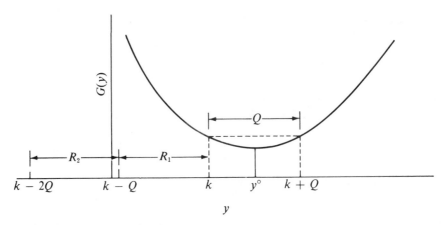

Figure 18.9 **Plot of the $G(y)$ function.**

placed whenever the inventory level reached the order point (or the trigger point). This ordering procedure is in contrast to the models considered in this section that assume stochastic demand and periodic review; i.e., the inventory is monitored at certain times, and orders are placed at only these times. The model considered now is analogous to the economic lot-size model (continuous review), but where the demand for the item is stochastic. Only (s,S) type policies[1] are considered, i.e., when the inventory falls to a level s, an order is placed to bring the inventory up to S (a quantity $Q = S - s$ is ordered). This model is often called a lot-size–reorder-point model; a quantity Q is ordered whenever the inventory level reaches the reorder level s.

The model can be described as follows. Inventory is stockpiled and used as demand dictates. When the stockpiled inventory level reaches s, an order is placed for Q units to bring the inventory position (the amount on hand plus the amount ordered less the backorders[2]) up to level S. There is a fixed delivery lead time of length λ before the order is received, and the demand for items from inventory during the time λ is assumed to be a continuous random variable, D, having probability density function denoted by $\varphi_D(\xi)$. The mean demand is assumed equal to $a\lambda$; i.e.,

$$E(D) = a\lambda,$$

where a is the number of items demanded per unit of time.

Figure 18.10 illustrates how the inventory level varies over time. Note that this diagram can be viewed as a series of cycles, with a cycle beginning when the order is received and ending just before the ensuing order is received. Note that if the demand during the period λ is large, it is possible to have a negative inventory

---

[1] Under *Remark 3* after the economic lot-size model, it was pointed out that these models can be viewed as a special case of an (s,S) policy.

[2] When demand is unsatisfied, it is assumed that it will be filled when the inventory is replenished, although a penalty cost will be incurred.

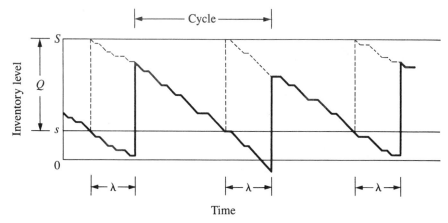

Figure 18.10 **Diagram of inventory level as a function of time.**

level. It is assumed that this unsatisfied demand will be backlogged. In Figure 18.10, the inventory position is represented by the dotted lines during the period of the delivery lead time, and by the solid lines at other times.

The costs to be considered are the ordering cost K, the cost of the units ordered, cQ (both charged at the time of the ordering), an inventory holding cost of h dollars per item per unit of time, and a shortage cost of p dollars for each unit of demand unfilled. The inventory policy is to track the inventory position so that when the inventory position reaches s, an order of size Q is placed; this order will be delivered after a period of length λ. The problem, then, is to determine when to place an order (find the order point or trigger point, s) and to determine what size it should be (find the order quantity, Q), so that the expected total cost per unit time is a minimum.

The expected total cost per unit time ($C(Q,s)$) consists of the sum of the following three components: the expected ordering costs per unit time ($E(OC)$), the expected holding cost per unit of time ($E(HC)$), and the expected shortage cost per unit of time ($E(SC)$); i.e.,

$$C(Q,s) = E(OC) + E(HC) + E(SC).$$

In order to evaluate the terms of this expression, we assume that there is never more than a single order outstanding and that the reorder point, s (based on the inventory position), is always nonnegative. The first assumption guarantees that the inventory on hand when an order is received will always fall above the reorder point because, otherwise, more than one order would be outstanding. If p/h is sufficiently large, as is usually the case in practice, these assumptions are generally satisfied.[1]

The expected ordering cost per unit time, $E(OC)$, is simply the ordering cost incurred per cycle times the expected number of cycles per unit of time. The

[1] The development that follows for the expression for the expected total cost per unit time is presented in a heuristic manner.

ordering cost incurred per cycle is

$$k + cQ.$$

In order to find the expected number of cycles per unit of time, assume that the unit of time is, say, a year. A cycle begins when an order is received and ends just before the ensuing order is received. Suppose that Q is 500 units, the lag in delivery time is 1 month (1/12 years), and the expected demand in 1 month is 100 units. These suppositions imply that $a = 1200$ or that the expected rate of demand is 1,200 units per year. It is evident that the expected time to deplete 500 units of inventory is 5/12 years (500/1,200). Therefore, the expected cycle length is equal to 5/12 years, so that in 1 year the expected number of cycles is $12/5 = 2.4$. In general, the expected number of cycles per unit time is given by a/Q. The expression for the expected ordering cost, $E(OC)$, is then given by

$$E(OC) = \left(\frac{a}{Q}\right)(K + cQ).$$

The expected holding cost per unit time is equal to the inventory holding cost per item per unit time, h, times the average inventory held over the unit of time. Assuming that a typical cycle is representative of the inventory holdings over the entire unit of time, the expected inventory held over a cycle will be obtained. From Figure 18.10, the inventory level at the beginning of the cycle is given by $S - a\lambda$, and the inventory level at the end of the cycle is $s - a\lambda$ (assuming the number of stockouts (negative inventory) can be neglected). Hence the expected holding cost per cycle (and, therefore, per unit of time) is given by

$$h[(S - a\lambda) + (s - a\lambda)]/2 = h[Q + s - a\lambda + s - a\lambda]/2 = h[Q/2 + s - a\lambda],$$

so that

$$E(HC) = h\left(\frac{Q}{2} + s - a\lambda\right).$$

The expected shortage cost per unit time, $E(SC)$, is simply the expected shortage cost incurred per cycle times the expected number of cycles per unit time (already obtained as a/Q). The expected shortage cost per cycle is just p times the expected number of shortages that occur during the lag period λ (because no shortages can occur until the inventory level reaches s); i.e.,

$$p \int_s^\infty (\xi - s)\varphi_D(\xi)\,d\xi,$$

$$E(PC) = \left[\left(\frac{a}{Q}\right)\left(p \int_s^\infty (\xi - s)\varphi_D(\xi)\,d\xi\right)\right].$$

Adding the expressions for $E(OC)$, $E(HC)$, and $E(PC)$ leads to

$$C(Q,s) = aK/Q + ac + h[(Q/2) + s - a\lambda] + (pa/Q)\int_s^\infty (\xi - s)\varphi_D(\xi)\,d\xi.$$

Because there are two decision variables (Q and s), the optimum values (Q^* and s^*) are found by minimizing $C(Q,s)$ with respect to the variables Q and s, i.e., setting the partial derivatives $\partial C(Q,s)/\partial Q$ and $\partial C(Q,s)/\partial s$ equal to zero. Thus

$$\frac{\partial C(Q,s)}{\partial Q} = \frac{-aK}{Q^2} + \frac{h}{2} - \frac{pa\left[\int_s^\infty (\xi - s)\varphi_D(\xi)\,d\xi\right]}{Q^2} = 0.$$

$$\frac{\partial C(Q,s)}{\partial s} = h - \frac{pa\left[\int_s^\infty \varphi_D(\xi)\,d\xi\right]}{Q}$$

Solving these equations simultaneously[1] leads to

(1)
$$Q^* = \sqrt{\frac{\left\{2a\left[K + p\int_{s^*}^\infty (\xi - s^*)\varphi_D(\xi)\,d\xi\right]\right\}}{h}},$$

(2)
$$\int_{s^*}^\infty \varphi_D(\xi)\,d\xi = \frac{hQ^*}{pa}.$$

Unfortunately, solving these equations simultaneously and obtaining a general closed form expression for Q^* and s^* is not possible, so an iterative procedure is desirable. Such a procedure is as follows:

1. As an initial step, assume that p equals zero and obtain a value of Q from equation (1). Note that this equation is just the expression for Q in the deterministic economic lot-size model when shortages are not permitted.
2. Solve for s in equation (2) using the value of Q found in step 1.
3. Using the value of s found in step 2, solve for a new Q using equation (1).
4. Repeat steps 2 and 3 until successive values of Q and s are sufficiently close.

In practice, this procedure will generally converge in just a few iterations.

Because there is no closed form solution, it is worth considering some special cases of distribution of demand. If the density function of demand is uniform over the range from 0 to t, i.e.,

$$\varphi_D(\xi) = \begin{cases} \dfrac{1}{t}, & \text{if } 0 \le \xi \le t \\[2mm] 0, & \text{otherwise,} \end{cases}$$

---

[1] Note that the optimum values of Q and s are independent of c, the unit cost of the items ordered. A little reflection indicates the total number of units ordered is independent of the values of Q and s, and, therefore, can be neglected in determining the optimum values of these parameters.

then equation (2) leads to

$$\int_s^\infty \varphi_D(\xi)\,d\xi = 1 - \frac{s}{t},$$

so that

$$s^* = \frac{t(pa - hQ^*)}{pa} = t\left(1 - \frac{hQ^*}{pa}\right).$$

Furthermore, from equation (1),

$$\int_s^\infty (\xi - s)\varphi_D(\xi)\,d\xi = \frac{t}{2} + \frac{s^2}{2t} - s$$

and

$$Q^* = \sqrt{\frac{(2aK + apt + aps^2/t - 2aps^*)}{h}}.$$

Finally, if the density function of demand is exponential, i.e.,

$$\varphi_D(\xi) = \left(\frac{1}{a\lambda}\right)e^{-\xi/a\lambda}, \quad \text{for } \xi > 0$$

then equation (2) leads to

$$\int_s^\infty \varphi_D(\xi)\,d\xi = e^{-s/a\lambda},$$

so that

$$s^* = -a\lambda \ln\left(\frac{hQ^*}{pa}\right).$$

Furthermore, from equation (1),

$$\int_s^\infty (\xi - s)\varphi_D(\xi)\,d\xi = a\lambda e^{-s/a\lambda},$$

and

$$Q^* = \sqrt{\frac{[2aK + 2a^2\lambda pe^{-s^*/a\lambda}]}{h}} = \sqrt{\left[\frac{2a}{h}\right](K + a\lambda pe^{-s^*/a\lambda})}.$$

EXAMPLE Consider the speaker example presented in Sec. 18.1. It was assumed that $K = 12{,}000$, $h = 0.30$ per speaker per month, and $a = 8{,}000$ per month. In this example, the demand was assumed to be fixed at the rate of 8,000 speakers per month. Now we assume that the demand is random and has a uniform density over the range from 0 to 16,000, with the unit of time considered to be 1 month and the delivery lead time also 1 month. Note that the expected demand is 8,000 speakers, so that a is again 8,000 and λ is 1. The penalty for unsatisfied demand will be $5 per speaker. Using the results just obtained for this distribution, with the iterative procedure step 1 leads to (setting p equal to 0)

$$Q = \sqrt{\frac{2(8,000)(12,000)}{0.30}} = 25,298.$$

Using this value of Q, solve for s; i.e.,

$$s = 16,000\left[1 - \frac{(0.30)(25,298)}{(5)(8,000)}\right] = 12,964.$$

Using this value of s, solve for Q; i.e.,

$$Q = \sqrt{\frac{(8,000)\left[2(12,000) + (5)(16,000) + \dfrac{5(12,964)^2}{16,000} - 2(5)(12,964)\right]}{0.30}}$$
$$= 26,773.$$

Using this value of Q, solve for s; i.e.,

$$s = 16,000\left[1 - \frac{(0.30)(26,773)}{(5)(8,000)}\right] = 12,787.$$

Three more iterations lead to $(Q = 26,945,\ s = 12,767)$, $(Q = 26,965,\ s = 12,764)$, and finally, to $(Q^* = 26,968,\ s^* = 12,764)$.

Consider this same example, but now assume that the distribution of demand is exponential with mean 8,000. Step 1 in the iterative procedure again leads to $Q = 25,298$. Using this value of Q, solve for s; i.e.,

$$s = -8,000\ln\frac{(0.30)(25,298)}{(5)(8,000)} = 13,297.$$

Using this value of s, solve for Q; i.e.,

$$Q = \sqrt{\frac{2(8,000)}{(0.30)}[12,000 + (8,000)(5)e^{-(13,297)/8,000}]} = 32,323.$$

Several further iterations lead to the final solution of $(Q^* = 34,532, s^* = 10,808)$.

MULTIPRODUCT INVENTORY MODELS The previous sections dealt with inventory systems for single-product models, but most real inventory systems involve many products with various types of interactions, such as joint storage and budget limitations and product substitutability. One important reason for studying single-product models first is that they provide insight into solving multiproduct problems, and, furthermore, it is often possible to "factor" an N-product problem into N one-product problems without loss of optimality. (This factoring can be done if the demand and cost for each product can be treated independently of the other products.) There has been some work on multiproduct models in which such factorization is not possible. In these models, stocks of a single product at different locations or echelons of a supply system can also be conveniently viewed as stocks of different products.[1] A multiproduct model proposed by A. F. Veinott, Jr.[2] is a direct analog of the single-product multiperiod inventory model with no setup cost as presented earlier. This multiproduct model considers N products and m different classes of demands for these products. The demand classes in a period may be classified by such characteristics as time of occurrence, essentiality, products desired, and acceptable substitutes. Under the usual restrictions on the form of the costs, the optimal policy is a single critical number policy for each product; i.e., if x_{ik} is the amount on hand of product k at period i, order up to y_{ik} if $x_{ik} < y_{ik}$; otherwise, do not order (assuming initially that $x_{1k} \leq y_{1k}$ for all k).

This model has many useful applications. For example, suppose there are two products, with product 1 serving as a substitute for product 2, and all unsatisfied demands are lost. If we choose for this model a stocking policy that supplies unsatisfied demand for product 2 with excess stock from product 1 (if available), we can obtain the optimal critical numbers. This example can be interpreted as a two-echelon inventory model with demands for a single product that cannot be satisfied at echelon 2 being transmitted up to echelon 1.

A second application concerns two products that serve as substitutes for each other. Again, all unsatisfied demands are assumed to be lost. The stocking policy supplies the unsatisfied demand for one product with the excess stock from the other (if available). This example can be interpreted as a two-location inventory model with an end-of-period redistribution of excess stock (if any) at one location to satisfy a shortage (if one exists) at the other location.

A different variation of the two-product inventory models was presented by D. Iglehart.[3] Inventories of product 2 are maintained to provide capability for production of product 1. For example, if product 1 is a car, product 2 might be machinery or labor. An optimal policy describes the amount of product 1 and product 2 that must be produced in period i to minimize the total cost, subject to certain constraints.

18.5 Conclusions

The inventory models presented here are rather simplified, but they serve the purpose of introducing the general nature of inventory models. Furthermore, they are sufficiently accurate representations of many actual inventory situations so that they frequently are useful in practice. For example, the economic lot-size formulas have been particularly widely used, although they are sometimes modified to include some type of stochastic demand. The multiperiod models with stochastic demand have been important in characterizing the types of

[1] An excellent summary is given in a paper by A. F. Veinott, Jr., "The Status of Mathematical Inventory Theory," *Management Science*, **12**(11): 745–777, 1966.

[2] A. F. Veinott, Jr., "Optimal Policy for a Multi-Product, Dynamic Non-Stationary Inventory Problem," *Management Science*, **12**(3): 206–222, 1965.

[3] D. Iglehart, "Capital Accumulation and Production for the Firm: Optimal Dynamic Policies," *Management Science*, **12**(3): 193–205, 1965.

policies to follow, for example, (s,S) policies, even though the optimal values of s and S are difficult to obtain. Nevertheless, many inventory situations possess complications that must still be taken into account, e.g., interaction between products. Several complex models have been formulated in an attempt to fit such situations, but they still leave a wide gap between practice and theory. Continued growth is occurring in the computerization of inventory data processing, along with accompanying growth in scientific inventory management.

SELECTED REFERENCES

1. Arrow, K.J., S. Karlin, and H. Scarf: *Studies in the Mathematical Theory of Inventory and Production*, Stanford Univ. Press. Stanford, Calif., 1958.
2. Brown, R. G.: *Decision Rules for Inventory Management*, Holt, Rinehart and Winston, New York, 1967.
3. Buchan, J., and E. Koenigsberg: *Scientific Inventory Management*, Prentice-Hall, Englewood Cliffs, N.J., 1963.
4. Buffa, E. S.: *Modern Production/Operations Management*, 6th ed. Wiley, New York, 1980.
5. Buffa, E. S., and J. G. Miller: *Production-Inventory Systems: Planning and Control*, 3d ed., Richard D. Irwin, Inc., Homewood, Ill., 1979.
6. Hadley, G., and T. Whitin: *Analysis of Inventory Systems*, Prentice-Hall, Englewood Cliffs, N.J., 1963.
7. Johnson, L. A., and D. C. Montgomery: *Operations Research in Production Planning, Scheduling and Inventory Control*, Wiley, New York, 1974.
8. Peterson, R., and E. A. Silver: *Decision Systems for Inventory Management and Production Planning*, Wiley, New York, 1979.
9. Starr, M., and D. Miller: *Inventory Control: Theory and Practice*, Prentice-Hall, Englewood Cliffs, N.J., 1962.
10. Veinott, A. F., Jr.: "The Status of Mathematical Inventory Theory," *Management Science*, **12**(11): 745–777, 1966.

PROBLEMS

1. Suppose that the demand for a product is 30 units per month, and the items are withdrawn uniformly. The setup cost each time a production run is made is $15. The production cost is $1 per item, and the inventory holding cost is $0.30 per item per month.

(a) Assuming shortages are not allowed, determine how often to make a production run and what size it should be.

(b) If shortages cost $3.00 per item per month, determine how often to make a production run and what size it should be.

2. The demand for a product is 650 units per week, and the items are withdrawn uniformly. The items are ordered, and the setup cost is $25. The unit cost of each item is $3, and the inventory holding cost is $0.05 per item per week.

(a) Assuming shortages are not allowed, determine how often to order and what size the order should be.

(b) If shortages cost $2 per item per week, determine how often to order and what size the order should be.

3. Solve Prob. 2 with shortages permitted and assume a delivery lag of 1 week.

4. Solve the economic lot-size model problem presented in Sec. 18.3 when shortages are permitted but when the cost is $5.00 per speaker.

5. A taxi company uses gasoline at the rate of 8,500 gallons/month. The gasoline costs $1.10/gallon, with a setup cost of $1,000. The inventory holding cost is 1 cent/gallon/month.

(*a*) Assuming shortages are not allowed, determine how often and how much to order.

(*b*) If shortages cost 50 cents/gallon/month, determine how often and how much to order.

6. Solve Prob. 5*a* by assuming that the cost of gasoline drops to $1.00/gallon if at least 50,000 gallons are purchased.

7. Solve Prob. 5*a* if the cost of gasoline is $1.20/gallon for the first 20,000 gallons purchased, $1.10 for the next 20,000 gallons, and $1.05/gallon thereafter.

8. Suppose the requirement for the next 5 months is given by $r_1 = 2$, $r_2 = 4$, $r_3 = 2$, $r_4 = 2$, and $r_5 = 4$. Items are ordered; the setup cost is $4, the purchase cost is $1, and the holding cost is $0.30. Determine the optimal production schedule, that satisfies the monthly requirements. Use dynamic programming.

9. Solve Prob. 8 by assuming that the production costs are given by $3 (1 + \log_e X)$, where X is the amount produced in a month.

10. Solve Prob. 8 by using the algorithm presented in Sec. 18.3.

11. Solve Prob. 9 by using the algorithm presented in Sec. 18.3.

12. Formulate Prob. 8 as an integer programming problem.

13. Solve the production planning model for the production of speakers when the requirements are increased by 1 unit in each period.

14. Solve the production planning model for the production of speakers when the unit costs during the first and third periods are increased to $1.50. Use dynamic programming.

15. Develop an algorithm to solve the production planning model that uses forward induction. (*Hint:* If an optimal policy is being followed and if the time of the *last* production is known for this optimal policy, the total cost of the previous periods must be a minimum for this reduced problem because the overall policy is optimal.)

16. Consider a situation where a particular product is produced and placed in-process inventory until it is needed in a subsequent production process. The number of units required in each of the next 3 months, as well as the setup cost and the regular-time unit production cost that would be incurred in each month, are

Month	Requirements	Setup cost ($)	Regular time unit cost ($)
1	1	5	8
2	3	10	10
3	2	5	9

There currently is 1 unit in inventory, and we want to have 2 units in inventory at the end of the 3 months. A maximum of 3 units can be produced on regular-time production in each month, although one additional unit can be produced on overtime at a cost that is $2 larger than the regular-time unit production cost. The cost of storage is $2 per unit for each extra month that it is stored.

Use dynamic programming to determine how many units should be produced in each month to minimize total cost.

17. A newspaper stand purchases newspapers for 20 cents and sells them for 25 cents. The shortage cost is 25 cents per newspaper (because the dealer buys papers at retail price to satisfy shortages). The holding cost is 0.1 cent. The demand distribution is a uniform distribution between 200 and 300. Find the optimal number of papers to buy.

18. Suppose the demand D for a spare airplane part has an exponential distribution with parameter $\frac{1}{50}$; that is,

$$\varphi_D(\xi) = \begin{cases} \dfrac{1}{50} e^{-\xi/50}, & \xi \geq 0 \\ 0, & \text{otherwise.} \end{cases}$$

This airplane will be obsolete in 1 year, hence all production is to take place at the present time. The production costs now are $1,000 per item—that is, $c = 1,000$—but they become $10,000 per item if they must be supplied at later dates—that is, $p = 10,000$. The holding costs, charged on the excess after the end of the period, are $300 per item. Determine the required number of spare parts.

19. A bread manufacturer distributes bread to grocery stores daily. The cost of the bread is 40 cents per loaf. The company sells the bread to the stores for 60 cents per loaf sold provided that it is disposed of as fresh bread (sold on the day it is baked). Bread not sold is returned to the company. The company has a store outlet that sells bread that is a day or more old for 30 cents per loaf. This salvage cost represents the holding cost. The unsatisfied demand cost is estimated to be 40 cents per loaf. If the demand has a uniform distribution between 1,000 and 2,000 loaves, find the optimal daily number of loaves that the manufacturer should produce.

20. A student majoring in operations research enjoys optimizing his personal decisions. He is analyzing one such decision currently, namely, how much money to take out of his savings account (if any) to buy travelers checks before leaving on a summer vacation trip to Europe.

He already has used the money he did have in his checking account to buy travelers checks worth $1,200, but this may not be enough. In fact, he has estimated the probability distribution of what he will need as shown in the following table:

Amount needed ($)	1,000	1,100	1,200	1,300	1,400	1,500	1,600	1,700
Probability	0.05	0.10	0.15	0.25	0.20	0.10	0.10	0.05

If he turns out to have less than he needs, then he would have to leave Europe 1 week early for every $100 short. Because he places a value of $150 on each week in Europe, each week lost would thereby represent a net imputed loss of $50 to him. However, every $100 travelers check costs an extra $1. Furthermore, *each* such check left over at the end of the trip (which would be redeposited in the savings account) represents a loss of $2 in interest that could have been earned in the savings account during the trip, so he does not want to purchase too many.

Using these data, determine the optimal decision on how many additional $100 travelers checks (if any) the student should purchase from his savings account money.

21.   Find the optimal ordering policy for a one-period model, where the demand has a probability density

$$\varphi_D(\xi) = \begin{cases} \dfrac{1}{20}, & \text{if } 0 \le \xi \le 20 \\ 0, & \text{otherwise,} \end{cases}$$

and the costs are

$$\text{Holding} = \$1 \text{ per item,}$$
$$\text{Shortage} = \$3 \text{ per item,}$$
$$\text{Setup} = \$1.50,$$
$$\text{Production} = \$2 \text{ per item.}$$

22.   Consider the following inventory model, which is a single-period model with known density of demand $\varphi_D(\xi) = e^{-\xi}$, for $\xi > 0$ and zero elsewhere. There are two costs connected with the model: The first is the purchase cost, given by $c \cdot (y - x)$; the second is the unsatisfied demand cost, which is just a constant, p (independent of the amount of unsatisfied demand).

(a)   If x units are available and goods are ordered up to y, write the expression for the expected loss, and describe completely the optimal policy.

(b)   If a fixed cost K is also incurred whenever an order is placed, describe the optimal policy.

23.   Using the approximation for finding the optimal policy for a single-period model when the density of demand has an exponential distribution, find this policy when

$$\varphi_D(\xi) = \begin{cases} \dfrac{1}{25} e^{-\xi/25}, & \text{if } \xi \ge 0 \\ 0, & \text{otherwise,} \end{cases}$$

and the costs are

$$\text{Holding} = 50 \text{ cents per item,}$$
$$\text{Shortage} = \$1.50 \text{ per item,}$$
$$\text{Purchase price} = \$1 \text{ per item,}$$
$$\text{Setup} = \$10.$$

24.   There are production processes for which the difference between the cost of producing the maximum number of units allowed by some capacity restriction and the cost of producing any number of units less than this maximum is negligible; i.e., ordering is by batches. Consider a one-stage model, where the only two costs are holding costs given by

$$h(y - D) = \left(\frac{3}{10}\right)(y - D),$$

and the penalty cost of unsatisfied demand given by

$$p(D - y) = 2.5(D - y).$$

The density function for demand is given by

$$\varphi_D(\xi) = \begin{cases} \dfrac{e^{-\xi/25}}{25}, & \text{for } \xi \geq 0 \\ 0, & \text{otherwise.} \end{cases}$$

If you order, you must order in batches of 100 units, and this quantity is delivered instantaneously. Thus, if x denotes the quantity on hand, and if you do not order, then $y = x$. If you order one batch, then $y = x + 100$. Let $G(y)$ denote the total expected cost of this inventory problem when there are y units available for the period (after you have ordered).

(a) Write the expression for $G(y)$.
(b) What is the optimal ordering policy?

25. Consider the following inventory situation. Demands are independent with common density given by the following:

$$\varphi_D(\xi) = \begin{cases} \dfrac{e^{-\xi/25}}{25}, & \text{for } \xi \geq 0 \\ 0, & \text{otherwise.} \end{cases}$$

Orders may be placed at the start of each period without setup cost at a price of $c = 10$. There are a holding cost of 7 per unit remaining in stock at the end of each period and a penalty cost of 15 per unit quantity backlogged.

(a) Find the optimal one-period policy.
(b) Find the optimal two-period policy.

26. Consider the following inventory situation. Demands are independent with common density $\varphi_D(\xi) = \frac{1}{50}$ $0 < \xi < 50$. Orders may be placed at the start of each period without setup cost at a price of $c = 10$. There are a holding cost of 7 per unit remaining in stock at the end of each period and a penalty cost of 15 per unit quantity backlogged.

(a) Find the optimal one-period policy.
(b) Find the optimal two-period policy.

27. Find the optimal inventory policy for the following two-period model by using a discount factor of $\alpha = 0.9$. Let the density of the demand D be given by

$$\varphi_D(\xi) = \begin{cases} \dfrac{1}{25}e^{-\xi/25}, & \text{if } \xi \geq 0 \\ 0, & \text{otherwise,} \end{cases}$$

and the costs are

$$\text{Holding} = 25 \text{ cents per item,}$$
$$\text{Shortage} = \$2.00 \text{ per item,}$$
$$\text{Purchase price} = \$1 \text{ per item.}$$

Stock left over at the end of the final period is salvaged for $1 per item, and shortages remaining at this time are also available at $1 per item.

28. Solve Prob. 27 for a two-period model assuming no salvage value, no backlogging at the end of the second period, and no discounting.

29. Solve Prob. 27 for an infinite-period model by using a discount factor of $\alpha = 0.90$.

30. Determine the optimum inventory policy when the goods are to be ordered at the end of every month from now on. The cost of ordering up to y when x is available is given by $2(y - x)$. Similarly, the cost of not satisfying a consumer demand of D is given by $5(D - y)$. The density function for the random variable, demand, is given by $\varphi_D(\xi) = e^{-\xi}$. The storage costs are given by $(y - D)$ and represent the expense of storing unsold stock. The losses at each succeeding stage are equivalent to a loss of 95 percent of that at the previous stage.

31. A supplier of high fidelity receiver kits is interested in using an optimal inventory policy. The distribution of demand per month is uniform between 2,000 and 3,000 kits. The cost of each kit is $150. The holding cost is estimated to be $3 per kit per month, and the unsatisfied demand cost is $30 per kit per month. Using a discount factor of $\alpha = 0.90$, find the optimal inventory policy for this "infinite" horizon problem.

32. The weekly demand for a certain type of electronic calculator is estimated to be given by

$$\varphi_D(\xi) = \begin{cases} \dfrac{1}{1,000} e^{-\xi/1,000}, & \xi \geq 0 \\ 0, & \text{otherwise.} \end{cases}$$

The cost of these calculators is $7.50. The holding cost is 7 cents per calculator per week. The unsatisfied demand cost is $2 per calculator per week. Using a discount factor of $\alpha = 0.95$, find the optimal inventory policy for this infinite-horizon problem.

33. Consider an infinite-period inventory model in which the demands are independent, identically distributed random variables. Denote the expected demand in a period by μ. Assume the cost of ordering z units $(z \geq 0)$ is $c \cdot z$ $(c > 0)$. Let α $(0 < \alpha < 1)$ be the discount factor. Assume that all unsatisfied demand is backlogged. Finally, suppose that when y is the inventory on hand after ordering but before the occurrence of a demand of size D in a period, a cost $(y - D)^2$ is incurred. When $y > D$, the cost is a charge for carrying the inventory; when $y < D$, the cost is a charge for backlogging demand. Describe the optimal ordering policy, and give simple formulas for its parameters in terms of c, α, and μ.

34. Find the optimal (k, Q) policy for Prob. 24 for an infinite-period model by using a discount factor of $\alpha = 0.90$.

35. For the case of linear shortage and holding costs, unit costs of p and h

respectively, show that the value of y^0 that satisfies

$$\Phi(y^D) = \frac{p - c(1 - \alpha)}{p + h}$$

is equivalent to the value of y that satisfies

$$\frac{dL(y)}{dy} + c(1 - \alpha) = 0$$

where $L(y)$, the expected shortage plus holding cost, is given by

$$L(y) = \int_y^\infty p(\xi - y)\varphi_D(\xi)\,d\xi + \int_0^y h(y - \xi)\varphi_D(\xi)\,d\xi.$$

36. Solve Prob. 1*b* assuming that the demand is random with uniform distribution over the interval (0,30) and that the delivery lead time is 1/2 month (2 weeks).

37. Solve Prob. 2*b* assuming that the demand is random with an exponential distribution with mean 650 and that the delivery lead time is one week.

38. Solve Prob. 5*b* assuming that the demand is random with uniform distribution over the interval (0,4250) and that the delivery lead time is 1/4 month (1 week).

39. Solve Prob. 5*b* assuming that the demand is random with an exponential distribution with mean 2125 and that the delivery lead time is 1/4 month (1 week).

CHAPTER 19

Forecasting

19.1 Introduction

Chapter 18, Inventory Theory, was concerned with finding optimal inventory policies. These policies were derived from inventory models and are, in part, dependent upon some forecast of sales or use of the items of interest. Forecasting is an essential component of any successful inventory system. However, forecasting need not be associated solely with problems of inventory control. Other examples where forecasting plays an important role in industry include marketing, financial planning, and production. Indeed, it is extremely rare to think of examples where managerial decisions are made in the absence of some form of forecasting. We should emphasize that a forecast is not the final product itself; it is to be used as a tool in making a managerial decision.

Forecasts can be obtained by using qualitative or quantitative techniques. In the former case, a forecast is usually the result of an expression of one or more experts' personal judgement or opinion, and it is often called a judgemental technique. For example, a major research university calls in its leading economists every September to obtain their judgement on what to expect as an inflation rate for the next academic year—a number crucial to the budgeting process. This number is generally arrived at by consensus after prolonged discussion by the economists.

Two distinct quantitative techniques are used in forecasting, both of which are conventional statistical techniques, i.e., time series analysis and regression analysis. A statistical time series is simply a series of numerical values that a random variable takes on over a period of time. For example, the daily market closing prices of a particular stock over the period of a year constitute a time series. Time series analysis exploits techniques that utilize these data for forecasting the values that the variable of interest will take on in a future period. For example, the West Coast distributor of 10-speed bicycles (Chap. 18) wants to make quarterly sales forecasts for planning purposes. He has data on sales during previous quarters; i.e., he has the values that the random variable quarterly sales takes on, and he wants to forecast the sales that will occur during the next quarter (or subsequent quarters).

In regression analysis,[1] the variable to be forecast (the dependent variable) is expressed as a mathematical function of other (independent) variables. For example, forecasting the total sales of a textbook in a given period may be functionally related to the mail order sales during the same period. Data on mail order sales and total sales over previous periods may be used to forecast total sales in a future period given the mail order sales for that period.

The three types of forecasts alluded to may be used in conjunction with one another. Indeed, the judgemental technique is often used together with an appropriate time series analysis.

19.2 Judgemental Techniques

Judgemental techniques are, by their very nature, subjective, and they may involve such qualities as intuition, expert opinion, and experience. They generally lead to forecasts that are based upon qualitative criteria. One commonly used technique is to bring together a group of experts who interact with each other and produce a consensus forecast. The example of the group of university economists who were asked to forecast the inflation rate is an example of the *Expert Group technique*.

Perhaps the most important judgemental technique is called the Delphi method. Like the Expert Group technique, the *Delphi method* utilizes a group of experts (not in a meeting setting). In addition to this group, there are one or more decision makers who ultimately are responsible for making the forecast. Finally, there is a staff who perform the duties associated with the method. These duties include the preparation of questionnaires and the analysis of their results.

The Delphi method first utilizes a questionnaire that is sent to the panel of experts and then analyzed. Based upon the results of the first questionnaire, a second questionnaire is developed and sent to the same panel of experts, together with the results of the first questionnaire. This second questionnaire is then completed by the panel of experts and returned for analysis. Based upon the results of the two questionnaires, and using their own expertise, the decision makers ultimately come forth with a forecast. The key to the Delphi method is the feedback of the information contained in the first questionnaire to the panel of

---

[1] Regression is simply an expression of the form of the function of the expected value of the dependent variable, given the values of the independent variables.

experts. Thus each member of the panel has access to information that he may have lacked originally, so that each member of the panel has all the same information when completing the second questionnaire.

Of course, the success of the Delphi method hinges on the quality of the design of the questionnaires. Occasionally, more than two iterations may be used if they are deemed desirable. This situation occurs when there appears to be sufficient divergence in the first two questionnaires to warrant a third round in the hope that the feedback from the results of the second round will lead to more convergence in the third.

19.3 Time Series

A *times series* can be viewed as the representation of the outcomes of a random variable of concern over a fixed period of time, usually taken at equally spaced intervals. The daily closing prices of AT&T stock taken over the last year comprise a time series. The quarterly unemployment rate from January 1980 to July 1984 comprises a time series. This time series is shown in Fig. 19.1. The quarterly sales of the West Coast distributor of 10-speed bicycles over the last three quarters also comprise a time series. The behavior of a time series can be displayed in graphical form, bar graphical form, or tabular form, where the first method is generally most descriptive of the pattern of behavior of the series.

Because a time series is a description of the past, a logical procedure for forecasting the future is to make use of this historical data. If history is to repeat itself—i.e., if the past data are indicative of what we can expect in the future—we can postulate an underlying mathematical model that is representative of the process. Indeed, if this model is known, except possibly for certain parameters, we can generate forecasts. Alternatively, if the model is not known, the past data may be suggestive of its form.

Suppose a model of a random variable of interest—e.g., a daily stock price—can be characterized by the following relationship,

$$X_t = h_t + e_t,$$

where X_t is the variable of interest at time t, h_t is a functional expression of the behavior of the time series, and e_t is a random error. The function h_t is a very general expression for the form of the time series. Let us consider some special cases.

Suppose that h_t takes on the form

$$h_t = \frac{1}{3}X_{t-1} + \frac{1}{3}X_{t-2} + \frac{1}{3}X_{t-3} = \frac{X_{t-1} + X_{t-2} + X_{t-3}}{3}.$$

This expression indicates that h_t is a moving average of the last three observations. Similarly, let h_t take on the form

$$h_t = \alpha X_{t-1} + (1 - \alpha)X_{t-2},$$

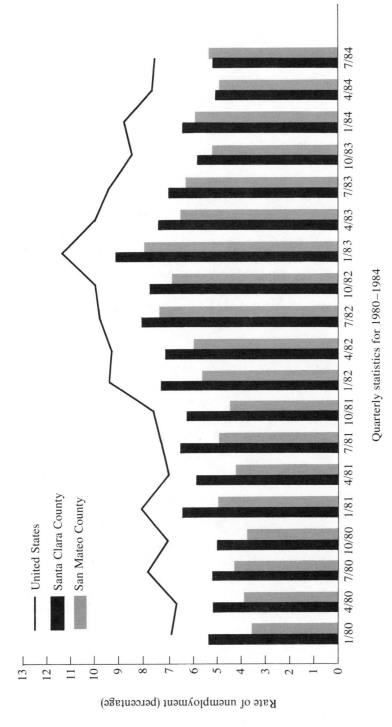

Figure 19.1 Unemployment rate (not seasonally adjusted).

so that h_t is a moving weighted average of the last two observations, with α being the weighting factor.

A final example is to let h_t take on the form

$$h_t = \alpha + \beta t.$$

This expression shows that h_t is a linear function of the time period with intercept α and slope β.

Other examples can be generated easily. Assuming that the parameters of the model are completely specified—e.g., α in the weighted average case—the past data, $X_1, X_2, \ldots, X_t$, can be used to generate the corresponding h values in each of the specific models mentioned. The differences,

$$X_i - h_i,$$

are called the *residuals*, and they should behave, in a probabilistic sense, like the random error e_t. Indeed, if these residuals do not behave like the random error, suspicion should be cast on the appropriateness of the form of the underlying model. The value, X_{t+1}, based upon knowledge of $X_1, X_2, \ldots, X_t$, is forecast by h_{t+1}.

In most realistic situations, knowledge of the exact form of the model is generally unknown. Even in those situations where the exact form is known, the parameters of the model remain unknown. For example, even if we assume that the underlying model is the moving weighted average, we generally do not know the weight α. In the forecasting process, if we assume the form of model, we can use the past data, $X_1, X_2, \ldots, X_t$, to estimate the unknown parameters in some optimal fashion. If we know neither the form nor the parameters exactly, we can use certain techniques to obtain a forecast. One such technique is called the Box-Jenkins method, and we shall discuss it later.

19.4 Forecasting Techniques

A distinction should be made between the underlying model of the process and the forecasting procedures to be used. It would make a great deal of sense to choose a procedure based on the underlying model, but such a choice is rarely made in industry. Instead, a forecasting procedure is chosen, often a simplistic one that is part of a computer routine, without any thought of the form of the actual underlying model. For example, a procedure using a simple moving average of the last four quarters of unemployment rate data may be used to make a forecast of the current unemployment rate, without regard to whether the time series based upon the model

$$X_t = \frac{X_{t-1} + X_{t-2} + X_{t-3} + X_{t-4}}{4}$$

is appropriate. Indeed, if a reasonable underlying model contains a seasonal adjustment, as is to be expected, the moving average forecasting procedure may be inadequate. The remainder of this section is devoted to the most commonly used forecasting procedures.

For a *time series*, the forecasting problem can be stated as follows. There exists a sequence of random variables $X_1, X_2, \ldots$ (a stochastic process) having expected values given by $E(X_1), E(X_2), \ldots$. The distribution of each of these random variables may be the same, or it may change (e.g., shift) according to some pattern. The random variables may be independent or dependent. Observations on these random variables $X_1, X_2, \ldots, X_t$ have been taken, and their values are denoted by $x_1, x_2, \ldots, x_t$. Based upon these previous outcomes, $E(X_t)$ is to be estimated; the estimate, which will be used as the forecast for subsequent periods, will be denoted by $\hat{E}(X_t)$.

For example, the West Coast distributor of 10-speed bicycles may make quarterly sales forecasts for planning purposes. He has data on sales during previous quarters; i.e., he has the values the random variable quarterly sales takes on, and he would like to forecast the sales that will occur in the forthcoming quarter or in subsequent quarters. Recognizing the fact that the sales in subsequent quarters are themselves random variables, accompanied by their associated variability, the distributor is willing to "settle" for an *estimate* of the expected sales in the present quarter, which will be used as the forecast of sales for future periods. In the absence of trends, seasonal adjustments, and so on, this estimate (presumably based upon many previous observations and not only on sales in the current quarter) will provide a "good" forecast for sales in subsequent quarters.

The following five forecasting procedures are often used in industry.

1. *Last value forecasting procedure.* The bicycle distributor may use the sales from the last quarter to estimate $E(X_t)$ and to serve as the forecast of the sales for future quarters. Hence $\hat{E}(X_t) = x_t$. This estimator has the disadvantage of being imprecise; i.e., its variance is large because it is based upon a sample of size 1. It is worth considering only if the conditional distribution has very small variance and/or the process is changing so rapidly that anything before time t is almost irrelevant or even misleading.

2. *Average forecasting procedure.* The bicycle distributor may use *all* his past quarterly data to forecast the sales for future quarters; i.e., he may choose

$$\hat{E}(X_t) = \sum_{i=1}^{t} \frac{x_i}{t}.$$

This estimate is an excellent one if the process is entirely stable. However, besides being too cumbersome when using large masses of data, we do not want to use data that are too old because occasional shifts are to be expected.

3. *Moving average forecasting procedure.* In using a moving-average estimate, the bicycle distributor uses only the last n periods; that is,

$$\hat{E}(X_t) = \sum_{t=t-n+1}^{t} \frac{x_t}{n}.$$

Not only does this estimator use all the relevant history in the last n periods, but it is easily updated from period to period; i.e., the first observation is lopped off and the last one added. The moving-average estimator combines the advantages of the previous estimators in that it uses only recent history and represents multiple observations. A disadvantage of this procedure is that it places as much weight on x_{t-n+1} as on x_t, and intuitively one would expect a good procedure to place more weight on the most recent observation.

4. *Exponential smoothing forecasting procedure.* If the bicycle distributor uses exponential smoothing, then

$$\hat{E}(X_t) = \alpha x_t + (1 - \alpha)\hat{E}(X_{t-1}),$$

where $0 < \alpha < 1$ is called the *smoothing constant*. Thus the forecast is just a weighted sum of the last observation and the previous forecast. The choice of α is discussed later. Note that the exponential smoothing technique represents a recursive relationship and can be expressed alternatively as

$$\hat{E}(X_t) = \alpha x_t + \alpha(1 - \alpha)x_{t-1} + \alpha(1 - \alpha)^2 x_{t-2} + \cdots.$$

In this form, it becomes evident that exponential smoothing gives the most weight to x_t and decreasing weights to earlier observations. Furthermore, the first form reveals that the forecast is simple to calculate because the data prior to period t need not be retained; all that is required is x_t and the previous forecast $\hat{E}(X_{t-1})$. Another alternative form for the exponential smoothing technique is given by

$$\hat{E}(X_t) = \hat{E}(X_{t-1}) + \alpha[x_t - \hat{E}(X_{t-1})],$$

which gives a heuristic justification for this procedure. Finally, a measure of effectiveness of exponential smoothing can be obtained under the assumption that the process is completely stable; that is, $X_1, X_2, \ldots$ are independent, identically distributed random variables with variance σ^2. It then follows that

$$\text{var}[\hat{E}(X_t)] \approx \frac{\alpha\sigma^2}{2 - \alpha} = \frac{\sigma^2}{(2 - \alpha)/\alpha},$$

so that the variance is statistically equivalent to a moving average with $(2 - \alpha)/\alpha$ observations. If α is chosen equal to 0.1, then $(2 - \alpha)/\alpha = 19$. Thus the exponential smoothing technique is "equivalent" to a moving-average procedure that uses 19 observations. However, it must be noted that when the aforementioned underlying assumptions are violated, exponential smoothing will react more quickly with superior "tracking."

An important drawback of exponential smoothing is that it lags behind a continuing trend; i.e., if the mean is increasing steadily, then the forecast will be several periods behind. However, the procedure can be easily adjusted for trend (and even seasonally adjusted). Another disadvantage of exponential smoothing is that it is difficult to choose an appropriate smoothing constant α. Exponential smoothing can be viewed as a statistical filter that inputs raw data from a stochastic process and outputs smoothed estimates of a mean that varies with time. If α is chosen to be small, response to change is slow, with resultant smooth estimators. Similarly if α is chosen to be large, response to change is fast, with resultant large variability in the output. Hence there is a need to compromise, depending upon the stability of the process. Furthermore, a "good" value of the smoothing constant depends upon the underlying stochastic process and the choice of a criterion to use in comparing constants. It has been suggested that α should not exceed 0.3 and that a reasonable choice for α is approximately 0.1. Of course it can be increased, perhaps temporarily, if an unusual change is expected or when starting. When starting, a reasonable approach is to choose $E(X_1)$ according to

$$\hat{E}(X_1) = \alpha x_1 + (1 - \alpha)(\text{initial estimate}).$$

In the case of past history, another procedure for choosing α is to run a restrospective simulation of the process; i.e., for a fixed value of α and using past history, compare the forecasted quantity with the actual outcome (look at the residual), and choose that value of α which is in some sense optimal. Hopefully, the process will behave in the future in the same manner as it has in the past.

5. *Exponential smoothing adjusted for trend forecasting procedure.* As we indicated earlier, the procedure outlined in (4) lags behind a continuing trend. Suppose that $E(X_t)$ is linear with *known* slope S. The slope is called the *trend factor*, and in the bicycle example it represents the units per period that the expected sales rate increases or decreases. Then instead of using the previous expression for $\hat{E}(X_t)$, the new expression,

$$\hat{E}(X_t) = \alpha x_t + (1 - \alpha)[\hat{E}(X_{t-1}) + S],$$

is substituted. However, S is usually not known, so S must also be estimated, and exponential smoothing can again be used for this purpose; that is,

$$\hat{E}(S_t) = \beta[\hat{E}(X_t) - \hat{E}(X_{t-1})] + (1 - \beta)\hat{E}(S_{t-1}),$$

where $0 < \beta < 1$ is another (possibly different from α) smoothing constant.[1] Hence $\hat{E}(X_t)$ can now be expressed as

$$\hat{E}(X_t) = \alpha x_t + (1 - \alpha)[\hat{E}(X_{t-1}) + \hat{E}(S_{t-1})],$$

and this estimate now becomes the estimate of $E(X_t)$. Unlike exponential smoothing without trend, $\hat{E}(X_t)$ is only a good estimate for $E(X_t)$ and is *not* a forecast for future periods. This phenomenon is caused by the increasing or decreasing trend, and hence the forecast of sales for the $(t + T)$th period, based upon past data through the tth period, is given by $X_{t,T}$, where

$$X_{t,T} = \hat{E}(X_t) + T\hat{E}(S_t)$$

and

$$T = 0, 1, 2, \ldots.$$

[1] The previous discussion concerning the choice of α is relevant to the choice of β.

The forecasting procedure (in the context of sales) can now be summarized as follows:

(a) Using the actual sales occuring in the tth period x_t, the estimate of the last period's expected sales $\hat{E}(X_{t-1})$, and trend rate $\hat{E}(S_{t-1})$, the estimate of the tth period's expected sales is given by

$$\hat{E}(X_t) = \alpha x_t + (1 - \alpha)[\hat{E}(X_{t-1}) + \hat{E}(S_{t-1})].$$

(b) From the estimate of this period's expected sales $\hat{E}(X_t)$ [calculated in (a)], the last period's estimate of expected sales $\hat{E}(X_{t-1})$, and the trend rate $\hat{E}(S_{t-1})$, the estimate of the tth period trend rate is given by

$$\hat{E}(S_t) = \beta[\hat{E}(X_t) - \hat{E}(X_{t-1})] + (1 - \beta)\hat{E}(S_{t-1}).$$

(c) Forecasts of sales for the $(t + T)$th period are given by

$$X_{t,T} = \hat{E}(X_t) + T\hat{E}(S_t).$$

EXAMPLE Suppose quarterly sales for bicycles were 2,800, 2,925, and 3,040, respectively. The initial estimate of the expected sales is 2,750, and the initial estimate of the trend is 100. Use exponential smoothing based upon the first three observations to forecast sales for the fifth period, using $\alpha = \beta = 0.1$. From (a), and using the initial estimates of expected sales and trend,

$$\hat{E}(X_1) = 0.1(2,800) + 0.9(2,750 + 100) = 2,845.$$

The initial estimate of sales can also be used to update the trend in (b); i.e.,

$$\hat{E}(S_1) = 0.1(2,845 - 2,750) + 0.9(100) = 99.5.$$

Repeating this procedure for the second observation leads to

$$\hat{E}(X_2) = 0.1(2,925) + 0.9(2,845 + 99.5) = 2,943$$

and

$$\hat{E}(S_2) = 0.1(2,943 - 2,845) + 0.9(99.5) = 99.4.$$

Finally, the third observation results in

$$\hat{E}(X_3) = 0.1(3,040) + 0.9(2,943 + 99.4) = 3,041$$

and

$$\hat{E}(S_3) = 0.1(3,041 - 2,943) + 0.9(99.4) = 99.3.$$

Therefore, the forecast of sales for the fifth period is

$$X_{3,2} = 3,041 + 2(99.3) = 3,240.$$

BOX-JENKINS METHOD

It has already been pointed out that procedures and models frequently are not coordinated in practice. The beauty of the Box-Jenkins method, a sophisticated and complex technique that requires a great amount of past data (a minimum of 50 time periods), is that the model and the procedure are coordinated. There is a systematic approach to identifying an appropriate model, chosen from a rich class of models. The historical data are used to test the validity of the model. The model also generates an appropriate forecasting procedure.

The Box-Jenkins method is iterative in nature. First, a model is chosen. To choose this model, we must compute autocorrelations and partial autocorrelations and examine their patterns. An autocorrelation measures the correlation between time series values separated by a fixed number of periods. This fixed number of periods is called the *lag*. Therefore, the autocorrelation for a lag of two periods measures the correlation between every other observation; i.e., it is the correlation between the original time series and the same series moved forward two periods. The partial autocorrelation is a conditional autocorrelation between the original time series and the same series moved forward a fixed number of periods, holding the effect of the other lagged times fixed. We can compute both the autocorrelations and the partial autocorrelations for all lags; we can do it easily with a computer. From the autocorrelations and the partial autocorrelations, we can identify the form of one or more possible models because a rich class of models is characterized by these parameters. Actually, we compute the sample autocorrelations and the sample partial autocorrelations, but these computations are "good" estimates, because we assume large amounts of data. Now that we have identified the model,—i.e., we have identified the h_t function—we must estimate the parameters associated with the model. This estimate is made using the historical data. The function h_t then becomes known (or approximately known) and we can compute the residuals and examine their behavior. Similarly, we can examine the behavior of the estimated parameters. If both the "residuals" and the "estimated parameters" behave as expected under the presumed model, the model appears to be validated. If they do not, then the model should be modified and the procedure repeated until a model is validated. At this point, we can obtain a forecast.

For example, suppose that the sample autocorrelations and the sample partial autocorrelations are calculated (usually by computer) as shown in Fig. 19.2. The sample autocorrelations appear to decrease exponentially as a function of the time lags, while the sample partial autocorrelations appear to have spikes at the first and second time lags of the observations followed by values that seem to be of negligible magnitude. This behavior of the sample autocorrelations and the sample partial autocorrelations is characteristic of the h_t function,

$$h_t = \beta_0 + \beta_1 X_{t-1} + \beta_2 X_{t-2}.$$

Assuming this functional form, we use the time series data to estimate β_0, β_1, and β_2 (usually by means of a computer program). Using these estimates, together with the time series data, we obtain the residuals

$$X_i - h_i.$$

If the assumed functional form of h_t is adequate, the residuals and the estimated

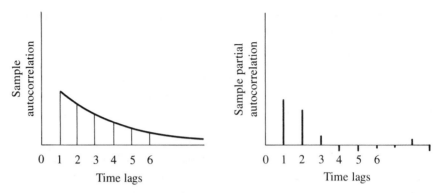

Figure 19.2 **Plot of sample autocórrelation and partial autocorrelation versus time lags.**

parameters should behave in a predictable manner. In particular, the sample residuals should behave as approximately independent, normally distributed random variables, each having mean zero and variance σ^2 (assuming that e_t, the random error at time period t, has mean zero and variance σ^2). The estimated parameters should be uncorrelated and significantly different from zero. Statistical tests are available for this diagnostic checking.

The Box-Jenkins procedure appears to be a complex one, and it is. Fortunately, software is available so the entire procedure is computerized. The programs calculate the sample autocorrelations and the sample partial autocorrelations necessary for identifying the form of the model. They also estimate the parameters of the model and do the diagnostic checking. These programs, however, cannot accurately identify one or more models that are compatible with the autocorrelations and the partial autocorrelations. This expertise can be acquired, but it is beyond the scope of this text. Although the Box-Jenkins method is complicated, the resultant forecasts are extremely accurate, and, when the time horizon is short, better than most other forecasting techniques. Further, the procedure produces a measure of the forecast error.

19.5 Linear Regression

Statistical problems often are concerned with data where there exists a relationship between two variables. This section highlights the results when the relationship is linear. For example, suppose that a publisher of textbooks is concerned about the initial press run for his books. He sells books both through bookstores and through mail orders. This latter method uses an extensive advertising campaign through publishing media and direct mail. The advertising campaign is conducted prior to the publication of the book. The sales manager has noted that there is a rather interesting linear relationship between the number of mail orders and the number sold through bookstores during the first year. He suggests that this relationship be exploited to determine the initial press run for subsequent books.

Thus, if the number of mail order sales for a book is denoted by X, and the number of bookstore sales by Y, then the random variables X and Y exhibit a **degree of association**. There is no functional relationship between these two random variables; i.e., given the number of mail order sales, one does not expect to determine *exactly* the number of bookstore sales. Note that for any given number of mail order sales, there is a range of possible bookstore sales, and vice versa. This variation may be partially due to measurement errors (incorrect counts, for example), but it can be attributed primarily to individual variation among published books. Thus no unique functional relationship between mail order sales and bookstore sales can be expected. However, it is anticipated that bookstore sales, for a given observed number of mail order sales, increase as mail order sales increase. If sales increase this way, what then is meant by the statement, "The sales manager has noted that there is a rather interesting linear relationship between the number of mail orders and the number sold through bookstores during the first year"? Such a statement implies that the *expected value* of the number of bookstore sales is linear with respect to the number of mail order sales; i.e.,

$$E[Y \mid X = x] = \alpha + \beta x.$$

Thus, if the number of mail order sales is x for many different books, the average number of corresponding bookstore sales would tend to be approximately $\alpha + \beta x$.

Other examples of this *degree-of-association model* can easily be found. An educator may be interested in the relationship between a student's performance on the college entrance examination and his subsequent performance in college. An engineer may be interested in the relationship between tensile strength and hardness of a material. An economist may wish to predict a measure of inflation as a function of the cost of living index, and so on.

The degree-of-association model is not the only model of interest. In some cases, there exists a **functional relationship** between two variables that may be linked linearly. In a forecasting context, one of the two variables is time, while the other is the variable of interest. In Section 19.3, such an example was alluded to when h_t was set equal to

$$h_t = \alpha + \beta t.$$

Therefore,

$$X_t^\dagger = \alpha + \beta t + e_t,$$

from which it follows that

$$E(X_t) = \alpha + \beta t.$$

Note that both the degree-of-association model and the *exact functional relationship* model lead to the same linear regression, and their subsequent

---

$\dagger$ The symbol X_t also can be read as X given t or as $X \mid t$.

treatment is almost identical. Hence the publishing example will be explored further to illustrate how to treat both kinds of models, although the special structure of the model,

$$h_t = \alpha + \beta t,$$

with t taking on integer values starting with 1 leads to certain simplified expressions. In regression analysis, standard notation uses X to represent the independent variable and Y to represent the dependent variable of interest. Consequently, the notational expression for this special time series model now becomes

$$Y_t = \alpha + \beta t + e_t.$$

METHOD OF LEAST SQUARES

Suppose that bookstore sales and mail order sales are given for 15 books. These data appear in Table 19.1, and the resulting plot is given in Figure 19.3.

It is evident that the points in Figure 19.3 do not lie on a straight line. Hence it is not clear where the line should be drawn to show the linear relationship. Suppose that an arbitrary line, given by the expression $\tilde{y} = a + bx$, is drawn through the data. A measure of how well this line fits the data can be obtained by computing the *sum of squares* of the vertical deviations of the actual points from the fitted line. Thus let y_i represent the bookstore sales of the ith book and x_i the corresponding mail order sales. Denote by $\tilde{y}_i$, the point on the fitted line corresponding to the mail order sales of x_i. The proposed measure of fit is then given by

$$Q = (y_1 - \tilde{y}_1)^2 + (y_2 - \tilde{y}_2)^2 + \cdots + (y_{15} - \tilde{y}_{15})^2 = \sum_{i=1}^{15} (y_i - \tilde{y}_i)^2.$$

Table 19.1 **Data for mail order and bookstore sales example**

Mail order sales	Bookstore sales
1,310	4,360
1,313	4,590
1,320	4,520
1,322	4,770
1,338	4,760
1,340	5,070
1,347	5,230
1,355	5,080
1,360	5,550
1,364	5,390
1,373	5,670
1,376	5,490
1,384	5,810
1,395	6,060
1,400	5,940

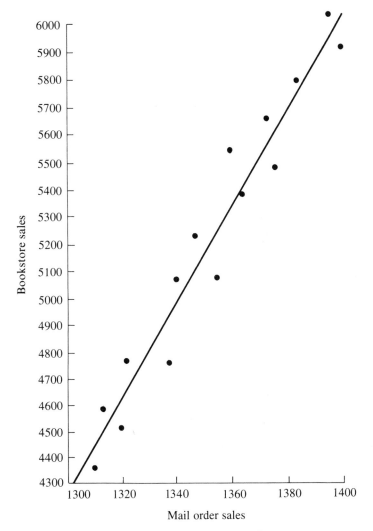

Figure 19.3 **Plot of mail order sales versus bookstore sales.**

The usual method for identifying the "best" fitted line is the **method of least squares**. This method chooses that line, $a + bx$, that makes Q a minimum. Thus a and b are obtained simply by setting the partial derivatives of Q with respect to a and b equal to zero, and solving the resultant equations. This method yields the solution,

$$b = \frac{\sum\limits_{i=1}^{n} (x_i - \bar{x})(y_i - \bar{y})}{\sum\limits_{i=1}^{n} (x_i - \bar{x})^2} = \frac{\sum\limits_{i=1}^{n} x_i y_i - \left(\sum\limits_{i=1}^{n} x_i \sum\limits_{i=1}^{n} y_i\right)\Big/ n}{\sum\limits_{i=1}^{n} x_i^2 - \left(\sum\limits_{i=1}^{n} x_i\right)^2 \Big/ n}$$

and

$$a = \bar{y} - b\bar{x},$$

where

$$\bar{x} = \sum_{i=1}^{n} x_i/n$$

and

$$\bar{y} = \sum_{i=1}^{n} y_i/n.$$

For the publishing example,

$$\bar{x} = 1{,}353.1,$$
$$\bar{y} = 5{,}219.3,$$
$$\sum_{i=1}^{15} (x_i - \bar{x})(y_i - \bar{y}) = 214{,}543.9$$
$$\sum_{i=1}^{15} (x_i - \bar{x})^2 = 11{,}966,$$

and $a = -19{,}041.9$, $b = 17.930$. Hence the least squares estimate of the book-store sales $\tilde{y}$, when the mail order sales is x, is given by

$$\tilde{y} = -19{,}041.9 + 17.930x,$$

and this line is drawn in Fig. 19.3.

This fitted line is useful for forecasting purposes. For a given value of x, the corresponding value of y represents the forecast. However, the decision maker may be interested in some measure of uncertainty that is associated with this forecast. This measure is easily obtained provided that certain assumptions can be made. Therefore, for the remainder of this section, it is assumed that

1. A random sample of n pairs $(x_1, Y_1), (x_2, Y_2), \ldots, (x_n, Y_n)$ is to be taken.
2. The Y_i are normally distributed with mean, $\alpha + \beta x_i$, and variance, σ^2 (independent of i).

The assumption that Y_i is normally distributed is not a critical assumption in determining the uncertainty in the forecast, but the assumption of constant variance is crucial. Furthermore, an estimate of this variance is required.

An unbiased estimate of σ^2 is given by $s_{y|x}^2$, where

$$s_{y|x}^2 = \sum_{i=1}^{n} \frac{(y_i - \tilde{y}_i)^2}{(n-2)}.$$

CONFIDENCE INTERVAL ESTIMATION OF $E(Y|x = x_*)$

A very important reason for obtaining the linear relationship between two variables is to use the line for future decision making. From the regression line, it is possible to estimate $E(Y|x)$ by a *point estimate* (the forecast) and a *confidence interval* estimate (a measure of forecast uncertainty). For example, the publisher might want to use this approach to estimate the expected number of bookstore sales corresponding to mail order sales of, say, 1,400, by both a point estimate and a confidence interval estimate. He may be interested in this approach for forecasting purposes. A point estimate corresponding to $x = x_*$ is given by

$$\tilde{y}_* = a + bx_*.$$

The end points of a $(100)(1 - \alpha)$ percent confidence interval are given by

$$a + bx_* - t_{\alpha/2;n-2} s_{y|x} \sqrt{\left[\frac{1}{n} + \frac{(x_* - \bar{x})^2}{\sum (x_i - \bar{x})^2} \right]}$$

and

$$a + bx_* + t_{\alpha/2;n-2} s_{y|x} \sqrt{\left[\frac{1}{n} + \frac{(x_* - \bar{x})^2}{\sum (x_i - \bar{x})^2} \right]},$$

where $s_{y|x}^2$ is the estimate of σ^2, and $t_{\alpha/2;n-2}$ is the $100\alpha/2$ percentage point of the t distribution with $n - 2$ degrees of freedom (see Table A5.2 of Appendix 5). It should be noted that the interval is narrowest where $x_* = \bar{x}$, and it becomes wider as x_* departs from the mean.

In the publishing example, $s_{y|x}^2$ is computed from the data in Table 19.1 to be 17,030. If a 95 percent confidence interval is required, Table A5.2 gives $t_{.025;13} = 2.160$. The results derived in the preceding section yield 6,060 as the point estimate of $E(Y|1{,}400)$, i.e., the forecast. Hence, the lower confidence limit corresponding to mail order sales of 1,400 is 5,918, and the upper confidence limit is 6,202. The fact that the confidence interval was obtained at a data point ($x = 1{,}400$) is purely coincidental.

PREDICTIONS

The confidence interval statement for the expected number of bookstore sales corresponding to mail order sales of 1,400 may be useful for budgeting purposes, but it is not too useful for making decisions about the *actual* press run. Instead of obtaining bounds on the *expected* number of bookstore sales, this kind of decision requires bounds on what the *actual* bookstore sales will be, i.e., a *prediction interval* on the value that the random variable (bookstore sales) takes on. This measure is a *different* measure of forecast uncertainty. The two end points of such an interval are given by the expressions

$$a + bx_+ - t_{\alpha/2;n-2} s_{y|x} \sqrt{\left[1 + \frac{1}{n} + \frac{(x_+ - \bar{x})^2}{\sum_{i=1}^{n} (x_i - \bar{x})^2} \right]}$$

and

$$a + bx_+ + t_{\alpha/2;n-2} s_{y|x} \sqrt{\left[1 + \frac{1}{n} + \frac{(x_+ - \bar{x})^2}{\sum_{i=1}^{n} (x_i - \bar{x})^2} \right]}$$

For a given value x_+, the probability is $1 - \alpha$ that the value of the future Y_+

associated with the x_+ will fall in this interval. Thus, if x_+ is 1,400, then the corresponding 95 percent prediction interval for the number of bookstore sales is given by $6,060 \pm 316$, which is naturally wider than the confidence interval for the expected number of bookstore sales.

Whereas the publisher can find an interval that will contain bookstore sales corresponding to particular mail order sales with probability $1 - \alpha$, he is unable to use this type of result over and over and still maintain a measure for making correct statements. The reason is that these statements would all be based upon the same statistical data, so that the statements would not be statistically independent. If the statements are independent, and if k future bookstore sales are to be predicted, with each statement being made with probability $1 - \alpha$, then the probability is $(1 - \alpha)^k$ that *all* k predictions of future bookstore sales are correct. However, if k is large or possibly unknown, even this technique based upon the (incorrect) assumption of independence would be useless. A solution to this problem can be obtained by using **simultaneous tolerance intervals**. Using this technique, the publisher can take the mail order sales of any book, find an interval (based on the previously determined fitted line) that will contain the actual bookstore sales with probability at least $1 - \alpha$, and repeat this for any number of books having the same or different mail order sales. Furthermore, the probability is P that all of these predictions are correct. An alternative interpretation is as follows. If every publisher followed this procedure, each using his own fitted line, then $100P$ percent of the publishers (on the average) would find that at least $100(1 - \alpha)$ percent of his bookstore sales would fall into the predicted intervals. This measure is the third measure of forecast uncertainty. The expression for the end points of each such interval is given by

$$a + bx_+ - c^{**}s_{y|x}\sqrt{\left[\frac{1}{n} + \frac{(x_+ - \bar{x})^2}{\sum\limits_{i=1}^{n}(x_i - \bar{x})^2}\right]}$$

and

$$a + bx_+ + c^{**}s_{y|k}\sqrt{\left[\frac{1}{n} + \frac{(x_+ - \bar{x})^2}{\sum\limits_{i=1}^{n}(x_i - \bar{x})^2}\right]},$$

where c^{**} is given in Table 19.2; c^{**} is clearly a function of n, P, and α.

Thus the publisher can state that the bookstore sales corresponding to known mail order sales will fall in the interval constructed using the expressions just given. Such statements can be made for as many books as the publisher desires. Furthermore, the probability is P that at least $100(1 - \alpha)$ percent of bookstore sales corresponding to mail order sales will fall in these intervals. If P is chosen as 0.90 and $\alpha = 0.05$, the appropriate value of c^{**} is 11,625. Hence the number of bookstore sales corresponding to mail order sales of 1,400 books will fall in the interval $6,060 \pm 759$. If another book had mail order sales of 1,353, the bookstore sales would fall in the interval $5,258 \pm 390$, and so on. At least 95

Table 19.2 **Values[†] of c^{**}**

n	$\alpha = 0.50$	$\alpha = 0.25$	$\alpha = 0.10$	$\alpha = 0.05$	$\alpha = 0.01$	$\alpha = 0.001$
			$P = 0.90$			
4	7.471	10.160	13.069	14.953	18.663	23.003
6	5.380	7.453	9.698	11.150	14.014	17.363
8	5.037	7.082	9.292	10.722	13.543	16.837
10	4.983	7.093	9.366	10.836	13.733	17.118
12	5.023	7.221	9.586	11.112	14.121	17.634
14	5.101	7.394	9.857	11.447	14.577	18.232
16	5.197	7.586	10.150	11.803	15.057	18.856
18	5.300	7.786	10.449	12.165	15.542	19.484
20	5.408	7.987	10.747	12.526	16.023	20.104
			$P = 0.95$			
4	10.756	14.597	18.751	21.445	26.760	32.982
6	6.652	9.166	11.899	13.669	17.167	21.266
8	5.933	8.281	10.831	12.484	15.750	19.568
10	5.728	8.080	10.632	12.286	15.553	19.369
12	5.684	8.093	10.701	12.391	15.724	19.619
14	5.711	8.194	10.880	12.617	16.045	20.050
16	5.771	8.337	11.107	12.898	16.431	20.559
18	5.848	8.499	11.357	13.204	16.845	21.097
20	5.937	8.672	11.619	13.521	17.272	21.652
			$P = 0.99$			
4	24.466	33.019	42.398	48.620	60.500	74.642
6	10.444	14.285	18.483	21.215	26.606	32.920
8	8.290	11.453	14.918	17.166	21.652	26.860
10	7.567	10.539	13.796	15.911	20.097	24.997
12	7.258	10.182	13.383	15.479	19.579	24.403
14	7.127	10.063	13.267	15.355	19.485	24.316
16	7.079	10.055	13.306	15.410	19.582	24.467
18	7.074	10.111	13.404	15.552	19.794	24.746
20	7.108	10.198	13.566	15.745	20.065	25.122

[†] Reprinted by permission from "Simultaneous Tolerance Intervals in Regression," by Lieberman, G. J., and R. G. Miller: *Biometrika*, **50**, 1 and 2, 164 (1963).

percent of the bookstore sales will fall into their predicted intervals, and these statements are made with confidence 0.90.

19.6 Conclusions

It is important to consider the entire forecasting system carefully. The need to obtain a forecast has to be identified at the appropriate management level. The historical data required must be compiled. By studying these data, an appropriate model can be structured. A forecasting procedure that behaves well under the model should be selected. The forecasting procedure may require choosing one or more parameters—e.g., the smoothing constant α in exponential smoothing—

Table 19.3 Basic forecasting techniques*

Technique	A. Qualitative methods		B. Times series analysis			C. Causal methods
	1. Delphi method	2. Panel consensus	1. Moving average	2. Exponential smoothing	3. Box-Jenkins	Regression model
Description	A panel of experts is interrogated by a sequence of questionnaires in which the responses to one questionnaire are used to produce the next questionnaire. Any set of information available to some experts and not others is thus passed on to the others, enabling all the experts to have access to all the information for forecasting. This technique eliminates the bandwagon effect of majority opinion.	This technique is based on the assumption that several experts can arrive at a better forecast than one person. There is no secrecy, and communication is encouraged. The forecasts are sometimes influenced by social factors, and may not reflect a true consensus.	Each point of a moving average of a time series is the arithmetic or weighted average of a number of consecutive points of the series, where the number of data points is chosen so that the effects of seasonals or irregularity or both are eliminated.	This technique is similar to the moving average, except that more recent data points are given more weight. Descriptively the new forecast is equal to the old one plus some proportion of the past forecasting error. Adaptive forecasting is somewhat the same except that seasonals are also computed. There are many variations of exponential smoothing: some are more versatile than others, some are computationally more complex, some require more computer time.	Exponential smoothing is a special case of the Box-Jenkins technique. The time series is fitted with a mathematical model that is optimal in the sense that it assigns smaller errors to history than any other model. The type of model must be identified and the parameters then estimated. This is apparently the most accurate statistical routine presently available but also one of the most costly and time consuming ones.	This functionally relates sales to other economic, competitive, or internal variables and estimates an equation using the least-squares technique. Relationships are primarily analyzed statistically, although any relationship should be selected for testing on a rational ground.
Accuracy: Short-term (0–3 mon)	Fair to very good	Poor to fair	Poor to good	Fair to very good	Very good to excellent	Good to very good
Medium-term (3 mon–2 yr)	Fair to very good	Poor to fair	Poor	Poor to good	Poor to good	Good to very good
Long-term (2 yr and over)	Fair to very good	Poor	Very poor	Very poor	Very poor	Poor

Identification of turning points	Fair to good	Poor to fair	Poor	Poor	Fair	Very good
Typical applications	Forecasts of long-range and new-product sales, forecasts of margins.	Forecasts of long-range and new-product sales, forecasts of margins.	Inventory control for low-volume items.	Production and inventory control, forecasts of margins and other financial data.	Production and inventory control for large-volume items, forecasts of cash balances.	Forecasts of sales by product classes, forecasts of margins.
Data required	A coordinator issues the sequence of questionnaires, editing and consolidating the responses.	Information from a panel of experts is presented openly in group meetings to arrive at a consensus forecast. Again, a minimum is two sets of reports over time.	A minimum of two years of sales history, if seasonals are present. Otherwise, less data. (Of course, the more history the better.) The moving average must be specified.	The same as for a moving average.	The same as for a moving average. However, in this case more history is very advantageous in model identification.	Several years' quarterly history to obtain good, meaningful relationships. Mathematically necessary to have two more observations than there are independent variables.
Cost of forecasting with a computer	$2,000+	$1,000+	$0.005	$0.005	$10.00	$100
Is calculation possible without a computer?	Yes	Yes	Yes	Yes	Yes	Yes
Time required to develop an application and make forecasts	2 months+	2 weeks	1 day	1 day	1–2 days	Depends on ability to identify relationship

and the historical data may prove useful in making this choice. Finally, the forecasting process should be viewed as dynamic, with the accumulated new data compared with their associated forecasts. These data may also be used to update the parameters and the form of the underlying model, as well as the parameters of the forecasting procedure itself.

Many forecasting procedures have been presented in this chapter. Each poses advantages and disadvantages that depend upon such factors as the underlying model, the time horizon for which the forecast is to be made, and the type of application. A summary of the properties of the procedures commonly used in practice is given in Table 19.3.

SELECTED REFERENCES

1. Box, G. E. P., and G. M. Jenkins: *Time Series Analysis, Forecasting and Control*, Holden-Day, San Francisco, 1976.
2. Brown, R. G.: *Statistical Forecasting for Inventory Control*, McGraw-Hill, New York, 1959.
3. Brown, R. G.: *Smoothing, Forecasting, and Prediction of Discrete Time Series*, Prentice-Hall, Englewood Cliffs, N.J., 1972.
4. Gilchrist, W. G.: *Statistical Forecasting*, Wiley, New York, 1976.
5. Hoff, J. C.: *A Practical Guide to Box-Jenkins Forecasting*, Lifetime Learning Publications, Belmont, Ca., 1983.
6. Montgomery, D. C., and L. A. Johnson: *Forecasting and Time Series Analysis*, McGraw-Hill, New York, 1976.

PROBLEMS

1. Suppose that the previous forecast was 2,083, the actual value of the variable of interest for the last period was 1,975, and the oldest value of the variable of interest was 1,945. Using the moving average technique based upon the most recent four observations, what is the new forecast for the next period?

2. Suppose that the previous forecast was 2,083, the actual value of the variable of interest for the last period was 1,975, and $\alpha = 0.2$. Using exponential smoothing, what is the new forecast for the next period?

3. Suppose that the previous forecast was 782, the actual value of the variable of interest for the last period was 794, and $\alpha = 0.1$ Using exponential smoothing, what is the new forecast for the next period?

4. Suppose that the previous forecast was 782, the actual value of the variable of interest for the last period was 794, and the oldest value of the variable of interest was 810. Using the moving average technique based upon the most recent three observations, what is the new forecast for the next period?

5. If α is set equal to zero or 1 in the exponential smoothing expression, what happens to the forecast?

6. Use the bicycle sales example presented in the section on exponential smoothing adjusted for trend, and solve the problem in this example using simple exponential smoothing with $\alpha = 0.1$.

7. Use the bicycle sales example presented in the section on exponential smoothing adjusted for trend, and solve the problem in this example using $\alpha = \beta = 0.2$.

8. The U.S. unemployment rate time series shown in Figure 19.1 can be represented in tabular form as follows:

Date	Unemployment rate (%)	Date	Unemployment rate (%)	Date	Unemployment rate (%)
1/80	6.9	1/81	8.2	1/82	9.4
4/80	6.7	4/81	7.0	4/82	9.2
7/80	7.9	7/81	7.3	7/82	9.8
10/80	7.1	10/81	7.5	10/82	9.9

Date	Unemployment rate (%)	Date	Unemployment rate (%)
1/83	11.4	1/84	8.8
4/83	10.0	4/84	7.6
7/83	9.4	7/84	7.5
10/83	8.4	10/84	—

(*a*) Starting with a forecast for 10/80, use the moving average technique based upon the past three periods to forecast each unemployment rate through 10/84.

(*b*) Examine the residuals for 10/80 through 7/84, and compute the mean of their absolute values, i.e.,

$$\frac{\sum |X_i - h_i|}{16}.$$

9. Use the unemployment data of Problem 8.

(*a*) Starting with a forecast for 10/80, use the exponential smoothing technique with an initial estimate of 6.8 percent and $\alpha = 0.1$, i.e.,

$$\text{Forecast for } 10/80 = (0.1)7.9 + (0.9)6.8,$$

to forecast each unemployment rate through 10/84.

(*b*) Examine the residuals for 10/80 through 7/84, and compute the mean of their absolute values, i.e.,

$$\frac{\sum |X_i - h_i|}{16}.$$

10. (*a*) Solve Prob. 9 using $\alpha = 0.2$.

(*b*) Which α ($\alpha = 0.1$ or 0.2) would you use to forecast the unemployment rate for 10/84?

11. Based upon the results of Probs. 8(*b*) and 9(*b*), which forecasting procedure would you choose, moving average or exponential smoothing?

12. Use the unemployment data of Prob. 8.

(a) Starting with a one-step forecast for 10/80, use the exponential smoothing technique adjusted for trend, with an initial estimate of 6.8 percent for unemployment and with an initial estimate of trend of 0.2 percent, to forecast each unemployment rate through 10/84. Use $\alpha = \beta = 0.1$.

(b) Examine the residuals for 10/80 through 7/84, and compute the mean of their absolute values, i.e.,

$$\frac{\sum |X_i - h_i|}{16}.$$

13. Based upon the results of Probs. 8(b), 9(b), and 12(b), which forecasting procedure would you choose, moving average, exponential smoothing, or exponential smoothing adjusted for trend?

14. In order to plan for a suitable labor force, you need to know the demand for a particular product. The following table presents demand over the past 11 quarters.

Quarter	Demand	Quarter	Demand	Quarter	Demand
1	546	5	647	9	736
2	528	6	594	10	724
3	530	7	665	11	813
4	508	8	630	12	—

(a) Starting with a forecast for quarter 5, use the moving average technique based upon the past 4 quarters to forecast each demand through quarter 12.

(b) Examine the residuals for quarter 5 through quarter 12, and compute the mean value of their absolute values, i.e.,

$$\frac{\sum |X_i - h_i|}{7}.$$

15. Use the quarterly demand data of Prob. 14.

(a) Starting with a forecast for quarter 3, use the exponential smoothing technique with an initial estimate of 546 and $\alpha = 0.1$, i.e.,

$$\text{Forecast for quarter 3} = (0.1)528 + (0.9)546,$$

to forecast each demand through quarter 12.

(b) Examine the residuals for quarter 3 through quarter 11, and compute the mean of their absolute values, i.e.,

$$\frac{\sum |X_i - h_i|}{9}.$$

16. (a) Solve Prob. 15 using $\alpha = 0.2$.

(b) Which α ($\alpha = 0.1$ or 0.2) would you use to forecast the demand for quarter 12?

17. Based upon the results of Probs. 14(b) and 15(b), which forecasting procedure would you choose, moving average or exponential smoothing?

18. Use the quarterly demand data of Prob. 14.

(a)   Starting with a one-step forecast for quarter 3, use the exponential smoothing technique adjusted for trend, with an initial estimate of 546 for demand and an initial estimate of trend of 18, to forecast each demand through quarter 12. Use $\alpha = \beta = 0.1$.

(b)   Examine the residuals for quarter 3 through quarter 11, and compute the mean of their absolute values, i.e.,

$$\frac{\sum |X_i - h_i|}{9}.$$

19.   Based upon the results of Probs. 14(b), 15(b), and 18(b), which forecasting procedure would you choose, moving average, exponential smoothing, or exponential smoothing adjusted for trend?

20.   Suppose that a time series behaves as follows:

t	Y	t	Y
1	430	6	514
2	446	7	532
3	464	8	548
4	480	9	570
5	498	10	591

(a)   Using the method of least squares, estimate the line $\alpha + \beta t$.

(b)   From the line found in (a), forecast Y_{11}.

(c)   Starting with a forecast in period 3, use the exponential smoothing technique with an initial estimate of 430 and $\alpha = 0.1$, i.e.,

$$\text{Forecast for period 3} = (0.1)446 + (0.9)430,$$

to forecast each demand through period 11.

(d)   Starting with a one-step forecast for period 3, use the exponential smoothing technique adjusted for trend, with an initial estimate of 430 for the variable of interest and an initial estimate of trend of 18, to forecast each demand through period 11. Use $\alpha = \beta = 0.2$.

21.   The following data relate road width x and accident frequency Y. Road width (in feet) was treated as the independent variable, and values of the random variable Y, in accidents per 10^8 vehicle miles, were observed.

Number of observations = 7.

x	y
26	92
30	85
44	78
50	81
62	54
68	51
74	40

$$\sum_{i=1}^{7} x_i = 354 \qquad \sum_{i=1}^{7} Y_i = 481$$

$$\sum_{i=1}^{7} x_i^2 = 19{,}956 \qquad \sum_{i=1}^{7} Y_i^2 = 35{,}451$$

$$\sum_{i=1}^{7} x_i Y_i = 22{,}200$$

Assume that Y is normally distributed with mean $\alpha + \beta x$ and constant variance for all x, and that the sample is random. Interpolate if necessary.

(a) Fit a least squares line to the data, and forecast the accident frequency when the road width is 55 feet.

(b) Construct a 95 percent prediction interval for Y_+, a future observation of Y, corresponding to $x_+ = 55$ feet.

(c) Suppose that two future observations on Y, both corresponding to $x_+ = 55$ feet, are to be made. Construct prediction intervals for both of these observations so that the probability is *at least* 95 percent that *both* future values of Y will fall into them simultaneously. *Hint:* If k predictions are to be made [such as given in (d) Construct a simultaneous tolerance interval for the future value of Y future observations will fall into their respective intervals.

(d) Construct a simultaneous tolerance interval for the future value of Y corresponding to $x_+ = 55$ feet with $P = 0.90$ and $1 - \alpha = 0.95$.

22. The following data are observations on a dependent random variable Y taken at various levels of an independent variable x. [It is to be assumed that $E(Y_i | x_i) = \alpha + \beta x_i$, and Y_i are independent normal random variables with mean zero and variance σ^2.] Suppose the data are as follows.

x_i	0	2	4	6	8
y_i	0	4	7	13	16

(a) Estimate the linear relationship by the method of least squares, and forecast the value of Y when $x = 10$.

(b) Find a 95 percent confidence interval for the expected value of Y at $x_* = 10$.

(c) Find a 95 percent prediction interval for a future observation to be taken at $x_+ = 10$.

(d) For $x_+ = 10$, $P = 0.90$, and $(1 - \alpha) = 0.95$, find a simultaneous tolerance interval for the future value of Y_+. Interpolate if necessary.

23. If a particle is dropped at time $t = 0$, physical theory indicates that the relationship between r, the distance traveled, and t, the time elapsed, is $r = gt^k$ for some positive constants g and k. A transformation to linearity can be obtained by taking logarithms:

$$\log r = \log g + k \log t.$$

Letting $y = \log r$, $A = \log g$, and $x = \log t$, this relation becomes $y = A + kx$. Due to random error in measurement, however, it can only be stated that $E(Y | x) = A + kx$. Assume Y is normally distributed with mean $A + kx$ and variance σ^2.

A physicist who wishes to estimate k and g performs the following experiment: At time 0 the particle is dropped. At time t the distance r is measured. He performs this experiment 5 times, obtaining the following data:

$y = logarithm\ r$	$x = logarithm\ t$
-3.95	-2.0
-2.12	-1.0
0.08	0.0
2.20	+1.0
3.87	+2.0

(a) Obtain least squares estimates for k and $\log g$, and forecast the distance traveled when $\log t = +3.0$.

(b) Starting with a forecast for $\log r$ when $\log t = 0$, use the exponential smoothing technique with an initial estimate of $\log r = -3.95$ and $\alpha = 0.1$, i.e.,

$$\text{Forecast of } \log r \text{ (when } \log t = 0) = (0.1)(-2.12) + (0.9)(-3.95),$$

to forecast each $\log r$ for all integer $\log t$ through $\log t = +3.0$.

(c) Repeat (b) using the exponential smoothing technique adjusted for trend and a one-step forecast. Use an initial estimate of trend equal to the slope found in (a). Let $\beta = 0.1$.

The following data have been calculated:

$$\bar{y} = 0.016$$
$$\sum (x_i - \bar{x})^2 = 10$$
$$\sum (x_i - \bar{x})(y_i - \bar{y}) = 19.96$$
$$\sum (y_i - \tilde{y}_i)^2 = 0.0858$$

$$\frac{s_{y|x}}{\sqrt{\sum (x_i - \bar{x})^2}} = 0.053$$

$$s_{y|z} \sqrt{\frac{1}{5}} = 0.076.$$

Note: All algorithms are to the base 10.

24. Suppose that the relation between Y and x is given by

$$E(Y \mid x) = \beta x,$$

where Y is assumed to be normally distributed with mean βx and *known* variance σ^2. n independent pairs of observations are taken and are denoted by $x_1, y_1; x_2, y_2; \ldots; x_n, y_n$. Find the least squares estimate of β.

CHAPTER 20

Markovian Decision Processes and Applications

20.1 Introduction

Section 15.2 introduced the concept of a dynamic system evolving over time. The behavior of such a system resulted in an analysis of a particular type of stochastic process. The ideas presented can be illustrated by considering the following maintenance-model example. A production process contains a machine that deteriorates rapidly in both quality and output under heavy usage, so that it is inspected periodically, say, at the end of each day. Immediately after inspection, the condition of the machine is noted and classified into one of four possible states:

State	Condition
0	Good as new
1	Operable— minor deterioration
2	Operable—major deterioration
3	Inoperable—output of unacceptable quality

Let X_t denote the observed state of the machine after inspection at the end of the tth day. It is reasonable to assume that the state of the system evolves according to some probabilistic "laws of motion," so that the sequence of states $\{X_t\}$ can be viewed as a stochastic process. Furthermore, it will be assumed that the stochastic process is a finite-state Markov chain (see Sec. 15.3), with known transition matrix given by

State	0	1	2	3
0	0	$\frac{7}{8}$	$\frac{1}{16}$	$\frac{1}{16}$
1	0	$\frac{3}{4}$	$\frac{1}{8}$	$\frac{1}{8}$
2	0	0	$\frac{1}{2}$	$\frac{1}{2}$
3	0	0	0	1

From this transition matrix, it becomes evident that once the machine becomes inoperable (enters state 3), it remains inoperable. Therefore, the analysis of this stochastic process is probably uninteresting because state 3 is an absorbing state, and eventually the machine will enter this state and just remain there; i.e., after some time period, X_t will always equal 3. Clearly, from a practical point of view, this model is intolerable because a machine that is inoperable cannot continue to remain in the production process and must be replaced (or repaired). This action of replacement alters the behavior of the system, so that the system now evolves over time according to the joint effect of the probabilistic laws of motion and the action of replacing an inoperable machine. Note that the action of replacing an inoperable machine can be thought of as defining a maintenance policy.

When a machine becomes inoperable and is replaced, the replacement machine is as good as new; i.e., the machine is found to be in state 0 at the time of the regular inspection at the end of the next day. As a practical matter, the replacement process can be thought of as taking 1 day to complete so that production is lost for this period.

The costs incurred while this system evolves contains several components. When the system is in states 0, 1, or 2, defective items may be produced during the next day, and the expected costs are given by

State	Expected cost due to producing defective items
0	0
1	$1,000
2	$3,000

If the machine is replaced, a replacement cost of $4,000 is incurred, together with a cost of lost production (lost profit) of $2,000. Hence the total cost incurred whenever the system is in state 3 is $6,000.

The stochastic process resulting from the system with the aforementioned maintenance policy, i.e., replacing an inoperable machine, is still a finite-state Markov chain, but with the transition matrix now given by

State	0	1	2	3
0	0	$\frac{7}{8}$	$\frac{1}{16}$	$\frac{1}{16}$
1	0	$\frac{3}{4}$	$\frac{1}{8}$	$\frac{1}{8}$
2	0	0	$\frac{1}{2}$	$\frac{1}{2}$
3	1	0	0	0

It may be interesting to evaluate the cost of this maintenance policy. If the (long run) expected average cost per day or the (long run) actual average cost per day is an appropriate measure, the results appearing in Sec. 15.7 (under the subsections on expected average cost per unit time or expected average cost per unit time for complex cost functions) are appropriate.

By noting that $p_{ij}^{(4)} > 0$ for all i and j, it is evident that every state is positive recurrent and belongs to one class. The steady-state equations can be written as

$$\pi_0 = \pi_3,$$

$$\pi_1 = \frac{7}{8}\pi_0 + \frac{3}{4}\pi_1,$$

$$\pi_2 = \frac{1}{16}\pi_0 + \frac{1}{8}\pi_1 + \frac{1}{2}\pi_2,$$

$$\pi_3 = \frac{1}{16}\pi_0 + \frac{1}{8}\pi_1 + \frac{1}{2}\pi_2,$$

$$1 = \pi_0 + \pi_1 + \pi_2 + \pi_3.$$

The simultaneous solution is

$$\pi_0 = \frac{2}{13},$$

$$\pi_1 = \frac{7}{13},$$

$$\pi_2 = \frac{2}{13},$$

$$\pi_3 = \frac{2}{13}.$$

Hence the long-run expected average cost per day is given by

$$0\pi_0 + 1{,}000\pi_1 + 3{,}000\pi_2 + 6{,}000\pi_3 = \frac{25{,}000}{13} = \$1{,}923.08,$$

and this cost represents the cost of this maintenance policy.

20.2 Markovian Decision Models

The previous section introduced an example of a maintenance model for a machine and presented a maintenance policy; i.e., when a machine becomes inoperable it is replaced; otherwise, the machine is left alone. In other words, a decision is made to take the action *replace the machine* when it is found to be in state 3, whereas a decision is made to take the action *leave the machine as is* when it is found to be in states 0, 1, or 2. Even when these two actions are the only permissible ones, there are still other policies that can be generated; e.g., when the machine becomes inoperable or is found to be operable but with major deterioration (machine is in states 2 or 3), replace it; otherwise leave the machine as is. Note that this policy generates a different transition matrix; i.e.,

State	0	1	2	3
0	0	$\dfrac{7}{8}$	$\dfrac{1}{16}$	$\dfrac{1}{16}$
1	0	$\dfrac{3}{4}$	$\dfrac{1}{8}$	$\dfrac{1}{8}$
2	1	0	0	0
3	1	0	0	0

To make the machine-maintenance example more realistic, suppose that a third action is permitted: overhaul. When a machine is overhauled, the machine is returned to state 1 (operable—minor deterioration) at the time of the regular inspection at the end of the next day. As a practical matter, like replacement, the overhaul process can be thought of as requiring a day to complete, so that production is lost for this period. Furthermore, overhauling the machine costs $2,000 and will not be considered as a viable decision when the machine becomes inoperable.

In viewing this dynamic system, it is evident that the system evolves over time according to the joint effect of the probabilistic laws of motion and the sequence of decisions made (actions taken). In particular, the machine is inspected at the end of each day and its state is recorded. A decision as to which action to take must be made, i.e.,

Decision	Action
1	Do nothing
2	Overhaul (return system to state 1)
3	Replace (return system to state 0)

For the general model it will be assumed that a system is observed at time $t = 0, 1, \ldots$ and classified into one of a finite number of states labeled $0, 1, \ldots, M$. Let $\{X_t, t = 0, 1, \ldots\}$ denote the sequence of observed states. After each observation, one of K (finite) possible decisions (actions), labeled 1, 2, ..., K, is taken.[1] Let $\{\Delta_t, t = 0, 1, \ldots\}$ denote the sequence of actual decisions made.

A policy, denoted by R, is a rule for making decisions at each point in time. In principle, a policy could use all the previously observed information up to time t, that is, the entire history of the system consisting of $X_0, X_1, \ldots, X_t$ and $\Delta_0, \Delta_1, \Delta_2, \ldots, \Delta_{t-1}$. However, for most problems encountered in practice, it is sufficient to confine consideration to those policies that depend upon only the observed state of the system at time t, X_t, and the possible decisions available. Hence a policy R can be viewed as a rule that prescribes decision $d_i(R)$ when the system is in state i, $i = 0, 1, \ldots, M$. Thus R is completely characterized by the values

$$\{d_0(R), d_1(R), \ldots, d_M(R)\}.$$

Note that this description assumes that whenever the system is in state i, the decision to be made is the same for all values of t. Policies possessing this property are called *stationary policies*.

In the example, the interesting policies are

Policy	Verbal description	$d_0(R)$	$d_1(R)$	$d_2(R)$	$d_3(R)$
R_a	Replace in state 3	1	1	1	3
R_b	Replace in state 3 overhaul in state 2	1	1	2	3
R_c	Replace in states 2, 3	1	1	3	3
R_d	Replace in states 1, 2, 3	1	3	3	3

Note that policy R_a is the policy described in the previous section, and R_c is the policy alluded to earlier in this section. Furthermore, recall that each policy results in a different transition matrix.

It has been noted that a system evolves over time according to the joint effect of the probabilistic laws of motion and the sequence of decisions made; its path is dependent upon its initial state, X_0. It is assumed that whenever the system is in state i and decision $d_i(R) = k$ is made, the system moves to a new state j, with known transition probability $p_{ij}(k)$, for all $i, j = 0, 1, \ldots, M$ and $k = 1, 2, \ldots, K$. Thus, if a given policy R is followed, the resultant stochastic process is a Markov chain with a known transition matrix (dependent upon the policy chosen). Unless otherwise noted, throughout this chapter it is assumed for technical reasons that the *Markov chain associated with every transition matrix is irreducible*.

---

[1] In general, the number of possible decisions may depend upon the state of the system. Such a case is considered in Sec. 20.7.

In the example, the following transition matrices are obtained:

R_a

State	0	1	2	3
0	0	$\frac{7}{8}$	$\frac{1}{16}$	$\frac{1}{16}$
1	0	$\frac{3}{4}$	$\frac{1}{8}$	$\frac{1}{8}$
2	0	0	$\frac{1}{2}$	$\frac{1}{2}$
3	1	0	0	0

R_b

State	0	1	2	3
0	0	$\frac{7}{8}$	$\frac{1}{16}$	$\frac{1}{16}$
1	0	$\frac{3}{4}$	$\frac{1}{8}$	$\frac{1}{8}$
2	0	1	0	0
3	1	0	0	0

R_c

State	0	1	2	3
0	0	$\frac{7}{8}$	$\frac{1}{16}$	$\frac{1}{16}$
1	0	$\frac{3}{4}$	$\frac{1}{8}$	$\frac{1}{8}$
2	1	0	0	0
3	1	0	0	0

R_d

State	0	1	2	3
0	0	$\frac{7}{8}$	$\frac{1}{16}$	$\frac{1}{16}$
1	1	0	0	0
2	1	0	0	0
3	1	0	0	0

To summarize, given a distribution $P\{X_0 = i\}$ over the initial states of the system and a policy R, a system evolves over time according to the joint effect of the probabilistic laws of motion and the sequence of decisions made (actions taken). In particular, when the system is in state i and decision $d_i(R) = k$ is made, then the probability that the system is in state j at the next observed time period is given by $p_{ij}(k)$. This situation results in a sequence of observed states $X_0, X_1, \ldots$ and a sequence of decisions made, $\Delta_0, \Delta_1, \ldots$. This sequence of observed states and sequence of decisions made is called a *Markovian decision process*. The term *Markovian* is used because of the underlying assumptions made about the probabilistic laws of motion.

Four maintenance policies have been described, but their properties have not been evaluated. Questions such as "Which one is 'best'?" remain to be answered. To pursue this avenue, it is necessary to introduce a cost structure. When the system is in state i and decision $d_i(R) = k$ is made following policy R, a known cost C_{ik} is incurred. This cost may represent an expected rather than an actual cost. For example, in the maintenance problem, the cost of leaving a machine as is depends upon the random variable, the number of defective items produced during the next time period. The expected value of this cost function taken with respect to the distribution of the number of defective items will result in the desired cost C_{ik}.[1] It is important to reiterate that this cost depends upon

[1] See Sec. 15.7 under the subsection on expected average cost per unit time for complex cost functions for an additional example.

only the state the system is found in and the decision made; that is,

$$C_{ik} = \text{known (expected) cost incurred during next transition}$$
$$\text{if system is in state } i \text{ and decision } k \text{ is made.}$$

For the four maintenance policies, the costs can be obtained from the following information:

Decision	State	Cost	Expected cost due to producing defective items	Maintenance cost	Cost (lost profit) of lost production	Total cost per day
1. Leave	0		0	0	0	0
machine	1		$1,000	0	0	$1,000
as is	2		$3,000	0	0	$3,000
	3		∞*	0	0	∞
2. Overhaul	0, 1, 2		0	$2,000	$2,000	$4.000
	3		0	∞*	$2,000	∞
3. Replace	0, 1, 2, 3		0	$4,000	$2,000	$6,000

* Because leaving the machine in an inoperable condition or overhauling it when it is inoperable is prohibited by assumption, a cost of infinity is assigned. An alternate approach would be to omit these decisions from the set of possible decisions when the machine is found to be in state 3.

Note that the costs incurred when the decision is made to replace the machine are independent of the state of the system. This fact is evident because no production takes place during the ensuing day when this action is taken. Finally, the total expected costs incurred per day are summarized as follows:

State	Decision	C_{ik} (in thousands of dollars)	
	1	2	3
0	0	4	6
1	1	4	6
2	3	4	6
3	∞	∞	6

To compare policies, we must settle on an appropriate cost measure. One such measure associated with a policy is the (long run) expected average cost per unit time; this measure will be the one used.[1] The results appearing in Sec. 15.7 are appropriate; i.e., for any policy, the (long run) expected average cost per unit time, $E(C)$, can be calculated from the expression

$$E(C) = \sum_{i=0}^{M} C_{ik}\pi_i,$$

where $k = d_i(R)$ for each i, and $(\pi_0, \pi_1, \ldots, \pi_M)$ represents the steady-state distribution of the state of the system under the policy R being evaluated. Thus the policy that minimizes $E(C)$ is sought. Using this criterion, it is evident that the distribution over the initial states of the system is not important, because the

---

[1] The ensuing results are also valid for the (long-run) actual average cost per unit time measure as noted in Sec. 15.7.

long-run effect of the cost of the initial decision is negligible. In the maintenance example, it is necessary to solve for $(\pi_0, \pi_1, \ldots, \pi_M)$ under each of the four policies of interest and then use these results to obtain $E(C)$. The necessary calculations for R_a are given in Sec. 20.1; all are now summarized:

Policy	$\pi_0, \pi_1, \pi_2, \pi_3$	$E(C)$
R_a	$\left(\dfrac{2}{13}, \dfrac{7}{13}, \dfrac{2}{13}, \dfrac{2}{13}\right)$	$\dfrac{1}{13}[2(0) + 7(1) + 2(3) + 2(6)] = \dfrac{25}{13} = 1.923$
R_b	$\left(\dfrac{2}{21}, \dfrac{5}{7}, \dfrac{2}{21}, \dfrac{2}{21}\right)$	$\dfrac{1}{21}[2(0) + 15(1) + 2(4) + 2(6)] = \dfrac{35}{21} = 1.667$ min.
R_c	$\left(\dfrac{2}{11}, \dfrac{7}{11}, \dfrac{1}{11}, \dfrac{1}{11}\right)$	$\dfrac{1}{11}[2(0) + 7(1) + 1(6) + 1(6)] = \dfrac{19}{11} = 1.727$
R_d	$\left(\dfrac{1}{2}, \dfrac{7}{16}, \dfrac{1}{32}, \dfrac{1}{32}\right)$	$\dfrac{1}{32}[16(0) + 14(6) + 1(6) + 1(6)] = \dfrac{96}{32} = 3$

It is evident that policy R_b is the best. Among the four policies considered, the policy that calls for replacing the machine when it is found to be in state 3 and overhauling it when it is found to be in state 2 is the best, and the (long-run) expected average cost per day is \$1,667.

The technique described here is just an exhaustive enumeration of a given set of possible policies. It is evident that direct enumeration becomes cumbersome when the number of policies is large and algorithms are desirable for finding optimal policies. The next three sections consider such algorithms.

20.3 Linear Programming and Optimal Policies

Section 20.2 defined a policy, and we saw that a policy R can be viewed as a rule that prescribes decision $d_i(R)$ when the system is in state i. Thus R is characterized by the values

$$\{d_0(R), d_1(R), \ldots, d_M(R)\}.$$

Alternatively, R can be characterized by assigning values $D_{ik} = 0$ or 1 in the matrix

$$
\text{State} \quad
\begin{array}{c}
0 \\ 1 \\ \vdots \\ M
\end{array}
\overset{\displaystyle \text{Decision, } k}{
\overset{\displaystyle
\begin{array}{cccc}
1 & 2 & \cdots & K
\end{array}}
{\begin{bmatrix}
D_{01} & D_{02} & \cdots & D_{0K} \\
D_{11} & D_{12} & \cdots & D_{1K} \\
\vdots & & & \vdots \\
D_{M1} & D_{M2} & \cdots & D_{MK}
\end{bmatrix}}},
$$

where each row must contain a single 1 with the rest of the elements zero (i.e., each row sums to 1). When an element $D_{ik} = 1$, it can be interpreted as calling for decision k when the system is in state i. In the maintenance-model example, policy

R_b can be characterized by the matrix

Decision, k

$$
\text{State} \quad
\begin{array}{c}
0 \\ 1 \\ 2 \\ 3
\end{array}
\begin{bmatrix}
\begin{array}{ccc}
1 & 2 & 3 \\
\end{array} \\
\begin{array}{ccc}
1 & 0 & 0 \\
1 & 0 & 0 \\
0 & 1 & 0 \\
0 & 0 & 1 \\
\end{array}
\end{bmatrix} ;
$$

i.e., replace the machine when it is in state 3, overhaul the machine when it is in state 2, and leave the machine as is when it is in states 0 or 1. This interpretation of the D_{ik} provides motivation for a linear programming formulation. Hopefully, the expected cost of a policy can be expressed as a linear function of the D_{ik} or a related variable, subject to linear constraints. Unfortunately, the D_{ik} are integers (zero or 1), and continuous variables are required for a linear programming formulation. This requirement can be handled by expanding the interpretation of a policy. The previous definition calls for making the same decision every time the system is in state i. The new interpretation of a policy will call for determining a probability distribution for the decision to be made when the system is in state i. Thus D_{ik} can now be viewed as

$$
D_{ik} = P\{\text{decision} = k | \text{state} = i\},^{\dagger} \quad k = 1, 2, \ldots, K,
$$
$$
i = 0, 1, \ldots, M.
$$

Such a policy is called a *randomized policy*, whereas the policy calling for $D_{ik} = 0$ or 1 can be called a *deterministic policy*. Randomized policies can again be characterized by the matrix

Decision, k

$$
\text{State} \quad
\begin{array}{c}
0 \\ 1 \\ \vdots \\ M
\end{array}
\begin{bmatrix}
\begin{array}{cccc}
1 & 2 & \cdots & K \\
\end{array} \\
\begin{array}{cccc}
D_{01} & D_{02} & \cdots & D_{0K} \\
D_{11} & D_{12} & \cdots & D_{1K} \\
 & & \vdots & \\
D_{M1} & D_{M2} & \cdots & D_{MK} \\
\end{array}
\end{bmatrix} ,
$$

where each row sums to 1, and now

$$
0 \le D_{ik} \le 1.
$$

Note that each row $(D_{i1}, D_{i2}, \ldots, D_{ik})$ is the probability distribution for the decision to be made when the system is in state i. As an example, suppose that a new policy, R_e, is to be used in the maintenance model. This policy is a

---

† The right-hand side of this equation is read as the conditional probability that the decision k is made, given the system is in state i.

randomized policy and is given by the matrix

$$\begin{array}{c} \text{Decision, } k \\ \begin{array}{ccc} 1 & 2 & 3 \end{array} \\ \text{State} \quad \begin{array}{c} 0 \\ 1 \\ 2 \\ 3 \end{array} \begin{bmatrix} 1 & 0 & 0 \\ 1 & 0 & 0 \\ \dfrac{1}{4} & \dfrac{1}{4} & \dfrac{1}{2} \\ 0 & \dfrac{1}{2} & \dfrac{1}{2} \end{bmatrix}. \end{array}$$

This policy calls for observing the state of the machine at the end of the day. If it is found to be in states 0 or 1, it is left as is. If it is found to be in state 2, it is left as is with probability $\frac{1}{4}$, overhauled with probability $\frac{1}{4}$, and replaced with probability $\frac{1}{2}$. Presumably, a random device with these probabilities (possibly a table of random numbers) can be used to make the actual decision. Finally, if the machine is found to be in state 3, it is overhauled with probability $\frac{1}{2}$ and replaced with probability $\frac{1}{2}$.

The *linear programming formulation* is best expressed in terms of a variable y_{ik}, which is related to D_{ik} as follows. Let y_{ik} be the steady-state unconditional probability that the system is in state i *and* decision k is made; that is,

$$y_{ik} = P\{\text{state} = i \text{ and decision} = k\}.$$

From the rules of conditional probability,

$$y_{ik} = \pi_i D_{ik}.$$

Furthermore,

$$\pi_i = \sum_{k=1}^{K} y_{ik},$$

so that

$$D_{ik} = \frac{y_{ik}}{\pi_i} = \frac{y_{ik}}{\sum_{k=1}^{K} y_{ik}}.$$

There exist several constraints on y_{ik}:

1. $\sum_{i=0}^{M} \pi_i = 1$, so that $\sum_{i=0}^{M} \sum_{k=1}^{K} y_{ik} = 1$.
2. From results on steady-state probabilities (see Sec. 15.7),

$$\pi_j = \sum_{i=0}^{M} \pi_i p_{ij}, \text{ so that } \sum_{k=1}^{K} y_{jk} = \sum_{i=0}^{M} \sum_{k=1}^{K} y_{ik} p_{ij}(k),^{\dagger} \quad \text{for } j = 0, 1, \ldots, M.$$

3. $y_{ik} \geq 0, i = 0, 1, \ldots, M$ and $k = 1, 2, \ldots, K.$

---

† The k is introduced in $p_{ij}(k)$ to indicate that the appropriate transition probability depends upon the decision k.

The long-run expected average cost per unit time is given by

$$E(C) = \sum_{i=0}^{M} \sum_{k=1}^{K} \pi_i C_{ik} D_{ik} = \sum_{i=0}^{M} \sum_{k=1}^{K} C_{ik} y_{ik}.$$

Hence the problem is to choose the y_{ik} that

$$\text{Minimizes} \quad \sum_{i=0}^{M} \sum_{k=1}^{K} C_{ik} y_{ik},$$

subject to the constraints

(1)
$$\sum_{i=0}^{M} \sum_{k=1}^{K} y_{ik} = 1.$$

(2)
$$\sum_{k=1}^{K} y_{jk} - \sum_{i=0}^{M} \sum_{k=1}^{K} y_{ik} p_{ij}(k) = 0, \quad \text{for } j = 0, 1, \ldots, M.$$

(3)
$$y_{ik} \geq 0 \quad i = 0, 1, \ldots, M; \quad k = 1, 2, \ldots, K.$$

This formulation is clearly a *linear programming problem* that can be solved by the simplex method. Once the y_{ik} are obtained, D_{ik} is easily found from

$$D_{ik} = \frac{y_{ik}}{\sum_{k=1}^{K} y_{ik}}.$$

The solution has some interesting properties. It will contain $(M + 1)$ basic variables $y_{ik} \geq 0$ (there is one redundant constraint). It can be shown that $y_{ik} > 0$ for at least one $k = 1, 2, \ldots, K$, for each $i = 0, 1, \ldots, M$. Therefore, it follows that $y_{ik} > 0$ for only *one* k for each $i = 0, 1, \ldots, M$; that is, $D_{ik} = 0$ or 1. In other words, the optimal policy is *deterministic rather than randomized*. Finally, since there are $(M + 2)$ functional constraints and $K(M + 1)$ original variables, "practical" problems tend to be large under this formulation, so that solutions may not be obtainable even with the simplex method.

EXAMPLE We can formulate the machine-maintenance problem as a *linear program*; i.e.,

Minimize $4{,}000y_{02} + 6{,}000y_{03} + 1{,}000y_{11} + 4{,}000y_{12} + 6{,}000y_{13}$
$+ 3{,}000y_{21} + 4{,}000y_{22} + 6{,}000y_{23} + M_1 y_{31} + M_2 y_{32}$
$+ 6{,}000y_{33},$

where M_1 and M_2 are taken to be large numbers, subject to

$$\sum_{i=0}^{3} \sum_{k=1}^{3} y_{ik} = 1,$$

$$\sum_{k=1}^{3} y_{0k} - (y_{03} + y_{13} + y_{23} + y_{33}) = 0,$$

$$\sum_{k=1}^{3} y_{1k} - \left(\frac{7}{8}y_{01} + y_{02} + \frac{3}{4}y_{11} + y_{12} + y_{22} + y_{32}\right) = 0,$$

$$\sum_{k=1}^{3} y_{2k} - \left(\frac{1}{16}y_{01} + \frac{1}{8}y_{11} + \frac{1}{2}y_{21}\right) = 0,$$

$$\sum_{k=1}^{3} y_{3k} - \left(\frac{1}{16}y_{01} + \frac{1}{8}y_{11} + \frac{1}{2}y_{21} + y_{31}\right) = 0,$$

and

$$y_{ik} \geq 0, \quad i = 0, 1, 2, 3 \quad \text{and} \quad k = 1, 2, 3.$$

This linear program can be solved by using the simplex method.

The results yield all y_{ik} equal to zero, except for $y_{01} = \frac{2}{21}$, $y_{11} = \frac{5}{7}$, $y_{22} = \frac{2}{21}$, and $y_{33} = \frac{2}{21}$. Note that these values are just the steady-state probabilities for policy R_b, which is now seen to be the optimal policy. The corresponding

$$D_{ik} = \frac{y_{ik}}{\sum_{k=1}^{3} y_{ik}}$$

are given by

$$D_{01} = D_{11} = D_{22} = D_{33} = 1,$$

and all the remaining $D_{ik} = 0$. This policy calls for leaving the machine as is when it is in states 0 or 1, overhauling it when it is in state 2, and replacing it when it is in state 3.

20.4 Policy-Improvement Algorithms for Finding Optimal Policies

A second algorithm for finding optimal policies is given by a *policy-improvement technique*. The algorithm to be presented is useful in that it often leads to finding the optimal policy quickly, and also it is applicable under more general conditions then previously specified; e.g., under certain assumptions, the number of states may be countably infinite rather than finite.

Following the model of Sec. 20.2, and as a joint result of the current state i of the system and the decision $d_i(R) = k$ when operating under policy R, two things occur. A (expected) cost C_{ik} that depends upon only the observed state of the system and the decision made is incurred. The system moves to a new state j at the next observed time period, with transition probability given by $p_{ij}(k)$. If, in fact, a cost that depends upon both the initial and transited states is incurred, it is treated as follows. Denote by $q_{ij}(k)$ the (expected) cost incurred when the system is in state i and decision k is made, and then evolves to state j at the next observed time period. Then

$$C_{ik} = \sum_{j=0}^{M} q_{ij}(k)p_{ij}(k).$$

When a system operates as just described under policy R, it can be shown that there exist values $g(R)$, $v_0(R)$, $v_1(R), \ldots, v_M(R)$ that satisfy

$$g(R) + v_i(R) = C_{ik} + \sum_{j=0}^{M} p_{ij}(k)v_j(R), \quad \text{for } i = 0, 1, 2, \ldots, M.$$

A heuristic justification for these relationships and an interpretation for these values are desirable. Denote by $v_i^n(R)$ the total expected cost of a system starting in state i (at the first observed time period) and evolving for n time periods. Then $v_i^n(R)$ consists of two components, namely, (1) C_{ik}, the cost incurred at the first observed time period as a result of the current state i and the decision $d_i(R) = k$ when operating under policy R, and (2) $\sum_{j=0}^{M} p_{ij}(k)v_j^{n-1}(R)$, the total expected cost of the system evolving over the remaining $n - 1$ time periods. Thus the recursive equation,

$$v_i^n(R) = C_{ik} + \sum_{j=0}^{M} p_{ij}(k)v_j^{n-1}(R),$$

for $i = 0, 1, 2, \ldots, M$ and $v_i^1(R) = C_{ik}$ for all i is obtained. It is of interest to explore the behavior of the total expected cost $v_i^n(R)$ as n gets large. Now, it is known that the long-run expected average cost *per unit time* following any policy R can be expressed as

$$g(R) = \sum_{i=0}^{M} \pi_i C_{ik},$$

which is independent of the starting state i. Hence $v_i^n(R)$ behaves approximately as $ng(R)$ for large n, and, in fact, can be expressed (neglecting certain fluctuations) as the sum of two components, one of which is independent of the initial state and one of which is dependent upon it; that is,

$$v_i^n(R) \approx ng(R) + v_i(R),$$

where $v_i(R)$ can be interpreted as the effect on the total expected cost due to starting in state i. Thus

$$v_i^n(R) - v_j^n(R) \approx v_i(R) - v_j(R),$$

so that $v_i(R) - v_j(R)$ is a measure of the effect of starting in state i rather than state j.

Substituting this linear approximation for $v_i^n(R)$ (assumed to be valid for large n) into the recursive equation for $v_i^n(R)$ leads to

$$g(R) + v_i(R) = C_{ik} + \sum_{j=0}^{M} p_{ij}(k)v_j(R),$$

for $i = 0, 1, \ldots, M$, so that these values satisfy the expressed equations.

Note that there are $M + 1$ equations with $M + 2$ unknowns, so that one of these variables may be chosen arbitrarily. By convention, $v_M(R)$ will be chosen equal to zero. Therefore, by solving a system of linear equations, the (long run) expected average cost per unit time following policy R, $g(R)$ can be obtained. In principle, all policies can be enumerated, and that policy which minimizes $g(R)$ can be found. However, even for a moderate number of states and decisions, this technique is cumbersome. Fortunately, there exists an algorithm that can be used to evaluate policies and find the optimum one without complete enumeration. The algorithm begins by choosing an arbitrary policy R_1 and calculates the values of $g(R_1), v_0(R_1), v_1(R_1), \ldots, v_{M-1}(R_1)$ [recall that $v_M(R_1)$ is chosen equal to zero]. This step is called *value determination*. A better policy, denoted by R_2, is then constructed. This step is called *policy improvement*. Using the new policy R_2, we repeat the value-determination step. These steps continue until two successive iterations lead to identical policies, which signifies that the optimal policy has been obtained. In particular, the following steps are to be followed:

Step 1 Value determination For an arbitrarily chosen policy R_1, use $p_{ij}(k_1)$, C_{ik_1}, and $v_M(R_1) = 0$ to solve the set of $(M + 1)$ equations,

$$g(R_1) = C_{ik_1} + \sum_{j=0}^{M} p_{ij}(k_1)v_j(R_1) - v_i(R_1), \quad i = 0, 1, \ldots, M.$$

for all $(M + 1)$ unknown values of $g(R_1), v_0(R_1), v_1(R_1), \ldots, v_{M-1}(R_1)$.

Step 2 Policy improvement Using the current values of $v_i(R_1)$ computed for policy R_1, find the alternative policy R_2 such that, for each state i, $d_i(R_2) = k_2$ is the decision that makes

$$C_{ik_2} + \sum_{j=0}^{M} p_{ij}(k_2)v_j(R_1) - v_i(R_1)$$

a minimum; that is, for *each* state i, find the appropriate value of k_2 that

$$\underset{k_2 = 1,2,\ldots,K}{\text{Minimizes}} \left\{ C_{ik_2} + \sum_{j=0}^{M} p_{ij}(k_2)v_j(R_1) - v_i(R_1) \right\},$$

and then set $d_i(R_2)$ equal to the minimizing value of k_2. This procedure defines a new policy, R_2.

If R_2 does not equal to R_1, then return to step 1, using R_2 instead of R_1, and solve for $g(R_2), v_0(R_2), v_1(R_2), \ldots, v_{n-1}(R_2)$. Using these values, go to step 2 and find R_3. Continue in this fashion until you find two successive R's to be equal. When you find them, the optimal policy is achieved, and the algorithm terminates. In fact, it can be shown that

1. $g(R_{j+1}) \le g(R_j)$, for $j = 1, 2, \ldots$, and
2. The algorithm terminates with the optimal solution in a finite number of iterations.

EXAMPLE We shall solve the maintenance model presented in Sec. 20.2 by the *policy-improvement algorithm*. Recall that the machine can be in one of four states: state 0, signifying the machine is as good as new; state 1, signifying the machine is operable with minor deterioration; state 2, signifying the machine is operable with major deterioration; and state 3, signifying the machine is inoperable. There exist three possible decisions: decision 1 implies leaving the machine as is; decision 2 implies overhaul, which returns it to state 1; and decision 3 implies replacement, which returns it to state 0. Each decision necessitates an action that affects the transition matrix, and there are costs C_{ik} associated with making decision k when the system is in state i. We want to find the optimal policy, and step 1 of the algorithm calls for choosing a policy arbitrarily. Choose the policy that calls for replacement of the machine when it is found to be in state 3; otherwise, leave the machine as is. Denote this policy by R_1. The transition matrix for this policy is given by

State	0	1	2	3
0	0	$\frac{7}{8}$	$\frac{1}{16}$	$\frac{1}{16}$
1	0	$\frac{3}{4}$	$\frac{1}{8}$	$\frac{1}{8}$
2	0	0	$\frac{1}{2}$	$\frac{1}{2}$
3	1	0	0	0

The costs incurred following policy R_1 are given by

State	C_{ik_1}
0	0
1	1,000
2	3,000
3	6,000

With this policy, the value-determination step requires solving the following four equations simultaneously for $g(R_1)$, $v_0(R_1)$, $v_1(R_1)$, and $v_2(R_1)$ [recall that $v_3(R_1)$ is arbitrarily taken to be zero]:

$$g(R_1) = C_{0k_1} + \sum_{j=0}^{3} p_{0j}(k_1)v_j(R_1) - v_0(R_1)$$

$$g(R_1) = C_{1k_1} + \sum_{j=0}^{3} p_{1j}(k_1)v_j(R_1) - v_1(R_1)$$

$$g(R_1) = C_{2k_1} + \sum_{j=0}^{3} p_{2j}(k_1)v_j(R_1) - v_2(R_1)$$

$$g(R_1) = C_{3k_1} + \sum_{j=0}^{3} p_{3j}(k_1)v_j(R_1) - v_3(R_1),$$

or alternatively [with $v_3(R_1) = 0$],

$$g(R_1) = \qquad + \frac{7}{8}v_1(R_1) + \frac{1}{16}v_2(R_1) - v_0(R_1)$$

$$g(R_1) = 1,000 + \frac{3}{4}v_1(R_1) + \frac{1}{8}v_2(R_1) - v_1(R_1)$$

$$g(R_1) = 3,000 \qquad + \frac{1}{2}v_2(R_1) - v_2(R_1)$$

$$g(R_1) = 6,000 + v_0(R_1).$$

The simultaneous solution to this system of equations yields

$$g(R_1) = \frac{25,000}{13} = 1,923$$

$$v_0(R_1) = -\frac{53,000}{13} = -4,077$$

$$v_1(R_1) = -\frac{34,000}{13} = -2,615$$

$$v_2(R_1) = \frac{28,000}{13} = 2,154.$$

Step 2 can now be applied. It is necessary to find the improved policy R_2, which has the property that $d_0(R_2) = k_2^0$, $d_1(R_2) = k_2^1$, $d_2(R_2) = k_2^2$, and $d_3(R_2) = k_2^3$ minimize the following expressions:

(0) $\quad C_{0k_2^0} - p_{00}(k_2^0)4,077 - p_{01}(k_2^0)2,615 + p_{02}(k_2^0)2,154 + 4,077$

(1) $\quad C_{1k_2^1} - p_{10}(k_2^1)4,077 - p_{11}(k_2^1)2,615 + p_{12}(k_2^1)2,154 + 2,615$

(2) $\quad C_{2k_2^2} - p_{20}(k_2^2)4,077 - p_{21}(k_2^2)2,615 + p_{22}(k_2^2)2,154 - 2,154$

(3) $\quad C_{3k_2^3} - p_{30}(k_2^3)4,077 - p_{31}(k_2^3)2,615 + p_{32}(k_2^3)2,154.$

To find k_2^0, the "best" decision when the machine is in state 0, it is necessary to evaluate the first expression for all possible decisions. Note that the appropriate transition probabilities and the costs C_{0k} depend upon the decisions made. A summary of the necessary calculations follows:

Decision	$p_{00}(k_2)$	$p_{01}(k_2)$	$p_{02}(k_2)$	$p_{03}(k_2)$	C_{0k_2}	Value of expression 0
1	0	$\frac{7}{8}$	$\frac{1}{16}$	$\frac{1}{16}$	0	1,923
2	0	1	0	0	4,000	5,462
3	1	0	0	0	6,000	6,000

It is clear that $d_0(R_2) = k_2^0 = 1$ minimizes this first expression, so that under R_2 the appropriate decision when the system is in state 0 is to leave the machine as is.

Similar calculations are required to find $d_1(R_2) = k_2^1$, $d_2(R_2) = k_2^2$, and $d_3(R_2) = k_2^3$; these calculations are summarized as follows:

State 1

Decision	$p_{10}(k_2)$	$p_{11}(k_2)$	$p_{12}(k_2)$	$p_{13}(k_2)$	C_{1k_2}	Value of expression 1
1	0	$\frac{3}{4}$	$\frac{1}{8}$	$\frac{1}{8}$	1,000	1,923
2	0	1	0	0	4,000	4,000
3	1	0	0	0	6,000	4,538

State 2

Decision	$p_{20}(k_2)$	$p_{21}(k_2)$	$p_{22}(k_2)$	$p_{23}(k_2)$	C_{2k_2}	Value of expression 2
1	0	0	$\dfrac{1}{2}$	$\dfrac{1}{2}$	3,000	1,923
2	0	1	0	0	4,000	-769
3	1	0	0	0	6,000	-231

State 3

Decision	$p_{30}(k_2)$	$p_{31}(k_2)$	$p_{32}(k_2)$	$p_{33}(k_2)$	C_{3k_2}	Value of expression 3
1	0	0	0	1	∞	∞
2	0	1	0	0	∞	∞
3	1	0	0	0	6,000	1,923

Thus $d_1(R_2) = k_2^1 = 1$, $d_2(R_2) = k_2^2 = 2$, and $d_3(R_2) = k_2^3 = 3$. Hence policy R_2 calls for leaving the machine alone when it is in states 0 or 1, overhauling it when it is in state 2, and replacing it when it is in state 3. Furthermore, because R_2 differs from R_1, at least one more iteration is required. The equations that must now be solved are given by [again setting $v_3(R_2) = 0$]

$$g(R_2) = \qquad\qquad +\frac{7}{8}v_1(R_2) + \frac{1}{16}v_2(R_2) - v_0(R_2)$$

$$g(R_2) = 1,000 \qquad\qquad +\frac{3}{4}v_1(R_2) + \frac{1}{8}v_2(R_2) - v_1(R_2)$$

$$g(R_2) = 4,000 \qquad\qquad + v_1(R_2) \qquad\qquad - v_2(R_2)$$

$$g(R_2) = 6,000 + v_0(R_2).$$

The simultaneous solution to these equations yields

$$g(R_2) = \frac{5,000}{3} = 1,667$$

$$v_0(R_2) = -\frac{13,000}{3} = -4,333$$

$$v_1(R_2) = \qquad\qquad -3,000$$

$$v_2(R_2) = -\frac{2,000}{3} = -667$$

Step 2 can now be applied. We seek an improved policy R_3 that has the property that $d_0(R_3) = k_3^0$, $d_1(R_3) = k_3^1$, $d_2(R_3) = k_3^2$, and $d_3(R_3) = k_3^3$ minimizes the following expressions:

(0) $C_{0k_3^0} - p_{00}(k_3^0)4,333 - p_{01}(k_3^0)3,000 - p_{02}(k_3^0)667 + 4,333$

(1) $C_{1k_3^1} - p_{10}(k_3^1)4,333 - p_{11}(k_3^1)3,000 - p_{12}(k_3^1)667 + 3,000$

(2) $C_{2k_3^2} - p_{20}(k_3^2)4,333 - p_{21}(k_3^2)3,000 - p_{22}(k_3^2)667 + 667$

(3) $C_{3k_3^3} - p_{30}(k_3^3)4,333 - p_{31}(k_3^3)3,000 - p_{32}(k_3^3)667.$

The first iteration provides most of the necessary data (the transition probabilities and C_{ik}) required for determining the new policy, except for the values of each of the four expressions. These values are found to be

Decision	Value of expression 0	Value of expression 1	Value of expression 2	Value of expression 3
1	1,667	1,667	3,333	∞
2	5,333	4,000	1,667	∞
3	6,000	4,667	2,334	1,667

Thus $d_0(R_3) = k_3^0 = 1$, $d_1(R_3) = k_3^1 = 1$, $d_2(R_3) = k_3^2 = 2$, and $d_3(R_3) = k_3^3 = 3$, so that this policy is identical to R_2. Because the policies on two successive iterations are the same, the optimal policy has been obtained. This optimal policy calls for leaving the machine as is when it is in states 0 or 1, overhauling it when it is in state 2, and replacing it when it is in state 3. Of course, this result is the same one found in Sec. 20.3.

20.5 Criterion of Discounted Costs

Throughout this chapter, we measured policies on the basis of the (long run) expected average cost per unit time or the (long run) actual average cost per unit time. An alternative measure is to find the expected long-run total discounted cost. A discount factor $\alpha < 1$ is specified, so that the present value of 1 unit of cost m periods in the future is α^m. α can be interpreted as equal to $1/(1 + i)$, where i is the current interest rate. This measure was used extensively in Chap. 18. We are seeking a policy that minimizes the expected long-run total discounted cost.

POLICY-IMPROVEMENT ALGORITHM

The description of the Markovian decision process is as described previously. Given a distribution $P\{X_0 = i)$ over the initial states of the system and a policy R, a system evolves over time according to the joint effect of the probabilistic laws of motion and the sequence of decisions made (actions taken). In particular, when the system is in state i and decision $d_i(R) = k$ is made, then the probability that the system is in state j at the next observed time period is given by $p_{ij}(k)$. Furthermore, a known expected cost C_{ik} is incurred. Denote by $V_i^n(R)$ the expected total discounted cost of a system starting in state i (at the first observed time period) and evolving for n time periods. Then $V_i^n(R)$ consists of two components, namely, (1) C_{ik}, the cost incurred at the first observed time period as a result of the current state i and the decision $d_i(R) = k$ when operating under policy R, and (2) $\alpha \sum_{j=0}^M p_{ij}(k) V_j^{n-1}(R)$, the expected total discounted cost of the system evolving over the remaining $n - 1$ time periods. Thus the recursive equation

$$V_i^n(R) = C_{ik} + \alpha \sum_{j=0}^M p_{ij}(k) V_j^{n-1}(R),$$

for $i = 0, 1, 2, \ldots, M$ and $V_i^1(R) - C_{ik}$ for all i is obtained. This policy can be evaluated by using the techniques associated with dynamic programming. It can be shown that as n approaches infinity, this expression converges to

$$V_i(R) = C_{ik} + \alpha \sum_{j=0}^{M} p_{ij}(k) V_j(R), \quad \text{for } i = 0, 1, \ldots, M,$$

where $V_i(R)$ can now be interpreted as the expected long-run total discounted cost for a system starting in state i and continuing indefinitely. There are $M + 1$ equations and $M + 1$ unknowns, and hence $V_i(R)$ may be obtained by standard methods. For example, the machine-maintenance model will be solved using the policy that calls for leaving the machine as is when in states 0 and 1, overhauling it when it is in state 2, and replacing it when it is in state 3—that is, policy R_b. The discount factor will be chosen to be $\alpha = 0.9$. The following set of equations is obtained:

$$V_0(R) = \quad\quad + 0.9 \left[\frac{7}{8} V_1(R) + \frac{1}{16} V_2(R) + \frac{1}{16} V_3(R) \right]$$

$$V_1(R) = 1{,}000 + 0.9 \left[\frac{3}{4} V_1(R) + \frac{1}{8} V_2(R) + \frac{1}{8} V_3(R) \right]$$

$$V_2(R) = 4{,}000 + 0.9 \left[\quad\quad V_1(R) \quad\quad\quad\quad\quad \right]$$

$$V_3(R) = 6{,}000 + 0.9 \left[V_0(R) \quad\quad\quad\quad\quad\quad \right].$$

The simultaneous solution to this system of equations yields

$$V_0(R) = 14{,}949$$
$$V_1(R) = 16{,}262$$
$$V_2(R) = 18{,}636$$
$$V_3(R) = 19{,}454.$$

Thus, assuming that the system started in state 0, the expected long-run total discounted cost is \$14,949.

The aforementioned procedure not only evaluates a given policy but also is suggestive of an algorithm to determine the optimal policy. The calculations are similar to those required in the value-determination step (step 1) of the policy-improvement technique presented in Sec. 20.4. Indeed, an algorithm very similar to that presented in Sec. 20.4 is available. In particular, these steps are to be followed:

Step 1   Value determination   For an arbitrarily chosen policy R_1, use $p_{ij}(k_1)$ and C_{ik_1} to solve the set of $(M + 1)$ equations

$$V_i(R_1) = C_{ik_1} + \alpha \sum_{j=0}^{M} p_{ij}(k_1) V_j(R_1), \quad i = 0, 1, \ldots, M$$

for all $(M + 1)$ unknown values of $V_i(R_1)$.

Step 2   Policy improvement   Using the current values of $V_i(R_1)$, find the alternative policy R_2 such that, for each state i, $d_i(R_2) = k_2$ is the decision that makes

$$C_{ik_2} + \alpha \sum_{j=0}^{M} p_{ij}(k_2)V_j(R_1)$$

a minimum; that is, for *each* state i, find the appropriate value of k_2 that

$$\underset{k_2 = 1,2,\ldots,K}{\text{Minimizes}} \left\{ C_{ik_2} + \alpha \sum_{j=0}^{M} p_{ij}(k_2)V_j(R_1) \right\},$$

and then set $d_i(R_2) =$ minimizing the value of k_2. This procedure defines a new policy R_2.

If R_2 does not equal R_1, then return to step 1 by using R_2 instead of R_1, and solve for $V_i(R_2)$, $i = 0, 1,\ldots, M$. Using these values, go to step 2 and find R_3. Continue in this fashion until you find two successive R's to be equal. When you find them, the optimal policy is achieved, and the algorithm terminates. In fact, it can be shown that

1. $V_i(R_{j+1}) \leq V_i(R_j)$, for $i = 0, 1,\ldots, M$ and $j = 1, 2,\ldots$,
2. The algorithm terminates with the optimal solution in a finite number of iterations, and
3. The algorithm is valid without the assumption that the Markov chain associated with every transition matrix is irreducible.

EXAMPLE We shall obtain the optimal policy for the machine-maintenance problem by the *policy improvement algorithm*. The discount factor is chosen to be 0.9. The first step, the value-determination step, has already been carried out earlier in this section if the arbitrary policy chosen, R_1, calls for leaving the machine as is when it is in states 0 or 1, overhauling it when it is in state 2, and replacing it when it is in state 3. The appropriate V's are

$$V_0(R_1) = 14,949$$
$$V_1(R_1) = 16,262$$
$$V_2(R_1) = 18,636$$
$$V_3(R_1) = 19,454.$$

Step 2 can now be applied. We are seeking an improved policy R_2 that has the property that $d_0(R_2) = k_2^0$, $d_1(R_2) = k_2^1$, $d_2(R_2) = k_2^2$, and $d_3(R_2) = k_2^3$ minimizes the following expressions:

(0) $C_{0k_2^0} + 0.9[p_{00}(k_2^0)14,949 + p_{01}(k_2^0)16,262 + p_{02}(k_2^0)18,636 + p_{03}(k_2^0)19,454]$

(1) $C_{1k_2^1} + 0.9[p_{10}(k_2^1)14,949 + p_{11}(k_2^1)16,262 + p_{12}(k_2^1)18,636 + p_{13}(k_2^1)19,454]$

(2) $C_{2k_2^2} + 0.9[p_{20}(k_2^2)14,949 + p_{21}(k_2^2)16,262 + p_{22}(k_2^2)18,636 + p_{23}(k_2^2)19,454]$

(3) $C_{3k_2^3} + 0.9[p_{30}(k_2^3)14,949 + p_{31}(k_2^3)16,262 + p_{32}(k_2^3)18,636 + p_{33}(k_2^3)19,454].$

Most of the necessary data can be taken from the first iteration of the example in Sec. 20.4 (the transition probabilities and C_{ik}). Using these data, the values of each of the four expressions are obtained as follows:

Decision	Value of expression 0	Value of expression 1	Value of expression 2	Value of expression 3
1	14,949	16,262	20,140	∞
2	18,636	18,636	18,636	∞
3	19,454	19,454	19,454	19,454

Thus $d_0(R_2) = k_2^0 = 1$, $d_1(R_2) = k_2^1 = 1$, $d_2(R_2) = k_2^2 = 2$, and $d_3(R_2) = k_2^3 = 3$, so that this policy is identical to R_1. Because the policies obtained on two successive iterations are the same, the optimal policy has been obtained. Again, the optimal policy calls for leaving the machine as is when it is in states 0 or 1, overhauling it when it is in state 2, and replacing it when it is in state 3—the same policy that was obtained by using the long-run expected average cost per day criterion.

LINEAR PROGRAMMING FORMULATION

Just as there is a policy-improvement algorithm for the expected long-run total discounted cost criterion, there is also a *linear programming formulation*. It can be shown that the statement of the linear programming problem is to choose the y_{ik} that

$$\text{Minimizes} \quad \sum_{i=0}^{M} \sum_{k=1}^{K} C_{ik} y_{ik},$$

subject to the constraints

1.
$$\sum_{k=1}^{K} y_{ik} - \alpha \sum_{i=0}^{M} \sum_{k=1}^{K} y_{ik} p_{ij}(k) = \beta_j, \quad \text{for } j = 0, 1, \dots, M,$$

where β_j are given constants such that $\beta_j > 0$ and $\sum_{j=0}^{M} \beta_j = 1$, and

2.
$$y_{ik} \geq 0, \qquad i = 0, 1, \dots, M \qquad k = 1, 2, \dots, K.$$

If we consider the policy defined by

$$D_{ik} = P\{\text{decision} = k \mid \text{state} = i\}$$

$$= \frac{y_{ik}}{\sum_{k=1}^{K} y_{ik}},$$

then the y_{ik} can be interpreted as a weighted (in a discounted sense) expected time of being in state i and making decision k, when $P\{X_0 = j\} = \beta_j$; that is, if

$$z_{ik}^n = P\{\text{at time } n, \text{ state} = i \text{ and decision} = k\},$$

then

$$y_{ik} = z_{ik}^0 + \alpha z_{ik}^1 + \alpha^2 z_{ik}^2 + \alpha^3 z_{ik}^3 + \cdots.$$

Again, it can be shown that the optimal policy is deterministic; that is, $D_{ik} = 0$ or 1. Furthermore, the technique is valid without the assumption that the Markov chain associated with every transition matrix is irreducible.

EXAMPLE Returning to the machine-maintenance model (with $\alpha = 0.9$), we can formulate the *linear program* as

Minimize $4{,}000y_{02} + 6{,}000y_{03} + 1{,}000y_{11} + 4{,}000y_{12} + 6{,}000y_{13}$
$$+ 3{,}000y_{21} + 4{,}000y_{22} + 6{,}000y_{23} + M_1 y_{31} + M_2 y_{32} + 6{,}000y_{33},$$

where M_1 and M_2 are taken to be large numbers, subject to

$$\sum_{k=1}^{3} y_{0k} - 0.9(y_{03} + y_{13} + y_{23} + y_{33}) = \frac{1}{4}$$

$$\sum_{k=1}^{3} y_{1k} - 0.9\left(\frac{7}{8}y_{01} + y_{02} + \frac{3}{4}y_{11} + y_{12} + y_{22} + y_{32}\right) = \frac{1}{4}$$

$$\sum_{k=1}^{3} y_{2k} - 0.9\left(\frac{1}{16}y_{01} + \frac{1}{8}y_{11} + \frac{1}{2}y_{21}\right) = \frac{1}{4}$$

$$\sum_{k=1}^{3} y_{3k} - 0.9\left(\frac{1}{16}y_{01} + \frac{1}{8}y_{11} + \frac{1}{2}y_{21} + y_{31}\right) = \frac{1}{4}$$

and

$$y_{ik} \geq 0, \qquad i = 0, 1, 2, 3; \qquad k = 1, 2, 3,$$

where $\beta_0, \beta_1, \beta_2$, and β_3 are arbitrarily chosen to be $\frac{1}{4}$.

The optimal solution yields all y_{ik} equal to zero, except for $y_{01} = 1.210$, $y_{11} = 6.656$, $y_{22} = 1.067$, and $y_{33} = 1.067$. The corresponding

$$D_{ik} = \frac{y_{ik}}{\sum_{k=1}^{3} y_{ik}}$$

are given $D_{01} = D_{11} = D_{22} = D_{33} = 1$, and all the remaining $D_{ik} = 0$. This solution is the same as that obtained earlier in this section and calls for leaving the machine as is when it is in states 0 or 1, overhauling it when it is in state 2, and replacing it when it is in state 3. The minimized value of the objective function is \$17,325, and it is seen to be related to the V's of the optimal policy found in the discussion of the discounted cost policy-improvement algorithm. Because $P\{X_0 = j\}$ was chosen to equal $\frac{1}{4}$ for all j,

$$17{,}325 = \frac{1}{4}[V_0(R) + V_1(R) + V_2(R) + V_3(R)]$$

$$= \frac{1}{4}[14{,}949 + 16{,}262 + 18{,}636 + 19{,}454].$$

FINITE-PERIOD MARKOVIAN DECISION PROCESSES AND THE METHOD OF SUCCESSIVE APPROXIMATIONS

Chapter 11 introduced the concept of dynamic programming and characterized deterministic dynamic programming problems and their solutions. Many of these concepts have analogous interpretations with Markovian decision processes. In particular, suppose we seek the expected total discounted cost of a system starting in state i and evolving for n time periods when an optimal policy is followed. Note that a finite number of time periods are now being considered. This problem is analogous to deterministic dynamic programming, except that the Markov system evolves according to some probabilistic laws of motion rather than evolving in a deterministic fashion. The deterministic dynamic programming solution is suggestive of the solution to this probabilistic dynamic programming problem. Denote by V_i^n the expected total discounted cost of a system starting in state i and evolving for n time periods when an optimal policy is followed.[1] Using the *principle of optimization*, it follows that this cost function satisfies the recursive relationship,

$$V_i^{n-1} = \min_k \left\{ C_{ik} + \alpha \sum_{j=0}^{M} p_{ij}(k) V_j^n \right\}, \qquad i = 0, 1, \dots, M.$$

Using this recursive relationship, the solution procedure moves backward period by period—each time finding the optimal policy for that period model—until it finds the optimal policy for the original problem. In particular, it is usually assumed that $V_0^0, V_1^0, \dots, V_M^0$ is zero, so that V_i^1 can be obtained from

$$V_i^1 = \min_k \{ C_{ik} \}, \qquad i = 0, 1, \dots, M,$$

with the corresponding optimal decisions becoming known. If this optimal policy is followed, V_i^1 is the minimum expected total discounted cost of a system starting in state i and evolving for one time period.

The V_i^2 can now be obtained from

$$V_i^2 = \min_k \left\{ C_{ik} + \alpha \sum_{j=0}^{M} p_{ij}(k) V_j^1 \right\}, \qquad i = 0, 1, \dots, M,$$

with the corresponding optimal decisions becoming known. If this optimal policy is followed, V_i^2 is the minimum expected total discounted cost of a system starting in state i and evolving for two time periods.

In a similar manner, the V_i^T can be obtained from

$$V_i^T = \min_k \left\{ C_{ik} + \alpha \sum_{j=0}^{M} p_{ij}(k) V_j^{T-1} \right\}, \qquad i = 0, 1, \dots, M,$$

---

[1] This notation V_i^n for cost is now being used instead of the notation introduced in Chap. 11 to be consistent with the material introduced in the current chapter. In accordance with the notation of Chap. 11, the subscript (i) is the state variable, and the superscript (n) is equivalent to the stage, except that the stage is now measured by the system having "n periods to go" rather than being in period n. This change is due to the need to treat the infinite-period problem also.

with the corresponding optimal decisions becoming known. If this optimal policy is followed, V_i^T is the minimum expected total discounted cost of a system starting in state i and evolving for T time periods. Thus, solving a five-period problem requires solving the four-, three-, two-, and one-period problems also. An example of a three-period version of the machine-maintenance model will be solved later in this section. It should be noted that α can be set equal to 1 (no discounting) for finite-period problems, in which case the cost criterion becomes the expected total cost.

Until now this section has dealt with a finite-period version of a Markov decision process. When the criterion of discounted costs is used, it can be shown that the V_i^n converges to V_i as n approaches infinity, where V_i is the expected (long run) total discounted cost of a system starting in state i and continuing indefinitely when an *optimal* policy is followed and satisfies

$$V_i = \min_k \left\{ C_{ik} + \alpha \sum_{j=0}^{M} p_{ij}(k) V_j \right\}, \qquad i = 0, 1, \ldots, M.$$

Furthermore, we obtain the optimal policy by making appropriate decisions to minimize the right-hand side of the preceding equation. This solution is, indeed, the solution to the Markov decision process considered throughout earlier sections of this chapter.

Finding V_i and the corresponding optimal decisions is generally difficult, but it is relatively simple to approximate V_i and obtain the corresponding policy. This is what the *method of successive approximations* does. It uses the recursive relationship of the finite-period problem presented earlier; that is,

$$V_i^{n+1} = \min_k \left\{ C_{ik} + \alpha \sum_{j=0}^{M} p_{ij}(k) V_j^n \right\}.$$

The first step is to choose arbitrarily a set of values, $V_0^0, V_1^0, V_2^0, \ldots, V_M^0$, usually taken to be zero (as will be assumed from here on). Using the expression for V_i^{n+1}, V_i^1 can be obtained from

$$V_i^1 = \min_k \{ C_{ik} \}, \qquad i = 0, 1, \ldots, M,$$

with the corresponding decisions becoming known. This step can be viewed as the first approximation to the optimal policy, and as noted earlier the V_i^1 can be interpreted as the expected total discounted cost of a system starting in state i and evolving for one period when an optimal policy is followed.

The next iteration uses the $V_0^1, V_1^1, V_2^1, \ldots, V_M^1$ found from the previous step. From the recurrence relationship presented, V_i^2 can be obtained from

$$V_i^2 = \min_k \left\{ C_{ik} + \alpha \sum_{j=0}^{M} p_{ij}(k) V_j^1 \right\},$$

with the corresponding decisions becoming known. This policy can be viewed as the second approximation to the optimal policy, and, as noted earlier, the V_i^2 can be interpreted as the expected total discounted cost of a system starting in state i and evolving for two periods when an optimal policy is followed.

Further iterations can be obtained by using the recursive relationship. For the Tth iteration, V_i^T can be interpreted as the expected total discounted cost of a system starting in state i and evolving for T periods when an optimal policy is followed. The number T can be made large, and V_i^T will become "close" to the optimal expected long-run total discounted cost, and, for sufficiently large T, the optimal policy will be obtained. However, there is no procedure for deciding when to terminate the method of successive approximations. A check can be made at any time to see whether the current iteration satisfies the policy-improvement equations; if it does, then an optimal policy has been obtained.

Although the *method of successive approximations* may not lead to an optimal policy (using a finite number of iterations), it has one distinct advantage over the policy-improvement and linear programming techniques; i.e., it never requires the solution of a system of simultaneous equations, and hence each iteration can be performed simply and quickly.

EXAMPLE We shall solve the machine-maintenance model $(\alpha = 0.9)$ by the *method of successive approximations*. Let $V_0^0 = V_1^0 = V_2^0 = V_3^0 = 0$. Then

$$V_0^1 = \min_k \{C_{0k}\} = 0 \qquad (k = 1)$$

$$V_1^1 = \min_k \{C_{1k}\} = 1{,}000 \quad (k = 1)$$

$$V_2^1 = \min_k \{C_{2k}\} = 3{,}000 \quad (k = 1)$$

$$V_3^1 = \min_k \{C_{3k}\} = 6{,}000 \quad (k = 3).$$

Thus the first approximation calls for making decision 1 (leave the machine alone) when the system is in states 0, 1, or 2. When the system is in state 3, decision 3 (replace) is made.

The second iteration leads to

$$V_0^2 = \min\left\{0 + 0.9\left[\frac{7}{8}(1{,}000) + \frac{1}{16}(3{,}000) + \frac{1}{16}(6{,}000)\right],\right.$$
$$\left. 4{,}000 + 0.9[1(1{,}000)], 6{,}000 + 0.9[1(0)]\right\} = 1{,}294 \ (k = 1)$$

$$V_1^2 = \min\left\{1{,}000 + 0.9\left[\frac{3}{4}(1{,}000) + \frac{1}{8}(3{,}000) + \frac{1}{8}(6{,}000)\right],\right.$$
$$\left. 4{,}000 + 0.9[1(1{,}000)], 6{,}000 + 0.9[1(0)]\right\} = 1{,}294 \ (k = 1)$$

$$V_2^2 = \min\left\{3{,}000 + 0.9\left[\frac{1}{2}(3{,}000) + \frac{1}{2}(6{,}000)\right],\right.$$
$$\left. 4{,}000 + 0.9[1(1{,}000)], 6{,}000 + 0.9[1(0)]\right\} = 4{,}900 \ (k = 2)$$

$$V_3^2 = \qquad\qquad\qquad 6{,}000 + 0.9[1(0)] = 6{,}000 \ (k = 3).$$

Thus the second approximation calls for leaving the machine as is when it is in states 0 or 1, overhauling it when it is in state 2, and replacing it when it is in state 3. Note that this policy is the optimal one, even though the optimal cost has not been obtained.

The third iteration leads to

$$V_0^3 = \min\left\{0 + 0.9\left[\frac{7}{8}(2,688) + \frac{1}{16}(4,900) + \frac{1}{16}(6,000)\right],\right.$$

$$\left. 4,000 + 0.9[1(2,688)], 6,000 + 0.9[1(1,294)]\right\} = 2,730 \ (k = 1)$$

$$V_1^3 = \min\left\{1,000 + 0.9\left[\frac{3}{4}(2,688) + \frac{1}{8}(4,900) + \frac{1}{8}(6,000)\right],\right.$$

$$\left. 4,000 + 0.9[1(2,688)], 6,000 + 0.9[1(1,294)]\right\} = 4,041 \ (k = 1)$$

$$V_2^3 = \min\left\{3,000 + 0.9\left[\frac{1}{2}(4,900) + \frac{1}{2}(6,000)\right],\right.$$

$$\left. 4,000 + 0.9[1(2,688)], 6,000 + 0.9[1(1,294)]\right\} = 6,419 \ (k = 2)$$

$$V_3^3 = \qquad\qquad\qquad 6,000 + 0.9[1(1,294)] = 7,165 \ (k = 3).$$

Again the optimal policy is achieved, and the costs are getting closer to those of the optimal policy. This procedure can be continued, and V_0^n, V_1^n, V_2^n, and V_3^n will converge to 14,949, 16,262, 18,636, and 19,454, respectively. It should be noted that termination of the method of successive approximations after the second iteration would have resulted in an optimal policy, although there is no way to know this fact without solving the problem by other methods.

As indicated earlier, the *method of successive approximation solves a finite-period Markovian decision problem*. In particular, the optimal solution to the one-period, machine-maintenance model calls for leaving the machine alone when it is in states 0, 1, or 2, and replacing it when it is in state 3. The minimum expected total discounted cost of the system starting in state i, $i = 0, 1, 2, 3$, and evolving for one period is given by 0, 1,000, 3,000, and 6,000, respectively. The optimal solution to the two-period, machine-maintenance model is

> *Period 1* Leave machine alone when it is in states 0 or 1.
> Overhaul machine when it is in state 2.
> Replace machine when it is in state 3.

> *Period 2* Leave machine alone when it is in states 0, 1, or 2.
> Replace machine when it is in state 3.

The minimum expected total discounted cost of the system starting in state i, $i = 0, 1, 2, 3$, and evolving for two periods, is given by 1,294, 2,688, 4,900, and

6,000, respectively. Finally, the optimal solution to the three-period model is

Period 1
and
Period 2

Leave machine alone when it is in states 0 or 1.
Overhaul machine when it is in state 2.
Replace machine when it is in state 3.

Period 3

Leave machine alone when it is in states 0, 1, or 2.
Replace machine when it is in state 3.

The minimum expected total discounted costs over three periods, if the system starts in state i, $i = 0, 1, 2, 3$, are given by 2,730, 4,041, 6,419, and 7,165, respectively.

20.6 A Water-Resource Model

A multipurpose dam is used for generating electric power, as well as for flood control. The capacity of the dam is 3 units. The probability distribution of the quantity of water, W_t, that flows into the dam during month t (for $t = 0, 1, \ldots$) is given by $P_W(m)$, where

$$P_W(0) = P\{W = 0\} = \frac{1}{6}$$

$$P_W(1) = P\{W = 1\} = \frac{1}{3}$$

$$P_W(2) = P\{W = 2\} = \frac{1}{3}$$

$$P_W(3) = P\{W = 3\} = \frac{1}{6}.$$

For the purpose of generating electric power, 1 unit of water is required. At the beginning of each month, water is released from the dam. The first unit is used to generate electric power and then used for irrigation purposes, the latter function being worth $100,000. If additional units are released, they can also be used for irrigation purposes, and each unit is worth $100,000. If the dam contains less than 1 unit at the beginning of a month, additional power must be purchased at a cost of $300,000. If at any time the water in the dam exceeds the capacity of 3 units, the excess water is released through the spillways at no cost or gain.

A release policy is sought. Policies are to be compared on the basis of expected discounted cost, with discount factor $\alpha = 0.99$. The **policy-improvement algorithm** will be used.

Let X_t denote the amount of water in the dam at time t. Then $X_t = 0, 1, 2, 3$. The natural laws of motion for this system (no water released) are given by the transition matrix

State	0	1	2	3
0	$\frac{1}{6}$	$\frac{1}{3}$	$\frac{1}{3}$	$\frac{1}{6}$
1	0	$\frac{1}{6}$	$\frac{1}{3}$	$\frac{1}{2}$
2	0	0	$\frac{1}{6}$	$\frac{5}{6}$
3	0	0	0	1

For example, the element in the second row and fourth column, p_{13}, is obtained as follows: If the dam contains 1 unit of water now, then for it to contain 3 units of water a month later, 2 or 3 units of water must flow into the dam during the month (recall that dam capacity is 3 units, so that a flow of 3 units will result in 1 unit being released through the spillways). This occurs with probability $\frac{1}{3} + \frac{1}{6} = \frac{1}{2}$.

There are three possible decisions that can be made at the beginning of each month:

Decision	Action
1	Release 1 unit
2	Release 2 units
3	Release 3 units

It is clear that releasing no units is not a sensible action because 1 unit is needed for electric power generation anyway. Thus a policy calls for determining how many units to release as a function of the quantity of water found in the dam. A typical policy R_1 might call for releasing all the water in the dam if it contains 0, 1, or 2 units, and releasing 2 units if it contains 3 units. The resultant transition matrix is given by

State	0	1	2	3
0	$\frac{1}{6}$	$\frac{1}{3}$	$\frac{1}{3}$	$\frac{1}{6}$
1	$\frac{1}{6}$	$\frac{1}{3}$	$\frac{1}{3}$	$\frac{1}{6}$
2	$\frac{1}{6}$	$\frac{1}{3}$	$\frac{1}{3}$	$\frac{1}{6}$
3	0	$\frac{1}{6}$	$\frac{1}{3}$	$\frac{1}{2}$

Of course, a policy that calls for releasing 3 units when there is only 1 unit in the dam is to be interpreted as calling for releasing all the available water. Necessary cost information can be obtained from the following data:

State	Decision	Cost (in hundred thousands)
0	1	3
	2	3
	3	3
1	1	−1
	2	−1
	3	−1
2	1	−1
	2	−2
	3	−2
3	1	−1
	2	−2
	3	−3

The policy R_1 will be used in the value-determination step (step 1) of the policy-improvement algorithm. Using the cost information just given, the values of C_{ik_1} are

$$C_{0k_1} = 3$$
$$C_{1k_1} = -1$$
$$C_{2k_1} = -2$$
$$C_{3k_1} = -2.$$

The following four equations must be solved:

$$V_0(R_1) = 3 + 0.99\left[\frac{1}{6}V_0(R_1) + \frac{1}{3}V_1(R_1) + \frac{1}{3}V_2(R_1) + \frac{1}{6}V_3(R_1)\right]$$

$$V_1(R_1) = -1 + 0.99\left[\frac{1}{6}V_0(R_1) + \frac{1}{3}V_1(R_1) + \frac{1}{3}V_2(R_1) + \frac{1}{6}V_3(R_1)\right]$$

$$V_2(R_1) = -2 + 0.99\left[\frac{1}{6}V_0(R_1) + \frac{1}{3}V_1(R_1) + \frac{1}{3}V_2(R_1) + \frac{1}{6}V_3(R_1)\right]$$

$$V_3(R_1) = -2 + 0.99\left[\frac{1}{6}V_1(R_1) + \frac{1}{3}V_2(R_1) + \frac{1}{2}V_3(R_1)\right].$$

The simultaneous solution of these equations results in the values

$$V_0(R_1) = -103.881, \quad V_1(R_1) = -107.881,$$

and

$$V_2(R_1) = -108.881, \quad V_3(R_1) = -110.358.$$

Step 2 can now be applied. We want to find an improved policy R_2 that has the property that $d_0(R_2) = k_2^0$, $d_1(R_2) = k_2^1$, $d_2(R_2) = k_2^2$, and $d_3(R_2) = k_2^3$

minimizes the following expressions:

(0) $C_{0k_2^0} + 0.99[-103.881 p_{00}(k_2^0) - 107.881 p_{01}(k_2^0)$
$- 108.881 p_{02}(k_2^0) - 110.358 p_{03}(k_2^0)]$

(1) $C_{1k_2^1} + 0.99[-103.881 p_{10}(k_2^1) - 107.881 p_{11}(k_2^1)$
$- 108.881 p_{12}(k_2^1) - 110.358 p_{13}(k_2^1)]$

(2) $C_{2k_2^2} + 0.99[-103.881 p_{20}(k_2^2) - 107.881 p_{21}(k_2^2)$
$- 108.881 p_{22}(k_2^2) - 110.358 p_{23}(k_2^2)]$

(3) $C_{3k_2^3} + 0.99[-103.881 p_{30}(k_2^3) - 107.881 p_{31}(k_2^3)$
$- 108.881 p_{32}(k_2^3) - 110.358 p_{33}(k_2^3)].$

To find k_2^0, the best decision when the system is in state 0, it is necessary to evaluate the first expression for all possible decisions. It is clear that when the system is in state 0 (dam empty), there is no choice among the decisions because they all are equivalent. The data for the necessary calculations for evaluating expression (0) follow:

State 0

Decision	$p_{00}(k_2)$	$p_{01}(k_2)$	$p_{02}(k_2)$	$p_{03}(k_2)$	C_{0k_2}	Total value of expression 0
1, 2, 3	$\frac{1}{6}$	$\frac{1}{3}$	$\frac{1}{3}$	$\frac{1}{6}$	3	-103.881

Similarly, for state 1 there is no choice among the decisions because they are all equivalent. The data for the necessary calculations for evaluating follow:

State 1

Decision	$p_{10}(k_2)$	$p_{11}(k_2)$	$p_{12}(k_2)$	$p_{13}(k_2)$	C_{1k_2}	Total value of expression 1
1, 2, 3	$\frac{1}{6}$	$\frac{1}{3}$	$\frac{1}{3}$	$\frac{1}{6}$	-1	-107.881

For the remaining two states, the appropriate transition probabilities and costs generally depend upon the decisions made. The data for the necessary calculations for finding the best decisions, given the dam is in states 2 and 3, follow:

State 2

Decision	$p_{20}(k_2)$	$p_{21}(k_2)$	$p_{22}(k_2)$	$p_{23}(k_2)$	C_{2k_2}	Total value of expression 2
1	0	$\frac{1}{6}$	$\frac{1}{3}$	$\frac{1}{2}$	-1	-109.358
2, 3	$\frac{1}{6}$	$\frac{1}{3}$	$\frac{1}{3}$	$\frac{1}{6}$	-2	-108.881

State 3

Decision	$p_{30}(k_2)$	$p_{31}(k_2)$	$p_{32}(k_2)$	$p_{33}(k_2)$	C_{3k_2}	Total value of expression 3
1	0	0	$\dfrac{1}{6}$	$\dfrac{5}{6}$	-1	-110.011
2	0	$\dfrac{1}{6}$	$\dfrac{1}{3}$	$\dfrac{1}{2}$	-2	-110.358
3	$\dfrac{1}{6}$	$\dfrac{1}{3}$	$\dfrac{1}{3}$	$\dfrac{1}{6}$	-3	-109.881

Thus $d_0(R_2) = k_2^0 = d_1(R_2) = k_2^1 = 1$, 2, or 3; $d_2(R_2) = k_2^2 = 1$; and $d_3(R_2) = k_2^3 = 2$. Hence policy R_2 calls for releasing all the water when there is 1 unit in the dam, 1 unit of water when there are 2 units available in the dam, and 2 units when there are 3 units available in the dam. This policy differs from R_1, so that another iteration is required. For the value-determination step, the equations that must now be solved are

$$V_0(R_2) = \quad 3 + 0.99\left[\frac{1}{6}V_0(R_2) + \frac{1}{3}V_1(R_2) + \frac{1}{3}V_2(R_2) + \frac{1}{6}V_3(R_2)\right]$$

$$V_1(R_2) = -1 + 0.99\left[\frac{1}{6}V_0(R_2) + \frac{1}{3}V_1(R_2) + \frac{1}{3}V_2(R_2) + \frac{1}{6}V_3(R_2)\right]$$

$$V_2(R_2) = -1 + 0.99\left[\frac{1}{6}V_1(R_2) + \frac{1}{3}V_2(R_2) + \frac{1}{2}V_3(R_2)\right]$$

$$V_3(R_2) = -2 + 0.99\left[\frac{1}{6}V_1(R_2) + \frac{1}{3}V_2(R_2) + \frac{1}{2}V_3(R_2)\right].$$

The simultaneous solution of these equations results in the values $V_0(R_2) = -119.642$, $V_1(R_2) = -123.642$, $V_2(R_2) = -125.119$, and $V_3(R_2) = -126.119$.

Step 2 can now be applied. We want to find an improved policy R_3 that has the property that $d_0(R_3) = k_3^0$, $d_1(R_3) = k_3^1$, $d_2(R_3) = k_3^2$, and $d_3(R_3) = k_3^3$ minimizes the following expressions:

(0) $\quad C_{0k_3^0} + 0.99[-119.642p_{00}(k_3^0) - 123.642p_{01}(k_3^0)$
$$- 125.119p_{02}(k_3^0) - 126.119p_{03}(k_3^0)]$$

(1) $\quad C_{1k_3^1} + 0.99[-119.642p_{10}(k_3^1) - 123.642p_{11}(k_3^1)$
$$- 125.119p_{12}(k_3^1) - 126.119p_{13}(k_3^1)]$$

(2) $\quad C_{2k_3^2} + 0.99[-119.642p_{20}(k_3^2) - 123.642p_{21}(k_3^2)$
$$- 125.119p_{22}(k_3^2) - 126.119p_{23}(k_3^2)]$$

(3) $\quad C_{3k_3^3} + 0.99[-119.642p_{30}(k_3^3) - 123.642p_{31}(k_3^3)$
$$- 125.119p_{32}(k_3^3) - 126.119p_{33}(k_3^3)].$$

The data on the transition matrices and the costs from the previous iteration can again be used; the resulting values of the expression are

Decision	Value of expression 0	Value of expression 1	Value of expression 2	Value of expression 3
1	−119.642	−123.642	−125.119	−125.693
2	−119.642	−123.642	−124.642	−126.119
3	−119.642	−123.642	−124.642	−125.642

Thus $d_0(R_3) = k_3^0 = d_1(R_3) = k_3^1 = 1$, 2, or 3; $d_2(R_3) = k_3^2 = 1$; and $d_3(R_3) = k_3^3 = 2$. Hence policy R_3 and policy R_2 are identical, and the optimal release policy calls for releasing all the water when there is 1 unit in the dam, 1 unit of water when there are 2 units available in the dam, and 2 units when there are 3 units available in the dam.

Of course, direct enumeration would have been just as simple a technique to use in this situation, but the policy-improvement algorithm was used for illustrative purposes.

20.7 Inventory Model

In Chap. 15 the following inventory problem was considered. A camera store stocks a particular model camera that can be ordered weekly. Let $D_1, D_2,\ldots,$ represent the demand for this camera during the first week, the second week,..., respectively. It is assumed that the D_i are independent, identically distributed random variables having a Poisson distribution with parameter λ equal to 1. Let X_0 represent the number of cameras on hand at the outset, X_1 the number of cameras on hand at the end of week one, X_2 the number of cameras on hand at the end of week two, and so forth. On Saturday night the store places an order that is delivered in time for the opening of the store on Monday. The store uses an (s,S) ordering policy. If the number of cameras on hand at the end of the week is less than $s = 1$ (no cameras in stock), the store orders up to $S = 3$. Otherwise, the store does not order (if there are any cameras in stock, no order is placed). It is assumed that sales are lost when demand exceeds the inventory on hand (no backlogging). The cost structure considered calls for incurring a penalty cost of $50 per unit for each unit of unsatisfied demand (lost sales). If $z > 0$ cameras are ordered, the cost incurred is $10 + 25z$ dollars. If no cameras are ordered, no ordering cost is incurred. Holding costs are to be neglected. In Sec. 15.7, this policy was evaluated by using the (long run) expected average cost per unit time as the criterion. It is not evident that this policy is optimal, and the purpose of this section is to find the optimal policy. Even though we know that the optimal policy must be of the (s,S) form, we will consider all possible policies, although we will assume that three cameras is the maximum number of cameras that the store will stock. The **policy-improvement algorithm** will be used first, followed by the **linear programming formulation**.

Because X_t represents the state of the system, i.e., the number of cameras on hand at the end of week t (before ordering), then $X_t = 0, 1, 2, 3$. Similarly, there are four possible decisions:

Decision	Action
0	Do not order
1	Order 1 camera
2	Order 2 cameras
3	Order 3 cameras

The possible transitions are given by[1]

Decision 0

State	0	1	2	3
0	1	0	0	0
1	$P\{D \geq 1\}$	$P\{D = 0\}$	0	0
2	$P\{D \geq 2\}$	$P\{D = 1\}$	$P\{D = 0\}$	0
3	$P\{D \geq 3\}$	$P\{D = 2\}$	$P\{D = 1\}$	$P\{D = 0\}$

Decision 1

State	0	1	2	3
0	$P\{D \geq 1\}$	$P\{D = 0\}$	0	0
1	$P\{D \geq 2\}$	$P\{D = 1\}$	$P\{D = 0\}$	0
2	$P\{D \geq 3\}$	$P\{D = 2\}$	$P\{D = 1\}$	$P\{D = 0\}$
3	Decision 1 not permitted			

Decision 2

State	0	1	2	3
0	$P\{D \geq 2\}$	$P\{D = 1\}$	$P\{D = 0\}$	0
1	$P\{D \geq 3\}$	$P\{D = 2\}$	$P\{D = 1\}$	$P\{D = 0\}$
2, 3	Decision 2 not permitted			

Decision 3

State	0	1	2	3
0	$P\{D \geq 3\}$	$P\{D = 2\}$	$P\{D = 1\}$	$P\{D = 0\}$
1, 2, 3	Decision 3 not permitted			

Recalling that the demand D is a Poisson random variable with parameter $\lambda = 1$, and using appendix Table A.5.4, these transitions can now be expressed as

Decision 0

State	0	1	2	3
0	1	0	0	0
1	0.632	0.368	0	0
2	0.264	0.368	0.368	0
3	0.080	0.184	0.368	0.368

Decision 1

State	0	1	2	3
0	0.632	0.368	0	0
1	0.264	0.368	0.368	0
2	0.080	0.184	0.368	0.368
3	Decision 1 not permitted			

[1] Note that in this example the set of possible decisions varies with the states.

Decision 2

State	0	1	2	3
0	0.264	0.368	0.368	0
1	0.080	0.184	0.368	0.368
2, 3	Decision 2 not permitted			

Decision 3

State	0	1	2	3
0	0.080	0.184	0.368	0.368
1, 2, 3	Decision 3 not permitted			

The cost information required is similar to that given in Sec. 15.7, and you are urged to review this material. A summary is given by

State	Decision	Actual cost per week	Expected cost per week, C_{ik}
0	0	$50D$	$50E(D) = 50$
	1	$35 + 50 \max\{(D-1),0\}$	$35 + 50[1P\{D=2\} + 2P\{D=3\} + \cdots] = 53.4$
	2	$60 + 50 \max\{(D-2),0\}$	$60 + 50[1P\{D=3\} + 2P\{D=4\} + \cdots] = 65.2$
	3	$85 + 50 \max\{(D-3),0\}$	$85 + 50[1P\{D=4\} + 2P\{D=5\} + \cdots] = 86.2$
1	0	$50 \max\{(D-1),0\}$	$50[1P\{D=2\} + 2P\{D=3\} + \cdots] = 18.4$
	1	$35 + 50 \max\{(D-2),0\}$	$35 + 50[1P\{D=3\} + 2P\{D=4\} + \cdots] = 40.2$
	2	$60 + 50 \max\{(D-3),0\}$	$60 + 50[1P\{D=4\} + 2P\{D=5\} + \cdots] = 61.2$
	3	Decision 3 not permitted	
2	0	$50 \max\{(D-2),0\}$	$50[1P\{D=3\} + 2P\{D=4\} + \cdots] = 5.2$
	1	$35 + 50 \max\{(D-3),0\}$	$35 + 50[1P\{D=4\} + 2P\{D=5\} + \cdots] = 36.2$
	2, 3	Decisions 2, 3 not permitted	
3	0	$50 \max\{(D-3),0\}$	$50[1P\{D=4\} + 2P\{D=5\} + \cdots] = 1.2$
	1, 2, 3	Decisions 1, 2, 3 not permitted	

Choose the (s,S) policy already introduced as the initial policy for carrying out the value-determination step (step 1) of the **policy-improvement algorithm**. This policy, R_1, calls for ordering up to 3 units whenever the system is in state 0 (no cameras on hand); otherwise, no order is placed. With this policy, the following four equations must be solved simultaneously for $g(R_1)$, $v_0(R_1)$, $v_1(R_1)$, and $v_2(R_1)$ [recall that $v_3(R_1)$ is arbitrarily taken to be zero]:

$$g(R_1) = C_{0k_1} + \sum_{j=0}^{3} p_{0j}(k_1)v_j(R_1) - v_0(R_1)$$

$$g(R_1) = C_{1k_1} + \sum_{j=0}^{3} p_{1j}(k_1)v_j(R_1) - v_1(R_1)$$

$$g(R_1) = C_{2k_1} + \sum_{j=0}^{3} p_{2j}(k_1)v_j(R_1) - v_2(R_1)$$

$$g(R_1) = C_{3k_1} + \sum_{j=0}^{3} p_{3j}(k_1)v_j(R_1) - v_3(R_1),$$

or alternatively,

$$g(R_1) = 86.2 + 0.080v_0(R_1) + 0.184v_1(R_1) + 0.368v_2(R_1) - v_0(R_1)$$
$$g(R_1) = 18.4 + 0.632v_0(R_1) + 0.368v_1(R_1) \qquad\qquad - v_1(R_1)$$

$$g(R_1) = 5.2 + 0.264v_0(R_1) + 0.368v_1(R_1) + 0.368v_2(R_1) - v_2(R_1)$$
$$g(R_1) = 1.2 + 0.080v_0(R_1) + 0.184v_1(R_1) + 0.368v_2(R_1).$$

The simultaneous solution of this system of equations yields

$$g_1(R_1) = 31.43$$
$$v_0(R_1) = 85.00$$
$$v_1(R_1) = 64.38$$
$$v_2(R_1) = 31.49.$$

Step 2 can now be applied. It is necessary to find the improved policy R_2, which has the property that $d_0(R_2) = k_2^0$, $d_1(R_2) = k_2^1$, $d_2(R_2) = k_2^2$, and $d_3(R_2) = k_2^3$ minimizes the following expressions:

(0) $C_{0k_2^0} + p_{00}(k_2^0)85 + p_{01}(k_2^0)64.38 + p_{02}(k_2^0)31.49 - 85$

(1) $C_{1k_2^1} + p_{10}(k_2^1)85 + p_{11}(k_2^1)64.38 + p_{12}(k_2^1)31.49 - 64.38$

(2) $C_{2k_2^2} + p_{20}(k_2^2)85 + p_{21}(k_2^2)64.38 + p_{22}(k_2^2)31.49 - 31.49$

(3) $C_{3k_2^3} + p_{30}(k_2^3)85 + p_{31}(k_2^3)64.38 + p_{32}(k_2^3)31.49.$

To find the optimal decisions, the following data are required:

State 0

Decision	$p_{00}(k_2)$	$p_{01}(k_2)$	$p_{02}(k_2)$	C_{0k_2}	Total value of expression 0
0	1	0	0	50	50
1	0.632	0.368	0	53.4	45.81
2	0.264	0.368	0.368	65.2	37.92
3	0.080	0.184	0.368	86.2	31.43

State 1

Decision	$p_{10}(k_2)$	$p_{11}(k_2)$	$p_{12}(k_2)$	C_{1k_2}	Total value of expression 1
0	0.632	0.368	0	18.4	31.43
1	0.264	0.368	0.368	40.2	33.54
2	0.080	0.184	0.368	61.2	27.05

State 2

Decision	$p_{20}(k_2)$	$p_{21}(k_2)$	$p_{22}(k_2)$	C_{2k_2}	Total value of expression 2
0	0.264	0.368	0.368	5.2	31.43
1	0.080	0.184	0.368	36.2	34.94

State 3

Decision	$p_{30}(k_2)$	$p_{31}(k_2)$	$p_{32}(k_2)$	C_{3k_2}	Total value of expression 3
0	0.080	0.184	0.368	1.2	31.43

Thus $d_0(R_2) = k_2^0 = 3$, $d_1(R_2) = k_2^1 = 2$, $d_2(R_2) = k_2^2 = d_3(R_2) = k_2^3 = 0$. Hence policy R_2 calls for ordering up to three cameras whenever there is 0 or 1 camera in stock; otherwise, no ordering is done; i.e., if the number of cameras on hand at the end of the week is less than $s = 2$ cameras, the store orders up to $S = 3$ cameras. Because policy R_2 differs from policy R_1, another iteration is required. The following four equations must be solved simultaneously for $g(R_2)$, $v_0(R_2)$, $v_1(R_2)$, and $v_2(R_2)$:

$$g(R_2) = 86.2 + 0.080v_0(R_2) + 0.184v_1(R_2) + 0.368v_2(R_2) - v_0(R_2)$$
$$g(R_2) = 61.2 + 0.080v_0(R_2) + 0.184v_1(R_2) + 0.368v_2(R_2) - v_1(R_2)$$
$$g(R_2) = 5.2 + 0.264v_0(R_2) + 0.368v_1(R_2) + 0.368v_2(R_2) - v_2(R_2)$$
$$g(R_2) = 1.2 + 0.080v_0(R_2) + 0.184v_1(R_2) + 0.368v_2(R_2).$$

The simultaneous solution of this system of equations yields

$$g_1(R_2) = 30.33$$
$$v_0(R_2) = 85.00$$
$$v_1(R_2) = 60.00$$
$$v_2(R_2) = 30.68.$$

Step 2 can now be applied. It is necessary to find the improved policy R_3, which has the property that $d_0(R_3) = k_3^0$, $d_1(R_3) = k_3^1$, $d_2(R_3) = k_3^2$, and $d_3(R_3) = k_3^3$ minimizes the following expressions:

(0) $\quad C_{0k_3^0} + p_{00}(k_3^0)85 + p_{01}(k_3^0)60 + p_{02}(k_3^0)30.68 - 85$

(1) $\quad C_{1k_3^1} + p_{10}(k_3^1)85 + p_{11}(k_3^1)60 + p_{12}(k_3^1)30.68 - 60$

(2) $\quad C_{2k_3^2} + p_{20}(k_3^2)85 + p_{21}(k_3^2)60 + p_{22}(k_3^2)30.68 - 30.68$

(3) $\quad C_{3k_3^3} + p_{30}(k_3^3)85 + p_{31}(k_3^3)60 + p_{32}(k_3^3)30.68.$

Using the data from the previous iteration, the relevant calculations are

Decision	Total value of expression 0	Total value of expression 1	Total value of expression 2	Total value of expression 3
0	50	34.20	30.33	30.33
1	44.20	36.01	34.65	—
2	36.01	30.33	—	—
3	30.33	—	—	—

Thus $d_0(R_3) = k_3^0 = 3$, $d_1(R_3) = k_3^1 = 2$, $d_2(R_3) = k_3^2 = d_3(R_3) = k_3^3 = 0$. Hence policy R_3 and policy R_2 are identical, so that the optimal policy calls for ordering up to three cameras when there is 0 or 1 camera in stock; otherwise, no ordering is done.

The **linear programming formulation** calls for finding the y_{ik} that

Minimize $\quad 50y_{00} + 53.4y_{01} + 65.2y_{02} + 86.2y_{03} + 18.4y_{10} + 40.2y_{11}$
$$+ 61.2y_{12} + 5.2y_{20} + 36.2y_{21} + 1.2y_{30},$$

subject to

$$y_{00} + y_{01} + y_{02} + y_{03} + y_{10} + y_{11} + y_{12} + y_{20} + y_{21} + y_{30} = 1,$$

$$y_{00} + y_{01} + y_{02} + y_{03} - [y_{00} + y_{01}(0.632) + y_{02}(0.264) + y_{03}(0.080)$$
$$+ y_{10}(0.632) + y_{11}(0.264) + y_{12}(0.080) + y_{20}(0.264)$$
$$+ y_{21}(0.080) + y_{30}(0.080)] = 0,$$

$$y_{10} + y_{11} + y_{12} - [y_{01}(0.368) + y_{02}(0.368) + y_{03}(0.184) + y_{10}(0.368)$$
$$+ y_{11}(0.368) + y_{12}(0.184) + y_{20}(0.368) + y_{21}(0.184) + y_{30}(0.184)] = 0,$$

$$y_{20} + y_{21} - [y_{02}(0.368) + y_{03}(0.368) + y_{11}(0.368) + y_{12}(0.368)$$
$$+ y_{20}(0.368) + y_{21}(0.368) + y_{30}(0.368)] = 0,$$

$$y_{30} - [y_{03}(0.368) + y_{12}(0.368) + y_{21}(0.368) + y_{30}(0.368)] = 0,$$

and

$$y_{00}, y_{01}, y_{02}, y_{03}, y_{10}, y_{11}, y_{12}, y_{20}, y_{21}, y_{30} \geq 0.$$

This linear program can be solved by using the simplex method. The results yield all y_{ik} equal to zero, except for

$$y_{03} = 0.148, \quad y_{12} = 0.252, \quad y_{20} = 0.368, \quad y_{30} = 0.233.$$

The corresponding D_{ik} are given by

$$D_{03} = D_{12} = D_{20} = D_{30} = 1,$$

and all the remaining $D_{ik} = 0$.

20.8 Conclusions

The material presented in this chapter represents a powerful tool for formulating models and finding the optimal policies for controlling a large **class** of systems—those that are **Markovian decision processes**. These techniques are applicable to the solution of problems in such areas as queueing theory, inventory, maintenance, and probabilistic dynamic programming, in general.

Two algorithms were presented, the **policy-improvement algorithm** and the **linear programming formulation**, for finding optimal policies. It is evident from the examples that data-collection requirements are high. Even if the solution converges rapidly in the policy-improvement algorithm, completing step 2 requires considerable calculation for systems with a large number of states. Using the linear programming formulation with, say, 50 states and 25 decisions leads to 1,250 variables and 51 constraints (excluding the nonnegativity constraints), which represents a large linear program. Nevertheless, these two solution methods are useful for solving real-world problems. When the cost criterion is the expected discounted cost, the **method of successive approximations** provides a valuable tool for approximating the optimal solution. Much simpler calculations are required for this algorithm than for the policy-improvement or linear programming methods.

Considerable research activities have been devoted to the field of

Markovian decision processes in recent years. C. Derman[1] has shown that in the expected average cost per unit time case, the optimal policy is deterministic (calls for always taking a particular action when the system is in a given state). Similarly, he has shown[2] that in the expected discounted cost case, the optimal policy is also deterministic. The policy-improvement algorithm is due to R. Howard.[3] For the expected average cost per unit time case, he presents not only the algorithm for the situation where all the states belong to one class but also an algorithm that is applicable when there is more than one (a finite number) class of states. He also considers the continuous-time case. The linear programming formulation using the expected average cost per unit time was first given by A. S. Manne,[4] who treated the case where all the states belong to one class. The linear programming formulation using the expected discounted cost was first given by F. d'Epenoux.[5] Finally, although the results presented in this chapter assumed the state space to be finite, most of the results are applicable to the case of a countable state space.

SELECTED REFERENCES

1. Bertsekas, D. P.: *Dynamic Programming and Stochastic Control*, Academic Press, New York, 1976.
2. Derman, C.: *Finite State Markovian Decision Processes*, Academic Press, New York, 1970.
3. Dreyfus, S., and A. Law: *The Art and Theory of Dynamic Programming*, Academic Press, New York, 1976.
4. Dynkin, E. B., and A. Yushkevich: *Controlled Markov Processes*, Springer-Verlag, 1979.
5. Heyman, D., and M. Sobel: *Stochastic Models in Operations Research, Vol. 2*, McGraw-Hill, New York, 1982.
6. Ross, S.: *Introduction to Stochastic Dynamic Programming*, Academic Press, New York, 1983.

PROBLEMS

1. During any period, a potential customer arrives at a certain facility with probability $\frac{1}{2}$. If there are already two people at the facility (including the one being served), the potential customer leaves the facility immediately and never returns. However, if there is one or fewer people, he enters the facility and becomes an actual customer. The manager of the facility has two types of service rates available. If he uses his "slow" service rate at a

---

[1] Derman, C.: "On Sequential Decisions and Markov Chains," *Management Science*, **9**: 16–24, 1962.

[2] Derman, C.: "Markovian Sequential Control Processes—Denumerable State Space," *Journal of Mathematical Analysis and Applications*, **10**: 295–302, 1965.

[3] Howard, R.: *Dynamic Programming and Markov Processes*, Technology Press, Cambridge, Mass., and Wiley, New York, 1960.

[4] Manne, A. S.: "Linear Programming and Sequential Decisions," *Management Science*, **6**: 259–267, 1960.

[5] d'Epenoux, F.: "Sur un Probleme de Production et de Stockage dans l'Aléatoire," *Rev. Française Information Recherche Opérationnelle*, **141**: 3–16, 1960; English translation: *Management Science*, **10**: 98–108, 1963.

cost of $3.00 during a period, a customer will be served and leave the facility with probability $\frac{3}{5}$. If he uses his "fast" service rate at a cost of $9.00 during a period, a customer will be served and leave the facility with probability $\frac{4}{5}$. Note that the probability of more than one customer arriving or more than one customer being served in a period is zero. A profit of $50 is earned when a customer is served. Use the *policy-improvement algorithm* to determine the policy the manager should follow to minimize his expected long-run average cost per period. (*Hint:* In computing the costs for services when two customers are at a facility, do not forget the opportunity cost of losing a potential customer.)

2. Formulate Prob. 1 as a *linear programming* problem.

3. A person often finds that she is up to 1 hour late for work. If she is from 1 to 30 minutes late, $5 is deducted from her paycheck; if she is from 31 to 60 minutes late for work, $10 is deducted from her paycheck. If she drives to work at her normal speed (which is well under the speed limit), she can arrive in 20 minutes. However, if she exceeds the speed limit a little here and there on her way to work, she can get there in 10 minutes, but she runs the risk of getting a speeding ticket. With probability $\frac{1}{8}$ she will get caught speeding and not only get fined $20 but also get delayed 10 minutes, so that it takes 20 minutes to reach work.

Let s be the time she finds she has to reach work before being late; that is, $s = 10$ means she has 10 minutes to get to work and $s = -10$ means she is already 10 minutes late for work. For simplicity, she considers s to be in one of four intervals: $(20,\infty)$, $(10,19)$, $(-10,9)$, and $(-20,-11)$.

The transition probabilities for s tomorrow if she does not speed today are given by

	$(20,\infty)$	$(10,19)$	$(-10,9)$	$(-20,-11)$
$(20,\infty)$	$\frac{3}{8}$	$\frac{1}{4}$	$\frac{1}{4}$	$\frac{1}{8}$
$(10,19)$	$\frac{1}{2}$	$\frac{1}{4}$	$\frac{1}{8}$	$\frac{1}{8}$
$(-10,9)$	$\frac{5}{8}$	$\frac{1}{4}$	$\frac{1}{8}$	0
$(-20,-11)$	$\frac{3}{4}$	$\frac{1}{4}$	0	0

The transition probabilities for s tomorrow if she speeds to work today are given by

	$(20,\infty)$	$(10,19)$	$(-10,9)$	$(-20,-11)$
$(20,\infty)$				
$(10,19)$	$\frac{3}{8}$	$\frac{1}{4}$	$\frac{1}{4}$	$\frac{1}{8}$
$(-10,9)$				
$(-20,-11)$	$\frac{5}{8}$	$\frac{1}{4}$	$\frac{1}{8}$	0

Note that there are no transition probabilities for $(20, \infty)$ and $(-10, 9)$, because she will get to work on time and from 1 to 30 minutes late, respectively, regardless of whether she speeds or not. Hence speeding when in these states would not be a logical choice.

Also note that the transition probabilities imply that the later she is for work and the more she has to rush to get there, the likelier she is to leave for work earlier the next day.

Use the *policy-improvement algorithm* to determine when she should speed and when she should take her time getting to work.

4. Formulate Prob. 3 as a *linear programming* problem.

5. Every Saturday night a man plays poker, much to the dismay of his wife. Regardless of the kind of mood his wife is in, if he takes her out to dinner (at an expected cost of \$14) before going to play poker, she will be in a good mood, with probability $\frac{7}{8}$, and a bad mood, with probability $\frac{1}{8}$, next Saturday night. However, if he goes to play poker without taking her out to dinner first, she will be in a good mood next Saturday, with probability $\frac{1}{8}$, and a bad mood, with probability $\frac{7}{8}$, regardless of her mood this week. Furthermore, if she happens to be in a bad mood and he does not take her to dinner, she will go to an exclusive store and buy a new outfit (at an expected cost of \$60). Use the *policy-improvement algorithm* to find the policy that the man should follow to minimize his long-run expected average cost per week.

6. Formulate Prob. 5 as a *linear programming* problem.

7. When a tennis player serves, he gets two chances to serve in bounds. If he fails to do so twice, he loses the point (1 unit). If he attempts to serve an ace, he serves in bounds, with probability $\frac{3}{8}$. If he serves a lob, he serves in bounds, with probability $\frac{7}{8}$. If he serves an ace in bounds, he wins the point (1 unit), with probability $\frac{2}{3}$. With an inbounds lob, he wins the point (1 unit), with probability $\frac{1}{3}$. Use the *policy-improvement algorithm* to determine the optimal strategy. (*Hint:* Let state 0 denote point over, two serves to go on next point; and let state 1 denote one serve left.)

8. Formulate Prob. 7 as a *linear programming* problem.

9. A student is concerned about her car and does not like to get it dented. When she drives to school she has a choice of parking it on the street in one space, parking it on the street and taking up two spaces, or parking in the lot. If she parks on the street in one space, her car gets dented, with probability $\frac{1}{10}$. If she parks on the street and takes two spaces, the probability of a dent is $\frac{1}{50}$ and the probability of a \$20 ticket is $\frac{3}{10}$. Parking in a lot costs \$5, but the car will not get dented. If her car gets dented, she can have it repaired at the dealer, in which case it is out of commission for a day and costs her \$50 in fees and cab fares. She can also drive her car dented, but she feels that the loss of pride and shame is worth about \$9 a day. Using the *policy-improvement algorithm*, determine the optimal policy.

10. Formulate Prob. 9 as a *linear programming* problem.

11. Each year Mr. Merrill has the chance to invest in two different no-load mutual funds: The Go-Go Fund or Go-Slow Mutual Fund. At the end of each year, Mr. Merrill liquidates his holdings, takes his profits, and then reinvests. The yearly profits of the mutual funds are dependent upon how the market reacts each year. Recently the market has been oscillating around the 1,000 mark, according to the probabilities given in the following matrix:

$$
\begin{array}{c c}
 & \begin{array}{c c c} 900 & 1{,}000 & 1{,}100 \end{array} \\
\begin{array}{c} 900 \\ 1{,}000 \\ 1{,}100 \end{array} &
\begin{bmatrix}
0.3 & 0.5 & 0.2 \\
0.1 & 0.5 & 0.4 \\
0.2 & 0.4 & 0.4
\end{bmatrix}
\end{array}
$$

Each year the market moves up (or down) 100 points, the Go-Go Fund has profits (or losses) of $20, while the Go-Slow Fund has profits (or losses) of $10. If the market moves up (or down) 200 points in a year, the Go-Go Fund has profits (or losses) of $50, while the Go-Slow Fund has profits (or losses) of only $20. If the market does not change, there is no profit or loss for either fund. Use the *policy-improvement algorithm* to determine how Mr. Merrill should invest each year.

12.   Formulate Prob. 11 as a *linear programming* problem.

13.   Suppose a person wants to dispose of a car. She receives an offer each month and must decide immediately whether or not to accept the offer. Once rejected, the offer is lost. The possible offers are $600, $800, and $1,000, made with probabilities $\frac{5}{8}$, $\frac{1}{4}$, and $\frac{1}{8}$, respectively (it may be assumed that successive offers are independent of each other). Suppose that there is a maintenance cost of $60 per month and that a discount factor of $\alpha = 0.95$ is specified. Using the *policy-improvement algorithm*, find a policy that minimizes the expected long-run total discounted cost. (*Hint*: There are two actions: accept or reject the offer. Let the state space at time t denote the offer at time t, augmented by the state ∞. The process goes to state ∞ whenever an offer is accepted, and it remains there at a monthly cost of 0.) Find the optimal policy using the *policy-improvement algorithm*.

14.   Formulate Prob. 13 as a *linear programming* problem.

15.   In Prob. 13, use three iterations of the *method of successive approximations* to approximate the optimal solution.

16.   The price of a certain stock is fluctuating among the prices $10, $20, and $30 from month to month. Market analysts have predicted that if the stock is at $10 during any month, it will be at $10 or $20 next month, with probabilities $\frac{4}{5}$ and $\frac{1}{5}$ respectively; if the stock is at $20, it will be at $10, $20, or $30 next month, with probabilities $\frac{1}{4}$, $\frac{1}{4}$, and $\frac{1}{2}$ respectively; and if the stock is at $30, it will be at $20 or $30 next month, with probabilities $\frac{3}{4}$ and $\frac{1}{4}$, respectively. Given a discount factor of 0.9, use the *policy-improvement algorithm* to determine when to sell and when to hold the stock to maximize the expected long-run total discounted profits. (*Hint*: Augment the state space with a state that is reached with probability 1 when the stock is sold and with probability 0 when the stock is held.)

17.   Formulate Prob. 16 as a *linear programming* problem.

18.   In Prob. 16, use three iterations of the *method of succcessive approximations* to approximate the optimal solution.

19.   A person is in the market for a house. Until he finds one he lives in a hotel for $75 a day. When he buys one, he pays immediately and moves in the next day. He can look at a house (if he chooses to) at most once a day, and when he does look at a house, he pays a broker's fee of $50. The houses can cost $140,000, $170,000, and $200,000, and these costs each occur with probability $\frac{1}{3}$ on any given day when he looks at a house. There is a daily discount factor of 0.999. Use the *policy-improvement algorithm* to find the optimal policy.

20. Formulate Prob. 19 as a *linear programming* problem.

21. In Prob. 19, use three iterations of the *method of successive approximations* to approximate the optimal solution.

22. A farmer raises corn. Each year that he has a successful crop he grosses $17,000 on expenses of $6,000 for seed and labor. Sometimes his crop fails and he grosses only $8,000. Each year the farmer has a chance of using two types of fertilizers: type A at a cost of $2,000 guarantees that there is a 60 percent chance of having a successful crop the next year, and type B at a cost of $3,000 guarantees that there is an 80 percent chance of a good crop next year. Using the *policy-improvement algorithm* with a discount factor of 0.5, determine when the farmer should use fertilizer A and B.

23. Formulate Prob. 22 as a *linear programming* problem.

24. In Prob. 22, use three iterations of the *method of successive approximations* to approximate the optimal solution.

25. A chemical company produces two chemicals, denoted by 0 and 1. Each month a decision is made as to which chemical to produce that month. Because the demand for each chemical is predictable, it is known that if 1 is produced this month, there is a 60 percent chance that it will also be produced again next month. Similarly, if 0 is produced this month, there is only a 20 percent chance that it will be produced again next month.

To combat the emissions of pollutants, the chemical company has two processes, process A, which is efficient in combating the pollution from the production of 1 but not from 0, and process B, which is efficient in combating the pollution from the production of 0 but not from 1. The amount of pollution from the production of each chemical under both processes is

	0	1
A	100	10
B	10	30

Unfortunately, there is a time delay in setting up the pollution-control processes, so that a decision as to which process to use must be made in the month prior to the production decision. Use the *policy-improvement algorithm* to determine a pollution-control policy that will minimize the present value of all future pollution at a discount factor of $\alpha = 0.5$.

26. Formulate Prob. 25 as a *linear programming* problem.

27. In Prob. 25, use two iterations of the *method of successive approximations* to approximate the optimal solution.

28. A man is playing a slot machine at $1 per play. Each time that he wins the jackpot of $10 he finds that if he pulls the lever hard, he has a 10 percent chance of winning on the next round. But if he pulls the lever gently, he has a 20 percent chance of hitting the jackpot on the next round. If he loses and then pulls the lever hard, he has an 80 percent chance of losing on the next round also. But if he pulls the lever gently, he has a 95 percent chance of losing again. Use the *policy-improvement algorithm* with a discount factor of 0.9 to determine whether the player should pull the lever hard or gently.

29. Formulate Prob. 28 as a *linear programming* problem.

30.   In Prob. 28, use two iterations of the *method of successive approximations* to approximate the optimal solution.

31.   Solve Prob. 19 as a *four-period model*.

32.   Solve Prob. 22 as a *four-period model*.

33.   Solve Prob. 25 as a *three-period model*.

34.   Solve Prob. 28 as a *three-period model*.

35.   Formulate the water-resource model presented in Sec. 20.6 as a *linear programming* problem.

36.   Use three iterations of the *method of successive approximations* to approximate the optimal solution to the water-resource model presented in Sec. 20.6.

37.   Solve the inventory model presented in Sec. 20.7 using the expected discounted cost as the cost criterion, with a discount factor of $\alpha = 0.95$.

38.   Use three iterations of the *method of successive approximations* to approximate the optimal solution to Prob. 37.

39.   Find the optimal solution to a *four-period* machine-maintenance model using the data from the example presented in this chapter. (Use a discount factor of $\alpha = 0.90$.)

40.   Solve the inventory model presented in Sec. 20.7 as a *four-period* problem.

41.   Solve the water-resource model presented in Sec. 20.6 as a *three-period* problem.

■ CHAPTER 21

Reliability

21.1 Introduction

The many definitions of reliability that exist depend upon the viewpoint of the user. However, they all have a common core that contains the statement that reliability, $R(t)$, is the probability that a device performs adequately over the interval $[0, t]$. In general, it is assumed that unless repair or replacement occurs, adequate performance at time t implies adequate performance during the interval $[0, t]$. The device under consideration may be an entire system, a subsystem, or a component.[1] Although this definition is simple, the systems to which it is applied are generally very complex. In principle, it is possible to break down the system into black boxes, with each black box being in one of two states: good or bad. Mathematical models of the system can then be abstracted from the physical processes and the theory of combinatorial probability used to predict the reliability of the system. The black boxes may be independent of, or be very dependent upon, each other. For any reasonable system, such a probability analysis generally becomes so cumbersome that it must be considered impractical. Hence we seek other methods that either simplify the calculations or provide bounds on the reliability of the entire complex system.

As an example, consider an automobile. There are a large number of functional parts, wiring, and joints. These may be broken into subsystems, with each subsystem having a reliability associated with it. Possible subsystems are the engine, transmission, exhaust, body, carburetor, and brakes. A mathematical

[1] A subsystem can be viewed as containing one or more components.

model of the automobile system can be abstracted and the theory of combinatorial probability used to predict the reliability of the automobile.

21.2 Structural Function of a System

Suppose an automobile can be divided into n components (subsystems). The performance of each component can be denoted by a random variable, X_i, that takes on the value $x_i = 1$ if the component performs satisfactorily for the desired time and $x_i = 0$ if the component fails during this time. In general, then, X_i is a binary random variable defined by

$$X_i = \begin{cases} 1, & \text{if component } i \text{ performs satisfactorily during time } [0, t] \\ 0, & \text{if component } i \text{ fails during time } [0, t]. \end{cases}$$

The performance of the system is measured by the binary random variable $\phi(X_1, X_2, \ldots, X_n)$,[1] where

$$\phi(X_1, X_2, \ldots, X_n) = \begin{cases} 1, & \text{if system performs satisfactorily during time } [0, t] \\ 0, & \text{if system fails during time } [0, t]. \end{cases}$$

The function ϕ is called the *structure function* of the system and is just a function of the n-component random variables. Thus the performance of the automobile is a function of its n components and takes on the value 1 if the automobile functions properly for the desired time and 0 if it does not. Because the performance of each component in the automobile takes on the value 1 or 0, then the function ϕ is defined over 2^n points, with each point resulting in a 1 if the automobile performs satisfactorily and a 0 if the automobile fails.

There are several important structure functions to consider, depending upon how the components are assembled. Three structure functions will be discussed in detail.

SERIES SYSTEM

The series system is the simplest and most common of all the configurations. For a series system, the system fails if any component of the system fails; i.e., it performs satisfactorily if and only if all the components perform satisfactorily. The structure function for a series system is given by

$$\phi(X_1, X_2, \ldots, X_n) = X_1 X_2 \cdots X_n = \min\{X_1, X_2, \ldots, X_n\}.$$

This equation holds because each X_i is either 1 or 0. Hence the structure function takes on the value 1 if each X_i equals 1 or, alternatively, if the minimum of the X_i equals 1. For example, suppose the automobile is divided into only two components: the engine (X_1) and the transmission (X_2). Then it is reasonable to assume that the automobile will perform satisfactorily for the desired time period

---

[1] Note that X_i and ϕ are functions of the time t, but t will be suppressed for ease of notation.

if and only if the engine and the transmission both perform satisfactorily. Hence

$$\phi(X_1, X_2) = X_1 X_2,$$

and

$$\phi(1, 1) = 1, \qquad \phi(1, 0) = \phi(0, 1) = \phi(0, 0) = 0.$$

PARALLEL SYSTEM

A parallel system of n components is defined to be a *system that fails if all components fail*, or alternatively, a *system that performs satisfactorily if at least one of the n components performs satisfactorily* (with all n components operating simultaneously). This property of parallel systems is often called *redundancy* (i.e., there are alternative components, existing within the system, to help the system operate successfully in case of failure of one or more components). The structure function for a parallel system is given by

$$\phi(X_1, X_2, \ldots, X_n) = 1 - (1 - X_1)(1 - X_2)\ldots(1 - X_n) = \max\{X_1, X_2, \ldots, X_n\}.$$

This equation again follows because each X_i is either 1 or 0. The structure function takes on the value 1 if at least one of the X_i equals 1 or, alternatively, if the largest X_i equals 1. In the automobile example, the car is equipped with front disk (X_1) and rear drum (X_2) brakes. The automobile will perform successfully if either the front or rear brakes operate properly.[1] If one is concerned with the structure function of the brake subsystem, then

$$\phi(X_1, X_2) = 1 - (1 - X_1)(1 - X_2) = X_1 + X_2 - X_1 X_2,$$

and

$$\phi(1, 1) = \phi(1, 0) = \phi(0, 1) = 1, \qquad \phi(0, 0) = 0.$$

k OUT OF n SYSTEM

Some systems are assembled such that the system operates if k out of n components function properly. Note that the series system is a k out of n system, with $k = n$, and the parallel system is a k out of n system, with $k = 1$. The structure function for a k out of n system is given by

$$\phi(X_1, X_2, \ldots, X_n) = \begin{cases} 1, & \text{if } \sum_{i=1}^{n} X_i \geq k \\ 0, & \text{if } \sum_{i=1}^{n} X_i < k. \end{cases}$$

In the automobile example, consider a large truck equipped with eight tires. The structure function for the tire system is an example of a four out of eight system.

---

[1] It is evident that the loss of the front or rear brakes will affect the braking capability of the automobile, but the definition of "perform successfully" may allow for either set working.

(Although the system's performance may be degraded if fewer than eight tires are operating, rearrangement of the tire configuration will result in adequate performance as long as at least four tires are useable.)

It is reasonable to expect the performance of an automobile to improve if the performance of one or more components is improved. This improvement can be reflected in the characterization of the structure function, where, for example, one would expect $\phi(1,0,0,1)$ to be no less than $\phi(1,0,0,0)$. Hence it will be assumed that if $x_i \leq y_i$, for $i = 1, 2, \ldots, n$, then

$$\phi(y_1, y_2, \ldots, y_n) \geq \phi(x_1, x_2, \ldots, x_n).$$

A system possessing this property (ϕ is an increasing function of x) is called a *coherent (or monotone) system*.

21.3 System Reliability

The structure function of a system containing n components is a binary random variable that takes on the value 1 or 0. Furthermore, the reliability of this system can be expressed as

$$R = P\{\phi(X_1, X_2, \ldots, X_n) = 1\}.[1]$$

Thus, for a series system, the reliability is given by

$$R = P\{X_1 X_2 \cdots X_n = 1\} = P\{X_1 = 1, X_2 = 1, \ldots, X_n = 1\}.$$

When the usual terms for conditional probability are employed,

$$R = P\{X_1 = 1\} P\{X_2 = 1 \mid X_1 = 1\} P\{X_3 = 1 \mid X_1 = 1, X_2 = 1\}$$
$$\cdots P\{X_n = 1 \mid X_1 = 1, \ldots, X_{n-1} = 1\}.$$

In general, such conditional probabilities require careful analysis. For example, $P\{X_2 = 1 \mid X_1 = 1\}$ is the probability that component 2 will perform successfully, given that component 1 performs successfully. Consider a system where the heat from component 1 affects the temperature of component 2 and thereby its probability of success. The performance of these components is then dependent, and the evaluation of the conditional probability is extremely difficult. If, on the other hand, the performance characteristics of these components do not interact, e.g., the temperature of one component does not affect the performance of the other component, then the components can be said to be independent. The expression for the reliability then simplifies and becomes

$$R = P\{X_1 = 1\} P\{X_2 = 1\} \cdots P\{X_n = 1\}.$$

When the components of a series system are assumed to be independent, it should be noted that the reliability is a function of the probability distribution of the X_i. This phenomenon is true for any system structure.

---

[1] The time t is now suppressed in the notation. Recall that the time is implicitly included in determining whether or not the ith component performs satisfactorily.

Unless otherwise specified, it will be assumed throughout the remainder of this chapter that the component performances are independent. Hence the probability distribution of the binary random variables X_i can be expressed as

$$P\{X_i = 1\} = p_i,$$

and

$$P\{X_i = 0\} = 1 - p_i.$$

Thus, for systems composed of independent components, the reliability becomes a function of the p_i; that is,

$$R = R(p_1, p_2, \ldots, p_n).$$

RELIABILITY OF SERIES SYSTEMS

As previously indicated, for a series structure

$$
\begin{aligned}
R(p_1, p_2, \ldots, p_n) &= P\{\phi(X_1, X_2, \ldots, X_n) = 1\} \\
&= P\{X_1 X_2 \cdots X_n = 1\} \\
&= P\{X_1 = 1, X_2 = 1, \ldots, X_n = 1\} \\
&= P\{X_1 = 1\} P\{X_2 = 1\} \cdots P\{X_n = 1\} \\
&= p_1 p_2 \cdots p_n.
\end{aligned}
$$

Thus, returning to the automobile example, if the probability that the engine performs satisfactorily is 0.95 and the probability that the transmission performs satisfactorily is 0.99, then the reliability of this automobile series subsystem is given by $R = (0.95)(0.99) = 0.94$.

RELIABILITY OF PARALLEL SYSTEMS

The structure function for a parallel system is

$$\phi(X_1, X_2, \ldots, X_n) = \max(X_1, X_2, \ldots, X_n),$$

and the reliability is given by

$$
\begin{aligned}
R(p_1, p_2, \ldots, p_n) &= P\{\max(X_1, X_2, \ldots, X_n) = 1\} \\
&= 1 - P\{\text{all } X_i = 0\} \\
&= 1 - P\{X_1 = 0, X_2 = 0, \ldots, X_n = 0\} \\
&= 1 - (1 - p_1)(1 - p_2) \cdots (1 - p_n).
\end{aligned}
$$

Thus, if the probability that the front disk brakes and the rear drum brakes perform satisfactorily is 0.99 for each, the subsystem reliability is given by

$$R = 1 - (0.01)(0.01) = 0.9999.$$

RELIABILITY OF k OUT OF n SYSTEMS

The structure function for a k out of n system is

$$\phi(X_1, X_2, \ldots, X_n) = \begin{cases} 1, & \text{if } \sum_{i=1}^{n} X_i \geq k \\ 0, & \text{if } \sum_{i=1}^{n} X_i < k, \end{cases}$$

and the reliability is given by

$$R(p_1, p_2, \ldots, p_n) = P\left\{ \sum_{i=1}^{n} X_i \geq k \right\}.$$

The evaluation of this expression is, in general, quite difficult except for the case of $p_1 = p_2 = \cdots = p_n = p$. Under this assumption, $\sum_{i=1}^{n} X_i$ has a binomial distribution with parameters n and p, so that

$$R(p, p, \ldots, p) = \sum_{i=k}^{n} \binom{n}{i} p^i (1 - p)^{n-i}.$$

For the truck tire example, if each tire has a probability of 0.95 of performing satisfactorily, then the reliability of a four out of eight system is given by

$$R = \sum_{i=4}^{8} \binom{8}{i} (0.95)^i (0.05)^{8-i} = 0.9999.$$

For general structures, the system reliability calculations can become quite tedious. A technique for computing reliabilities for this general case will be presented in the next section. However, the final result of this section is to indicate that the reliability function of a system of independent components can be shown to be an increasing function of the p_i; that is, if $p_i \leq q_i$ for $i = 1, 2, \ldots, n$, then

$$R(q_1, q_2, \ldots, q_n) \geq R(p_1, p_2, \ldots, p_n).$$

This result is analogous to, and dependent upon, the assumption that the structure function of the system is coherent. The implication of this intuitive result is that the reliability of the automobile will improve if the reliability of one or more components is improved.

21.4 Calculation of Exact System Reliability

A representation of the structure of a system can be expressed in terms of a network, and some of the material presented in Chap. 10 is relevant. For example, consider the system that can be represented by the network in Fig. 21.1. This system consists of five components, connected in a somewhat complex manner. According to the network diagram, the system will operate successfully if there exists a flow from A (source) to D (sink) through the directed graph, i.e., if components 1 and 4 operate successfully, or components 2 and 5 operate successfully, or components 1, 3, and 5 operate successfully. In fact, each arc can be viewed as having capacity 1 or 0, depending upon whether or not the

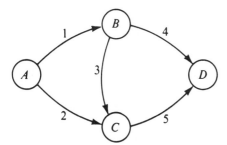

Figure 21.1 **A five-component system.**

component is operating. If an arc has a 0 attached to it (the component fails), then the network would lose that arc, and the system would operate successfully if and only if there was a path from the source to the sink in the resultant network. This situation is illustrated in Fig. 21.2, where the system still operates if components 3 and 4 fail but becomes inoperable if components 2, 3, and 4 fail. This suggests a possible method for computing the exact system reliability. Again, denote the performance of the ith component by the binary random variable X_i. Then X_i takes on the value 1 with probability p_i and 0 with probability $(1 - p_i)$. For each realization, $X_1 = x_1, X_2 = x_2, X_3 = x_3, X_4 = x_4$, and $X_5 = x_5$ (there are 2^5 such realizations), it is determined whether or not the system will operate, i.e., whether or not the structure function equals 1. The network consisting of those arcs with X_i equal to 1 contains at least one path if and only if the corresponding structure function equals 1. If a path is formed, the probability of obtaining this configuration is obtained. For the realization in Fig. 21.2a, a path is formed, and

$$P\{X_1 = 1, X_2 = 1, X_3 = 0, X_4 = 0, X_5 = 1\} = p_1 p_2 (1 - p_3)(1 - p_4) p_5.$$

Because each realization is disjoint, the system reliability is just the sum of the probabilities of those realizations that contain a path. Unfortunately, even for this simple system, 32 different realizations must be evaluated, and other techniques are desirable.

Another possible procedure for finding the exact reliability is to note that the

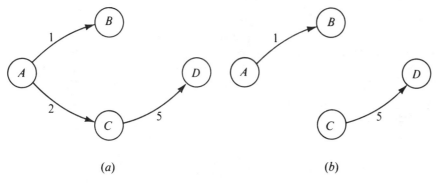

(a) (b)

Figure 21.2 **(a) System with components 3, 4 failed; (b) system with components 2, 3, 4 failed.**

reliability $R(p_1, p_2, \ldots, p_n)$ can be expressed as

$$R(p_1, p_2, \ldots, p_n) = P\{\text{maximum flow from source to sink} \geq 1\}.$$

This identity allows the concept of paths and cuts presented in Chap. 10 to be used. In reliability theory, the terminology of minimal paths and minimal cuts is introduced. A **minimal path** is a *minimal set of components that, by functioning, ensures the successful operation of the system*. For the example in Fig. 21.1, components 2 and 5 are a minimal path. A **minimal cut** is a *minimal set of components that, by failing, ensures the failure of the system*. In Fig. 21.1, components 1 and 2 are a minimal cut. For the system given in Fig. 21.1, the minimal paths and cuts are

Minimal paths	Minimal cuts
$X_1 X_4$	$X_1 X_2$
$X_1 X_3 X_5$	$X_4 X_5$
$X_2 X_5$	$X_2 X_3 X_4$
	$X_1 X_5$

If we use all the **minimal paths**, there are **two ways** to obtain the **exact system reliability**. Because the system will operate if all the components in at least one of the minimal paths operate, the system reliability can be expressed as

$$R(p_1, p_2, p_3, p_4, p_5) = P\{\phi(X_1, X_2, X_3, X_4, X_5) = 1\}$$
$$= P\{(X_1 X_4 = 1) \cup (X_1 X_3 X_5 = 1) \cup (X_2 X_5 = 1)\}.$$

Using the algebra of sets,

$$R(p_1, p_2, p_3, p_4, p_5) = P\{X_1 X_4 = 1\} + P\{X_1 X_3 X_5 = 1\}$$
$$+ P\{X_2 X_5 = 1\} - P\{X_1 X_3 X_4 X_5 = 1\}$$
$$- P\{X_1 X_2 X_4 X_5 = 1\} - P\{X_1 X_2 X_3 X_5 = 1\}$$
$$+ P\{X_1 X_2 X_3 X_4 X_5 = 1\}$$
$$= p_1 p_4 + p_1 p_3 p_5 + p_2 p_5 - p_1 p_3 p_4 p_5$$
$$- p_1 p_2 p_4 p_5 - p_1 p_2 p_3 p_5 + p_1 p_2 p_3 p_4 p_5$$
$$= 2p^2 + p^3 - 3p^4 + p^5, \text{ when } p_i = p.$$

Notice that there are $2^3 - 1 = 7$ terms in the expansion of the reliability function (in general, if there are r paths, then there are $2^r - 1$ terms in the expansion), so that this calculation is not simple.

The second method of determining the system reliability from paths is as follows: For the minimal path containing components 1 and 4, $X_1 X_4 = 1$ if and only if both components function. This fact is similarly true for the other two minimal paths. However, the system will operate if all the components in at least one of the minimal paths operate. Hence paths operate as a parallel system, so that

$$\phi(X_1, X_2, X_3, X_4, X_5) = \max[X_1 X_4, X_1 X_3 X_5, X_2 X_5]$$
$$= 1 - (1 - X_1 X_4)(1 - X_1 X_3 X_5)(1 - X_2 X_5).$$

Because $X_i^2 = X_i$, then

$$\phi(X_1, X_2, X_3, X_4, X_5) = {}_1X_4 + X_1X_3X_5 + X_2X_5 - X_1X_3X_4X_5$$
$$- X_1X_2X_4X_5 - X_1X_2X_3X_5 + X_1X_2X_3X_4X_5.$$

Noting that ϕ is a binary random variable taking on the values 1 and 0,

$$E[\phi(X_1, X_2, X_3, X_4, X_5)] = P\{\phi(X_1, X_2, X_3, X_4, X_5) = 1\}$$
$$= R(p_1, p_2, p_3, p_4, p_5).$$

Therefore,

$$R(p_1, p_2, p_3, p_4, p_5)$$
$$= E[X_1X_4 + X_1X_3X_5 + X_2X_5 - X_1X_3X_4X_5 - X_1X_2X_4X_5$$
$$- X_1X_2X_3X_5 + X_1X_2X_3X_4X_5]$$
$$= p_1p_4 + p_1p_3p_5 + p_2p_5 - p_1p_3p_4p_5 - p_1p_2p_4p_5 - p_1p_2p_3p_5$$
$$+ p_1p_2p_3p_4p_5.$$

This result is the same as the one obtained earlier and requires essentially the same amount of calculation.

If we use all the **minimal cuts**, there are also *two ways* to obtain the **exact system reliability**. Because the system will fail if and only if all the components in at least one of the minimal cuts fail, the system reliability can be expressed as

$$R(p_1, p_2, p_3, p_4, p_5) = 1 - P\{\phi(X_1, X_2, X_3, X_4, X_5) = 0\}$$
$$= 1 - P\{(X_1 = 0, X_2 = 0) \cup (X_4 = 0, X_5 = 0)$$
$$\cup (X_2 = 0, X_3 = 0, X_4 = 0) \cup (X_1 = 0, X_5 = 0)\}$$
$$= 1 - P\{X_1 = 0, X_2 = 0\} - P\{X_4 = 0, X_5 = 0\}$$
$$- P\{X_2 = 0, X_3 = 0, X_4 = 0\} - P\{X_1 = 0, X_5 = 0\}$$
$$+ P\{X_1 = 0, X_2 = 0, X_4 = 0, X_5 = 0\}$$
$$+ P\{X_1 = 0, X_2 = 0, X_3 = 0, X_4 = 0\}$$
$$+ P\{X_1 = 0, X_2 = 0, X_5 = 0\}$$
$$+ P\{X_2 = 0, X_3 = 0, X_4 = 0, X_5 = 0\}$$
$$+ P\{X_1 = 0, X_4 = 0, X_5 = 0\}$$
$$+ P\{X_1 = 0, X_2 = 0, X_3 = 0, X_4 = 0, X_5 = 0\}$$
$$- P\{X_1 = 0, X_2 = 0, X_3 = 0, X_4 = 0, X_5 = 0\}$$
$$- P\{X_1 = 0, X_2 = 0, X_4 = 0, X_5 = 0\}$$
$$- P\{X_1 = 0, X_2 = 0, X_3 = 0, X_4 = 0, X_5 = 0\}$$
$$- P\{X_1 = 0, X_2 = 0, X_3 = 0, X_4 = 0, X_5 = 0\}$$
$$+ P\{X_1 = 0, X_2 = 0, X_3 = 0, X_4 = 0, X_5 = 0\}$$
$$= 1 - q_1q_2 - q_4q_5 - q_2q_3q_4 - q_1q_5 + q_1q_2q_3q_4$$
$$+ q_1q_2q_5 + q_2q_3q_4q_5 + q_1q_4q_5 - q_1q_2q_3q_4q_5,$$

where

$$q_i = 1 - p_i.$$

This result is, of course, algebraically equivalent to the same one obtained previously, and it involves $2^4 - 1 = 15$ terms in the expansion of the reliability function. In general, if there are s cuts, there are $2^s - 1$ terms in the expansion.

The second method of determining the system reliability from cuts is: For the minimal cut containing components 1 and 2, $1 - (1 - X_1)(1 - X_2) = 0$ if and only if both components fail. This fact is similarly true for the other three cuts. However, the system will operate if at least one of the components in *each* cut operates. Hence cuts operate as a series system, so that

$$
\begin{aligned}
\phi(X_1, X_2, X_3, X_4, X_5) = {}& \min[1 - (1 - X_1)(1 - X_2), \, 1 - (1 - X_4)(1 - X_5), \\
& 1 - (1 - X_2)(1 - X_3)(1 - X_4), \, 1 - (1 - X_1)(1 - X_5)] \\
= {}& ([1 - (1 - X_1)(1 - X_2)][1 - (1 - X_4)(1 - X_5)] \\
& [1 - (1 - X_2)(1 - X_3)(1 - X_4)][1 - (1 - X_1)(1 - X_5)]) \\
= {}& 1 - (1 - X_1)(1 - X_2) - (1 - X_4)(1 - X_5) \\
& - (1 - X_2)(1 - X_3)(1 - X_4) - (1 - X_1)(1 - X_5) \\
& + (1 - X_1)(1 - X_2)(1 - X_3)(1 - X_4) \\
& + (1 - X_1)(1 - X_2)(1 - X_5) \\
& + (1 - X_2)(1 - X_3)(1 - X_4)(1 - X_5) \\
& + (1 - X_1)(1 - X_4)(1 - X_5) \\
& - (1 - X_1)(1 - X_2)(1 - X_3)(1 - X_4)(1 - X_5).
\end{aligned}
$$

Taking expectations on both sides leads to the desired expression for the reliability. *Again*, this method requires essentially the same amount of calculation as required for the first procedure using cuts.

Although the results presented in this section were based upon the example, an extension to any system can be easily obtained. All minimal paths and/or cuts must be found and one of the four methods presented chosen.

As previously mentioned, if there are r paths and s cuts in the network, then calculating the exact reliability using paths will involve summing $2^r - 1$ terms, and using cuts will involve $2^s - 1$ terms. Hence the method using paths should be used if and only if $r \leq s$. Generally, however, it is simpler to find minimal paths rather than minimal cuts, so that the method using paths may have to be used because finding all cuts may be computationally infeasible. It is evident that finding the exact reliability of a system is quite difficult and that bounds are desirable, provided that the calculations are substantially reduced.

21.5 Bounds on System Reliability

It is evident that the calculations required to compute exact system reliability are numerous, and that other methods, such as obtaining upper and lower bounds, are desirable.

There exists a well-known result concerning binary random variables, i.e.,

If $X_1, X_2, \ldots, X_n$ are independent binary random variables that take on the values 1 or 0, and $Y_i = \prod_{j \in J_i} X_j$, where the product ranges over all j that are elements in the set J_i, $i = 1, 2, \ldots, r$, then

$$P\{Y_1 = 0, Y_2 = 0, \ldots, Y_r = 0\} \geq P\{Y_1 = 0\} P\{Y_2 = 0\} \cdots P\{Y_r = 0\}.$$

Returning to the example of Sec. 21.4, it was pointed out that the system will operate if all the components in at least one of the minimal paths operate, so that

$$
\begin{aligned}
R(p_1, p_2, p_3, p_4, p_5) &= P\{\phi(X_1, X_2, X_3, X_4, X_5) = 1\} \\
&= 1 - P\{\text{all paths fail}\} \\
&= 1 - P\{X_1 X_4 = 0, X_1 X_3 X_5 = 0, X_2 X_5 = 0\}.
\end{aligned}
$$

From the aforementioned result on binary random variables,

$$
\begin{aligned}
R(p_1, p_2, p_3, p_4, p_5) &\leq 1 - P\{X_1 X_4 = 0\} P\{X_1 X_3 X_5 = 0\} P\{X_2 X_5 = 0\} \\
&= 1 - (1 - p_1 p_4)(1 - p_1 p_3 p_5)(1 - p_2 p_5) \\
&= 1 - (1 - p^2)^2 (1 - p^3),
\end{aligned}
$$

when

$$p_i = p,$$

so that an upper bound is obtained. Similarly, in Sec. 21.4 it was pointed out that the system will operate if at least one of the components in *each* cut operates, so that

$R(p_1, p_2, p_3, p_4, p_5)$

$\quad = P\{\phi(X_1, X_2, X_3, X_4, X_5) = 1\} = P\{\text{at least one of } X_1, X_2 \text{ operates; at}$
$\quad \text{least one of } X_4, X_5 \text{ operates; at least one of } X_2, X_3, X_4 \text{ operates; at}$
$\quad \text{least one of } X_1, X_5 \text{ operates}\}$

$\quad = P\{[1 - (1 - X_1)(1 - X_2)] = 1, [1 - (1 - X_4)(1 - X_5)] = 1,$
$\qquad\qquad [1 - (1 - X_2)(1 - X_3)(1 - X_4)] = 1, [1 - (1 - X_1)(1 - X_5)] = 1\}$

$\quad = P\{(1 - X_1)(1 - X_2) = 0, (1 - X_4)(1 - X_5) = 0,$
$\qquad\qquad (1 - X_2)(1 - X_3)(1 - X_4) = 0, (1 - X_1)(1 - X_5) = 0\}.$

Now $(1 - X_i)$ are independent binary random variables that take on the values 1 and 0, so that the result on binary random variables is again applicable; that is,

$R(p_1, p_2, p_3, p_4, p_5)$

$\quad \geq (P\{(1 - X_1)(1 - X_2) = 0\} P\{(1 - X_4)(1 - X_5) = 0\}$
$\qquad\qquad P\{(1 - X_2)(1 - X_3)(1 - X_4) = 0\} P\{(1 - X_1)(1 - X_5) = 0\})$

$\quad = ([1 - (1 - p_1)(1 - p_2)][1 - (1 - p_4)(1 - p_5)]$
$\qquad\qquad [1 - (1 - p_2)(1 - p_3)(1 - p_4)][1 - (1 - p_1)(1 - p_5)])$

$\quad = [1 - (1 - p)^2]^3 [1 - (1 - p)^3],$

when

$$p_i = p,$$

so that a lower bound is obtained.

Thus we obtain an upper bound on the reliability based upon paths and a lower bound based upon cuts. For example, if $p_i = p = 0.9$, then

$$0.9693 = [1 - (0.1)^2]^3[1 - (0.1)^3] \le R(0.9, 0.9, 0.9, 0.9, 0.9)$$
$$\le 1 - [1 - (0.9)^2]^2[1 - (0.9)^3] = 0.9902.$$

Furthermore, the exact reliability obtained from the expressions in Sec. 21.4 is given by

$$R(0.9, 0.9, 0.9, 0.9, 0.9) = .9)^2 + (0.9)^3 - 3(0.9)^4 + (0.9)^5 = 0.9712.$$

In general, this technique provides useful results in that the bounds are frequently quite narrow.

21.6 Bounds on Reliability Based upon Failure Times

The previous sections considered systems that performed successfully during a designated period or failed during this same period. An alternative way of viewing systems is to view their performance as a function of time.

Consider a component (or system) and its associated random variable, the time to failure, T. Denote the probability distribution of the time to failure of the component by F and its density function by f. In terms of the previous discussion, the random variables X and T are related in that X takes on the values

$$1, \quad \text{if } T \ge t$$
$$0, \quad \text{if } T < t.$$

Then

$$R(t) = P\{X = 1\} = 1 - F(t) = \int_t^{\infty} f(y)\,dy.$$

An appealing intuitive property in reliability is the failure rate. The failure rate $r(t)$ is defined for those values of t for which $F(t) < 1$ by

$$r(t) = \frac{f(t)}{R(t)}.$$

This function has a useful probabilistic interpretation; namely, $r(t)\,dt$ represents the conditional probability that an object surviving to age t will fail in the interval $[t, t + dt]$. This function is sometimes called the *hazard rate*.

In many applications, there is every reason to believe that the failure rate tends to increase because of the inevitable deterioration that occurs. Such a failure rate that remains constant or increases with age is said to have an *increasing failure rate* (IFR).

In some applications, the failure rate tends to decrease. It would be expected to decrease initially, for instance, for materials that exhibit the phenomenon of work hardening. Certain solid-state electronic devices are also believed to have a decreasing failure rate. Thus a failure rate that remains constant or decreases with age is said to have a *decreasing failure rate* (DFR).

The failure rate possesses some interesting properties. The time to failure distribution is completely determined by the failure rate. In particular, it is easily shown that

$$R(t) = 1 - F(t) = \exp\left[-\int_0^t r(\xi)\,d\xi\right].$$

Thus an assumption made about the failure rate has direct implications on the time to failure distribution. As an example, consider a component whose failure distribution is given by the exponential; that is,

$$F(t) = P\{T \le t\} = 1 - e^{-t/\theta}.$$

Thus $R(t)$ is given by $e^{-t/\theta}$, and the failure rate is given by

$$r(t) = \frac{\frac{1}{\theta}e^{-t/\theta}}{e^{-t/\theta}} = \frac{1}{\theta}.$$

Note that the exponential has a constant failure rate and hence has both IFR and DFR. In fact, using the expression relating the time to failure distribution and the failure rate, it is evident that a component having a constant failure rate must have a time to failure distribution that is exponential.

BOUNDS FOR IFR DISTRIBUTIONS

Under either IFR or DFR assumptions, it is possible to obtain sharp bounds on the reliability in terms of moments and percentiles: In particular, such bounds can be derived from statements based upon the *mean time to failure*. This fact is particularly important because many design engineers present specifications in terms of mean time to failure.

Because the exponential distribution with constant failure rate is the boundary distribution between IFR and DFR distributions, it provides natural bounds on the survival probability of IFR and DFR distributions. In particular, it can be shown that if all that is known about the failure distribution is that it is IFR and has mean μ, then the greatest lower bound on the reliability that can be given is

$$R(t) \ge \begin{cases} e^{-t/\mu}, & \text{for } t < \mu \\ 0, & \text{for } t \ge \mu, \end{cases}$$

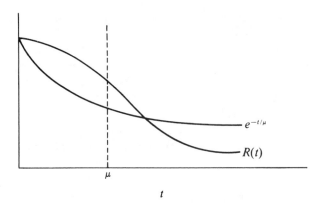

Figure 21.3 A lower bound on reliability for IFR distributions.

and the inequality is sharp; i.e., the exponential distribution with mean μ attains the lower bound for $t < \mu$, and the degenerate distribution concentrating at μ attains the lower bound for $t \geq \mu$. This situation can be represented graphically as shown in Fig. 21.3.

The least upper bound on $R(t)$ that can be obtained if we know only that F is IFR with mean μ is given by

$$R(t) \leq \begin{cases} 1, & \text{for } t \leq \mu \\ e^{-\omega t}, & \text{for } t > \mu, \end{cases}$$

where ω depends on t and satisfies $1 - \omega\mu = e^{-\omega t}$. It is important to note that the ω in the term $e^{-\omega t}$ is a function of t, so that a different ω must be found for each t. For fixed t and μ, this ω is obtained by finding the intersection of the linear function $(1 - \omega\mu)$ and the exponential function $e^{-\omega t}$. It can be shown that for $t > \mu$, such an intersection always exists.

Thus $R(t)$ for an IFR distribution with mean μ can be bounded above and below, as shown in Fig. 21.4. Note that the lower bound is the only one of consequence for $t < \mu$, and that the upper bound is the only one of consequence for $t > \mu$.

INCREASING FAILURE-RATE AVERAGE

Now that bounds on the reliability of a component have been obtained, what can be said about the preservation of *monotone failure rate*; i.e., what structures have the IFR property when their individual components have this property? Series structures of independent IFR (DFR) components are also IFR (DFR). k out of n structures consisting of n identical independent components, each having an IFR failure distribution, are also IFR; however, parallel structures of independent IFR components are not IFR unless they are composed of identical compo-

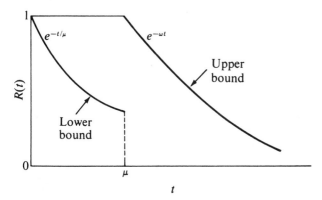

Figure 21.4 **Upper and lower bounds on reliability for IFR distributions.**

nents. Thus it is evident that, even for some simple systems, there may not be a preservation of the monotone failure rate.

Instead of using the failure rate as a means for characterizing the reliability,

$$R(t) = \exp\left[-\int_0^t r(\xi)\,d\xi \right],$$

a somewhat less appealing characterization can be obtained from the failure-rate average function,

$$\int_0^t \frac{r(\xi)\,d\xi}{t} = -\frac{\log R(t)}{t}.$$

A distribution F such that $F(0) = 0$ is called IFRA (increasing failure-rate average) if and only if

$$\int_0^t \frac{r(\xi)\,d\xi}{t}$$

is nondecreasing in $t \geq 0$. A similar definition is given for DFRA. It can be shown that a coherent system of independent components, each of which has an IFRA failure distribution, has a system failure distribution that is also IFRA.

As with IFR systems, there are bounds for IFRA systems. It can be easily shown that IFR distributions are also IFRA distributions (but not the reverse), and the same upper bound as given for IFR distributions is applicable here. A sharp lower bound for IFRA distributions with mean μ is given by

$$R(t) \geq \begin{cases} 0, & \text{for } t \geq \mu \\ e^{-bt}, & \text{for } t < \mu, \end{cases}$$

where b depends upon t and is defined by $e^{-bt} = b(\mu - t)$.

As an example, a monotone system containing only independent components, each of which is exponential (thereby IFRA), is itself IFRA, and the aforementioned bounds are applicable. Furthermore, these bounds are dependent only upon the system mean time to failure.

21.7 Conclusions

In recent years, the delivery of systems that perform adequately for a specified period of time in a given environment has become an important goal for both industry and government. In the space program, higher system reliability means the difference between life and death. In general, the cost of maintaining and/or repairing electronic equipment during the first year of operation often exceeds the purchase cost, giving impetus to the study and development of reliability techniques.

This chapter has been concerned with determining system reliability (or bounds) from a knowledge of component reliability or characteristics of components, such as failure rate or mean time to failure. Even the desirable state of knowing these values may lead to cumbersome and sometimes crude results. However, it must be emphasized that these values, e.g., component reliability or mean time to failure, are *not* known and are often just the design engineers' educated guesses. Furthermore, except in the case of the exponential distribution, knowledge of the mean time to failure leads to nothing but bounds. Also, it is evident that the reliability of components or systems depends heavily upon the failure rate, and the assumption of constant failure rate, which appears to be used frequently in practice, should not be made without careful analysis.

The contents of the chapter have not been concerned with the statistical aspects of reliability, i.e., estimating reliability from test data. This subject was omitted because our emphasis is on probability models, but this is not a reflection on its importance. The statistical aspects of reliability may very well be the important problem. Statistical estimation of component reliability is well in hand, but estimation of system reliability from component data is virtually an unsolved problem.

SELECTED REFERENCES

1. Barlow, R., J. Fussell, and N. Singpurwalla, eds.: *Reliability and Fault Tree Analysis*, SIAM Publications, 1975.
2. Barlow, R. E., and F. Proschan: *Mathematical Theory of Reliability*, Wiley, New York, 1965.
3. ———— and ————: *Statistical Theory of Reliability and Life Testing*, Holt, Reinhart & Winston, New York, 1974.
4. Gnedenko, B. V., Yu. K. Belyayev, and A. D. Solovyev: *Mathematical Methods of Reliability Theory*, Academic Press, New York, 1969.
5. Kapur, K., and L. Lamberson: *Reliability in Engineering Design*, Wiley, New York, 1977.

6. Lieberman, G. J.: "The Status and Impact of Reliability Methodology," *Naval Research Logistics Quarterly*, **16**(1): 17–35, 1969.

7. Ross, S.: *Introduction to Probability Models*, Academic Press, New York, 1972.

8. Shooman, M. L.: *Probabilistic Reliability—An Engineering Approach*, McGraw-Hill, New York, 1968.

PROBLEMS

1. Show that the structure function for a 3-component system that functions if and only if component 1 functions *and* at least one of components 2 or 3 functions, is given by

$$\phi(X_1 X_2 X_3) = X_1 \max(X_2, X_3)$$
$$= X_1[1 - (1 - X_2)(1 - X_3)].$$

2. Show that the structure function for a 4-component system that functions if and only if components 1 and 2 function *and* at least one of components 3 or 4 functions, is given by

$$\phi(X_1, X_2, X_3, X_4) = X_1 X_2 \max(X_3, X_4).$$

3. Find the reliability of the structure function given in Prob. 1 when each component has probability p_i of performing successfully.

4. Find the reliability of the structure function given in Prob. 2 when each component has probability p_i of performing successfully.

5. Suppose that there exist three different type components, with two units of each type. Each unit operates independently, and each type has probability p_i of performing successfully. Either one or two systems can be built. One system can be assembled as follows: The two units of each type component are put together in parallel, and the three types are then assembled to operate in series. Alternatively, two subsystems are assembled, each consisting of the three different type components assembled in series. The final system is obtained by putting the two subsystems together in parallel. Which system has higher reliability?

6. Consider the following network.

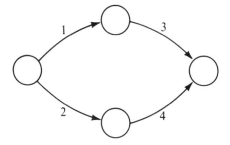

Assume that each component is independent with probability p_i of performing satisfactorily.

(*a*) Find all the minimal paths and cuts.

(*b*)   Compute the exact system reliability, and evaluate it when $p_i = p = 0.90$.

(*c*)   Find upper and lower bounds on the reliability, and evaluate them when $p_i = p = 0.90$.

7.   Solve Prob. 6 by using the following network.

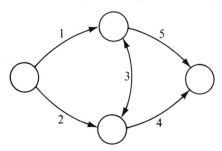

Note that component 3 flows in both directions.

8.   Solve Prob. 6 by using the following network.

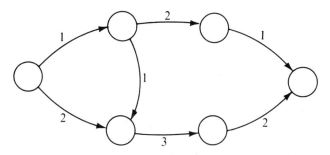

9.   Solve Prob. 6 by using the following network.

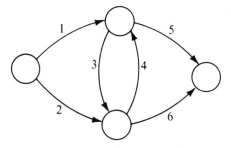

10.   Suppose F is IFR, with $\mu = 0.5$. Find upper and lower bounds on $R(t)$ for (*a*) $t = \frac{1}{4}$ and (*b*) $t = 1$.

11.   A time to failure distribution is said to have a Weibull distribution if the cumulative distribution function is given by

$$F(t) = 1 - e^{-t^\beta / \eta}, \eta, \beta > 0.$$

Find the failure rate, and show that the Weibull distribution is IFR when $\beta \geq 1$ and DFR when $0 < \beta \leq 1$.

12. Consider a parallel system consisting of two independent components whose time to failure distributions are exponential with parameters μ_1 and μ_2, respectively ($\mu_1 \neq \mu_2$). Show that the time to failure distribution of the system is not IFR. *Hint*:

$$R(t) = P\{T_1 > t \text{ or } T_2 > t\} = 1 - P\{T_1 \leq t \text{ and } T_2 \leq t\}$$
$$= 1 - (1 - e^{-t/\mu_1})(1 - e^{-t/\mu_2}).$$

13. For Prob. 12, show that the time to failure distribution is IFRA.

■ CHAPTER 22

Decision Analysis

22.1 Introduction

In recent years, decision analysis has become an important technique in business, industry, and government. Decision analysis provides a rational methodology for decision making in the face of uncertainty. It enables a manager to choose among alternatives in an optimal fashion, taking into account the worth of acquiring experimental data to reduce the uncertainty.

This chapter presents a framework for making decisions when (1) experimentation is infeasible and (2) experimentation is possible, resulting in the availability of sample data. The criterion of optimality used to select among alternatives will be the minimization of expected cost. Among the problems considered in this chapter are the following: What is the decision that minimizes expected cost, given the result of an experiment (if indeed an experiment is performed)? By following the optimal policy, what is the expected cost? If an experiment is performed, will it be worthwhile; that is, will the decrease in expected cost be more than the cost of the experiment? Finally, what is the maximum amount of money that might be spent in order to eliminate all of the uncertainty?

EXAMPLE Consider the following problem. An oil company owns some land that is purported to contain oil. The company classifies such land into four categories by the total number of barrels that are expected to be obtained from the well, i.e., a 500,000-barrel well, a 200,000-barrel well, a 50,000-barrel well, or a dry well.

Table 22.1 **Table of profits for oil company**

	500,000-barrel well	200,000-barrel well	50,000-barrel well	Dry well
Drill for oil	650,000	200,000	−25,000	−75,000
Unconditional lease	45,000	45,000	45,000	45,000
Conditional lease	250,000	100,000	0	0

The company is faced with deciding whether to drill for oil, to unconditionally lease the land to an independent oil driller, or to conditionally lease the land at a rate depending upon the oil strike. The cost of drilling a producing well is $100,000, and the cost of drilling a dry well is $75,000. For producing wells, the profit per barrel of oil is $1.50 (after deducting all production costs). Under the unconditional lease agreement, the company receives $45,000 for the land, whereas under the conditional lease arrangement, the company receives 50 cents for each barrel of oil extracted, provided the land yields a 200,000- or 500,000-barrel strike; otherwise, it receives nothing.

The possible profits for the oil company are shown in Table 22.1.

22.2 Decision Making without Experimentation

GENERAL FRAMEWORK

Before seeking a solution to the aforementioned problem, it is worthwhile to formulate a general framework for decision making. The decision maker must choose an action a from a set A of possible actions. In the oil-drilling example, the set A consists of three points, a_1, a_2, and a_3, that correspond to drilling for oil, unconditionally leasing the land, and conditionally leasing the land, respectively. In taking an action, the decision maker must be aware of its consequences, which will usually also be a function of the "state of nature." A state of nature θ is a representation of the actual real-world situation to which the action will apply. Generally, the states of nature are an enumeration, within the model according to some set of indices, of possible alternative representations of the physical phenomenon being studied. The set of possible values that θ can assume will be denoted by Θ. In the oil-drilling example, Θ consists of four points, θ_1, θ_2, θ_3, and θ_4, with θ_1 corresponding to the land yielding a 500,000-barrel well, θ_2 corresponding to a 200,000-barrel well, θ_3 corresponding to a 50,000-barrel well, and θ_4 corresponding to a dry well. Very often the states of nature are characterized by a parameter of a family of probability distributions. In the context of the oil-drilling example, the potential strikes might be viewed as the expected value of the random variable, oil yield, having some assumed form of probability distribution. Thus a representation of the model of this oil-drilling problem is that the oil yield in the site is a random variable with an unknown expected value. The company is willing to approximate this expected value by one of four values: 500,000 barrels, 200,000 barrels, 50,000 barrels, and no barrels

Table 22.2 **Loss function for oil-drilling example**

Action \ State of nature	θ_1:500,000- barrel well	θ_2:200,000- barrel well	θ_3:50,000- barrel well	θ_4 dry well
a_1: drill for oil	−650,000	−200,000	25,000	75,000
a_2: unconditionally lease	−45,000	−45,000	−45,000	−45,000
a_3: conditionally lease	−250,000	−100,000	0	0

(dry). Thus the states of nature become these possible values of the expected value of the random variable, oil yield.

To measure the consequences of a decision maker's action, we assume that there exists a *loss function* $l(a, \theta)$ that reflects the loss from taking action a when the state of nature is θ; it is defined for each combination of a and θ. If the problem is formulated in terms of gains, a gain can be termed as a negative loss. The loss function is generally measured in monetary terms, although other utility functions can be used. Note that $l(a, \theta)$ is assumed to be a function only of a and θ. The loss function for the oil-drilling example is easily obtained from Table 22.1 and is given in Table 22.2.[1] Although the loss function is easily obtained directly from the action and the state of nature in this example, occasionally the loss depends upon the outcome of a random variable whose probability distribution depends upon the true state of nature. For example, this situation would occur in the oil-drilling example if the profit were expressed directly in terms of the random variable, oil yield. The loss would then be a random variable, and $l(a, \theta)$ would then be interpreted as the expected value of the loss incurred when action a is taken and the true state of nature is θ. Hence even here the loss function depends upon only a and θ. In general, in formulating the problem, if the state of nature is defined so broadly that observing its value resolves all uncertainty relevant to the decision at hand, then the loss can always be expressed as a (deterministic) function of θ and the action a. If this case is not true, meaning that the observation of θ would still leave some uncertainty as to the ultimate consequence of a given action a, the loss function $l(a, \theta)$ is computed as the expected loss, given state θ and action a.

MINIMAX CRITERION

If the true state of nature were known, it would be simple to choose the correct action, i.e., that action which has minimum loss. Unfortunately, the true state of nature is not generally known, and choosing a correct action is not simple. In the oil-drilling example, if $\theta = \theta_1$, a 500,000-barrel well, the best action is to drill for oil, whereas if $\theta = \theta_4$, a dry well, the best action is to lease unconditionally. This decision-theory formulation has the appearance of game theory as described in detail in Chap. 12, with the two players being the decision maker and nature. The

---

[1] In discussing this example throughout the chapter, many negative values appear. These are to be interpreted as gains or profit and should not cause the reader any trouble.

actions correspond to the pure strategies of the decision maker, and the states of nature correspond to the pure strategies of nature. The payoff matrix in game theory is analogous to the loss table. An approach for obtaining solutions to game theory problems is through the *minimax principle*. This principle tells the decision maker to find the maximum loss for each of his actions and to choose that action which has the smallest maximum loss. Similarly, the decision maker's opponent, nature in this case, should find the minimum loss to the decision maker for each one of her possible states of nature and present to the decision maker that state of nature which maximizes this minimum loss. If these loss values are equal, the game is said to have a *value*. If a game has a value, and if each player follows his optimal strategy, the decision maker can guarantee that his loss will never exceed the value. Furthermore, if the decision maker follows his optimal strategy and if nature deviates from hers, the loss to the decision maker can only be decreased. Unfortunately, in this context a value does not always exist. However, it does exist in the oil-drilling example. Using the minimax criterion, the decision maker should choose action a_2 and guarantee that his loss will not exceed $-45,000$. Similarly, nature should choose state $\theta = \theta_3$ or $\theta = \theta_4$ and guarantee that the decision maker's loss will be at least $-45,000$. Thus this "game" does indeed have a value, and the minimax strategy for the decision maker is to lease unconditionally.

A fundamental theorem in the theory of games states that if mixed strategies are allowed, and if the minimax principle is followed, the game always has a value. A mixed strategy for the decision maker is a probability distribution defined over the action space. The actual choice of strategy is dependent upon the outcome of a random device having a probability distribution associated with the action space. Thus choosing a mixed strategy is equivalent to choosing a probability distribution. Similarly, a mixed strategy for nature is a probability distribution defined over the possible states of nature. Pure strategies are just special cases of mixed strategies, where the probability assigned to the chosen action is 1 and the probability assigned to the other action is zero. Because both the action and the state of nature are random variables, the loss incurred is also a random variable, and again expected loss is the criterion.

However, even though the minimax principle has some attractive properties, it is seldom used in games against nature because it is an extremely conservative criterion in this context. The actions taken when this principle is used assume that nature is a conscious opponent that wants to inflict as much damage as possible on the decision maker. Generally, nature is not a malevolent opponent, and it is unlikely that the decision maker has to guard against such an occurrence.

BAYES' CRITERION

The previous section pointed out that the minimax principle says to proceed as if nature will select a probability distribution, defined over the possible states of nature, which is least favorable to the decision maker. It was also noted that this approach is very conservative because there is no reason to expect nature to use this distribution. As a matter of fact, in some situations the decision maker will actually have some advance information about θ that contradicts this assumption about what nature will do. When the decision maker has such information, he certainly should take it into account. Such information can usually be translated into a probability distribution, acting as though the state of nature is a random variable, in which case this distribution is referred to as a *prior distribution*. Prior distributions are often subjective in that they may depend upon the experience or intuition of an individual.

For example, in the oil-drilling problem, the company has had some experience with wells in similar geographic areas and has concluded that about 10 percent of the strikes are 500,000-barrel wells, 15 percent are 200,000-barrel wells, 25 percent are 50,000-barrel wells, and 50 percent are dry wells. Hence these data can be translated into the prior distribution as follows:

$$P\{\theta = \theta_1\} = P_\theta(1) = 0.10$$
$$P\{\theta = \theta_2\} = P_\theta(2) = 0.15$$
$$P\{\theta = \theta_3\} = P_\theta(3) = 0.25$$
$$P\{\theta = \theta_4\} = P_\theta(4) = 0.50.$$

A procedure for using the prior distribution to aid in the selection of an action is the Bayes' criterion. The *Bayes' principle* tells the decisions maker to select that action (called the *Bayes' decision procedure*) which minimizes the expected loss. The expected loss $l(a)$ is evaluated with respect to the prior distribution, which is defined over the possible states of nature; that is,

$$l(a) = E[l(a, \theta)] = \begin{cases} \sum_{\text{all } k} l(a, k) P_\theta(k), & \text{if } \theta \text{ is discrete} \\ \int_{-\infty}^{\infty} l(a, y) P_\theta(y) \, dy, & \text{if } \theta \text{ is continuous.} \end{cases}$$

Thus, for the oil-drilling example, the expected loss $l(a)$ for each action is given by

$$l(a_1) = E[l(a_1, \theta)] = -650,000(0.10) - 200,000(0.15) + 25,000(0.25)$$
$$+ 75,000(0.50)$$
$$= -\$51,250,$$

$$l(a_2) = E[l(a_2, \theta)] = -45,000(0.10) - 45,000(0.15) - 45,000(0.25)$$
$$- 45,000(0.50)$$
$$= -\$45,000,$$

$$l(a_3) = E[l(a_3, \theta)] = -250,000(0.10) - 100,000(0.15)$$
$$= -\$40,000.$$

Hence using the Bayes' principle leads to selecting action a_1, that is, drill for oil, and the associated expected loss is $-\$51,250$ (profit). It is interesting to speculate as to whether the decision maker could have improved upon this expected loss by making use of a mixed strategy rather than a pure strategy (because nature is using the mixed strategy specified by the prior distribution). It can be shown that the decision maker cannot improve his position by using mixed strategies, so that it is sufficient for him to consider only pure strategies.

22.3 Decision Making with Experimentation

The previous sections assumed that the decision maker was to make his decision without experimentation. However, if some experimentation is possible (perhaps at a cost), the data derived from this experimentation should be incorporated into the decision-making process. For example, returning to the oil-drilling example, suppose that it is possible to obtain seismic soundings at a cost of $12,000. This information leads to four possible seismic classifications, denoted by (1), (2), (3), and (4). Classification (1) denotes that there is definitely a closed geologic structure to the site (a very favorable condition if the presence of oil is desired); classification (2) denotes that there is probably a closed structure to the site; classification (3) denotes that there is a nonclosed structure to the site (a relatively unfavorable condition); and classification (4) denotes that there is no structure to the site (an unfavorable condition). Based upon past examination of similar geologic areas (100 such examinations), the company obtains the data presented in Table 22.3.[1] The values in parentheses in each cell can be interpreted as conditional probabilities, given the state of nature: e.g., if the well is a 200,000-barrel well, then $\frac{3}{16}$ can be interpreted as the conditional probability that the seismic reading is classified as (2) (probably a closed structure to the site); if the well is dry, then $\frac{15}{48}$ can be interpreted as the conditional probability that the seismic reading is classified as (3) (a nonclosed structure to the site); and so on. Before proceeding with the example, we shall discuss a general method for incorporating these data.

Let X denote the information made available by experimentation obtained from a random sample. X is then a random variable and may be viewed as a

Table 22.3 Frequency of seismic classifications

Seismic classification	θ_1:500,000-barrel well	θ_2:200,000-barrel well	θ_3:50,000-barrel well	θ_4: dry well
1	$7\left(\dfrac{7}{12}\right)$	$9\left(\dfrac{9}{16}\right)$	$11\left(\dfrac{11}{24}\right)$	$9\left(\dfrac{9}{48}\right)$
2	$4\left(\dfrac{4}{12}\right)$	$3\left(\dfrac{3}{16}\right)$	$6\left(\dfrac{6}{24}\right)$	$13\left(\dfrac{13}{48}\right)$
3	$1\left(\dfrac{1}{12}\right)$	$2\left(\dfrac{2}{16}\right)$	$3\left(\dfrac{3}{24}\right)$	$15\left(\dfrac{15}{48}\right)$
4	$0\left(\dfrac{0}{12}\right)$	$2\left(\dfrac{2}{16}\right)$	$4\left(\dfrac{4}{24}\right)$	$11\left(\dfrac{11}{48}\right)$

[1] Although the actual fraction of wells falling historically into the four categories differs slightly from the prior distribution, the prior probabilities given under Bayes' criterion in Sec. 22.2 are thought to be more representative of what to expect for this particular site and will be used subsequently.

function of the sample data; for example, X may denote a sample mean, the maximum of the sample, a vector of the sample observations, the third observation in a sample, and so forth. The decision maker is to choose a decision procedure rule, or strategy, which tells him the form and amount of experimentation and what action to take for each possible value that X may take on. Denote this function to be chosen as $d[x]$, so that if the random variable X takes on the value x, then $a = d[x]$ would be the action to be taken. The decision maker, then, is interested in choosing a function d, from among the many possible decision functions, that is, in some sense, optimal. (Indeed, part of the problem here is to choose a good working definition for the term *optimal*.) To evaluate a decision function, we must explore its consequences. Because the action taken, a, is a function of the outcome of the random variable X, then $d[X]$ is also a random variable, and the loss associated with that action also depends upon the outcome of this random variable. An appropriate measure of the consequences of taking action $a = d[X]$, when the true state of nature is θ, is then given by the expected value of the loss. This quantity will be known as the *risk function* $R(d, \theta)$; that is

$$R(d, \theta) = E[l(d[X], \theta)],$$

where the expectation is taken with respect to the probability distribution of the random variable X, and the loss function includes the cost of experimentation.

Now consider how to apply this approach to the oil-drilling example. Suppose the following decision rule, d_1, is to be evaluated. If the seismic reading is classified as (1), take action a_1; if the seismic reading is classified as (2) or (3), take action a_3; and if the seismic reading is classified as (4), take action a_2; that is,

$$d_1[x] = a_1, \quad \text{for } x = 1$$
$$d_1[x] = a_2, \quad \text{for } x = 4$$
$$d_1[x] = a_3, \quad \text{for } x = 2 \text{ or } x = 3.$$

Therefore,

$$R(d_1, \theta_1) = -650,000\left(\frac{7}{12}\right) - 45,000(0) - 250,000\left(\frac{4}{12} + \frac{1}{12}\right) + 12,000$$
$$= -\$471,333,$$

$$R(d_1, \theta_2) = -200,000\left(\frac{9}{16}\right) - 45,000\left(\frac{2}{16}\right) - 100,000\left(\frac{3}{16} + \frac{2}{16}\right) + 12,000$$
$$= -\$137,375,$$

$$R(d_1, \theta_3) = 25,000\left(\frac{11}{24}\right) - 45,000\left(\frac{4}{24}\right) + 0\left(\frac{6}{24} + \frac{3}{24}\right) + 12,000$$
$$= \$15,958,$$

$$R(d_1, \theta_4) = 75,000\left(\frac{9}{48}\right) - 45,000\left(\frac{11}{48}\right) + 0\left(\frac{13}{48} + \frac{15}{48}\right) + 12,000$$
$$= \$15,750.$$

Note that the 12,000 represents the cost of obtaining the seismic data.

Thus it is evident how the risk function for a given decision procedure is evaluated. The risk function provides a means for defining *optimality*. An optimal decision function might be defined as one that will minimize the risk for every value of θ. However, it is evident that an optimal decision function (in this sense) may not always exist and, in fact, does not exist in most cases. Thus the preceding definition is inadequate. Hence another definition of optimality is considered in the next section.

BAYES' PROCEDURES

Even when data are available, there is no best definition of *optimal procedures*. With data, it is still possible to use a minimax criterion or a minimax decision function, but it too suffers from the same disadvantages as it does when no data are available; i.e., it assumes that nature will act as a conscious opponent and confront the decision maker with the least favorable distribution of θ.

If the decision maker has some advance information about the states of nature that can be described in terms of a prior distribution, then the *Bayes' principle* can be applied to the *risk function*. If the states of nature are discrete, the **Bayes' risk** corresponding to a decision function d and a prior probability distribution of θ, $P_\theta(k)$, is given by

$$B(d) = \sum_{\text{all } k} R(d, k) P_\theta(k).$$

If the states of nature are continuous, the Bayes' risk corresponding to a prior probability density function of θ, $P_\theta(y)$, is given by

$$B(d) = \int_{-\infty}^{\infty} R(d, y) P_\theta(y) \, dy.$$

The Bayes' risk provides another means for defining optimality for decision rules using the *Bayes' principle*. The *Bayes' principle* tells the decision maker to select that function d (called the *Bayes' decision procedure*) which minimizes $B(d)$. A method for finding Bayes' decision procedures follows.

When no data were available, using the Bayes' procedure lead us to select that action which minimized the expected loss; this expectation was evaluated with respect to the prior distribution of θ. Now that data are available, additional information is available about the state of nature. For example, if the seismic data are classified as (4), they are evidence that the strike will not be a 500,000-barrel well and probably not a 200,000-barrel well. Hence, after observing the experimental data, we should update the prior distribution by using more timely information about the probability distribution of the state of nature. Such updated information is called the *posterior distribution* of θ, given the prior distribution and the data $X = x$. The posterior distribution of θ is just the conditional distribution of θ, given $X = x$. If θ is discrete, the posterior distribution will be denoted by $h_{\theta|X=x}(k)$, and, if θ is continuous, then the

Table 22.4 **Values of $h_{\theta|X=x}(k)$, the posterior distribution of θ**

x \ k	θ_1	θ_2	θ_3	θ_4
1	0.166	0.240	0.327	0.267
2	0.129	0.108	0.241	0.522
3	0.039	0.087	0.146	0.728
4	0	0.107	0.238	0.655

posterior distribution will be denoted by $h_{\theta|X=x}(y)$. The method for calculating the posterior distribution is given later. However, if the method used for calculating the Bayes' procedure when no data are available is followed (selecting that action which minimizes the *expected loss*) with this expectation now evaluated with respect to the *posterior distribution* of θ, given $X = x$, this decision procedure minimizes $B(d)$. Hence it is the Bayes' procedure. This statement is not obvious, but it can easily be proved. Thus, to find the Bayes' procedure, the decision maker computes the posterior distribution of θ, given $X = x$. He then chooses that action which minimizes the expected loss[1] $l_h(a)$ (including the cost of experimentation)[2] with this expectation evaluated with respect to the *posterior* distribution of θ, given $X = x$, where

$$l_h(a) = E[l(a,\theta)] = \begin{cases} \sum_{\text{all } k} l(a,k)h_{\theta|X=x}(k), & \text{if } \theta \text{ is discrete} \\ \int_{-\infty}^{\infty} l(a,y)h_{\theta|X=x}(y)\,dy, & \text{if } \theta \text{ is continuous.} \end{cases}$$

In the oil-drilling example, the *posterior distribution* can be calculated by methods to be discussed later in this section and is given in Table 22.4.

Suppose that the seismic reading is classified as (3) (the geologic site has a nonclosed structure). To obtain the Bayes' procedure, we compute the expected loss with respect to the posterior distribution of θ, given $X = 3$, for each of the actions as follows:

$$l_h(a_1) = E[l(a_1,\theta)] = -650{,}000(0.039) - 200{,}000(0.087) + 25{,}000(0.146)$$
$$+ 75{,}000(0.728) + 12{,}000$$
$$= \$27{,}500,$$

$$l_h(a_2) = E[l(a_2,\theta)] = -45{,}000 + 12{,}000 = -\$33{,}000,$$

$$l_h(a_3) = E[l(a_3,\theta)] = -250{,}000(0.039) - 100{,}000(0.087) + 12{,}000$$
$$= -\$6{,}450.$$

The Bayes' procedure selects action a_2 (because this action minimizes the expected loss), which implies that the company should unconditionally lease the

---

[1] Note that loss is used rather than risk.

[2] Although the notation $l_h(a)$ does not show it, one should remember that this quantity does indeed depend upon the experimental outcome, x.

land. Thus we see that the experimental data change the action of the decision maker. Without experimentation, using the Bayes' procedure recommended drilling for oil, whereas the information obtained from the seismic data recommends that the company unconditionally lease the land. Incidentally, although Table 22.4 was obtained for all values of x, it was necessary to obtain the values for only $x = x_3$. In fact, this method of computing Bayes' procedures has the important advantage that it is necessary to compute only the optimal $d[x]$ for the single point that corresponds to the outcome of the experiment. Using the basic formula for $B(d)$ to find the Bayes' procedure requires the determination of the entire optimal decision function, which is generally more difficult.

CALCULATION OF THE POSTERIOR DISTRIBUTION

Denote by (θ, X) a bivariate random variable having a joint probability distribution. Consider the case where (θ, X) is a discrete bivariate random variable, with joint probability distribution given by $P_{\theta X}(k, j)$. Each random variable θ and X has a marginal distribution. In fact, $P_\theta(k)$, the prior distribution of θ, is the marginal distribution of θ. The usual expression given as the probability distribution of the random variable X actually corresponds to the conditional probability distribution of X, given θ. For example, if X has a Poisson distribution with parameter $\theta = 24$, then $e^{-24}24^j/j!$ is just the conditional probability distribution function of X, given $\theta = 24$.[1] To indicate that this distribution is a conditional distribution, we introduce the notation

$$Q_{X|\theta=k}(j) = P\{X = j \mid \theta = k\}.$$

Thus, in the Poisson example,

$$Q_{X|\theta=24}(j) = P\{X = j \mid \theta = 24\} = \frac{e^{-24}24^j}{j!}$$

represents the conditional probability distribution of X, given that $\theta = 24$, and it has the form of a Poisson distribution with parameter $\theta = 24$.

If the joint distribution of (θ, X) is of interest, the expression

$$P_{\theta X}(k, j) = Q_{X|\theta=k}(j)P_\theta(k)$$

can be used to evaluate it. $Q_X(j)$, the marginal distribution of X, can also be obtained; that is,

$$Q_X(j) = \sum_{\text{all } k} P_{\theta X}(k, j) = \sum_{\text{all } k} Q_{X|\theta=k}(j)P_\theta(k).$$

Finally, the only remaining probability distribution that has not been discussed is the conditional distribution of θ, given $X = j$, that is, the posterior distribution of θ, given $X = j$, $h_{\theta|X=j}(k)$. An alternative expression for the joint

---

[1] In order to be consistent with the notation introduced in this chapter, θ is used instead of the more usual symbol λ to denote the parameter of the Poisson distribution.

probability distribution of (θ, X) is given by

$$P_{\theta X}(k, j) = h_{\theta | X = j}(k) Q_X(j).$$

Equating the two expressions for $P_{\theta X}(k, j)$, and letting $j = x$ (the outcome of the experiment), leads to the important result from which the posterior distribution can be calculated; that is,

$$h_{\theta | X = x}(k) = \frac{Q_{X | \theta = k}(x) P_\theta(k)}{Q_X(x)}.$$

Thus, in summary, the posterior distribution can be calculated by using the preceding expression. $P_\theta(k)$ is the prior distribution. $Q_{X | \theta = k}(x)$ is the ordinary expression for the probability distribution of the random variable X evaluated at $X = x$, but it is written in this form to show its dependence upon the value of the parameter θ. The function $Q_X(x)$ is the marginal distribution of the random variable X, evaluated at $X = x$, and is obtained from

$$Q_X(x) = \sum_{\text{all } k} Q_{X | \theta = k}(x) P_\theta(k).$$

Returning to the oil-drilling example, suppose that the seismic reading is classified as 3 (the geologic site has a nonclosed structure). Recall that the prior distribution of the classification of the land is assumed to be

$$P\{\theta = \theta_1\} = P_\theta(1) = 0.10$$
$$P\{\theta = \theta_2\} = P_\theta(2) = 0.15$$
$$P\{\theta = \theta_3\} = P_\theta(3) = 0.25$$
$$P\{\theta = \theta_4\} = P_\theta(4) = 0.50.$$

It is necessary to evaluate the expressions $h_{\theta | X = 3}(1)$, $h_{\theta | X = 3}(2)$, $h_{\theta | X = 3}(3)$, and $h_{\theta | X = 3}(4)$, where

$$h_{\theta | X = 3}(k) = \frac{Q_{X | \theta = k}(3) P_\theta(k)}{Q_X(3)}, \quad \text{for } k = 1, 2, 3, \text{ and } 4.$$

In this case, $Q_{X | \theta = k}(3) = P\{X = 3 | \theta = k\}$ is just the probability that the seismic reading will be classified as (3), given that the well is a θ_k-barrel well, and these values can be obtained directly from Table 22.3. Hence

$$Q_{X | \theta = 1}(3) = \frac{1}{12}, \quad Q_{X | \theta = 2}(3) = \frac{1}{8}, \quad Q_{X | \theta = 3}(3) = \frac{1}{8}, \quad Q_{X | \theta = 4}(3) = \frac{5}{16}.$$

The marginal distribution of the random variable X evaluated at $X = 3$ can now be obtained; that is,

$$Q_X(3) = Q_{X | \theta = 1}(3) P_\theta(1) + Q_{X | \theta = 2}(3) P_\theta(2) + Q_{X | \theta = 3}(3) P_\theta(3) + Q_{X | \theta = 4}(3) P_\theta(4)$$

$$= \left(\frac{1}{12}\right)(0.1) + \frac{1}{8}(0.15) + \frac{1}{8}(0.25) + \frac{5}{16}(0.50) = 0.2147,$$

so that the posterior distribution can now be calculated; that is,

$$h_{\theta|X=3}(1) = \frac{(\frac{1}{12})(0.1)}{0.2147} = 0.039$$

$$h_{\theta|X=3}(2) = \frac{(\frac{1}{8})(0.15)}{0.2147} = 0.087$$

$$h_{\theta|X=3}(3) = \frac{(\frac{1}{8})(0.25)}{0.2147} = 0.146$$

$$h_{\theta|X=3}(4) = \frac{(\frac{5}{16})(0.50)}{0.2147} = 0.728.$$

There exists a simple tabular algorithm that will yield Table 22.4, i.e., the posterior distribution of θ. Table 22.5(a)(b)(c) is such a table. The entries in the top row of Table 22.5(a) are simply the prior probabilities of the well sizes, whereas the entries in the bottom four rows are the conditional probabilities of a seismic classification given the size of a well. The entries in the first four columns of Table 22.5(b) are the entries of the corresponding elements of Table 22.5(a), multiplied by the appropriate prior probability (e.g., $0.0583 = (\frac{7}{12})(0.10)$). The entries in the last column of Table 22.5(b) are simply the sum of the four elements in the corresponding row (e.g., $0.3511 = 0.0583 + 0.0844 + 0.1146 + 0.0938$). The entries in Table 22.5(c), the conditional probabilities of obtaining a particular well size given a seismic classification, are the entries of the corresponding elements of Table 22.5(b), divided by the appropriate element $Q_X(x)$, in the last column of Table 22.5(b) (e.g., $0.166 = 0.0583/0.3511$).

The expression for the posterior distribution has been given, where θ and X are both discrete random variables. If θ is discrete and X is continuous, the posterior distribution $h_{\theta|X=x}(k)$ is given by

$$h_{\theta|X=x}(k) = \frac{f_{X|\theta=k}(x)P_{\theta}(k)}{f_X(x)},$$

where $P_{\theta}(k)$ is the prior distribution of θ, and $f_{X|\theta=k}(x)$ is the ordinary expression for the density function of the random variable X, but it is written in this form to show its dependence upon the value of the parameter θ. The function $f_X(x)$ is the marginal density of the random variable X, and it is obtained from

$$f_X(x) = \sum_{\text{all } k} f_{X|\theta=k}(x)P_{\theta}(k).$$

If both θ and X are continuous, the posterior distribution $h_{\theta|X=x}(y)$ is given by

$$h_{\theta|X=x}(y) = \frac{f_{X|\theta=y}(x)P_{\theta}(y)}{f_X(x)},$$

where $P_{\theta}(y)$ is the prior density function of θ. The function $f_{X|\theta=y}(x)$ has been defined previously. $f_X(x)$ is the marginal density of the random variable X, and it

Table 22.5 **Tabular algorithm for computation of posterior distribution—oil-drilling example**

(a)

		Prior dist. $P_\theta(k)$			
		0.10	0.15	0.25	0.50
		$Q_{X\vert\theta=k}(x)$			
Seismic classification x	k	θ_1	θ_2	θ_3	θ_4
	1	$\frac{7}{12}$	$\frac{9}{16}$	$\frac{11}{24}$	$\frac{9}{48}$
	2	$\frac{4}{12}$	$\frac{3}{16}$	$\frac{6}{24}$	$\frac{13}{48}$
	3	$\frac{1}{12}$	$\frac{2}{16}$	$\frac{3}{24}$	$\frac{15}{48}$
	4	$\frac{0}{12}$	$\frac{2}{16}$	$\frac{4}{24}$	$\frac{11}{48}$

(b)

Seismic classification x	k	$Q_{X\vert\theta=k}(x)P_\theta(k)$				$Q_X(x)$
		θ_1	θ_2	θ_3	θ_4	
	1	0.0583	0.0844	0.1146	0.0938	0.3511
	2	0.0333	0.0281	0.0625	0.1354	0.2593
	3	0.0083	0.0188	0.0313	0.1563	0.2147
	4	0.0	0.0188	0.0417	0.1146	0.1751

(c)

Seismic classification x	k	Posterior distribution of θ $h_{\theta\vert X=x}(k)$			
		θ_1	θ_2	θ_3	θ_4
	1	0.166	0.240	0.327	0.267
	2	0.129	0.108	0.241	0.522
	3	0.039	0.087	0.146	0.728
	4	0.0	0.107	0.238	0.655

is obtained from

$$f_X(x) = \int_{-\infty}^{\infty} f_{X|\theta=y}(x) P_\theta(y) \, dy.$$

Finally, if θ is continuous and X is discrete, the posterior distribution $h_{\theta|X=x}(y)$ is given by

$$h_{\theta|X=x}(y) = \frac{Q_{X|\theta=y}(x) P_\theta(y)}{Q_X(x)},$$

where $P_\theta(y)$ is the prior density function of θ. The function $Q_{X|\theta=y}(x)$ is the ordinary expression for the probability distribution of the random variable X, that is, $P\{X = x \,|\, \theta = y\}$, but it is written in this form to show its dependence upon the value of the parameter θ. $Q_X(x)$ is the marginal distribution of the random variable X, and it is obtained from

$$Q_X(x) = \int_{-\infty}^{\infty} Q_{X|\theta=y}(x) P_\theta(y) \, dy.$$

VALUE OF EXPERIMENTATION

Before performing any experiment, we should determine its potential value. Suppose the experiment can lead to perfect information about the state of nature. What is this perfect information worth? In the oil-drilling example, seismic information that is *imperfect* costs $12,000. If perfect information saves, say, only $10,000, seismic information should be forgone because it is too expensive. If we knew that the strike would be a 500,000-barrel well (state of nature is θ_1), then the best action to take clearly would be a_1, drill for oil. We can see from Table 22.2 that this action would lead to a loss of $-\$650,000$. Similarly, if we knew that the strike would be a 200,000-barrel well (state of nature is θ_2), the best action again would be a_1, with a corresponding loss of $-\$200,000$. However, if we knew that the strike would be a 50,000-barrel well (state of nature is θ_3), the best action would be a_2, unconditionally lease the land, with a corresponding loss of $-\$45,000$. Finally, if we knew that the well was dry (state of nature is θ_4), the best action again would be a_2, also with a corresponding loss of $-\$45,000$. Because the (prior) probabilities of each of these states are known, the expected loss with perfect information available about the state of nature $E(PI)$ is given by

$$E(PI) = -650,000(0.1) - 200,000(0.15) - 45,000(0.25) - 45,000(0.50)$$
$$= -\$128,750.$$

The Bayes' solution (without any data) provided for an expected loss of $-\$51,250$, which is substantially more than the expected loss with perfect information, so that experimentation can lead to potential savings. In fact, the decision maker should be willing to pay a cost of up to $-51,250 + 128,750 = \$77,500$ for perfect information.

Table 22.6 **Bayes' actions, expected losses, and marginal distribution for oil example**

x	Bayes' action	Expected loss	Marginal distribution $Q_X(x)$
1	a_1	−115,700	0.351
2	a_1	−48,275	0.259
3	a_2	−33,000	0.215
4	a_2	−33,000	0.175

Now that experimentation may be desirable, it is useful to determine the value of obtaining seismic data. It has been shown that if the seismic data are classified as (3), the optimal (Bayes) action is a_2, with a corresponding loss of − \$33,000. Using the same techniques, the optimal (Bayes) actions can be obtained if the seismic data are classified as (1), (2), or (4). These results are summarized in Table 22.6. Because the entries for the expected loss depend upon the outcome of the experiment, x, the overall measure of the effectiveness of the experiment requires obtaining a weighted sum that is weighted with respect to the marginal probability distribution of the random variable, X, of the Bayes' losses. The calculations required for obtaining this marginal distribution, $Q_X(x)$, are described earlier in the section dealing with the calculation of the posterior distribution, where we obtained $Q_X(3)$. Other values are given in Table 22.6. Hence the weighted sum of the Bayes' losses, called the *unconditional expected loss with experimentation*, is given by

$$-115{,}700(0.351) - 48{,}275(0.259) - 33{,}000(0.215) - 33{,}000(0.175) = -\$65{,}984.$$

The value of the experiment (beyond its cost of \$12,000) is then given by the difference between this weighted sum and the Bayes' loss without data; that is,

$$-65{,}984 + 51{,}250 = -\$14{,}734,$$

indicating an expected savings of \$14,734 due to following an optimal decision procedure with experimentation. Hence obtaining seismic soundings does reduce the total expected cost.

In fact, if the nonoptimal procedure, d_1, presented earlier in this section, is followed, its weighted risk is given by

$$-471{,}333(0.1) - 137{,}375(0.15) + 15{,}958(0.25) + 15{,}750(0.50) = -\$55{,}875.$$

Thus an expected savings of \$10,109 (−65,984 + 55,875) is obtained by using the (optimal) Bayes' procedure rather than the procedure d_1.

22.4 Decision Trees

An alternative method to the analysis presented in this chapter is the use of *decision trees*. A decision tree is a graphical method of expressing, in chronological order, the alternative actions that are available to the decision maker and the choices determined by chance. Decision trees consist of forks (nodes) and branches. There are two types of forks: decision forks represented by squares □ and chance forks represented by circles ○. Branches are straight lines that emanate from decision forks or chance forks. When a decision maker encounters a decision fork, he must choose one of the alternative branches to travel on. When a decision maker encounters a chance fork, he has no control over which branch to travel on. Instead, his path is determined by chance events whose probabilities are those associated with the branches that emanate from the chance fork.

For example, the decision tree for the oil-drilling problem is given in Fig. 22.1, and you are urged to refer to this figure throughout the ensuing discussion. Initially the decision maker has a choice of not using seismic soundings or using seismic soundings. Either action triggers some consequences. If the decision not to use seismic soundings is made, the decision maker is led down the appropriate path, arriving at a fork (node) with branches marked: drill, unconditionally lease, and conditionally lease. He must choose one of these branches on which to continue. If he chooses to drill, he is led down the appropriate path, arriving at a fork with branches marked: 500,000-barrel well, 200,000-barrel well, 50,000-barrel well, and dry well. The choice of the branch on which to continue is a chance event.

Depending upon the outcome of this chance event, he reaches a terminating point. Similarly, if the initial decision is to use seismic soundings, the decision maker is led down the appropriate path, arriving at a fork with branches marked: definitely closed structure, probably closed structure, nonclosed structure, no structure. The choice of the branch on which to continue is a chance event. If by chance the data reveal a nonclosed structure, then this branch is chosen, and he arrives at a fork with branches marked: drill, unconditionally lease, and conditionally lease. The decision maker must choose one of these branches on which to continue. If he chooses to drill, he is led down the appropriate branch, arriving at a fork with branches marked: 500,000-barrel well, 200,000-barrel well, 50,000-barrel well, and dry well. The choice of the branch on which to continue is again a chance event. Depending upon the outcome of this chance event, he reaches a terminating point. The entire tree can be completed in this fashion.[1]

The previous discussion presents a graphical method for representing the decision problem. However, nothing was said about how to choose the optimal path to travel on. Basically, the calculations described in the earlier sections of this chapter are required, namely, finding posterior probabilities, marginal probabilities, and Bayes' risks. For each possible path that can be followed, the loss is specified at the terminal point. Working *backward* from each terminal point to the nearest fork (a chance fork), we place a loss at that fork, this cost being the expected cost taken with respect to the probabilities associated with the branches. These probabilities represent the probability of a certain state of nature, indicated by the terminal branch, being chosen, given the path followed to the last fork. For example, for the no-seismic data drill path, the probability of the

---

[1] In Fig. 22.1 only part of the tree is presented, but all other branches can be easily drawn.

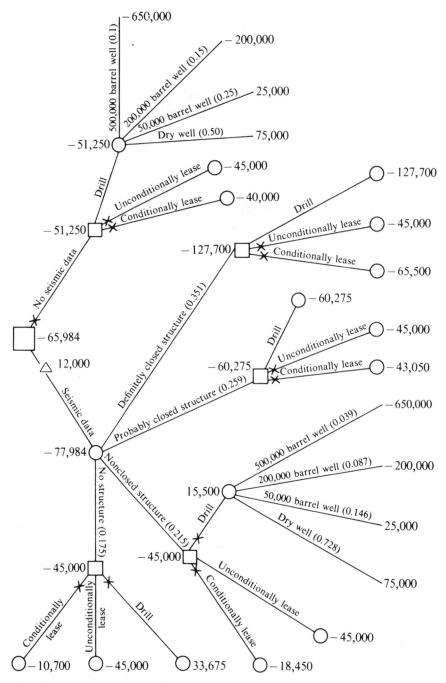

Figure 22.1 Decision tree for oil-drilling example.

500,000-barrel branch is just the prior probability that the well is a 500,000-barrel well—that is, 0.1. For the seismic-data nonclosed structure drill path, the probability of the 500,000-barrel branch is just the posterior probability that the well is a 500,000-barrel well, given the seismic reading was classified as a nonclosed structure—that is, 0.039. Again, working backward, we find that the next fork is a decision fork. The loss associated with this fork is the minimum loss over the branches associated with that node. On the no-seismic data path, −51,250 represents the minimum of −51,250, −45,000, and −40,000 and is associated with the action *drill*. Hence, this action is the best one to take, given that the decision maker is at that fork. The symbol (×) through the other two branches eliminates the actions *unconditionally lease* and *conditionally lease* from further consideration on that path. Similarly, on the seismic data, nonclosed structure path, −45,000 represents the minimum of 15,500, −45,000, and −18,450 and is associated with the action *unconditionally lease*. Hence, this action is the best one to take, given that the decision maker is at that fork. The symbol (×) through the other two branches eliminates the other two actions from further consideration on that path. The next fork on the seismic data path is a chance fork. The loss associated with this fork is the expected cost taken with respect to the probabilities associated with the branches. These probabilities represent the (unconditional) probability that the seismic reading, indicated by the branch, is obtained, given the path followed to this fork. For the seismic data path, the probability that the seismic reading will lead to the nonclosed structure branch is just the unconditional probability that it will be classified as a nonclosed structure—that is, 0.215. Finally, the beginning fork has a loss associated with it of −65,984. This loss is the minimum of −51,250 that is associated with the no-seismic data branch and −65,984, which is associated with the seismic data branch (and obtained by adding the cost of taking seismic soundings, 12,000, to the −77,984 attached to the branch). Note that the cost of taking seismic soundings is denoted by the symbol △ on the branch. Hence the no-seismic data branch is eliminated, and the optimal procedure is to follow the seismic data path, leading to an expected profit of 65,984, which is, of course, the solution obtained earlier. Again, it is worthwhile to note that the calculations required by using decision-tree analysis are identical to those required by using the previously described analytical methods.

22.5 Utility Function

The oil-drilling example assumed that an expected loss (profit) in monetary terms was the appropriate measure of the consequences of taking an action, given a state of nature. However, there are many situations where this assumption is inappropriate. For example, suppose that an individual was offered the choice of (1) accepting a 50–50 chance of winning $10,000 or nothing or (2) receiving $4,000 with certainty. Many people would prefer the $4,000 even though the expected payoff on the 50–50 chance of winning $10,000 is $5,000. A company may be unwilling to invest a large sum of money in a new product even if the expected profit is substantial if there is a risk of losing their investment and thereby becoming bankrupt. People buy insurance even though it is a poor investment; the insurance company must pay expenses *and* make a profit. Do these examples invalidate the previous material? Fortunately, the answer is no, because there is a way of transforming monetary values into an appropriate scale that reflects the decision makers' preferences. This scale is called the *utility scale*, and it becomes the appropriate measure of the consequences of taking an action, given a state of nature. A detailed discussion of **utilities** can be found in the references at the end of this chapter.

22.6 Carnival Example

A carnival is scheduled to appear in a city on a given date. The profits that will be obtained depend heavily upon the weather. In particular, if the weather is rainy, the carnival loses $15,000; if it is cloudy, the carnival loses $5,000; and if it is sunny, the carnival makes a profit of $10,000. The carnival has to set up equipment for its show, but it can cancel the show prior to setting up its equipment. This action results in a loss of $1,000. Furthermore, by incurring an additional cost of $1,000, the carnival can postpone its setup decision until the day before the scheduled performance. At this time, the carnival can obtain the local weather report. The Weather Bureau has compiled data based upon its predictions; these data are given in Table 22.7. Furthermore, the Weather Bureau has compiled a prior distribution of the weather. In particular, the probabilities of rain, clouds, and sun are 0.1, 0.3, and 0.6, respectively.

We will analyze this example by first using decision-tree analysis. The unevaluated decision tree is shown in Fig. 22.2, and it is a graphical representation of the decision problem.[1] Note that the lower part of the tree represents the *no data case* while the upper part uses additional information from *experimentation*. The first decision fork to confront the decision maker requires making a choice between using or not using the Weather Bureau's report (fork 1). If the choice is not to use the Weather Bureau's information, the decision maker is led down the path that arrives at decision fork 2 with branches marked *setup* and *no setup* (cancel). The selection of one of these branches results in a flow into a chance fork (either fork 3 or fork 4). The choice of the branch on which to

Table 22.7 **Weather Bureau data for carnival example**

Probability that forecast is	Actual weather		
	Rain	Clouds	Sun
Rain (*RF*)	0.7	0.2	0.1
Clouds (*CF*)	0.2	0.6	0.2
Sun (*SF*)	0.1	0.2	0.7

[1] The forks are numbered arbitrarily for discussion purposes.

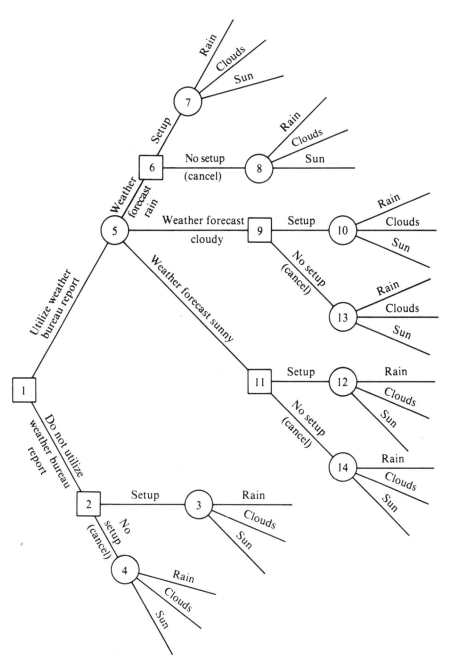

Figure 22.2 Unevaluated decision tree for carnival example.

continue is a chance event, and, depending upon the outcome of this chance event, the decision maker reaches one of the terminating points: rain, clouds, or sun. Associated with each of these terminating points is a monetary consequence.

If, at initial decision fork 1, the decision maker chooses to use the Weather Bureau's information, he is led down the path that arrives at fork 5, with branches marked: weather forecast rain, weather forecast cloudly, weather forecast sunny. The choice of the branch on which to continue is a chance event. If (by chance) the Weather Bureau forecasts a sunny day, then the decision maker chooses this branch, and it leads to decision fork 11, which has subsequent branches identical to those described for fork 2.

This discussion has been concerned with a graphical method for representing the decision problem, and it has not been concerned with how to choose the optimal path to travel on. Determining the optimal path requires calculations similar to those described for the oil-drilling example. In particular, the posterior distribution of the states of nature (rain, clouds, or sun) is required, given the weather forecast. This posterior distribution is given in Table 22.7, and the details will be presented later in this section. These posterior probabilities are necessary for the evaluation of the decision tree.

Figure 22.3 is the evaluated decision tree for the carnival example. For each possible path that can be followed, the loss is specified at the terminal point. If we work *backward* from each terminal point to the nearest fork (a chance fork), the loss placed at that fork is the expected cost taken with respect to the probabilities associated with the branches. These probabilities represent the probability of the state of nature (indicated by the terminal branch) being chosen, given the path followed to the last fork. For example, for the *Do not utilize weather bureau report Setup path*, the probability of reaching the sun branch is just the prior probability that a day will be sunny—that is, 0.6 (this probability is shown on the branch). The expected cost at fork 3 is −$3,000 (profit). For the *Utilize weather bureau report Weather forecast sunny Setup path*, the probability of reaching the sun branch is just the posterior probability that a day will be sunny, given that the weather forecast is for a sunny day—that is, 0.857 (this posterior probability is shown on the branch). The expected cost at fork 12 is −$7,655 (profit). Working backward from fork 12 leads to fork 11, a decision fork. Fork 14 also leads into fork 11. The loss associated with fork 11 is the minimum loss over the two branches that emanated from that fork. The loss of −$7,655 represents the minimum of −$7,655 and $1,000, and it is associated with the action *setup*. Hence this action is the best one to take, given that the decision maker is at fork 11. The symbol (×) through the other branch eliminates that branch from further consideration on that path. Again, working *backward* from fork 11 leads to fork 5, a chance fork. The loss associated with this fork is the expected cost taken with respect to the probabilities associated with the branches. These probabilities represent the (unconditional) probability that the Weather Bureau's forecast, indicated by the branch, is obtained, given the path followed to this fork. For the *Utilize weather bureau report path*, the probability that the weather forecast will be sunny is simply the *unconditional* probability that the forecast will call for

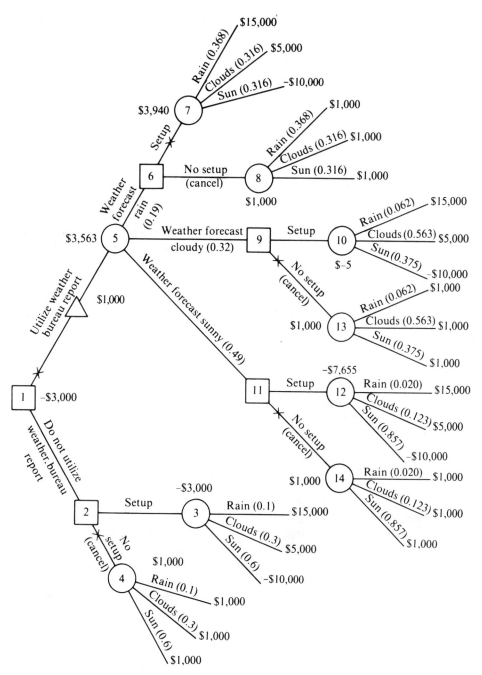

Figure 22.3 **Evaluated decision tree for carnival example.**

sun—that is, 0.49. This probability appears on the appropriate branch in Fig. 22.3, and its calculation will be discussed later in this section.[1] The expected cost at fork 5 is $-\$3,563$ ($-7,655(0.49) + -5(0.32) + 1,000(0.19)$). Continuing to work backward from fork 5 leads to fork 1, the initial decision fork. Fork 2 also leads into this initial decision fork. The loss associated with fork 1 is the minimum loss over the (two) branches that emanate from that fork. The loss of $-\$3,000$ represents the minimum of $-3,000$ and $-2,563$ (after adding the $\$1,000$ cost of using the Weather Bureau's forecast), and it is associated with the action that calls for not using the Weather Bureau's forecast. Indeed, the optimal decision is not to use the Weather Bureau's forecast and to set up for the carnival, leading to an expected profit of $\$3,000$.

Although incurring a cost of $\$1,000$ to use the Weather Bureau's report was not worthwhile, a cost of $\$563$ or less would be worthwhile. Finally, what is the most that the carnival should be willing to pay for any type of information about the weather? The expected loss with perfect information is given by

$$E(PI) = 1,000(0.1) + 1,000(0.3) - 10,000(0.6) = -\$5,600,$$

so that some type of experimentation may lead to potential savings, with a decision maker being willing to pay a cost for perfect information up to

$$-3,000 + 5,600 = \$2,600.$$

CALCULATION OF THE POSTERIOR DISTRIBUTION FOR THE CARNIVAL EXAMPLE

To calculate the posterior distribution, we need to use the same tabular algorithm that was presented for the oil-drilling example. The results are given in Table 22.8.

The entries in the top row of Table 22.8(a) are simply the prior probabilities of the weather conditions, whereas the entries in the bottom three rows are the conditional probabilities of a forecast type, given a particular weather condition. The entries in the first three columns of Table 22.8(b) are the entries of the corresponding elements of Table 22.8(a) multiplied by the appropriate prior probability (e.g., $0.07 = (0.70)(0.10)$). The entries in the last column of Table 22.8(b) are simply the sum of the three elements in the corresponding row (e.g., $0.19 = 0.07 + 0.06 + 0.06$). The entries in Table 22.8(c), the conditional probabilities of obtaining a particular weather condition given a particular forecast type, are the entries of the corresponding elements of Table 22.8(b) divided by the appropriate element, $Q_X(x)$, in the last column of Table 22.8(b) (e.g., $0.368 = 0.07/0.19$).

NON-DECISION-TREE ANALYSIS OF THE CARNIVAL EXAMPLE

An alternative (but equivalent) method for solving the carnival example is to use the techniques given in Secs. 22.2 and 22.3. There are two potential actions (other

[1] These probabilities are also obtained from the tabular algorithm for the computation of the posterior distribution (the last column of Table 22.8(b)).

Table 22.8 Tabular algorithm for computation of posterior distribution for the carnival example

(a)

Prior distribution $P_\theta(k)$	0.10	0.30	0.60
	$Q_{x|\theta=k}(x)$		
k \ x	Rain θ_1	Clouds θ_2	Sun θ_3
Rain forecast (RF)	0.70	0.20	0.10
Cloudy forecast (CF)	0.20	0.60	0.20
Sunny forecast (SF)	0.10	0.20	0.70

(b)

	$Q_{x|\theta=k}(x)P_\theta(k)$			$Q_x(x)$
k \ x	Rain θ_1	Clouds θ_2	Sun θ_3	
RF	0.07	0.06	0.06	0.19
CF	0.02	0.18	0.12	0.32
SF	0.01	0.06	0.42	0.49

(c)

Posterior distribution of θ			
	$h_{\theta|X=x}(k)$		
k \ x	Rain θ_1	Clouds θ_2	Sun θ_3
RF	0.368	0.316	0.316
CF	0.062	0.563	0.375
SF	0.020	0.123	0.857

Table 22.9 Loss function for
carnival example

| | State of nature | | |
Action	Rain	Clouds	Sun
a_1: setup	15,000	5,000	−10,000
a_2: no setup	1,000	1,000	1,000

than deciding whether or not to use the Weather Bureau's data), namely, *setup*
(a_1) and *no setup* (a_2). There are three states of nature: Rain (R), Clouds (C),
and Sun (S). The loss function is presented in Table 22.9. The problem will be
solved by first assuming the local Weather Bureau's report is not available
(no data). The expected loss $l(a)$ for each action is given by

$$l(a_1) = 15,000(0.1) + 5,000(0.3) - 10,000(0.6) = -\$3,000,$$
$$l(a_2) = 1,000(0.1) + 1,000(0.3) + 1,000(0.6) = \$1,000.$$

Hence the Bayes' principle leads to selecting action a_1, that is, setting up, and the
associated expected loss is −\$3,000 (profit).

Now, the Weather Bureau's report will be assumed to be available but at a
cost of \$1,000. The posterior distribution can be obtained and is given in Table
22.8(c). This table was obtained by using the tabular algorithm. Entries can also
be obtained directly from the usual expressions for posterior probabilities. For
example, the posterior distribution that the weather will be sunny, given that the
forecast is for rain, is given by

$$\frac{(0.1)(0.6)}{(0.7)(0.1) + (0.2)(0.3) + (0.1)(0.6)} = 0.316.$$

The optimal Bayes' actions, given the various forecasts, are presented in
Table 22.10. A typical entry in Table 22.10 will be obtained next. Given that the
forecast is for rain,

$$l_h(a_1) = (0.368)(15,000) + (0.316)(5,000) - (0.316)(10,000) + 1,000$$
$$= \$4,940,$$
$$l_h(a_2) = \$1,000 + 1,000 = \$2,000.$$

Hence the recommended Bayes' action is a_2, and the corresponding expected loss

Table 22.10 Table of Bayes' actions, expected losses, and
marginal distribution for carnival example

Forecast	Bayes' action	Expected loss	Marginal distribution
RF	a_2	2,000	0.19
CF	a_1	995	0.32
SF	a_1	−6,655	0.49

is $2,000. Similarly, the marginal probability that the forecast will be sun is given by

$$(0.1)(0.1) + (0.2)(0.3) + (0.7)(0.6) = 0.49.$$

This result is also obtained in the last column of Table 22.8(*b*). Hence, if the Weather Bureau's reports are to be used, the Bayes' actions call for *setting up* if the forecast is for clouds or sun but for *not setting up* if the forecast is for rain.

Is it desirable to use the Weather Bureau's data? The answer to this question calls for computing the unconditional expected loss with experimentation (weighted sum of the Bayes' losses); that is,

$$2,000(0.19) + 995(0.32) - 6,655(0.49) = -2,563.$$

Thus the value of Weather Bureau's data is given by

$$-2,563 + 3,000 = 437,$$

(which is an actual loss relative to the no-data case), so that the Weather Bureau's data are not worth the $1,000 cost.

22.7 Conclusions

Decision analysis has become an important technique in the solution of business problems. It can be applied to broad problems facing management, such as determining whether to enter a new product field, or it can be used to solve smaller problems, such as the one illustrated by the oil-drilling example. It is characterized by the decision maker enumerating all the available courses of action, expressing his utilities, and quantifying his subjective probabilities. When these data are available, decision analysis becomes a powerful tool in determining an optimal course of action.

SELECTED REFERENCES

1. Brown, R. V., A. S. Kahr, and C. Peterson: *Decision Analysis for the Manager*, Holt, New York, 1974.
2. Holloway, C.A.: *Decision Making under Uncertainty*, Prentice-Hall, Englewood Cliffs, N.J., 1979.
3. Keeney, R. L. and H. Raiffa: *Decisions with Multiple Objectives*, Wiley, New York, 1976.
4. LaValle, I. H.: *Fundamentals of Decision Analysis*, Holt, New York, 1978.
5. Raiffa, H.: *Decision Analysis*, Addison-Wesley, Reading, Mass., 1968.
6. Schlaifer, R. O.: *Analysis of Decisions under Uncertainty*, McGraw-Hill, New York, 1969.
7. Winkler, R. L.: *Introduction to Bayesean Inference and Decision*, Holt, New York, 1972.

PROBLEMS

1. A new type of airplane is to be purchased by the Air Force, and the number of *spare* engines to be ordered must be determined. The Air Force must order these spare engines in batches of 5, and it can choose among only 15, 20, or 25 spares. The supplier of

these engines has two plants, and the Air Force must make its decision prior to knowing which plant will be used. From past experience, the Air Force knows that the number of spare engines required when production takes place at plant A is approximated by a Poisson distribution with parameter $\theta = 21$, whereas the number of spare engines required when production takes place at plant B is approximated by a Poisson distribution with parameter $\theta = 24$. The cost of a spare engine purchased now is $400,000, whereas the cost of a spare engine purchased at a later date is $900,000. Holding costs and interest are to be neglected. Spares must always be supplied if they are demanded, and unused engines will be scrapped when the airplanes become obsolete. From these data, the loss function can be computed as

Action	State of nature $\theta_1:\theta = 21$	$\theta_2:\theta = 24$
a_1: order 15	1.155×10^7	1.414×10^7
a_2: order 20	1.012×10^7	1.207×10^7
a_3: order 25	1.047×10^7	1.135×10^7

The Air Force knows from past experience that $\frac{2}{3}$ of all types of airplane engines are produced in plant A, and only $\frac{1}{3}$ are produced in plant B. Furthermore, it knows that a similar type of engine was produced for an earlier version of the current airplane under consideration. The order size for this earlier type was the same as for the current model. Furthermore, its nonobsolete life is identical with that planned for the present version. The engine for the current order will be produced in the same plant as the previous model, although the Air Force does not know which of the two plants this is. The Air Force does have access to the data on the number of spares actually required for the older version (which had a Poisson distribution), but it does not have time to determine the production location.

(a) What action does the Bayes' procedure recommend, assuming that the information on the old airplane model is not available?

(b) How much money is it worthwhile to pay for "perfect information"?

(c) Assuming that cost of data on the old airplane model is free and that 30 spares were required, determine the Bayes' action.

2. A large mill is faced with the problem of extending $100,000 credit to a new customer, a dress manufacturer. The mill classifies typical companies into the following categories: poor risk, average risk, and good risk. Their experience indicates that 25 percent of similar companies are poor risks, 45 percent are average risks, and 30 percent are good risks. If credit is extended, the expected profit for poor risks is $-$15,000, for average risks $10,000, and for good risks $20,000. If credit is not extended, the dress manufacturer will turn to another mill. The mill is able to consult a credit-rating organization for a fee of $2,000. Their experience with this credit-rating company is as follows:

Credit company evaluation	Actual credit rating, % Poor	Average	Good
Poor	50	40	20
Average	40	50	40
Good	10	10	40

(a) What action does the Bayes' procedure recommend, assuming the credit-rating company is not used?

(b) How much money is it worthwhile to pay for "perfect information"?

(c) What is the optimal expected loss if the credit-rating company data are used? Does it pay to use these data?

(d) What action does the Bayes' procedure recommend if the credit-rating company determines the dress manufacturer to be a poor risk?

3. Use the scenario given in Prob. 2.

(a) Draw and properly label the decision tree.
(b) Evaluate the decision tree.
(c) Determine the optimal policy.
(d) How much money is it worthwhile to pay for "perfect information"?

4. A manufacturer produces items that have a probability p of being defective. These items are formed into lots of 150. Past experience indicates that p is either 0.05 or 0.25, and, furthermore, in 80 percent of the lots produced, p equals 0.05 (and, in 20 percent of the lots, p equals 0.25). These items are then used in an assembly, and ultimately their quality is determined before the final assembly leaves the plant. Initially the manufacturer can *either* screen each item in a lot at a cost of $15 per item and replace defective items *or* use the items directly without screening. If the latter action is chosen, the cost of rework is ultimately $100/defective item. For these data, the costs per lot can be calculated as:

	$p = 0.05$	$p = 0.25$
Screen	1,500	1,500
Do not screen	750	3,750

Because screening requires scheduling of inspectors and equipment, the decision to screen or not screen must be made 2 days before the potential screening takes place. However, one item can be taken from the lot and sent to a laboratory, and its quality (defective or nondefective) can be reported before the screen/no-screen decision must be made. The cost of this initial inspection is $125.

(a) What action does the Bayes' procedure recommend without looking at the single item?

(b) How much money is it worthwhile to pay for "perfect information"?

(c) What is the optimal expected cost if the quality of items is determined before the screen/no-screen decision is made?

(d) What action does the Bayes' procedure recommend if the quality of one of the items is determined and found to be defective?

5. Use the scenario given in Prob. 4.

(a) Draw and properly label the decision tree.
(b) Evaluate the decision tree.
(c) Determine the optimal policy.
(d) How much money is it worthwhile to pay for "perfect information"?

6. Assume that there are two weighted coins. Coin 1 has a probability of 0.3 of turning up heads, and coin 2 has a probability of 0.6 of turning up heads. A coin is tossed once. The decision maker must decide which coin was tossed. The probability that coin 1 was tossed is 0.6, and the probability that coin 2 was tossed is 0.4. The loss matrix is as follows:

	Coin 1 tossed	Coin 2 tossed
a_1: say coin 1 tossed	0	1
a_2: say coin 2 tossed	1	0

(a)   What is the Bayes' procedure (action) before the coin is tossed?

(b)   What is the Bayes' procedure if the outcome is heads? What if it is tails?

7.   Use the scenario given in Prob. 6.

(a)   Draw and properly label the decision tree.

(b)   Evaluate the decision tree.

(c)   Determine the optimal policy.

8.   A company has developed a new chip that will enable it to enter the microcomputer field if it so desires. Alternatively, it can sell its rights for $800,000. If it chooses to build computers, the profitability of the venture depends upon the company's ability to market the microcomputer during the first year. It has sufficient access to retail outlets so that it can guarantee sales of 1,000 computers. On the other hand, if this computer catches on, it can sell 10,000 machines. The company believes that both sales alternatives are equally likely and that all other alternatives are negligible. The cost of setting up the assembly line is $600,000. The difference between the selling price and the variable cost is $600. Market research can be performed at a cost of $400,000 to determine which of the two levels of demand is more realistic. Previous experience indicates that such market research is correct two-thirds of the time.

(a)   What action does the Bayes' procedure recommend, assuming market research is not used?

(b)   How much money "is it worthwhile to pay for perfect information"?

(c)   What is the optimal expected loss if market research is used? Does it pay to use market research?

(d)   What action does the Bayes' procedure recommend if market research determined that only 1,000 computers will be sold?

9.   Use the scenario given in Prob. 8.

(a)   Draw and properly label the decision tree.

(b)   Evaluate the decision tree.

(c)   Determine the optimal policy.

(d)   How much money is it worthwhile to pay for "perfect information"?

10.   A new type of camera film has been developed. It is packaged in sets of 5 sheets, each sheet providing an instantaneous snapshot. Because this process is new, the manufacturer has attached an additional sheet to the package, so that the store may test 1 sheet before it sells the package of 5. In promoting the film, the manufacturer offers to refund the entire purchase price of the film if 1 of the 5 is defective. This refund must be paid by the camera store, and the selling price has been fixed at $1 if this guarantee is to be valid. The camera store may sell the film for 50 cents if the preceding guarantee is replaced by one that pays 10 cents for each defective sheet. The cost of the film to the camera store is 20 cents, and the film is not returnable. The store may take three actions:

a_1: scrap the film,

a_2: sell the film for $1,

a_3: sell the film for 50 cents.

(a)   If the six states of nature correspond to 0, 1, 2, 3, 4, 5 defective sheets in the package, complete the following loss table:

a \ θ	0	1	2	3	4	5
a_1	0.20					
a_2	−0.80		0.20			
a_3	−0.30	−0.20		0.00		

(b)   The store has accumulated the following information on sales of 60 such packages:

Quality of attached sheet	Defectives in box					
	0	1	2	3	4	5
Good	10	8	6	4	2	0
Bad	0	2	4	6	8	10
Total	10	10	10	10	10	10

These data indicate that each state of nature is equally likely, so that this prior can be assumed. What is the Bayes' procedure (before testing the attached sheet) for a package of film?

(c)   What is the optimal expected loss for a package of film if the attached sheet is tested? What action does the Bayes' procedure recommend if the sheet is good? If it is bad?

11.   Solve the oil-drilling example if the profit per barrel of oil is increased to $4.

12.   Solve the oil-drilling example by using the prior distribution formed from the data in Table 22.3.

13.   Solve the carnival example if the cost of using the Weather Bureau's data is reduced to $400.

14.   Refer to the scenarios in the appropriate problems and assume that no experimental data are available; draw, properly label, and evaluate the decision tree:

(a)   for Prob. 2,
(b)   for Prob. 4,
(c)   for Prob. 6,
(d)   for Prob. 8.

■ CHAPTER 23

Simulation

■ The technique of **simulation** has long been an important tool of the designer, whether it be for simulating airplane flight in a wind tunnel, simulating plant layouts with scale models of machines, or simulating lines of communication with an organization chart. With the advent of the high-speed digital computer for conducting simulated experiments, this technique also has become very important to operations researchers. Thus *simulation* has become an *experimental arm of operations research.*

The emphasis in the preceding chapters was on formulating and solving mathematical models that represent real systems. One of the main strengths of this approach is that it abstracts the essence of the problem and reveals its underlying structure, thereby providing insight into the cause-and-effect relationships within the system. Therefore, if it is possible to construct a mathematical model that is both a reasonable idealization of the problem and amenable to solution, this analytical approach usually is superior to simulation. However, many problems are so complex that they cannot be solved analytically. Thus, even though simulation tends to be a relatively expensive procedure, it often provides the only practical approach to a problem.

Within operations research, simulation typically involves the construction of a model that is also largely mathematical in nature. Rather than describing the overall behavior of the system directly, the *simulation model* describes the operation of the system in terms of *individual events* of the individual components of the system. In particular, the system is divided into elements whose behavior can be predicted, at least in terms of probability distributions, for each of the various possible states of the system and its inputs. The interrelationships among the elements also are built into the model. Thus simulation provides a means of dividing the model-building job into smaller component parts that can be formulated more readily (e.g., a component part might be a simple queueing system) and then combining these component parts in their natural order. After constructing the model, we can then activate it by using random numbers to generate simulated events over time according to the appropriate probability distributions. The result is a simulation of the actual operation of the system over time, and we can record its aggregate behavior. By repeating this process for the various alternative configurations for the design and operating policies of the system, and by comparing their performances, we can identify the most promising configurations. Because of statistical error, it is impossible to guarantee that the configuration yielding the best simulated performance is indeed the optimal one, but it should be at least near optimal if the simulated experiment was designed properly.

Thus simulation typically is nothing more or less than the technique of performing *sampling experiments* on the model of the system. The experiments are done on the model rather than on the real system itself only because the latter would be too inconvenient, expensive, and time consuming. Otherwise, simulated experiments should be viewed as virtually indistinguishable from ordinary statistical experiments, so that they also should be based upon sound statistical theory. Simulated experiments usually are executed on a computer because of the vast amount of data being generated and processed rather than because of any inherent relationship between the experiment and the computer.

23.1 Illustrative Examples

EXAMPLE 1

Suppose you were offered a chance to play a game whereby you would repeatedly flip an unbiased coin until the *difference* between the number of heads tossed and the number of tails tossed is *three*. You would be required to pay $1 for each flip of the coin, but you would receive $8 at the end of each play of the game. You are not allowed to quit during a play of the game. Thus you win money if the number of flips required is fewer than eight, but you lose money if more than eight flips are required. How would you decide whether or not to play this game?

Many people would base this decision on simulation, although they probably would not call it by that name. (There is also an analytical solution for this game, but it is not a particularly elementary one.) In this case, simulation amounts to nothing more than playing the game alone many times until it becomes clear whether it is worthwhile playing for money. Half an hour spent in repeatedly flipping a coin and recording the earnings or losses that would have resulted might be sufficient.

How would this simulated experiment be executed on a computer? Although the computer cannot flip coins, it can generate numbers. Therefore, it would generate (or be given) a sequence of random digits, each of which would correspond to a flip of a coin. (The generation of random numbers is discussed in Sec. 23.2.) The probability distribution for the outcome of a flip is that the probability of a head is $\frac{1}{2}$ and the probability of a tail is $\frac{1}{2}$, whereas there are 10 possible values of a random digit, each having a probability of $\frac{1}{10}$. Therefore, five of these values (say, 0, 1, 2, 3, 4) would be assigned an association with a *head* and the other five (say, 5, 6, 7, 8, 9) with a *tail*. Thus the computer would simulate the playing of the game by examining each new random digit generated and labeling it a *head* or a *tail*, according to its value. It would continue doing this, recording the outcome of each simulated play of the game, as long as desired.

To illustrate the computer approach to this simulated experiment, we suppose that the computer generated the following sequence of random digits:

8, 1, 3, 7, 2, 7, 1, 6, 5, 5, 7, 9, 0, 0, 3, 4, 3, 5, 6, 8, 5,
8, 9, 4, 8, 0, 4, 8, 6, 5, 3, 5, 9, 2, 5, 7, 9, 7, 2, 9, 3, 9,
8, 5, 8, 9, 2, 5, 7, 6, 9, 7, 6, 0, 7, 3, 9, 8, 2, 7, 1, 0, 3,
2, 6, 2, 7, 1, 3, 7, 0, 4, 4, 1, 8, 3, 2, 1, 3, 9, 5, 9, 0, 5,
0, 3, 8, 7, 8, 9, 5, 4, 0, 8, 3, 8, 0, 1.

Thus, denoting a head by *H* and a tail by *T*, the first simulated play of the game is *THHTHTHTTTT*, requiring 11 simulated flips of a coin. The subsequent simulated plays of the game require 5, 5, 9, 7, 7, 5, 3, 17, 5, 5, 3, 9, and 7 simulated flips, respectively. This experiment has a sample size of 14 (14 simulated plays of the game), where the individual observations are the number of flips required for a play of the game. One useful statistic is

$$\text{Sample average} = \frac{11 + 5 + \cdots + 7}{14} = 7,$$

because the sample average provides an *estimate* of the true *mean* of the underlying probability distribution.

This sample average of 7 would seem to indicate that, on the average, you should win about \$1 each time you play the game. Therefore, if you do not have a relatively high aversion to risk, it appears that you should choose to play this game, preferably a large number of times. However, beware! One of the common errors in the use of simulation is that conclusions are based on overly small samples, because statistical analysis was inadequate or totally lacking. In this case, the *sample standard deviation* is 3.67, so that the estimated *standard deviation* of the *sample average* is $3.67/\sqrt{14} \approx 0.98$. Therefore, even if it is assumed that the probability distribution of the number of flips required for a play of the game is a *normal distribution* (which is a gross assumption because the true distribution is *skewed*), any reasonable *confidence interval* for the true *mean* of this distribution would extend far above 8. Hence a much larger sample size is required before we can draw a valid conclusion at a reasonable level of statistical significance. Unfortunately, because the standard deviation of a sample average is inversely proportional to the *square root* of the sample size, a large increase in the sample size is required to yield a relatively small increase in the precision of the estimate of the true mean. In this case, it appears that an additional 100 simulated plays of the game might be adequate.

It so happens that the true *mean* of the number of flips required for a play of this game is 9. Thus, in the long run, you actually would lose about $1 each time you played the game.

EXAMPLE 2

Consider the M/M/1 queueing theory model (Poisson input, exponential service times, and single server) that was discussed at the beginning of Sec. 16.6. Although this model already has been solved analytically, it will be instructive to consider how to study it using simulation.

To summarize the physical operation of the system, arriving customers enter the queue, eventually are serviced by the server, and then leave. Thus it is necessary for the simulation model to describe and synchronize the arrival of customers and the servicing of customers. The two methods for handling such synchronization in a digital computer are *fixed-time incrementing* and *next-event incrementing*. They will be described in turn.

With **fixed-time incrementing**, the following two-step procedure is used, beginning with the system in its initial state at a given point in time. First, *advance time* by a small *fixed amount*; add 1 to a register that serves as the master clock for the system to record the passage of this time. Second, *update the system* by determining what events occurred during this elapsed time unit and what the resulting state of the system is. Repeat these two steps for as many time units as desired.

For the queueing-theory model under consideration, only two types of events can occur during each of these elapsed time units, namely, one or more *arrivals* and one or more *service completions*. Furthermore, the probability of two or more arrivals or of two or more service completions during a time unit is negligible for this model if the time unit is relatively short. Thus the only two possible events during such a time unit that need to be investigated are the arrival of one customer and the service completion for one customer. Each of these events has a known probability. Therefore, just as in Example 1, to simulate whether an event occurs the computer only needs to generate a random number. For example, suppose that the probability that a customer will arrive during an elapsed time unit is 0.007. The computer would need to generate 1 of the 1,000 possible three-digit numbers $(000, 001, \ldots, 999)$ at random. By associating seven of the possible numbers (say, $000, \ldots, 006$) with the event occurring, and the remaining numbers with the event not occurring, the random number generated determines the actual simulated outcome for that time unit. If a customer were in the process of being served, the computer would be programmed to use this same method to determine if a simulated service completion occurs during the elapsed time unit, given the probability of such a completion. However, if no customer were being served, the computer would decide automatically that no service completion had occurred during the elapsed time unit. To implement this procedure, the computer would use an indicator that would be given one of two numerical values, depending upon whether the server was busy serving a customer. Similarly, a counter would be used to record the current number of customers in the queue (waiting to be served).

Thus updating the system after an elapsed time unit amounts to updating the numbers that should be inserted into the indicator and the counter. At the same time, the computer would record the desired information about the aggregate behavior of the system during this time unit. For example, it could record the *number of customers* in the queueing system and the *waiting time* of any customer who just completed his wait. If it is sufficient to estimate only the mean rather than the probability distribution of each of these random variables, the computer would merely add the value (if any) for the current time unit to a cumulative sum. The sample averages would be obtained after the simulation run was completed by dividing these sums by the sample sizes involved, namely, the total elapsed time (number of time units) and the total number of customers, respectively.

Next-event incrementing differs from fixed-time incrementing in that the master clock is incremented by a *variable* amount rather than by a fixed amount each time. Conceptually, the next-event incrementing procedure keeps the simulated system running without interruption until an event occurs, at which point the computer pauses momentarily to record the change in the system. To implement this conceptual idea, the computer actually proceeds by keeping track of when the next few simulated events are scheduled to occur, jumping in simulated time to the first of these events, and updating the system. This cycle is repeated as many times as desired.

For this example the computer needs to keep track of two future events, namely, the next arrival and the next service completion (if a customer currently is being served). These times are obtained by taking a random observation from the probability distribution of interarrival and service times, respectively. As before, the computer takes such a random observation by generating and using a random number. (This technique is discussed subsequently in Sec. 23.2.) Thus, each time an arrival or service completion occurs, the computer first determines how long it will be until the next time this event will occur and then adds this time to the current clock time.[1] This sum is then stored in a computer file. To determine which event will occur next, the computer finds the minimum of the clock times stored in the file. This procedure will be illustrated in Sec. 23.4 (see Table 23.8) for a specific single-server queueing system.

Several pertinent questions about how to conduct a simulation study of this type still remain to be answered. These answers are presented in a broader context in subsequent sections.

---

[1] If the service completion leaves no customers in the system, then the generation of the time until the next service completion is postponed until the next arrival occurs.

23.2 Formulating and Implementing a Simulation Model

CONSTRUCTING THE MODEL

The first step in a simulation study is to develop a model representing the system to be investigated. This step requires the analyst to become thoroughly familiar with the operating realities of the system and the objectives of the study. Given this requirement, the analyst probably would attempt to reduce the real system to a logical flow diagram. The system is thereby broken down into a set of components linked together by a master flow diagram, where the components themselves may be broken down into subcomponents, and so on. Ultimately the system is decomposed into a set of elements for which operating rules may be given. These operating rules predict the events that will be generated by the corresponding elements, perhaps in terms of probability distributions. After specifying these elements, rules, and logical linkages, the analyst needs to test the model thoroughly piece by piece. This testing can be done partially by performing a gross version of the simulation on a calculator and checking whether each input is received from the appropriate source and whether each output is acceptable to the next submodel. However, the individual components of the model also should be tested alone to verify that their internal performance is reasonably consistent with reality.

It should be emphasized that, like any operations research model, the simulation model need not be a completely realistic representation of the real system. In fact, it appears that most simulation models err on the side of being overly realistic rather than overly idealized. With the former approach, the model easily degenerates into a mass of trivia and meandering details, so that a great deal of programming and computer time is required to obtain a small amount of information. Furthermore, failing to strip away trivial factors to get down to the core of the system may obscure the significance of those results that are obtained.

If the behavior of an element cannot be predicted exactly, given the state of the system, it is better to take random observations from the probability distributions involved than to use averages to simulate the performance of this element. This statement is true even when one is interested in only the average aggregate performance of the system, because combining average performances for the individual elements may result in something far from average for the overall system.

One question that may arise when choosing probability distributions for the model is whether to use frequency distributions of historical data or to seek the theoretical probability distribution that best fits these data. The latter alternative usually is preferable because it avoids reproducing the idiosyncrasies of a certain period in the past.

GENERATING RANDOM NUMBERS

As the examples in Sec. 23.1 demonstrated, implementing a simulation model requires random numbers to obtain random observations from probability

Table 23.1 **Table of random digits**[†]

09656	96657	64842	49222	49506	10145	48455	23505	90430	04180
24712	55799	60857	73479	33581	17360	30406	05842	72044	90764
07202	96341	23699	76171	79126	04512	15426	15980	88898	06358
84575	46820	54083	43918	46989	05379	70682	43081	66171	38942
38144	87037	46626	70529	27918	34191	98668	33482	43998	75733
48048	56349	01986	29814	69800	91609	65374	22928	09704	59343
41936	58566	31276	19952	01352	18834	99596	09302	20087	19063
73391	94006	03822	81845	76158	41352	40596	14325	27020	17546
57580	08954	73554	28698	29022	11568	35668	59906	39557	27217
92646	41113	91411	56215	69302	86419	61224	41936	56939	27816
07118	12707	35622	81485	73354	49800	60805	05648	28898	60933
57842	57831	24130	75408	83784	64307	91620	40810	06539	70387
65078	44981	81009	33697	98324	46928	34198	96032	98426	77488
04294	96120	67629	55265	26248	40602	25566	12520	89785	93932
48381	06807	43775	09708	73199	53406	02910	83292	59249	18597
00459	62045	19249	67095	22752	24636	16965	91836	00582	46721
38824	81681	33323	64086	55970	04849	24819	20749	51711	86173
91465	22232	02907	01050	07121	53536	71070	26916	47620	01619
50874	00807	77751	73952	03073	69063	16894	85570	81746	07568
26644	75871	15618	50310	72610	66205	82640	86205	73453	90232

[†] Reproduced with permission from The Rand Corporation, *A Million Random Digits with 100,000 Normal Deviates*. Copyright, The Free Press, Glencoe, Ill., 1955, top of p. 182.

distributions. One method for generating such random numbers is to use a physical device such as a spinning disk or an electronic randomizer. Several tables of random numbers have been generated in this way, including one containing 1 million random digits, published by the Rand Corporation. An excerpt from the Rand table is given in Table 23.1.

Various relatively sophisticated statistical procedures have been proposed for testing whether a sequence of numbers constitutes a sample of random numbers or not.[1] Basically the requirements are that each successive number in the sequence must have an equal probability of taking on any one of the possible values, and it must be statistically independent of the other numbers in the sequence. In other words, the numbers need to be random observations from a discrete version of the *uniform distribution.*

If a computer is to be used for executing the simulation, the random numbers it needs could be fed into the computer from one of the available tables. However, it is more common for the computer itself to generate the random numbers. There are a number of methods for generating them, of which the most popular are the *congruential methods* (additive, multiplicative, and mixed). The *mixed congruential method* has become probably the most widely used in recent years, so we shall focus on this approach.

---

[1] See Selected References 4 and 11 for further information about these tests and the generation of random numbers.

The **mixed congruential method** generates a *sequence* of random numbers by always calculating the next random number from the last one obtained, given an initial random number x_0 (called the *seed*), which may be obtained from some published source such as the Rand table. In particular, it calculates the $(n + 1)$st random number, x_{n+1}, from the nth random number, x_n, by using the recurrence relation

$$x_{n+1} \equiv (ax_n + c)(\text{modulo } m),$$

where a, c, and m are positive integers ($a < m, c < m$). This mathematical notation signifies that x_{n+1} is the *remainder* when $(ax_n + c)$ is divided by m. Thus the *possible* values of x_{n+1} are $0, 1, \ldots, m - 1$, so that m represents the desired number of *different* values that could be generated for the random numbers. To illustrate, suppose that $m = 8$, $a = 5$, $c = 7$, and $x_0 = 4$. The resulting sequence of random numbers is calculated in Table 23.2. (The sequence cannot be continued further because it would just begin repeating the numbers in the same order.) Note that this sequence includes each of the eight possible numbers exactly once. This property is desirable, but it does not occur with some choices of a and c. (Try $a = 4$, $c = 7$, $x_0 = 3$.) Fortunately, there are rules available for choosing values of a and c that will guarantee this property. (There are no restrictions on the seed, x_0, because it affects only where the sequence begins and not the progression of numbers.)

For a binary computer with a word size of b bits, the usual choice for m is

Table 23.2 Illustration of mixed congruential method

n	x_n	$5x_n + 7$	$\dfrac{5x_n + 7}{8}$	x_{n+1}
0	4	27	$3 + \dfrac{3}{8}$	3
1	3	22	$2 + \dfrac{6}{8}$	6
2	6	37	$4 + \dfrac{5}{8}$	5
3	5	32	$4 + \dfrac{0}{8}$	0
4	0	7	$0 + \dfrac{7}{8}$	7
5	7	42	$5 + \dfrac{2}{8}$	2
6	2	17	$2 + \dfrac{1}{8}$	1
7	1	12	$1 + \dfrac{4}{8}$	4

$m = 2^b$; this is the total number of nonnegative integers that can be expressed within the capacity of the word size. (Any undesired integers that arise in the sequence of random numbers are just not used.) With this choice of m, we can ensure that each possible number occurs exactly once before any number is repeated by selecting any of the values $a = 1, 5, 9, 13, \ldots$ and $c = 1, 3, 5, 7, \ldots$. For a decimal computer with a word size of d digits, the usual choice for m is $m = 10^d$, and the same property is ensured by selecting any of the values $a = 1, 21, 41, 61, \ldots$ and $c = 1, 3, 7, 9, 11, 13, 17, 19, \ldots$ (that is, all positive *odd* integers *except* those ending with the digit 5). The specific selection can be made on the basis of the *serial correlation* between successively generated numbers, which differs considerably among these alternatives.[1]

Frequently, random numbers with only a relatively small number of digits are desired. For example, suppose that only three digits are desired, so that the possible values can be expressed as $000, 001, \ldots, 999$. In such a case, the usual procedure still is to use $m = 2^b$ or $m = 10^d$, so that an extremely large number of random numbers can be generated before the sequence starts repeating itself. However, except for purposes of calculating the next random number, all but three digits of each random number would be discarded. One convention is to take the *last* three digits (i.e., the three trailing digits).

The **multiplicative congruential method** is just the special case of the mixed congruential method where $c = 0$. The *additive congruential method* also is similar, but it sets $a = 1$ and replaces c by some random number preceding x_n in the sequence, for example, x_{n-1} (so that more than one seed is required to start calculating the sequence).

Strictly speaking, the numbers generated by the computer should not be called random numbers because they are predictable and reproducible (which sometimes is advantageous). Therefore, they are sometimes given the name *pseudorandom numbers*. However, the important point is that they satisfactorily play the role of random numbers in the simulation if the method used to generate them is valid.

GENERATING RANDOM OBSERVATIONS FROM A PROBABILITY DISTRIBUTION

Given a sequence of random numbers, how can one generate a sequence of random observations from a given probability distribution?

For simple discrete distributions, one answer is quite evident, as demonstrated by the examples of Sec. 23.1. Merely allocate the possible values of a random number to the various numbers in the probability distribution in direct proportion to the respective probabilities of those numbers. For example, consider the probability distribution of the outcome of a throw of two dice. It is known that the probability of throwing a 2 is $\frac{1}{36}$ (as is the probability of throwing

---

[1] See Coveyou, R. R.: "Serial Correlation in the Generation of Pseudo-Random Numbers," *Journal of the Association of Computing Machinery*, 7:72–74, 1960.

a 12), the probability of throwing a 3 is $\frac{2}{36}$, and so on. Therefore, $\frac{1}{36}$ of the possible values of a random number should be associated with throwing a 2, $\frac{2}{36}$ of the values with throwing a 3, and so forth. Thus, if two-digit random numbers are being used, 72 of the 100 values would be selected for consideration, so that a random number would be rejected if it took on any one of the other 28 values. Then 2 of the 72 possible values (say, 00 and 01) would be assigned an association with throwing a 2, 4 of them (say, 02, 03, 04, and 05) would be assigned to throwing a 3, and so on.

For more complicated distributions, the answer still is essentially the same although the procedure is slightly more involved. The *first step* is to construct the cumulative distribution function $F(x) = P\{X \leq x\}$, where X is the random variable involved. This step can be done by *writing the equation* for this function, or by *graphically plotting* the function, or by *developing a table* giving the value of x for uniformly spaced values of $F(x)$ from 0 to 1. The *second step* is to generate a random decimal number between 0 and 1. This step is done by obtaining a random integer number having the desired number of digits (including any leading zeros) and then placing a decimal point in front of it. The *final step* is to set $P\{X \leq x\}$ equal to the random decimal number and solve for x. This value of x is the desired random observation from the probability distribution. This procedure is illustrated in Fig. 23.1 for the case where the cumulative distribution function is plotted graphically and the random decimal number happens to be 0.5269.

When the given probability distribution is continuous, the procedure just outlined actually approximates this continuous distribution by a discrete distribution whose irregularly spaced points have equal probabilities. However, this situation is not particularly serious because the approximation can be made as accurate as desired if we use a sufficiently large number of digits for the random number. Perhaps the greatest danger is that the approximation will be

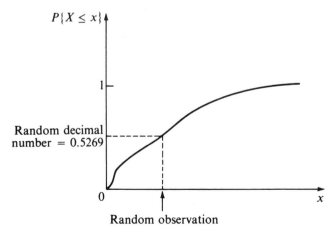

Figure 23.1 **Illustration of procedure for obtaining a random observation from a given probability distribution.**

adequate everywhere *except* in the extreme tails of the distribution. For example, suppose that three-digit random numbers are being used. Then the values of $P\{X \leq x\}$ that will be sampled range from 0.000 to 0.999.[1] However, it may be that those rare occurrences when the actual value taken on by X falls outside the range permitted in the simulation would have a critical impact on the system. One refinement that would rectify this problem is to generate a second random number, whenever the first one is (for the case of three-digit random numbers) 000 or 999, to select a value of $P\{X \leq x\}$ within the range from 0.000000 to 0.000999 or from 0.999000 to 0.999999.

Although the graphical procedure illustrated by Fig. 23.1 is convenient if the simulation is done manually, the computer must revert to some alternative approach such as the two mentioned earlier. One of these involved using a table of the cumulative distribution function. Having the computer use such a table is essentially equivalent to using the graphical procedure manually. The disadvantages of this *table look-up approach* are the great amount of work required to develop the table and the limitations on accuracy because of computer storage limitations. The other approach mentioned earlier requires *writing the equation* for the cumulative distribution function and then solving for the point where this function equals the random decimal number. This approach leads to a simple explicit solution for several important probability distributions, to be illustrated soon for the exponential and Erlang distributions. For other cases, time-consuming numerical methods would be required to obtain the solution in this way. Fortunately, for certain important probability distributions, special techniques have been developed for efficiently generating random observations from that particular distribution. Two of the simplest of these techniques, which are applicable to the normal distribution and the chi-square distribution, respectively, are described at the end of this section.

Consider the *exponential distribution* (see Sec. 16.4) that has the cumulative distribution function

$$P\{X \leq x\} = 1 - e^{-\alpha x}, \quad \text{for } x \geq 0,$$

where $1/\alpha$ is the mean of the distribution. Applying the *equation approach* just discussed, set this function equal to a *random decimal number* (denoted by r) between 0 and 1. Thus

$$1 - e^{-\alpha x} = r,$$

so

$$e^{-\alpha x} = 1 - r.$$

Therefore, taking the natural logarithm of both sides,

$$\ln(e^{-\alpha x}) = \ln(1 - r),$$

---

[1] A slight refinement is to add a 5 in the next decimal place of each value to center the range, 0.0005 to 0.9995.

so that

$$-\alpha x = \ln{(1-r)},$$

which yields

$$x = \frac{\ln{(1-r)}}{-\alpha}$$

as the desired random observation from the exponential distribution. (It should be noted that other, more complicated, techniques have also been developed for the exponential distribution,[1] and some of these techniques may be faster for the computer than calculating a logarithm.)

Because a random decimal number between 0 and 1 is just a random observation from a discrete form of the *uniform distribution* between 0 and 1, $(1-r)$ is itself a random decimal number. Therefore, to save a subtraction, it is common in practice simply to use the *original* random decimal number r directly in place of $(1-r)$.

A natural extension of this procedure for the exponential distribution also can be used to generate a random observation from an *Erlang* (gamma) *distribution* (see Sec. 16.7). The sum of k independent exponential random variables, each with mean $1/k\alpha$, has the Erlang distribution with shape parameter k and mean $1/\alpha$. Therefore, given a sequence of k random decimal numbers between 0 and 1, say, $r_1, r_2, \ldots, r_k$, the desired random observation from the Erlang distribution is

$$x = \sum_{i=1}^{k} \frac{\ln{(1-r_i)}}{-k\alpha},$$

which reduces to

$$x = -\frac{1}{k\alpha} \ln{\left\{ \prod_{i=1}^{k} (1-r_i) \right\}},$$

where Π denotes multiplication. Once again, the subtractions may be eliminated simply by using the r_i directly in place of the $(1-r_i)$.

A particularly simple technique for generating a random observation from a *normal distribution* is obtained by applying the central limit theorem. Because a random decimal number essentially has a *uniform distribution* from 0 to 1, it has mean $\frac{1}{2}$ and standard deviation $1/\sqrt{12}$. Therefore, this theorem implies that the sum of n random decimal numbers has approximately a normal distribution with mean $n/2$ and standard deviation $\sqrt{n/12}$. Thus, if $r_1, r_2, \ldots, r_n$ are a sample of random decimal numbers, then

$$x = \frac{\sigma}{\sqrt{n/12}} \sum_{i=1}^{n} r_i + \left(\mu - \frac{n}{2} \frac{\sigma}{\sqrt{n/12}} \right)$$

[1] For example, see Knuth, D. E.: *The Art of Computer Programming*, Vol. 2, *Semi-Numerical Algorithms*, chap. 3, Addison-Wesley, Reading, Mass., 1969.

is a random observation from an approximately normal distribution with mean μ and standard deviation σ. This approximation is an excellent one (except in the tails of the distribution), even with small values of n. Thus values of n from 5 to 10 often are used; $n = 12$ also is a convenient value, because it eliminates the square root terms from the preceding expression.

Various other approximate or exact techniques for generating random observations from a normal distribution have also been developed.

A simple method for handling the *chi-square distribution* is to use the fact that it is obtained by summing squares of standardized normal random variables. Thus, if $y_1, y_2, \ldots, y_n$ are a sample of random observations from a normal distribution with mean 0 and standard deviation 1, such as could be obtained (approximately) by the technique just described, then

$$x = \sum_{i=1}^{n} y_i^2$$

is a random observation from a chi-square distribution with n degrees of freedom.

PREPARING A SIMULATION PROGRAM

A number of detailed decisions confront the person who must write the computer program for executing a simulation. Although an extensive discussion of these issues is beyond the scope of this book, we shall mention several major considerations.

The basic purpose of most simulation studies is to compare alternatives. Therefore, the simulation program must be flexible enough to accommodate readily the alternatives that will be considered. Because it often is impossible to predict exactly what interesting alternatives will be uncovered during the course of the study, it is essential that flexibility and provision for rapid, simple modifications be built into the program.

Most of the instructions in a simulation program are logical operations, whereas the relatively little actual arithmetic work required is usually of a very simple type. This consideration should be reflected in the choice of computer equipment and programming language to be used.

The considerations just mentioned actually provided part of the motivation for an important breakthrough in the art of simulation that occurred during the early 1960s, namely, the development of general *simulation programming languages*. For example, two early languages that continue to be widely used are GPSS[1] and SIMSCRIPT.[2] A third that is widely used outside the United States is SIMULA.[3] These languages are designed especially to expedite the type of programming (and reprogramming) unique to simulation. Their specific pur-

[1] See Schriber, T: *Simulation Using GPSS*, Wiley, New York, 1974.
[2] See Kiviat, P. J., R. Villanneva, and H. M. Markowitz: *The SIMSCRIPT 11.5 Programming Language*, Consolidated Analysis Centers, Inc., Los Angeles, 1973.
[3] See Birtwistle, G., O.-J. Dahl, B. Myhrhaug, and K. Nygaard: *SIMULA BEGIN*, Auerbach, Philadelphia, 1973.

poses include the following. One objective is to provide a convenient means of describing the elements that commonly appear in simulation models. A second is to expedite changing the design and operating policies of the system being simulated, so that a large number of configurations (including some suggested during the course of the study) can be considered easily. Another service provided by the simulation languages is some type of internal timing and control mechanism, with related commands, to assist in the kind of bookkeeping that is required when executing a simulation run. They also are designed to obtain data and statistics conveniently on the aggregate behavior of the system being simulated. Finally, these languages provide simple operational procedures, such as introducing changes into the simulation model, initializing the state of the model, altering the kind of output data to be generated, and stacking a series of simulation runs.

For all these reasons a simulation program almost always should be written in one of these simulation languages rather than in a general programming language. The tremendous savings in programming time ordinarily provided by the simulation languages usually compensate for any slight loss in computer running time.

Finally, it should be emphasized that the strategy of the simulation study should be planned carefully before finishing the simulation program. Merely letting the computer compile masses of data in a blind search for attractive alternatives is far from adequate. Simulation basically is a means for conducting an experimental investigation. Therefore, just as with a physical experiment, careful attention should be given to the construction of a theory of formal hypotheses to be tested and to the skillful design of a statistical experiment that will yield valid conclusions. This subject is discussed in Secs. 23.3 and 23.4.

VALIDATING THE MODEL

The typical simulation model consists of a high number of elements, rules, and logical linkages. Therefore, even when the individual components have been carefully tested, numerous small approximations can still cumulate into gross distortions in the output of the overall model. Consequently, after writing and debugging the computer program, it is important to test the *validity* of the model for reasonably predicting the aggregate behavior of the system being simulated.

When some form of the real system has already been in operation, its performance data should be compared with the corresponding output data from the model. Standard statistical tests can sometimes be used to determine whether the differences in the means, variances, and probability distributions generating the two sets of data are statistically significant. The time-dependent behavior of the data might also be compared statistically. If the data are not amenable to statistical analysis, another approach is to ask personnel familiar with the behavior of the real system if they can discriminate between the two sets of data.

If the model is intended to simulate alternative design configurations or operating policies for a proposed system for which no actual data are available, it may be worthwhile to conduct a *field test* to collect some real data to compare with the output of the model. Conducting such a test might involve constructing a small prototype of some version of the proposed system and placing it into operation. Another possibility might be to alter temporarily an existing system to correspond to one of the proposals.

However, field tests frequently are too expensive and time consuming to be used. Without any real data as a standard of comparison, the only way to validate the overall model is to have knowledgeable people carefully check the credibility of output data for a variety of situations. Even when no basis exists for checking the reasonableness of the data for a *single* situation, some conclusions usually can be drawn about how the *relative* performance of the system should change as various parameters are changed. It is especially important to convince the *decision maker* of the credibility of the model, so he will be willing to use it at least to *aid* his decisions. If the model may be used again in the future, careful records of its predictions and of actual results should be kept to continue the validation process.

23.3 Experimental Design for Simulation

SELECTING A STATISTICAL PROCEDURE[1]

The underlying statistical theory applicable to *simulated* experimentation is essentially indistinguishable from that for *physical* experimentation. Thus the design of a simulated experiment should be based upon the large body of knowledge comprising the science of statistics.

There are, however, differences between physical and simulated experimentation regarding the emphasis placed on using the various types of statistical procedures. Physical experiments frequently involve testing hypotheses about the value of a population parameter or about the equality of several population means. Simulated experiments typically place more emphasis on *optimization*. It probably is taken for granted that alternative design configurations have different population means for the index of performance of the system. Instead, the objective of the simulation study often is to find the alternative yielding the greatest mean index of performance.[2] Hence *multiple decision tests* and complete or partial *ordering procedures* frequently are appropriate for simulated experiments. Furthermore, *sequential procedures* tend to be useful, both because the evolution of the experiments may be difficult to predict and because a simulated experiment often can be resumed relatively easily.

---

[1] This subsection assumes some knowledge of statistical procedures.

[2] In some cases, however, the objective is just to *describe* the performance of proposed systems or policies for management's evaluation and decision making, so *point estimates* and *confidence intervals* probably would be obtained. Simulated experiments also are occasionally conducted to determine which factors significantly influence the performance of the system (perhaps to guide subsequent experimentation), in which case *analysis of variance* probably would be used.

Another difference between these two types of experiments is the degree to which the experimental conditions can be held constant when comparing alternatives. Only simulated experiments can control the variability in the behavior of the elements of the system during the course of the experiment. By reproducing the same sequence of random numbers for each alternative simulated, it often is possible to reproduce an identical sequence of events. This reproduction sharpens the contrast between alternatives by reducing the residual variation in the differences in the aggregate performance of the system, so that much smaller sample sizes are required to detect statistically significant differences. Therefore, this approach usually is far superior to generating new random numbers for each alternative. The fact that reproducing the same random numbers does not yield statistically independent results should not be of great concern. The correct procedure for comparing only two alternatives is to pair the results regarding the aggregate performance of the system that were produced by the same events. Because these pairs of results are obtained under the same experimental conditions, the differences between them become the relevant sample observations. This sample would be used to test the hypothesis that the mean of these differences is zero and to obtain a confidence interval estimate of this mean. This result would thereby indicate whether there is a statistically significant difference between the means of the performance index of the system for the two alternatives. If more than two alternatives need to be compared, the *Bonferroni inequality* can be used to construct *simultaneous confidence intervals* on the means of the differences for the various pairs of alternatives.[1]

Often it is possible to express the alternatives in terms of the values of one or more continuous design variables. In these cases, there actually is an infinite number of alternatives (although the differences among some of them are minute). Because it would be impossible to simulate all of them, it is necessary to take a selective sample of these alternatives and then estimate the value of the design variables that will maximize some index of performance for the system. There exists considerable literature that gives efficient procedures for experimentally determining the maximum of a mathematical function to within a specified accuracy.[2]

VARIANCE-REDUCING TECHNIQUES

Because considerable computer time usually is required for simulation runs, it is important to obtain as much and as precise information as possible from the amount of simulation that can be done. Unfortunately, there has been a tendency in practice to apply simulation uncritically without giving adequate thought to

[1] See Bowker, Albert H. and Gerald J. Lieberman: *Engineering Statistics*, 2d ed., pp. 304–308, Prentice-Hall, Englewood Cliffs, N.J., 1972.

[2] A survey of the procedures available for this problem is given by Wilde, Douglass J.: *Optimum Seeking Methods*, Prentice-Hall, Englewood Cliffs, N.J., 1964.

the efficiency of the experimental design. This tendency has occurred despite the fact that considerable progress has been made in developing special techniques for increasing the precision (i.e., decreasing the variance) of sample estimators.

These variance-reducing techniques often are called **Monte Carlo techniques** (a term sometimes applied to simulation in general). Because they tend to be rather sophisticated, it is not possible to explore them deeply here. However, we shall attempt to impart the flavor of these techniques and the great increase in precision they sometimes provide by presenting two of them in the following example.

Consider the *exponential distribution* whose parameter has a value of 1. Thus its probability density function is $f(x) = e^{-x}$, as shown in Fig. 23.2, and its cumulative distribution function is $F(x) = 1 - e^{-x}$. It is known that the mean of this distribution is 1. However, suppose that this mean were not known and that we want to estimate this mean by using simulation.

To provide a standard of comparison for the two variance-reducing techniques, we consider first the straightforward simulation approach, sometimes called the *crude Monte Carlo technique*. This approach involves generating some *random observations* from the exponential distribution under consideration and then using the *average* of these observations to estimate the mean. As described in Sec. 23.2, these random observations would be

$$x_i = -\ln(1 - r_i), \quad \text{for } i = 1, 2, \ldots, n,$$

where $r_1, r_2, \ldots, r_n$ are random decimal numbers between 0 and 1. If we use a portion of Table 23.1 to obtain 10 such random decimal numbers, the resulting random observations are shown in Table 23.3. (These same random numbers also are used to illustrate the variance-reducing techniques to sharpen the comparison.) Notice that the sample average is 0.779, as opposed to the true mean of 1.000. However, because the standard deviation of the sample average happens to be $1/\sqrt{n}$, or $1/\sqrt{10}$ in this case (as could be estimated from the sample), an error of this amount or larger would occur approximately one-half of the time. Furthermore, because the standard deviation of a sample average is always

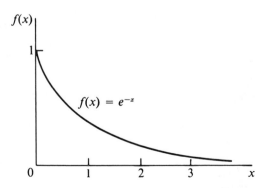

Figure 23.2 **Probability density function for example.**

Table 23.3 **Example for crude Monte Carlo technique**

i	Random number r_i[†]	Random observation $x_i = -\ln(1 - r_i)$
1	0.495	0.684
2	0.335	0.408
3	0.791	1.568
4	0.469	0.633
5	0.279	0.328
6	0.698	1.199
7	0.013	0.014
8	0.761	1.433
9	0.290	0.343
10	0.693	1.183

Total = 7.793
Estimate of mean = 0.779

[†] Actually, 0.0005 was added to the indicated value for each of the r_i, so that the range of their possible values would be from 0.0005 to 0.9995 rather than from 0.000 to 0.999.

inversely proportional to $\sqrt{n}$, this sample size would need to be quadrupled to reduce this standard deviation by one-half. These somewhat disheartening facts suggest the need for other techniques that would obtain such estimates more precisely and more efficiently.

A relatively simple Monte Carlo technique for obtaining better estimates is **stratified sampling**. There are two shortcomings of the crude Monte Carlo approach that are rectified by stratified sampling. First, by the very nature of randomness, a random sample may not provide a particularly uniform cross section of the distribution. For example, the random sample given in Table 23.3 has no observations between 0.014 and 0.328, even though the probability that a random observation will fall inside this interval is greater than $\frac{1}{4}$. Second, certain portions of a distribution may be more critical than others for obtaining a precise estimate, but random sampling gives no special priority to obtaining observations from these portions. For example, the tail of an exponential distribution is especially critical in determining its mean. However, the random sample in Table 23.3 includes no observations larger than 1.568, even though there is at least a small probability of *much* larger values. This explanation is the basic one for this particular sample average being far below the true mean. Stratified sampling circumvents these difficulties by dividing the distribution into portions called *strata*, where each stratum would be sampled individually with disproportionately heavy sampling of the more critical strata.

To illustrate, suppose that the distribution is divided into *three* strata in the manner shown in Table 23.4. These strata were chosen to correspond to

Table 23.4 **Formulation of stratified sampling example**

Stratum	Portion of distribution	Stratum random no.	Sample size	Sampling weight
1	$0 \leq F(x) \leq 0.64$	$r'_i = 0 + 0.64 r_i$	4	$w_i = \dfrac{4/10}{0.64} = \dfrac{5}{8}$
2	$0.64 \leq F(x) \leq 0.96$	$r'_i = 0.64 + 0.32 r_i$	4	$w_i = \dfrac{4/10}{0.32} = \dfrac{5}{4}$
3	$0.96 \leq F(x) \leq 1$	$r'_i = 0.96 + 0.04 r_i$	2	$w_i = \dfrac{2/10}{0.04} = 5$

observations approximately from 0 to 1, from 1 to 3, and from 3 to infinity, respectively. To ensure that the random observations generated for each stratum actually lie in that portion of the distribution, the random decimal numbers must be converted into the indicated range for $F(x)$, as shown in the third column of Table 23.4. The number of observations to be generated from each stratum is given in the fourth column.[1] The last column then shows the resulting *sampling weight* for each stratum, i.e., the *ratio* of the *sampling proportion* (the fraction of the total sample to be drawn from the stratum) to the *distribution proportion* (the probability of a random observation falling inside the stratum). These sampling weights roughly reflect the relative importance of the respective strata in determining the mean.

Given the formulation of the stratified sampling approach shown in Table 23.4, the same random numbers used in Table 23.3 yield the observations given in the fifth column in Table 23.5. However, it would not be correct to use the unweighted average of these observations to estimate the mean, because certain portions of the distributions have been sampled more than others. Therefore, before taking the average, divide the observations from each stratum by the sampling weight for that stratum to give proportionate weightings to the different portions of the distribution, as shown in the last column of Table 23.5. The resulting *weighted* average of 0.948 provides the desired estimate of the mean.

The second variance-reducing technique we shall mention is the method of **complementary random numbers**.[2] The motivation for this method is that the "luck of the draw" on the random decimal numbers generated may cause the average of the resulting random observations to be substantially on one side of the true mean, whereas the *complements* of those random decimal numbers (which are themselves random decimal numbers) would have tended to yield a nearly opposite result. (For example, the random decimal numbers in Table 23.3 average less than 0.5, and none are as large as 0.8, which led to an estimate substantially

---

[1] These sample sizes are roughly based on a recommended guideline that they be proportional to the *product* of the *probability* of a random observation falling inside the corresponding stratum *times* the *standard deviation* within this stratum.

[2] This method is a special case of the method of *antithetic variates*, which attempts to generate *pairs* of random observations having a high *negative* correlation, so that the combined average will tend to be closer to the mean.

Table 23.5 **Example for stratified sampling**

Stratum	i	Random number r_i	Stratum random no. r_i'	Stratum random observation $x_i' = -\ln(1 - r_i')$	Sampling weight w_i	$\dfrac{x_i'}{w_i}$
1	1	0.495	0.317	0.381	$\dfrac{5}{8}$	0.610
	2	0.335	0.215	0.242	$\dfrac{5}{8}$	0.387
	3	0.791	0.507	0.707	$\dfrac{5}{8}$	1.131
	4	0.469	0.300	0.357	$\dfrac{5}{8}$	0.571
2	5	0.279	0.729	1.306	$\dfrac{5}{4}$	1.045
	6	0.698	0.864	1.995	$\dfrac{5}{4}$	1.596
	7	0.013	0.644	1.033	$\dfrac{5}{4}$	0.826
	8	0.761	0.884	2.154	$\dfrac{5}{4}$	1.723
3	9	0.290	0.9716	3.561	5	0.712
	10	0.693	0.9877	4.398	5	0.880

Total = 9.481
Estimate of mean = 0.948

below the true mean.) Therefore, using *both* the original random decimal numbers *and* their complements to generate random observations and then calculating the *combined* sample average should provide a more precise estimator of the mean. This approach is illustrated in Table 23.6,[1] where the first three columns come from Table 23.3 and the last two columns use the complementary random decimal numbers, which results in a combined sample average of 0.920.

This example has suggested that the variance-reducing techniques provide a much more precise estimator of the mean than does straightforward simulation. These results definitely were not a coincidence, as a derivation of the variance of the estimators would show. In comparison with straightforward simulation, these techniques (including several more complicated ones not presented here) do indeed provide a much more precise estimator with the same amount of computer time, or they provide as precise an estimator with much less computer time. Despite the fact that additional analysis may be required to incorporate one

---

[1] It should be noted that 20 calculations of a logarithm were required in this case, in contrast to the 10 that were required by each of the preceding techniques.

Table 23.6 **Example for method of complementary random numbers**

i	Random number r_i	Random observation $x_i = -\ln(1 - r_i)$	Complementary random number $r_i' = 1 - r_i$	Random observation $x_i' = -\ln(1 - r_i')$
1	0.495	0.684	0.505	0.702
2	0.335	0.408	0.665	1.092
3	0.791	1.568	0.209	0.234
4	0.469	0.633	0.531	0.756
5	0.279	0.328	0.721	1.275
6	0.698	1.199	0.302	0.359
7	0.013	0.014	0.987	4.305
8	0.761	1.433	0.239	0.272
9	0.290	0.343	0.710	1.236
10	0.693	1.183	0.307	0.366

Total: 7.793   10.597

Estimate of mean $= \frac{1}{2}(0.779 + 1.060) = 0.920$

or more of these techniques into the simulation study, the rewards should not be forgone readily.

Although this example was a particularly simple one, it is often possible, though more difficult, to apply these techniques to much more complex problems. For example, suppose that the objective of the simulation study is to estimate the mean waiting time of customers in a queueing system (such as those described in Sec. 17.1). Because both the probability distribution of time between arrivals and the probability distribution of service times are involved, and because consecutive waiting times are not statistically independent, this problem may appear to be beyond the capabilities of the variance-reducing techniques. However, as has been described in detail elsewhere,[1] these techniques and others can indeed be applied to this type of problem very advantageously. For example, the method of *complementary random numbers* can be applied simply by repeating the original simulation run, substituting the complements of the original random decimal numbers to generate the corresponding random observations.

TACTICAL PROBLEMS

There are several special *tactical* issues that arise in connection with gathering the data from simulated experiments. We shall briefly describe these here and then subsequently elaborate on certain ways of dealing with them.

Many simulation studies are concerned with investigating systems that operate continually in a steady-state condition. Unfortunately, a simulation model cannot be operated this way; it must be started and stopped. Because of the artificiality introduced by the abrupt beginning of operation, the perfor-

[1] Ehrenfeld, S. and S. Ben-Tuvia: "The Efficiency of Statistical Simulation Procedures," *Techno-metrics*, **4**(2):257–275, 1962. Also see Selected References 6, 7, and 11 for a general discussion of the theory and application of various variance-reducing techniques.

mance of the simulated system does not become representative of the corresponding real-world system until it too has essentially reached a steady-state condition (i.e., until the probability distribution of the state of the simulated system has essentially reached a limiting *equilibrium* distribution). Thus one tactical problem is how to obtain data that are relevant for predicting the *steady-state* behavior of the real system.

The traditional way of dealing with this problem is to run the simulation model for some time without collecting data until it is believed that the simulated system has essentially reached a steady-state condition. Unfortunately, it is difficult to estimate just how long this *stabilization period* needs to be. Furthermore, available analytical results suggest that a surprisingly long period is required, so that a great deal of unproductive computer time must be expended. Section 23.4 presents a relatively new statistical approach that eliminates these difficulties.

A related tactical issue is the selection of the *starting conditions* for the simulated system. The traditional recommendation is that the simulated system should be started in a state as representative of steady-state conditions as possible to minimize the required length of the stabilization period. However, the underlying objective of the simulated experiment is to *estimate* these conditions, so little advance information may be available to guide the selection in this way. The procedure in Sec. 23.4 also eliminates this difficulty.

Most statistical sampling procedures assume that the experimental output data are in the form of a collection of distinct and statistically independent random observations from some underlying probability distribution. By contrast, because of the nature of the problems for which simulation is used, the observations from a simulated experiment are likely to be highly correlated. For example, there is a high correlation between the waiting times of consecutive customers in a queueing system. Furthermore, many measures of performance are such that the simulated experiment yields this measure continuously as a function of time rather than as a sequence of separate observations. Thus another tactical problem is how to collect the data so as to circumvent these difficulties.

One traditional method is to execute a series of completely separate and independent simulation runs of equal length and to use the average measure of performance for each run (excluding the initial stabilization period) as an individual observation. The main disadvantage is that each run requires an initial stabilization period for approaching a steady-state condition, so that much of the simulation time is unproductive. The second traditional method eliminates this disadvantage by making the runs consecutively, using the ending condition of one run as the steady-state starting condition for the next run. In other words, one continuous overall simulation run (except for the one initial stabilization period) is divided for bookkeeping purposes into a series of equal portions (runs). The average measure of performance for each portion is then treated as an individual observation. The disadvantage of this method is that it does not eliminate the correlation between observations entirely, even though it may reduce it considerably by making the portions sufficiently long.

Once again, these difficulties are eliminated by the statistical approach described in Sec. 23.4.

23.4 The Regenerative Method of Statistical Analysis

We have just described several difficult *tactical* problems in gathering data from simulated experiments and the shortcomings of traditional statistical procedures in dealing with these problems. We now present an innovative statistical approach that is especially designed to eliminate these problems.

The basic concept underlying this approach is that for many systems a simulation run can be divided into a series of **cycles** such that the behavior of the system during different cycles is both *statistically independent* and *identically distributed*. Thus, if we calculate some *statistic* to summarize the behavior of interest within each cycle, these statistics for the respective cycles constitute a series of independent and identically distributed observations that can be analyzed by standard statistical procedures. Because the system keeps going through these independent and identically distributed cycles whether or not it is in a steady-state condition, these observations are directly applicable from the outset for estimating the steady-state behavior of the system.

For cycles to possess these properties, they must each *begin* at the same **regeneration point**, i.e., at the point where the system again enters a certain special state from which the simulation can proceed without any knowledge of its past history. The system can be viewed as *regenerating* itself at this point in the sense that the probabilistic structure of the future behavior of the system depends upon being at this point and not on anything that happened previously. (This property is the *Markovian property* described in Sec. 15.2 for Markov chains.) A cycle *ends* when the system again reaches the regeneration point (when the next cycle begins). Thus the **length of a cycle** is just the elapsed time between consecutive occurrences of the regeneration point, which is a random variable that depends upon the evolution of the system.

When *next-event incrementing* is used, a typical regeneration point is a point at which an event has just occurred but no future events have yet been scheduled. Thus nothing needs to be known about the history of previous schedulings, and the simulation can start from scratch in scheduling future events. When *fixed-time incrementing* is used, a regeneration point is a point at which the probabilities of possible events occurring during the next unit of time do not depend upon when any past events occurred, but only on the current state of the system.

Not every system possesses regeneration points, so this **regenerative method** of collecting data cannot always be used. Furthermore, even when there are regeneration points, the one chosen to define the beginning and ending points of the cycles must recur frequently enough so that a substantial number of cycles will be obtained with a reasonable amount of computer time.[1] Thus some care must be taken to choose a suitable regeneration point.

---

[1] The theoretical requirements for the method are that the expected cycle length be *finite* and that the number of cycles would go to infinity if the system continued operating indefinitely.

Table 23.7 **Correspondence between random numbers and random observations for queueing system example**

Random number	Interarrival time	Service time
0	6	1
1	8	3
⋮	⋮	⋮
9	24	19

Perhaps the most important application of the regenerative method to date has been to the simulation of *queueing systems,* including *queueing networks* (see Sec. 16.9) such as the ones that arise in computer modeling.[1]

EXAMPLE Suppose that information needs to be obtained about the steady-state behavior of a system that can be formulated as a *single-server queueing system* (see Sec. 16.2). However, both the interarrival and service times have a *uniform distribution* with a range from 5 to 25 and from 0 to 20, respectively, so that analytical results are not available. Therefore, simulation with *next-event incrementing* is to be used to obtain the desired results.

Except for the distributions involved, the general approach is the same as described in Sec. 23.1 for Example 2. Suppose that *one-digit* random numbers are used to generate the random observations from the distributions, as shown in Table 23.7. Beginning the simulation run with *zero* customers in the system then yields the results summarized in Table 23.8 and Fig. 23.3, where the random numbers are obtained sequentially as needed from the tenth row of Table 23.1.[2]

For this system, one *regeneration point* is where an *arrival* occurs with *no* previous customers left. At this point, the probabilistic structure of when future arrivals and service completions will occur is completely independent of any previous history. The only relevant information is that the system has just entered the special state of having had *zero* customers *and* having the time until the next arrival reach *zero.* The simulation run would not previously have scheduled any future events but would now generate *both* the next interarrival time and the service time for the customer that just arrived.

The only other regeneration points for this system are where an arrival and a service completion occur simultaneously, with a prespecified number of customers in the system. These points would occur only rarely[3] for the real system

---

[1] See, for example, Iglehart, Donald L., and Gerald S. Shedler, "Regenerative Simulation of Response Times in Networks of Queues," *Journal of the Association for Computing Machinery,* **25**(3):449–460, 1978.

[2] When both an interarrival time and a service time need to be generated at the same time, the interarrival time is obtained first.

[3] More precisely, the probability is *zero* that an arrival and a service completion will occur at exactly the same time.

Table 23.8 **Simulation run for queueing system example**

Time	Number of customers	Random number	Next arrival	Next service completion
0	0	9	24	—
24	1	2, 6	34	37
34	2	4	48	37
37	1	6	48	50
48	2	4	62	50
50	1	1	62	53
53	0	—	62	—
62	1	1, 1	70	65
65	0	—	70	—
70	1	3, 9	82	89
82	2	1	90	89
89	1	4	90	98
90	2	1	98	98
98	2	1, 5	106	109
106	3	6	124	109
109	2	2	124	114
114	1	1	124	117
117	0	—	124	—
124	1	5, 6	140	137
137	0	—	140	—
140	1	9, 3	164	147
147	0	—	164	—
164	1			

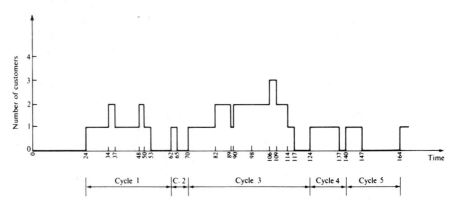

Figure 23.3 **Outcome of the simulation run for the queueing system example.**

because its distributions for interarrival and service times are *continuous*. However, they would occur with some frequency in the simulation run because Table 23.7 makes discrete the distributions that are actually used to generate the random observations. Therefore, one of these points actually could be chosen to define a *cycle*. However, the regeneration point described in the preceding paragraph occurs much more frequently and thus is a better choice. With this selection, the first five complete cycles of the simulation run are those shown in Fig. 23.3. (In most cases, you should have a considerably larger number of cycles in the entire simulation run in order to have sufficient precision in the statistical analysis.)

Various types of information about the steady-state behavior of the system can be obtained from this simulation run, including *point estimates* and *confidence intervals* for the expected number of customers in the system, the expected waiting time, and so on. In each case, it is necessary to use only the corresponding statistics from the respective cycles and the lengths of the cycles. We shall first present the general statistical expressions for the regenerative method and then apply them to this example.

STATISTICAL FORMULAS

Formally speaking, the statistical problem for the regenerative method is to obtain estimates of the expected value of some random variable X of interest. This estimate is to be obtained by calculating a statistic Y for each cycle such that

$$E(X) = \frac{E(Y)}{E(Z)},$$

where the random variable Z is an appropriate measure of the *size* of the cycle. Thus, if n complete cycles are generated during the simulation run, the data gathered are $Y_1, Y_2, \ldots, Y_n$ and $Z_1, Z_2, \ldots, Z_n$ for the respective cycles.

Letting $\bar{Y}$ and $\bar{Z}$, respectively, denote the sample averages for these two sets of data, the corresponding *point estimate* of $E(X)$ would be obtained from the formula

$$\text{Est}\{E(X)\} = \frac{\bar{Y}}{\bar{Z}}.$$

To obtain a *confidence interval estimate* of $E(X)$, we must first calculate several quantities from the data. These quantities include the *sample variances*

$$s_{11}^2 = \frac{1}{n-1} \sum_{i=1}^{n} (Y_i - \bar{Y})^2 = \frac{1}{n-1} \sum_{i=1}^{n} Y_i^2 - \frac{1}{n(n-1)} \left(\sum_{i=1}^{n} Y_i \right)^2,$$

$$s_{22}^2 = \frac{1}{n-1} \sum_{i=1}^{n} (Z_i - \bar{Z})^2 = \frac{1}{n-1} \sum_{i=1}^{n} Z_i^2 - \frac{1}{n(n-1)} \left(\sum_{i=1}^{n} Z_i \right)^2,$$

and the combined *sample covariance*

$$s_{12}^2 = \frac{1}{n-1} \sum_{i=1}^{n} (Y_i - \bar{Y})(Z_i - \bar{Z})$$

$$= \frac{1}{n-1} \sum_{i=1}^{n} Y_i Z_i - \frac{1}{n(n-1)} \left(\sum_{i=1}^{n} Y_i \right) \left(\sum_{i=1}^{n} Z_i \right).$$

Also let

$$s^2 = s_{11}^2 - 2 \left(\frac{\bar{Y}}{\bar{Z}} \right) s_{12}^2 + \left(\frac{\bar{Y}}{\bar{Z}} \right)^2 s_{22}^2.$$

Finally, let α be the constant such that $(1 - 2\alpha)$ is the desired *confidence coefficient* for the confidence interval, and look up K_α in Table A5.1 (see Appendix 5) for the normal distribution. If n is not too small, a close approximation[1] of the desired *confidence interval estimate* of $E(X)$ is then given by

$$\frac{\bar{Y}}{\bar{Z}} - \frac{K_\alpha s}{\bar{Z}\sqrt{n}} \leq E(X) \leq \frac{\bar{Y}}{\bar{Z}} + \frac{K_\alpha s}{\bar{Z}\sqrt{n}};$$

that is, the probability is approximately $(1 - 2\alpha)$ that the end points of an interval generated in this way will surround the actual value of $E(X)$.

APPLICATION OF THE STATISTICAL FORMULAS TO THE EXAMPLE

Consider first how to estimate the *expected waiting time* for a customer *before* beginning service (denoted by W_q in Chap. 16). Thus the random variable X now would represent a customer's waiting time excluding service, so

$$W_q = E(X).$$

The corresponding information gathered during the simulation run is the *actual* waiting time (excluding service) incurred by the respective customers. Therefore, for each cycle, the summary statistic Y would be the *sum of the waiting times*, and the size of the cycle Z would be the *number of customers*, so that

$$W_q = \frac{E(Y)}{E(Z)}.$$

For cycle 1, a total of three customers are processed, so $Z_1 = 3$. The first customer incurs no waiting before beginning service, the second waits 3 units of time (from 34 to 37), and the third waits 2 units of time (from 48 to 50), so $Y_1 = 5$.

---

[1] This is an approximation only because the probability distributions of $\bar{Y}$ and $\bar{Z}$ are only approximately *normal*. Therefore, n must be sufficiently large that, by applying the central limit theorem, these approximations to the normal distribution will be sufficiently close.

We proceed similarly for the other cycles. The data for the problem are

$$
\begin{aligned}
Y_1 &= 5, & Z_1 &= 3 \\
Y_2 &= 0, & Z_2 &= 1 \\
Y_3 &= 34, & Z_3 &= 5 \\
Y_4 &= 0, & Z_4 &= 1 \\
Y_5 &= 0, & Z_5 &= 1 \\
\bar{Y} &= 7.8, & \bar{Z} &= 2.2.
\end{aligned}
$$

Therefore, the *point estimate* of W_q is

$$
\text{Est}\{W_q\} = \frac{\bar{Y}}{\bar{Z}} = \frac{7.8}{2.2} = 3\frac{6}{11}.
$$

To obtain a 95 percent *confidence interval estimate* of W_q, the preceding formulas are first used to calculate

$$
s_{11}^2 = 219.20, \qquad s_{22}^2 = 3.20, \qquad s_{12}^2 = 24.80, \qquad s = 9.14.
$$

Because $(1 - 2\alpha) = 0.95$, $\alpha = 0.025$, so that $K_\alpha = 1.96$ from Table A5.1. The resulting confidence interval is

$$
-0.09 \le W_q \le 7.19;
$$

that is,

$$
W_q \le 7.19.
$$

The reason that this confidence interval is so wide (even including impossible negative values) is that the number of sample observations (cycles), $n = 5$, is so small. Note in the general formula that the width of the confidence interval is *inversely proportional* to the *square root* of n, so that, e.g., quadrupling n reduces the width by half (assuming no change in s or $\bar{Z}$). Given preliminary values of s and $\bar{Z}$ from a short preliminary simulation run (such as the preceding run), this relationship makes it possible to estimate in advance the width of the confidence interval that would result from any given choice of n for the full simulation run. The final choice of n can then be made based on the tradeoff between computer time and the precision of the statistical analysis.

Now suppose that this simulation run is to be used to estimate P_0, the probability of having *zero* customers in the system. (The theoretical value is known to be $P_0 = 1 - \lambda/\mu = 1 - (\frac{1}{15})/(\frac{1}{10}) = \frac{1}{3}$.) The corresponding information obtained during the simulation run is the fraction of time during which the system is empty. Therefore, the summary statistic Y for each cycle would be the *total time* during which *no* customers are present, and the size Z would be the *length* of the cycle, so that

$$
P_0 = \frac{E(Y)}{E(Z)}.
$$

The length of cycle 1 is 38 (from 24 to 62), so that $Z_1 = 38$. During this time, the system is empty from 53 to 62, so that $Y_1 = 9$. Proceeding in this manner for the other cycles, the following data are obtained for the problem:

$$
\begin{aligned}
Y_1 &= 9, & Z_1 &= 38 \\
Y_2 &= 5, & Z_2 &= 8 \\
Y_3 &= 7, & Z_3 &= 54 \\
Y_4 &= 3, & Z_4 &= 16 \\
Y_5 &= 17, & Z_5 &= 24 \\
\bar{Y} &= 8.2, & \bar{Z} &= 28.
\end{aligned}
$$

Thus the *point estimate* of P_0 is

$$
\text{Est}\{P_0\} = \frac{8.2}{28} = 0.293.
$$

By calculating

$$
s_{11}^2 = 29.20, \qquad s_{22}^2 = 334, \qquad s_{12}^2 = 17, \qquad s = 6.92,
$$

a 95 percent *confidence interval estimate* of P_0 is found to be

$$
0.076 \le P_0 \le 0.510.
$$

(The wide range of this interval indicates that a much longer simulation run would be needed to obtain a relatively precise estimate of P_0.)

If we redefine Y appropriately, the same approach also can be used to estimate other probabilities involving the number of customers in the system. However, because this number never exceeded 3 during this simulation run, a much longer run will be needed if the probability involves larger numbers.

The other basic queueing theory expected values defined in Sec. 16.2 (W, L_q, L) can be estimated from the estimate of W_q by using the relationships among these four expected values given near the end of Sec. 16.2. However, they can also be estimated directly from the results of the simulation run. For example, because the *expected number of customers waiting to be served* is

$$
L_q = \sum_{n=2}^{\infty} (n - 1) P_n,
$$

it can be estimated by defining

$$
Y = \sum_{n=2}^{\infty} (n - 1) T_n,
$$

where T_n is the *total time* that exactly n customers are in the system during the cycle. (This definition of Y actually is *equivalent* to the definition used when estimating W_q.) In this case, Z would be defined as it would be when estimating any P_n, namely, the *length* of the cycle. The resulting *point estimate* of L_q then turns out to be simply the *point estimate* of W_q multiplied by the actual *average arrival rate* for the complete cycles observed.

It is also possible to estimate *higher moments* of these probability distributions by redefining Y accordingly. For example, the *second moment* about the origin of the *number of customers waiting to be served* (N_q),

$$E(N_q^2) = \sum_{n=2}^{\infty} (n-1)^2 P_n,$$

can be estimated by redefining

$$Y = \sum_{n=2}^{\infty} (n-1)^2 T_n.$$

This point estimate, along with the point estimate of L_q (the first moment of N_q) just described, can then be used to estimate the *variance of N_q*. Specifically, because of the general relationship between variance and moments, this variance is

$$\mathrm{Var}(N_q) = E(N_q^2) - L_q^2.$$

Therefore, its point estimate is obtained by substituting in the point estimates of the quantities on the right-hand side of this relationship.

Finally, we should mention that it was unnecessary to generate the first *interarrival* time (24) for the simulation run summarized in Table 23.8 and Fig. 23.3 because this time played no role in the statistical analysis. It is more efficient with the regenerative method just to start the run at the regeneration point.

Selected References 3 and 11 (Chap. 6) provide considerably more information about the regenerative method, including how it can be applied to more complicated kinds of problems than those considered here.

23.5 Conclusions

There have been numerous applications of simulation in a wide variety of contexts. Some examples are listed here to illustrate the great versatility of this technique:

1. Simulation of the operations at a large airport by an airline company to test changes in company policies and practices (e.g., amounts of maintenance capacity, berthing facilities, spare aircraft, and so on).
2. Simulation of the passage of traffic across a junction with time-sequenced traffic lights to determine the best time sequences.
3. Simulation of a maintenance operation to determine the optimal size of repair crews.
4. Simulation of the flux of uncharged particles through a radiation shield to determine the intensity of the radiation that penetrates the shield.
5. Simulation of steel-making operations to evaluate changes in operating practices and the capacity and configuration of the facilities.

6. Simulation of the United States economy to predict the effect of economic policy decisions.
7. Simulation of large-scale military battles to evaluate defensive and offensive weapons systems.
8. Simulation of large-scale distribution and inventory control systems to improve the design of these systems.
9. Simulation of the overall operation of an entire business firm to evaluate broad changes in the policies and operation of the firm and also to provide a business game for training executives.
10. Simulation of a telephone communications system to determine the capacity of the respective components that are required to provide satisfactory service at the most economic level.
11. Simulation of the operation of a developed river basin to determine the best configuration of dams, power plants, and irrigation works that will provide the desired level of flood control and water-resource development.
12. Simulation of the operation of a production line to determine the amount of in-process storage space that should be provided.

We have focused in this chapter on the use of simulation for predicting the *steady-state* behavior of systems whose states change only at discrete points in time. However, by having a series of runs begin with the prescribed *starting conditions*, we can also use simulation to describe the *transient* behavior of a proposed system. Furthermore, if we use differential equations, simulation can be applied to systems whose states change *continuously* with time.

Simulation is indeed a very versatile tool. However, it is by no means a panacea. Simulation is inherently an imprecise technique. It provides only *statistical estimates* rather than exact results, and it *compares alternatives* rather than generating an optimal one. Furthermore, simulation is a *slow and costly* way to study a problem. It usually requires a large amount of time and expense for analysis and programming, in addition to considerable computer running time. Simulation models tend to become unwieldy, so that the number of cases that can be run and the accuracy of the results obtained often turn out to be very inadequate. Finally, simulation yields only *numerical data* about the performance of the system, so that it provides no additional insight into the cause-and-effect relationships within the system except for the clues that can be gleaned from these numbers (and from the analysis required to construct the simulation model). Therefore, it is very expensive to conduct a sensitivity analysis of the parameter values assumed by the model. The only possible way would be to conduct new series of simulation runs with different parameter values, which would tend to provide relatively little information at a relatively high cost.

Simulation provides a way of *experimenting* with proposed systems or policies without actually implementing them. Sound statistical theory should be used in designing these experiments. Surprisingly long simulation runs often are needed to obtain *statistically significant* results. However, *variance-reducing techniques* can be very helpful in reducing the length of the runs needed.

Several *tactical* problems arise when we apply traditional statistical estimation procedures to simulated experiments. These problems include prescribing appropriate *starting conditions*, determining when a *steady-state condition* has essentially been reached, and dealing with *statistically dependent* observations. These problems can be eliminated by using the *regenerative method* of statistical analysis. However, there are some restrictions on when this method can be applied.

Simulation unquestionably has an important place in the theory and practice of operations research. It is an invaluable tool for use on those problems where analytical techniques are inadequate.

SELECTED REFERENCES

1. Banks, Jerry, and John S. Carson, II: *Discrete-Event System Simulation*, Prentice-Hall, Englewood Cliffs, N. J., 1984.

2. Bratley, Paul, Bennett L. Fox, and Linus Schrage: *A Guide to Simulation*, Springer-Verlag, New York and Secaucus, N. J., 1983.

3. Crane, M. A., and A. J. Lemoine: *An Introduction to the Regenerative Method for Simulation Analysis*, Springer-Verlag, Berlin, 1977.

4. Fishman, George S.: *Principles of Discrete Event Simulation*, Wiley, New York, 1978.

5. Franta, W. R.: *The Process View of Simulation*, Elsevier, New York, 1977.

6. Hammersley, J. M., and D. C. Handscombe: *Monte Carlo Methods*, Methuen, London, 1964.

7. Kleijnen, J. P. C.: *Statistical Techniques in Simulation*, Marcel Dekker, New York, *Part I*, 1974; *Part II*, 1975.

8. Law, Averill M., and W. David Kelton: *Simulation Modeling and Analysis*, McGraw-Hill, New York, 1982.

9. Pritsker, A. Alan B.: *Introduction to Simulation and SLAM II*, 2d ed., Systems Publishing Corp., West Lafayette, Ind., 1984.

10. Pritsker, A. Alan B., and C. Elliott Sigal: *Management Decision Making*: *A Network Simulation Approach*, Prentice-Hall, Englewood Cliffs, N. J., 1983.

11. Rubenstein, Reuven Y.: *Simulation and the Monte Carlo Method*, Wiley, New York, 1981.

PROBLEMS

(Random numbers needed to do these problems manually should be obtained from Table 23.1. For each part, use the digits *consecutively* starting from the front of the top row to form *three-digit* random numbers 096, 569, 665, and so on.)

1. Use the *mixed congruential method* to generate the following sequences of random numbers:

(*a*) A sequence of 10 *one-digit* random numbers such that $x_{n+1} \equiv (x_n + 3)(\text{modulo } 10)$ and $x_0 = 2$.

(b) A sequence of eight random numbers between 0 and 7 such that $x_{n+1} \equiv (5x_n + 1)(\text{modulo } 8)$ and $x_0 = 1$.
(c) A sequence of five *two-digit* random numbers such that $x_{n+1} \equiv (61x_n + 27)(\text{modulo } 100)$ and $x_0 = 10$.

2. Use the *mixed congruential method* to generate a sequence of five *two-digit* random numbers such that $x_{n+1} = (41x_n + 33)(\text{modulo } 100)$ and $x_0 = 48$.

3. Use the *mixed congruential method* to generate the following sequences of random numbers:

(a) A sequence of five random numbers between 0 and 31 such that $x_{n+1} \equiv (13x_n + 15)(\text{modulo } 32)$ and $x_0 = 14$.
(b) A sequence of three *three-digit* random numbers such that $x_{n+1} \equiv (201x_n + 503)(\text{modulo } 1{,}000)$ and $x_0 = 485$.

4. Use the one-digit random numbers—5, 2, 4, 9, 7—to generate random observations for each of the following situations:

(a) Throwing an unbiased coin.
(b) Throwing a die.
(c) The color of a traffic light found by a randomly arriving car when it is green 40 percent of the time, yellow 10 percent of the time, and red 50 percent of the time.

5. Generate five random observations from a *uniform distribution* between -10 and $+40$.

6. Suppose that random observations are needed from the *triangular distribution* whose probability density function is

$$f(x) = \begin{cases} 2x, & \text{if } 0 \le x \le 1 \\ 0, & \text{otherwise.} \end{cases}$$

(a) Derive an expression for each random observation as a function of the random decimal number r.
(b) Generate five random observations.

7. Generate three random observations from each of the following probability distributions:

(a) The *uniform distribution* from 25 to 75.
(b) The distribution whose probability density function is

$$f(x) = \begin{cases} \dfrac{1}{4}(x + 1)^3, & \text{if } -1 \le x \le 1 \\ 0, & \text{otherwise.} \end{cases}$$

(c) The distribution whose probability density function is

$$f(x) = \begin{cases} \dfrac{1}{200}(x - 40), & \text{if } 40 \le x \le 60 \\ 0, & \text{otherwise.} \end{cases}$$

8. Generate three random observations from each of the following probability distributions:

(a) The random variable X has $P\{X = 0\} = \frac{1}{2}$. Given $X \neq 0$, it has a uniform distribution between -5 and 15.

(b) The distribution whose probability density function is

$$f(x) = \begin{cases} x - 1, & \text{if } 1 \leq x \leq 2 \\ 3 - x, & \text{if } 2 \leq x \leq 3. \end{cases}$$

(c) The *geometric distribution* with parameter $p = 1/3$, so that

$$P\{X = k\} = \begin{cases} \dfrac{1}{3}\left(\dfrac{2}{3}\right)^{k-1}, & \text{if } k = 1, 2, \ldots \\ 0, & \text{otherwise.} \end{cases}$$

9. Generate three random observations from a *normal distribution* with mean $= 10$ and standard deviation $= 5$. (Use $n = 3$ for each observation.)

10. Generate four random observations from a *normal distribution* with mean $= 0$ and standard deviation $= 1$. (Use $n = 3$ for each observation.) Then use these four observations to generate two random observations from a *chi-square distribution* with 2 degrees of freedom.

11. Generate two random observations from each of the following probability distributions:

(a) The exponential distribution with mean $= 4$.

(b) The *Erlang* distribution with mean $= 4$ and shape parameter $k = 2$ (that is, standard deviation $= 2\sqrt{2}$).

(c) The normal distribution with mean $= 4$ and standard deviation $= 2\sqrt{2}$. (Use $n = 6$ for each observation.)

12. Generate four random observations from an *exponential distribution* with mean $= 1$. Then use these four observations to generate one random observation from an *Erlang distribution* with mean $= 4$ and shape parameter $k = 4$.

13. The weather can be considered a stochastic system, because it evolves in a probabilistic manner from one day to the next. Suppose for a certain location that this probabilistic evolution satisfies the following description:

The probability of rain tomorrow is 0.6 if it is raining today.

The probability of being clear (no rain) tomorrow is 0.8 if it is clear today.

Simulate the evolution of the weather for 10 days, beginning the day after a clear day.

14. The game of craps requires the player to throw two dice one or more times until a decision has been reached as to whether he wins or loses. He wins if the first throw results in a sum of 7 or 11, or, alternatively, if the first sum is 4, 5, 6, 8, 9, or 10 and the same sum reappears before a sum of 7 has appeared. Conversely, he loses if the first throw results in a sum of 2, 3, or 12, or, alternatively, if the first sum is 4, 5, 6, 8, 9, or 10 and a sum of 7 appears before the first sum reappears.

(a) Simulate five plays of this game to start the process of estimating the probability of winning.

(b) For a large number of plays of the game, the proportion of wins has *approximately* a *normal distribution* with mean = 0.493 and standard deviation = $0.5/\sqrt{n}$. Use this information to calculate the number of simulated plays that would be required to have a probability of at least 0.95 that the proportion of wins will be less than 0.5.

15. Consider the M/M/1 queueing theory model that was discussed in Sec. 16.6 and Example 2, Sec. 23.1. Suppose that the mean arrival rate is 3 per hour, the mean service rate is 5 per hour, and you are required to estimate the expected waiting time before service begins by using simulation.

(*a*) Starting with the system empty, use *next-event incrementing* to perform the simulation until two service completions have occurred.

(*b*) Starting with the system empty, use *fixed-time incrementing* (with 6 minutes as the time unit) to perform the simulation until two service completions have occurred.

(*c*) Write a computer simulation program with *next-event incrementing* for this problem. Use the *regenerative method* with 100 cycles to obtain a point estimate and 95 percent confidence interval for the steady-state expected waiting time before service begins. Compare these results with the theoretical value.

(*d*) Write a computer simulation program with *fixed-time incrementing* and 0.1 minute as the time unit. Use the *regenerative method* with 100 cycles to obtain a point estimate and 95 percent confidence interval for the steady-state expected waiting time before service begins. Compare these results with the theoretical value.

16. Consider the probability distribution whose probability density function is

$$f(x) = \begin{cases} \dfrac{1}{x^2}, & \text{if } 1 \le x \le \infty \\ 0, & \text{otherwise.} \end{cases}$$

The problem is to perform a simulated experiment, with the help of variance-reducing techniques, for estimating the mean of this distribution. To provide a standard of comparison, also derive the mean analytically.

For each of the following cases, generate 10 observations and calculate the resulting estimate of the mean:

(*a*) Use the *crude Monte Carlo method*.

(*b*) Use *stratified sampling* with *three* strata: $0 \le F(x) \le 0.6$, $0.6 < F(x) \le 0.9$, $0.9 < F(x) \le 1$, with 3, 3, and 4 observations, respectively.

(*c*) Use the *method of complementary random numbers*.

17. One product produced by a certain company requires that bushings be drilled into a metal block and that cylindrical shafts be inserted into the bushings. The shafts are required to have a radius of at least 1.0000 inch, but the radius should be as little larger than this as possible. In actuality, the probability distribution of what the radius of a shaft will be (in inches) has the probability density function

$$f_s(x) = \begin{cases} 400e^{-400(x-1.0000)}, & \text{if } x \ge 1.0000 \\ 0, & \text{otherwise.} \end{cases}$$

Similarly, the probability distribution of what the radius of a bushing will be (in inches) has the probability density function

$$f_B(x) = \begin{cases} 100, & \text{if } 1.0000 \le x \le 1.0100 \\ 0, & \text{otherwise.} \end{cases}$$

The clearance between a bushing and a shaft is the difference in their radii. Because they are selected at random, there occasionally is interference (i.e., negative clearance) between a bushing and a shaft that were to be mated. The objective is to determine how frequently this interference will happen under the current probability distributions.

Perform a simulated experiment for estimating the probability of interference. Notice that almost all cases of interference will occur when the radius of the bushing is much closer to 1.0000 inch than to 1.0100 inches. Therefore, it appears that an efficient experiment would generate most of the simulated bushings from this critical portion of the distribution. Take this observation into account in part (b). For each of the following cases, generate 10 observations and calculate the resulting estimate of the probability of interference:

    (a)   Use the *crude Monte Carlo method.*
    (b)   Develop and apply a *stratified sampling* approach to this problem.
    (c)   Use the *method of complementary random numbers.*

    18.   Simulation is being used to study a system whose measure of performance X will be partially determined by the outcome of a certain external factor. This factor has three possible outcomes (unfavorable, neutral, and favorable) that will occur with equal probability $(1/3)$. Because the favorable outcome would greatly increase the spread of possible values of X, this outcome is more critical than the others for estimating the mean and variance of X. Therefore, a *stratified sampling* approach has been adopted, with six random observations of the value of X generated under the favorable outcome, three generated under the neutral outcome, and one generated under the unfavorable outcome—as follows:

Outcome of external factor	Simulated values of X
Favorable	$8, 5, 1, 6, 3, 7$
Neutral	$3, 5, 2$
Unfavorable	2

    (a)   Develop the resulting estimate of $E(X)$.
    (b)   Develop the resulting estimate of $E(X^2)$.

    19.   A certain single-server system has been simulated, with the following sequence of waiting times before service for the respective customers. Use the *regenerative method* to obtain a point estimate and 90 percent confidence interval for the steady-state expected waiting time before service.

    (a)   0, 5, 4, 0, 2, 0, 3, 1, 6, 0.
    (b)   0, 3, 2, 0, 3, 1, 5, 0, 0, 2, 4, 0, 3, 5, 2, 0.

    20. Consider the queueing system example presented in Sec. 23.4 for the regenerative method. Explain why the point where a *service completion* occurs with *no* other customers left is *not* a regeneration point.

21. A company has been having a maintenance problem with a certain complex piece of equipment. This equipment contains four identical vacuum tubes that have been the cause of the trouble. The problem is that the tubes fail fairly frequently, thereby forcing the equipment to be shut down while a replacement is made. The current practice is to replace tubes only when they fail. However, a proposal has been made to replace all four tubes whenever any one of them fails to reduce the frequency with which the equipment must be shut down. The objective is to compare these two alternatives on a cost basis.

The pertinent data are the following. For each tube, the operating time until failure has approximately a *uniform distribution* from 1,000 to 2,000 hours. The equipment must be shut down for 1 hour to replace one tube or for 2 hours to replace all four tubes. The total cost associated with shutting down the equipment and replacing tubes is $100/hour plus $20 for each new tube.

(a) Starting with four new tubes, simulate the operation of the two alternative policies for 5,000 hours of simulated time.

(b) Use the data from part (a) to make a preliminary comparison of the two alternatives on a cost basis.

(c) For the *proposed* policy, describe an appropriate *regeneration point* for defining cycles that will permit applying the *regenerative method* of statistical analysis. Explain why the regenerative method cannot be applied to the *current* policy.

(d) For the *proposed* policy, use the *regenerative method* to obtain a point estimate and 95 percent confidence interval for the steady-state *expected cost per hour* from the data obtained in part (a).

(e) Write a computer simulation program for the two alternative policies. Then repeat parts (a), (b), and (d) on the computer, with 100 cycles for the *proposed* policy and 55,000 hours of simulated time (including a stabilization period of 5,000 hours) for the current policy.

22. A manufacturing company has two planers for cutting flat surfaces in large work pieces of two different types. The time required to perform each job varies somewhat, depending largely upon the number of passes that must be made. In particular, for both types of work pieces, the time required by a planer has approximately the following probability distribution:

Time, in min	Probability
10	0.30
20	0.25
30	0.18
40	0.12
50	0.08
60	0.045
70	0.015
80	0.007
90	0.003

Every half-hour one work piece of *both* types is brought to the planer department.

Unfortunately, the planer department has had a difficult time keeping up with its work load. Frequently there are a number of work pieces waiting for a free planer. This waiting has seriously disrupted the production schedule for the subsequent operations, thereby greatly increasing the cost of in-process inventory as well as the cost of idle equipment and resulting lost production. Therefore, a proposal has been made to obtain one additional planer to relieve this bottleneck.

It is estimated that the total incremental cost (including capital recovery cost) associated with obtaining and operating another planer would be \$30/hour. (This estimate takes into account the fact that, even with an additional planer, the total running time for all the planers will remain the same.) It is also estimated that the total cost associated with work pieces having to wait to be processed is \$200 per work piece per hour and \$100 per work piece per hour for work pieces of the first and second types, respectively. Because of this difference in costs, work pieces of the first type always are given priority over those of the second type. In other words, if a planer becomes free when work pieces of both types are waiting, a work piece of the first type always is chosen to be processed next.

> (*a*) Starting with all planers idle waiting for work pieces to arrive momentarily, use *next-event incrementing* to simulate the operation of the two alternative policies (the status quo or obtaining one additional planer) for 3 hours of simulated time.
>
> (*b*) Describe an appropriate *regeneration point* for defining cycles that will permit applying the *regenerative method* of statistical analysis to this problem.
>
> (*c*) Write a computer simulation program for the two alternative policies. Use the *regenerative method* with 100 cycles each to compare the two alternatives on a cost basis.

23. Select any of the typical applications of simulation listed in Sec. 23.5 and develop a simulation model for this type of problem.

■ Appendixes

■ APPENDIX 1

Convexity

The concept of *convexity* is frequently used in operations research work. Therefore, we introduce the properties of convex (or concave) functions and convex sets.

DEFINITION   A *function* of a single variable, $f(x)$, is a **convex function** if, for each pair of values of x, say, x' and x'',

$$f[\lambda x'' + (1 - \lambda)x'] \le \lambda f(x'') + (1 - \lambda)f(x')$$

for all values of λ such that $0 \le \lambda \le 1$. It is a **strictly convex function** if $\le$ can be replaced by $<$. It is a **concave function** (or a **strictly concave function**) if this statement holds when $\le$ is replaced by $\ge$ (or by $>$).

This definition has an enlightening geometric interpretation. Consider the graph of the function $f(x)$ drawn as a function of x. Then $[x', f(x')]$ and $[x'', f(x'')]$ are two points on the graph of $f(x)$, and $[\lambda x'' + (1 - \lambda)x', \lambda f(x'') + (1 - \lambda)f(x')]$ represents the various points on the line segment between these two points when $0 < \lambda \le 1$. Thus the original inequality in the definition indicates that this line segment lies entirely above or on the graph of the function. Therefore, $f(x)$ is convex if, for each pair of points on the graph of $f(x)$, the line segment joining these two points lies entirely above or on the graph of $f(x)$. In other words, $f(x)$ is convex if it is "always bending upward." (This condition is sometimes referred to as "concave upward," as opposed to "concave downward" for a concave function.) To be more precise, if $f(x)$ possesses a second derivative everywhere, then $f(x)$ is convex if and only if $d^2f(x)/dx^2 \ge 0$ for all values of x [for which $f(x)$ is defined]. Similarly, $f(x)$ is strictly convex when $d^2f(x)/dx^2 > 0$, concave when $d^2f(x)/dx^2 \le 0$, and strictly concave when $d^2f(x)/dx^2 < 0$. Some examples are given in Figs. A1.1 to A1.4.

The concept of a convex function also generalizes to functions of more than one variable. Thus if $f(x)$ is replaced by $f(x_1, x_2, \ldots, x_n)$, the definition just given still applies if

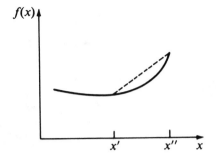

Figure A1.1 **A convex function.**

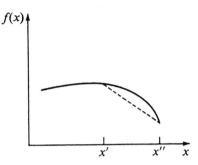

Figure A1.2 **A concave function.**

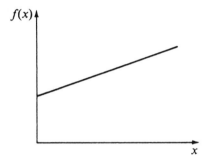

Figure A1.3 **A function that is both convex and concave.**

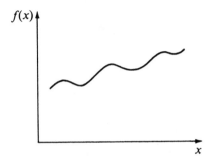

Figure A1.4 **A function that is neither convex nor concave.**

x is replaced everywhere by $(x_1, x_2, \ldots, x_n)$. Similarly, the corresponding geometric interpretation is still valid after generalizing the concepts of *points* and *line segments*. Thus, just as a particular value of (x, y) is interpreted as a point in two-dimensional space, each possible value of $(x_1, x_2, \ldots, x_m)$ may be thought of as a point in m-dimensional (Euclidean) space. By letting $m = n + 1$, the points on the graph of $f(x_1, x_2, \ldots, x_n)$ become the possible values of $(x_1, x_2, \ldots, x_n, f(x_1, x_2, \ldots, x_n))$. Another point, $(x_1, x_2, \ldots, x_n, x_{n+1})$, is said to lie above, on, or below the graph of $f(x_1, x_2, \ldots, x_n)$, according to whether x_{n+1} is larger, equal to, or smaller than $f(x_1, x_2, \ldots, x_n)$, respectively.

DEFINITION   The **line segment** joining any two points $(x_1', x_2', \ldots, x_m')$ and $(x_1'', x_2'', \ldots, x_m'')$ is the collection of points

$$(x_1, x_2, \ldots, x_m) = [\lambda x_1'' + (1 - \lambda)x_1', \lambda x_2'' + (1 - \lambda)x_2', \ldots, \lambda x_m'' + (1 - \lambda)x_m'],$$

such that $0 \leq \lambda \leq 1$.

Thus a line segment in m-dimensional space is a direct generalization of a line segment in two-dimensional space. For example, if

$$(x_1', x_2') = (2, 6), \qquad (x_1'', x_2'') = (3, 4)$$

then the line segment joining them is the collection of points

$$(x_1, x_2) = [3\lambda + 2(1 - \lambda), 4\lambda + 6(1 - \lambda)],$$

where $0 \leq \lambda \leq 1$.

DEFINITION $f(x_1, x_2, \ldots, x_n)$ is a **convex function** if, for each pair of points on the graph of $f(x_1, x_2, \ldots, x_n)$, the line segment joining these two points lies entirely above or on the graph of $f(x_1, x_2, \ldots, x_n)$. It is a **strictly convex function** if this line segment actually lies entirely above this graph except at the end points of the line segment. **Concave functions** and **strictly concave functions** are defined in exactly the same way, except that *above* is replaced by *below*.

Just as the second derivative can be used (when it exists everywhere) to check whether a function of a single variable is convex, so second partial derivatives can be used to check functions of several variables, although in a more complicated way. For example, if there are two variables, then $f(x_1, x_2)$ is convex if and only if

(1)
$$\frac{\partial^2 f(x_1, x_2)}{\partial x_1^2} \frac{\partial^2 f(x_1, x_2)}{\partial x_2^2} - \left[\frac{\partial^2 f(x_1, x_2)}{\partial x_1 \partial x_2} \right]^2 \geq 0,$$

(2)
$$\frac{\partial^2 f(x_1, x_2)}{\partial x_1^2} \geq 0,$$

and

(3)
$$\frac{\partial^2 f(x_1, x_2)}{\partial x_2^2} \geq 0,$$

for all possible values of (x_1, x_2), assuming that these partial derivatives exist everywhere. It is strictly convex if $\geq$ can be replaced by $>$ in all three conditions [but now condition (3) is superfluous and can be omitted because it is implied by the other two conditions], whereas $f(x_1, x_2)$ is concave if $\geq$ can be replaced by $\leq$ in conditions (2) and (3). When there are more than two variables, the conditions for convexity are a generalization of the ones just shown. In mathematical terminology, $f(x_1, x_2, \ldots, x_n)$ is convex if and only if its $n \times n$ Hessian matrix is positive semidefinite for all possible values of $(x_1, x_2, \ldots, x_n)$.

Thus far convexity has been treated as a general property of a function. However, many nonconvex functions do satisfy the conditions for convexity over certain intervals for the respective variables. Therefore, it is meaningful to talk about a function being convex over a certain region. For example, a function is said to be convex within a neighborhood of a specified point if its second derivative or partial derivatives satisfy the conditions for convexity at that point. This concept is useful in Appendix 2.

Finally, two particularly important properties of convex functions should be mentioned. First, if $f(x_1, x_2, \ldots, x_n)$ is a convex function, then $g(x_1, x_2, \ldots, x_n) = -f(x_1, x_2, \ldots, x_n)$ is a concave function, and vice versa. Second, the sum of convex functions is a convex function. To illustrate,

$$f_1(x_1) = x_1^4 + 2x_1^2 - 5x_1$$

and

$$f_2(x_1, x_2) = x_1^2 + 2x_1 x_2 + x_2^2$$

are both convex functions, as you can verify by calculating their second derivatives. Therefore, the sum of these functions,

$$f(x_1, x_2) = x_1^4 + 3x_1^2 - 5x_1 + 2x_1x_2 + x_2^2,$$

is a convex function, whereas its negative,

$$g(x_1, x_2) = -x_1^4 - 3x_1^2 + 5x_1 - 2x_1x_2 - x_2^2,$$

is a concave function.

The concept of a convex function leads quite naturally to the related concept of a **convex set**. Thus, if $f(x_1, x_2, \ldots, x_n)$ is a convex function, then the collection of points that lie above or on the graph of $f(x_1, x_2, \ldots, x_n)$ form a convex set. Similarly, the collection of points that lie below or on the graph of a concave function is a convex set. These cases are illustrated in Figs. A1.5 and A1.6 for the case of a single independent variable. Furthermore, convex sets have the important property that, for any given group of convex sets, the collection of points that lie in all of them (i.e., the intersection of these convex sets) is also a convex set. Therefore, the collection of points that lie both above or on a convex function and below or on a concave function is a convex set, as illustrated in Fig. A1.7. Thus convex sets may be viewed intuitively as a collection of points whose bottom boundary is a convex function and whose top boundary is a concave function. To be a bit

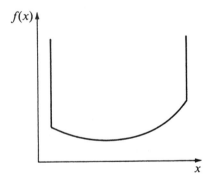

Figure A1.5 **Example of a convex set determined by a convex function.**

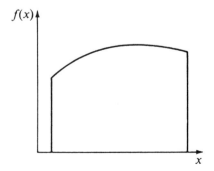

Figure A1.6 **Example of a convex set determined by a concave function.**

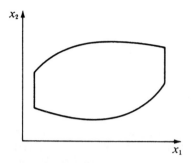

Figure A1.7 **Example of a convex set determined by both convex and concave functions.**

more precise, a convex set may be defined as follows:

> DEFINITION   A **convex set** is a collection of points such that, for each pair of points in the collection, the entire line segment joining these two points is also in the collection.

The distinction between nonconvex sets and convex sets is illustrated in Figs. A1.8 and A1.9. Thus the set of points shown in Fig. A1.8 is not a convex set because there exist

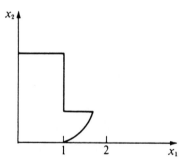

Figure A1.8 **Example of a set that is not convex.**

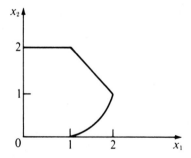

Figure A1.9 **Example of a convex set.**

many pairs of these points, for example $(1, 2)$ and $(2, 1)$, such that the line segment between them does not lie entirely within the set. This is not the case for the set in Fig. A1.9, which is convex.

In conclusion, the useful concept of an *extreme point* of a convex set needs to be introduced.

DEFINITION   An **extreme point** of a convex set is a point in the set that does not lie on any line segment that joins two other points in the set.

Thus the extreme points of the convex set in Fig. A1.9 are $(0, 0)$, $(0, 2)$, $(1, 2)$, $(2, 1)$, $(1, 0)$, and all the infinite number of points on the boundary between $(2, 1)$ and $(1, 0)$. If this particular boundary were a line segment instead, then the set would have only the five listed extreme points.

Classical Optimization Methods

This appendix reviews the classical methods of calculus for finding a solution that maximizes or minimizes (1) a function of a single variable, (2) a function of several variables, and (3) a function of several variables subject to constraints on the values of these variables. It is assumed that the functions considered possess continuous first and second derivatives and partial derivatives everywhere. Some of the concepts discussed next have been introduced briefly in Secs. 14.2 and 14.3.

Consider a function of a single variable, such as that shown in Fig. A2.1. A necessary condition for a particular solution, $x = x^*$, to be either a minimum or a maximum is that

$$\frac{df(x)}{dx} = 0 \quad \text{at } x = x^*.$$

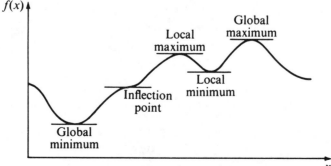

Figure A2.1 A function having several maxima and minima.

Thus in Fig. A2.1 there are five solutions satisfying these conditions. To obtain more information about these five so-called *critical points*, it is necessary to examine the second derivative. Thus, if

$$\frac{d^2f(x)}{dx^2} > 0 \quad \text{at } x = x^*,$$

then x^* must be at least a *local minimum* [that is, $f(x^*) \le f(x)$ for all x sufficiently close to x^*]. Using the language introduced in Appendix 1, we can say that x^* must be a local minimum if $f(x)$ is *strictly convex* within a neighborhood of x^*. Similarly, a sufficient condition for x^* to be a *local maximum* (given that it satisfies the necessary condition) is that $f(x)$ is *strictly concave* within a neighborhood of x^* (that is, the second derivative is *negative* at x^*). If the second derivative is zero, the issue is not resolved (the point may even be an *inflection point*), and it is necessary to examine higher derivatives.

To find a *global minimum* [i.e., a solution x^* such that $f(x^*) \le f(x)$ for all x], it is necessary to compare the local minima and identify the one that yields the smallest value of $f(x)$. If this value is less than $f(x)$ as $x \to -\infty$ and as $x \to +\infty$ (or at the end points of the function, if it is only defined over a finite interval), then this point is a global minimum. Such a point is shown in Fig. A2.1, along with the global maximum, which is identified in an analogous way.

However, if $f(x)$ is known to be either a convex or concave function (see Appendix 1 for a description of such functions), the analysis becomes much simpler. In particular, if $f(x)$ is a *convex* function, such as the one shown in Fig. A1.1, then any solution x^*, such that

$$\frac{df(x)}{dx} = 0 \quad \text{at } x = x^*,$$

is known automatically to be a *global minimum*. In other words, this condition is not only a *necessary* but a *sufficient* condition for a global minimum of a convex function. If this function actually is strictly convex, then this solution must be the only global minimum. (However, if the function is either always decreasing or always increasing, so the derivative is nonzero for all values of x, then there will be no global minimum at a finite value of x.) Otherwise, there could be a tie for the global minimum over a single interval where the derivative is zero. Similarly, if $f(x)$ is a *concave* function, then having

$$\frac{df(x)}{dx} = 0 \quad \text{at } x = x^*$$

becomes both a *necessary* and *sufficient* condition for x^* to be a *global maximum*.

The analysis for an unconstrained function of several variables, $f(\mathbf{x})$ where $\mathbf{x} = (x_1, x_2, \ldots, x_n)$ is similar. Thus a *necessary* condition for a solution $\mathbf{x} = \mathbf{x}^*$ to be either a minimum or a maximum is that

$$\frac{\partial f(\mathbf{x})}{\partial x_j} = 0 \quad \text{at } \mathbf{x} = \mathbf{x}^*, \quad \text{for } j = 1, 2, \ldots, n.$$

After identifying the critical points that satisfy this condition, each such point is then classified as a local minimum or maximum if the function is *strictly convex* or *strictly concave*, respectively, within a neighborhood of the point. (Additional analysis is required if the function is neither one.) The *global minimum* and *maximum* would be found by comparing the relative minima and maxima and then checking the value of the function as some of the variables approach $-\infty$ or $+\infty$. However, if the function is known to be *convex* or *concave*, then a critical point must be a *global minimum* or a *global maximum*, respectively.

Now consider the problem of finding the *minimum* or *maximum* of the function $f(\mathbf{x})$, subject to the restriction that $\mathbf{x}$ must satisfy all the equations

$$g_1(\mathbf{x}) = b_1$$
$$g_2(\mathbf{x}) = b_2$$
$$\vdots$$
$$g_m(\mathbf{x}) = b_m,$$

where $m < n$. For example, if $n = 2$ and $m = 1$, the problem might be to

$$\text{Maximize} \quad f(x_1, x_2) = x_1^2 + 2x_2,$$

subject to

$$g(x_1, x_2) = x_1^2 + x_2^2 = 1.$$

In this case (x_1, x_2) is restricted to be on the circle of radius 1, whose center is at the origin, so that the goal is to find the point on this circle that yields the largest value of $f(x_1, x_2)$. This example is soon solved after a general approach to the problem is outlined.

A classical method of dealing with this problem is the **method of Lagrange multipliers**. This procedure begins by formulating the **Lagrangean function**

$$h(\mathbf{x}, \lambda) = f(\mathbf{x}) - \sum_{i=1}^{m} \lambda_i [g_i(\mathbf{x}) - b_i],$$

where the new variables $\lambda = (\lambda_1, \lambda_2, \ldots, \lambda_m)$ are called *Lagrange multipliers*. Notice the key fact that for the *feasible* values of $\mathbf{x}$,

$$g_i(\mathbf{x}) - b_i = 0, \quad \text{for all } i.$$

Thus $h(\mathbf{x}, \lambda) = f(\mathbf{x})$. Therefore, it can be shown that if $(\mathbf{x}, \lambda) = (\mathbf{x}^*, \lambda^*)$ is a *local or global minimum* or *maximum* for the unconstrained function $h(\mathbf{x}, \lambda)$, then $\mathbf{x}^*$ is a corresponding *critical point* for the original problem. As a result, the method now reduces to analyzing $h(\mathbf{x}, \lambda)$ by the procedure just described for unconstrained functions. Thus the $(n + m)$ partial derivatives would be set equal to zero; that is,

$$\frac{\partial h}{\partial x_j} = \frac{\partial f}{\partial x_j} - \sum_{i=1}^{m} \lambda_i \frac{\partial g_i}{\partial x_j} = 0, \quad \text{for } j = 1, 2, \ldots, n,$$

$$\frac{\partial h}{\partial \lambda_i} = -g_i(\mathbf{x}) + b_i = 0, \quad \text{for } i = 1, 2, \ldots, m,$$

and then the critical points would be obtained by solving these equations for $(\mathbf{x}, \lambda)$. Notice that the last m equations are equivalent to the constraints in the original problem, so only feasible solutions are considered. After further analysis to identify the *global minimum* or *maximum* of $h(\cdot)$, the resulting value of $\mathbf{x}$ is then the desired solution to the original problem.

It should be pointed out that from a practical computational viewpoint, the method of Lagrange multipliers is not a particularly powerful procedure. It is often essentially impossible to solve the equations to obtain the critical points. Furthermore, even when they can be obtained, the number of critical points may be so large (often infinite) that it is impractical to attempt to identify a global minimum or maximum. However, for certain types of small problems, this method can sometimes be used successfully. To illustrate, consider the example introduced earlier. In this case,

$$h(x_1, x_2) = x_1^2 + 2x_2 - \lambda[x_1^2 + x_2^2 - 1],$$

so that

$$\frac{\partial h}{\partial x_1} = 2x_1 - 2\lambda x_1 = 0,$$

$$\frac{\partial h}{\partial x_2} = 2 - 2\lambda x_2 = 0, \qquad \frac{\partial h}{\partial \lambda} = -[x_1^2 + x_2^2 - 1] = 0.$$

The first equation implies that either $\lambda = 1$ or $x_1 = 0$. If $\lambda = 1$, then the other two equations imply that $x_2 = 1$ and $x_1 = 0$. If $x_1 = 0$, then the third equation implies that $x_2 = \pm 1$. Therefore, the two critical points for the original problem are $(x_1, x_2) = (0, 1)$ and $(0, -1)$. Thus it is apparent that these points are the *global maximum* and *minimum*, respectively.

In presenting the classical optimization methods just described, we have assumed that you are already familiar with derivatives and how to obtain them. However, there is a special case of importance in operations research work that warrants additional explanation, namely, the derivative of an integral. In particular, consider how to find the derivative of the function

$$F(y) = \int_{g(y)}^{h(y)} f(x, y) \, dx,$$

where $g(y)$ and $h(y)$ are the limits of integration expressed as functions of y. To begin, suppose that these limits of integration are constants, so that $g(y) = a$ and $h(y) = b$, respectively. For this special case, it can be shown that, given the regularity conditions assumed at the beginning of this appendix, the derivative is simply

$$\frac{d}{dy} \int_a^b f(x, y) \, dx = \int_a^b \frac{\partial f(x, y)}{\partial y} \, dx.$$

For example, if $f(x, y) = e^{-xy}$, $a = 0$, and $b = \infty$, then

$$\frac{d}{dy} \int_0^\infty e^{-xy} \, dx = \int_0^\infty (-x)e^{-xy} \, dx = -\frac{1}{y^2}$$

at any positive value of y. Thus the intuitive procedure of interchanging the order of differentiation and integration is valid for this case. However, finding the derivative becomes a little more complicated than this when the limits of integration are functions. In particular,

$$\frac{d}{dy} \int_{g(y)}^{h(y)} f(x, y) \, dx = \int_{g(y)}^{h(y)} \frac{\partial f(x, y)}{\partial y} \, dx + f(h(y), y) \frac{dh(y)}{dy} - f(g(y), y) \frac{dg(y)}{dy},$$

where $f(h(y), y)$ is obtained by writing out $f(x, y)$ and then replacing x by $h(y)$ wherever it appears, and similarly for $f(g(y), y)$. To illustrate, if $f(x, y) = x^2 y^3$, $g(y) = y$, and $h(y) = 2y$, then

$$\frac{d}{dy} \int_y^{2y} x^2 y^3 \, dx = \int_y^{2y} 3x^2 y^2 \, dx + (2y)^2 y^3(2) - y^2 y^3(1) = 14y^5$$

at any positive value of y.

Matrices and Matrix Operations

A **matrix** is defined to be a *rectangular array of numbers*. For example,

$$\mathbf{A} = \begin{bmatrix} 2 & 5 \\ 3 & 0 \\ 1 & 1 \end{bmatrix}$$

is a 3×2 matrix (where 3×2 denotes "3 by 2") because it is a rectangular array of numbers with three rows and two columns. (Matrices are denoted in this book by **bold-faced capital letters.**) The numbers in the rectangular array are called the **elements** of the matrix. For example,

$$\mathbf{B} = \begin{bmatrix} 1 & 2.4 & 0 & \sqrt{3} \\ -4 & 2 & -1 & 15 \end{bmatrix}$$

is a 2×4 matrix whose elements are $1, 2.4, 0, \sqrt{3}, -4, 2, -1$, and 15. Thus, in more general terms,

$$\mathbf{A} = \begin{bmatrix} a_{11} & a_{12} & \cdots & a_{1n} \\ a_{21} & a_{22} & \cdots & a_{2n} \\ \vdots & \vdots & & \vdots \\ a_{m1} & a_{m2} & & a_{mn} \end{bmatrix} = \|a_{ij}\|$$

is an $m \times n$ matrix, where $a_{11}, \ldots, a_{mn}$ represent the numbers that are the elements of this matrix; $\|a_{ij}\|$ is shorthand notation for identifying the matrix whose element in row i and column j is a_{ij} for every $i = 1, 2, \ldots, m$ and $j = 1, 2, \ldots, n$.

Because matrices do not possess a numerical value, they cannot be added, multiplied, and so on as if they were individual numbers. However, it is sometimes desirable to perform certain manipulations on arrays of numbers. Therefore, rules have been developed for performing operations on matrices that are analogous to arithmetic operations. To describe these, let $\mathbf{A} = \|a_{ij}\|$ and $\mathbf{B} = \|b_{ij}\|$ be two matrices having the same number of rows and the same number of columns. Then $\mathbf{A}$ and $\mathbf{B}$ are said to be equal ($\mathbf{A} = \mathbf{B}$) if and only if *all* of the corresponding elements are equal ($a_{ij} = b_{ij}$ for all i and j). The operation of multiplying a matrix by a number (denote this number by k) is performed by multiplying each element of the matrix by k, so that

$$k\mathbf{A} = \|ka_{ij}\|.$$

For example,

$$3\begin{bmatrix} 1 & \dfrac{1}{3} & 2 \\ 5 & 0 & -3 \end{bmatrix} = \begin{bmatrix} 3 & 1 & 6 \\ 15 & 0 & -9 \end{bmatrix}.$$

To add $\mathbf{A}$ and $\mathbf{B}$, simply add the corresponding elements, so that

$$\mathbf{A} + \mathbf{B} = \|a_{ij} + b_{ij}\|.$$

To illustrate,

$$\begin{bmatrix} 5 & 3 \\ 1 & 6 \end{bmatrix} + \begin{bmatrix} 2 & 0 \\ 3 & 1 \end{bmatrix} = \begin{bmatrix} 7 & 3 \\ 4 & 7 \end{bmatrix}.$$

Similarly, subtraction is done as

$$\mathbf{A} - \mathbf{B} = \mathbf{A} + (-1)\mathbf{B},$$

so that

$$\mathbf{A} - \mathbf{B} = \|a_{ij} - b_{ij}\|.$$

For example,

$$\begin{bmatrix} 5 & 3 \\ 1 & 6 \end{bmatrix} - \begin{bmatrix} 2 & 0 \\ 3 & 1 \end{bmatrix} = \begin{bmatrix} 3 & 3 \\ -2 & 5 \end{bmatrix}.$$

Note that, with the exception of multiplication by a number, all the preceding operations are defined only when the two matrices involved are of the same size. However, all of them are straightforward because they involve performing only the same comparison or arithmetic operation on the corresponding elements of the matrices.

There exists one additional elementary operation that has not been defined, **matrix multiplication**, but it is considerably more complicated. To find the element in row i, column j of the matrix resulting from multiplying $\mathbf{A}$ times $\mathbf{B}$, it is necessary to multiply each element in row i of $\mathbf{A}$ by the corresponding element in column j of $\mathbf{B}$ and then to add these products. Therefore, this matrix multiplication is defined if and only if the number of columns of $\mathbf{A}$ equals the number of rows of $\mathbf{B}$, because this condition is required if we are to perform the specified element-by-element multiplication. Thus, if $\mathbf{A}$ is an $m \times n$ matrix and $\mathbf{B}$ is an $n \times r$ matrix, then their product is

$$\mathbf{AB} = \left\| \sum_{k=1}^{n} a_{ik}b_{kj} \right\|.$$

To illustrate,

$$\begin{bmatrix} 1 & 2 \\ 4 & 0 \\ 2 & 3 \end{bmatrix} \begin{bmatrix} 3 & 1 \\ 2 & 5 \end{bmatrix} = \begin{bmatrix} 1(3) + 2(2) & 1(1) + 2(5) \\ 4(3) + 0(2) & 4(1) + 0(5) \\ 2(3) + 3(2) & 2(1) + 3(5) \end{bmatrix} = \begin{bmatrix} 7 & 11 \\ 12 & 4 \\ 12 & 17 \end{bmatrix}.$$

On the other hand, if one attempts to multiply these matrices in the reverse order, the resulting product

$$\begin{bmatrix} 3 & 1 \\ 2 & 5 \end{bmatrix} \begin{bmatrix} 1 & 2 \\ 4 & 0 \\ 2 & 3 \end{bmatrix}$$

is not even defined. Even when both **AB** and **BA** are defined,

$$\mathbf{AB} \neq \mathbf{BA}$$

in general. Thus *matrix multiplication* should be viewed as a specially designed operation whose properties are quite different from those of *arithmetic multiplication*. To understand why this special definition was adopted, consider the following system of equations:

$$2x_1 - x_2 + 5x_3 + x_4 = 20$$
$$x_1 + 5x_2 + 4x_3 + 5x_4 = 30$$
$$3x_1 + x_2 - 6x_3 + 2x_4 = 20.$$

Rather than writing these equations out as shown here, they can be written much more concisely in matrix form as

$$\mathbf{Ax} = \mathbf{b},$$

where

$$\mathbf{A} = \begin{bmatrix} 2 & -1 & 5 & 1 \\ 1 & 5 & 4 & 5 \\ 3 & 1 & -6 & 2 \end{bmatrix}, \quad \mathbf{x} = \begin{bmatrix} x_1 \\ x_2 \\ x_3 \\ x_4 \end{bmatrix}, \quad \mathbf{b} = \begin{bmatrix} 20 \\ 30 \\ 20 \end{bmatrix}.$$

It is this kind of multiplication for which matrix multiplication is designed.

Carefully note that *matrix division* is not defined.

Although the matrix operations described here do not possess certain of the properties of arithmetic operations, they do satisfy the following laws:

$$\mathbf{A} + \mathbf{B} = \mathbf{B} + \mathbf{A},$$
$$(\mathbf{A} + \mathbf{B}) + \mathbf{C} = \mathbf{A} + (\mathbf{B} + \mathbf{C}),$$
$$\mathbf{A}(\mathbf{B} + \mathbf{C}) = \mathbf{AB} + \mathbf{AC},$$
$$\mathbf{A}(\mathbf{BC}) = (\mathbf{AB})\mathbf{C},$$

when the relative sizes of these matrices are such that the indicated operations are defined.

Another type of matrix operation, which has no arithmetic analog, is the **transpose operation**. This operation involves nothing more than interchanging the rows and columns of the matrix, which is frequently useful for performing the multiplication operation in the desired way. Thus, for any matrix $\mathbf{A} = \|a_{ij}\|$, its transpose $\mathbf{A}^T$ is

$$\mathbf{A}^T = \|a_{ji}\|.$$

For example, if

$$A = \begin{bmatrix} 2 & 5 \\ 1 & 3 \\ 4 & 0 \end{bmatrix},$$

then

$$A^T = \begin{bmatrix} 2 & 1 & 4 \\ 5 & 3 & 0 \end{bmatrix}.$$

Zero and 1 are numbers that play a special role in arithmetic. There also exist special matrices that play a similar role in matrix theory. In particular, the matrix that is analogous to 1 is the **identity matrix I**, which is a square matrix whose elements are zeros except for ones along the main diagonal. Thus

$$I = \begin{bmatrix} 1 & 0 & 0 & \cdots & 0 \\ 0 & 1 & 0 & \cdots & 0 \\ 0 & 0 & 1 & \cdots & 0 \\ \vdots & \vdots & \vdots & & \vdots \\ 0 & 0 & 0 & \cdots & 1 \end{bmatrix}.$$

The number of rows or columns of I can be specified as desired. The analogy of I to 1 follows from the fact that for any matrix A,

$$IA = A = AI,$$

where I is assigned the appropriate number of rows and columns in each case for the multiplication operation to be defined. Similarly, the matrix that is analogous to zero is the so-called **null matrix 0**, which is a matrix of any size whose elements are *all zeros*. Thus

$$0 = \begin{bmatrix} 0 & 0 & \cdots & 0 \\ 0 & 0 & \cdots & 0 \\ \vdots & \vdots & & \vdots \\ 0 & 0 & \cdots & 0 \end{bmatrix}.$$

Therefore, for any matrix A,

$$A + 0 = A, \qquad A - A = 0, \qquad \text{and} \qquad 0A = 0 = A0,$$

where 0 is the appropriate size in each case for the operations to be defined.

On certain occasions, it is useful to partition a matrix into several smaller matrices called **submatrices**. For example, one possible way of partitioning a 3×4 matrix would be

$$A = \begin{bmatrix} a_{11} & a_{12} & a_{13} & a_{14} \\ a_{21} & a_{22} & a_{23} & a_{24} \\ a_{31} & a_{32} & a_{33} & a_{34} \end{bmatrix} = \begin{bmatrix} a_{11} & A_{12} \\ A_{21} & A_{22} \end{bmatrix},$$

where

$$A_{12} = [a_{12} \ \ a_{13} \ \ a_{14}], \qquad A_{21} = \begin{bmatrix} a_{21} \\ a_{31} \end{bmatrix}, \qquad A_{22} = \begin{bmatrix} a_{22} & a_{23} & a_{24} \\ a_{32} & a_{33} & a_{34} \end{bmatrix}$$

all are submatrices. Rather than perform operations element by element on such partitioned matrices, we can instead do them in terms of the submatrices, provided the partitionings are such that the operations are defined. For example, if **B** is a partitioned 4×1 matrix such that

$$\mathbf{B} = \begin{bmatrix} b_1 \\ b_2 \\ b_3 \\ b_4 \end{bmatrix} = \begin{bmatrix} b_1 \\ \mathbf{B}_2 \end{bmatrix},$$

then

$$\mathbf{AB} = \begin{bmatrix} a_{11} & b_1 + \mathbf{A}_{12}\mathbf{B}_2 \\ \mathbf{A}_{21} & b_1 + \mathbf{A}_{22}\mathbf{B}_2 \end{bmatrix}.$$

A special kind of matrix that plays an important role in matrix theory is the kind that has either a *single row* or a *single column*. Such matrices are often referred to as **vectors**. Thus

$$\mathbf{x} = [x_1, x_2, \ldots, x_n]$$

is a **row vector**, and

$$\mathbf{x} = \begin{bmatrix} x_1 \\ x_2 \\ \vdots \\ x_n \end{bmatrix}$$

is a **column vector**. (Vectors are denoted in this book by **bold-faced lower case letters**.) These vectors also are sometimes called *n-vectors* to indicate that they have n elements. For example,

$$\mathbf{x} = \left[1, 4, -2, \frac{1}{3}, 7 \right]$$

is a 5-vector. A **null vector 0** is either a row vector or a column vector whose elements are *all zeros*, i.e.,

$$\mathbf{0} = [0, 0, \ldots, 0], \qquad \mathbf{0} = \begin{bmatrix} 0 \\ 0 \\ \vdots \\ 0 \end{bmatrix}.$$

(Although the same symbol **0** is used for either kind of *null vector*, as well as for a *null matrix*, the context normally will identify which it is.)

One reason vectors play an important role in matrix theory is that any $m \times n$ matrix can be partitioned into either m row vectors or n column vectors, and important properties of the matrix can be analyzed in terms of these vectors. To amplify, consider a set of n-vectors, $\mathbf{x}_1, \mathbf{x}_2, \ldots, \mathbf{x}_m$, of the same type (i.e., they are either all row vectors or all column vectors).

DEFINITION   A set of vectors $\mathbf{x}_1, \mathbf{x}_2, \ldots, \mathbf{x}_m$ is said to be **linearly dependent** if there exist m numbers (denoted by $c_1, c_2, \ldots, c_m$), some of which are not zero, such that

$$c_1 \mathbf{x}_1 + c_2 \mathbf{x}_2 + \cdots + c_m \mathbf{x}_m = \mathbf{0}.$$

Otherwise, the set is said to be **linearly independent**.

To illustrate, if $m = 3$ and

$$\mathbf{x}_1 = [1, 1, 1]$$
$$\mathbf{x}_2 = [0, 1, 1]$$
$$\mathbf{x}_3 = [2, 5, 5],$$

then

$$2\mathbf{x}_1 + 3\mathbf{x}_2 - \mathbf{x}_3 = \mathbf{0},$$

so that

$$\mathbf{x}_3 = 2\mathbf{x}_1 + 3\mathbf{x}_2.$$

Thus $\mathbf{x}_1, \mathbf{x}_2, \mathbf{x}_3$ would be linearly dependent because one of them is a linear combination of the others. However, if $\mathbf{x}_3$ were changed to

$$\mathbf{x}_3 = [2, 5, 6]$$

instead, then $\mathbf{x}_1, \mathbf{x}_2, \mathbf{x}_3$ would be linearly independent.

DEFINITION   The **rank** of a *set* of vectors is the largest number of *linearly independent vectors* that can be chosen from the set.

Continuing the preceding example, the rank of the set of vectors $\mathbf{x}_1, \mathbf{x}_2, \mathbf{x}_3$ was 2, but it became 3 after changing $\mathbf{x}_3$.

DEFINITION   A **basis** for a *set* of vectors is a *collection* of linearly independent vectors taken from the set such that every vector in the set is a linear combination of the vectors in the collection (i.e., every vector in the set equals the sum of certain multiples of the vectors in the collection).

To illustrate, $\mathbf{x}_1$ and $\mathbf{x}_2$ constituted a basis for $\mathbf{x}_1, \mathbf{x}_2, \mathbf{x}_3$ in the preceding example before $\mathbf{x}_3$ was changed.

THEOREM A3.1   A *collection* of r linearly independent vectors chosen from a set of vectors is a *basis* for the set if and only if the set has rank r.

Given the preceding results regarding vectors, it is now possible to present certain important concepts regarding matrices.

DEFINITION   The **row rank** of a matrix is the *rank* of its set of *row vectors*. The **column rank** of a matrix is the *rank* of its *column vectors*.

For example, if the matrix $\mathbf{A}$ is

$$\mathbf{A} = \begin{bmatrix} 1 & 1 & 1 \\ 0 & 1 & 1 \\ 2 & 5 & 5 \end{bmatrix},$$

then its row rank was shown to be 2. Note that the column rank of $\mathbf{A}$ is also 2. This fact is no coincidence, as the following general theorem indicates.

THEOREM A3.2   The *row rank* and *column rank* of a matrix are *equal*.

Thus it is only necessary to speak of *the rank* of a matrix.

The final concept to be discussed is that of the **inverse of a matrix**. For any nonzero number k, there exists a reciprocal or inverse, $k^{-1} = 1/k$, such that

$$kk^{-1} = k^{-1}k = 1.$$

Is there an analogous concept that is valid in matrix theory? In other words, for a given matrix **A** other than the null matrix, does there exist a matrix $\mathbf{A}^{-1}$ such that

$$\mathbf{AA}^{-1} = \mathbf{A}^{-1}\mathbf{A} = \mathbf{I}?$$

If **A** is not a square matrix (i.e., if the number of rows and columns of **A** differ), the answer is *never*, because these matrix products would necessarily have a different number of rows for the multiplication to be defined (so that the equality operation would not be defined). However, if **A** is square, then the answer is *under certain circumstances*, as indicated in Theorem A3.3.

DEFINITION   A matrix is called **nonsingular** if its rank equals both the number of rows and the number of columns. Otherwise, it is called **singular**.

Thus only square matrices can be *nonsingular*. A useful way of testing for nonsingularity is provided by the fact that a square matrix is nonsingular if and only if *its determinant is nonzero*.

THEOREM A3.3   (a)   If **A** is *nonsingular*, there is a unique nonsingular matrix $\mathbf{A}^{-1}$, called the **inverse** of **A**, such that $\mathbf{AA}^{-1} = \mathbf{I} = \mathbf{A}^{-1}\mathbf{A}$.
(b)   If **A** is *nonsingular* and **B** is a matrix for which either $\mathbf{AB} = \mathbf{I}$ or $\mathbf{BA} = \mathbf{I}$, then $\mathbf{B} = \mathbf{A}^{-1}$.
(c)   *Only nonsingular* matrices have *inverses*.

To illustrate, consider the matrix

$$\mathbf{A} = \begin{bmatrix} 5 & -4 \\ 1 & -1 \end{bmatrix}.$$

Notice that the rank of **A** is 2, so it is *nonsingular*. Therefore, **A** must have an *inverse*, which happens to be

$$\mathbf{A}^{-1} = \begin{bmatrix} 1 & -4 \\ 1 & -5 \end{bmatrix}.$$

Hence,

$$\mathbf{AA}^{-1} = \begin{bmatrix} 5 & -4 \\ 1 & -1 \end{bmatrix} \begin{bmatrix} 1 & -4 \\ 1 & -5 \end{bmatrix} = \begin{bmatrix} 1 & 0 \\ 0 & 1 \end{bmatrix},$$

and

$$\mathbf{A}^{-1}\mathbf{A} = \begin{bmatrix} 1 & -4 \\ 1 & -5 \end{bmatrix} \begin{bmatrix} 5 & -4 \\ 1 & -1 \end{bmatrix} = \begin{bmatrix} 1 & 0 \\ 0 & 1 \end{bmatrix}.$$

Simultaneous Linear Equations

Consider the system of simultaneous linear equations

$$a_{11}x_1 + a_{12}x_2 + \cdots + a_{1n}x_n = b_1,$$
$$a_{21}x_1 + a_{22}x_2 + \cdots + a_{2n}x_n = b_2,$$
$$\vdots$$
$$a_{m1}x_1 + a_{m2}x_2 + \cdots + a_{mn}x_n = b_m.$$

It is commonly assumed that this system has a solution, and a unique solution, if and only if $m = n$. However, this assumption is an oversimplification. It raises the questions: Under what conditions will these equations have a simultaneous solution? Given that they do, when will there be only one such solution? If there is a unique solution, how can it be identified in a systematic way? These questions are the ones we explore in this appendix. The discussion of the first two questions assumes that you are familiar with the basic information about matrices in Appendix 3.

The preceding system of equations can also be written in matrix form as

$$\mathbf{Ax} = \mathbf{b},$$

where

$$\mathbf{A} = \begin{bmatrix} a_{11} & a_{12} & \cdots & a_{1n} \\ a_{21} & a_{22} & \cdots & a_{2n} \\ & & \vdots & \\ a_{m1} & a_{m2} & \cdots & a_{mn} \end{bmatrix}, \quad \mathbf{x} = \begin{bmatrix} x_1 \\ x_2 \\ \vdots \\ x_n \end{bmatrix}, \quad \mathbf{b} = \begin{bmatrix} b_1 \\ b_2 \\ \vdots \\ b_m \end{bmatrix}.$$

The first two questions can be answered immediately in terms of the properties of these matrices. First, the system of equations possesses at least one solution if and only if the *rank* of **A** equals the *rank* of [**A, b**]. (Notice that equality is guaranteed if the *rank* of **A** equals *m*.) This result follows immediately from the definitions of *rank* and *linear independence* given in Appendix 3, because if the *rank* of [**A, b**] exceeds the *rank* of **A** by 1 (the only other possibility), then **b** is *linearly independent* of the column vectors of **A** (that is, **b** cannot equal any linear combination **Ax** of these vectors.

Second, given that these ranks are equal, there are then two possibilities. If the *rank* of **A** is *n* (its maximum possible value), then the system of equations will possess exactly *one* solution. [This result follows from Theorem A3.1, the definition of a *basis*, and part (*b*) of Theorem A3.3.] If the *rank* of **A** is *less* than *n*, then there will exist an *infinite number of solutions*. (This result follows from the fact that for any *basis* of the column vectors of **A**, the x_j corresponding to column vectors not in this basis can be assigned any value, and there will still exist a solution for the other variables as before.)

Finally, it should be noted that if **A** and [**A, b**] have a *common rank r* such that $r < m$, then $(m - r)$ of the equations must be linear combinations of the other ones, so that these $(m - r)$ *redundant* equations can be deleted without affecting the solution(s). It then follows from the preceding results that this system of equations (with or without the redundant equations) possesses at least one solution, where the number of solutions is *one* if $r = n$ or *infinite* if $r < n$.

Now consider how to find a solution to the system of equations. Assume for the moment that $m = n$ and **A** is nonsingular, so that a unique solution exists. This solution can be obtained by the **Gauss-Jordan method of elimination** (commonly called **Gaussian elimination**), which proceeds as follows. To begin, eliminate the first variable from all but one (say, the first) of the equations by adding an appropriate multiple (positive or negative) of this equation to each of the others. (For convenience, this one equation would be divided by the coefficient of this variable, so that the final value of this coefficient is 1.) Next, proceed in the same way to eliminate the second variable from all equations except one new one (say, the second). Then repeat this procedure for the third variable, the fourth variable, and so on, until each of the *n* variables remains in only one of the equations and each of the *n* equations contains exactly one of these variables. The desired solution can then be read from the equations directly.

To illustrate the *Gauss-Jordan method of elimination*, we consider the following system of linear equations:

(1) $$x_1 - x_2 + 4x_3 = 10$$
(2) $$-x_1 + 3x_2 \qquad = 10$$
(3) $$2x_2 + 5x_3 = 22.$$

The method begins by eliminating x_1 from all but the first equation. This first step is executed simply by adding Eq. (1) to Eq. (2), which yields

(1) $$x_1 - x_2 + 4x_3 = 10$$
(2) $$2x_2 + 4x_3 = 20$$
(3) $$2x_2 + 5x_3 = 22.$$

The next step is to eliminate x_2 from all but the second equation. Begin this step by dividing Eq. (2) by 2, so that x_2 will have a coefficient of $+1$, as follows:

(1) $$x_1 - x_2 + 4x_3 = 10$$
(2) $$x_2 + 2x_3 = 10$$
(3) $$2x_2 + 5x_3 = 22.$$

Then add Eq. (2) to Eq. (1), and subtract two times Eq. (2) from Eq. (3), which yields

(1) $$x_1 \qquad + 6x_3 = 20$$
(2) $$x_2 + 2x_3 = 10$$
(3) $$x_3 = 2.$$

The final step is to eliminate x_3 from all but the third equation. This step requires subtracting six times Eq. (3) from Eq. (1) and subtracting two times Eq. (3) from Eq. (2), which yields

(1) $$x_1 \qquad\qquad = 8$$
(2) $$x_2 \qquad = 6$$
(3) $$x_3 = 2.$$

Thus the desired solution is $(x_1, x_2, x_3) = (8, 6, 2)$, and the procedure is completed.

Now consider briefly what happens if the Gauss-Jordan method of elimination is applied when $m \neq n$ and/or $\mathbf{A}$ is singular. As we discussed earlier, there are three possible cases to consider. First, if the rank of $[\mathbf{A}, \mathbf{b}]$ exceeds the rank of $\mathbf{A}$ by 1, then *no solution* to the system of equations will exist. In this case, the Gauss-Jordan method obtains an equation where the left-hand side has vanished (i.e., all the coefficients of the variables are zero), whereas the right-hand side is nonzero. This signpost indicates that no solution exists, so there is no reason to proceed further.

The second case is where both of these ranks are equal to n, so that a *unique solution* exists. This case implies that $m \geq n$. If $m = n$, then the previous assumptions must hold and no difficulty arises. Therefore, suppose that $m > n$, so that there are $(m - n)$ redundant equations. In this case, all these redundant equations are eliminated (i.e., both the left-hand and right-hand sides would become zero) during the process of executing the Gauss-Jordan method, so the unique solution is identified just as it was before.

The final case is where both these ranks are equal to r, where $r < n$, so that the system of equations possesses an *infinite number of solutions*. In this case, at the completion of the Gauss-Jordan method, each of r variables remains in only one of the equations, and each of the r equations (any additional equations have vanished) contains exactly one of these variables. However, each of the other $(n - r)$ variables either vanishes or remains in some of the equations. Therefore, any solution obtained by assigning arbitrary values to the $(n - r)$ variables, and then identifying the respective values of the r variables from the single final equation in which each one appears, is a solution to the system of simultaneous equations. Equivalently, the transfer of these $(n - r)$ variables to the right-hand side of the equations (either before or after the method is executed) identifies the solution for the r variables as a function of these extra variables.

■ APPENDIX 5

Tables

Table A5.1[†] **Areas under the normal curve from K_α to ∞**

$$P\{\text{normal} \geq K_\alpha\} = \int_{K_\alpha}^{\infty} \frac{1}{\sqrt{2\pi}} e^{-x^2/2}\, dx = \alpha$$

K_α	.00	.01	.02	.03	.04	.05	.06	.07	.08	.09
0.0	.5000	.4960	.4920	.4880	.4840	.4801	.4761	.4721	.4681	.4641
0.1	.4602	.4562	.4522	.4483	.4443	.4404	.4364	.4325	.4286	.4247
0.2	.4207	.4168	.4129	.4090	.4052	.4013	.3974	.3936	.3897	.3859
0.3	.3821	.3783	.3745	.3707	.3669	.3632	.3594	.3557	.3520	.3483
0.4	.3446	.3409	.3372	.3336	.3300	.3264	.3228	.3192	.3156	.3121
0.5	.3085	.3050	.3015	.2981	.2946	.2912	.2877	.2843	.2810	.2776
0.6	.2743	.2709	.2676	.2643	.2611	.2578	.2546	.2514	.2483	.2451
0.7	.2420	.2389	.2358	.2327	.2296	.2266	.2236	.2206	.2177	.2148
0.8	.2119	.2090	.2061	.2033	.2005	.1977	.1949	.1922	.1894	.1867
0.9	.1841	.1814	.1788	.1762	.1736	.1711	.1685	.1660	.1635	.1611
1.0	.1587	.1562	.1539	.1515	.1492	.1469	.1446	.1423	.1401	.1379
1.1	.1357	.1335	.1314	.1292	.1271	.1251	.1230	.1210	.1190	.1170
1.2	.1151	.1131	.1112	.1093	.1075	.1056	.1038	.1020	.1003	.0985
1.3	.0968	.0951	.0934	.0918	.0901	.0885	.0869	.0853	.0838	.0823
1.4	.0808	.0793	.0778	.0764	.0749	.0735	.0721	.0708	.0694	.0681
1.5	.0668	.0655	.0643	.0630	.0618	.0606	.0594	.0582	.0571	.0559
1.6	.0548	.0537	.0526	.0516	.0505	.0495	.0485	.0475	.0465	.0455
1.7	.0446	.0436	.0427	.0418	.0409	.0401	.0392	.0384	.0375	.0367
1.8	0359	.0351	.0344	.0336	.0329	.0322	.0314	.0307	.0301	.0294
1.9	.0287	.0281	.0274	.0268	.0262	.0256	.0250	.0244	.0239	.0233
2.0	.0228	.0222	.0217	.0212	.0207	.0202	.0197	.0192	.0188	.0183
2.1	.0179	.0174	.0170	.0166	.0162	.0158	.0154	.0150	.0146	.0143
2.2	.0139	.0136	.0132	.0129	.0125	.0122	.0119	.0116	.0113	.0110
2.3	.0107	.0104	.0102	.00990	.00964	.00939	.00914	.00889	.00866	.00842
2.4	.00820	.00798	.00776	.00755	.00734	.00714	.00695	.00676	.00657	.00639
2.5	.00621	.00604	.00587	.00570	.00554	.00539	.00523	.00508	.00494	.00480
2.6	.00466	.00453	.00440	.00427	.00415	.00402	.00391	.00379	.00368	.00357
2.7	.00347	.00336	.00326	.00317	.00307	.00298	.00289	.00280	.00272	.00264
2.8	.00256	.00248	.00240	.00233	.00226	.00219	.00212	.00205	.00199	.00193
2.9	.00187	.00181	.00175	.00169	.00164	.00159	.00154	.00149	.00144	.00139

K_α	.0	.1	.2	.3	.4	.5	.6	.7	.8	.9
3	.00135	$.0^3968$	$.0^3687$	$.0^3483$	$.0^3337$	$.0^3233$	$.0^3159$	$.0^3108$	$.0^4723$	$.0^4481$
4	$.0^4317$	$.0^4207$	$.0^4133$	$.0^5854$	$.0^5541$	$.0^5340$	$.0^5211$	$.0^5130$	$.0^6793$	$.0^6479$
5	$.0^6287$	$.0^6170$	$.0^7996$	$.0^7579$	$.0^7333$	$.0^7190$	$.0^7107$	$.0^8599$	$.0^8332$	$.0^8182$
6	$.0^9987$	$.0^9530$	$.0^9282$	$.0^9149$	$.0^{10}777$	$.0^{10}402$	$.0^{10}206$	$.0^{10}104$	$.0^{11}523$	$.0^{11}260$

[†] From Frederick E. Croxton, *Tables of Areas in Two Tails and in One Tail of the Normal Curve.* Copyright 1949 by Prentice-Hall, Inc., Englewood Cliffs, N. J.

Table A5.2[†] **100 α percentage points of student's t distribution**
P{student's t with v degrees of freedom ≥ tabled value} = α

α \ ν	0.40	0.25	0.10	0.05	0.025	0.01	0.005	0.0025	0.001	0.0005
1	0.325	1.000	3.078	6.314	12.706	31.821	63.657	127.32	318.31	636.62
2	.289	0.816	1.886	2.920	4.303	6.965	9.925	14.089	22.327	31.598
3	.277	.765	1.638	2.353	3.182	4.541	5.841	7.453	10.214	12.924
4	.271	.741	1.533	2.132	2.776	3.747	4.604	5.598	7.173	8.610
5	0.267	0.727	1.476	2.015	2.571	3.365	4.032	4.773	5.893	6.869
6	.265	.718	1.440	1.943	2.447	3.143	3.707	4.317	5.208	5.959
7	.263	.711	1.415	1.895	2.365	2.998	3.499	4.029	4.785	5.408
8	.262	.706	1.397	1.860	2.306	2.896	3.355	3.833	4.501	5.041
9	.261	.703	1.383	1.833	2.262	2.821	3.250	3.690	4.297	4.781
10	0.260	0.700	1.372	1.812	2.228	2.764	3.169	3.581	4.144	4.587
11	.260	.697	1.363	1.796	2.201	2.718	3.106	3.497	4.025	4.437
12	.259	.695	1.356	1.782	2.179	2.681	3.055	3.428	3.930	4.318
13	.259	.694	1.350	1.771	2.160	2.650	3.012	3.372	3.852	4.221
14	.258	.692	1.345	1.761	2.145	2.624	2.977	3.326	3.787	4.140
15	0.258	0.691	1.341	1.753	2.131	2.602	2.947	3.286	3.733	4.073
16	.258	.690	1.337	1.746	2.120	2.583	2.921	3.252	3.686	4.015
17	.257	.689	1.333	1.740	2.110	2.567	2.898	3.222	3.646	3.965
18	.257	.688	1.330	1.734	2.101	2.552	2.878	3.197	3.610	3.922
19	.257	.688	1.328	1.729	2.093	2.539	2.861	3.174	3.579	3.883
20	0.257	0.687	1.325	1.725	2.086	2.528	2.845	3.153	3.552	3.850
21	.257	.686	1.323	1.721	2.080	2.518	2.831	3.135	3.527	3.819
22	.256	.686	1.321	1.717	2.074	2.508	2.819	3.119	3.505	3.792
23	.256	.685	1.319	1.714	2.069	2.500	2.807	3.104	3.485	3.767
24	.256	.685	1.318	1.711	2 064	2.492	2.797	3.091	3.467	3.745
25	0.256	0.684	1.316	1.708	2.060	2.485	2.787	3.078	3.450	3.725
26	.256	.684	1.315	1.706	2.056	2.479	2.779	3.067	3.435	3.707
27	.256	.684	1.314	1.703	2.052	2.473	2.771	3.057	3.421	3.690
28	.256	.683	1.313	1.701	2.048	2.467	2.763	3.047	3.408	3.674
29	.256	.683	1.311	1.699	2.045	2.462	2.756	3.038	3.396	3.659
30	0.256	0.683	1.310	1.697	2.042	2.457	2.750	3.030	3.385	3.646
40	.255	.681	1.303	1.684	2.021	2.423	2.704	2.971	3.307	3.551
60	.254	.679	1.296	1.671	2.000	2.390	2.660	2.915	3.232	3.460
120	.254	.677	1.289	1.658	1.980	2.358	2.617	2.860	3.160	3.373
∞	.253	.674	1.282	1.645	1.960	2.326	2.576	2.807	3.090	3.291

[†] Reproduced from Table 12 of *Biometrika Tables for Statisticians*, vol. I, 3d ed., 1966, by permission of the Biometrika Trustees.

Table A5.3[†] **100 α percentage points of chi-square distribution**
   P{chi square with v degrees of freedom ≥ tabled value} = α

α ν	0.995	0.99	0.975	0.95	0.90	0.75	0.50
1	.0⁴393	.0³157	.0³982	.00393	.0158	.102	.455
2	.0100	.0201	.0506	.103	.211	.575	1.386
3	.0717	.115	.216	.352	.584	1.213	2.366
4	.207	.297	.484	.711	1.064	1.923	3.357
5	.412	.554	.831	1.145	1.610	2.675	4.351
6	.676	.872	1.237	1.635	2.204	3.455	5.348
7	.989	1.239	1.690	2.167	2.833	4.255	6.346
8	1.344	1.646	2.180	2.733	3.490	5.071	7.344
9	1.735	2.088	2.700	3.325	4.168	5.899	8.343
10	2.156	2.558	3.247	3.940	4.865	6.737	9.342
11	2.603	3.053	3.816	4.575	5.578	7.584	10.341
12	3.074	3.571	4.404	5.226	6.304	8.438	11.340
13	3.565	4.107	5.009	5.892	7.042	9.299	12.340
14	4.075	4.660	5.629	6.571	7.790	10.165	13.339
15	4.601	5.229	6.262	7.261	8.547	11.036	14.339
16	5.142	5.812	6.908	7.962	9.312	11.912	15.338
17	5.697	6.408	7.564	8.672	10.085	12.792	16.338
18	6.265	7.015	8.231	9.390	10.865	13.675	17.338
19	6.844	7.633	8.907	10.117	11.651	14.562	18.338
20	7.434	8.260	9.591	10.851	12.443	15.452	19.337
21	8.034	8.897	10.283	11.591	13.240	16.344	20.337
22	8.643	9.542	10.982	12.338	14.041	17.240	21.337
23	9.260	10.196	11.688	13.091	14.848	18.137	22.337
24	9.886	10.856	12.401	13.848	15.659	19.037	23.337
25	10.520	11.524	13.120	14.611	16.473	19.939	24.337
26	11.160	12.198	13.844	15.379	17.292	20.843	25.336
27	11.808	12.879	14.573	16.151	18.114	21.749	26.336
28	12.461	13.565	15.308	16.928	18.939	22.657	27.336
29	13.121	14.256	16.047	17.708	19.768	23.567	28.336
30	13.787	14.953	16.791	18.493	20.599	24.478	29.336
40	20.707	22.164	24.433	26.509	29.051	33.660	39.335
50	27.991	29.707	32.357	34.764	37.689	42.942	49.335
60	35.535	37.485	40.482	43.188	46.459	52.294	59.335
70	43.275	45.442	48.758	51.739	55.329	61.698	69.334
80	51.172	53.540	57.153	60.391	64.278	71.145	79.334
90	59.196	61.754	65.647	69.126	73.291	80.625	89.334
100	67.328	70.065	74.222	77.929	82.358	90.133	99.334
K_α	−2.576	−2.326	−1.960	−1.645	−1.282	−0.6745	0.000

[†] Abridged from Table 8 of *Biometrika Tables for Statisticians*, vol. I, 3d ed., 1966, by permission of the Biometrika Trustees.

Table A5.3 (*continued*)

0.25	0.10	0.05	0.025	0.01	0.005	0.001	α $\Big/$ ν
1.323	2.706	3.841	5.024	6.635	7.879	10.828	1
2.773	4.605	5.991	7.378	9.210	10.597	13.816	2
4.108	6.251	7.815	9.348	11.345	12.838	16.266	3
5.385	7.779	9.488	11.143	13.277	14.860	18.467	4
6.626	9.236	11.070	12.832	15.086	16.750	20.515	5
7.841	10.645	12.592	14.449	16.812	18.548	22.458	6
9.037	12.017	14.067	16.013	18.475	20.278	24.322	7
10.219	13.362	15.507	17.535	20.090	21.955	26.125	8
11.389	14.684	16.919	19.023	21.666	23.589	27.877	9
12.549	15.987	18.307	20.483	23.209	25.188	29.588	10
13.701	17.275	19.675	21.920	24.725	26.757	31.264	11
14.845	18.549	21.026	23.337	26.217	28.300	32.909	12
15.984	19.812	22.362	24.736	27.688	29.819	34.528	13
17.117	21.064	23.685	26.119	29.141	31.319	36.123	14
18.245	22.307	24.996	27.488	30.578	32.801	37.697	15
19.369	23.542	26.296	28.845	32.000	34.267	39.252	16
20.489	24.769	27.587	30.191	33.409	35.718	40.790	17
21.605	25.989	28.869	31.526	34.805	37.156	43.312	18
22.718	27.204	30.144	32.852	36.191	38.582	43.820	19
23.828	28.412	31.410	34.170	37.566	39.997	45.315	20
24.935	29.615	32.671	35.479	38.932	41.401	46.797	21
26.039	30.813	33.924	36.781	40.289	42.796	48.268	22
27.141	32.007	35.172	38.076	41.638	44.181	49.728	23
28.241	33.196	36.415	39.364	42.980	45.558	51.179	24
29.339	34.382	37.652	40.646	44.314	46.928	52.620	25
30.434	35.563	38.885	41.923	45.642	48.290	54.052	26
31.528	36.741	40.113	43.194	46.963	49.645	55.476	27
32.620	37.916	41.337	44.461	48.278	50.993	56.892	28
33.711	39.087	42.557	45.722	49.588	52.336	58.302	29
34.800	40.256	43.773	46.979	50.892	53.672	59.703	30
45.616	51.805	55.758	59.342	63.691	66.766	73.402	40
56.334	63.167	67.505	71.420	76.154	79.490	86.661	50
66.981	74.397	79.082	83.298	88.379	91.952	99.607	60
77.577	85.527	90.531	95.023	100.425	104.215	112.317	70
88.130	96.578	101.879	106.629	112.329	116.321	124.839	80
98.650	107.565	113.145	118.136	124.116	128.299	137.208	90
109.141	118.498	124.342	129.561	135.807	140.169	149.449	100
+0.6745	+1.282	+1.645	+1.960	+2.326	+2.576	+3.090	K_α

For $\nu > 100$ take

$$\chi^2 = \nu \left\{ 1 - \frac{2}{9\nu} + K_\alpha \sqrt{\frac{2}{9\nu}} \right\}^2 \quad \text{or} \quad \chi^2 = \frac{1}{2} \{ K_\alpha + \sqrt{(2\nu - 1)} \}^2,$$

according to the degree of accuracy required. K_α is the standardized normal deviate corresponding to α and is shown in the bottom line of the table.

Table A5.4† Summation of terms of the Poisson distribution: $1,000P$ {Poisson with parameter $\lambda \leq c$}

c \ λ	0.01	0.02	0.03	0.04	0.05	0.06	0.07	0.08	0.09	
0	990	980	970	961	951	942	932	923	914	
1	1000	1000	1000	999	999	998	998	997	996	
2				1000	1000	1000	1000	1000	1000	

c \ λ	0.10	0.15	0.20	0.25	0.30	0.35	0.40	0.45	0.50	
0	905	861	819	779	741	705	670	638	607	
1	995	990	982	974	963	951	938	925	910	
2	1000	999	999	998	996	994	992	989	986	
3		1000	1000	1000	1000	1000	999	999	998	
4							1000	1000	1000	

c \ λ	0.55	0.60	0.65	0.70	0.75	0.80	0.85	0.90	0.95	1.00
0	577	549	522	497	472	449	427	407	387	368
1	894	878	861	844	827	809	791	772	754	736
2	982	977	972	966	959	953	945	937	929	920
3	998	997	996	994	993	991	989	987	984	981
4	1000	1000	999	999	999	999	998	998	997	996
5			1000	1000	1000	1000	1000	1000	1000	999
6										1000

c \ λ	1.05	1.10	1.15	1.20	1.25	1.30	1.35	1.40	1.45	1.50
0	350	333	317	301	287	273	259	247	235	223
1	717	699	681	663	645	627	609	592	575	558
2	910	900	890	879	868	857	845	833	821	809
3	978	974	970	966	962	957	952	946	940	934
4	996	995	993	992	991	989	988	986	984	981
5	999	999	999	998	998	998	997	997	996	996
6	1000	1000	1000	1000	1000	1000	999	999	999	999
7							1000	1000	1000	1000

c \ λ	1.55	1.60	1.65	1.70	1.75	1.80	1.85	1.90	1.95	2.00
0	212	202	192	183	174	165	157	150	142	135
1	541	525	509	493	478	463	448	434	420	406
2	796	783	770	757	744	731	717	704	690	677
3	928	921	914	907	899	891	883	875	866	857
4	979	976	973	970	967	964	960	956	952	947
5	995	994	993	992	991	990	988	987	985	983
6	999	999	998	998	998	997	997	997	996	995
7	1000	1000	1000	1000	1000	999	999	999	999	999
8						1000	1000	1000	1000	1000

† Reproduced by permission from *Tables for Multiple-Server Queueing Systems Involving Erlang Distributions*, Frederick S. Hillier and Frederick D. Lo, Technical Report #14, NSF GK-2925, Department of Operations Research, Stanford University, December 28, 1971.

Table A5.4 (*continued*)

c \ λ	2.10	2.20	2.30	2.40	2.50	2.60	2.70	2.80	2.90	3.00
0	122	111	100	091	082	074	067	061	055	050
1	380	355	331	308	287	267	249	231	215	199
2	650	623	596	570	544	518	494	469	446	423
3	839	819	799	779	758	736	714	692	670	647
4	938	928	916	904	891	877	863	848	832	815
5	980	975	970	964	958	951	943	935	926	916
6	994	993	991	988	986	983	979	976	971	966
7	999	998	997	997	996	995	993	992	990	988
8	1000	1000	999	999	999	999	998	998	997	996
9			1000	1000	1000	1000	999	999	999	999
10								1000	1000	1000	1000

c \ λ	3.10	3.20	3.30	3.40	3.50	3.60	3.70	3.80	3.90	4.00
0	045	041	037	033	030	027	025	022	020	018
1	185	171	159	147	136	126	116	107	099	092
2	401	380	359	340	321	303	285	269	253	238
3	625	603	580	558	537	515	494	473	453	433
4	798	781	763	744	725	706	687	668	648	629
5	906	895	883	871	858	844	830	816	801	785
6	961	955	949	942	935	927	918	909	899	889
7	986	983	980	977	973	969	965	960	955	949
8	995	994	993	992	990	988	986	984	981	979
9	999	998	998	997	997	996	995	994	993	992
10	1000	1000	999	999	999	999	998	998	998	997
11			1000	1000	1000	1000	1000	999	999	999
12								1000	1000	1000

c \ λ	4.10	4.20	4.30	4.40	4.50	4.60	4.70	4.80	4.90	5.00
0	017	015	014	012	011	010	009	008	007	007
1	085	078	072	066	061	056	052	048	044	040
2	224	210	197	185	174	163	152	143	133	125
3	414	395	377	359	342	326	310	294	279	265
4	609	590	570	551	532	513	495	476	458	440
5	769	753	737	720	703	686	668	651	634	616
6	879	867	856	844	831	818	805	791	777	762
7	943	936	929	921	913	905	896	887	877	867
8	976	972	968	964	960	955	950	944	938	932
9	990	989	987	985	983	980	978	975	972	968
10	997	996	995	994	993	992	991	990	988	986
11	999	999	998	998	998	997	997	996	995	995
12	1000	1000	999	999	999	999	999	999	998	998
13			1000	1000	1000	1000	1000	1000	999	999
14									1000	1000

Table A5.4 (continued)

c \ λ	5.10	5.20	5.30	5.40	5.50	5.60	5.70	5.80	5.90	6.00
0	006	006	005	005	004	004	003	003	003	002
1	037	034	031	029	027	024	022	021	019	017
2	116	109	102	095	088	082	077	072	067	062
3	251	238	225	213	202	191	180	170	160	151
4	423	406	390	373	358	342	327	313	299	285
5	598	581	563	546	529	512	495	478	462	446
6	747	732	717	702	686	670	654	638	622	606
7	856	845	833	822	809	797	784	771	758	744
8	925	918	911	903	894	886	877	867	857	847
9	964	960	956	951	946	941	935	929	923	916
10	984	982	980	977	975	972	969	965	961	957
11	994	993	992	990	989	988	986	984	982	980
12	998	997	997	996	996	995	994	993	992	991
13	999	999	999	999	998	998	998	997	997	996
14	1000	1000	1000	1000	999	999	999	999	999	999
15					1000	1000	1000	1000	1000	1000

c \ λ	6.10	6.20	6.30	6.40	6.50	6.60	6.70	6.80	6.90	7.00
0	002	002	002	002	002	001	001	001	001	001
1	016	015	013	012	011	010	009	009	008	007
2	058	054	050	046	043	040	037	034	032	030
3	143	134	126	119	112	105	099	093	087	082
4	272	259	247	235	224	213	202	192	182	173
5	430	414	399	384	369	355	341	327	314	301
6	590	574	558	542	527	511	495	480	465	450
7	730	716	702	687	673	658	643	628	614	599
8	837	826	815	803	792	780	767	755	742	729
9	909	902	894	886	877	869	860	850	840	830
10	953	949	944	939	933	927	921	915	908	901
11	978	975	972	969	966	963	959	955	951	947
12	990	989	987	986	984	982	980	978	976	973
13	996	995	995	994	993	992	991	990	989	987
14	998	998	998	997	997	997	996	996	995	994
15	999	999	999	999	999	999	998	998	998	998
16	1000	1000	1000	1000	1000	999	999	999	999	999
17						1000	1000	1000	1000	1000

Table A5.4 *(continued)*

c \ λ	7.10	7.20	7.30	7.40	7.50	8.00	8.50	9.00	9.50	10.00
0	001	001	001	001	001	000	000	000	000	000
1	007	006	006	005	005	003	002	001	001	000
2	027	025	024	022	020	014	009	006	004	003
3	077	072	067	063	059	042	030	021	015	010
4	164	156	147	140	132	100	074	055	040	029
5	288	276	264	253	241	191	150	116	089	067
6	435	420	406	392	378	313	256	207	165	130
7	584	569	554	539	525	453	386	324	269	220
8	716	703	689	676	662	593	523	456	392	333
9	820	810	799	788	776	717	653	587	522	458
10	894	887	879	871	862	816	763	706	645	583
11	942	937	932	926	921	888	849	803	752	697
12	970	967	964	961	957	936	909	876	836	792
13	986	984	982	980	978	966	949	926	898	864
14	994	993	992	991	990	983	973	959	940	917
15	997	997	996	996	995	992	986	978	967	951
16	999	999	999	998	998	996	993	989	982	973
17	1000	1000	999	999	999	998	997	995	991	986
18			1000	1000	1000	999	999	998	996	993
19						1000	999	999	998	997
20							1000	1000	999	998
21									1000	999
22										1000

c \ λ	10.5	11.0	11.5	12.0	12.5	13.0	13.5	14.0	14.5	15.0
0	000	000	000	000	000	000	000	000	000	000
1	000	000	000	000	000	000	000	000	000	000
2	002	001	001	001	000	000	000	000	000	000
3	007	005	003	002	002	001	001	000	000	000
4	021	015	011	008	005	004	003	002	001	001
5	050	038	028	020	015	011	008	006	004	003
6	102	079	060	046	035	026	019	014	010	008
7	179	143	114	090	070	054	041	032	024	018
8	279	232	191	155	125	100	079	062	048	037
9	397	341	289	242	201	166	135	109	088	070
10	521	460	402	347	297	252	211	176	145	118
11	639	579	520	462	406	353	304	260	220	185
12	742	689	633	576	519	463	409	358	311	268
13	825	781	733	682	628	573	518	464	413	363
14	888	854	815	772	725	675	623	570	518	466
15	932	907	878	844	806	764	718	669	619	568
16	960	944	924	899	869	835	798	756	711	664
17	978	968	954	937	916	890	861	827	790	749
18	988	982	974	963	948	930	908	883	853	819
19	994	991	986	979	969	957	942	923	901	875
20	997	995	992	988	983	975	965	952	936	917
21	999	998	996	994	991	986	980	971	960	947
22	999	999	998	997	995	992	989	983	976	967
23	1000	1000	999	999	998	996	994	991	986	981
24			1000	999	999	998	997	995	992	989
25				1000	999	999	998	997	996	994
26					1000	1000	999	999	998	997
27							1000	999	999	998
28								1000	999	999
29									1000	1000

Table A5.4 (*continued*)

c \ λ	16	17	18	19	20	21	22	23	24	25
1	000	000	000	000	000	000	000	000	000	000
2	000	000	000	000	000	000	000	000	000	000
3	000	000	000	000	000	000	000	000	000	000
4	000	000	000	000	000	000	000	000	000	000
5	001	001	000	000	000	000	000	000	000	000
6	004	002	001	001	000	000	000	000	000	000
7	010	005	003	002	001	000	000	000	000	000
8	022	013	007	004	002	001	001	000	000	000
9	043	026	015	009	005	003	002	001	000	000
10	077	049	030	018	011	006	004	002	001	001
11	127	085	055	035	021	013	008	004	003	001
12	193	135	092	061	039	025	015	009	005	003
13	275	201	143	098	066	043	028	017	011	006
14	368	281	208	150	105	072	048	031	020	012
15	467	371	287	215	157	111	077	052	034	022
16	566	468	375	292	221	163	117	082	056	038
17	659	564	469	378	297	227	169	123	087	060
18	742	655	562	469	381	302	232	175	128	092
19	812	736	651	561	470	384	306	238	180	134
20	868	805	731	647	559	471	387	310	243	185
21	911	861	799	725	644	558	472	389	314	247
22	942	905	855	793	721	640	556	472	392	318
23	963	937	899	849	787	716	637	555	473	394
24	978	959	932	893	843	782	712	635	554	473
25	987	975	955	927	888	838	777	708	632	553
26	993	985	972	951	922	883	832	772	704	629
27	996	991	983	969	948	917	877	827	768	700
28	998	995	990	980	966	944	913	873	823	763
29	999	997	994	988	978	963	940	908	868	818
30	999	999	997	993	987	976	959	936	904	863
31	1000	999	998	996	992	985	973	956	932	900
32		1000	999	998	995	991	983	971	953	929
33			1000	999	997	994	989	981	969	950
34				999	999	997	994	988	979	966
35				1000	999	998	996	993	987	978
36					1000	999	998	996	992	985
37						999	999	997	995	991
38						1000	999	999	997	994
39							1000	999	998	997
40								1000	999	998
41									999	999
42									1000	999
43										1000

Answers to Selected Problems

Chapter 3

1. (*b*) Maximize $Z = 4{,}500x_1 + 4{,}500x_2$,

subject to
$$
\begin{aligned}
x_1 &&\leq&\; 1 \\
x_2 &\leq&\; 1 \\
5{,}000x_1 + 4{,}000x_2 &\leq&\; 6{,}000 \\
400x_1 + 500x_2 &\leq&\; 600 \\
x_1 \geq 0,\; x_2 &\geq&\; 0.
\end{aligned}
$$

3. $(x_1, x_2) = (13, 5);\; Z = 31.$

4. $(x_1, x_2, x_3) = (0, 10, 6\frac{2}{3});\; Z = 70.$
10. $(x_1, x_2) = (2, 1);\; Z = 7.$
13. $(x_1, x_2) = (-\frac{8}{7}, \frac{18}{7});\; Z = \frac{80}{7}.$
18. $(x_1, x_2, x_3) = (\frac{4}{5}, \frac{9}{5}, 0),$ with $Z = 7.$

1. (*a*) $(x_1, x_2) = (2, 2)$ is optimal. Other corner-point feasible solutions are $(0, 0), (3, 0),$ and $(0, 3).$
10. $(x_1, x_2, x_3) = (0, \frac{5}{2}, \frac{5}{2})$ is optimal.
14. $(x_1, x_2, x_3, x_4, x_5) = (0, 5, 0, \frac{5}{2}, 0)$ with $Z = 50$ is optimal.
20. (*a*) Right side is $Z = 8,\; x_2 = 14,\; x_6 = 5,\; x_3 = 11.$
    (*b*) $x_1 = 0,\; 2x_1 - 2x_2 + 3x_3 = 5,\; x_1 + x_2 - x_3 = 3.$

Chapter 6

2. (a) Minimize $y_0 = 25y_1 + 20y_2 + 75y_3,$
subject to $-y_1 + y_2 + 5y_3 \geq 5$
$$2y_1 + y_2 + 3y_3 \geq 10$$
$$y_1 \geq 0, y_2 \geq 0, y_3 \geq 0.$$

7. (c)

Complementary basic solutions

| Primal problem | | | Dual problem | |
Basic solution	Feasible?	$Z = y_0$	Feasible?	Basic solution
$(0,0,20,10)$	yes	0	no	$(0,0,-6,-8)$
$(4,0,0,6)$	yes	24	no	$(1\frac{1}{5},0,0,-5\frac{3}{5})$
$(0,5,10,0)$	yes	40	no	$(0,4,-2,0)$
$(2\frac{1}{2},3\frac{3}{4},0,0)$	yes & optimal	45	yes & optimal	$(\frac{1}{2},3\frac{1}{2},0,0)$
$(10,0,-30,0)$	no	60	yes	$(0,6,0,4)$
$(0,10,0,-10)$	no	80	yes	$(4,0,14,0)$

18. Maximize $y_0 = 8y_1 + 6y_2,$
subject to $y_1 + 3y_2 \leq 2$
$$4y_1 + 2y_2 \leq 3$$
$$2y_1 \qquad \leq 1$$
$$y_1 \geq 0, y_2 \geq 0.$$

20. (a) Minimize $y_0 = 30y_1 + 20y_2 + 25y_3,$
subject to $y_2 - 3y_3 = -1$
$$3y_1 - y_2 + y_3 = 2$$
$$y_1 - 4y_2 + 2y_3 = 1$$
$$y_1 \geq 0, y_2 \geq 0, y_3 \geq 0.$$

23. (d) Not optimal since $2y_1 + 3y_2 \geq 3$ violated for $y_1^* = 1/5, y_2^* = 3/5.$
(f) Not optimal since $3y_1 + 2y_2 \geq 2$ violated for $y_1^* = 1/5, y_2^* = 3/5.$

30.

Part	New basic solution $(x_1, x_2, x_3, x_4, x_5)$	Feasible?	Optimal?
(a)	$(0,30,0,0,-30)$	No	No
(b)	$(0,20,0,0,-10)$	No	No
(c)	$(0,10,0,0,60)$	Yes	Yes
(d)	$(0,20,0,0,10)$	Yes	Yes
(e)	$(0,20,0,0,10)$	Yes	Yes
(f)	$(0,10,0,0,40)$	Yes	No
(g)	$(0,20,0,0,10)$	Yes	Yes
(h)	$(0,20,0,0,10,x_6=-10)$	No	No
(i)	$(0,20,0,0,0)$	Yes	Yes

31. $-10 \leq \theta \leq 10/9.$

Chapter 7

1. Let x_{ij} be the shipment from plant i to distribution center j. Then $x_{13} = 2, x_{14} = 10,$
$x_{22} = 9, x_{23} = 8, x_{31} = 10, x_{32} = 1$; cost = \$20,200.

4. (Answer in millions of acres) England $\to$ 70 oats; France $\to$ 110 wheat; Spain $\to$ 15 wheat, 60 barley, 5 oats.

10. (a) $x_{11} = 3, x_{12} = 2, x_{22} = 1, x_{23} = 1, x_{33} = 1, x_{34} = 2$; three iterations to reach optimality.

(b) and (c) $x_{11} = 3, x_{12} = 0, x_{13} = 0, x_{14} = 2, x_{23} = 2, x_{32} = 3$; already optimal.

15. $x_{11} = 10, \ x_{12} = 15, \ x_{22} = 0, \ x_{23} = 5, \ x_{25} = 30, \ x_{33} = 20, \ x_{34} = 10, \ x_{44} = 10$; cost = 77.30. Also have other tied optimal solutions.

20. $x_{14} = 20, x_{16} = 50, x_{23} = 10, x_{24} = 10, x_{25} = 60, x_{37} = 60.$

27. Back $\to$ David, breast $\to$ Tony, butterfly $\to$ Chris, freestyle $\to$ Carl; time = 126.2.

33.

Master problem	Subproblem 1	Subproblem 2
$3x_1 + 2x_2 \le 18$	$x_1 \le 4$	$2x_2 \le 12$

Chapter 8

7. $(x_1, x_2) = (10, 5)$ is optimal.

Chapter 9

3. $(x_1, x_2, x_3) = (1, 3, 1)$ with $Z = 8$ is optimal.

8. $(x_1, x_2, x_3) = (\frac{2}{3}, 2, 0)$ with $Z = \frac{22}{3}$ is optimal.

12.

Part	New optimal solution	Value of Z
(a)	$(x_1, x_2, x_3, x_4, x_5) = (0, 0, 9, 3, 0)$	117
(b)	$(x_1, x_2, x_3, x_4, x_5) = (0, 5, 5, 0, 0)$	90

15. (b)

Range of θ	Optimal solution	$Z(\theta)$
$0 \le \theta \le 2$	$(x_1, x_2) = (0, 5)$	$120 - 10\theta$
$2 \le \theta \le 8$	$(x_1, x_2) = (\frac{10}{3}, \frac{10}{3})$	$\dfrac{320 - 10\theta}{3}$
$8 \le \theta$	$(x_1, x_2) = (5, 0)$	$40 + 5\theta$

16.

Range of θ	Optimal solution x_1	x_2	$Z(\theta)$
$0 \le \theta \le 1$	$10 + 2\theta$	$10 + 2\theta$	$30 + 6\theta$
$1 \le \theta \le 5$	$10 + 2\theta$	$15 - 3\theta$	$35 + \theta$
$5 \le \theta \le 25$	$25 - \theta$	0	$50 - 2\theta$

Chapter 10

1. (a) $O \to A \to B \to D \to T$ or $O \to A \to B \to E \to D \to T$, with length = 16.

5. (a) $\{(O, A); (A, B); (B, C); (B, E); (E, D); (D, T)\}$, with length = 18.

8. (a)

Arc	(1,2)	(1,3)	(1,4)	(2,5)	(3,4)	(3,5)	(3,6)	(4,6)	(5,7)	(6,7)
Flow	4	4	1	4	1	0	3	2	4	5

11.

Event	1	2	3	4	5	6	7	8	9	10
Earliest time	0	6	3	5	10	10	11	14	13	20
Latest time	0	7	3	6	11	10	13	14	15	20
Slack	0	1	0	1	1	0	2	0	2	0

Critical path: $1 \to 3 \to 6 \to 8 \to 10$.

14. $t_e = 37, \sigma^2 = 9$.

Chapter 11

3.

	Store		
	1	*2*	*3*
Allocations	1	2	2
	3	2	0

8.

	(a)	(b)
Phase 1	2 M	2.945 M
2	1 M	1.055 M
3	1 M	0
Market share:	6%	6.302%

13. $x_1 = -2 + \sqrt{13} \approx 1.6056, x_2 = 5 - \sqrt{13} \approx 1.3944; Z = 98.233$.

19. Produce 2 on first production run; if none acceptable, produce 2 on second run. Expected cost = $575.

Chapter 12

1. (a) Player I: strategy 2; player II: strategy 1.

6. (a) Politician I: issue 2; politician II: issue 2.

   (b) Politician I: issue 1; politician II: issue 2.

   (c) Minimax criterion says politician I can use any issue, but issue 1 offers him his only chance of winning if politician II is not "smart."

10. (a) $(x_1, x_2) = (\frac{2}{5}, \frac{3}{5}); (y_1, y_2, y_3) = (\frac{1}{5}, 0, \frac{4}{5}); v = \frac{8}{5}$.

13. Minimize $-x_4$,

subject to
$$5x_1 + 2x_2 + 3x_3 - x_4 \geq 0$$
$$4x_2 + 2x_3 - x_4 \geq 0$$
$$3x_1 + 3x_2 \qquad - x_4 \geq 0$$
$$x_1 + 2x_2 + 4x_3 - x_4 \geq 0$$
$$-x_1 - x_2 - x_3 \qquad = -1$$
$$x_1 \geq 0, x_2 \geq 0, x_3 \geq 0, x_4 \geq 0.$$

Chapter 13

8. (b) (long, medium, short) = (14,0,16), with profit of $9,560,000.

14.

Assignment	1	2	3	4	5
Assignee	1	3	2	4	5

19. $(x_1, x_2, x_3, x_4) = (0, 1, 1, 0)$ with $Z = 36$.

22. $(x_1, x_2, x_3, x_4, x_5) = (0, 0, 1, 1, 1)$, with $Z = 6$.
27. (b) $(x_1, x_2, x_3) = (0, 0, 2)$, with $Z = 14$.

Chapter 14

8. (a) Concave.
16. Approximate solution $= 1.0125$.
25. Exact solution is $(x_1, x_2) = (2, -2)$.
28. (a) Approximate solution is $(x_1, x_2) = (0.75, 1.875)$.
32. $(x_1, x_2) = (1, 2)$ cannot be optimal.
35. (a) $(x_1, x_2) = (1 - 3^{-1/2}, 3^{-1/2})$.
42. (a) $(x_1, x_2) = (2, 0)$ is optimal.
　　(b) Minimize $Z = Z_1 + Z_2$,

$$
\begin{aligned}
\text{subject to} \quad 2x_1 \quad\quad + u_1 - y_1 \quad\quad\quad + z_1 \quad\quad &= 8 \\
2x_2 + u_1 \quad\quad - y_2 \quad\quad\quad + z_2 &= 4 \\
x_1 + x_2 \quad\quad\quad\quad + v_1 \quad\quad &= 2 \\
x_1 \geq 0, x_2 \geq 0, u_1 \geq 0, y_1 \geq 0, y_2 \geq 0, v_1 \geq 0, z_1 \geq 0, z_2 \geq 0.
\end{aligned}
$$

　　(c) $(x_1, x_2, u_1, y_1, y_2, v_1, z_1, z_2) = (2, 0, 4, 0, 0, 0, 0, 0)$ is optimal.
47. (b) Maximize $Z = 3x_{11} - 3x_{12} - 15x_{13} + 4x_{21} - 4x_{23}$,

$$
\begin{aligned}
\text{subject to} \quad x_{11} + x_{12} + x_{13} + 3x_{21} + 3x_{22} + 3x_{23} &\leq 8 \\
5x_{11} + 5x_{12} + 5x_{13} + 2x_{21} + 2x_{22} + 2x_{23} &\leq 14 \\
0 \leq x_{ij} \leq 1, \text{ for } i = 1, 2 \text{ and } j = 1, 2, 3.
\end{aligned}
$$

54. (a) $(x_1, x_2) = (\frac{1}{3}, \frac{2}{3})$.
57. $(x_1, x_2) = \left[3 + \left(\dfrac{r}{2}\right)^{1/3}, 3 + \left(\dfrac{r}{2}\right)^{1/2} \right]$ maximizes $P(\mathbf{x}; r)$, so that $(x_1, x_2) = (3, 3)$ is optimal.

Chapter 15

2. (a) All states belong to the same recurrent class.
6. (b) $\pi_0 = \pi_1 = \pi_2 = \pi_3 = \pi_4 = \frac{1}{5}$.
8. (a) $\pi_0 = 0.182, \pi_1 = 0.285, \pi_2 = 0.368, \pi_3 = 0.165$.
　　(b) 31.42.

Chapter 16

1. Input source: population having hair; customers: customers needing haircuts; queue: customers waiting for a barber; queue discipline: first-come-first-served; service mechanism: barber(s).
4. (a) 0.135.
　　(b) 0.270.
　　(c) 0.0527.
7. (b) $P_0 = \frac{2}{5}, P_n = (\frac{3}{5})(\frac{1}{2})^n$.
　　(c) $L = \frac{6}{5}, L_q = \frac{3}{5}, W = \frac{1}{25}, W_q = \frac{1}{50}$.
11. $\frac{31}{32}$.
18. (a) 0.429.
　　(b) 0.154.
　　(c) 0.072.

20.

Part	P_0	P_1	P_2	P_3	E(not running)
(a)	0.493	0.329	0.146	0.032	0.718
(b) (i)	0.333	0.222	0.148	0.099	2.000
(b) (ii)	0.415	0.277	0.185	0.123	1.015
(c)	0.546	0.364	0.081	0.009	0.553

24. (a) W_q (exponential) $= 2W_q$ (constant) $= \frac{8}{5}W_q$ (Erlang).
   (b) W_q(new) $= \frac{1}{2}W_q$(old) and L_q(new) $= L_q$(old) for all distributions.
26. Current policy: $L = 1$; proposed policy: $L = \frac{13}{16}$.
32. (a) $W = \frac{1}{2}$.
   (b) $W_1 = 0.20$, $W_2 = 0.35$, $W_3 = 1.10$.
   (c) $W_1 = 0.125$, $W_2 = 0.3125$, $W_3 = 1.250$.

36.

Service distribution	P_0	P_1	P_2	L
Erlang	0.561	0.316	0.123	0.561
Exponential	0.571	0.286	0.143	0.571

Chapter 17

2. (a) $E[WC] = 16$.
   (c) $E[WC] = 26\frac{1}{2}$.
8. Status quo: $E[TC] = 50$; proposal: $E[TC] = 75.75$; keep status quo.
11. (a) Crew size $= 2$.
   (b) Crew size $= 3$.
12. $\mu = 1.15$ minimizes $E[TC]$.
18. (a) $E[T] = \dfrac{6.8r}{v}$.

   (c) $E[T] = \dfrac{67r}{21v}$.
21. One doctor: $E[TC] = 624.80$; two doctors: 92.95; have two doctors.

Chapter 18

1. (a) $t = 1.83$, $Q = 54.77$.
   (b) $t = 1.91$, $Q = 57.45$, $S = 52.22$.
4. $t = 3.26$, $Q = 26{,}046$, $S = 24{,}572$.
13. Produce 7 units in period 1 and 7 units in period 3.
16. Produce 3 units in period 1 and 4 units in period 3.
19. Produce 1857 loaves.
21. $(s, S) = (1, 5)$.
24. (a) $G(y) = (\frac{3}{10})y + 70e^{-y/25} - 15/2$.
   (b) $(k, Q) = (21, 100)$ policy.
27. If $x \le 46$, order $46 - x$ units; otherwise, do not order.
30. If $x \le 2$, order $2 - x$ units; otherwise, do not order.
33. If $x \le y^0$, order $y^0 - x$ units; otherwise, do not order.
   $y^0 = \mu - c(1 - \alpha)/2$.
36. $s = 24$, $Q = 58$, $(s, S) = (24, 82)$

Chapter 19

1. 2090.5
3. 783.2
8. (a)

10/80	7.167							
1/81	7.233	1/82	7.267	1/83	9.633	1/84	9.267
4/81	7.733	4/82	8.067	4/83	10.367	4/84	8.867
7/81	7.433	7/82	8.700	7/83	10.433	7/84	8.267
10/81	7.500	10/82	9.467	10/83	10.267	10/84	7.967

   (b) 0.890
12. (a)

10/80	7.299						
1/81	7.486	1/82	8.182	1/83	9.429	1/84	10.349
4/81	7.772	4/82	8.511	4/83	9.878	4/84	10.405
7/81	7.901	7/82	8.794	7/83	10.143	7/84	10.307
10/81	8.041	10/82	9.119	10/83	10.314	10/84	10.181

   (b) 1.152
20. (a) $410.333 + 17.630t$

   (b) 604.267

   (c)

3	431.6	6	445.220	9	468.880
4	434.84	7	452.098	10	478.992
5	439.356	8	460.089	11	490.193

   (d)

3	465.52	6	517.405	9	567.864
4	483.075	7	534.236	10	585.671
5	500.196	8	551.212	11	604.329

Chapter 20

1. Use slow service when no or one customers are present and fast service when two customers are present.
2. Minimize $3y_{01} + 9y_{02} + 3y_{11} + 9y_{12} + 28y_{21} + 34y_{22}$,
   subject to $y_{01} + y_{02} - (\frac{1}{2}y_{01} + \frac{3}{10}y_{11} + \frac{1}{2}y_{02} + \frac{2}{5}y_{12}) = 0$
   $y_{11} + y_{12} - (\frac{1}{2}y_{01} + \frac{1}{2}y_{11} + \frac{3}{5}y_{21} + \frac{1}{2}y_{02} + \frac{1}{2}y_{12} + \frac{4}{5}y_{22}) = 0$
   $y_{21} + y_{22} - (\frac{2}{10}y_{11} + \frac{2}{5}y_{21} + \frac{1}{10}y_{12} + \frac{1}{5}y_{22}) = 0$
   $y_{01} + y_{02} + y_{11} + y_{12} + y_{21} + y_{22} = 1$
   $y_{ik} \geq 0$ for $i = 0, 1, 2$, and $k = 1, 2$.
7. State 1: attempt ace; state 2: attempt lob.
8. Minimize $-\frac{1}{8}y_{01} + \frac{7}{24}y_{02} + \frac{1}{2}y_{11} + \frac{5}{12}y_{12}$,
   subject to $y_{01} + y_{02} - (\frac{3}{8}y_{01} + y_{11} + \frac{7}{8}y_{02} + y_{12}) = 0$
   $y_{11} + y_{12} - (\frac{5}{8}y_{01} \qquad + \frac{1}{8}y_{02}) \qquad = 0$
   $y_{01} + y_{02} + y_{11} + y_{12} = 1$
   $y_{ik} \geq 0$ for $i = 0, 1$ and $k = 1, 2$.
13. Reject $600 offer, accept any of the other two.
14. Minimize $60(y_{01} + y_{11} + y_{21}) - 600y_{02} - 800y_{12} - 1,000y_{22}$,
   subject to $y_{01} + y_{02} - (0.95)(\frac{5}{8})(y_{01} + y_{11} + y_{21}) = \frac{5}{8}$
   $y_{11} + y_{12} - (0.95)(\frac{1}{4})(y_{01} + y_{11} + y_{21}) = \frac{1}{4}$
   $y_{21} + y_{22} - (0.95)(\frac{1}{8})(y_{01} + y_{11} + y_{21}) = \frac{1}{8}$
   $y_{ik} \geq 0$ for $i = 0, 1, 2$ and $k = 1, 2$.
15. After three iterations, approximation is, in fact, the optimal policy given in 13.

22. Use fertilizer B regardless of crop quality.

23. Minimize $-5400(y_{01} + y_{11}) - 6200(y_{02} + y_{12})$,

subject to $y_{01} + y_{02} - (\frac{1}{2})(\frac{3}{5}y_{01} + \frac{3}{5}y_{11} + \frac{4}{5}y_{02} + \frac{4}{5}y_{12}) = \frac{1}{2}$

$y_{11} + y_{12} - (\frac{1}{2})(\frac{2}{5}y_{01} + \frac{2}{5}y_{11} + \frac{1}{5}y_{02} + \frac{1}{5}y_{12}) = \frac{1}{2}$

$y_{ik} \geq 0$ for $i = 0, 1$ and $k = 1, 2$.

24. After three iterations, approximation is optimal policy given in Prob. 22.

32. Use fertilizer B in all four periods regardless of crop quality.

39. In periods 1 to 3 do nothing when the machine is in states 0 or 1, overhaul when machine is in state 2, and replace when in state 3. In period 4 do nothing when machine is in state 0, 1, or 2, and replace when in state 3.

Chapter 21

1. Paths are $\{x_1, x_2\}$ and $\{x_1, x_3\}$.

$\Phi(x_1, x_2, x_3) = \max[x_1 x_2, x_1 x_3] = x_1 \max[x_2, x_3] = x_1[1 - (1 - x_2)(1 - x_3)]$.

3. $R(p_1, p_2, p_3) = p_1[1 - (1 - p_2)(1 - p_3)]$.

6. *(a)* Minimal paths are $\{x_1, x_3\}$ and $\{x_2, x_4\}$.

Minimal cuts are $\{x_1, x_2\}$, $\{x_1, x_4\}$, $\{x_2, x_3\}$, and $\{x_3, x_4\}$.

(b) $R(p_1, p_2, p_3) = 1 - (1 - p_1 p_3)(1 - p_2 p_4) = 0.9639$ when $p_i = 0.90$.

(c) Upper bound = exact system reliability.

Lower bound = $(1 - q_1 q_2)(1 - q_1 q_4)(1 - q_2 q_3)(1 - q_3 q_4) = 0.9606$ when $p_i = 0.90$, $q_i = 0.10$.

10. *(a)* $0.659 \leq R(t) \leq 1$

(b) $0 \leq R(1) \leq 0.324$.

Chapter 22

1. *(a)* a_3.

(b) Up to $230,000.

(c) a_3.

6. *(a)* Guess coin 1.

(b) Heads: coin 2; tails: coin 1.

8. *(a)* Produce the chip.

(b) Up to $400,000.

(c) $-$2,300,000. It doesn't pay to use market research.

(d) Produce the chip.

12. Bayes' procedure without seismic soundings is a_1 with expected loss of $-$68,000.

Seismic sounding	Bayes' action	E(loss)	$Q_x(x)$
1	a_1	$-137,700$	0.360
2	a_1	$-67,925$	0.260
3	a_2	$-33,000$	0.210
4	a_2	$-33,000$	0.170

Value of seismic soundings is $781, so they should not be used.

Chapter 23

1. *(a)* 5, 8, 1, 4, 7, 0, 3, 6, 9, 2.

4. *(a)* Assigning numbers 0, 1, 2, 3, 4 to heads and 5, 6, 7, 8, 9 to tails gives the sequence *THHTT*.

6. (*a*) $x = \sqrt{r}$.

11. (*a*) $x = -4 \ln(1 - r)$.

    (*b*) $x = -2 \ln[(1 - r_1)(1 - r_2)]$.

    (*c*) $x = 4 \sum\limits_{i=1}^{6} r_i - 8$.

16. Use first 10 three-digit decimals from Table 23.1 and generate observations from

$$x_i = \frac{1}{1 - r_i}.$$

Method:	Analytic	Monte Carlo	Stratified sampling	Complementary numbers
Mean:	∞	4.3969	8.7661	3.812

19. (*a*) $\text{Est}\{W_q\} = 2\frac{1}{3}$ and $P\{1.572 \leq W_q \leq 3.094\} = 0.90$.

Index